KRAFT

CHAPTER TEN:
PRODUCT PRICING

CHAPTER TWELVE:
THE MASTER BUDGET

THE PLACERS, INC.

CHAPTER ELEVEN:
MANAGERIAL ASPECTS
OF BUDGETING

HARLEY DAVIDSON

CHAPTER THIRTEEN:
PRODUCTION AND
INVENTORY
MANAGEMENT TECHNIQUES

TRAVEL COSTS

CHAPTER FOURTEEN:
CONTROLLING
NONINVENTORY
COSTS

ALCOA

CHAPTER FIFTEEN:
DECENTRALIZATION
AND RESPONSIBILITY
ACCOUNTING

CHAPTER SIXTEEN:
RELEVANT COSTING

Cadbury Schweppes

CHAPTER EIGHTEEN:
LEGAL REQUIREMENTS
AND ETHICAL BEHAVIOR
IN BUSINESS

CHAPTER SEVENTEEN:
CAPITAL ASSET
SELECTION AND
CAPITAL BUDGETING

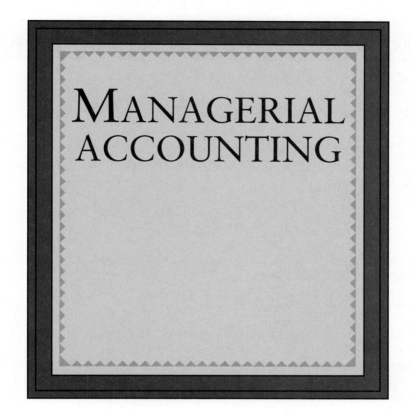

MANAGERIAL ACCOUNTING

ACCOUNTING TEXTBOOKS FROM WEST EDUCATIONAL PUBLISHING

Listed alphabetically by author

Jesse T. Barfield, Cecily A. Raiborn, and Michael A. Dalton: *Cost Accounting: Traditions and Innovations*

William H. Hoffman, Jr., William A. Raabe, and James E. Smith: *West's Federal Taxation: Corporations, Partnerships, Estates, and Trusts, 1993 Edition*

William H. Hoffman, Jr., James E. Smith, and Eugene Willis: *West's Federal Taxation: Individual Income Taxes, 1993 Edition*

Michael C. Knapp: *Contemporary Auditing: Issues and Cases*

Joseph G. Louderback, G. Thomas Friedlob, and Franklin J. Plewa: *Survey of Accounting*

William A. Raabe, Gerald E. Whittenburg, and John C. Bost: *West's Federal Tax Research, 2E*

Cecily A. Raiborn, Jesse T. Barfield, and Michael R. Kinney: *Managerial Accounting*

James E. Smith: *West's Internal Revenue Code of 1986 and Treasury Regulations: Annotated and Selected, 1993 Edition*

Lanny M. Solomon, Larry M. Walther, and Richard J. Vargo: *Financial Accounting, 3E*

Lanny M. Solomon, Larry M. Walther, Linda Plunkett, Richard J. Vargo: *Accounting Principles, 4E*

Gerald E. Whittenburg, Ray Whittington, and Martha Altus: *Income Tax Fundamentals, 1993 Edition*

Eugene Willis, William H. Hoffman, Jr., David Maloney, and William A. Raabe: *West's Federal Taxation: Comprehensive Volume, 1993 Edition*

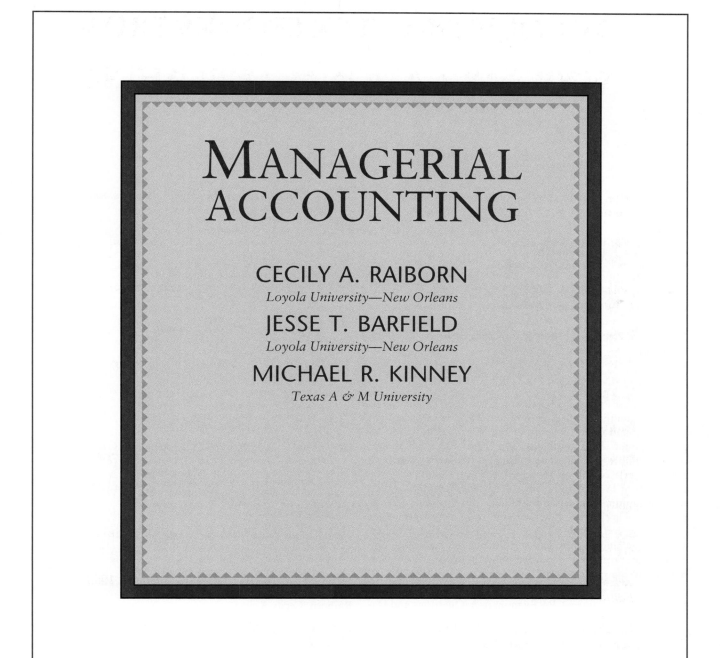

MANAGERIAL ACCOUNTING

CECILY A. RAIBORN
Loyola University—New Orleans

JESSE T. BARFIELD
Loyola University—New Orleans

MICHAEL R. KINNEY
Texas A & M University

West Publishing Company
Minneapolis/St. Paul   New York   Los Angeles   San Francisco

Copyediting: Joan Torkildson
Composition: Parkwood Composition
Art: Randy Miyake
Cover Design: John Rokusek
Cover Image: Wendy Chan, Image Bank

Production, Prepress, Printing and Binding by West Publishing Company.

WEST'S COMMITMENT TO THE ENVIRONMENT

In 1906, West Publishing Company began recycling materials left over from the production of books. This began a tradition of efficient and responsible use of resources. Today, up to 95 percent of our legal books and 70 percent of our college and school texts are printed on recycled, acid-free stock. West also recycles nearly 22 million pounds of scrap paper annually—the equivalent of 181,717 trees. Since the 1960s, West has devised ways to capture and recycle waste inks, solvents, oils, and vapors created in the printing process. We also recycle plastics of all kinds, wood, glass, corrugated cardboard, and batteries, and have eliminated the use of styrofoam book packaging. We at West are proud of the longevity and the scope of our commitment to our environment.

Material from Uniform CPA Examination, Questions and Unofficial Answers, Copyright © 1977, 1978, 1981, 1983, 1985 by American Institute of Certified Public Accountants, is reprinted (or adapted) with permission.

Material from Certified Management Accountant Examination, Copyright © 1974, and 1976 through 1991 by Institute of Certified Management Accountants, is reprinted (or adapted) with permission.

Photo credits follow index.

COPYRIGHT © 1993 By WEST PUBLISHING COMPANY
610 Opperman Drive
P.O. Box 64526
St. Paul, MN 55164-0526

Printed in the United States of America

00 99 98 97 96 95 94 93   8 7 6 5 4 3 2 1 0

Library of Congress Cataloging-in-Publication Data

Raiborn, Cecily A.
    Managerial accounting / Cecily A. Raiborn, Jesse T. Barfield, Michael R. Kinney.
        p. cm.
    Includes bibliographical references and indexes.
    ISBN 0-314-01169-2
    1. Managerial accounting.   I. Barfield, Jesse T.   II. Kinney, Michael R.   III. Title.
HF5657.4.R34   1992
658.15′11—dc20   92-29592
                                                    CIP

CONTENTS

PART 1

MANAGERIAL ACCOUNTING BASICS   1

CHAPTER 1   INTRODUCTION TO MANAGEMENT ACCOUNTING   2

Learning Objectives   2
On Site—Southwest Airlines: Conservative Financially   3
Managerial Functions   4
Changes in the American Business Environment   6
    Type of Businesses   6
    News Note—Maquiladoras Are Thriving   7

International Marketplace   8
News Note—The Computerized Bank   9
Product Variety   9

Stages of Production   9

Relationship of Financial and Management Accounting   12
Financial Accounting   12
Management Accounting   12
News Note—Design the Information System to Meet the Information Needs   13

Management Accounting Standards   14
News Note—Why Have a CASB?   15

Management Accounting and Ethics   16
News Note—Fraud in Business   19

Management Accounting Professionals   19

Site Analysis   19

Chapter Summary   20
Appendix—Organizational Structure   20
Glossary   22
Selected Bibliography   23
End-of-Chapter Materials   24
Questions   24
Case   25
Ethics Discussion   26

CHAPTER 2   COST TERMINOLOGY AND COST FLOWS   30

Learning Objectives   30
On Site—The Cost of Satellites   31
Cost Behavior   33
News Note—The Costs of Duck Hunting   34
News Note—Trading Variable and Fixed Costs   36

News Note—Let Someone Else Do It! 37
News Note—Change the Process—Change the Cost 38

Product Costs and Period Costs 39
The Conversion Process 39
Product Costs 40
Period Costs 41

Components of Product Cost 44
Direct Materials 44
Direct Labor 45
News Note—Consider the Facts 47
Overhead 47
News Note—Employee Health-Care Costs Are Skyrocketing 48
News Note—Quality Cost Behavior 49
Prime and Conversion Costs 49
News Note—Allen-Bradley's Costing Methods Are Radically Different 50

Accumulation of Product Costs 51

Cost of Goods Manufactured and Sold 53

Site Analysis 55

Chapter Summary 55
Appendix—Income Statement Comparisons 56
Glossary 58
Selected Bibliography 59
Solution Strategies 59
End-of-Chapter Materials 60
Questions 60
Exercises 61
Problems 64
Cases 66
Ethics Discussion 70

CHAPTER 3   SETTING PREDETERMINED OVERHEAD RATES   72

Learning Objectives 72

On Site—Don Larousse's Trucking Empire 73

Predetermined Overhead Rates 74

Analyzing Mixed Costs 77
    Cost Behavior 77
    High-Low Method 79

Preparing Flexible Budgets 81

Developing and Using Predetermined Overhead Rates 82
    Variable Overhead Rate 82
    News Note—Using Cost Drivers for Better Cost Information 84
    News Note—Distorted Information Breeds Distorted Decisions 85
    Fixed Overhead Rate 86

Overhead Application 88
    Under- and Overapplied Overhead 89
    Disposition of Under- and Overapplied Overhead 89

Combined Overhead Rates 91
    News Note—What Causes the Lack of Information? 94

Site Analysis 94
    Applications Strategies 95

Chapter Summary 95
Appendix 1—Least Squares Regression Analysis 96
Appendix 2—Allocation of Service Department Costs 99
Glossary 102
Selected Bibliography 104
Solution Strategies 104
End-of-Chapter Materials 105
    Questions 105
    Exercises 107
    Problems 112
    Cases 118
    Ethics Discussion 120

CHAPTER 4   ACTIVITY–BASED MANAGEMENT   124

Learning Objectives   124

On Site—Caterpillar's Costs Are Built on ABC   125

Why Product Cost Information Is Developed   126

Activity Analysis   127
    Value-Added and Non-Value-Added Activities   127
    News Note—What Steps Are Involved?   130
    Manufacturing Cycle Efficiency   131
    News Note—Non-Value-Added Activities Are Everywhere!   133

Cost Driver Analysis   133
    News Note—How to Choose a Cost Driver   134
    News Note—Immaterial Organizational Level Costs Can Be Assigned   138

Activity-Based Costing   139
    Two-Stage Allocation   139
    Short-Term and Long-Term Variable Costs   139
    Horizontal Flow of Activities   140

Determining When an ABC System Is Appropriate   141
    News Note—The Cost System Can Affect Behavior   144

Activity-Based Costing Illustrated   144

Operational Control Under Activity-Based Costing   146

Performance Evaluation Using ABM   148
    News Note—Knowledge of Real Costs Will Affect Decisions   149
    News Note—The High Cost of Non-Quality Work   150

Theory of Constraints   150
    Applications Strategies   152

Site Analysis   152

Chapter Summary   153
Glossary   154
Selected Bibliography   155
Solution Strategies   155
End-of-Chapter Materials   156
    Questions   156
    Exercises   156
    Problems   161
    Cases   166
    Ethics Discussion   170

P A R T   2

USING MANAGERIAL ACCOUNTING INFORMATION IN COSTING   171

CHAPTER 5   INTRODUCTION TO PRODUCT COSTING AND A STANDARD
COST SYSTEM   172

Learning Objectives   172

On Site—Old Rosebud: A Horse Farm with Standards   173

Methods of Product Costing   173
    Costing Systems   174
    Valuation Methods   174

Development of a Standard Cost System   176
    Target Costing   176
    News Note—Determine the Cost Before Production   178
    Setting Standards   178
    Material Standards   179
    Labor Standards   180
    Overhead Standards   182

Variance Computations   183
    Materials Variances   186
    Preferred Material Variances Model   187
    Labor Variances   187
    News Note—Separating Quality Problems from Efficiency Problems   189
    Overhead Variances   189

Cost Control and Variance Responsibility   193
    Materials   193
    News Note—Understand the Critical Nature of Reporting Frequency   194
    Labor   195

Overhead   195
News Note—The Relationship of Activity-Based and Standard Costing   197
Considerations in Establishing Standards   198
Appropriateness   199
News Note—Change the Process—Change the Standard   200
Attainability   200
News Note—The "Full Figure" Standard Game   201
Changes in Standards Usage   202
News Note—When to Investigate Variances   203
Site Analysis   203
Chapter Summary   204
Applications Strategies   205
Appendix—Standard Cost System Journal Entries   205
Glossary   207
Selected Bibliography   209
Solution Strategies   209
Demonstration Problem   210
End-of-Chapter Materials   212
Questions   212
Exercises   214
Problems   216
Cases   223
Ethics Discussion   228

CHAPTER 6   JOB ORDER PRODUCT COSTING   230

Learning Objectives   230
On Site—Dinamation: That's a Big Job   231
Job Order Costing System   231
News Note—Conner Peripherals Produces To Order   232
Job Order Costing: Details and Documents   234

Materials Requisitions 234
Job Order Cost Sheet 237
Employee Time Sheets 237
News Note—Bar Coding: Not Just for Grocery Stores Anymore 239
Overhead 239
News Note—Uncompensated Overtime for Managers & Professionals 240
Completion of Production 240

Job Order Costing Illustration 241
News Note—An Elaborate Time Clock 245

Job Order Costing Using Standard Costs 246
News Note—Job Order Costing—What More Do You Need? 247

Job Order Costing to Assist Management 248
Wainwright & Trumbley 248
Seawind Company 249
FM Corporation 250

Job Order Product Costing in High-Tech Environments 250
News Note—Implementing JIT Requires Change in Mindset 252

Site Analysis 252
Applications Strategies 253

Chapter Summary 253
Glossary 254
Selected Bibliography 254
Solution Strategies 254
Demonstration Problem 254
End-of-Chapter Materials 257
Questions 257
Exercises 258
Problems 261
Cases 266
Ethics Discussion 269

CHAPTER 7   PROCESS COSTING   272

Learning Objectives 272

On Site—E. McIlhenny Sons: A Spicy Process 273

Introduction to Process Costing 273
    The Numerator 276
    The Denominator 277

Weighted Average and FIFO Process Costing Methods 278
    News Note—FIFO EUP More Common Than Weighted Average 279
    The Production Process 279
    Weighted Average Method 282
    FIFO Method 286

Process Costing with Standard Costs 291

Process Costing in a Multidepartment Setting 292

Repetitive Manufacturing 294
    News Note—H-P Makes Some Significant Accounting Changes 295
    Applications Strategies 296

Site Analysis 296

Chapter Summary 297
Appendix—Journal Entries Related to Avery Island Glass 298
Glossary 299
Selected Bibliography 300
Solution Strategies 300
Demonstration Problem 301
End-of-Chapter Materials 304
    Questions 304
    Exercises 305
    Problems 308
    Cases 313
    Ethics Discussion 317

CHAPTER 8   ABSORPTION AND VARIABLE COSTING   318

Learning Objectives   318
On Site—All Businesses Need Good Cost Management   319
An Overview of the Two Methods   320
    Absorption Costing   321
    Variable Costing   322
Absorption and Variable Costing Illustrations   324
Comparison of the Two Approaches   329
    News Note—Cost Systems Need Overhauls   330
    News Note—Income Manipulation Not Possible Under Variable Costing
        334
Uniform Capitalization for Tax Purposes   335
    News Note—Unicap Rules Mean New Decisions   336
Site Analysis   336
Chapter Summary   337
    Applications Strategies   338
Appendix—Theoretical Justifications for Absorption and Variable Costing   339
Glossary   341
Selected Bibliography   341
Solution Strategies   342
Demonstration Problem   343
End-of-Chapter Materials   345
    Questions   345
    Exercises   346
    Problems   349
    Cases   355
    Ethics Discussion   358

P A R T 3

USING MANAGERIAL ACCOUNTING INFORMATION FOR PLANNING   359

CHAPTER 9   BREAKEVEN AND COST–VOLUME–PROFIT ANALYSIS   360

Learning Objectives   360

On Site—The New England Patriots: Full Stadium, But No Profits   361

The Breakeven Point   361

Formula Approach to Breakeven   364

Definition of CVP Analysis   365

Using CVP Analysis   366
   News Note—Understand Your Cost-Volume-Profit Relationships   367
   Specified Amount of Profit   367
   Net Margin on Sales   369

The Income Statement Approach   371

Incremental Analysis for Short-Run Changes   373
   News Note—When Prices Are Down, Volume Needs To Be Up   374

Margin of Safety   377

Operating Leverage   378
   News Note—The Relationship Between Postal Rates and Postal Volume   380

CVP Analysis in a Multiproduct Environment   380

Underlying Assumptions of CVP Analysis   383
   News Note—The Longer You Keep a Customer, The Less It Costs You   385
Costs and Quality   385
   News Note—Quality at Coca-Cola   386
   Applications Strategies   388
Site Analysis   388

Chapter Summary   389
Appendix 1—Cash Breakeven Point   390
Appendix 2—Graphic Approaches to Breakeven   392
   Breakeven Chart   392
   News Note—Can We Make It Up in Volume?   394
   Profit-Volume Graph   394
Glossary   395
Selected Bibliography   396
Solution Strategies   396
Demonstration Problem   397
End-of-Chapter Materials   399
   Questions   399
   Exercises   399
   Problems   403
   Cases   407
   Ethics Discussion   409

CHAPTER 10 PRODUCT PRICING   410

Learning Objectives   410
On Site—Kraft General Foods: Competitors' Prices Are Important   411

Product Life Cycle 412
    News Note—Cost Reductions Can Bring Price Reductions 414

Pricing Objectives and Strategies 414
    Cost-Plus Pricing 416
    Time and Material Pricing 418
    Special Order Pricing 419
    Penetration Pricing and Price Skimming 421
    Multiple Product Pricing 421
    Price Reductions 422
    Regulated Prices 422

Operating Environment 422
    Market Structure 422
    News Note—Regulated Prices Can Cost Consumers 423
    International Dimensions 424
    News Note—The Efficiency of Japanese Automakers Is Worldclass 425
    Regulation 425
    News Note—Do Doctors Fix Prices 426
    Consumer Behavior 426
    News Note—Rising Prices Don't Curb Demand for Pharmaceuticals 427
    Supply 427

Transfer Pricing 428
    Cost-Based Transfer Prices 430
    Market-Based Transfer Prices 430
    Negotiated Transfer Prices 430
    Dual Pricing 431
    Multinational Settings 432
    News Note—Ethical Issues in Pricing 433

Pricing Ethics 433

Site Analysis 433

Chapter Summary 434
    Applications Strategies 435

Appendix—Transfer Prices for Service Departments 436
    Setting Transfer Prices 436
    News Note—Transfer Pricing Systems Need to Look for Cost Drivers 438
    Advantages of Transfer Prices 439
    Disadvantages of Transfer Prices 440

Glossary 440

Selected Bibliography 442

Solution Strategies 442

End-of-Chapter Materials 443
    Questions 443
    Exercises 444
    Problems 449
    Cases 455
    Ethics Discussion 459

CHAPTER 11 MANAGERIAL ASPECTS OF BUDGETING   462

Learning Objectives   462

On Site—Financial Planning at The Placers Inc.   463

Budgeting and Management Functions   464
  Purposes of Budgeting   464
  News Note—Even Accountants Can't Always Budget for Profits   466
  Strategic and Tactical Planning   466
  News Note—Life Cycle Stage of Product Affects Budgeting Process   469
  News Note—Different Stages of Life, Different Ways of Budgeting   470

The Budgeting Process   470
  Participation   471
  News Note—Participation Is Important   473
  Timing   474
  Budget Manuals   475
  Implementation and Control   476
  Sales Price and Sales Volume Variances   477
  Analyzing Cost Variances   479
  Budget Revisions   480
  Performance Evaluation   480

Site Analysis   484

Chapter Summary   484
  News Note—Budgets Should Direct, Not Control, the Organization   485
  Applications Strategies   486

Appendix—Zero-Based Budgeting   486
Glossary   487
Selected Bibliography   488
Solution Strategies   489
End-of-Chapter Materials   489
  Questions   489

Exercises 490
Cases 495
Ethics Discussion 498

CHAPTER 12 THE MASTER BUDGET 500

Learning Objectives 500

On Site—U.S. Catholic Church Benefits from Budgets 501

The Master Budget 501

The Master Budget Illustrated 505

    Sales Budget 506

    *News Note—Budgeting Sales on an International Basis Is a Complex Task
    507*

    Production Budget 507

    Purchases Budget 508

    Overhead Budget 509

    Selling, General, Administrative (SG&A) Budget 509

    Personnel Compensation Budget 510

    Capital Budget 510

    Cash Budget 511

    News Note—A Corporation's Oxygen Is Its Cash! 512

    News Note—Who Pays When? 515

    Budgeted Financial Statements 519

    News Note—Negative Cash Flow Takes Its Toll at Chrysler 524

Concluding Comments 524
  News Note—Loan Officers Aren't Receptive to Cold Calls 525

Site Analysis 525

Chapter Summary 525
  Applications Strategies 526
Glossary 527
Selected Bibliography 527
Solution Strategies 527
End-of-Chapter Materials 528
    Questions 528
    Exercises 529
    Problems 532
    Cases 541
    Ethics Discussion 547

P A R T   4

USING MANAGERIAL ACCOUNTING INFORMATION FOR CONTROLLING   549

CHAPTER 13 PRODUCTION AND INVENTORY MANAGEMENT TECHNIQUES   550

Learning Objectives 550
On Site—Harley-Davidson Gets Help From JIT 551
Costs Associated with Inventory 552
Economic Order Quantity 554
  News Note—Does Government Really Need All This Inventory? 555

Materials Requirements Planning   557
    News Note—MRP Helps in Inventory Planning   *559*

Just-In-Time Systems   561
    News Note—The Big Box Theory   *563*
    News Note—We Could Have It To You Quicker But . . .   *564*

Changes Needed to Implement JIT   565
    Purchasing, Supplier Relationships, and Distribution   565
    News Note—Team Up With Your Suppliers   *567*
    Production Processing   568
    Plant Layout   569
    News Note—Moving Furniture for Production Increases   *570*

Accounting Implications of JIT   571
    News Note—Implement JIT with a Charitable Donation!   *572*
    ABC Inventory Analysis   574
    News Note—Can JIT Help Prevent Recessions?   *575*

Site Analysis   *576*

Chapter Summary   577
    Applications Strategies   *578*

Appendix—Order Point and Safety Stock   579
Glossary   *580*
Selected Bibliography   *581*
Solution Strategies   *582*
End-of-Chapter Materials   *583*
    Questions   *583*
    Exercises   *584*
    Problems   *587*
    Cases   *593*
    Ethics Discussion   *595*

CHAPTER 14 CONTROLLING NONINVENTORY COSTS   598

Learning Objectives 598

On Site—Corporate Travel Costs Are Flying High 599
Cost Control Systems 599
    Cost Understanding 600
    Cost Containment 603
    Cost Avoidance 605
    Cost Reduction 605
    News Note—"Face-to-Face" No Longer Necessarily Means Travel 606
    News Note—Just Cutting Costs Won't "Cut" It 607

Committed versus Discretionary Costs 608
    Committed Costs 608
    News Note—Cost Cutting with No Layoffs 609
    Discretionary Costs 610
    News Note—"Naked" Planes Are Less Costly 611
    Benefits from Discretionary Cost Incurrence 611
    Measuring Discretionary Cost Efficiency and Effectiveness 614
    News Note—The Surrogate Measure Is Absenteeism 616

Budgeting Discretionary Costs 617
    News Note—No Checking, Less Cheating 618

Controlling Engineered Costs 618

Controlling Discretionary Costs Using the Budget 620

Site Analysis 624

Chapter Summary 625
    Applications Strategies 626

Appendix—Program Budgeting 626
Glossary 628
Selected Bibliography 628
Solution Strategies 629
End-of-Chapter Materials 630
    Questions 630
    Exercises 630
    Problems 634
    Cases 638
    Ethics Discussion 642

CHAPTER 15 DECENTRALIZATION AND RESPONSIBILITY ACCOUNTING 644

Learning Objectives 644

On Site—Alcoa Decentralizes for "Freedom" 645

Decentralization 646
  News Note—Loosening the Reins 647
  Advantages of Decentralization 647
  News Note—Hanson Prefers a "Hands Off" Structure 649
  Disadvantages of Decentralization 649
  News Note—$8 Million Worth of Haircuts! 650

Responsibility Accounting 651

Responsibility Accounting and Control Systems 652
  News Note—Credit Cards Need Volume to be Profitable 653

Types of Responsibility Centers 655
  Cost Centers 655
  News Note—Performance Measurements Must Correlate with Jobs 657
  Revenue Centers 658
  Profit Centers 659
  Investment Centers 659

Measuring Performance Toward the Ultimate Goal 659
  News Note—Quality Means Zero Defects at Senco 660

Performance Measurements 660
  *News Note—Even More Than One Financial Performance Measure Exists
    664*
  Divisional Income 666
  Cash Flow 666
  Return on Investment 667
  Residual Income 671

Limitations of Return on Investment and Residual Income 672

Performance Evaluation in Multinational Settings 675
  News Note—Use Transfer Prices—But Don't Abuse Them 676

Throughput as a Performance Measure   676
Site Analysis   678

Chapter Summary   679
Appendix—Performance Measurement Areas and Cost Drivers   680
Glossary   680
Selected Bibliography   684
Solution Strategies   684
Demonstration Problem   686
End-of-Chapter Materials   687
  Questions   687
  Exercises   688
  Problems   691
  Cases   699
  Ethics Discussion   704

P A R T   5

USING MANAGERIAL ACCOUNTING INFORMATION FOR DECISION MAKING   707

CHAPTER 16 RELEVANT COSTING   708

Learning Objectives   708
On Site—Gateway 2000 Believes in Buying, Not Making   709
The Concept of Relevance   710
  Association with Decision   710
  Importance to Decision Maker   711

News Note—Let's Incur the Cost Now 712
Bearing on the Future 712

Sunk Costs 712

Relevant Costs for Specific Decisions 715
Equipment Replacement Decisions 716
News Note—Are the Profits Worth the Costs? 717
Make-or-Buy Decisions 719
Scarce Resources Decisions 722
News Note—Is Make-or-Buy a Short-Run Decision? 723
News Note—Dollars Pour in from Barbie Accessory Sales 725
Sales Mix Decisions 725
*News Note—Make Sure Your "Base Case" Is an Appropriate Comparison
730*
Product Line Decisions 731
News Note—Consider the Potential as Well as the Costs 734

Site Analysis 735

Chapter Summary 735
Applications Strategies 736

Appendix—Linear Programming 737
Glossary 738
Selected Bibliography 739
Solution Strategies 740
Demonstration Problem 741
End-of-Chapter Materials 743
Questions 743
Exercises 744
Problems 747
Cases 755
Ethics Discussions 759

CHAPTER 17 CAPITAL ASSET SELECTION AND CAPITAL BUDGETING 760

Learning Objectives 760

On Site—Wellness Programs Are Businesses' Newest Investments 761

The Investment Decision 762
    Is the Activity Worth an Investment? 762
    Which Assets Can Be Used for the Activity? 763
    Of the Available Assets for Each Activity, Which Is the Best Investment? 763
    Of the "Best Investments" for All Worthwhile Activities, In Which Ones
        Should the Company Invest? 766

Use of Cash Flows in Capital Budgeting 767
    Cash Flows Illustrated 768
    Timelines 769

Discounting Future Cash Flows 770

Discounted Cash Flow Methods 771
    Net Present Value Method 771
    News Note—Use Cost of Capital Cautiously 772
    Present Value Index 775
    Internal Rate of Return 776
    News Note—Japan Must Now Begin to Consider Hurdle Rates 778

Nondiscounting Methods 779
    Payback Period 779
    News Note—Investment's Payback Occurs in Less Than a Half-Year 780
    Accounting Rate of Return 780
    News Note—Comparing American, Korean, and Japanese Techniques 782

Assumptions and Limitations of Methods 782

The Effect of Depreciation on After-Tax Cash Flows 784

Illustration of After-Tax Cash Flows in Capital Budgeting 785

Link Between Payback Period and Accounting Rate of Return 788

High-Tech Investments 789
    News Note—IBM Knew the Rate of Return Wouldn't Justify the Project 791
    News Note—High Hurdle Rates Bias Investment Decisions 792

Post-Investment Audit 795
    News Note—Flexibility Means Profitability 796
    News Note—Why Do Post-Investment Audits? 798

Site Analysis 798

Chapter Summary 799

Applications Strategies 800

Appendix—Time Value of Money 801
    Present Value of a Single Cash Flow 801
    Present Value of an Annuity 802
    Nested Annuities 803

Glossary 804
Selected Bibliography 805
Solution Strategies 806
Demonstration Problem 808
End-of-Chapter Materials 810
    Questions 810
    Exercises 811

Problems 814
Cases 822
Ethics Discussion 825

CHAPTER 18 LEGAL REQUIREMENTS AND ETHICAL BEHAVIOR IN BUSINESS 828

Learning Objectives 828

On Site—Cadbury Owner Faced Many Ethical Dilemmas 829

Distinguishing Legal from Ethical Behavior 830

Basic Ethical Theories 831
    Utilitarianism 831
    Kantian Analysis 831
    News Note—Managers Need to Perform Ethical Analysis 832

Concern for Legality Is Essential 833
    Foreign Corrupt Practices Act 833
    News Note—How Much to "Buy" Business? 836
    News Note—Internal Controls for Small Business 839
    Racketeer Influenced and Corrupt Organizations Act 839
    News Note—An Attempt to Alter RICO 841
    The Securities Exchange Act of 1934 842
    News Note—Is Insider Trading Not a Crime? 843
    Legislation Related to Employees 843
    News Note—Mandatory Protection No Longer an Employer Option 846
    Environmental Legislation 847
    News Note—Cleanup Costs Can Create Credit Concerns 849
    Whistleblowing 850

Computer Software Piracy 851

Codes of Conduct 851
    News Note—The Good in Whistleblowing 852

Site Analysis   856

Chapter Summary   856
Appendix—Summary of United Nations Code of Conduct   857
Glossary   859
Selected Bibliography   860
End-of-Chapter Materials   861
  Questions   861
  Exercises   862
  Cases   865
  Ethics Discussion   868

APPENDIX—PRESENT VALUE TABLES   871

END OF TEXT GLOSSARY   876

AUTHOR INDEX   886

ORGANIZATION INDEX   891

SUBJECT INDEX   894

PREFACE

Accounting is often referred to as the "language of business." However, managers must be able to communicate their needs to accountants effectively and understand the resulting answers. Thus, this text stresses the techniques and procedures that will be of most importance to managers. The perspective taken by *Managerial Accounting* is that managers and accountants must understand when accounting information is needed, what techniques are available to provide that information, what details are needed to perform the techniques, and the benefits and limitations of the information provided by the various techniques in response to the manager's needs.

While the text's primary focus is on the *users* of accounting information, it is equally important that providers understand user needs so that appropriate questions can be asked and details obtained. An integrated approach to information flow will create an atmosphere of trust, sharing, and cooperation.

Managerial Accounting, then, is intended to provide a context for dialogue among all of the business disciplines. The text emphasizes the practical rather than the theoretical. However, including some basic conceptual issues is necessary so that readers are better able to understand the benefits and limitations of techniques and information. For example, managers who attempt to use cost-volume-profit analysis without recognizing its underlying assumptions will have difficulty understanding CVP's application limitations.

Our belief is that it is critical for readers to understand that accounting is a cross-functional discipline that provides information useful to all management areas. It is also essential that readers recognize that managerial accounting information is necessary in all types of businesses (manufacturing, service, and not-for-profit) whether large or small. Substantial effort has been taken to illustrate all of these types of enterprises, in both the domestic and the international arenas. Rapid changes in the global business environment, such as the introduction in previously communist countries of profit-making operations, will create new demands for management information, and this information will have to be prepared in the international language of business: accounting.

Audience

This text is primarily directed toward students who have completed a basic financial accounting course. The text can be used in the second semester of a financial/

managerial accounting sequence or in a separate managerial accounting course. Students should have a basic familiarity with the mechanics of accounting and the preparation and informational content of the basic financial statements. The text may be used in a course under either the semester or the quarter system.

This text has three central themes. The first is to discuss the managerial accounting tools and models available to managers for use in their planning, controlling, and decision-making functions. The second is to illustrate the computations necessary to obtain the desired information from the tools and models. The third is to illustrate the managerial applicability of these tools in business situations and, in some instances such as budgeting, the behavioral consequences that may result from use of the various tools.

Structure

The text approaches the three basic themes through the use of On-Site chapter opening vignettes about real companies. These vignettes address a variety of functional areas (such as marketing, economics, finance, and personnel) and discuss management planning, control, or decision-making situations. At the end of each chapter, additional comments about the opening vignette are provided in the section entitled "Site Analysis." This section indicates how the company reacted to, or resolved, the On-Site situation or problem.

Part 1 of *Managerial Accounting* introduces the reader to important managerial accounting concepts and definitions. One very important and current topical area (activity-based costing) is addressed early in the text (chapter 4). Placing this topic early in the text allows readers to understand the dynamic nature of managerial accounting and the manner in which nonaccountants can have an impact on how accounting information is gathered, analyzed, and used. Part 2 provides product costing accounting techniques essential for cost of goods sold and inventory account valuations on the financial statements. While these chapters contain techniques that are more appropriate for preparers than users of managerial accounting information, users should have a basic understanding of the components of product and service costs and how these costs are developed. Much of the information in these chapters is covered more extensively for accounting majors in a subsequent cost accounting course. Parts 3–5 present a logical progression of the basic management functions (planning, controlling, and decision making). Some of the topics covered under one of the three functions could just as easily be included in another. For example, standard costing is necessary for planning (especially as related to budgeting), but it is also essential in the control function.

Flexibility

The chapters in the text are written so as to be relatively self-contained. This feature allows faculty to cover the text chapters in a variety of ways without affecting the student's ability to comprehend the material. Some alternative chapter sequences are provided in the Instructor's Manual.

Style

The authors have endeavored to make the text readable and current and to provide numerous real company examples, models, and illustrations. Footnotes are used throughout the text not only for the typical purpose of reference citations but also, in some cases, to supplement textual material. Material is relegated to footnote status for one of the following reasons: (1) it provides a definition or term that is covered at length in another part of the text; (2) it provides an additional example to the one provided in the text proper; or (3) it provides information that is not crucial to, but elaborates on, material contained in the text proper.

Pedagogy

This text is extremely student-oriented. In an effort to make managerial accounting interesting and relevant, real companies have been used to illustrate key concepts throughout the text. With over 200 references to actual organizations, *Managerial Accounting* reflects the real world of business students will encounter. The following text features have been designed to promote an ease of learning and provide a high interest level.

Learning Objectives   The beginning of each chapter provides students with an orderly framework for the material to be covered.

On-Site Openers   Each chapter begins with a vignette about an aspect of a real-world organization that is related to chapter materials. This is in keeping with the goal of illustrating managerial applications of accounting tools. Through these chapter openers, students are shown how the topics included in the chapter affect businesses on a daily basis. The On-Sites have been selected to illustrate both profit and not-for-profit organizations as well as manufacturing and service industries. The On-Sites include Southwest Airlines, Office of Technology Assessment, Caterpillar, Dinamation International, E. McIlhenny & Sons, The New England Patriots, Kraft General Foods, plus many more.

News Notes   In keeping with the practical orientation of this text there are a series of News Notes that provide current selections from the popular business press in each chapter. Like the On-Site chapter openers, the News Notes are grounded in real-world applications with over 125 references to organizations such as Allen Bradley, Hewlett-Packard, U.S. Postal Service, Mattel, and Baylor University Medical Center.

These topics are important because they reflect the contemporary world of business activity. Seven themes (behavioral, high-tech, service or small business, general business, international, quality, and ethical) are used in the News Notes to illustrate how managerial accounting concepts affect various aspects of business. Logos are used to inform the reader of the News Note theme.

Site Analysis   This section of the chapter presents students with the organization's reaction to or resolution of the topic discussed in the On-Site opener.

Applications Strategies   A set of Application Strategies follows the Site Analysis section. These strategies indicate to the students how the chapter tools are applicable to various functional business disciplines like finance, management, economics, or marketing.

Chapter Summaries   Each chapter includes a summary to promote student retention of primary chapter points.

Key Terms   When a new term is introduced in the text, it is listed in boldface type and defined at that point.

Glossaries   A glossary is given at the end of each chapter so students are aware of the new terms and definitions included in the chapter material. In addition, an end-of-text glossary is also provided for all terms defined in the text.

Selected Bibliographies   Each chapter features a selected bibliography of current articles or books for students who want to pursue their interest in chapter topics.

Solution Strategies   In this section, students are provided with all relevant formulae and major computational formats from the chapter. These strategies may be used as guides to work end-of-chapter materials or to refresh the memory.

Demonstration Problems   At the end of appropriate chapters, a demonstration problem and solution are given so that students can check their understanding of chapter computations before doing end-of-chapter assignments.

End-of-Chapter Materials   Each chapter contains a variety of end-of-chapter materials (at different levels of difficulty) that include questions, exercises, problems, essays, cases, and ethical discussion situations. The Ethical Discussion items can be used to prompt in-class discussion or as homework assignments. An introduction to various ethical theories is provided for the instructor in the solutions manual which can be drawn upon to further the ethics discussions. End-of-chapter materials that are computer-solvable are indicated with a computer icon. Students can use these materials to check their level of comprehension of the chapter topics.

Instructor Support Materials

The text is accompanied by a full range of support materials for the instructor.

Annotated Instructor's Edition   This special edition has been prepared by the authors and, in each chapter, contains a variety of margin notes designed to improve and enhance teaching effectiveness and efficiency. These notes include the following:

- Teaching Notes—These notes indicate potential areas that may affect student learning progress in the course or may be interrelated with other college courses with which students have familiarity.
- Points to Emphasize—These points provide some logical "checkpoints" to ensure student clarity on subject matter.
- Points to Consider—These points indicate questions that can be asked to generate student responses that indicate understanding of the material or critical thinking skills; some of these points also provide alternative examples to those given in the text.
- Teaching Transparencies—These notations refer to points at which selected teaching transparencies can be used. The masters for these transparencies are included in the Instructor's Manual. These transparency masters are not duplicates of textual exhibits, but rather provide additional perspectives on the

text materials. The transparencies are also available on SoftCraft Presenter™ software, which allows the instructor to alter the transparencies and customize them for individualized course usage.

- Check Figures—Final answers are provided for all numerical end-of-chapter exercises, problems, and cases.
- Video Vignettes—Vignettes are indicated by icons at points where it would be appropriate to show one or more of the videos that accompany the text. In line with the practical orientation of the text, substantial effort has gone into developing a leading-edge video program, available to adopters upon request.

Videos   Unique to this text is the provision of many video vignettes that illustrate text concepts. For example, one tape provides the students with a tour that illustrates the concepts of job order and process costing. Part of the video contains a walk-through of the highly automated West Publishing facility. This video enables students, especially those in nonmanufacturing locales, to understand how the conversion process occurs and the components needed to develop product costs. Other videos are tied directly to text examples and relate to companies (such as E. McIlhenny & Sons, Nissan, and United Telecom/US Sprint) introduced in the On-Site vignettes or News Notes. The Association for Manufacturing Excellence video (AME) "On the Road to Manufacturing Excellence" contains four segments that illustrate automated processes and just-in-time/total quality management philosophies. Two other AME videos ("We're Getting Closer," and "Managing the Supply Chain") accompany the text. As in the On the Road video, segments are provided that illustrate how American companies are increasing their competitive stance through process and quality changes. Lastly, a selection of tapes entitled "The Blue Chip Enterprise Initiative" is available, which feature small businesses and how they met their individual challenges to become profitable and competitive components of the U.S. business environment. The four-volume video library, "Strengthening America's Competitiveness: Resource Management Insights for Small Business Success," was developed by the Blue Chip Enterprise Initiative, sponsored by Connecticut Mutual Life Insurance Company, the U.S. Chamber of Commerce, and *Nation's Business* magazine. Almost every chapter in the text has one or more videos to accompany it; points of reference for classroom use are fully integrated in the Annotated Instructor's Edition. These tapes are provided free to qualified adopters.

Video Guide   Instructors choosing to use the videos are provided a set of instructor notes. These notes provide a brief overview, length, and key points of the segment as well as some questions for classroom discussion.

Instructor's Manual   This manual (developed with the assistance of Gregory K. Lowry at Fort Valley State College) contains sample syllabi, a listing of chapter terminology, chapter lecture outlines, an assignment/classification table indicating the level of difficulty of all end-of-chapter materials, and some CMA exam multiple-choice questions for use as additional test materials or for quizzes. Masters for approximately forty teaching transparencies referenced in the Annotated Instructor's Edition as well as masters for some of the text exhibits are included in the transparency package.

Solutions Manual   This volume, prepared by the authors, has been independently reviewed and checked for accuracy. Every effort has been made to provide an error-free Solutions Manual. It contains complete solutions to each question, exercise, problem, essay, and case in the text. The beginning of the manual also includes a brief overview of the various ethical theories; this section can be duplicated and provided to the students to help them answer the ethics discussion questions. Some suggested discussion points or (if from professional exams) complete answers are provided for the ethics questions, but no distinct right-or-wrong answer is given. This volume also contains the Student Check Figures that may be obtained by instructors for free distribution to students.

Solution Transparency Acetates   Acetates are provided from the solutions manual for all numerical end-of-chapter materials.

Test Bank   The test bank has been prepared by the authors and contains over one thousand multiple-choice, short exercise, and short discussion questions with related solutions.

WesTest™   This supplement is a computerized version of the multiple-choice and short problem portions of the hard-copy test bank. WesTest includes edit and word processing features that allow test customization through the addition, deletion, or scrambling of test selections.

SoftCraft Presenter™   This supplement is a state-of-the-art presentation graphics program for Microsoft Windows™. This exciting new program is available from West Publishing Company, in conjunction with SoftCraft, Inc. Qualified adopters of the text will receive all transparency material preloaded onto the program. The program gives instructors the opportunity to customize transparencies so they are specific to classroom needs. Illustrations include charts, graphs, figures, and other visual support. SoftCraft Presenter's animation allows for curve editing, scalable type, type manipulation, shape and color blends, rotation and skewing, and variable zoom.

Student Support Materials

Students are also provided with a comprehensive support package to enhance their learning experience.

Working Papers   This student supplement contains a set of forms for all numerical end-of-chapter problems and cases. These working papers are partially completed and help guide the student in problem solutions.

Study Guide   The student study guide contains chapter learning objectives, chapter overviews, detailed chapter notes, and self-test questions. This volume has been prepared by Alan Campbell of Arkansas State University.

MICROSTUDY   The study guide is also available in a computerized format from Delta Software, Inc. The computerized version offers immediate feedback for students as they work the questions. Students can study at their own speed and practice taking tests with MICROSTUDY's practice quizzes.

Student Check Figures   For instructors who wish to provide students with answers to end-of-chapter materials, this list has been prepared by the authors from the solutions contained in the solutions manual. The check figures provide a reference point answer for all numerical end-of-chapter materials, except those for which the provision of a check figure would be inappropriate. These check figures are available free of charge upon instructor request.

Spreadsheet Applications for Managerial Accounting   This package has been developed by James T. Doak of Vulcan Technology. It allows students to use Lotus® 1-2-3® or Quattro Pro® software to solve over fifty in-text problems (which have been indicated with a computer disk icon). The package includes a brief introduction to spreadsheets for those students with little or no experience with Lotus or Quattro Pro. The exercises and problems chosen for the applications workbook have been selected to cover a range of difficulties, beginning with simple features of spreadsheet software and moving to more advanced topics, including graphics. The package includes a disk with exercise and problem templates in 5¼-inch or 3½-inch format. A solutions manual is available for instructors. Please contact your local West Representative or West Publishing Company for more information.

Practice Sets   Two practice sets have been provided with the text.

- *Pennsylvania Containers: An Activity-Based Costing Case,* developed by Mark Bettner of Bucknell University, illustrates activity-based costing using a manufacturing company which produces garbage dumpsters and customized trash receptacles. This practice set concentrates on determination of cost drivers and their use in assigning overhead costs to products. It can be used when teaching chapter 4 (Activity-Based Management) or in conjunction with several chapters from the text to show the student the impact of activity-based costing on decision making. A solutions manual is available for instructors. Please contact your local West Representative or West Publishing Company for more information.

- *Pet Polygon Manufacturing Company* is a computerized practice set that was written by L. Murphy Smith and Dana Forgione of Texas A&M University. It provides students with the opportunity to develop a complete master budget. The practice set emphasizes preparing a master budget, and the use of budgeting information to make managerial decisions. A solutions manual indicates how the practice set can be used in conjunction with the master budgeting chapters (11 and 12) or as a continuing problem for the entire term. The student workbook is available in IBM compatible format with a 5¼-inch and 3½-inch disk.

Our goal has been to produce a text that highlights the importance of the influence of accounting techniques on business decision making and behavior, illustrates the significance of all functional disciplines to the creation and development of accounting information, is comprehensible to all readers and, finally, is applicable for college learning as well as long-term reference. To achieve such a goal, this text stresses the view that internal accounting information is most useful when it directly meets management's information needs.

Acknowledgments

We would like to thank the many people who have helped us during the writing of this text. The constructive comments and suggestions made by the following reviewers were instrumental in developing, rewriting, and improving the quality and readability of this book.

Rubik Atamian	University of Texas–Pan American
Urton Anderson	University of Texas–Austin
Roy E. Baker	University of Missouri–Kansas City
Frank Barton	Memphis State University
Kurt Buerger	Angelo State University
Richard Calvasina	University of West Florida
Gordon Chapman	Eastern Washington University
Ken Cherney	Wisconsin Lutheran College
Jack Christie	Lakehead University (Canada)
Joanne A. Collins	California State University–Los Angeles
Michael F. Cornick	University of North Carolina–Charlotte
Frank P. Daroca	Loyola Marymount University
Lee Dexter	Moorhead State University
Roger K. Doost	Clemson University
David Dunsdon	Oregon State University
Robert C. Elmore	Tennessee Tech University
James M. Emig	Villanova University
Dale L. Flesher	University of Mississippi
Leslie B. Fletcher	Louisiana State University
Margaret Gagne	University of Colorado–Colorado Springs
Jackson F. Gillespie	University of Delaware
Rosalie C. Hallbauer	Florida International University
Santhi C. Harvey	Central State University
Michael Haselkorn	Bentley College
Bambi Hora	University of Central Oklahoma
Richard D. Hulme	California State Polytechnic University–Pomona
Lyle Jacobsen	California State University–Hayward
Richard Keith	University of Massachusetts–Boston
Marsha H. Kertz	San Jose State University
Ilene K. Kleinsorge	Oregon State University
Robert W. Koehler	Pennsylvania State University
Diane O. Kuhlmann	Mankato State University
Amy H. Lau	Oklahoma State University
Donald Leaphart	Pennsylvania State University–Fayette
Wallace Leese	California State University–Chico
Greg K. Lowry	Fort Valley State College
James Makofski	Fresno City College
Donald D. Martin	Central Missouri State University
Otto Martinson	Old Dominion University
John R. McIntyre	Bemidji State University
Roland A. Minch	State University of New York–Albany
Robert G. Morgan	East Tennessee State University
Sylvia Ong	Scottsdale Community College

Jeffrey J. Phillips	University of Dayton
Franklin J. Plewa	Idaho State University
Peter Poznanski	Cleveland State University
Virginia Roe	University of New Orleans
Debra Salvucci	Stonehill College
Jeffrey W. Schatzberg	University of Arizona
Jan Sebastian	Florida State University
Carolyn M. Shankel	Johnson County Community College
Ann Snodgrass	Pellissippi State Technical Community College
Jeff Tsay	University of Texas–Arlington
John M. Virchick	Chapman University
Audrey Warren	San Francisco State University
Michael Werner	University of Miami
Patricia Williams	Boston College
James E. Williamson	San Diego State University
Neil Wilner	University of North Texas

Special mention must be given to Jim Emig and Ann Snodgrass for all their hard work as problem checkers, to Caroline Fisher and Michael Saliba of Loyola University–New Orleans for their input on the application strategies, to Dinah Payne of the University of New Orleans for her assistance in the legal and ethical areas, and to Joel Ridenour for his long hours of valuable assistance.

Special thanks must also be made to the Institute of Management Accountants. This organization has been extremely generous in its permission to use numerous CMA problems and excerpts from its *Management Accounting* periodical and other publications. The people at IMA have been wonderful to work with.

We also acknowledge the American Institute of Certified Public Accountants for permission to use material from Uniform CPA Examinations and the many publishers who granted permissions for use of their materials as On-Site/Site Analysis/News Note excerpts.

Lastly, thanks must be given to all of the people at West Publishing who have helped us on this project and to our families and friends who have encouraged and supported us in this endeavor.

Cecily Raiborn
Jesse Barfield
Mike Kinney

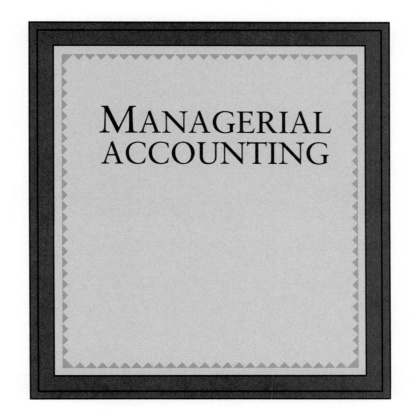

MANAGERIAL ACCOUNTING

PART ONE

MANAGERIAL ACCOUNTING BASICS

C H A P T E R   1

INTRODUCTION TO MANAGEMENT ACCOUNTING

LEARNING OBJECTIVES

After completing this chapter, you should be able to do the following:

1. Explain why management accounting information is important to managers
2. Relate management accounting to the various managerial functions
3. Understand how the changes that have occurred in the business environment have affected business operations
4. Differentiate among the stages of production
5. Compare financial and management accounting
6. Understand how the Cost Accounting Standards Board and the Institute of Management Accountants influence management accounting standards
7. Explain why the ethical standards for management accountants affect all managers
8. (Appendix) Discuss organizational structure relationships

Southwest Airlines: Conservative Financially

Southwest Airlines' revenues have grown from $81 million to $1.2 billion since deregulation allowed it to extend its routes out of Texas in 1978, but Herb Kelleher's scrappy, offbeat airline hasn't lost its Texas touch. Southwest was one of the handful of airlines profitable in 1990, when even American lost money. This strength is not an accident or the product of luck. "We may be flamboyant marketers, but we're conservative financially," Kelleher explains.

Southwest tightly controls costs. [According to one source, the company] has the lowest costs in the industry by far. In the first quarter of 1991, Southwest's operating cost per available seat mile was 15% lower than those of its nearest competitor, America West, 29% lower than Delta's, 32% lower than United's, and 39% lower than USAir's.

Southwest achieves those lower costs in a number of ways. Since it flies short distances, all of Southwest's aircraft are Boeing 737s. Using a single aircraft type saves significantly on training, maintenance and inventory costs. And, since a plane earns revenues only when it is in the air, Southwest gets its aircraft into and out of the gate faster than anyone else. Fully 70% of Southwest's flights have a turnaround time of 15 minutes.

Southwest flights offer peanuts and drinks but no meals. Besides adding to costs, meal service is impractical on short hops. To save boarding time, there is no assigned seating. To cut costs even more, Southwest doesn't subscribe to any centralized reservation system. To save investment in labor and equipment, Southwest doesn't even transfer baggage to other carriers. That's the passengers' responsibility.

SOURCE: Subrata N. Chakravarty, "Hit 'em Hardest with the Mostest," *Forbes* (September 16, 1991), pp. 48ff. Adapted by permission of FORBES Magazine, September 16, 1991. © Forbes Inc.

T he lead-in to the previous article was, "Great management is not easy to define. But if you want to see what it looks like, come with us and visit Southwest Airlines." Herb Kelleher, like all great managers, is concerned with costs—costs associated with every aspect of the business. How much does it cost to hold inventory parts? How much does it cost to sit at the gate five extra minutes? How much does it cost to subscribe to a reservation system or transfer baggage? These types of cost information are usually provided by the management accounting information system.

According to the Institute of Management Accountants (IMA),[1] **management accounting** refers to the "process of identification, measurement, accumulation, analysis, preparation, interpretation, and communication of financial information used by management to plan, evaluate, and control within an organization and to assure appropriate use of and accountability for its resources."[2] Thus, management account-

management accounting

---

[1]The IMA was called the National Association of Accountants (NAA) prior to 1991.
[2]Institute of Management Accountants (formerly National Association of Accountants), *Statements on Management Accounting, Number 2: Management Accounting Terminology* (New York: June 1, 1983), p. 65.

ing focuses on information needs of an organization's managers. Managers are decision makers and, as such, face uncertainty about the factors that affect their decisions. The best way to overcome uncertainty is with information.

In a business organization, information comes in various forms: qualitative, quantitative, factual, and estimated. Some information may reflect the contents of a plan prior to beginning certain activities. Other information may provide answers during the activities to questions such as "Where are we?" "How did we get here?" and "How are we doing?" Yet another type of information may report the results of activities, so that such results can be analyzed and evaluated and used in future planning. Some of the needed information may be historical, monetary, and based on generally accepted accounting principles, but managers also often require forecasted information. Some of that forecasted information will be qualitative in nature, developed for managers' specific needs, and related to their planning, controlling, evaluating, and decision-making functions.

MANAGERIAL FUNCTIONS

goals

Managers, in focusing on the future, set goals and objectives. **Goals** are desired results or conditions contemplated in qualitative terms. Targets expressed in quantitative terms that can be achieved during a preestablished period or by a specified date are referred to as **objectives.** Objectives should logically result from goals. For example, a goal of Southwest Airlines might be to get all persons traveling a distance of one hundred to five hundred miles to board a Southwest plane rather than drive cars. A related objective might be to cut each plane's turnaround time at the gate by two minutes, so that passengers would experience less "airport delay."

objectives

planning

Translating goals and objectives into the specific activities and resources required to achieve those goals and objectives is called **planning.** Companies develop short-term, intermediate-term, and long-term plans. Short-term plans are prepared in more detail than longer-term plans and are used by managers as one basis for the control and performance evaluation functions. For example, Southwest had a two-for-one travel policy during the spring of 1992. Company management might have decided that getting someone to fly with a partner did not create any substantial cost increase for the airline and could possibly create a frequent flyer out of the second person. Developing such a program required a knowledge of the costs related to flying planes.

controlling

The exerting of managerial influence on operations so that they will conform to plans is called **controlling.** The control process uses standards or norms against which actual results are compared. Control involves setting performance standards, measuring performance, periodically comparing actual performance with standards, and taking corrective action when operations do not conform with established standards. Southwest uses a standard of fifteen minutes at the gate as one of its performance measures.

performance evaluations

Using management accounting information, managers can conduct **performance evaluations** to determine if operations are proceeding according to plan or if actual results differ significantly from those that were expected. If the latter case exists, adjustments to operating activities may be needed. Southwest, for instance, could use plane arrival and departure time information to determine whether the standard of fifteen minutes was achieved. Managerial performance evaluation considers both ef-

Southwest's low fares and profit picture can partially be explained by the company's commitment to low-cost service. Low cost in this case means no-frills but not low quality. Passengers are extremely pleased with SW's on-time record and frequent flights to desired destinations.

fectiveness and efficiency. The successful accomplishment of a task reflects **effectiveness,** while performing tasks to produce the best outcome at the lowest cost from the resources used is **efficiency.** For example, it is *effective* for cleaning crews to board a plane and pick up the trash left by passengers, but it is more *efficient* to use flight attendants to perform this task. The efficiency comes from the cost reduction produced by the quickness in turnaround time. Many airlines could not perform in this manner, however, because of inflexible work rules. The best performance maximizes both effectiveness and efficiency.

    A manager's ability to manage depends on good **decision making,** or choosing the best alternative among the solutions available for a particular course of action. For instance, Herb Kelleher made wise decisions after the airline industry was deregulated, not only to expand Southwest's routes but also to refrain from adding European flights and competing directly with the larger airlines. To make proper and valid choices, managers need information related to alternative solutions. Managers, then, are the information users and accountants are the information providers. The quantity of information needed by managers is related both to the expected consequences of the decision and to the complexity of activities performed by the organization. More important decisions and more complex activities require more information. Managers currently desire and need more information than in the past because of the many ways in which business is changing.

effectiveness

efficiency

decision making

EXHIBIT 1–1
▼▼▼▼▼▼▼▼▼▼▼▼

CHANGES IN
AMERICAN BUSINESS

	"The Old Days"	"The New Age"
Major Type of Business	Manufacturing	Service
Wage Rates	Low	High
Major Work Force	Human	Machine
View of Market	Domestic	International
Performance Measurement Focus	Production	Consumer
Product Variety	Limited	Virtually unlimited
Size of Production Runs	Mass	Limited
Profit Margins	Fairly stable	Squeezed

CHANGES IN THE AMERICAN BUSINESS ENVIRONMENT

As shown in Exhibit 1–1, American business has gone through dramatic changes over the past fifty years. These changes, which are expected to continue, have occurred in the types of businesses, markets, and products which U.S. companies have pursued.

Type of Businesses

First, a major shift has occurred in the type of business conducted in the United States. This country was, for many years, recognized as the world leader in manufacturing. While manufacturing is still prevalent in the American economy, a shift toward more service businesses has occurred. In the last twenty-five years, jobs in the service sector increased from 55 percent to over 70 percent of U.S. employment.[3] It is predicted that by the year 2000, about 80 percent of the work force will be employed in service occupations.[4] Much of this shift has been created by a consumer perception that goods manufactured in some foreign countries provide higher quality *for the cost* than goods manufactured domestically. Whether this generalization is true or not will continuously be debated, but it is true that foreign manufacturers do have some cost advantages over American manufacturers. One of these advantages is in the form of labor costs.

Wage rates and fringe benefits for workers have increased substantially in the United States relative to other countries. Fringe benefit costs are currently estimated to be between 30 and 40 percent of base-pay wages. As costs to employ labor have increased, companies have had three primary choices: emigrate to other countries where the wage rates are lower, leave the market, or automate. For example, Falcon Products, Inc., of St. Louis and approximately 1,900 other companies have chosen Mexico as the new "favorite" location spot for some manufacturing operations. (See the following News Note.)

[3]John W. Wright, *The American Almanac of Jobs and Salaries,* 1987–88 ed. (New York: Avon Books, 1988), p. xxii.
[4]Marvin Cetron, "Long-Term Trends Affecting the Institute of Industrial Launderers into the Twenty-first Century," *Industrial Launderer* (January 1989), p. 36.

NEWS NOTE

Maquiladoras Are Thriving

With Mexican free trade in the wind and U.S. labor costs continuing to climb, many mid-sized manufacturers are considering setting up assembly operations in Mexico under the maquiladora program.

With this program, a manufacturer can bring in materials to his Mexican plant free of Mexican tariffs, assemble the product, and ship it back to the country of origin, only paying duty on the value-added due to manufacturing.

The duty-free environment is attractive, but the primary benefit of maquiladoras is the low-wage rate of the Mexican workforce. Mexican workers earn, on average, $1.50 an hour, including vacations and benefits. This compares to an average of $8.50 an hour for similar work and benefits for workers in the United States.

Many Fortune 500 companies have huge maquiladora operations in Mexico. They have invested millions of dollars in their plants. But mid-sized manufacturers can also take advantage of the maquiladora program without investing the money in constructing a plant. They can do this through the so-called "shelter operations."

[Persons running shelter operations] provide everything for a manufacturer, from a building to labor," says Gregg McCumber, a partner with Grant Thornton's office in Brownsville, Texas. "All the manufacturer has to do is pay a fixed rate. It's an excellent way for a mid-sized company to set up a maquiladora."

SOURCE: "Instant Manufacturing with Maquiladoras," *Manufacturing Issues* (Grant Thornton: Summer 1991), p. 7.

While the first two alternatives—emigration or leaving the market—have been adopted by some U.S. companies, other companies did not consider these options to be the most feasible. Some companies declined to emigrate, in part because of the devastating effect that such decisions would have on the American economy. Thus, many manufacturers opted to automate, which created a change from a labor-intensive economy to a machine-intensive economy. Such a decision would reduce the amounts spent for employee wages, but would increase the capital investments required by the firms.

The evolution from labor-intensive to machine-intensive operations has occurred both in the work area and in the area of information technology. Highly automated machines are used for many jobs and, as shown in Exhibit 1–2, robots are becoming more and more commonplace. Disciplines such as accounting have been dramatically affected by the use of computers that provide less costly and more flexible data analyses. Data can now be easily formatted in a variety of ways to suit internal and external reporting purposes as well as regulatory needs. Information can be provided to users in the form and presentation most suited to their needs. Even companies, such as banks, that are primarily viewed as service organizations have automated more and more of their operations, as discussed in the following News Note.

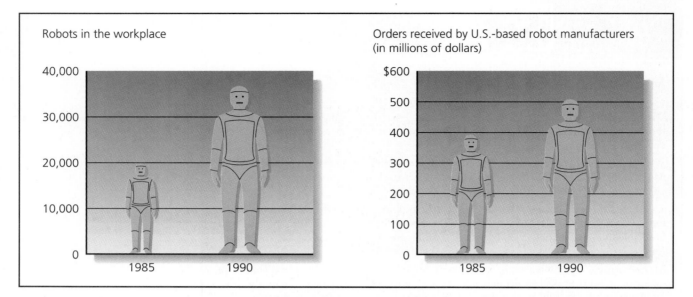

EXHIBIT 1–2
▼▼▼▼▼▼▼▼▼▼▼▼▼

MORE ROBOTS ON
THE JOB

SOURCE: Robotic Industries Association (as shown in *The New Orleans Times-Picayune*, June 17, 1990, p. G1).

International Marketplace

As technology has developed, the world has essentially become smaller. U.S. companies and consumers have begun to realize that alternative choices exist for the sale and purchase of products and services. The market view has become international rather than domestic. Choices, especially those of consumers, are made on consumer-oriented bases of price, quality, and design rather than on the question of domestic or foreign production. Often foreign goods win on all consumer-oriented counts. While exports have risen from the mid-1980s, imports are also up. While exports almost doubled from 1980 to 1990 and, by 1989, had increased by 70 percent over 1985, imports had increased almost three times during the decade of the 1980s.[5]

Many industries, such as airlines, trucking, and telecommunications, were previously regulated. Several of these industries were heavily impacted by the opening of world markets. The government and public believed that deregulation might stimulate competition, both in service and in price. But with all of its benefits, deregulation has created many casualties. Deregulation allowed Southwest Airlines to achieve national prominence through being able to compete on price for markets served, even though those markets were only domestic ones. Other companies that previously competed in international arenas, such as Eastern and Pan Am, could not survive the deregulated atmosphere and have been eliminated from their previous "positions of honor" in the airline industry.

Deregulation has also affected the companies that served the deregulated industries. For instance, when trucking was deregulated, Continental Traffic Service (CTS) in Memphis was severely harmed. CTS audited and paid freight bills for companies and, after deregulation, found itself with few customers and almost no revenue. Like SW Airlines, however, CTS cut its costs and increased its volume to push the company into a position of industry leadership.

---

[5] "U.S. Manufactured Export Growth," *Deloitte & Touche Review* (January 28, 1991), pp. 3–4.

NEWS
NOTE

The Computerized Bank

The LaPorte State Bank of LaPorte, Texas, is going high-tech. By the end of the first quarter of 1990, the $30 million bank will have 24 personal computers and the equivalent of 22 full-time employees. Such heavy automation in banking is called "platform automation." It means that one person can do everything and that the customer need not even walk across the hall to a credit department. The computer integrates all systems into one. Before platform automation, a loan officer or a bank employee would have to print out a report on data they needed, then use that report to work with other reports on the computer. Now, everything is instantly on the screen.

The new system will also give managers much greater control over the bank, since they will have access to better and completely up-to-date information. The bank will also have better credit control with its new system and will have excellent tracking of its loan portfolio. By investing in automation, W. Randolph Woodard, the chairman and CEO, says the bank will "be able to expand and take on more business easily and in a cost-effective manner."

SOURCE: Adapted from "Automating to Increase Productivity," *Currency* (Grant Thornton: Spring 1990), pp. 3–4.

Product Variety

In addition to the factors mentioned earlier, consumers also demand product variety. Companies have begun offering hundreds of alternative choices in product selection. To accomplish this, companies need to be able to change rapidly from one production run to another and to produce limited quantities of a wide variety of items. However, to a manufacturer, high variety causes many additional costs related to ordering and stocking components.

Each of these changes has affected the production process or the provision of service, the information needs of managers, and the cost of doing business. To remain in business, a company must make a reasonable profit on its operating activities. To do so, it must determine which of its products and services are the most attractive to consumers and at what price. At the same time, the company must concern itself with the cost of making the product or performing the service. Selling prices of many goods are set by the marketplace rather than by the individual producer. Thus, if companies are to generate reasonable profit margins, it must be through containing costs rather than by raising selling prices. If a company is a manufacturer, its managers must understand how product costs are incurred in the various stages of the production process.

STAGES OF PRODUCTION

Most merchandising companies do not have stages of production, because products are purchased ready for sale to customers or in the form of finished goods. Manufacturers and service companies, however, must convert raw materials and supplies into a different form. This conversion requires a production flow that, for accounting purposes, must be traced through the organization.

In making a product or performing a service, processing or performance flows through three stages: (1) pre-production or work not started (raw materials and supplies), (2) work in process, and (3) finished work. Costs are associated with each stage. The stages of production in a manufacturing firm and some costs associated with each stage are illustrated in Exhibit 1–3. In the first stage of processing, the cost incurred reflects the prices paid for purchasing materials and/or supplies. To begin the second stage, materials are issued into the production process. Other costs are then incurred to convert the raw materials into finished products. These costs include the wages paid to people producing the goods as well as **overhead** charges, which are the indirect or supporting costs of converting materials and supplies into finished products or services. Overhead costs are incurred for items such as electricity, depreciation, cleanup, supervision, and equipment maintenance. The total accumulated production costs for materials, labor, and overhead equal the cost of goods in the

EXHIBIT 1–3
▼▼▼▼▼▼▼▼▼▼▼

STAGES AND COSTS
OF PRODUCTION

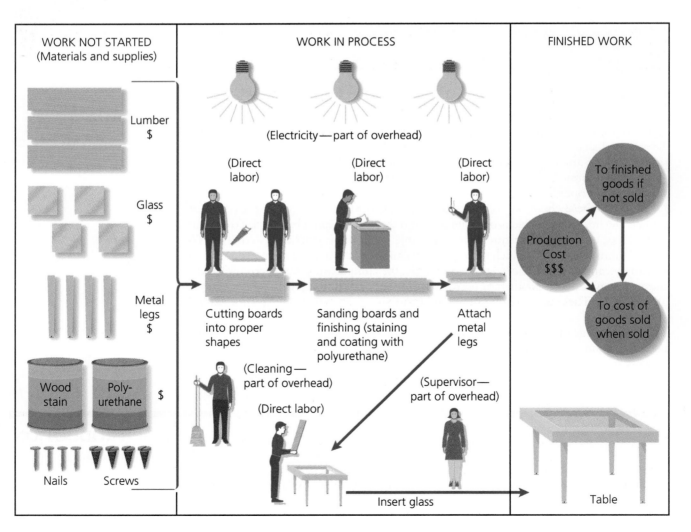

Textbook production begins with a manuscript as a raw material. Direct labor and overhead are added as the manuscript enters the Work in Process stage. The completed texts are the Finished Goods of the publishing company.

third stage (finished work). Thus, the primary accounts involved in the cost accumulation process are: (1) Materials and/or Supplies, (2) Work in Process, and (3) Finished Goods. These accounts relate to the three stages of production shown in Exhibit 1–3.

Service firms ordinarily do not have the same degree of cost complexity as manufacturers. The work-not-started stage of processing normally consists only of the cost of supplies that are necessary for performing services. Supplies are inventoried until they are placed into a work-in-process stage. At that point, labor and overhead are added to achieve finished results. Service firms cannot normally inventory finished work until a future point in time. The service is rendered and delivered to the client in a single step.

Despite the differences among merchandising companies, manufacturers, and service firms, each type of organization can use management accounting concepts and techniques, although to different degrees. Management accounting and financial accounting use a common data base to provide internal and external information, respectively.

RELATIONSHIP OF FINANCIAL AND MANAGEMENT ACCOUNTING

Although the objectives and nature of financial and management accounting differ, all accounting information tends to rely on the same basic accounting system and set of accounts. Accounting information is supposed to address four different functions: (1) provide information to external parties (stockholders, creditors, and various regulatory bodies); (2) help estimate the cost of products and services; (3) help control operations; and (4) help in product/service pricing. Each of these functions truly requires different information and, therefore, should justify different accounting information systems. This idea of different systems for different purposes is discussed in the News Note on page 13.

While technology has improved to the point that a company could have different accounting systems designed for different purposes, most companies still rely on a single system to supply the basic accounting information. The single system is typically focused on providing information for financial accounting purposes, but its informational output can be adapted to meet most internal management requirements.

Financial Accounting

Financial accounting focuses on external users and, as such, must comply with generally accepted accounting principles. The information used in financial accounting is typically historical, verifiable, quantifiable, and monetary. These characteristics are essential to the uniformity and consistency needed for external financial statements. Financial accounting information is usually quite aggregated and related to the organization as a whole. In some cases, a regulatory agency such as the Securities and Exchange Commission (SEC) or an industry commission (such as banking or insurance) may mandate financial accounting practices. In other cases, financial accounting information is a basic essential of business because it is necessary for obtaining loans, preparing tax returns, and understanding how well or poorly the business is performing.

Management Accounting

Management accounting provides information for internal users. Managers are often concerned with individual parts or segments of the business rather than the organization as a whole. Management accounting information therefore commonly addresses such concerns rather than the "big picture" of financial accounting. For example, Southwest Airlines needs information about the profitability of each of its routes in addition to knowing the overall company profitability.

Management accountants are expected to be flexible in serving management's needs. This means that providing forecasted, qualitative, and nonmonetary information is often necessary. For instance, a manager debating whether to sell a piece of land now or in three years is not likely to rely on the land's historical cost to make the decision. Instead, the manager will need estimates about changes in land prices for the next three years and information on events that are expected to occur, such as the possibility of a shopping center being built on property that adjoins the company land because of recent zoning changes.

cost accounting Organizations that are engaged in significant conversion processes have a distinct need for one specific area of management accounting, called **cost accounting**. Cost

NEWS NOTE

Design the Information System to Meet the Information Needs

Many companies now recognize that their cost systems are inadequate for today's powerful competition. Systems designed mainly to value inventory for financial and tax statements are not giving managers the accurate and timely information they need to promote operating efficiencies and measure product costs.

No single system can adequately answer the demands made by the diverse functions of cost systems. While companies can use one method to capture all their detailed transactions data, the processing of this information for diverse purposes and audiences demands separate, customized development. Companies that try to satisfy all the needs for cost information with a single system have discovered they can't perform important managerial functions adequately. Moreover, systems that work well for one company may fail in a different environment. Each company has to design methods that make sense for its particular products and processes.

SOURCE: Reprinted by permission of *Harvard Business Review*. An excerpt from "One Cost System Isn't Enough," by Robert S. Kaplan (January–February 1988). Copyright © 1988 by the President and Fellows of Harvard College; all rights reserved.

accounting focuses on determining the cost of making products or performing services and creates an overlap between financial accounting and management accounting. It integrates with financial accounting by providing product cost valuations for inventories and cost of goods sold on the financial statements. Cost accounting also integrates with management accounting by providing some of the quantitative, cost-based information managers need to plan and control operations, prepare budgets, and make decisions about product profitability. Exhibit 1–4 depicts the relationship of cost accounting to the larger systems of financial and management accounting.

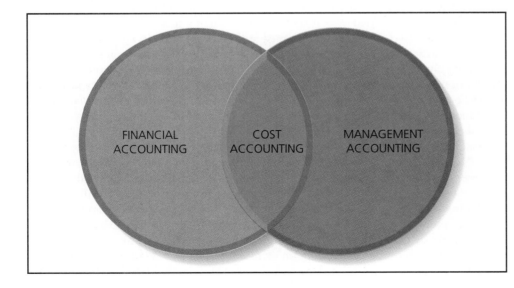

EXHIBIT 1–4
▼▼▼▼▼▼▼▼▼▼

FINANCIAL, MANAGEMENT, AND COST ACCOUNTING OVERLAP

EXHIBIT 1–5
▼▼▼▼▼▼▼▼▼▼▼▼

FINANCIAL AND
MANAGEMENT
ACCOUNTING
DIFFERENCES

	Financial	Management
Primary users	External	Internal
Primary organizational focus	Whole	Parts
Information characteristics	Must be	May be
	Historical	Forecasted
	Quantitative	Quantitative or qualitative
	Monetary	Monetary or nonmonetary
	Accurate	Timely
Overriding criteria	Consistency	Situation relevant (useful)
	Verifiability	Benefits in excess of cost
	Uniformity	Flexibility
Recordkeeping	Mandatory	Combination of formal and informal

Exhibit 1–5 details the differences between financial and management accounting. Management accounting is not generally required by any organization or regulatory body, such as the Financial Accounting Standards Board (FASB) or the SEC. With the exception of the rules set forth by the Cost Accounting Standards Board (which are discussed next), management accounting is optional and, thus, more flexible than financial accounting in meeting managers' needs.

MANAGEMENT ACCOUNTING STANDARDS

Accountants do not have to adhere to generally accepted accounting principles in providing information for managers' internal purposes. A primary criterion for internal information is that it serve management's needs by being useful to managers' functions. A related criterion is a cost/benefit consideration that information should be developed and provided only if the cost of producing it is less than the benefit of having it. These two criteria, though, must still be considered in light of the criteria mentioned earlier in the chapter for financial accounting information—verifiability, uniformity, and consistency. These three characteristics are also important in preparing internal reports, because basing any document simply on whim and flexibility would be counterproductive. But from a management accounting perspective, meeting managerial needs is more important than being confined by financial accounting requirements.

Cost Accounting Standards Board

Financial accounting standards are established by the FASB, a private-sector body. No similar board exists to define universal management accounting standards. However, a public-sector board entitled the **Cost Accounting Standards Board** (CASB) was established in 1970 by the U.S. Congress to promulgate uniform cost accounting standards for defense contractors and federal agencies. Twenty cost accounting standards (of which one has been withdrawn) were issued by the CASB. These standards do not constitute a comprehensive set of rules, and compliance is *required* only for companies bidding on or pricing cost-related contracts for the federal government. Reasons behind the board's existence are described in the following News Note.

NEWS NOTE

Why Have a CASB?

Those not familiar with the federal government procurement process might wonder why the government is concerned with contractor (company) cost accounting practices. If the government could buy all the goods and services it requires in an open competitive marketplace, then contractor cost accounting practices would not be of significant interest. The problem is that the majority of defense procurement dollars are based on negotiated contracts. Due to the nature of the product (such as high-risk technology development programs) and the lack of competition (it is not economical to have more than one supplier of an F-18 fighter, for example), the government must negotiate with contractors based on the estimated cost of the product. Law and regulation require such estimates to be supported by adequate cost or pricing data. Thus, costs are used to establish prices and, on some contracts, the actual reimbursement of the contractor by the government. These costs are computed based on the contractor's cost accounting system and practices.

The objectives of the Board were to:

- Increase the degree of uniformity in cost accounting practices among government contractors in like circumstances,
- Establish consistency in cost accounting practices in like circumstances by each individual contractor over periods of time, and
- Require contractors to disclose their cost accounting practices in writing.

SOURCE: Robert B. Hubbard, "Return of the Cost Accounting Standards Board," *Management Accounting* (October 1990), p. 56. Published by Institute of Management Accountants, Montvale, N.J.

The CASB was discontinued in 1980 because of a lack of funding, but was recreated in 1988 as an independent board of the Office of Federal Procurement Policy, rather than an agency of Congress. The board met for the first time in July 1990 and faces numerous controversial issues at a time when there is extreme interest in the abilities of defense contractors to predict project costs. One issue that is being discussed is whether to extend the authority of the CASB to civilian government agency contracts. Such an extension would primarily affect the computer and consulting industries. At the time this text went to print, the CASB had not adopted any new standards, but it had issued a proposed recodification of the standards, rules, and regulations that were set by the original CASB.

In contrast to the CASB, the Institute of Management Accountants (IMA) issues non–legally binding guidelines in the areas of cost and management accounting called **Statements on Management Accounting** (SMAs). These pronouncements are developed by the Management Accounting Practices (MAP) committee[6] of the IMA after a rigorous developmental and exposure process to assure their wide support. The first

Statements on Management Accounting

---

[6]An earlier program of the IMA's MAP committee produced Statements on Management Accounting Practices (SMAPs). These statements also provide guidance in the practice of management accounting and deal with issues including fixed asset accounting, guidelines for inventory measurement, and criteria for decisions about whether to make or purchase product components.

Unlike FASB Standards, which must be complied with for corporate external financial statements, Statements on Management Accounting (SMAs) provide non-mandatory guidelines for internal reporting. SMAs are issued by the Institute of Management Accountants.

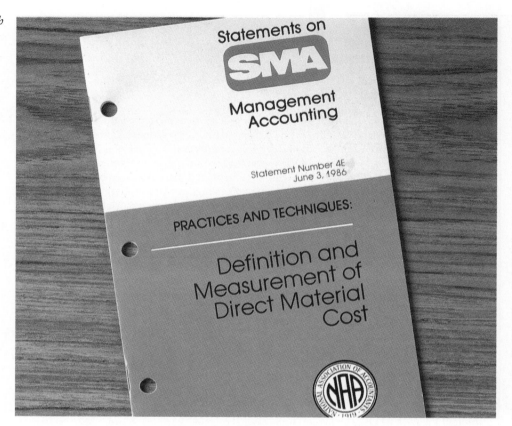

SMAs concentrated on the development of a framework for management accounting and include objectives and terminology. Later SMAs address management accounting practices and techniques such as determining direct labor cost, computing the cost of capital, and measuring entity performance. These statements are important to all managers and are covered at appropriate points throughout the remainder of the text.

MANAGEMENT ACCOUNTING AND ETHICS

While the IMA cannot issue universal standards for management and cost accounting techniques, it can issue professional standards that are binding upon its members. Because of the pervasive nature of management accounting and the upper organizational levels at which many management accountants work, the IMA decided, in the interests of its members and their organizations, to formalize some basic ethical values held by the accounting profession. The standards included in the IMA's Code of Ethics (Exhibit 1–6) reflect the areas of competence, confidentiality, integrity, and objectivity.

Managers are, to some degree, affected by these standards. For matters in which management accountants are expected to adhere to these standards, the ethical options of associated managers are influenced. A manager's ability to improperly record information, commit fraud, or "manage" earnings is lessened if he or she has no

Competence

Management accountants have a responsibility to:

- Maintain an appropriate level of professional competence by ongoing development of their knowledge and skills.
- Perform their professional duties in accordance with relevant laws, regulations, and technical standards.
- Prepare complete and clear reports and recommendations after appropriate analyses of relevant and reliable information.

Confidentiality

Management accountants have a responsibility to:

- Refrain from disclosing confidential information acquired in the course of their work except when authorized, unless legally obligated to do so.
- Inform subordinates as appropriate regarding the confidentiality of information acquired in the course of their work and monitor their activities to assure the maintenance of that confidentiality.
- Refrain from using or appearing to use confidential information acquired in the course of their work for unethical or illegal advantage either personally or through third parties.

Integrity

Management accountants have a responsibility to:

- Avoid actual or apparent conflicts of interest and advise all appropriate parties of any potential conflict.
- Refrain from engaging in any activity that would prejudice their ability to carry out their duties ethically.
- Refuse any gift, favor, or hospitality that would influence or would appear to influence their actions.
- Refrain from either actively or passively subverting the attainment of the organization's legitimate and ethical objectives.
- Recognize and communicate professional limitations or other constraints that would preclude responsible judgment or successful performance of an activity.
- Communicate unfavorable as well as favorable information and professional judgments or opinions.
- Refrain from engaging in or supporting any activity that would discredit the profession.

Objectivity

Management accountants have a responsibility to:

- Communicate information fairly and objectively.
- Disclose fully all relevant information that could reasonably be expected to influence an intended user's understanding of the reports, comments, and recommendations presented.

SOURCE: Institute of Management Accountants (formerly National Association of Accountants), *Statements on Management Accounting: Objectives of Management Accounting* (New York: June 17, 1982).

EXHIBIT 1–6
▼▼▼▼▼▼▼▼▼▼▼▼

STANDARDS OF ETHICAL CONDUCT FOR MANAGEMENT ACCOUNTANTS

accounting personnel support. As the News Note on page 19 indicates, ethical standards in business are sometimes not as high as they should be.

Top managers should be the individuals who understand, interpret, and communicate the corporate value system to other employees. If managers shun their responsibilities in this area, other employees will often be quick to follow such a lead. Should managers not adhere to honest business practices voluntarily, laws and regulations will be adopted to mandate such practices. One example of the government's stand on ethics is the Foreign Corrupt Practices Act (FCPA). This law makes it illegal for a company to engage in various "questionable" foreign payments and also *mandates* that a company maintain accurate accounting records and a reasonable system

internal control

of **internal control**.[7] Ethics-related *laws* (rather than voluntary compliance) could produce more complications than benefits because of the specificity that would be required.

As with all codes of ethics, the IMA code should be viewed as a goal for professional behavior. Every potential situation cannot be addressed in such a code. Each individual operates under a personal code of ethics; those persons lacking high standards will not be deterred from unethical behavior by either a mandated or a voluntary code. However, the IMA code does provide a benchmark by which managers and management accountants can judge their conduct.

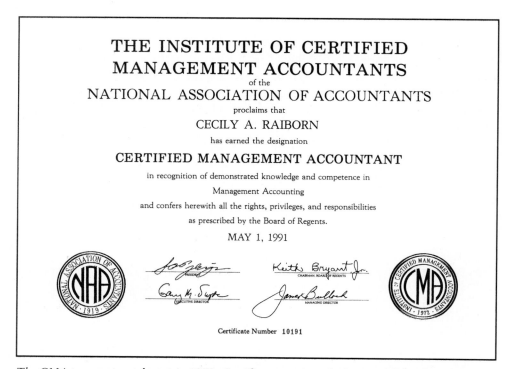

The CMA program was begun in 1972. Certificates are issued after a candidate has passed a 2-day examination and met a specified experience requirement. Exam questions reflect the interdisciplinary focus of the profession of management accounting.

---

[7]An **internal control** is any measure used by management to protect assets, promote the accuracy of records, ensure adherence to company policies, or promote operational efficiency.

MANAGEMENT ACCOUNTING PROFESSIONALS

Over eleven thousand members of the IMA are Certified Management Accountants. The CMA (Certificate in Management Accounting) is a professional designation that recognizes the successful accomplishment of a two-day examination, acceptable work experience, and continuing education requirements. The examination consists of four parts (Economics, Finance, and Management; Financial Accounting and Reporting; Management Reporting, Analysis, and Behavioral Issues; and Decision Analysis and Information Systems). CMA "questions are constructed to measure not only technical knowledge and awareness of principles but to assess the individual's ability to analyze information and communicate the results in a meaningful and understandable manner." [8] Some of the end-of-chapter materials in this text are taken from the CMA exam and are so indicated.

SITE ANALYSIS

Management accounting is important in every type of business. Managers at Southwest Airlines, for example, need to understand where costs are incurred and make decisions about whether those costs are necessary (value-added) or unnecessary (non-value-added). Southwest, like all companies, seeks to eliminate non-value-added costs to improve its profitability and to provide better customer service.

Southwest managers need information about individual route profitability to determine whether to continue that route. They need budget information to make decisions about

continued

---

[8]Keith Bryant, Jr., "A New Beginning for the CMA Program," *Management Accounting* (August 1990), p. 47.

current and future expenditures. They need information about industry standard costs for fuel and salaries to know how their costs compare to the norms of the industry. Managers need to know how many passengers need to be on a plane to cover the costs of making that flight and make a profit. All of these types of information and more are produced by the management accounting system, which has been designed with managers' needs in mind.

CHAPTER SUMMARY

Management accounting refers to the development, analysis, and presentation of information used by managers in performing their functions of planning, controlling, evaluating, and decision making. The information provided by management accounting can be quantitative, qualitative, factual, and/or estimated. The overriding criterion of management accounting information is that it meets the needs of its users. In contrast, the primary criteria of financial accounting are verifiability, uniformity, and consistency.

Numerous changes have occurred in the business environment that have affected the way business is conducted and the types of information needed by and available to managers. These changes are related to production, marketing, and customer issues.

The three basic stages of production are: pre-production (materials and supplies), work in process, and finished work. Labor and overhead are added to materials and supplies to convert those inputs to finished outputs. The costs that flow through these stages are accumulated to determine the cost of making a product or performing a service.

The Cost Accounting Standards Board was established to set standards for determining costs of cost-based contracts with the federal government. Other than this governmental board, management accounting has no regulatory agency to define standards. The Institute of Management Accountants does promulgate non–legally binding guidelines called Statements on Management Accounting. This organization has also established a code of ethics that is binding on IMA members. The code is concerned with the competence, confidentiality, integrity, and objectivity of management accountants. Thus, managers who have IMA members working in their organizations are, to some degree, affected by these ethical standards.

APPENDIX

Organizational Structure

An organization is a system comprising humans, nonhuman resources, and commitments configured to achieve certain explicit and implicit goals and objectives. This appendix provides some general information regarding organizational structure. The structure or design of an entity normally evolves from its nature, policies, and goals, because certain designs are more conducive to certain types of operations. For example, a manufacturer will have an organizational segment known as the production center while a wholesaler will not.

An **organization chart** illustrates the functions, divisions, and positions in a company and how these are related. An important part of reviewing an organization chart is the determination of line and staff employees. **Line employees** are directly responsible for achieving the organization's goals and objectives, while **staff employees** are responsible for providing advice, guidance, and service to line personnel.

In some organizations, accountants may be viewed as line personnel and part of the management group. Such a classification depends upon the firm's size and structure. Accountants are more often considered as staff employees and are, therefore, responsible for providing line managers with timely, complete, and relevant information to improve decision making and reduce uncertainty.

The organization chart also indicates the lines of authority and responsibility. The right (usually by virtue of position or rank) to use resources to accomplish a task or achieve an objective is called **authority.** This concept differs from **responsibility,** which is the obligation to accomplish a task or achieve an objective. Authority can be delegated or assigned to others; ultimate responsibility cannot be delegated.

Although organization charts permit visualization of a company's structure, they do not present all factors necessary to understand how an organization functions. At any given level of the organization, it is impossible to see from the organization chart who wields more power, has more status, or has more informal authority and responsibility. Nonetheless, an organization chart does provide a basic diagram of certain official chains of command and channels of communication.

Exhibit 1–7 presents an organization chart for the Freeman Corporation, a firm that constructs and operates sporting goods stores. The Freeman organization chart indicates two positions under the vice-president of finance: treasurer and controller. The duties of these two individuals are often confused. A corporation's **treasurer** gen-

organization chart

line employees

staff employees

authority

responsibility

treasurer

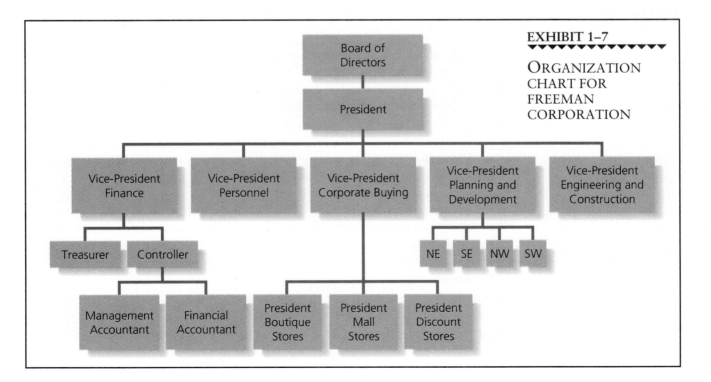

EXHIBIT 1–7

ORGANIZATION CHART FOR FREEMAN CORPORATION

controller

erally handles the actual resources and does not have access to the accounting records. Specific duties of the treasurer normally include directing activities for the following: handling cash receipts, disbursements, and balances; managing credit and collections; maintaining bank relations and arranging financing; managing investments; and insuring company assets. The treasurer's functions are in contrast to the **controller,** who supervises operations of the accounting system but does not handle or negotiate changes in actual resources.

In many organizations, the controller is the chief accountant and is responsible for maintaining and reporting on both the cost and financial sets of accounts. The controller should ensure that the accounting system provides the maximum amount of detail needed for internal and external purposes, while having a minimum amount of redundancy within the accounts. The controller is responsible for designing and maintaining the company's internal control system as well as helping management interpret accounting information. Interpreting accounting information allows the controller to exercise his or her technical abilities by assisting managers in determining the relevance certain information has to a decision, the need for additional accounting data, and the financial consequences of potential actions.

matrix structures

In addition to the traditional hierarchal line-staff organization structure just discussed, some companies have adopted **matrix structures.** In these organizational structures, functional departments and project teams exist simultaneously. Thus, an individual reports to two managers (one in the functional area and one in the project team), which provides a dual authority system. This structure is often used in organizations such as R&D companies and consulting firms that require significant coordination of personnel and that must respond to a rapidly changing environment.

GLOSSARY

Authority   the right (usually by virtue of position or rank) to use resources to accomplish a task or achieve an objective (from appendix)

Controller   the person who supervises operations of the accounting system, but does not handle or negotiate changes in actual resources (from appendix)

Controlling   the exerting of managerial influence on operations so that they will conform to plans

Cost accounting   an area of management accounting that focuses on determining the cost of making products or performing services

Cost Accounting Standards Board (CASB)   a public-sector board first established in 1970 (terminated in 1980; reestablished in 1988) that has the power to promulgate uniform cost accounting standards for defense contractors and federal agencies

Decision making   a process of choosing among the alternative solutions available for a particular course of action

Effectiveness   the successful accomplishment of a task

Efficiency   performing tasks to produce the best outcome at the lowest cost from the resources used

Goal   a desired result or condition, contemplated in qualitative terms

Internal control any measure used by management to protect assets, promote the accuracy of records, ensure adherence to company policies, or promote operational efficiency

Line employee a person who is directly responsible for achieving an organization's goals and objectives (from appendix)

Management accounting the process of identification, measurement, accumulation, analysis, preparation, interpretation, and communication of financial information used by management to plan, evaluate, and control within an organization and to assure appropriate use of and accountability for its resources

Matrix structure an organizational structure in which functional departments and project teams exist simultaneously so that the resulting lines of authority resemble a grid (from appendix)

Objective a target that can be expressed in quantitative terms to be achieved during a preestablished period or by a specified date

Organization chart an illustration of the functions, divisions, and positions in a company and how these are related (from appendix)

Overhead the indirect or supporting costs of converting materials or supplies into finished products or services

Performance evaluation determining the degree of success in accomplishing a task; relates to both effectiveness and efficiency

Planning translating goals and objectives into the specific activities and resources required to achieve those goals and objectives

Responsibility the obligation to accomplish a task or achieve an objective (from appendix)

Staff employee a person who is responsible for providing advice, guidance, and service to line personnel (from appendix)

Statements on Management Accounting (SMAs) nonbinding guidelines for cost and management accounting issued by the Institute of Management Accountants

Treasurer the person who generally handles the actual resources in an organization but who does not have access to the accounting records (from appendix)

SELECTED BIBLIOGRAPHY

Blanchard, Kenneth, and Norman Vincent Peale. *The Power of Ethical Management.* New York: Fawcett Crest, 1988.

Elliott, Robert K., and Peter D. Jacobson. "U.S. Accounting: A National Emergency." *Journal of Accountancy* (November 1991), pp. 54–58.

Hager, Bruce. "What's Behind Business' Sudden Fervor for Ethics." *Business Week* (September 22, 1991), p. 65.

Kanter, Rosabeth Moss. "The New Managerial Work." *Harvard Business Review* (November–December 1989), pp. 85–92.

Kaplan, Robert S. "The Evolution of Management Accounting." *The Accounting Review* (July 1984), pp. 390–418.

Sellers, Patricia. "What Customers Really Want." *Fortune* (June 4, 1990), pp. 58ff.

Shenkir, William G. "A Perspective from Education: Business Ethics." *Management Accounting* (June 1990), pp. 30–33.

Siers, Howard L., and Robert B. Sweeney. "Ethics and the CMA," *Management Accounting* (April 1992), pp. 47–50.

Sourwine, Darrel A. "Putting the Pieces Together." *Management Accounting* (July 1991), pp. 44–49.

Zellner, Wendy, and Eric Schine. "Striking Gold in the California Skies," *Business Week* (March 30, 1992), p. 48.

END-OF-CHAPTER MATERIALS

Questions

1. What are the primary management functions, and how are they supported by management accounting?

2. Differentiate between effectiveness and efficiency. Give an example related to your college experience.

3. Why would operating in a global (rather than in a strictly domestic) marketplace cause a need for additional information? Discuss some of the additional information you think managers would need and why such information would be valuable.

4. Choose any product (such as calendars) that is produced in at least ten varieties. What kinds of additional costs would be caused by variety?

5. What are the stages of production? What kinds of costs are incurred in each stage, and why do such costs need to be accumulated?

6. Define management accounting. How is it related to financial and cost accounting?

7. What are the criteria to evaluate the worthiness of financial accounting information? Why do these differ from the primary criteria for management accounting?

8. Why is flexibility in management accounting important to managers? How can management accounting provide such flexibility?

9. To what situations are the standards of the CASB limited? Why are standards necessary in such situations?

10. Of what value is a corporate code of ethics? Discuss this question in relationship to the various stakeholders (employees, creditors, stockholders) of the organization.

11. What are the four major topics encompassed by the IMA's Code of Ethics, and why do you believe that these specific topical areas were chosen?

12. (Appendix) Differentiate between authority and responsibility. Can you have one without the other? Explain.

13. (Appendix) Discuss your reaction to the following statement: "An organization chart represents the manner in which a company operates."

14. (Appendix) Briefly explain the duties of the controller and the treasurer.

15. (Appendix) In a matrix organization, one individual will have two "bosses." Discuss the problems that such an organizational structure might create.

16. *(Essay)* "Every manager must think cross-functionally because every department has to play a strategic role, understanding and contributing to other facets of the business." (Rosabeth Moss Kanter, "The New Managerial Work," *Harvard Business Review* [November–December 1989], p. 89. Copyright © 1989 by the President and Fellows of Harvard College; all rights reserved.) State your major and discuss why you will need to understand all the other business disciplines.

17. *(Essay) (Appendix)* Coordination is the organizational integration of tasks and activities. In general, effective coordination can be attained by the proper assignment of responsibility and delegation of authority within the context of the formal organizational structure.

    a. Discuss some basic principles that you think would allow the delegation of authority to be effective.
    b. Identify some actions of a superior that would undermine the effectiveness of the delegation of authority.
    c. Identify some actions of subordinates that would undermine the effectiveness of the delegation of authority.

    (CMA adapted)

▍ Case

18. The Arvee Corporation has manufactured recreational vehicles for nearly ten years. During this time Arvee bought existing older buildings near the founder's home to expand its facilities as needed. Now, new competition and rapid sales growth to an annual level of nearly $300 million have made management realize that the company needs to consolidate its locations, reorganize its operations, and modernize its equipment to bring costs into line and to maintain traditional profit margins.

    Five existing plant locations service the three operating divisions: Van Division (small motorized travel vans), Home Division (large motorized homes), and Trailer Division (nonmotorized hitch-on trailers). Several warehouses service the various plant locations, and the corporate office is at a location separate from the production and warehouse facilities. All buildings are within a five-mile radius. Some plant locations include production facilities for two divisions; the overlap that has developed is creating inefficiencies and additional costs. Corporate management has decided that it should take one of the following two courses of action:

    • Alternative 1 is to consolidate the facilities into fewer existing locations.
    • Alternative 2 is to consolidate all facilities into one new location.

    With either of these two alternatives, each division would have exclusive management, production, and warehouse areas. A central warehouse would house common production materials and components; each division's production locations would house other inventories unique to its vehicle models.

The manufacturing operations at most of the plant locations need to be reorganized for greater production efficiency. Frequently, the planning for the production facilities required to meet the increased sales was not well conceived. This is now adversely affecting the current work activities as well as materials and production flow. Moreover, the technology for this kind of production is changing. Thus, many of the equipment items need to be replaced because they are obsolete or worn out. In general, management has come to realize that a complete plant modernization is needed to survive the emerging market challenges.

Tony Pratt, corporate controller, is charged with the responsibility for presenting a summary report on the proposed plant modernization for an upcoming meeting of the Modernization Committee that will oversee the implementation of the project.

Required:

a. Discuss the types of information Tony needs to prepare his report and from what sources such information would be obtained.
b. Design a report format that you think would provide the information to the committee in an understandable and useful way.

(CMA adapted)

Ethics Discussion

19. Many maquiladoras have been opened directly across the border from U.S. cities. Such businesses operate in an environment of inexpensive and plentiful labor and loose laws about worker safety and the environment. Discuss the ethics of operating such businesses in both the United States and Mexico.

20. The Long Branch Bakery is known countywide for its excellent bread and donuts. Sales have, however, been falling because of small but continuous price increases. The increases have been warranted because of increased ingredient costs. The vice-president of marketing wants to substitute low-grade animal fat for 95 percent of the vegetable shortening currently used and reduce the selling prices of the products to their old levels. She does not, however, want to change the slogan on the package from "Made with Pure Vegetable Shortening," since some vegetable shortening will still be used. You are the marketing manager for the bakery. How would you react to this proposal?

21. It has been determined that middle managers and employees often feel pressure to conform to the ethical standards set by upper management, even if this means compromising personal principles. Discuss the following:

a. Why would such compromises occur?
b. What are the advantages and disadvantages of such compromises?
c. What are some ways to avoid making such compromises?

22. In a recent poll on the perceived ethical standards of twelve professional groups, commercial bankers ranked last. They had previously ranked third. And another recent survey found that "while 90 percent of the financial services companies surveyed have a code of conduct or other policy statement, only 30 percent have any ethics training in place." (Gary Edwards, "Banking Ethics Today," *Ethics Journal* [September/October 1991], p. 4)

a. What reasons can you give for such a tremendous drop in public opinion of bankers?

b. Justify the idea of banks having ethics codes but no training.

c. What kind(s) of ethics training programs would you provide for bank employees and why?

23. A primary area of expansion for Wal-Mart is small-town U.S.A. But when Wal-Mart moves in, many local retailers are forced to close their doors because they cannot compete. According to the *Wall Street Journal,* "more than 80% of a Wal-Mart's sales can come at the expense of other local businesses, which can mean a loss of as much as $8 million in sales to area stores." (Barbara Marsh, "Merchants Mobilize to Battle Wal-Mart in a Small Community," *Wall Street Journal* [June 5, 1991], p. A1.)

a. Explain Wal-Mart's reasoning behind expanding to small towns.

b. Assume that you are a senior citizen on a fixed income. Write a short letter to your local small-town newspaper on your feelings about a new Wal-Mart opening in your town.

c. Assume that you are the owner of Small Town Pharmacy. Since the new Wal-Mart opened, your customers have almost disappeared. Discuss your feelings about the Wal-Mart store.

d. Do the benefits received by the members of the local community outweigh the costs to the local retailers? Explain the reasons for your answer.

24. EraTech Corporation, a developer and distributor of business applications software, has been in business for five years. The company's sales have increased steadily to the current level of $25 million per year.

Andrea Nolan joined EraTech about one year ago as accounting manager. Her duties include supervision of the company's accounting operations and preparation of the company's financial statements. Nolan has noticed that in the past six months, EraTech's sales have ceased to rise and have actually declined in the two most recent months. This unexpected downturn has resulted in cash shortages. Compounding these problems, EraTech has had to delay the introduction of a new product line because of delays in documentation preparation.

EraTech contracts most of its printing requirements to Web Graphic, Inc., a small company owned by Ron Borman. Borman has dedicated a major portion of his printing capacity to EraTech's requirements because EraTech's contracts represent approximately 50 percent of Web Graphic's business. Andrea Nolan has known Borman for many years; in fact, she learned of EraTech's need for an accounting manager from Borman.

While preparing EraTech's most recent financial statements, Nolan became concerned about the company's ability to maintain steady payments to its suppliers; she estimated that payments to all vendors, normally made within thirty days, could exceed seventy-five days. Nolan is particularly concerned about payments to Web Graphic; she knows that EraTech had recently placed a large order with Web for printing the new product documentation.

Nolan is considering telling Borman about EraTech's cash problems; however, she is aware that a delay in the printing of the documentation would jeopardize EraTech's new product.

Required:

a. Describe Andrea Nolan's ethical responsibilities in the previous situation. Refer to specific standards of the IMA's Code of Ethics to support your answer.

b. Without prejudice to your answer in part (a), assume that Andrea Nolan learns that Ron Borman has decided to postpone the special paper order for

EraTech's printing job; Nolan believes that Borman must have heard rumors about EraTech's financial problems from some other source because she has not talked with Borman. Should Andrea Nolan tell the appropriate EraTech officials that Borman has postponed the paper order? Explain your answer using the IMA Code of Ethics for support.

c. Without prejudice to your answers in parts (a) and (b), assume that Ron Borman has decided to postpone the special paper order for EraTech's printing job because he has learned of EraTech's financial problems from some source other than Nolan. In addition, Nolan realizes that Jim Grason, EraTech's purchasing manager, knows of her friendship with Ron Borman. Now Nolan is concerned that Grason may suspect she told Borman of EraTech's financial problems when Grason finds out Borman postponed the order. Describe the steps that Andrea Nolan should take to resolve this situation. Use the IMA Code of Ethics to support your answer.

(CMA)

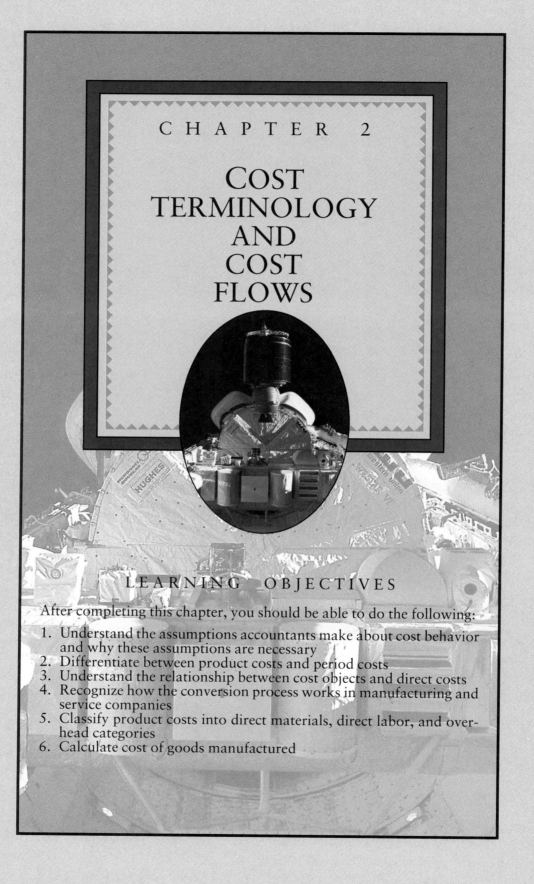

C H A P T E R   2

COST TERMINOLOGY AND COST FLOWS

LEARNING OBJECTIVES

After completing this chapter, you should be able to do the following:

1. Understand the assumptions accountants make about cost behavior and why these assumptions are necessary
2. Differentiate between product costs and period costs
3. Understand the relationship between cost objects and direct costs
4. Recognize how the conversion process works in manufacturing and service companies
5. Classify product costs into direct materials, direct labor, and overhead categories
6. Calculate cost of goods manufactured

The Cost of Satellites

A report by the Office of Technology Assessment, a research arm of Congress, underscores how difficult it is to reduce the cost of space exploration. Military and scientific satellites cost hundreds of millions of dollars each, as do the rockets they ride into space. A single spy satellite can cost $750 million—more than the Central Intelligence Agency spends on covert activities annually. A proposed National Aeronautics and Space Administration satellite to study Earth will cost $5 billion—twice the annual budget of the National Science Foundation.

SOURCE: Bob Davis, "Will Space Program Find Itself Shrinking Or on the Rocks?" *Wall Street Journal* (February 27, 1990), p. A12.

E veryone, including the government, is concerned about costs. Students are concerned about the cost of a Saturday night dinner and movie. Parents are concerned about the cost of their child's college education. Airline managers are concerned about the monthly fuel cost for scheduled flights. Manufacturing managers are concerned about the cost of product quality control. It is not appropriate, however, to simply refer to "the cost," because numerous conditions must be specified before "the cost" can be determined. Is the student considering a fast-food or a four-star restaurant? Will the child want to attend a public or private college, in-state or out-of-state? Fuel cost can change dramatically in a short period of time because of unforeseen conditions in the oil-producing economy. The cost of product quality control can be increased or decreased depending on the level of reliability a manufacturer wants its products to have, or on the quality of the components making up the product.

Communication requires that both the sender and receiver of the message understand the terms being used. Cost is a word that requires clarification of type.

EXHIBIT 2–1
▼▼▼▼▼▼▼▼▼▼▼▼

COST
CLASSIFICATION
CATEGORIES

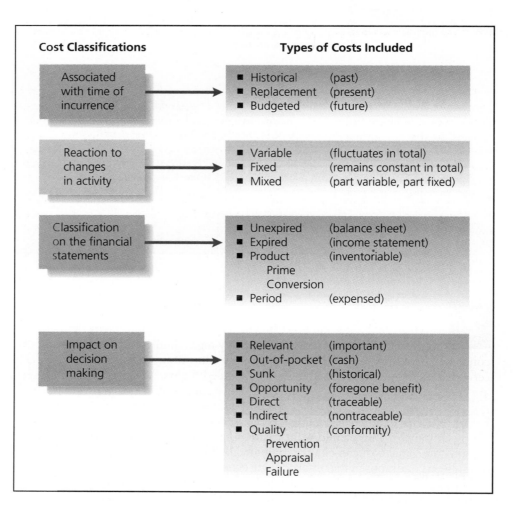

Cost Classifications	Types of Costs Included	
Associated with time of incurrence	■ Historical ■ Replacement ■ Budgeted	(past) (present) (future)
Reaction to changes in activity	■ Variable ■ Fixed ■ Mixed	(fluctuates in total) (remains constant in total) (part variable, part fixed)
Classification on the financial statements	■ Unexpired ■ Expired ■ Product Prime Conversion ■ Period	(balance sheet) (income statement) (inventoriable) (expensed)
Impact on decision making	■ Relevant ■ Out-of-pocket ■ Sunk ■ Opportunity ■ Direct ■ Indirect ■ Quality Prevention Appraisal Failure	(important) (cash) (historical) (foregone benefit) (traceable) (nontraceable) (conformity)

Effective managers must be able to clearly understand and communicate commonly used management accounting terminology. Cost is an often-used word in organizations and reflects a monetary measure of the resources given up to acquire a good or service. However, the term *cost* is seldom used without a preceding adjective to specify the type of cost being considered. Different types of costs are used in different situations. For example, the historical or acquisition cost of an asset is used to prepare a balance sheet, but replacement cost is used to estimate an asset's value for insurance purposes.

A cost can be viewed in a variety of ways depending on the objective or information desired. Exhibit 2–1 presents a number of different cost categories and the types of costs included in each. These categories are not mutually exclusive; a cost may be defined in one way at one point in time and in another way at a different point in time. Different types of costs will be addressed at various points throughout the text. At this time, it is merely important to understand that cost can have many different meanings.

COST BEHAVIOR

In any period, a cost may change in direction or in magnitude (or both) with corresponding changes in activity levels. Activity measures can include sales and production volume, machine hours, number of purchase orders sent, or number of miles traveled in space. The way a *total cost* (rather than unit cost) reacts to changes in activity reflects that cost's behavior pattern. Every cost will change if activity levels are shifted in extremes and given a long enough span of time. Therefore, to properly identify, analyze, and use cost behavior information, a time frame must be specified to indicate how far into the future a cost should be examined, and a particular range of activity must be assumed. The assumed range of activity is referred to as the **relevant range,** which generally reflects the normal operating range of the company. Within the relevant range, the two most common cost behaviors are variable and fixed.

relevant range

Costs that vary *in total* in direct proportion to changes in activity are classified as **variable costs.** Examples include the costs of materials, hourly wages, and sales commissions. Variable costs can be extremely important in regard to the total profit picture of a company, because every time a product is produced or a service is rendered, a corresponding amount of each variable cost is incurred. Since the total cost varies in direct proportion to the changes in activity levels, a variable cost must be a constant amount *per unit.*[1]

variable costs

On the other hand, a cost that remains constant *in total* within the relevant range of activity is considered a **fixed cost.** Such costs vary inversely on a per-unit basis with changes in the level of activity. This means that the *per-unit* fixed cost decreases with increases in the activity level, and increases with decreases in the activity level. Fixed costs include supervisors' salaries, depreciation (other than that computed under the units of production method), and insurance. Note that "in the long run all costs are variable at the total business unit level. If you were to stop producing all products, then obviously, all other costs can, in time, be eliminated."[2]

fixed cost

An apt analogy about the difference between variable and fixed costs is made for Soviet managers in the News Note on the next page.

To illustrate the need for a relevant range of activity, assume that the Hilo Hallie Company, a Hawaiian muumuu manufacturer, has the cost structure for materials and building depreciation shown in the graphs in Exhibit 2–2. The exhibit indicates that actual variable cost for materials is curvilinear rather than linear and that over the long run, several levels of cost exist for machinery depreciation.

---

[1]An accountant's view of a variable cost is, in fact, a slight distortion of reality. Variable costs usually increase at a changing rate until a range of activity is reached in which the average variable cost rate per unit becomes fairly constant. Within this range, the slope of the cost line becomes less steep because the firm benefits from operating efficiencies such as price discounts on materials, improved worker skills, and increased productivity. Beyond this range, the slope becomes quite steep as the firm enters an activity range in which some operating inefficiencies (such as worker crowding and material shortages) cause the average variable cost rate to trend sharply higher. Because of the curves on each end of the graph, accountants choose as the relevant range that range of activity in which the variable costs are constant per unit.
[2]Robert A. Howell and Stephen R. Soucy, "Cost Accounting in the New Manufacturing Environment," *Management Accounting* (August 1987), p. 46.

NEWS NOTE

The Costs of Duck Hunting

Vodka, sex, and ammunition. . . . The ingredients of the lecture on cost accounting made 20 Soviet managers sit up and pay attention. They were attending a three-week course at Wake Forest University's Babcock Graduate School of Management, where professor Kendall Middaugh explained the difference between the fixed and variable costs of duck hunting. A certain amount of vodka was a fixed cost; you would drink it on a weekend, hunting or not. But shells and extra vodka, swallowed for warmth since you [would be alone], should be considered variable costs.

SOURCE: Colin Leinster, "We Need Yuppies in Moscow," *FORTUNE* (November 20, 1989), p. 153. © 1989 The Time Inc. Magazine Company. All rights reserved.

EXHIBIT 2–2
▼▼▼▼▼▼▼▼▼▼▼▼

RELEVANT RANGE
OF ACTIVITY FOR
HILO HALLIE
COMPANY

Note: The two graphs on the left present bases of activity (yards and production) unique to the specific costs being graphed (materials and depreciation, respectively). Once a relevant range of activity is chosen, total variable cost will change at the same rate for all changes in activity and total fixed cost will not change, regardless of changes in activity.

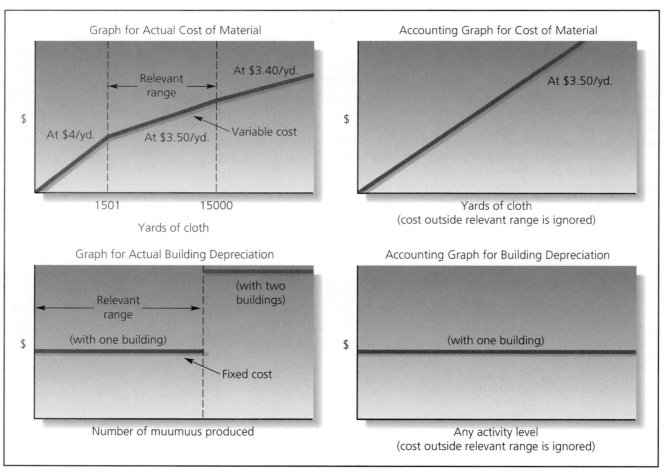

The curves on the material cost graph reflect pricing policies by material suppliers. If Hilo Hallie's purchasing agent buys cloth in less than 1,500-yard lots, the price per yard is $4. If cloth is purchased in lots between 1,501 and 15,000 yards, the price is $3.50 per yard. Quantities over 15,000 yards may be purchased for $3.40 per yard. Because the company always buys in quantities of 6,000 to 15,000 yards, this is the relevant range of activity for material purchases. The cloth cost is variable because total cost will vary in direct proportion to the quantity purchased within the relevant range. If Hilo Hallie Company buys 8,000 yards, it will pay $28,000 for its purchases; if it buys 12,000 yards, the cost will be $42,000. In each instance, because both volumes were within the relevant range, the cost remains constant at $3.50 per yard and exemplifies a variable cost that is truly linear over the relevant range.

A decision about the relevant range must also be made for fixed costs. The fixed cost shown in Exhibit 2–2 is for building depreciation. Hilo Hallie management has determined that one building, depreciated at $1,500 per month, can house enough equipment to produce between 1 and 15,000 muumuus per month. However, when production exceeds 15,000 muumuus, additional facilities will be required. If another similar building is acquired, there will be an additional $1,500 of building depreciation per month. Since the company always produces between 2,000 and 5,000 muumuus per month, the fixed cost for building depreciation is $1,500 per month.

In some businesses and for some items, variable and fixed costs may be "traded" for one another depending upon managerial decisions. An example is given in the News Note on page 36, in which company management determined it was less expensive to incur the fixed costs of machinery depreciation than the variable costs of postage.

Other costs exist that are not strictly variable or fixed. For example, a **mixed cost** has both a variable and a fixed component. It does not fluctuate in direct proportion with changes in activity, nor does it remain constant with changes in activity. An example of a mixed cost is electricity that is computed as a flat charge (the fixed component) for basic service plus a stated rate for each kilowatt hour (kwh) of electricity used (the variable component). Exhibit 2–3 shows a graph for the Hilo Hallie Company's electricity charge from Honolulu Power & Light, which consists of a flat rate of $100 per month plus $.018 per kwh. If Hilo Hallie Company uses 50,000 kwhs of electricity in a month, its total electricity bill is $1,000 [$100 + ($.018 × 50,000)]. If 60,000 kwhs are used, the electricity bill is $1,180.

mixed cost

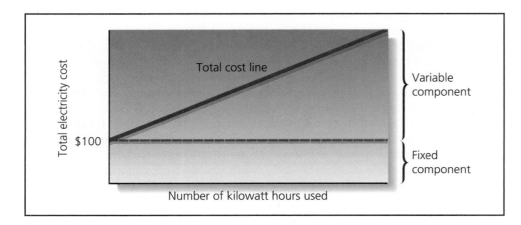

EXHIBIT 2–3

GRAPH OF A MIXED COST

Some companies, such as Kodak, National Car Rental Systems, and Cummins Engine, hire other firms such as IBM, Andersen Consulting, AT&T, and KPMG Peat Marwick to do their data processing. This process of "outsourcing" can create another type of mixed cost. In such cases, there is a trade-off of costs. Oftentimes, substantial fixed costs are eliminated and are replaced by a mixed cost, as indicated in the next News Note. Whether a company exchanges variable for fixed or fixed for mixed costs, shifting costs from one type of cost behavior to another changes the basic cost structure of the company and can have a significant impact on profits.

Another type of cost shifts upward or downward when activity changes by a certain interval or "step." These step costs can be variable or fixed. Step variable costs have small steps, and step fixed costs have large steps. For example, a water bill computed as $.002 per gallon for 1 to 1,000 gallons, $.003 per gallon for 1,001 to 2,000 gallons, $.005 per gallon for 2,001 to 3,000 gallons, and so on, is an example of a step variable cost. Telephone operator salaries, where one operator is paid $2,500 per month and is needed for every 150 calls received per day by the company, is an example of a step fixed cost.

Managers who understand the types of behavior exhibited by costs can better estimate total costs at various levels of activity. Although all costs do not strictly conform to the previous categories, the categories represent the types of cost behavior typically encountered in business. Management accountants generally separate mixed costs into their variable and fixed components so that behavior of these costs is more readily apparent.[3] This separation allows managers to focus on the two basic types of costs: variable and fixed. When step variable or step fixed costs exist, accountants must choose a specific relevant range of activity that will allow step variable costs to be treated as variable and step fixed costs to be treated as fixed.

By separating mixed costs and by specifying a relevant range for step costs, *accountants are treating their perception of the cost behavior that occurs in the relevant range as fact.* A variable cost is assumed to be perfectly linear and equal to the average variable unit cost within the relevant range, while a fixed cost is assumed to be constant in total within the relevant range. These treatments of variable and fixed costs can be justified for two reasons. First, the conditions that are assumed by accountants approximate reality and, if the company operates only within the relevant range of

---

[3]Methods for analyzing mixed costs are discussed in chapter 3.

NEWS NOTE

Let Someone Else Do It!

Computers typically gobble 3% to 5% of an industrial company's operating budget, and often more at service companies. For companies that lay out hundreds of millions of dollars each year for data processing, outsourcing has powerful appeal.

Generally, the [company providing the service] buys a customer's computer hardware and hires all or most of the employees who have been running it. For example, EDS paid Enron some $6 million for its computers, software, and data-transmission network. The Dallas computer services giant also hired some 550 Enron employees—mostly computer operators and programmers—at comparable wages and benefits.

None of the companies FORTUNE spoke with would reveal details of their contracts, but normally an outsourcer charges a fixed annual amount, plus additional fees based on processing volume. Says John McGeachie, an information management consultant for Arthur D. Little: "In an uncertain world, people want to be able to control their costs. That's very hard to do if you own lots of mainframes. Outsourcing lets you pay each time you process a piece of data."

The customer can also save on taxes: While hardware must be depreciated over three to five years, outsourcing fees are deductible as a current business expense. Enron expects to save $200 million in this decade—20% to 24% of total computing costs.

SOURCE: David Kirkpatrick, "Why Not Farm Out Your Computing?" *FORTUNE* (September 23, 1991), pp. 103–4. © 1991 The Time Inc. Magazine Company. All rights reserved.

---

activity, the cost behaviors selected are the appropriate ones. Second, selection of a constant variable cost per unit and a constant fixed cost in total provides a convenient, stable measurement for use in planning and decision making.

To make these generalizations about variable and fixed costs, accountants need to find a valid predictor for cost changes. A **predictor** is an activity measure that, when changed, is accompanied by consistent, observable changes in a cost item. However, simply because the two items change together does not necessarily prove that the predictor causes the change in the other item. For instance, assume that every time your professor wears blue, you have a quiz. If this is consistent, observable behavior, you may use the color of clothing to predict quizzes—but clothes color does not cause quizzes!   **predictor**

In contrast to predictors, **cost drivers** are measures of activity that are believed to have a direct cause-effect relationship to a cost. For example, production volume has a direct effect on the total cost of raw material used and can be said to "drive" that cost. Thus, production volume can be used as a valid predictor of that cost. The following News Note illustrates the idea of a cost driver; IBM determined that the method of laser mirror construction, rather than production quantity, caused testing costs. Changing the way the mirrors were constructed dramatically changed the cost associated with the product. Thus, knowing cost drivers is extremely important information.   **cost drivers**

In most situations, the cause-effect relationship is less clear, since costs are commonly caused by multiple factors. For example, quality control costs are affected by a variety of factors such as production volume, quality of materials used, skill level

NEWS NOTE

Change the Process—Change the Cost

International Business Machines Corp. said it developed a low-cost way to make tiny lasers, a technology now dominated by Japanese electronics companies.

[The new process] allows IBM to test the lasers in batches of as many as 20,000 units; testing is a major expense in laser-making. IBM estimated that its method will be 50% cheaper than current processes, and said it will also be faster and more efficient.

IBM said it used a chip-making process to etch small trenches into 2-inch-diameter wafers of laser material. Then it covered the trenches with a reflective material that turned them into tiny mirrors. After each wafer was tested, it was cut into as many as 20,000 separate lasers.

By contrast, current laser-making methods form mirrors by breaking the wafer into tiny pieces; the broken edges then act as reflecting surfaces. Since the lasers aren't finished until their mirrors are made, devices must then be tested one at a time.

Daniel Wilt, a technical supervisor at AT&T's Bell Laboratories . . . estimated that IBM's method, if done well, could cut the cost of each semiconductor laser from $10 to $1.

SOURCE: Laurence Hooper, "IBM Finds Way to Reduce Costs of Small Lasers," *Wall Street Journal* (January 31, 1991), p. B5. Reprinted by permission of *The Wall Street Journal,* © 1991 Dow Jones & Company, Inc. All rights reserved worldwide.

of workers, and level of automation. While it may be difficult to determine which factor actually caused a specific change in quality control cost, any of these factors could be chosen to predict that cost if confidence exists about the factor's relationship with cost changes. To be used as a predictor, the predictor and the cost need only change together in a foreseeable manner.

In a florist shop, one labor cost driver is the type of arrangement to be made. Making bouquets will require more labor time and skill than will putting cut flowers into a vase.

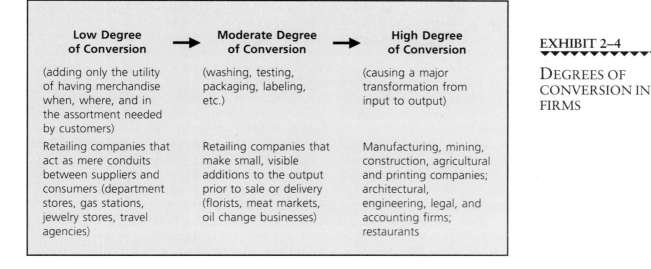

Low Degree of Conversion	→	Moderate Degree of Conversion	→	High Degree of Conversion
(adding only the utility of having merchandise when, where, and in the assortment needed by customers)		(washing, testing, packaging, labeling, etc.)		(causing a major transformation from input to output)
Retailing companies that act as mere conduits between suppliers and consumers (department stores, gas stations, jewelry stores, travel agencies)		Retailing companies that make small, visible additions to the output prior to sale or delivery (florists, meat markets, oil change businesses)		Manufacturing, mining, construction, agricultural and printing companies; architectural, engineering, legal, and accounting firms; restaurants

EXHIBIT 2–4
▼▼▼▼▼▼▼▼▼▼▼▼

DEGREES OF CONVERSION IN FIRMS

PRODUCT COSTS AND PERIOD COSTS

In addition to a designation as to cost behavior, costs are also classified as either product or period costs. Costs associated with making or acquiring inventory are **product** (or inventoriable) **costs,** while all other costs are period costs. In general, product costs are incurred in the production or conversion area, and period costs are incurred in nonproduction or nonconversion areas.[4]

product costs

The Conversion Process

To some extent, all organizations convert inputs into outputs. Inputs typically consist of materials, labor, and overhead. The outputs of a conversion process include both products and services. Exhibit 2–4 compares the conversion activities of different types of organizations. Note that many service companies engage in a high degree of conversion. Firms of professionals (such as accountants, architects, attorneys, engineers, and surveyors) convert labor and other resource inputs (materials and overhead) into completed jobs (audit reports, building plans, contracts, blueprints, and property survey reports).

Firms that engage in only a low-to-moderate degree of conversion can conveniently expense insignificant costs of labor and overhead related to conversion. The clerical cost saved by expensing outweighs the value of any slightly improved information that might result from assigning such costs to products or services. For example, when employees in a grocery store cut open shipping containers and stock individual packages on shelves, a labor cost for conversion has been incurred. Grocery stores, however, do not try to attach the stockpeople's wages to inventory; such labor costs are treated as period costs and are expensed as they are incurred.

---

[4]Although less common, it is possible for a cost to be physically incurred outside the production area but still be in direct support of production and, therefore, considered a product cost. An example of this situation is the salary of a product cost analyst who is based at company headquarters.

In contrast, in high-conversion firms, the informational benefits gained from assigning the labor and overhead costs to the output produced significantly exceed the clerical costs of maintaining the necessary accounting system. No one would presume to expense the labor costs incurred for workers constructing a bridge; these costs would be treated as product costs and inventoried as part of the cost of the construction job until the bridge was completed for the client.

Exhibit 2–5 compares the basic input/output relationships of a merchandising (retail) company and those of a manufacturing/service company.[5] This exhibit illustrates that the primary difference between these companies is the absence or presence of the area labeled "the production center." This center involves the conversion of physical inputs to final products. Input factors flow into the production center and are transformed to completed goods or services. If the output is a product, it can be warehoused or displayed (or both) after it is completed until it is sold to a customer. Service outputs are simply provided to the client commissioning the work.

Technically, conversion does occur in merchandising businesses, but it is not as significant in terms of time, effort, or cost as it is in manufacturing or service companies. Merchandising conversion includes tagging merchandise with sales tickets and, as is done at Neiman Marcus, adding store-name labels to goods. The costs of such activities should conceptually be treated as additional costs of merchandise, and the department adding these costs could be viewed as a "mini" production center. Most often, however, merchandising companies have no designated production center.

Product Costs

Because most retailers do not specify "production centers" and because goods are purchased in finished or almost finished condition, the product costs associated with inventory are easy to determine. Basically the only product cost is the purchase cost (including any associated freight charges) of the unsold merchandise that has been purchased for resale. Such firms ordinarily have only a single inventory account called Merchandise Inventory, which represents the unexpired product cost (or asset). As the merchandise is sold, the product cost is transferred to Cost of Goods Sold, which represents an expired product cost (or expense).

On the other hand, manufacturers and service companies engage in many activities that involve the physical change of inputs into finished products and services. The costs of all of these activities must be gathered and assigned to the outputs as product costs. This assignment allows the determination of inventory cost and cost of goods sold or services rendered.

Manufacturers must account for raw materials and supplies, work in process for partially completed goods, and finished goods inventory if control is to be maintained over the production process. Each type of inventory requires its own account. The costs are considered unexpired until the goods are sold. While service firms have an inventory account for the supplies used in the conversion process and may have a Work in Process account, these firms do not normally have a Finished Goods account

---

[5]For convenience, the term *manufacturer* refers to a company engaged in a high degree of conversion of raw material input into other tangible output. Manufacturers typically convert inputs to outputs through the use of people and machines to produce large quantities of output that can be physically inspected. The term *service company* refers to an individual or firm engaged in a high or moderate degree of conversion using few raw material inputs and, often, a significant amount of effort (either human or machine). Service output may be tangible (an audit report) or intangible (health care) and normally cannot be inspected prior to its use. Service firms may be profit-making businesses or not-for-profit organizations.

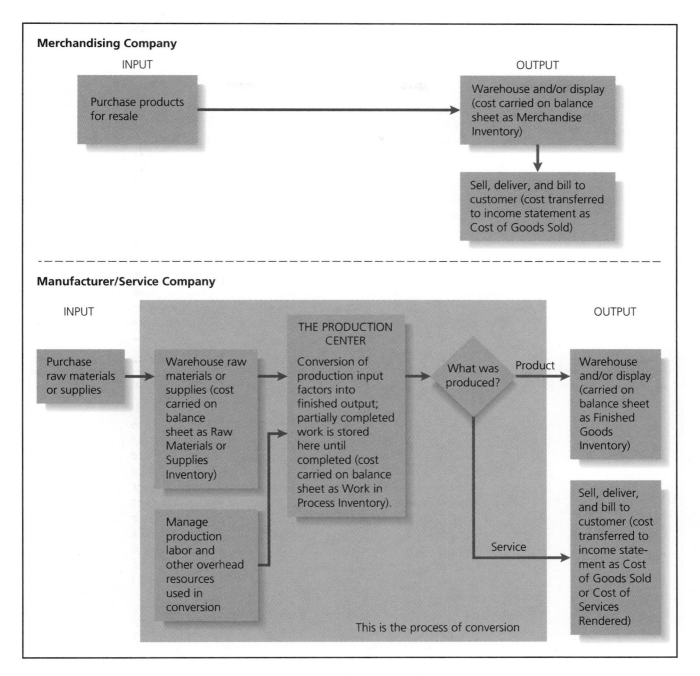

Merchandising Company

INPUT

Purchase products for resale

OUTPUT

Warehouse and/or display (cost carried on balance sheet as Merchandise Inventory)

Sell, deliver, and bill to customer (cost transferred to income statement as Cost of Goods Sold)

Manufacturer/Service Company

INPUT

Purchase raw materials or supplies

Warehouse raw materials or supplies (cost carried on balance sheet as Raw Materials or Supplies Inventory)

Manage production labor and other overhead resources used in conversion

THE PRODUCTION CENTER

Conversion of production input factors into finished output; partially completed work is stored here until completed (cost carried on balance sheet as Work in Process Inventory).

What was produced?

Product

Service

OUTPUT

Warehouse and/or display (carried on balance sheet as Finished Goods Inventory)

Sell, deliver, and bill to customer (cost transferred to income statement as Cost of Goods Sold or Cost of Services Rendered)

This is the process of conversion

because services cannot be warehoused. When the services are accepted by the client, the product costs are then expensed on the income statement in a Cost of Services Rendered account.

Period Costs

Costs that are associated with periods of time rather than being related to making or acquiring a product or performing a service are **period costs.** These costs are related

EXHIBIT 2–5
▼▼▼▼▼▼▼▼▼▼▼

BUSINESS INPUT/ OUTPUT RELATIONSHIPS

period costs

to business operations other than production, such as in the selling, general, and administrative areas. Period costs that have been incurred and have future benefit are unexpired and are classified as assets. Period costs (such as secretaries' salaries and current period advertising) having no determinable future benefit are expensed as incurred. Prepaid insurance on an administration building represents an unexpired period cost; as the premium period passes, the insurance becomes an expired period cost (insurance expense).

Note that if insurance cost is incurred for a manufacturing building at General Foods, for example, that cost is considered overhead and a type of product cost. On the other hand, when insurance costs are incurred at General Foods' administrative offices, they are period costs. Thus, the distinction between product and period cost is primarily made on the basis of *where* the cost was incurred rather than the *type* of cost incurred. Exhibit 2–6 provides some additional examples of product and period costs.

Mention must be made of one specific type of period cost—that associated with distribution. A **distribution cost** is any cost incurred to market a product or service. Distribution costs include all amounts spent on advertising, warehousing, and delivering or shipping products to customers. While distribution costs must be expensed as incurred for financial accounting purposes, managers must remember that these costs are related directly to products and services. Distribution costs will change rel-

distribution costs

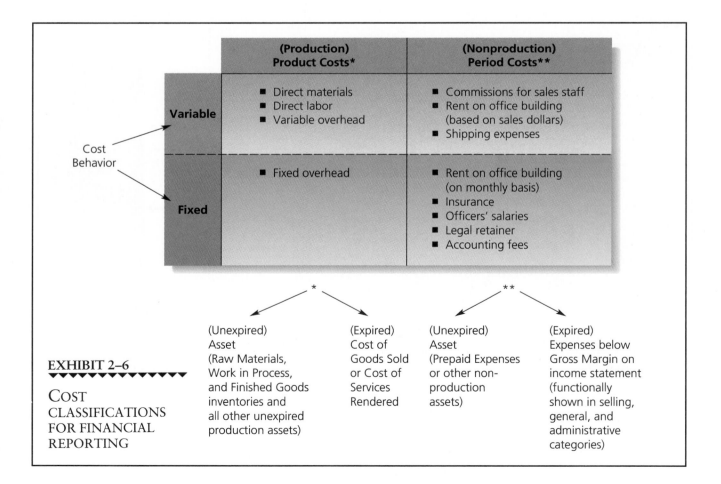

EXHIBIT 2–6
▼▼▼▼▼▼▼▼▼▼▼

COST CLASSIFICATIONS FOR FINANCIAL REPORTING

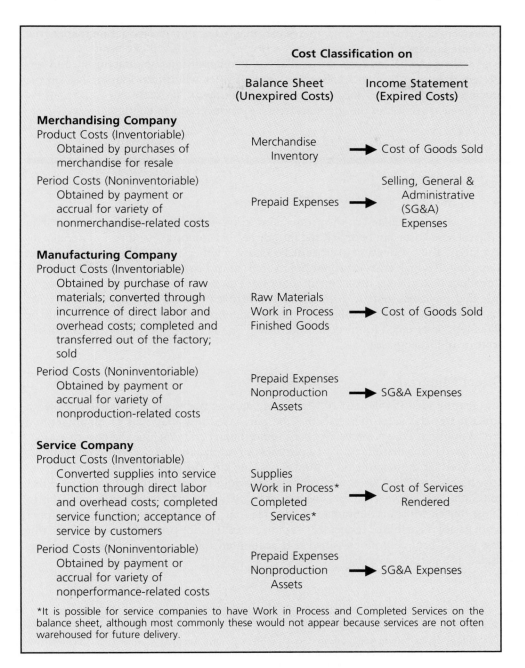

EXHIBIT 2–7

COMPARISON OF
PRODUCT AND
PERIOD COSTS

Cost Classification on

	Balance Sheet (Unexpired Costs)	Income Statement (Expired Costs)
Merchandising Company		
Product Costs (Inventoriable) Obtained by purchases of merchandise for resale	Merchandise Inventory	→ Cost of Goods Sold
Period Costs (Noninventoriable) Obtained by payment or accrual for variety of nonmerchandise-related costs	Prepaid Expenses →	Selling, General & Administrative (SG&A) Expenses
Manufacturing Company		
Product Costs (Inventoriable) Obtained by purchase of raw materials; converted through incurrence of direct labor and overhead costs; completed and transferred out of the factory; sold	Raw Materials Work in Process Finished Goods	→ Cost of Goods Sold
Period Costs (Noninventoriable) Obtained by payment or accrual for variety of nonproduction-related costs	Prepaid Expenses Nonproduction Assets	→ SG&A Expenses
Service Company		
Product Costs (Inventoriable) Converted supplies into service function through direct labor and overhead costs; completed service function; acceptance of service by customers	Supplies Work in Process* Completed Services*	→ Cost of Services Rendered
Period Costs (Noninventoriable) Obtained by payment or accrual for variety of nonperformance-related costs	Prepaid Expenses Nonproduction Assets	→ SG&A Expenses

*It is possible for service companies to have Work in Process and Completed Services on the balance sheet, although most commonly these would not appear because services are not often warehoused for future delivery.

ative to changes in product/service volume. Therefore, when making decisions, managers cannot take an "out-of-sight, out-of-mind" attitude about these costs simply because they have been expensed for financial accounting purposes. A study several years ago found that storage and warehousing costs were "20–30% of a company's typical distribution or logistics costs and that logistics overall may represent as much as 20% of the U.S. Gross National Product." [6] Selling prices must be set high enough

[6]Gene R. Tyndall and John R. Busher, "Warehouse Accounting and Control: Guidelines for Distribution and Financial Managers," *Management Accounting* (September 1985), p. 68.

to recover such costs and, thus, these costs may have a major impact on managerial decision making.[7]

Product and period costs are similar for merchandising, manufacturing, and service companies, although some of the account titles will differ. Exhibit 2–7 on the previous page compares these costs and account titles.

The next section of the chapter discusses product costs in depth.

COMPONENTS OF PRODUCT COST

Product costs are related to the products or services that generate the revenues of an entity. These costs can be separated into three cost components: direct materials, direct labor, and production overhead. To know whether a cost is direct, a **cost object** (anything to which costs attach or are related) must be specified. A cost object can be a product or service, a department, a division, or a territory. Once the cost object is specified, any costs that are distinctly traceable to it are called **direct costs.** Those costs that cannot be traced are called **indirect** (or common) **costs.** These costs can only be **allocated,** or assigned to the cost object using one or more appropriate predictors or arbitrarily chosen bases.[8]

cost object

direct costs
indirect costs
allocated

Direct Materials

Any readily identifiable part of a product, such as the wood in a table, is called a **direct material.** Direct materials may be purchased raw materials or manufactured subassemblies.[9] Direct materials cost should theoretically include the cost of all materials used in the manufacture of a product or performance of a service. For example, when Monogram manufactures model airplane kits, the cost of the plastic, glue, decals, paint, propeller, box, and cellophane would theoretically make up the direct materials cost. However, direct costs must be *distinctly and conveniently traceable* to a cost object. Most accountants would agree that the cost of the cellophane wrapper is not easily traceable or monetarily significant to the kit's production cost. Thus, this cost would probably be classified and accounted for as indirect materials and included as a part of overhead.

direct material

---

[7]The uniform capitalization rules (unicap rules) of the Tax Reform Act of 1986 caused many manufacturers, wholesalers, and retailers to expand the types and amounts of nonproduction-area costs that are treated as product costs for tax purposes. The unicap rules require that distribution costs for warehousing be considered part of product cost, but not distribution costs for marketing and customer delivery. The rationale for such treatment is that such costs are incident to production or acquisition.

[8]Different cost objects may be designated for different decisions. As the cost object changes, the direct and indirect costs may also change. For instance, if a production division is specified as the cost object, the division manager's salary is direct. If, instead, the cost object is a sales territory and the production division operates in more than one territory, the division manager's salary is indirect.

[9]Outside processing cost may also be considered a direct material cost. For example, a furniture manufacturer may want a special plastic laminate on tables. Rather than buying the necessary equipment, the manufacturer may send the tables to another company that specializes in this process. The amount paid for this process may be considered a direct material cost by the manufacturer.

Similarly, in a service business, the cost of some direct materials may be insignificant or may not be easily traceable to a designated cost object. For instance, each advertising campaign in a marketing firm would require the separate accumulation of costs to know the full cost of developing the campaign. In designing ads, various colored pens or pencils would be used. The cost of the pens and pencils would be relatively insignificant to trace and would be treated as overhead.

The distinction between direct and indirect costs is not as clear-cut as it may seem. Some costs that may be distinctly traceable would not, from an accounting standpoint, be conveniently or practically traceable. Such costs are treated and classified as indirect costs. At Levi Strauss, if the product (jeans) is considered the cost object, a direct materials cost is the cost of the denim used in production. The cost, however, of thread (a very important production material) *could* be traced to jeans production, but probably would not be because of the insignificance of the amount and the cost of attempting to do so. Thread cost is, therefore, considered an indirect cost of production.

Direct Labor

Direct labor refers to the time spent by individuals who work specifically on manufacturing a product or performing a service. The seamstresses at Haggar Apparel and the nurse at Aurora Hospital represent direct labor workers.

direct labor

Direct labor cost consists of wages or salaries paid to employees who work on a product or perform a service, if that labor transforms raw materials or supplies into finished goods or completed services. Such wages and salaries must also be conveniently traceable to the product or service. Another perspective of direct labor is that it directly adds value to the final product or service. Because much production activity

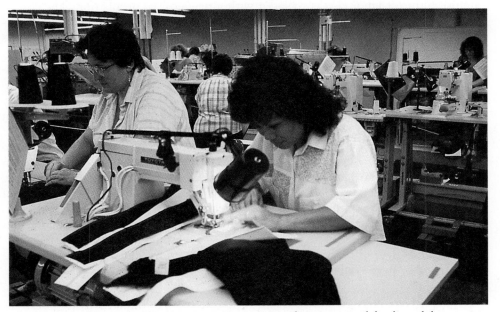

The wages paid to workers sewing garment pieces together are part of the direct labor cost. Direct labor is a product cost along with direct materials and overhead.

NEWS NOTE

Consider the Facts

The U.S. harbors a long tradition of thinking that costs, particularly labor costs, are all that matter. Recently Robert Hayes, a manufacturing expert at the Harvard business school, got an SOS from the head of a company making integrated circuits. The company had poured $250 million into a plant bejeweled with statistical process controls, computer-integrated manufacturing, the works. Though labor is less than 5% of the product's cost, labor was the problem: The workers, a quarter of them illiterate, couldn't handle the new machines.

"Why did you hire them?" Hayes asked. Because, the executive explained, he needed several hundred workers and could not find enough literate ones in the new location. "Then why put the plant there?" Hayes asked. Came the reply: "Because it has one of the cheapest labor costs in the country."

SOURCE: Thomas A. Stewart, "Lessons From U.S. Business Blunders," *FORTUNE* (April 23, 1990), pp. 128–29. © 1990 The Time Inc. Magazine Company. All rights reserved.

was once performed by individuals, direct labor once represented a primary production cost. Now, in the more highly automated production environments, "[i]t is not uncommon to find that direct labor accounts for only 8%–12% of total cost at many manufacturers. This trend is even more pronounced when one considers current forecasts relating to the factory of the future." [10] Eventually, managers may find that almost all direct labor cost is replaced with a new cost of production—the cost of robots and other fully automated machinery that is used in manufacturing operations. Thus, while labor is an essential element of production, the News Note above indicates that managers should not overstate the importance of labor cost.

Direct labor cost should include basic compensation, production efficiency bonuses, and the employer's share of social security taxes. In addition, when a company's operations are relatively stable, direct labor cost should include all employer-paid insurance costs, holiday and vacation pay, and pension and other retirement benefits. [11]

As with some materials, some labor costs that should theoretically be considered direct are treated as indirect. Two reasons exist for this treatment: (1) inefficiency in tracing the particular labor costs specifically or (2) erroneous information resulting from handling such costs in the "theoretically" correct manner. The treatment of some employee fringe benefits as indirect is related to the concept of cost inefficiencies. While fringe benefit costs should be treated as direct labor cost, many companies do not have stable work forces that would allow a reasonable estimate of fringe benefit cost to be developed, or, alternatively, the time, effort, and cost such an assignment could require might not be worth the additional accuracy it would provide.

---

[10]James A. Brimson, "How Advanced Manufacturing Technologies Are Reshaping Cost Management," *Management Accounting* (March 1986), p. 27.
[11]Institute of Management Accountants (formerly National Association of Accountants), *Statements on Management Accounting: Definition and Measurement of Direct Labor Cost* (Montvale, N.J.: June 13, 1985), p. 4.

NEWS NOTE

Employee Health-Care Costs Are Skyrocketing

Health-care costs have risen so fast in the last two years that many American corporations now spend an amount equal to one-fourth of their net earnings to provide medical coverage to their employees. . . . [A] survey by Foster Higgins & Co., a benefits consulting firm, shows that the average company spent 21.6 percent more last year to provide doctor and hospital care to their employees than the year before. Over the past two years, the cost to employers has risen 46.3 percent.

The annual survey of 1,955 employers is one of the largest of its kind, covering primarily large and medium-sized corporations. On average, companies spent $3,161 per employee to cover their medical costs [in 1990], up from $2,600 per employee in 1989.

SOURCE: Frank Swoboda, "Health-care Costs Strangling Business," [*New Orleans*] *Times Picayune* (January 29, 1991), p. D3.

However, as indicated in the News Note above, when fringe benefit costs are as large as the ones discussed, tracing them to direct labor may provide more useful management information.

Treating certain labor costs as direct can provide improper information about product or service costs. Assume that Simoneaux Company employs thirty workers to refinish furniture. Each employee earns $8 per hour. If the employees work overtime, they receive time-and-a-half pay, or $12 per hour. Furniture is refinished based on the color of stain, expected time to complete, and level of job difficulty. One week prior to a holiday, the employees worked a total of 1,430 hours, or 230 hours of overtime to complete all refinishing jobs at the warehouse. If the overtime premium of $4 per hour were assigned to the items refinished specifically during the overtime hours, these items would appear to have a labor cost 50 percent greater than items refinished during regular working hours. Since scheduling is random, the items that *happened* to be refinished during overtime hours should not be forced to bear the overtime charges. Therefore, amounts incurred for costs such as overtime or shift premiums are usually considered overhead rather than direct labor cost, and are indirectly allocated to all units. Thus, of the total employee labor payroll of $12,360, only $11,440 (1,430 hours × $8 per hour) would be classified as direct labor cost. The remaining $920 (230 hours × $4 per hour) would be considered overhead.

There are occasions, however, when allocating costs such as overtime to all units is not appropriate. If a customer requests a job to be scheduled during overtime hours or is in a rush and requests overtime to be worked, overtime or shift premiums should be considered direct labor and be attached to the job that created the costs.

Overhead

Overhead costs are essential to the conversion process but simply cannot be traced directly to output. **Overhead** is any factory or production cost that is indirect to man-   **overhead** ufacturing a product or providing a service and, accordingly, does not include direct materials and direct labor.[12] It does include indirect materials and indirect labor as well as any and all other costs incurred in the production area. "The great part of most companies' costs (other than those for purchased materials) typically occur in overhead categories. Even in manufacturing, more than two-thirds of all nonmaterial costs tend to be indirect or overhead expenses." [13]

While direct materials and direct labor are always variable costs, overhead costs may be either variable or fixed. Variable overhead includes the cost of indirect materials and of indirect labor paid on an hourly basis, such as wages for forklift operators, material handlers, and others who support the production, assembly, and/or service process. Also included in variable overhead is the cost of oil and grease used for machine maintenance, paper towels used in the factory rest rooms, and the variable portion of utility charges (or any other mixed cost) in the conversion area. Depreciation calculated using the units of production method is a variable overhead cost. This type of depreciation method reflects declines in machine utility as a function of usage rather than time passage and is very appropriate in an automated plant.

Fixed overhead comprises costs such as depreciation (other than units-of-production depreciation) on production/service-providing assets, license fees, and insurance and property taxes. Fixed indirect labor cost includes salaries for management personnel such as supervisors, shift superintendents, and the production/service manager. The fixed portion of mixed costs (such as maintenance and utilities) incurred in the conversion area is also part of fixed overhead.

A final category of overhead cost is that of quality costs. These costs are significant in amount, often totaling 20 to 25 percent of sales.[14] The categories of quality costs are prevention, appraisal, and failure costs. **Prevention costs** are those that are incurred to improve quality by preventing defects from occurring. Amounts spent on training programs, researching customer needs, and improved production equipment are considered prevention costs. Expenditures made for prevention will minimize the costs that will be incurred for appraisal and failure. **Appraisal costs** are incurred for monitoring or inspection; these costs compensate for mistakes not eliminated through prevention. **Failure costs** may be internal (such as scrap and rework) or external (such as product returns due to quality problems, warranty costs, and complaint department costs).

As indicated in the following News Note, some quality costs are variable, some are step fixed, and some are fixed. But, regardless of the type of cost behavior, companies are learning that spending money on prevention is easier than having to pay to correct problems later. Lifeline Systems, Inc. of Watertown, Massachusetts is one company that firmly believes in quality. After installing a total quality program, profits increased by 600 percent on a 30 percent increase in revenues.

The sum of direct materials, direct labor, variable overhead, and fixed overhead costs makes up total product cost.[15] Product costs can also be classified as either prime or conversion costs.

prevention costs

appraisal costs

failure costs

---

[12]Another term used for overhead is *burden*. The authors believe that this term is unacceptable, as it connotes costs that are extra, unnecessary, or oppressive.

[13]James Brian Quinn et al., "Beyond Products: Services-based Strategy," *Harvard Business Review* (March–April 1990), p. 65. Copyright © by the President and Fellows of Harvard College; all rights reserved.

[14]"Measuring the Cost of Quality Takes Creativity," *Manufacturing Issues* (Grant Thornton: Spring 1991), p. 1.

[15]This definition of product cost is the traditionally accepted one that is also referred to as absorption costing. Another product costing method, called variable costing, excludes the fixed overhead component. Absorption and variable costing are compared in depth in chapter 8.

NEWS NOTE

Quality Cost Behavior

If the relationship of quality cost information to the organization's level of quality control is to be identified and understood, the behavior of the cost category must be analyzed. This analysis requires that the reporting mechanism segregates the data according to the following dimensions:

- Variable costs: Costs that vary in proportion to the quantity of defective output (e.g., scrap, rework, customer complaints).
- Semi-fixed costs: Costs that remain stable over some relevant range, then "step up" to a higher level beyond a critical value of defective output (e.g., inspection, testing, audits).
- Fixed costs: Costs that remain the same regardless of the quantity of defective output produced (e.g., planning, process control, and training).

Consider scrap and rework costs, for example. These costs approach zero if the quantity of defective output is also nearly zero. However, scrap and rework costs would be extremely high if the number of defective parts produced were high. Training expenditures, on the other hand, would not vary regardless of the quantity of defective output produced in a given time period.

SOURCE: Lawrence A. Poneman, "Accounting for Quality Costs," (Fall 1990), p. 46. Reprinted with permission from *The Journal of Cost Management for the Manufacturing Industry*. Warren, Gorham & Lamont, a division of Research Institute of America, 210 South Street, Boston, MA 02111. All rights reserved.

Doing quality inspections on submersible pool lights creates an appraisal cost for the manufacturer. However, this cost will be substantially less than an external failure cost faced by the company in the event of a defective light.

Prime and Conversion Costs

The total cost of direct materials and direct labor is referred to as **prime cost** because these costs are most convincingly associated with and traceable to a specific product. According to the IMA, **conversion cost** is "the sum of direct labor . . . and factory overhead which is directly or indirectly necessary for transforming raw materials and purchased parts into a salable finished product."[16] Since direct labor is included as part of both prime cost and conversion cost, prime cost plus conversion cost does not sum to product cost, because direct labor would be double-counted.

Exhibit 2–8 shows the typical components of product cost for a manufacturing company. The following News Note about Allen-Bradley, however, indicates that some companies have alternative concepts about product cost.

prime cost

conversion cost

---

[16]Institute of Management Accountants (formerly National Association of Accountants), *Statements on Management Accounting: Management Accounting Terminology* (Montvale, N.J.: June 1, 1983), p. 24.

NEWS NOTE

Allen-Bradley's Costing Methods Are Radically Different

One of the most talked about factories of the future is the Allen-Bradley "factory within a factory" in Milwaukee. Based on volume estimates and market prices, this business generates approximately $40 million a year in sales. It is capable of taking an order on one day, producing upwards of 500 different parts the following day, and shipping all of the order on the following day. There is some plastic and steel raw material inventory but virtually no work-in-process or finished goods inventory. At the end of the day, the flow line is empty and orders have been shipped. Material is the prime component of product cost. There are some variable expenses but a major portion of the costs, including the few factory technicians and the physical plant, are fixed. Allen-Bradley chose to expense labor and overhead as period costs. For one thing, there is virtually no labor. For another, there is no inventory to attach costs to.

SOURCE: Robert A. Howell and Stephen R. Soucy, "Allen-Bradley: Today's Factory of the Future," *Management Accounting* (August 1987), p. 45. Published by Institute of Management Accountants, Montvale, N.J.

EXHIBIT 2–8
▼▼▼▼▼▼▼▼▼▼▼▼

COMPONENTS OF PRODUCT COST

PRIME COST   Direct Materials

CONVERSION COST   Direct Labor

Factory Overhead
    Variable Overhead Components
        Indirect Materials
        Indirect Labor—Hourly Wages
        Variable portion of mixed costs
        Other variable factory costs
    Fixed Overhead Components
        Rent
        Depreciation
        Indirect Labor—Salaried Employees
        Licenses
        Taxes
        Insurance
        Fixed portion of mixed costs
        Other fixed factory costs

ACCUMULATION OF PRODUCT COSTS

Product costs can be accumulated using either a perpetual or a periodic inventory system. In a perpetual inventory system, all product costs flow through Work in Process to Finished Goods and, ultimately, to Cost of Goods Sold. The perpetual system continuously provides current information for financial statement preparation and for inventory and cost control. Because the costs of maintaining a perpetual system have diminished significantly as computerized production, bar-coding, and information processing have become more pervasive, this text will assume that all companies discussed use this inventory method.

The Whitehead Corporation is used to illustrate the flow of product costs in a manufacturing organization. The May 1, 1993, inventory account balances for Whitehead were as follows: Raw Materials (all direct), $5,500; Work in Process, $17,500; and Finished Goods, $7,890. Whitehead uses separate variable and fixed accounts to record the incurrence of overhead. Actual overhead costs are transferred at the end of the month to the Work in Process Inventory account. The following transactions, keyed to the journal entries in Exhibit 2–9, represent Whitehead's activity for a month.

(1)	Raw Materials Inventory	49,000	
	Accounts Payable		49,000
	To record cost of direct materials purchased on account		
(2)	Work in Process Inventory	53,500	
	Raw Materials Inventory		53,500
	To record direct materials transferred to production		
(3)	Work in Process Inventory	117,500	
	Variable Overhead	48,000	
	Salaries and Wages Payable		165,500
	To accrue factory wages for direct and indirect labor		
(4)	Fixed Overhead	4,000	
	Salaries and Wages Payable		4,000
	To accrue production supervisor's salary		
(5)	Variable Overhead	7,000	
	Fixed Overhead	5,000	
	Utilities Payable		12,000
	To record mixed utility cost in its variable and fixed proportions		
(6)	Variable Overhead	1,300	
	Supplies Inventory		1,300
	To record indirect materials used		
			(continued)

EXHIBIT 2–9
▼▼▼▼▼▼▼▼▼▼

WHITEHEAD CORPORATION—MAY 1993 FLOW OF PRODUCT COSTS THROUGH ACCOUNTS

EXHIBIT 2–9 *continued*
▼▼▼▼▼▼▼▼▼▼▼▼▼▼

WHITEHEAD
CORPORATION—
MAY 1993 FLOW OF
PRODUCT COSTS
THROUGH
ACCOUNTS

(7) Fixed Overhead	2,500	
Cash		2,500
To record payments for factory property taxes for the period		
(8) Fixed Overhead	92,500	
Accumulated Depreciation—Equipment		92,500
To record depreciation on factory assets for the period		
(9) Fixed Overhead	1,000	
Prepaid Insurance		1,000
To record expiration of prepaid insurance on factory assets		
(10) Work in Process Inventory	161,300	
Variable Overhead		56,300
Fixed Overhead		105,000
To record the transfer of actual overhead costs to Work in Process Inventory		
(11) Finished Goods Inventory	324,875	
Work in Process Inventory		324,875
To record the transfer of work completed during the period		
(12) Accounts Receivable	446,750	
Sales		446,750
To record the selling price of goods sold on account during the period		
(13) Cost of Goods Sold	327,125	
Finished Goods Inventory		327,125
To record cost of goods sold for the period		

During May, Whitehead's purchasing agent bought $49,000 of direct materials on account (entry 1), and the warehouse manager transferred $53,500 of materials into the production area (entry 2). Production wages for the month totaled $165,500; direct labor accounted for $117,500 of that amount (entry 3). May salary for the production supervisor was $4,000 (entry 4). The total utility cost for May was $12,000; analyzing this cost indicated that $7,000 of this amount was variable and $5,000 was fixed (entry 5). Indirect materials costing $1,300 were removed from the Supplies Inventory and placed into the production process (entry 6). Whitehead also paid $2,500 for May's property taxes on the factory (entry 7), depreciated the factory assets $92,500 (entry 8), and recorded the expiration of $1,000 of prepaid insurance on the factory assets (entry 9). Entry 10 shows the transfer of actual overhead to Work in Process Inventory. During May, $324,875 of goods were completed and transferred to Finished Goods (entry 11). Sales on account of $446,750 were recorded during the month (entry 12); the goods that were sold had a total cost of $327,125 (entry 13).

COST OF GOODS MANUFACTURED AND SOLD

In merchandising businesses, cost of goods sold (CGS) is computed as beginning merchandise inventory plus net purchases minus ending merchandise inventory. Manufacturing businesses cannot use such a simplistic approach to calculate cost of goods sold. The production costs incurred during the period relate both to goods that were completed and to goods that are still in process. Therefore, a manufacturer prepares a schedule of cost of goods manufactured (CGM) as a preliminary step to the computation of CGS. The CGM and CGS schedules for the Whitehead Corporation are shown in Exhibit 2–10; these schedules use the information given in the previous section.

Whitehead Corporation
Schedule of Cost of Goods Manufactured
for Month Ended May 31, 1993

Beginning balance of Work in Process, 5/1/93			$ 17,500
Manufacturing costs for the period			
Raw materials (all direct)			
Beginning balance	$ 5,500		
Purchases of materials	49,000		
Raw materials available			
for use	$54,500		
Ending balance	1,000		
Total raw materials used		$ 53,500	
Direct labor		117,500	
Variable overhead			
Indirect labor	$48,000		
Utilities	7,000		
Supplies	1,300	56,300	
Fixed overhead			
Utilities	$ 5,000		
Supervisor's salary	4,000		
Factory property taxes	2,500		
Factory asset depreciation	92,500		
Factory insurance	1,000	105,000	
Total current period manufacturing costs			332,300
Total costs to account for			$349,800
Ending balance of Work in Process, 5/31/93			24,925
Cost of goods manufactured			$324,875

Whitehead Corporation
Schedule of Cost of Goods Sold for Month Ended May 31, 1993

Beginning balance of Finished Goods, 5/1/93	$ 7,890
Cost of goods manufactured	324,875
Cost of goods available for sale	$332,765
Ending balance of Finished Goods, 5/31/93	5,640
Cost of goods sold	$327,125

EXHIBIT 2–10
▼▼▼▼▼▼▼▼▼▼▼▼

COST OF GOODS MANUFACTURED AND COST OF GOODS SOLD SCHEDULES

The schedule of cost of goods manufactured starts with the beginning balance of work in process and details all product cost components (direct materials, direct labor, variable overhead, and fixed overhead). The cost of materials used in production during the period is equal to beginning balance of Raw Materials Inventory plus raw materials purchased minus the ending inventory of Raw Materials. Direct labor cost is then added to the cost of direct materials used. Since direct labor cannot be warehoused, all charges for direct labor during the period are part of Work in Process Inventory. Variable and fixed overhead costs are added to the costs of direct materials and direct labor to determine total current period manufacturing costs.

Beginning Work in Process Inventory is added to total current period manufacturing costs to obtain a subtotal amount that can be referred to as "total costs to account for." The value of ending Work in Process Inventory is calculated (through techniques discussed later in the text) and subtracted from the subtotal to provide the **cost of goods manufactured** (CGM) during the period. CGM represents the total production cost of the goods that were completed and transferred to Finished Goods during the period. This amount does not include the cost of work still in process at the end of the period. The schedule of cost of goods manufactured allows managers to see the relationships among the various production costs and to trace cost flows through the inventory accounts. It is usually prepared only as an internal schedule and is not provided to external parties.

cost of goods manufactured

Cost of goods manufactured is added to the beginning balance of Finished Goods to find the cost of goods available for sale during the period. The ending inventory of Finished Goods is calculated by multiplying a physical unit count times a unit cost. Under a perpetual inventory, the actual amount of ending Finished Goods Inventory can be compared to that which should be on hand, based on the Finished Goods account balance recorded at the end of the period. Any differences can be attributed to a loss factor.

When a manufacturer makes a sale, the cost of the goods that were sold is removed from the Finished Goods Inventory account as the goods themselves are removed from the warehouse.

SITE ANALYSIS

When the cost of one unit of production (a spy satellite) is $750 million or (a NASA satellite) $5 billion, it is important that those paying for it understand the elements that compose that cost. For a spy or space exploration vehicle, the direct materials costs would include all of the metal and equipment costs composing the readily identifiable components that are contained in the satellite. Direct labor cost would include the payroll for designers, engineers, and construction workers who physically worked on the satellite. Overhead costs would include all indirect materials, indirect labor, other production costs, and the cost of security protecting the construction site.

Numerous companies are typically involved in the production of satellites. While each company could calculate the CGM for its satellite components, all production costs incurred by all the companies would need to be totaled to determine the satellite's total cost of goods manufactured.

The government would also be interested in knowing what type of cost behavior was exhibited by the different costs. This interest would extend beyond the basic production cost to other related costs, such as those of the launch. For example, the Strategic Defense Initiative (SDI) Office began looking into building a laser to launch small satellites, those weighing less than twenty-five pounds. To determine the launch expense, the SDI estimated that a laser "could launch 100 [microspacecraft] into orbit a day at a cost of $200 per pound."[17] Thus, the SDI has recognized a variable cost of launching—for every additional pound of weight, there will be an additional $200 of cost. Knowledge of this cost behavior should indicate that lighter materials should be used, if possible and if the appropriate quality can be obtained.

According to an article in *FORTUNE,* "U.S. manufacturers are generally doing a better job keeping costs down than foreign competitors are."[18] But controlling costs requires an ability to recognize what kind of cost is being incurred and how changes in activity affect the total cost for each production or performance element, as well as understanding the relationships among costs. Managers must realize that the term *cost* means different things to different people and then take care to determine how cost is being defined.

CHAPTER SUMMARY

This chapter introduces many different cost terms used by managers and management accountants and presents the flow of costs in a manufacturing environment.

Within the relevant range, variable costs are constant per unit, but fluctuate in total with changes in activity levels. Fixed costs remain constant in total as activity levels change within the relevant range, meaning that fixed costs on a per-unit basis vary inversely with activity level changes. The relevant range is generally the normal operating range of the company. Mixed costs, such as maintenance, have both a variable and a fixed element.

---

[17]Bob Davis, "Will Space Program Find Itself Shrinking Or on the Rocks?" *Wall Street Journal* (February 27, 1990), p. A12.
[18]Alex Taylor III, "The U.S. Gets Back in Fighting Shape," *FORTUNE* (April 24, 1989), p. 48.

A predictor is an activity measure that, when changed, is accompanied by consistent, observable changes in a cost. A cost driver is an activity measure that has a direct causal effect on a cost.

The process of converting raw materials or supplies to finished goods is what distinguishes manufacturers and service companies from merchandising companies. This process requires the accumulation of all costs incurred in the production area as product costs.

Product (inventoriable) costs include direct materials and conversion costs (direct labor and overhead). These costs are unexpired until finished goods are sold. Period costs are those costs incurred outside the production or conversion area for selling, general, and administrative functions. These costs are expensed when they expire, which is often in the period in which they were incurred.

Direct costs are so defined based on their traceability to a specific cost object. While indirect costs cannot be explicitly traced to a cost object, allocation techniques can be used to assign such costs to a related object.

Cost of goods manufactured is the total cost of the goods that were completed and transferred to finished goods during the period. This computation is prepared for internal management information and is presented on a schedule that supports the cost of goods sold computation on the income statement.

APPENDIX

Income Statement Comparisons

The income statements of merchandising, manufacturing, and service businesses are basically the same except for differences in the cost of goods sold section. A merchandising company has only one inventory account and, thus, cost of goods sold reflects only changes within the merchandise inventory account. A manufacturing organization has three inventory accounts, and the cost of goods sold section of its income statement depicts the changes in Finished Goods Inventory. A manufacturer supports its cost of goods sold computation with a schedule of cost of goods manufactured for the period. This schedule is not normally presented in the company's external financial statements. The CGM replaces the purchases amount used by merchandisers. A service company computes the cost of services rendered instead of cost of goods sold. Illustrations of income statements for each type of business follow. Balance sheets are not shown because the only differences are in the number and titles of inventory accounts.

DELUXE DEPARTMENT STORE
Income Statement
for the Year Ended December 31, 1993

Net Sales		$5,840,000
Cost of Goods Sold		
Merchandise inventory, 1/1/93	$ 922,000	
Cost of purchases	4,040,000	
Total merchandise available for sale	$4,962,000	
Less: Merchandise inventory, 12/31/93	900,000	
Cost of goods sold		4,062,000
Gross Margin on Sales		$1,778,000
Operating Expenses		
Selling expenses	$ 898,000	
Administrative expenses	628,000	1,526,000
Income from Operations		$ 252,000

Other Income			
Dividend income	$ 17,000		
Rental income	5,820	$ 22,820	
Other Expenses			
Interest on bonds & notes		(52,120)	29,300
Income before Taxes			$ 222,700
Income Taxes			86,680
Net Income			$ 136,020

Earnings per share (assume 100,000 shares outstanding) $1.36

RIVET MANUFACTURING COMPANY
Income Statement
for the Year Ended December 31, 1993

Sales			$9,000,000
Cost of Goods Sold			
Beginning inventory of finished goods	$ 180,000		
Cost of goods manufactured (see below)	6,000,000		
Cost of goods available for sale	$6,180,000		
Less: Ending inventory of finished goods	164,000		
Cost of goods sold			6,016,000
Gross Margin on Sales			$2,984,000
Operating Expenses			
Selling expenses (similar to items detailed for merchandising company)	$ 900,000		
Administrative expenses (similar to items detailed for merchandising company)	540,000		1,440,000
Income from Operations			$1,544,000
Other Expenses			
Interest on notes			44,000
Income before Taxes			$1,500,000
Income Taxes			680,000
Net Income			$ 820,000

Earnings per share (assume 500,000 shares outstanding) $1.64

RIVET MANUFACTURING COMPANY
Schedule of Cost of Goods Manufactured
for the Year Ended December 31, 1993

Beginning Work in Process			$ 600,000
Manufacturing costs for the period			
Raw Materials (all direct)			
Beginning inventory	$ 350,000		
Purchases	3,400,000		
Total materials available	$3,750,000		
Ending inventory	400,000		
Direct materials used		$3,350,000	
Direct Labor		1,800,000	
Variable Overhead		400,000	
Fixed Overhead		350,000	5,900,000
Total Costs to Account For			$6,500,000
Ending Work in Process			500,000
Cost of Goods Manufactured			$6,000,000

FISHER ADVERTISING AGENCY
Income Statement
for the Year Ended December 31, 1993

Service Revenue		$3,600,000
Cost of Services Rendered		
Direct labor	$1,350,000	
Supplies	67,500	
Service department overhead	355,500	1,773,000
Gross Margin on Services		$1,827,000
Operating Expenses		
Selling expenses (similar to items detailed		
for merchandising company)	$ 262,500	
Administrative expenses (similar to items		
detailed for merchandising		
company)	780,000	1,042,500
Income from Operations		$ 784,500
Interest Expense		123,000
Income before Taxes		$ 661,500
Income Taxes		185,220
Net Income		$ 476,280
Earnings per share (assume 100,000 shares outstanding)		$4.76

GLOSSARY

Allocate   to assign based on the use of a cost predictor or an arbitrary method

Appraisal costs   quality control costs that are incurred for monitoring or inspection; compensate for mistakes not eliminated through prevention

Conversion cost   the sum of direct labor and factory overhead costs; the cost incurred in changing direct materials or supplies into finished products or services

Cost driver   a factor that has a direct cause-effect relationship to a cost

Cost object   anything to which costs attach or are related

Cost of goods manufactured   the total cost of the goods that were completed and transferred to Finished Goods Inventory during the period

Direct cost   a cost that is distinctly traceable to a particular cost object

Direct labor   the time spent by individuals who work specifically on manufacturing a product or performing a service

Direct material   a readily identifiable part of a product

Distribution cost   any cost incurred to market a product or service; includes all money spent on advertising, warehousing, and shipping products to customers

Failure costs   quality control costs that are associated with goods or services that have been found not to conform or perform to the required standards, as well as all related costs (such as that of the complaint department); may be internal or external

Fixed cost   a cost that remains constant in total within a specified range of activity

Indirect cost   a cost that cannot be traced explicitly to a particular cost object; common cost

Inventoriable cost   see product cost

Mixed cost   a cost that has both a variable and a fixed component; it does not fluctuate in direct proportion to changes in activity, nor does it remain constant with changes in activity

Overhead   any factory or production cost that is indirect to the product or service; does not include direct materials or direct labor

Period costs   any costs other than those associated with making or acquiring inventory

Predictor   an activity measure that, when changed, is accompanied by consistent, observable changes in another item

Prevention costs   quality control costs that are incurred to improve quality by preventing defects from occurring

Prime cost   the sum of direct materials costs and direct labor costs

Product cost   any cost associated with making or acquiring inventory

Relevant range   the specified range of activity over which a variable cost remains constant per unit or a fixed cost remains fixed in total

Variable cost   a cost that varies in total in direct proportion to changes in activity

---

SELECTED BIBLIOGRAPHY

Brimson, James A. "Technology Accounting." *Management Accounting* (March 1989), pp. 47–53.

Calonius, Erik. "Smart Moves by Quality Champs." *FORTUNE 1991: The New American Century* (1991), pp. 24–28.

Cooper, Robin, and Robert S. Kaplan. "How Cost Accounting Distorts Product Costs." *Management Accounting* (April 1988), pp. 20–27.

Kaplan, Robert S. "One Cost System Isn't Enough." *Harvard Business Review* (January–February 1988), pp. 61–66.

Krantz, K. Theodor. "How Velcro Got Hooked on Quality." *Harvard Business Review* (September–October 1989), p. 34ff.

Swift, Paul. "Cost Calculation and Flow in the Manufacturing Environment." *Production & Inventory Management Review* (November 1989), pp. 38–39.

SOLUTION STRATEGIES

Cost of Goods Manufactured

Beginning balance of Work in Process Inventory	XXX
Manufacturing costs for the period	
Raw Materials (all direct)	
Beginning balance	X
Purchases of materials	+ XX

```
         Raw materials available
           for use                            XXX
         Ending balance              −    XX
              Total raw materials used          XXX
       Direct labor                           +   XX
       Variable overhead                      +   XX
       Fixed overhead                         + XXX
   Total current period manufacturing costs              + XXXX
   Total costs to account for                              XXXX
   Ending balance of Work in Process Inventory           −   XX
   Cost of goods manufactured                             XXXX
```

Cost of Goods Sold
```
   Beginning balance of Finished Goods Inventory          XX
   Cost of goods manufactured                           + XXXX
   Cost of goods available for sale                       XXXX
   Ending balance of Finished Goods Inventory               X
   Cost of goods sold                                     XXXX
```

END-OF-CHAPTER MATERIALS

Questions

1. Why is the relevant range important to managers?

2. What is a mixed cost? How do accountants treat mixed costs in analyzing cost behavior? What information is essential in such a treatment of mixed costs?

3. How do predictors and cost drivers differ? Why is such a distinction important?

4. What is a product cost? What types of costs are included in product costs for merchandising companies, manufacturers, and service companies?

5. What activity distinguishes manufacturing and service companies from merchandising companies? Describe this activity.

6. What are the accounting and reporting implications that accompany the use of a high degree of conversion?

7. List six types of companies that engage in a high degree of conversion. Describe their conversion processes.

8. Why would Finished Goods Inventory seldom appear on the balance sheet of a service company?

9. What is a period cost? What types of costs are included in period costs for merchandising companies, manufacturers, and service companies?

10. Can you determine whether a cost is a product or period cost if you simply know for what purpose the cost was incurred (for example, depreciation, wages, property taxes, etc.)? If so, indicate how. If not, indicate why not and what other information is needed.

11. How is the concept of a direct cost related to that of a cost object?

12. "Prime costs and conversion costs compose product cost; therefore, the sum of these two cost categories is equal to product cost." Is this statement true or false? Explain.

13. What is included on the cost of goods manufactured schedule? Why is it said that this schedule shows the flow of costs in a manufacturing company?

Exercises

14. *(Cost classifications)* Indicate whether each of the following items is a variable (V), fixed (F), or mixed (M) cost, and whether it is a product or service (PT) cost or a period (PD) cost. If some items have alternative answers, indicate the alternatives and the reasons for them.

    a. Wages of forklift operators who move materials along the assembly line
    b. Hand soap used in factory rest rooms
    c. Utility costs incurred at manufacturing company headquarters
    d. Drafting paper used in an architectural firm
    e. Cost of company labels attached to shirts made by the firm
    f. Wages of factory quality control inspectors
    g. Insurance premiums on raw materials warehouse
    h. Salaries of staff auditors in a CPA firm
    i. Freight costs of delivering products to customers
    j. Cost of clay to make pottery
    k. Wages of carpenters of a construction company

15. *(Cost behavior)* Ellerd Company produces flag stand sets. The company incurred the following costs to produce 1,000 flag stand sets last month:

Flags	$ 1,000
Bases	2,000
Flagpoles	3,000
Straight-line depreciation	1,200
Supervisors' salaries	3,600
Utilities	600
Total	$11,400

    a. What did each flag stand set component cost? What did each flag stand set cost?
    b. What is the probable type of behavior that each of the costs exhibits?
    c. This month, the company expects to produce 500 flag stand sets. Would you expect each type of cost to increase or decrease? Why? What will be the total cost of 500 sets?

16. *(Total cost determination with mixed cost)* The managers of Quick Oil Change pay $300 per month for a machine maintenance contract. In addition, variable charges average $2.50 for every auto oil change or lube job.

    a. Determine the total cost and the cost per unit if Quick Oil Change does the following number of oil changes or lube jobs in May 1993:
       1. 100
       2. 180
       3. 300
    b. Why does the cost per unit change in each of the three previous cases?

17. *(Predictors and cost drivers)* To explain or predict the behavior of costs, accountants often use factors that change in a consistent pattern with the costs in question. What are some factors you might select to predict or explain the behavior of the following costs? Would these same factors be considered cost drivers as well as predictors? If not, why not? What other items could be used as cost drivers?

    a. Inspection costs
    b. Equipment maintenance
    c. Salespersons' travel expenses
    d. Indirect factory labor

18. *(Financial statement classifications)* Bluejay Enterprises purchased a plastics extruding machine for $200,000 to make rigid beach umbrellas. During its first operating year, the machine produced 50,000 umbrellas and depreciation was calculated to be $25,000 on the machine. Bluejay sold 30,000 umbrellas.

    a. What part of $200,000 is expired?
    b. Where would all amounts related to this machine appear on the financial statements?

19. *(Direct vs. indirect costs)* Bordelon Company makes aluminum canoes. Following are some costs incurred in the factory in 1993:

    Material Costs

Aluminum	$381,000
Equipment oil and grease	2,000
Chrome rivets to assemble canoes	12,600
Wooden ribbing and braces	12,400

    Labor Costs

Equipment operators	$120,000
Equipment mechanics	34,000
Factory supervisors	48,000

    a. What is the direct materials cost for 1993?
    b. What is the direct labor cost for 1993?
    c. What are the indirect labor and indirect materials costs for 1993?

20. *(Direct vs. indirect costs)* Hagen State University's College of Business has five departments: Accounting, Finance, Management, Marketing, and Decision Sciences. Each department chairperson is responsible for the department's budget preparation. The following costs are incurred in the Management Department:

    a. Management faculty salaries
    b. Chairperson's salary
    c. Cost of computer time of campus mainframe used by members of the department
    d. Cost of equipment purchased by the department from allocated state funds
    e. Cost of travel by department faculty paid from externally generated funds contributed directly to the department
    f. Cost of secretarial salaries (secretarial salaries are shared by the entire college)
    g. Depreciation allocation of the college building cost for the number of offices used by department faculty
    h. Cost of periodicals/books purchased by the department

    Indicate whether each of the previous costs is direct or indirect to the Management Department.

21. *(Labor cost classification)* Purple Pens, Inc., operates two shifts, paying a late-shift premium of 10 percent and an overtime premium of 50 percent. Labor premiums are included in overhead. The June 1994 factory payroll is as follows:

Total wages for June for 14,000 hours	$93,600
Normal hourly wage for early-shift employees	$6
Total regular hours worked, split evenly between the early and late shifts	12,000

All overtime was worked by the early shift during June.

a. How many overtime hours were worked in June?
b. How much of the total labor cost should be charged to direct labor? To overhead?
c. What amount of overhead was for late-shift premiums? For overtime premiums?

22. *(CGM and CGS)* Loya Manufacturing had the following inventory balances at the beginning and end of May 1994:

	5/1/94	5/31/94
Raw Materials	$ 6,000	$ 8,000
Work in Process	34,000	42,000
Finished Goods	16,000	12,000

All raw materials are direct to the production process. The following information is also available about manufacturing costs incurred during May:

Costs of raw materials used	$64,000
Direct labor costs	81,000
Factory overhead	58,000

a. Calculate the cost of goods manufactured for May.
b. Determine the cost of goods sold for May.

23. *(CGM and CGS)* Meadows Company's July 1995 cost of goods sold was $700,000. July 31 work in process was 95 percent of the July 1 work in process. Overhead was 80 percent of direct labor cost. During July, $220,000 of direct materials were purchased. Other July information follows:

Inventories	July 1	July 31
Direct materials	$ 44,400	$ 38,000
Work in process	80,000	?
Finished goods	217,000	210,000

a. Prepare a schedule of the cost of goods sold for July.
b. Prepare the July cost of goods manufactured schedule.
c. What are the July prime costs incurred?
d. What are the July conversion costs incurred?

24. *(Missing information on CGM)* The accounting records of the Alt Company re-flected inventory balances and cost data related to manufacturing in April 1994:

	April 1	April 30
Direct materials	$35,000	$57,000
Work in process	22,000	43,000
Finished goods	27,000	36,000
Cost of goods manufactured during April		$180,000
Direct materials used		53,000
Factory overhead incurred		54,000

a. What is the amount of direct materials purchased in April?

b. What was April's cost of goods sold?

25. *(Cost of services rendered)* The following information is related to the Edwards Medical Practice for June 1994, the firm's first month in operation:

Doctors' salaries for June	$12,000
Nurses' salaries for June	4,200
Medical supplies purchased in June	1,800
Utilities for month (80 percent related to patient treatment)	900
Office salaries for June (50 percent related to patient treatment)	2,600
Medical supplies at June 30	800
Depreciation on medical equipment for June	600
Building rental (80 percent related to patient treatment)	700

Compute the cost of services rendered.

26. *(Terminology)* Match the following definitions on the right with the terms on the left. Definitions may be used more than once.

Terms	Definitions
a. Cost of goods manufactured	1. Sum of direct labor and factory overhead
b. Expired cost	2. Costs outside the conversion area
c. Overhead	3. Inventoriable costs
d. Allocation	4. A type of cost that has both a variable and a fixed component
e. Mixed cost	5. Assets
f. Unexpired costs	6. Sum of direct materials and direct labor
g. Indirect cost	7. Cost that cannot be traced to a particular cost object
h. Product costs	8. Cost that has no future benefit
i. Period costs	9. Total cost of products finished during the period
j. Distribution cost	10. Cost distinctly traceable to a particular object
k. Direct cost	11. All nontraceable costs necessary to make a product or perform a service
l. Prime cost	12. Any cost incurred to market a product or promote a service
m. Conversion cost	13. Expenses and losses
	14. Assigning indirect costs to products or services

■ Problems

27. *(Cost behavior)* Shirley Smith has been elected to handle the local little theatre summer play. She is trying to determine the price to charge little theatre members for attendance at this year's presentation of *My Fair Lady*. She has developed the following cost estimates associated with the play:

Cost of printing invitations will be $260 for 100 to 499; cost to print between 500 and 600 will be $280.

Cost of readying and operating the theatre for three evenings will be $1,000.

Postage to mail invitations will be $.30 each.
Cost of building stage sets will be $1,200.
Cost of printing up to 1,000 programs will be $250.
Cost of security will be $110 plus $30 per hour; five hours will be needed
each night.
Costumes will be donated by several local businesses.

The little theatre has 200 members, and each member is allowed two guests. Ordinarily, only 75 percent of the members attend the summer offering, each bringing the two allowed guests. The play will be presented from 8:00 P.M. to 11:00 P.M. Invitations are mailed to those members calling to say they plan to come and also to each of the guests they specify.

Required:

a. Indicate the type of behavior exhibited by all the items Shirley needs to consider.
b. If Shirley's estimate of attendance is correct, what will be the total cost of the summer offering of the play?
c. If Shirley's estimate of attendance is correct, what will be the cost per person attending?
d. If 90 percent of the members attend and each invites two guests, what will be the total cost of the play? The cost per person? What primarily causes the difference in the cost per person?

28. *(Cost behavior)* Heavenly Chefs prepares dinners for several airlines, and sales average 300,000 meals per month. The significant costs of each dinner prepared are for the meat, vegetables, and plastic trays and utensils. (No desserts are provided because passengers are more calorie conscious than in the past.) The company prepares meals in batches of 1,000. The following data are shown in the company's accounting records for June 1994:

Cost of meat for 1,000 dinners	$800
Cost of vegetables for 1,000 dinners	60
Cost of plastic trays and utensils for 1,000 dinners	220
Direct labor for 1,000 dinners	750

Overhead charges total $800,000 per month; these are considered fully fixed for purposes of cost estimation.

Required:

a. What is the cost per dinner based on average sales and June prices?
b. If sales increase to 400,000 dinners per month, what will be the cost per dinner (assuming that cost behavior patterns remain the same as in June)?
c. If sales are 400,000 dinners per month but Heavenly does not want the cost per dinner to exceed its current level [based on (a) above], what amount can the company pay for meat, assuming all other costs are the same as the June levels?
d. Heavenly's competitor, Cumulus Caterers, has bid a price of $8.60 per dinner to the airlines. The profit margin in the industry is 100 percent of total cost. If Heavenly is to retain the airlines' business, how many dinners must the company produce each period to reach the bid price of Cumulus? Assume June cost patterns will not change and dinners must be produced in batches of 1,000.

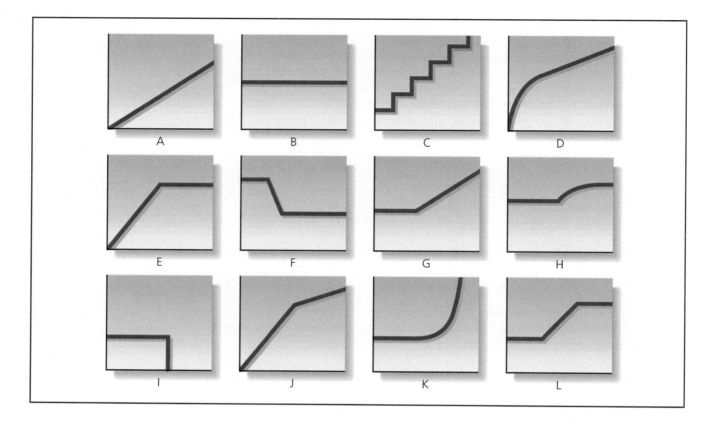

29. *(Cost behavior)* A company's cost structure may contain numerous different cost behavior patterns. The following are descriptions of several different costs; match these to the appropriate graphs above. On each graph, the vertical axis represents cost and the horizontal axis represents level of activity or volume.

Required:

Identify, by letter, the graph that illustrates each of the following cost behavior patterns. Graphs may be used more than once.

1. Cost of raw materials, where the cost decreases by $.06 per unit for each of the first 150 units purchased, after which it remains constant at $2.75 per unit.
2. City water bill, which is computed as follows:

First 750,000 gallons or less	$ 1,000 flat fee
Next 15,000 gallons	.002 per gallon used
Next 15,000 gallons	.005 per gallon used
Next 15,000 gallons	.008 per gallon used
Etc.	Etc.

3. Rent on a factory building donated by the city, where the agreement provides for a fixed-fee payment, unless 250,000 labor hours are worked, in which case no rent needs to be paid.
4. Cost of raw materials used.
5. Electricity bill—a flat fixed charge of $250 plus a variable cost after 150,000 kilowatt hours are used.
6. Salaries of maintenance workers if one maintenance worker is needed for every 1,000 hours or less of machine time.

7. Depreciation of equipment using the straight-line method.
8. Rent on a factory building donated by the county, where the agreement provides for a monthly rental of $100,000 less $1 for each labor hour worked in excess of 200,000 hours. However, a minimum rental payment of $20,000 must be made each month.
9. Rent on a machine that is billed at $1,000 for up to 500 hours of machine time. After 500 hours of machine time, an additional charge of $1 per hour is paid up to a maximum charge of $2,500 per period.

(AICPA adapted)

30. *(Cost classifications)* Leonard Ashe is a painter and incurred the following costs during April 1994 when he painted three houses. He spent $600 on paint, $50 on mineral spirits, and $65 on brushes. He also bought two pair of coveralls for $12 each; he wears coveralls only while he works. During the first week of April, Leonard placed a $10 ad for his business in the classifieds. Leonard had to hire an assistant for one of the painting jobs; he paid her $8 per hour, and she worked 25 hours.

　　Being a very methodical person, Leonard kept detailed records of his mileage to and from each painting job. His average operating cost per mile for his van is $.25. He found a $15 receipt in his van for a Mapsco that he purchased in April, which he uses to find addresses when he is first contacted to give an estimate on a painting job. He also had $6 in receipts for bridge tolls ($1 per trip) for a painting job he did across the river.

　　Near the end of April, Leonard decided to go camping, and he turned down a job on which he had bid $1,800. He called the homeowner long-distance (at a cost of $3.60) to explain his reasons for declining the job.
Required:
Using the following headings, indicate how each of the April costs incurred by Leonard would be classified. Assume that the cost object is a house-painting job.

　　Type of Cost
　　Variable
　　Fixed
　　Direct
　　Indirect
　　Period
　　Product

31. *(Cost flows)* Cartwright, Inc., had the following November 1993 inventory balances:

	November 1	November 30
Raw Materials	$18,100	$20,300
Work in Process	24,400	22,800
Finished Goods	20,000	20,500

During November, Cartwright purchased $46,000 of raw materials. All raw materials are considered direct materials. Total labor payroll for the month was $50,600. Direct labor employees were paid $6 per hour and worked 7,200 hours in November. Total factory overhead charges for the period were $70,000.
Required:

a. Determine the prime cost added to production during November.
b. Determine the conversion cost added to production in November.
c. Determine the cost of goods manufactured in November.
d. Determine the cost of goods sold in November.

32. *(Journal entries)* Dunes, Inc., makes only one product. The following data represent transactions and balances for May 1994, the company's first month of operations:

Direct materials purchased on account	$116,000
Direct materials issued to production	80,000
Direct labor payroll accrued	52,000
Indirect labor payroll paid	17,200
Factory insurance expired	400
Factory utilities paid	4,600
Factory depreciation recorded	8,200
Ending work in process (4,000 units)	28,000
Ending finished goods	3,100 units
Sales on account	$212,000 ($40 per unit)

Required:

a. How many units were sold in May? How many units were manufactured in May?
b. What was the total cost of goods manufactured in May?
c. What was the per-unit cost of goods manufactured in May?
d. Prepare the journal entries to record the flow of costs in Dunes, Inc., for May using the perpetual inventory system.

33. *(Journal entries)* At the beginning of April 1995, the East Company account balances were as follows:

Raw Materials Inventory	$1,250
Work in Process Inventory	4,350
Finished Goods Inventory	1,500

Transactions during April were:

a. Raw materials were purchased on account, $8,000.
b. Direct materials of $2,675 and indirect materials of $400 were issued to production.
c. Factory payroll was $7,500 for direct labor and $3,500 for indirect labor.
d. Office salaries were $6,000 for April.
e. Utilities were accrued for $1,250; 80 percent of this was for the factory.
f. Depreciation on company assets was $1,500; 60 percent of this was for factory assets.
g. Building rent of $2,000 was paid; the factory occupies 70 percent of the rented space.
h. Products costing $12,280 were completed in April.
i. Products costing $9,350 were sold on account for $12,500 in April.

Required:

a. Prepare journal entries for the previous transactions, assuming a perpetual inventory system. (Hint: One necessary journal entry has not been listed.)
b. What product costs are included in the financial statements for April? Where will the costs appear at the end of April?

34. *(CGM and CGS)* Barnes, Inc., produces American flags for department stores. The raw materials account includes both direct and indirect materials. The account balances at the beginning and end of August 1994 are as follows:

	August 1	August 31
Raw Materials Inventory	$14,000	$15,300
Work in Process Inventory	20,500	18,800
Finished Goods Inventory	7,000	5,200

During the month, Barnes purchased $46,000 of raw materials; direct materials used in August were $34,400. Factory payroll costs for March were $85,200, of which 72 percent was related to direct labor. Overhead charges for depreciation, insurance, utilities, and maintenance were $55,300 for the month.

Required:

a. Determine total overhead for August. (Hint: Include indirect material.)
b. Prepare a schedule of the cost of goods manufactured.
c. Prepare a schedule of the cost of goods sold.

35. *(Missing figures)* For each of the following cases, compute the missing figures:

	Case #1	Case #2	Case #3
Sales	$5,900	?	$17,300
Direct materials used	400	?	5,000
Direct labor	?	$ 900	500
Prime cost	2,400	?	?
Conversion cost	3,700	?	9,200
Overhead	?	4,000	?
Cost of goods manufactured	3,200	4,600	?
Beginning work in process	300	700	200
Ending work in process	?	2,600	4,100
Beginning finished goods	?	1,000	1,800
Ending finished goods	1,000	?	?
Cost of goods sold	?	5,200	9,000
Gross profit	3,100	?	?
Operating expenses	?	4,400	2,600
Net income (loss)	1,100	(5,000)	?

 Cases

36. The Charles Company experienced a flood on May 21 of the current year, which destroyed the company's Work in Process Inventory. For the purposes of submitting an insurance claim, the company needs an estimate of the inventory value. Management found the following information:

Raw materials, 5/1	$1,000
Work in process, 5/1	5,000
Accounts payable, 5/1	5,500
Accounts payable, 5/20	8,000
Direct labor hours from 5/1 to 5/20	1,750
Direct labor hourly rate	6
Estimated fixed overhead, 5/1 to 5/20	3,500
Estimated variable overhead, 5/1 to 5/20	5,250

On 5/22, the company took a physical inventory and found $2,500 of raw materials on hand. The accounts payable account is used only for purchases of raw materials. Payments made on account from 5/1 through 5/20 were $6,500.

a. Determine the value of Work in Process Inventory that was destroyed by the flood if $16,000 of goods had been transferred to finished goods from 5/1 to 5/20.

b. What other information might the insurance company require? How would management determine or estimate this information?

37. A portion of the costs incurred by business organizations is designated as "direct labor costs." As used in practice, the term *direct labor cost* has a wide variety of meanings. Unless the meaning intended in a given context is clear, misunderstanding and confusion are likely to ensue. If a user does not understand the elements included in direct labor cost, erroneous interpretations of the numbers may occur and could result in poor management decisions.

   In addition to understanding the conceptual definition of direct labor cost, management accountants must understand how direct labor cost should be measured.

   a. Distinguish between direct labor and indirect labor.
   b. Discuss why some nonproductive labor (e.g., coffee breaks, personal time) can be and often is treated as direct labor, while other nonproductive time (e.g., downtime, training) is treated as indirect labor.
   c. Presented next are labor cost elements that a company has classified as direct labor, manufacturing overhead, or either direct labor or manufacturing overhead, depending on the situation.

   • Direct labor: Included in the company's direct labor are cost production efficiency bonuses and certain benefits for direct labor workers such as FICA (employer's portion), group life insurance, vacation pay, and workers' compensation insurance.
   • Manufacturing overhead: Included in the company's overhead are costs for wage continuation plans in the event of illness, the company-sponsored cafeteria, the personnel department, and recreational facilities.
   • Direct labor or manufacturing overhead: Included in the "situational" category are maintenance expense, overtime premiums, and shift premiums.
   Explain the rationale used by the company in classifying the cost elements in each of the three presented categories.
   d. The two aspects of measuring direct labor costs are (1) the quantity of labor effort that is to be included, that is, the types of hours that are to be counted, and (2) the unit price by which each of these quantities is multiplied to arrive at monetary cost. Why are these considered separate and distinct aspects of measuring labor cost?

   (CMA adapted)

▌ Ethics Discussion

38. An extremely important variable cost per employee is health care provided by the employer. As mentioned in the chapter, in 1990 the average annual cost per employee was $3,161. This figure is expected to continue to rise each year as more and more expensive technology is used on patients and the costs of that technology must be passed along through the insurance company to the employer. One simple way to reduce these variable costs is to cut back on employee insurance coverage.

   a. Discuss the ethical implications of reducing employee health-care coverage to cut back on the variable costs incurred by the employer.
   b. Assume that you are an employer with 500 employees. You are forced to cut back on some insurance benefits. Your coverage currently includes the follow-

ing items: mental-health coverage, long-term disability, convalescent facility care, nonemergency but medically necessary procedures, dependent coverage, and life insurance. Select the two you would eliminate or dramatically reduce and provide reasons for your selections.

c. Prepare a plan that might allow you to "trade" some of the variable employee health-care costs for a fixed or a mixed cost.

39. You are the chief financial officer for a small manufacturing company that has applied for a bank loan. In speaking with the bank loan officer, you are told that two minimum criteria for granting loans are (1) a 40 percent gross margin and (2) income of at least 15 percent of sales. Looking at the last four months' income statements, you find that gross margin has been between 30 and 33 percent, but income has ranged from 18 to 24 percent of sales. You discuss these relationships with the company president, who suggests that some of the product costs included in Cost of Goods Sold be moved to the selling, general, and administrative categories so that the income statement will conform to the bank's criteria.

a. Which types of product costs might be easiest to reassign to period cost classifications?

b. Since the president is not suggesting that any expenses be kept off the income statement, do you see any ethical problems with the request? Discuss.

c. Write a short memo to convince the banker to loan the company the funds in spite of noncompliance with the loan criteria.

40. A cost of operating any organization in this day and age is computer software. Most software can be purchased on either a per-unit basis (making it a variable cost) or a site license basis (making it a fixed cost). You are a manager in a marketing company that engages in substantial market research. You have asked for a copy of a statistical analysis package that costs $400 per package for each of the 20 people in your department. The software company will allow a site license at a cost of $12,000. The package is essential to the organization's ability to perform research, but the controller does not have funds in the budget for 20 copies. Therefore, the controller purchases 4 copies and tells you to duplicate the other necessary copies. You resist, saying that to do so would be in violation of the copyright law, which allows only 1 copy to be made for backup purposes.

a. Since the fixed cost for the site license exceeds the amount that would be paid for the 20 copies, can you think of any reason to incur that $12,000 cost? Discuss.

b. Assume you are currently working on a research project for Mighty Midget Toy Company. Proper analysis requires the use of this software package. Is the cost of the software a direct or an indirect cost to the Mighty Midget project? If direct, what amount do you believe could be attached to the project? If indirect, should the cost be allocated to the project in some way? If so, how?

c. How would you handle this situation? What might be the consequences of your actions?

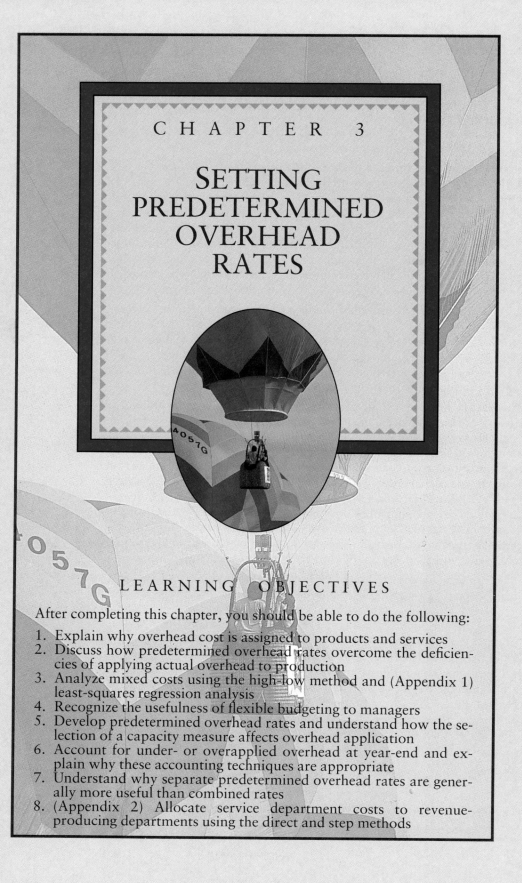

CHAPTER 3

SETTING PREDETERMINED OVERHEAD RATES

LEARNING OBJECTIVES

After completing this chapter, you should be able to do the following:

1. Explain why overhead cost is assigned to products and services
2. Discuss how predetermined overhead rates overcome the deficiencies of applying actual overhead to production
3. Analyze mixed costs using the high-low method and (Appendix 1) least-squares regression analysis
4. Recognize the usefulness of flexible budgeting to managers
5. Develop predetermined overhead rates and understand how the selection of a capacity measure affects overhead application
6. Account for under- or overapplied overhead at year-end and explain why these accounting techniques are appropriate
7. Understand why separate predetermined overhead rates are generally more useful than combined rates
8. (Appendix 2) Allocate service department costs to revenue-producing departments using the direct and step methods

Don Larousse's Trucking Empire

Nestled amid the junk car yards and abandoned lots littered with rusting shipping containers in eastern New Orleans is the hub of Don Larousse's trucking empire. It fits the landscape: three adjoining mobile homes and a parking lot that quickly puddles when it pours. From here he runs three trucking-related companies, the most prominent being Trans Gulf Inc., a container hauling line that brings in $4 million in revenue annually. The other two bring in another $7 million. Larousse is proud of his Spartan surroundings. "Eight hundred bucks for a trailer with central air and heat—you can't beat those kind of deals," he said. Low overhead are words to live by in the cutthroat—but growing—container hauling business.

SOURCE: Mike Hughlett, "The Little Business of Trucking," [*New Orleans*] *Times Picayune* (February 3, 1991), p. G1.

L ike Don Larousse, most businesspeople are concerned with overhead costs. Until recently for many companies, direct materials and direct labor were the largest costs of producing a product or providing a service. Overhead was merely another cost that was necessary but not exceptionally significant in amount. In manufacturing operations, automation and product variety have caused overhead costs to increase tremendously, while direct labor cost has declined to less than 10 percent in many companies. In service businesses, overhead costs for marketing, distribution, bonding, and storage continue to rise.

To determine the profitability of various products, managers must understand the factors that drive the overhead costs related to those products. Such information is also needed so that managers are better able to control overhead costs. Understanding the activities that cause costs to be incurred may help managers make better decisions about product pricing and company strategies.

No one could ever accuse Don Larousse of having lavish headquarters for his Trans Gulf company. Low overhead translates into high profits after direct costs are covered.

73

Don Larousse, for example, understands the impact that changing locations would have on his business costs and, therefore, profitability. The overhead impacts of increasing the number of long-haul versus short-haul jobs might not be so obvious. (Long-haul jobs require more prorated state license plate fees, more time spent at weight-check stations and, possibly, more costs to add truck amenities that would make his drivers more comfortable.) If Mr. Larousse knew the specific factors that cause overhead costs to be incurred, he might choose to accept or decline additional long-haul business (a strategic business decision). If more long-haul business were accepted and more overhead costs incurred, the additional overhead *should* be assigned to the business that generated the overhead costs so that an appropriate selling price could be set. Spreading the additional overhead costs to both short- and long-haul runs would make the short-haul runs seem less profitable than they actually are and the long-haul runs more profitable. Thus, finding the best method to assign overhead to units produced or services rendered is critical.

PREDETERMINED OVERHEAD RATES

actual cost system

The three elements of production cost are direct materials, direct labor, and overhead. Accountants can use an actual or a normal cost system (see Exhibit 3–1) to accumulate product cost.[1] In an **actual cost system,** all cost elements are actual costs. Actual direct materials and direct labor costs are accumulated in Work in Process Inventory (WIP) as they are incurred. Actual overhead costs are accumulated separately from materials and labor and are assigned to WIP at the end of a period. Actual cost systems are less than desirable because they require that all overhead cost information be known before any cost assignment can be made to products or services. Waiting for the information reduces management's ability to make timely operating decisions.

normal cost system

predetermined overhead rate

Most companies choose to employ a **normal cost system** that accumulates actual direct materials and labor costs, but uses a predetermined overhead rate (or rates) to assign overhead cost to WIP Inventory. A **predetermined overhead rate** (or OH application rate) is an estimated, average constant charge per unit of activity for a group of related overhead amounts. It is calculated by dividing total estimated annual overhead cost in each group by a related estimated measure of volume or activity of the cost driver. The formula for a predetermined overhead rate is:

$$\text{Predetermined OH rate} = \frac{\text{Total estimated overhead costs}}{\text{Estimated level of related volume or activity}}$$

The time frame over which to estimate the overhead cost and level of activity is typically one year. "An annual period is appropriate for the predetermination of overhead rates unless the production/marketing cycle of the entity is such that the use of a longer or shorter period would clearly provide more useful information."[2] For ex-

---

[1]Another alternative also exists. This type of system is called a standard cost system and is covered in chapter 5.
[2]Institute of Management Accountants (formerly National Association of Accountants), *Statements on Management Accounting: Accounting for Indirect Production Costs* (Montvale, N.J.: June 1, 1987), p. 11.

	Actual Cost System	**Normal Cost System**
Direct materials	Actual cost	Actual cost
Direct labor	Actual cost	Actual cost
Overhead	Actual cost assigned	Predetermined rate used to assign cost

EXHIBIT 3–1

ACTUAL VERSUS NORMAL COST SYSTEM

ample, the use of a longer period of time would be appropriate in companies such as Avondale Shipyards (which builds military ships) or Boh Bros. Construction Company (which constructs roads, bridges, and office buildings).

To illustrate the calculation of a predetermined OH rate, assume that the Don Larousse companies have total estimated overhead costs for 1993 of $1,550,000. Company accountants should determine which of these overhead costs are created by the same cost driver and separate the costs into **cost pools**. Assume that the cost driver of one overhead cost pool of $650,000 is total number of truck miles. Estimated truck miles for 1993 are 250,000. The predetermined OH rate for mileage-related costs is $2.60 per mile ($650,000 ÷ 250,000). The remaining $900,000 of overhead costs should be divided into related cost pools, and appropriate cost drivers should be used to establish predetermined rates.

cost pools

There are three primary reasons for using predetermined OH rates rather than actual overhead costs for product costing. First, a predetermined overhead rate allows overhead to be assigned to the goods produced or services rendered *during* the period rather than at the *end* of the period. If actual overhead costs are assigned, all overhead costs must be known before any assignment can be made. Total overhead costs cannot be determined until all overhead cost transactions of the period have occurred. Thus, use of a predetermined rate increases the availability of timely information for use in planning, controlling, and decision making.

A second reason to use predetermined OH rates is that they can compensate for fluctuations in actual overhead costs that have nothing to do with activity levels. Overhead may vary on a monthly basis because of seasonal or calendar factors. For instance, factory utility costs may be higher during the summer than at other times of the year. If production were constant each month and actual overhead were assigned to production, the increase in utilities would cause product cost per unit to be greater during the summer months than in other months.

Assume that Blake, Inc., has overhead costs of $220,000 per month, excluding utilities. Utility costs for two months (March and July) are $20,000 and $30,000, respectively. This company makes a single product and defines activity as units of production. Production each month is 20,000 units. The actual overhead cost per unit is calculated as follows:

	March	**July**
$\dfrac{\text{Actual Overhead}}{\text{Actual Units Produced}}$	$\dfrac{\$240,000}{20,000} = \$12$ per unit	$\dfrac{\$250,000}{20,000} = \$12.50$ per unit

The $.50 cost differential between these two months is related solely to the $10,000 difference in the numerators—not to any difference in the product itself.

Third, predetermined overhead rates can overcome the problem of fluctuations in activity levels that have no impact on actual fixed overhead costs. Activity levels may vary because of seasons or monthly calendar differences, including holiday periods. Even if total overhead costs were equal each period, changes in activity would cause a per-unit change in cost because of the fixed cost element of overhead.

Suppose that Snowden Manufacturing has $357,000 of actual fixed overhead cost in both January and February. Like Blake, Inc., Snowden produces only one type of product and, therefore, defines activity as units of production. The company produces 17,500 and 17,000 units in January and February, respectively. Actual fixed overhead per unit increases by $.60 from January to February:

	January	**February**
$\dfrac{\text{Actual Fixed Overhead}}{\text{Actual Units Produced}}$	$\dfrac{\$357,000}{17,500} = \$20.40$ per unit	$\dfrac{\$357,000}{17,000} = \$21$ per unit

Fixed overhead cost per unit changes inversely with changes in activity levels. It is important to realize that this type of fluctuation occurs only in relation to fixed overhead costs. Total variable overhead costs rise in direct proportion to increases in production levels, but the per unit variable cost does not change.

Since variable and fixed overhead costs behave differently, separate predetermined overhead rates should be developed for the variable and fixed elements of overhead cost. Remember that variable costs increase in total with changes in activity and remain constant on a per-unit basis. Fixed costs, on the other hand, remain constant in total with increases in activity but vary inversely on a per-unit basis with activity changes. Additionally, since costs are caused or "driven" by different factors, separate predetermined rates should be developed for the various cost pools of an organization.

The labor portion of the groundskeeping costs to maintain Nottoway Plantation is a mixed cost. A small permanent staff is retained year-round, creating a fixed charge. Because of natural conditions and an increase in visitation, additional workers are hired part-time during the summer months for a variable element.

ANALYZING MIXED COSTS

The first step in computing separate variable and fixed predetermined overhead rates is to examine the behavior of each cost incurred by the company.

Cost Behavior

Costs may be variable, fixed, or mixed. Exhibit 3–2 illustrates a survey of the types of cost behavior of various categories of costs. Behavior may be related to the type of cost (almost all respondents indicated that taxes, insurance and depreciation were fixed costs). But behavior often depends on the business itself rather than on the type of cost (almost equal numbers of respondents indicated tooling, quality control, and energy costs as being variable, mixed, and fixed, respectively).

EXHIBIT 3–2

COST BEHAVIOR BY CATEGORY

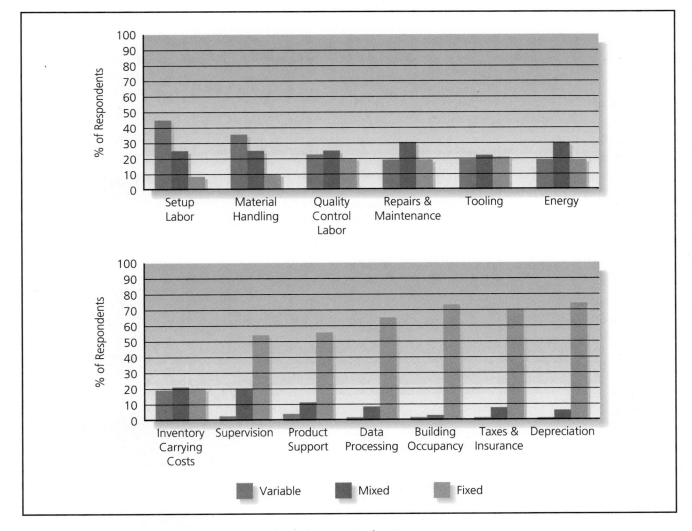

SOURCE: Robert A. Howell et al., *Management Accounting in the New Manufacturing Environment* (Montvale, N.J.: National Association of Accountants, 1987), pp. 42–43.

Like variable and fixed costs, mixed costs are assumed by accountants to be linear rather than curvilinear. Because of this linearity assumption, the general formula for a straight line can be used to describe any type of cost (i.e., variable, fixed, or mixed) within a relevant range of activity. The straight-line formula is:

$$y = a + bX$$

where y = total cost
a = fixed portion of total cost
b = variable portion of total cost (the rate at which total cost changes in relation to changes in X; when a graph is prepared to depict the straight line, b represents the slope of the line)
X = activity base to which y (the cost driver) is being related

Exhibit 3–3 illustrates the use of the straight-line formula for each type of cost behavior. An entirely variable cost is represented as $y = \$0 + bX$. A zero is shown as the value for a because there is no fixed cost. A purely fixed cost would be formulated as: $y = a + \$0X$. Zero is substituted in the formula for b since there is no cost component that varies with the activity base in that case. A mixed cost has formula values for both the a and b unknowns.

Since mixed costs contain amounts for both values, mixed costs must be separated into their variable and fixed components before separate overhead rates can be calculated. The simplest method of separation is the high-low method.

EXHIBIT 3–3
▼▼▼▼▼▼▼▼▼▼▼▼▼

USES OF THE
STRAIGHT LINE COST
FORMULA

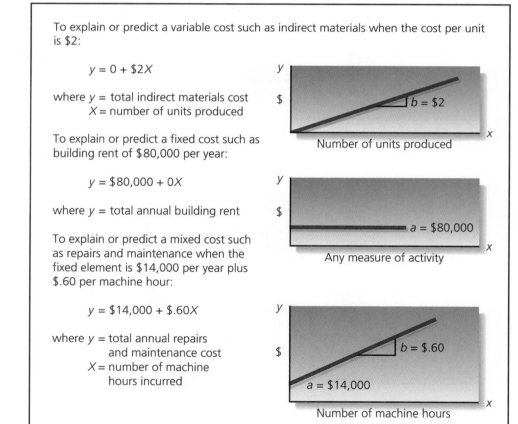

To explain or predict a variable cost such as indirect materials when the cost per unit is $2:

$y = 0 + \$2X$

where y = total indirect materials cost
X = number of units produced

$b = \$2$

Number of units produced

To explain or predict a fixed cost such as building rent of $80,000 per year:

$y = \$80,000 + 0X$

where y = total annual building rent

$a = \$80,000$

Any measure of activity

To explain or predict a mixed cost such as repairs and maintenance when the fixed element is $14,000 per year plus $.60 per machine hour:

$y = \$14,000 + \$.60X$

where y = total annual repairs and maintenance cost
X = number of machine hours incurred

$b = \$.60$

$a = \$14,000$

Number of machine hours

High-Low Method

The **high-low method** is a separation technique that uses actual total cost observations at two levels of activity and calculates the change in both activity and cost. The observations selected are the highest and lowest activity levels *if* these are representative of costs within the relevant range. Note that the selections of "high" and "low" are made on the basis of activity levels rather than costs. The reason for this selection is that the analysis is undertaken to estimate how costs change in relation to activity changes. Activities cause costs to change; costs do not cause activities to change.

The changes in activity and cost are determined by subtracting the low observation values from the high values. These differences are then used to calculate the b (variable cost) value in the $y = a + bX$ formula as follows:

$$b = \frac{\text{Change in total cost}}{\text{Change in activity level}}$$

The b value is the unit variable cost per measure of activity. At either level of activity, the b value can be multiplied by the activity level to determine the amount of total variable cost contained in total cost.

Total variable cost plus total fixed cost is equal to total mixed cost. Thus, the fixed portion of a mixed cost is found by subtracting total variable cost from total cost: $a = y - bX$. Either the high or low level of activity can be used to determine the fixed portion of the mixed cost, since fixed cost is constant at all activity levels within the relevant range.

The computations for separating mixed costs are illustrated in Exhibit 3–4 using equipment usage time and water cost information for Dauterive's Car Wash.

The following equipment time and water cost information is available:

Month	Level of Activity in Machine Hours	Water Cost
January	210	$4,050
February	208	4,027
March	150	2,750
April	228	4,386
May	240	4,605
June	245	4,730
July	239	4,643
August	241	4,680

Step 1: Select the highest and lowest levels of activity within the relevant range and obtain the costs associated with those levels. These levels and costs are 208 and 245 hours and $4,730 and $4,027, respectively.

Step 2: Calculate the change in cost compared to the change in activity.

	Machine Hours	Associated Total Cost
High activity	245	$4,730
Low activity	208	4,027
Changes	37	$ 703

(continued)

EXHIBIT 3–4

DAUTERIVE'S CAR WASH ANALYSIS OF MIXED WATER COST

Step 3: Determine the relationship of cost change to activity change to find the variable cost element.

$$b = \$703 \div 37 \text{ MH} = \$19 \text{ per machine hour}$$

Step 4: Compute total variable cost (TVC) at either level of activity.

High level of activity: TVC = $19 (245) = $4,655
Low level of activity: TVC = $19 (208) = $3,952

Step 5: Subtract total variable cost from total cost at either level of activity to determine fixed cost.

High level of activity: a = $4,730 − $4,655 = $75
Low level of activity: a = $4,027 − $3,952 = $75

Step 6: Substitute the fixed and variable cost values in the straight-line formula to get an equation that can be used to estimate total cost at any level of activity within the relevant range.

$$y = \$75 + \$19X$$

where X = equipment (machine) hours

Dauterive's normal operating range of activity is between 200 and 250 hours per month. The data for March is outside the relevant range, so this observation should be disregarded in analyzing the water cost.

Total mixed cost increases or decreases with changes in activity. The change in cost is equal to the change in activity multiplied by the unit variable cost; the fixed cost element does not fluctuate with changes in activity. The variable cost per unit of activity reflects the average change in cost for each additional unit of activity. For Dauterive's Car Wash, this average cost is $19 per hour of equipment use. The fixed cost is then calculated at $75 per month.

As mentioned earlier, the high-low method is the easiest method of separating mixed costs into their variable and fixed elements. Another separation technique (regression analysis) is discussed in Appendix 1 to this chapter. Regression provides better information about mixed costs, but it is tedious to perform by hand. Many software packages are amenable to regression analysis and, thus, it is highly useful in today's computer-oriented environment. Regardless of which method is used to separate mixed costs, it is important to recognize the following two points. First, high-low and regression are simply estimation techniques that will not provide exact costs of future activities. Second, the appropriateness of the resulting cost formula from either technique will depend on the validity of the activity measure chosen as the predictor of the variable cost.

PREPARING FLEXIBLE BUDGETS

Using the various cost formulae developed through high-low or regression analysis, managers can estimate overhead costs at various activity levels. Estimated overhead costs are presented in a **flexible budget,** which is a series of financial plans that detail the individual cost factors composing total cost and present those costs at different levels of activity. Costs are treated as either variable or fixed, meaning that mixed costs are separated into their variable and fixed components. Flexible budgets can be prepared for both product costs and period costs.

flexible budget

The activity levels shown on a flexible budget usually cover management's contemplated range of activity for the upcoming period. If all activity levels are within the relevant range, costs at each successive level should equal the amount of the previous level plus a uniform dollar increment for each variable cost factor. The increment is the variable cost per unit of activity multiplied by the quantity of additional activity.

To prepare the budget, all costs are analyzed as to their cost behavior. The straight-line formula ($y = a + bX$) is used to determine total cost at any level of activity for each variable and fixed cost. In Exhibit 3–5, the individual overhead costs

	a = Fixed Cost	b = Variable Cost
Purely Variable Costs		
Indirect labor		
Support workers		$ .45
Idle time		.03
Fringe benefits		.05
Indirect materials		.30
Total variable		$ .83
Purely Fixed Costs		
Supervision (X < 75,000 hours)	$ 80,600*	
Depreciation	26,700	
Maintenance contract (X < 75,000)	10,000**	
Insurance	3,600	
Total fixed (X < 75,000)	$120,900	
Mixed		
Power	1,800	10.50
Totals for flexible budget formula		
(for X < 75,000 machine hours)	$122,700	$11.33

*Supervision is expected to be $95,400 when X ≥ 75,000.
**Machine maintenance contracts will increase to $14,000 when X ≥ 75,000.

Flexible budget formulae (where y = total manufacturing overhead):

(If X < 75,000 MH)	$y = \$122,700 + \$11.33 \text{ MH}$
(If X ≥ 75,000 MH)	$y = \$141,500 + \$11.33 \text{ MH}$

EXHIBIT 3–5
▼▼▼▼▼▼▼▼▼▼▼▼▼

PALO CORPORATION MACHINING DEPARTMENT ANALYSIS OF OH COSTS (FORMULA BASED ON MACHINE HOURS)

of Palo Corporation's Machining Department are used to illustrate the preparation of a flexible budget. The department's activity base is machine hours, and its contemplated range is between 60,000 and 90,000 machine hours per year.

Analyzing the individual overhead cost factors has provided Palo's cost accountant with the information presented in Exhibit 3–5, which shows all cost factors in terms of the a (fixed) and b (variable) values of the straight-line formula. While total fixed costs are assumed to remain constant over management's contemplated range of activity, situations may arise when a fixed cost component increases as activity increases within the contemplated range. Such changes would reflect the existence of a step fixed cost. For example, supervision may be a step fixed cost. One supervisor may be able to manage up to fifteen people; if sixteen to thirty people are to be supervised, another supervisor is necessary. The increased need for the supervisor would cause payroll cost to increase by a "step."

According to the information in Exhibit 3–5, supervision and machine maintenance contract costs both contain steps at an activity level of 75,000 machine hours. At that level, supervision and maintenance contract costs increase by $14,800 and $4,000, respectively. Thus, Palo Corporation's Machining Department needs two flexible budget formulae, since the analysis indicates the existence of steps in the fixed costs. The flexible budget formulae for the Machining Department are given at the bottom of Exhibit 3–5.

Using the formulae derived in Exhibit 3–5, a flexible budget (Exhibit 3–6) can be prepared for Palo Corporation's Machining Department overhead costs. A flexible budget is a good way to see any steps that exist for the categories of expected fixed costs. Exhibit 3–6 also illustrates the stable behavior of variable cost per machine hour compared to the irregular behavior of fixed cost per machine hour.

Two factors cause the irregular behavior in Palo's fixed cost per hour: a change in activity level and the steps in the fixed costs. As machine hours (MHs) increase, fixed cost per machine hour *should* decrease, assuming total fixed cost does not change. However, in the Machining Department, total fixed cost increases by $18,800 at 75,000 MHs. Such irregular behavior of fixed cost per unit requires that one specific level be chosen to calculate a predetermined fixed overhead rate per unit for product costing purposes.

DEVELOPING AND USING PREDETERMINED OVERHEAD RATES

With the detailed information specified in the flexible budget, companies can compute separate overhead rates for variable and fixed overhead costs.

Variable Overhead Rate

Variable overhead (VOH) is that amount of overhead which changes proportionately in total with some measure of volume or activity. It includes indirect materials, variable indirect labor costs, and the variable portion of any mixed cost. A predetermined overhead rate should be computed for each variable overhead cost pool that is caused by a different cost driver. The information needed for these computations can be taken from any level of activity shown on the flexible budget that is within the relevant range. Total cost for each cost pool is then divided by the level of activity on

EXHIBIT 3–6
▼▼▼▼▼▼▼▼▼▼▼▼▼▼

PALO CORPORATION
MACHINING
DEPARTMENT
VARIABLE AND
FIXED OVERHEAD
FLEXIBLE BUDGET

	Machine Hours (MHs)		
	60,000	70,000	80,000
Variable Costs			
Indirect materials	$ 18,000	$ 21,000	$ 24,000
Indirect labor			
Support workers	27,000	31,500	36,000
Idle time	1,800	2,100	2,400
Fringe benefits	3,000	3,500	4,000
Power	630,000	735,000	840,000
Total variable costs	$679,800	$793,100	$ 906,400
Variable costs per hour	$ 11.33	$ 11.33	$ 11.33
Fixed Costs			
Supervision	$ 80,600	$ 80,600	$ 95,400
Maintenance contract	10,000	10,000	14,000
Depreciation	26,700	26,700	26,700
Insurance	3,600	3,600	3,600
Power	1,800	1,800	1,800
Total fixed costs	$122,700	$122,700	$ 141,500
Fixed costs per hour	$ 2.05	$ 1.75	$ 1.77
Total cost	$802,500	$915,800	$1,047,900
Total cost per machine hour	$ 13.38	$ 13.08	$ 13.10

which the estimate was based. Variable overhead will be applied to production using the related activity base.

Since VOH is assumed to be constant per unit at all activity levels within the relevant range, the activity level chosen to estimate total variable cost is unimportant. For example, assume that at a production level of 25,000 units, a company estimates that $2,500 of cost will be incurred for indirect materials. These estimates give a predetermined variable overhead rate for indirect materials of $.10 per unit ($2,500 ÷ 25,000). Correspondingly, if indirect materials cost is truly variable, the company would have estimated a total cost of $3,600 for 36,000, or the same $.10 per unit.

The Quaker State product line has evolved and increased over many years in response to consumer demand and changing engine and driving conditions. Increased product variety increases the type and amount of overhead costs, such as those for packaging.

NEWS NOTE

Using Cost Drivers for Better Cost Information

In the mid-1980s, people at the Roseville Networks Division (RND) of Hewlett-Packard didn't believe the numbers the accounting system produced. Now they do. Over 5 years, RND has developed a new accounting system that measures the factors that truly drive costs. The cost-driver system is more accurate, more timely, and ultimately more useful to its "customers"—the people who rely on the information it provides.

RND makes about 250 products (mostly printed-circuit assemblies), each of which has various options—for a total of about 1,100 different items. Overhead costs are divided into three cost pools: procurement, production, and support. Procurement overhead includes the costs of buying materials and of receiving, storing, handling, and documenting them. Production overhead includes the cost of activities required to assemble and test products. Support overhead includes production engineering, central data-processing support, process engineering, and manufacturing management. Support overhead is first allocated to the first two categories and then RND assigns the two remaining overhead categories to products using [appropriate] cost drivers.

RND recognizes that costs cannot be traced with surgical precision. But the company is convinced that at least for now, cost drivers have been found that produce more accurate costs than before.

The activity base or cost driver selected should be one that provides a logical relationship between the driver and overhead cost incurrence. The cost driver that generally first comes to mind is production volume. However, unless a company makes only one type of output, production volume is not really a feasible activity measure for any overhead cost. If multiple products or services are produced, overhead costs will be incurred because of numerous factors, including the differing nature of the items, product variety, and product complexity. Consider, for example, the above News Note related to Hewlett-Packard's use of differing cost drivers.

The concept of homogeneity underlies all cost allocation. Some measure of activity that is common to all costs in a given cost pool must be determined to allocate overhead to heterogeneous products. The "volume measures used most frequently and appropriately include direct labor hours, direct labor dollars, machine hours, production orders, engineering change orders, or some product-related physical measure such as tons [or] gallons."[3] Direct labor hours and direct labor dollars have traditionally been the most commonly used measures of activity. In addition, companies often use only a single total overhead cost pool or two overhead cost pools (total variable and total fixed).

As technology and the manufacturing environment change, companies such as Hewlett-Packard and its Roseville Networks Division recognize that changes may need to be made in their cost information systems. Using a less-than-appropriate al-

---

[3]Ibid.

location base and a minimal number of cost pools can result in poor managerial information, as discussed in the following News Note. The failure of the traditional labor-based, single/double pool systems to accurately assign costs is becoming more apparent as companies automate, increase the number and variety of product lines, and incur higher overhead costs than ever before.

For example, using direct labor to allocate overhead costs in highly automated plants results in extremely large overhead rates because the costs are applied over an ever-decreasing number of labor hours (or dollars). When automated plants allocate overhead on the basis of labor, managers are frequently concerned about the high rates per labor hour. Often, they conclude that the way to reduce overhead is to reduce labor. Such a conclusion is erroneous. The overhead charge is high because labor is low; further reducing labor will simply increase the overhead rate! In highly automated plants, if only one activity base is to be used for overhead allocations, machine hours would be a more appropriate base than either direct labor hours or direct labor dollars.

NEWS NOTE

Distorted Information Breeds Distorted Decisions

Managers in companies selling multiple products are making important decisions about pricing, product mix, and process technology based on distorted cost information. What's worse, alternative information rarely exists to alert these managers that product costs are badly flawed. Most companies detect the problem only after their competitiveness and profitability have deteriorated.

Distorted cost information is the result of sensible accounting choices made decades ago, when most companies manufactured a narrow range of products. Back then, the costs of direct labor and materials, the most important production factors, could be traced easily to individual products. Distortions from allocating factory and corporate overhead by burden rates on direct labor were minor. And the expense of collecting and processing data made it hard to justify more sophisticated allocation of these and other indirect costs.

Today, product lines and marketing channels have proliferated. Direct labor now represents a small fraction of corporate costs, while expenses covering factory support operations, marketing, distribution, engineering, and other overhead functions have exploded. But most companies still allocate these rising overhead and support costs by their diminishing direct labor base or, as with marketing and distribution costs, not at all.

These simplistic approaches are no longer justifiable—especially given the plummeting costs of information technology. They can also be dangerous. Intensified global competition and radically new production technologies have made accurate product cost information crucial to competitive success.

Many companies are looking at multiple cost pools and new activity measures for overhead allocation, including number or time of machine setups, number of different parts, material handling time, and quantity of product defects.[4] Regardless of how many cost pools are created or which activity base is chosen, the method of overhead application is the same. The predetermined overhead rate is used in a normal costing system to apply or assign overhead to Work in Process Inventory based on the *actual quantity of the activity base used.* At this time, for simplicity, separate cost pools for variable and fixed overhead will be assumed, as will a single activity measure to allocate each.

To illustrate the calculation of a predetermined variable overhead rate, information for the Keller Corporation is given in Exhibit 3–7. Keller uses machine hours to compute its predetermined variable OH rate, because the company is highly automated and most variable OH costs are created through machinery usage. Computation of the predetermined rate is made in 1993, using estimated variable overhead costs and machine hours for 1994. *Predetermined overhead calculations are always made in advance of the year of application.* As machine hours are used in 1994, charges will be made to Work in Process Inventory to record overhead cost using the predetermined rate. The process of making this assignment is shown after the discussion of fixed overhead rates.

Fixed Overhead Rate

Fixed overhead (FOH) is that portion of total overhead that remains constant in total with changes in activity within the relevant range. Fixed overhead includes factory supervisors' salaries, straight-line depreciation on factory buildings and equipment, and the fixed portion of mixed factory costs. Estimates must be made for all fixed overhead costs, and these estimates are then assigned to appropriate cost pools to make up the numerator of the predetermined overhead rate calculations.

Since fixed overhead is constant in total, it varies inversely on a per-unit basis with changes in activity; therefore, a different unit cost will result at every different

---

[4]Use of such nontraditional activity measures to allocate overhead and the resultant activity-based costs are discussed in chapter 4.

Progressive die metal stamping presses produce thousands of parts per minute at Masco Industries, with minimal operator involvement. It is highly unlikely that direct labor is an appropriate basis upon which to assign overhead costs to products in such a situation.

EXHIBIT 3–7
▼▼▼▼▼▼▼▼▼▼▼▼▼
KELLER
CORPORATION
PREDETERMINED
VARIABLE
OVERHEAD RATE
CALCULATION

1. Estimate total cost of each component at a selected level of 1994 activity:

	Total Estimated Cost at 100,000 MHs
Estimated variable indirect labor	$ 40,000
Estimated indirect materials	20,000
Estimated variable utilities and variable portion of other mixed costs	260,000
Total estimated variable overhead cost	$320,000

2. Divide the total estimated variable overhead cost by the selected level of activity to find the total predetermined variable overhead rate:

$$\frac{\text{Total estimated variable overhead cost at 100,000 machine hours}}{100,000 \text{ machine hours}} = \frac{\$320,000}{100,000} = \$3.20 \text{ per MH}$$

Note: The above computation produces the necessary information for product costing purposes, but it does not provide the detail needed by managers. For example, to plan or control variable overhead costs, managers need the individual costs per unit of activity shown below.

Estimated variable indirect labor	$ 40,000	÷	100,000 =	$ .40
Estimated indirect materials	20,000	÷	100,000 =	.20
Estimated variable utilities and variable portion of other mixed costs	260,000	÷	100,000 =	2.60

level of activity. Thus, a particular level of activity must be specified to calculate the predetermined fixed overhead rate per measurement unit. This level of activity is usually stated at the **expected activity** for the firm for the upcoming period. Expected activity is a short-run concept representing the anticipated level of activity for the upcoming year. If actual results are close to expected results (both dollar and volume), this capacity measure should result in product costs that most closely reflect actual historical costs.

expected activity

Companies may choose to use some activity level other than expected activity to compute their predetermined fixed overhead rates. Alternative measurement bases include theoretical, practical, and normal capacity.

The estimated absolute maximum potential activity that could occur during a specified time frame is called **theoretical capacity.** This measure assumes that all production factors are operating perfectly and, as such, disregards realities such as machinery breakdowns and reduced or halted plant operation on holidays. Because of its unrealistic assumptions, theoretical capacity is generally considered an unacceptable basis for overhead application. Reducing theoretical capacity by ongoing, regular operating interruptions (such as holidays, downtime, and start-up time) provides the **practical capacity** that could be achieved during normal working hours. This measure is a more reasonable basis of activity measurement than theoretical capacity, but it is still not probable to consistently attain practical capacity.

theoretical capacity

practical capacity

Sometimes managers wish to give consideration to historical and estimated future production levels and to cyclical and seasonal fluctuations. Therefore, they may

EXHIBIT 3–8
▼▼▼▼▼▼▼▼▼▼▼▼

KELLER
CORPORATION
PREDETERMINED
FIXED OVERHEAD
RATE CALCULATION

Estimated machine-related fixed overhead costs for 1994:	
Straight-line depreciation on machines	$ 62,000
Machine lease payments	13,000
Machine insurance	16,000
Machine maintenance workers' salaries	53,000
Fixed portion of utilities	34,000
Total budgeted fixed costs	$178,000

$$\frac{\text{Total estimated machine-related fixed overhead}}{100,000 \text{ machine hours}} = \frac{\$178,000}{100,000} = \$1.78 \text{ per MH}$$

normal capacity

use a **normal capacity** measure that encompasses the long-run (five to ten years) average activity of the firm. This measurement does represent a reasonably attainable level of activity, but still will not provide costs that are most similar to actual costs. Distortions of cost could arise if activity levels varied significantly within the long-run period.

To continue the Keller Corporation example, information on the company's estimated machine-related fixed overhead costs is given in Exhibit 3–8. Total estimated fixed overhead for this cost pool for 1994 is $178,000; expected activity is 100,000 machine hours. Using these estimates, the predetermined fixed overhead rate is calculated as $1.78 per machine hour.

OVERHEAD APPLICATION

Once the variable and fixed predetermined overhead rates are calculated, they are used throughout the following year to apply overhead to Work in Process. Overhead may be applied as production occurs, when goods or services are transferred out of Work in Process Inventory, or at the end of each month. **Applied overhead** is the amount of overhead assigned to Work in Process as a result of incurring the activity that was used to develop the application rate. Application is made using the predetermined rates and the actual level of activity.

applied overhead

To illustrate the application process, assume that during January 1994, Keller's machines run 3,000 hours. Using the calculation from Exhibit 3–7, variable overhead is applied at the rate of $3.20 per machine hour. Thus, variable machine-related overhead for the month is $9,600 (3,000 × $3.20). Using the fixed OH rate computed in Exhibit 3–8, $5,340 (3,000 × $1.78) of fixed machine-related overhead is applied to WIP Inventory. When overhead is applied to work in process, Work in Process Inventory is debited and the appropriate overhead account is credited. Thus the journal entries to apply January machine-related overhead for Keller Corporation are:

Work in Process Inventory	9,600	
Variable Overhead		9,600
To apply machine-related variable		
overhead for January		

Work in Process Inventory	5,340	
Fixed Overhead		5,340
To apply machine-related fixed		
overhead for January		

Under- and Overapplied Overhead

While companies may be able to estimate future overhead costs and expected activity with some degree of accuracy, there is simply a human inability to precisely project future events. Thus, actual overhead incurred during a period will rarely, if ever, equal applied overhead. This inequality of amounts represents under- or overapplied overhead. When the amount of overhead applied to Work in Process is less than actual overhead, the overhead is said to be **underapplied.** The opposite situation (applying more overhead to Work in Process than was actually incurred) is referred to as **overapplied overhead.**

underapplied overhead

overapplied overhead

Applied overhead is only indirectly related to the amount of *actual overhead cost* incurred by the company. Overhead is applied to Work in Process as a representation of actual costs incurred, but the incurrence of actual costs does not affect overhead application. On the other hand, applied overhead is directly related to the amount of *actual activity* incurred. This direct relationship exists because application is based on the estimated rate multiplied by the actual activity.

The amount of under- or overapplied overhead must be closed at the end of the period because expected activity was used to develop the predetermined rate. Since expected activity refers to a one-year time frame, disposition of the balance of under- or overapplied overhead should take place at year-end.

Disposition of Under- and Overapplied Overhead

In a normal costing system, when actual overhead costs are incurred, they are debited to the variable and fixed overhead general ledger accounts and credited to the various sources of overhead costs. (These entries are presented in chapter 2.) Applied overhead is debited to Work in Process using the predetermined rates and credited to the variable and fixed overhead general ledger accounts. The end-of-period balance in each overhead general ledger account represents underapplied (debit) or overapplied (credit) overhead. Applied overhead is added to actual direct materials and direct labor costs in the development of cost of goods manufactured.

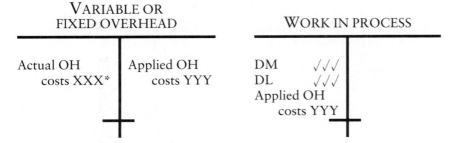

*Offsetting these debits are credits to various sources of OH costs, such as Accumulated Depreciation, Accounts Payable, Supplies Inventory, Wages Payable, etc.

Overhead accounts are temporary accounts and any balances in them are closed at year-end. Proper disposition of under- or overapplied overhead depends upon the materiality of the amount involved. If the amount is immaterial, it is closed to the Cost of Goods Sold account. When underapplied (debit balance) overhead is closed, it causes Cost of Goods Sold to increase since not enough overhead was applied to production during the year. Alternatively, closing overapplied (credit balance) overhead causes Cost of Goods Sold to decrease because too much overhead was applied to production during the year.

If the amount of under- or overapplied overhead is significant, it should be allocated among the accounts containing applied overhead. These accounts are Work in Process, Finished Goods, and Cost of Goods Sold. A significant amount of under- or overapplied overhead means that the balances in each of these accounts are quite different from what they would have been if actual overhead costs had been assigned to production. The under- or overapplied amount is allocated among the affected accounts to restate their balances to conform more closely with actual historical costs. Such conformity is required by generally accepted accounting principles for external financial statements.

Exhibit 3–9 uses assumed amounts to illustrate the technique of apportioning overapplied variable overhead among the necessary accounts. Had the amount been underapplied, the accounts debited and credited in the journal entry would have been reversed. The computations would not have differed if the overhead had been fixed rather than variable.

EXHIBIT 3–9
▼▼▼▼▼▼▼▼▼▼▼

APPORTIONING
OVERAPPLIED
OVERHEAD

Variable Overhead		Amount of VOH in Account Balance	
Actual	$293,600	Work in Process	$234,000
Applied	377,800	Finished Goods	390,000
Overapplied	$ 84,200	Cost of Goods Sold	936,000

1. Add overhead amounts in accounts and determine proportional relationships:

	VOH Balance	Proportion	Percentage
Work in Process	$ 234,000	$234,000 ÷ $1,560,000	15%
Finished Goods	390,000	$390,000 ÷ $1,560,000	25%
Cost of Goods Sold	936,000	$936,000 ÷ $1,560,000	60%
Total	$1,560,000		100%

2. Multiply percentages times overapplied variable overhead amount to determine the amount of adjustment needed:

	%	×	Overapplied VOH	=	Adjustment Amount
Work in Process	15%	×	$84,200	=	$12,630
Finished Goods	25%	×	$84,200	=	21,050
Cost of Goods Sold	60%	×	$84,200	=	50,520

3. Prepare journal entry to close variable overhead account and assign adjustment amount to appropriate accounts:

Variable Overhead	84,200	
Work in Process		12,630
Finished Goods		21,050
Cost of Goods Sold		50,520

Using predetermined overhead rates (if based on valid cost drivers) provides a rational and systematic manner of assigning overhead costs to products for external financial statement preparation. Separate variable and fixed overhead rates and accounts developed using separate cost pools provide more refined information for planning, controlling, and decision making. In spite of this fact, companies may (and commonly do) choose to use combined overhead rates rather than separate ones for variable and fixed overhead.

COMBINED OVERHEAD RATES

Companies may use a single overhead application rate rather than separate rates for the numerous variable and fixed overhead cost pools. The single rate can be related to a particular cost pool (such as machine-related overhead) or to overhead costs in general. Combined overhead rates are traditional in businesses for three reasons: clerical ease, cost savings, and no requirement to separate overhead costs by cost behavior.

The calculation of a combined predetermined overhead rate requires specification of an expected activity level because of the behavior of fixed costs. All variable and fixed overhead costs at the expected activity level are estimated and totaled. The summation is divided by the expected activity level to derive the single overhead application rate.

Assume that the Keller Corporation (from Exhibits 3–7 and 3–8) decides to use a combined predetermined overhead rate for machine-related overhead costs. The company designates 100,000 machine hours as its expected activity level. Keller's combined predetermined machine-related overhead rate is calculated as follows:

Total estimated machine-related VOH at 100,000 MH (from Exhibit 3–7)	$320,000
Total estimated machine-related FOH (from Exhibit 3–8 and the same at any number of machine hours within the relevant range)	178,000
Total estimated machine-related OH cost	$498,000
Divided by expected activity in machine hours	100,000
Predetermined overhead rate per machine hour	$4.98

For each machine hour used in 1994, Keller's Work in Process account will be charged with $4.98 of overhead. (This single rate is equal to the sum of the variable and fixed rates calculated earlier.) Thus, when Keller uses 3,000 machine hours in January, it would apply overhead as follows:

Work in Process Inventory	14,940	
Machine-Related Overhead		14,940
To apply machine-related overhead for January		

While this particular entry provides the same total application to Work in Process Inventory as did the variable and fixed entries, Keller managers have eliminated an important source of information about overhead costs. Assume that the total machine usage during 1994 was 95,000 hours and the actual overhead costs were exactly as estimated: $3.20 per machine hour for variable and $178,000 in total for fixed. Total actual overhead costs would be $482,000 ($304,000 + $178,000), but total applied overhead would be $473,100 ($4.98 × 95,000). Had separate rates been used, applied overhead would have been $304,000 ($3.20 × 95,000) of variable and $169,100 ($1.78 × 95,000) of fixed. The $8,900 ($482,000 − $473,100) of underapplied overhead is specifically caused by fixed overhead, not by variable overhead—a fact not observable from the combined rate.

As the degree of aggregation increases from simply combining related cost pools to combining all factory overhead, information may become more and more distorted. Boudreaux Company information is used to provide a simple example of the differing results obtained between using a departmental and plantwide overhead rate. The company has two departments: Assembly and Finishing. Assembly work is performed by robots, and a large portion of this department's overhead cost consists of depreciation and electricity charges. Finishing work is performed manually by skilled laborers, and most charges in this department are for labor, fringe benefits, indirect materials, and supplies.

Boudreaux Company makes two products: A and B. Product A requires five machine hours in Assembly and one direct labor hour in Finishing; Product B requires two machine hours in Assembly and three direct labor hours in Finishing. Exhibit 3–10 provides information about estimated overhead costs and activity measures, and shows the computations of departmental and plantwide overhead rates. Product overhead application amounts for A and B are also given.

Note the significant difference in the overhead applied to each product using departmental versus plantwide rates. If departmental rates are used, product cost more clearly reflects the different amounts and types of machine/labor work performed on the two products. If a plantwide rate is used, essentially each product only absorbs

EXHIBIT 3–10
▼▼▼▼▼▼▼▼▼▼▼▼▼

BOUDREAUX COMPANY DEPARTMENTAL VERSUS PLANTWIDE OVERHEAD RATES

	Assembly	Finishing
Estimated annual overhead	$300,200	$99,800
Estimated annual direct labor hours (DLH)	5,000	20,000
Estimated annual machine hours (MH)	38,000	2,000

Departmental overhead rates:
Assembly (automated) $300,200 ÷ 38,000 = $7.90 per MH
Finishing (manual) $99,800 ÷ 20,000 = $4.99 per DLH

Total plantwide overhead = $300,200 + $99,800 = $400,000
Plantwide overhead rate (using MH) ($400,000 ÷ 40,000 = $10.00)
Plantwide overhead rate (using DLH) ($400,000 ÷ 25,000 = $16.00)

	To Product A	To Product B
Overhead assigned using departmental rates:		
Assembly	5($7.90) = $39.50	2($7.90) = $15.80
Finishing	1($4.99) = 4.99	3($4.99) = 14.97
Total	$44.49	$30.77
using plantwide rate:		
based on MH	5($10.00) = $50.00	2($10.00) = $20.00
based on DLH	1($16.00) = $16.00	3($16.00) = $48.00

overhead from a single department—from Assembly if machine hours are used and from Finishing if direct labor hours are used. Use of either plantwide rate ignores the dissimilarity of work performed in the departments.

Use of plantwide overhead rates rather than departmental rates may also contribute to problems in product pricing. While selling prices must be reflective of market conditions, management typically uses cost as a starting point for setting prices. If plantwide rates distort the true cost of a product, selling prices might be set too low or too high, causing management to make incorrect decisions.

Assume in the case of Boudreaux Company that direct materials and direct labor costs for Product A are $5 and $35, respectively. Adding the various overhead amounts to these prime costs gives the total product cost under each method. Exhibit 3–11 shows these product costs and the profit or loss that would be indicated if Product A has a normal market selling price of $105.

Use of the product costs developed from plantwide rates could cause Boudreaux management to make erroneous decisions about Product A. If the cost figure developed from a plantwide direct labor hour basis is used, management may think that Product A is significantly more successful than it actually is. Such a decision could cause resources to be diverted from other products. If the cost containing overhead based on the plantwide machine hour allocation is used, management may believe that Product A should not be produced, since it appears not to be generating a very substantial gross profit. In either instance, assuming that machine hours and direct labor hours are the best possible allocation bases for Assembly and Finishing, respectively, the only cost that gives management the necessary information upon which to make resource allocation and product development/elimination decisions is the one produced by using the departmental overhead rates.

While clerical cost savings may result from the use of a combined rate, the ultimate costs of poor information are significantly greater than the savings that are generated. Combined rates result in a lack of detail that hinders managers' abilities to plan operations, control costs, and make decisions. Additionally, cause-effect relationships between costs and activities are blurred when combined rates are used. This factor may contribute to an inability to reduce costs or improve productivity. As detailed in the News Note on page 94, a major effect of using a single overhead rate is the lack of the ability to understand cost behavior.

Since most companies produce a wide variety of products or perform a wide variety of services, different activity measures are normally necessary in different departments of the same company and for different types of overhead costs. Machine

	Departmental Rates	Plantwide Rate (MH)	Plantwide Rate (DLH)
Direct materials	$ 5.00	$ 5.00	$ 5.00
Direct labor	35.00	35.00	35.00
Overhead	44.49	50.00	16.00
Total cost	$ 84.49	$ 90.00	$ 56.00
Selling price	$105.00	$105.00	$105.00
Gross profit	$ 20.51	$ 15.00	$ 49.00
Rate of profit	19.5%	14.3%	46.7%

EXHIBIT 3–11
▼▼▼▼▼▼▼▼▼▼▼▼

BOUDREAUX COMPANY TOTAL PRODUCT COSTS AND PROFITS

NEWS NOTE

What Causes the Lack of Information?

Soviet accounting follows cost accounting principles but does not distinguish fixed costs from variable costs. Costs are accumulated only to determine output costs. The company keeps two sets of figures: one tracing a predicted annual plan, the other recording actual income and expenditures.

Economists have attributed the inefficiency of the Soviet economy to the paucity of information that [the] accounting system provides. Managers have few hard numbers on which to base their decisions. Gorbachev has publicly criticized the cost accounting system and has asked his ministry of finance to create one that's more effective.

SOURCE: Glenn Alan Cheney, "Soviet-American Financial Coexistence," *Journal of Accountancy* (January 1990), p. 70.

hours may be the most appropriate activity base for many costs in a department that is highly automated. Direct labor hours may be the best basis for assigning the majority of overhead costs in a labor-intensive department. In the quality control area, number of defects may provide the best allocation base. Separate departmental and cost pool activity bases are generally thought to be superior to the use of a combined plantwide base, because they allow cost accumulation and cost application to be more homogeneous. Different rates will provide better information for planning, control, performance evaluation, and decision making.

SITE ANALYSIS

An understanding of overhead costs is essential to operating a business. As indicated in the opening On-Site vignette, "low overhead are words to live by." Since overhead is now such a high proportion of most companies' costs, it is essential to keep them as low as possible because "customers have no allegiance to anything but rock-bottom rates [or prices]."[5] Most businesses, however, cannot keep their overhead costs quite as low as Mr. Larousse can.

Knowing how overhead costs behave, being able to estimate costs at various levels of activity, and assigning overhead to products and services are essential techniques in successful business planning and control. Direct attachment of costs to products and services should be the rule to the extent feasible and possible. By directly attaching as many costs as possible, companies will be minimizing the role of direct labor as a basis on which to assign costs—making the costs that are developed more accurate and appropriate. As indicated in the following Applications Strategies, the concepts contained in this chapter are important to all disciplines so that managers can make more effective and efficient resource allocations and can understand what profits are being generated by which products and services.

---

[5]Mike Hughlett, "The Little Business of Trucking," [*New Orleans*] *Times Picayune* (February 3, 1991), p. G-2.

Discipline	Application
Accounting	Allows timely financial statement valuations; provides more stable product costs; provides a means to assist managers in making future plans, controlling costs, and solving problems
Economics	Helps in analyzing and predicting costs in the quest for efficiency in a competitive market environment; provides a real-world measure of economic concept of "marginal cost" in decision making
Finance	Helps in estimating costs for future periods; provides more timely knowledge of gross profit margins
Management	Helps in OH cost analysis and control; provides a basis for planning, controlling, and decision making; provides an indication of product/service profitability; forces recognition of cause-effect relationships between costs and activities or cost drivers
Marketing	Allows bid prices to be estimated more easily because underlying costs are understood

APPLICATIONS STRATEGIES OF PREDETERMINED OVERHEAD RATES AND MIXED COST SEPARATION

CHAPTER SUMMARY

Predetermined overhead rates are calculated in advance of a period by dividing estimated overhead costs by a selected level of activity. Such rates allocate equal amounts of overhead to goods or services based on the actual activity associated with the goods or services. Use of predetermined rates to apply overhead costs to production and/or services is usually more advantageous than applying actual overhead costs, because predetermined rates eliminate the delays and distortions that occur when actual overhead is applied.

Preparing a flexible budget helps management understand how costs behave at various levels of activity within the relevant range. All costs in the flexible budget can be calculated using the formula $y = a + bX$, where y = total cost, a = fixed cost, b = variable cost per unit of activity, and X = the level of activity. This formula requires that costs be classified as either variable or fixed, so mixed costs must be separated into their variable and fixed components. The high-low method is one way to make this separation; it uses two points of actual activity data (the highest and lowest) and determines the change in cost and activity. Dividing the cost change by the activity change gives the per unit variable cost portion of the mixed cost. Fixed cost is determined by subtracting total variable cost from total cost at either the high or the low level of activity.

Use of predetermined rates will normally result in either under- or overapplied overhead at year-end. Year-end disposition of under- or overapplied overhead depends on the magnitude of the amount. If the total amount is small, it is closed to Cost of Goods Sold or Cost of Services Rendered. If the amount is large, it is allocated to Work in Process, Finished Goods, and Cost of Goods Sold/Services Rendered.

While some companies use a combined predetermined overhead rate to determine product costs, use of separate rates according to cost behavior and multiple rates for different cost pools will yield costs that better reflect the resources sacrificed to make a product or perform a service. Since variable costs remain constant per unit over the relevant range of activity, total variable overhead can be divided by any level of activity to compute the predetermined rate. To compute a fixed overhead rate, however, a specific level of activity must be chosen; most companies select the expected annual capacity level. Estimated fixed overhead is then divided by the chosen level of activity to obtain the predetermined rate.

APPENDIX 1

Least-Squares Regression Analysis

The chapter illustrates the high-low method of separating mixed costs into their variable and fixed elements. This appendix provides an introduction to regression analysis as an additional method of mixed cost analysis.

outliers

A potential weakness of the high-low method is that **outliers** (nonrepresentative points) may be inadvertently used in the calculation. Outliers fall outside the relevant range of activity or are distortions of normal cost within the relevant range. Any estimates of future costs calculated from a line drawn using an outlier point will not be representative of actual costs and are probably not good predictors.

least-squares regression analysis

A statistical technique, known as **least-squares regression analysis,** is available that mathematically determines the cost formula of a mixed cost by considering all representative data points rather than only two points. Like the high-low method, this technique separates the variable and fixed cost elements of any type of mixed cost. Least-squares regression analysis is used to develop an equation that predicts an unknown value of a dependent variable from the known values of one or more independent variables. When multiple independent variables exist, least-squares regression also helps to select the independent variable that is the best predictor of the dependent variable. For example, least squares can be used by managers trying to decide if machine hours, direct labor hours, or number of parts per product best explain and predict changes in a certain overhead cost pool.

simple regression
multiple regression

Using only one independent variable to predict the dependent variable is known as **simple regression** analysis; in **multiple regression,** two or more independent variables are used to predict the dependent variable. All chapter examples assume that a linear relationship exists between variables. In a linear relationship, each one-unit change in an independent variable produces a specific unit change in the dependent variable.

Simple linear regression employs the same straight-line ($y = a + bX$) formula that was used in the high-low method. From the available data, a regression line is mathematically developed that minimizes the sum of the *squares* of the vertical deviations between the actual observation points and the regression line. This line represents the line that best fits the data observations.

Exhibit 3–12 illustrates how least-squares regression would appear visually. Graph A of Exhibit 3–12 presents an assumed set of observations. Graph B indicates that many regression lines could be drawn for the data set. Of the many lines that could be drawn through the data set, most would provide a poor fit. Actual observation values from the data set are designated as *y* values. The regression line represents computed values for all activity levels, and the points on a regression line are desig-

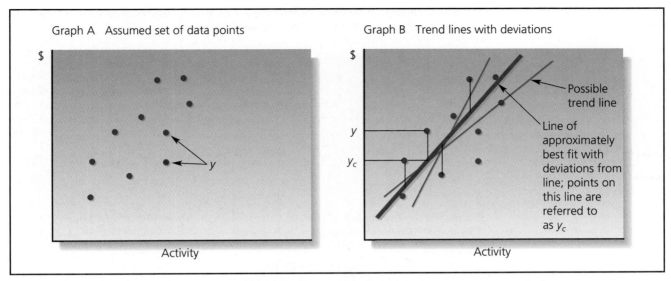

Graph A Assumed set of data points

Graph B Trend lines with deviations

EXHIBIT 3–12

ILLUSTRATION OF
LEAST-SQUARES
REGRESSION LINE

nated as y_c values. Note that the y values do not generally fall directly on the regression line. The vertical line segments from the observation points to the regression line in Graph B of Exhibit 3–12 are deviations. The amount of a deviation is determined by subtracting the y_c value at an activity level from its related y value. Deviations above the regression line are positive amounts, while deviations below the line are negative. Minimizing the sum of the *squared* deviations eliminates the problem of having both positive and negative differences for $(y - y_c)$. Least squares is used to estimate the values for a and b in an equation for the regression line that uses the y_c values rather than the y values:

$$y_c = a + bX$$

This equation can then be used by the cost analyst for predictions and analytical purposes.

The Dauterive Car Wash data for machine hours and water cost from Exhibit 3–4 are used to calculate the regression line. The equations necessary to compute b and a values using the method of least squares are as follows:[6]

$$b = \frac{\Sigma xy - n\bar{x}\bar{y}}{\Sigma x^2 - n\bar{x}^2}$$

$$a = \bar{y} - b\bar{x}$$

where $\bar{x}$ = mean of the independent variable
$\bar{y}$ = mean of the dependent variable
n = number of observations

The **mean** of a variable is its arithmetic average and is calculated by dividing the sum of the observations by the number of observations.

mean

---

[6]These equations are derived from mathematical computations beyond the scope of this text, but which are found in many statistics books. The symbol Σ means "the summation of."

The Dauterive data need to be restated in an appropriate form for substitution into the equations for b and a. These restatements are:

x	y	xy	x^2
210	$ 4,050	$ 850,500	$ 44,100
208	4,027	837,616	43,264
228	4,386	1,000,008	51,984
240	4,605	1,105,200	57,600
245	4,730	1,158,850	60,025
239	4,643	1,109,677	57,121
241	4,680	1,127,880	58,081
1,611	$31,121	$7,189,731	$372,175

(Note that the outlier for March of 150 machine hours has once again been ignored.) The mean values for these data are $(1,611 \div 7)$ and $(\$31,121 \div 7)$, or 230 and $4,446, respectively.

Substituting appropriate amounts into the formulae yields the a (fixed) and b (variable) cost values. The b value is calculated first, since it is used to compute a.

$$b = \frac{\Sigma xy - n\overline{x}\,\overline{y}}{\Sigma x^2 - n\overline{x}^2}$$

$$= \frac{[7,189,731 - 7(230)(\$4,446)]}{[372,175 - 7(230)(230)]}$$

$$= \frac{\$31,671}{1,875} = \$16.89$$

$$a = \overline{y} - b\overline{x}$$

$$a = \$4,446 - \$16.89(230)$$

$$a = \$4,446 - \$3,885 = \$561$$

Thus, the cost formula under least-squares regression is:

$$\text{Total water cost} = \$561 + \$16.89 \text{ per machine hour}$$

Notice that the least-squares method gives a fixed cost (a value) that is significantly higher than that provided by the high-low method ($y = \$75 + \$19$ MH) of analyzing mixed costs. Such information is very important when managers seek to understand and control costs based on reaction to changes in activity. Because of the many computer packages that are able to do least-squares regression quickly and accurately, it has become virtually costless to do this type of analysis using a variety of possibilities as the independent variable. While least squares provides a way to predict the value of one variable by using values of another variable, this technique does not indicate how well the known independent variables are suited to predicting the unknown, dependent one. Deciding how strongly variables are related requires the use of correlation analysis—a topic discussed in statistics texts.

Allocation of Service Department Costs

Organizations incur costs for two basic types of activities: those that generate revenue (products and services) and those that do not. Organizational support areas consist of both service and administrative departments. **Service departments** (such as central purchasing and central computing) provide one or more specific functional tasks for other internal units; **administrative departments** (including top management personnel and organization headquarters) perform management activities that benefit the entire organization. Costs of service and administrative departments are referred to collectively as "service department costs," since company administration provides service to the rest of the company.

service departments

administrative departments

Managers understand that the selling prices charged for the organization's goods or services must cover both the costs of revenue-generating activities and the costs of support activities before profits can be achieved. Non-revenue-producing activities are conducted merely to support revenue-producing activities. Thus, service department costs are, in essence, simply another form of overhead that must be allocated to revenue-generating departments and, finally, to units of product or service.

To make managers of revenue-producing areas more aware that their activities are responsible for covering all organizational costs, service department costs are often allocated or charged to user departments. A rational and systematic allocation base for service department costs should reflect the management accountant's consideration of four criteria: 1) the benefits received by the revenue-producing department from the service department; 2) a causal relationship between factors in the revenue-producing department and costs incurred in the service department; 3) the fairness or equity of the allocations between or among revenue-producing departments; and 4) the ability of revenue-producing departments to bear the allocated costs.

Benefits received and causal relationships are the two criteria that are used most often to decide on allocation bases. These two criteria are reasonably objective and will produce rational allocations. Fairness is a valid theoretical basis for allocation, but it is difficult to implement since everyone does not have the same perception of what is fair or equitable. The ability-to-bear criterion is not normally used to allocate service department costs to revenue-producing departments because it often results in unrealistic or profit-detrimental actions. For example, managers might employ financial and logistical manipulations in an attempt to minimize the basis on which costs are to be allocated to their departments.

Applying the two primary criteria (benefits and causes) to the allocation of service department costs can help to specify some acceptable allocation bases. It is essential that the allocation base selected be valid because an improper base will always yield improper information regardless of how complex or precise the allocation process appears to be.

Methods of Service Department Cost Allocation

When service department costs are going to be allocated to revenue-producing areas, the basic cost pools are comprised of all revenue-producing and service departments and their direct costs. These costs can be gathered and specified in terms of cost behavior (variable and fixed) or in total. Intermediate pools are then developed in the allocation process. There may be one or more layers of intermediate pools; however, the last layer will consist of only revenue-producing departments. The number of layers and the costs shown in the intermediate pools depend upon the type of allocation method selected. The costs of the intermediate pools are then distributed to final cost objects (such as products, programs, or functional areas).

There are two basic methods of allocating the pooled costs of the service departments to revenue-producing departments: the direct method and the step method.[7]

direct method

The **direct method** of allocation is the easiest method. Service department costs are assigned directly to the revenue-producing areas using one specific basis for each department. There are no intermediate cost allocations. For example, Personnel Department costs might be assigned to production departments based on the number of people in each production department.

step method

The **step method** of cost allocation assigns indirect costs to cost objects after considering the interrelationships of the cost objects. A specific base is also utilized in this method, but the step method employs a ranking for the quantity of services provided by each service department to other areas. This **"benefits-provided" ranking** lists service departments in an order that begins with the one providing the most service to all other corporate areas (both non-revenue and revenue-producing). The ranking ends with the service department that provides the least service to all but the revenue-producing areas. After the ranking is developed, service department costs are allocated down the list until all costs have ultimately been assigned to the revenue-producing areas. This ranking sequence is recommended because the step method partially recognizes the reciprocal relationships among the service departments. For example, since Personnel provides services for all areas of the company, Personnel might be the first department listed in the ranking and all other areas would receive a proportionate allocation of the Personnel Department's costs.

"benefits provided" ranking

Illustration of Service Department Cost Allocation

Koontz Enterprises has two production divisions (Black Cat Sportswear and Magic Products) and three service departments (Administration, Personnel, and Public Relations). Budgeted costs are as follows:

Administration	$ 600,000
Personnel	280,000
Public Relations	320,000
Black Cat Sportswear	940,000
Magic Products	1,125,000

The service departments above are listed in the order of their benefits-provided ranking. Selected potential allocation bases are presented below.

	Number of Employee Hours	Number of Employees	$s of Assets Employed
Administration	9,400	4	$380,000
Personnel	6,240	3	140,000
Public Relations	4,160	2	90,000
Black Cat Sportswear	11,250	5	400,000
Magic Products	16,875	6	600,000

---

[7]The algebraic or reciprocal approach to service department cost allocation considers all interrelationships of departments and reflects these in simultaneous equations. This technique is covered in any standard cost accounting text.

	Base	% of Total Base	Amount To Allocate	Amount Allocated
Administration Costs (employee hours)				
Black Cat Sportswear	11,250	40	$600,000	$ 240,000
Magic Products	16,875	60	600,000	360,000
Totals	28,125	100		$ 600,000
Personnel Costs (# of employees)				
Black Cat Sportswear	5	46	$280,000	$ 128,800
Magic Products	6	54	280,000	151,200
Totals	11	100		$ 280,000
Public Relations Costs ($s of assets employed)				
Black Cat Sportswear	$ 400,000	40	$320,000	$ 128,000
Magic Products	600,000	60	320,000	192,000
Totals	$1,000,000	100		$ 320,000
Grand total of allocated departmental costs:				
Black Cat Sportswear				$ 496,800
Magic Products				703,200
Total allocated				$1,200,000

EXHIBIT 3–13

KOONTZ ENTERPRISES DIRECT METHOD ALLOCATION OF SERVICE DEPARTMENT COSTS

Koontz' management thinks that administration costs should be allocated on the basis of employee hours, personnel costs on the basis of number of employees, and public relations costs on the basis of dollars of assets employed.

Use of the direct method of service department allocation produces the total budgeted costs for Black Cat Sportswear and Magic Products shown in Exhibit 3–13.

To apply the step method of allocation, the "benefits-provided" ranking specified by Koontz Enterprises is used. Departments are first listed in the order designated by Koontz and costs are assigned using an appropriate, specified allocation base to the departments receiving service. Once costs have been assigned from a department, no additional costs are charged back to that department. Step allocation of Koontz Enterprises service costs is shown in Exhibit 3–14.

For simplicity, cost behavior in all departments has been ignored. A more appropriate allocation process would specify different bases in each department for the variable and fixed costs. Costs would then be assigned in a manner more reflective of their behavior. Such differentiation would not change the process of allocation, but would change the results for each of the two methods (direct and step). Separation of variable and fixed costs would, however, provide better allocations. Again, use of the computer would now make this process more practical than it has been in the past.

EXHIBIT 3–14
▼▼▼▼▼▼▼▼▼▼▼▼▼

KOONTZ
ENTERPRISES STEP
METHOD
ALLOCATION OF
SERVICE
DEPARTMENT COSTS

Administration Costs (employee hours)	Base	% of Total Base	Amount To Allocate	Amount Allocated
Personnel	6,240	16	$600,000	$ 96,000
Public Relations	4,160	11	600,000	66,000
Black Cat Sportswear	11,250	29	600,000	174,000
Magic Products	16,875	44	600,000	264,000
Totals	38,525	100		$ 600,000
Personnel Costs (# of employees)				
Public Relations	2	15	$376,000	$ 56,400
Black Cat Sportswear	5	39	376,000	146,640
Magic Products	6	46	376,000	172,960
Totals	13	100		$ 376,000
Public Relations Costs ($s of assets employed)				
Black Cat Sportswear	$ 400,000	40	$442,400	$ 176,960
Magic Products	600,000	60	442,400	265,440
Totals	$1,000,000	100		$ 442,400

Grand total of allocated departmental costs:

Black Cat Sportswear	$ 497,600
Magic Products	702,400
Total allocated	$1,200,000

GLOSSARY

Actual cost system   a method of accumulating product or service costs that uses actual direct materials, actual direct labor, and actual overhead costs

Administrative department   an organizational unit that performs management activities that benefit the entire organization (from appendix)

Applied overhead   the amount of overhead assigned to Work in Process Inventory as a result of incurring the activity that was used to develop the application rate; the amount is computed by multiplying the quantity of actual activity by the predetermined rate

Benefits-provided ranking   a listing of service departments in an order that begins with the one providing the most service to all other organizational areas; the ranking ends with the service department that provides the least service to all but the revenue-producing areas (from appendix)

Capacity   a measure of production volume or of some other cost driver

Cost pool   a grouping of all costs that are associated with the same activity or cost driver

Direct method (of service department allocation)   a method that uses a specific base to assign service department costs directly to revenue-producing departments with no other intermediate cost allocations (from appendix)

Expected activity   a short-run concept representing the anticipated level of activity for the upcoming year

Flexible budget   a series of financial plans that detail the individual cost factors composing total cost and present those costs at different levels of activity according to cost behavior

High-low method   a mixed cost separation technique that uses actual observations of a total cost at the highest and lowest levels of activity and calculates the change in both activity and cost; the levels chosen must be within the relevant range

Least-squares regression analysis   a statistical technique that mathematically determines the cost line of a mixed cost by considering all representative data points; it investigates the association or relationship between or among dependent and independent variables

Mean   the arithmetic average, calculated by dividing the sum of the observations by the number of observations

Multiple regression   a method of using two or more independent variables to predict the dependent variable in the least-squares regression

Normal capacity   the long-run (5 to 10 years) average activity of the firm that gives effect to historical and estimated future production levels and to cyclical and seasonal fluctuations

Normal cost system   a method of accumulating product or service costs that uses actual direct materials and direct labor cost, but assigns overhead costs to Work in Process through the use of a predetermined overhead rate

Outlier   a nonrepresentative point that either falls outside the relevant range or is a distortion of typical cost within the relevant range

Overapplied overhead   an occurrence that results when the overhead applied to Work in Process is greater than actual overhead

Practical capacity   the activity level that could be achieved during normal working hours giving consideration to ongoing, regular operating interruptions, such as holidays, downtime, and start-up time

Predetermined overhead rate   an estimated constant charge per unit of activity used to assign overhead costs to production or services based on the actual quantity of the related activity base incurred

Regression line   a line that represents the cost formula for a set of cost observations

Service department   an organizational unit that provides one or more specific functional tasks for other internal units (from appendix)

Simple regression   a method of using only one independent variable to predict the dependent variable in least-squares regression

Step method (of service department cost allocation)   a method that assigns service department costs to cost objects using a specific base after considering the interrelationships of the service departments and the revenue-producing departments (from appendix)

Theoretical capacity   some estimated absolute maximum potential activity that could occur during a specific time frame

Underapplied overhead   an occurrence that results when the overhead applied to Work in Process Inventory is less than actual overhead

SELECTED BIBLIOGRAPHY

Brunton, Nancy M. "Evaluation of Overhead Allocations." *Management Accounting* (July 1988), pp. 22–26.

Callan, John P., et al. "Elgin Sweeper Company's Journey Toward Cost Management." *Management Accounting* (July 1991), pp. 24–27.

Clausing, Neal. "But What's My Cost?" *Journal of Cost Management for the Manufacturing Industry* (Fall 1990), pp. 52–56.

Miller, John A. "Designing and Implementing a New Cost Management System." *Journal of Cost Management for the Manufacturing Industry* (Winter 1992), pp. 41–53.

Roth, Harold P., and A. Faye Borthick. "Are You Distorting Costs by Violating ABC Assumptions?" *Management Accounting* (November 1991), pp. 39–42.

Schlesinger, Jacob M. "GM to Reduce Capacity to Match Its Sales." *Wall Street Journal* (April 25, 1988), p. 2.

SOLUTION STRATEGIES

High-low Method (using assumed amounts)

	(Independent Variable) Activity	(Dependent Variable) Associated Total Cost	=	Total Variable Cost (Rate × Activity)	+	Total Fixed Cost
"High" level	28,000	$36,000		$22,400	+	$13,600
"Low" level	18,000	28,000		14,400	+	13,600
Differences	10,000	$ 8,000				

$.80 variable cost per unit of activity

Flexible Budget
(at any activity level within the relevant range)

$$y = a + bX$$

or

Total Cost = Total Fixed Cost +
(Variable Cost Per Unit of Activity × Level of Activity)

Predetermined Overhead Rate

$$\text{Predetermined OH rate} = \frac{\text{Estimated overhead}}{\text{Estimated level of activity}}$$

(Should be separated into variable and fixed rates and by related cost pools)

Under- and Overapplied Overhead

Variable/Fixed Overhead	XXX	
Various accounts		XXX

Actual overhead is debited to the overhead general ledger account and credited to the sources of the overhead costs

Work in Process*	YYY	
Variable/Fixed Overhead		YYY

Applied overhead is debited to WIP and credited to the overhead general ledger account

*Could be debited directly to Cost of Services Rendered (CSR) in a nonmanufacturing company

A debit balance in Variable/Fixed Overhead at the end of the period is underapplied overhead; a credit balance is overapplied overhead. An immaterial under- or overapplied balance in the OH account is closed at the end of the period to CGS or CSR; a material amount is prorated to WIP, FG, and CGS or CSR.

Service Department Cost Allocation

Direct method:
1. Determine rational and systematic allocation base for each service department.
2. Assign costs from each service department directly to revenue-producing areas using specified allocation bases.

Step method:
1. Determine rational and systematic allocation base for each service department.
2. List service departments in order from the one which provides the *most* service to all other areas (both revenue and non-revenue producing) to the one which only provides service to revenue-producing areas (benefits-provided ranking).
3. Beginning with the first service department listed, allocate the costs from that department to all remaining departments; repeat the process until only revenue-producing departments remain.

END-OF-CHAPTER MATERIALS

Questions

1. What are the overhead implications with regard to expanding automation and product variety in American industry?

2. Why are direct labor hours losing favor as an activity base in some manufacturing companies? Would direct labor still be a valid basis for applying overhead in service companies? Discuss the reasoning behind your answer.

3. Why would the question of whether overhead was assigned using actual rates or predetermined rates make a difference in costing a product?

4. List three reasons to use predetermined overhead rates rather than actual costs to apply indirect costs to products. Why would these reasons be of importance to managers? To marketers? To accountants?

5. Why is it necessary to separate mixed costs into their variable and fixed cost elements for product costing purposes?

6. List six or more mixed costs and provide at least two possible cost drivers for the variable cost element in each type of mixed cost. In what cases would each of the two bases provide better cost information?

7. Why is it necessary to separate mixed costs to prepare a flexible budget?

8. When using a flexible budget, how does fixed cost per unit change as production increases within the relevant range? Variable cost per unit?

9. Why must a particular level of activity be specified to calculate a predetermined fixed overhead rate? Why is such specificity not required to calculate a predetermined variable overhead rate?

10. A company might use one of four different measures of capacity to compute its predetermined fixed overhead rate. What are these four capacity measures, and what differences exist between them? Under what conditions would each provide the best product cost information?

11. How would overhead that was materially underapplied at the end of a year be treated? How might this underapplication affect product costs and annual profits?

12. In a multiproduct company, the number of different products cannot be meaningfully added together to represent production. How can the cost accountant represent production in a single physical quantity?

13. *(Appendix 1)* The high-low method uses only two observation points to separate mixed costs. How does this differ from least-squares regression analysis? Are there any ways in which these two methods are the same or similar?

14. *(Appendix 1)* Differentiate between a dependent variable and an independent variable.

15. *(Appendix 1)* You are trying to project your total college expenses for next year. If you use simple regression analysis, which variable would you choose as the independent variable? If you use multiple regression analysis, which six variables might you choose as the independent variables? Which method would provide better information and why?

16. *(Appendix 2)* Why are service department costs often allocated to revenue-producing departments?

17. *(Appendix 2)* How does service department cost allocation create a feeling of cost responsibility among revenue-producing area managers?

18. *(Appendix 2)* What similarities and differences exist between the direct and step methods of allocating service department costs?

19. *(Appendix 2)* Why is a "benefits-provided" ranking used in the step method of allocation?

Exercises

20. *(Mixed cost analysis)* Celeste Productions makes several different products. Its repairs and maintenance costs have been identified as a mixed cost, and the company wants to develop a budget formula for this mixed cost using machine hours as an activity base. The only historical data the company has is that when 20,000 machine hours were incurred (one-third of expected capacity), repairs and maintenance were $405,000. During 1996, when the company produced at expected capacity, the mixed cost was $510,000. Using this data, develop a budget formula for repairs and maintenance.

21. *(High-low method)* Pretty Cakes Bakery had the following utilities bills during January through September of the current year:

Month	Oven Hours	Utilities
January	1,375	$760
February	1,510	822
March	1,750	835
April	1,484	772
May	1,400	768
June	1,600	820
July	1,625	823
August	1,650	829
September	1,500	810

   a. Using the high-low method, determine the *a* and *b* values.
   b. If it is expected that the company will incur 1,640 hours of baking in October, predict that month's utility costs.

22. *(Flexible budget)* Finks, Inc., used the following values of *a* and *b* in the formula $y = a + bX$ for preparing its flexible budget during the past year: $a = \$3,700$ and $b = \$1.85$ per unit. Frank Finks, president, believes the company will expand to a new relevant range. Fixed costs are expected to remain at $3,700 until the company reaches a level of 8,000 units of production volume, when fixed costs are expected to increase by $1,500. The variable rate is expected to drop at the 9,000 unit volume by $.05 per unit because of volume buying.

   a. Prepare a flexible budget for the new relevant range at the 7,000, 8,000, and 9,000 units of output levels.
   b. Calculate the unit costs at each level.

23. *(Flexible budget)* Loving Touch Pet Salon is in the business of dog grooming. It has determined the following cost formulae for its costs:

$$\text{Supplies (variable): } y = \$0 + \$4.00X$$
$$\text{Direct labor (variable): } y = \$0 + \$12.00X$$
$$\text{Overhead (mixed): } y = \$8,000 + \$1.00X$$

Cheryl Fourcade, the owner, has determined that because the business is intensely labor-oriented, all costs are related to DLHs.

   a. Prepare a flexible budget for each of the following activity levels: 550, 600, 650, and 700 DLHs.
   b. Determine the total cost per direct labor hour at each of the levels of activity.
   c. Loving Touch groomers normally work a total of 650 direct labor hours during a month. Each grooming job typically takes a groomer one and one-

quarter hours. Cheryl wants to earn 40 percent on her costs. What should she charge each pet owner for grooming?

24. *(Predetermined OH rates using different bases)* Monique Dué Enterprises prepared the following 1995 abbreviated flexible budget:

	Machine Hours			
	10,000	11,000	12,000	13,000
Factory Costs				
Variable	$40,000	$44,000	$48,000	$52,000
Fixed	15,000	15,000	15,000	15,000

Monique has set 11,000 machine hours as the 1995 expected annual capacity. It takes two machine hours to produce each product. The company plans to operate at one-twelfth of the expected annual capacity each month.

a. Calculate separate variable and fixed rates using (1) machine hours and (2) units of products.
b. Calculate the combined overhead rate using (1) machine hours and (2) units of products.

25. *(OH application)* Use the information from Exercise 24. In April 1995, the company produced 442 units. During the month, Monique Dué incurred $3,360 of variable overhead and $1,310 of fixed overhead and had 884 actual machine hours.

a. What amount of fixed factory overhead should be applied to production in April 1995?
b. What amount of variable factory overhead should be applied to production in April 1995?
c. Calculate the over- or underapplied variable and fixed overhead for April 1995.

26. *(Predetermined OH rates and under/overapplication)* Cukamora Products applies overhead at a combined rate for fixed and variable overhead of 175 percent of direct labor cost. During the first three months of 1995, actual costs were incurred as follows:

	Direct Labor Cost	Actual Overhead
January	$360,000	$640,000
February	330,000	570,400
March	340,000	600,000

a. What amount of overhead was applied to production in each of the above months?
b. What was the under- or overapplied overhead for each month and in total for the quarter?

27. *(Predetermined OH rates and under/overapplied OH)* Bardfeld, Inc., had the following information in its Work in Process account for April 1995:

WORK IN PROCESS

Beginning balance	5,000	Transferred out	167,500
Materials added	75,000		
Labor (10,000 DLHs)	45,000		
Applied overhead	60,000		
Ending balance	17,500		

All labor is paid the same rate per hour. Overhead is applied to Work in Process on the basis of direct labor hours. The only work left in process at the end of the month had a total of 1,430 direct labor hours accumulated to date.

a. What is the total predetermined overhead rate per direct labor hour?
b. What amounts of material, labor, and overhead are included in the ending Work in Process balance?
c. If actual total overhead for April were $59,350, what is the amount of under- or overapplied overhead?

28. *(Disposition of under/overapplied OH)* Matt Reed Company has an overapplied overhead balance at the end of 1994 of $27,975. The amount of overhead contained in other selected account balances at year-end are:

Work in Process	$ 45,000
Finished Goods	84,000
Cost of Goods Sold	171,000

a. Prepare the necessary journal entries to close the overapplied overhead balance under two alternative approaches.
b. Which approach is the better choice, and why?

29. *(Disposition of under/overapplied OH)* Casey Company's books reflected the following 1996 balances:

	January 1	December 31
Raw Materials	$18,000	$11,000
Work in Process	8,700	11,000
Finished Goods	38,000	22,500

During 1996, $54,000 of direct materials were added to manufacturing and $36,000 of direct labor (6,000 hours at $6 per hour). Total machine hours run in 1996 were 75,000. The firm charges a fixed overhead rate of $.60 per machine hour and a variable overhead rate of $.04 per machine hour. During 1996, actual overhead costs were $47,500.

a. Prepare a schedule of cost of goods manufactured for 1996.
b. Calculate Cost of Goods Sold before closing over- or underapplied overhead.
c. By what amount would the closing of over- or underapplied overhead affect cost of goods sold? (Hint: Without knowing the amount of overhead contained in each account balance, you must use the relationships of the totals to allocate under- or overapplied OH.)

30. *(Predetermined OH rates and capacity measures)* Caruso, Inc., makes blenders. Management has decided to apply overhead to products using a predetermined rate. To determine the rates, management estimated the following budgeted data:

Variable factory overhead at 10,000 direct labor hours	$43,500
Variable factory overhead at 15,000 direct labor hours	65,250
Fixed factory overhead at all levels between 10,000 and 18,000 direct labor hours	40,500

Practical capacity is 18,000 direct labor hours; expected capacity is two-thirds of practical capacity.

   a. What is Caruso, Inc.'s predetermined variable overhead rate?
   b. What is the most common activity measure used to calculate a predetermined overhead rate? Using this measure, calculate the predetermined fixed overhead rate.
   c. Use your answers to (a) and (b). If the firm incurred 11,500 direct labor hours during a period, how much total overhead would be applied? If actual overhead during the period were $90,000, what would be the annual amount of under- or overapplied overhead?

31. *(Predetermined OH rates with flexible budgets)* The Diamond Company expects the following overhead amounts at each of the following activity levels:

	Machine Hours			
	1,000	*1,250*	*1,500*	*1,750*
Total variable costs	$2,000	$2,500	$3,000	$3,500
Total fixed costs	2,000	2,000	2,000	2,400
Total overhead	$4,000	$4,500	$5,000	$5,900

   a. Calculate the predetermined overhead rate at the expected capacity of 1,500 machine hours.
   b. If the total predetermined rate were $3.60, what was the capacity level used for overhead rate calculation?
   c. Analyze and explain the rate differences calculated in parts (a) and (b).

32. *(Appendix 1)* Use the data in Exercise 21 on the Pretty Cakes Bakery.

   a. Apply least-squares analysis to determine the *a* and *b* values.
   b. If it is expected that the company will incur 1,640 hours of baking in October, predict that month's utility costs.
   c. Which method (high-low or regression) do you think will provide better information on which to forecast future costs? Why?

33. *(High-low; Appendix 1)* Kase Dairy specializes in making cheese. Management wants to improve its budgeting of overhead costs and provides you with the following data:

	Monthly Production of Pounds of Cheese	Cheese-making Facility Overhead
January	1,000	$12,000
February	1,250	10,900
March	2,000	13,300
April	1,500	12,100
May	2,125	16,500
June	1,750	13,000
July	1,800	13,700

a. Determine the *a* and *b* values for the equation $y = a + bX$ using the high-low method.

b. Determine the *a* and *b* values for the equation $y = a + bX$ using the regression formula.

c. Provide four other possible independent variables that management might consider using to forecast overhead costs. When might each of these bases provide better information?

34. *(Appendix 2)* Premiere Bank has three revenue-generating areas: checking accounts, savings accounts, and loans. The bank also has three service areas: administration, personnel, and accounting. The direct costs per month and the interdepartmental service structure are shown below in a benefits-provided ranking.

% of Service Used by

Department	Direct Costs	Admin.	Pers.	Acctg.	Check.	Sav.	Loans
Administration	$ 60,000	—	10	10	40	20	20
Personnel	40,000	10	—	10	20	40	20
Accounting	60,000	10	10	—	20	20	40
Checking accounts	60,000						
Savings accounts	50,000						
Loans	100,000						

a. Compute the total cost for each revenue-generating area using the direct method.

b. Compute the total cost for each revenue-generating area using the step method.

35. *(Appendix 2)* Barkman Corp. allocates its service department costs to its producing departments using the direct method. Information for September 1994 follows:

Services provided to other departments:	Personnel	Maintenance
Personnel		10%
Maintenance	15%	
Fabricating	45%	60%
Finishing	40%	30%
Service department costs	$68,000	$50,000

a. What amount of personnel and maintenance costs should be assigned to Fabricating for September?

b. What amount of personnel and maintenance costs should be assigned to Finishing for September?

36. *(Appendix 2)* Michelle Hogg operates a restaurant and catering business. She wants to allocate administrative cost to the two revenue-producing areas. Administrative costs for the period were $43,650. Michelle believes that direct labor hours of each department are the proper basis for allocation. Direct labor hours incurred by each department are: administrative, 5,100; restaurant, 21,000; and catering, 12,000. What amount of administrative cost should be allocated to the restaurant and the catering areas?

Problems

37. *(Mixed cost analysis and predetermined OH rate)* Mimi Manufacturing's predetermined total overhead rate is $6.70, of which $6.30 is variable. Costs at two production levels are:

Overhead Items	8,000 MH	10,000 MH
Indirect materials	$12,800	$16,000
Indirect labor	27,000	33,000
Maintenance	3,700	4,500
Utilities	4,000	5,000
All other	6,700	8,300

Required:

a. Determine the variable and fixed values for each item and give the total overhead formula.
b. What is Mimi's expected activity if the predetermined rate given is based upon expected activity?
c. Determine the expected OH costs at the expected activity.
d. If the firm raises its expected activity level by 3,000 machine hours from that found in part (b), calculate a new predetermined total overhead rate. Draft a memo to management to explain why the rate has changed.

38. *(Analyzing OH costs)* The Lacy Company's predetermined total overhead rate for product costing purposes is $23.00 per unit. Of this amount, $18.00 is the variable portion. Cost information for two levels of activity is as follows:

Overhead components	800 units	1,200 units
Indirect materials	$6,400	$9,600
Indirect labor	5,600	8,400
Handling	2,600	3,800
Maintenance	2,000	3,000
Utilities	2,000	2,800
Supervision	4,000	4,000

Required:

a. Determine the fixed and variable values for each of the preceding components of overhead and determine the total overhead cost formula.
b. What is the company's expected volume level if the predetermined rate is based on expected capacity?
c. Determine the expected overhead costs at the expected activity level.
d. Lacy Company management decides to revise its expected activity level to be 100 units greater than the present level. Determine the new total predetermined overhead rate for product costing purposes.

39. *(Choice of application base)* Cristin Company uses the formula $y = a + bX$ to predict and analyze overhead costs. In the previous year, Cristin used $1,750 per month for the a factor and $.35 for the b factor in applying overhead. Cristin has used direct labor hours in the past, but is wondering whether overhead behavior is more closely associated with machine hours. The following data have been generated for consideration:

Month	Machine Hours	Overhead Costs
1	425	$2,525
2	460	2,961
3	410	2,484
4	480	2,649
5	502	2,705
6	418	2,496

Required:

a. Determine the fixed and variable values using machine hours.
b. For April of the coming year, Cristin expects 3,150 direct labor hours and 492 machine hours. Predict overhead costs using (1) direct labor hours and (2) machine hours.
c. If April's actual fixed overhead costs are $1,525 and actual variable overhead costs are $1,200, which activity base appears better?
d. Discuss criteria in choosing the best activity base for Cristin Company.

40. *(High-low method and flexible budget)* Gary Enterprises tests prospective employees for its management team with the following flexible overhead budget at several levels of activity; some of the amounts are intentionally missing:

	Direct Labor Hours (X)				
Overhead Accounts	8,000	10,000	12,000	14,000	16,000
Indirect materials	$2,400			$4,200	
Indirect labor		$50,000			$80,000
Insurance	600			600	
Depreciation	3,000				3,000
Repairs & maintenance		3,800	$4,300		
Utilities			2,700	3,100	

Required:

a. Using the high-low method, determine the *a* and *b* values for the formula $y = a + bX$, where X is direct labor hours for each item presented.
b. Complete the overhead flexible budget presented in the problem.
c. Assume that 10,000 direct labor hours is expected capacity. Determine:
   1. The predetermined variable OH application rate.
   2. The predetermined fixed OH application rate.
   3. The total predetermined OH application rate.

41. *(Mixed cost analysis and capacity measures)* Kevin Enterprises has two departments: Framing and Covering. Framing is highly automated, and machine hours are used as the activity base there. Covering is labor-intensive, causing the use of direct labor hours as the activity base. A flexible budget is provided below for each department:

	Machine Hours (MHs)			
Framing Overhead	3,000	4,000	5,000	6,000
Variable	$ 6,600	$ 8,800	$11,000	$13,200
Fixed	4,200	4,200	4,200	4,200
Total	$10,800	$13,000	$15,200	$17,400

	Direct Labor Hours (DLHs)			
Covering Overhead	*9,000*	*12,000*	*15,000*	*18,000*
Variable	$45,000	$60,000	$75,000	$90,000
Fixed	3,000	3,000	3,000	3,000
Total	$48,000	$63,000	$78,000	$93,000

The firm produces one style of sofa, which can be covered in a variety of fabrics. Each sofa requires one hour of machine time and three hours of direct labor. Next year Kevin Enterprises plans to produce 5,200 sofas, which is 600 more than normal capacity.

Required:

a. Give the *a* and *b* values for the straight-line cost formula for each department.
b. Predict next year's overhead for each department.
c. Using normal capacity, calculate the predetermined total overhead per sofa. Using expected activity, calculate the predetermined total overhead per sofa.
d. Management wants to earn a gross margin of 50 percent on cost. Which of the two activity measures used in part (c) would you select to determine total cost per sofa, and why?

42. *(Capacity measures and under/overapplied OH)* Howington Enterprises makes only one product. It has a theoretical capacity of 50,000 units annually. Practical capacity is 80 percent of theoretical capacity, while normal capacity is 80 percent of practical capacity. The firm is expecting to produce 36,000 units next year. The following are the estimated factory overhead costs budgeted by the company president, Michael Howington, for the coming year:

Indirect materials: $2.00 per unit
Indirect labor: $144,000 plus $2.50 per unit
Utilities: $6,000 plus $.04 per unit
Repairs and maintenance: $20,000 plus $.34 per unit
Material handling costs: $16,000 plus $.12 per unit
Depreciation: $.06 per unit
Building rent: $50,000 per year
Insurance: $12,000 per year

Required:

a. Determine the straight-line formula for total overhead.
b. Assume that Howington produced 35,000 units during the year and that actual costs were exactly as budgeted. Calculate the over- or underapplied overhead for each possible measurement base.
c. Which information determined in part (b) would be the most beneficial to management, and why?

43. *(Plantwide vs. departmental OH rates)* Kendall, Inc., has two departments: Mixing and Fabricating. Mixing has two workers and twelve machines. Fabricating has twenty-two direct laborers and two machines. One product that the company makes uses both departments and requires machine and labor times as follows:

	Mixing	Fabricating
Machine hours	6.00	.30
Direct labor hours	.04	4.00

Estimated volumes and overhead costs for each department for the coming year are:

	Mixing	Fabricating
Estimated machine hours	36,000	4,650
Estimated direct labor hours	4,800	48,000
Estimated overhead	$312,120	$162,000

Required:

a. Calculate a plantwide rate using machine hours.
b. Given your answer to part (a), how much overhead would be assigned to each product unit?
c. Calculate departmental rates. Using these rates, how much overhead would be assigned to each unit of product?
d. Which rate provides a better representation of the costs of production, and why?

44. *(Plantwide vs. departmental OH rates)* Thompson Manufacturing is composed of a Cutting Department and an Assembly Department. The Cutting Department is staffed by one person who runs fifteen machines. The Assembly Department, on the other hand, is highly labor-intensive, having twenty direct laborers and three machines. All products manufactured by Thompson pass through both departments. Product KL85 uses the following quantities of machine time and direct labor hours:

	Cutting	Assembly
Machine hours	9.00	.12
Direct labor hours	.03	3.00

Thompson has estimated the following total overhead costs and activity levels for each department for 1994:

	Cutting	Assembly
Estimated overhead	$862,200	$432,000
Estimated machine hours	72,000	9,200
Estimated direct labor hours	5,200	50,000

Required:

a. Thompson Manufacturing's accountant uses a plantwide rate for overhead application based on machine hours. What is the rate that will be used for 1994?
b. How much overhead would be assigned to each unit of Product KL85 under the method currently in use?
c. The company's auditors inform Thompson that the method being used to apply overhead is inappropriate. They indicate that machine hours should be used for an application base in Cutting and direct labor hours should be used in Assembly. Using these bases, what would be the departmental rates for 1994? How much overhead would be assigned to each unit of Product KL85 using departmental rates?

45. *(Appendix 1)* David Enterprises has compiled the following data to analyze its utility costs in an attempt to obtain better cost control:

	Machine Hours	Utility Cost
January	200	$150
February	325	220
March	400	240
April	410	245
May	525	310
June	680	395
July	820	420
August	900	450

Required:

a. Determine the *a* and *b* values for the straight-line cost formula using the high-low method.

b. Determine the *a* and *b* values for the straight-line cost formula using the least-squares regression analysis.

c. If September's machine hours are expected to be 760, what are the expected utility costs based on your answers to (a) and (b)? Why do these answers differ?

d. Which of the two sets of values is preferable, and why?

e. As a manager, what questions might you ask about the data just compiled?

46. *(Appendix 2)* Brookhaven Hospital is a small country hospital that wants to determine its full costs of operating its three revenue-producing programs: surgery; in-patient care; and out-patient services. The hospital wants to allocate budgeted costs of administration, public relations, and maintenance to the three revenue-producing programs. The costs budgeted for each service department are: administration, $872,500; public relations, $210,000; and maintenance, $326,500. Total assets employed is chosen as the allocation base for administration; number of employees is to be used for public relations; and number of square feet assigned is used for maintenance costs. The expected utilization of these activity bases is as follows:

	$ of Assets Employed	# of Employees	Sq. Ft. Assigned
Administration	$ 767,800	15	12,000
Public relations	188,000	7	2,200
Maintenance	372,200	12	3,500
Surgery	2,875,000	8	1,800
In-patient care	1,770,000	35	30,600
Out-patient services	1,050,000	14	18,000

Required:

a. Using the direct method, allocate the expected service department costs to the revenue-producing areas.

b. Assuming that the areas are listed in a benefits-provided ranking, allocate the expected service department costs to the revenue-producing areas.

47. *(Appendix 2)* Dixon Cooper owns and manages DHC Realty. The company generates revenue through three departments: commercial sales, residential sales, and property management. Mr. Cooper wants to determine the total costs (including support department costs) of each revenue-generating department. Each

of the company department's direct costs and several associated allocation bases are presented below.

Department	Direct Costs	Available Allocation Bases # of Employees/ Salespersons	$ of Assets Employed	$ of Revenue
Administration	$ 980,000	12	$1,760,000	N/A
Accounting	477,000	7	682,000	N/A
Promotion	381,000	4	470,000	N/A
Commercial Sales	5,245,000	26	620,000	$6,760,000
Residential Sales	4,589,510	105	910,000	8,230,000
Property Management	199,200	6	420,000	498,000

Mr. Cooper has listed the service departments in their benefits-provided ranking. He has selected the following allocation bases on which to allocate service department costs: number of employees/salespersons for administration; dollars of assets employed for accounting; and dollars of revenue for promotion.

Required:

a. Using the direct method, allocate the service department costs to the revenue-generating departments.
b. Using the step method, allocate the service department costs to the revenue-generating departments.
c. Under each method, which department is most profitable?

48. *(Essay)* Jennifer Regan, an economics major, was concentrating diligently on her managerial accounting homework when her younger brother, Jeffrey, came into the room. Jeffrey, a rather advanced thirteen year-old, wanted Jennifer to explain the subject she was studying. Jennifer patiently explained to Jeffrey about predetermined overhead rates and confessed to having difficulty understanding the topic. Jeffrey listened intently, left the room, and came back a few minutes later with the following picture:

Explain the analogy that Jeffrey's picture represents.

Cases

49. Martin Charity Hospital wants to budget its expected costs for each month of the upcoming year in its psychiatric ward. The hospital's management accountant has determined that bed occupancy is the best predictor of cost behavior. The ward has a total of 100 beds, which are generally 70 percent occupied. At 70 percent occupancy, the following costs are incurred per patient day:

	Cost per Patient Day	Per-Day Cost	Total Fixed Cost Per Month
Variable Costs			
Linens	$ 4.00	$ 280	
Food	7.50	525	
Drugs	30.00	2,100	
Doctors	60.00	4,200	
Mixed Costs			
Orderlies (one full-time)		768	$2,880
Nurses (two full-time)		2,700	8,000
Maintenance		100	4,000
Fixed Costs			
Depreciation			1,800
Utilities			960

Except for the three full-time employees, nurses and orderlies are hired from a pool from the hospital by the ward; this is the reason their salaries can be computed on a daily basis. If such hirings are made, they will result in the costs shown in the "per-day" column. One additional full-time nurse and orderly will be necessary if occupancy reaches 85 percent.

Utilities generally cost a fixed fee of $960 per month; this would, however, increase to approximately $1,140 if occupancy reaches 85 percent. Depreciation charges are computed on a straight-line basis at $1,800 per month.

Doctors charges are entirely variable, based on number of patients and assuming one visit for thirty minutes per day. Variable costs are based on a thirty-day month.

Required:

a. What costs are expected for the ward for a month at 60 percent, 80 percent, and 90 percent occupancy?

b. What criticisms might be leveled at the previous 90 percent occupancy budget? Or, because of the organizational type, at any of the expected budgets?

50. Rose Bach has recently been hired as controller of Empco, Inc., a sheet metal manufacturer. Empco has been in the sheet metal business for many years and is currently investigating ways to modernize its manufacturing process. At the first staff meeting Bach attended, Bob Kelley, chief engineer, presented a proposal for automating the Drilling Department. Kelley recommended that Empco purchase two robots that would have the capability of replacing the eight direct labor workers in the department.

The cost savings outlined in Kelley's proposal included the elimination of direct labor cost in the Drilling Department plus a reduction of manufacturing overhead cost in the department to zero, because Empco charges manufacturing overhead on the basis of direct labor dollars using a plantwide rate.

The president of Empco was puzzled by Kelley's explanation of cost savings, believing it made no sense. Bach agreed, explaining that as firms become more automated, they should rethink their manufacturing overhead systems. The president then asked Bach to look into the matter and prepare a report for the next staff meeting.

To refresh her knowledge, Bach reviewed articles on manufacturing overhead allocation for an automated factory and discussed the matter with some of her peers. Bach also gathered the following historical data on the manufacturing overhead rates experienced by Empco over the years.

Date	Average Annual Direct Labor Cost	Average Annual Manufacturing Overhead Cost	Average Manufacturing Overhead Application Rate
1940s	$1,000,000	$ 1,000,000	100%
1950s	1,200,000	3,000,000	250%
1960s	2,000,000	7,000,000	350%
1970s	3,000,000	12,000,000	400%
1980s	4,000,000	20,000,000	500%

Bach also wanted to have some departmental data to present at the meeting and, using Empco's accounting records, was able to estimate the following annual averages for each manufacturing department in the 1980s:

	Cutting Department	Grinding Department	Drilling Department
Direct labor	$ 2,000,000	$1,750,000	$ 250,000
Manufacturing overhead	11,000,000	7,000,000	2,000,000

Required:
a. Disregarding the proposed use of robots in the Drilling Department, describe the shortcomings of the system for applying overhead that is currently used by Empco, Inc.
b. Explain the misconceptions underlying Bob Kelley's statement that manufacturing overhead cost in the Drilling Department would be reduced to zero if the automation proposal was implemented.
c. Recommend ways to improve Empco, Inc.'s method for applying overhead by describing how it should revise its overhead accounting system:
    1. in the Cutting and Grinding Departments; and
    2. to accommodate the automation of the Drilling Department.

(CMA)

51. Moss Manufacturing has just completed a major change in its quality control (QC) process. Previously, products had been reviewed by QC inspectors at the end of each major process, and the company's ten QC inspectors were charged as direct labor to the operation or job. In an effort to improve efficiency and quality, a computerized video QC system was purchased for $250,000. The system consists of a minicomputer, fifteen video cameras, other peripheral hardware, and software.

The new system uses cameras stationed by QC engineers at key points in the production process. Each time an operation changes or there is a new operation, the cameras are moved, and a new master picture is loaded into the computer by a QC engineer. The camera takes pictures of the units in process, and the computer compares them to the picture of a "good" unit. Any differences are sent to a QC engineer who removes the bad units and discusses the flaws with the production supervisors. The new system has replaced the ten QC inspectors with two QC engineers.

The operating costs of the new QC system, including the salaries of the two QC engineers, have been included as factory overhead in calculating the company's plantwide factory overhead rate, which is based on direct labor dollars.

The company's president is confused. His vice-president of production has told him how efficient the new system is, yet there is a large increase in the factory overhead rate. The computation of the rate before and after automation is as follows:

	Before	After
Budgeted overhead	$1,900,000	$2,100,000
Budgeted direct labor	1,000,000	700,000
Budgeted overhead rate	190%	300%

"Three hundred percent," lamented the president. "How can we compete with such a high factory overhead rate?"

Required:

a. (1) Define "factory overhead," and cite three examples of typical costs that would be included in factory overhead.

(2) Explain why companies develop factory overhead rates.

b. Explain why the increase in the overhead rate should not have a negative financial impact on Moss Manufacturing.

c. Explain, in the greatest detail possible, how Moss Manufacturing could change its overhead accounting system to eliminate confusion over product costs.

(CMA)

█   Ethics Discussion

52. From Maria Shao, "The Cracks in Stanford's Ivory Tower," *Business Week* (March 11, 1991), p. 64: "Stanford gets some $175 million a year in direct research funding from the federal government. Like other schools that receive these grants, it also gets reimbursed by Uncle Sam for overhead or indirect costs associated with the research. In Stanford's case, that's an additional $85 million or so a year, or roughly 20% of its operating budget." Some of the items that were charged to the government for research included:

$2,000 a month in floral arrangements
$2,500 to refurbish a grand piano
$3,000 for a cedar-lined closet
$184,000 in depreciation on a yacht donated to Stanford's sailing program

The rate charged to Uncle Sam for overhead varies among universities. According to *Newsweek* (Sharon Begley, et al., "Milking the Laboratories for Dollars" [May 6, 1991], p. 58), the following are overhead "add-ons" per dollar of research money:

Harvard Medical	$.88	(and, in 1992, hopes for $.96)
Yale and Johns Hopkins	$.60	
Massachusetts Institute of Technology	$.575	

After investigations, Stanford returned almost $700,000 to the government, and MIT returned $731,000 for inappropriate charges. In April 1991, "Harvard Med said it would withdraw $500,000 from its request for reimbursement of indirect costs incurred in fiscal 1991; the school admits that it may not have been proper to charge the government $3,100 for a dean's retirement party and $140,000 for upkeep on the president's house and dean's office." (Begley)

a. Discuss the rationale for allowing colleges and universities to charge the government for overhead costs related to research grants.

b. Discuss the ethical implications of allowing colleges and universities to "liberally" decide what overhead costs should be included in research-related overhead.

c. Discuss the budgetary implications of allowing colleges and universities to "liberally" decide what overhead costs should be included in research-related overhead.

d. What is your reaction as a taxpayer to a college or university's including costs such as those listed earlier in "research-related overhead"?

e. If one of the previously mentioned universities were a research firm rather than a university and you had engaged it to perform a research task for your company, discuss how you would want to set policy for what costs could be considered as part of research-related overhead for which you could be charged.

53. Assigning overhead costs to products is necessary to more accurately estimate the cost of producing a good or performing a service. One "product" that takes on an exceptional number of additional charges for overhead is an aspirin dose (two units) in a hospital. Following is an estimate of why a patient is charged $7 for a dose of aspirin. Some costs are referred to as "shared and shifted costs"; others are called overhead. In all cases, this simply means that these costs are not covered by revenue dollars elsewhere and must then be covered by doing all of the things a hospital charges for—including administering aspirin.

COUNTY COMMUNITY HOSPITAL PRODUCT COSTING SHEET

	Unit	Unit Cost	Total Units	Total Cost
Raw Material				
Aspirin	ea.	$ 0.006	2	$0.012
Direct Labor				
Physician	hr.	60.000	0.0083	0.500
Pharmacist	hr.	30.000	0.0200	0.603
Nurse	hr.	20.000	0.0056	0.111
Indirect Labor				
Orderly	hr.	12.000	0.0167	0.200
Recordkeeping	hr.	12.000	0.0167	0.200
Supplies				
Cup	ea.	0.020	1	0.020
Shared & Shifted Costs				
Unreimbursed Medicare		0.200	1	0.200
Indigent Care		0.223	1	0.223
Uncollectible Receivables		0.084	1	0.084
Malpractice Insurance		0.034	2	0.068

Excess Bed Capacity	0.169	1	0.169
Other Operating Costs	0.056	1	0.056
Other Administrative Costs	0.112	1	0.112
Excess Time Elements	0.074	1	0.074

HOSPITAL OVERHEAD COSTS @32.98%	.868
FULL COST (including Overhead)	$3.500
PROFIT (@50%)	3.500
PRICE (per dose)	$7.000

SOURCE: David W. McFadden, "The Legacy of the $7 Aspirin," *Management Accounting* (April 1990), p. 39. Published by Institute of Management Accountants, Montvale, N.J.

(Note that the dose is charged twice for malpractice insurance—once for each aspirin!)

a. Discuss the reasons why such cost shifting is necessary.

b. What other kinds of costs might be included in the additional "overhead" charge at the rate of 32.98 percent?

c. Discuss the ethical implications of shifting costs such as those for indigent care, uncollectible receivables, and excess bed capacity to a patient receiving a dose of aspirin.

d. Are you willing to accept a $7 charge for a dose of aspirin, knowing what costs are considered in developing such a charge if you are (1) a paying customer or (2) the hospital manager? Discuss the reasons behind your answers.

54. Bordelee Machine Corporation is bidding on a contract with the government of Mosquel for 200,000 units of gizzels. The contract calls for payment of costs plus a profit margin of 50 percent. Costs are estimated as follows:

Direct materials and direct labor	$60 per unit
Variable overhead	$12 per unit
Total fixed overhead	$2,400,000

By acquiring the machinery and supervisory support needed to produce the 200,000 units, Bordelee will obtain the capacity to produce 250,000 units.

a. Should the price bid by Bordelee include a fixed overhead cost of $12 per unit or $9.60? How were these two amounts determined? Which of these two amounts would be more likely to cause the company to obtain the contract? Why?

b. Assume that Bordelee set a bid price of $122.40 and obtained the contract. After producing the units, Bordelee submitted an invoice to the government of Mosquel for $25,200,000. The minister of finance for the country requests an explanation. Can you provide one?

c. Bordelee uses the excess machine capacity to produce an additional 50,000 units for another buyer while making the units for Mosquel. Is it ethical to present a $25,200,000 bill to Mosquel? Discuss.

d. Bordelee does not use the excess machine capacity while making the units for Mosquel. However, several months after that contract was completed, the company begins production of additional units. Was it ethical to present a $25,200,000 bill to Mosquel? Discuss.

e. Bordelee does not use the excess capacity, because no other buyer exists for units of this type. Was it ethical to make a bid of $122.40 based on a fixed overhead rate per unit of $9.60? Discuss.

55. Tom Savin has recently been hired as a cost accountant by the Offset Press Company, a privately held company that produces a line of offset printing presses and lithograph machines. During his first few months on the job, Savin discovered that Offset has been underapplying factory overhead to the Work in Process account, while overstating expense through the general and administrative accounts. This practice has been going on since the start of the company six years ago. The effect in each year has been favorable, having a material impact on the company's tax position. No internal audit function exists at Offset, and the external auditors have not yet discovered the underapplied factory overhead.

   Prior to the sixth-year audit, Savin had pointed out the practice and its effect to Mary Brown, the corporate controller, and had asked her to let him make the necessary adjustments. Brown directed him not to make adjustments but to wait until the external auditors had completed their work and see what they uncovered.

   The sixth-year audit has now been completed, and the external auditors have once more failed to discover the underapplication of factory overhead. Savin again asked Brown if he could make the required adjustments and was again told not to make them. Savin, however, believes that the adjustments should be made and that the external auditors should be informed of the situation.

   Since there are no established policies at Offset Press Company for resolving ethical conflicts, Savin is considering following one of the three alternative courses of action that follow:

   • Follow Brown's directive and do nothing further.
   • Attempt to convince Brown to make the proper adjustments, and advise the external auditors of her actions.
   • Tell the Audit Committee of the Board of Directors about the problem and give them the appropriate accounting data.

   a. For each of the three alternative courses of action that Tom Savin is considering, explain whether or not the action is appropriate. You may want to refer to the "Standards of Ethical Conduct for Management Accountants" given in chapter 1.
   b. Without prejudice to your answer in part (a), assume that Tom Savin again approaches Mary Brown to make the necessary adjustments and is unsuccessful. Describe the steps that Tom Savin should take in proceeding to resolve this situation.

   (CMA adapted)

CHAPTER 4

ACTIVITY-BASED MANAGEMENT

LEARNING OBJECTIVES

After completing this chapter, you should be able to do the following:

1. Differentiate between value-added and non-value-added activities
2. Understand why non-value-added activities cause costs to increase unnecessarily
3. Determine when the use of activity-based costing is appropriate
4. Distinguish between activity-based costing and conventional overhead allocation methods
5. Designate the cost drivers in an activity-based costing system
6. Recognize how installing an activity-based costing system affects performance and behavior
7. Know how the theory of constraints can assist in determining production flow
8. Recognize the benefits that can be achieved with the use of activity-based costing

Caterpillar's Costs Are Built on ABC

Today's competitive environment makes it imperative for manufacturers competing globally to know their costs. They need to understand costs at several levels, the activities that are driving costs, the link between management decisions and subsequent costs incurred, and the areas where improvement opportunities lie.

Simple cost systems are accurate enough for assigning costs that are easily traceable to the production process, such as production material and direct labor, but they don't specifically assign costs such as machine tool energy consumption, setup, machine repair, durable tooling, and manufacturing support activities. Such systems also fail to recognize the product-by-product cost effects of volume, product and process complexity, product design, and the different values of capital assets used in the production process.

A good cost system mirrors the manufacturing process and related support activities and quantifies them product by product. The more complex and inconsistent these processes are, the more difficult it is to assign costs to products accurately. Thus, the cost system becomes more complex as it attempts to compensate for the lack of simplicity of the manufacturing processes.

Such considerations led Caterpillar to develop a product costing system . . . [designed] to identify the activities consumed by products and, through a logical, reliable, and consistent process, assign the related costs properly to each.

SOURCE: Lou F. Jones, "Product Costing at Caterpillar," *Management Accounting* (February 1991), pp. 34–35. Published by Institute of Management Accountants, Montvale, N.J.

aterpillar dismissed the use of a single plantwide overhead rate based on direct labor in the late 1940s, because company managers found that such a method did not provide good product cost information. Now, many companies have complex, automated processes that produce a wide variety of products. If plantwide, direct labor-based rates could not provide good cost information in those far simpler times, many cost information systems currently using such a basis must be providing less-than-adequate information.

As indicated in Exhibit 4–1, both users and preparers of product cost information are concerned about its accuracy and relevance to decision making. The reasons for dissatisfaction with some traditionally available information are many, but are summarized by the following quote: "Today's management accounting information, driven by the procedures and cycles of the organization's financial reporting system, is too late, too aggregated, and too distorted to be relevant for managers' planning and control decisions."[1] The cost element causing the problem is overhead, and the failure lies in the manner in which overhead is allocated or attached to products.

---

[1]H. Thomas Johnson and Robert S. Kaplan, *Relevance Lost* (Boston: Harvard Business School Press, 1987), p. 1.

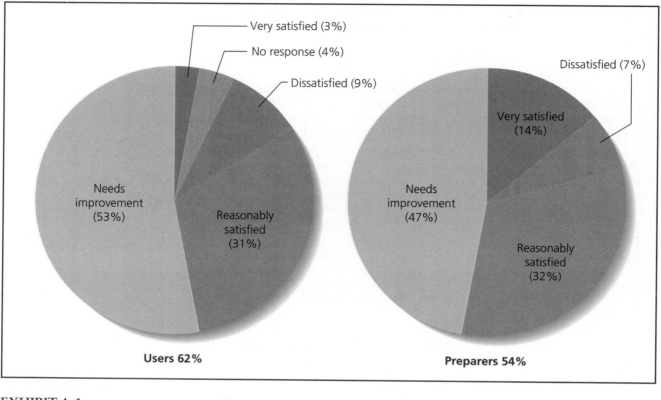

EXHIBIT 4–1
▼▼▼▼▼▼▼▼▼▼▼▼▼▼

LEVEL OF
DISSATISFACTION
WITH PRODUCT
COST INFORMATION

SOURCE: Robert Howell et al., *Management Accounting in the New Manufacturing Environment* (Montvale, N.J.: National Association of Accountants, 1987), pp. 146 and 160.

WHY PRODUCT COST INFORMATION IS DEVELOPED

Product (or service) cost information is developed for three purposes: (1) to report to various external parties; (2) to help in pricing decisions; and (3) to allow managerial control over operations. In many organizations, the first purpose has often overwhelmed the other two. This circumstance has arisen partially because the external parties (Securities Exchange Commission, Internal Revenue Service, and other regulatory agencies) to which the company reports have established rules about what will be considered appropriate inclusions in determining cost.

For instance, the Financial Accounting Standards Board has mandated that research and development costs be expensed as incurred and, therefore, cannot be considered product costs for audited financial statements. Because external parties desire conformity in information reporting, and because no one has mandated how product costs should be developed for the other two purposes, it is often easier to use the same product costing system for all three purposes. The degree of ease resulting from the use of such information may not, however, be directly related to the usefulness of the resulting decisions.

While it is impossible to determine the *exact* cost of a product, managers should try to develop the best possible estimate of that cost. This best estimate arises when the most costs can be traced directly to products using valid measures of resource consumption (cost drivers) and when the fewest costs are assigned arbitrarily. Direct materials and direct labor costs have always been traced easily to products because these costs are variable in relation to volume. Thus, volume was and is a valid measure of direct materials and direct labor consumption.

In the past, when direct labor was a more significant part of product cost than it is currently, overhead was often attached to products using a direct labor hour (DLH) base. While DLHs may not have been the *most* accurate measure of resource consumption, it was generally considered a reasonable allocation base. The modern manufacturing environment, though, is highly machine-intensive with high overhead costs and low direct labor costs. Incurrence of overhead, however, is not solely related to machine hours; it is often related to product variety or other cost drivers. Such an environment requires more sophisticated measures of overhead cost allocation. Some techniques that fall under the umbrella heading of activity-based management and which help managers obtain the best possible estimate of product or service costs are covered in this chapter.

ACTIVITY ANALYSIS

Product cost determination, although specifically designated as an accounting function, is a major concern of all managers. For example, product costs impact decisions on corporate strategy (is it profitable to be in a particular market?), marketing (how much does this product cost and how should it be priced?), and finance (should we invest in additional plant assets to manufacture this product?). In theory, it would not matter what a product or service cost to produce or perform if enough customers were willing to buy that product or service at a price set by the company to cover costs and provide a reasonable profit margin. In reality, customers usually only purchase a product or service that provides acceptable value for the price being charged.

Management, then, should be concerned about whether customers perceive an equality relationship between selling price and value. The concept of **activity-based management** focuses on the activities incurred during the production/performance process as the way to improve the value received by a customer and the resulting profit achieved by providing this value. The concepts covered by activity-based management are shown in Exhibit 4–2 and are discussed in this chapter. These concepts help companies to produce more efficiently, determine costs more accurately, and control and evaluate performance more effectively.

activity-based management

Value-Added and Non-Value-Added Activities

In the context of business, **activities** are considered to be repetitive actions that are performed to fulfill a business function. Each activity can be judged as value-added or non-value-added. An activity may increase the worth of a product or service to the

EXHIBIT 4–2
▼▼▼▼▼▼▼▼▼▼

THE ACTIVITY-
BASED
MANAGEMENT
UMBRELLA

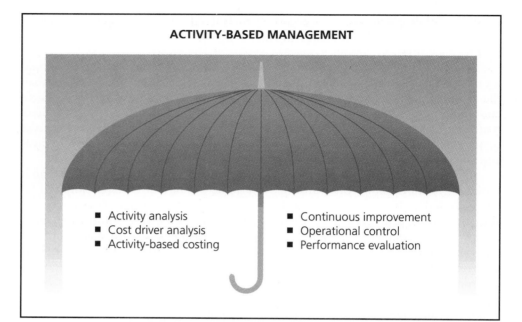

ACTIVITY-BASED MANAGEMENT

- Activity analysis
- Cost driver analysis
- Activity-based costing

- Continuous improvement
- Operational control
- Performance evaluation

value-added activities

non-value-added activities

customer; in this case the customer is willing to pay for that activity and it is considered **value-added**. Some activities, though, simply increase the time spent on a product or service but do not increase its worth to the customer; these activities are **non-value-added.** The additional time creates additional costs that are unnecessary. If

Getting luggage on the proper flights is definitely a value-added activity for airlines. Using bar code scanners makes this process easier and faster for baggage handlers.

non-value-added activities were eliminated, costs would decrease without affecting the market value or quality of the product or service.

Exhibit 4–3 of a televised football game provides a simplified example of value-added and non-value-added activities. While the quarter-hour spent in the huddle or lined up on the field is value-added from the players' and coaches' perspectives, the viewer merely sees people standing on the field. That time is often considered by the viewer (the customer) as non-value-added. The two hours taken up by commercials, the half-time show, instant replays, and so on, also may be value-added from certain perspectives, but possibly not from the viewer's, who may not even watch these portions of the telecast.

As in a televised football game, significant amounts of non-value-added activities exist in business. In analyzing activities, managers should prepare a **process map** that indicates *every* step that goes into making or doing something. It is critical that all steps be included, not just the obvious ones. For example, storing newly purchased parts would not be on a typical list of "Steps in Making Product X," but when materials and supplies are purchased, they are commonly warehoused until needed. Such storage uses facilities that cost money and time for moving the items into and out of storage. As indicated in the News Note on the next page, General Electric is quite familiar with process mapping.

process map

Once the process map has been developed, a **value chart** can be constructed that highlights value-added and non-value-added activities and the time spent in those activities from the beginning to end of a process. Essentially four types of time compose the entire processing time of an entity: production (or performance), inspection, transfer, and idle. The actual time that it takes to perform the functions necessary to manufacture the product or perform the service is the **production** or performance **time.** This quantity of time is value-added. Performing quality control results in **inspection time,** and moving products or components from one place to another constitutes **transfer time.** Lastly, storage time and time spent waiting at the production operation for processing are referred to as **idle time.** Inspection time, transfer time, and idle time are all considered non-value-added time. Thus, the lead or cycle time from the receipt of an order to completion of a product or performance of a service is equal to production time plus non-value-added time.

value chart

production time
inspection time

transfer time
idle time

While it is theoretically correct to view inspection time and transfer time as non-value-added, it is important to realize that very few companies can completely eliminate all quality control functions and that it is impossible to eliminate all transfer

EXHIBIT 4–3
▼▼▼▼▼▼▼▼▼▼▼▼

VALUE-ADDED AND
NON-VALUE-ADDED
ACTIVITIES

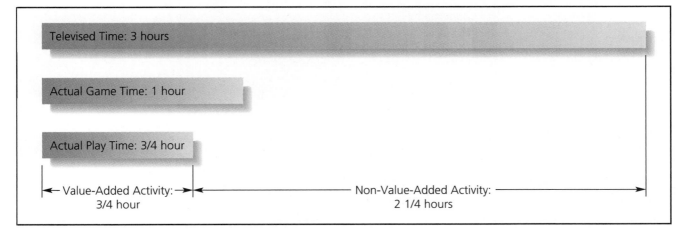

Televised Time: 3 hours

Actual Game Time: 1 hour

Actual Play Time: 3/4 hour

←— Value-Added Activity: —→|←——————— Non-Value-Added Activity: —————————→
        3/4 hour   2 1/4 hours

NEWS NOTE

What Steps Are Involved?

Elaborate process maps use diamonds, circles, and squares to distinguish work that adds value from work that doesn't, like inspection. These are furbelows, not really necessary. What's essential is that every step be mapped, from the order clerk picking up the phone to the deliveryman getting a signed receipt.

Process mapping sounds simple, but it's not. To do it right, managers, employees, suppliers, and customers must work on the map together to make sure that what the company thinks happens really does. When a team from GE's Evendale, Ohio, plant mapped the process of making turbine shafts for jet engines, the job took more than a month, and the map went all around a conference room.

When a process is mapped, GE has—often for the first time—the ability to manage an operation in a coherent way from start to finish. For example, in pursuit of 100% machine utilization, all rotating parts used to go to a central steam-cleaning facility between operations; now the shaftmakers have their own cleaning booths because the process map revealed that the time saved more than paid for the additional equipment.

SOURCE: Thomas A. Stewart, "GE Keeps Those Ideas Coming," *FORTUNE* (August 12, 1991), p. 48. © 1991 The Time Inc. Magazine Company. All rights reserved.

EXHIBIT 4–4
▼▼▼▼▼▼▼▼▼▼▼

TILTON COMPANY VALUE CHART

Compounding

Operations	Receiving	Quality control	Storage	Move to production facility	Waiting for use	Machine setup	Compounding	Quality control	Move to packaging
Average Time (Days)	1	2	15–20	.5	5	.5	3.5	1	.5

Packaging

Operations	Receiving	Storage	Move to production facility	Waiting for use	Machine setup	Packaging	Quality control	Move to finished goods warehouse	Storage	Move to shipping dock	Sitting on shipping dock	Ship to customer
Average Time (Days)	.5	5–15	.5	5	.5	.5	2	.5	0–20	1	.5	1–3

Total time in compounding:	29.0 – 34.0 days	Total value-added time:	3.5 days
Total time in packaging:	17.0 – 49.0 days	Total value-added time:	.5 days
Total processing time:	46.0 – 83.0 days	Total value-added time:	4.0 days
	Non-value-added time:	**42–79 days**	

Non-Value-Added Activities

Value-Added Activities

time. Understanding the non-value-added nature of these functions, however, should help managers strive to minimize such activities to the extent possible.

A value chart for the Tilton Company (Exhibit 4–4) illustrates the various activities of its manufacturing process. Note the excessive amounts of time that are consumed by storing and moving materials. Only four days of value-added production time are in the entire sequence and, in some instances, the company may also question the time spent in packaging. Packaging is essential for some products but unnecessary for others and, since packaging takes up about a third of the U.S. landfills and creates a substantial cost, many companies and consumers are focusing their attention on reducing or eliminating packaging.

Manufacturing Cycle Efficiency

Dividing value-added production time by total lead time indicates **manufacturing cycle efficiency** (MCE), or how well a firm's manufacturing capabilities use time resources. In a manufacturing environment, "[t]ypically, value is added to the product only 10% of the time from receipt of the parts until shipment to the customer. Ninety percent of the cycle time is waste. A product is much like a magnet. The longer the cycle time, the more the product attracts and creates cost." [2] In a "perfect" production environment, the manufacturing cycle efficiency "would be 100%, since the goal is to eliminate non-value-added time by producing the exact needs at the exact time at every stage of production." [3] One method that moves a company toward such an optimized manufacturing environment is a just-in-time inventory system. **Just-in-time** (JIT) refers to the idea that inventory is manufactured (or purchased) only as the need for it arises or in time to be sold or used. The use of JIT concepts would eliminate a significant portion of the idle time occurring from storage and wait processes.

In a retail environment, lead time relates to the time from ordering an item to the sale of that item to a customer; non-value-added activities in retail refer to shipping time from the supplier, receiving department delays for counting merchandise, and any storage time between receipt and sale. In a service company, lead time refers to the time between the service order and service completion. All activities that are not incurred in actual service performance and unproductive nonactivities (such as delays in beginning a job) are considered non-value-added *for that job*. Washington D.C.'s Transamerica Telemarketing Inc. recognized that there were substantial time inefficiencies in the organization after the loss of a major client. An analysis of job functions indicated the causes of the inefficiencies; removing those causes increased the efficiency of both marketing and account service personnel.

NVA activities are illustrated in the following example. On Monday at 9:00 A.M., a plumber receives a phone call to replace a leaking pipe. The plumber schedules the job for Tuesday at 3:30 P.M.; upon arriving at the house, he spends twenty minutes repairing the pipe, five minutes writing an invoice, and five minutes chatting with the homeowner. The total lead time is thirty-one hours (9:00 A.M. Monday to 4:00 P.M. Tuesday)—of which only twenty to twenty-five minutes is value-added for that particular job! The five minutes spent writing the invoice could be perceived as value-added by the customer, because if the pipe breaks again within

manufacturing cycle efficiency

just-in-time

---

[2]Tom E. Pryor, "Activity Accounting: The Key to Waste Reduction," *The Accounting Systems Journal* (Fall 1990), p. 38.
[3]Callie Berliner and James A. Brimson, eds., *Cost Management for Today's Advanced Manufacturing* (Boston: Harvard Business School Press, 1988), p. 4.

the warranty period, there is evidence that the additional work is under warranty. As the following News Note indicates, even in service businesses non-value-added activities have to be identified to be eliminated.

Non-value-added activities can be attributed to systemic, physical, and human factors. For example, the system may require that products be manufactured in large batches to minimize costs of setting up machinery or that service jobs be taken in order of cruciality. Physical factors contribute to non-value-added activities, since, in many instances, building layouts do not provide for the most efficient transfer of products. This factor is especially apparent in multistory buildings in which receiving and shipping must be on the ground floor, but storage and production are on other floors. People may also be responsible for non-value-added activities because of improper skills or training or of a need to be sociable (production workers discussing weekend sports events during production Monday morning). Attempts to reduce non-value-added activities should be directed at all of these causes and should focus on those that create the most unnecessary costs.

Although doing process mapping and constructing a value chart for *each* product or service could be quite time-consuming, a few such charts can quickly indicate where a company is losing time and money through non-value-added activities. Using amounts such as depreciation on storage facilities, wages for employees who handle warehousing, and an "interest charge" on tied-up working capital funds can provide an estimate of cost reduction provided by the elimination of non-value-added activities.

Moving and storing are two types of non-value-added activities. While all NVA activities cannot be eliminated, process analysis should highlight the time these activities take so that action can be implemented to reduce that time.

NEWS NOTE

Non-Value-Added Activities Are Everywhere!

A Pittsburgh car dealer learned what is possible when he messed up the repairs on a Westinghouse executive's car. The manager offered the dealer a choice between a day in court or a review by Westinghouse's quality center. He chose the second—and now repairs that took 28 individual steps, seven forms, and three days require 12 steps, two forms, and two hours.

SOURCE: Thomas A. Stewart, "The New American Century: Where We Stand," *FORTUNE* (Special edition 1991), p. 21. © 1991 The Time Inc. Magazine Company. All rights reserved.

COST DRIVER ANALYSIS

Because companies engage in various activities, company resources are consumed and, in turn, costs are incurred. All activities have related cost drivers, defined in chapter 2 as factors having direct cause-effect relationships to a cost. It may be possible to identify many cost drivers for an individual business unit. For example, some cost drivers for the purchasing area are number of purchase orders, number of supplier contacts, and number of shipments received. The number of cost drivers that can be identified is not necessarily the same number as should be used. Management should keep the cost drivers selected for use to a reasonable number and be certain that the cost of measuring the cost driver is not excessive. As indicated in the News Note on page 134, cost drivers should be easy to understand, directly related to the activity being performed, and appropriate for performance measurement.

Costs have traditionally been accumulated into one or two cost pools (total factory overhead or variable and fixed factory overhead). Furthermore, one or two cost drivers (direct labor hours and/or machine hours) have been used to assign costs to products. As indicated in the opening vignette about Caterpillar, however, the use of single cost pools and single cost drivers may produce illogical product or service costs in complex production (or service) environments.

To reflect the more complex environments, the accounting system must first recognize that costs are created and incurred because their drivers occur at different levels. This recognition requires the use of **cost driver analysis,** which investigates, quantifies, and explains the relationships of drivers and their related costs. Traditionally, cost drivers were viewed only at the unit level: how many hours of labor or machine time does it take to produce a product or render a service? While some costs are **unit level costs** that are caused by the production or acquisition of a single unit of product or the delivery of a single unit of service, other costs occur at "higher" levels of activity. These higher activity levels include batch, product or process, and organizational or facility levels. Some examples of the kinds of costs occurring at the various levels are given in Exhibit 4–5.

cost driver analysis

unit level costs

NEWS NOTE

How to Choose a Cost Driver

In principle, every cost is the product of a price . . . and a quantity of something—which could be regarded as the activity. However, the number of different activities that can be practically accommodated in cost systems, and hence the number of cost pools, is limited. The art in designing an ABC system is in choosing a limited number of activity measures that can satisfactorily proxy for a wide range of the actual activities carried on [in] the firm. An activity measure is a satisfactory proxy if it is highly correlated with an activity. For example, it is likely that the engineering cost pool isn't just a function of the number of engineering change orders. Nevertheless, if the various activities that generate those costs are highly correlated with the number of engineering change orders, then the number of engineering change orders is likely to be a satisfactory proxy for the real cost drivers.

SOURCE: Eric Noreen, "Conditions Under Which Activity-Based Cost Systems Provide Relevant Costs," *Journal of Management Accounting Research* (Fall 1991), p. 164.

EXHIBIT 4–5
▼▼▼▼▼▼▼▼▼▼▼▼▼

LEVELS OF COSTS

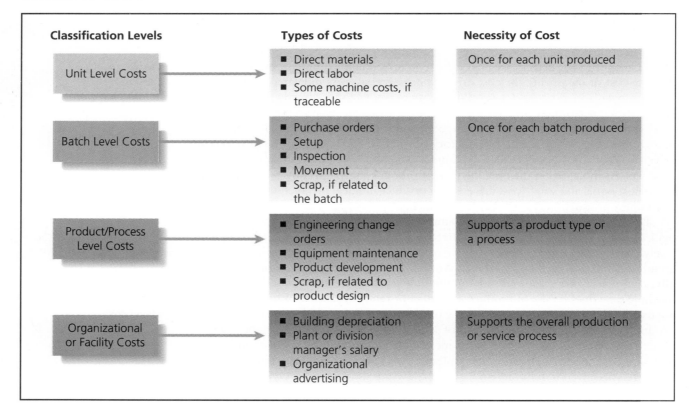

Classification Levels	Types of Costs	Necessity of Cost
Unit Level Costs	■ Direct materials ■ Direct labor ■ Some machine costs, if traceable	Once for each unit produced
Batch Level Costs	■ Purchase orders ■ Setup ■ Inspection ■ Movement ■ Scrap, if related to the batch	Once for each batch produced
Product/Process Level Costs	■ Engineering change orders ■ Equipment maintenance ■ Product development ■ Scrap, if related to product design	Supports a product type or a process
Organizational or Facility Costs	■ Building depreciation ■ Plant or division manager's salary ■ Organizational advertising	Supports the overall production or service process

Costs that are caused by a group of things being made, handled, or processed at a single time are called **batch level costs.** A good example of a batch level cost is the cost of setting up a machine. Assume that setting up a machine to cast product parts costs Caterpillar $500. Two different parts are to be manufactured during the day; therefore, two setups will be needed at a total cost of $1,000. The first run will generate 500 Type A parts, while the second run will generate 100 Type B parts. These quantities are specifically needed for production because the company is on a just-in-time production system. If a unit-based cost driver were used, the total setup cost of $1,000 would be divided by 600 parts, giving a cost per part of $1.67. This method would assign the majority of the cost to Type A parts (500 × $1.67 = $835). However, because the cost is actually a batch level cost, $500 should be spread over 500 Type A parts for a cost of $1 per part, and $500 should be spread over 100 Type B parts for a cost of $5 per part. Using a batch level perspective indicates the commonality of the cost to the units within the batch and is more indicative of the relationship between the activity (setup) and the driver (different production runs).

batch level costs

A cost caused by the development, production, or acquisition of different items is called a **product** or **process level cost.** To illustrate this level of cost, assume that the engineering department of Caterpillar issued ten engineering change orders (ECOs) during May. Of these ECOs, eight related to Product X, two related to Product Y, and none related to Product Z. Each ECO costs $2,700 to issue. During May, the company produced 2,000 units of Product X, 3,000 units of Product Y, and 10,000 units of Product Z. If ECO costs were treated as unit level costs, the total ECO cost of $27,000 would be spread over the 15,000 units produced at a cost per unit of $1.80. However, this method inappropriately assigns $18,000 of ECO cost to Product Z, which had no engineering change orders issued for it! Treating ECO costs as product/process level would assign $21,600 of costs to Product X and $5,400 to Product Y. These amounts would be assigned *not* to current month production, but

product or process level cost

Under activity-based costing, the total research and development cost of developing each Nintendo game would be considered a product level cost. ABC would average that amount over all the estimated units to be produced—from introduction to product demise—of each specific game.

to all units of Products X and Y produced during the time that these ECOs are in effect, because the costs theoretically benefit all current and future production.

organizational level

Some costs (**organizational level**) are incurred only to support the ongoing facility operations. These costs are common to many different activities and products or services and can only be prorated to products on an arbitrary basis. Activity-based costing would not try to assign such costs to products.

Traditionally, accounting has assumed that if costs did not vary with changes in production at the unit level, those costs were fixed rather than variable. Such an assumption is not true. Batch level, product level, and organizational level costs are all variable, but these types of costs vary for reasons other than changes in production volume. For this reason, to determine an accurate estimate of product or service cost, costs should be accumulated at each successively higher level of costs. Because unit, batch, and product level costs are all related to units of products (merely at different levels), these costs can be gathered together at the product level to match with the revenues generated by product sales. Organizational level costs, however, are not product related and, thus, should only be subtracted in total from net product revenues.

Exhibit 4–6 indicates how cost accumulation at the various levels can be used to determine a total product cost. Each product cost would be multiplied by the number of units sold, and that amount of cost of goods sold would be subtracted from total product revenues to obtain a product line profit or loss item. These computations would be performed for each product line and summed to determine net product revenues, from which the unassigned organizational level costs would be subtracted to find company profit or loss. In this model, the traditional distinction (discussed in chapter 2) between product and period costs is not visible, because the emphasis is on product profitability analysis for internal management rather than financial statement presentations.

While it would be most appropriate not to assign organizational level costs to products at all, some companies do attach them to goods produced or services rendered. The News Note on page 138 indicates that Caterpillar performs this type of assignment because it believes the amount is insignificant relative to all other costs.

Data from Carson Manufacturing Company are used to illustrate the difference in information that would result from recognizing multiple cost levels. Before recognizing that some costs were incurred at the batch, product, and organizational levels, Carson totaled its factory overhead costs and allocated them among its three types of products on a direct labor hour basis. Each product requires one direct labor hour, but Product B is a low-volume, special order line. As shown in the first section of Exhibit 4–7, cost information indicated that Product B was a profitable product for Carson Manufacturing. After analyzing its activities, Carson began accumulating costs at the different levels and assigning them to products based on appropriate cost drivers. While the individual details for this overhead assignment are not shown, the final assignments and resulting product profitability figures are presented in the second section of Exhibit 4–7. Prior to this analysis, management believed that the company was generating a reasonable profit on Product B. However, this more refined approach to assigning costs shows results contrary to that belief.

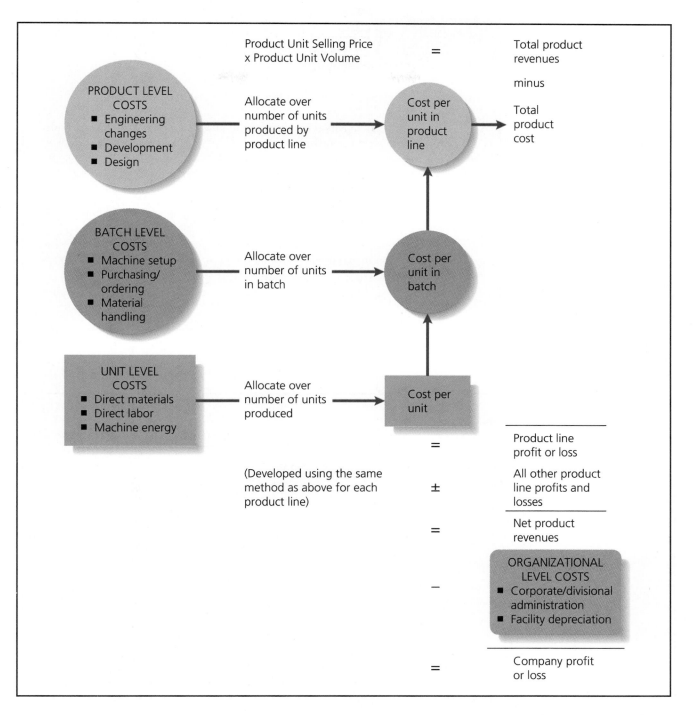

EXHIBIT 4–6
▼▼▼▼▼▼▼▼▼▼▼

DETERMINING
PRODUCT
PROFITABILITY AND
COMPANY PROFIT

EXHIBIT 4–7

▼▼▼▼▼▼▼▼▼▼▼▼▼▼

PROFITABILITY
ANALYSIS FOR
CARSON
MANUFACTURING
COMPANY

	Product A (10,000 units)		Product B (3,000 units)		Product C (200,000 units)		
Total OH cost = $5,782,950 Total DLHs = 213,000 OH rate per DLH = $27.15	Unit	Total	Unit	Total	Unit	Total	Total
Product Revenue	$100.00	$1,000,000	$ 90.00	$270,000	$80.00	$16,000,000	$17,270,000
Product Costs							
Direct	$ 40.00	$ 400,000	$ 40.00	$ 120,000	$18.00	$ 3,600,000	
OH per DLH	27.15	271,500	27.15	81,450	27.15	5,430,000	
Total	$ 67.15	$ 671,500	$ 67.15	$ 201,450	$45.15	$ 9,030,000	9,902,950
Profit or (Loss)		$ 328,500		$ 68,550		$ 6,970,000	$ 7,367,050

	Product A (10,000 units)		Product B (3,000 units)		Product C (200,000 units)		
	Unit	Total	Unit	Total	Unit	Total	Total
Product Revenue	$100	$1,000,000	$ 90	$ 270,000	$80	$16,000,000	$17,270,000
Product Costs							
Direct	$ 40	$ 400,000	$ 40	$ 120,000	$18	$ 3,600,000	
Overhead							
Unit level	15	150,000	25	75,000	12	2,400,000	
Batch level	18	180,000	37	111,000	7	1,400,000	
Product level	7	70,000	31	93,000	3	600,000	
Total	$ 80	$ 800,000	$133	$ 399,000	$40	$ 8,000,000	9,199,000
Product Line							
Profit or (Loss)		$ 200,000		$(129,000)		$ 8,000,000	$ 8,071,000
Organizational Level Costs							703,950
Company Profit							$ 7,367,050

ACTIVITY-BASED COSTING

Recognizing that various levels of costs exist, gathering costs into related cost pools, and using multiple cost drivers to assign costs to products and services are the three underlying elements of **activity-based costing** (ABC). ABC is an accounting information system that identifies the various activities performed in an organization and collects costs on the basis of the underlying nature and extent of those activities. Activity-based costing focuses on attaching costs to products and services based on the activities performed to produce, perform, distribute, or support those products and services.

activity-based costing

Two-Stage Allocation

After being initially recorded, costs are accumulated in activity center cost pools using first-stage cost drivers that reflect the appropriate level of cost incurrence (unit, batch, or product/process). An **activity center** is a segment of the production or service process for which management wants to separately report the costs of the activities performed. In defining these centers, management should consider geographical proximity of equipment, defined centers of managerial responsibility, magnitude of product costs, and the need to keep the number of activity centers manageable. The fact that a relationship exists between a cost pool and a cost driver indicates that, if the cost driver can be reduced or eliminated, the related cost should also be reduced or eliminated.

activity center

After accumulation, costs are allocated out of the activity center cost pools and applied to products and services using a second-stage cost driver. The process is the same as the overhead application process illustrated in chapter 3. The driver chosen for each cost pool attempts to measure the amount of a specific type of resource consumed by the product or service. Exhibit 4–8 illustrates this two-stage process of tracing costs to products and services in an ABC system.

As noted in the exhibit, the cost drivers for the collection stage may differ from those for the allocation stage, since some activity center costs are not traceable to lower levels of activity. Costs at the lowest (unit) level of activity should be allocated to products using volume-related cost drivers. Costs incurred at higher (batch and product/process) levels should be allocated to products using non-volume-related cost drivers; costs at these levels have traditionally been viewed as fixed costs. Often, however, activity-based costing systems do not use the traditional definitions of variable and fixed costs. Instead, costs are referred to as being either short-term variable or long-term variable.

Short-Term and Long-Term Variable Costs

Short-term variable costs change in direct relation to changes in business volume. Costs that do not change in relation to volume have traditionally been viewed as fixed. "Generally [however], as a business expands, costs tend to be far more variable than they should be, and when it contracts, they are far more fixed than they should be."[4] Professor Robert Kaplan of Harvard University views this ability of "fixed"

---

[4]B. Charles Ames and James D. Hlavacek, "Vital Truths About Managing Your Costs," *Harvard Business Review* (January–February 1990), p. 145.

long-term variable costs

costs to change under the "Rule of One," which suggests that having more than one unit of a resource makes that resource variable. Thus, many people have come to view fixed costs as **long-term variable costs,** for which the appropriate cost drivers simply need to be identified.

product variety
product complexity

Two cost drivers that cause long-term variable costs to change are product variety and product complexity. **Product variety** refers to the number of different types of products produced, while **product complexity** refers to the number of components or operations included in a product or the number of processes through which a product flows. Long-term variable costs tend to increase as the number and types of products increase because of the additional overhead support that is needed, such as warehousing, purchasing, setups, and inspections.

Horizontal Flow of Activities

Activity-based costing also allows managers to recognize the horizontal flow of activities through an organization. The process focuses on the numerous cost impacts created by making a product or performing a service. For example, an electrician in an electrical repair company has been assigned a schedule for the day. On his way to his

EXHIBIT 4–8
▼▼▼▼▼▼▼▼▼▼▼

TRACING COSTS IN
AN ACTIVITY-BASED
COSTING SYSTEM

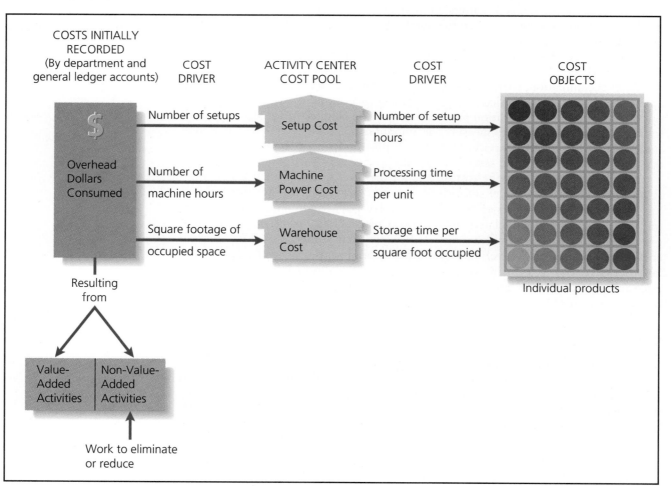

first client, the office receives a call from a customer who has had a total power outage in her home. Because of the critical nature of this job, the scheduler phones the electrician telling him to change his schedule. The receptionist must call all the other customers to inform them of the delay; the electrician may have to return to the office to obtain different parts; an invoice must be sent to the new customer. On a vertical-function basis, everyone in the organization worked their regular number of hours and performed their regular functions. On a cross-functional basis, however, there is a particular cost driver (emergency telephone calls) that causes additional activity and creates additional costs. ABC would focus on these additional activities and costs, while a conventional accounting system (using, for example, electrician labor hours as the cost driver) would not recognize the added activities or costs because, from a vertical-function aspect, nothing changed.

This discussion indicates that a vital loss of information may occur in an accounting system that ignores activity and cost relationships. Not every accounting system that uses direct labor or machine hours as the cost driver is providing inadequate or inaccurate cost information. There are, however, some general clues that may signal managers to review the costs being provided by the conventional accounting system. Some of these clues are more relevant to manufacturing entities, but others are equally appropriate for both manufacturing and service businesses.

DETERMINING WHEN AN ABC SYSTEM IS APPR

If a company's process or product/service line has undergone one or more significant changes, managers and accountants need to investigate whether the existing cost system still provides a reasonable estimate of product or service cost. Many companies

Caterpillar's use of automated equipment causes direct labor costs to decline, but increases electricity and depreciation charges. Overhead application rates using a direct labor base are no longer appropriate.

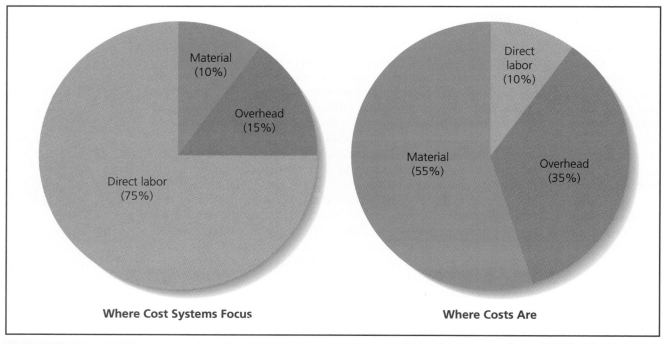

Where Cost Systems Focus   **Where Costs Are**

EXHIBIT 4–9
▼▼▼▼▼▼▼▼▼▼▼▼

ACCOUNTING
SYSTEMS DO NOT
REFLECT COST
COMPONENTS

SOURCE: Tom E. Pryor, "Precisely Correct But Totally Useless." Reprinted from *Today's CPA* (November/December 1989), p. 51, published by the Texas Society of CPAs.

have recently experienced large reductions in direct labor because of automation, which also creates increased overhead charges. As shown in Exhibit 4–9, current accounting systems often focus on the wrong components of a company's cost by continuing to use direct labor as an overhead allocation base. If direct labor becomes a small part of total cost, it is unlikely that labor is the primary overhead cost driver. Continuing to use direct labor as the overhead application base will create extraordinarily high application rates. Products made using automated equipment will tend to be charged an insufficient amount of overhead, while products made using high proportions of direct labor will tend to be overcharged.

Many companies now produce a wide variety of products (or perform numerous services) in very small quantities. These companies should review their cost systems carefully because (as indicated in Exhibit 4–10) product (and service) variety creates additional overhead costs that should ultimately be traced to specific products. Using one or two overhead pools will cause the overhead related to the specific products to be spread over all products. This process results in increased costs for products that are not responsible for the increased overhead. "If production volumes are fairly similar—say, volume of one product is no more than five times that of any other—product costs will probably be accurate. Accuracy falls off rapidly as the range grows to more than 10 to 1."[5]

A change in the competitive environment in which a company operates may also mean a need for better cost information. Increased competition may occur because other companies have recognized a particular product or service's profit potential,

---

[5]Robin Cooper, "You Need a New Cost System When . . . ," *Harvard Business Review* (January–February 1989), p. 80.

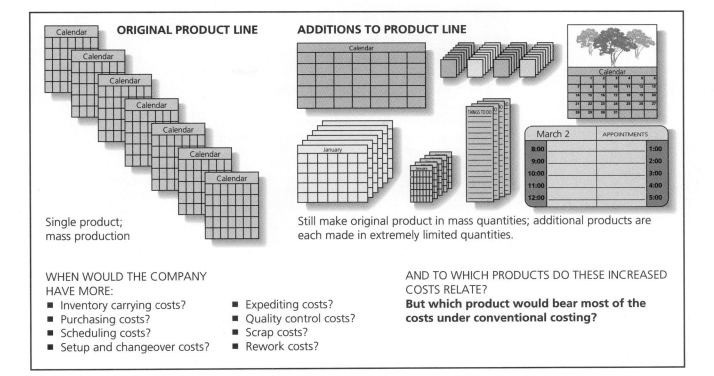

ORIGINAL PRODUCT LINE

Single product;
mass production

ADDITIONS TO PRODUCT LINE

Still make original product in mass quantities; additional products are
each made in extremely limited quantities.

WHEN WOULD THE COMPANY
HAVE MORE:
- Inventory carrying costs?
- Purchasing costs?
- Scheduling costs?
- Setup and changeover costs?

- Expediting costs?
- Quality control costs?
- Scrap costs?
- Rework costs?

AND TO WHICH PRODUCTS DO THESE INCREASED
COSTS RELATE?
**But which product would bear most of the
costs under conventional costing?**

EXHIBIT 4–10

PRODUCT VARIETY
CREATES OVERHEAD
COSTS

the product or service has become cost-feasible to make or perform, or an industry
has been deregulated. If many new companies are competing for old business, management must know the cost to produce or perform the company's products and
services, so that profit margins and prices can be reasonably set.

Changes in management strategy can also signal a need for a new cost system.
For example, if management wants to begin new operations, the cost system must be
able to provide information on how costs will change. Viewing costs in the traditional
variable versus fixed classifications does not allow such information to be effectively
developed. Viewing costs as short-term versus long-term variable focuses on cost
drivers and the changes the new operations will have on activities and costs.

Another management strategy might be to change employee behavior. The traditional cost system might not encourage such a change, while an activity-based costing system would—as indicated in the following News Note.

One behavior that many companies are currently encouraging is continuous improvement. This behavior relates to improving how employees perform their tasks,
the level of quality achieved by a product, and the level of service generated by the
company. Continual improvement recognizes the concept of eliminating non-value-
added activities to reduce lead time, making products (or performing services) with
zero defects, reducing product costs on an ongoing basis, and simplifying products
and processes.

Continuous improvement focuses on including employees in the process, since
they are often the source of the best ideas. For example, when KL Spring & Stamping
Corporation (a supplier of auto parts in Chicago, Illinois) needed to upgrade its product, employees formed quality circles to address and resolve problems related to late
deliveries or defective products.

NEWS NOTE

The Cost System Can Affect Behavior

One company was successful because of its technological innovation. When the market sent signals that cost—not just technical superiority—was important, the company decided to pay more attention to efficient designs. It urged its engineers to stop designing from the ground up and to incorporate some of the parts already in use. The old cost system couldn't track such things as how many part numbers were used, so there was no way to identify expensive products made with low-volume or unique components. The company designed its new system with this important new variable in mind.

Another company bought an expensive piece of test equipment to improve product quality. But the old cost system treated the machine as overhead. The work force took advantage of this "free" work center by building complex products on it. A new cost system ensured that workers put the new equipment to best use by making the test area a cost center and charging products an hourly rate for using it.

SOURCE: Reprinted by permission of *Harvard Business Review*. An excerpt from "You Need a New Cost System When . . . ," by Robin Cooper (January–February 1989), p. 80. Copyright © 1989 by the President and Fellows of Harvard College; all rights reserved.

Regardless of the reason or reasons behind the need for a change in costing systems, companies now have the ability to implement ABC systems. In the past, such implementation would have been technologically unfeasible. Introduction of the personal computer, numerically controlled (NC) machines, and bar coding allows significantly more information to be more readily available much more cost effectively.

ACTIVITY-BASED COSTING ILLUSTRATED

A brief illustration of activity-based costing in an inventory control department is shown in Exhibit 4–11. First, information is gathered about the activities and costs of an area. Costs are then assigned to specific products based on activities. The department has allocated its total cost among the three activities performed using the number of employees working in those areas. This allocation is based on the fact that occurrences, rather than volume, are indicative of work performed in the department.

Two of the products manufactured by this company are Product A and Product B. Product A is a rather complex unit that is not in extremely high demand; Product B is a simple unit that is produced in mass quantities. The difference in cost allocated to Product A between the traditional allocation system using direct labor hours ($1.25) and the activity accounting system ($2.88) is 230 percent more! For Product B, the difference between the traditional ($.75) and ABC ($.049) allocations is 1,531 percent less!

A primary consequence of relying on the inaccurate traditional cost figures might be that Product A would be underpriced, while Product B might be overpriced. Such improper pricing might cause sales of Product A to increase, which in turn would

- 12 employees in department; 400,000 budgeted total direct labor hours
- $500,000 total budgeted annual departmental overhead cost
- Product A: estimated production for year, 1,000 units @ 1 DLH per unit
- Product B: estimated production for year, 25,000 units @ .6 DLH per unit
- Other products use the remaining 384,000 DLHs

Traditional Allocation System—Based on DLHs
$500,000 ÷ 400,000 DLHs = $1.25 per DLH
Product A: 1,000 × 1 DLH = 1,000; 1,000 × $1.25 = $1,250; $1,250 ÷ 1,000 = $1.25 per unit OH cost
Product B: 25,000 × .6 DLH = 15,000; 15,000 × $1.25 = $18,750; $18,750 ÷ 25,000 = $.75 per unit OH cost

Activity-Based Costing Allocation System
Costs for each type of activity performed in the department are most reasonably related to number of times of occurrence; volume is not a significant factor.

Stage 1—Assign costs to cost pools related to the three departmental activities; first stage driver for all activities is assumed to be # of employees
Receiving purchased parts—requires 6 (of 12) employees; activity consumes $250,000 of cost; second stage allocation basis is number of shipments of purchased parts—estimated at 25,000 for year
Receiving raw material—requires 3 (of 12) employees; activity consumes $125,000 of cost; second stage allocation basis is number of shipments of raw materials—estimated at 10,000 for year
Disbursing material—requires 3 (of 12) employees; activity consumes $125,000 of cost; second stage allocation basis is number of production runs—estimated at 5,000 for year

Stage 2—Remove costs from activity cost pools and assign to products using second stage cost drivers for each activity

Cost Allocation to Activities
Receiving purchased parts: $250,000 ÷ 25,000 = $10 per shipment
Receiving raw material: $125,000 ÷ 10,000 = $12.50 per shipment
Disbursing material: $125,000 ÷ 5,000 = $25 per production run

Cost Allocation to Product
Product A: 1,000 units manufactured required 200 purchased parts shipments, 50 raw material shipments, and 10 production runs; allocation using ABC: (200 × $10) + (50 × $12.50) + (10 × $25) = $2,875 for 1,000 units or $2.88 per unit OH cost
Product B: 25,000 units manufactured required 100 purchased parts shipments, 8 raw materials shipments, and 5 production runs; allocation using ABC: (100 × $10) + (8 × $12.50) + (5 × $25) = $1,225 for 25,000 units or $.049 per unit

EXHIBIT 4–11
▼▼▼▼▼▼▼▼▼▼▼▼

ILLUSTRATION OF ACTIVITY-BASED COSTING ALLOCATION— INVENTORY CONTROL DEPARTMENT

increase costs even more. Sales of Product B would probably decline, resulting in lower total revenues and, more than likely, would not significantly lower total overhead costs.

Discrepancies in costs between traditional and activity-based costing are not uncommon. Studies have shown that after activity-based costing has been implemented, the costs of high-volume, standard products have declined anywhere from 10 to 30 percent. Low-volume, specialty product costs tend to increase from 100 to 500 percent, although in some cases costs have risen by 1,000 percent to 5,000 percent! [6]

Although the illustration in Exhibit 4–11 used costs normally included in product costing, activity-based costing is just as applicable to service department costs. Weyerhaeuser Company, for example, uses an activity-based costing system (referred to as a "charge-back" system) to allocate corporate overhead costs to its revenue-producing units. Some of the costs incurred are assigned on the basis of hours, but others are on the basis of reports, paychecks, documents, customers, and transactions. [7]

OPERATIONAL CONTROL UNDER ACTIVITY-BASED COSTING

The list of companies using activity-based costing is impressive and includes Hewlett-Packard, Cal Electronic Circuits, Hughes Aircraft, IBM, Tektronix, GenCorp Polymer Products, and Owens Corning Fiberglass, among many others. Most companies use activity-based costing in a stand-alone fashion, separate and apart from their conventional cost accounting systems—although some companies have partially integrated ABC with their conventional systems. While activity-based costing could be used to generate product costs for financial statements, this system is more often employed to improve performance and enhance management's ability to make better product profitability analyses. Activity-based costing should not be perceived as a substitute or alternative for conventional systems, but a means by which to provide additional, more accurate information. As discussed in the following News Note, the costs of operating both systems need to be weighed against the benefits provided.

While activity-based costing provides more long-term than short-term information, it can still be useful in short-term decisions. Activity-based management and costing provide many benefits for both production and service organizations. Since ABC systems more accurately assign overhead costs to products and services, the information generated from such systems should allow companies to better control costs; adjust product, process, or marketing strategy; affect behavior; and evaluate performance.

To control costs, managers must understand where costs are being incurred and for what purpose. Some of this understanding will come from differentiating between value-added and non-value-added activities. Some will come from the better information generated by more appropriate tracing of overhead costs to products and services. Some will come from viewing fixed costs as long-term variable costs and recognizing that certain activities will cause those costs to change. Understanding costs allows managers to visualize what needs to be done to control those costs, to implement cost reduction activities, and to plan resource utilization.

---

[6]Peter B. B. Turney, *An Introduction to Activity-based Costing* video (ABC Technologies, Inc.: 1990).
[7]H. Thomas Johnson and Dennis A. Loewe, "How Weyerhaeuser Manages Corporate Overhead Costs," *Management Accounting* (August 1987), pp. 20–26.

NEWS NOTE

Always Consider Cost-Benefit

Although a company probably wants a system that perfectly mirrors the business, the detail and EDP resources needed to achieve perfection come at a great cost. As an ABC system becomes more complex and detailed, the cost of added detail ultimately outweighs the benefits gained from increased accuracy.

The axiom that "it is more important to be approximately right than precisely wrong" is appropriate to ABC implementation. . . . For example, [a distribution center might find] that eight cost drivers add 1 percent to the cost structure and provide enough data and control to reduce total costs by 5 percent, for a net tangible reduction of 4 percent. Adding another eight drivers to the system (thus bringing the total to sixteen cost drivers) might conceivably bring about another 5 percent reduction in cost. However, the incremental cost of data needed for the additional eight drivers is likely to cost much more than the incremental 5 percent saved. The point is to expend effort on those activities where significant rewards are possible.

SOURCE: Ilene K. Kleinsorge and Ray D. Tanner, "Activity-Based Costing: Eight Questions to Answer Before You Implement" (Fall 1991), p. 87. Reprinted with permission from *The Journal of Cost Management for the Manufacturing Industry*. Warren, Gorham & Lamont, a division of Research Institute of America, 210 South Street, Boston, Mass. 02111. All rights reserved.

Activity-based management techniques have given managers of these firms a better idea of the profit margins provided by different products. This information improves the ability of corporate management to make strategic and, possibly, pricing decisions.

Traditional accounting systems concentrate on controlling cost incurrence, while ABC focuses on controlling the source of the cost incurrence. "Businesses become competitive and efficient by eliminating waste in operational activities, not by managing recorded costs." [8] Thus, by concentrating controls on the causes of costs, more costs become controllable because cost reduction efforts can be directed at specific cost drivers. It is "important to note, however, that a reduction in drivers, which results in a reduced dependency on activities, does not lower costs until the excess resources are reduced or redeployed into more productive areas." [9]

Activity-based costing systems indicate that significant resources are consumed by low-volume products and complex production operations. A recent study of the 3,200-member Controllers Council showed that 78 percent of the respondents "believe their existing cost systems frequently understate profits on high-volume products and overstate profits on specialty items." [10]

By better understanding the underlying cost of making a product or performing a service, managers obtain new insight into product or service profitability. Such insight could result in management decisions about expanding or contracting product variety, raising or reducing prices, and entering or leaving a market. For example, managers may decide to raise selling prices or discontinue production of low-volume specialty output, since that output consumes more resources than does high-volume output. Managers may decide to discontinue manufacturing products that require complex operations. Or, managers may reap the benefits from low-volume or complex production through implementing high-technology processes. The following News Note indicates that the costs generated from ABC will affect decisions.

ABC information can even affect decisions about plant and equipment investments. Installing computerized equipment may cause a reduction of production activities and an increase in efficiency. Activity-based costing, in a variety of ways, "provides an understanding of the impact of new and different activities required for the advanced manufacturing technologies of today [and] provides flexibility to systems designed to cope with changing and restructured manufacturing environments." [11] Activity-based costing indirectly changes the cost accumulation process, but directly changes the cost assignment process to be more realistic regarding how and why costs are incurred.

PERFORMANCE EVALUATION USING ABM

Activity-based management encourages and rewards workers for developing new skills, accepting greater responsibilities, and making suggestions for improvements in plant layout, product design, and worker utilization. Each of these improvements

---

[8] H. Thomas Johnson, "A Blueprint for World-Class Management Accounting," *Management Accounting* (June 1988), p. 30.
[9] Michael R. Ostrenga, "Activities: The Focal Point of Total Cost Management," *Management Accounting* (February 1990), p. 43.
[10] "Poll: 50% of Cost Systems Obsolete," *Accounting Today* (August 28, 1989), p. 14.
[11] Patrick L. Romano, "Activity Accounting," *Management Accounting* (May 1988), pp. 73–74.

Knowledge of Real Costs Will Affect Decisions

ABM pins the costs of overhead functions—from design and field maintenance to payroll and public relations—on the products and services that use them. This presents a clear picture of priorities for quality and cost-reduction efforts. By using ABM in its plants, for example, a major soft-drink producer has found that the costs of its array of brands vary as much as 400% from what traditional cost-accounting methods reported. Knowing this, says a finance officer of the company, will be pivotal in decisions on discontinuing some brands and trying to boost sales of others.

SOURCE: Kevin Kelly, "A Bean-Counter's Best Friend," *Business Week/The Quality Imperative Issue* (October 25, 1991), p. 43.

reduces non-value-added time and cost. In addition, by focusing on activities and costs, ABM is better able to provide more appropriate measures of performance than are found in more traditional systems.

"Performance measurements must be externally focused. They . . . must be linked to and support the business goals. They must measure what is of value to the customer." [12] Focusing on the idea of value-added activities underlies activity-based management. Measures can be quantitative or qualitative, nonfinancial or financial. Selection of the measurement should definitely be related to the performance that management wishes to either encourage or discourage. Probably the two most important performance measures of U.S. businesses at this time are quality and service.

A commitment to quality requires that companies make major adjustments in the way they design products, train and develop their work force, make decisions on acquisition and utilization of plants and equipment, and interact with suppliers and customers. Products should be designed to provide the maximum quality possible for the forecasted selling price. Spoilage and defects should not be built into product or service costs. ABM, with its focus on value-added and non-value-added activities, helps to eliminate building such costs into a product. According to Philip B. Crosby, quality itself is free. Unfortunately, as seen in the News Note on the next page, the cost of nonquality work is very expensive.

One measure of service is how quickly the customer receives the goods needed or requested. The appropriate performance measure is a nonfinancial one: lead time. If lead time is measured, products should be available to customers more rapidly. In addition, a manufacturer would tend to make products that would have fewer parts, parts that are more interchangeable, and parts that require few or no engineering changes after the production process is begun. Lead time measurement should also force rearrangement of building layout, increase work force productivity, and reduce defects and reworks, because these changes would minimize lead time. Lastly, lead

[12]Thomas O'Brien, "Measurements in the New Era of Manufacturing," Proceedings from *Cost Accounting for the '90s: Responding to Technological Change* (Montvale, N.J.: Institute of Management Accountants, formerly National Association of Accountants, 1988), p. 72.

The High Cost of Nonquality Work

[The cost of nonquality work encompasses the costs of] (1) all efforts involved in doing work over, including clerical work; (2) all scrap; (3) warranty (including in-plant handling of returns); (4) after-service warranty; (5) complaint handling; (6) inspection and test; and (7) other costs of error, such as engineering change notices, purchasing change orders, etc. It is normal to obtain only one-third of the real cost the first time you try [to measure] it.

SOURCE: Philip B. Crosby, *Quality Is Free* (New York: New American Library, 1979), p. 103.

time measurement should cause managers to observe and correct any phenomena that are creating production, performance, or processing delays. These phenomena are caused by non-value-added activities or by constraints in the system.

THEORY OF CONSTRAINTS

constraint

Anything (whether human or machine) that confines or limits the ability to perform a project or function is a **constraint.** Human constraints occur because of an inability to understand, react, or perform at some higher rate of speed. These constraints cannot be totally overcome, but can be reduced through proper hiring and training. Since the labor content contained in products is rapidly declining as automation increases, constraints caused by machines are generally of more concern than human constraints in reducing lead time.

bottlenecks

Machine constraints create **bottlenecks,** or inabilities to process at the necessary speed. Bottlenecks cause an activity that is to be processed through them to be slowed down. Plant capacity is equal to the capacity of the bottlenecks within the plant, because production cannot move through the plant at a faster rate than that allowed by the constraining resources. The **theory of constraints** states that production or performance cannot take place at a rate faster than the slowest machine in the process.[13] Even in a totally automated (or "lights-out") process, there will always be constraints, because all machines do not operate at the same speed nor do they handle the same capacity. Therefore, it is necessary to identify the constraints and work around them.

theory of constraints

Exhibit 4–12 provides a simplified illustration of a production process constraint. While Machine 1 can process 120,000 pounds of raw material in an hour, Machine 2 can only handle 65,000 pounds. Of an input of 100,000 pounds, 35,000 pounds of

---

[13]The theory of constraints was introduced to business environments by Eliyahu Goldratt and Jeff Cox in the book *The Goal* (Croton-on-Hudson, N.Y.: North River Press, Inc., 1986).

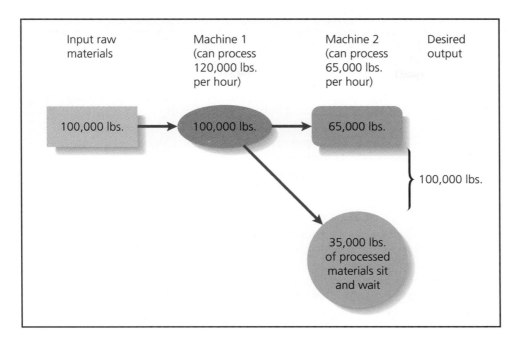

EXHIBIT 4–12
▼▼▼▼▼▼▼▼▼▼▼▼

PRODUCTION
CONSTRAINT

processed material must wait on the constraining machine at the end of an hour of processing.

While the effect of the constraint on production is obvious, the implication is not quite as clear. Managers have a tendency to want to see machines *working,* not sitting idle. Consider what this tendency would mean if the desired output were 600,000 pounds rather than 100,000. If Machine 1 were kept in continual use, all 600,000 pounds would be processed through Machine 1 in five hours. However, there would now be a backlog of 275,000 pounds [600,000 − 5(65,000)] of processed material in front of Machine 2! All this material would require handling and storage space and create the additional costs related to those non-value-added activities.

Machine constraints also have an implication for quality control. Managers normally choose quality control points to follow the completion of some particular process. When constraint points are known, quality control points should be placed in front of them. "Make sure the bottleneck works only on good parts by weeding out the ones that are defective. If you scrap a part before it reaches the bottleneck, all you have lost is a scrapped part. But if you scrap the part after it's passed through the bottleneck, you have lost time that cannot be recovered." [14]

Once constraints are known, care should be taken to make the best use of the time they provide. Subsequently, "after having made the best use of the existing constraints, the next step is to reduce their limitations on the system's performance." [15] Determine what options are available to reduce those limitations, such as adding more machines to perform the functions of the constraint or processing materials through a different machine.

[14]Eliyahu M. Goldratt and Jeff Cox, *The Goal* (Croton-on-Hudson, N.Y.: North River Press, Inc., 1986), p. 156.
[15]Robert E. Fox, "The Constraint Theory," Proceedings from *Cost Accounting for the '90s: Responding to Technological Change* (Montvale, N.J.: Institute of Management Accountants, formerly National Association of Accountants, 1988), p. 51.

APPLICATIONS STRATEGIES OF ACTIVITY-BASED MANAGEMENT	Discipline	Application
	Accounting	Use of cost drivers provides natural accumulation and allocation techniques; more realistic costs help indicate those products that should be "outsourced" (purchased rather than produced)
	Economics	More realistic costs provide better indication of marginal costs and marginal revenues; facilitate cost reduction efforts on non-value-added activities to create higher profits
	Finance	More realistic costs help in evaluating true profitability of products for decisions such as product or product line elimination or expansion
	Management	Creates higher awareness of causes of costs; promotes closer relationships with suppliers and customers; encourages product redesign for standardization; promotes management of cross-functional processes; helps provide more relevant performance measurements
	Marketing	More realistic costs help to establish more realistic bid prices; help to plan market strategy for product promotion; highlight the cost of product variety and product complexity

SITE ANALYSIS

Caterpillar's cost system objectives are to identify activities consumed by production and, using a "logical, reliable, and consistent process," to properly assign the costs to the related products. These objectives are satisfied using activity-based costing as part of the company's desire to improve operational controls. As noted at the beginning of the chapter, adjusting the cost system to reflect the factory's operating conditions is not a new phenomenon at Caterpillar. The system that was implemented in the 1940s was developed by former CEO William H. Franklin.

Mr. Franklin believed that a good cost system was beneficial in several respects:

> We were setting our parts prices much better. We found we were selling some parts way below cost. When we got [the parts] really costed right, some were [priced] way above cost. If you don't look out, you'll be wondering why you're not making any money on these parts or not getting any of the business. It costs quite a bit to have a good cost system. The investment in the system and in the people to support it ought to bring back more than its cost. I'm afraid most companies don't appreciate the value of what accounting can do for them.[16]

Caterpillar management has not deviated from Mr. Franklin's concepts. The company understands that activity-based costing is designed to provide better information about product and service activities and their related costs "so that management can focus its attention on the products and processes with the most leverage for increasing profits."[17]

continued

---

[16]Interview by Stephen Soucy and Marcus Moore, "Caterpillar's Accounting Visionary," *Management Accounting* (February 1991), p. 35. Published by Institute of Management Accountants, Montvale, N.J.
[17]Robin Cooper and Robert S. Kaplan, "Measure Costs Right: Make the Right Decisions," *Harvard Business Review* (September–October 1988), p. 103.

One of the company's recent adjustments after looking at ABC figures that quantified in dollars the value of higher quality and shorter lead time was a $2 billion plant modernization and redesign plan.

their various Caterpillar believes that the whole company should be involved with and "own" the cost system, because the system is more than simply a responsibility of accountants or accounting. As shown in the Applications Strategies, activity-based management concepts can provide useful information for all disciplines in performing managerial functions.

CHAPTER SUMMARY

In a highly competitive business environment, companies need to reduce costs to make profits. One way to reduce costs without reducing quality is to decrease the number of non-value-added organizational activities. Value is added to products only during production (manufacturing company), performance (service company), or display (retail company). All other activities, such as storage, moving, and waiting, are considered non-value-added.

Activity-based management views organizational processes as value-added and non-value-added activities. Process mapping can be performed to see all the activities that take place when producing a product or performing a service. Each activity is designated as value-added or non-value-added on a value chart. Management should strive to minimize or eliminate non-value-added activities because they cause unnecessary costs and longer lead times without providing extra "worth" for customers.

Traditional costing systems often accumulate costs in one cost pool (or a very few cost pools) and allocate those costs to products using one cost driver (generally related to direct labor or machine hours). Activity-based costing accumulates costs for activity centers in multiple cost pools at a variety of levels (unit, batch, product, and organizational). This system then allocates these costs using multiple cost drivers (both volume- and non-volume-related). Thus, costs are assigned more accurately, and managers can focus on controlling activities that cause costs rather than trying to control the costs that result from the activities.

Activity-based management concepts highlight interrelationships among functional areas. Costs incurred in one area are often the result of activities engaged in by other areas (for instance, the potential relationship of poor product quality or defects to engineering design). Activity-based management provides feedback about product design and potential candidate areas for process improvements or waste elimination. It allows and encourages the use of nonfinancial measures, such as lead time, as indicators of activity and performance. Finally, activity-based costing provides a more accurate way to assign overhead costs to products than what has been used traditionally.

The theory of constraints, which states that work cannot occur at a rate faster than the slowest machine or person in a process, is useful in identifying the causes of some of the non-value-added wait time in a system. Management should examine operating bottlenecks to determine what can be done to cost effectively eliminate or reduce the effects of the bottlenecks.

GLOSSARY

Activity   a repetitive action performed in fulfillment of business functions

Activity-based costing   an accounting information system that identifies the various activities performed in an organization and collects costs on the basis of the underlying nature and extent of those activities

Activity-based management   a discipline that focuses on the activities incurred during the production/performance process as the way to improve the value received by a customer and the resulting profit achieved by providing this value

Activity center   a segment of the production or service process for which management wants to separately report the costs of the activities performed

Batch level cost   a cost that is caused by a group of things made, handled, or processed at a single time

Bottleneck   any resource whose ability to process is less than the need for processing

Constraint   anything that confines or limits the ability to perform a project or function

Cost driver analysis   the process of investigating, quantifying, and explaining the relationships of cost drivers and their related costs

Idle time   storage time and time spent waiting at a production operation for processing

Inspection time   the time taken to perform quality control

Just-in-time (JIT)   the idea that inventory is manufactured (or purchased) only as the need for it arises or in time to be sold or used

Long-term variable cost   a cost that has traditionally been viewed as a fixed cost

Manufacturing cycle efficiency (MCE)   actual production time divided by total lead time; provides a measure of processing efficiency

Non-value-added activity   an activity that increases the time spent on a product or service but does not increase its worth

Organizational level cost   a cost incurred to support ongoing facility operations

Process map   a flowchart or diagram that indicates every step that goes into making a product or providing a service

Product complexity   refers to the number of components or operations included in a product or the number of processes through which a product flows

Product level cost   a cost that is caused by the development, production, or acquisition of a type of product

Product variety   the number of different types of products produced

Production time   the actual time it takes to perform the functions necessary to manufacture a product

Theory of constraints   a concept stating that production or performance cannot take place at a rate faster than the slowest machine or person in the process

Transfer time   the time it takes to move products or components from one place to another

Unit level cost   a cost that is caused by the production or acquisition of a single unit of product or the delivery of a single unit of service

Value-added activity   an activity that increases the worth of a product or service to the customer and for which the customer is willing to pay

Value chart   a visual representation that indicates the value-added and non-value-added activities and time spent in each of those activities from the beginning to the end of a process

---

SELECTED BIBLIOGRAPHY

Brausch, John M. "Selling ABC." *Management Accounting* (February 1992), pp. 42–46.

Brimson, James. *Activity Accounting: An Activity-Based Costing Approach.* New York: John Wiley & Sons, 1991.

Caminiti, Susan. "The Payoff from a Good Reputation." *FORTUNE* (February 10, 1992), pp. 74–77.

Collins, Frank, ed. *Implementing Activity-Based Costing.* New York: Executive Enterprises Publishing Company, 1991.

Hirsch, Maurice L., Jr., and Michael C. Nibbelin. "Incremental, Separable, Sunk, and Common Costs in Activity-Based Costing." *Journal of Cost Management for the Manufacturing Industry* (Spring 1992), pp. 39–47.

Raffish, Norm, and Peter B. B. Turney, eds. "Glossary of Activity-Based Management." *Journal of Cost Management for the Manufacturing Industry* (Fall 1991), pp. 53–63.

Turney, Peter B. B. *Common Cents: The ABC Performance Breakthrough.* Portland, Ore.: Cost Technology, 1991.

SOLUTION STRATEGIES

1. Determine the activity centers of the organization.
2. Determine departmental activities and efforts needed to conduct those activities—the cost drivers.
3. Determine resources consumed in conducting activities and the level at which those resources are consumed (unit, batch, product, organizational).
4. Allocate the resources to the activity centers based on the cost drivers.
5. Allocate unit, batch, and product costs to products and services based on activities and cost drivers involved.
6. Treat organizational level costs as nonattachable to products.

END-OF-CHAPTER MATERIALS

■ Questions

1. Why is product cost information necessary?
2. Describe the system known as activity-based management.
3. Define value-added and non-value-added activities. Compare these types of activities and give examples of each.
4. Why is the concept of value-added activities a customer-oriented notion?
5. To what factors can non-value-added activities be attributed? Why would customers perceive these factors as non-value-added activities?
6. Define the manufacturing cycle efficiency (MCE) measure and explain how it is calculated. In an optimized manufacturing environment, where MCE = 100 percent, what would be the status of non-value-added activities?
7. Explain the meaning and usage of cost drivers.
8. Does conventional cost accounting use cost drivers? If so, explain how. If not, explain why.
9. Briefly describe the cost accumulation and assignment process in an ABC system.
10. Why do the more traditional methods of overhead assignment "overload" standard products with overhead costs, and how does ABC improve overhead assignments?
11. What operating characteristics of a company might indicate that ABC could provide improved managerial information?
12. The chapter identified several underlying *causes* of a company's need for a new cost system. Using these causes as a basis, list and discuss some *symptoms* that might be visible reflections of these underlying causes.
13. Why can control in an activity-based management system be more effective than in a conventional system?
14. Explain the comment, "Identifying non-value-added activities provides management with a distinct control opportunity."
15. What is the underlying concept of the theory of constraints? Of what benefit is this theory to manufacturing and service companies?
16. Evaluate the comment, "Quality control points should be placed after bottlenecks."

■ Exercises

17. *(Terminology)* Find the item in the right-hand column that goes with the term in the left-hand column:

    a. Activity-based costing
    b. Theory of constraints

    1. Increases worth of a product to the customer
    2. Has a cause-effect relationship to a cost

c. Process map	3. A resource whose ability to process is less than the need for processing
d. Cost driver	4. Increases time and cost but not worth to customer
e. Manufacturing cycle efficiency	5. A measure of processing efficiency
f. Long-term variable costs	6. Inventory is purchased only as needed for sale or use
g. Value-added activity	7. Costs that have been traditionally viewed as fixed
h. Just-in-time	8. A flowchart indicating all steps taken in producing a product or service
i. Non-value-added activity	9. Production cannot occur faster than slowest machine or person
j. Bottleneck	10. System that collects costs according to nature and extent of activities

18. *(VA and NVA activities)* Howard, Howard & Howard is a law firm that is considering implementing activity-based costing. Following is a list of the activities performed by the attorneys in a typical day.

Activities	Time
Take depositions	1.0 hr.
Research	3.0 hrs.
Conference calls	.5 hr.
Travel time (to and from court)	1.0 hr.
Actual litigation time	1.5 hrs.
Correspondence	1.0 hr.
Lunch	.5 hr.
Contemplating litigation strategy	2.0 hrs.

   a. List the value-added activities and explain why they are value-added.
   b. List the non-value-added activities and explain why they are non-value-added.

19. *(VA and NVA activities)* Lief Erickson Company constructs alpine-style homes in the Catskill Mountains for its customers. As its consultant, you have developed the following value chart:

Operations	Average # of Days
Receiving materials	1
Storage of materials	8
Measuring and cutting materials	4
Handling materials	4
Setting up and moving scaffolding	5
Assembling materials	7
Building fireplace	4
Framing structure	3
Cutting and framing doors and windows	2
Attaching siding and sealing joints	4
County inspection	1

   a. What are the value-added activities and their total time?
   b. What are the non-value-added activities and their total time?
   c. Calculate the manufacturing cycle efficiency of the process.

20. *(VA and NVA activities)* The Porter Company is investigating the costs of schedule changes in its factory. Following is a list of the activities, estimated times, and average costs required for a single schedule change.

Activity	Estimated Time	Average Cost
Review impact of orders	30 min.–2 hrs.	$ 300
Reschedule orders	15 min.–24 hrs.	800
Lost sales		
Unreliable customer service		
Reschedule production orders	15 min.–1 hr.	75
Contact production supervisor	5 min.	5
Stop production and change over		
Generate paperwork to return materials		
Return and locate materials (excess inventory)	20 min.–6 hrs.	1,500
Generate new production paperwork	15 min.–4 hrs.	500
Change routings		
Change bill of materials		
Change procurement schedule	10 min.–8 hrs.	2,100
Purchase orders		
Inventory		
Collect paperwork from the floor	15 min.	75
Review new line schedule	15 min.–30 min.	100
Overtime premiums	3 hrs.–10 hrs.	1,000
Total		$6,455

a. Which of the previous activities, if any, are value-added?

b. What is the cost driver in this situation?

c. How can the cost driver be controlled and the activities eliminated?

(Coopers & Lybrand)

21. *(Cost of non-value-added activities)* Refer to the value chart for each lot or production run shown in Exhibit 4–4. Jill Tilton, the company president, asked her management accountant for and received the following information so that the company could try to determine the total cost of non-value-added activities for one lot of its product.

Annual salary for receiving clerks	$24,000
Annual salary for quality control personnel	38,000
Annual salary for materials/products handlers (movers)	16,000
Annual salary for person who does setup	26,000

Each unit requires 1 square foot of storage space in a storage building containing 100,000 square feet. Depreciation per year on the building is $125,000, and property taxes and insurance total $35,000. Assume a 365-day year for plant assets and a 240-day year for personnel. Where a range of time is indicated, assume an average. Waiting time (all time, other than production and storage time, at Tilton Company) is estimated at $50 per lot per day. Each day of delay in customer receipt (shipping time) is estimated to cost $150 per unit per day. The average production lot size is 500 units.

Determine the total cost of non-value-added activities per unit per day for each lot.

22. *(Lead time and MCE)* Billy Brewer is the manager of the Mill House Brewery. Mill House employees perform the following functions when making the company's nonalcoholic beer:

Receiving and transferring ingredients	1 hr.
Mixing the ingredients and cooking	3 hrs.
Bottling the beer	5 hrs.
Transferring the bottled beer to trucks	2 hrs.

a. Calculate the lead time of this manufacturing process.
b. Calculate the manufacturing cycle efficiency of this process.

23. *(Cost drivers)* Following is a list of all of the cost pools in the Menard Company to which overhead costs are assigned.

Maintenance
Utilities
Computer operations
Quality control
Material handling
Material storage
Factory rent

For each of these cost pools, identify a cost driver and explain why it is appropriate.

24. *(Activity-based costing)* Eloquence Publishing Company is concerned about the profit generated by its regular paperback dictionaries. Company managers are considering only producing the top-quality, hand-sewn dictionaries with gold-edged pages. Eloquence is currently assigning the $1,000,000 of overhead costs to both types of dictionaries based on machine hours. Some additional data follow.

	Regular	Hand-sewn
Revenues	$3,200,000	$2,800,000
Direct costs	$2,500,000	$1,200,000
Number produced	1,000,000	700,000
Machine hours	85,000	15,000
Inspection hours	5,000	25,000

The $1,000,000 of overhead is composed of $400,000 of utilities and $600,000 of quality control inspectors' salaries.

a. Determine the overhead cost that should be assigned to each type of dictionary using cost drivers appropriate for each type of overhead cost.
b. Should Eloquence stop producing the regular dictionaries? Explain.

25. *(Activity-based costing)* The Silvernagel Company is attempting to institute an activity-based accounting system to cost products. The Purchasing Department incurs costs of $473,500 per year and has five people working in it. Because finding the best supplier takes the majority of the effort in the department, most of the costs are allocated to this area.

Activity	Allocation Measure	# of People	Total Cost
Finding best suppliers	# of telephone calls	3	$300,000
Issuing purchase orders	# of purchase orders	1	100,000
Reviewing receiving reports	# of receiving reports	1	73,500

During the year, 150,000 telephone calls are made in the Purchasing Department, 10,000 purchase orders are issued, and 7,000 shipments are received and reports filed. Many of the purchase orders are received in the same shipment.

A complex product manufactured by the company required the following activities in the Purchasing Department over the year: 115 telephone calls, 36 purchase orders, and 29 receipts.

a. What amount of Purchasing Department cost should be assigned to the manufacturing of this product?

b. If 200 units of the product are manufactured during the year, what is the Purchasing Department cost per unit?

26. *(Product profitability)* Langly Company manufactures products A and B. Product A is a relatively simple product that is made in large quantities. Product B is a complicated product that is made according to customer specifications. Langly annually sells 50,000 units of Product A and 25,000 units of Product B. The costs incurred for each of the two products are:

	Product A	**Product B**
Revenue	$800,000	$800,000
Direct labor	300,000	500,000
Direct materials	200,000	100,000
Overhead	?	?

Both products require the same amount and kind of material. Labor is paid $20 per hour. Overhead consists of $200,000 of depreciation and $150,000 of headquarters expenses.

a. Calculate the profit (loss) on both products if overhead is assigned according to direct labor hours.

b. Calculate the profit (loss) on both products if headquarters expenses are deducted from total company income from both products and not allocated.

c. Does your answer in part (a) or part (b) provide a better representation of the profit contributed by each product? Explain.

27. *(Terminology)* Find the item in the right-hand column that goes with the term in the left-hand column.

a. Cost driver analysis	1. Confines or limits ability to perform or function
b. Value chart	2. Those costs that have traditionally been viewed as fixed costs
c. Product complexity	3. Number of components, operations, or processes to produce a product
d. Transfer time	4. Costs caused by a group of things being processed at a single time
e. Long-term variable costs	5. Storage time and time waiting for processing
f. Constraint	6. Time it takes to move products or components from one place to another
g. Batch level costs	7. A repetitive action performed to fulfill a business function
h. Activity	8. Investigating, quantifying, and explaining relationships of cost drivers and their related costs

i. Idle time

j. Product variety

9. The number of different types of products produced

10. Representation of value-added and non-value-added activities and times of each in a process

28. *(Constraint)* Flow Corporation has two departments. Department 1 is labor-intensive, while Department 2 is composed of a robot. The output of Department 1 averages 45 units per hour. The units are then transferred to Department 2, where they are finished by the robot. The robot can finish 45 units an hour at a maximum. Flow Corporation needs to complete 180 units this afternoon for an order that has been backlogged for four months.

The production manager has informed the people in Department 1 that they are to work on nothing else except this order from 1:00 P.M. until 5:00 P.M. The supervisor in Department 2 has scheduled the same times for the robot to work on the order. Following is the activity of Department 1 for each hour of the afternoon:

Time	1:00–2:00	2:00–3:00	3:00–4:00	4:00–5:00
Production	39 units	40 units	49 units	52 units

Assume that each unit moves directly from Department 1 to Department 2 with no lag time. Did Flow Corporation complete the 180 units by 5:00 P.M.? If not, explain and provide detailed computations.

▅ Problems

29. *(VA and NVA activities; MCE)* Larry Larson, who was recently elected mayor, is concerned about the deficit spending by the City of New Orleans. As a manager of the city's road construction workers, you have been asked to evaluate their performance in an effort to reduce costs. After spending some time secretly observing your workers, you noted the following activities:

Activities	Time (in hours)
Driving to the work location	.5
Blocking off the road	1.0
Setting up the road stripper	2.0
Drinking coffee	13.0
Stripping the road	10.0
Setting up the asphalt layer	6.0
Talking	4.0
Laying asphalt on the road	5.0
Unblocking the road	2.0
Loading equipment and leaving site	1.0

Required:

a. What are the value-added activities and times?

b. What are the non-value-added activities and times?

c. Calculate the manufacturing cycle efficiency.

30. *(Using ABC to price)* The budgeted manufacturing overhead costs of Beaver Window Company for 1993 are as follows:

Type of Costs	Cost Pools
Electric power	$ 500,000
Work cells	3,000,000
Materials handling	1,000,000
Quality control inspections	1,000,000
Product runs (machine setups)	500,000
Total budgeted overhead costs	$6,000,000

For the last five years, the cost accounting department has been charging overhead production costs based on machine hours. The estimated budgeted capacity for 1993 is 1,000,000 machine hours.

Phil Stolzer, president of Beaver Window, recently attended a seminar on activity-based costing. He now believes that ABC results in more reliable cost data that, in turn, will give the company an edge in pricing over its competitors. Upon the president's request, the production manager provided the following data regarding expected 1993 activity for the cost drivers of the budgeted overhead costs listed earlier.

Type of Costs	Activity-Based Cost Drivers
Electric power	100,000 kilowatt hours
Work cells	600,000 square feet
Materials handling	200,000 material moves
Quality control inspections	100,000 # of inspections
Product runs (machine setups)	50,000 product runs

Linda Ryan, the VP of Marketing, received an offer to sell 5,000 windows to a local construction company. Linda asks the head of cost accounting to prepare cost estimates for producing the 5,000 windows. The head of cost accounting accumulated the following data concerning production of 5,000 windows:

Direct materials cost	$100,000
Direct labor cost	$300,000
Machine hours	10,000
Direct labor hours	15,000
Electric power—kilowatt hours	1,000
Work cells—square feet	8,000
# of material handling moves	100
# of quality control inspections	50
# of product runs (setups)	25

Required:

a. What is the predetermined overhead rate if the traditional measure of machine hours is used?

b. What is the manufacturing cost per window under the present cost accounting system?

c. What is the manufacturing cost per window under the proposed ABC method?

d. If the prior two cost systems will result in different cost estimates, which cost accounting system is preferable as a pricing policy and why?

(From Nabil Hassa, Herbert E. Brown, and Paula M. Saunders, "Management Accounting Case Study: Beaver Window Inc.," *Management Accounting Campus Report,* Fall 1990. Copyright © 1990 IMA [formerly NAA].)

31. *(Determine product cost)* Drextel Chemical Company has identified activity centers to which overhead costs are assigned. The cost pools and cost drivers for these centers are as follows:

Activity Center	Cost Pool	Cost Driver
Utilities	$300,000	50,000 machine hours
Setup	100,000	700 setups
Materials handling	800,000	200,000 lbs. of material

The company's products and related statistics follow:

	Product A	Product B
Machine hours	35,000	15,000
Direct materials	75,000 lbs.	125,000 lbs.
Direct labor hours	20,000	25,000
Number of setups	200	500
Number of units produced	10,000	5,000

Additional data: One direct labor hour costs $10, and the 200,000 lbs. of material were purchased for $360,000.

Required: Determine the total cost for each product and the cost per unit.

32. *(Determine product cost)* Howell Manufacturing has identified activity centers to which overhead costs are assigned. The cost pools for these centers and their selected cost drivers for 1993 are as follows:

Activity Centers	Cost Pools	Selected Cost Drivers
Utilities	$278,000	60,000 machine hours
Scheduling and setup	260,000	780 setups
Materials handling	640,000	1,600,000 lbs. of materials

The company's products and other operating statistics follow:

	Products		
	A	B	C
Direct costs	$80,000	$80,000	$90,000
Machine hours	30,000	10,000	20,000
Number of setups	130	380	270
Pounds of materials	500,000	300,000	800,000
Number of units produced	40,000	20,000	60,000
Direct labor hours	40,000	20,000	60,000

Required:

a. Determine unit product cost using the appropriate cost drivers for each of the products.

b. Prior to installing an ABC system, Howell management had been pricing its products on the basis of conventional costing using direct labor hours to allocate total overhead. Because the firm operates in a competitive market, it sets prices on only a 20 percent markup on cost.
   1. Calculate unit costs based on conventional costing.
   2. Determine selling prices based on unit costs for conventional costing and for ABC costs.

c. Discuss the problems related to setting prices based on conventional costing and how ABC improves the information.

33. *(Cost assignment)* John Gun, CPA, was not entirely convinced that his fees for different types of services were based on accurate costs. His son, Sam, was home for the summer and had just completed his managerial accounting course where he learned about ABC. John and Sam were discussing costing for the firm's services (accounting and auditing, tax, and management services) and they decided to apply ABC to find more accurate costs for these services. That summer, they identified the following activity centers, assigned costs to cost pools, and selected respective cost drivers for the second-stage assigning of costs to services for the fiscal year ended May 31:

Activity Center	Cost Pool	Quantities	Cost Drivers
Planning and review	$ 66,000	93,200 hrs.	Billable time
EDP	70,000	7,200 hrs.	Computational time
Clerical	56,000	52	Number of professionals
Library	22,000	186	Books and periodicals purchased
Programming	56,000	4,160 hrs.	Programmer time
Building costs	88,000	15,000	Square feet
Administration	150,000	500	Number of clients
Total	$508,000		

Also, they compiled the following statistics for each of the services provided clients during the past year:

	A & A	Tax	Mgmt. Serv.
Direct costs	$1,952,000	$1,610,000	$732,000
Billable time (hours)	48,800	32,200	12,200
EDP (hours)	4,320	2,400	480
Clerical (number of professionals)	30	16	6
Library (new purchases)	51	99	36
Programming (hours)	1,200	520	2,440
Building (square feet)	8,800	4,875	1,325
Administration (number of clients)	170	280	50

Required:

a. Make the second-stage assignment of cost pools to the cost of services.

b. Determine the total cost of each class of service.

c. Assume that John Gun had used a predetermined overhead rate of $5.45 per billable hour for all services, found by dividing last year's budgeted overhead ($508,000) by last year's estimated billable hours (93,200). Had Mr. Gun budgeted the same costs assigned under ABC in part (a) above and estimated the same billable hours as were actually incurred, respectively, what predetermined overhead rates would he have used for each separate class of service? Mr. Gun doubles his costs in job pricing. Discuss the implications of using the latter overhead rates.

34. *(Activity-based costing)* Ainsworth Company produces office desks. The desks typically produced are five-drawer and made of gray metal. However, Ainsworth does take custom orders for desks. Ainsworth's overhead costs for a month in which no custom desks are produced are as follows:

Purchasing Department for raw materials and supplies
   (10 purchase orders per month) $ 5,000
Setting up machines for production runs (4 times per month after
   maintenance checks)   400
Utilities (based on 3,200 machine hours)   160
Supervisors (2)   8,000
Machine and building depreciation (fixed)   5,500
Quality control and inspections (performed on random selection
   of desks each day; one quality control worker)   2,500
Total overhead costs $21,560

Ainsworth's factory operations are highly automated, and the management accountant is allocating overhead to products based on machine hours. This allocation process has resulted in an overhead allocation rate of $6.7375 per machine hour ($21,560 ÷ 3,200 MHs).

In June 1993, six orders were filled for custom desks. The custom order sale prices were based on charges for actual direct materials, actual direct labor, and the $6.7375 per machine hour for an estimated 200 hours of machine time. During that month, the following costs were incurred for 3,200 hours of machine time:

Purchasing Department for raw materials and supplies
   (22 purchase orders) $ 6,200
Setting up machines for production runs (18 times)   1,800
Utilities   160
Supervisors (2)   8,000
Machine and building depreciation (fixed)   5,500
Quality control and inspections   2,980
Engineering design and specification costs   3,000
Total overhead costs $27,640

Required:

a. What part of the Purchasing Department cost is variable and what part is fixed? Indicate what types of Purchasing Department costs would fit into each of these categories.

b. Why might the number of machine setups have increased from 4 to 18 when only six custom orders were received?

c. Why might the cost of quality control and inspections have increased?

d. Why were engineering design and specification costs included during June but not in the original overhead cost listing?

e. If Ainsworth were to adopt activity-based costing, what should the management accountant consider as the cost drivers for each of the previous items?

f. Do you think the custom orders should have been priced using an overhead rate of $6.7375 per machine hour? Indicate the reasoning behind your answer.

35. *(Essay)* You are the new controller of a small job shop that manufactures special-order desk nameplate stands. As you review the records, you find that all the orders are shipped late; the average process time for any order is three weeks; and the time actually spent in production operations is two days. The president of the company has called you in to discuss missed delivery dates.

Required:

a. What possible considerations might you suggest to the company president for the problems?

b. Discuss how a value chart could be used to alleviate the problem.

36. *(Essay)* Sherrill Industrial Paints has engaged you to help the company analyze and update their costing and pricing practices. The company product line has changed over time from general paints to specialized marine coatings. Although some large commodity orders are received, the majority of business is now generated from small lot sizes of products that are designed and produced to meet specifically detailed environmental and technical requirements.

The company has experienced tremendous overhead growth, including costs in customer service, production scheduling, inventory control, and laboratory work. Overhead has essentially doubled since the shift in product lines. Management believes that large orders are being penalized and small orders are receiving favorable cost (and therefore selling price) treatment.

Required:

a. Indicate why the shift in product lines would have caused such major increases in overhead.

b. Is it possible that management is correct in its belief about large and small order costs? If so, why?

c. What would you suggest to management to reflect the change in business?

37. *(Essay)* Many companies now recognize that their cost systems are inadequate for today's powerful global competition. Managers in companies selling multiple products are making important product decisions based on distorted cost information, as most cost systems designed in the past focused on inventory valuation. In order to elevate the level of management information, current literature suggests that companies should have as many as three cost systems for (1) inventory valuation, (2) operational control, and (3) activity-based costing, which is also known as individual product cost measurement.

Required:

a. Discuss why the traditional cost information system, developed to value inventory, distorts product cost information.

b. Identify the purpose and characteristics of each of the following cost systems:
   1. Inventory valuation
   2. Activity-based costing

c. 1. Describe the benefits that management can expect from activity-based costing.
   2. List the steps that a company, using a traditional cost system, would take to implement activity-based costing.

(CMA adapted)

▎ Cases

38. *(Activity-based costing)* Roth and Borthick Company manufactures two products. Following is a production and cost analysis for each product for the year 1993.

Cost Component	Product A	Product B	Both Products	Cost
Units produced	10,000	10,000	20,000	
Raw materials used (units)				
Material X	50,000	50,000	100,000	$ 800,000
Material Y		100,000	100,000	1,200,000

Labor used

Department 1				$	681,000
Direct labor ($375,000)	20,000	5,000	25,000		
Indirect labor					
Inspection	2,500	2,500	5,000		
Machine operations	5,000	10,000	15,000		
Setups	200	200	400		
Department 2				$	462,000
Direct labor ($200,000)	5,000	5,000	10,000		
Indirect labor					
Inspection	2,500	5,000	7,500		
Machine operations	1,000	4,000	5,000		
Setups	200	400	600		

Machine hours used

Department 1	5,000	10,000	15,000	$	400,000
Department 2	5,000	20,000	25,000	$	800,000

Power used (kwh) $ 400,000

Department 1	1,500,000
Department 2	8,500,000

Other activity data

Building occupancy	$1,000,000
Purchasing	$ 100,000
# of purchase orders	
Material X	200
Material Y	300
Square feet occupied	
Purchasing	10,000
Power	40,000
Department 1	200,000
Department 2	250,000

Faye Harold, the management accountant, has just returned from a seminar on activity-based costing. To apply the concepts she has learned, she decides to analyze the costs incurred for Products A and B from an activity basis. In doing so, she specifies the following first and second allocation processes:

First Stage: Allocations to Departments

Cost Pool	Cost Object	Activity Allocation Basis
Building occupancy	Departments	Square feet occupied
Purchasing	Materials	# of purchase orders
Power	Departments	Kilowatt hours

Second Stage: Allocation to Products

Cost Pool	Cost Object	Activity Allocation Basis
Departments		
Indirect labor	Products	Hours worked
Power	Products	Machine hours
Machinery related	Products	Machine hours
Building occupancy	Products	Machine hours
Materials		
Purchasing	Products	Materials used

Required:

a. Determine the total overhead for Roth and Borthick Company.

b. Determine the plantwide overhead rate for the company, assuming the use of direct labor hours.

c. Determine the cost per unit for Product A and for Product B using the overhead application rate found in (b).

d. Using activity-based costing, determine the cost allocations to departments (first-stage allocations). Allocate in the following order: building occupancy, purchasing, and power.

e. Using the allocations found in (d), determine the overhead cost allocations to products (second-stage allocations).

f. Determine the cost per unit for Product A and Product B using the overhead allocations found in (e).

(From Harold P. Roth and A. Faye Borthick, "Getting Closer to *Real* Product Costs," *Management Accounting* [May 1989], pp. 28–33. Published by Institute of Management Accountants, Montvale, N.J.)

39. CarryAll Company produces briefcases from leather, fabric, and synthetic materials in a single production department. The basic product is a standard briefcase that is made from leather, lined with fabric. CarryAll has a good reputation in the market because the standard briefcase is a high-quality item and has been well produced for many years.

Last year, the company decided to expand its product line and produce specialty briefcases for special orders. These briefcases differ from the standard in that they vary in size; they contain both leather and synthetic materials; and they are imprinted with the buyer's logo, whereas the standard briefcase is simply imprinted with the CarryAll name in small letters. The decision to use some synthetic materials in the briefcase was made to hold down the materials cost. To reduce the labor costs per unit, most of the cutting and stitching on the specialty briefcases is done by automated machines, which are used to a much lesser degree in the production of the standard briefcases. Because of these changes in the design and production of the specialty briefcases, CarryAll believed that they would cost less to produce than the standard briefcases. However, because they are specialty items, they were priced slightly higher—standards are priced at $30, specialty briefcases at $32.

After reviewing last month's results of operations, CarryAll's president became concerned about the profitability of the two product lines, because the standard briefcase showed a loss while the specialty briefcase showed a greater profit margin than expected. The president is wondering whether the company should drop the standard briefcase and focus entirely on specialty items. The cost data for last month's operations as reported to the president are as follows:

	Standard		Speciality	
Units Produced		10,000		2,500
Direct Materials				
Leather	1.0 sq. yd.	$15.00	0.5 sq. yd.	$ 7.50
Fabric	1.0 sq. yd.	5.00	1.0 sq. yd.	5.00
Synthetic				5.00
Total materials		$20.00		$17.50
Direct Labor	0.5 hr. @ $12.00	6.00	0.25 hr. @ $12.00	3.00
Factory Overhead	0.5 hr. @ $ 8.98	4.49	0.25 hr. @ $ 8.98	2.24
Cost per unit		$30.49		$22.74

Factory overhead is applied on the basis of direct labor hours. The rate of $8.98 per DLH was calculated by dividing the total overhead of $50,500 for the month by the direct labor hours of 5,625. As shown above, the cost of a standard briefcase is $.49 higher than its $30 sales price, whereas the specialty briefcase has a cost of only $22.74 for a gross profit of $9.26. The problem with these costs is that they do not accurately reflect the activities involved in manufacturing each product. Determining the costs using activity-based costing should provide better product costing data to help gauge the actual profitability of each product line.

The factory overhead costs must be analyzed to determine the activities causing the costs. Assume that the following costs and cost drivers have been identified:

- *Purchasing Department cost is $6,000.* The major activity driving the Purchasing Department costs is the number of purchase orders processed. During the month, Purchasing prepared the following number of purchase orders: for leather, 20; for fabric, 30; and for synthetic material, 50.
- *Receiving and inspecting materials cost is $7,500.* Receiving and inspecting costs are driven by the number of deliveries. During the month, the following number of deliveries were made: for leather, 30; for fabric, 40; and for synthetic materials, 80.
- *Setting up production line cost is $10,000.* Setup activities involve changing the machines to produce the different types of briefcases. A setup for production of the standard briefcases requires one hour, while setup for the specialty briefcases requires two hours. Standard briefcases are produced in batches of 200; specialty briefcases are produced in batches of 25. During last month, there were 50 setups for the standard items and 100 setups for the specialty items.
- *Inspecting finished goods cost is $8,000.* All briefcases are inspected to ensure that quality standards are met. However, the final inspection of standard briefcases takes very little time because the employees identify and correct quality problems as they do the hand-cutting and stitching. A survey of the personnel responsible for inspecting the final products showed that they spent 150 hours on the standard briefcases and 250 hours on the specialty ones during the month.
- *Equipment-related costs are $6,000.* Equipment-related costs include repairs, depreciation, and utilities. Management has determined that a logical basis for assigning these costs to products is machine hours. A standard briefcase requires ½ hour of machine time, and a specialty briefcase requires 2 hours. Thus, during the last month, 5,000 hours of machine time relate to the standard line, and 5,000 hours relate to the specialty line.
- *Plant-related costs are $13,000.* Plant-related costs include property taxes, insurance, administration, and others. These costs are to be assigned to products using machine hours.

a. Using activity-based costing concepts, what overhead costs are assigned to the two products?
b. What is the unit cost of the two products using activity-based costing concepts?
c. Reevaluate the president's concern about the profitability of the two product lines.

(IMA)

▉ **Ethics Discussion**

40. Cost allocation is a pervasive problem. Nearly every organization must cope with cost allocation in some manner when measuring and reporting costs for purposes such as performance evaluation, product costing, and cost justification or reimbursement. The telecommunications industry has had a cost allocation problem since its inception.

Currently, costs incurred by telecommunications companies may be classified as either *nontraffic sensitive costs* (NTS costs) or as *traffic sensitive costs* (TS costs). NTS costs do not fluctuate with traffic volume over a relevant range of call volumes and hence have a fixed cost behavior pattern. TS costs are costs of providing telecommunication services that have a direct relationship to the number of messages or volume of traffic handled by the network. TS costs tend to exhibit a "step" cost behavior pattern. NTS costs are substantial in amount and in relation to TS costs.

Most NTS costs for a local exchange company are common to all major services provided by the company. Thus, the allocation of NTS costs will affect local telephone rates and intrastate and interstate toll rates. A large portion of NTS costs can be directly identified with geographic areas and often with specific customers. Despite this fact, regulators generally do not allow telephone companies to vary rates by geographic area or customer by basing rates on recovery of NTS costs that can be directly identified with specific geographic regions or customers.

(From J. Patrick Cardullo and Richard A. Moellenberndt, "The Cost Allocation Problem in a Telecommunications Company," *Management Accounting* [September 1987], pp. 39–44. Published by the Institute of Management Accountants, Montvale, N.J.)

a. Would activity-based costing be useful in a telecommunications company? Would ABC be feasible in the current regulatory environment? Discuss.

b. Is it ethical to spread all charges (even those that can be identified with specific regions and/or customers) among all customers? Take *both* a positive and a negative standpoint and justify each answer.

PART TWO

USING MANAGERIAL ACCOUNTING INFORMATION IN COSTING

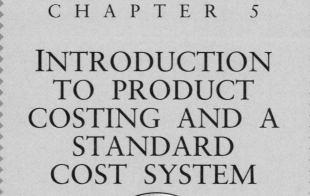

CHAPTER 5

INTRODUCTION TO PRODUCT COSTING AND A STANDARD COST SYSTEM

LEARNING OBJECTIVES

After completing this chapter, you should be able to do the following:

1. Distinguish a job order product costing system from a process costing system
2. Differentiate among actual, normal, and standard costing systems
3. Understand how standards for material and labor are set
4. Explain why standard cost systems are used
5. Calculate materials, labor, and overhead variances
6. Analyze variances for control and performance evaluation purposes
7. Recognize how organizational evolution and desired level of attainability affect standard setting
8. Understand how standard setting and standard usage are changing in modern business

Old Rosebud: A Horse Farm with Standards

Old Rosebud is a 400-acre Kentucky farm that specializes in boarding brood mares and their foals. Old Rosebud's owners estimated the following costs to be incurred for each mare per day: $3 for feed (direct materials), $3 for veterinary fees (direct labor), and $.40 for variable overhead costs per mare per day, and $8.70 for remaining fixed overhead expenses ($190,530 estimated fixed overhead divided by an estimated 21,900 boarding days). As actual expenses were incurred during the year, they were compared to expectations to determine how well costs were being controlled and the causes of the differences.

Adapted from Hans Sprohge and John Talbott, "New Applications for Variance Analysis," *Journal of Accountancy* (April 1989), pp. 137–141.

A primary objective of cost accounting is to determine the cost of the products made or the services performed by an organization. Just as a variety of methods (first-in, first-out; last-in, first-out; average; specific identification) exist to determine inventory valuation and cost of goods sold for a retailer, different methods are available to value inventory and calculate product cost in a manufacturing or service environment. The method chosen will depend on the nature of the product or service and the company's conversion process.

This chapter begins a sequence of chapters presenting various methods of product costing. The chapter first distinguishes between two basic costing systems (job order and process) and then discusses three methods of valuation that can be used within these systems (actual, normal, and standard). The remainder of the chapter focuses on the nature and use of a standard costing system, like that used by Old Rosebud. A standard costing system can be used with either system of product costing and provides important information for managerial planning, controlling, and decision-making functions.

METHODS OF PRODUCT COSTING

Before products can be costed, a determination must be made about (1) the type of product costing system and (2) the method of valuation to be used. Product costing systems differ markedly, and the system employed indicates what is to be the cost object and how costs are assigned to production. The method of valuation specifies how product costs will be measured. Companies must have both a cost system and a method of valuation, meaning that six possible combinations exist (shown in Exhibit 5–1).

	METHOD OF VALUATION		
COST SYSTEM	**Actual**	**Normal**	**Standard**
JOB ORDER	Actual DM Actual DL Actual OH assigned to job after end of period	Actual DM Actual DL OH applied at completion of job or end of period (predetermined rate x actual input)	Standard DM and/or Standard DL OH applied when goods are completed or at end of period (predetermined rate x standard input)
PROCESS	Actual DM, DL, and OH costs using FIFO or weighted average cost flow	Actual DM and DL and predetermined OH rates using FIFO or weighted average cost flow	Standard DM, DL and OH; will always be FIFO cost flow

EXHIBIT 5–1
▼▼▼▼▼▼▼▼▼▼▼▼▼

COSTING SYSTEMS
AND INVENTORY
VALUATION

job order costing

process costing

Costing Systems

Job order and process costing are the two basic cost systems. **Job order costing** is the costing system used by entities that produce tailor-made goods or services in limited quantities which conform to specifications designated by the purchaser of those goods or services. Examples of companies in which job order costing is appropriate include a printing company that prepares advertisements for numerous clients, an attorney who has her own practice, and a research firm that performs product development studies. Services in general are typically highly user-specific, so job order costing systems are usually appropriate for such businesses. Job order costing systems are discussed in depth in chapter 6.

The other primary product costing system, **process costing,** is used by entities that produce large quantities of homogeneous goods. Process costing is used in companies manufacturing bricks, saltwater taffy, and breakfast cereal. Because the output of a single process in a company utilizing a process costing system is homogeneous, specific units of output cannot be readily identified with specific input costs within a given time frame. This characteristic of process costing systems makes a cost flow assumption necessary. Cost flow assumptions provide a way for accountants to assign costs to products while ignoring the actual physical flow of units. Process costing systems use either the FIFO or the weighted average cost flow assumption; these types of process costing systems are covered in chapter 7.

Valuation Methods

The three basic methods of valuation are actual, normal, and standard costing. When a company uses the costs of actual direct materials, direct labor, and overhead to determine the cost of work in process inventory, that company is employing an actual costing system. Because of the reasons discussed in chapter 3, many companies mod-

Accounting for the construction of the Glen Canyon Dam hydropower facility required the use of job order costing. This type of accounting system is appropriate when goods are produced in limited quantities conforming to customer specifications.

ify actual cost systems to use predetermined overhead rates rather than actual overhead costs. Combining actual direct materials and labor costs with predetermined overhead rates is called normal costing. If the predetermined rate is substantially equivalent to what the actual rate would have been, its use provides an acceptable and useful costing system.

Companies using either job order or process costing may employ **standards** (or predetermined benchmarks) for costs to be incurred and/or quantities to be used. In a **standard cost system,** unit norms or standards are developed for direct material and direct labor quantities and/or costs. Overhead is applied to production using the predetermined rate, which is considered the standard. Both actual and standard costs are recorded in the accounting records to provide an essential element of cost control—having norms against which actual costs of operations can be compared. These standards may then be used to plan for future activities and cost incurrence and to value inventories.

In planning, standards are the building blocks used to assemble plans more quickly and easily than otherwise would be possible. A charity might set a standard for the amount of annual contributions to be raised from various individuals or companies, or a sales manager might set a standard for employee travel expenses per month. Or, if Old Rosebud plans to have 50 mares boarded for 30 days next month, it should expect to spend $4,500 (50 mares × $3 per day × 30 days) for feed.

Standards can also be used for control purposes. One requirement for control is that managers be aware of how much actual activities and actual consumption of resources differ from expectations. A standard cost system helps companies recognize deviations or variances from expected production costs and correct problems resulting from excess costs or usage. Actual costing systems do not provide this benefit, and normal costing systems cannot provide it in relation to materials and labor.

standards

standard cost system

If the deviations from standard are large, managers can exert influence to correct whatever is causing the difference. For example, if the actual cost for feed for the 50 mares discussed earlier is $5,000, management should investigate the $500 difference to determine its cause. Several possibilities could exist: the price paid for feed was greater than that which was expected; several mares could have been in foal and consumed more feed; or rats could have been in the barn consuming feed, causing the need to purchase more.

Note that the explanations of the $500 difference suggest that there are two underlying causes of the variance. One relates to the cost of the feed, while the other relates to the quantity of feed used. These causes can exist separately or together. Managers need to be able to determine which part of the total variance relates to which cause to properly evaluate performance.

The availability of standards speeds up and improves decision making because managers have a predetermined, rigorous set of expectations upon which to make decisions, such as setting prices. For example, managers at Old Rosebud used the expected $15.10 daily cost ($3 + $3 + $.40 + $8.70) to set a boarding rate of $25 per day per mare. Performance evaluation is also improved through comparing actual costs of operations to standard costs and highlighting significant differences.

DEVELOPMENT OF A STANDARD COST SYSTEM

Although standard cost systems were initiated by manufacturing entities, such systems can also be used by service organizations. In any organization, however, it is critical that the standards development process be handled in a knowledgeable and thorough manner.

Target Costing

In developing products to market, U.S. manufacturers have traditionally confined their approach to the following sequence. A product is designed; its costs are determined; and a selling price is set based, to some extent, on the costs involved. If the market will not bear the resulting selling price, the company either does not make as much profit as hoped for or attempts to lower production costs.

target costing

Some manufacturing companies are now beginning to employ a Japanese technique known as **target costing** before a product is ever designed, engineered, or produced. This method determines an "allowable" product cost by using market research to estimate what the market will pay for a product with specific characteristics. An acceptable profit margin rate is subtracted from the estimated selling price, leaving an implied maximum per-unit cost for the product. The target cost is then continuously reduced in an effort to achieve "continuous improvement." The difference between the way the Japanese and Americans view the costing process is illustrated in Exhibit 5–2.

The implied maximum or target cost is compared to the expected product cost. If the target cost is less than the expected cost, the company has several alternatives. First, the product design and/or production process can be changed to reduce costs.

cost tables

Preparation of **cost tables** helps in determining how such adjustments can be made. These tables are data bases that provide information about the impact on product

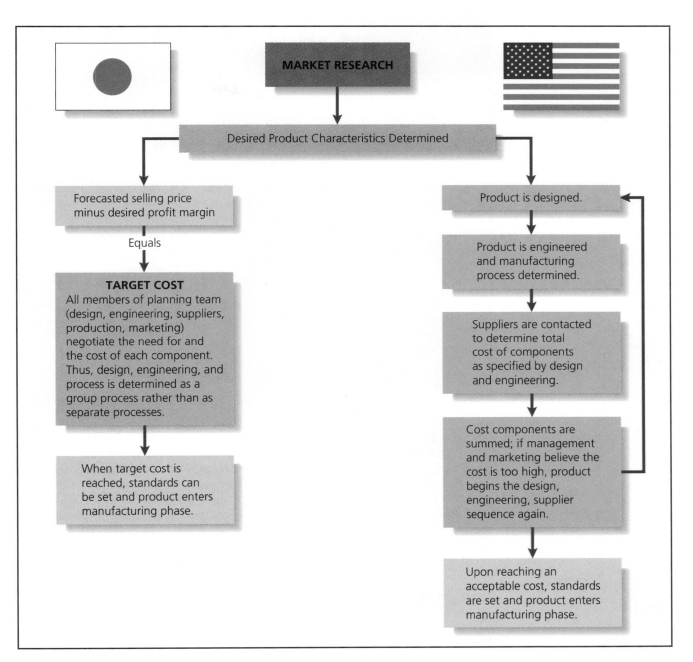

EXHIBIT 5–2
▼▼▼▼▼▼▼▼▼▼▼▼

DEVELOPING
PRODUCT COSTS

costs of using different input resources, manufacturing processes, and design specifications. Second, a less-than-desired profit margin can be accepted. Or, third, the company can decide that it does not want to enter this particular product market at the current time because it cannot make the profit margin it desires.

The process of developing a target cost is discussed in the following News Note. Target costs should be used *prior* to the production phase of operations, because about 80 percent of product cost is determined during the design stage for a product when the materials, manufacturing process, and engineering specifications are made.

Determine the Cost Before Production

The team in charge of bringing a new product idea to market determines the price at which the product is most likely to appeal to potential buyers. From this crucial judgment all else follows. After deducting the desired profit margin from the forecasted sales price, the planners develop estimates for each of the elements that make up a product's costs: design and engineering, manufacturing, sales and marketing. Each of these is further subdivided to identify and estimate the cost of each component that goes into the finished product.

Every part or function is treated as a component—not only windshields and engine blocks but spaces such as the trunk—and each is assigned a target cost. Says [a former consultant for Nissan], "This is where the battle begins." The battle is an intense negotiating process between the company and its outside suppliers, and among departments that are responsible for different aspects of the product. The sum of the initial estimates may exceed the overall target cost by 20% or more. By the time the battle is over, however, compromises and tradeoffs by product designers, process engineers, and marketing specialists generally produce a projected cost that is within close range of the original target.

SOURCE: Ford S. Worthy, "Japan's Smart Secret Weapon," *FORTUNE* (August 12, 1991), pp. 73–74. © The Time Inc. Magazine Company. All rights reserved.

Thus, by designing the product to meet an allowable cost, companies can try to eliminate as many non-value-added activities (and, therefore, costs) from the production process as possible. In addition, because suppliers provide valuable input, engineering may find that, with few modifications to the original design, regularly stocked supplier components rather than more costly, special-order items can be used in the production stage. Once the target cost is determined, standards can be set that indicate the allowable costs and quantities specified by the target cost. Actual production costs and activities can then be monitored to indicate their level of conformity to the target standards.

Setting Standards

standard cost

The estimated cost to manufacture a single unit of product or perform a service is called the **standard cost.** Thus, the $15.10 cost per boarding day estimated by Old Rosebud would be its standard cost. Standards are traditionally established for each component (material, labor, and overhead) of product cost. Developing a standard cost involves judgment and practicality in identifying the types of material and labor to be used and their related quantities and prices. Developing standards for overhead requires that costs have been appropriately classified according to cost behavior, valid allocation bases have been chosen, and a reasonable level of activity has been specified.

A primary objective in manufacturing a product or performing a service is to minimize unit cost while achieving certain quality specifications. Almost all products can be manufactured with a variety of inputs (materials, labor, and overhead) that

Regardless of the type of product or service provided, most organizations can determine standards for one or more cost components. Old Rosebud uses a standard cost system to predict the costs of feeding and caring for the brood mares which it boards.

would generate the same basic output. Even after output quality is specified, there still is often a wide spectrum of input factors that would achieve the quality objective. The input choices that are ultimately made affect the standards that are set.

Once management has established the design and manufacturing process that will produce the desired output quality and has determined which input resources will be used, quantity and price standards can be developed. Like the determination of target costs, standards should be developed by a group, composed of representatives from the following areas: management accounting, product design, industrial engineering, personnel, data processing, purchasing, and management. It is especially important to involve managers and, to some extent, employees whose performance will be compared to the standards. This involvement helps assure credibility of the standards and helps motivate personnel to operate as closely as possible to the standards. In some instances, information from suppliers can also be useful, especially in the area of setting material price standards.

Material Standards

The first step in developing material standards is to identify and list the specific direct material components used to manufacture the product or to perform the service. It is essential that three things be known about the materials inputs: what inputs are used; the quality of those inputs; and the quantity of those inputs.

In making quality decisions, managers should seek the advice of materials experts, engineers, accountants, and marketing personnel. There are many cost-benefit trade-offs involved in making quality decisions. In most cases, as the quality of raw material rises, so does the cost. Decisions about material input components usually attempt to balance the interrelationships of cost, quality, quantity, and selling prices.

For example, since Old Rosebud uses a complete-diet pellet feed rather than an oat-based feed, the cost per gallon is higher, but the number of gallons of feed used is less and it does not have to be supplemented with hay. Therefore, quantity and cost estimates become direct functions of quality decisions.

Given the quality selected for each component, physical quantity estimates can be made in terms of weight, size, volume, or other measure. These estimates can be based on results of engineering tests, opinions of people using the materials, or historical data. Information about material components, their specifications (including quality), and quantities needed are compiled on a document called the **bill of materials.** Even a company that does not have a formal standard cost system is likely to develop a bill of materials for each of its products simply as a guide for production activity.

bill of materials

Exhibit 5–3 illustrates a bill of materials for a pair of women's pumps produced by Tran Shoes. Some additional materials, such as thread and cobbler nails, are not shown on this document because they are considered to be indirect costs and are included in variable overhead.

After the standard quantities of material components are developed, prices are determined for each component. The purchasing agent is the person most likely to have the expertise to estimate standard prices. Prices should reflect factors such as desired component quality, reliability and physical proximity of the supplier, and quantity and purchase discounts allowed. If purchasing agents are involved in setting reasonable price standards for materials, those individuals are more likely to be able to explain the cause(s) of future variations from the standards.

When all quantity and price information is available, component quantities are multiplied by unit prices to get the total cost of each component. These totals are summed to determine the total standard materials cost of one unit of product, as shown (after the section on overhead standards) in Exhibit 5–5 for one pair of pumps produced by Tran Shoes.

Labor Standards

Developing labor standards requires the same basic procedures as those used for materials. Each worker operation, such as bending, reaching, lifting, moving materials, turning screws, sanding, and packing, should be identified. In specifying operations and movements, activities such as setup and rework must be considered because they

EXHIBIT 5–3
▼▼▼▼▼▼▼▼▼▼▼▼

TRAN SHOES BILL OF
MATERIALS

| Product: Women's Pump—Size 7 | | Revision Date: 8/1/93 | |
| Product Number: 262 | | Standard Lot Size: 5,000 | |
Component ID#	Quantity Required	Description of Component	Comments
L-15	2 sq. ft.	Fine-grained domestic cowhide	Tanned & dyed in-house
A-7	1 sq. ft.	Highly polished, two-ply shoe sole grade leather	
H-21	2	Hard rubber, reinforced heels	
C-5	2	Cushion inserts	

are performed during the production process. All unnecessary movements by workers and of materials should be disregarded when time standards are set and should be minimized or eliminated as non-value-added activities.

Each production operation must be converted to quantitative information to be a usable standard. Time and motion studies may be performed by the company,[1] or times that have been developed from industrial engineering studies for various movements can be used. Another way to set a time standard is to use the average time needed to perform the task during the past year. Such information can be calculated from employees' past time sheets.[2] Using historical data may, however, include past inefficiencies or may not consider technologically advanced machinery that was recently added or training workers received. For example, employees at Delta Wire Company in Clarksdale, Mississippi became substantially more proficient at their jobs after receiving training courses in the production processes of their manufacturing plant. Managers can compensate for such inefficiencies by making subjective adjustments to the available data.

After the analysis of labor tasks is complete, an **operations flow** (or routing) **document** can be prepared. This document lists all the necessary tasks to make a product or perform a service and the time allowed for each task. All specified activities should be analyzed as to their ability to add value to the product or service. Any non-value-added activities that are included should be targeted for reduction or elimination. Exhibit 5–4 presents a simplified operations flow document that reflects the manufacturing process for a pair of women's pumps at Tran Shoes. This document reflects 11 minutes (6.50 + 4.50) of move time that is non-value-added.

Labor rate standards should reflect the wages paid to employees who perform the various production tasks. In the simplest situation, all personnel working in a given department are paid the same wage rate; this could occur, for example, when

operations flow document

Product: Women's Pump—Size 7 Product Number: 262		Revision Date: 8/1/93 Standard Lot Size: 5,000	
Operation ID#	Department	Standard Minutes per Pair	Description of Task
27	Cutting	15.00	Cut leather uppers and soles; drill holes for sewing
		6.50	*Move to next department*
33	Sewing	12.50	Stitch uppers and attach to soles
34	Sewing	5.00	Nail heels to soles
		4.50	*Move to next department*
45	Finishing	9.50	Stain and polish soles, heels, and uppers

EXHIBIT 5–4
▼▼▼▼▼▼▼▼▼▼▼▼

TRAN SHOES OPERATIONS FLOW DOCUMENT

---

[1] In performing internal time and motion studies, observers need to be aware that employees may engage in "slowdown" tactics when they are being clocked. The purpose of such tactics is to have a longer time set as the standard, which would make employees appear more efficient when actual results are measured.
[2] An employee time sheet indicates what jobs were worked on and for what period of time. "Time sheets" can also be prepared for machines by using machine clocks or counters. Bar-coding is another way to track work flow through an organization.

wages are tied specifically to the job description or a labor contract. If employees performing the same or similar tasks are paid different wage rates, a weighted average rate must be computed and used as the standard. The average rate is computed as the total wage cost per hour divided by the number of workers. As the composition of a labor team changes, it is possible that the time needed to make a product will also change. For instance, workers who have been doing the job longer are likely to be paid more and be able to do that job more quickly than those who were just hired. There will often be trade-offs between rates and times for labor similar to those between price and quality for material.

Overhead Standards

Overhead standards are simply the predetermined overhead application rates discussed in chapter 3. Separate variable and fixed rates or a combined overhead rate can be found from the overhead flexible budget. Management may consider the use of either a standard plantwide rate or standard departmental rates. Alternatively, activity-based costing concepts employing multiple cost pools and multiple cost drivers may be used to determine standard overhead cost rates.

The Cutting and Finishing Departments in Tran Shoes rely heavily on direct labor. The predetermined overhead rate for these two departments is $8.50 per direct labor hour. These two departments work a total of 24.5 (15 + 9.5) minutes on each pair of pumps, so the total overhead applied per pair is $3.47 [(24.5 ÷ 60) × $8.50]. The Sewing Department is machine-intensive, and the predetermined overhead rate has been set at $5.70 per machine hour. Each pair of shoes is worked on 17.5 (12.5 + 5) minutes in Sewing, indicating that $1.66 [(17.5 ÷ 60) × $5.70] of overhead should be applied in that department. The costs associated with the 11 minutes of move time are considered as part of overhead. The overhead costs caused by move time are included in the predetermined overhead rate.

standard cost card

After the bill of materials, operations flow document, and standard overhead costs have been developed, a **standard cost card** is prepared. This document (shown in Exhibit 5–5) summarizes all the standard quantities and costs needed to complete one pair of women's pumps.

Standard costs and quantities are used during the period to assign costs to inventory accounts. In actual or normal cost systems, actual material and labor costs are debited to Work in Process as production occurs. In most standard cost systems, *standard* (rather than actual) costs of production are debited to Work in Process.[3] The difference between actual and standard costs or quantities is referred to as a **variance**.

variance

Variance discussions often use either direct labor hours or machine hours as the measure of inputs. These measures are used and referred to in the models for illustrative purposes. Alternative cost drivers such as setup time and material costs (or, more specifically from the Old Rosebud example, number of mares boarded) may be more appropriately related to cost incurrence. If such drivers exist, better information will be achieved from their use.

---

[3]The standard cost of each cost element (direct materials, direct labor, variable overhead, and fixed overhead) is said to be *applied* to the goods produced. This terminology is the same as that used when overhead is *applied* to inventory based on a predetermined rate.

Product: Women's Pump—Size 7   **Product Number: 262**

Direct Materials

			Departments			
			Cutting	Sewing	Finishing	
ID#	Unit Cost	Total Quantity	Cost	Cost	Cost	Total Cost
L-15	$4.00/sq. ft.	2.00 sq. ft.	$ 8.00			$ 8.00
A-7	$5.00/sq. ft.	1.20 sq. ft.	6.00	(All indirect)		6.00
H-21	$ .70 each	2 per pair			$1.40	1.40
C-5	$ .60 each	2 per pair			1.20	1.20
DIRECT MATERIALS TOTALS			$14.00		$2.60	$16.60

Direct Labor

	Avg. Wage	Total	Cutting	Sewing	Finishing	Total
ID#	Per Minute*	Minutes	Cost	Cost	Cost	Cost
27	$.16	15.00	$2.40			$2.40
33	.18	12.50		$2.25		2.25
34	.12	5.00		.60		.60
45	.18	9.50			$1.71	1.71
DIRECT LABOR TOTALS			$2.40	$2.85	$1.71	$6.96

Production Overhead

Cost Driver	Standard Time	Standard Dept'l Rate	Total Cost
Direct Labor Hours	24.5 minutes	$8.50 per DLH	$3.47
Machine Hours	17.5 minutes	$5.70 per MH	1.66
OVERHEAD TOTAL			$5.13

Total cost = $16.60 + $6.96 + $5.13 = $28.69

*Note: Labor costs per minute are found by dividing hourly rates by 60.

EXHIBIT 5–5
▼▼▼▼▼▼▼▼▼▼▼

TRAN SHOES
STANDARD COST
CARD

VARIANCE COMPUTATIONS

The most basic variance computation is a **total variance,** or the difference between   **total variance**
total actual cost incurred and total standard cost for the output produced during the
period. This variance can be diagrammed as follows:

Actual cost of actual   Standard cost of actual
production inputs   production outputs

Total Variance

A total variance can be computed for each cost element of production. Although total variances indicate differences between actual and expected production costs, they do not provide useful information for determining *why* such differences occurred. For example, the chapter earlier mentioned that if Old Rosebud had a $500 variance related to feed, it could have been related to a variety of causes. To help managers in their control objectives, total variances for materials and labor are subdivided into price and usage variances.

A price variance reflects the difference between what was actually paid for inputs and what should have been paid for inputs during the period. A usage variance shows the difference between the quantity of actual inputs and the quantity of standard inputs for the actual output (or quantity of products made or services rendered) of the period. A quantity difference is multiplied by a standard price or rate to provide a monetary measure that can be recorded in the accounting records. Usage variances focus on the efficiency of results—the relationship of inputs to outputs.

The basic diagram used to calculate a total variance can be expanded to provide a general model indicating the subvariances:

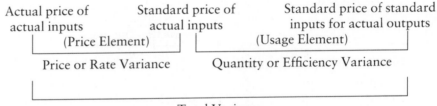

Actual price of   Standard price of   Standard price of standard
actual inputs   actual inputs   inputs for actual outputs

(Price Element)   (Usage Element)

Price or Rate Variance   Quantity or Efficiency Variance

Total Variance

standard quantity allowed

The far-right column uses a measure of output known as the **standard quantity allowed.** This measure of quantity translates the actual output into the standard quantity of input that should have been used to achieve the actual level of output. The right-hand column is computed as the standard quantity allowed times the standard price of the input resources.

The diagram can be simplified by using the abbreviated notations shown in Exhibit 5–6. This model progresses from the *actual* price of *actual* input on the left to the *standard* price of *standard* quantity allowed on the right. The middle measure of input is a hybrid of *actual* quantity and *standard* price.

Old Rosebud farm is used to illustrate the basic variance computations. Old Rosebud's standard costs are presented at the top of Exhibit 5–7. Also shown in the exhibit are the actual quantity and cost data for 1994 when fifty-two mares were boarded for a total of 18,980 days. This information is used to compute the materials, labor, and overhead variances for 1994.[4] Variance computations must indicate whether the amount of the variance is unfavorable (U) or favorable (F).

---

[4]Variance computations should be performed significantly more often than once per year. This period was chosen because it reflects the data provided by Sprohge and Talbott in their previously referenced article.

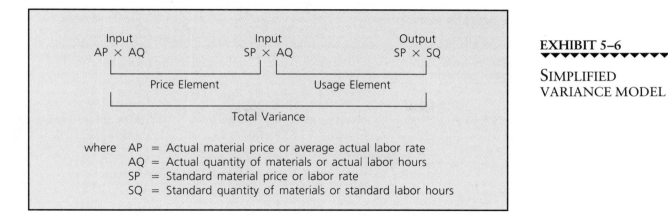

EXHIBIT 5–6
▼▼▼▼▼▼▼▼▼▼▼

SIMPLIFIED
VARIANCE MODEL

Standards for one day's boarding of one mare:

1.5 gallons of feed pellets at $2 per gallon	$ 3.00
1/10 hour of veterinary fees at $30 per hour	3.00
10 ounces of rubdown supplies per mare per day at $.04 per ounce	.40
Applied fixed overhead (based on estimated total FOH of $190,530 and 21,900 boarding days)	8.70
Total standard cost per day	$15.10

Actual data for 1994:
- Number of boarding days—18,980
- Gallons of feed used—29,400
- Price per gallon of feed used—$2.30
- Veterinary hours incurred—1,681
- Veterinary fee per hour—$35
- Number of ounces of supplies—148,040
- Price per ounce of supplies—$.05
- Total fixed overhead—$185,000

Standard Quantities Allowed

DIRECT MATERIALS: Standard quantity allowed for feed = 18,980 days × 1.5 gallons per day = 28,470 gallons

DIRECT LABOR: Standard quantity allowed for veterinary hours = 18,980 days × 1/10 hour per day = 1,898 hours

VARIABLE OVERHEAD: Standard quantity allowed for ounces of rubdown supplies = 18,980 days × 10 ounces = 189,800 ounces

EXHIBIT 5–7
▼▼▼▼▼▼▼▼▼▼▼

OLD ROSEBUD
STANDARD/ACTUAL
COST DATA FOR 1994

Materials Variances

Using the model and inserting information concerning material quantities and prices provides the following computations. (Note that the standard quantity for feed is taken from the bottom of Exhibit 5–7.)

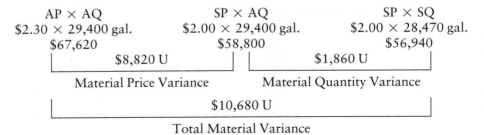

The subvariances for materials are known as the materials price and materials quantity variances, respectively. The **material price variance** (MPV) indicates the amount of money spent below (*F* for favorable) or above (*U* for unfavorable) the standard price for the quantity of materials purchased. For Old Rosebud, the actual price paid for feed was $2.30 per gallon, while the standard was $2.00, giving an unfavorable material price variance of $8,820. This variance can also be calculated as:

$$\begin{aligned} \text{MPV} &= \text{AQ (AP} - \text{SP)} \\ &= 29,400\ (\$2.30 - \$2.00) \\ &= 29,400\ (\$.30) \\ &= \$8,820\ U \end{aligned}$$

The positive sign reflects the increased price paid over the standard price and, therefore, the unfavorable nature of the variance.

The **material quantity variance** (MQV) indicates the standard cost saved (F) or expended (U) because of the difference between the actual quantity of material used and the standard quantity of material allowed for the goods produced or services rendered during the period. If the actual quantity used is less than the standard quantity allowed, the company has been more efficient than expected; if a greater quantity has been used than allowed, the company has been less efficient in its activities. Old Rosebud used 930 more gallons of feed than the standard allowed for the 18,980 boarding days. This inefficient usage results in an unfavorable materials quantity variance:

$$\begin{aligned} \text{MQV} &= \text{SP (AQ} - \text{SQ)} \\ &= \$2.00\ (29,400 - 28,470) \\ &= \$2.00\ (930) \\ &= \$1,860\ U \end{aligned}$$

The total material feed variance ($10,680 U) can be calculated by taking the difference between $67,620 total actual cost of inputs and $56,940 total standard cost of the output or service provided. The total variance also represents the summation of the individual variances. Thus, an alternative computation for the total material variance is to add the price and quantity subvariances ($8,820 U + $1,860 U = $10,680 U).

(margin notes)
material price variance

material quantity variance

Preferred Materials Variance Model

A total variance for a cost component is *generally* equal to the sum of the price and usage variances of the component used. A modification of the variance model occurs when the quantity of material *purchased* is not the same as the quantity of material *used* during a period. In such cases, the general model is altered slightly to provide better information for management control purposes.

In the preferred model illustrated next, the materials price variance is calculated based on the quantity of materials *purchased* rather than the quantity of materials *used*. A materials price variance relates more closely to the purchasing, rather than the production, function. The variation in the model allows the materials price variance to be more quickly isolated. The materials usage variance is still computed on the basis of the actual quantity of materials used in production.

If Old Rosebud farm had actually purchased 30,000 gallons of feed in 1994 and only used 29,400, the material price variance would be calculated as:

AP × AQ		SP × AQ
\$2.30 × 30,000 gal.		\$2.00 × 30,000 gal.
\$69,000		\$60,000

$$\underset{\text{Material Purchase Price Variance}}{\rule{0pt}{0pt}}\quad \text{\$9,000 U}$$

This variance is often referred to as the material **purchase price variance**, while the previously presented variance could be referred to as the material **usage price variance**. The material purchase price variance can also be calculated by multiplying the actual quantity purchased by the difference between the actual and standard prices, or [30,000 gallons (\$2.30 − \$2.00)] = 30,000 (\$.30) = \$9,000 U.

The materials quantity variance is calculated as presented earlier, because the actual quantity of feed used is not determined by the amount that is purchased. Old Rosebud would simply have 600 gallons of feed on hand to use the following year. This change in the general model is shown below using subscripts to indicate actual quantity purchased (p) and used (u).

purchase price variance

usage price variance

$$AP \times AQ_p \qquad\qquad SP \times AQ_p$$

Material Purchase Price Variance

$$SP \times AQ_u \qquad\qquad SP \times SQ_u$$

Material Quantity Variance

A total materials variance should not be calculated in this model because each subvariance calculation is made using a different measurement base.

Labor Variances

The price and usage elements of the total labor variance are the labor rate and labor efficiency variances. The model for and computations of the labor variances for Old Rosebud follow. The standard quantity is taken from the bottom of Exhibit 5–7 for veterinary hours.

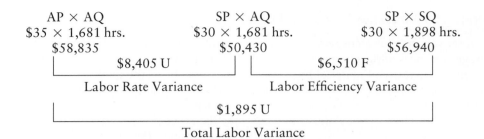

$$\underset{\text{Labor Rate Variance}}{\underbrace{\begin{array}{c}\text{AP} \times \text{AQ}\\ \$35 \times 1{,}681 \text{ hrs.}\\ \$58{,}835\end{array}\qquad\qquad\begin{array}{c}\text{SP} \times \text{AQ}\\ \$30 \times 1{,}681 \text{ hrs.}\\ \$50{,}430\end{array}}_{\$8{,}405 \text{ U}}}\qquad\underset{\text{Labor Efficiency Variance}}{\underbrace{\qquad\begin{array}{c}\text{SP} \times \text{SQ}\\ \$30 \times 1{,}898 \text{ hrs.}\\ \$56{,}940\end{array}}_{\$6{,}510 \text{ F}}}$$

$$\underset{\text{Total Labor Variance}}{\underbrace{\qquad\qquad\qquad\$1{,}895 \text{ U}\qquad\qquad\qquad}}$$

labor rate variance

The **labor rate variance** (LRV) shows the difference between the actual rate (or actual weighted average rate) paid to the veterinarians for the period and the standard rate for all hours actually worked during the period. The labor rate variance can also be computed as:

$$
\begin{aligned}
\text{LRV} &= \text{AQ (AP } - \text{ SP)}\\
&= 1{,}681 \text{ (\$35 } - \text{ \$30)}\\
&= 1{,}681 \times \text{(\$5)}\\
&= \$8{,}405 \text{ U}
\end{aligned}
$$

labor efficiency variance

The **labor efficiency variance** (LEV) compares the number of actual direct labor hours worked with the standard hours allowed for the actual number of boarding days (or work actually achieved). This difference is multiplied by the standard labor rate to establish a dollar value for the efficiency (F) or inefficiency (U) of the direct labor workers. The labor efficiency variance can also be calculated as:

$$
\begin{aligned}
\text{LEV} &= \text{SP (AQ } - \text{ SQ)}\\
&= \$30 \text{ (1,681 } - \text{ 1,898)}\\
&= \$30 \times \text{(}-217\text{)}\\
&= -\$6{,}510 \text{ (F)}
\end{aligned}
$$

The negative sign reflects the reduced cost per pound and, therefore, the favorable nature of the variance. The variance is favorable because the standard hours allowed were greater than the actual hours worked.

The total labor variance ($1,895 U) can be determined by taking the difference between the total actual labor cost ($58,835) and the total standard labor cost for the actual boarding days ($56,940). It may also be determined by adding the two labor variances [$8,405 U + (−$6,510 F) = $1,895 U].

The following News Note provides a slightly different perspective on efficiency variances. It suggests that the efficiency variance is truly composed of two elements (quality problems and efficiency problems) that should be accounted for separately.

As the News Note points out, it is possible that reductions in labor time (and, thus, favorable efficiency variances) may be obtained by producing defective or poor quality units. For example, assume that workers at Lipple Manufacturing are paid $9 per hour and can produce one unit of product in 2 hours. During the period, 1,500 units are made in 2,610 hours. The standard quantity of time allowed for production is 3,000 hours. The labor efficiency variance is $9 (2,610 − 3,000) or $3,510 F. However, 80 of the units produced were unacceptable because of defects. The quality variance would be computed as follows: 80 units × 2 hours per unit × $9 per hour = $1,440 U.

NEWS NOTE

Separating Quality Problems from Efficiency Problems

Historically, efficiency variances have been computed by multiplying excess inputs by the standard price. In recent years, this approach has been criticized for motivating managers to ignore quality concerns to avoid unfavorable efficiency variances. In other words, there is an incentive to produce a low-quality product by minimizing the amount of material used or the time spent in production.

[An approach could be taken that] separates the efficiency variance from the quality variance. Inputs consisting of conversion time or material used in defective units [would be] captured in the quality variance.

Separating the two variances allows production decision makers to evaluate the trade-offs between efficiency and quality. They can minimize production time to gain a favorable efficiency variance but this probably will increase the number of defective units and result in an unfavorable quality variance. Likewise, trying to minimize the number of defective units may result in investing more time and more material and therefore having an unfavorable efficiency variance.

SOURCE: Carole Cheatham, "Updating Standard Cost Systems," *Journal of Accountancy* (December 1990), pp. 59–60.

Overhead Variances

The use of separate variable and fixed overhead application rates and accounts allows the computation of separate variances for each type of overhead. These separate computations provide managers with the greatest detail and, thus, the greatest flexibility for control and performance evaluation purposes. Also, because of increased use of nonsimilar bases for various overhead allocations, each different cost pool for variable and fixed overhead may require separate price and usage computations. Because of the business's nature, all overhead calculations for Old Rosebud are based on number of boarding days.

As with materials and labor, total variable and total fixed overhead variances can be divided into specific price and usage subvariances for each type of overhead. The different overhead subvariances are referred to as follows:

Variable overhead price element → Variable Overhead Spending Variance

Variable overhead usage element → Variable Overhead Efficiency Variance

Fixed overhead price element → Fixed Overhead Spending Variance

Fixed overhead usage element → Volume Variance

Variable Overhead The total variable overhead (VOH) variance is the difference between actual variable overhead costs incurred for the period and standard variable overhead cost applied to the period's actual production or service output. The difference at year-end is the total variable overhead variance, which is also the amount of under- or overapplied variable overhead. The following diagram illustrates the computation of the total variable overhead variance.

Actual Variable   Variable Overhead Cost
Overhead Cost   Applied to Production

|_____|

Total Variable Overhead (VOH) Variance
(Under- or Overapplied Variable Overhead)

The following variable overhead variance computations use 1994 data for Old Rosebud farm. It is assumed that the only variable overhead item is rubdown supplies for the mares. The actual cost of these supplies for the year was $7,402 for 148,040 ounces. In this case, the standard number of boarding days is equal to the actual number of boarding days. For each day a mare was boarded, she should have been rubbed down with a total of 10 ounces of supplies (as shown in Exhibit 5–7). Thus, the standard ounces allowed were 189,800. Each ounce of supplies was expected to cost the farm $.04 in variable overhead. The variable overhead variances for Old Rosebud are computed as follows using the input and output measures:

(Input Measure =   (Output Measure =
Actual Ounces of Supplies)   Standard Cost × Standard
                                      Quantity Allowed)

$(AP \times AQ)$ $(SP \times AQ)$ $(SP \times SQ)$
($.05 × 148,040 oz.)   ($.04 × 148,040 oz.)   ($.04 × 10 oz. × 18,980)
$7,402 $5,921.60 $7,592

|_____$1,480.40 U_____|_____$1,670.40 F_____|

VOH Spending Variance   VOH Efficiency Variance

|_____$190 F_____|

Total VOH Variance

variable overhead spending variance

variable overhead efficiency variance

The **variable overhead spending variance** is the difference between actual variable overhead and budgeted variable overhead based on actual input. The **variable overhead efficiency variance** is the difference between budgeted VOH at the actual input activity and budgeted VOH at standard input allowed. This variance quantifies the effect of using more or less actual input than the standard allowed for the actual output. When actual input exceeds standard input allowed, operations appear inefficient. Excess input also means that more variable overhead is needed to support the additional input.

Fixed Overhead   The total fixed overhead (FOH) variance is the difference between actual FOH costs incurred and standard FOH cost applied to the period's actual production. This difference is also the amount of under- or overapplied fixed overhead for the period. The following model shows the computation of the total fixed overhead variance.

Actual Fixed   Fixed Overhead Cost
Overhead Cost   Applied to Production

|_____|

Total Fixed Overhead (FOH) Variance
(Under- or Overapplied Fixed Overhead)

The total fixed overhead variance is subdivided into its price and usage elements by inserting *budgeted* fixed overhead as a middle column into the model.

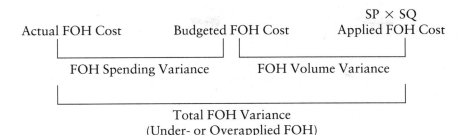

In the model, the left column is simply labeled "actual FOH cost" and is not computed as a price times quantity measure, because fixed overhead is generally acquired in lump-sum amounts rather than on a per-unit input basis. The **fixed overhead spending variance** is the difference between actual and budgeted fixed overhead. The fixed overhead **volume variance** is the difference between budgeted and applied fixed overhead. Budgeted fixed overhead is a constant amount throughout the relevant range; thus, *the middle column is a constant figure regardless of the actual quantity of input or the standard quantity of input allowed.* This concept is a key element in computing FOH variances. The budgeted amount of fixed overhead is equal to the standard FOH rate times the estimated capacity measure used to compute the standard rate.

fixed overhead spending variance

volume variance

Applied fixed overhead equals the FOH application rate times the standard input allowed for the production achieved. In regard to fixed overhead, the standard input allowed for the production achieved measures capacity utilization for the period. The standard input for Old Rosebud is one boarding day per mare; thus, the number of boarding days also represents the standard quantity of input allowed for the output achieved. This type of relationship is true of many organizations that provide services on a daily basis. In a manufacturing environment, a conversion of inputs to standard quantity of outputs normally needs to be made, as indicated in the demonstration problem at the end of the chapter.

Inserting the data for Old Rosebud farm into the model gives the following:

Actual FOH Cost	Budgeted FOH Cost ($8.70 × 21,900 boarding days)	Applied FOH Cost ($8.70 × 18,980 boarding days)
$185,000	$190,530	$165,126

$5,530 F	$25,404 U
FOH Spending Variance	FOH Volume Variance

$19,874 U
Total FOH Variance

Actual 1994 fixed overhead cost for the farm was $185,000, while the budgeted amount was $190,530. This difference is the FOH spending variance, which could be related to a decrease in property taxes for the farm, not replacing a salaried worker who quit during the year, or a decline in the fixed portion of utility costs.

For Old Rosebud farm, the FOH application rate is $8.70 per boarding day ($190,530 ÷ 21,900). This rate exists because the farm chose an expected annual capacity level of 21,900 boarding days. Had any other capacity level been chosen, the rate would have differed, even though the total amount of budgeted fixed overhead ($190,530) would have been the same. *If any level of capacity is experienced other than that which was used in determining the application rate, a volume variance will occur.* For example, if Old Rosebud had chosen 18,980 boarding days as the denominator level of activity to set the predetermined FOH rate, there would be no volume variance for 1994. If any number of boarding days less than 18,980 had been chosen as the denominator level of activity, the volume variance would have been favorable.

The difference between the $190,530 budgeted FOH and the $165,126 applied FOH gives the $25,404 unfavorable volume variance for the year. The $19,874 unfavorable total fixed overhead variance is the underapplied balance in the fixed overhead account at year-end.

Exhibit 5–8 compares the actual costs incurred by Old Rosebud farm with the flexible budget at the actual level of activity. This cost report is for an annual period, but it could just as easily be prepared for any other time period.

EXHIBIT 5–8
▼▼▼▼▼▼▼▼▼▼▼▼

OLD ROSEBUD ACTUAL/FLEXIBLE BUDGET COMPARISON FOR THE YEAR ENDED DECEMBER 31, 1994

| Budgeted number of boarding days | | 21,900 | | | |
| Actual number of boarding days | | 18,980 | | | |

	(1)	(2)	(3)	(4)	(5)	(6)
		Input	Standard Cost Allowed	Total Variance	Price Variance	Usage Variance
	Actual Cost	Flexible Budget	Based on Actual Output	Column (3) − (1)	Column (2) − (1)	Column (3) − (2)
Variable Cost Components*						
Feed	$ 67,620	$ 58,800.00	$ 56,940	$10,680U	$ 8,820.00U	$1,860.00U
Veterinary fees	58,835	50,430.00	56,940	1,895U	8,405.00U	6,510.00F
Rubdown supplies	7,402	5,921.60	7,592	190F	1,480.40U	1,670.40F
Total variable	$133,857	$115,151.60	$121,472	$12,385U	$18,705.40U	$6,320.40F

	(1)	(2)	(3)	(4)	(5)	(6)
			Standard Cost Allowed	Total Variance	Price Variance	Usage Variance
	Actual Cost	Fixed Cost Budget	Based on Actual Output	Column (3) − (1)	Column (2) − (1)	Column (3) − (2)
Fixed Cost Components**						
Depreciation	$ 45,000	$ 45,000	$ 39,000	$ 6,000U	$ 0	$ 6,000U
Insurance	11,000	11,000	9,547	1,453U	0	1,453U
Utilities	12,000	14,500	12,565	565F	2,500F	1,935U
Repairs & maintenance	10,000	11,000	9,547	453U	1,000F	1,453U
Labor	88,000	96,000	83,201	4,799U	8,000F	12,799U
Advertisements	11,000	8,000	6,933	4,067U	3,000U	1,067U
Entertainment	8,000	5,030	4,333	3,667U	2,970U	697U
Total fixed	$185,000	$190,530	$165,126	$19,874U	$5,530F	$25,404U

*For variable costs, amounts in column (3) are calculated by multiplying the number of actual boarding days times the rate per unit.
**For fixed costs, the amounts in column (3) are calculated as follows: 1) divide each budgeted amount in column (2) by the expected annual capacity (21,900 boarding days); and 2) multiply the result by the actual number of boarding days (18,980).

COST CONTROL AND VARIANCE RESPONSIBILITY

Cost control focuses on the variances between actual costs incurred for a period and the standard costs that should have been incurred based on actual output. To exercise any type of control, managers first must be provided with detailed information on the various cost components. Second, a well-designed system of cost control and variance analysis should capture variances as early as possible.

Variance analysis is the process of categorizing the nature (favorable or unfavorable) of the differences between standard and actual costs and seeking the reasons for those differences. The system should help managers determine who or what is responsible for the variance and who is best able to explain it. As indicated in the News Note on page 194, when variances reflect poor performance, an early measurement system may allow operational performance to be improved. The longer the reporting of a variance is delayed, the more difficult it becomes to determine its cause.

variance analysis

Material price and labor rate variances are not as controllable at the production or service level as are material quantity and labor efficiency variances. Price and rate standards tend to be predictive in nature and are more dependent on outside forces than are usage standards.

Materials

Material price variances are normally determined at the point of purchase. Purchasing agents cannot always *control* prices, but given adequate lead time and resources, these individuals should be able to *influence* those prices. This influence is exerted through knowing what suppliers are available and choosing suppliers that provide

The continuous flow processing in a petroleum refinery may not be conducive to the calculation of variances during the period. It may be more appropriate to calculate variances for this type of production environment when goods are completed.

NEWS NOTE

Understand the Critical Nature of Reporting Frequency

Comparisons [of actual results against standard or budgeted levels] can be made periodically or each time a unit of work is finished. To be most useful, however, the frequency of reported information should follow the cycle of the production process being measured. In departments producing hundreds of parts per hour, the per-unit materials, labor, machine time, and utility consumption should be reported daily or even hourly. The system for control in a support department or a research lab could report on a much longer cycle.

Obviously, it is not much help to get monthly cost reports for an operation that turns out many parts per second. A manager controlling work hourly and daily does not want to receive an aggregate variance report in the middle of the subsequent month. Equally as obvious, daily or weekly cost reports would confuse departments taking several months to assemble a complex machine or performing basic research.

SOURCE: An excerpt from "One Cost System Isn't Enough," by Robert S. Kaplan (January–February 1988). Reprinted by permission of *Harvard Business Review*. Copyright © 1988 by the President and Fellows of Harvard College; all rights reserved.

the appropriate material in the most reasonable time span at the most reasonable cost. The purchasing agent can also influence material prices by purchasing in quantities that provide price discounts or by engaging in contractual arrangements such as long-term purchase contracts. The purchasing agent is usually the person who is best able to explain why a materials price variance occurs. Also, by being part of the team that originally set the materials price standard, the purchasing agent is usually the individual to whom responsibility for material price variances is assigned.

Materials quantity variances can be determined when materials are issued or used. Such variances are considered the responsibility of the person in charge of the job or department. Materials are ordinarily requisitioned based on the number of actual units to be produced times the standard quantity per unit. Excess material requisition slips are filled out when additional materials are taken out of inventory. Using excess requisition slips allows control to take place while work is under way rather than at the end of the period or when production is completed. Monitoring requisition slips for significant excess material withdrawals alerts managers to seek causes for the excesses and, if possible, take timely corrective action.

Some production settings, such as chemical and petroleum processing, involve a continuous flow process. In these cases, it may not be practical or reasonable to isolate quantity variances when materials are placed into production. The material quantity variance is more feasibly measured when production is complete and the total quantity of production is known. Measuring usage for relatively short time periods and reporting quantity variances after production is complete can still assist management in controlling operations. (Labor efficiency variances are also more appropriately measured at the end of production in these types of manufacturing operations.)

There are exceptions to the normal assignment of responsibility for materials price and quantity variances. Assume that Old Rosebud's farm manager asked the purchasing agent to acquire, without adequate lead time, additional quantities of feed. This request was made because there was an unexpected increase in mares being boarded during a vacation period. Such a spur-of-the-moment acquisition could result in paying a price higher than standard. Price variances from these types of causes should be assigned to the service (or production) activity, not to purchasing. In contrast, assume the purchasing agent acquires inferior quality feed that results in excess consumption and an unfavorable quantity variance. This quantity variance should be assigned to purchasing rather than to service or production. Such situations are likely to be identified from continuous, rather than end-of-period, reporting.

Labor

Labor rate and labor efficiency variances are commonly identified as a part of the payroll process and assigned to the person in charge of the service or production area. This assignment assumes that those managers have the ability to influence the type of labor personnel used. For instance, Old Rosebud could use a veterinarian's assistant for many duties rather than a DVM (Doctor of Veterinary Medicine). As with material variances, correlations may exist between labor variances. For example, using highly skilled, highly paid individuals for lower-level jobs could cause an unfavorable labor rate variance, accompanied by a favorable labor efficiency variance.

Sometimes a common factor may influence both material and labor and, thus, cause both a material and a labor variance. For instance, in a manufacturing situation, the purchase of inferior quality materials could result in a favorable materials price variance, an unfavorable materials usage variance, and an unfavorable labor efficiency variance. The efficiency variance could reflect increased production time, since many units were rejected as substandard because of the inferior materials. In another common situation, the use of lower-paid, less-skilled workers results in a favorable rate variance, but causes excessive materials usage.

The probability of detecting relationships among variances is improved, but not assured, by timely variance reporting. The accounting and reporting process should highlight interrelationships of variances, and managers should be aware of the possibility of such relationships when reviewing variance reports.

Overhead

The difference between actual and applied overhead is the amount of under- or overapplied overhead or the total overhead variance that must be explained. Control purposes differ for variable and fixed overhead because of the types of costs that make up the two categories as well as the ability of managers to influence those costs.

Variable Overhead   Variable overhead (VOH) costs are incurred on an ongoing basis as work is performed and are directly related to that work. Because of this direct relationship to activity, control of VOH costs is similar to that for materials and labor. Variable overhead is controlled by (1) keeping actual costs in line with planned costs for the actual level of activity and (2) getting the planned output yield from the overhead resources placed into production.

Variable overhead spending variances are commonly caused by price differences—paying higher or lower average actual prices than the standard prices allowed. Such fluctuations often occur because price changes have not been reflected in the standard rate. For instance, average indirect labor wage rates, supply costs, or utility rates could have increased or decreased since the standard VOH rate was computed. In such instances, the standard rate should be adjusted. If managers have no control over prices charged by external parties, they should not be held accountable for var-

The cost of shoeing a horse would probably be considered overhead. The cost is often variable because many owners and trainers hire self-employed farriers and pay those individuals on a per-horse basis.

iances arising because of such price changes. However, if managers could influence prices through, for example, long-term purchase arrangements, such options should be investigated as to their long-term costs and benefits before making a decision to change the standard. Waste or spoilage of resources, such as indirect materials, is another possible cause of the VOH spending variance.

The VOH efficiency variance reflects the managerial control implemented or needed in regard to yield of output as related to input. If overhead is applied on the basis of direct labor hours, the signs (favorable or unfavorable) of the variable overhead and direct labor efficiency variances will be the same, since the actual and standard hours compared in the two calculations are the same. However, because alternate overhead application bases are often used, the signs of these two variances are often no longer related to one another. Use of any alternative basis, including those provided under activity-based costing, does not affect the implementation of a standard costing system, as indicated in the following News Note.

Fixed Overhead   Control of fixed overhead (FOH) is distinctly different from that of variable overhead because fixed overhead may not necessarily be directly related to current activity. Because managers must commit to many types of fixed costs in lump-sum amounts before current period activity takes place, managers may have

NEWS NOTE

The Relationship of Activity-Based and Standard Costing

In typical manufacturers today, the emphasis is shifting sharply away from labor. Instead, overhead is now the cost component emphasized in developing accurate standards. To a large degree, this is the motivation behind the development of activity-based costing. The development and maintenance of accurate standards, therefore, hinges on the degree to which overhead can be analyzed and overhead rates adjusted for more fair distributions. From a systems perspective, activity-based costing is the way the system is developed and designed structurally and mechanically. Standard costing is the way the system is used to manage costs.

SOURCE: Robert A. Bonsack, "Does Activity-Based Costing Replace Standard Costing?" (Winter 1991), p. 47. Reprinted with permission from the *Journal of Cost Management for the Manufacturing Industry*. Warren, Gorham & Lamont, a division of Research Institute of America, 210 South Street, Boston, Mass. 02111. All rights reserved.

only limited ability to control FOH costs in the short run. Once managers commit to a fixed cost, it becomes unchangeable for some period of time *regardless of whether actual work takes place.* Thus, control of many fixed overhead costs must occur at the *time of commitment* rather than at the *time of activity.*

The FOH spending variance normally represents a weighted average price variance of the components of fixed overhead, although it can also reflect mismanagement of resources. Control over the FOH spending variance often must take place on a transaction-by-transaction basis when managers arrange for facilities. For example, Old Rosebud farm's budgeted fixed overhead costs were shown in Exhibit 5–8 and consisted of the following items:

Depreciation	$ 45,000
Insurance	11,000
Utilities	14,500
Repairs & maintenance	11,000
Labor	96,000
Advertisement	8,000
Entertainment	5,030
Total	$190,530

Of the previous costs, managers could, in the short run, probably influence the insurance and advertising charges by "shopping" for prices when the insurance coverage and promotional campaigns were negotiated. Entertainment costs can be controlled to some extent, but are significantly affected by the location in which the entertainment occurs (Memphis is less expensive than New York) and the type of entertainment involved (lunch is less expensive than dinner).

The remaining costs are basically uncontrollable in the short run. Depreciation expense is based on the factory's historical cost, salvage value, and expected life. Utility costs are set by rate commissions and are influenced by the size and type of the physical plant. Even a "turn-off-the-lights" program can only reduce utilities by a limited amount. Repairs and maintenance can be controlled to some extent, but are highly affected by the type of operation involved. For example, Old Rosebud could not simply allow its pasture fences or barns to deteriorate. Labor salaries are contractual obligations that were set at the time of employment or salary review.

A total FOH spending variance amount would not provide management with enough specific information to decide whether corrective action would be possible or desirable. Individual cost variances for each component need to be reviewed. Such a review will help managers determine the actual cause(s) of and responsibility for the several components of the total fixed overhead spending variance.

In addition to controlling spending, utilizing capacity is another important aspect of managerial control. Capacity utilization is reflected in the volume variance. The volume variance is a direct function of the capacity level chosen for the computation of the standard fixed overhead application rate. Although utilization is controllable to some degree, the volume variance is the one variance over which managers have the least influence and control, especially in the short run. But it is important that managers exercise what ability they do have to influence and control capacity utilization properly.

An unfavorable volume variance indicates less-than-expected utilization of capacity. If available capacity is currently being used at a level below (or above) that which was anticipated, managers should recognize that condition, investigate its reasons, and (if possible and desirable) initiate appropriate action. The degree of capacity utilization should always be viewed in relationship to inventory and sales. If capacity is overutilized (a favorable volume variance) *and* inventory is stockpiling, managers should decrease capacity utilization. A favorable volume variance could, however, be due to increased sales demand with no stockpiling of inventory—in which case no adjustments should be made to reduce utilization.

If capacity is underutilized (an unfavorable volume variance) *and* sales are back-ordered or going unfilled, managers should try to increase capacity utilization. However, managers *must* understand that underutilization of capacity is not always an undesirable condition. In a manufacturing company, it is more appropriate for managers to *not produce* than to produce goods that will simply end up in inventory stockpiles. Unneeded inventory production, although it will serve to utilize capacity, will generate substantially more costs for materials, labor, and overhead (including storage and handling costs). The positive impact that such unneeded production will have on the fixed overhead volume variance is unimportant because it is outweighed by the other unnecessary costs caused by accumulating excess inventory.

Managers can sometimes influence capacity utilization by modifying work schedules, taking measures to relieve production constraints, eliminating non-value-added activities, and carefully monitoring the movement of resources through the production or service process. Such actions should be taken during the period rather than after the period has ended. Efforts made after work is completed may improve next period's operations, but will have no impact on past work.

CONSIDERATIONS IN ESTABLISHING STANDARDS

When standards are established, appropriateness and attainability need to be considered. Appropriateness, in relation to a standard, refers to the basis on which the standards are developed and how long they are expected to last. Attainability refers to management's belief about the degree of difficulty or rigor that should be incurred in achieving the standard.

Appropriateness

While standards are developed from past and current information, they should reflect technical and environmental factors expected for the period in which the standards

Standards must change to reflect changed conditions. Labor time standards for document preparation in the manual environment would have been substantially longer than in the current PC-oriented office.

NEWS NOTE

Change the Process—Change the Standard

Labor and material usage standards normally are set by the industrial engineering department. Material price normally is considered the responsibility of purchasing. Similarly, the labor rates are set by the personnel department. As the production processes change (improve), past standards become less than realistic, and should be revised. It is the responsibility of departments that originally created the standard to inform the accounting department about the need for revising the standards.

But, unfortunately, some managers prefer to keep the old standards because the new improved production process makes their performance look better with old standards.

SOURCE: Lakshmi U. Tatikonda, "Production Managers Need a Course in Cost Accounting," *Management Accounting* (June 1987), p. 27. Published by Institute of Management Accountants, Montvale, N.J.

are to be applied. Factors such as materials quality, normal ordering quantities, employee wage rates, degree of plant automation, facility layout, and mix of employee skills should be considered. Management should not think that, once standards are set, they will remain useful forever. Standards must evolve over the organization's life to reflect its changing methods and processes. As suggested in the preceding News Note, out-of-date standards will produce variances that do not provide logical bases for planning, controlling, decision making, or evaluating performance. Current operating performance is not comparable to out-of-date standards.

To illustrate the previous point, assume that a computer manufacturer set price standards for computer chips in 1990 and did not change that standard for three years. By 1993, the price of chips had declined drastically. The consistently favorable material price variances for the chips should have been noticed, and managers should have realized that the price variance was not relevant to evaluating the purchasing agent's performance, inventory valuation, or any product pricing decisions. The price reductions occurring since the standard was set have made the standard obsolete and worthless.

Another example of appropriateness relates to changes in facility layout. Assume that a company set its labor time standards in 1990; in 1993, the company made major changes in the plant layout that eliminated many non-value-added labor movements. If the labor time standard is not reduced to reflect these changes, labor efficiency variances will not be meaningful.

Attainability

Standards provide a target level of performance and can be set at various levels of rigor. The level of rigor invested in the standard affects motivation, and one reason for using standards is to motivate employees. Standards can be classified by their degree of rigor and, thus, their motivational value ranges from easy to difficult. The classifications are as follows: expected, practical, and ideal.

NEWS NOTE

The "Full Figure" Standard Game

A standard cost system has three basic functions: collecting the actual costs of a manufacturing operation, determining the achievement of that manufacturing operation, and evaluating performance through the reporting of variances from standard. These variances provide managers with the information that directs them to areas that are not performing according to budget. Sometimes, however, the standards that are set do more to hinder the manager than to help.

In the "Full Figure" Standard Game, the standard amounts for material, labor, and overhead costs may have been set realistically in the preliminary stages of the standard-setting process, but, somewhere along the line, a little extra is added here and there so that "achievable" standards are established. The sure sign that this game is being played to the hilt is that all variances reported for material, labor, and overhead are favorable. Also, if these "full figure standards" are used to establish selling prices, then the inventories of these overpriced goods increase rapidly.

SOURCE: Richard V. Calvasina and Eugene J. Calvasina, "Standard Costing Games that Managers Play," *Management Accounting* (March 1984), pp. 49, 51. Published by Institute of Management Accountants, Montvale, N.J.

Expected standards are those set at a level that reflects what is actually expected to occur in the future period. Such standards anticipate future waste and inefficiencies and allow for them. As such, expected standards are not of significant value for motivation, control, or performance evaluation. Any variances from expected standards should be minimal. As seen in the preceding News Note, managers should take care that expected standards are not set to be "too achievable." **expected standards**

Standards that can be reached or slightly exceeded approximately 60 to 70 percent of the time with reasonable effort by workers are called **practical standards**. These standards allow for normal, unavoidable time problems or delays such as machine downtime and worker breaks. Practical standards represent an attainable challenge and have traditionally been thought to be the most effective at inducing the best worker performance and at determining the effectiveness and efficiency of workers at performing their tasks. Both favorable and unfavorable variances result from the use of such moderately rigorous standards. **practical standards**

Standards that provide for no inefficiency of *any* type are called **ideal standards**. Ideal standards encompass the highest level of rigor and do not allow for normal operating delays or human limitations such as fatigue, boredom, or misunderstanding. Unless a plant is entirely automated (and then there is still the possibility of human or power failure), it is impossible for ideal standards to be attained. Most attempts to use such standards result in discouraged and resentful workers who, ultimately, ignore the standard. Variances from ideal standards will always be unfavorable and traditionally have not been considered useful for constructive cost control or performance evaluation. **ideal standards**

management by exception

Depending on the type of standard in effect, the acceptable ranges used to apply the **management by exception** principle will differ.[5] This difference is especially notable for those deviations on the unfavorable side. If a company uses expected standards, the ranges of acceptable variances should be extremely small, since actual cost should closely conform to the standard. A company using ideal standards would expect variances to fall within a very wide range of acceptability, since managers would know that the standards could not be met. The News Note on the next page about a recent study of manufacturing company controllers provides some reasons why managers are using more formalized methods of judging when to investigate variance than those used in the past.

Variances large enough to fall outside the ranges of acceptability are generally indicative of trouble. The variances themselves, though, do not reveal the cause of the trouble or the person or group responsible. To determine variance causes, managers must investigate problems through observation, inspection, and inquiry. Such investigations will involve the time and effort of people at the operating level as well as accounting personnel. Operations personnel should be alert in spotting variances as they occur and record the reasons for the variances to the extent those causes can be determined. For example, operating personnel could readily detect and report causes such as machine downtime or material spoilage.

The ability to determine causes of variances is often proportional to how much time, effort, and money a company spends in gathering information about variances during the period. Managers must be willing and able to accumulate variance information regularly and consistently to evaluate the evidence, isolate the cause(s), and (if possible) influence performance to improve the process. If variances are ignored when they occur, it is often impossible or extremely costly to determine the relevant data at a later point in time.

CHANGES IN STANDARDS USAGE

Standard cost systems have been used since the early 1900s to determine the causes and controllability of deviations from specified norms. Once ability to control can be assigned, performance can be evaluated. In using variances for performance evaluation, however, many accountants currently believe that incorrect measurements are sometimes being used. For example, oftentimes the determination of materials standards includes a factor for waste or spoilage. In setting labor standards, the practical level of attainment is most often used even though it includes time for downtime and human error. Use of standards that are not aimed at the highest possible level of attainment is now being questioned.

The questions being asked have become more prevalent with the Japanese productivity of recent years. The Japanese management philosophy is a notable exception to the traditional disbelief in the use of ideal standards for performance evaluation. The just-in-time (JIT) inventory system developed by the Japanese has goals of zero defects, zero inefficiency, and zero downtime. Under such a system, ideal standards become expected standards. There is, basically, no level of acceptable deviation

---

[5]Management by exception allows managers to set upper and lower limits of tolerance for deviations and only investigate those deviations that fall outside those tolerance ranges.

NEWS NOTE

When to Investigate Variances

Variance investigation policies [for materials and labor at large companies] are moving away from pure judgment and toward the use of structured or formalized exception procedures.

[One] explanation is that the results are being driven by manufacturing innovations that lead to shorter production runs and shorter product life cycles. In such an environment, monthly variance reports may be so untimely as to be virtually useless. In a flexible manufacturing environment, production runs can be extremely short—only days or perhaps even hours. To provide timely feedback in an environment where the nature of operations and the products being produced change rapidly, more accounts and greater reporting frequency are required.

[Another] explanation relates to the increasing globalization of markets rather than to the characteristics or individual operating policies of the firm. When competing internationally, companies face more competitors, are less likely to be the lowest-cost producers, and face more uncertainties than in domestic markets. . . . By reducing production cost surprises, intensified management accounting (in the frequency of reports and the details of variance composition) can compensate for these additional uncertainties.

SOURCE: Bruce R. Gaumnitz and Felix P. Kollaritsch, "Manufacturing Variances: Current Practice and Trends," (Spring 1991), pp. 63–64. Reprinted with permission from the *Journal of Cost Management for the Manufacturing Industry*. Warren, Gorham & Lamont, a division of Research Institute of America, 210 South Street, Boston, Mass. 02111. All rights reserved.

from standard. As mentioned previously, ideal standards should only be considered for use in automated plants.

With the use of the management by exception principle, managers permit inefficient uses of resources and improper production. Setting standards at the tightest possible (ideal) level would provide the most useful performance evaluation information and help ensure that the highest quality goods are produced at the lowest possible cost. If no inefficiencies are built into or tolerated in the system, deviations from standard should be minimized and performance improved.

Whether setting standards at the ideal level will become the norm of American companies cannot be determined at this time. However, the authors expect that the level of attainability for standards will move away from the practical and much closer to the ideal. This conclusion is made based on the fact that many companies must now compete in global markets. When a competitor uses the highest possible standards and when prices are based to some extent on cost, a company using anything less than those same tight standards will be put at a competitive disadvantage.

SITE ANALYSIS

As shown by Exhibit 5–8, Old Rosebud farm was plagued with some rather large variances. While farm management had virtually no control over the depreciation, insurance, and utility variances, analysis of the other variances found the following under-

continued

lying causes. A drought in Kentucky and the rest of the nation caused feed prices to rise substantially and, additionally, a mineral supplement was added to the feed that increased its cost but helped to minimize skeletal bone disease. Old Rosebud farm had lost a major client during the year, which lowered its expected boarding days and caused management not to replace a salaried worker who quit early in the year. Without this skilled individual, however, the remaining employees worked many more hours than normally would be required to do their jobs. Lastly, a new farm brochure was developed to give to potential clients and, in hopes of increasing boarding days, more clients were entertained.[6]

Regardless of whether an organization is Old Rosebud, Citicorp, the city of Houston, or Chrysler Corporation, standard costing will help managers more effectively understand what costs should be and provide a foundation from which to analyze the reasons for nonconformity of costs. The following Applications Strategies present some important uses for all discipline areas of this highly versatile tool.

CHAPTER SUMMARY

A standard cost is a budget for one unit of product or service output. Standards provide norms against which actual costs can be compared to control costs and evaluate performance. In a true standard cost system, standards are derived for prices and quantities of each product component (materials, labor, variable overhead, and fixed overhead). Standards should be developed by a team composed of professional staff and managers as well as employees whose performance will be evaluated by such standards. A standard cost card is used to accumulate and record specific information about components, processes, quantities, and costs that form the standard for a product. The materials and labor sections of the standard cost card are derived from the bill of materials and the operations flow document, respectively.

In a standard costing system, both actual and standard costs are accumulated, and then variances are computed and analyzed. Each total variance is separated into subvariances relating to price and usage (efficiency) elements.

Variance analysis provides a basis for management planning, control, and performance evaluation. Using standard costs, managers can forecast what costs should be at various levels of activity and can compare these forecasts with actual results. When large variances are observed, the responsible manager attempts to determine the cause(s) and, if possible, takes corrective action. Variances should be recorded as early in the production/service process as is feasible so that their causes will be more discoverable.

Standards should be established that are appropriate and attainable. Current, up-to-date standards should be used that reflect the relevant technical and operational expectations for the period in which the standards are to be applied. Attainability refers to the degree of rigor built into the standards. The level of rigor chosen should be based on realistic expectations and motivational effects on employees. The prac-

---

[6]Hans Sprohge and John Talbott, "New Applications for Variance Analysis," *Journal of Accountancy* (April 1989), pp. 137–41.

Discipline	Application	**APPLICATIONS STRATEGIES OF STANDARD COSTING**
Accounting	Permits accountants to integrate both budgetary and actual costs into the information system; promotes clerical ease and efficiency in record-keeping; captures variances in the accounts	
Economics	Standard costs, when based on ideal standards, represent an effort to maximize the efficiency with which resources are used and, thereby, to minimize the cost per unit for a given quality of product or service	
Finance	Facilitates planning and decision making; budgeting for future periods can be done more efficiently and effectively when standard costs are available	
Management	Used in budgeting, cost analysis and control, performance evaluation, and problem solving to enhance management's performance	
Marketing	Improves price setting because of appropriate cost estimation; when costs have been kept at their lowest, the company can keep prices competitive, and the sales force has a strong advantage; helps to determine if a company can be competitive in a given market for a given product (can the volume needed to reduce costs be attained?)	

tical level has typically been thought to have the best motivational impact; however, some Japanese firms use ideal standards to indicate their goals of minimum cost and zero defects.

APPENDIX

Standard Cost System Journal Entries

Journal entries for the Old Rosebud farm information are given in Exhibit 5–9. The feed price variance in this exhibit is accounted for using the secondary information of 30,000 pounds purchased. Note that all unfavorable variances have debit balances and favorable variances have credit balances. Unfavorable variances represent excess costs, while favorable variances represent cost reductions. Since standard costs are shown in Work in Process (a debit-balanced account), it is reasonable that excess costs are also debits.

While standard cost systems are useful for internal reporting, such costs are not acceptable for external reporting unless they are *substantially equivalent* to those that would have resulted from using an actual cost system.[7] If standards are achievable and updated periodically, this equivalency should exist. Using standards for financial statements should provide fairly conservative inventory valuations because the effects of excess prices and/or inefficient operations are minimized.

If actual costs are used in financial statements, the standard cost information shown in the accounting records must be adjusted at year-end to approximate actual

---

[7]Actual product costs should not include extraordinary charges for such items as waste, spoilage, and inefficiency. Such costs should be written off as period expenses.

Feed Inventory*	60,000.00	
Materials Price Variance	9,000.00	
Accounts Payable		69,000.00
To record the purchase of 30,000 gallons of feed at $2.30 per pound		
Cost of Services Rendered**	56,940.00	
Materials Quantity Variance	1,860.00	
Feed Inventory		58,800.00
To record the issuance and usage of 29,400 gallons of feed for 18,980 boarding days		
Cost of Services Rendered**	56,940.00	
Labor Rate Variance	8,405.00	
Wages Payable		58,835.00
Labor Efficiency Variance		6,510.00
To record the usage of 1,681 hours of veterinary time at a wage rate of $35 per hour for 18,980 boarding days		

During period:
Variable Overhead	7,402.00	
Accounts Payable***		7,402.00
To record actual variable overhead costs incurred for rubdown supplies		

During period:
Fixed Overhead	185,000.00	
Various Accounts		185,000.00
To record actual fixed overhead costs incurred for depreciation, insurance, repairs & maintenance, etc.		

At end of period (or upon completion of production or performance):
Cost of Services Rendered**	172,718.00	
Variable Overhead		7,592.00
Fixed Overhead		165,126.00
To apply overhead at $.40 (variable) and $8.70 (fixed) per actual boarding days (18,980)****		

At year-end:
VOH Spending Variance	1,480.40	
Variable Overhead	190.00	
VOH Efficiency Variance		1,670.40
To close the variable overhead account		
FOH Volume Variance	25,404.00	
FOH Spending Variance		5,530.00
Fixed Overhead		19,874.00
To close the fixed overhead account		

*In a manufacturing company, this debit would have been to Raw Materials Inventory.

**In a manufacturing company, this debit would have been to Work in Process Inventory. Service companies rarely use such an account.

***In a manufacturing company, there would be a variety of variable overhead costs, and this credit would be to "various accounts" such as Accounts Payable, Wages Payable, Supplies Inventory, etc.

****In a manufacturing company, this computation would be for the standard quantity of the activity base allowed for actual production achieved.

EXHIBIT 5–9
▼▼▼▼▼▼▼▼▼▼▼▼▼

OLD ROSEBUD
JOURNAL ENTRIES
FOR 1994

cost information. The nature of the year-end adjusting entries depends on whether the variance amounts are significant or not.

All manufacturing variances (materials, labor, and overhead) are considered together to determine the appropriate year-end disposition. If the combined impact of these variances is considered to be insignificant, standard costs are approximately the same as actual costs, and the variances are closed to Cost of Services Rendered or Cost of Goods Sold. Unfavorable variances, having debit balances, are closed by crediting them; favorable variances, having credit balances, are closed by debiting them. In a manufacturing company, although all production of the period has not yet been sold, this treatment of insignificant variances is justified on the basis of the immateriality of the amounts involved.

In contrast, if the total variance amount is significant, the overhead variances are prorated at year-end to ending inventories and Cost of Goods Sold in proportion to the relative size of those account balances. This proration disposes of the variances and presents the financial statements in a way that approximates the use of actual costing. Proration is based on the relative size of the account balances. Disposition of significant variances is similar to the disposition of large amounts of under- or over-applied overhead shown in chapter 3. The materials price variance would be prorated among Raw Materials Inventory, Work in Process Inventory, Finished Goods Inventory, and Cost of Goods Sold/Cost of Services Rendered. All other variances occur as part of the conversion process and are prorated only to the Work in Process, Finished Goods, and Cost of Goods Sold/Cost of Services Rendered accounts.

GLOSSARY

Bill of materials a document that contains information about product material components, their specifications (including quality), and the quantities needed for production

Cost tables data bases that provide information about the effects on product costs of using different input resources, manufacturing processes, and product designs

Expected standards standards that reflect what is actually expected to occur in the future period

Fixed overhead spending variance the difference between actual and budgeted fixed overhead

Ideal standards standards that allow for no inefficiency of *any* type and are, therefore, sometimes also called perfection or theoretical standards

Job order product costing the product costing system used by entities that produce tailor-made goods or services in limited quantities that conform to specifications designated by the purchaser of those goods or services

Labor efficiency variance the difference between the number of actual direct labor hours worked and the standard hours allowed for the actual output times standard labor rate per hour

Labor rate variance the difference between the total actual direct labor wages for the period and the standard rate for all hours actually worked during the period

Management by exception   a technique in which managers set upper and lower limits of tolerance for deviations and only investigate deviations that fall outside those tolerance ranges

Materials price variance   the amount of money spent below (favorable) or above (unfavorable) the standard price for the quantity of materials

Materials quantity variance   the standard cost saved (favorable) or expended (unfavorable) because of the difference between the actual quantity of material that was used and the standard quantity of material allowed for the goods produced during the period

Operations flow document   a listing of all tasks necessary to make a unit of product or perform a service and the corresponding time allowed for each operation

Practical standards   standards that allow for normal, unavoidable time problems or delays such as machine downtime and worker breaks; can be reached or slightly exceeded approximately 60 to 70 percent of the time with reasonable effort by workers

Process costing system   the product costing system used by entities that produce large quantities of homogeneous goods

Purchase price variance   the materials price variance when calculated based on the quantity of materials *purchased* during the period rather than the quantity of materials *used*

Standard   a benchmark or norm against which actual results may be compared

Standard cost   a budgeted or estimated cost to manufacture a single unit of product or perform a single service

Standard cost card   a document that summarizes the direct material and direct labor standard quantities and prices needed to complete one unit of product as well as the overhead allocation bases and rates

Standard cost system   a product costing system that uses norms for direct materials and direct labor quantities and/or costs and a predetermined rate as the standard for overhead; these standards are used to value inventories and to compare with actual costs to determine deviations; a system in which standards are developed and used for planning and control purposes; a system in which both standard and actual costs are recorded in the accounting records

Standard quantity allowed   a measure of quantity that translates the actual output achieved into the standard input quantity that should have been used to achieve that output

Target costing   a Japanese method of determining the maximum allowable cost of a product before it is designed, engineered, or produced by subtracting an acceptable profit margin rate from a forecasted selling price

Total variance   the difference between total actual cost incurred and total standard cost applied for the output produced during the period; can also be designated by cost components (DM, DL, VOH and FOH)

Usage price variance   the materials price variance when calculated based on the quantity of materials *used* during the period

Variable overhead efficiency variance   the difference between budgeted variable overhead at actual input activity and budgeted variable overhead at standard input allowed

Variable overhead spending variance   the difference between actual variable overhead and budgeted variable overhead based on actual input

Variance   any difference between actual and standard costs

Variance analysis   the process of categorizing the nature (favorable or unfavorable) of the differences between standard and actual costs and seeking the reasons for those differences

Volume variance   the difference between budgeted and applied fixed overhead

SELECTED BIBLIOGRAPHY

Boer, Germain B. "Making Accounting a Value-Added Activity." *Management Accounting* (August 1991), pp. 36–41.

Doost, Robert K., and Evans Papas. "Frozen-to-Current Cost Variance." *Management Accounting* (March 1988), pp. 41–43.

Edwards, James Don, et al. "How Milliken Stays On Top." *Journal of Accountancy* (April 1989), pp. 63–68 ff.

Harrell, Horace W. "Materials Variance Analysis and JIT: A New Approach." *Management Accounting* (May 1992), pp. 33–36.

Jaouen, Pauline R., and Bruce R. Neumann. "Variance Analysis, Kanban, and JIT: A Further Study." *Journal of Accountancy* (June 1987), pp. 164–166 ff.

Pederson, R. Brian. "Weyerhaeuser: Streamlining Payroll." *Management Accounting* (October 1991), pp. 38–41.

Sakurai, Michiharu. "Target Costing and How to Use It." *Journal of Cost Management for the Manufacturing Industry* (Summer 1989), pp. 39–50.

Walden, Steven. "Beyond the Variance: Cost Accounting Challenges for the 1990s." In *Emerging Practices in Cost Management,* edited by Barry J. Brinker. Boston: Warren, Gorham & Lamont, 1990, pp. 181–185.

SOLUTION STRATEGIES

Variances in Formula Format

Materials price variance = AQ (AP − SP)
   (Note that it is preferable to use actual quantity purchased.)
Materials quantity variance = SP (AQ − SQ)
Labor rate variance = AQ (AP − SP)
Labor efficiency variance = SP (AQ − SQ)
Variable overhead spending variance = Actual VOH − (SR × AQ)
Variable overhead efficiency variance = SR (AQ − SQ)
Fixed overhead spending variance = Actual FOH − Budgeted FOH
Fixed overhead volume variance = Budgeted FOH − (SR × SQ)

Variances in Diagram Format

Actual Price ×   Standard Price ×
Actual Quantity Purchased   Actual Quantity Purchased

Materials Purchase Price Variance

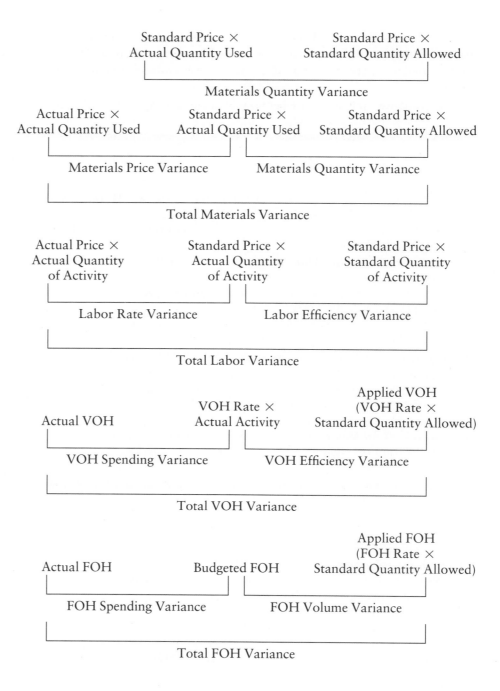

DEMONSTRATION PROBLEM

Accessories Unlimited manufactures "slap" bracelets—thin strips of plastic that wrap around the wrist to form a bracelet. The production operation is a simple process requiring only one material and very little labor. Variable overhead is applied on a machine hour (MH) basis. Fixed overhead is applied on a per-unit basis; the predetermined rate was calculated using a production estimate of 75,000 bracelets per month. The following standard costs and quantities have been developed for one bracelet:

Direct material (8 inches of 1-inch-wide plastic)	$ .01 per inch	$.08
Direct labor (1 minute)	$ 9.00 per hour	.15
Variable OH (15 seconds per bracelet)	$12.00 per MH	.05
Fixed OH (per bracelet)		.10
Total cost per bracelet		$.38

During August, company records indicated the following actual cost and production information:

Purchases of 1-inch-wide plastic: 48,000 ft. @ $.11 per ft.
Usage of 1-inch-wide plastic: 46,900 ft.
Direct labor: 1,180 hrs. @ $9.05 per hour
Machine time: 288 hrs.
Variable overhead: $3,602
Fixed overhead: $7,650
Production: 70,260 bracelets

Required: Compute all materials, labor, and overhead variances.

Solution to Demonstration Problem

1.   Determine appropriate standards for all cost elements.

70,260 bracelets × 8" = 562,080 in.; 562,080 ÷ 12 = 46,840 ft. of DM

70,260 bracelets × 1 min. = 70,260 min.; 70,260 ÷ 60 = 1,171 hrs. of DL time

70,260 bracelets × 15 sec. = 1,053,900 sec.;
1,053,900 ÷ 60 = 17,565 min.; 17,565 ÷ 60 = 292.75 hrs. of machine time

2.   Make computations.

Direct Materials:

AQ × AP   AQ × SP
48,000 × $.11   48,000 × $.12
$5,280 $5,760

$480 F

Materials Price Variance

AQ × SP   SQ × SP
46,900 × $.12   46,840 × $.12
$5,628 $5,620.80

$7.20 U

Materials Quantity Variance

Direct Labor:

AH × AR	AH × SR	SH × SR
1,180 × $9.05	1,180 × $9	1,171 × $9
$10,679	$10,620	$10,539

$59 U	$81 U
Labor Rate Variance	Labor Efficiency Variance

$140 U
Total Labor Variance

Variable Overhead:

Actual VOH	AH × SR	SH × SR
	288 × $12	292.75 × $12
$3,602	$3,456	$3,513

$146 U	$57 F
VOH Spending Variance	VOH Efficiency Variance

$89 U
Total VOH Variance

Fixed Overhead:

Actual FOH	Budgeted FOH	SQ × SR
		70,260 × $.10
$7,650	$7,500	$7,026

$150 U	$474 U
FOH Budget Variance	FOH Volume Variance

$624 U
Total FOH Variance

END-OF-CHAPTER MATERIALS

 Questions

1. Given that different product costing methods can be used (e.g., job order costing and process costing), what are the primary factors that influence the choice of a method?

2. In what kind of a production environment are you likely to find job order costing in use? What are the major differences between the production environments in which job order costing is used and the production environments in which process costing is used?

3. What are the three alternative methods for valuing products? How do these methods differ?

4. Would normal or standard product costing provide the greatest opportunity to evaluate the control of costs for a period? Explain.

5. What is a standard cost and how are the various management functions facilitated by using standards?

6. What individuals should make up the standards development team and why should they be included?

7. What is a bill of materials and how is it used in a standard cost system?

8. Sometimes the quantities shown on the bill of materials differ from those shown on the standard cost card. Explain why this could happen.

9. What is an operations flow document? How is it used in a standard cost system?

10. Why is a standard cost system known as a dual recording system?

11. What is a variance and what does it measure?

12. What does the term *standard hours allowed* mean?

13. What is variance analysis?

14. For the following list of variances indicate (a) when each variance should be calculated and (b) to whom responsibility for the variance should be assigned and why:

    a. material price variance
    b. material quantity variance
    c. labor rate variance
    d. labor efficiency variance
    e. variable overhead spending variance
    f. fixed overhead volume variance

15. Paul Bodette, management accountant for Energetics, noticed that the plant has experienced several large unfavorable material quantity variances during the prior quarter. Before starting his probe of the matter, he has requested that you list some possible reasons for this type of variance.

16. Is fixed overhead controlled by management on a per-unit basis? Explain your answer.

17. Of what importance is capacity utilization to managers? When they control utilization, are they always controlling costs? Explain.

18. Why is it important for managers to periodically update standards?

19. How can the manner in which standards are set be motivating or unmotivating to employees?

20. Assume you are managing each of the following organizations. Indicate several bases upon which you might decide to set standards for materials and labor.

    a. UA Cinema
    b. Department of Economics at a university
    c. Election campaign for a gubernatorial candidate
    d. Domino's Pizza
    e. Dr. Seuss's Pediatric Clinic

21. *(Appendix)* Unfavorable variances are recorded as debits, and favorable variables are recorded as credits. Explain why this is true, if it is, or why it is false.

Exercises

22. *(Job order vs. process costing usage)* The following is a list of different types of firms. Indicate for each firm, based on the type of production process and the nature of the product or service, whether its costing system would more likely be based on job order costing (JOC) or process costing (PC).
This firm:

a. manufactures jet airplanes to customer specifications
b. manufactures household paints
c. produces three different types of soft drinks
d. is an automobile repair shop
e. is a corporate law firm
f. manufactures hair spray and hand lotion
g. is a hospital
h. cans salmon and tuna

23. *(Actual vs. normal costing system)* For fiscal year 1993, the Pratlow Machining Company estimated it would incur total overhead costs of $200,000 and work 10,000 direct labor hours. During January 1993, the company worked exclusively on one job, Job 2233. It incurred January costs as follows:

Direct materials used		$38,000
Direct labor (1,800 hours)		36,000
Manufacturing overhead:		
Rent	$ 900	
Utilities	4,200	
Insurance	3,100	
Labor	6,500	
Depreciation	2,000	
Maintenance	2,900	19,600

a. Assuming the Pratlow Company uses an actual costing system, compute the January costs assigned to Job 2233.
b. Assuming the Pratlow Company uses a normal costing system with a predetermined overhead rate based on its estimates, compute the January costs assigned to Job 2233.
c. What is the major factor driving the difference between your answers in parts (a) and (b)?

24. *(Material variances)* Walt Newmann and Company makes large bronze statues of the American eagle in flight as objets d'art for shopping centers, courthouses, and other public buildings. In June 1996, the purchasing agent, Jane Newmann, bought 26,400 pounds of scrap copper and tin at an average price of $4.10 per pound in the correct proportions to make bronze. In June, the company used 23,500 pounds and produced 125 statues. Each eagle requires a standard quantity of 192 pounds of alloy at a standard cost of $4.00 per pound. Calculate the material purchase price variance and indicate who has responsibility for it. Calculate the material quantity variance and indicate who has responsibility for it.

25. *(Material variances)* Rick's Raincoats experienced the following costs related to direct materials during August 1996:

Actual quantity purchased	37,500 pounds
Actual unit price	$19
Actual quantity used	40,000 pounds
Standard quantity allowed	35,000 pounds
Standard unit price	$17.50

Rick Boatman, company president, has requested that you determine the material purchase price variance and the material quantity variance.

26. *(Material variances)* Teri's Toons incurred the following direct material costs in November 1995 for printing sheet music:

Actual unit purchase price	$.165 per sheet
Quantity purchased in November	100,000 sheets
Quantity used in November	90,000 sheets
Standard quantity allowed for good production	89,800 sheets
Standard unit price	$.168 per sheet

Calculate the materials purchase price variance and the materials quantity variance.

27. *(Labor variances)* Jack's Cabinets builds kitchen cabinets in uniform sets. Each set requires a standard quantity of 16.5 direct labor hours. The average standard hourly wage of the crew of cabinetmakers is $13.50. During October 1995, the company built 250 sets. The direct labor was 4,210 hours, and gross pay was $55,993. Jack has asked you to analyze direct labor for him.

28. *(Labor variances)* Cathy's Corner makes school uniforms. During February 1995, the business experienced the following direct labor costs:

Efficiency variance (unfavorable)	$8,690
Actual direct labor rate per hour	$3.75
Standard direct labor rate per hour	$3.95
Standard hours allowed for production	10,000

Determine (a) the actual hours worked during February, (b) the total payroll, and (c) the labor rate variance.

29. *(Labor variances)* Tyson Towels uses a standard cost system. The company experienced the following results related to direct labor in December 1995:

Actual hours worked	13,750
Actual direct labor rate	$7.25
Standard hours allowed for production	13,500
Standard direct labor rate	$6.75

Calculate (a) the total payroll, (b) the labor rate variance, and (c) the labor efficiency variance.

30. *(OH variances)* Cooper Company, which makes copper barrel stays, uses a standard cost system. For 1995, budgeted overhead is $160,000 based on 240,000 expected annual machine hours. The standard time per stay is .20 machine hours. The following are data for production in June 1995:

Number of finished stays produced	100,400
Actual machine hours	21,000
Actual overhead incurred	$13,100

a. Ed Cooper, company president, wants to know what the total overhead variance for June is.

b. Mr. Cooper wants you to analyze overhead in as much detail as possible. Investigation reveals the following data:

Budgeted variable overhead for 1995	$96,000
Budgeted fixed overhead for 1995	64,000
Actual variable overhead for June	7,600
Actual fixed overhead for June	5,500

Fixed overhead was expected to be incurred at an even rate throughout the year.

31. *(OH variances)* David Watts Manufacturing Company's overhead costs are as follows:

Actual variable overhead	$ 96,000
Actual fixed overhead	41,000
Standard variable overhead applied	100,000
Standard fixed overhead applied	42,105
Budgeted fixed overhead	40,000
Standard variable overhead based on actual machine hours	95,000

Calculate as many overhead variances as possible.

Problems

32. *(Material & labor variances)* Christopher Company makes high-quality loose-leaf binders for conventions. Standard quantities and costs follow:

Direct materials	¼ lb. at $1.00 per lb.
Direct labor	2 minutes at $6.00 per hour

In May 1993, 70,000 binders were produced. Christopher's purchasing agent bought 26,000 pounds of material in May at $1.02 per pound. The May factory payroll reflected $13,420 of direct labor for 2,200 hours. In May, 17,700 pounds of direct materials were placed in production.
Required: Calculate materials and labor variances.

33. *(Material & labor variances)* Phoenix Manufacturers makes blank computer disks. It takes one-eighth of a pound of direct materials and one minute of direct labor at standard per disk. Direct materials cost $2.60 per pound at standard, and the standard direct labor rate is $6.00 per hour.

During April, 35,200 disks were made, and the company experienced a $260 unfavorable material quantity variance. The purchasing agent had purchased 400 pounds of material more than the company used, incurring a favorable price variance of $200. Six hundred total direct labor hours were incurred in making disks, and a total unfavorable labor variance of $120 occurred.
Required: Determine the following:

a. Standard quantity of materials allowed
b. Actual quantity of materials used
c. Actual quantity of materials purchased
d. Actual price of materials purchased
e. Standard hours allowed for production

    f. Labor efficiency variance
    g. Labor rate variance
    h. Actual labor rate paid

34. *(Missing amounts)* For each of the following independent cases, supply the missing amounts:

	Case 1	Case 2	Case 3	Case 4
Units produced	300	(d)	640	625
Standard hours per unit	2	.6	(g)	(j)
Standard hours allowed	(a)	1,200	960	(k)
Standard rate per hour	$5	(e)	$3.50	$6
Actual hours worked	615	1,160	(h)	2,550
Actual labor cost	(b)	(f)	$3,230	$15,300
Labor rate variance	$62 U	$80 U	$95 F	(l)
Labor efficiency variance	(c)	$120 F	(i)	$300 U

35. *(OH variances)* Buchholz Boots makes popular western boots. Standard time and costs for a pair of boots are as follows:

Machine time (hours)	1.20
VOH rate per machine hour	$.75
FOH rate per machine hour	$.40

During 1995, the following operating statistics were compiled:

Total fixed overhead applied to production	$232,000
Volume variance	12,000 F
Actual variable overhead	439,000
Actual fixed overhead	224,000
Variable overhead spending variance	2,500 U

Required:

a. For fixed overhead, calculate the following:
    1. Standard machine hours allowed
    2. Pairs of boots made
    3. Budgeted FOH
    4. Expected annual capacity in machine hours
    5. Fixed overhead spending variance
    6. Fixed overhead total variance
b. For variable overhead, calculate the following:
    1. Total applied variable overhead
    2. Total variable overhead variance
    3. Actual machine hours incurred
    4. Variable overhead efficiency variance

36. *(All variances)* Lucky Finn Company makes snow skis using three materials: fiberglass, lacquer, and a prepurchased accessories set including boot locks, guides, and decals. Standards for the materials and labor for one pair of snow skis are as follows:

10 lbs. of fiberglass at $1.10 per lb.	$11.00
1 qt. of lacquer @ $8.00 per gallon	2.00
1 set of accessories	8.00
5 hours of direct labor @ $5.00 per hour	25.00
Variable overhead @ $.80 per direct labor hour	4.00
Fixed overhead at $.20 per direct labor hour*	1.00
Total	$51.00

Based on budgeted annual FOH of $12,000 and expected annual capacity of 60,000 hours.

During November 1995, the firm had the following actual data related to the production of 1,000 pair of skis:

Purchase of Material
    Fiberglass—12,000 lbs. @ $1.05
    Lacquer—260 gallons @ $8.10
    Sets of accessories—1,100 @ $7.80

Materials Used
    Fiberglass—9,900 lbs.
    Lacquer—240 gallons
    Sets of accessories—1,005 sets

Direct Labor Used
    5,400 hours @ $4.90
    Actual variable overhead in November—$4,120
    Actual fixed overhead in November—$1,160

Required: Calculate materials, labor, and overhead variances.

37. *(Deviations from standards)* As part of its cost control program, Tracer Company uses a standard cost system for all manufactured items. The standard cost for each item is established at the beginning of the fiscal year, and the standards are not revised until the beginning of the next fiscal year. Changes in costs, caused during the year by changes in material or labor inputs or by changes in the manufacturing process, are recognized as they occur by the inclusion of planned variances in Tracer's monthly operating budgets.

Presented next is the labor standard that was established for one of Tracer's products, effective June 1, 1993, the beginning of the fiscal year.

Assembler A labor (5 hours @ $10 per hour)	$ 50
Assembler B labor (3 hours @ $11 per hour)	33
Machinist labor (2 hours @ $15 per hour)	30
Standard cost per 100 units	$113

The standard was based on the labor being performed by a team consisting of five persons with Assembler A skills, three persons with Assembler B skills, and two persons with machinist skills; this team represents the most efficient use of the company's skilled employees. The standard also assumed that the quality of material that had been used in prior years would be available for the coming year.

For the first seven months of the fiscal year, actual manufacturing costs at Tracer have been within the standards established. However, the company has received a significant increase in orders, and there is an insufficient number of skilled workers available to meet the increased production. Therefore, beginning in January, the production teams will consist of eight persons with Assembler A skills, one person with Assembler B skills, and one person with machinist skills. The reorganized teams will work more slowly than the normal teams, and as a result, only 80 units will be produced in the same time period that 100 units would normally be produced. Faulty work has never been a cause for units to be rejected in the final inspection process, and it is not expected to be a cause for rejection with the reorganized teams.

Furthermore, Tracer has been notified by its material supplier that a lower-quality material will be supplied beginning January 1. Normally, one unit of raw material is required for each good unit produced, and no units are lost due to defective material. Tracer estimates that 6 percent of the units manufactured after January 1 will be rejected in the final inspection process due to defective material.

Required:

a. Determine the number of units of lower-quality material that Tracer Company must enter into production to produce 35,720 good finished units.

b. Without prejudice to your answer in part (a), assume that Tracer must manufacture a total of 50,000 units in January to have sufficient good units to fill the order received.

   1. Determine how many hours of each class of labor will be needed to manufacture a total of 50,000 units in January.

   2. Determine the amount that should be included in Tracer's January operating budget for the planned labor variance caused by the reorganization of the labor teams and the lower-quality material, and indicate how much of the planned variance can be attributed to (a) the change in material and (b) the reorganization of the labor teams.

(CMA)

38. *(Comprehensive; multiple materials)* The Lieto Stamping Company manufactures a variety of products made of plastic and aluminum components. During the winter months, substantially all production capacity is devoted to the production of lawn sprinklers for the following spring and summer seasons. Because a variety of products are made throughout the year, factory volume is measured by direct labor hours rather than units of product.

The company has developed the following standards for the production of a lawn sprinkler:

Direct materials:		
Aluminum	0.2 lbs. at $0.40 per lb.	$0.08
Plastic	1.0 lbs. at $0.38 per lb.	0.38
Direct labor	0.3 hrs. at $4.00 per hr.	1.20
Overhead:		
Variable	0.3 hrs. at $1.60 per hr.	0.48
Fixed	0.3 hrs. at $1.20 per hr.	0.36

   (Overhead is calculated using 30,000 direct labor hours as expected annual capacity.)

During February 1993, 8,500 good sprinklers were manufactured, and the following costs were incurred and charged to production:

Materials requisitioned for production:

Aluminum	1,900 lbs. at $0.40 per lb.	$ 760
Plastic		
Regular grade	6,000 lbs. at $0.38 per lb.	2,280
Low grade*	3,500 lbs. at $0.38 per lb.	1,330

Direct labor:

Regular time	2,300 hrs. at $4.00 per hr.	9,200
Overtime	400 hrs. at $6.00 per hr.	2,400

Overhead:

Variable		5,200
Fixed		3,100
Total costs charged to production		$24,270

Material price variations are not charged to production but to a material price variance account at the time the invoice is entered. All materials are carried in inventory at standard prices. Material purchases for February were:

Aluminum	1,800 lbs. at $0.48 per lb.	$ 864
Plastic		
Regular grade	3,000 lbs. at $0.50 per lb.	1,500
Low grade*	6,000 lbs. at $0.29 per lb.	1,740

Because of plastic shortages, the company was forced to purchase lower-grade plastic than called for in the standards. This increased the number of sprinklers rejected on inspection.

Required: Answer the following multiple-choice questions. Present all calculations in good form.

a. The total variation from standard cost of the costs charged to production for February 1993 is
   1. $3,080 unfavorable.
   2. $3,020 unfavorable.
   3. $3,140 favorable.
   4. $3,020 favorable.
b. The standard material quantities already include an allowance for acceptable material scrap loss. In this situation, the material usage variance would most likely be caused by
   1. defective aluminum.
   2. improper processing by labor.
   3. inadequate allowance for scrap loss.
   4. substitute plastic.
c. The spending or budget variance for the fixed portion of the overhead costs is
   1. $100 unfavorable.
   2. $60 favorable.
   3. $0.
   4. not calculable from the problem.
d. The labor efficiency variance is the difference between standard labor hours of output and
   1. 2,300 hours.
   2. 2,700 hours.
   3. 2,900 hours.
   4. 2,500 hours.

 e. The labor rate variance is
  1. $0.
  2. $600 unfavorable.
  3. $800 unfavorable.
  4. $1,400 unfavorable.
 f. The manufacturing overhead volume variance is
  1. the result of inadequate cost control.
  2. the result of actual direct labor hours exceeding standard direct labor hours allowed for the output achieved.
  3. the result of the overapplication of fixed cost to output.
  4. not the result of any of the reasons listed in 1–3.
 g. The total variable overhead budget variance is
  1. $1,120 unfavorable.
  2. $1,220 unfavorable.
  3. $1,160 unfavorable.
  4. $1,280 unfavorable.
 h. The standard cost system employed by this company has as its primary benefit
  1. cost reduction.
  2. cost control.
  3. inventory valuation for tax returns.
  4. simplification of bookkeeping.

(CMA adapted)

39. *(Essay)* Mark-Wright, Inc. (MWI) is a specialty frozen food processor located in the midwestern states. Since its founding in 1982, MWI has enjoyed a loyal local clientele that is willing to pay premium prices for the high-quality frozen foods it prepares from specialized recipes. In the last two years, the company has experienced rapid sales growth in its operating region and has had many inquiries about supplying its products on a national basis. To meet this growth, MWI expanded its processing capabilities, which resulted in increased production and distribution costs. Furthermore, MWI has been encountering pricing pressure from competitors outside its normal marketing region.

 As MWI desires to continue its expansion, Jim Condon, CEO, has engaged a consulting firm to assist MWI in determining its best course of action. The consulting firm concluded that, while premium pricing is sustainable in some areas, if sales growth is to be achieved, MWI must make some price concessions. Also, in order to maintain profit margins, costs must be reduced and controlled. The consulting firm recommended the institution of a standard cost system to better accommodate the changes in demand that can be expected when serving an expanding market area.

 Condon met with his management team and explained the recommendations of the consulting firm. Condon then assigned the task of establishing standard costs to his management team. After discussing the situation with their respective staffs, the management team met to review the matter.

 Jane Morgan, purchasing manager, advised that meeting expanded production would necessitate obtaining basic food supplies from other than MWI's traditional sources. This would entail increased raw material and shipping costs and may result in lower-quality supplies. Consequently, these increased costs would need to be made up by the processing department if current cost levels are to be maintained or reduced.

Stan Walters, processing manager, countered that the need to accelerate processing cycles to increase production, coupled with the possibility of receiving lower-grade supplies, can be expected to result in a slip in quality and a greater product rejection rate. Under these circumstances, per-unit labor utilization cannot be maintained or reduced, and forecasting future unit labor content becomes very difficult.

Tom Lopez, production engineer, advised that if the equipment is not properly maintained, and thoroughly cleaned at prescribed daily intervals, it can be anticipated that the quality and unique taste of the frozen food products will be affected. Jack Reid, vice-president of sales, stated that if quality cannot be maintained, MWI cannot expect to increase sales to the levels projected.

When Condon was apprised of the problems encountered by his management team, he advised them that if agreement could not be reached on appropriate standards, he would arrange to have them set by the consulting firm, and everyone would have to live with the results.

a. 1. List the major advantages of using a standard cost system.
   2. List disadvantages that can result from using a standard cost system.
b. 1. Identify those who should participate in setting standards and describe the benefits of their participation in the standard-setting process.
   2. Explain the general features and characteristics associated with the introduction and operation of a standard cost system that make it an effective tool for cost control.
c. What could be the consequences if Jim Condon has the standards set by the outside consulting firm?

(CMA)

40. *(Essay)* Some executives believe that it is extremely important to manage "by the numbers." This form of management requires that all employees with departmental or divisional responsibilities spend time understanding the company's operations and how they are reflected by the company's performance reports. Managers are then expected to transmit to their employees a need to be attuned to important signposts that can be detected in performance reports. One of the various numerical measurement systems used by companies is standard costs.

a. Discuss the characteristics that should be present in a standard cost system to encourage positive employee motivation.
b. Discuss how a standard cost system should be implemented to positively motivate employees.
c. The use of variance analysis often results in "management by exception." Discuss the meaning and behavioral implications of "management by exception." Explain how employee behavior could be adversely affected when "actual to standard" comparisons are used as the basis for performance evaluation.

(CMA adapted)

41. *(Essay)* Standard cost accounting systems are generally considered to be among the best features of modern management accounting. Standard cost systems are employed widely, and management depends on such systems for a variety of functions.

Portfolio management is a powerful concept that is important in finance and marketing. The marketing application of the concept is to develop and manage a balanced portfolio of products. Market share and market growth can be used to classify products for portfolio purposes, and the product classifications are often extended to the organizational units that make the product. The market share/growth classifications can be depicted in the following manner.

		MARKET SHARE	
		High	Low
MARKET GROWTH RATE	High	Rising Star	Question Mark
	Low	Cash Cow	Dog

Question marks are products that show high growth rates but have relatively small market shares, such as new products that are similar to their competitors. Rising stars are high-growth, high-market-share products that tend to mature into cash cows. Cash cows are slow-growing established products that can be "milked" for cash to help the question marks and introduce new products. The dogs are low-growth, low-market-share items that are candidates for elimination or segmentation.

Understanding where a product falls within this market share/growth structure is important when applying a standard cost system.

a. Discuss the major advantages of using a standard cost accounting system.
b. Describe the kinds of information that are useful in setting standards and the conditions that must be present to support the use of standard costing.
c. Discuss the applicability or nonapplicability of using standard costing for a product classified as a
   1. cash cow.
   2. question mark.

(CMA)

Cases

42. Day-Mold was founded several years ago by two designers who had developed several popular lines of living room, dining room, and bedroom furniture for other companies. The designers believed that their design for dinette sets could be standardized and would sell well. They formed their own company and soon had all the orders they could complete in their small plant in Dayton, Ohio.

    From the beginning the firm was successful. The owners bought a microcomputer and software that produced financial statements, which an employee prepared. The owners thought that the information they needed was contained in these statements.

Recently, however, the employees have been requesting raises. The owners wonder how to evaluate the employees' requests. At the suggestion of Day-Mold's CPA, the owners have hired a consultant to implement a standard cost system. The consultant believes that the calculation of variances will aid management in setting responsibility for labor's performance.

The supervisors believe that under normal conditions, a dinette set can be assembled with five hours of direct labor at a cost of $20 per hour. The consultant has assembled labor cost information for the most recent month and would like your advice in calculating direct labor variances.

During the month, the actual direct labor wages paid were $127,600 to employees who worked 5,800 hours. The factory produced 1,200 dinette sets during the month.

a. Using the previous information, prepare variance computations for management's consideration. Hint: Under the conventional approach, there will be a direct labor efficiency variance, a direct labor rate variance, and a total direct labor variance. Under a different logical approach, there will be a direct labor efficiency variance, a direct labor rate variance, a direct labor "joint" variance, and a total direct labor variance.

b. Contrast these two approaches and make some recommendations to management.

From Nabil Hassan and Sarah Palmer, "Management Accounting Case Study: Day-Mold," *Management Accounting Campus Report* (Spring 1990). Copyright © 1990 IMA (formerly NAA).

43. ColdKing Company is a small producer of fruit-flavored frozen desserts. For many years, ColdKing's products have had strong regional sales on the basis of brand recognition; however, other companies have begun marketing similar products in the area, and price competition has become increasingly important. John Wakefield, the company's controller, is planning to implement a standard cost system for ColdKing and has gathered considerable information from his co-workers on production and material requirements for ColdKing's products. Wakefield believes that the use of standard costing will allow ColdKing to improve cost control and make better pricing decisions.

ColdKing's most popular product is raspberry sherbet. The sherbet is produced in 10-gallon batches, and each batch requires six quarts of good raspberries. The fresh raspberries are sorted by hand before they enter the production process. Because of imperfections in the raspberries and normal spoilage, one quart of berries is discarded for every four quarts of acceptable berries. Three minutes is the standard direct labor time for the sorting that is required to obtain one quart of acceptable raspberries. The acceptable raspberries are then blended with 10 gallons of the other ingredients; blending requires 12 minutes of direct labor time per batch. During blending, there is some loss of materials. After blending, the sherbet is packaged in quart containers. Wakefield has gathered the following cost information:

- ColdKing purchases raspberries at a cost of $.80 per quart. All other ingredients cost a total of $.45 per gallon.
- Direct labor is paid at the rate of $9.00 per hour.
- The total cost of material and labor required to package the sherbet is $.38 per quart.

a. Develop the standard cost for each direct cost component and the total cost of a 10-gallon batch of raspberry sherbet. The standard cost should identify the
   1. standard quantity,
   2. standard rate, and
   3. standard cost per batch.
b. As part of the implementation of a standard cost system at ColdKing, John Wakefield plans to train those responsible for maintaining the standards on how to use variance analysis. Wakefield is particularly concerned with the causes of unfavorable variances.
   1. Discuss the possible causes of unfavorable material price variances, and identify the individual(s) who should be held responsible for these variances.
   2. Discuss the possible causes of unfavorable labor efficiency variances, and identify the individual(s) who should be responsible for these variances.

(CMA)

44. NuLathe Company produces a turbo engine component for jet aircraft manufacturers. A standard cost system has been used for years with good results.

Unfortunately, NuLathe has recently experienced production problems. The source for its direct material went out of business. The new source produces a similar but higher-quality material. The price per pound from the original source had averaged $7, while the price from the new source is $7.77. The use of the new material results in a reduction of scrap. This scrap reduction reduces the actual consumption of direct material from 1.25 to 1.00 pound per unit. In addition, the direct labor is reduced from 24 to 22 minutes per unit because there is less scrap labor and machine setup time.

The direct material problem was occurring at the same time that labor negotiations resulted in an increase of over 14 percent in hourly direct labor costs. The average rate rose from $12.60 per hour to $14.40 per hour. Production of the main product requires a high level of labor skill. Because of a continuing shortage in that skill area, an interim wage agreement had to be signed.

NuLathe started using the new direct material on April 1, the same date that the new labor agreement went into effect. NuLathe has been using standards that were set at the beginning of the calendar year. The direct material and direct labor standards for the turbo engine component are as follows:

Direct material	1.2 lbs. at $6.80 per lb.	$ 8.16
Direct labor	20 min. at $12.30 per DLH	4.10
Standard prime cost per unit		$12.26

Howard Foster, management accounting supervisor, had been examining the following performance report that he had prepared at the close of business on April 30. Jane Keene, assistant controller, came into Foster's office, and Foster said, "Jane, look at this performance report! Direct material price increased 11 percent, and the labor rate increased over 14 percent during April. I expected greater variances, yet prime costs decreased over 5 percent from the $13.79 we experienced during the first quarter of this year. The proper message just isn't coming through."

"This has been an unusual period," said Keene. "With all the unforeseen changes, perhaps we should revise our standards based on current conditions and start over."

Foster replied, "I think we can retain the current standards but expand the variance analysis. We could calculate variances for the specific changes that have occurred to direct material and direct labor before we calculate the normal price and quantity variances. What I really think would be useful to management right now is to determine the impact the changes in direct material and direct labor had in reducing our prime costs per unit from $13.79 in the first quarter to $13.05 in April—a reduction of $.74."

PERFORMANCE REPORT

Standard Cost Variance Analysis for April 1995

	Standard	Price Variance		Quantity Variance		Actual
DM	$ 8.16	($ .97 × 1.0)	$.97 U	($ 6.80 × .2)	$1.36 F	$ 7.77
DL	4.10	[$2.10 × (22/60)]	.77 U	[$12.30 × (2/60)]	.41 U	5.28
	$12.26					$13.05

Comparison of 1995 Actual Costs

	1st Quarter Costs	April Costs	% Increase (Decrease)
DM	$ 8.75	$ 7.77	(11.2)%
DL	5.04	5.28	4.8 %
	$13.79	$13.05	(5.4)%

a. Discuss the advantages of (1) immediately revising the standards and (2) retaining the current standards and expanding the analysis of variances.

b. Prepare an analysis that reflects the impact the new direct material and new labor contract had on reducing NuLathe's prime costs per unit from $13.79 to $13.05. The analysis should show the changes in prime costs per unit that are due to (1) the use of new direct materials and (2) the new labor contract. This analysis should be in sufficient detail to identify the changes due to direct material price, direct labor rate, the effect of direct material quality on direct material usage, and the effect of direct material quality on direct labor usage.

(CMA adapted)

45. Funtime, Inc., manufactures video game machines. Market saturation and technological innovations have caused pricing pressures, which have resulted in declining profits. To stem the slide in profits until new products can be introduced, top management has turned its attention to both manufacturing economies and increased production. To realize these objectives, an incentive program has been developed to reward managers who contribute to an increase in the number of units produced and effect cost reductions.

The production managers have responded to the pressure of improving manufacturing in several ways, which have resulted in increased completed units over normal production levels. The video game machines are put together by the Assembly Group, which requires parts from both the Printed Circuit Boards (PCB) and the Reading Heads (RH) groups. To attain increased production levels, the PCB and RH groups commenced rejecting parts that previously would have been tested and modified to meet manufacturing standards. Preventive maintenance on machines used in the production of these parts has been postponed with only emergency repair work being performed to keep production lines moving. The Maintenance Department is concerned that there will be serious breakdowns and unsafe operating conditions.

The more aggressive Assembly Group production supervisors have pressured maintenance personnel to attend to their machines at the expense of other groups. This has resulted in machine downtime in the PCB and RH groups, which, when coupled with demands for accelerated parts delivery by the Assembly Group, has led to more frequent parts rejections and increased friction among departments.

Funtime operates under a standard cost system. The standard costs for video game machines are as follows:

Cost Item	Standard Cost per Unit		
	Quantity	Cost	Total
Direct material			
Housing unit	1	$20	$ 20
Printed circuit boards	2	15	30
Reading heads	4	10	40
Direct labor			
Assembly group	2 hours	8	16
PCB group	1 hour	9	9
RH group	1.5 hours	10	15
Variable overhead	4.5 hours	2	9
Total standard cost per unit			$139

Funtime prepares monthly reports based on standard costs. Presented next is the report for May 1993, when production and sales both reached 2,200 units.

	Budget	Actual	Variance
Units	2,000	2,200	200 F
Variable costs			
Direct material	$180,000	$220,400	$40,400 U
Direct labor	80,000	93,460	13,460 U
Variable overhead	18,000	18,800	800 U
Total variable costs	$278,000	$332,660	$54,660 U

Funtime's top management was surprised by the unfavorable variances. Jack Rath, management accountant, was assigned to identify and report on the reasons for the unfavorable variances as well as the individuals or groups responsible. After review, Rath prepared the following usage report:

Cost Item	Quantity	Actual Cost
Direct material		
Housing units	2,200 units	$ 44,000
Printed circuit boards	4,700 units	75,200
Reading heads	9,200 units	101,200
Direct labor		
Assembly	3,900 hours	31,200
Printed circuit boards	2,400 hours	23,760
Reading heads	3,500 hours	38,500
Variable overhead	9,900 hours	18,800
Total variable cost		$332,660

Rath reported that the PCB and RH groups supported the increased production levels but experienced abnormal machine downtime. This, in turn, caused idle time, which required the use of overtime to keep up with the accelerated demand for parts. The idle time was charged to direct labor. Rath also reported that the production managers of these two groups resorted to parts rejections, as opposed to testing and modification procedures formerly applied. Rath determined that the Assembly Group met management's objectives by increasing production while utilizing lower than standard hours.

a. For May 1993, Funtime, Inc.'s labor rate variance was $5,660 unfavorable, and the labor efficiency variance was $200 favorable. By using these two variances and calculating the following variances, prepare an explanation of the $54,660 unfavorable variance between budgeted and actual costs for May 1993.
   1. Material price variance
   2. Material quantity variance
   3. Variable overhead efficiency variance
   4. Variable overhead spending variance
b. 1. Identify and briefly explain the behavioral factors that may promote friction among the production managers and the maintenance manager.
   2. Evaluate Jack Rath's analysis of the unfavorable results in terms of its completeness and its effect on the behavior of the production groups.

(CMA)

▉ Ethics Discussion

46. Mera Catlett was hired a month ago at the Inola Division of the Tulsa Manufacturing Company. Ms. Catlett supervises plant production and is paid $6,500 per month. In addition, her contract calls for a percentage bonus based on cost control. The company president has defined cost control as "the ability to obtain favorable cost variances from the standards provided."

   After one month, Ms. Catlett realized that the standards that were used at the Inola Division were outdated. Since the last time the standards had been revised, the Inola Division had undergone some significant plant layout changes and installed some automated equipment, both of which reduced labor time considerably. However, by the time she realized the errors in the standards, she had received her first month's bonus check of $5,000.

a. Since the setting of the standards and the definition of her bonus arrangement were not her doing, Ms. Catlett does not feel significantly compelled to discuss the errors in the standards with the company president. Besides, Ms. Catlett is a single woman who wants to buy a red turbo-Porsche. Discuss the ethics of her not discussing the errors in the standards and/or the problems with the definition of cost control with the company president.
b. Assume instead that Ms. Catlett has an elderly mother who has just been placed in a nursing home. The elderly Ms. Catlett is quite ill and has no income. The younger Ms. Catlett lives in an efficiency apartment and drives a six-year-old car so that she can send the majority of her earnings to the nursing home to provide for her mother. Discuss the ethics of her not discussing the errors in the standards and/or the problems with the definition of cost control with the company president.

c. Assume again the facts in part (b) and that the company president plans to review and revise, if necessary, all production standards at the Inola Division next year. Discuss what may occur if Ms. Catlett does not inform the president of the problems with the standards at the current time. Discuss what may occur if Ms. Catlett informs the president of all the facts, both professional and personal. Can you suggest a way in which she may keep a bonus and still have the standards revised? (Consider the fact that the standard cost has implications for sales prices.)

47. Flower Mound Corporation needs to hire four people to work in the factory who can run robotic equipment and route products through processing. All factory space is on a single floor. Labor standards have been set for product manufacturing.

At this time, the company has had ten experienced people apply for the available jobs. One of the applicants for the jobs is Darrell Bulls. Darrell is paralyzed and must use a wheelchair. He does have several years' experience using the robotic equipment, but for him to use the equipment, the controls must be placed on a special panel and lowered for him to access. Willie Roberts, the personnel director, has interviewed Darrell and has decided against hiring him because Willie does not believe Darrell can work "up to the current labor standard."

a. How, if at all, would hiring the physically disabled affect labor variances (both rate and hours) if the standards had been set based on the nondisabled?
b. If a supervisor has decided to hire the physically disabled, how (if at all) should his/her performance evaluations be affected?
c. What are the ethical implications of hiring the physically disabled in preference to the nondisabled? What are the ethical implications of hiring the nondisabled in preference to the disabled? (You may want to consider the 1992 Americans with Disabilities Act in developing your answer.)
d. On what bases should Willie Roberts make his decision to hire or not hire Darrell Bulls? Discuss what you believe to be the appropriate decision process.

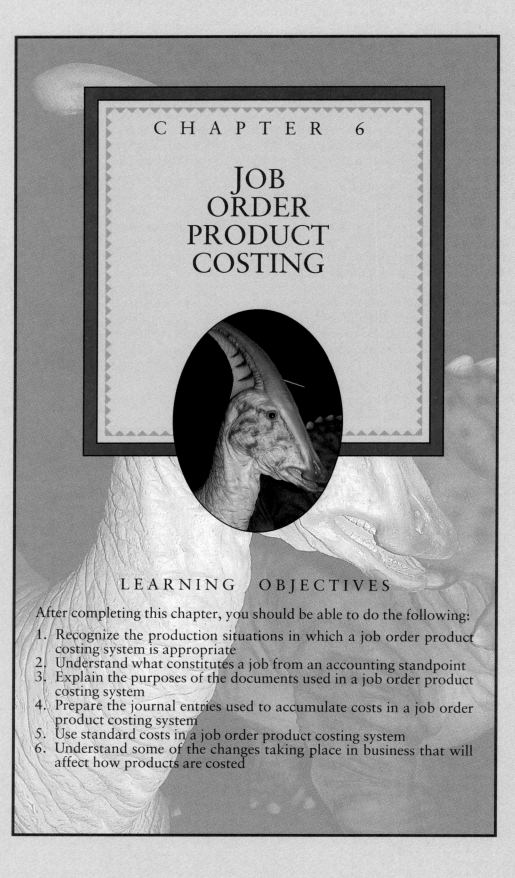

C H A P T E R   6

JOB ORDER PRODUCT COSTING

LEARNING OBJECTIVES

After completing this chapter, you should be able to do the following:

1. Recognize the production situations in which a job order product costing system is appropriate
2. Understand what constitutes a job from an accounting standpoint
3. Explain the purposes of the documents used in a job order product costing system
4. Prepare the journal entries used to accumulate costs in a job order product costing system
5. Use standard costs in a job order product costing system
6. Understand some of the changes taking place in business that will affect how products are costed

Dinamation: That's a Big Job

Tongues, flippers, and eyeballs? One look at the spare-parts inventory tells you this is no ordinary manufacturer. In fact, Dinamation International Corporation, based in San Juan Capistrano, California, is a dream come true for Chris Mays, who heads this company that creates robotic dinosaurs. Mays began in 1982 by importing life-sized reptilian replicas manufactured in Japan. The models were highly unrealistic, however, so he decided to strike out on his own. He assembled a renowned board of scientific advisors and opened the first Dinamation plant in the U.S. in 1986. Now Mays' creations are so highly regarded that he outbid the old company for a project on its home turf, a park in Kasaoka, Japan.

When Dinamation unveils a new dinosaur, it represents the efforts of a group of at least 20 people, called a "New Creature Team." Paleontologists, artists, sculptors, engineers, welders, moldmakers, and computer experts all work together. The entire process, from concept to completion, often takes as long as a year. The process isn't inexpensive either—counting fabrication, the mechanics, and their lifelike resin skins, mobile models cost more than $100,000 each to build.

SOURCE: Michele Burgess, "Prehistory at Play," *SKY* (July 1990), p. 10ff. This article has been excerpted by permission of Michele Burgess and through the courtesy of Halsey Publishing Company, publishers of Delta Airlines *SKY* magazine.

aking one robotic dinosaur a year is not what could be called mass manufacturing! But, like making any other product, it requires converting raw materials to a finished product through the use of direct labor and overhead. Since each dinosaur is substantially different from any other dinosaur, it would be very difficult to develop a set of standard costs for this process. Thus, Dinamation would use a method of cost accounting called job order product costing to record its conversion process.

JOB ORDER COSTING SYSTEM

Product costing is concerned with (1) cost identification, (2) cost management, and (3) product cost assignment. In a job order product costing system, costs are accumulated individually by **job**—defined as a single unit[1] or group of like units identifiable as being produced to distinct customer specifications. The following News Note provides an example of production-to-order for a job order system.

---

[1]To eliminate the need for repetition, units should be read to mean either products or services, since job order product costing is applicable to both manufacturing and service companies. For the same reason, *produced* can mean *manufactured* or *performed*.

Conner Peripherals Produces To Order

Conner Peripherals is currently the fastest-growing major manufacturer in America. The company has leaped into the vanguard of the $8.9-billion-a-year compact disk drive industry, along with other hot companies such as Seagate Technology and Quantum Corp.

Each new Conner disk drive is a premium-priced product engineered to specifications negotiated with Compaq or some other key customer. The buyer may want a drive to be thinner, or have more capacity, or retrieve data more quickly, or use less power—the feature Compaq wanted recently in the drive for its hugely popular notebook computer, the LTE. The only customers Conner turns away are those looking for a cut-rate product.

Each job in a job cost system is treated as a unique "cost entity" or cost object. Job order costing would be useful in companies like Ohio's Norton Manufacturing Inc., North Dakota's Richtman's Printing, or Virginia's BTG Inc. Norton decided to concentrate on high-quality, low-volume production of crankshafts—especially for race cars. Richtman's does a variety of printing jobs. In both instances, job order costing allows the costs and profits of each job to be known and repeat jobs to be bid appropriately. BTG, a computer manufacturer, decided it wanted the government as a customer but could not produce in the $50 million contract-range typical of government contracts. The company instead makes prototypes for the government, generating almost $30 million per year in sales.

Costs of different jobs are maintained in separate subsidiary ledger accounts and are not added together or commingled in those ledger accounts. The logic of separating costs for individual jobs is shown by the following example. During March, Richard Sandow, an artist, made drawings and small to-scale clay models of three dinosaurs for Prehistoric Beasts, Inc.: a Tyrannosaurus rex, a Pachycephalosaurus, and a Pteranodon. When completed, the "Rex" will be thirty-three feet high, the "Pachy" will be twelve feet, and the Pteranodon (really a bird rather than a dinosaur) will have a wing span of twenty-seven feet. To total all Richard's business costs for June and divide by three projects would produce a meaningless average cost for each project. This type of average cost per job would be equally meaningless in any other entity that manufactures products or provides services geared to unique customer specifications. Since job results are heterogeneous and distinctive in nature, the costs of those jobs are, logically, not averageable.

Exhibit 6–1 provides the Work in Process control and subsidiary ledger accounts for Sandow's job order product costing system. The usual production costs of direct materials, direct labor, and overhead are accumulated for each job. The typical job order inventory accounts use actual direct materials and direct labor cost combined

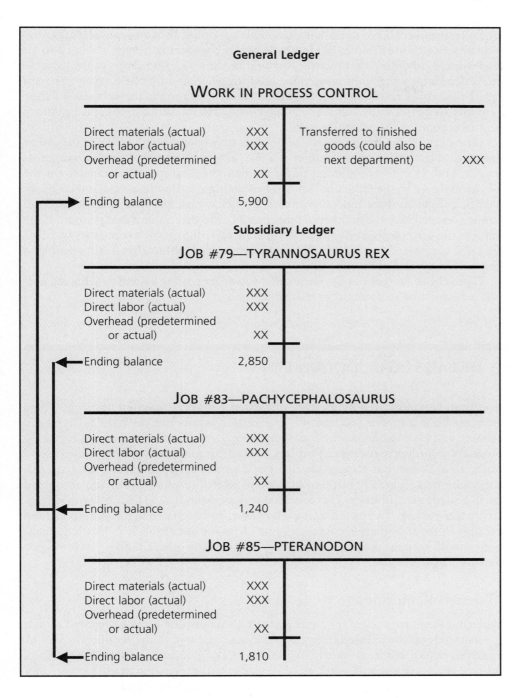

EXHIBIT 6–1
▼▼▼▼▼▼▼▼▼▼▼▼

SEPARATE
SUBSIDIARY LEDGER
ACCOUNTS FOR JOBS

with predetermined overhead rates multiplied by some actual cost driver (such as direct labor hours, cost or quantity of materials used, or number of materials requisitions). The normal costing method of valuation is used because actual direct material and direct labor costs are fairly easy to identify and are associated with a particular job.[2] Overhead costs are not usually traceable to specific jobs and must be allocated to production. For example, Sandow's electricity cost during March is related to all jobs worked on during that month. It would be difficult, if not impossible, to accurately determine which jobs created the need for what amount of electricity. To help assure the proper recording of costs, the amounts appearing in the subsidiary ledger accounts are periodically compared and reconciled to the Work in Process Inventory control account in the general ledger.

The output of a given job can be a single unit or multiple similar or dissimilar units. For example, Sandow's output is a clay model of each customer's contracted-for dinosaur. If a job's output is a single product, the total costs accumulated for the job are assigned to the individual unit. When multiple output results, a unit cost may only be computed if the units are similar. In such a case, the total accumulated job cost is averaged over the number of units produced to determine a cost per unit. If the output consisted of dissimilar units (for instance, if all Sandow's dinosaurs were for the same customer), no cost per unit can be determined, although it is still possible to know the total cost of the job.

These basic facts about the nature of a job order costing system provide the necessary foundation to account for individual jobs.

JOB ORDER COSTING: DETAILS AND DOCUMENTS

A job can be categorized by its stage of existence in its production life cycle. There are three basic stages of production: (1) agreed upon but not yet started, (2) jobs in process, and (3) completed jobs. Since job order costing is used by companies making products according to user specifications, unique raw materials may be required. Raw materials are often not acquired until a job is agreed upon. The materials acquired, although often separately distinguishable and related to specific jobs, are accounted for in a single general ledger control account (Raw Materials Inventory) with subsidiary ledger backup. The materials may, however, be designated in the storeroom (and possibly in the subsidiary records) as being "held for use in Job XX." Such designations should keep the materials from being used on a job other than the one for which they were acquired.

Materials Requisitions

materials requisition

When materials are needed for a job, a materials requisition form is prepared so that the materials can be released from the warehouse and sent to the production area. A **materials requisition** form (shown in Exhibit 6–2) is a source document that indicates the types and quantities of materials to be placed into production or used in performing a service. The form provides a way to trace responsibility for materials cost and links materials to specific jobs. Material requisitions release warehouse personnel from further responsibility for the issued materials and assign responsibility to the department that issued the requisition. As materials are issued, their costs are released

---

[2]While actual overhead may be assigned to jobs, such an approach would be less frequent because total overhead would not be known until the period was over, causing an unwarranted delay in overhead assignment. Activity-based costing can increase the validity of tracing overhead costs to specific products or jobs.

Most construction projects require the use of a job order costing system. The costs of materials and labor can be directly attached to the job, but predetermined rates are typically used to apply overhead.

from Raw Materials Inventory and, if the materials are direct to the job, are sent to Work in Process Inventory. If the Raw Materials Inventory account also contains indirect materials, those costs are assigned to Overhead when the indirect materials are issued.

Completed materials requisition forms are important documents in the audit trail of company records because they provide the ability to verify the flow of materials from the warehouse to the department and job that received the materials. Such doc-

EXHIBIT 6–2
▼▼▼▼▼▼▼▼▼▼▼

MATERIALS
REQUISITION FORM

No. 341

Date _____

Job Number _____   Department _____

Authorized by _____   Issued by _____

Received by _____   Inspected by _____

Item No.	Part No.	Description	Unit of Measure	Quantity Required	Quantity Issued	Unit Cost	Total Cost

Job Number ___186___

Customer Name and Address:

Austin Museum of Natural History
3497 Brazos Blvd.
Austin, Texas 78701

Contract Agreement Date: _____3/25/93_____
Scheduled Starting Date: _____4/5/93_____
Agreed Completion Date: _____3/1/94_____
Actual Completion Date: _____
Delivery Instructions: Crate and deliver to museum

Description of Job:

1 Tyrannosaurus rex—33 ft. high; 40 ft. long
Weight—approx. 2 tons   Include universal
eye movement; 500-watt sound system

Contract Price: _$182,521_

Department A—Art

Direct Materials (Est. $10,900)			Direct Labor (Est. $3,969)			Overhead based on					
						# of Req. (@ $15)			# of DLH (@ $8)		
Date	Source	Amount	Date	Source	Amount	Date	Source	Amount	Date	Source	Amount

Department B—Molding & Covering
(same format as above but with different OH rates)

Department C—Robotics
(same format as above but with different OH rates)

SUMMARY

	Art Dept. Actual	Art Dept. Budget	Molding & Covering Dept. Actual	Molding & Covering Dept. Budget	Robotics Dept. Actual	Robotics Dept. Budget
Direct materials	_____	$10,900	_____	$24,500	_____	$17,640
Direct labor	_____	3,969	_____	24,118	_____	3,310
Overhead (req.)	_____	180	_____	4,804	_____	2,940
Overhead (DLH)	_____	1,056	_____	3,783	_____	1,460
Totals	_____	$16,105	_____	$57,205	_____	$25,350

Final Costs:	Actual	Budget
Art Dept.	_____	$16,105
Molding & Covering Dept.	_____	57,205
Robotics Dept.	_____	25,350
Total	_____	$98,660

EXHIBIT 6–3
▼▼▼▼▼▼▼▼▼▼▼▼

PREHISTORIC BEASTS, INC. JOB ORDER COST SHEET

uments are usually prenumbered and come in multicopy sets so that completed copies can be maintained in the warehouse and the department, and for each job.

When direct materials are first issued to production, a job moves from the first stage of its production life cycle into the second: jobs in process. When a job enters this stage, it is necessary to begin the process of cost accumulation using the primary accounting document in a job order system—the job order cost sheet (also called a job cost record).

Job Order Cost Sheet

The source document that provides virtually all financial information about a particular job is the **job order cost sheet.** The set of all job order cost sheets for uncompleted jobs composes the Work in Process Inventory subsidiary ledger. The total costs contained in all job order cost sheets for uncompleted jobs should reconcile to the Work in Process Inventory control account balance in the general ledger, as shown in Exhibit 6–1.

job order cost sheet

The top portion of a job order cost sheet includes a job number, a description of the task, customer identification, various scheduling information, delivery instructions, and contract price. The remainder of the form details actual costs for materials and labor and applied overhead costs. The form might also include budgeted cost information, especially if such information had been used to estimate the job's selling price.

Exhibit 6–3 illustrates a job cost record for Prehistoric Beasts, Inc. The company has been contacted to produce one Tyrannosaurus rex for the Austin Museum of Natural History. All of the company's job cost sheets include a section for budgeted data so that budget-to-actual comparisons can be made for planning and control purposes. Direct materials and direct labor costs are assigned to jobs, and the amounts are indicated on the job order cost sheet as work on the job is performed. Direct materials information is gathered from the materials requisition forms, while direct labor information is found on employee time sheets or employee labor tickets. (Employee time sheets are discussed in the next section.)

Overhead is applied to production at Prehistoric Beasts using two predetermined overhead rates.[3] The first rate is based on the number of materials requisitions, and the second is based on direct labor hours. Prehistoric Beasts' management has found that these two activity bases better reflect the incurrence of costs than would a single base. Using the number of materials requisitions reflects management's determination that numerous parts create substantially more of some types of overhead support costs, such as warehousing and purchasing. Direct labor hours provides a reasonable allocation base for overhead costs such as electricity, indirect labor, and indirect materials.

Employee Time Sheets

An **employee time sheet** (Exhibit 6–4) indicates, for each employee, what jobs were worked on during the day and for what amount of time. These time sheets are most reliable if the employee fills them out as the day progresses. As work arrives at an employee station, it is accompanied by a tag specifying its job order number. The

employee time sheet

---

[3]If actual overhead is used in product costing, the overhead section could also have a source column similar to those included under direct materials and direct labor.

EXHIBIT 6–4
▼▼▼▼▼▼▼▼▼▼

EMPLOYEE TIME
SHEET

For Week Ending _____
Department _____
Employee Name _____
Employee I.D. Number _____

| Type of Work | | Job | Start | Stop | Day (circle) | Total |
Code	Description	Number	Time	Time		Hours
					M T W Th F S	
					M T W Th F S	
					M T W Th F S	
					M T W Th F S	
					M T W Th F S	
					M T W Th F S	

Employee Signature   Supervisor's Signature (for overtime)

times that work was started and stopped are noted on the time sheet.[4] These time sheets should be collected and reviewed by supervisors to ensure that the information is as accurate as possible.

In today's highly automated factories, employee time sheets may not be extremely useful or necessary documents. However, machine time can be tracked in the same way as human labor through the use of machine clocks or counters. As jobs are transferred from one machine to another, the clock or counter can be reset to mark the start and stop times. Machine times can then be equated to employee-operator time. Another convenient way to track employee time is through bar coding, as indicated in the following News Note. Using bar coding also provides the ability to trace machine depreciation to specific products by using a time-related depreciation measure (such as depreciation per hour of use).

Transferring employee time sheet (or alternative source document) information to the job order cost sheet requires a knowledge of employee labor rates. Wage rates are found in the employees' personnel files. The employee time spent on the job is multiplied by the employee's wage rate. The amounts are summed to find total direct labor cost for the period, and the summation is recorded on the cost sheet. Time sheet information is also used for payroll preparation. After these uses, time sheets are filed and retained because they are basic documents that can be referenced to satisfy various future information needs. If total actual labor costs for the job differ significantly from the original estimate, the manager responsible for labor cost control can be asked to clarify the reasons underlying the situation.

---

[4]One alternative to a time sheet prepared for the day is an individual time ticket for each job. These forms could be handed out by supervisors to employees as employees are assigned new jobs. Another alternative is to have supervisors maintain a record of which employees worked on what jobs for what period of time. This alternative is extremely difficult, however, if a supervisor is overseeing a large number of employees or when the employees are dispersed through a large section of the plant.

NEWS NOTE

Bar Coding: Not Just for Grocery Stores Anymore

Bar coding is among the most accurate data collection technologies. Aside from point-of-sale applications, bar code systems were initially implemented to track and control product movement through the receipt, storage, and shipping functions of large warehouse facilities. [But,] carefully designed pilot projects in visible, highly successful applications enable bar coding to reveal its many benefits to management and systems users. For example, one large plumbing manufacturer in the Midwest recently implemented time-and-attendance and shop-floor-control systems that use bar coding. The pilot project was begun in a rather simple two-stage labor process involving furnace heating and quality inspection. In less than two years, the company eliminated eleven different forms that were used when time and inspection data were recorded manually. Inspector efficiency improved by 10 to 12 percent, in part because the inspector *never* touched a piece of paper other than a bar code label.

In addition, if a job is being billed at cost plus a specified profit margin (a cost-plus job), the number of hours worked may be checked by the buyer. This situation is quite common and especially important when dealing with government contracts. Hours not worked directly on the contracted job cannot be arbitrarily or incorrectly charged to the cost-plus job without the potential for detection.

Lastly, time sheets provide information on overtime hours. Under the Fair Labor Standards Act, overtime must be paid at a time-and-a-half rate to all nonmanagement employees. The News Note on the next page addresses a problem relative to management or professional labor costs and bidding on jobs. The important thing to remember is to keep good records on all costs, including those related to employees.

Overhead

Actual overhead incurred during production is included in an overhead control account. If actual overhead is applied to jobs, the cost accountant will wait until the end of the period and divide actual overhead incurred by some related measure of activity or cost driver. Actual overhead would be applied to jobs by multiplying the actual overhead rate times the actual measure of activity associated with each job.

More commonly, overhead is applied to job order cost sheets by using one or more annualized predetermined overhead application rates. Overhead is assigned to jobs by multiplying the predetermined rate times the actual measure of the activity base that was incurred during the period and was associated with each job. If predetermined rates are used, overhead is applied at the end of the period or at completion of production, whichever is earlier. Overhead is applied at the end of each period so that the Work in Process Inventory account contains costs for all three product ele-

Uncompensated Overtime for Managers and Professionals

Uncompensated overtime has a significant impact on any firm employing professionals whose salaries are assigned directly to final cost [objects] on the basis of the number of hours worked. Concerns having to do with uncompensated overtime include cost assignment and allocation, inequities in bidding practices, pricing strategies, quality of output, hiring, and [workforce] retention as well as employee morale.

The use of uncompensated overtime has become common when firms are bidding or preparing proposals for work that will be priced and billed at an hourly rate. This scenario is true particularly in the highly competitive fields of accounting, consulting, and engineering services. The competitive advantage for a company using uncompensated overtime derives from the fact that such a company can propose a $20-per-hour rate for an employee earning $1,000 per week for a 50-hour week, while a company basing its bid or proposal on a standard 40-hour week would have to quote an hourly rate of $25 per hour to cover its cost.

Uncompensated overtime also affects the distribution of indirect overhead costs. If uncompensated overtime is not recorded, then overhead that was applied on a direct labor hour basis would be applied only for 40 hours. Such a procedure would cause an underallocation of overhead to jobs on which professionals worked during their uncompensated overtime hours.

SOURCE: Adapted from Richard F. Berk, "Uncompensated Overtime," *Management Accounting* (August 1991), pp. 31–32. Published by Institute of Management Accountants, Montvale, N.J.

ments (direct materials, direct labor, and overhead). When jobs are completed during a period, overhead is applied to Work in Process Inventory upon completion so that a proper product cost can be transferred to Finished Goods Inventory.

Completion of Production

When a job is completed, its total cost is transferred to the Finished Goods Inventory account. Job cost sheets for completed jobs are removed from the WIP subsidiary ledger and are transferred to a Finished Goods file, and serve as a subsidiary ledger for that account. When goods are sold, the cost shown on the job order cost sheet is transferred to Cost of Goods Sold. Such a cost transfer presumes the use of a perpetual inventory system, since goods are generally easily identified and tracked in a job order costing environment.

Job cost sheets for sold jobs are kept in a company's permanent files. A completed job cost sheet provides management with a historical summary about total costs and, if appropriate, the cost per finished unit for a given job. The cost per unit may be helpful for planning and control purposes as well as for bidding on future contracts. If a job was exceptionally profitable, management might decide to pursue additional similar jobs. If a job was unprofitable, the job cost sheet may provide indications of areas in which cost control was lax. Such indications are more readily determinable if the job cost sheet presents the original, budgeted cost information.

In any job order product costing system, the individual job is the focal point. The next section of the chapter presents a comprehensive job order costing illustration using Prehistoric Beasts, Inc., the company introduced earlier.

JOB ORDER COSTING ILLUSTRATION

Prehistoric Beasts, Inc., normally sets selling prices at cost plus 85 percent. The sales price ($182,521) of the Tyrannosaurus rex was established by multiplying the total estimated cost information shown in Exhibit 6–3 ($98,660) by 185 percent. This sales price is agreed to by the Austin Museum of Natural History in a contract dated March 25, 1993. Company managers schedule the job to begin on April 5 and be completed by March 1 of the following year. The job is assigned the number 186 for identification purposes. Following is a description of the process.

> The artists first make careful drawings followed by a small clay model. By measuring this model, the engineers can plan a movable robot that will act as the skeleton of the finished dinosaur. While the engineers are building the robot, sculptors are busy making a full-size clay statue of the dinosaur. This takes several months. When the large clay sculpture is finished, it's turned over to mold-makers who cover the clay with a liquid plastic that hardens into a shell. This shell is called a mold and can be removed in several pieces. The hollow mold is then reassembled and a special liquid foam rubber is poured into it. After the foam rubber dries, the mold is removed and the newly formed "skin" is wrapped around the finished robotic skeleton. Movements of the robot are created by pushing compressed air through small tubes into cylinders that contain a piston. The base of the creature contains air valves, a sound system, and a small computer that controls the flow of air to all parts of the robotic skeleton, causing the creature to move in a lifelike way. Mouth movements are synchronized with sounds emanating from a hidden speaker.[5]

The following journal entries illustrate the flow of costs for the Art Department of Prehistoric Beasts, Inc., during April 1993. Several jobs were worked on in the Art Department during that month, including Job #186. Although costs would be accounted for individually for each job worked on during the month, only the detail for Job #186 is shown.

In entries 1, 2, and 4 (following), Work in Process Inventory—Art Dept. has been debited twice to highlight the costs associated with Job #186 versus those associated with other jobs. In practice, the WIP control account for a given department would be debited only once for total costs assigned to it. The details for posting to the individual job cost records would be presented in the journal entry explanations.

1. During April 1993, material requisition forms #628–641 indicated that $4,995 of raw materials were issued from the warehouse to the Art Department. This amount included $160 of direct materials used on Job #186 (issued on April 5 and 21) and $4,245 of direct materials used on other jobs. The remaining $590 of raw materials issued during April were indirect materials.

Work in process at Dinamation is unusual to say the least. Custom fitting the tongue into the mouth of this Pachycephalosaurus is one direct labor activity during the production process.

[5]Michele Burgess, "Prehistory at Play," *SKY* (July 1990), p. 12.

Work in Process Inventory—Art Dept. (Job #186)	160	
Work in Process Inventory—Art Dept. (other jobs)	4,245	
Manufacturing Overhead—Art Dept. (indirect materials)	590	
Raw Materials Inventory		4,995

To record direct and indirect materials issued per
requisitions during April

2. The April time sheets and payroll summaries of the Art Department were used to trace direct and indirect labor to that department. Total labor cost for the Art Department for April was $15,075. Job #186 required $1,349 of direct labor cost during the two biweekly pay periods of April 9 ($368) and April 23 ($981). The remaining jobs in process required $12,576 of direct labor costs. Indirect labor costs for April totaled $1,150.

Work in Process Inventory—Art Dept. (Job #186)	1,349	
Work in Process Inventory—Art Dept. (other jobs)	12,576	
Manufacturing Overhead—Art Dept. (indirect labor)	1,150	
Salaries and Wages Payable		15,075

To record salaries and wages associated with Art Dept.
during April

3. In addition to indirect materials and indirect labor, the Art Department incurred other overhead costs during April. Repairs and maintenance costs were paid in cash. Overhead costs were also incurred from some items not detailed; these costs have been credited to various other accounts. The following entry summarizes the accumulation of these other actual overhead costs in the Manufacturing Overhead account:

Manufacturing Overhead—Art Dept.	846	
Accumulated Depreciation		285
Prepaid Insurance		50
Utilities Payable		325
Cash		110
Various other accounts		76

To record actual overhead costs of the Art Dept. during
April exclusive of indirect materials and indirect labor

4. Prehistoric Beasts, Inc., prepares financial statements at the end of each month. To do so, Work in Process Inventory must include all production costs—direct materials, direct labor, and overhead. Prehistoric Beasts allocates overhead to the Art Department Work in Process Inventory based on two predetermined overhead rates: $15 per material requisition and $8 per direct labor hour. In April, materials for Job #186 required two material requisitions, and the artists had worked a total of forty-five hours. The other jobs worked on during the month received total applied overhead of $1,493 (19 requisitions × $15 and 151 DLH × $8).

Work in Process Inventory—Art Dept. (Job #186)	390	
Work in Process Inventory—Art Dept. (other jobs)	1,493	
Manufacturing Overhead—Art Dept.		1,883

To apply overhead to Art Dept. Work in Process for April
using predetermined application rates

Notice that the amount of overhead actually incurred during April in the Art Department ($590 + $1,150 + $846 = $2,586) is not equal to the amount of overhead applied to that department's Work in Process Inventory ($1,883). This $703 difference is the underapplied overhead for the month. Because the predetermined

Job Number ___186___

Customer Name and Address:

Austin Museum of Natural History
3497 Brazos Blvd.
Austin, Texas 78701

Contract Agreement Date: _____3/25/93_____
Scheduled Starting Date: _____4/5/93_____
Agreed Completion Date: _____3/1/94_____
Actual Completion Date: _____
Delivery Instructions: Crate and deliver to museum

Description of Job:

1 Tyrannosaurus rex—33 ft. high; 40 ft. long
Weight—approx. 2 tons   Include universal
eye movement; 500-watt sound system

Contract Price: ___$182,521___

Department A—Art

Direct Materials (Est. $10,900)			Direct Labor (Est. $3,969)			Overhead based on # of Req. (@ $15)			# of DLH (@ $8)		
Date	Source	Amount	Date	Source	Amount	Date	Source	Amount	Date	Source	Amount
4/5	MR#630	$ 35	4/9	wk ended	$368	4/30	2MRs	$30	4/30	45DLH	$360
4/21	MR#637	125	4/23	wk ended	981						

(other similar entries would be made throughout production)

Department B—Molding & Covering
(same format as above but with different OH rates)

Department C—Robotics
(same format as above but with different OH rates)

SUMMARY

	Art Dept.		Molding & Covering Dept.		Robotics Dept.	
	Actual	Budget	Actual	Budget	Actual	Budget
Direct materials	$11,034	$10,900	$23,176	$24,500	$22,639	$17,640
Direct labor	3,890	3,969	22,985	24,118	3,421	3,310
Overhead (req.)	193	180	4,987	4,804	2,995	2,940
Overhead (DLH)	1,029	1,056	3,952	3,783	1,347	1,460
Totals	$16,146	$16,105	$55,100	$57,205	$30,402	$25,350

		Actual	Budget
Final Costs:	Art Dept.	$ 16,146	$16,105
	Molding & Covering Dept.	55,100	57,205
	Robotics Dept.	30,402	25,350
	Total	$101,648	$98,660

EXHIBIT 6–5
▼▼▼▼▼▼▼▼▼▼▼

PREHISTORIC
BEASTS, INC.
COMPLETED JOB
ORDER COST SHEET

rates are based on annual estimates, differences in actual and applied overhead will accumulate during the year. Under- or overapplied overhead will be closed at year-end, as shown in chapter 3, to either Cost of Goods Sold (if the under- or overapplied amount is immaterial) or to WIP, FG, and CGS (if significant).

These Dinamation dinosaurs are ready for shipment to the Smithsonian exhibit (from left: Allosaurus, Tyrannosaurus rex, Parasaurolophus, and Triceratops). The Allosaurus is full-scale, while the others are half-scale.

The preceding summarizations indicate the types of entries each department of Prehistoric Beasts, Inc., would make. Direct materials and direct labor data are posted to each job order cost sheet on a continuous basis (usually daily); entries are posted to the general ledger control accounts at less frequent intervals (usually monthly).

Similar entries for the Tyrannosaurus rex are made throughout the production process. Exhibit 6–5 shows the completed cost sheet for Job #186 for Prehistoric Beasts. Note that direct material requisitions, direct labor cost, and applied overhead shown earlier in items 1, 2, and 4 are posted on the job cost sheet. Other entries are not detailed.

Job #186 will be worked on by all departments, sometimes concurrently. When the job is completed, its costs are transferred to Finished Goods Inventory. The journal entries related to completion and sale are as follows:

Finished Goods Inventory—Job #186	101,648	
Work in Process Inventory—Art Dept.		16,146
Work in Process Inventory—Molding &		
Covering Dept.		55,100
Work in Process Inventory—Robotics		30,402
Cost of Goods Sold—Job #186	101,648	
Finished Goods Inventory—Job #186		101,648
Accounts Receivable—Austin Museum	182,521	
Sales		182,521

The completed job cost sheet can be used by managers in all departments to determine how well costs were controlled. While the Art Department experienced higher direct materials cost than budgeted, direct labor in that department was under budget. In the Molding and Covering Department, actual direct materials and direct

NEWS NOTE

An Elaborate Time Clock

Many of the robots in the E.T. ride and other attractions at MCA Universal Studios were built at Sally Industries, Inc. People are Sally's most valuable asset, and management of their time is at the core of Sally's production control system.

As production workers arrive in the morning, each one logs onto a dedicated PC in the middle of the shop floor. The screen displays a menu of projects available to be worked on. The employee chooses a project, and a menu of tasks for that project is displayed. The employee then logs onto one of the tasks, and the start time for the task is written to the database. If the employee stops working on that task, he or she logs off that one and onto another one until departure time. The budgeted hours for the first task have been updated for this morning's work, and the budgeted hours remaining on all tasks are displayed on the terminal. This information is summarized in a Lotus spreadsheet weekly and then posted to Sally's payroll module in its accounting system. There it is automatically transferred to the job cost module and the general ledger accounts.

For a relatively small company such as Sally, the time management and production control system represents a significant investment in resources. Nevertheless, the system has paid for itself in a number of ways:

- Workers are very conscious of how they use their time—especially as they log themselves in and out—and they can see how their time fits into the time budgeted for the project. They "work smarter."

- Because the system is on-line, real-time, shop management knows the work status of each task and project at any instant. Managers can "manage smarter."

- The system flags on the main screen any task and project that is over budget. Management can give these items special attention.

- Time records are more accurate. Workers don't have to rely on their memories to complete a time sheet daily or weekly.

SOURCE: Thomas L. Barton and Frederick M. Cole, "Accounting for Magic," *Management Accounting* (January 1991), p. 27ff. Published by Institute of Management Accountants, Montvale, N.J.

labor costs were slightly below budget. Robotics experienced a rather substantial unfavorable difference in materials costs. Overall, costs were controlled relatively well on this job, since total costs were only 3 percent above budget.

Managers are interested in controlling costs on each job as well as by department for each time period. Actual direct materials, direct labor, and factory overhead costs are accumulated in departmental accounts and are periodically compared to budgets so that managers can respond to significant deviations. Transactions must be recorded in a consistent, complete, and accurate manner to have information on actual costs available for periodic comparisons. Managers may stress different types of cost control in different types of businesses. The preceding News Note illustrates one business that is intensely interested in labor costs.

The Prehistoric Beasts, Inc., example assumed the use of predetermined overhead rates. Attempting to use actual overhead costs for determination of job cost is difficult

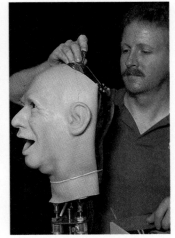

The bones and muscles of Sally Industries characters are made of steel and plastics operated by a computer. Painstaking adjustments ensure that complex eye and mouth mechanisms function smoothly. Here Luigi is fine-tuned prior to final assembly and finish art.

because of the delayed timing of overhead information and differences in periodic activity levels. The delay in information may be critical when a job is being provided for a customer on a cost-plus basis. Atypical variations in periodic activity could cause management to make incorrect assumptions about the cost per job. A manager might mistakenly determine that a particular job's cost was significantly higher or lower than it would have been in a period of normal activity. In a cost-plus contract, incorrect assumptions about costs could result in overcharging some customers while undercharging others. Such problems are overcome by using predetermined overhead rates.

A predetermined overhead rate is a type of standard. It establishes a constant amount of overhead assignable as a component of product cost and eliminates any immediate need for actual overhead information in the calculation of product cost. Standard costs can also be used for direct materials and/or direct labor in a job order environment.

JOB ORDER COSTING USING STANDARD COSTS

The Prehistoric Beasts, Inc., example illustrated the use of actual historical cost data for direct materials and direct labor in a job order product costing system. Using actual costs for direct materials and direct labor may cause the cost of similar units to fluctuate from period to period or job to job because of changes in component costs. The use of standard costs for direct materials and direct labor can minimize the effects of such cost fluctuations in the same way that predetermined rates do for overhead costs.

A standard costing system determines product cost by using predetermined estimates for prices and quantities of component elements. These estimates are used instead of actual costs in the inventory accounts. After production is complete, the standard production cost is compared to the actual production cost to determine the efficiency of the production process. Differences between standard and actual costs are called variances.

Standards can be used in a job order system only if a company typically engages in jobs that produce fairly similar products. One type of standard job order product costing system uses standards only for input prices of materials and/or rates for labor. This process is reasonable if all output relies on basically the same kinds of materials and/or labor. It may, however, not be feasible to develop standards for quantities of materials and/or labor, since each job may be distinctly different from others with regard to those elements. If standards are used for price or rate amounts only, the debits to Work in Process Inventory become a combination of actual and standard information: actual quantities at standard prices or rates.

Brush Strokes is a house-painting company located in the Southwest. Management has decided that, because of the climate, one specific brand of paint is the best brand of paint to use. Each gallon of paint costs $25. The painters employed by Brush Strokes are paid $7.95 per hour. These two amounts can be used as price and rate standards for the company. No standards can be set for the quantity of paint that will be used on a job or the amount of time the job will require, because those items will vary with the size and quantity of wood on the structure being painted.

Assume that Brush Strokes paints a house that required 50 gallons of paint and 40 hours of labor time. The standard cost for the paint is $1,250 (50 × $25) and for labor is $318 (40 × $7.95). Brush Strokes bought the paint when it was on sale, so

Job Order Costing—What More Do You Need?

A job-order production process is usually the setting where it is easy to install a cost system and where its value is seen as highest, since many such companies need frequent cost information.

Consider a cold-drawn steel company that processes steel bars to customer specifications. These bars may be drawn through a die, heat-treated, ground, polished, straightened, and cut in 10 or 15 operations. Since each operation requires enough labor that recording time by job and by work station is a minor inconvenience, a job-order cost system is appropriate. Material scrap can also be recorded by job and by work station. This kind of system provides actual cost by operation and by product. If companies establish standard costs, they can easily compare actual costs with those standards.

A job-order cost system provides detailed cost control and accurate product costs. Since managers have a choice of using standard or actual costs, there is little else that one could want from a cost system.

SOURCE: An excerpt from "What Kind of Cost System Do You Need?" by Michael J. Sandretto (January–February 1985). Reprinted by permission of *Harvard Business Review*. Copyright © 1985 by the President and Fellows of Harvard College; all rights reserved.

the actual price paid was $21 per gallon, or a total of $1,050. Comparing this price to the standard results in a $200 favorable material price variance (50 gallons at $4 per gallon). If labor were paid $8.25 per hour to paint the house, there would be a $12 unfavorable (40 hours at $.30 per hour) labor rate variance.

Other job order companies produce output that is homogeneous enough to allow standards to be developed for both quantities and prices for materials and labor. Such companies usually use distinct production runs for numerous similar products. In such circumstances, the output is homogeneous for each run, unlike the heterogeneous output of Brush Strokes. Quantity standards are more easily determined for direct materials and direct labor when output is homogeneous.

Ventura Company is a job order manufacturer that uses both price and quantity material and labor standards. Ventura manufactures photomasks, which are chrome-coated glass or quartz plates that have tiny images of computer circuits etched on their surfaces. They are used to manufacture semiconductor chips. Since each computer requires a different set of circuits, the photomasks are manufactured in distinct batches each month for each computer manufacturer. Price and quantity standards for direct materials and direct labor have been established and are used to compare the estimated and actual costs of monthly production runs of the same manufacturer's photomasks. These computations would be the same as those given in chapter 5.

Variances can be computed for actual-to-standard differences regardless of whether standards have been established for both quantities and prices or only for prices. Standard costs for materials and labor provide the same types of benefits as predetermined overhead rates: more timely information and comparisons against actual amounts.

As indicated in the preceding News Note, standard costing job order systems are reasonable substitutes for actual or normal costing systems as long as they provide managers with useful information. Any type of product costing system is acceptable in practice if it is effective and efficient in serving the company's unique production needs, provides the information desired by management, and can be implemented at a cost that is reasonable when compared to the benefits to be received. These criteria apply equally well to both manufacturers and service companies.

The major difference in job order costing for a service organization and a manufacturing firm is that a service organization may use an insignificant amount of direct materials on each job. In such cases, direct materials may be treated (for the sake of convenience) as part of overhead rather than accounted for separately. The accountant in the service company may only need to trace direct labor to jobs and allocate all other production costs to jobs. Allocations of these costs may be accomplished most effectively by using a predetermined rate per direct labor hour or, if wage rates are approximately equal throughout the firm, per direct labor dollar. Other alternative cost drivers may also be used as possible overhead allocation bases.

Whether the entity is a manufacturer or a service organization that tailors its output to customer specifications, company management will find that job order costing techniques will help in the managerial functions.

JOB ORDER COSTING TO ASSIST MANAGEMENT

Job order costing is useful to managers in planning, controlling, decision making, and evaluating performance. Knowing the costs of individual jobs will allow managers to better estimate future job costs and establish realistic selling prices. The use of budgets and standards in a job order product costing system provides information against which actual costs can be compared at reasonable time intervals for control purposes. These comparisons can also furnish some performance evaluation information. The following examples demonstrate the usefulness to managers of job order costing.

Wainwright & Trumbley

Wainwright & Trumbley is a large brokerage firm with a diversified set of clients and types of jobs. Ms. Wainwright, the firm's managing partner, wanted to know which clients were the most profitable and which were the least profitable. To determine this information, she requests a breakdown of profits per job measured on both a percentage and an absolute dollar basis.

Ms. Wainwright found that the firm did not maintain records of costs per client job. Costs had been accumulated only by type—travel, entertainment, and so forth. Mr. Mumford, a partner in the firm, was certain that the largest profits came from the firm's largest accounts. A careful job cost analysis was performed. It was found that the largest accounts contributed the most revenue to the firm, but the smallest percentage and absolute dollars of incremental profits. Until Ms. Wainwright requested this information, no one had totaled all the costs spent on obtaining each client and on the communications, entertainment, and other costs associated with maintaining each client.

When a company has a large number of jobs that vary in size, time, or effort, it may be difficult to know which jobs are responsible for disproportionately large amounts of costs. Job order costing can assist in determining which jobs are truly profitable and can help managers to better monitor costs. As a result of the cost anal-

Manufacturing custom boats requires commitment to detail—so does pricing the boats. Information about the costs for direct materials, direct labor, and overhead can be gathered from a job order costing system. The profit margin must then be negotiated between seller and buyer.

ysis, Ms. Wainwright changed the firm's strategy. The firm began concentrating its efforts on smaller clients who were located in closer proximity to the primary office. These efforts caused profits to increase substantially because significantly fewer costs were incurred for travel and entertainment. A job order cost system was implemented to track the per-period and total costs associated with each client. Unprofitable accounts were dropped, and account managers felt more responsibility to monitor and control costs related to their particular accounts.

Seawind Company

The Seawind Company manufactures three types of boats built to customer specifications.[6] Before job order costing was instituted, the owner (Ronnie Trump) had no means of determining the costs associated with the production of each type of boat. When a customer provided boat specifications and asked what the selling price would be, Ronnie merely estimated costs in what he felt was a reasonable manner. In fact, during the construction process, Ronnie did not assign any costs to Work in Process Inventory; all production costs were sent to the Finished Goods Inventory account.

After implementing a job order costing system, Seawind Company had better control over its inventory, better inventory valuations for financial statements, and better information with which to prevent part stockouts (not having parts in inventory) and production stoppages. The job order costing system provided Mr. Trump

---

[6]This example is based on an article by Leonard A. Robinson and Loudell Ellis Robinson, "Steering a Boat Maker Through Cost Shoals," *Management Accounting* (January 1983), pp. 60–66. Published by Institute of Management Accountants, Montvale, N.J.

with information on what work was currently in process and at what cost. From this information, Ronnie was better able to judge whether additional work could be accepted and when current work would be completed. Since job order costing assigns costs to Work in Process Inventory, balance sheet figures were more accurate. As materials were used in the production system, the use of materials requisitions to transfer goods from Raw Materials Inventory to Work in Process produced inventory records that were more current and reflective of raw materials quantities on hand. Finally, the use of a job order product costing system gave Mr. Trump an informed means by which to estimate costs and more adequately price future jobs.

FM Corporation

FM Corporation of Rogers, Arkansas is another company that needed good product costing information. FM produces custom-molded structural plastics for limited volume orders. Although orders were high, profits were negative and the company was forced into Chapter 11 bankruptcy. A new costing system was instituted to help track inventory, and profit margins were required of all jobs. This system, and an emphasis on quality improvements, allowed FM to pull out of Chapter 11 in only 14 months.

JOB ORDER PRODUCT COSTING IN HIGH-TECH ENVIRONMENTS

Wainwright & Trumbley, Seawind Company, and FM Corporation represent the kinds of businesses usually linked with job order product costing systems—businesses with limited volume, high direct labor involvement, and the need for frequent cost information. Although it is unusual to think of job order costing with "high-tech" manufacturing concepts, they are not incompatible.

Automated production and its influence on manufacturing and cost accounting are discussed at length in chapter 13. This section of the chapter is included to illustrate that cost accounting systems must reflect the manufacturing environment in which they are being used. No one system can be designed for use in all companies. It is the production situation that dictates the type of costing system to be used and that may provide the impetus for change in that system.

Companies manufacturing customized goods have often scheduled production in batches that emphasized "smoothing the work flow, specializing the work force, and minimizing the average unit cost of setups." [7] By batching production, job shops often had long lead times and significant inventory buildup. Many job shops are increasingly headed toward automation, as shown in Exhibit 6–6. The reasons behind this move generally center on competitiveness and quality, as illustrated by the following quote. "Major U.S. manufacturers know their competitiveness ultimately depends on the components bought from subcontractors, so if American job shops can't match the quality and cost of overseas suppliers, the large companies will be compelled to turn to offshore sources." [8]

---

[7] James E. Ashton and Frank X. Cook, Jr., "Time to Reform Job Shop Manufacturing," *Harvard Business Review* (March–April 1989), p. 107.
[8] Richard Brandt and James B. Treece, "Retool or Die: Job Shops Get a Fix on the Future," *Business Week* (June 16, 1986), p. 108.

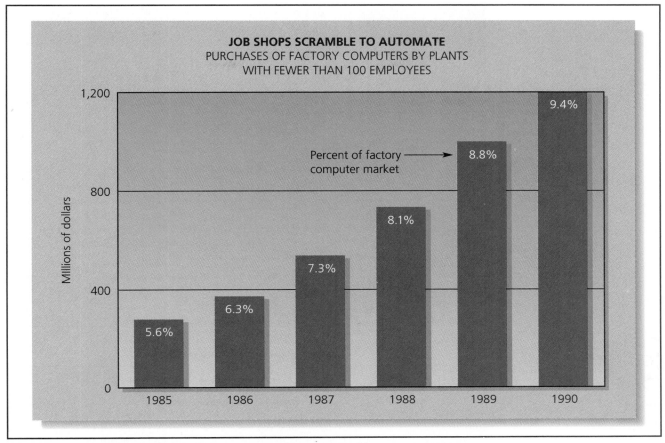

SOURCE: "Retool or Die: Job Shops Get a Fix on the Future," p. 106; reprinted from June 16, 1986 issue of *Business Week* by special permission, copyright © 1986 by McGraw-Hill, Inc.

EXHIBIT 6–6
▼▼▼▼▼▼▼▼▼▼▼

JOB SHOP
AUTOMATION

Another concept associated with high-technology environments is **just-in-time inventory,** or JIT, which refers to manufacturing inventory only as the need for it arises. Some job order environments are amenable to JIT implementation. Companies would need to separate repetitive types of production from truly unique orders. It is the repetitive type of production that is compatible to a JIT outlook. For example, the production of photomasks by Ventura Company (discussed earlier) reflects a situation in which just-in-time inventory might be appropriate, while the production of boats by Seawind Company would not.

When attempting to implement a JIT system, equipment should be managed for efficiency and to reduce the "travel" time of products between work stations. Companies need to identify any constraints in the production process and eliminate these to the extent possible so that production may flow more rapidly. The theory of constraints (TOC) suggests that throughout an organization there are bottlenecks that keep a system from achieving higher performance. The constraints are the critical points of the system, and product flow through the constraint(s) should be smooth and constant. In the following News Note, the plant controller for Valmont/ALS (a job shop steel fabricator in Brenham, Texas) discusses that company's decision to implement a just-in-time system and its consideration of the theory of constraints.

just-in-time inventory

Implementing JIT Requires Change in Mindset

"Why produce inventory to stock rather than only to customer order?" Our old school of thought had been that it was not possible to manufacture a new order on a consistent basis in less than the standard lead time, so a large inventory of manufactured parts and finished goods were required.

Our new challenge now would be to produce only to customer order while substantially reducing the amount of time it took to produce an order. It would be necessary to identify our constraint(s) in our operation and to use it as the heartbeat of our entire plant. Our scheduling system would allow for strategically sized inventory buffers placed directly in front of our constraints. The size of the inventory buffer required would depend on an analysis of the average downtime of the nonconstraint resources (cost centers with overcapacity) that feed the constraint.

SOURCE: David S. Koziol, "How the Constraint Theory Improved a Job-Shop Operation," *Management Accounting* (May 1988), p. 46. Published by Institute of Management Accountants, Montvale, N.J.

Dinamation, the company in the opening vignette, does not really sell its dinosaurs. It enters a partnership with museums or other entities to allow the creatures to be used in exhibits for three to four months. Sponsor cost can be high ($150,000 for fourteen weeks at Pittsburgh's Carnegie Museum of Natural History), but attendance certainly increases—it has been known to rise by as much as 1,400 percent when the dinosaurs "are in town." Exhibit proceeds are then split between the sponsoring organization and Dinamation. But lack of sales does not disqualify Dinamation from the use of job order product costing. The company must still determine how much each beast costs to make so that it knows how much to charge for lease arrangements to recoup costs.

Job order costing is still a primary product costing technique in use in business. But discussion at the end of the chapter briefly introduces the implementation of just-in-time inventory processes as one change occurring in American industry product manufacturing, technology, and philosophy. The introduction of JIT and other changes is having an impact on the way product costs are determined.

Traditional cost accounting defines product cost as consisting of direct materials, direct labor, and overhead. Direct materials and direct labor are considered the prime costs of production. However, as production becomes more automated, the quantity of direct labor shrinks while the amount of overhead increases. Overhead allocations based on direct labor bases (either hours or cost) are becoming less appropriate. New and, hopefully, more appropriate ways to determine product cost (such as activity-based costing) are being tried by more and more businesses. Businesses must adapt to the changes taking place around them to meet increasing competition.

As indicated in the Applications Strategies, job order product costing is used by the various business disciplines to provide useful information for managerial decision making.

Discipline	Applications
Accounting	Helps assign costs to products and services in a way that reflects business operations for most service companies and for manufacturers that produce to customers' specifications; may, in highly automated manufacturing companies, require that only direct materials be traced to each job and the insignificant cost of direct labor be combined with overhead and allocated to jobs using predetermined rate(s)
Economics	Provides information that helps determine the product demands placed on resources; helps measure the cost of operating activities
Finance	Provides information for valuing inventory and cost of goods sold for financial statements, tax returns, and regulatory agencies
Management	Provides information for differentiating between profitable and unprofitable jobs and customers; allows for a comparison of actual costs with budgeted costs and/or standards to determine cost overruns and the reasons thereof; affords opportunities to increase efficient and economical business operations
Marketing	Provides information that can be used to more accurately determine job costs (including marketing and distribution costs) so that better decisions can be made regarding output pricing and the customers to target

APPLICATIONS STRATEGIES FOR JOB ORDERING COSTING

CHAPTER SUMMARY

Job order product costing is a traditional cost accounting system used in companies that make a limited quantity of products or provide a limited number of services uniquely tailored to customer specifications. A job order costing system considers the "job" as the cost object for which costs are accumulated. A job can consist of one or more units of output, and job costs are accumulated in a job order cost sheet. Job cost sheets for uncompleted jobs serve as the Work in Process Inventory subsidiary ledger. Completed job cost records for jobs not yet delivered to customers constitute the Finished Goods Inventory subsidiary ledger.

In an actual or normal cost job order system, direct materials and direct labor are traced specifically (during the period and for each department) to the individual jobs in process. Direct materials are traced through materials requisition forms; direct labor is traced through employee time sheets. An actual cost system would apply actual overhead to jobs. More commonly, a normal costing system is used in which overhead is assigned using one or more predetermined overhead rates multiplied by the actual activity base incurred. Overhead is applied to Work in Process Inventory at the end of the month or when the job is complete, whichever is earlier.

Job order costing is especially appropriate and useful for many service businesses, such as advertising, legal, and architectural firms. In contrast to manufacturers, service companies often do not attempt to trace direct materials to jobs, but consider them a part of overhead cost. Tracing is not considered necessary when the materials cost is insignificant in relation to the job's total cost.

Job order costing assists management in planning, controlling, decision making, and evaluating performance. It allows managers to trace costs specifically associated with current jobs to better estimate costs for future jobs. Additionally, managers using job order costing can better control the costs associated with current production, especially if comparisons with budgets or standards are used. Attachment of costs to specific jobs is also necessary to price jobs that are contracted on a cost-plus basis. Lastly, since costs are accumulated by specific jobs, managers can more readily determine which jobs or types of jobs are most profitable to the organization.

A cost accounting system should be compatible with the manufacturing environment in which it is used. Job order costing can sometimes be used in a business that wishes to implement just-in-time (JIT) inventory procedures if repetitive types of production are identified.

GLOSSARY

Employee time sheet a source document that indicates, for each employee, what jobs were worked on during the day and for what amount of time

JIT (just-in-time) inventory the process of manufacturing inventory only as the need for it arises

Job a single unit or group of like units identifiable as being produced to distinct customer specifications

Job order cost sheet a source document that provides virtually all the financial information about a particular job; the set of all job order cost sheets for uncompleted jobs composes the Work in Process subsidiary ledger

Materials requisition a source document that indicates the types and quantities of materials to be placed into production or used in performing a service; causes materials and their costs to be released from the raw materials warehouse and sent to Work in Process

SELECTED BIBLIOGRAPHY

Brignall, T. J., et al. "Product Costing in Service Organizations." *Management Accounting Research* (December 1991), pp. 227–48.

Coulter, Carlton III. "Computer Solutions: Better Estimating with Computerized Job Cost Data." *Highway & Heavy Construction* (April 1991), p. 15.

Doney, Lloyd D. "Using Expert Systems for Job Cost Estimates." *Management Accounting* (December 1987), pp. 63–64.

Fordham, Gregory L. "Computerized Job Cost Considerations for Government Contractors." *The CPA Journal* (July 1988), pp. 79–81.

Walleigh, Richard C. "What's Your Excuse for Not Using JIT?" *Harvard Business Review* (March–April 1986), pp. 38–40ff.

SOLUTION STRATEGIES

Basic Journal Entries in a Job Order Costing System:

Raw Materials Inventory	XX	
Accounts Payable		XX
To record the purchase of raw materials		

Work in Process Inventory—Dept. (Job #)	XXX	
Raw Materials Inventory		XXX
To record the issuance of materials requisitioned for a specific job		

Work in Process Inventory—Dept. (Job #)	XXX	
Wages Payable		XXX
To record direct labor payroll for employees working on a specific job		

Manufacturing Overhead	XXX	
Various accounts		XXX
To record the incurrence of actual overhead costs. (Account titles to be credited must be specified in an actual journal entry.)		

Work in Process Inventory—Dept. (Job #)	XXX	
Manufacturing Overhead		XXX
To apply overhead to a specific job. (This may be actual OH or OH applied using a predetermined rate. Predetermined OH is applied at job completion or end-of-period, whichever is earlier.)		

Finished Goods Inventory (Job #)	XXX	
Work in Process Inventory		XXX
To record the transfer of completed goods from WIP to FG		

DEMONSTRATION PROBLEM

Precision Metalworks is a newly formed firm that builds towers for equipment used in radio, television, and communications transmission. Each tower is custom-engineered based on the site conditions and height requirements. The towers are built in sections in the firm's factory and then hauled by rail or truck to the site location where they are assembled.

Organizationally, the firm is comprised of two departments: Construction and Assembly. The Construction Department is responsible for engineering and manufacturing each tower; the Assembly Department assembles and erects the towers.

In its first year of operations (1993), Precision Metalworks obtained contracts for the construction of three towers:

Tower 1: a 1,500-foot tower for public television in Idaho;
Tower 2: a 300-foot radio tower in Cleveland; and
Tower 3: a 500-foot radio tower in Atlanta.

The firm uses a job order costing system based on normal costs. Overhead is applied in the Construction Department at the predetermined rate of $40 per ton of metal processed. In the Assembly Department, overhead is applied at the predetermined rate of $100 per foot of tower that is erected.

For 1993, significant transactions are summarized as follows:

1. Raw materials (metal) were purchased on account: 2,000 tons at $100 per ton.

2. Materials were requisitioned for use in the three towers (all materials used are regarded as direct materials): Tower 1—1,300 tons; Tower 2—200 tons; and Tower 3—300 tons. All of the materials were issued to the Construction Department.

3. The time sheets and payroll summaries indicated the following direct labor costs were incurred:

	Construction Dept.	% Complete	Assembly Dept.	% Complete
Tower 1	$200,000	100%	$300,000	100%
Tower 2	25,000	100%	40,000	50%
Tower 3	30,000	40%	0	0%

4. Indirect manufacturing costs were incurred in each department:

	Construction Dept.	Assembly Dept.
Labor	$20,000	$ 40,000
Utilities	10,000	5,000
Depreciation	40,000	110,000

5. Manufacturing overhead was applied based on the predetermined overhead rates in effect in each department.

6. Tower 1 was completed and sold at a price equal to cost plus $400,000.

7. Any under- or overapplied overhead is assigned to Cost of Goods Sold.
   Required:

   a. Record the journal entries for items 1 through 7.
   b. As of the end of 1993, determine the total cost assigned to Tower 2 and Tower 3.

Solution to Demonstration Problem

a. 1.	Raw Materials	200,000	
	Accounts Payable		200,000
	To record purchase of materials		
2.	WIP—Construction (Tower 1)	130,000	
	WIP—Construction (Tower 2)	20,000	
	WIP—Construction (Tower 3)	30,000	
	Raw Materials		180,000
	To record requisition and issuance of materials		
3.	WIP—Construction (Tower 1)	200,000	
	WIP—Construction (Tower 2)	25,000	
	WIP—Construction (Tower 3)	30,000	
	WIP—Assembly (Tower 1)	300,000	
	WIP—Assembly (Tower 2)	40,000	
	Wages Payable		595,000
	To record direct labor costs		

4. Manufacturing Overhead—Construction	70,000	
Manufacturing Overhead—Assembly	155,000	
Wages Payable		60,000
Utilities Payable		15,000
Accumulated Depreciation		150,000
To record indirect manufacturing costs		
5. WIP—Construction (Tower 1)	52,000	
WIP—Construction (Tower 2)	8,000	
WIP—Construction (Tower 3)	12,000	
Manufacturing Overhead—Construction		72,000
To record application of Construction Dept. manufacturing overhead		
WIP—Assembly (Tower 1)	150,000	
WIP—Assembly (Tower 2)	15,000	
Manufacturing Overhead—Assembly		165,000
To record application of Assembly Dept. manufacturing overhead		
6. Finished Goods	832,000	
WIP—Construction (Tower 1)		382,000
WIP—Assembly (Tower 1)		450,000
To record completion of Tower 1		
Cost of Goods Sold	832,000	
Finished Goods		832,000
To record cost of tower sold		
Accounts Receivable	1,232,000	
Sales		1,232,000
To record sale of Tower 1		
7. Manufacturing Overhead—Construction	2,000	
Manufacturing Overhead—Assembly	10,000	
Cost of Goods Sold		12,000
To close OH to CGS		

b.

	Tower 2	Tower 3
Direct materials—Construction	$ 20,000	$30,000
Direct labor—Construction	25,000	30,000
Manufacturing overhead—Construction	8,000	12,000
Direct materials—Assembly	0	0
Direct labor—Assembly	40,000	0
Manufacturing overhead—Assembly	15,000	0
Totals	$108,000	$72,000

END-OF-CHAPTER MATERIALS

Questions

1. In the context of job order product costing, what is a job?

2. If the costs in all of the subsidiary ledgers for all work that has been started but not yet completed were summed, the total would equal the balance in which control account? Why?

3. When materials are used in the production process, their costs are charged to one of two accounts. What are the two accounts and how is it determined which account should be charged?

4. If job order product costing is in use, what is the primary document for tracking the costs associated with individual jobs? What information is shown on this document?

5. What is the primary source document for determining how much of an employee's time should be charged to a specific job? When should this document be prepared?

6. Once a job is completed, in which account are the costs associated with the job found? What constitutes the support for the information in this control account?

7. The sum of all costs on the job costs sheets for all the products that are sold during a period would equal the balance in which account? Would this account balance typically be determined using a perpetual or a periodic inventory system? Why?

8. For identical products produced in different periods, which costing method (actual, normal, or standard) is likely to show the greatest interperiod fluctuation in the costs assigned to the products? Why?

9. What is the primary difference between job order costing for a manufacturing firm and job order costing for a service organization? Why does this difference arise?

10. What types of service organizations are likely to use job order costing?

11. For each of the following types of organizations, indicate whether you think standards for materials and labor could be used for prices and quantities:

   a. an automobile body repair shop
   b. a medical lab that performs a variety of blood tests
   c. a print shop
   d. a company offering executive education courses in numerous cities in the United States

12. What changes are occurring in manufacturing job shop environments that may induce many organizations to change the product costing system?

13. Why would a change from a labor-intensive production system to a machine-driven production system likely necessitate changes in the job order costing system?

14. Assume that you work part-time in a restaurant to help support your college education. Each customer's or table's order could be considered a "job." What constraints exist in the restaurant that might hinder the prompt "completion" of the job?

Exercises

15. *(Missing numbers)* The Throckmorton Auto Shop uses a job order costing system based on normal costs. Overhead is applied at the rate of 80 percent of direct labor costs. Jobs in process at the end of November are as shown:

	Job No. 313	Job No. 318	Job No. 340
Direct materials	$ 5,000	$ 7,000	$ 9,400
Direct labor	12,000	b	c
Overhead	a	10,000	d
Total	e	f	27,400

Find the values for a through f.

16. *(Overhead application; total cost; WIP balance)* The Baltimore Bridge Company constructs bridges for the interstate highway system. In its first year of operations, the firm worked on three bridges. Each bridge is built on-site and treated as a separate job. Overhead is applied to jobs based on the number of tons of direct material consumed. On average, direct materials cost $50 per ton. Some relevant information on the jobs follows:

	Bridge 1	Bridge 2	Bridge 3	Total
Direct materials	$ 45,000	$ 54,000	$135,000	$234,000
Direct labor	180,000	213,000	599,000	992,000
Overhead				439,920

a. Compute the overhead rate per ton of direct materials.
b. Compute the amount of overhead assigned to each bridge.
c. Compute the total costs assigned to each bridge for the first year.
d. Assuming Bridge 3 is the only one that was finished during the year, compute the year-ending balance in Work in Process.

17. *(Total cost & sales price)* The Denver Blacksmith Shop is a small firm whose specialty is the production of custom metal products. The firm employs a job order costing system based on normal costs. Overhead is applied to production at the rate of $12 per direct labor hour. During August, the firm finished Job 129, a batch of metal steps for mobile homes. The total direct material and direct labor costs assigned to Job 129 were $14,000 and $18,000, respectively. The firm's direct labor rate is $9 per hour.

a. Compute the total cost of Job 129.
b. Record the journal entry to transfer the job to the Finished Goods Inventory.
c. Compute the sales price of Job 129 if the job is priced to yield a gross margin equal to 40 percent of the sales price.

18. *(Journal entries)* Bradly Heavy Industries is a newly formed firm that manufactures various items of equipment used in handling products made of concrete. For its first month of operations, it recorded the following activity:

- Purchased direct materials on account, $400,000.
- Used $325,000 of the purchased materials in production operations.
- Incurred direct labor costs: 8,000 hours @ $12 per hour.
- Incurred manufacturing overhead costs: indirect labor—$200,000, utilities—$150,000, rent—$100,000, and depreciation—$150,000.

The firm employs a job order costing system based on actual costs.

a. Prepare the journal entries to record the previous transactions.
b. Prepare the journal entry that would be recorded at the end of January to charge production for the overhead costs.
c. Assuming no products were completed during the period, compute the ending balances in the Raw Material and Work in Process Inventory accounts.

19. *(Journal entries; standard costs)* Southwood Manufacturing Company employs a job order costing system based on standard costs. For one of its products, Part No. 307, the standard costs per unit are as follows:

Direct materials	$ 9
Direct labor	20
Manufacturing overhead	8

Standard costs are used in the inventory accounts, and there were no differences between standard and actual costs relative to the production of Part No. 307.

a. Record the journal entry for the transfer of direct materials into production for 1,000 units of Part No. 307.
b. Compute the total cost assigned to the 1,000 units of Part No. 307 and record the journal entry to recognize the completion of the 1,000 units.
c. Record the journal entries associated with the sale of the 1,000 units of Part No. 307 for $50,000.

20. *(Journal entries)* The California Hattery uses a perpetual inventory system. The firm maintains one inventory account for various materials that are used to make hats as well as the supplies that are used to lubricate and maintain its production machinery. For the month of August, the firm had the following transactions that affected its materials inventory account:

- Purchased felt material on account, $80,000.
- Issued felt for hat production, $38,000.
- Issued lubricants for machinery maintenance, $2,000.

Record the journal entries for the three prior transactions.

21. *(Budgeted & actual cost comparisons)* West Coast Fabrics produces men's suits to the specifications of various wholesaling customers. Each suit that is produced passes through two departments: Cutting and Assembly. For one recent order, Job 418, the company produced 500 wool suits and budgeted the following costs for the order:

	Cutting Department	Assembly Department	Total
Direct materials	$12,500	$1,000	$13,500
Direct labor	2,000	8,000	10,000
Factory overhead	1,500	500	2,000
Totals	$16,000	$9,500	$25,500

The actual cost of Job 418 was $29,000, as indicated in the following:

	Cutting Department	Assembly Department
Direct materials	$15,000	$1,050
Direct labor	2,000	8,650
Factory overhead	1,700	600

a. Where was the biggest difference between the budgeted cost and the actual cost of Job 418?
b. List two plausible explanations for this difference.

22. *(Actual vs. standard costs)* The Hot Air Creations Company manufactures blimps that are used for various promotions and commercial advertising. The company can produce four blimps per year. Since the company has a standard design and construction process, the firm uses a standard costing system. The standard costs to produce a single blimp follow:

Direct materials	$360,000
Direct labor (16,000 hours @ $20)	320,000
Overhead	200,000
Total standard cost	$880,000

For the first blimp produced in 1994, the actual costs were:

Direct materials	$340,000
Direct labor (20,000 hours @ $20.10)	402,000
Overhead	207,000
Total actual cost	$949,000

a. Compute the variance between actual and standard cost for each of the following: direct materials, direct labor, and manufacturing overhead for the first blimp produced in 1994.

b. Is the large direct labor variance found in part (a) driven primarily by the number of hours worked or the cost per hour? Explain.

Problems

23. *(Journal entries)* The Shetland Publishing Company recorded the following transactions for October 1993:

- Purchased materials on account, $900,000.
- Issued materials into production, $700,000. Of the total materials issued, $500,000 could be traced directly to specific jobs.
- Factory labor costs in the amount of $650,000 were incurred. Only $500,000 of this amount could be attributed to specific jobs.
- Overhead was applied to jobs on the basis of 110 percent of direct labor cost.
- Job #807 costing $250,000 was completed.
- Job #807 was sold on account for $400,000.

Required: Record all necessary journal entries to account for the previous transactions.

24. *(Journal entries; total costs; sales prices)* Bart's Landscaping, Inc., employs a job order costing system based on actual costs. Overhead cost is assigned to jobs based on the hours Bart works on each job (overhead is assigned weekly). Bart is the only employee. During the first week in May, Bart performed work for three homeowners: Jones, Alinaba, and Brown. The following transactions occurred during the week:

- Trees were purchased for Jones, $500.
- Brick pavers were purchased for Alinaba, $2,000.
- Materials for a sprinkler system were purchased for Brown, $1,800.
- Overhead expenses were incurred as follows:

Fuel	$ 40
Depreciation	200
Utilities	60
Insurance	100
Repairs/maintenance	200

- Bart worked the following hours (Bart's Landscaping, Inc., pays Bart $25 per hour for his labor):

    20 hours installing the sprinkler system for Brown
    10 hours planting the trees for Jones
    30 hours installing the brick pavers for Alinaba

All three jobs were completed during the week.

Required:

a. Record the journal entries for each of the previous transactions.

b. Determine the total costs assigned to each job.

c. If Bart prices each job at 180 percent of cost, determine the price charged for each landscaping job.

25. *(Journal entries)* Technotronix, Inc., custom manufactures robots that are used in repetitive production tasks. At the beginning of 1993, three jobs were in process. The costs assigned to the jobs as of January 1, 1993, are as follows:

	Job 114J	Job 117N	Job 128P
Direct materials	$200,000	$1,400,000	$100,000
Direct labor	150,000	800,000	60,000
Overhead	100,000	600,000	42,000
Totals	$450,000	$2,800,000	$202,000

During the course of 1993, two more jobs were started, 133I and 134P, and the following transactions occurred:

- Materials were purchased, $1,200,000.
- Direct materials were issued to production:

Job 114J	$212,000
Job 117N	158,000
Job 128P	410,000
Job 133I	160,000
Job 134P	125,000

- Indirect materials were issued to production, $111,900.
- Labor costs were incurred as follows:

Job 114J	$175,000
Job 117N	302,000
Job 128P	450,000
Job 133I	205,000
Job 134P	110,000
Indirect labor	300,000

- Other overhead costs were incurred, $500,000.
- Actual overhead costs were applied to jobs on the basis of machine hours. The machine hours consumed on each job were:

Job 114J	1,200
Job 117N	1,800
Job 128P	3,400
Job 133I	900
Job 134P	700

Required:

a. Prepare the journal entries to record the previous events.

b. Assume that Jobs 114J and 117N were completed during the year. Prepare the journal entries to record the completion of these jobs.

c. Assume Job 117N was sold during the year for $3,000,000. Prepare the necessary journal entries to record the sale.

26. *(Missing numbers)* Bill's Custom Cabinetry is a small firm that manufactures cabinets for various residential uses. The firm applies overhead to jobs at a rate of 90 percent of direct labor cost. On December 31, 1993, an unfortunate chain saw incident destroyed some of the firm's cost records. The following information for 1993 was extracted from the grisly scene:

DIRECT MATERIALS

Beginning	$1,200		?
Purchases	?		
Ending	$4,800		

WORK IN PROCESS

Beginning	$34,000		?
DM	?		
DL	80,000		
OH	?		
Ending	$16,000		

FINISHED GOODS

Beginning	$18,000		
Goods compl.	?	$340,000
Ending	$42,000		

COST OF GOODS SOLD

?

Required: As Bill's close friend, you have been asked to find the following:

a. Cost of Goods Sold for the year
b. Cost of cabinets completed during the year
c. Cost of direct material used
d. Amount of applied factory overhead
e. The cost of direct materials purchased during the year

27. *(Flow of costs)* After preparing for your managerial accounting exam, you confidently turn to your roommate and declare, "I think I've finally figured out how product costs flow through the various accounts and how they are reflected on income statements and balance sheets."

   Upon hearing this wonderful news, your roommate responds, "Hey, if you really want to test your understanding of product costing, try working a problem my old prof gave me." After rummaging for fifteen minutes through various files, folders, and shelves, your roommate slaps a sheet of paper in front of you and explains that the sheet contains information pertaining to one year of operations for the Elios Manufacturing Company.

   The sheet contains the following information:

Beginning inventory, direct material	$ 10,000
Ending inventory, direct material	20,000
Direct material used	200,000
Sales	500,000
Beginning Work in Process Inventory	50,000
Ending Work in Process Inventory	80,000
Cost of products completed during the year	400,000
Actual factory overhead costs incurred	120,000
Selling and administrative expenses	70,000
Beginning Finished Goods Inventory	100,000

Ending Finished Goods Inventory	85,000
Beginning balance—property, plant & equip.	225,000
Ending balance—property, plant, & equip.	240,000
Applied factory overhead	60 percent of direct labor cost

At the bottom of the sheet was the following information: Elios uses a normal costing system.

Required: Using the information just given, compute the following:

a. The cost of direct materials purchased
b. The cost of direct labor
c. Applied factory overhead
d. The Cost of Goods Sold before closing underapplied overhead
e. The net income or net loss before closing underapplied overhead

28. *(Applied OH; total cost)* The Steelworks Safety Company manufactures metal shields for various pieces of power equipment to protect machine operators. The shields are created in a two-step process. First, materials are cut and formed in the Stamping Department. This department is very machine-intensive and highly automated. Overhead in this department is applied based on machine time ($12 per machine hour). The second department, the Finishing Department, welds the materials received from the Stamping Department and then applies either a paint or galvanized finish. The Finishing Department is very labor-intensive, and consequently overhead is applied based on direct labor hours ($8 per direct labor hour).

During June 1993, the firm worked on three separate jobs. Information on the three jobs follows:

	Department	
Job # 8721	*Stamping*	*Finishing*
Direct labor hours	1,600	2,000
Machine hours	4,000	800
Direct labor cost	$16,000	$18,000
Direct materials cost	$88,000	$ 4,000
Job # 8722		
Direct labor hours	3,600	5,000
Machine hours	9,000	1,200
Direct labor cost	$ 36,000	$45,000
Direct materials cost	$190,000	$ 9,000
Job # 8723		
Direct labor hours	400	1,300
Machine hours	2,000	300
Direct labor cost	$ 4,000	$11,700
Direct materials cost	$28,000	$ 1,000

The firm employs a job order product costing system based on normal costs. Actual overhead costs in the Stamping and Finishing Departments for the month were, respectively, $200,000 and $65,000.

Required:

a. Determine the total amount of overhead to be applied to each of the three jobs.
b. Calculate the total cost of each job.
c. Calculate the difference between the amount of overhead applied from each department and the amount of overhead incurred in each department.

29. *(Cost of FG & WIP; cost variances)* Haswell Music, Inc., produces brass musical instruments. In late March 1994, Haswell received an order to produce 2,000 trumpets.

Given that the company had no other work in process and no other immediate orders, production of the trumpets was set to begin on April 1. Management determined that the trumpets would be produced in four batches of 500 units. The company utilizes a job order costing system based on standard costs. According to current standards, the cost of one trumpet is:

Direct materials	$ 35
Direct labor	30
Overhead	35
Total	$100

All materials are introduced at the outset of the production process. Direct labor and overhead costs are incurred evenly from the beginning of the production process to the end. By the end of April, 1,000 of the trumpets were complete, another 500 trumpets were (on average) 60 percent of the way through the production process, and the last 500 trumpets were (on average) only 10 percent of the way through the production process.

Required:

a. As of the end of April, determine the cost of trumpets in the Finished Goods Inventory.

b. As of the end of April, determine the ending balance in the Work in Process Inventory. (Hint: The 500 trumpets that are 60 percent through the production process have all the necessary materials, but would be considered to be the equivalent of 300 fully completed trumpets as to labor and overhead.)

c. If the actual costs incurred during the month of April for direct materials, direct labor, and overhead were, respectively, $73,000, $43,000, and $47,000, compute the cost variance for each cost component.

30. *(OH application rate; applied OH; methods)* Priscilla's Pottery produces a variety of finely crafted porcelain products. The products range from residential commodes to very delicate figurines. Production is sequenced in three departments. Production begins in the Sculpting Department where clay materials are mixed and then hand-formed (some products are formed using molds) into the required products. Next, the products go to the Glazing Department where various protective coatings and paints are applied to the products. Lastly, the products move through the Curing Department where the products are "fired" in a kiln.

The Sculpting and Glazing Departments are very labor-intensive operations. Virtually no high-tech equipment is in use in either department.

Two years ago, the Curing Department underwent a transformation. One computer-driven kiln was installed to replace seven gas-fired kilns that were manually operated by 15 employees. Now, the entire department consists of two individuals who sequence materials into the computerized kiln, maintain the kiln, and place finished products in storage. The computerization of the Curing Department has vastly enhanced the quality of the finished products.

The company uses a job order costing system in which actual overhead costs are assigned to products using a plantwide overhead rate based on direct labor hours. For the most recent period, the total costs in each department were as follows:

	Sculpting	Glazing	Curing
Overhead:			
Indirect labor	$100,000	$ 50,000	$ 15,000
Utilities	5,000	4,000	40,000
Depreciation	20,000	8,000	90,000
Repairs & maintenance	2,000	2,500	20,000
Taxes & insurance	2,500	1,000	15,000
Total overhead	$129,500	$ 65,500	$180,000
Direct materials	25,000	40,000	1,000
Direct labor	912,000	588,000	20,000

The actual direct labor hours worked in each department for the same period were:

	Sculpting	Glazing	Curing
Direct labor hours	114,000	84,000	2,000

Required:

a. Based on the previous information, compute the overhead application rate for the company.
b. The direct labor time expended in each department to complete two different products is as follows:

	Sculpting	Glazing	Curing
Product 1	6 hrs.	3 hrs.	1 hr.
Product 2	3 hrs.	5 hrs.	2 hrs.

Compute the amount of overhead that would be applied to each product based on the rate you computed in part (a).
c. The company is considering a change in its product costing system to allow departmental application of overhead rather than plantwide application of overhead. First, compute departmental overhead rates based on the departmental costs and direct labor information given earlier. Then, for the two products in (b), recompute the amount of overhead that would be assigned to them if overhead were applied at the departmental level based on direct labor hours. Compare these answers to your answers in part (b); does this method provide a more accurate determination of costs? Why or why not?
d. Is direct labor hours the best base for applying overhead in the Curing Department? Explain. If your answer is no, what alternative might be preferable?

31. *(Essay)* For each of the following, write a brief paragraph describing the role of the document in product costing:

a. Employee time sheet
b. Material requisition form
c. Job order cost sheet

▉ Cases

32. Valport Company employs a job order cost system based on actual costs. Manufacturing overhead is applied on the basis of machine hours (MH) using a predetermined overhead rate. The current fiscal year rate of $15.00 per MH is based on an estimated manufacturing level of 80,000 machine hours. Valport's policy is to close the over/under application of manufacturing overhead to Cost of Goods Sold.

Operations for the year ended November 30, 1994, have been completed. All of the accounting entries have been made for the year except the following: application of manufacturing overhead to the jobs worked on during November; the transfer of costs from Work in Process to Finished Goods for the jobs completed in November; and the transfer of costs from Finished Goods to Cost of Goods Sold for the jobs that have been sold during November. Summarized data that have been accumulated from the accounting records as of October 31, 1994, and for November 1994, follow.

Jobs N11-007, N11-013, and N11-015 were completed during November 1994. All completed jobs except Job N11-013 had been turned over to customers by the close of business on November 30, 1994.

| | Work in Process | November 1994 Activity | | |
| | Balance | Direct | Direct | Machine |
Job No.	10/31/94	Materials	Labor	Hours
N11-007	$ 87,000	$ 1,500	$ 4,500	300
N11-013	55,000	4,000	12,000	1,000
N11-015	–0–	25,600	26,700	1,400
D12-002	–0–	37,900	20,000	2,500
D12-003	–0–	26,000	16,800	800
Totals	$142,000	$95,000	$80,000	6,000

Operating Activity	Activity Through 10/31/94	November 1994 Activity
Manufacturing overhead incurred		
Indirect materials	$ 125,000	$ 9,000
Indirect labor	345,000	30,000
Utilities	245,000	22,000
Depreciation	385,000	35,000
Total incurred overhead	$1,100,000	$96,000
Other items		
Material purchases*	$965,000	$98,000
Direct labor costs	$845,000	$80,000
Machine hours	73,000	6,000

	Account Balances at Beginning of Fiscal Year 12/01/93
Materials Inventory*	$105,000
Work in Process Inventory	60,000
Finished Goods Inventory	125,000

*Material purchases and materials inventory consist of both direct and indirect materials. The balance of the Materials Inventory account as of November 30, 1994, is $85,000.

a. Valport Company uses a predetermined overhead rate to apply manufacturing overhead to its jobs. When overhead is accounted for in this manner, there may be over- or underapplied overhead.
   1. Explain why a business uses a predetermined overhead rate to apply manufacturing overhead to its jobs.
   2. How much manufacturing overhead would Valport have applied to jobs through October 31, 1994?

3. How much manufacturing overhead would be applied to jobs by Valport during November 1994?

4. Determine the amount by which the manufacturing overhead is over- or underapplied as of November 30, 1994. Be sure to indicate whether the overhead is over- or underapplied.

5. Over- or underapplied overhead must be eliminated at the end of the accounting period. Explain why Valport's method of closing over- or underapplied overhead to Cost of Goods Sold is acceptable in this case.

b. Determine the balance in Valport Company's Finished Goods Inventory at November 30, 1994.

c. Prepare a Statement of Cost of Goods Manufactured for Valport Company for the year ended November 30, 1994.

(CMA)

33. Constructo, Inc., is a manufacturer of furnishings for infants and children. The company uses a job order cost system for cost accumulation. Constructo's Work in Process Inventory at April 30, 1994, consisted of the following jobs:

Job No.	Items	Units	Accumulated Cost
CBS102	Cribs	20,000	$ 900,000
PLP086	Playpens	15,000	420,000
DRS114	Dressers	25,000	250,000
			$1,570,000

The company's finished goods inventory, which Constructo values using the FIFO (first-in, first-out) method, consisted of five items:

Item	Quantity and Unit Cost	Accumulated Cost
Cribs	7,500 units @ $64 each	$ 480,000
Strollers	13,000 units @ $23 each	299,000
Carriages	11,200 units @ $102 each	1,142,400
Dressers	21,000 units @ $55 each	1,155,000
Playpens	19,400 units @ $35 each	679,000
		$3,755,400

Constructo applies factory overhead on the basis of direct labor hours. The company's factory overhead budget for the fiscal year ending May 31, 1994, totals $4,500,000, and the company plans to incur 600,000 direct labor hours during this period. Through the first eleven months of the year, a total of 555,000 direct labor hours were worked, and total factory overhead amounted to $4,273,500.

At the end of April, the balance in Constructo's Materials Inventory account, which includes both raw materials and purchased parts, was $668,000. Additions to and requisitions from the materials inventory during the month of May included the following:

	Raw Materials	Purchased Parts
Additions	$242,000	$396,000
Requisitions:		
Job CBS102	51,000	104,000
Job PLP086	3,000	10,800
Job DRS114	124,000	87,000
Job STR077		
(10,000 strollers)	62,000	81,000
Job CRG098		
(5,000 carriages)	65,000	187,000

During the month of May, Constructo's factory payroll consisted of the following:

Account	Hours	Cost
CBS102	12,000	$122,400
PLP086	4,400	43,200
DRS114	19,500	200,500
STR077	3,500	30,000
CRG098	14,000	138,000
Indirect labor	3,000	29,400
Supervision		57,600
		$621,100

Listed below are the jobs that were completed and the unit sales for the month of May:

Job No.	Items	Quantity Complete
CBS102	Cribs	20,000
PLP086	Playpens	15,000
STR077	Strollers	10,000
CRG098	Carriages	5,000

Items	Quantity Shipped
Cribs	17,500
Playpens	21,000
Strollers	14,000
Dressers	18,000
Carriages	6,000

a. Describe when it is appropriate for a company to use a job order cost system.
b. Calculate the dollar balance in Constructo's Work in Process Inventory account as of May 31, 1994.
c. Calculate the dollar amount related to the playpens in Constructo's Finished Goods Inventory as of May 31, 1994.
d. Explain the proper accounting treatment for overapplied or underapplied overhead balances when using a job order cost system.

(CMA)

Ethics Discussion

34. In March 1989, the Federal Aviation Administration began investigating allegations that some maintenance supervisors for a U.S. airline company had been signing off on maintenance work that actually was not performed on individual aircraft.

a. Why could an individual airplane be considered a "job" for an airline company?
b. One of the maintenance tasks that was allegedly not completed was the washing of a cabin head air exchanger. Assume the following facts. Some of the airline's mechanics are on strike. The task is considered routine; the plane was only one year old and in excellent condition. The plane was scheduled to depart the airport in 30 minutes on a fully booked flight; washing the exchange filter would have taken a minimum of one hour. The airline is currently having problems with on-time departures and arrivals. The plane arrived safely at its destination. Discuss the possible perceptions and thoughts of the maintenance supervisor at the time that this maintenance should be performed.

   c. Discuss the perceptions and thoughts of the passengers at the terminal if the maintenance were performed.
   d. Discuss the ethical issues involved.

35. Dr. Acikalin is a plastic surgeon who treats both paying and charity patients. In the past month, there have been several very wealthy patients in for tummy tucks, face lifts, and liposuction. One other patient, on whom Dr. Acikalin has worked countless hours for over a year, is a young boy who had been in a motorcycle accident; the child is a charity case.

   a. Discuss the practical aspects of shifting some appropriately assigned overhead costs from the child's case to the wealthy patients.
   b. Discuss the ethical aspects of shifting some appropriately assigned overhead costs from the child's case to the wealthy patients.
   c. By accepting charity patients who require such extensive treatment, Dr. Acikalin is not making a reasonable income from his profession. He is considering closing his practice and working only for a for-profit hospital. Do you have any suggestions on how he might be able to continue serving both charity and wealthy patients and still earn a reasonable income?

36. Gillespie Enterprises uses a job order costing system that employs standards for materials and labor. These standards were set last year. Gillespie management has entered into a fixed-price contract with the federal government to provide uniforms for military personnel. The accepted bid price was determined using last year's standards. Since the bid was made, production operations related to uniforms was moved from the Northeast to a small town in Mississippi. Wage rates were substantially reduced, as were many overhead costs such as property taxes and utilities.

   a. Discuss the benefits and drawbacks of entering into fixed-price versus cost-plus contracts for customer-specified jobs.
   b. Discuss your feelings about holding the government to the fixed-price contract assuming you are
      1. the salesperson who obtained the job and is paid commission related to sales dollars.
      2. a major stockholder of Gillespie Enterprises.
      3. a taxpayer.
   c. How would the accounting concept of lower-of-cost-or-market be useful in this situation?

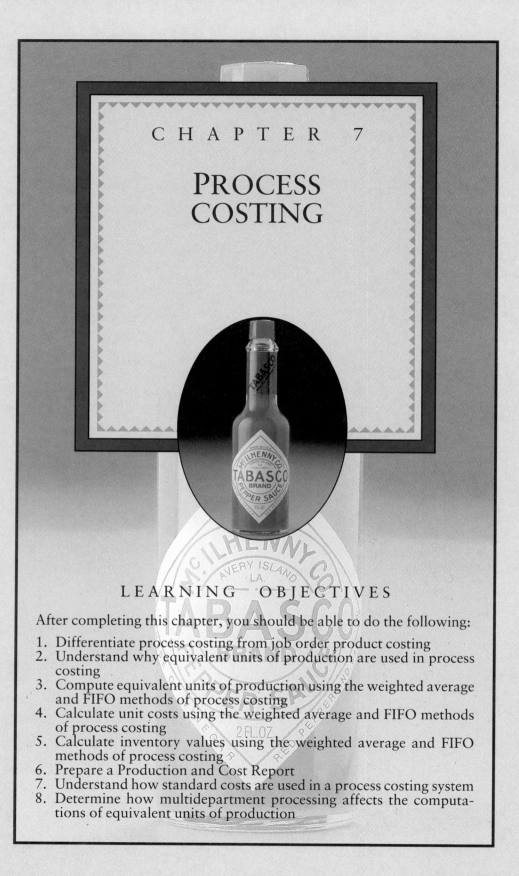

C H A P T E R   7

PROCESS COSTING

LEARNING OBJECTIVES

After completing this chapter, you should be able to do the following:

1. Differentiate process costing from job order product costing
2. Understand why equivalent units of production are used in process costing
3. Compute equivalent units of production using the weighted average and FIFO methods of process costing
4. Calculate unit costs using the weighted average and FIFO methods of process costing
5. Calculate inventory values using the weighted average and FIFO methods of process costing
6. Prepare a Production and Cost Report
7. Understand how standard costs are used in a process costing system
8. Determine how multidepartment processing affects the computations of equivalent units of production

T he mass production of McIlhenny's Tabasco sauce is totally unlike the production process used by Dinamation International (discussed in chapter 6). Because the process itself differs, so must the method of accounting for that process. E. McIlhenny Sons would use **process costing** to determine the product cost of its Tabasco sauce. This costing method accumulates and assigns costs to units of production in companies that make large quantities of homogeneous products. Process costing is used by manufacturers of many food products, as well as bricks, gasoline, and paper. In addition, manufacturers of automobiles and appliances can use process costing.

process costing

  This chapter illustrates the two methods of calculating unit cost in a process costing system: the weighted average and FIFO methods. Once unit cost is determined, total costs are assigned to the units transferred out of a department and to that department's ending Work in Process Inventory.

INTRODUCTION TO PROCESS COSTING

In some ways, the cost accumulation in a process costing system is similar to job order product costing procedures. In a **process costing system,** as in a job order system, costs are accumulated by cost component in each production department. As units are transferred from one department to the next, unit costs are also transferred so

process costing system

273

that a total production cost is accumulated by the end of production. In a job order system, accumulated departmental costs are assigned to specific jobs, which may be a single unit or a batch of units. In contrast, in a process costing system, accumulated departmental costs are spread or assigned to all units produced that flowed through that department during the period. As indicated in chapter 5 (Exhibit 5–1), the valuation method chosen (actual, normal, or standard) affects which costs are included in the inventory accounts.

The two basic differences between job order and process costing are (1) the *quantity* of production for which costs are being accumulated at any one time and (2) the cost *object* to which the costs are assigned. For example, an entrepreneur who bakes cookies at home for specific orders would use a job order product costing system, gather the direct materials and direct labor costs associated with production of each baking job, and assign those costs to the individual jobs. After all costs are accumulated and the cookies are completed, the cost per cookie can be determined if all the cookies baked for the job were similar.

In contrast, bakeries such as Entenmann's, which produces over 2 million cookies a week, could not use a job order system because the volume is simply too great. At Entenmann's, direct materials and direct labor costs could be gathered during the

Process costing is the appropriate cost system to use in most food production environments. Materials and labor may be direct costs for a particular type of Cadbury candy, but overhead costs would be averaged among all Cadbury product lines.

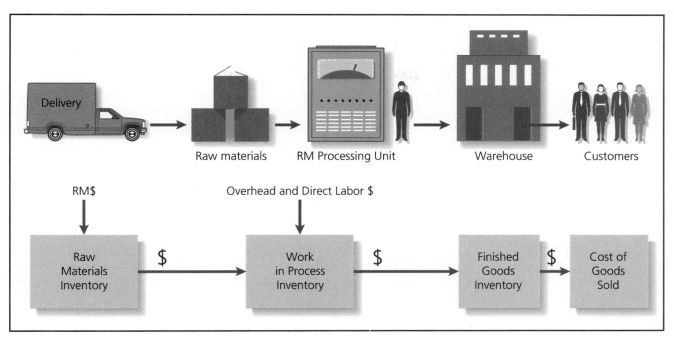

| Delivery | Raw materials | RM Processing Unit | Warehouse | Customers |

RM$ Overhead and Direct Labor $

| Raw Materials Inventory | $\$$ | Work in Process Inventory | $\$$ | Finished Goods Inventory | $\$$ | Cost of Goods Sold |

EXHIBIT 7–1
▼▼▼▼▼▼▼▼▼▼▼
FLOW OF COSTS
THROUGH
PRODUCTION

period for each department and each product. Since a variety of cookies are produced in any department during a period, the costs assignable to each type of product must be individually designated and attached to each type of cookie. Costs are then assigned to the products worked on during the period. Production does not have to be complete for costs to be assigned in a process costing system. Such cost assignment is discussed in this chapter.

In addition to the two primary differences between job order and process costing, there are three other differences. A process costing system would: (1) produce homogeneous rather than heterogeneous products; (2) use continuous processing rather than specific processing; and (3) use a production and cost report (discussed later in the chapter) rather than a job order cost sheet.

In a production environment, the cost of the inventory components is moved through and accumulated in the accounts as the inventory flows through the production process. Exhibit 7–1 illustrates this flow of costs following the units being produced. At the end of production, the costs that have been accumulated must be assigned to all the units produced to determine the cost per unit for inventory valuation and cost of goods sold purposes.

Cost assignment in any production environment is essentially an averaging process. In general, and in the simplest of situations, a product's actual unit cost is found by dividing a period's departmental production costs by that period's departmental quantity of production. This average is expressed by the following formula:

$$\text{Unit Cost per Period} = \frac{\text{Sum of Production Costs}}{\text{Quantity of Production}}$$

Production costs include direct material, direct labor, and overhead.

The Numerator

The formula numerator is obtained by accumulating departmental costs incurred for a single time period. Since most companies manufacture more than one product, costs must be accumulated by product, not just by department.

Exhibit 7–2 presents the source documents and records used to initially assign costs to production departments during a period. The three products in the exhibit are started in the Mixing Department. Products A and B are transferred to Baking so that they will harden into their proper shapes. Product C, however, is made of a material that hardens without baking and, therefore, does not need to be processed in the second department. Production costs incurred in Mixing for Products A and B are transferred to Baking as the goods are transferred. Additional costs in the Baking Department will attach to the products before they are sent to Finished Goods. Product C will contain only material, labor, and overhead costs from the Mixing Department.

As was true in job order costing, the direct materials and direct labor components of product cost present relatively few problems for cost accumulation and assignment. Direct materials cost can be measured from the materials requisition slips and invoiced prices; direct labor cost can be determined from the employee time sheets and wage rates for the period. These costs are assigned at the end of the period (usually each month) from the departments to the units produced. In contrast to direct

EXHIBIT 7–2
▼▼▼▼▼▼▼▼▼▼

COST FLOWS AND COST ASSIGNMENTS

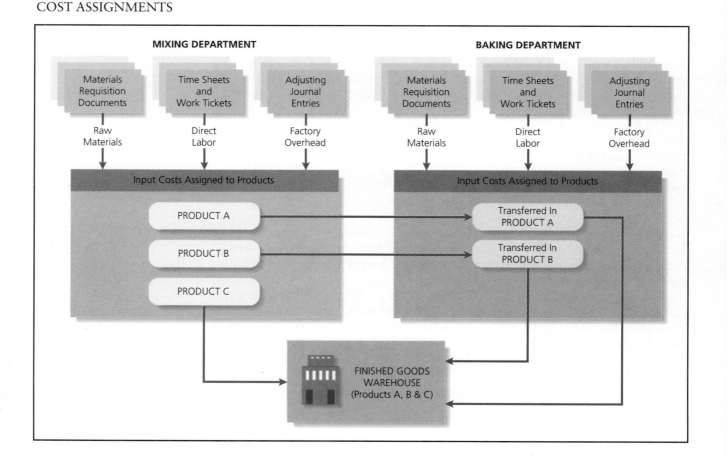

materials and direct labor, which are easily traced to products, overhead must be allocated in some manner to production.

Overhead may be assigned to products through the use of predetermined application rates, although actual costs are often used for product costing in process costing systems. If total actual overhead costs are relatively constant each period and production volume is relatively steady over time, using actual overhead costs will provide a fairly stable production cost. If such conditions do not exist, application of actual overhead will yield fluctuating product costs, and predetermined application rates should be used.

To summarize, the numerator in the average product cost fraction is the sum of the: (1) actual direct materials cost; (2) actual direct labor cost; and (3) actual or predetermined overhead cost. Costs are accumulated in individual departments and relate to the units of product worked on in those departments during the period.

The Denominator

The unit cost formula denominator represents total departmental production for the period. If all units were 100 percent complete at the end of each accounting period, units could simply be counted to obtain the denominator. But in most production processes, a Work in Process Inventory of partially completed units exists at the end of each period. Any partially completed ending inventory of the current period becomes the partially completed beginning inventory of the next period. Process costing assigns costs to both fully and partially completed units by converting partially completed units to equivalent whole units or **equivalent units of production.**

**equivalent units of
production**

Because of the aging process involved in making Tabasco pepper sauce, raw materials started during the current period cannot be fully completed by the end of the period. This condition necessitates the use of equivalent units of production to account for the work performed each period.

Equivalent units of production (EUP) are an approximation of the number of whole units of output that could have been produced during a period from the actual effort expended during that period. EUP are necessary because using only completed units to determine unit cost would not clearly reflect all the work accomplished during a period. Equivalent units of production are calculated by multiplying the number of actual, but incomplete, units produced by the respective percentage degree of completion and adding the results to the fully completed units for the period.

For example, assume the Mixing Department had no beginning inventory. During January, the Mixing Department produced 100,000 complete units and 10,000 units that were 20 percent complete. These partially complete units are in ending Work in Process Inventory. The period's equivalent units of production are 102,000 [(100,000 × 100%) + (10,000 × 20%)]. This quantity is the denominator of the formula used to calculate departmental unit product costs.

Use of equivalent units of production provides for the recognition of two facts. First, units in beginning WIP were started last period, but they will be completed during the current period. This two-period production sequence means that some costs related to these units were incurred last period and additional costs will be incurred in the current period. Second, partially completed units in the ending WIP Inventory were started in the current period, but they will not be completed until the next period. Thus, current period production efforts on the ending WIP Inventory caused costs to be incurred in this period and will cause additional costs to be incurred next period.

Qualified production personnel should inspect ending work in process units to determine the proportion of work that was completed during the current period. The mathematical complement to this proportion represents the amount of work that needs to be performed next period. Physical inspection at the end of last period provided the information about the work to be performed in the current period on the beginning inventory.

WEIGHTED AVERAGE AND FIFO PROCESS COSTING METHODS

A primary purpose of any costing system is to determine product costs for financial statement purposes. When goods are transferred from Work in Process Inventory to another department or to Finished Goods Inventory, a cost must be assigned to those goods. In addition, at the end of any period, a value must be assigned to goods that are only partially complete and still remain in Work in Process Inventory.

There are two alternative methods of accounting for cost flows in process costing: (1) the weighted average method and (2) the FIFO (first-in, first-out) method. These methods relate to the way in which cost flows are assumed to occur in the production process. In a very general way, it is helpful to relate these process costing approaches to the cost flow methods used in financial accounting.

In a retail business, the weighted average method is used to determine an average cost per unit of inventory. This cost is computed by dividing the total cost of goods available by total units available. Total cost and total units are found by adding purchases and beginning inventory. Costs and units of the current period are not distinguished in any way from those of the prior period. On the other hand, the FIFO method, in retail accounting, separates goods by when they were purchased and by their cost. Unit costs of beginning inventory are the first to be sent to Cost of Goods Sold; units in ending inventory are costed at the most recent purchase prices.

NEWS NOTE

FIFO EUP More Common Than Weighted Average

Many [textbook] authors construe the methodological simplicity of the [weighted] average cost approach as a genuine practical advantage. On the contrary, the computerization of cost accounting systems in manufacturing and access to personal computers with spreadsheet applications eliminate the computational disadvantages of learning FIFO.

The results of a recent survey of 112 manufacturing corporations indicate that 52% of these companies are using process costing in their basic cost accounting systems. Furthermore, 58% of the companies surveyed are using the FIFO cost flow assumption, whereas only 21% are using average cost.

The major shortcoming of the average method is that the costs of different periods are mixed together, and, as a result, interperiod variations in unit costs are concealed. The fact that process costing under the FIFO method is more informative than under the average approach reduces the likelihood of incorrect decisions by management with regard to controlling costs.

SOURCE: Rex C. Hauser, Frank R. Urbancic, and Donald E. Edwards, "Process Costing: Is It Relevant?" *Management Accounting* (December 1989), p. 53. Published by Institute of Management Accountants, Montvale, N.J.

The use of these methods in costing manufactured goods is similar to their use in costing retail purchases. The **weighted average method** computes an average cost per unit of production, while the **FIFO method** keeps beginning inventory and current period production and costs separate. The denominator used in the unit cost formula differs depending on which of the two methods is used. Both methods, however, generally result in approximately the same unit costs.

As in retail inventory, cost assignment is easier for the weighted average method than for the FIFO method. For this reason, weighted average is presented first in the following discussion. However, as discussed in the News Note above, simplicity does not always provide the best information. The FIFO method better reflects the actual physical flow of goods through production and, when period costs do fluctuate, provides managers better information with which to control costs and base decisions by not combining costs of different periods. In addition, the FIFO method focuses on current period cost. Managerial performance is evaluated on the basis of costs incurred only in the current period.

weighted average method
FIFO method

The Production Process

To begin a production operation, there must be an introduction of some direct material. Without any direct material, there would be no need for labor or overhead to be incurred. The material added at the start of production is 100 percent complete throughout the process regardless of the percentage of completion of labor and overhead. For example, to make Tabasco sauce, the pepper pods and salt must be added in full at the start of production.

Most production processes require more than one direct material. Additional materials may be added at any point or, possibly, continuously during processing. Materials may even be added at the end of processing. For example, the bottle and box for the Tabasco sauce are direct materials added at the end of processing. Thus, the Tabasco is 0 percent complete as to the bottle and the box (two direct materials) at any point in the production process, although other materials and some labor and overhead may have been incurred. The following production flow for the Tabasco-making process visually illustrates the need for separate EUP computations for each cost component.

The materials "pepper pods and salt" are 100 percent complete at any point in the previous process after the start of production; no additional peppers or salt are added later in production. When enough time, labor, and overhead have been added to reach the 80 percent completion point, a second material (vinegar) is added. Prior to 80 percent completion, the material "vinegar" was 0 percent complete; after the 80 percent point, the vinegar is 100 percent complete. After additional aging, more labor and overhead costs are incurred and, after inspection, the product is bottled and boxed at approximately a 99 percent completion point. More labor is needed to pack the boxes in cases for storage as a finished good. Thus, at the end of a month, any unbottled amounts of Tabasco remaining in Work in Process Inventory might be at least 80 percent complete as to labor and overhead. If this were true, the product would be 100 percent complete as to pepper pods, salt, and vinegar, but 0 percent complete as to bottles and boxes.

If all materials are at the same degree of completion, a single materials computation may be made. If multiple materials are used and are placed into production at

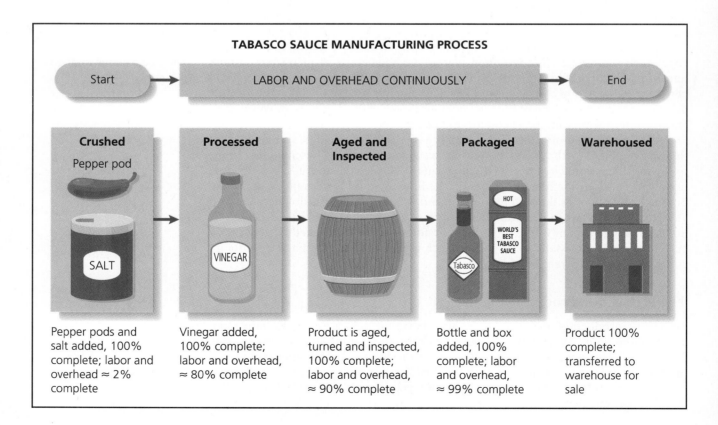

TABASCO SAUCE MANUFACTURING PROCESS

Start → LABOR AND OVERHEAD CONTINUOUSLY → End

Crushed	Processed	Aged and Inspected	Packaged	Warehoused
Pepper pod / SALT	VINEGAR		Tabasco / HOT WORLD'S BEST TABASCO SAUCE	
Pepper pods and salt added, 100% complete; labor and overhead ≈ 2% complete	Vinegar added, 100% complete; labor and overhead, ≈ 80% complete	Product is aged, turned and inspected, 100% complete; labor and overhead, ≈ 90% complete	Bottle and box added, 100% complete; labor and overhead, ≈ 99% complete	Product 100% complete; transferred to warehouse for sale

different points, it will be necessary to make multiple EUP calculations for materials. When overhead is applied on a direct labor basis or when direct labor and overhead are added to the product at the same rate, one percentage of completion estimate may be made and used for both conversion cost components.

For example, in the Tabasco discussion, the same number of equivalent units results for peppers and salt, for bottles and boxes, and for labor and overhead. However, separate calculations of unit cost may be desirable for each component. These separate calculations would give managers more information for planning and control purposes. Managers must weigh the costs of making separate calculations against the benefits from having the additional information. For illustrative purposes, however, single computations are made when cost components are always at equal percentages of completion.

Currently, overhead costs are more likely to be caused by cost drivers other than direct labor. Therefore, companies will probably begin making single computations for "conversion EUP" less often than in the past. For example, the cost driver of overhead in the production of Tabasco might be aging time. The longer the product ages, the more costs will be incurred for items such as storage building depreciation, insurance, and inspection. In such a case, it would be highly unlikely that the degrees of completion of direct labor and aging time will be equal.

The calculation of equivalent units of production requires that a cost flow be specified—either weighted average or FIFO. There is only one difference between the weighted average and FIFO process costing methods of *calculating* EUP. A comparison of the two methods demonstrates that this difference in the EUP calculations lies in the treatment of beginning inventory.

A company less complex than E. McIlhenny Sons is used to illustrate the steps for computing EUP and cost assignment for the weighted average and FIFO methods of process costing. Exhibit 7–3 provides selected production and cost information for the May 1993 operations of Avery Island Glass, which supplies the bottles used by E. McIlhenny Sons. The majority of the direct materials are added at the start of the process; these are referred to as a single component (Material A). Material B represents the boxes used to ship the bottles. Because the plant is highly automated, direct labor activity is limited and primarily occurs at the end of production. Overhead is

Beginning work in process (Material A, 100%; Material B, 0%; Labor, 20%; Overhead, 45%)		180,000 bottles
Units started during May		4,223,000
Units completed and transferred to finished goods		4,210,000
Ending work in process (Material A, 100%; Material B, 0%; Labor, 10%; Overhead, 30%)		193,000
Cost of beginning inventory:		
Material A	$ 37,315.00	
Material B	0	
Direct labor	24,566.50	
Overhead	78,330.40	$ 140,211.90
Current period costs:		
Material A	$358,955.00	
Material B	84,200.00	
Direct labor	398,363.50	
Overhead	519,175.60	1,360,694.10

EXHIBIT 7–3
▼▼▼▼▼▼▼▼▼▼▼

AVERY ISLAND GLASS PRODUCTION AND COST INFORMATION— MAY 1993

Mass production techniques are used by McIlhenny Co. to make Tabasco pepper sauce. A process costing system is used to accumulate all the costs of production and, at the end of each period, to average those costs over the units completed and the units still in process.

applied on the basis of machine hours. Thus, labor and overhead are not combined into a single conversion cost category. The percentage figures after the production information in Exhibit 7–3 refer to the degree of completion for that particular cost component.

Weighted Average Method

The weighted average method of computing equivalent units of production adds the units in beginning Work in Process Inventory to the new units started during the current period to determine the potential quantity of production for the period. The work performed during the period does not necessarily always result in complete, whole units. The weighted average method is *not* concerned about what quantity of work was performed in the prior period on the units in beginning inventory. This method focuses only on units that are *completed* in the current period and units that remain in ending inventory.

Step 1: Calculate the **total units to account for.**   **total units to account for**
    The total units to account for reflects all physical units worked on in the department during the current period—beginning inventory units plus units started.

Beginning inventory	180,000
Units started during current period	4,223,000
Units to account for	4,403,000

Step 2: Calculate the total units accounted for.
    This step reflects what happened to the units to account for (as determined in Step 1) during the period and also requires the use of physical units. At the end of the period, units are either completed and transferred out, or they are partially completed and remain in ending Work in Process Inventory.[1] This step verifies that the total units for which the department was responsible is equal to the total units that were accounted for. If these amounts are not equal, any additional computations will be incorrect.

Units completed and transferred out	4,210,000
Units in ending WIP inventory	193,000
Units accounted for	4,403,000

    The types of units detailed at this point (transferred out and in ending inventory) indicate the categories that will be assigned costs in the final step. The units accounted for in Step 2 equal the units to account for in Step 1.
    Completed units are either (1) beginning inventory units that have been completed during the current period or (2) units started and completed during the period. The number of **units started and completed** equals the total units completed during   **units started and completed** the period minus the units in beginning inventory. For Avery Island Glass, the number of units started and completed in May is 4,030,000 (4,210,000 − 180,000).

Step 3: Determine the equivalent units of production for each cost component (materials, labor, and overhead).
    The weighted average method does not distinguish between units in beginning inventory and units entering production during this period. This step uses the number of whole units in beginning inventory and the number of units started and completed (S&C) during the period. In this manner, the weighted average method is treating beginning inventory units as though they were started and completed in the current period. The weighted average computations for equivalent units of production are as follows:

---

[1]Another category, that of spoilage or damaged units, does exist. It is assumed, for purposes of simplicity in this text, that such happenings do not occur. Reference to any standard cost accounting text can be made for the treatment of spoilage and damaged units.

	Mat. A	Mat. B	DL	OH
BI (whole units)	180,000	180,000	180,000	180,000
Units S&C	4,030,000	4,030,000	4,030,000	4,030,000
EI (whole units × % complete)	193,000	0	19,300	57,900
EUP	4,403,000	4,210,000	4,229,300	4,267,900

Note that the first two lines of this schedule (BI and Units S&C) are equal to the total units completed and transferred out (4,210,000) given in Step 2 above.

Ending inventory is 100 percent complete as to Material A, but 0 percent complete as to Material B because boxes are not added until the end of the process. The ending inventory is 10 percent complete as to labor and 30 percent complete as to overhead cost. Only when all product components are placed into production at the same time and at the same rate will materials, labor, and overhead all be at equal percentages of completion. Generally, each cost component is at a different degree of completion. For this reason, the completion percentage must be separately determined *for each cost component*. If the percentages of completion differ, separate EUP calculations must be made for each cost component.

Step 4:   Determine the total cost to account for.

total cost to account for

The **total cost to account for** equals the costs included in beginning inventory plus current period costs. For Avery Island Glass, the total cost to account for is $1,500,906.

	Mat. A	Mat. B	DL	OH	Total
BI cost	$ 37,315	$ 0	$ 24,566.50	$ 78,330.40	$ 140,211.90
Current period costs	358,955	84,200	398,363.50	519,175.60	1,360,694.10
Total cost to account for	$396,270	$84,200	$422,930.00	$597,506.00	$1,500,906.00

Information is given on total costs for *each element of production:* direct materials (separated because A and B are at a different degree of completion), direct labor, and overhead. Total cost will be assigned in Step 6 to the goods transferred out to finished goods (or the next department) and to ending Work in Process Inventory in relation to the whole or equivalent whole units contained in each category.

Step 5:   Calculate the cost per equivalent unit of production.

A cost per equivalent unit of production must be computed for each cost component for which a separate calculation of EUP is made. Since the weighted average method does not distinguish between units in beginning inventory and units started during this period, neither does it differentiate between beginning inventory costs and current period costs. The costs of beginning inventory and the current period are summed for each cost component and averaged over that component's respective weighted average equivalent units of production. This calculation for unit cost for each cost component at the end of the period is as follows:

$$\text{Unit Cost} = \frac{\text{Beginning Inventory Cost} + \text{Current Period Cost}}{\text{Weighted Average Equivalent Units of Production}}$$

$$= \frac{\text{Total Cost Incurred}}{\text{Total Equivalent Units of Production}}$$

Under the weighted average method, costs and units (respectively) from two different periods are totaled to form the numerator and denominator used to calculate the average unit cost. This computation allows total costs to be divided by total units—the common weighted average approach that produces an average component cost per unit. Avery Island Glass's weighted average calculations for cost per EUP for materials, labor, and overhead are as follows:

	Mat. A	Mat. B	DL	OH	Total
BI cost	$37,315	$ 0	$ 24,566.50	$ 78,330.40	$ 140,211.90
Current period costs	358,955	84,200	398,363.50	519,175.60	1,360,694.10
Total cost to account for	$396,270	$84,200	$422,930.00	$597,506.00	$1,500,906.00
÷ EUP (Step 3)	4,403,000	4,210,000	4,229,300	4,267,900	
Cost per EUP	$.09	$.02	$.10	$.14	$.35

The unit costs for the four product cost components (Materials A and B, labor, and overhead) are summed to find the total production cost for all whole units completed during May. For Avery Island Glass, this cost is $.35 ($.09 + $.02 + $.10 + $.14).

Step 6:   Assign costs to inventories and prepare a cost reconciliation.

This step assigns total production costs to units of product. Cost assignment in a department involves determining the cost of (1) goods completed and transferred out during the period and (2) the units in ending Work in Process Inventory.

The cost of goods transferred out using the weighted average method is found by multiplying the total number of units transferred by the total cost per EUP, which combines all component costs. Because this method is based on an averaging technique that combines both prior and current period work, the period in which the transferred units were started is not important. All units and all costs have been commingled. The total cost transferred out for Avery Island Glass for May is $1,473,500 ($.35 × 4,210,000).

Ending WIP inventory cost is calculated using the equivalent units of production for each cost component. The EUP are multiplied by the component cost per unit calculated in Step 5. Cost of ending inventory using the weighted average method is:

Ending WIP inventory:	
Material A (193,000 × 100% × $.09)	$17,370
Material B (193,000 × 0% × $.02)	0
Direct labor (193,000 × 10% × $.10)	1,930
Overhead (193,000 × 30% × $.14)	8,106
Total cost of ending inventory	$27,406

Note that Material B does not need to be in the schedule because the ending inventory was 0 percent complete as to this cost element. The quantities that result from multiplying whole units by the percentage of completion are equal to the equivalent units of production.

The total costs assigned to transferred-out units and units in ending inventory must equal the total cost to account for. For Avery Island Glass, total cost to account for (Step 4) was determined as $1,500,906, which equals transferred-out cost ($1,473,500) plus ending work in process cost ($27,406).

The steps just discussed can be combined into a **Production and Cost Report.** This document details all manufacturing quantities and costs, shows the computation of cost per EUP, and indicates the cost assignment to goods produced during the period. Exhibit 7–4 shows the Production and Cost Report for Avery Island Glass using the weighted average method process costing method.

FIFO Method

The FIFO method of determining EUP more realistically reflects the way in which most goods actually flow through the production system. The FIFO method does *not* commingle units and costs of different periods. Equivalent units and costs of beginning inventory are withheld from the computation of average current period cost. FIFO focuses specifically on the work performed *during the current period.*

Using the data from Exhibit 7–3, steps 1 and 2 are the same for the FIFO method as for the weighted average method because these two steps involve the use of physical units. Therefore, the total units to account for and accounted for are 4,403,000.

Step 3: Determine the equivalent units of production.

Under FIFO, the work performed last period is *not* commingled with work of the current period. The EUP schedule for FIFO is:

	Mat. A	Mat. B	DL	OH
BI (EUP *not* completed in the prior period)	0	180,000	144,000	99,000
Units S&C	4,030,000	4,030,000	4,030,000	4,030,000
EI (whole units × % complete)	193,000	0	19,300	57,900
EUP	4,223,000	4,210,000	4,193,300	4,186,900

Under FIFO, only the work performed on the beginning inventory *during the current period* is shown in the EUP schedule. This work equals the whole units in beginning inventory multiplied by (1 − the percentage of work done in the prior period). Thus, if a unit was 40 percent complete as to labor at the end of last period, an additional 60 percent of the total needs to be added during the current period for that unit to be complete.

In the Avery Island Glass example, no additional Material A is needed in May to complete the 180,000 units in the beginning inventory. However, no boxes (Material B) were included in that beginning inventory, so all beginning inventory needed to be boxed. Since beginning inventory was only 20 percent complete as to

Production Data		Equivalent Units of Production			
	Whole Units	Mat. A	Mat. B	DL	OH
BI	180,000*	180,000	0	36,000	81,000
Units started	4,223,000				
To account for	4,403,000				
BI completed	180,000	0	180,000	144,000	99,000
S&C	4,030,000	4,030,000	4,030,000	4,030,000	4,030,000
Units completed	4,210,000				
EI	193,000**	193,000	0	19,300	57,900
Accounted for	4,403,000	4,403,000	4,210,000	4,229,300	4,267,900

Cost Data

	Total	Mat. A	Mat. B	DL	OH
BI cost	$ 140,211.90	$ 37,315	$ 0	$ 24,566.50	$ 78,330.40
Current					
period costs	1,360,694.10	358,955	84,200	398,363.50	519,175.60
Total cost to					
account for	$1,500,906.00	$396,270	$84,200	$422,930.00	$597,506.00
Divided by EUP		4,403,000	4,210,000	4,229,300	4,267,900
Cost per EUP	$.35	$.09	$.02	$.10	$.14

Cost Assignment

Transferred out (4,210,000 × $.35)				$1,473,500	
Ending inventory:					
Material A (193,000 × $.09)			$17,370		
Direct labor (19,300 × $.10)			1,930		
Overhead (57,900 × $.14)			8,106	27,406	
Total cost accounted for				$1,500,906	

*Fully complete as to Material A; 0% as to Material B; 20% as to labor; 45% as to overhead.
**Fully complete as to Material A; 0% as to Material B; 10% as to labor; 30% as to overhead.

EXHIBIT 7–4
▼▼▼▼▼▼▼▼▼▼▼▼

AVERY ISLAND
GLASS PRODUCTION
AND COST REPORT
FOR MONTH ENDED
MAY 31, 1993
(WEIGHTED
AVERAGE METHOD)

labor, the company needs to do 80 percent more labor work on the goods during May. Overhead was estimated at the beginning of the period to be 45 percent complete, so 55 percent more of the overhead work must be accomplished during the current period, or the equivalent of 99,000 units (55% × 180,000).

The remaining figures in the FIFO EUP schedule are the same as those of the weighted average method. The *only* difference between the weighted average and FIFO EUP computations is that the work performed in the prior period on beginning inventory is not included in current period EUP. This difference is equal to the number of units in beginning inventory multiplied by the percentage of work performed in the prior period, as follows:

	Mat. A	Mat. B	DL	OH
FIFO EUP	4,223,000	4,210,000	4,193,300	4,186,900
Plus the EUP in BI (work completed in the prior period: Mat. A, 100%; Mat. B, 0%; Labor, 20%; Overhead, 45%)	180,000	0	36,000	81,000
Weighted Average EUP	4,403,000	4,210,000	4,229,300	4,267,900

Step 4:   Determine the total cost to account for.

This step is the same as it was under the weighted average method. The total cost to account for is $1,500,906.

Step 5:   Calculate the cost per equivalent unit of production.

Since cost determination is made on the basis of equivalent units of production, different results will be obtained for the weighted average and FIFO methods. The calculations for cost per equivalent unit reflect the difference in the quantity that each method uses for beginning inventory. Since the EUP calculation for FIFO ignores work performed on beginning inventory during the prior period, the FIFO cost per EUP computation also ignores prior period costs and uses only costs incurred in the current period. The FIFO cost per EUP calculation is:

$$\text{Unit Cost} = \frac{\text{Current Period Cost}}{\text{FIFO Equivalent Units of Production}}$$

Calculations for Avery Island Glass are:

	Mat. A	Mat. B	DL	OH	Total
Current period costs	$358,955	$84,200	$398,363.50	$519,175.60	$1,360,694.10
÷ EUP (Step 3)	4,223,000	4,210,000	4,193,300	4,186,900	
Cost per EUP	$.085	$.02	$.095	$.124	$.324

The production cost for each whole unit produced during May under the FIFO method is $.324 ($.085 + $.02 + $.095 + $.124).

It is useful to recognize the difference between the two total cost computations. The weighted average total cost of $.35 is the average total cost of each unit completed during May, *regardless of when production was begun.* The FIFO total cost of $.324 is the total cost of each unit that was produced *(both started and completed)* during the current period. The $.026 difference ($.350 − $.324) is caused by the difference in treatment of beginning Work in Process Inventory costs.

Step 6:   Assign costs to inventories and prepare a cost reconciliation.

The FIFO method assumes that the units in beginning inventory are the first units completed during the current period and, thus, are the first units transferred out. The remaining units transferred out during the period were both started and completed in the current period. As shown in the Production and Cost Report in Exhibit 7–5, the two-step computation needed to determine the cost of goods transferred out distinctly presents this FIFO logic.

The first part of the cost assignment for units transferred out relates to the units that were in beginning inventory. These units had Material A and some labor and overhead costs attached to them at the start of the period. These prior period costs were *not* included in the cost per EUP calculations in Step 5 above. Finishing these units required current period work and, therefore, current period costs. To determine the total cost of producing the units in beginning inventory, the costs associated with the beginning inventory are added to the current period costs needed to complete the goods.

EXHIBIT 7–5

AVERY ISLAND GLASS PRODUCTION AND COST REPORT FOR MONTH ENDED MAY 31, 1993 (FIFO METHOD)

Production Data		Equivalent Units of Production			
	Whole Units	Mat. A	Mat. B	DL	OH
BI	180,000*	180,000	0	36,000	81,000
Units started	4,223,000				
To account for	4,403,000				
BI completed	180,000	0	180,000	144,000	99,000
S&C	4,030,000	4,030,000	4,030,000	4,030,000	4,030,000
Units completed	4,210,000				
EI	193,000**	193,000	0	19,300	57,900
Accounted for	4,403,000	4,223,000	4,210,000	4,193,300	4,186,900

Cost Data

	Total	Mat. A	Mat. B	DL	OH
BI cost	$ 140,211.90				
Current period costs	1,360,694.10	$358,955	$84,200	$398,363.50	$519,175.60
Total cost to account for	$1,500,906.00				
Divided by EUP		4,223,000	4,210,000	4,193,300	4,186,900
Cost per EUP	$.324	$.085	$.02	$.095	$.124

Cost Assignment

Transferred out:
BI costs .... $ 140,211.90
Cost to complete:
Material B (180,000 × $.02) 3,600.00
Direct labor (144,000 × $.095) 13,680.00
Overhead (99,000 × $.124) 12,276.00
Cost of BI transferred .... $ 169,767.90
Started & completed (4,030,000 × $.324) 1,305,720.00 $1,475,487.90
Ending inventory:
Material A (193,000 × $.085) .... $ 16,405.00
Direct labor (19,300 × $.095) 1,833.50
Overhead (57,900 × $.124) 7,179.60   25,418.10
Total cost accounted for $1,500,906.00

*Fully complete as to Material A; 0% as to Material B; 20% as to labor; 45% as to overhead. Note: The quantities under EUP for this line are *not* included in the final EUP summation.
**Fully complete as to Material A; 0% as to Material B; 10% as to labor; 30% as to overhead.

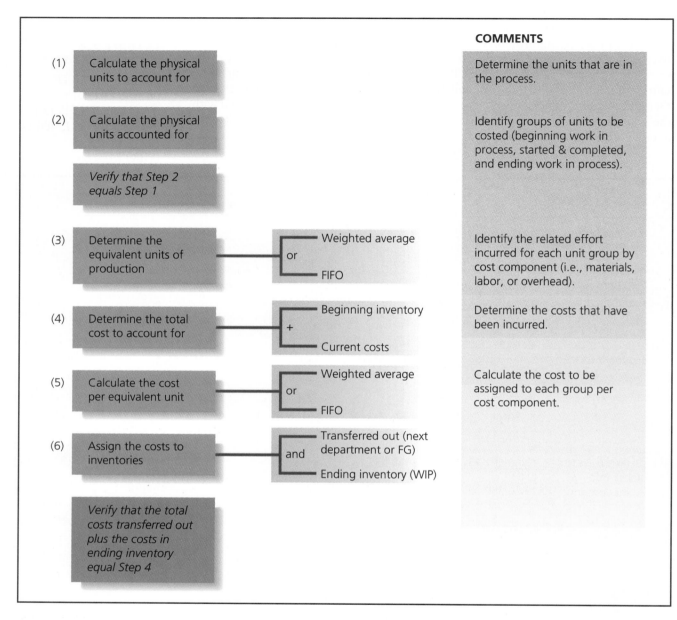

COMMENTS

(1) Calculate the physical units to account for — Determine the units that are in the process.

(2) Calculate the physical units accounted for

Verify that Step 2 equals Step 1 — Identify groups of units to be costed (beginning work in process, started & completed, and ending work in process).

(3) Determine the equivalent units of production — Weighted average or FIFO — Identify the related effort incurred for each unit group by cost component (i.e., materials, labor, or overhead).

(4) Determine the total cost to account for — Beginning inventory + Current costs — Determine the costs that have been incurred.

(5) Calculate the cost per equivalent unit — Weighted average or FIFO — Calculate the cost to be assigned to each group per cost component.

(6) Assign the costs to inventories — Transferred out (next department or FG) and Ending inventory (WIP)

Verify that the total costs transferred out plus the costs in ending inventory equal Step 4

EXHIBIT 7–6

▼▼▼▼▼▼▼▼▼▼▼▼

STEPS IN PROCESS COSTING

The second part of the cost assignment for units transferred out relates to the units that were started and completed in the current period. The cost of these units is computed using current period costs.

This two-step transferred-out cost assignment process is shown next using the Avery Island Glass information. The company had 180,000 units in the beginning May inventory and transferred out a total of 4,210,000 units during the month.

Transferred out:
    (1) Beginning inventory (prior period costs) $ 140,211.90
        Completion of beginning inventory:
            Material A (180,000 × 0% × $.085)   0

Material B (180,000 × 100% × $.02)   3,600.00
Direct labor (180,000 × 80% × $.095)   13,680.00
Overhead (180,000 × 55% × $.124)   12,276.00
Total cost of beginning inventory transferred $ 169,767.90
(2) Units started & completed (4,030,000 × $.324)   1,305,720.00
Total cost of units transferred out $1,475,487.90

Since the beginning inventory units were 100 percent complete as to Material A, no additional Material A needed to be added during the month. None of the beginning inventory units contained Material B, so 100 percent was added during May. Labor and overhead at the start of the month were only 20 percent and 45 percent complete, respectively, so 80 percent and 55 percent of the labor and overhead work are added during May at current period costs. The units started and completed are costed at the total current period FIFO cost of $.324, since all work on these units was performed during the current period.

Calculation of the cost of ending Work in Process Inventory is the same under both the FIFO and weighted average methods. Although cost per unit differs, the number of equivalent units of production is the same under both methods. Ending work in process cost using FIFO is as follows:

Ending inventory:
Material A (193,000 × 100% × $.085) $16,405.00
Material B (193,000 × 0% × $.02)   0
Direct labor (193,000 × 10% × $.095)   1,833.50
Overhead (193,000 × 30% × $.124)   7,179.60
Total cost of ending inventory $25,418.10

The total cost of the units transferred ($1,475,487.90) plus the cost of the ending inventory units ($25,418.10) equals the total cost to be accounted for ($1,500,906). These computations are included in the FIFO Production and Cost Report shown on page 289.

Exhibit 7–6 summarizes the six computational steps just discussed. These steps are necessary to determine the costs assignable to the units completed and to those still in ending inventory at the end of a period in a process costing system.

PROCESS COSTING WITH STANDARD COSTS

All examples in the chapter use historical actual costs to assign values to products under either the weighted average or the FIFO method. Companies may prefer to use standard rather than actual costs for inventory valuation purposes. The use of standard costs simplifies process costing and allows variances to be measured during the period. Actual costing requires that a new production cost be computed each production period. Standard costing eliminates such recomputations, although standards do need to be reviewed (and possibly revised) at a minimum of once a year in order to keep the amounts current.

Calculations for equivalent units of production for standard process costing are identical to those of FIFO process costing. Unlike the weighted average method, the emphasis of both standard costing and FIFO is on the measurement and control of current production and current period costs. The weighted average method commingles both units and costs of the prior period with those of the current period. This commingling reduces the emphasis on current effort that standard costing is intended to represent and measure.

In a standard cost process costing system, actual costs of the current period are compared to the standard costs of the equivalent units of production. If actual costs are less than standard, there is a favorable variance; unfavorable variances arise if the actual costs are greater than the standard. Units are transferred out of a department at the standard cost of each production element.

PROCESS COSTING IN A MULTIDEPARTMENT SETTING

Most companies have multiple, rather than single, processing facilities. In a multi-department processing environment, goods are transferred from a predecessor department to a successor department. For example, the production of Tabasco sauce could not be completed in a single department primarily because of the aging process.

As illustrated in Exhibit 7–1, manufacturing costs always follow the physical flow of goods. Therefore, the costs of the completed units of predecessor departments are treated as an input material cost in successor departments. This treatment requires the use of an additional cost component element called *transferred-in*. This element always has a percentage of completion factor of 100 percent, since the goods would not have been transferred from the predecessor department without being fully com-

Aged red pepper mash and vinegar are the raw materials in this unfinished Tabasco pepper sauce slurry. When properly filtered, this mixture is the finished product of one department and becomes the transferred-in cost product of the bottling department.

plete. The transferred-in element is handled the same as any other cost element in the calculations of EUP and cost per EUP.

A successor department may add additional raw materials to the units that have been transferred in or may simply provide additional labor with the corresponding incurrence of overhead. Anything added in the successor department requires its own cost element column for calculating equivalent units of production and cost per equivalent unit (unless the additional elements have the same degree of completion, at which point they can be combined).

Occasionally, successor departments may change the unit of measure from predecessor departments. For example, E. McIlhenny Sons may consider the measure in the first department (Crushing) to be in pounds. After crushing the peppers and salt, the mixture is then aged in 400-pound barrels. Thus, the Aging Department measure is probably in barrels. If the Crushing Department showed 16,000 pounds of mixture as the EUP transferred out, the Aging Department would need to record it as 40 barrels (16,000 ÷ 400) of EUP transferred in.

Exhibit 7–7 provides a Production and Cost Report illustration for the Aging Department at the Tabasco sauce plant. No materials are added in the Aging Department. The beginning inventory is assumed to be fully complete as to transferred-in

EXHIBIT 7–7
▼▼▼▼▼▼▼▼▼▼▼▼

MULTIDEPARTMENT
SETTING—AGING
DEPARTMENT
(WEIGHTED
AVERAGE METHOD)

Production Data		Equivalent Units of Production		
	Whole Units	Transferred-In	DL	OH
BI (in barrels)	600	600	480	360
Units transferred-in	10,000			
To account for	10,600			
BI completed	600	0	120	240
S&C	9,300	9,300	9,300	9,300
Units completed	9,900			
EI	700	700	490	560
Accounted for	10,600	10,600	10,390	10,460

Cost Data				
	Total	Transferred-In	DL	OH
BI cost	$ 1,450,310	$ 998,000	$ 61,560	$ 390,750
Current period costs	28,898,490	16,640,400	1,268,360	10,989,730
Total cost to account for	$30,348,800	$17,638,400	$1,329,920	$11,380,480
Divided by EUP		10,600	10,390	10,460
Cost per EUP	$2,880	$1,664	$128	$1,088

Cost Assignment				
Transferred out (9,900 × $2,880)			$28,512,000	
Ending inventory:				
Transferred-in (700 × $1,664)		$1,164,800		
Direct labor (490 × $128)		62,720		
Overhead (560 × $1,088)		609,280	1,836,800	
Total cost accounted for			$30,348,800	

materials and cost, 80 percent complete as to labor, and 60 percent complete as to overhead. These 10,000 barrels represent 4,000,000 pounds of mixture. The per-unit cost of the mixture that left the Crushing Department was multiplied by 400 to determine the cost per barrel in the Aging Department. Each pound of mixture can make 8 bottles of Tabasco; bottles will be used as the unit of measure in the next department. The ending inventory is assumed to be fully complete as to transferred-in materials and cost, 70 percent complete as to labor, and 80 percent complete as to overhead. The Aging Department uses the weighted average process costing method. Assumed information is provided for costs.

REPETITIVE MANUFACTURING

Manufacturing techniques have traditionally been of two types: job order and process. But because of the rapidly changing manufacturing environment, many new process technologies are emerging. One of these is **repetitive manufacturing,** in which company output is a large volume of homogeneous products that have been fabricated, machined, assembled, and tested. Exhibit 7–8 presents the comparative characteristics of each type of manufacturing system.

Job order costing is not appropriate in a repetitive manufacturing environment because it is not designed to account for continuous processing of large volumes of like products. Process costing, while designed for large volumes of like products, is best employed for continuous flows of products such as liquids or powders. Repetitive manufacturing produces discrete units of products rather than continuous flows. In a repetitive manufacturing operation, direct labor cost is usually a minimal amount of total product cost. In addition, repetitive manufacturing often makes use of the

EXHIBIT 7–8
▼▼▼▼▼▼▼▼▼▼▼

COMPARATIVE
CHARACTERISTICS
OF
MANUFACTURING
PROCESSING

Characteristic	Job Order	Process	Repetitive Manufacturing
Volume	Low	High	High
Nature of product	Each job is different	Uniform product such as fluids or powders produced continuously	Standard products in discrete units
Process time	Long	Long	Short
Direct labor content	High	Varies; large enough to require accounting for	Very small
Work in process levels	High	Varies; large enough to require accounting for	Minimal

SOURCE: Rick Hunt, Linda Garrett, and C. Mike Merz, "Direct Labor Cost Not Always Relevant at H-P," *Management Accounting* (February 1985), p. 59. Published by Institute of Management Accountants, Montvale, N.J.

NEWS NOTE

H-P Makes Some Significant Accounting Changes

Job order costing is not appropriate for repetitive manufacturing because the job order system is not suited for controlling a very high volume of standardized products. Attempted use of a job order costing system at Hewlett-Packard frustrated line managers and production workers because they could not physically differentiate between the products in different orders that were being worked on. In order to keep the process flowing efficiently, workers and materials were frequently traded between orders which confounded the cost accounting system's attempt to track the costs of each order.

In order to adapt its manufacturing environment and to provide useful management information, some Hewlett-Packard divisions made the following changes in their cost accounting systems:

1. Eliminate Direct Labor Cost Category. Because direct labor comprises such a small percent of total product cost—only 3% to 5%—the continual effort to prepare standard labor costs and then variances from these standards had little potential impact upon overall cost control.

2. Treat Manufacturing Overhead as an Expense. Implementing the JIT concept drastically lowered inventory levels and reduced the time between the start of production and delivery of finished goods. Virtually all of the manufacturing overhead incurred each month, now including direct labor, flowed through to cost of goods sold in the same month. Tracking overhead through work-in-process and finished goods provided no useful information.

The net result of these changes is that Hewlett-Packard realized significant savings in staff time and costs without any significant changes in costs reported on their financial statements, or costs used in planning and controlling production, or costs analyzed for pricing or [other] decisions.

SOURCE: Rick Hunt, Linda Garrett, and C. Mike Merz, "Direct Labor Cost Not Always Relevant at H-P," *Management Accounting* (February 1985), p. 58ff. Published by Institute of Management Accountants, Montvale, N.J.

just-in-time inventory concept of maintaining minimal levels of Work in Process Inventory. The preceding News Note provides some information on the use of repetitive manufacturing techniques at Hewlett-Packard and the resulting impacts on the accounting system.

Product costing systems will continue to evolve as production environments evolve. Job order and process costing really represent two ends of a continuum of product costing methods. The new manufacturing techniques are likely to eliminate direct labor as a separate cost component in many companies and use, in its place, a cost of technology. Activity-based costing will be of great import in repetitive environments because of the mass production of highly differentiated products. This differentiation will, in turn, cause significant increases in overhead costs and, therefore, will necessitate the use of better overhead allocation techniques and cost drivers that focus on changeovers and customer specifications.

SITE ANALYSIS

At E. McIlhenny Sons, production costs cannot be traced directly to individual bottles of Tabasco. Costs, however, can be traced in total, department by department, to the production output that flowed through each department. As the Tabasco (in pounds, barrels, or bottles) flows through the process, the costs of the various elements of production are accumulated and averaged over the completed and incomplete output at the end of the period. Because cost assignment is based on equivalent units, the estimate of the degree of completion must be as accurate as possible. If such estimates are inaccurate, the resulting costs will be less than useful to managers.

In addition, for costs to be most accurate, overhead costs should be accumulated in multiple cost pools—each with its most appropriate cost driver. E. McIlhenny Sons may find that one overhead EUP computation per department is not enough because multiple cost pools are included within a department. For example, some overhead costs in the "Turning" department might be related to the direct labor inspections by a McIlhenny family member, while others are related to the automated equipment that turns the aged slurry.

A costing system should provide four basic functions: estimate product cost, provide information to external parties (through financial statements and other necessary forms), permit operational control, and help in decision making such as product pricing. To do these things, a costing system should reflect the production environment in which that system operates. Even at McIlhenny, where the company philosophy is "Don't change anything that you don't have to," management recognizes the need to update production techniques. Such updates will, for most companies, affect the accounting and costing systems.

The Applications Strategies for process costing follows.

APPLICATIONS STRATEGIES FOR PROCESS COSTING	Discipline	Applications
	Accounting	Used for mass production in long processing runs of fluids and powders; short runs of discrete units with little direct labor and minimal work in process should use a variation of process costing for repetitive manufacturing.
	Economics	Can provide accurate product costs for economic decisions based on the best information available; competitive pricing depends on having good information from a costing system that reflects the underlying economic nature of the production process.
	Finance	Helps in preparing accurate financial reports for companies engaging in mass production of homogeneous output; capital analysis is partially dependent upon the ability to generate and predict accurate unit costs.
	Management	Helps in conducting planning, controlling, problem solving, and evaluating functions.
	Marketing	Useful for competitive pricing and for making rational decisions about which products to promote (based on the relative profitability of products).

CHAPTER SUMMARY

Process costing is used in manufacturing companies producing large quantities of homogeneous products. It is essentially an averaging method used to assign manufacturing costs to units of production for purposes of planning, controlling, decision making, and preparing financial statements.

Either the weighted average or the FIFO method can be used to compute equivalent units of production and assign costs in a process costing system. The difference between the two methods lies solely in the treatment of the work performed in the prior period on the beginning Work in Process Inventory. Under the weighted average method, work performed in the prior period is combined with current period work and the total costs are averaged over all units. Using the FIFO method, work done in the last period on beginning Work in Process Inventory is not commingled with current period work, nor are costs of beginning Work in Process added to current period costs to derive unit production cost. With FIFO, current period costs are divided by current period production to generate a unit production cost related entirely to work actually performed in the current period.

The six basic steps necessary in deriving and assigning product cost under a process costing system are listed in Exhibit 7–6 and in the Solution Strategies at the end of the chapter. Calculations of equivalent units of production must be made for each cost component. The cost components include transferred-in costs (if multidepartmental), direct materials, direct labor, and overhead. In cases of multiple materials having different degrees of completion, each material is considered a separate cost component. If overhead is applied on a direct labor basis or is incurred at the same rate as direct labor, labor and overhead may be combined as a single cost component and referred to as "conversion."

Companies in multidepartment process environments will need to track costs continuously throughout each department as the goods move from one department to the next. The tracking is handled through the use of a transferred-in cost component for purposes of EUP and cost per EUP computations.

A new type of manufacturing environment, repetitive manufacturing, is becoming a part of the U.S. economy. Repetitive manufacturing involves significant automation, which has affected company costs and costing processes.

APPENDIX

Journal Entries Related to Avery Island Glass

Summary journal entries and T-accounts for the Avery Island Glass month of May example given in the chapter follow. For these entries, the following four assumptions are made: sales for May were 4,000,000 bottles; all sales were on account for $.73 per unit; a perpetual FIFO inventory system is used; and Avery Island Glass began May with no Finished Goods Inventory.

1. Work in Process Inventory	358,955.00	
Raw Materials Inventory—A		358,955.00
To record issuance of Material A to production		
2. Work in Process Inventory	398,363.50	
Wages Payable		398,363.50
To accrue wages for direct labor		
3. Manufacturing Overhead	519,175.60	
Various accounts		519,175.60
To record actual overhead costs for May		
4. Work in Process Inventory	84,200.00	
Raw Materials Inventory—B		84,200.00
To record issuance of Material B to production		
5. Work in Process Inventory	519,175.60	
Manufacturing Overhead		519,175.60
To apply actual overhead to production in May		
6. Finished Goods Inventory	1,475,487.90	
Work in Process Inventory		1,475,487.90
To transfer cost of completed units to finished goods. (Entry would be for $1,473,500 if weighted average were used.)		
7. Cost of Goods Sold	1,407,447.90	
Finished Goods Inventory		1,407,447.90
To transfer cost of goods sold from FG to expense account, using FIFO:		

First 180,000 units $ 169,767.90
Remaining 3,820,000
   units at $.324   <u>1,237,680.00</u>
            <u>$1,407,447.90</u>

(Entry would be for $1,400,000 if weighted average were used—4,000,000 × $.35)

8. Accounts Receivable	2,920,000.00	
Sales		2,920,000.00
To record May sales on account ($4,000,000 × $.73)		

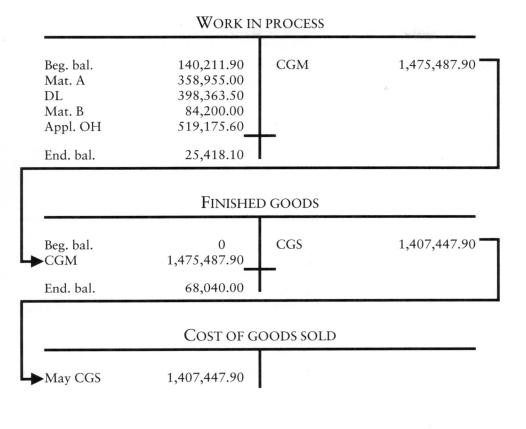

AVERY ISLAND GLASS T-ACCOUNTS

WORK IN PROCESS

Beg. bal.	140,211.90	CGM	1,475,487.90
Mat. A	358,955.00		
DL	398,363.50		
Mat. B	84,200.00		
Appl. OH	519,175.60		
End. bal.	25,418.10		

FINISHED GOODS

Beg. bal.	0	CGS	1,407,447.90
CGM	1,475,487.90		
End. bal.	68,040.00		

COST OF GOODS SOLD

May CGS	1,407,447.90

GLOSSARY

Equivalent units of production an approximation of the number of whole units of output that could have been produced during a period from the actual effort expended during that period

FIFO method a method of process costing that computes an average cost per equivalent unit of production using only current period production and cost information; units and costs in beginning inventory are separately sent to the next department or to Finished Goods Inventory, as appropriate

Process costing a method of accumulating and assigning costs to units of production in companies that make large quantities of homogeneous products

Process costing system a costing system in which costs are accumulated for each cost component in each department and assigned to all of the units that flow through the department

Production and Cost Report a document used in a process costing system; details all manufacturing quantities and costs, shows the computation of cost per EUP, and indicates the cost assignment to goods produced during the period

Repetitive manufacturing   a new manufacturing process in which company output consists of a large volume of homogeneous products that have been fabricated, machined, assembled, and tested

Total cost to account for   the balance in Work in Process at the beginning of the period plus all current costs for direct materials, direct labor, and overhead

Total units to account for   all units that were worked on in the department during the current period; consists of beginning inventory units plus units started

Units started and completed   the total units completed during the period minus the units in beginning inventory

Weighted average method   a method of process costing that computes an average cost per equivalent unit of production; combines beginning inventory units and costs with current production and costs, respectively, to compute that average

SELECTED BIBLIOGRAPHY

Collins, Don E. "How Borg-Warner Made the Transition from Pile Accounting to JIT." *Management Accounting* (October 1990), pp. 32–35.

Falhaber, Thomas A., et al. "Building a Process Cost Management System from the Bottom Up." *Management Accounting* (May 1988), pp. 58–62.

SOLUTION STRATEGIES

1. Compute whole units to account for:

    Beginning inventory in whole units
    + Units started (or transferred in) during period

2. Compute whole units accounted for:

    Units completed and transferred out
    + Ending inventory in whole units

3. Compute equivalent units of production per cost component:

    a. Weighted average

       Beginning inventory in whole units
       + Units started and completed*
       + (Ending inventory × % complete)

    b. FIFO

       (Beginning inventory × % not complete at start of period)
       + Units started and completed*
       + (Ending inventory × % complete)

4. Compute total costs to account for:

    Costs in beginning inventory
    + Costs of current period

5. Compute cost per equivalent unit per cost component:

a. Weighted average

Cost of component in beginning inventory
+ Cost of component for current period
= Total cost
÷ EUP for component

b. FIFO

Cost of component for current period
÷ EUP for component

6. Assign costs to inventories:

a. Weighted average
   1. Transferred out
      Whole units transferred × (Total cost per EUP for all components)
   2. Ending inventory
      EUP for each component × Cost per EUP for each component

b. FIFO
   1. Transferred out:
      Beginning inventory costs
      + (Beginning inventory × % not complete at beginning of period for each
         component × Cost per EUP for each component)
      + (Units started and completed × Total cost per EUP for all components)
   2. Ending inventory:
      EUP for each component × Cost per EUP for each component

*Units started and completed = (Units transferred out − Units in beginning inventory)

DEMONSTRATION PROBLEM

The Big Muddy Brick Company, located near St. Louis, Missouri, manufactures a
high-quality brick which is used in residential and commercial construction. The firm
is small but highly automated and typically produces about 300,000 bricks per
month. A brick is formed in a continuous production operation. In the initial step, a
tightly controlled mixture of soils and water is forced into a brick mold that travels
on a continuous conveyor belt. No other materials are required to produce a brick.
The conveyor belt moves at a snail's pace, and each brick spends two to three days
on the conveyor belt before it emerges at the end of the factory as a finished brick.
Approximately the last thirty-six hours on the conveyor belt are spent inside a gigan-
tic oven which removes a substantial portion of the moisture from the product. The
actual time each brick spends on the conveyor is dependent upon temperature and
humidity conditions inside and outside of the plant building. The speed of the conveyor is controlled and monitored by a computer. The firm uses a process costing
system based on actual costs to assign production costs to output. Costs are accumulated in three cost pools: materials, direct labor, and overhead. The following are
cost and production data for the month of November 1993.

Beginning Work in Process Inventory	25,000 bricks
This inventory is 100% complete as to materials, 60% complete as to direct labor, and 36% complete as to overhead.	
Started this period	305,000 bricks
Ending Work in Process Inventory	30,000 bricks
This inventory is 100% complete as to materials, 50% complete as to direct labor, and 40% complete as to overhead.	

Costs:	Materials	Direct Labor	Overhead
Beginning inventory	$ 1,330	$ 435	$ 852
Costs incurred in November	12,200	15,000	18,180

Required:

a. Using the six steps discussed in the text (and summarized in the Solution Strategies), determine the cost of the bricks in ending WIP and the cost of bricks transferred to Finished Goods Inventory for November 1993. Assume the company uses the weighted average method.

b. Repeat part (a), assuming the company uses the FIFO method.

Solution to Demonstration Problem

a. Weighted average:

Step 1: Calculate total units to account for:

Beginning inventory	25,000
Units started during current period	305,000
Units to account for	330,000

Step 2: Calculate the total units accounted for:

Units completed and transferred out	300,000
Units in ending WIP inventory	30,000
Units accounted for	330,000

Step 3: Determine the equivalent units of production:

	Materials	Direct Labor	Overhead
BI (whole units)	25,000	25,000	25,000
Units started and completed	275,000	275,000	275,000
EI (whole units × % complete)	30,000	15,000	12,000
EUP	330,000	315,000	312,000

Step 4: Determine the total cost to account for:

	Materials	Direct Labor	Overhead
BI cost	$ 1,330	$ 435	$ 852
Current period cost	12,200	15,000	18,180
Total cost to account for	$13,530	$15,435	$19,032

Total all cost pools = $13,530 + $15,435 + $19,032 = $47,997

Step 5: Calculate the cost per equivalent unit of production:

	Materials	Direct Labor	Overhead
Total cost	$13,530	$15,435	$19,032
Divide by EUP	330,000	315,000	312,000
Cost per EUP	$.041	$.049	$.061

Total cost per EUP = $.041 + $.049 + $.061 = $.151

Step 6: Assign costs to inventories and goods transferred out:

Cost of goods transferred ($0.151 × 300,000)		$45,300
Cost of ending inventory:		
Materials ($0.041 × 30,000)	$ 1,230	
Direct labor ($0.049 × 15,000)	735	
Overhead ($0.061 × 12,000)	732	2,697
Total cost assigned		$47,997

b. FIFO method:

Step 1: Calculate total units to account for:

Beginning inventory	25,000
Units started during current period	305,000
Units to account for	330,000

Step 2: Calculate the total units accounted for:

Units completed and transferred out	300,000
Units in ending WIP inventory	30,000
Units accounted for	330,000

Step 3: Determine the equivalent units of production:

	Materials	Direct Labor	Overhead
BI (EUP not completed in October, the prior period)	0	10,000	16,000
Units started and completed	275,000	275,000	275,000
EI (whole units × % complete)	30,000	15,000	12,000
EUP	305,000	300,000	303,000

Step 4: Determine the total cost to account for:

	Materials	Direct Labor	Overhead
BI cost	$ 1,330	$ 435	$ 852
Current period cost	12,200	15,000	18,180
Total cost to account for	$13,530	$15,435	$19,032

Total all cost pools = $13,530 + $15,435 + $19,032 = $47,997

Step 5: Calculate the cost per equivalent unit of production:

	Materials	Direct Labor	Overhead
Current period cost	$12,200	$15,000	$18,180
Divide by EUP	305,000	300,000	303,000
Cost per EUP	$0.04	$0.05	$0.06

Total cost per EUP = $0.04 + $0.05 + $0.06 = $0.15

Step 6: Assign costs to inventories and goods transferred out:

Cost of goods transferred:		
Beginning inventory costs	$ 2,617	
Costs to complete beginning WIP:		
Materials ($0.04 × 0)	0	
Direct labor ($0.05 × 10,000)	500	
Overhead ($0.06 × 16,000)	960	
Total cost of beginning inventory	$ 4,077	
Started and completed ($0.15 × 275,000)	41,250	
Total cost of goods transferred		$45,327

Cost of ending inventory:

Materials ($0.04 × 30,000)	$ 1,200	
Direct labor ($0.05 × 15,000)	750	
Overhead ($0.06 × 12,000)	720	2,670
Total cost assigned		$47,997

END-OF-CHAPTER MATERIALS

Questions

1. Describe the characteristics of a production environment in which process costing would likely be found.

2. What is the major difference between job order and process costing in the way departmental costs are assigned to products? How does this affect product costs?

3. What are the two methods used in process costing to assign an "average" cost to products? How do these methods differ?

4. What are the two important source documents for determining, respectively, the costs of direct materials and direct labor to be assigned to products for a period in a department? What information does each of these provide?

5. What is meant by the term *equivalent units of production,* and what is its role in process costing?

6. Briefly describe the six steps involved in assigning product costs in a process costing environment.

7. At the end of a period, the total production costs accumulated in a department are assigned to two groups of products; identify the two groups. Where do the costs in each group appear on the accounting records?

8. What is meant by the term *transferred-out costs*? How does calculation of transferred-out cost differ under the weighted average and the FIFO methods?

9. Arrange the following four terms in an equation such that both sides of the equation contain two terms, and the right-hand side is equal to the left-hand side:

Cost of the beginning inventory	(BI)
Costs transferred out	(TO)
Cost of the ending inventory	(EI)
Costs incurred this period	(TP)

10. Arrange the following terms, which relate to a period's production, in an equation such that the two sides are equal, one side represents total units to account for, and the other side represents total units accounted for:

Units in the beginning inventory	(BI)
Units in the ending inventory	(EI)
Units started and completed	(S&C)
Units started but not completed	(SNC)
Units transferred out	(TO)

11. In computing the cost per equivalent unit of production, is one equivalent unit computation sufficient for all of the cost categories (direct materials, direct labor, and overhead)? Explain.

12. Which process costing method, FIFO or weighted average, provides the better picture of the actual amount of work accomplished in a period? Explain.

13. In an inflationary environment (costs are rising from period to period), which process costing method, FIFO or weighted average, would assign the higher cost to the ending Work in Process in a department? (Assume production is stable from period to period.) Explain.

14. Describe a circumstance (or circumstances) in which the FIFO and weighted average costs per equivalent unit of production would be identical or nearly identical.

15. In a firm where the process costing system is used as a primary tool to evaluate periodic cost control as well as to assign costs to products, would the firm more likely opt to use FIFO or weighted average? Explain.

16. What document is used in process costing to detail all manufacturing quantities and costs and indicate cost assignments? Discuss the information provided to managers by this document.

17. In the process costing context, what are transferred-in costs? Why might the cost per unit transferred out of one department be different from the transferred-in cost per unit shown on the Production and Cost Report of the next department?

18. When products are assigned a standard cost in a process costing system, does the cost assignment approach more closely resemble the FIFO or weighted average approach? Explain.

19. How does the process costing environment vary from the emerging high-tech repetitive manufacturing environment?

Exercises

20. *(Total units; WA EUP)* The Great Northwestern Paint Company uses a process costing system to account for its production costs (based on the weighted average method). All materials are added at the start of the process while labor and overhead costs are incurred evenly throughout the production process. The company's records for the month of September contained the following information:

Beginning inventory	8,000 gallons
Started during September	200,000 gallons
Transferred to finished goods	202,000 gallons

As of September 1, the beginning inventory was 40 percent complete as to conversion. On September 30, the ending inventory was 60 percent complete as to conversion.

a. Determine the total number of units to account for.
b. Determine the equivalent units of production for direct materials.
c. Determine the equivalent units of production for direct labor and manufacturing overhead.

21. *(Total units; FIFO EUP)* Repeat Exercise 20 assuming that the Great Northwestern Paint Company uses the FIFO method of process costing. Why is the FIFO number of equivalent units smaller than the weighted average equivalent units for each cost category?

22. *(WA EUP & cost per EUP)* The Sun Block Company produces tanning gel in a continuous flow production process. The company uses process costing based on the weighted average method to assign production costs to products. Direct labor

costs are incurred evenly throughout the process while all material is added at the beginning of the process. The following is information on the direct labor costs and physical unit activity for the month of July.

	Pounds of Gel
Beginning inventory	14,000
Transferred out this period	50,000
Ending inventory	10,000

	Direct Labor Costs
Beginning inventory	$ 2,000
Incurred this period	12,000

The beginning and ending inventories for July are, respectively, 75 percent and 10 percent complete as to direct labor costs.

a. Determine the equivalent units of production for direct labor in the month of July.

b. Determine the cost per equivalent unit of production for direct labor in July.

23. *(FIFO EUP & cost per EUP)* Repeat Exercise 22 assuming the Sun Block Company uses the FIFO method rather than the weighted average method. Why does the unit cost vary between the two methods?

24. *(WA EUP; cost per EUP; cost distribution)* The GoldFinch Company produces ice cream and employs a process costing system based on the weighted average method to assign costs to production. Various materials are added at discrete stages in the production process while direct labor and factory overhead are incurred evenly throughout the process. For the first week in May, the company experienced the following results:

Gallons of ice cream in beginning inventory	4,000
Gallons of ice cream started	30,000
Gallons of ice cream completed	24,000

For the same week, the relevant costs were as follows:

	Direct Labor	Factory Overhead
Beginning inventory	$ 2,000	$1,800
Costs this period	10,000	4,500

Also for this week, the beginning inventory was 25 percent complete as to direct labor and overhead. The ending inventory was 60 percent complete as to direct labor and overhead.

a. Compute equivalent units of production for direct labor and overhead.

b. For direct labor and overhead, compute the cost per equivalent unit of production.

c. For direct labor and overhead, determine the cost of the ending inventory and the cost transferred to finished goods.

25. *(FIFO EUP; cost per EUP; cost distribution)* The Panama Sugar Company employs a process costing system based on the FIFO method. For the month of January, the following information was extracted from the company's records for direct labor costs:

Beginning inventory (40% complete as to labor)	10,000 lbs.
Direct labor cost in beginning inventory	$ 900

Ending inventory (80% complete as to labor)   20,000 lbs.
Total direct labor costs incurred $20,000
Cost per equivalent unit for direct labor $0.10

Compute:

a. Total equivalent units (pounds) for direct labor in January.
b. The cost of direct labor in goods completed and transferred out.
c. The cost of direct labor in the ending WIP inventory.

26. *(WA EUP; cost per EUP; cost distribution)* The Hansen Oil Refinery uses a process costing system based on the FIFO method. Some summary information for the month of April on direct labor costs in the Chemical Department follows:

Beginning inventory (40% complete as to labor)   3,000,000 gallons
Units started   15,000,000 gallons
Ending inventory (30% complete as to labor)   5,000,000 gallons
Direct labor cost per equivalent unit $0.05
Direct labor costs transferred out $737,000

If the company had used the weighted average method, rather than the FIFO method, compute:

a. the direct labor cost per equivalent unit of production.
b. the direct labor cost assigned to the ending inventory.

27. *(FIFO EUP; cost per EUP; cost distribution)* In a single-process production system, the Teddy Company manufactures a rabies vaccine for animals. The company uses a process costing system based on standard costs. The company's standard costs for a single vial follow:

	Standard Cost Per Vial
Direct materials	$2
Direct labor	3
Manufacturing overhead	4
Total	$9

In the production process, materials are added at the beginning of the process and conversion costs are applied evenly throughout the process. Production and WIP inventory information for the month of February is as shown:

Beginning inventory   3,000 vials (30% complete)
Started this period   12,000 vials
Ending inventory   2,000 vials (80% complete)

For February 1993, compute:

a. equivalent units of production for direct materials and conversion costs.
b. the cost of the ending inventory and goods completed and transferred out.

28. *(Missing numbers; multidepartment)* The Hawaiian Fruit Company produces a limited variety of fruit drinks in a three-stage sequential production process. Each stage of the production process (sequentially the departments are: Steaming, Mixing, and Packaging) is organized as a separate department, and each maintains a separate Work in Process account to track and assign costs to production. Limited information for the company's inventory accounts follows for the month of March:

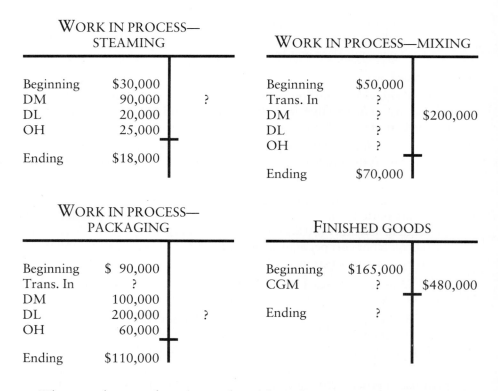

WORK IN PROCESS—STEAMING

Beginning	$30,000	
DM	90,000	?
DL	20,000	
OH	25,000	
Ending	$18,000	

WORK IN PROCESS—MIXING

Beginning	$50,000	
Trans. In	?	
DM	?	$200,000
DL	?	
OH	?	
Ending	$70,000	

WORK IN PROCESS—PACKAGING

Beginning	$ 90,000	
Trans. In	?	
DM	100,000	?
DL	200,000	
OH	60,000	
Ending	$110,000	

FINISHED GOODS

Beginning	$165,000	
CGM	?	$480,000
Ending	?	

a. What was the cost of goods transferred from the Steaming Department to the Mixing Department in March?

b. Collectively, what was the cost for direct materials, direct labor, and overhead in the Mixing Department for March?

c. What was the Cost of Goods Manufactured for March?

29. *(Description of production systems)* The following are brief phrases that characterize certain production environments. To the right of the phrases are three columns that correspond to three different production systems. For each phrase, put a check mark in the column if the phrase describes that production system.

	Job Order	Process	Repetitive Manufacturing
a. High volume production			
b. Low direct labor content			
c. High levels of WIP			
d. Short process time			
e. Continuous production			
f. Batch production			
g. Great product diversity			

Problems

30. *(WA EUP & cost assignment)* Murphy's Company produces a single product, which is a chemical used in the manufacture of SPUD missiles. The company employs a process costing system based on the weighted average cost flow assumption. The following information pertains to the company's operations for the month of October 1993:

Unit Data

Beginning work in process	6,000 gallons
(70% complete as to conversion)	
Started this period	24,000 gallons
Ending work in process	8,500 gallons
(40% complete as to conversion)	

Cost Data	Direct Materials	Conversion Costs
Beginning WIP	$ 9,500	$14,700
Incurred this period	35,500	72,450

All materials are introduced at the start of the process.
Required:

a. Determine the total number of units to account for.
b. Compute the total costs to account for in each cost pool.
c. Compute the cost per equivalent unit for direct materials and conversion.
d. Compute the cost assigned to the goods transferred to finished goods and the cost of the ending work in process.

31. *(FIFO EUP; cost assignment)* The following information has been extracted from the Cooking Department cost records of the San Francisco Canning Company for the month of October 1993. The information pertains to direct materials used in the Cooking Department. The company utilizes a process costing system based on the FIFO method.

Beginning inventory (20% complete as to direct materials)	100,000 lbs.
Ending inventory (70% complete as to direct materials)	80,000 lbs.
Direct material costs incurred in October	$ 93,600
Direct material costs transferred out	90,400
Cost per equivalent unit for October	$ 0.10

Required: Compute the following:

a. Equivalent units of production for direct materials in October.
b. Cost per equivalent unit for direct materials in September 1993.
c. Cost of direct materials assigned to the ending WIP inventory for October.

32. *(FIFO; cost assignment)* The Iowa Chemical Company produces anhydrous ammonia that is used as a farm fertilizer. In its plant, the firm accounts for the product costs using a process costing system based on the FIFO method. The following information pertaining to direct labor costs has been extracted from the company's cost records for the month of March:

Beginning inventory (60% complete as to direct labor)	1,000,000 lbs.
Beginning inventory cost	$ 54,000
Direct labor costs incurred this period	$800,000
Direct labor cost per equivalent unit (pound)	$0.10
Ending inventory (40% complete as to direct labor)	500,000 lbs.

Required:

a. Compute the cost of direct labor in the goods transferred out.
b. Compute the cost of direct labor in the ending inventory.
c. For the month of March, what was the denominator that was used in computing the cost per equivalent unit for direct labor?

33. *(FIFO method)* The Big Brewsky employs a process costing system (based on the FIFO method) in its beer production plants. In the company's small Milwaukee plant, beer is packaged in 16-gallon kegs. Materials are added at the beginning of the process, and conversion costs are incurred evenly throughout the process. Unit information for a recent period follows:

Beginning inventory	900 kegs (40% complete)
Units started	4,000 kegs
Ending inventory	1,000 kegs (80% complete)

The following are relevant costs for the same period.

	Direct Materials	Conversion Costs
Beginning inventory	$1,900	$ 1,000
Current period costs	7,200	11,718

Required:

a. Determine the total units to account for.
b. Determine the equivalent units of production.
c. Determine the cost per equivalent unit.
d. Determine the cost of the ending inventory and the cost of goods completed and transferred out.
e. Prepare the journal entry for the transfer of goods from Work in Process to Finished Goods.

34. *(FIFO; two materials)* Haydel's Bakery produces carrot cakes in mass quantities and uses a process costing system to account for its costs. The bakery production line is set up in one department. Batter is mixed first, with all necessary ingredients added at the start of production. The batter is poured into pans, baked, and cooled. Then the cake is iced with a confectionary sugar/water mixture. The last step in the process is to let the icing harden and move the cake into a display case. Icing is added approximately when the cakes have had 85 percent of the total labor and overhead.

Production and cost data for April 1993 follow. Beginning inventory consisted of 20 cakes, which were approximately 80 percent complete as to labor and overhead. The batter associated with beginning inventory has a cost of $60, and related conversion costs totaled $32.

A total of 430 cakes were started during April and 440 were completed. The ending inventory was 90 percent complete. Costs for the month were: batter, $1,324.40; icing, $31.50; and conversion, $857.34.
Required:

a. Using the FIFO method, determine the equivalent units of production for each cost component for April for Haydel's Bakery.
b. Calculate the cost per unit for each cost component for the bakery for April.
c. Determine the appropriate valuation for April's ending Work in Process Inventory and the units transferred to the display case for sale.
d. The bakery sells its carrot cakes for $7.75 and, during April, 427 cakes were sold. What was the total gross profit margin on the sale of the cakes?

35. *(FIFO & WA methods)* The West Virginia Tobacco Company produces cans of smokeless tobacco (chewing tobacco). The company employs a process costing system to assign production costs to the units produced. For the second week in July, the firm had a beginning inventory of 20,000 cans that were 20 percent complete as to materials and 50 percent complete as to conversion costs. During the week an additional 100,000 cans were started in production. At the end of

the week, 25,000 cans remained in the Work in Process Inventory, and were 70 percent complete as to materials and 80 percent complete as to conversion costs.
Required: For the second week in July,

a. compute the total units to account for.
b. determine how many units were started and completed.
c. determine the equivalent units of production for each cost component based on the FIFO method.
d. determine the equivalent units of production for each cost component based on the weighted average method.
e. reconcile your answers in parts (c) and (d).

36. *(Production & cost report; WA & FIFO methods)* In a single process production system, the Era-Tatum Corporation produces plastic harmonicas. For the month of September 1993, the company's accounting records reflected the following:

Beginning Work in Process Inventory	10,000 units
100% complete as to Material A	
0% complete as to Material B	
40% complete as to direct labor	
60% complete as to overhead	
Units started during the month	80,000 units
Ending Work in Process Inventory	15,000 units
100% complete as to Material A	
0% complete as to Material B	
30% complete as to direct labor	
40% complete as to overhead	

Cost Data	Beginning Inventory	September Costs
Material A	$10,000	$ 75,000
Material B	0	35,000
Direct labor	5,000	100,000
Overhead	4,000	70,000

Required: For the month of September, prepare

a. a production and cost report assuming the company uses the weighted average method.
b. a production and cost report assuming the company uses FIFO.

37. *(Multiproduct)* Gregg Industries manufactures a variety of plastic products including a series of molded chairs. The three models of molded chairs, which are all variations of the same design, are Standard (can be stacked), Deluxe (with arms), and Executive (with arms and padding). The company uses batch manufacturing and has a process costing system.

Gregg has an extrusion operation and subsequent operations to form, trim, and finish the chairs. Plastic sheets are produced by the extrusion operation, some of which are sold directly to other manufacturers. During the forming operation, the remaining plastic sheets are molded into chair seats and the legs are added; the Standard model is sold after this operation. During the trim operation, the arms are added to the Deluxe and Executive models and the chair edges are smoothed. Only the Executive model enters the finish operation where the padding is added. All of the units produced receive the same steps within each operation.

The May production run had a total manufacturing cost of $898,000. The units of production and direct material costs incurred were as follows:

	Units Produced	Extrusion Materials	Form Materials	Trim Materials	Finish Materials
Plastic sheets	5,000	$ 60,000			
Standard model	6,000	72,000	$24,000		
Deluxe model	3,000	36,000	12,000	$ 9,000	
Executive model	2,000	24,000	8,000	6,000	$12,000
	16,000	$192,000	$44,000	$15,000	$12,000

Manufacturing costs applied during the month of May were:

	Extrusion Operation	Form Operation	Trim Operation	Finish Operation
Direct labor	$152,000	$60,000	$30,000	$18,000
Factory overhead	240,000	72,000	39,000	24,000

Required:

a. For each product produced by Gregg Industries during the month of May, determine the
   1. unit cost.
   2. total cost.
   Be sure to account for all costs incurred during the month, and support your answer with appropriate calculations.
b. Without prejudice to your answer in part (a), assume that 1,000 units of the Deluxe model remained in Work in Process at the end of the month. These units were 100 percent complete in the trim operation. Determine the value of the 1,000 units of the Deluxe model in Gregg Industries' Work in Process Inventory at the end of May.

(CMA)

38. *(WA; second department)* The Bangor Company produces desktop calendars in a two-process, two-department operation. In the first process (the Printing Department), the materials are printed and cut. In the second process (the Assembly Department), materials received from the Printing Department are assembled into individual calendars and then bound. Each department maintains its own Work in Process account, and costs are assigned using process costing and the weighted average method. In the Assembly Department, conversion costs are incurred evenly throughout the process, while direct materials are applied at the end of the process. For the month of November 1993, the following costs were recorded in the Assembly Department:

	Transferred In	Conversion	Materials
Beginning inventory	$25,000	$ 4,000	$ 0
Incurred this period	80,000	15,000	10,000

For November, the beginning inventory contained 20,000 calendars, and an additional 80,000 calendars were transferred in from the Printing Department. The ending inventory consisted of 30,000 calendars that were 60 percent of the way through the conversion process. Compute for the Assembly Department in November:

a. the cost per equivalent unit of production for all three cost pools.
b. the cost transferred to finished goods.
c. the cost of the ending WIP inventory.

39. *(WA & FIFO EUP; second department)* The Stiglits Company employs a process costing system in its chemical products plants. One particular plant produces a single chemical that is packaged in 55 gallon drums and flows through two dis-

tinct processes (grinding and mixing). Some materials, including the drum, enter production at the beginning of the first process (grinding). The balance of the materials are added at the beginning of the second process (mixing). Conversion costs are incurred and applied uniformly throughout both processes. Unit volume data relating to the mixing process for the month of November 1993 follow:

Beginning inventory	500 drums (30% complete)
Drums transferred in during November	1,000
Drums transferred out during November	900
Ending inventory in process	600 drums (40% complete)

Required:

a. Assuming a weighted average method, compute equivalent units for materials, conversion costs, and transferred-in costs for November in the Mixing Department.
b. Repeat part (a) using the FIFO method.

Cases

40. Hi-Fri, Inc., manufactures "bug zappers" for the control of mosquitos and other outside pests around patios and gardens. The bug zappers are sold to various major department stores under private labels. At the beginning of February 1993, Hi-Fri, Inc., had 4,000 bug zappers in beginning inventory, which were 90 percent complete as to material and 75 percent complete as to conversion. During the month, 22,000 units were started, and at the end of February, 5,000 remained in ending inventory. The ending inventory was 60 percent complete as to material and 40 percent complete as to conversion.

Actual cost data for the month were as follows:

	Material	Conversion	Total
Beginning inventory	$ 78,000	$ 42,000	$120,000
Current costs	400,000	220,000	620,000
Total costs	$478,000	$262,000	$740,000

a. Prepare EUP schedules for FIFO and weighted average.
b. Prepare Production and Cost Reports for FIFO and weighted average.
c. Discuss the differences in the two reports prepared for part (b). Which would provide better information to departmental managers and why?

41. The Spring Water Company is a small concern that provides water to approximately 200 rural households in western Wyoming. The company is organized into two departments. In the Screening Department, water is pulled from a local river and then pushed through a series of screens to remove large particulates. In the Chemical Department, the water is run through a series of fine filters, and then chemicals such as chlorine and fluoride are added. For the month of November, the company experienced the following results:

		Percentages of Completion		
	Gallons	Transferred In	Materials	Conversion
Screening Department				
Beginning inventory	100,000	NA	100%	40%
Transferred out	2,000,000			
Ending inventory	200,000	NA	100%	60%

Chemical Department

Beginning inventory	80,000	100%	0%	40%
Transferred in	?			
Ending inventory	100,000	100%	0%	70%

Costs	Transferred In	Materials	Conversion
Screening Department			
Beginning inventory	NA	$ 300	$ 100
November costs	NA	3,000	2,000
Chemical Department			
Beginning inventory	$480	$ 0	$ 64
November costs	?	2,000	1,800

a. Prepare a production report for the Screening Department for November assuming the company uses the weighted average method.

b. Prepare a production report for the Chemical Department for November assuming the company uses the weighted average method.

c. Prepare the journal entries for the transfer of goods in November from the Screening Department to the Chemical Department, and from the Chemical Department to the potable water storage tank (Finished Goods Inventory).

42. The Bass Grabber Company produces rubber worms in a variety of colors. The worms are used for recreational fishing. Each worm passes through three separate departments before it is complete and ready for shipment to sporting goods wholesalers. The worm begins in the Molding Department, then passes into the Vulcanizing Department and is finished in the Packaging Department. Product costs are separately tracked by department and assigned via a process costing system. Overhead is applied to production in each department at a rate of 70 percent of the department's direct labor cost. The following information pertains to departmental operations for the second complete year of the company's existence.

WORK IN PROCESS—MOLDING

Beginning	$50,000		
DM	80,000		?
DL	80,000		
OH	?		
Ending	$25,000		

WORK IN PROCESS—VULCANIZING

Beginning	$80,000		
Trans. In	?		
DM	40,000		$320,000
DL	?		
OH	?		
Ending	$50,000		

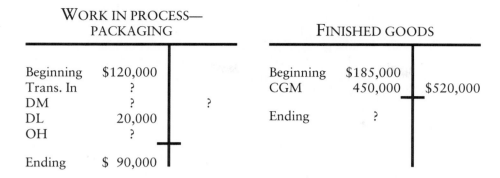

WORK IN PROCESS—PACKAGING				FINISHED GOODS		
Beginning	$120,000			Beginning	$185,000	
Trans. In	?			CGM	450,000	$520,000
DM	?	?				
DL	20,000			Ending	?	
OH	?					
Ending	$ 90,000					

a. What was the cost of goods transferred from the Molding Department to the Vulcanizing Department for the year?

b. How much direct labor cost was incurred in the Vulcanizing Department? How much overhead?

c. How much direct material cost was charged to products passing through the Packaging Department?

d. Prepare the journal entries for all interdepartmental transfers of products, including the transfer from the Packaging Department to the Finished Goods Inventory.

43. Wood Glow Manufacturing Company produces a single product, a wood refinishing kit that sells for $17.95. The final processing of the kits occurs in the Packaging Department. An internal quilted wrap is applied at the beginning of the packaging process. A compartmented outside box printed with instructions and the company's name and logo is added when units are 60 percent through the process. Conversion costs, consisting of direct labor and applied overhead, occur evenly throughout the packaging process. The following data pertain to the activities of the Packaging Department during October.

- Beginning Work in Process Inventory was 10,000 units, 40 percent complete as to conversion costs.
- 30,000 units were started and completed in the month.
- There were 10,000 units in ending work in process, 80 percent complete as to conversion costs.

The Packaging Department's October costs were:

Quilted wrap	$80,000
Outside boxes	50,000
Direct labor	22,000
Applied overhead ($3.00 per direct labor dollar)	66,000

The costs transferred in from prior processing were $3.00 per unit. The cost of goods sold for the month was $240,000, and the ending Finished Goods Inventory was $84,000. Wood Glow uses the first-in, first-out method of inventory valuation.

Wood Glow's controller, Mark Brandon, has been asked to analyze the activities of the Packaging Department for the month of October. Brandon knows that in order to properly determine the department's unit cost of production, he must first calculate the equivalent units of production.

a. Prepare an equivalent units of production schedule for the October activity in the Packaging Department. Be sure to account for the beginning Work in Process Inventory, the units started and completed during the month, and the ending Work in Process Inventory.

b. Determine the cost per equivalent unit of the October production.

c. Assuming that the actual overhead incurred during October was $5,000 more than the overhead applied, describe how the value of the ending Work in Process Inventory would be determined.

(CMA)

44. Kristina Company, which manufactures quality paint sold at premium prices, uses a single production department. Production begins with the blending of various chemicals, which are added at the beginning of the process, and ends with the canning of the paint. Canning occurs when the mixture reaches the 90 percent stage of completion. The gallon cans are then transferred to the Shipping Department for crating and shipment. Labor and overhead are added continuously throughout the process. Factory overhead is applied at the rate of $3.00 per direct labor hour.

Prior to May, when a change in the process was implemented, work in process inventories were insignificant. The change in process enables greater production but results in substantial amounts of work in process for the first time. The company has always used the weighted average method to determine equivalent production and unit costs. Now, production management is considering changing from the weighted average method to the first-in, first-out method.

The following data relate to actual production during the month of May:

Costs for May:

Work in Process Inventory, May 1 (4,000 gallons, 25% complete)

Direct materials—chemicals	$ 45,600
Direct labor ($10 per hour)	6,250
Factory overhead	1,875

May costs added

Direct materials—chemicals	228,400
Direct materials—cans	7,000
Direct labor ($10 per hour)	35,000
Factory overhead	10,500

	Units for May (Gallons)
Work in Process Inventory, May 1 (25% complete)	4,000
Sent to Shipping Department	20,000
Started in May	21,000
Work in Process Inventory, May 31 (80% complete)	5,000

a. Prepare a schedule of equivalent units for each cost element for the month of May using the
   1. weighted average method.
   2. FIFO method.

b. Calculate the cost (to the nearest cent) per equivalent unit for each element for the month of May using the
   1. weighted average method.
   2. FIFO method.

c. Discuss the advantages and disadvantages of using the weighted average method versus the FIFO method, and explain under what circumstances each method should be used.

(CMA)

Ethics Discussion

45. FulRange, Inc., produces complex printed circuits for stereo amplifiers. The circuits are sold primarily to major component manufacturers, and any production overruns are sold to small manufacturers at a substantial discount. The small manufacturer segment appears very profitable because the basic operating budget assigns all fixed expenses to production for the major manufacturers, the only predictable market.

A common product defect that occurs in production is a "drift," caused by failure to maintain precise heat levels during the production process. Rejects from the 100 percent testing program can be reworked to acceptable levels if the defect is drift. However, in a recent analysis of customer complaints, George Wilson, the cost accountant, and the quality control engineer have ascertained that normal rework does not bring the circuits up to standard. Sampling shows that about one-half of the reworked circuits will fail after extended, high-volume amplifier operation. The incidence of failure in the reworked circuits is projected to be about 10 percent over one to five years' operation.

Unfortunately, there is no way to determine which reworked circuits will fail, because testing will not detect this problem. The rework process could be changed to correct the problem, but the cost/benefit analysis for the suggested change in the rework process indicates that it is not practicable. FulRange's marketing analyst has indicated that this problem will have a significant impact on the company's reputation and customer satisfaction if it is not corrected. Consequently, the board of directors would interpret this problem as having serious negative implications on the company's profitability.

Wilson has included the circuit failure and rework problem in his report for the upcoming quarterly meeting of the board of directors. Due to the potential adverse economic impact, Wilson has followed a long-standing practice of highlighting this information.

After reviewing the reports to be presented, the plant manager and her staff were upset and indicated to the controller that he should control his people better. "We can't upset the board with this kind of material. Tell Wilson to tone that down. Maybe we can get it by this meeting and have some time to work on it. People who buy those cheap systems and play them that loud shouldn't expect them to last forever."

The controller called Wilson into his office and said, "George, you'll have to bury this one. The probable failure of reworks can be referred to briefly in the oral presentation, but it should not be mentioned or highlighted in the advance material mailed to the board."

Wilson feels strongly that the board will be misinformed on a potentially serious loss of income if he follows the controller's orders. Wilson discussed the problem with the quality control engineer, who simply remarked, "That's your problem, George."

a. Discuss the ethical considerations that George Wilson should recognize in deciding how to proceed in this matter.

b. Explain what ethical responsibilities should be accepted in this situation by
   1. The controller.
   2. The quality control engineer.
   3. The plant manager and her staff.

c. What should George Wilson do in this situation? Explain your answer.

(CMA)

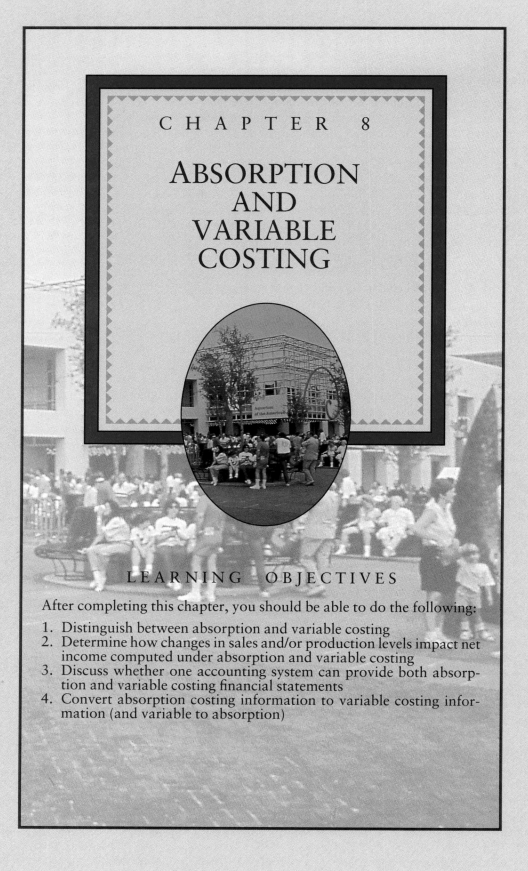

C H A P T E R   8

ABSORPTION AND VARIABLE COSTING

LEARNING OBJECTIVES

After completing this chapter, you should be able to do the following:

1. Distinguish between absorption and variable costing
2. Determine how changes in sales and/or production levels impact net income computed under absorption and variable costing
3. Discuss whether one accounting system can provide both absorption and variable costing financial statements
4. Convert absorption costing information to variable costing information (and variable to absorption)

To answer any of the questions just asked, it is necessary to know certain information about product cost. First, the type of costing system in use by the company must be understood. Second, the valuation method being used for products must be understood. Third, the way product cost is defined by the company must be known. Fourth, the method of presentation desired by the company must be considered.

Job order and process costing are two costing *systems* that allow costs to be accumulated in specific ways. Job order costing is distinctly appropriate for companies that make products or perform services in compliance with customer specifications. Process costing is appropriate for manufacturers producing large quantities of homogeneous output. (Repetitive manufacturing may soon necessitate a new product costing system to account for manufacturers producing mass quantities of customer-specific products.)

Actual, normal, and standard costs are three methods of cost *valuation*. Actual costing uses actual direct materials, direct labor, and overhead costs to compute product or service cost. Normal costing includes actual direct materials and direct labor costs, but uses predetermined overhead rates to apply overhead to production.

Standard costing assigns direct materials, direct labor, and overhead to products or services using established per-unit norms. Standard costs may be used for external reporting only if the resulting valuations closely reflect actual costs.

This chapter discusses the third and fourth dimensions of product costs—cost accumulation and cost presentation. The method of accumulation specifies which manufacturing cost components are recorded as part of product cost. While one method of cost accumulation is used and may be appropriate for both external reporting and internal budgeting purposes, that same method is not necessarily the best method for internal management decision making.

The method of *presentation* focuses on how costs are shown on external financial statements or internal management reports. Accumulation and presentation procedures are accomplished using one of two methods: absorption costing or variable costing. Each method uses the same basic data but structures and processes that data differently. Either method can be used in job order or process costing and with actual, normal, or standard costs.

AN OVERVIEW OF THE TWO METHODS

absorption costing

The most common approach to product costing is **absorption costing,** which treats the costs of all manufacturing components (direct materials, direct labor, variable overhead, and fixed overhead) as inventoriable or product costs. This method has been used consistently in earlier chapters on product costing systems. In fact, the product cost definition given in chapter 2 specifically fits the absorption costing method. On the other hand, **variable costing** is a cost accumulation method that includes only variable production costs (direct materials, direct labor, and variable overhead) as product or inventoriable costs. In variable costing, fixed overhead is

variable costing

Hospitals commonly use full absorption costing because of the necessity to cover numerous costs in non-revenue-producing areas. Such costs include indigent care, malpractice insurance, excess bed capacity, and other administrative costs.

treated as a period cost. Both absorption and variable costing consider costs incurred in the nonmanufacturing (selling, general, and administrative) areas of the organization as period costs and expense these costs in a manner that properly matches them with revenues.

With regard to presentation, absorption costing presents expenses on an income statement or a financial report according to their **functional classifications.** A functional classification is a group of costs that were all incurred for the same basic purpose. Functional classifications include categories such as cost of goods sold, selling expenses, and general and administrative expenses. In contrast, a variable costing statement typically presents expenses according to cost behavior (variable versus fixed), although it may also present expenses by functional classifications within the behavioral categories.

functional classifications

This discussion indicates that there are two basic differences between the absorption and variable costing. The first difference is the way that fixed overhead (FOH) is treated for product costing purposes. Under absorption costing, FOH is considered a product cost; under variable costing, it is considered a period cost. The second difference is the way in which costs are presented on external or internal reports. Absorption costing classifies costs by function, while variable costing categorizes costs by behavior and, then potentially, by function.

Absorption Costing

Absorption costing is also known as full costing, since all types of manufacturing costs are included as product costs. An organization incurs costs for direct materials (DM), direct labor (DL), and variable overhead (VOH) only when goods are produced or services are rendered. Since total DM, DL, and VOH costs increase with each additional product made or service rendered, these costs are considered product costs and inventoried until the product or service is sold. Fixed overhead (FOH) costs, however, may be incurred even when production or service facilities are idle. Although total FOH cost does not vary with units of production or level of service, this cost provides the basic capacity necessary for production or service to occur. Without the incurrence of fixed overhead, production could not take place. Therefore, absorption costing considers FOH to be inventoriable.[1] Exhibit 8–1 depicts an absorption costing model.

Major authoritative bodies of the accounting profession, such as the Financial Accounting Standards Board and the Securities and Exchange Commission, apparently believe that absorption costing provides external parties with a more informative picture of earnings than does variable costing. This belief is indicated by the fact that the accounting profession has unofficially disallowed the use of variable costing as a generally accepted inventory valuation method for external reporting purposes since the IRS began requiring absorption costing for tax purposes.[2]

On external absorption costing financial reports, Work in Process Inventory, Finished Goods Inventory, and Cost of Goods Sold accounts include variable per-unit production costs as well as a per-unit allocation of fixed factory overhead. Nonfac-

---

[1]There is significant controversy about the theoretical justification and practical application of absorption and variable costing. Without attempting to cover all the background issues surrounding these methods, the appendix to this chapter provides some insight into the cases made for both absorption and variable costing.

[2]Robert W. Koehler, "Triple-Threat Strategy," *Management Accounting* (October 1991), p. 34.

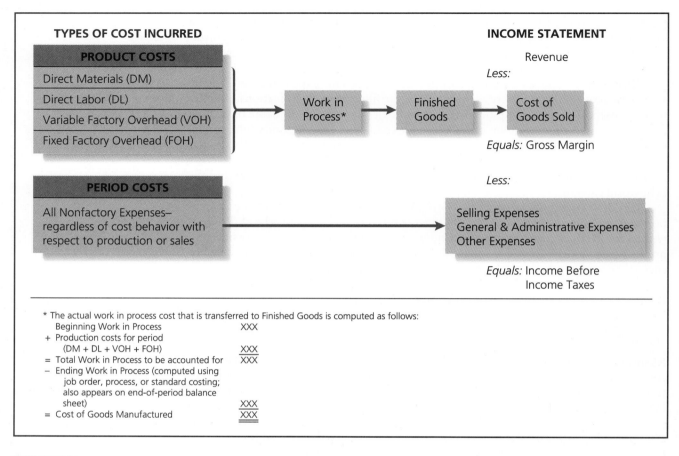

TYPES OF COST INCURRED

INCOME STATEMENT

PRODUCT COSTS
Direct Materials (DM)
Direct Labor (DL)
Variable Factory Overhead (VOH)
Fixed Factory Overhead (FOH)

Work in Process* → Finished Goods → Cost of Goods Sold

Revenue

Less:

Cost of Goods Sold

Equals: Gross Margin

PERIOD COSTS
All Nonfactory Expenses– regardless of cost behavior with respect to production or sales

Less:

Selling Expenses
General & Administrative Expenses
Other Expenses

Equals: Income Before Income Taxes

* The actual work in process cost that is transferred to Finished Goods is computed as follows:

Beginning Work in Process	XXX	
+ Production costs for period (DM + DL + VOH + FOH)	XXX	
= Total Work in Process to be accounted for	XXX	
– Ending Work in Process (computed using job order, process, or standard costing; also appears on end-of-period balance sheet)	XXX	
= Cost of Goods Manufactured	XXX	

EXHIBIT 8–1
▼▼▼▼▼▼▼▼▼▼▼▼

ABSORPTION
COSTING MODEL

tory expenses are presented by functional account classifications that indicate the reasons for the cost incurrence. These nonfactory costs may vary in proportion to sales level, be fixed in amount, or be mixed or step costs.

Cost behavior (relative to changes in activity) is not observable from an absorption costing income statement or management report. However, cost behavior is extremely important for a variety of managerial activities including cost-volume-profit analysis, budgeting, and relevant costing.[3] While companies must prepare external statements using absorption costing, internal reports often show cost behavior to facilitate management analysis and decision making. Variable costs are more controllable than fixed costs for ongoing operations; thus, variable costs may figure more prominently into short-run decisions.

Variable Costing

Variable costing is also known as direct costing and is illustrated in Exhibit 8–2.[4] This illustration indicates that variable costing includes, as inventoriable, only vari-

---

[3]Cost-volume-profit analysis is discussed in chapter 9, budgeting in chapters 11 and 12, and relevant costing in chapter 16.
[4]Direct costing is, however, a misnomer for variable costing. All variable *manufacturing* costs, whether direct or indirect, are considered product costs under variable costing.

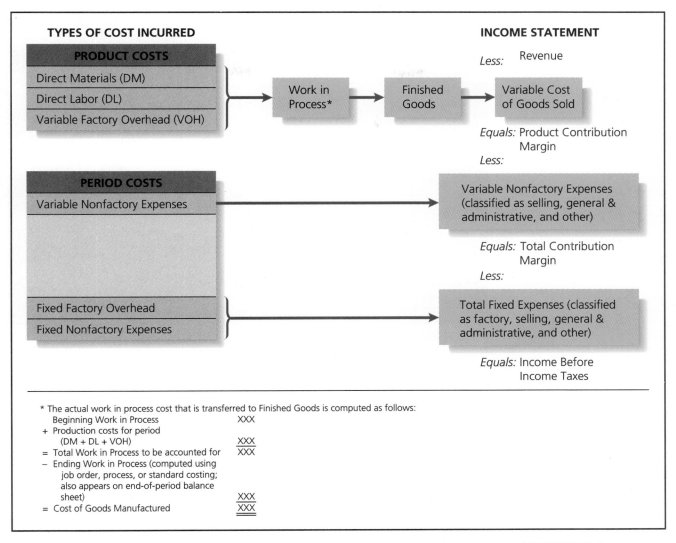

EXHIBIT 8–2
▼▼▼▼▼▼▼▼▼▼▼▼

VARIABLE COSTING
MODEL

able production costs. Variable costing defines product costs solely as "costs of *actual production.*" Since fixed manufacturing overhead will be incurred even if there is no production, variable costing proponents believe that fixed manufacturing overhead does not qualify as a product cost. Thus, fixed overhead costs are treated as period expenses by being charged against revenue in the period they are incurred.

A variable costing income statement or management report separates costs by cost behavior. Under variable costing, Cost of Goods Sold is more appropriately called *Variable* Cost of Goods Sold because it is composed of only the variable production costs related to the units sold. Revenue minus variable cost of goods sold is called **product contribution margin** and indicates how much revenue is available to cover all period expenses and to potentially provide net income.

product contribution margin

Variable, nonfactory period expenses (such as a sales commission set at 10 percent of product selling price) are deducted from product contribution margin to determine the amount of **total contribution margin.** Total contribution margin is the difference between total revenues and total variable expenses. This amount indicates

total contribution margin

The Aquarium of the Americas engaged in a unique method of covering some of the fixed costs of construction. Individual bricks, costing less than $5 each, were sold at $50 apiece to produce a $45 "product" contribution margin.

the dollar figure available to "contribute" to the coverage of all fixed expenses, both factory and nonfactory.[5] After fixed expenses are covered, any remaining contribution margin provides income to the company. Variable costing financial statements are also known as contribution income statements.

Even with their differences, the two costing methods have some underlying similarities. First, both methods use the same basic cost information. Second, the treatment of direct materials, direct labor, and variable factory overhead is the same under absorption and variable costing; these costs are always considered product costs. Third, selling, general, and administrative expenses are considered period costs under both costing methods. Fourth, there are no differences between accounts other than in Work in Process Inventory, Finished Goods Inventory, and the expense accounts under the two methods. The next section of the chapter provides a detailed illustration using both absorption and variable costing.

ABSORPTION AND VARIABLE COSTING ILLUSTRATIONS

Perfect Pens, Inc., produces high-quality executive pens. The company employs a standard costing system, has negotiated long-term contracts for all materials and labor, and has automated the majority of the production processes. For the last two

---

[5]Contribution margin can also be computed on a per-unit basis as selling price per unit minus total variable cost per unit. Unit contribution margin is a significant factor in determining the level of sales at which a company breaks even (or incurs no profit or loss) and in analyzing the relationships among costs, sales volumes, and profit levels (cost-volume-profit analysis).

reasons, actual material and labor costs differed little from standard costs in any year. Any variable overhead variances that might arise are insignificant in amount and are written off through Cost of Goods Sold as incurred. For purposes of this illustration, all actual and standard costs for each year shown are assumed to be equal. Exhibit 8–3 provides the standard production costs per unit and the annual budgeted non-production costs for Perfect Pens, Inc. These costs are used to compare absorption and variable costing procedures and presentations. All standard and budgeted costs are assumed to remain constant over the three years 1993–1995.

Perfect Pens, Inc., computes its standard predetermined fixed overhead application rate by dividing estimated annual fixed factory overhead (FOH) by expected annual capacity utilization in units as shown in Exhibit 8–3. This calculation provides a standard fixed overhead rate of $5 per unit. Using a single fixed overhead application rate based on units is considered acceptable for Perfect Pens, Inc., because the company makes only one type of product.

Assume that Perfect Pens began its 1993 operations with no Finished Goods Inventory. Actual production and sales information for the years 1993 through 1995 are shown in Exhibit 8–4. In 1993, Perfect Pens also ends the year with no Finished Goods Inventory, since all units produced that year were also sold. In the other two years, production and sales differ; such a situation is common because production frequently "leads" sales figures as a company stockpiles inventory for a later period.

Exhibit 8–5 presents absorption costing income statements for Perfect Pens, Inc., for 1993–1995. Selling price per unit is $50. The standard absorption cost per unit is $29, which is composed of the standard costs of direct materials ($13), direct labor ($4), variable overhead ($7), and fixed overhead ($5). Cost of goods manufactured is equal to the $29 standard production cost per unit multiplied by the number of units produced that year. Ending inventory cost is calculated as the units in ending inventory multiplied by the $29 standard cost per unit.

Note that in each year when production volume was not equal to the estimated volume used to compute the FOH application rate, a volume variance exists. As dis-

---

EXHIBIT 8–3

**PERFECT PENS, INC.
BASIC DATA**

Standard variable cost per unit:

Direct materials	$13
Direct labor	4
Variable factory overhead	7
Total variable cost per unit	$24

$$\text{Fixed Overhead Application Rate} = \frac{\text{Estimated Annual Fixed OH}}{\text{Estimated Annual Capacity in Units}}$$

$$= \frac{\$1,250,000}{250,000} = \$5$$

Total absorption cost per unit:

Standard variable cost	$24
Standard fixed overhead application rate	5
Total absorption cost per unit	$29

Budgeted nonproduction costs:

Selling expenses (mixed cost)	$75,000 + $3.00 per unit sold
General & administrative expenses (fixed)	$450,000

EXHIBIT 8–4
▼▼▼▼▼▼▼▼▼▼

PERFECT PENS, INC.
ACTUAL
PRODUCTION, SALES
INFORMATION
(1993–1995)

Year	Units Produced	Units Sold
1993	250,000	250,000
1994	240,000	220,000
1995	280,000	300,000
Totals	770,000	770,000

EXHIBIT 8–5
▼▼▼▼▼▼▼▼▼▼

PERFECT PENS, INC.
ABSORPTION
COSTING
COMPARATIVE
INCOME
STATEMENTS (Income
Statement information in
$000s)

cussed in chapter 5, a volume variance is the difference between estimated and applied fixed overhead. Fixed overhead is applied to production based on the actual output of the period. If production is less than expected, the volume variance is unfavorable; if production is greater than expected, the volume variance is favorable.

In Exhibit 8–5, each year's volume variance is shown as an adjustment to Cost of Goods Sold. An unfavorable volume variance causes Cost of Goods Sold to increase, whereas a favorable volume variance causes Cost of Goods Sold to be reduced. Gross margin is the difference between sales revenue and the adjusted Cost of

	1993	1994	1995	Total
Units produced	250,000	240,000	280,000	770,000
Sales volume	250,000	220,000	300,000	770,000
Sales ($50 × # of units sold)	$12,500	$11,000	$15,000	$38,500
Cost of Goods Sold:				
Beginning inventory ($29 × # of units in BI)	$ 0	$ 0	$ 580	$ 0
Cost of goods manufactured ($29 × # of units produced)	7,250	6,960	8,120	22,330
Cost of goods available	$ 7,250	$ 6,960	$ 8,700	$22,330
Ending inventory ($29 × # of units in EI)	0	580	0	0
Cost of goods sold ($29 × # of units sold)	$ 7,250	$ 6,380	$ 8,700	$22,330
Volume variance*	0	50	(150)	(100)
Adjusted CGS	$ 7,250	$ 6,430	$ 8,550	$22,230
Gross Margin	$ 5,250	$ 4,570	$ 6,450	$16,270
Operating Expenses:				
Selling [$75,000 + ($3 × # of units sold)]	$ 825	$ 735	$ 975	$ 2,535
G&A (fixed cost)	450	450	450	1,350
Total	$ 1,275	$ 1,185	$ 1,425	$ 3,885
Income before Taxes	$ 3,975	$ 3,385	$ 5,025	$12,385
*Volume Variance:	**1993**	**1994**	**1995**	**Total**
Actual production	250,000	240,000	280,000	770,000
× Predetermined FOH rate	× $5	× $5	× $5	× $5
Applied FOH	$1,250,000	$1,200,000	$1,400,000	$3,850,000
Estimated annual FOH	1,250,000	1,250,000	1,250,000	3,750,000
Volume variance	$ 0	$ 50,000U	$ 150,000F	$ 100,000F

Goods Sold. The nonfactory costs shown in Exhibit 8–5 are grouped by functional areas (selling, general, and administrative). As indicated in Exhibit 8–3, selling expenses are mixed costs and contain both a variable and a fixed cost element. These different elements are not apparent from the absorption costing income statement.

Exhibit 8–6 provides the variable costing income statements for Perfect Pens, Inc., for the years 1993–1995. Under variable costing, the standard cost per unit is $24 rather than $29. This $5 difference reflects the fact that fixed overhead is included as a period cost rather than being allocated on a per-unit basis as part of product cost. Notice also that no volume variance is shown on the variable costing income statements. A volume variance arises in absorption costing when actual production activity does not equal the estimated activity level used in setting the application rate. Since no fixed overhead application rate exists under variable costing, no volume variance can occur.

Cost of goods manufactured (CGM) in Exhibit 8–6 equals the $24 standard variable production cost multiplied by the number of units produced. Ending inventory is equal to the units *not* sold multiplied by the standard cost of $24 per unit. Product contribution margin each year is a constant amount of $26 multiplied by the number

	1993	1994	1995	Total
Units produced	250,000	240,000	280,000	770,000
Sales volume	250,000	220,000	300,000	770,000
Sales ($50 × # of units sold)	$12,500	$11,000	$15,000	$38,500
Cost of Goods Sold:				
Beginning inventory ($24 × # of units in BI)	$ 0	$ 0	$ 480	$ 0
Cost of goods manufactured ($24 × # of units produced)	6,000	5,760	6,720	18,480
Cost of goods available	$ 6,000	$ 5,760	$ 7,200	$18,480
Ending inventory ($24 × # of units in EI)	0	480	0	0
Variable CGS ($24 × # of units sold)	$ 6,000	$ 5,280	$ 7,200	$18,480
Product contribution margin ($26 PCM per unit × # of units sold)	$ 6,500	$ 5,720	$ 7,800	$20,020
Variable selling expenses ($3 × # of units sold)	750	660	900	2,310
Total contribution margin ($23 CM × # of units sold)	$ 5,750	$ 5,060	$ 6,900	$17,710
Fixed Expenses:				
Factory	$ 1,250	$ 1,250	$ 1,250	$ 3,750
Selling	75	75	75	225
G&A	450	450	450	1,350
Total	$ 1,775	$ 1,775	$ 1,775	$ 5,325
Income before Taxes	$ 3,975	$ 3,285	$ 5,125	$12,385

EXHIBIT 8–6

PERFECT PENS, INC. VARIABLE COSTING COMPARATIVE INCOME STATEMENTS (Income Statement information in $000s)

At the Knotts Berry Farm amusement park, entrance fees are established using an estimated volume of attendance. If attendance at the park exceeds or falls short of the expectation, there will be a volume variance related to fixed overhead costs.

of units sold. The $26 is the difference between the selling price of $50 and the standard variable production cost of $24. Since this per-unit amount is constant, all years having equal sales volumes would also have equal amounts of product contribution margin.

Because of the emphasis on cost behavior, the next subtotal on a variable costing income statement is total contribution margin. All variable *nonfactory* expenses are subtracted from product contribution margin to compute total contribution margin. For Perfect Pens, Inc., the only variable nonfactory expense is selling cost of $3 per unit sold. The contribution margin percentage is equal to total contribution margin divided by total sales. This percentage is constant at 46 percent each year as shown:

Sales price per unit	$50	100%
Variable production costs per unit	24	48%
Product contribution margin per unit	$26	52%
Variable selling expenses per unit	3	6%
Total contribution margin per unit	$23	46%

The contribution margin percentage indicates that $.46 of each $1.00 of sales can be used toward covering fixed costs and to generate a profit for the firm.

Next on the variable costing income statements, all fixed expenses are deducted from the total contribution margin to determine income before taxes for the year. The fixed expenses include the fixed factory overhead of $1,250,000, the fixed selling expenses of $75,000, and the fixed G&A expenses of $450,000.

Note that all nonfactory expenses for each year are *always* shown as period costs on both sets of income statements. For example, total 1993 selling expenses are shown in Exhibit 8–5 as a single amount of $825,000. Under variable costing, these amounts are merely rearranged on the income statement into their separate variable and fixed component amounts. In Exhibit 8–6, this $825,000 amount is shown as $750,000 of variable selling expenses and $75,000 of fixed selling expenses. The variable selling expenses are included in determining the total contribution margin, while the fixed portion is deducted from total contribution margin.

Variable costing income statements are more useful internally for planning, controlling, and decision making than are absorption costing statements. The benefit of variable costing income statements exists because, to effectively carry out their various functions, managers need to understand and be able to project how different costs will change in reaction to changes in activity levels. Variable costing, through its emphasis on cost behavior, provides needed information to managers. As the News Note on page 330 indicates, a single cost system may not provide all of the information managers need.

The income statements in Exhibits 8–5 and 8–6 show that absorption and variable costing provide different income figures when sales are not equal to production. This difference in income arises solely from what components are included in or excluded from product cost for each method rather than from the method of presentation. If the 1993 absorption costing income statement were recast using cost behavior categories, income between the recast absorption costing statement and the one shown in Exhibit 8–5 would not differ. Likewise, if the 1993 variable costing income statement were recast using functional categories, income between that recast statement and the one shown in Exhibit 8–6 would be the same. Thus, it is specification of product cost components that causes the difference between absorption and variable costing incomes, *not* that the form of presentation differs. This specification refers to the fact that fixed overhead is included as a product cost under absorption costing, but it is considered a period cost under variable costing.

COMPARISON OF THE TWO APPROACHES

Exhibit 8–7 compares Perfect Pen's yearly product cost flows using absorption costing to those occurring under variable costing. The right-hand column of Exhibit 8–7 indicates a single difference in product cost flows, caused by assigning fixed overhead to products under absorption costing rather than to the period under variable costing. The amount of fixed overhead that is included in product cost will ultimately affect the income statement when the products are sold. Product sales, however, may take place in a different time period than that in which the costs are actually incurred.

In 1993, the $1,250,000 difference between the $7,250,000 cost of goods manufactured (CGM) under absorption and the $6,000,000 CGM under variable costing is equal to 250,000 units produced multiplied by the unit fixed overhead application rate of $5. Since all units produced in 1993 are also sold, this $1,250,000 differential is reflected on both methods' income statements in the same time period. Using absorption costing, this $1,250,000 is shown as part of Cost of Goods Sold. The $1,250,000 is expensed on the variable costing income statement as part of the fixed overhead period cost. Since all fixed overhead is expensed in one place or another on the 1993 income statements of both methods, there is no difference in income for that year. In a standard costing system, in which standard costs are constant over time, when production and sales volumes are equal, income under absorption costing will be equal to that computed under variable costing.

EXHIBIT 8–7
▼▼▼▼▼▼▼▼▼▼▼▼

PERFECT PENS INC.
COMPARISON OF
PRODUCT COST
FLOWS

	Units	Absorption Costing ($29/unit)	Variable Costing ($24/unit)	Fixed Cost Differential
1993				
Beginning inventory	0	$ 0	$ 0	$ 0
Cost of goods manufactured	250,000	7,250,000	6,000,000	1,250,000
Cost of goods available	250,000	$7,250,000	$6,000,000	$1,250,000
Cost of goods sold	250,000	7,250,000	6,000,000	1,250,000
Ending inventory	0	$ 0	$ 0	$ 0
(Change from BI to EI = Fixed Cost Differential)				$ 0
1994				
Beginning inventory	0	$ 0	$ 0	$ 0
Cost of goods manufactured	240,000	6,960,000	5,760,000	1,200,000
Cost of goods available	240,000	$6,960,000	$5,760,000	$1,200,000
Cost of goods sold	220,000	6,380,000	5,280,000	1,100,000
Ending inventory	20,000	$ 580,000	$ 480,000	$ 100,000
(Change from BI to EI = Fixed Cost Differential)				$+ 100,000
1995				
Beginning inventory	20,000	$ 580,000	$ 480,000	$ 100,000
Cost of goods manufactured	280,000	8,120,000	6,720,000	1,400,000
Cost of goods available	300,000	$8,700,000	$7,200,000	$1,500,000
Cost of goods sold	300,000	8,700,000	7,200,000	1,500,000
Ending inventory	0	$ 0	$ 0	$ 0
(Change from BI to EI = Fixed Cost Differential)				$ (100,000)

In 1994, there are differences under absorption and variable costing in the values of ending inventories and cost of goods manufactured. In addition, the absorption and variable costing beginning inventories differ in 1995. In these years, the fixed overhead application rate multiplied by the change in the number of units in inventory explains the differences in net income between the two methods. Whenever production and sales volumes differ, resulting in increases or decreases in inventory, income under the two methods will differ. If standard costs are used and variances are expensed as immaterial, the amount of the difference can be computed as follows:

$$\begin{array}{c} \text{Change in} \\ \text{number of units} \\ \text{in inventory} \end{array} \times \begin{array}{c} \text{Fixed overhead} \\ \text{application rate} \end{array} = \begin{array}{c} \text{\$ difference between} \\ \text{absorption \& variable} \\ \text{costing incomes} \end{array}$$

Using this formula for the 1993–1995 data of Perfect Pens, Inc. gives the following:

Year	Units in EI	−	Units in BI	=	Change in # of units	×	FOH application rate	=	Difference in incomes
1993	0		0		0		$5		0
1994	20,000		0		+ 20,000		$5		+ $ 100,000
1995	0		20,000		− 20,000		$5		$(100,000)

If no beginning or ending inventories exist, the cumulative total income under both methods will be identical. For Perfect Pens, Inc., over the three-year period, 770,000 units are produced and 770,000 units are sold. All of the costs incurred (whether variable or fixed) are expensed in one year or another under both methods. The income difference in each year is solely caused by the period of time in which fixed overhead is expensed.

Whether absorption costing income is greater or less than variable costing income depends on the relationship of production and sales and two basic assumptions: (1) unit product costs are constant over time and (2) all variances from standard costs are immaterial. Exhibit 8–8 shows the possible relationships between production and sales levels and the effects of these relationships on net income. These relationships are as follows:

- If production is equal to sales, absorption costing income will equal variable costing income.
- If production is greater than sales, absorption costing income is greater than variable costing income. This result occurs because some fixed overhead cost is deferred as part of inventory cost on the balance sheet under absorption costing, while the total amount of fixed overhead cost is expensed as a period cost under variable costing.
- If production is less than sales, absorption costing income is less than variable costing income. In this case, absorption costing expenses all of the current period fixed overhead cost as well as releases some fixed overhead cost from inventory, where it had been deferred in a prior period. Only current period fixed overhead is shown on the variable costing income statement, so the additional amount released from beginning inventory makes absorption costing income lower.

EXHIBIT 8–8
▼▼▼▼▼▼▼▼▼▼▼▼

PRODUCTION TO
SALES
RELATIONSHIPS AND
EFFECTS*

where P = Production and S = Sales
       AC = Absorption Costing and VC = Variable Costing

	Absorption vs. Variable Income Statement Income before Taxes	**Absorption vs. Variable Balance Sheet Ending Inventory**
P = S	No difference from beginning inventory	No additional difference
P > S (Stockpiling inventory)	AC > VC By amount of fixed OH in ending inventory minus fixed OH in beginning inventory	Ending inventory difference increased (by fixed OH in EI for period plus any BI difference)
P < S (Selling off beginning inventory)	AC < VC By amount of fixed OH released from balance sheet beginning inventory	Ending inventory difference reduced (by fixed OH from BI charged to cost of goods sold)

*The effects of the relationships presented here are based on two qualifying assumptions:
 (1) that unit costs are constant over time; and
 (2) that any fixed cost variances from standard are written off when incurred rather than being prorated to inventory balances.

A convention center incurs tremendous fixed operating costs that are not related to the meetings which are held in the facilities. The fixed costs are truly more related to time than to usage.

This process of deferring and releasing fixed overhead costs in and from inventory makes income manipulation possible under absorption costing, as discussed in the News Note on the next page. For this reason, some people believe that variable costing might be more useful for external purposes than absorption costing is.

Exhibit 8–9 summarizes the differences between absorption and variable costing into four categories: composition of product cost, structure of the chart of accounts, process of accumulating costs, and format of the income statement. Although these differences are set out into four categories, there are not really four distinct differences between the methods—there are only two. The major difference lies in the treatment of fixed overhead for each method: FOH is a product cost for absorption costing and a period cost for variable costing. The second difference is that absorption costing "ignores" cost behavior in presentations, while variable costing focuses on such be-

Absorption Costing	Variable Costing
(1) Composition of Product Cost	
Fixed factory overhead is attached, in separate measurable amounts, to the units being produced. Only if the firm were to sell all inventory produced in a period and all inventory on hand at the beginning of the period would all previously incurred fixed factory overhead be recognized on the income statement as part of cost of goods sold.	Fixed factory overhead is recognized as a period cost (expense) when it is incurred. It does not attach in separate measurable amounts to the units produced. Each period, all fixed factory overhead incurred is recognized on the income statement as an expense, but not through cost of goods sold.
(2) Structure of the Chart of Accounts	
Costs are classified according to functional categories (such as production, selling, general and administrative).	Costs are classified according to both type of cost behavior (fixed or variable) and functional categories (factory and nonfactory). Mixed costs are separated into their fixed and variable components.
(3) Process of Accumulating Costs	
Costs are assigned to functional categories without the necessity of making prior analysis of behavior. All factory costs are considered product costs. All nonfactory costs are considered period costs.	Costs are classified and accumulated according to behavior on the basis of previous analysis. Only variable factory costs are considered product costs. Fixed factory costs are considered period costs. All nonfactory costs are considered period costs.
(4) Format of the Income Statement	
Costs are presented on the income statement according to functional categories. This format highlights gross margin (as illustrated in Exhibit 8–1). The various functional categories present costs without regard to cost behavior. Nonfactory period costs are deducted from gross margin to determine income before taxes.	Costs are presented on the income statement separately according to cost behavior. This format highlights contribution margin (as illustrated in Exhibit 8–2). Fixed costs are deducted from contribution margin to determine income before taxes. Costs may be further categorized by functional classifications.

EXHIBIT 8–9
▼▼▼▼▼▼▼▼▼▼▼

DIFFERENCES BETWEEN ABSORPTION AND VARIABLE COSTING

NEWS NOTE

Income Manipulation Not Possible Under Variable Costing

Conceptually, variable costing always has given a more realistic income. Any "full" method of costing (absorption costing or activity-based costing) permits management to manipulate income by adjusting inventory. A company can increase income by producing more units and thus deferring more fixed costs of this period. In this way it even is possible for a company to report a profit when its sales are lower than the breakeven point. If planned income is more than sufficient in the current period, production could be reduced so that fewer fixed costs could be deferred. Accordingly, income can be reported higher or lower than in the previous period even if unit sales, prices, and costs are the same. Variable costing would eliminate this avenue for income manipulation. It is a purer system because costs are charged off as incurred.

SOURCE: Robert W. Koehler, "Triple-Threat Strategy," *Management Accounting* (October 1991), p. 34. Published by Institute of Management Accountants, Montvale, N.J.

EXHIBIT 8–10
▼▼▼▼▼▼▼▼▼▼▼▼

PERFECT PENS, INC.
CONVERTING
VARIABLE COSTING
TO ABSORPTION
COSTING

1993	Cost of Goods Sold	1,250,000	
	Fixed Overhead		1,250,000
	To reclassify factory FOH as CGS since all production was sold during period		
1994	Finished Goods (20,000 × $5)	100,000	
	Cost of Goods Sold (220,000 × $5)	1,100,000	
	FOH Volume Variance	50,000	
	Fixed Overhead		1,250,000
	To reclassify factory FOH with an increase in ending inventory cost and CGS and establish the unfavorable volume variance for the year		
1995	Cost of Goods Sold	1,500,000	
	Fixed Overhead		1,250,000
	FOH Volume Variance		150,000
	Retained Earnings		100,000
	To reclassify factory FOH as CGS, establish the favorable volume variance for the year, and record the increase in income from the previous year through RE		

havior. Because of this focus, different charts of accounts, processes of accumulating costs, and formats for income statements are needed in variable costing.

These differences do have an impact on the accounting process. Accounting information must be gathered and recorded somewhat differently under the two product costing methods. However, to maintain two sets of accounting records is unnecessary. Oftentimes, the accounting system is maintained on a variable costing basis, and working paper entries are made at the end of the period to convert the internal information to an appropriate external form. These entries provide for the recognition of a fixed overhead volume variance and attach fixed overhead to Work in Process Inventory, Finished Goods Inventory, and Cost of Goods Sold. An illustration of such a conversion is provided in Exhibit 8–10, using the earlier information from the Perfect Pens, Inc. example.

If a company kept its accounts on a variable costing basis, it would need to make working paper entries at year-end to increase its inventory and Cost of Goods Sold accounts for the fixed overhead cost per unit. Additionally, a volume variance would need to be recorded if the actual fixed overhead allocation base differed from the estimated base. The separate variable and fixed accounts for each of the functional classifications could be added together and shown as a single amount on the absorption costing income statement.

Uniform capitalization for tax purposes

As mentioned earlier, the Internal Revenue Service established absorption costing as the method required for tax returns, which, in turn, promoted absorption costing to the unofficial method used for financial statements. The Tax Reform Act of 1986 began requiring the use of **uniform capitalization** (unicap) **rules** for all manufacturers and many wholesalers and retailers. The unicap rules require the inclusion in inventory of many previously expensed indirect costs; these inclusions for manufacturers cover all costs that directly benefit or are incurred because of production, including some general and administrative costs. Wholesalers and retailers that previously did not need to include any indirect costs in inventory now must inventory costs for items such as off-site warehousing, purchasing agents' salaries, and repackaging.

uniform capitalization rules

The following News Note indicates that the unicap rules will have significant impacts on management decisions. It is estimated that the unicap rules will have cost manufacturers approximately $35 billion in taxes between 1987 and 1992, since fewer nonfactory costs may initially be written off as period costs for tax purposes.[6] To comply with these regulations, many manufacturers have had to modify their cost accounting systems to identify and accumulate the designated indirect costs in a way that permits assigning such costs to production.

The material in this chapter is not intended to reflect the IRS unicap rules. However, if the financial community ultimately accepts the additional nonfactory costs as credible product costs, the IRS Code and Treasury Regulations may, once again, have influenced the generally accepted accounting definitions and procedures.

---

[6]Joseph V. Richards and James C. Godbout, "GASP—It's Super Full Absorption," *Ernst & Whinney Ideas* (Fall/Winter 1987–88), p. 2.

NEWS NOTE

Unicap Rules Mean New Decisions

The Tax Reform Act of 1986 added a new specialty to cost accounting. A UNICAP specialist will [need to] work with management in making key decisions such as:

- Should the company maintain a lower level of inventory so that less cost need be capitalized at year-end under the new rules?
- To facilitate the allocation process, can certain departments be divided along production versus non-production (or inventoriable versus noninventoriable) lines?
- Could the accounting or data processing department help standardize the division of costs in departments that have both inventoriable and noninventoriable costs?
- Will tax methods be used for financial and other purposes, or should multiple records be kept for inventory?

SOURCE: Joseph R. Oliver, "A New Dimension for Cost Accounting," *New Accountant* (November 1989), p. 42. © 1989 New DuBois Corporation, excerpted with permission.

SITE ANALYSIS

Cost accounting systems in businesses tend to develop over time. They typically begin by providing the minimal amount of information in the easiest-to-come-by format. They advance to a point where they can totally meet external reporting demands, but do not necessarily provide managers with the most appropriate information in the most appropriate format. Absorption costing meets external demands; variable costing tends to meet internal needs. While everyone in the organization will never agree on what the "real" cost of a product is, "the goal is to provide management with the most accurate cost information available." [7]

For a company making a single product on a discrete basis, the determination of product cost is fairly easy: divide current period costs by current period production. For a company engaged in continuous-flow production, the same basic method holds true: divide current period costs by current period equivalent production for each cost component. However, when the variety of products is high and the processes are complex, the answers to the questions at the beginning of the chapter are much more difficult.

> There is no one best way to design a successful cost management system. Moreover, cost management is an art, not a science. Since there is no single answer, cost managers must design the best system for their companies through a continually evolving process. [8]

continued

---

[7] Neal Clausing, "But What's My Cost?" *Journal of Cost Management for the Manufacturing Industry* (Fall 1990), p. 55.
[8] Ibid., p. 56.

That evolutionary process should seek to merge the best aspects of both absorption and variable costing with many other concepts presented in this text. The final stage of evolution for a cost system should result in one that is:

- simple—so that all who use it can understand it and that errors are minimized;
- comparable—so that it will be acceptable for external reporting;
- amenable to new manufacturing technologies;
- reflective of cost behaviors (and will, therefore, use multiple drivers to allocate overhead costs); and
- able to influence employee behaviors to increase productivity, efficiency, and product quality.

Can one cost system do all of these things? Professor Robert Kaplan of the Harvard Business School does not believe it can:

> No single system can adequately answer the demands made by the diverse functions of cost systems. While companies can use one method to capture all their detailed transactions data, the processing of this information for diverse purposes and audiences demands separate, customized development. Companies that try to satisfy all the needs for cost information with a single system have discovered they can't perform important managerial functions adequately. Moreover, systems that work well for one company may fail in a different environment. Each company has to design methods that make sense for its particular products and processes.[9]

No one knows what the cost systems of the future will look like. It is possible that many costs currently called "fixed" will be designated as long-term variable costs and, thus, be traced through appropriate cost drivers to products. The more costs that are deemed variable, the less of a distinction there will be between the results of absorption and variable costing. Managers and accountants alike can only hope that cost systems will develop that accomplish the objectives set forth earlier and, in doing so, will provide a prompt and accurate answer to the question, "But what's my cost?"

Applications related to cost systems and presentations are given on the next page.

CHAPTER SUMMARY

Two methods that businesses can use to determine product costs are absorption and variable costing. Under absorption costing, all factory costs (both variable and fixed) are treated as product costs. The absorption costing income statement reflects a full production cost approach for cost of goods sold, computes gross margin, and classifies nonfactory costs according to functional areas rather than by cost behavior.

Variable costing computes product cost using only the variable costs of production (direct materials, direct labor, and variable factory overhead). Fixed overhead charges are considered period costs and are expensed when they are incurred. The variable costing income statement presents cost of goods sold as composed of only

---

[9]An excerpt from "One Cost System Isn't Enough," by Robert S. Kaplan (January–February 1988), p. 66. Reprinted by permission of *Harvard Business Review*. Copyright © by the President and Fellows of Harvard College; all rights reserved.

APPLICATIONS STRATEGIES OF COSTING METHODS AND PRESENTATIONS	Discipline	Applications
	Accounting	Need to help inform users of costing information about the differences in product costing methods and how those differences will affect analysis—for example, since cost-volume-profit analysis focuses on variable costing, ''breakeven'' sales may not cause the company to break even on its absorption costing income statement; separating costs into their fixed and variable elements makes preparing flexible budgets and providing relevant costing information easier
	Economics	Absorption costing focuses on short-run profit figures rather than on long-run profit contribution figures; if absorption costing were a true ''full'' costing method, it would provide an accurate cost and profit picture for each product; variable costing approaches provide managers with costs that come close to the economist's notion of marginal costs and, thus, improve decision making
	Finance	Need to relate the information from both methods to standard industry-related financial statement guidelines for normal cost and profit ranges to determine if the company's basic costs and expense structure are reasonable and fall within the normal ranges—if they do not, it will be difficult to be profitable in the long run; financial analysts generally estimate a firm's value using external financial statements that are based on absorption costing
	Management	Understanding and being able to project how different costs will change in reaction to changes in activity levels is essential for effective operational planning, controlling, and decision making; management can keep its accounts on a variable costing basis for all of its managerial advantages and convert the numbers to absorption costing for external reporting purposes; variable costing might lead to underpricing and lowered profits
	Marketing	As product diversity increases, more overhead costs are incurred and, if these are not appropriately attached to products, a distorted product profit picture may arise and lead marketing personnel to believe that product proliferation is ''free''

the variable production cost per unit, shows product and total contribution margin figures, and classifies costs according to their cost behavior (variable or fixed). While variable costing can potentially provide management with better information for internal purposes than can absorption costing, variable costing is not considered an acceptable method of inventory valuation for external reporting or tax returns.

Absorption costing income differs from variable costing income for any period in which production and sales volumes differ. The difference between the two income amounts reflects the amount of fixed overhead that is either attached to or released from inventory in absorption costing as opposed to being immediately expensed in variable costing. Assuming that standard cost variances are immaterial and product cost is consistent over time, the following generalizations can be made:

1. If production is equal to sales, absorption costing income is equal to variable costing income because all fixed overhead is expensed under either method in the period incurred.

2. If production is greater than sales, absorption costing income is greater than variable costing income because absorption costing attaches a per-unit fixed overhead cost to each unit produced but not sold during the period. This inventorying of fixed overhead is in contrast to the expensing of all fixed overhead incurred during the period under variable costing.

3. If production is less than sales, absorption costing income is less than variable costing income because some fixed overhead deferred in a previous period (because of units being produced but not sold) will be released from inventory as part of Cost of Goods Sold. This release of fixed overhead means that there will be a greater amount of fixed overhead expensed on the absorption costing income statement than on the variable costing income statement.

APPENDIX

Theoretical Justifications for Absorption and Variable Costing

The basic underlying difference between absorption and variable costing is perceived by most accounting professionals to be a single issue: the decision as to which production costs should be treated as assets (product costs) and which should be treated as expenses (period costs). Accounting literature defines *asset* as an expected future economic benefit and *product cost* as one that is incurred because of production activity. Thus, the relevant question for determining whether absorption or variable costing is more "appropriate" centers on which costs must be incurred to produce inventory and, thus, provide future economic benefits. A future economic benefit means that something has "service potential to the extent that [it averts] the necessity for incurring costs in the future." [10]

The two basic parties interested in the output of accounting information systems are external users and internal users. Each group has different needs and would prefer that information be organized in a way that would best help accomplish that group's particular objectives. In general, financial accounting focuses on the needs of external users of accounting information, while cost/managerial accounting focuses on the needs of internal or management users.

External users make evaluations about an entity based on its long-term track record and use these evaluations in deciding whether to provide or withhold capital to that entity. The accountant is seen by external readers primarily as a special type of historian who measures past conditions and performance of the entity and who reports these events in a consistent, standardized format. The use of absorption costing financial statements provides a broad-based perspective in that product cost includes all factory costs. The profession has made a commitment to uniformity and standardization in preparing and reporting external financial statements. Absorption costing, through its similar treatment of all types of overhead costs, is amenable to a standardized presentation format.

---

[10]James M. Fremgen, "The Direct Costing Controversy—An Identification of the Issues," *Accounting Review* (January 1964), pp. 43–45, reprinted in Louis Geller and Jae K. Shim, eds., *Readings in Cost and Managerial Accounting* (Dubuque, Iowa: Kendall/Hunt, 1980), p. 49.

A basic proposition of absorption costing is that fixed overhead costs are necessary to produce inventory. Most fixed overhead costs provide the basic manufacturing capacity necessary to produce. It is obvious that products cannot be produced without basic capacity. Therefore, the underlying premise of absorption costing has theoretical merit. On this basis, fixed overhead should be included as part of product cost.

If the idea is accepted that fixed overhead is a product cost, then the matching concept used in external reporting requires that period expenses (through Cost of Goods Sold) include only the portion of fixed overhead relating to the units sold during the period. Consequently, the remaining fixed overhead attaches to units that have not been sold and is carried as part of inventory cost until a future period when those units are sold.

In contrast, internal users seem to prefer the information detail and format generated by variable costing. Variable costing advocates do not consider fixed factory overhead to be an asset or part of product cost. The premise underlying this philosophy is that fixed overhead is incurred to provide capacity regardless of whether production takes place. Fixed overhead is, then, not caused by production and should not be inventoried. Since some fixed overhead costs must be incurred every period, proponents of variable costing view fixed overhead as a period, rather than a product, cost. Period costs are expensed when incurred and do not attach to the units produced.

Variable costing is viewed as more adequately assisting managers in performing their planning, controlling, and decision-making functions. Most managers believe that effective control of current costs is important because they are held accountable for those costs. In attempting to control costs, managers prefer to receive reports that present fixed costs in a lump-sum manner similar to the way in which those fixed costs are incurred—rather than having fixed costs spread over production on a per-unit basis. Furthermore, the magnitude of many fixed costs (for example, depreciation and management salaries) can only be influenced in the long run rather than in the short run. Reporting fixed costs on a per-unit basis tends to contradict their true behavior and, thus, may hinder a manager's ability to control those costs.

For planning, controlling, and decision making, managers are not often interested in information based on the externally imposed criteria of uniformity and standardization. Managers want information that is useful and relates to a specific task at hand. Since managers are charged with the best use of scarce resources within an organization, they seek to use decision models and information that clearly depict relationships among independent and dependent variables. Because variable costing focuses on the relationship of costs to levels of activity, managers can more easily predict the future consequences of present actions using variable costing information.

Although absorption and variable costing are two distinct product costing methods, the chapter indicates the fact that they definitely overlap. Conclusions about the "rightness" or "wrongness" of absorption or variable costing depends upon one's perspective and belief in what constitutes an asset cost. Each method is valuable in relation to needs of the particular set of statement users it is intended to satisfy.

GLOSSARY

Absorption costing a cost accumulation method that treats the costs of all manufacturing components (direct materials, direct labor, variable overhead, and fixed overhead) as inventoriable or product costs; is also known as full costing

Functional classification a group of costs that were all incurred for the same basic purpose

Product contribution margin revenue minus variable cost of goods sold

Total contribution margin revenue minus all variable costs regardless of the area of incurrence (production or nonproduction)

Uniform capitalization rules IRS rules that require the inclusion in inventory of many previously expensed indirect costs; these inclusions for manufacturers cover all costs that directly benefit or are incurred because of production, including some general and administrative costs; wholesalers and retailers that previously did not need to include any indirect costs in inventory now must inventory costs for items such as off-site warehousing, purchasing agents' salaries, and repackaging; is also known as super-full absorption costing

Variable costing a cost accumulation method that includes only variable production costs (direct materials, direct labor, and variable overhead) as product or inventoriable costs; treats fixed overhead as a period cost; is also known as direct costing

SELECTED BIBLIOGRAPHY

Cornick, Michael, et al. "How Do Companies Analyze Overhead?" *Management Accounting* (June 1988), pp. 41–43.

Moore, L. Ted. "Manufacturing Cost Estimation." *Cost Engineering* (May 1990), pp. 17–21.

Paegelow, Richard S. "Management Accounting: Don't Base Product Decisions on Variable Costs." *Bank Accounting & Finance* (Summer 1991), pp. 55–59.

Santori, Peter. "Measuring Product Profitability in Today's Manufacturing Environment." *Emerging Practices in Cost Management*, Barry J. Brinker, ed. (Boston: Warren, Gorham & Lamont, 1990), pp. 327–32.

Sharman, Paul. "Time to Re-Examine the P&L." *CMA* (September 1991), pp. 22–25.

Sharp, Douglas, and Linda F. Christensen. "A New View of Activity-Based Costing." *Management Accounting* (September 1991), pp. 32–34.

Weber, Joseph V., et al. "Inventory Costing Under TRA 86—Part I." *CPA Journal* (May 1988), pp. 66–70.

SOLUTION STRATEGIES

1. Which method is being used (absorption or variable)?

   a. If absorption:
   - What is the fixed overhead application rate?
   - What denominator capacity was used in determining the fixed overhead application rate?
   - Is production equal to the denominator capacity used in determining fixed overhead application rate? If not, there is a fixed overhead volume variance that must be assigned, at least in part, to the income statement.
   - What is the cost per unit of product? (DM + DL + VOH + FOH)

   b. If variable:
   - What is the cost per unit of product? (DM + DL + VOH)
   - What is total fixed overhead? Assign to income statement in total as a period cost.

2. What is the relationship of production to sales?

   a. Production = Sales
   Absorption costing income = Variable costing income
   b. Production > Sales
   Absorption costing income > Variable costing income
   c. Production < Sales
   Absorption costing income < Variable costing income

3. Dollar difference between absorption costing income and variable costing income = FOH application rate × Change in inventory units

4. Use dollar difference determined in #3 to convert income figures as follows:

	From Absorption to Variable	From Variable to Absorption
No change in inventory	No adjustment	No adjustment
Increase in inventory	Subtract difference	Add difference
Decrease in inventory	Add difference	Subtract difference

DEMONSTRATION PROBLEM

The Silver Key Corporation began operations on January 14, 1993. The firm manufactures a computer keyboard that is sold to various computer producers. The firm's product costing system is based on actual costs and assumes a FIFO cost flow. Work in Process inventories are always minimal and are ignored for product costing purposes. Following are the firm's published income statements (based on absorption costing) for its first two years of operations, 1993 and 1994.

	1993		1994	
Sales		$625,000		$891,000
Cost of Goods Sold				
Beginning FG	$ 0		$ 60,000	
Cost of goods manufactured	300,000		382,500	
Goods available	$300,000		$442,500	
Ending FG	60,000	240,000	25,500	417,000
Gross margin		$385,000		$474,000
Less SG&A expenses				
Selling	$ 90,000		$126,000	
General & administrative	145,000	235,000	180,000	306,000
Net income		$150,000		$168,000

In regard to the 1993 and 1994 operations, other information from the accounting records indicated the following:

	1993	1994
Production in units	25,000	30,000
Sales in units	20,000	33,000
Production costs		
Direct materials per unit	$4.00	$4.00
Direct labor per unit	$3.00	$3.50
Variable overhead per unit	$1.00	$1.50
Annual fixed overhead cost	$100,000	$112,500
Other variable costs		
Selling costs per unit	$2.00	$2.00
Other fixed costs		
Annual selling costs	$ 50,000	$ 60,000
Annual G&A costs	$145,000	$180,000

Required:

a. Based on the previous data, recast the 1993 and 1994 income statements in the variable costing format.
b. Reconcile the costs assigned to the ending inventories for 1993 and 1994 in part (a) with the costs assigned to the ending inventories in the income statements presented earlier.
c. Reconcile the net incomes determined in part (a) with the net incomes shown in the original income statements.

Solution to Demonstration Problem

a. Recast the income statements for 1993 and 1994:

	1993		1994	
Sales		$625,000		$891,000
Cost of Goods Sold				
Beginning FG	$ 0		$ 40,000	
Cost of goods manufactured	200,000		270,000	
Goods available	$200,000		$310,000	
Ending FG	40,000	160,000	18,000	292,000
Production contribution margin		$465,000		$599,000
Less variable selling expenses		40,000		66,000
Total contribution margin		$425,000		$533,000
Fixed expenses				
Overhead	$100,000		$112,500	
Selling	50,000		60,000	
General & administrative	145,000	295,000	180,000	352,500
Net income		$130,000		$180,500

b. Reconcile ending Finished Goods Inventory costs:

	1993	1994
Ending inventory (variable costing)	$ 40,000	$ 18,000
Add back inventoriable portion of fixed factory overhead under the use of absorption costing:		
1993: ($100,000 ÷ 25,000) × 5,000	20,000	
1994: ($112,500 ÷ 30,000) × 2,000		7,500
Ending inventory (absorption costing)	$ 60,000	$ 25,500

c. Reconcile the net income for 1993 and 1994 under variable costing with the net income reported under absorption costing:

	1993	1994
Net income (variable costing, part a)	$130,000	$180,500
For 1993, add back the portion of fixed overhead that would be inventoried under absorption costing		
[($100,000 ÷ 25,000) × 5,000]	20,000	
For 1994, deduct the portion of fixed overhead that would be charged against this period's income under absorption costing*		(12,500)
Net income (absorption costing)	$150,000	$168,000

*Fixed overhead deducted under variable costing $112,500

Fixed overhead deducted under absorption costing with a FIFO cost flow:		
First 5,000 units sold (from beginning inventory)	$ 20,000	
Next 28,000 units sold [($112,500/30,000) × 28,000]	105,000	125,000
Additional fixed overhead deducted under absorption costing		$ 12,500

END-OF-CHAPTER MATERIALS

Questions

1. Which of the following are defined as product costs when absorption costing is used? When variable costing is used?

direct materials	direct labor
variable factory overhead	fixed factory overhead
selling expenses	administrative expenses

2. What is a functional classification of expenses? Give examples of functional classifications.

3. What is a behavioral classification of expenses? What are the behavioral classifications?

4. Which approach (variable or absorption) classifies costs by behavior? Which classifies by functional category?

5. For each of the terms that follow, indicate whether the term would be found on an absorption income statement (A), a variable costing income statement (V), or both (B).

    cost of goods sold
    contribution margin
    gross margin
    selling expenses
    variable expenses
    administrative expenses
    fixed expenses

6. What is the difference between absorption and variable costing in the treatment of fixed factory overhead?

7. Is it true that variable costing cannot be used in conjunction with a costing system that is based on standard costs? Explain.

8. Which approach, variable or absorption, is unofficially required by the Financial Accounting Standards Board and the Securities and Exchange Commission for external financial reporting? Why do you think this requirement exists?

9. Would a volume variance ever be found on a variable costing income statement? Explain.

10. Define product contribution margin and total contribution margin. What is the difference between the product and total contribution margins?

11. For a specific firm in a year in which production and sales volume are equal, both an absorption and a variable costing income statement are prepared. Would you normally expect that the gross margin on the absorption costing statement would be equal to the total contribution margin on the variable costing statement? Explain.

12. Which costing approach (variable or absorption) provides the clearer picture as to how costs will change as activity changes? Explain.

13. If the net incomes for a company computed under the variable and absorption approaches are different, which of the following cost(s) is (are) responsible for the difference?

a. the variable cost of direct materials
b. the variable cost of factory overhead
c. the variable selling expenses
d. the fixed selling expenses
e. the fixed factory overhead

14. In the following expressions, let S = sales volume, P = production volume, and f = function of. Which of the following expressions are true?

> Net Income(absorption) = $f(S,P)$
> Net Income(absorption) = $f(S)$
> Net Income(variable) = $f(S,P)$
> Net Income(variable) = $f(S)$

15. Describe a circumstance in which net income computed under the absorption costing method will exceed the net income computed under the variable costing method. What is the reason that this condition exists?

16. (Appendix) Why does the definition of an "asset" affect an analysis of which costing method (variable or absorption) is theoretically superior?

17. (Appendix) Why do proponents of variable costing view fixed factory overhead as a period cost?

18. (Appendix) Evaluate the merits of the following statement: "Relative to variable costing, absorption costing is a superior product costing method."

■ Exercises

19. *(Product cost under AC & VC)* The Blue Suede Shoe Company produced 100,000 pairs of shoes and sold 70,000 in its first year of operations. There was no Work in Process Inventory at year-end. Its costs for that year were:

Direct materials	$ 400,000
Direct labor	300,000
Variable factory overhead	150,000
Variable selling & administrative	210,000
Fixed factory overhead	250,000
Fixed selling & administrative	175,000
Total	$1,485,000

For this company's first year of operations, compute

a. the cost of one unit of product if the company uses variable costing.
b. the cost of one unit of product if the company uses absorption costing.

20. *(Product cost under AC & VC)* The Toronto Telephone Company produces telephones that it sells to a variety of electronics wholesalers. Its operating costs for 1993 are summarized:

Variable costs	
Selling & administration (per unit sold)	$2
Production (per unit produced)	8
Fixed Costs	
Selling & administration	$1,000,000
Production	2,000,000
Selling price (per unit)	$50

In 1993, the company produced 100,000 units and sold 80,000. It had no beginning inventories for 1993 and no ending Work in Process Inventory.

a. If the company uses absorption costing, compute the cost assigned to the ending inventory.

b. If the company uses variable costing, compute the cost assigned to the ending inventory.

21. *(Missing numbers)* An incomplete 1993 income statement for the Holloway Company follows:

Sales ($40 per unit)	$1,000,000
Variable cost of goods sold	?
Product contribution margin	?
Variable selling & administrative costs	100,000
Total contribution margin	600,000
Fixed production costs	250,000
Fixed administrative costs	?
Net income	150,000

Based on the prior information, compute the following:

a. the cost to produce one unit of product
b. the total product contribution margin
c. fixed administrative costs

22. *(Missing numbers)* Shortly after the end of its first year of operations, a fire destroyed nearly all cost and production records of the Safe Living Products Company, a producer of quality smoke alarms. Having been hired to piece together the fragments of the records that were salvaged from the blaze, you have determined the following regarding the first-year operations:

Production in units	?
Sales in units	9,500
Total sales	$109,250.00
Gross margin	54,625.00
Total fixed factory overhead costs incurred	22,500.00
Variable production costs (per unit)	3.50
Total selling and administrative costs	38,000.00

a. From the previous information, prepare an income statement in the absorption costing format.
b. Determine how many units were produced in the first year.

23. *(Volume variance)* The Holstein Milk Company produces evaporated milk. The firm uses an absorption costing system based on standard costs. Overhead is applied to production at a rate of $.10 per unit. The standard costs per unit for 1993 were:

Direct materials	$0.07
Direct labor	$0.05
Variable overhead	$0.04
Fixed overhead	$?

The expected level of production for 1993 is 4,000,000 units.

a. For 1993, how much fixed manufacturing overhead did the company expect to incur?

b. If actual production was 4,200,000 units, compute the volume variance.

c. Prepare the journal entry to dispose of the volume variance.

24. *(NI under AC & VC)* The following information pertains to the operations of the Fillmore Manufacturing Company for 1993:

Sales (2,000 units @ $20)	$40,000
Variable costs of production	10,000
Fixed costs of production	5,000
Variable selling costs (per unit sold)	1
Fixed selling costs	3,000
Beginning WIP and Finished Goods Inventories (units)	0
Ending WIP Inventory (units)	0
Total number of units produced	2,500

For the Fillmore Company for 1993, determine

a. net income if absorption costing is used,

b. net income if variable costing is used, and

c. reconcile your answers in parts (a) and (b).

25. *(Income under AC & VC)* The CC Company manufactures Mexican bonnets. Information pertaining to its first year of operations follows:

Sales in dollars	$?
Production in units	5,000
Sales in units	4,500
Variable costs per unit	
Direct materials	$3
Direct labor	4
Factory overhead	2
Selling & administrative	1
Fixed costs (per year)	
Factory overhead	$200,000
Selling & administrative	100,000

The company had no work in process at the end of its first year of operations. Determine how much higher (or lower) the reported first-year net income would have been if the CC Company used absorption costing rather than variable costing.

26. *(Convert to VC)* The ClipIt Company produces and sells boxes of assorted household fasteners. Included with its published 1993 financial statements was the following income statement:

Sales (1,000,000 boxes @ $4.00)	$4,000,000
Cost of goods sold	2,000,000
Gross margin	$2,000,000
Selling & administrative expenses	1,500,000
Net income	$ 500,000

From carefully scanning the company records you were able to obtain additional information regarding the company's operations for 1993:

- The company had no beginning or ending inventories of work in process.
- The company had no beginning Finished Goods Inventory.

- Production in 1993 was 1,250,000 units.
- Total fixed production costs were $400,000.
- Variable selling costs were $1 per unit.

a. Determine the ClipIt Company's net income for 1993 under variable costing.
b. Reconcile the net income computed in part (a) with the net income reported in the previous income statement.

27. *(Convert to AC)* In its first year of operations, the Jayhawk Company reported the following operating results (on production of 12,000 units and sales of 10,000 units):

Sales	$500,000
Total contribution margin	250,000
Net income	100,000

From an examination of the cost records, you have also determined that variable selling and administrative costs amounted to $2 per unit, and fixed selling and administrative costs were $30,000.

Using the previous information, prepare an income statement for the Jayhawk Company using absorption costing.

28. *(Convert to AC)* The Canadian Beverage Company has been in operation for two years. It is a privately held firm and produces no external financial information. It employs the variable costing method for preparing internal financial statements. Selected information from its first two years of operations follows:

	Year 1	Year 2
Quarts of product produced	500,000	500,000
Quarts of product sold	400,000	550,000
Fixed production costs	$1,000,000	$1,000,000
Variable production costs	1,500,000	1,500,000
Net income (variable costing)	400,000	1,300,000

a. Had the company used absorption costing in year 1, how much net income would it have reported?
b. Had the company used absorption costing in both years 1 and 2, how much net income would it have reported in year 2?

Problems

29. *(Product costs under VC & AC; CM; GM)* The Leisure Equipment Company produces and sells electric golf carts. The company uses a costing system based on actual costs. Selected accounting and production information for fiscal 1993 follows:

Net income (absorption costing)	$ 400,000
Sales	$3,400,000
Beginning inventories (WIP & Finished Goods) (units)	0
Ending WIP (units)	0
Fixed factory overhead cost incurred	$ 600,000
Selling & administrative costs, variable	$ 400,000
Selling & administrative costs, fixed	$ 500,000
Net income (variable costing)	$ 310,000
Units produced	2,000
Units sold	?

Required: Compute each of the following:

a. number of units sold
b. the cost of one unit of product under variable costing
c. the cost of one unit of product under absorption costing
d. the total contribution margin under variable costing
e. the gross margin under absorption costing

30. *(Determine income & FG under AC & VC)* In 1993 (its first year of operations), the William Tell Archery Company, a producer of bow sets (bows and arrows), reported the following results:

Sales	88,000 units @ $100 = $8,800,000
Production	100,000 units
Ending WIP	0 units

Variable costs incurred:		Fixed costs incurred:	
Direct materials	$1,500,000	Factory overhead	$ 750,000
Direct labor	2,000,000	General overhead	1,300,000
Factory overhead	500,000	Selling & administrative	
Selling & administrative costs	616,000 –	costs	450,000

vary w/ Sales

Required:

a. Using the prior information, prepare an income statement for the year ended December 31, 1993, based on absorption costing.
b. Using the prior information, prepare a variable costing income statement.
c. Compute the cost of the ending Finished Goods Inventory under absorption costing.
d. Compute the cost of the ending Finished Goods Inventory using variable costing.
e. Reconcile your answers in parts (c) and (d).

31. *(Convert to AC; explain differences)* In 1984, Bill Clemens invented and patented a lawn edger. After saving enough funds to form a company to produce the lawn edger, Bill began production of the machines in 1993. An income statement for his first year of operations follows:

Sales (1,900 units)		$190,000
Variable cost of goods sold		
Beginning inventory	$ 0	
Cost of goods manufactured (3,000 units)	195,000	
Cost of goods available for sale	$195,000	
Less ending inventory	71,500	123,500
Product contribution margin		$ 66,500
Variable selling & administrative expenses		9,500
Total contribution margin		$ 57,000
Less fixed expenses		
Factory overhead	$ 60,000	
Selling & administrative	40,000	100,000
Net loss		$(43,000)

It is apparent from the form of the income statement that Bill has elected to use variable costing.

Required:

a. Recast the previous income statement in the absorption costing format.
b. Assuming Bill knows very little about accounting, prepare a memo to Bill explaining the differences in the net loss and inventory amounts under the variable and absorption approaches.

32. *(Income statement information)* Spirit Apparel is a firm that manufactures t-shirts that bear the insignias of various sports teams. The company has just completed its third year of operations. The firm employs a standard costing system. The standard costs per unit that follow have remained constant for all three years.

	Standard Unit Costs
Direct materials	$4.00
Direct labor	2.00
Variable overhead	1.50
Fixed overhead	2.00

Variable selling and administrative costs run $1.25 per unit, and fixed selling and administrative costs were $300,000 for year 3. The fixed overhead costs of $2.00 per unit are based on expected production of 50,000 units. Inventory and production information for year 3 follows:

Beginning inventory	10,000 units
Production	50,000 units
Ending inventory	4,000 units

Required:

a. Is the company using variable or absorption costing? How can you tell?
b. If there were no cost variances in year 3, how much factory overhead was incurred?
c. Ignoring any cost variances, how much fixed factory overhead was expensed in year 3?
d. What amount of cost is assigned to the ending inventory in year 3?
e. Assuming year 3 production was only 45,000 units, compute the year 3 volume variance.

33. *(Income under AC & VC)* The Hydraulic Hose Company manufactures hoses that are used to transfer hydraulic oil between hydraulic pumps and hydraulic power cylinders. The hoses are built to withstand pressure up to 1,000 pounds per square inch. The firm's hoses are found on a variety of industrial, commercial, and agricultural equipment. On January 1, 1990, the firm switched to a standard costing system based on absorption costs. The standard costs per unit are reassessed each January and are then set for the following year. The firm measures its output in feet of hose produced. Work in Process Inventories are typically so negligible that they can be ignored. The firm compiles financial statements on a monthly basis, and information for the month of July 1992 follows:

Beginning Finished Goods Inventory	200,000 feet
Planned production	1,000,000 feet
Actual production	1,000,000 feet
Number of feet sold in July	1,050,000 feet
Standard variable production costs	$0.50 per foot
Standard fixed production costs	.20 per foot
Average July sales price	1.30 per foot

Fixed selling and administrative expenses were $200,000, and variable selling and administrative expenses were $105,000 in July.

Required:

a. Using the previous information, compile Hydraulic Hose Company's income statement for the month of July.

b. Assuming that actual fixed overhead and standard fixed overhead were equal in July, recast the income statement in the variable costing format.

c. Why is the net income higher when variable costing is used?

34. *(Income under AC & VC)* Talbot, Inc., has been working on the development of models to predict its costs and revenues. As a result of its work, three models have been developed. There is a revenue, a production cost, and a period cost (selling, general, and administration expense) model:

Revenue Model

$$Y = \$30X$$

where Y is total revenue and X is the number of units sold.

Production Cost Model

$$Y = \$40,000 + \$10X$$

where Y is total production cost and X is the number of units produced.

Period Cost Model

$$Y = \$20,000 + \$5X$$

where Y is total period costs and X is the number of units sold.

Required:

a. Based on the previous models, compute the projected net income for a period where Talbot produces 10,000 units and sells 8,000. Assume that Talbot uses absorption costing.

b. Repeat part (a), but this time assume that Talbot uses variable costing.

35. *(Income under AC & VC)* The Bird Tub, Inc., is a small firm (formed in 1990) that manufactures a combination outdoor bird feeder/water basin. The product is sold exclusively in Canada and northern parts of the United States. Its main appeal to bird enthusiasts is that it has an electric heating element that keeps liquids from freezing, even in the cold winter months. Information on its operations for 1993 and 1994 follows:

	1993	1994
Production in units	10,000	12,000
Sales in units	8,000	14,000
Beginning Finished Goods Inventory (units)	0	?
Beginning and ending WIP inventories (units)	0	0
Average sales price per unit	$ 15	$ 16
Average direct material cost per unit	2	2
Average direct labor cost per unit	3	3
Variable overhead cost per unit	1	1
Actual fixed factory overhead	50,000	48,000
Selling expenses		
Total variable	10,000	17,500
Total fixed	20,000	18,000

Required:

a. Assuming the company uses an absorption costing system based on actual costs, compile income statements for 1993 and 1994.

b. How much total net income is generated under absorption costing for the two-year period?

c. Assuming the company uses a variable costing system based on actual costs, compile income statements for 1993 and 1994.

d. How much total net income is generated under variable costing for the two-year period?

e. Does the choice of variable or absorption costing affect the timing for the recognition of expenses, or the actual amount of expenses incurred?

36. *(Missing numbers; VC income statement)* The following information was extracted from cost records of the Sly Fox Company for 1993. For 1993, the company had no beginning Finished Goods Inventory, and it had no beginning or ending WIP inventories. The company uses variable costing.

	Variable Costs	**Fixed Costs**
Direct materials	$3 per unit	
Direct labor	5 per unit	
Factory overhead	2 per unit	$200,000
Selling & administrative	2 per unit	350,000

The product contribution margin in 1993 was $8 per unit and net income was $200,000.

Required:

a. What was the company's sales price per unit?

b. What were total revenues?

c. How many units were sold?

d. Prepare a variable costing income statement for 1993.

37. *(Missing numbers)* Consistent with the firm's wacky reputation, the new controller of the Car Games Company was presented with a puzzler on her first day of work. She was simply told to examine the two income statements that follow, which pertain to the same firm over the same period of time.

	Variable	**Absorption**
Sales	$3,000	?
Cost of goods sold	1,500	?
Total contribution margin	1,200	NA
Total nonproduct costs incurred	NA	$1,200
Net income	?	200
Beginning Finished Goods & WIP	0	?
Ending WIP inventory	?	0
Ending Finished Goods Inventory	0	?
Units produced	?	?
Units sold	?	?

After examining the statements, she asked for your help.

Required: Determine the following amounts:

a. gross margin

b. variable selling and administrative expense

c. fixed selling and administrative costs

  d. the amount of fixed factory overhead cost incurred
  e. the net income under variable costing

38. *(Income under VC & AC; cost of FG)* The High CL Company manufactures deep fat fryers that are sold for use in restaurants, nightclubs, and snack bars. The company employs a standard variable costing system. However, because the company has common stock that is publicly traded, it must convert the variable costing data to an absorption basis for external financial statements. The following information pertains to fiscal years 1993 and 1994:

	1993	1994
Average sales price per unit	$40	$41
Production in units	25,000	30,000
Sales in units	25,000	25,000
Beginning Finished Goods Inventory (units)	2,000	?
Work in Process (beginning & ending)	0	0

Standard costs per unit for both 1993 and 1994:

Materials	$8.00
Labor	6.50
Overhead	3.50

Annual fixed costs (actual and standard were the same):

Factory	$240,000
Selling & administrative	100,000

Also, for both 1993 and 1994, variable selling and administrative costs amounted to 20 percent of total sales. In converting the variable costing data to absorption, the company applies the fixed overhead based on the practical capacity of 30,000 units. Any resulting volume variance is treated as an adjustment to Cost of Goods Sold. Variable overhead is applied based on the actual number of units produced in the period.

Required:

  a. Prepare an income statement based on standard variable costing for 1994.
  b. Prepare an income statement based on standard absorption costing for 1994.
  c. Reconcile your answers in parts (a) and (b).
  d. Compute the cost assigned to the ending Finished Goods Inventory for 1994 under standard absorption costing.

39. *(Essay)* Which of the following dimensions of product costing would be affected by a switch from absorption to variable costing: the product costing system, the valuation method, cost accumulation, or financial statement presentation? Why and how?

40. *(Essay)* Your neighbor, Tim Allen, wants to do some home improvements, but finds that the power drill he owns is ill-equipped for the job. You are a vice-president of the Zoomby Corporation, which manufactures the Zoomby Power Drill 2000. Tim knows that you can purchase tools from the company at "cost plus 10 percent"—a tremendous discount from what he would have to pay in a retail store. Discuss the variety of ways that Zoomby could compute "cost" in selling tools to company employees and which one or ones would be the most appropriate.

Cases

41. The Daniels Tool & Die Corporation has been in existence for a little over three years. The company's sales have been increasing each year as it builds a reputation. The company manufactures dies to its customers' specifications; as a consequence, a job order cost system is employed. Factory overhead is applied to the jobs based on direct labor hours, utilizing the absorption (full) costing method. Overapplied or underapplied overhead is treated as an adjustment to Cost of Goods Sold. The company's income statements for the last two years are as follows:

DANIELS TOOL & DIE CORPORATION
1992–1993 COMPARATIVE INCOME STATEMENTS

	1992	1993
Sales	$840,000	$1,015,000
Cost of goods sold		
Finished goods, 1/1	$ 25,000	$ 18,000
Cost of goods manufactured	548,000	657,600
Total available	$573,000	$ 675,600
Finished goods, 12/31	18,000	14,000
Cost of goods sold before overhead		
adjustment	$555,000	$ 661,600
Underapplied factory overhead	36,000	14,400
Cost of goods sold	$591,000	$ 676,000
Gross profit	$249,000	$ 339,000
Selling expenses	$ 82,000	$ 95,000
Administrative expenses	70,000	75,000
Total operating expenses	$152,000	$ 170,000
Operating income	$ 97,000	$ 169,000

DANIELS TOOL & DIE CORPORATION
INVENTORY BALANCES

	1/1/92	12/31/92	12/31/93
Raw Material	$22,000	$30,000	$10,000
Work in Process			
Costs	$40,000	$48,000	$64,000
Direct labor hours	1,335	1,600	2,100
Finished Goods			
Costs	$25,000	$18,000	$14,000
Direct labor hours	1,450	1,050	820

Daniels used the same predetermined overhead rate in applying overhead to production orders in both 1992 and 1993. The rate was based on the following estimates:

Fixed factory overhead	$ 25,000
Variable factory overhead	$155,000
Direct labor hours	25,000
Direct labor costs	$150,000

In 1992 and 1993, actual direct labor hours expended were 20,000 and 23,000, respectively. Raw materials put into production were $292,000 in 1992 and $370,000 in 1993. Actual fixed overhead was $42,300 for 1992 and $37,400 for 1993, and the planned direct labor rate was the direct labor rate achieved.

For both years, all of the reported administrative costs were fixed, while the variable portion of the reported selling expenses results from a commission of 5 percent of sales revenue.

a. For the year ended December 31, 1993, prepare a revised income statement for Daniels Tool & Die Corporation utilizing the variable costing method. Be sure to include the contribution margin on your statement.

b. Prepare a numerical reconciliation of the difference in operating income between Daniels Tool & Die Corporation's 1993 income statement prepared on the basis of absorption costing and the revised 1993 income statement prepared on the basis of variable costing.

c. Describe both the advantages and disadvantages of using variable costing.

(CMA)

42. Portland Optics, Inc., specializes in manufacturing lenses for large telescopes and cameras used in space exploration. As the specifications for the lenses are determined by the customer and vary considerably, the company uses a job order cost system. Factory overhead is applied to jobs on the basis of direct labor hours, utilizing the absorption (full) costing method. Portland's predetermined overhead rates for 1992 and 1993 were based on the following estimates:

	1992	1993
Direct labor hours	32,500	44,000
Direct labor cost	$325,000	$462,000
Fixed factory overhead	130,000	176,000
Variable factory overhead	162,500	198,000

Jim Bradford, Portland's controller, would like to use variable costing for internal reporting purposes as he believes statements prepared using variable costing are more appropriate for making product decisions. In order to explain the benefits of variable costing to the other members of Portland's management team, Bradford plans to convert the company's income statement from absorption costing to variable costing. He has gathered the following information for this purpose, along with a copy of Portland's 1992–93 comparative income statement.

PORTLAND OPTICS, INC.
COMPARATIVE INCOME STATEMENT
FOR THE YEARS 1992–93

	1992	1993
Net sales	$1,140,000	$1,520,000
Cost of goods sold		
Finished goods at January 1	$ 16,000	$ 25,000
Cost of goods manufactured	720,000	976,000
Total available	$ 736,000	$1,001,000
Finished goods at December 31	25,000	14,000

Cost of goods sold before overhead		
adjustment	$ 711,000	$ 987,000
Overhead adjustment	12,000	7,000
Cost of goods sold	$ 723,000	$ 994,000
Gross profit	$ 417,000	$ 526,000
Selling expense	$ 150,000	$ 190,000
Administrative expense	160,000	187,000
Total operating expenses	$ 310,000	$ 377,000
Operating income	$ 107,000	$ 149,000

- Portland's actual manufacturing data for the two years are as follows:

	1992	1993
Direct labor hours	30,000	42,000
Direct labor cost	$300,000	$435,000
Raw materials used	140,000	210,000
Fixed factory overhead	132,000	175,000

- The company's actual inventory balances were:

	12/31/91	12/31/92	12/31/93
Raw Materials	$32,000	$36,000	$18,000
Work in Process			
Costs	$44,000	$34,000	$60,000
Direct labor hours	1,800	1,400	2,500
Finished Goods			
Costs	$16,000	$25,000	$14,000
Direct labor hours	700	1,080	550

- For both years, all administrative costs were fixed, while a portion of the selling expense resulting from an 8 percent commission on net sales was variable. Portland reports any over- or underapplied overhead as an adjustment to Cost of Goods Sold.

a. For the year ended December 31, 1993, prepare the revised income statement for Portland Optics, Inc., utilizing the variable costing method. Be sure to include the contribution margin on the revised income statement.

b. Describe two advantages of using variable costing rather than absorption costing.

(CMA)

43. Sun Company, a wholly owned subsidiary of Guardian, Inc., produces and sells three main product lines. The company employs a standard cost accounting system for recordkeeping purposes. At the beginning of 1993, the president of Sun Company presented the budget to the parent company and accepted a commitment to contribute $15,800 to Guardian's consolidated profit in 1993. The president has been confident that the year's profit would exceed the budget target, since the monthly sales reports that she has been receiving have shown that sales for the year will exceed budget by 10 percent. The president is both disturbed and confused when the controller presents an adjusted forecast as of November 30, 1993, indicating that profit will be 11 percent under budget. The two forecasts are as follows:

	1/1/93	11/30/93
Sales	$268,000	$294,800
Cost of sales at standard*	212,000	233,200
Gross margin at standard	$ 56,000	$ 61,600
(Under-) overapplied fixed overhead	0	(6,000)
Actual gross margin	$ 56,000	$ 55,600
Selling expenses	$ 13,400	$ 14,740
Administrative expenses	26,800	26,800
Total operating expenses	$ 40,200	$ 41,540
Earnings before tax	$ 15,800	$ 14,060

*Includes fixed manufacturing overhead of $30,000.

There have been no sales price changes or product mix shifts since the 1/1/93 forecast. The only cost variance on the income statement is the underapplied manufacturing overhead. This amount arose because the company produced only 16,000 standard machine hours (budgeted machine hours were 20,000) during 1993 as a result of a shortage of raw materials while its principal supplier was closed for a strike. Fortunately, Sun Company's Finished Goods Inventory was large enough to fill all sales orders received.

a. Analyze and explain why the profit has declined in spite of increased sales and good control over costs.
b. What plan, if any, could Sun Company adopt during December to improve its reported profit at year-end? Explain your answer.
c. Illustrate and explain how Sun Company could adopt an alternative internal cost reporting procedure that would avoid the confusing effect of the present procedure.
d. Would the alternative procedure described in part (c) be acceptable to Guardian, Inc., for financial reporting purposes? Explain.

(CMA adapted)

Ethics Discussion

44. Peter Klein is the sales representative for a heavy construction equipment manufacturer. He is compensated by a moderate fixed salary plus an 8 percent bonus on sales. Klein is aware that some of the higher-priced items earn the company a lower contribution margin and some of the lower-priced items earn the company a higher contribution margin. He learned this information from the variable costing financial statements produced by the company for management-level employees. One of Klein's best friends is a manager at the company.

Klein has recently started pushing sales only of the high-priced items by generously entertaining receptive customers and offering them gifts through the company's promotion budget. He feels that management has not given him adequate raises in the twenty years he has been with the company, and now he is too old to find a better job.

a. Are Klein's actions legal?
b. What are the ethical issues involved in the case from Klein's standpoint?
c. Are there ethical issues to the case from company management's standpoint?
d. What do you believe Klein should do? Why?

PART THREE

USING MANAGERIAL ACCOUNTING INFORMATION FOR PLANNING

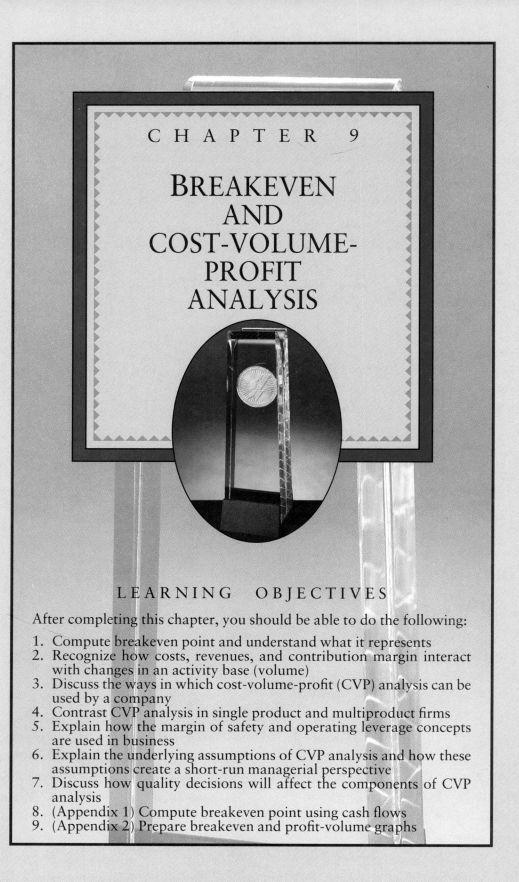

C H A P T E R   9

BREAKEVEN AND COST-VOLUME-PROFIT ANALYSIS

LEARNING OBJECTIVES

After completing this chapter, you should be able to do the following:

1. Compute breakeven point and understand what it represents
2. Recognize how costs, revenues, and contribution margin interact with changes in an activity base (volume)
3. Discuss the ways in which cost-volume-profit (CVP) analysis can be used by a company
4. Contrast CVP analysis in single product and multiproduct firms
5. Explain how the margin of safety and operating leverage concepts are used in business
6. Explain the underlying assumptions of CVP analysis and how these assumptions create a short-run managerial perspective
7. Discuss how quality decisions will affect the components of CVP analysis
8. (Appendix 1) Compute breakeven point using cash flows
9. (Appendix 2) Prepare breakeven and profit-volume graphs

The New England Patriots: Full Stadium, But No Profits

Professional sports is a capital-intensive, high fixed cost industry. In order to make a profit the stadiums and arenas must be at or near capacity for most of the season. Yet, there are teams that continue to lose money although every game is sold out. [As of 1988], the New England Patriots have had a sold-out stadium for every game and still have lost money for the last seven years. Breakeven points for even the lower-cost franchises continue to rise. The Pittsburgh Pirates, with a low total salary of approximately $6 million, [had] a breakeven point of 1.4 million fans [as of 1988].

SOURCE: William Wucinich, "Profit Is the Name of the Game," *Management Accounting* (February 1991), p. 58. Published by Institute of Management Accountants, Montvale, N.J.

A chieving the right combination of volume level and selling price that will generate enough revenue to cover all variable and fixed costs is a problem faced by all organizations. Regardless of whether you are the manager of a professional sports team, a rock concert promoter, or a dentist with your own practice, covering costs is a matter of operational survival. The level of activity, in units or dollars, at which total revenues equal total costs is called the **breakeven point** (BEP). At breakeven, the organization experiences neither profit nor loss on its operating activities. As the manager, promoter, or dentist, however, you would most likely not want to operate at a level of volume that simply covered costs; you would want to make profits. Knowing the "break even" level of operations provides a point of reference from which you would be better able to plan for volume goals that should generate income rather than produce losses.

breakeven point

THE BREAKEVEN POINT

Finding the breakeven point requires an understanding of an organization's revenue and cost functions. As noted in chapters 2 and 3, certain assumptions are made about cost behavior so that the information can be used in accounting computations. The following list summarizes these simplifying assumptions about revenue and cost functions.

Revenue: Total revenue fluctuates in direct proportion to units sold. Revenue per unit is assumed to remain constant, and fluctuations in per-unit revenue for factors such as quantity discounts are ignored.

Variable costs: Total variable costs fluctuate in direct proportion to level of activity or volume. On a per-unit basis, variable costs remain constant within the relevant range. This assumed variable cost behavior is the same as the assumed revenue behavior. Variable costs exist in all functional business areas including production, distribution, selling, and administration.

Having enough volume to fill Foxboro Stadium does not guarantee profits. Profits only occur after all variable and fixed costs are covered.

Fixed costs: Total fixed costs remain constant within the relevant range. Per-unit fixed cost decreases as volume increases, and it increases as volume decreases. Fixed costs include *both* fixed factory overhead and fixed selling and administrative expenses.

Mixed costs: Mixed costs must be separated into their variable and fixed elements before they can be used in breakeven analysis. Any method (such as high-low) that validly separates these costs in relation to one or more predictors may be used.

One very important amount in breakeven analysis is contribution margin. On a per-unit basis, **contribution margin** (CM) is defined as selling price minus the per-unit variable production, selling, and administrative costs. Contribution margin reflects

contribution margin

EXHIBIT 9–1
▼▼▼▼▼▼▼▼▼▼▼▼

FOOTBALL FANS,
INC. 1993 INCOME
STATEMENT

	Total	Per Unit	Percent
Sales (7,000 pom-poms)	$49,000	$7.00	100%
Variable Costs:			
Production	$ 3,430	$ .49	7%
Selling	17,150	2.45	35%
Total variable cost	20,580	$2.94	42%
Contribution Margin	$28,420	$4.06	58%
Fixed Costs:			
Production	$10,000		
Selling & administrative	12,000		
Total fixed cost	22,000		
Income Before Income Taxes	$ 6,420		

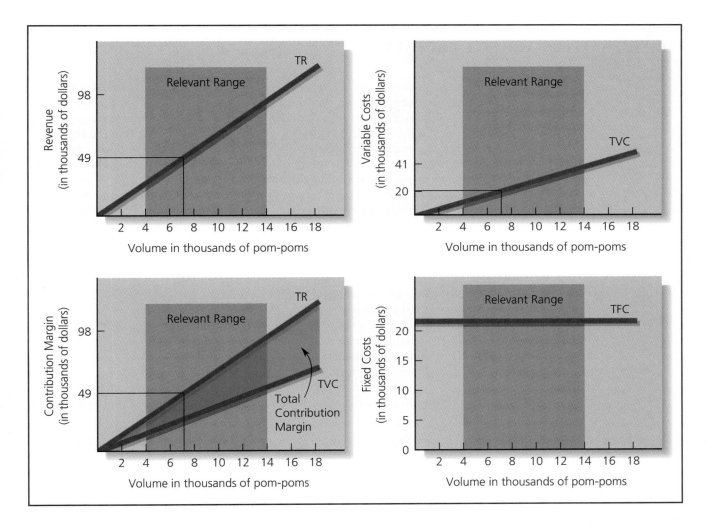

the revenue remaining after covering all variable costs. It is this amount that *contrib-utes* to the coverage of all fixed costs and to the generation of profits. Contribution margin per unit is constant because both revenue and variable costs have been defined as being constant per unit. As defined in chapter 8, total contribution margin is the difference between total revenues and total variable costs for all units sold. Total contribution margin fluctuates in direct proportion to sales volume.

To illustrate the computation of breakeven point, 1993 income statement information for Football Fans, Inc., is given in Exhibit 9–1. The company began producing and selling pom-poms at football stadiums this year. The current relevant range of production and sales for the company is between 4,000 and 14,000 pom-poms per year. The costs given in the exhibit are standard costs for all product elements.

The income statement items for Football Fans, Inc., are graphed in Exhibit 9–2. These graphs provide visual representations of the company's revenue, costs, and contribution margin behaviors.

EXHIBIT 9–2
▼▼▼▼▼▼▼▼▼▼

FOOTBALL FANS, INC. GRAPHICAL PRESENTATION OF INCOME STATEMENT ITEMS

FORMULA APPROACH TO BREAKEVEN

The formula approach uses an algebraic equation to calculate the breakeven point. It is important to note, however, that the answer to the equation is not always an "acceptable" solution. For example, partial units cannot be sold, or some items may be sold only in specified lot sizes. Thus, the answers provided by solving the equations may need to be rounded to whole numbers. Rounding is always done upward in breakeven analysis because this will provide a small profit rather than the small loss that would be shown from rounding downward.

Algebraic breakeven computations use an equation representing the income statement. This equation groups costs by behavior and shows the relationships among revenue, fixed cost, variable cost, volume, and profit as follows:

$$R(X) - VC(X) - FC = P$$

where R = revenue (selling price) per unit
   X = number of units sold or to be sold
  $R(X)$ = total revenue
   FC = total fixed cost
   VC = variable cost per unit
  $VC(X)$ = total variable cost
   P = before-tax profit

Slightly reformatting this equation shows that total revenues are equal to total cost plus profit:

$$R(X) = VC(X) + FC + P$$

Since the equation represents an income statement, P can be set equal to zero for the formula to indicate a breakeven situation. At the point where $P = \$0$, total revenues equal total costs, and breakeven point (BEP) *in units* to be sold can be found by solving the equation for X.

$$R(X) = VC(X) + FC$$
$$R(X) - VC(X) = FC$$
$$(R - VC)(X) = FC$$
$$X = FC \div (R - VC)$$

Breakeven point volume is equal to total fixed cost divided by (revenue per unit minus variable cost per unit). Since revenue minus variable cost is equal to contribution margin, the formula can be abbreviated as follows using contribution margin to find BEP.

$$X = FC \div CM$$

where CM = contribution margin per unit

The information shown in Exhibit 9–1 for Football Fans, Inc., indicates the following: a $7 unit selling price, $2.94 unit variable cost, and $22,000 of total fixed costs. The company's contribution margin is $4.06 per unit ($7 − $2.94). Breakeven point for the company is calculated as:

$$\$7X = \$2.94X + \$22,000$$
$$\$7X - \$2.94X = \$22,000$$
$$\$4.06X = \$22,000$$
$$X = \$22,000 \div \$4.06$$
$$X = 5,418.7 \text{ pom-poms}$$

Since it is not possible to sell seven-tenths of a pom-pom, this answer must be rounded to the next whole number, or 5,419.

Breakeven point can be expressed either in units or in dollars of revenue. One way to convert a unit breakeven point to dollars is to multiply the breakeven point in units by the selling price per unit. For Football Fans, Inc., the breakeven point in sales dollars is $37,933 (5,419 units × $7 per unit). Another method of computing breakeven point in sales dollars requires the computation of a contribution margin ratio.

Rather than using contribution margin per unit to calculate BEP, the **contribution margin ratio** (CM%) may be used. This ratio is equal to contribution margin divided by revenue. CM ratio can be calculated using either per-unit or total revenue minus total variable cost information. This ratio indicates what proportion of selling price remains after variable costs have been covered and allows BEP to be determined even if unit selling price and unit variable cost are not known. Dividing total fixed cost by the CM ratio gives the breakeven point *in sales dollars.*

contribution margin ratio

$$CM\% = (R - VC) \div R$$
$$X_\$ = FC \div CM\%$$

where $CM\%$ = contribution margin ratio
        $X_\$$ = breakeven point in sales dollars

The contribution margin for Football Fans, Inc., is given in Exhibit 9–1 as 58 percent ($4.06 ÷ $7). The company's computation of dollars of breakeven sales is $22,000 ÷ .58, or $37,931. The $2 difference between this sales dollar answer and the one computed earlier ($37,933) is caused by using a rounded-up whole number of breakeven units. The BEP in units can be determined by dividing the BEP in sales dollars by the unit selling price, or $37,931 ÷ $7 = 5,418.7 (or a rounded 5,419 units).

The breakeven point provides a starting point for planning future operations. Managers want to earn profits, not just cover costs, so the BEP formula can be used by substituting an amount other than zero for the profit (P) term. This substitution converts breakeven analysis to cost-volume-profit analysis.

DEFINITION OF CVP ANALYSIS

Cost-volume-profit (CVP) **analysis** is the process of examining the relationships among revenues, costs, and profits for a relevant range of activity and for a particular time frame. This technique is applicable in all economic sectors (manufacturing, wholesaling, retailing, and service industries) because the same types of managerial functions are performed in each type of organization.

cost-volume-profit analysis

Two essential managerial functions discussed in chapter 1 were planning and controlling. Planning emphasizes a goal orientation for the *future,* which means there is an associated uncertainty or risk. Having information related to the task or prob-

Managers must understand the underlying relationships of costs, volume, and selling prices to profits if good business decisions are to be made. While an increase in selling price will provide a higher contribution margin, sales volume may also decline.

lem under consideration reduces uncertainty. In contrast, the control function is performed *currently* by comparing actual performance to preestablished plans. Such comparisons use information on company objectives and achievements.

To plan and control effectively, managers must understand the behavior of costs and revenues as they change in reaction to changes in sales volume. This understanding can be used to predict future conditions (plan) and to explain, evaluate, and act on past results (control). The cost-volume-profit model helps link cost behavior and sales volume in a way that assists managers to plan and control as shown in the News Note at the top of the next page.

All costs are considered in the CVP model, regardless of whether they are product, period, variable, or fixed. The analysis is usually performed on a firm- or company-wide basis and is valid for only the short term because of its basic assumptions of *known* and *constant* selling prices and costs. If CVP were a long-range planning tool, it would need to recognize the possibilities of price and cost fluctuations. The same basic CVP model and calculations can be applied to a single or multiproduct business.

USING CVP ANALYSIS

CVP analysis uses the same algebraic income statement formula given earlier for the calculation of breakeven point, but includes a profit amount. By using known amounts for selling price per unit, variable cost per unit, volume of units, and fixed costs, the formula can be solved to find the amount of profit generated under specified conditions.

NEWS NOTE

Understand Your Cost-Volume-Profit Relationships

"When you start in a business, you tend to do anything for volume without thinking how it's going to affect the bottom line." Now Jane and Bob Phipps, co-owners of Fresh From Texas, a San Antonio vegetable firm, know better.

[In 1987, the Phippses decided to begin making and distributing tofu.] "We bought all the equipment without saying 'What percentage of our sales is tofu?' And, 'If sales increase, what percentage are they going to have to increase to justify [the investment]?' We've been losing money every month."

To offset the loss, they've balanced costs and volume elsewhere to increase profits. For example, before agreeing to supply items such as fresh, cut broccoli in bulk to a large grocery chain in 1989, the Phippses carefully analyzed all costs. They had five employees cut up a crate of broccoli, and the Phippses calculated their waste from cutting the broccoli heads into florets. They estimated the time spent bagging the products and multiplied that by the average wage rate to approximate labor costs. They also added up costs of product packaging, including artwork and printing of bags and shipping boxes. Finally, they calculated delivery costs.

All those little steps kept them from repeating their big tofu mistake. "In our market, the processing part of it is very competitive," Jane Phipps says, but "you have to quote a price where you can make a profit."

SOURCE: Bradford McKee, "Impressive Volume, But Does It Make Money?" *Nation's Business* (November 1991), p. 10. Reprinted by permission. Copyright 1991, U.S. Chamber of Commerce.

A more frequent and significant application of CVP analysis is to set a desired target profit and focus on the relationships between it and specified income statement amounts to find an unknown. Volume is a common unknown in such applications because managers want to achieve a particular amount of profit and need to know what quantity of sales needs to be generated to accomplish this objective. Selling price is not as common an unknown as volume because selling price is often market-related rather than being set solely by company management. Additionally, since selling price and volume are often directly related and certain costs are considered fixed, managers may use CVP to determine how high the variable cost can be and still provide a given amount of profit. Variable cost may be manipulated by modifying product design specifications, the manufacturing process, or material quality.

Profits may be stated as either a fixed or a variable amount and on either a before- or an after-tax basis. The following examples continue the Football Fans example using different statements of desired profit.

Specified Amount of Profit

Contribution margin represents the amount of sales dollars that remain after variable costs are covered. Each dollar of contribution margin generated by product sales goes first to cover fixed costs and, succeeding at that, will produce profits. *After the breakeven point is reached, each dollar of contribution margin is a dollar of profit.*

Before Taxes   Profit is treated in the breakeven formula as an additional cost to be covered. The inclusion of a desired profit changes the formula from a breakeven to a CVP equation.

$$R(X) = VC(X) + FC + PBT$$
$$R(X) - VC(X) = FC + PBT$$
$$X = (FC + PBT) \div (R - VC)$$
$$OR$$
$$X = (FC + PBT) \div CM$$

where PBT = specified amount of profit before taxes

The two solutions above will be in units. However, a third solution can be obtained for sales dollars. That formula is:

$$R(X) = (FC + PBT) \div CM\%$$

Assume that Football Fans, Inc., wants to produce a before-tax profit of $14,540. To do so, the company must sell 9,000 pom-poms, which will generate $63,000 of revenue. These calculations are shown in Exhibit 9–3.

After Taxes   Income taxes represent a significant aspect of business decision making. Managers need to be aware of the effects of income tax in choosing a specified profit amount. A company desiring to have a particular amount of *net income* must first determine the amount of income that must be earned on a *before-* tax basis, given the applicable tax rate. The CVP formula that designates a specified after-tax net income amount is:

$$R(X) = VC(X) + FC + PAT$$

where PAT = specified amount of profit after taxes

EXHIBIT 9–3
▼▼▼▼▼▼▼▼▼▼▼▼

FOOTBALL FANS INC. CVP ANALYSIS— SPECIFIED AMOUNT OF PROFIT BEFORE TAXES

PBT desired = $14,540

In Units:

$$R(X) = VC(X) + FC + PBT$$
$$\$7X = \$2.94X + \$22,000 + \$14,540$$
$$\$7X - \$2.94X = \$22,000 + \$14,540$$
$$X = \$36,540 \div (\$4.06)$$
$$= 9,000 \text{ pom-poms}$$

In Sales Dollars:

$$Sales = (FC + PBT) \div CM\%$$
$$= \$36,540 \div .58$$
$$= \$63,000$$

The profit after tax is equal to the profit before tax minus the applicable tax. Thus, PAT is further defined so that it can be integrated into the original before-tax CVP formula:

$$PAT = PBT - [(TR)(PBT)] \text{ or}$$
$$PBT = PAT \div (1 - TR)$$

where PBT = specified amount of profit before taxes
     TR = tax rate

Substituting into the formula,

$$R(X) = VC(X) + FC + [PAT \div (1 - TR)]$$
$$R(X) - VC(X) = FC + [PAT \div (1 - TR)]$$
$$CM(X) = FC + PBT$$
$$X = (FC + PBT) \div CM$$

Assume that Football Fans, Inc., wants to earn $18,704 of profit after taxes and the company's tax rate is 30 percent. The number of pom-poms and dollars of sales needed are calculated in Exhibit 9–4.

Net Margin on Sales

Rather than specifying a particular amount of profit to be earned, managers may state profits as a net margin on sales so that, as units sold or sales dollars increase, profits will increase at a constant rate. Net margin on sales may be stated on either a before- or an after-tax basis and either as a percentage of revenues or as a per-unit profit. If

---

PAT desired = $18,704; tax rate = 30%

In Units:

$$PBT = PAT \div (1 - \text{Tax rate})$$
$$= \$18,704 \div (1 - .30)$$
$$= \$18,704 \div .70$$
$$= \$26,720$$

$$CM(X) = FC + PBT$$
$$\$4.06X = \$22,000 + \$26,720$$
$$\$4.06X = \$48,720$$
$$X = \$48,720 \div \$4.06$$
$$= 12,000 \text{ pom-poms}$$

In Sales Dollars:

$$\text{Sales} = (FC + PBT) \div CM\%$$
$$= (\$22,000 + \$26,720) \div .58$$
$$= \$48,720 \div .58$$
$$= \$84,000$$

EXHIBIT 9–4
▼▼▼▼▼▼▼▼▼▼▼▼

FOOTBALL FANS, INC. CVP ANALYSIS—SPECIFIED AMOUNT OF PROFIT AFTER TAXES

net margin is stated as a percentage, it is convenient to convert that rate into a per-unit amount so that the formula does not appear overly complex. The CVP formula must be adjusted to recognize that profit is related to volume of activity.

Before Taxes   This situation assumes that the desired profit is equal to a specified net margin on sales. As sales in units or dollars increase, so will the amount of profit at a constant rate. The adjusted CVP formula for computing the necessary unit volume of sales to earn a specified net margin on sales or per-unit profit before taxes is:

$$R(X) = VC(X) + FC + PBT(X)$$

where PBT = desired profit per unit before taxes

Solving for X (or volume) gives the following:

$$
\begin{aligned}
R(X) - VC(X) - PBT(X) &= FC \\
X &= FC \div (R - VC - PBT) \\
X &= FC \div (CM - PBT)
\end{aligned}
$$

The profit is treated in the CVP formula as if it were an additional variable cost to be covered. If the profit is viewed in this manner, the original contribution margin and contribution margin ratio are *effectively* adjusted downward to reflect the desired net margin or profit per unit.

When setting the desired profit as a percentage of selling price, that percentage cannot exceed the contribution margin ratio. If it does, an infeasible problem is created, since the "effective" contribution margin is a negative percentage. In such a case, the actual contribution margin percentage plus the desired profit percentage would exceed 100 percent of the selling price—a condition that cannot occur.

Assume that the president of Football Fans, Inc., wants to know what level of sales (in units and dollars) would be required to earn a 25 percent before-tax profit on sales. The calculations shown in Exhibit 9–5 provide the answers to these questions.

After Taxes   Adjusting the CVP formula to determine a return on sales on an after-tax basis involves stating profits in relation to both volume and the tax rate. The algebraic manipulations are as follows:

$$
\begin{aligned}
R(X) &= VC(X) + FC + PBT(X) \\
&\text{and} \\
PBT(X) &= [PAT \div (1 - TR)](X) \\
PAT(X) &= PBT(X) - [TR \text{ times } PBT(X)]
\end{aligned}
$$

where PBT = desired profit per unit before taxes
PAT = desired profit per unit after taxes

$$
\begin{aligned}
R(X) &= VC(X) + FC + [PAT \div (1 - TR)](X) \\
R(X) - VC(X) &= FC + PBT(X) \\
CM(X) &= FC + PBT(X) \\
CM(X) - PBT(X) &= FC \\
X(CM - PBT) &= FC \\
X &= FC \div (CM - PBT)
\end{aligned}
$$

PBT desired = 25% on sales revenues

EXHIBIT 9–5
▼▼▼▼▼▼▼▼▼▼▼▼▼▼
FOOTBALL FANS,
INC. CVP ANALYSIS—
RETURN ON SALES
BEFORE TAXES

This is equal to the following per unit net margin:

$$\text{PBT per unit} = .25(\$7) = \$1.75$$

In Units:

$$R(X) = VC(X) + FC + PBT(X)$$
$$\$7X = \$2.94X + \$22{,}000 + \$1.75X$$
$$\$7X - \$2.94X - \$1.75X = \$22{,}000$$
$$X = \$22{,}000 \div (\$4.06 - \$1.75)$$
$$= \$22{,}000 \div \$2.31$$
$$= 9{,}524 \text{ pom-poms (rounded)}$$

In Sales Dollars:

The following relationships exist

	Per Unit	**Percent**
Selling price	$7.00	100%
Variable costs	(2.94)	(42%)
25% net margin on sales	(1.75)	(25%)
"Effective" contribution margin	$2.31	33%

$$\text{Sales} = FC \div \text{"Effective" } CM \text{ ratio*}$$
$$= \$22{,}000 \div .33 = \$66{,}667$$

*Note that it is not necessary to have per-unit data; all computations can be made with percentage information only.

Assume that Football Fans, Inc., wishes to earn a profit after taxes of 20 percent on revenue and has a 30 percent tax rate. The necessary sales in units and dollars are computed in Exhibit 9–6.

All the previous illustrations of CVP analysis were made using a variation of the formula approach. Solutions were not accompanied by mathematical proofs. The income statement model is also an effective means of developing and presenting solutions and/or proofs for solutions to CVP applications.

THE INCOME STATEMENT APPROACH

The income statement approach to CVP analysis allows the preparation of pro forma (or budgeted) statements from available information. Income statements can be used to prove the accuracy of computations made under the formula approach to CVP analysis, or the statements can simply be prepared to determine the impact of various

EXHIBIT 9–6
▼▼▼▼▼▼▼▼▼▼▼

FOOTBALL FANS,
INC. CVP ANALYSIS—
DESIRED PROFIT
AFTER TAXES

PAT desired = 20% of revenue = .20($7) = $1.40; tax rate = 30%

In Units:

$$PBT(X) = [\$1.40 \div (1 - .3)](X)$$
$$= [\$1.40 \div .7]X$$
$$= \$2X$$

$$CM(X) = FC + PBT(X)$$
$$\$4.06X = \$22,000 + \$2X$$
$$\$2.06X = \$22,000$$
$$X = \$22,000 \div \$2.06$$
$$= 10,680 \text{ pom-poms (rounded)}$$

In Sales Dollars:

	Per Unit	Percent
Selling price	$7.00	100.0%
Variable costs	(2.94)	(42.0%)
Net margin sales before taxes	(2.00)	(28.6%)
"Effective" contribution margin	$2.06	29.4%

$$X = FC \div \text{"Effective" } CM \text{ ratio}$$
$$= \$22,000 \div .294$$
$$= \$74,830 \text{ (rounded)}*$$

*10,680 pom-poms @ $7 selling price = $74,760. The difference between the answer in units and the answer in sales dollars is because of the rounding in both the unit answer and the contribution margin percentage answer.

sales levels on profits either before or after taxes. Since the formula and income statement approaches are based on the same relationships, each should be able to prove the other.[1]

Exhibit 9–7 proves each of the computations made in the preceding exhibits for Football Fans, Inc. The answers provided by either the algebraic or income statement approaches to breakeven and CVP analysis are valid only in relation to *specific* selling prices and cost relationships. Changes that occur in the company's selling price or cost structure will cause a change in the breakeven point or in the sales needed to obtain a desired profit figure. How revenue and cost changes will affect a company's breakeven point or sales volume required to realize desired profits can be determined through incremental analysis.

---

[1]The income statement approach can be readily adapted to a computerized spreadsheet format. The spreadsheets can be used to quickly see the results of many different combinations of the CVP factors.

Previous Computations
Breakeven point: 5,419 pom-poms
Specified profit ($14,540) before taxes: 9,000 pom-poms
Specified profit ($18,704) after taxes: 12,000 pom-poms
Net margin on sales (25%) before taxes: 9,524 pom-poms
Net margin on sales (20%) after taxes: 10,680 pom-poms

R = $7 per unit; VC = $2.94 per unit; FC = $22,000; tax rate (when applicable) = 30%

	Basic Data	Exhibit 9–3	Exhibit 9–4	Exhibit 9–5	Exhibit 9–6
Pom-poms sold	5,419	9,000	12,000	9,524	10,680
Sales	$37,933	$63,000	$84,000	$66,668	$74,760
Total variable costs	15,932	26,460	35,280	28,001	31,399
Contribution margin	$22,001	$36,540	$48,720	$38,667	$43,361
Total fixed costs	22,000	22,000	22,000	22,000	22,000
Profit before taxes	$ 1*	$14,540	$26,720	$16,667**	$21,361
Taxes (30%)			8,016		6,408
Profit after taxes (NI)			$18,704		$14,953***

*Off due to rounding
**Desired profit before taxes = 25% on revenue; .25 × $66,668 = $16,667
***Desired profit after taxes = 20% on revenue; .20 × $74,760 = $14,952

EXHIBIT 9–7
▼▼▼▼▼▼▼▼▼▼▼▼▼

FOOTBALL FANS,
INC. INCOME
STATEMENT
APPROACH TO CVP—
PROOF OF
COMPUTATIONS

INCREMENTAL ANALYSIS FOR SHORT-RUN CHANGES

Breakeven point may increase or decrease, depending on the particular changes that occur in the revenue and cost factors. This point is illustrated in the News Note on the next page about Freeport-McMoRan's Crystal project. When gas selling prices are high, drilling wells and incurring substantial costs can be justified by the total dollars of revenue that can be generated. However, when selling prices decline, the only way to make profits is to increase sales volume or reduce costs.

Other things being equal, breakeven point will increase if there is an increase in total fixed cost, a decrease in selling price per unit, or an increase in variable costs. A decrease in selling price, an increase in variable costs, or a combination of the two will cause a decrease in unit contribution margin. These relationships are indicated in Exhibit 9–8. The breakeven point will decrease if there is a decrease in total fixed cost or an increase in unit or percentage contribution margin. Any factor that causes a change in breakeven point will also cause a shift in total profits or losses at any level of activity.

NEWS NOTE

When Prices Are Down, Volume Needs to be Up

Eight wells and 621 feet of water don't mix economically with conventional offshore platforms. Crystal is a new design for production platforms created [for Freeport McMoRan] in New Orleans. Price and volume determine whether investment will be made in such an expensive project.

"At these $2 gas (per thousand cubic feet) prices, you've got to find a whole lot of gas," James R. Moffett (Freeport's Chairman) said. Traditionally, you can get there with either $4 gas or twice as [much volume]. But there is another way, he said: Cut the costs. Crystal's design did just that by saving up to 20% of the steel required—although it still requires 9,675 tons of $800–$900 per ton steel. But the savings totaled to approximately $3–$4 million or 12–16%.

SOURCE: Adapted from John Hall, "Crystal Oil Rig to Boost Drilling," [*New Orleans*] *Times Picayune* (January 30, 1991), p. D1.

incremental analysis

   Incremental analysis is a process that focuses only on factors that change from one course of action or decision to another. As related to CVP situations, incremental analysis is based on changes occurring in revenues, costs, and/or volume. Following are some examples of changes that may occur in a company and the incremental computations that can be used to determine the effects of those changes on breakeven point or profits.

EXHIBIT 9–8
▼▼▼▼▼▼▼▼▼▼▼▼▼

FOOTBALL FANS, INC. EFFECTS OF CHANGES FROM ORIGINAL DATA

Original Data:	Revenue per unit	$7.00
	Variable cost per unit	2.94
	Contribution margin per unit	$4.06

Fixed costs = $22,000
Breakeven point = 5,419 pom-poms

If fixed costs increase to $23,954, BEP rises to 5,900 pom-poms.

$4.06X = \$23,954; X = \$23,954 \div \$4.06; X = 5,900$

If revenue per unit falls to $6.90, BEP rises to 5,556 pom-poms.

$\$6.90 - \$2.94 = \$3.96$ new *CM;* $\$3.96X = \$22,000; X = 5,556$ (rounded)

If variable cost per unit rises to $3.15, BEP rises to 5,715 pom-poms.

$\$7.00 - \$3.15 = \$3.85$ new *CM;* $\$3.85X = \$22,000; X = 5,715$ (rounded)

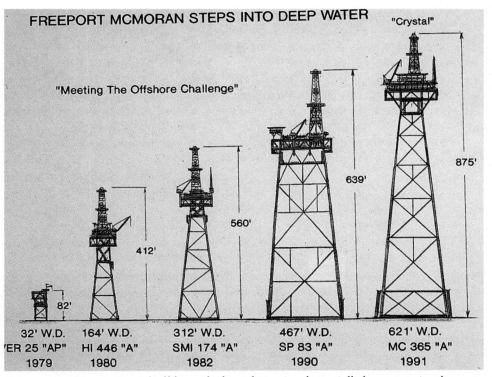

Freeport McMoran's Crystal offshore platform design is substantially less expensive than other designs. Using less steel reduces the total platform cost which, in turn, lowers the fixed depreciation cost.

The basic facts related to Football Fans, Inc., are continued:

Selling price		$7.00
Variable cost per unit		
Production	$ .49	
Selling	2.45	2.94
Contribution margin per unit		$4.06
Contribution margin ratio	58%	
Fixed costs per year	$22,000	
Breakeven point	5,419 pom-poms	

All of the following examples use before-tax information to simplify the computations. After-tax analysis would require the application of a (1 − tax rate) factor to all profit figures.

Case #1: The company wishes to earn a profit before taxes of $20,300. How many pom-poms does it need to sell?

Since BEP is known, this question simply addresses the *additional* pom-poms above the breakeven point needed to generate $20,300 of before-tax profits. Each dollar of contribution margin after the BEP is a dollar of profit. The answer is a total of 10,419 pom-poms:

$$\$20,300 \div \$4.06 = 5,000 \text{ pom-poms above BEP}$$
$$\text{BEP} = 5,419 \text{ units}$$
$$\text{Total pom-poms} = 10,419$$

Case #2: Football Fans, Inc., estimates that it can sell an additional 1,000 pom-poms if it spends $500 more on advertising. Should the company incur this extra fixed cost?

The contribution margin from the additional pom-poms must first cover the additional fixed cost before profits can be generated.

Increase in contribution margin	
(1,000 pom-poms × $4.06 *CM* per unit)	$4,060
Increase in fixed cost	(500)
Net incremental benefit	$3,560

Since the net incremental benefit is positive, the advertising campaign would result in an increase in profits and, thus, should be undertaken.

Case #3: The company estimates that, if the selling price of each pom-pom is reduced to $6, an additional 1,500 pom-poms can be sold per year. Should the company reduce the price of pom-poms? Current sales volume, given in Exhibit 9–1, is 7,000 units.

If the selling price is reduced, the contribution margin per unit will decrease to $3.06 per unit ($6 *SP* − $2.94 *VC*). Sales volume is estimated to increase to 8,500 units (7,000 + 1,500).

Total new contribution margin	
(8,500 units × $3.06 *CM* per unit)	$26,010
Total fixed costs (unchanged)	(22,000)
New profit before taxes	$ 4,010
Current profit before taxes (from Exhibit 9–1)	(6,420)
Reduction in profit before taxes	$(2,410)

Since the company will have less profit before taxes than is currently being generated, the company should not reduce its selling price.

Case #4: Because the home team has gotten into the playoffs, Football Fans, Inc., has an opportunity to sell 500 pom-poms at a $5 selling price to Boston Sports, a shop in the Copley Place Mall. Variable materials costs will increase by $.06 per unit because a more expensive plastic stick will be used. If the opportunity is accepted, an additional $250 fixed commission will be made to the salesperson generating this order. This sale is not expected to interfere with current sales. Should Football Fans, Inc., make this sale?

The new total variable cost per unit is $3 ($2.94 total current *VC* + $.06 increase in direct materials). The $5 selling price minus the $3 new total variable cost provides a contribution margin of $2 per unit sold to the sports shop.

Total contribution margin provided by this sale
    (500 units × $2 *CM* per unit) $1,000
Additional fixed cost related to this sale   (250)
Net incremental benefit $ 750

The total contribution margin generated by the sale not only covers the additional fixed cost of the commission, but also provides a net incremental benefit or profit to the firm and, therefore, should be made.

As with all proposals, however, this one should be evaluated on the basis of its long-range potential. Is the commission a one-time payment or will additional commissions have to be paid for future sales to Boston Sports? Is it possible that sales in the shop could affect stadium sales and, if so, to what extent? If the home team advances further in the playoffs, are there opportunities for additional sales to Boston Sports?

These are just a few examples of possible changes that may occur in a company's revenue and cost structure. In most situations, a complete income statement need not be prepared to determine the effects of changes. The contribution margin or incremental approach will often be sufficient to decide on the monetary merits of proposed or necessary changes. In making decisions, however, management must also consider the qualitative and long-run effects of the changes.

MARGIN OF SAFETY

When making decisions about various business opportunities that are presented, managers often consider the size of the company's margin of safety. The **margin of safety** is the excess of a company's budgeted or actual sales over its breakeven point. It is the amount that sales can drop before reaching the breakeven point and, thus, provides a certain amount of "cushion" from losses.

margin of safety

The margin of safety can be expressed as units, dollars, or a percentage. The following formulae are applicable:

Margin of safety in units = Actual units − Breakeven units

Margin of safety in dollars = Actual sales $ − Breakeven sales $

$$\text{Margin of safety \%} = \frac{\text{Margin of Safety in Units or \$}}{\text{Actual Sales in Units or \$}}$$

The breakeven point for Football Fans, Inc., is 5,419 units or $37,933 of sales. The company's income statement presented in Exhibit 9–1 showed actual sales for the year ended January 31, 1994, of 7,000 units or $49,000. The margin of safety for Football Fans, Inc., is quite high, since it is operating far above its breakeven point (see Exhibit 9–9).

The margin of safety calculation allows management to determine how close to a danger level the company is operating and, as such, provides an indication of risk. The lower the margin of safety, the more carefully management must watch sales figures and control costs so that a net loss will not be generated. At low margins of safety, managers are less likely to take advantage of opportunities that, if incorrectly analyzed, could send the company into a loss position.

EXHIBIT 9–9
▼▼▼▼▼▼▼▼▼▼▼▼▼▼▼

FOOTBALL FANS,
INC. MARGIN OF
SAFETY

In units:	7,000 actual − 5,419 BEP = 1,581 units
In sales $:	$49,000 actual − $37,933 BEP = $11,067
Percentage:	(7,000 − 5,419) ÷ 7,000 = .226
	or
	($49,000 − $37,933) ÷ $49,000 = .226

OPERATING LEVERAGE

operating leverage

Another measure that is closely related to the margin of safety and also provides useful management information is the company's degree of operating leverage. The relationship of a company's variable and fixed costs is reflected in its **operating leverage.** Typically, highly labor-intensive organizations, such as McDonald's and Domino's Pizza, have high variable costs and low fixed costs and, thus, have low operating leverage and a relatively low breakeven point. (An exception to this rule is sports teams, which are highly labor-intensive, but the labor costs are fixed rather than variable.) In companies with low operating leverage, wide swings in volume levels can occur and still allow the company to show a profit.

Conversely, organizations that are highly capital-intensive, such as Delta Air Lines and Texas Power & Light, have a cost structure that includes low variable and high fixed costs. Such a structure reflects high operating leverage. Because variable costs are low, the breakeven point is relatively high; if selling prices are predomi-

Most of the costs at Bearings Inc. (in Cleveland) are fixed. In an August 1991 Barrons article, CFO Raymond Smiley estimated that every additional $2 million in revenues resulted in almost $300,000 of after-tax income.

nantly set by the market, volume has the primary impact on profitability. Companies, as they become more automated, will face this type of cost structure and become more dependent on volume to add profits. In the News Note on page 380, the plight of the United States Postal Service illustrates what an impact volume can make on profitability in a high-fixed cost environment.

Companies with high operating leverage also have high contribution margin ratios. While such companies have to establish fairly high sales volumes to initially cover fixed costs, once those costs are covered, each unit sold after breakeven produces large profits. Thus, a small increase in sales can have a major impact on a company's profits. The **degree of operating leverage** (DOL) measures how a *percentage* change in sales, from the current level, will affect company profits. In other words, it indicates how sensitive the company is to sales increases and decreases. The computation providing the degree of operating leverage factor is:

degree of operating leverage

$$\text{Degree of Operating Leverage} = \frac{\text{Contribution Margin}}{\text{Profit Before Taxes}}$$

This calculation assumes that fixed costs do not increase when sales increase.

Assume that Football Fans, Inc., is currently selling 5,500 pom-poms. Exhibit 9–10 provides the income statement that reflects this sales level. At sales of 5,500 pom-poms, the company has an operating leverage factor of 67.7. If the company increases sales by 20 percent, the change in profits is equal to the degree of operating leverage multiplied by the percentage change in sales, or 1,354 percent! If sales decrease by the same 20 percent, there is a negative 1,354 percent impact on profits. Exhibit 9–10 confirms these computations.

The degree of operating leverage diminishes the farther a company moves from its breakeven point. Thus, when the margin of safety is small, the degree of operating leverage is large. In fact, at breakeven, the degree of operating leverage is infinite,

	(5,500 pom-poms) Current	(6,600 pom-poms) 20% Increase	(4,400 pom-poms) 20% Decrease
Sales	$38,500	$46,200	$30,800
Variable costs	16,170	19,404	12,936
Contribution margin	$22,330	$26,796	$17,864
Fixed costs	22,000	22,000	22,000
Profit before taxes	$ 330	$ 4,796	$(4,136)

Degree of operating leverage:
Contribution margin ÷ Profit before taxes
($22,330 ÷ $330)   67.7
($26,796 ÷ $4,796)   5.59
[$17,864 ÷ $(4,136)]   Not applicable

Profit increase at 6,600 pom-poms = $4,796 − $330
= $4,466 (or 1,354% of original profit)
Profit decrease at 4,400 pom-poms = $(4,136) − $330
= $(4,466) (or −1,354% of original profit)

EXHIBIT 9–10

FOOTBALL FANS, INC. DEGREE OF OPERATING LEVERAGE

NEWS NOTE

The Relationship Between Postal Rates and Postal Volume

The United States Postal Service is required by law to break even over time, and do so even though it cannot set its own prices.

[In 1992,] the price of a first-class stamp went up by 4 cents. That 16% increase was five times the overall rate of inflation [and] the fifth rate increase in ten years. This kind of price-raising inevitably reduces volume. Yet the Postal Service needs volume to support its enormous and steadily growing fixed costs. When mail volume slipped just 0.3% in 1991, a prospective $1 billion surplus was more than sliced in half. Most of the volume drop came in third-class mail.

The loss of the huge (62 billion pieces a year) third-class market to private carriers is of more than theoretical concern. A decline in the Postal Service's third-class mail market could have a devastating effect on the rest of the Service's business, especially its first class service.

More and more, third-class mail is emerging as the bedrock of the postal system [and] is pure gold in the economics of mail processing. It is easier to handle [than first-class mail], and so has an inherently lower cost. It is generally presorted at a savings and it probably generates a good 20% of first-class volume. By providing a base volume, it helps maintain the economics of mechanized and automated processing and helps cover the cost of maintaining the USPS' universal delivery system. But every time third-class rates rise, businesses have that much more incentive to find alternative ways of delivery.

SOURCE: James Cook, "A Mailman's Lot Is Not a Happy One," *Forbes* (April 27, 1992), p. 82ff.

since any increase from zero is an infinite percentage change. If a company is operating close to the breakeven point, each percentage increase in sales can make a dramatic percentage impact on net income. As the company moves away from breakeven sales, the margin of safety increases, but the degree of operating leverage declines.

All of the previous examples assume a single product company. Most businesses do not produce and/or sell a single product. The next section of the chapter deals with the more realistic multiproduct entity.

CVP ANALYSIS IN A MULTIPRODUCT ENVIRONMENT

Companies typically produce and sell a variety of products or services, some of which may be related to one another (such as baseballs and baseball bats or visual and print media advertisements using the same promotional campaign). To perform CVP analysis in a multiproduct company, it is necessary to assume a constant product sales mix or, alternatively, an average contribution margin ratio. The constant mix assumption can be referred to as the "bag" or "package" assumption. The analogy is that sales mix represents a bag or package of items that are sold together. For example, whenever some of Product A is sold, specified quantities of Products B and C are also sold.

Use of an assumed constant sales mix allows the computation of a weighted average contribution margin ratio, which is useful for CVP analysis for the group of items being sold. The CM ratio is *weighted* on the basis of the quantities of each item included in the group. The contribution margin ratio of the item that makes up the largest proportion of the bag has the greatest impact on the average contribution margin of the "bag" mix. Without the assumption of a constant sales mix, breakeven point cannot be calculated, nor can CVP analysis be used effectively.[2]

Let's continue with the Football Fans, Inc., example. Because of the success of the pom-poms, company management has decided to also produce T-shirts for the team. The vice-president of marketing estimates that for every five pom-poms sold, the company will sell one T-shirt. Therefore, the "bag" of products has a 5:1 ratio. The company must incur $14,000 in additional fixed costs related to plant assets (depreciation, insurance, etc.) to support a higher relevant range of production and additional licensing fees. Exhibit 9–11 provides relevant company information and shows the breakeven computations.

Any shift in the proportion of sales mix of products will change the weighted average contribution margin and, as such, the breakeven point. If the sales mix shifts toward products with lower contribution margins, there will be an increase in the BEP; furthermore, there will be a decrease in profits unless there is corresponding increase in total revenues. A shift toward higher margin products without a corresponding decrease in revenues will cause increased profits and a lower breakeven point.

The weighted average contribution margin ratio can also be calculated by multiplying the sales mix percentages (relative to sales dollars) by the CM ratios for each product respectively and summing the results. The information in the note on Exhibit 9–11 provides the sales mix relationship of 70:30 as to dollars of sales for pom-poms and T-shirts. Using this information, the CM ratio for the "bag" of products is computed as follows:

$$\begin{array}{ll} \text{Pom-poms: } 70\% \times 58\% = & .406 \\ \text{T-shirts: } 30\% \times 70\% \quad = & \underline{.210} \\ \qquad \text{Total CM ratio} & \underline{.616} \end{array}$$

To break even at the level indicated, Football Fans, Inc., must sell the products in exactly the relationships specified in the original sales mix. If sales are at the specified level but not in the specified mix, the company will experience either a profit or a loss, depending upon whether the mix is shifted toward the product with the higher or the lower contribution margin ratio.

Exhibit 9–12 shows the financial results if Football Fans, Inc., sells the souvenir merchandise in a sales mix proportion different from that assumed in the breakeven computation. The company had 1,169 "bags" of sales, but the mix was 4:2 pom-poms to T-shirts instead of a 5:1 ratio. Income of $7,534 is generated because the company sold a higher proportion of the T-shirts, which have a higher contribution margin.

---

[2]Once the constant percentage contribution margin in a multiproduct firm is determined, all of the situations regarding profit points can be treated the same as they were earlier in the chapter—remembering that the answers reflect the "bag" assumption.

	Pom-Poms		T-shirts	
Product Cost Information				
Selling price	$7.00	100%	$15.00	100%
Total variable cost	2.94	42%	4.50	30%
Contribution margin	$4.06	58%	$10.50	70%

Total Fixed Costs ($22,000 previous + $14,000 additional) = $36,000

	Pom-Poms		T-shirts		Total	Percentage
Proportion of units	5		1			
Revenue per unit	$7.00		$15.00			
Total revenue per "bag"		$35.00		$15.00	$50.00	100.0%
Variable cost per unit	2.94		4.50			
Total variable cost per "bag"		14.70		4.50	19.20	38.4%
Contribution margin per unit	$4.06		$10.50			
Contribution margin per "bag"		$20.30		$10.50	$30.80	61.6%

BEP in units: $CM(B) = FC$

where B = "bag" of products

$$\$30.80B = \$36,000$$
$$B = 1,169 \text{ "bags" to breakeven (rounded)}$$

Note: Each "bag" is made up of 5 pom-poms; thus, it will take 5,845 pom-poms and 1,169 T-shirts to break even assuming the constant 5:1 sales mix.

BEP in sales $: $B = FC \div CM\%$

where $CM\%$ = weighted average CM for "bag"

$$B = \$36,000 \div .616$$
$$= \$58,442 \text{ (rounded)}$$

Note: The breakeven sales dollars also represent the assumed constant sales mix of $35 of sales of pom-poms to $15 of sales of T-shirts, or a 70% to 30% ratio. Thus, the company must have approximately $40,909 ($58,442 × 70%) of sales of pom-poms and $17,533 of sales of T-shirts to break even.

Proof of above computations using the income statement approach:

	Pom-Poms	T-shirts	Total
Sales	$40,909	$17,533	$58,442
Variable Costs	17,184	5,261	22,445
Contribution Margin	$23,725	$12,272	$35,997
Fixed Costs			36,000
Net Income (Loss)			$ (3)*

*Off due to rounding

EXHIBIT 9–11
▼▼▼▼▼▼▼▼▼▼▼▼▼▼

FOOTBALL FANS, INC. CVP ANALYSIS—
MULTIPLE PRODUCTS

	Pom-Poms		T-shirts		Total	Percentage
Proportion of units	4		2			
Revenue per unit	$7.00		$15.00			
Total revenue per "bag"		$28.00		$30.00	$58.00	100.0%
Variable cost per unit	2.94		4.50			
Total variable cost per "bag"		11.76		9.00	20.76	35.8%
Contribution margin per unit	$4.06		$10.50			
Contribution margin per "bag"		$16.24		$21.00	$37.24	64.2%

BEP in units: $CM(B) = FC$
     where B = "bag" or mix of products

$37.24B = $36,000
          B = 967 "bags" to break even

Actual results: 1,169 "bags" with 4 pom-poms and 2 T-shirts in each bag; thus, the company sold 4,676 pom-poms and 2,338 T-shirts (4:2 proportion).

	Pom-Poms	T-shirts	Total
Sales	$32,732	$35,070	$67,802
Variable Costs	13,747	10,521	24,268
Contribution Margin	$18,985	$24,549	$43,534
Fixed Costs			36,000
Net Income			$ 7,534

EXHIBIT 9–12

▼▼▼▼▼▼▼▼▼▼▼

FOOTBALL FANS,
INC. EFFECTS OF
PRODUCT MIX SHIFT

UNDERLYING ASSUMPTIONS OF CVP ANALYSIS

The cost-volume-profit model is a useful planning tool that can provide information on the impact on profits when changes are made in the costing system or in sales levels. As with any model, however, it reflects reality but does not duplicate it. CVP is a tool that focuses on the short run partially because of the assumptions that underlie the computations. While these assumptions are necessary, they limit the accuracy of the results. These assumptions follow; some of these were also provided at the beginning of the chapter.

1. All variable cost and revenue behavior patterns are constant per unit and linear within the relevant range.

2. Total contribution margin (total revenue − total variable costs) is linear within the relevant range and increases proportionally with output. This assumption follows directly from assumption 1.

3. Total fixed cost is a constant amount within the relevant range.

4. Mixed costs can be accurately separated into their fixed and variable elements. *Accuracy* of this separation is particularly unrealistic, but reliable estimates can be developed from the high-low method or regression analysis (discussed in chapter 3 and its appendix).

5. Sales and production are equal; thus there is no material fluctuation in inventory levels. This assumption is necessary because of the allocation of fixed costs to inventory at potentially different rates each year. This assumption is more realistic as companies begin to use just-in-time inventory systems.

6. There will be no capacity additions during the period under consideration. If such additions were made, fixed (and, possibly, variable) costs would change. Any changes in fixed or variable costs would invalidate assumptions 1–3.

7. In a multiproduct firm, the sales mix will remain constant. If this assumption were not made, no useful weighted average contribution margin could be computed for the company for purposes of CVP analysis.

8. There is either no inflation, inflation affects all cost factors equally, or, if factors are affected unequally, the appropriate effects are incorporated into the CVP figures.

9. Labor productivity, production technology, and market conditions will not change. If any of these changes occur, costs would change correspondingly, and it is possible that selling prices would change. Such changes would invalidate assumptions 1–3.

These nine premises are the traditional assumptions associated with cost-volume-profit analysis and reflect an ad hoc disregard of possible (and probable) future changes. Accountants have generally assumed that cost behavior, once classified, remained constant over periods of time as long as operations remained within the relevant range and in the absence of evidence to the contrary. Thus, for example, once a cost was determined to be "fixed," it would be fixed next year, the year after, and ten years from now.

As mentioned in chapter 4, however, it is more realistic to regard fixed costs as long-term variable costs. Companies can, over the long run through managerial decisions, lay off supervisors and sell plant and equipment items. Fixed costs are not fixed forever. In fact, in many companies, some overhead costs considered to be fixed "have been the most variable and rapidly increasing costs." [3] Part of this cost "misclassification" problem has been because of improper specification of the cost drivers. As companies become less focused on production and sales volumes as cost drivers, they will begin to recognize that fixed costs only exist under a short-term reporting period perspective.

In addition, certain costs may arise that are variable in the first year of providing a product or service to a customer that will not arise in future years. As the following News Note shows, differing current and future period costs are very important in various service businesses. Failure to consider such changes in costs can provide a very distorted picture on how profits are generated and, therefore, present an improper analysis of the relationships of costs, volume, and profits.

---

[3]Robin Cooper and Robert S. Kaplan, "How Cost Accounting Distorts Product Costs," *Management Accounting* (April 1988), p. 27.

The Longer You Keep a Customer, the Less It Costs You

It may be obvious that acquiring a new customer entails certain one-time costs for advertising, promotions, and the like. In credit cards, for example, companies spend an average of $51 to recruit a new customer and set up the new account. But there are many more pieces to the profitability puzzle.

As purchases rise, operating costs decline. Checking customers' credit histories and adding them to the corporate database is expensive, but those things need be done only once. Also, as the company gains experience with its customers, it can serve them more efficiently. One small financial consulting business that depends on personal relationships with clients has found that costs drop by two-thirds from the first year to the second because customers know what to expect from the consultant and have fewer questions or problems.

Also, companies with long-time customers can often charge more for their products or services. Many people will pay more to stay in a hotel they know or to go to a doctor they trust than to take a chance on a less expensive competitor.

Yet another economic boon from long-time customers is the free advertising they provide. One of the leading home builders in the United States, for example, has found that more than 60% of its sales are the result of referrals.

These cost savings and additional revenues combine to produce a steady stream of profits over the course of the customer's relationship with the company. While the relative importance of these effects varies from industry to industry, the end result is that longer term customers generate increasing profits.

SOURCE: An excerpt from "Zero Defections: Quality Comes to Services," by Frederick F. Reichheld and W. Earl Sasser, Jr. (September–October 1990), pp. 106–7. Reprinted by permission of *Harvard Business Review*. Copyright © 1990 by the President and Fellows of Harvard College; all rights reserved.

COSTS AND QUALITY

While cost, price, and volume are the three major factors in determining a company's profits, it is necessary to recognize that these three factors work hand-in-hand with a fourth factor: quality. The quality specifications of a product and its components will play an important part in influencing costs. But, while costs may be affected, a Gallup Poll in 1988 also showed that quality products are typically able to command higher selling prices.[4] And often volume increases simply through quality recognition. For example, the following News Note indicates that part of Coca-Cola's popularity is quality-based.

[4]George Melloan, "Computers Elevate Product Quality Standards," *Wall Street Journal* (October 11, 1988), p. A25.

NEWS NOTE

Quality at Coca-Cola

"Very simply, Coca-Cola means quality in the minds of consumers and retailers the world over," says chairman and CEO Roberto C. Goizueta. "And it is the standard of product quality that the people of The Coca-Cola Company have maintained for more than a century that gives the brand its ubiquity. If we did not have, make, market, and perpetuate a product of unquestionable quality, all the other manifestations of quality within our organization simply would not exist."

Company executives stress that Coca-Cola did not become the world standard for soft drink quality overnight; rather, this success is the result of a firm commitment made to consumers in the 1920s that every Coca-Cola would taste exactly alike. To deliver on that promise, the company instituted some of the toughest quality control standards and procedures around.

SOURCE: Jerry G. Bowles, "World Class Quality: The Challenge of the 1990s," *FORTUNE* (September 23, 1991), p. 140ff. © 1991 The Time Magazine Company. All rights reserved.

Another reason for quality recognition currently comes from the Malcolm Baldrige National Quality Awards, which were established by Congress in 1987. Each year judges can choose two winners from each of three categories: large manufacturers, large service companies, and businesses with less than 500 full-time employees. However, of over 200 applicants during 1988–1991, only 12 have been selected. The winners are listed in Exhibit 9–13. However, winning the award is not a "guarantee that a company's products are superior" or that the winners have "solved their busi-

Numerous American companies seek Baldrige recognition for their quality achievements since the institution of the award in 1987. Raymond Marlow, President and CEO of Marlow Industries, was extremely pleased with his company's success in 1991.

Year	Company	Location
1988	Globe Metallurgical	Cleveland, Ohio
	Motorola	Schaumburg, Ill.
	Commercial Nuclear Fuel Division (Westinghouse)	Pittsburgh, Pa.
1989	Milliken	Spartenburg, S.C.
	Business Products and Systems Group (Xerox)	Rochester, N.Y.
1990	Cadillac Motor Car (General Motors)	Detroit, Mich.
	AS/400 Unit (IBM)	Rochester, Minn.
	Federal Express*	Memphis, Tenn.
	Wallace Co.	Houston, Tex.
1991	Solectron	San Jose, Calif.
	Zytec Corp.	Eden Prairie, Minn.
	Marlow Industries, Inc.	Dallas, Tex.

*For the four years available at print, Federal Express is the first and only service company to win the Baldrige Award.

EXHIBIT 9–13

MALCOLM BALDRIGE AWARD WINNERS 1988–1991

ness problems and gone to capitalist heaven." [5] Even after obtaining the award, some winners (such as Motorola) have had quality problems and others (such as Commercial Nuclear Fuel and Federal Express) have had declines in profitability. As of early 1992, Federal Express made a decision to eliminate service between European destinations, and Wallace Co. (a family-owned business) was operating in Chapter 11 bankruptcy.

While the Baldrige Award may not be a perfect indicator of quality, it seems that many American companies aspire for the award and are, therefore, inspired to try to achieve better quality. Achieving better quality, however, will affect costs. Some costs could decline because of redesigning products for parts simplification or standardizing components. Other costs may increase—some of which could be variable (such as higher-quality materials and components, training courses for employees, and preventive maintenance), while others (such as supplier certification programs, investments in computer-integrated or numerically controlled machines to better monitor quality, and implementation of quality-circle programs) may be "fixed" or long-term variable.

It would seem that the costs of ensuring quality should, in the long run, outweigh the costs of having poor quality. While the increased costs could cause higher variable or fixed costs currently, other costs (such as those attributable to rework, redesign, and product failure) should fall. Breakeven point and volume levels needed to achieve desired profits will not necessarily rise because it may be possible to charge higher selling prices to maintain a constant contribution margin. And even if the needed volume levels *do* rise, higher volumes of sales may be attainable with the higher-quality products than would have been with lower-quality products. All in all, considering the implications of quality changes on cost, price, and volume should help focus managers' attention more on the long run and less on the short run.

---

[5] Jeremy Main, "Is the Baldrige Overblown?" *FORTUNE* (July 1, 1991), p. 62.

APPLICATIONS STRATEGIES OF BREAKEVEN AND CVP ANALYSIS

Discipline	Application
Accounting	Shows relationships among all factors involved in profitability throughout the relevant range and seeks the best combination of those factors; helps determine the sales volume needed to meet desired profit figures (before or after tax); must understand how the various tax structures will impact the computation of desired profits
Economics	Makes companies aware of importance of volume (a high CM but no sales will not allow a company to break even); multiple CVP calculations will help to pinpoint the volume at which profits will be maximized; allows use of marginal or incremental analysis for decision making; promotes recognition of sensitivity of profits to price changes; useful in making decisions about alternative systems of production because of differing cost structures; assists in analyzing how total costs and profits will vary depending on the level of automation; aids in choosing the optimal price, cost, and output levels for each product
Finance	Indicates the profit impacts of company operating structure (low vs. high leverage) before and after new product or service introductions or changes in sales mix; difference between BEP and cash BEP (appendix) indicates the importance of depreciation (and other noncash) deductions for tax purposes; helps influence choice of product lines to emphasize; can be used to determine profit impact of volume changes which equals [(unit contribution × change in units produced and sold) − changes in fixed costs]
Management	Helps identify various cost and pricing strategies and what effects they will have on profits; shows dollar-for-dollar effect of contribution margin on profits after BEP; relationship of margin of safety and degree of operating leverage helps indicate the overall company health and the significance of volume increases on total profits
Marketing	Helps justify advertising budgets (the higher the CM percentage, the more dollar-for-dollar benefit of advertising); BEP or calculated CVP point can be compared to sales forecast to check for reasonableness (can sales level be achieved at stated price and with estimated marketing expenditure level?); if fixed advertising expenditures are increased, can needed sales increases be achieved based on market share?; consider unit contribution margin (or percentage) with capacity utilization to determine which products to promote (market, promote, advertise) and which to demarket (raise price, harvest, cut advertising expenditures)

SITE ANALYSIS

Revenues, costs, and profits are all integrally related with an underlying base of quality. For a sports team, primary revenues are generated from ticket sales and broadcast rights. Since payments for ticket prices and broadcast rights are typically set in advance of a season, ticket sales volume and cost control are the two key elements of profitability. Ticket sales volume is generally a function of the quality of play by team members and winning record.

continued

Payroll is the primary expense for professional sports teams. For football teams, this expense typically makes up between 60 percent to 65 percent of total cost. "In 1987, the payroll of the New England Patriots was $19 million, the third highest in the league." [6] Salary costs are critical in sports because most players are paid regardless of whether or not they are playing—due either to termination clauses or to injuries.

The CVP concepts in the chapter could be used to answer questions such as the following for any sports team. If ticket prices are increased and the team owner wants profits to remain the same, how much will ticket volume have to be? What will be the effects on forecasted profits if forecasted sales volumes for different ticket categories do not materialize? If player salaries and stadium costs increase, volume remains constant, and ticket prices cannot be raised, by how much will other costs have to be reduced for profits to remain at the current level?

While all businesses do not face the same situations as major-league sports teams, in most instances, product and service prices are set by the market's willingness to pay and the availability of product substitutes. Volume, costs, and product or service quality play the leading roles in determining whether a company wins or loses in the game of making money. The business you are involved in (manufacturing, service, or retailing) is unimportant when you consider the relationships of the profit-making factors. In addition, regardless of the discipline area in which you work, there are numerous ways in which you can help increase revenues, decrease costs, and raise profitability, as shown in the Applications Strategies.

CHAPTER SUMMARY

Management planning for company success includes planning for price, volume, fixed and variable costs, quality, contribution margins, and breakeven point. The interrelationships of these factors are studied in breakeven and cost-volume-profit (CVP) analysis.

The breakeven point (BEP) uses linear relationships to determine that quantity of sales volume at which the company will experience zero profit or loss. Total contribution margin (sales minus all variable costs) is equal to total fixed costs at the breakeven point. BEP will change if the company's selling price(s) or costs change.

Since most companies want to operate at above breakeven, CVP analysis extends the BEP computation by introducing a desired profit factor. The sales necessary to generate a desired amount of profit are computed by adding the desired profit to fixed costs and dividing that total by contribution margin or contribution margin ratio. After fixed costs are covered, each dollar of contribution margin generated by company sales will produce a dollar of before-tax profit.

The margin of safety for a firm indicates how far (in units, sales dollars, or a percentage) a company is operating from its breakeven point. A company's degree of operating leverage shows what percentage change in profit would occur given a specified percentage change in sales from the current level.

In a multiproduct firm, all breakeven and cost-volume-profit analyses are performed using an assumed constant sales mix of products or services. This sales mix is

[6]William Wucinich, "Profit Is the Name of the Game," *Management Accounting* (February 1991), p. 58.

referred to as the "bag" or "package" assumption, and it requires the computation of a weighted average contribution margin (and, thus, contribution margin ratio) for the "bag" of products being sold. Answers to breakeven or CVP computations are in units or dollars of "bags" of products. The number of bags can be converted to individual items by using the sales mix relationship.

CVP analysis is short-range in focus because it assumes linearity of all functions. Managers need to include in their considerations the effect of quality (and other types of) changes on both current and future costs to make better, more realistic decisions. While CVP analysis provides one way for a manager to reduce the risk of uncertainty, the model is based on several assumptions that limit its ability to reflect reality.

APPENDIX 1

Cash Breakeven Point

cash breakeven point

Companies that have limited funds available may want to compute a breakeven point that indicates a sales volume necessary to cover all cash expenses for a period. Such a point is called the **cash breakeven point** and is calculated as follows:

$$\text{Cash BEP} = \text{Cash } FC \div (SP - VC) \qquad OR \qquad \text{Cash BEP} = \text{Cash } FC \div CM$$

where
FC = fixed costs
SP = selling price per unit
VC = variable cost per unit
CM = contribution margin per unit

If a company wanted to compute its cash BEP on a before-tax basis, the cash fixed costs in the formula are equal to total fixed costs minus total depreciation or other noncash charges. (Other noncash charges would include things such as patent, goodwill, and bond premium or discount amortization.) On an after-tax basis, cash fixed costs are equal to total fixed costs minus total noncash charges minus the tax shield provided by the noncash charges. These calculations are shown next using depreciation as the only noncash charge.

The Wichita Wildcats are a football team owned by the Busch Company. The Busch Company also owns several other businesses. Assume that the Wichita Wildcats have the following fixed costs:

Salaries for office personnel, players, and management	$13,900,000
Insurance	1,250,000
Lease payments	3,450,000
Depreciation	2,578,000
Total	$21,178,000

The team sells its tickets for $20, and total variable costs per unit are $5. The applicable tax rate for the Busch Company is 30 percent.

Since depreciation is a noncash cost, the cash breakeven point ignores it as part of the numerator. On a before-tax basis, cash BEP in units is computed as follows:

$$\text{Cash Breakeven Point} = \frac{\text{Cash } FC}{(SP - VC)}$$

$$= \frac{\$21,178,000 - \$2,578,000}{\$20 - \$5}$$

$$= \frac{\$18,600,000}{\$15}$$

$$= 1,240,000 \text{ tickets}$$

At this level of ticket sales, the Wildcats are operating below the breakeven point of 1,411,867 tickets ($21,178,000 ÷ $15). Thus, there would be no taxable income for the Wildcats. Cash BEP for any company or segment of a company will always be less than actual BEP because the numerator has been lowered by the amount of the noncash expenses.

Depreciation, while not a cash expense, is deductible for tax purposes when a company has profits. This tax deduction produces a **tax benefit** that equals the amount of the depreciation multiplied by the tax rate. Assuming that the Busch Company as a whole is profitable, the company is better off for tax purposes by having depreciation than by not having depreciation. The company's taxable income is decreased by the amount of the depreciation deduction. Thus, the company has to pay fewer dollars in cash for taxes—causing the net cash costs to decrease. The after-tax cash breakeven point is as follows:

tax benefit

Total fixed costs		$21,178,000
Less depreciation	$2,578,000	
Less depreciation tax shield ($2,578,000 × 30%)	773,400	3,351,400
Net cash fixed costs		$17,826,600

$$\text{Cash BEP} = \frac{\text{Net cash fixed costs}}{\text{Selling price} - \text{Variable costs}}$$

$$= \frac{\$17,826,600}{\$20 - \$5}$$

$$= \$1,188,440 \text{ tickets}$$

While the cash breakeven computation may serve as a guide for companies concerned about making certain that cash expenditures can be met, this calculation has some additional assumptions over the standard breakeven computations. Those assumptions are that all revenues are collected and all costs are paid in the period of the sale. Unfortunately for many companies, collections and payments are not made at the same time as a sale, purchase, or expense may be recorded. Large distortions in the collection and payment patterns could have a significant impact on the validity of the cash breakeven point computation.

APPENDIX 2

Graphic Approaches to Breakeven

The graphs presented in Exhibit 9–2 illustrate individual cost classification behaviors, but are not very useful for determining how revenues, costs, and volume are related.

breakeven chart

Breakeven Chart

To graphically depict the relationships among revenues, variable costs, fixed costs, and profits (or losses) a **breakeven chart** is used. The breakeven point is located at the point where the total cost and total revenue lines cross. The following steps are necessary to preparing a breakeven chart.

Step 1: Label the x-axis as volume and the y-axis as dollars. Plot the variable cost line as a linear function with a slope equal to total variable cost per unit. Next, plot the revenue line with a slope equal to the unit sales price. The area between the variable cost and revenue lines represents total contribution margin at each level of volume.

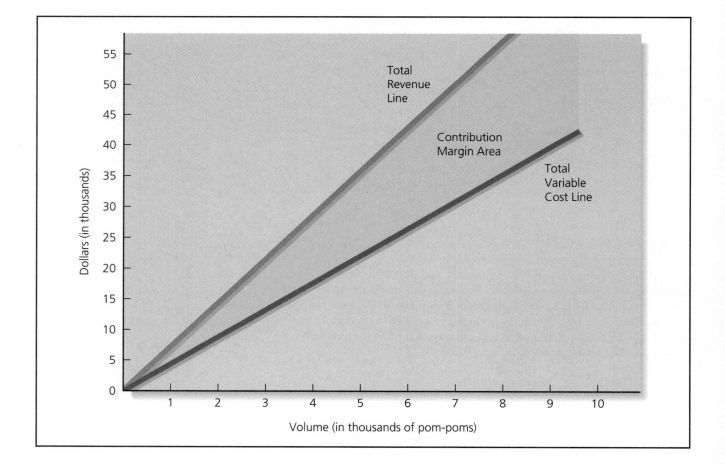

Step 2: Total cost is graphed by adding a line parallel to the total variable cost line. The distance between the total and variable cost lines is the amount of fixed cost. The total cost line is above and to the left of the total variable cost line. Breakeven point is located where the revenue and total cost lines intersect. If exact readings could be taken on the graph, the breakeven point for Football Fans, Inc., would be $37,933 of sales and 5,419 pom-poms (both figures are rounded).

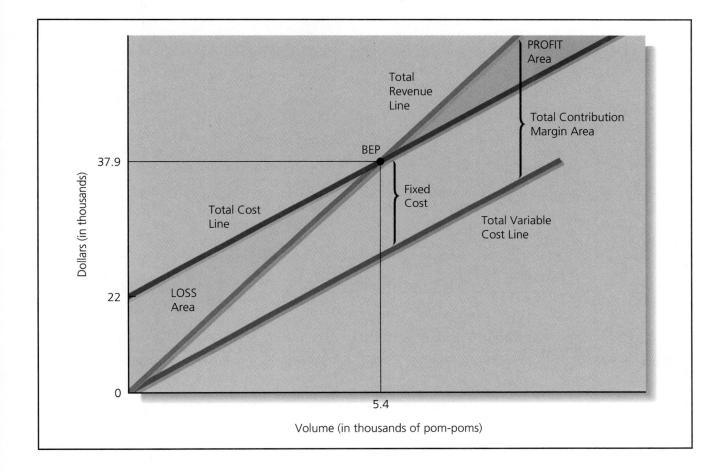

The format of this breakeven graph allows the following important observations to be made.

1. Contribution margin is created by the excess of revenues over *variable* costs. As indicated in the following News Note, if variable costs are greater than revenues, no quantity of volume will ever allow a profit to be made.

2. Total contribution margin is *always* equal to total fixed cost plus profit or minus loss.

3. Before profits can be generated, contribution margin must exceed fixed costs.

Closely related to the breakeven chart is the profit-volume graph.

Can We Make It Up in Volume?

John Palmer, a University of Western Ontario economics professor, says the Canadian pennies have long outlived their usefulness and are nothing but a nuisance. Mr. Palmer is campaigning to have the penny banned altogether for the following reasons:

- Depending on copper prices, it costs the Royal Canadian Mint as much as two cents to produce every penny.
- On average, the mint produces 700 million pennies a year just to keep up with the high rate of disappearance caused by people who toss them in piggy banks, ponds or wishing wells. There are about seven billion pennies out there.
- In 1989, more than one billion pennies were produced.

The Mint has tried to reduce the costs of production by cutting the weight. The penny is 98% copper, 1.5% zinc, and .05% tin. Given that copper is so expensive, why not switch to mostly zinc with a copper coating, like the Americans have? The vice-president of manufacturing at the Mint says that by the time the mint switches to zinc, which is about three-fourths the cost of copper, and adds another step to copper-plate the penny, any cost savings will likely be wiped out by the cost of making the change.

SOURCE: Adapted from Canadian Press, "Professor Seeks Total Ban on No-Longer-Useful Penny," [*Toronto*] *Globe & Mail* (August 7, 1990), A8.

Profit-Volume Graph

profit-volume graph

Another method of visually presenting income statement information is the **profit-volume** (PV) **graph,** which reflects the amount of profit or loss at each sales level. The horizontal axis on the PV graph represents unit sales volume, and the vertical axis represents dollars. Amounts shown above the horizontal axis are positive and represent profits, while amounts below the horizontal axis are negative and represent losses.

To draw the graph, two points are first located: total fixed costs and breakeven point. Total fixed costs are shown on the vertical axis as a negative amount (or below the sales volume line). If no pom-poms were sold, fixed costs of $22,000 would still be incurred and a loss of the entire amount would result. Location of the breakeven point may be determined either using a breakeven chart or algebraically. Breakeven point in units is shown on the horizontal axis because there is no profit or loss at that point. With these two points plotted, a line is drawn that passes between and extends through the breakeven point. This line can be used to read, from the vertical axis, the amount of profit or loss for any sales volume. This line represents total contribution margin, and its slope is determined by the unit contribution margin. The line shows that no profit is earned until the contribution margin covers the fixed costs.

The PV graph for Football Fans, Inc., is shown in Exhibit 9–14. Total fixed costs are $22,000, and breakeven point is 5,419 pom-poms. The profit line reflects the original Exhibit 9–1 income statement data in that, at sales of 7,000 pom-poms, the company will earn $6,420.

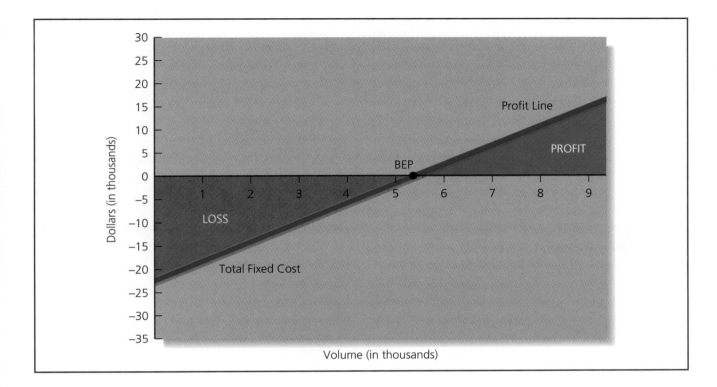

While graphic approaches to breakeven provide detailed visual displays, they do not provide precise breakeven solutions since exact points cannot be read from the graphs. Exact computations of breakeven points must be found using an algebraic formula approach.

EXHIBIT 9–14
▼▼▼▼▼▼▼▼▼▼▼▼

FOOTBALL FANS, INC. PROFIT-VOLUME GRAPH

GLOSSARY

Breakeven chart   a graphical depiction of the relationships among revenues, variable costs, fixed costs, and profits (or losses) [from appendix]

Breakeven point   that level of activity, in units or dollars, at which total revenues equal total costs

Cash breakeven point   a sales volume necessary to cover all cash expenses for a period [from appendix]

Contribution margin   selling price per unit minus all variable production, selling, and administrative costs per unit

Contribution margin ratio   contribution margin divided by revenue; indicates what proportion of selling price remains after variable costs have been covered

Cost-volume-profit analysis   a process of examining the relationships among revenues, costs, and profits for a relevant range of activity and for a particular time frame

Degree of operating leverage   a measure of how a percentage change in sales, from the current level, will affect company profits

Incremental analysis a process that focuses only on factors that change from one course of action or decision to another

Margin of safety the excess of the budgeted or actual sales of a company over its breakeven point

Operating leverage a factor that reflects the relationship of a company's variable and fixed costs

Profit-volume graph a graphical presentation that reflects the amount of profit or loss associated with each level of sales [from appendix]

Tax benefit the reduction in taxes provided by noncash deductions; the amount is equal to the noncash charge multiplied by the tax rate [from appendix]

SELECTED BIBLIOGRAPHY

Ames, B. Charles, and James D. Hlavacek. "Vital Truths About Managing Your Costs." *Harvard Business Review* (January–February 1990), pp. 140–47.

Dudick, Thomas S. "Pricing Strategies for Manufacturers." *Management Accounting* (November 1989), pp. 30–31ff.

Main, Jeremy. "How to Win the Baldrige Award." *FORTUNE* (April 23, 1990), p. 101ff.

Mendes, Joshua. "The Prince of Smart Pricing." *FORTUNE* (March 23, 1992), pp. 107–8.

Youde, Richard Y. "Cost-of-Quality Reporting: How We See It." *Management Accounting* (January 1992), pp. 34–38.

SOLUTION STRATEGIES

Cost-Volume-Profit

Most CVP problems are solvable by using a numerator/denominator approach. All numerators and denominators and the type of problem each relate to are listed below. The formulae relate to both single- and multiple-product firms, but results for multi-product firms are per bag and must be converted to units of individual products.

where FC = fixed cost
CM = contribution margin per unit
$CM\%$ = contribution margin percentage
P = total profit (can be on before-tax or on an after-tax basis converted to before-tax)
P_u = profit per unit
$P_u\%$ = profit percentage per unit

To convert after-tax profit to before-tax profit, divide after-tax profit by $(1 - \text{tax rate})$.

Problem Situation	Numerator	Denominator
Simple BEP (in units)	FC	CM
Simple BEP (in dollars)	FC	CM%
CVP with lump-sum profit (in units)	FC + P	CM
CVP with lump-sum profit (in dollars)	FC + P	CM%
CVP with desired net margin on sales (in units)	FC	$CM - P_u$
CVP with desired net margin on sales (in dollars)	FC	$CM\% - P_u\%$

Margin of Safety

$$\text{Margin of safety in units} = \text{Actual units} - \text{Breakeven units}$$

$$\text{Margin of safety in dollars} = \text{Actual sales \$} - \text{Breakeven sales \$}$$

$$\text{Margin of safety \%} = \frac{\text{Margin of safety in Units or \$}}{\text{Actual Sales in Units or \$}}$$

Degree of Operating Leverage

$$\text{Degree of operating leverage} = \frac{\text{Contribution Margin}}{\text{Profit before Taxes}}$$

$$\text{Predicted additional profit} = \text{Degree of Operating Leverage} \times \text{Percent change in sales} \times \text{Current profit}$$

DEMONSTRATION PROBLEM

TabbyWorld makes and sells scratch posts for cats. Cost information for one scratch post is as follows:

Direct materials	$2.00
Direct labor	1.00
Variable overhead	.50
Variable selling expenses	.10
Total variable costs	$3.60
Total fixed overhead	$388,800

Each scratch post sells for $9.00. Current annual production and sales volume is 75,000 posts.

Required:

a. Compute the contribution margin and contribution margin ratio for Tabby-World's product.

b. Compute the breakeven point in units for TabbyWorld, using contribution margin.

c. Compute the breakeven point in sales dollars for TabbyWorld, using contribution margin ratio.

d. What is TabbyWorld's margin of safety in units? In sales dollars?

e. What is TabbyWorld's degree of operating leverage? If sales increase by 20 percent, by how much will before-tax income increase?

f. If TabbyWorld wants to earn $43,200 of before-tax profits, how many posts will have to be sold?

g. If TabbyWorld wants to earn $40,500 after taxes and is subject to a 25 percent tax rate, how many units will have to be sold?

h. If TabbyWorld's fixed costs increased by $7,560, how many units would need to be sold to break even? (Use original data.)

i. TabbyWorld can sell an additional 6,000 scratch posts overseas for $8.50. Variable costs will increase by $.30 for shipping expenses, and fixed costs will increase by $25,000 because of the purchase of a new machine. This is a one-time-only sale and will not affect domestic sales this year or in the future. Should TabbyWorld sell the additional units?

Solution to Demonstration Problem

a. CM = Selling Price − Variable Cost = $9.00 − $3.60 = $5.40
   CM% = Selling Price − Variable Cost ÷ Selling Price = $5.40 ÷ $9.00 = 60%

b. BEP = Fixed Cost ÷ CM = $388,800 ÷ $5.40 = 72,000

c. BEP = Fixed Cost ÷ CM% = $388,800 ÷ 60% = $648,000
   [Note: This answer is also equal to 72,000 units × $9 per unit selling price.]

d. Margin of safety = Current units of sales − Breakeven sales = 75,000 − 72,000 = 3,000 units
   Margin of safety = Current revenues − Breakeven revenues = $675,000 − $648,000 = $27,000

e. Current CM = 75,000 × $5.40 = $405,000; current before-tax profit = $405,000 − $388,800 = $16,200
   Degree of operating leverage = $405,000 ÷ $16,200 = 25
   Increase in income = 25 × 20% = 500%
   Proof: 75,000 × 1.2 = 90,000 units; 90,000 × $5.40 = $486,000 CM − $388,800 FC = $97,200 PBT; ($16,200 current PBT × 500%) + $16,200 = $97,200

f. BEP = (FC + Desired Profit) ÷ CM = ($388,800 + $43,200) ÷ $5.40 = 80,000 units

g. Profit after tax ÷ (1 − Tax rate) = Profit before tax
   $40,500 ÷ .75 = $54,000
   BEP = (FC + Desired Profit) ÷ CM = ($388,800 + $54,000) ÷ $5.40 = 82,000 units

h. Additional units to break even = Increase in FC ÷ CM = $7,560 ÷ $5.40 = 1,400; new BEP = 72,000 + 1,400 = 73,400 units

i. New CM for these units = $8.50 − $3.90 = $4.60; 6,000 × $4.60 = $27,600, which is $2,600 above the additional $25,000 fixed cost. Yes, TabbyWorld should sell the additional units.

END-OF-CHAPTER MATERIALS

Questions

1. Since managers in commercial entities aspire to make a profit, why would these managers care about the breakeven point?

2. Of what value is cost-volume-profit analysis to managers?

3. How is breakeven analysis related to CVP?

4. What is contribution margin and how is it used?

5. Why does contribution margin fluctuate in direct proportion with sales volume?

6. How can contribution margin be used to determine breakeven in both units and dollars?

7. If the variable costs associated with a product increase per unit, but selling price and fixed costs remain constant, what will happen to (a) contribution margin and (b) breakeven point?

8. Why is the formula approach to breakeven analysis a more effective tool than a graphical approach?

9. The CVP model works directly with profit before taxes. How can you solve a problem in which profit is presented as an after-tax statistic?

10. How are operating leverage and automation related?

11. Is high operating leverage always beneficial? Why or why not?

12. The president of Henry's Hamburgers has just been informed that the chain is operating at an 8 percent margin of safety with a degree of operating leverage of 52. What should his reaction be and why?

13. What is the bag assumption and why is it necessary in a multiproduct company?

14. What effect would specifying the quality of a product be likely to have on each of the CVP factors?

15. What are the basic CVP assumptions? Why do managers who use CVP analysis keep these assumptions in mind when using the answers provided by the model?

16. Why is it necessary to also consider qualitative factors when solving problems using CVP?

17. Why is the perspective by managers using CVP a short-term one and what are the implications of such a perspective?

18. (Appendix 1) Of what value is the cash breakeven point to managers? What limits its significance?

Exercises

19. *(BEP)* Black Enterprises has the following revenue and cost functions:

$$\text{Revenue} = \$60 \text{ per unit}$$
$$\text{Fixed costs} = \$200,000$$
$$\text{Variable costs} = \$8 \text{ per unit}$$

What is the breakeven point in units? In dollars?

20. *(BEP)* Joseph McKeever Enterprises publishes inspirational paperback books in which the selections are cartoon-illustrated. The following operational data relate to a typical month:

Unit sales price	$8.00
Unit variable cost	$1.60
Fixed costs	$18,000
Current volume	3,200 books

The company is considering expansion that would cost another $4,000 in monthly fixed cost. If it does, production and sales will increase by 2,000 books.

   a. Without considering the expansion, what is the firm's breakeven point and its monthly before-tax profit?
   b. Recalculate breakeven point in books and monthly before-tax profit assuming that the company undertakes the expansion.

21. *(BEP)* The Flyer Company manufactures and sells a toy train set called the Woo-Woo. The company's annual fixed costs are $340,000. Its variable cost is $62 per Woo-Woo, and each set is sold for $190.

   a. What is the breakeven point in Woo-Woos and in dollars?
   b. How many Woo-Woos must be sold for the company to earn $1,000,000 in before-tax profit?

22. *(CVP with before-tax profit)* Whoppie Dog House Builders is planning to make and sell 10,000 of its finest canine palaces. The fixed costs are $400,000, and the variable costs are 60 percent of the selling price. What must the selling price be to earn $100,000 profit before tax?

23. *(CVP with after-tax profit)* Jeff Walker manufactures riding lawnmowers that sell for $800. The unit costs are:

Direct materials	$275
Direct labor	150
Variable overhead	70
Variable selling expense	45

Fixed factory overhead is $100,000 annually and fixed general, selling, and administrative expenses are $120,000. Jeff is in a 30 percent tax bracket.

   a. How many lawnmowers does Mr. Walker have to make and sell to earn $140,000 in after-tax income?
   b. How much revenue is needed to earn an after-tax income of 12 percent of sales?

24. *(Incremental analysis)* Hi-Tec Auto Parts has annual sales of $1,800,000 with variable expenses of 60 percent of sales and fixed expenses of $60,000 monthly. How much will sales have to increase so that Hi-Tec will have pretax income of 15 percent of sales?

25. *(CVP, alternatives)* Randy New is an architect who charges $100 per client hour. His monthly expenses are:

Office rent	$ 800
Office staff	1,200
Utilities	400
Total fixed expenses	$2,400

He is required to have sixty hours of continuing education annually to maintain his license and has determined that this costs him $800 monthly. Monthly variable costs average $15 per client hour, and Mr. New is in a 30 percent tax bracket.

a. How many client hours per month must Mr. New have to break even?

b. How many client hours per month must Mr. New have to earn $8,000 per month after tax?

c. Mr. New enjoys tennis and flying his private plane and wonders if he could work six-hour days and four-day weeks and still earn $8,000 after tax. Show computations and prove your answer.

26. *(BEP, margin of safety)* John Brown has a street lunch vending business in which he sells quiche and a soda as a package for $3.00. The variable costs of each package lunch are $1.20. His annual fixed costs are $50,000.

a. What is his breakeven point in revenue and number of lunches?

b. If the business is currently selling 32,400 lunches annually, what is John's margin of safety in units, percentage, and dollars?

27. *(BEP, operating leverage)* Paula's Pet-Do specializes in washing and grooming pets. Paula charges $12 per pet visit and has the following costs:

Variable costs per visit	
Direct materials	$ .50
Direct labor	$2.00
Fixed monthly costs	
Rent of shop	$400
Insurance	50
Licenses	25
Equipment depreciation	50
Promotion	100
Utilities	150

a. How many pet visits are needed to break even? How many dollars of revenues?

b. Paula feels that she should earn 25 percent of revenues before tax. How many pet visits would this require?

c. If Paula has 140 pet visits a month, what is her operating leverage?

d. If Paula can increase pet visits by 20 percent over the current 140 visits, how much will income increase? What will be the new total income? Prove your answer.

28. *(Margin of safety, operating leverage)* Crescent City Hot Sauce, Inc., sells its four-ounce bottle of pepper sauce for $2.90. Variable costs are $.52 per bottle, and fixed costs are $288,000 annually. The firm is currently selling 320,000 bottles annually.

a. What is the company's margin of safety in units?

b. Calculate the degree of operating leverage.

c. If the company can increase sales by 25 percent, by what percentage will its income increase? Prove your answer.

29. *(BEP, margin of safety, operating leverage)* In early 1990, Stephen King received from his publisher, Viking Penguin, a $9 million advance for a new book. This advance is against future royalties of 15 percent of retail selling price of $18.95.

However, should the book fail to sell enough to cover the advance, King is not liable for repayment. Viking expects the cost of printing 1.5 million hardcover copies of the book to be $3 million because of the extremely large print run. Advertising costs for the book are expected to be $200,000, and other fixed costs are budgeted at $4.5 million. Selling price from Viking Penguin to booksellers is 60 percent of retail price.

a. To justify the amount of the advance, how many copies of the book would Viking Penguin need to sell?

b. If the printing costs are considered fixed for the 1.5 million copies, and variable costs of production are $.01 per copy, what is Viking Penguin's break-even point?

c. Using the original data, how much profit before taxes will Viking earn selling only the 1.5 million copies from the first run?

d. Using the original data, if the hardback goes into a second printing of 1.5 million copies, how much will Viking Penguin earn if the entire second printing is sold?

e. Using the original data, if Viking Penguin sells 1,475,000 copies, what is its margin of safety in sales dollars? In units? What is the company's degree of operating leverage? If sales increased 1.5 percent, what would be the percentage increase in profits? Prove this increase.

(Original data based on John Pickering, "Blockbuster Advances Shake Up Book Business," *Accounting Today* [February 5, 1990], p. 6.)

30. *(Multiproduct BEP)* Lights-R-Us sells only flashlights and batteries at the entrance to a local cave. The firm sells two batteries to each flashlight. The flashlight sells for $3.00 and costs $1.00. Each battery sells for $.50 and costs $.20. The company's monthly fixed costs are $2,400. How many batteries will the company sell at the BEP? Prove your answer.

31. *(Multiproduct CVP)* The Music Box sells CD players, speakers, and discs in the ratio of 1:2:5. Each player has a $40 contribution margin, each speaker has a $15 contribution margin, and each disc has a contribution margin of $2. Fixed expenses are $140,000 annually. Unit selling prices are $200 for players, $50 for speakers, and $5 for discs. Melody Chason, owner, is in a 30 percent tax bracket.

a. What is the breakeven revenue? How many players, speakers, and discs does this represent?

b. How much revenue is necessary to earn a pretax profit of $100,000?

c. How much revenue is necessary to earn an after-tax profit of $100,000?

d. If the firm earns the revenue determined in (c), but it sells four speakers to each player and five discs, what would the company's profit be? Why is this amount not $100,000?

32. *(Appendix 1)* Genevieve's Kitchen makes and sells boxes of Cajun candies. The firm's income statement for 1994 follows:

Sales (25,000 boxes @ $12)		$300,000
Variable costs		
Production (25,000 × $3)	$75,000	
Sales commissions (25,000 × $1.20)	30,000	105,000
Contribution margin		$195,000
Fixed costs		
Production	$28,000	
General, selling, and administrative	15,000	43,000
Income before taxes		$152,000
Income taxes (30%)		45,600
Net income		$106,400

Fixed production costs include $4,000 of depreciation, and fixed general, selling, and administrative costs include $2,000 of depreciation.

a. Determine the firm's cash breakeven point before taxes.
b. Determine the firm's cash breakeven point on an after-tax basis.
c. Prove your answer to (b).

Problems

33. *(BEP, CVP before & after taxes)* Bill Rigby has a shop that makes and sells class rings for local high schools. Operating statistics follow:

Average selling price per ring	$250
Variable costs per ring	
Rings and stones	$ 90
Sales commissions	18
Variable overhead	8
Annual fixed costs	
Selling expenses	$42,000
General and administrative expenses	56,000
Production	30,000

Mr. Rigby's tax rate is 30 percent.
Required:

a. What is Mr. Rigby's breakeven point in rings? In revenue?
b. How much revenue is needed to yield $140,000 pretax profit?
c. How much revenue is needed to yield an after-tax profit of $120,000?
d. How much revenue is needed to yield an after-tax profit of 20 percent of revenue?
e. Mr. Rigby's marketing manager believes that by spending an additional $12,000 in advertising and lowering his price by $20 per ring, he can increase the number of rings sold by 25 percent. He is currently selling 2,200 rings. Should he do this?

34. *(BEP, CVP, margin of safety)* Boudreaux Company makes small flat-bottomed boats called pirogues. The president, Bayou Boudreaux, enlists your help in predicting the effects of some changes she is contemplating and gives you the following information:

Variable costs to produce each pirogue	
Direct materials	$ 90
Direct labor	100
Variable factory overhead	20
Average variable selling cost per pirogue	30
Average variable general and administrative cost per pirogue	10
Annual fixed production overhead	$660,000
Annual fixed selling expenses	190,000
Annual fixed general and administrative expenses	300,000

Bayou advises you that each pirogue sells for $400 and that demand for the current year is 14,400 pirogues or $5,760,000 of sales.

The following are some of the changes Bayou is considering:

1. The sales staff believes that demand will increase 15 percent if price is reduced 10 percent.
2. The engineering design staff believes that spending $30 on each pirogue to strengthen the hull will cause demand to increase 20 percent because consumers will believe the pirogue to be superior to any other product on the market.
3. The sales manager believes that increasing advertising by $25,000 will increase demand by 20 percent.

Required:

a. Calculate the breakeven point in units and dollars.
b. Calculate the margin of safety in units, dollars, and percentage.
c. Calculate the effects on profit and dollar breakeven point of the independent propositions (ignore tax implications). For each proposition, advise the president about the proposal.

35. *(Incremental analysis)* Ansel Needeys has her own travel agency in which her fees are 20 percent on hotel bookings, 15 percent on car rentals, and 10 percent on airline flights. Her normal monthly operating statistics are:

Costs		Gross Bookings	
Advertising	$1,000	Hotel bookings	$10,800
Rent	800	Car rentals	3,600
Utilities	300	Airline fares	14,200
Other expenses	1,400		$28,600

Required:

a. Given the previous commission percentages, what are her normal monthly fees? The normal monthly pretax profit?
b. Ansel can increase her hotel bookings by 40 percent if she spends an additional $200 on advertising. Should she do this?
c. Hillary Westin has offered to merge his bookings with Ansel's and become her employee. He would receive a base salary of $600 a month plus 20 percent of the fees on his bookings which, for a normal month, follow:

Hotel bookings	$5,000
Car rentals	2,000
Airline fares	2,000

Should Ansel accept the proposal?

d. Use the information in (c). During Hillary's first month, he generated $10,000 of bookings, but they were as follows:

Hotel bookings	$3,000
Car rentals	2,000
Airline fares	5,000

Would Ansel be pleased? Why?

36. *(BEP, CVP with before- & after-tax profits)* The Wind Finder Company sells weathervanes for $18 each. Variable manufacturing costs are $8, and variable selling, general, and administrative costs are $3 per unit. Fixed costs incurred uniformly throughout the year are $840,000.
    Required:
    a. Calculate the breakeven point in units and dollars.
    b. How many units must be sold to earn $80,000 in pretax profits?
    c. Assume a tax rate of 35 percent. How many units have to be sold to yield an after-tax profit of $140,000?
    d. If labor costs are 35 percent of variable manufacturing costs and 20 percent of the total fixed costs, by how much would an 8 percent decrease in labor costs decrease the breakeven point in dollars?

37. *(CVP with before- & after-tax profits)* Paul Dué Enterprises makes two types of travel bags: hanging bags and case-type bags. The firm sells these in the ratio of one hanging bag to two case-type bags. Selling prices are $54 and $38, respectively, and variable costs are $22 and $15, respectively. Fixed costs are $860,000. The firm is in the 35 percent tax bracket.
    Required: Calculate the number of each type of bag necessary to achieve each of the following:
    a. Breakeven point
    b. $200,000 of pretax profit
    c. $200,000 of after-tax profit
    d. Pretax profit of 20 percent of revenue
    e. After-tax profit of 15 percent of revenue

38. *(Multiproduct company)* Norman Hill Manufacturing makes carved wooden mallard hens and their ducklings. For every hen the firm sells, it also sells three ducklings. The following are the company's revenues and costs:

	Hens	Ducklings
Selling price	$14	$8
Variable cost	4	2
Contribution margin	$10	$6

Fixed costs each month are $12,000.
Required:

a. What is the average contribution margin ratio?
b. Calculate the breakeven point in units of each type of duck and in sales dollars for each type of duck.
c. If the company wants to earn $25,000 in pretax profits per month, how many hens and ducklings must it sell?

d. The company specifies $20,000 of after-tax profits as its objective, is in a 30 percent tax bracket, and believes that the mix has changed to one hen for every five ducklings. How much revenue is needed, and in what proportions, to achieve its profit objective?

39. *(Multiproduct company)* Revere Sounds, Inc., makes portable CD players, CDs, and batteries, which follow a normal pattern for sales mix of 1:3:6, respectively. The following reflects the company's costs:

	CD Players	CDs	Batteries
Variable product costs	$62.00	$1.20	$.22
Variable selling expenses	14.00	.50	.05
Variable G&A	.10	.04	.03
Annual fixed factory overhead	$610,000		
Annual fixed selling expense	160,000		
Annual fixed G&A	180,000		

Selling prices are $140 for CD players, $5 for CDs, and $.50 for batteries. The firm is in a 40 percent tax bracket.

Required:

a. What is the annual dollar breakeven point?
b. How many CD players, CDs, and batteries are expected to be sold at the BEP?
c. If the firm desires a pretax profit of $240,000, how much total revenue and how many of each item would be needed?
d. If the firm desires an after-tax profit of $200,000, how much total revenue and how many of each item would be needed?
e. If the firm achieves the revenue determined in (d), what is its margin of safety in dollars and percentage?

40. *(Income effects of different products)* The Able Company has one department that produces three replacement parts for the company. However, only one part can be produced in any month because of the adjustments that must be made to the equipment. The department can produce up to 15,000 units of any one of the three parts in each month. The company expresses the monthly after-tax CVP relationships for each part using an equation method. The format of the equations and the equations for each replacement part are as follows:

$$ATR \times [(SP - VC) \times U - FC]$$

where ATR = after-tax rate
         SP = selling price
         VC = variable cost
         U = units
         FC = fixed costs

Part	Part Equation
AL45	$.6[(\$4.00 - \$1.25)U - \$33,400]$
BT62	$.6[(\$4.05 - \$2.55)U - \$15,000]$
GM17	$.6[(\$4.10 - \$2.00)U - \$22,365]$

Required: Determine each of the following:

a. the contribution margin per unit for Part BT62
b. the breakeven volume in units for Part GM17
c. the amount of Able's after-tax net income if Able Company produces and sells 13,000 units of Part AL45

d. the number of units of Part BT62 required to be produced and sold to contribute $4,140 to Able's after-tax net income

e. the production and unit sales volume level at which Able Company will be indifferent between Parts BT62 and GM17

f. the maximum effect on Able's after-tax net income that can be realized when production in this department is at capacity

(CMA adapted)

41. *(Appendix 2)* The Clemson Boy Scout Council has enlisted your help in developing a presentation to a group of local business executives who have previously given generously to support the council's efforts. Investigation reveals that each boy is charged $7 per month, that monthly variable costs per scout are $1, and that the council's monthly fixed expenses are $2,800. Most of the council's workers are volunteers.

Required:

a. Prepare a breakeven chart for the council.

b. Prepare a profit-volume graph for the council.

c. Which graph would you recommend that the council use in its presentation?

42. *(Essay)* A company is currently using breakeven analysis, but the president is uncertain as to the uses of this analytical tool.

a. Define breakeven point for the president and explain how it is computed.

b. Discuss the major uses of breakeven analysis.

(AICPA adapted)

43. *(Essay)* Daly Company has determined the number of car sunshades it will need to sell to break even. Daly wishes to earn a 20 percent profit on revenues rather than break even selling the sunshades.

a. Explain how breakeven analysis can be used to determine the number of sunshades Daly would have to sell to attain a 20 percent profit on sales.

b. If variable cost per unit increases as a percentage of the sales price, how would that affect the number of sunshades that Daly would have to sell to break even, and why?

c. Identify the limitations of breakeven analysis in management decision making.

(AICPA adapted)

Cases

44. Kalifo Company manufactures a line of electric garden tools that are sold in general hardware stores. The company's controller, Sylvia Harlow, has just received the sales forecast for the coming year for Kalifo's three products: hedge clippers, weeders, and leaf blowers. Kalifo has experienced considerable variations in sales volumes and variable costs over the past two years, and Harlow believes the forecast should be carefully evaluated from a cost-volume-profit viewpoint. The preliminary forecast information for 1994 is as follows:

	Weeders	Hedge Clippers	Leaf Blowers
Unit sales	50,000	50,000	100,000
Unit selling price	$28	$36	$48
Variable manufacturing cost per unit	13	12	25
Variable selling cost per unit	5	4	6

For 1994, Kalifo's fixed factory overhead is estimated at $2,000,000, and the company's fixed selling and administrative expenses are forecasted to be

$600,000. Kalifo has an effective tax rate of 40 percent.

a. Determine Kalifo Company's forecasted net income for 1994.
b. Assuming the sales mix remains as budgeted, determine how many units of each product Kalifo Company must sell to break even in 1994.
c. Determine the total dollar sales Kalifo Company must sell in 1994 to earn an after-tax profit of $450,000.
d. After preparing the original estimates, Kalifo Company determined that its variable manufacturing cost of leaf blowers would increase 20 percent, and the variable selling cost of hedge clippers could be expected to increase $1 per unit. However, Kalifo has decided not to change the selling price of either product. In addition, Kalifo has learned that its leaf blower has been perceived as the best value on the market, and it can expect to sell three times as many leaf blowers as any other product. Under these circumstances, determine how many units of each product Kalifo Company would have to sell to break even in 1994.
e. Explain the limitations of cost-volume-profit analysis that Sylvia Harlow should consider when evaluating Kalifo Company's 1994 forecast.

(CMA)

45. Mountain Airways is a small local carrier that flies among the northern midcontinent states. All seats are coach, and the following data are available:

Average full passenger fare	$150
Number of seats per plane	120
Average load factor (seats occupied)	70%
Average variable cost per passenger	$40
Fixed operating costs per month	$1,800,000

a. What is breakeven point in passengers and revenues?
b. What is breakeven point in number of flights?
c. If Mountain raises its average full passenger fare to $200, it is estimated that the load factor will decrease to 55 percent. What will be the breakeven point in number of flights?
d. The cost of fuel is a significant variable cost to any airline. If fuel charges increase $8 per barrel, it is estimated that variable cost per passenger will rise to $60. In this case, what would be the new breakeven point in passengers and in number of flights (refer back to original data)?
e. Mountain Airways has experienced an increase in variable cost per passenger to $50 and an increase in total fixed costs to $2,000,000. The company has decided to raise the average fare to $180. What number of passengers are needed to generate an after-tax profit of $600,000 if the tax rate is 40 percent?
f. (Using the original data) Mountain is considering offering a discounted fare of $120 that the company feels would increase the load factor to 80 percent. Only the additional seats would be sold at the discounted fare. Additional monthly advertising costs would be $100,000. How much pretax income would the discounted fare provide Mountain if the company has 40 flights per day, 30 days per month?
g. Mountain has an opportunity to obtain a new route. The company feels it can sell seats at $175 on the route, but the load factor would be only 60 percent. The company would fly the route 20 times per month. The increase in fixed costs for additional crew, additional planes, landing fees, maintenance, and so on, would total $100,000 per month. Variable cost per passenger would remain at $40.

1. Should the company obtain the route?
2. How many flights would Mountain need to earn pretax income of $57,500 per month on this route?
3. If the load factor could be increased to 75 percent, how many flights would be needed to earn pretax of $57,500 per month on this route?
4. What qualitative factors should be considered by Mountain in making its decision about acquiring this route?

46. In 1989, First State Bank of Lake Lillian (Minnesota) issued and cleared nearly 70% of all rebate checks from manufacturers. In a single day, First State cleared up to 1 million rebate checks. In the previous thirteen years, the bank had sent out more than 500 million checks—and only had $18 million in assets! In 1988, the bank paid out about $1 billion in rebates; average checks were for under $10. The way First State obtained all this business was to offer to clear each check for $.022 rather than the $.06 wanted by the big commercial banks.

   a. Discuss why First State Bank of Lake Lillian could process checks for almost one-third of what large commercial banks wanted.
   b. Discuss some cost-volume-profit effects the clearing of rebate checks would have on the bank.

   (Facts from Bill Richards, "The Hero in All This Is the Person Who Balances First State's Books," *Wall Street Journal* [June 7, 1989], p. B1. Reprinted with permission of *The Wall Street Journal.* © 1989 Dow Jones & Company, Inc. All rights reserved worldwide.)

Ethics Discussion

47. Killoway Chemical Company's new president has learned that for the past four years, the company has been dumping its industrial waste into the local river and falsifying reports to authorities about the levels of suspected cancer-causing materials in that waste. His plant manager says that there is no sure proof that the waste causes cancer, and there are only a few fishing towns within a hundred miles down river. If the company has to treat the substance to neutralize its potentially injurious effects and then transport it to a legal dumpsite, the company's variable and fixed costs would rise to a level that might make the firm uncompetitive. If the company loses its competitive advantage, 10,000 local employees could become unemployed and the town's economy could collapse.

   a. What kinds of variable and fixed costs can you think of that would increase (or decrease) if the waste were treated rather than dumped? How would these costs affect product contribution margin?
   b. What are the ethical conflicts the president faces?
   c. What rationalizations can you detect that have been devised by plant employees?
   d. What options and suggestions can you offer the president?

48. Women often receive reports of positive Pap smears when, in actuality, these results are negative. Newspaper accounts detail an industry utilizing overworked, undersupervised, poorly paid technicians to perform Pap smear tests. Some labs allow workers to analyze up to four times as many specimens per year as experts recommend for accuracy. Workers may be paid $.45 to analyze a smear when patients are charged $35.

   a. Discuss the cost-volume-profit relationships that exist in this case.
   b. Discuss the ethics of the laboratories' owners who allow technicians to be paid piecework for such analysis work.
   c. Discuss the ethics of the workers who rush through Pap smear analyses.

C H A P T E R   10

PRODUCT PRICING

L E A R N I N G   O B J E C T I V E S

After completing this chapter, you should be able to do the following:

1. Understand how a product's life cycle stage affects price
2. Differentiate among various definitions of product cost
3. Recognize why setting the right price is important
4. Explain various pricing strategies that exist and when they are used
5. Understand how the environment in which businesses operate affects prices
6. Understand how and why transfer prices for products are used internally in organizations
7. Understand how and why transfer prices for services are used internally in organizations

Kraft General Foods: Competitors' Prices Are Important

Philip Morris acquired General Foods in 1985 and Kraft in 1988. [But,] the food business is not the staple it used to be. Recession-battered consumers have changed their shopping habits. The combination of price-sensitive buyers and a narrowing of the quality gap between private-label and brand-name goods means slower sales for Kraft General Foods [the single unit result of the two acquisitions]. KGF's North American revenues rose only 1% in 1991.

Kraft's cheese division turned soft, the aftermath of bad pricing decisions made under Mike Miles's leadership. [In 1990 and 1991], prices for milk—*the* cost of goods in cheese, of course—turned volatile, and while private-label cheese producers kept their prices down, Kraft priced its products much higher.

The private-label brands devoured chunks of the U.S. cheese market. By the time Kraft started slicing prices in 1991—as much as 14% on Cracker Barrel—retailers were living quite nicely off their store brands. In some cases, say industry analysts, [retailers] refused to pass on Kraft's price cuts to consumers. The pricing foibles led to 1991's $125 million—at least 20%— shortfall in expected cheese profits.

Now the food marketers, like the folks at Philip Morris U.S.A., acknowledge that pricing their way to high profits is a luxury of the past.

SOURCE: Patricia Sellers, "Can He Keep Philip Morris Growing?" *FORTUNE* (April 6, 1992), pp. 87, 90. © 1992 The Time Inc. Magazine Company. All rights reserved.

T he prices that a company charges for its products depend upon those products' life cycle stage, ingredients' or components' costs, and the company's objectives, strategies, and operating environment. Kraft General Foods, for example, would not price a new breakfast cereal in the same way as an older product brand. And, as indicated in the opening On Site, when ingredient costs decline, companies having substantially equivalent products must meet competitors' price reductions or risk losing market share. Philip Morris has also realized that the operating environment currently consists of consumers who are much more health conscious than in the past. This recognition has created an onslaught of "light" cheeses and lunch meats.

Each of the previous factors is related, and managers must concurrently analyze all the factors to help in pricing. Finding the right price is an art, not a science. Pricing decisions affect planning because sales are the starting point of the budgeting process. Proper pricing of a firm's products or services is essential to a firm's survival and profitability. Management's goal is to set prices so that long-run profits will be maximized.

PRODUCT LIFE CYCLE

Products and services, like people, go through a series of sequential life cycle stages. It is not easy to determine how "old" a product must be before it moves from one stage to another. Products (such as hula hoops and miniskirts) have been known to revitalize or "come back from the dead" with renewed vigor.

The specific product life cycle stages are: development, introduction, growth, maturity, and harvest; sales in each stage are shown in Exhibit 10–1. Companies must be aware of the life cycle stage that their products are in, because the stage may have a tremendous impact on costs, sales, and pricing strategies. During the development stage, costs exist with no corresponding offsetting revenues. High costs are also incurred during the introduction stage, but sales are merely beginning; therefore, profits are still nonexistent. Costs tend to level off during the remaining three stages as the standards are stabilized and production becomes routine. Sales increase through growth, level off in maturity, and then decline during the harvest stage.

Once a product idea has been formulated, the market is researched to determine the features customers desire. As discussed in chapter 5, it is at this time that engineering, design, and suppliers should discuss the production process and the types of components. It is often helpful to have suppliers participate in the design phase or, alternatively, to provide product specifications to the supplier who would draft a design for approval.

Awareness of a forecasted selling price that the market will bear allows managers to determine a target production cost. Decisions made during the design stage can affect product sales, design, costs, and quality for the remainder of the product's life cycle. Most studies have indicated that about 80 to 90 percent of a product's life cycle cost is determined by decisions made before production ever begins. Products should be designed for the quality and cost desired. For example, Germany's Braun sells a coffeemaker with vertical lines on the side that are not there for decoration, but to

EXHIBIT 10–1
▼▼▼▼▼▼▼▼▼▼▼

PRODUCT LIFE CYCLE

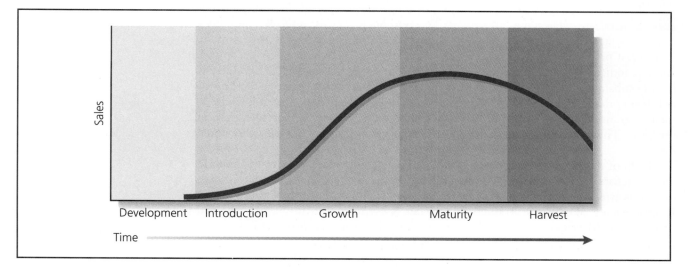

Development   Introduction   Growth   Maturity   Harvest

Sales

Time

add strength and hide any imperfections caused by using a less expensive plastic. "Adding the lines reduced Braun's plastic costs by nearly 70%."[1]

Products need to be designed to use the fewest number of parts, and parts should be standardized to the greatest extent possible. For example, Black & Decker found that it produced one hundred different motors for its power tools. Since recognizing that fact, B&D has reduced the number of motors to fewer than twenty and wants to make only five. As indicated in the News Note on the next page about Philips Industries, changes can be made after original design, but think of the profits the company would have had since product origination if the product had been designed the "new way" first!

If products are designed properly during development, they should require only a minimal number of engineering changes after being released to production. Each time an engineering change is made, one or more of the following problems occurs and creates additional costs: the operations flow document must be reprinted; workers must relearn tasks; machine dies or setups must be changed; and parts currently ordered or in stock may be made obsolete. If costs are to be affected significantly, any design changes must be made early in process.

Many successful companies "make sure the designer works as an equal partner in a product-development team that includes engineering, marketing, and manufacturing. This way the designer gets in on a project from the beginning and can influence almost every aspect of the product—how it works, how many parts it has, whether it's recyclable."[2]

Product introduction is essentially a "start-up" phase. Sales are usually quite low, and selling prices often are set in some relationship (equal to, above, or below) to the market price of similar **substitute goods** or services, if such goods or services are available. Costs, however, can be quite substantial in the introduction phase. For example, in a 1990 survey, a grocery industry task force determined that on the average, "manufacturers paid $5.1 million to get a new product or line extension on grocery store shelves nationwide. The cheapest [product introduction] studied cost $378,000; the most expensive, $21.2 million."[3] Costs incurred during this phase are typically related to product design, market research, advertising, and promotion.

substitute goods

The growth stage begins when the product first breaks even. During the growth stage, the product has been accepted by the market and profits begin to rise. Product quality also may improve during this stage of the life cycle because competitors have improved on original production designs. Prices are fairly stable during this period because many substitutes may exist or because consumers have become "attached" to the product and are willing to pay a particular price for it rather than buy a substitute.

In the maturity stage, sales begin to stabilize or slowly decline, and firms often compete on the basis of selling price. Costs are often at their lowest level during this period, so profits may be high. Kraft General Foods' products such as Jell-o and Kool-Aid are in their maturity stage. Some products, like these, seem to remain at this stage "forever."

---

[1]Brian Dumaine, "Design That Sells and Sells and . . . ," *FORTUNE* (March 11, 1991), p. 90.
[2]Ibid., p. 92.
[3]Richard Gibson, "Marketing—Pinning Down Costs of Product Introductions," *Wall Street Journal* (November 26, 1990), p. B1.

Cost Reductions Can Bring Price Reductions

Philips Industries Inc. brainstormed to improve one of the company's 2,000 products—a diffuser that distributes air from ceiling ducts. It decided the number of parts could be reduced to 8 from 31, resulting in a $250,000 annual saving in material and labor costs. That permitted the company to raise the profit margin on the product while cutting its price 15%. Sales of the ceiling diffuser have jumped 39% and market share has gone from 12% to 15%.

SOURCE: Lynn Adkins, "Philips Industries' Cost-Cutting Mavens," *Business Monthly* (November 1986), p. 47. Reprinted with permission, *Business Monthly* magazine. Copyright © 1986 by Goldhirsh Group, Inc., 38 Commercial Wharf, Boston, Mass. 02110.

The decline stage reflects waning sales. For example, KGF's Louis Rich products, which increased in popularity so rapidly, are now experiencing such a downturn in demand that Philip Morris is closing down one plant in California and not completing another plant in Missouri. During the decline stage, prices are often cut dramatically to stimulate business.

Customers are concerned with obtaining a quality product or service for a perceived "reasonable" price. Product prices change, however, over the product life cycle because customer sensitivity "to performance versus price varies over the product life cycle."[4] Producers of goods and providers of service should be concerned with maximizing profits over a product's or service's life cycle because, to be profitable, revenues must be generated in excess of total (not period) product costs.

PRICING OBJECTIVES AND STRATEGIES

A firm's pricing objectives should follow from its goals. Therefore, pricing decisions should relate to considerations such as profitability, market share, and growth and should be part of a total plan to achieve overall success in the market. One of the most widely read studies on pricing objectives indicated that four primary goals exist: (1) achieving a target return on investment; (2) achieving a target market share; (3) stabilizing prices; and (4) meeting the competition.[5] These goals reflect different planning horizons (number 1 is long-range; number 4 is short-range) and different abilities (number 3 may be possible for a **price maker** but not for a **price taker**).[6] Some

price maker   **price taker**

[4]Gerald I. Susman, "Product Life Cycle Management," in *Emerging Practices in Cost Management,* ed. Barry J. Brinker (Boston: Warren, Gorham & Lamont, 1990), p. 226.
[5]Robert F. Lanzillotti, "Pricing Objectives in Large Companies," *American Economic Review* (December 1958), pp. 921–40.
[6]A price maker is a firm that determines the level of output and the corresponding price that will maximize its profits. A price taker accepts the market price as given by industry supply and demand.

goals may be in conflict with others; for example, it may be difficult to achieve a target market share while also achieving a target return on investment. At different points in time and for different companies, some of these goals may be primary and others secondary. And, while none of these goals specifies profit maximization, each of the four can be viewed as an alternative, more measurable, goal.

To increase volume and profits, Jack Hadley decided to become a price maker when he took over the Kiamichi Railroad of Hugo, Oklahoma. Mr. Hadley recognized that profits were unattainable with the existing employee union wage structure. Thus he reduced company costs by lowering pay scales and replacing the lost wages with a profit-sharing incentive plan for employees. Then, Jack Hadley took an innovative approach to pricing by disregarding the market price and pricing the railroad's services at the lowest possible amount that would still allow for profits.

Price times volume equals revenue, but price often directly affects volume. Setting too high a price (like Kraft General Foods did with its cheese) can limit volume, reducing revenue to less than it could have been. Setting too low a price can also reduce revenue because (1) low prices may be associated with inferior products, causing a volume reduction; or, if number 1 is not true, (2) the additional volume created will not necessarily be enough to compensate for the low price. Thus, management must consider both what demand will exist at various selling price levels and the prices at which competitors will offer substitute products. Financial difficulties will arise if production costs are greater than the selling price that consumers can or will pay or if competitors can price an equivalent product below the firm's costs. The latter situation indicates that (1) other firms produce goods more efficiently or (2) these competing firms have substantially higher volumes over which to allocate fixed costs and, thus, have a lower fixed cost per unit.

Exhibit 10–2 indicates the primary stakeholders setting or influencing the setting of prices. Their influences may affect different companies differently; for example, companies in food production are more highly regulated than companies engaged in carpet cleaning services.

Many government contracts are performed on a cost-plus basis. At the NASA Michoud Assembly Facility, costs of producing space shuttle components are accumulated using a job order system that provides the documentation to support the prices billed.

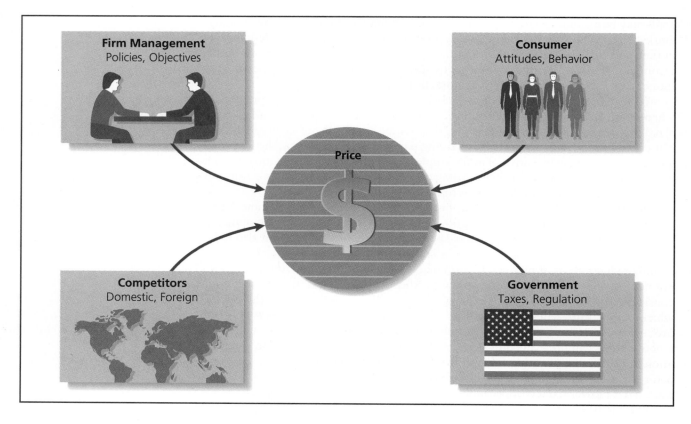

EXHIBIT 10–2
▼▼▼▼▼▼▼▼▼▼

WHO SETS OR
INFLUENCES PRICES

A variety of strategies may be used to achieve the pricing objectives decided on by company management. Eight of these are discussed in the following sections: cost-plus pricing; time and material pricing; special order pricing; penetration pricing and price skimming; multiple product pricing; price reductions; and regulated prices.

Cost-Plus Pricing

cost-plus pricing

In **cost-plus pricing**, selling price is calculated by adding a designated markup to a defined cost. In cost-plus arrangements, the term *cost* must be carefully defined and clearly understood by both parties to the contract.

Cost-plus pricing is used in many situations that have low profit margins and many substitute products. For instance, grocery retailers, such as Food Lion, often use cost-plus pricing. Cost is defined as the variable purchasing cost, and a markup is added to cover fixed costs and provide a profit margin. In such instances, if all stores could buy at the same cost, the stores that keep their overhead and profit margins the lowest would be the ones with the lowest selling prices.

In addition, many construction firms and government contractors (such as Martin Marietta) also use cost-plus contracts. Use in these industries is appropriate because of the specialized nature of the products and the limited quantities in which those products will be produced.

Because of its emphasis on "cost," this method of pricing would seem to be one of the most logical and appropriate. There are, however, numerous ways to compute cost. Product cost is defined in chapter 2 as including direct materials, direct labor, variable production overhead, and fixed production overhead. This definition reflects the concept of absorption costing. An alternative computation of product cost, known as variable costing, considers only those cost components that change in relationship to volume (direct materials, direct labor, and variable production overhead) as product cost. Variable costing treats fixed production overhead as a period expense.

Computations for the Metzer Company variable and absorption costs are shown in Exhibit 10–3, with information needed for alternative product cost definitions. Fixed production overhead cost is allocated on a per-unit basis for purposes of simplicity in this example.

While absorption and variable costing are the two most widely recognized methods of determining product cost, other definitions can be used in conjunction with pricing situations. A true "full" cost would be defined as total product cost plus assigned per-unit period expenses plus an opportunity cost. An **opportunity cost** represents a potential benefit that is given up because one course of action is chosen over another. Opportunity costs are not recorded in the accounting records because they are related to transactions that did not occur rather than to those that did occur. Such costs, however, are very important in making decisions.

opportunity cost

Assume that Metzer can either use its production facilities to make the product discussed in Exhibit 10–3 or rent the facilities for $860,000 per period. The rent indicates an opportunity cost of $1 per unit. If Metzer produced and sold the expected 860,000 units during the period, the fixed period expense per unit would be $.45 ($387,000 ÷ 860,000 units). Thus, total period cost per unit is $5.45 ($5.00 variable period cost + $.45 fixed period cost). The full cost per unit that would need to be covered by the selling price would be $33.45 ($27 absorption cost + $1.00 opportunity cost + $5.45 period cost).

Managers might alternatively choose to define cost from a variable costing basis. This definition would result in a $30 total variable cost—the sum of the $24 variable production cost, the $5 per-unit variable period expenses, and the $1 of opportunity cost. The total fixed costs of $2,967,000 ($2,580,000 + $387,000) and any desired profit would have to be covered by the markup on total variable cost.

Product Costs (per unit)		
a. Direct materials	$16	
b. Direct labor	6	
c. Variable production overhead	2	
d. Total variable product cost	$24	← variable cost
e. Allocated fixed production overhead		
($2,580,000 ÷ 860,000 units)	3	
f. Total production cost	$27	← absorption cost
Period Expenses		
g. Per-unit variable period expenses	$5	
h. Fixed period expenses	$387,000	
Opportunity Cost		
i. Foregone benefits of facilities (averaged over all units produced) (per unit)	$1	

EXHIBIT 10–3
▼▼▼▼▼▼▼▼▼▼▼▼

METZER COMPANY
PRODUCT COST
INFORMATION

While cost-plus pricing is apparently a fairly simple method of price determination, its simplicity may be misleading. Trying to use any type of absorption cost as a basis for pricing would require a reasonable allocation of total overhead charges to the product. If the company makes a variety of products, such an allocation may be difficult, if not impossible. Also, if the company is gathering its overhead in a single cost pool and/or using a single cost driver for allocation, the allocations may be inaccurate or inappropriate.

In trying to set a long-term selling price using cost as a basis, company managers would be likely to use one of the concepts of full cost as a starting point. In contrast, if an already profitable company has an opportunity to bid on a sale outside of its normal, ongoing business, it may choose one of the smaller cost bases upon which to calculate its price in hopes of obtaining the additional business. The tighter the competition for the business, the lower the basis that may be chosen. Depending upon the objective, a number of other pricing strategies may be chosen.

Time and Material Pricing

time and material pricing

The use of **time and material pricing** is quite common in service organizations, such as repair companies and professional firms. This method allows prices to be set using separate rates for the direct labor time involved and the direct materials used. Each rate is developed by including direct costs, a markup to cover selling and administrative charges, and a markup for profit.

Estimated 1994 cost and pricing information for Ron's Electrical Service is given in Exhibit 10–4. Ron Schorg, the owner, has found that his costs can be divided between those that relate to the electricians and their service area and those that relate

EXHIBIT 10–4
▼▼▼▼▼▼▼▼▼▼▼▼

ESTIMATED 1994
COSTS FOR RON'S
ELECTRICAL SERVICE

	Labor-related Costs	Parts-related Costs
Manager's salary (duties split 60:40 between service work and parts work)	$27,000	$18,000
Benefits (25% of electricians' wages and salary)	36,750	4,500
Bookkeeping service	4,250	1,820
Supplies	1,000	3,900
Utilities	1,200	4,600
Depreciation & property taxes	1,800	3,730
Total	$72,000	$36,550
Electricians' wages (3 electricians working 40-hours per week, 50 weeks per year = 6,000 hours; wages divided by 6,000 hours = $20 per hour)	$120,000	
Repair parts		$85,000
Desired profit rates (per hour and per dollar of parts' cost)	$10	20%

Labor loading charge = $72,000 ÷ 6,000 hours = $12; $12 + $10 profit = $22 per hour billed
Materials loading charge = $36,550 ÷ $85,000 = $.43; $.43 + $.20 profit = $.63 for each dollar of parts' cost

to the parts (materials) area. All costs have been assigned in Exhibit 10–4 to one of these two areas. Ron has also set desired profit rates of $10 per hour for electricians' time and 20 percent of parts' cost. Using the $10 per hour desired profit rate indicates that Ron should charge $42 per labor hour for electrician services ($20 hourly wage plus $22 **labor loading charge**). He will charge customers the cost of parts plus a **materials loading charge** of $.63 per dollar of cost. The materials charge is designed to cover Ron's ordering, handling, and carrying costs for the parts inventory plus provide a profit margin. Using these rates, a job that required five hours of electrician's time and $20 of parts would be billed to the customer as follows:

labor loading charge
materials loading charge

Labor cost (5 hours @ $42)	$210.00
Materials cost [$20 + ($20 × $.63)]	32.60
Total price to customer	$242.60

Special Order Pricing

In **special order pricing,** management must determine a sales price to charge for manufacturing or service jobs that are outside the company's normal production/service realm. Special order situations include jobs that require a bid, are taken during slack periods, or are made to a specific buyer's specifications. Typically, the sales price quoted on a special order job should be high enough to cover the variable costs of the job and any incremental (additional) fixed costs caused by the job and to generate a profit.

special order pricing

Special order pricing requires knowledge of the **relevant costs,** or the costs that are logically associated with the specific problem or decision at hand. For a cost to be relevant, it must have a connection or bearing on some future endeavor and must be an out-of-pocket or a differential cost. **Out-of-pocket costs** involve current or near-current cash expenditures, while **differential costs** are those that vary in amount among the alternatives being considered.

relevant costs

out-of-pocket costs
differential costs

To illustrate the concept of a differential cost, assume that you are planning to go downtown to see a specific movie this evening, but you have no car. You have three possible methods of transportation: the city bus, the city streetcar, or a cab. Both the bus and the streetcar cost $1 each way; the cab trip costs $2.50 each way. The movie costs $5. The costs of the bus and the streetcar are not differential costs with respect to each other, but the cab alternative involves a $1.50 ($2.50 − $1.00) differential cost with respect to the other alternatives. The cost of the movie, while an out-of-pocket cost, is irrelevant to the decision since it does not differ among any of the alternatives.

Faust Corporation, a shoe manufacturer, is used to illustrate a special price decision. The company has been given the opportunity to bid on a special order for 1,000 pairs of men's leather shoes for Alpha Beta Airlines. Faust's management wants to obtain the order as long as the additional business will provide a satisfactory contribution to profit. The company has machine and labor hours that are not currently being used, and raw materials can be obtained from the supplier. Also, Faust has no immediate opportunity to use its currently unused capacity in another way, so an opportunity cost is not a factor.

Exhibit 10–5 presents information that management has gathered to determine a price to bid on the shoes. Direct materials, direct labor, and variable factory overhead costs are relevant to setting the bid price because these variable production costs will be incurred for each additional pair of shoes produced. While all variable costs

EXHIBIT 10–5
▼▼▼▼▼▼▼▼▼▼▼▼

FAUST
CORPORATION
PRODUCT COST
INFORMATION

	Normal Costs	Relevant Costs
Per-unit cost for one pair of men's shoes:		
Direct materials	$ 6	$ 6
Direct labor	5	5
Variable overhead	3	3
Variable selling expenses (commissions)	3	0
Total variable cost	$17	$14
Fixed factory overhead (allocated)	2	
Fixed selling & administrative expense	1	
Total cost per pair of shoes	$20	

are normally relevant to a special pricing decision, the variable selling expense is irrelevant in this instance because no sales commission will be paid on this sale. Fixed production overhead and fixed selling and administrative expenses are not expected to increase because of this sale, so these expenses are not included in the pricing decision.

Using the available cost information, the relevant cost used to determine the bid price for the shoes is $14 (direct materials, direct labor, and variable overhead). This cost is the minimum price at which the company should sell a pair of shoes. If the existing fixed costs have been covered by regular sales, any price set higher than $14 will provide the company some profit.

Assume Faust is currently experiencing a $10,000 net loss. Company managers want to set a bid price that would cover the net loss generated by other sales and create a $3,000 before-tax profit. In this case, Faust Corporation would spread the total $13,000 desired amount over the 1,000 pair of shoes at $13 per pair. This would give a bid price of $27 per pair ($14 variable cost + $13). However, *any* price above the $14 variable cost will contribute toward reducing the $10,000 loss.

In setting the bid price, management must decide how much profit it would consider reasonable on the special order. As another example, if Faust Corporation's usual selling price for a pair of shoes is $30, each sale provides a normal profit margin of $10 per pair, or 50 percent of the $20 total cost. Setting the bid price for the special order at $21 would cover the variable production costs of $14 and provide a normal 50 percent profit margin. This computation illustrates a simplistic cost-plus approach to pricing, but ignores both product demand and market competition. Faust Corporation's bid price should also reflect these considerations. In addition, company management should consider the effect that the additional job will have on the activities engaged in by the company and whether these activities will create additional, unforeseen costs.

Sometimes a company will depart from its typical price-setting routine and "low-ball" bid jobs. A low-ball bid may only cover variable costs or it may be below such costs. The rationale behind low-ball bids is to obtain the job to have the opportunity to introduce company products or services to a particular market segment. Special pricing of this nature may provide work for a period of time, but cannot be continued for the long run. To remain in business, a company must set product or service selling prices to cover total variable costs, to cover an appropriate amount of fixed and selling/administrative costs, and to provide a reasonable profit margin. An exception to this general rule, however, may occur when a company produces related or complementary products. For instance, a company such as Nintendo might sell video hardware at or below cost and use the ancillary software games programs as the primary source of profit.

Special prices may also be justified when orders are of an unusual nature (because of the quantity, method of delivery, or packaging) or because the products are being tailor-made to customer instructions. Lastly, special pricing can be used when producing goods for a one-time job, such as an overseas order that will not affect domestic sales.

When setting a special order price, management must consider the qualitative issues as well as the quantitative ones. For instance, will setting a low bid price cause this customer (or others) to feel that a precedent has been established for future prices? Will the contribution margin on a bid, set low enough to acquire the job, earn a sufficient amount to justify the additional burdens placed on management or employees by this activity? How, if at all, will special order sales affect the company's normal sales? If the job is taking place during a period of low business activity (off-season or recession), is management willing to take the business at a lower contribution or profit margin simply to keep a trained work force employed?

Penetration Pricing and Price Skimming

Penetration pricing and price skimming are two common pricing strategies that are used most often with products in the introduction stage of their life cycle. When a company sets a price that is significantly below the current market price for a similar product or service, it is known as **penetration pricing**. The lower price is then often raised as the product moves into its growth stage. This tactic is designed to entice customers to use the product and, hopefully, become loyal to it. Texas Instruments employed this strategy when it introduced its semiconductor chips for computers.

penetration pricing

An alternative to penetration pricing is **price skimming**, which means that an introductory price is set higher than what exists for similar (but potentially lower-quality) products. A high price may also be set because there are no similar products or services in the market—as in the case of IBM's first personal computer or Sony's camcorders. With this strategy, the price will generally fall at later stages of the product life cycle, as other competitors enter the market and/or as better production technology is developed.

price skimming

Multiple Product Pricing

Since most companies sell a variety of products and services, company management must consider how the pricing of a newly introduced item will relate to its current prices. If a new product is to become part of an existing product family, management should appropriately position the new product's price within the context of the family's current pricing structure. For example, if a company adds a five-drawer file cabinet to its line of one-, two-, three-, and four-drawer file cabinets, the new product's price should be somewhat consistent with, but perhaps lower than, the sum of the prices of a two- plus a three-drawer cabinet. If the five-drawer price is higher than that sum, sales of the new item may be less than expected because some consumers may buy a two-drawer and a three-drawer cabinet to meet their needs.

Price Reductions

ad hoc discounts

Sellers commonly give other businesses trade discounts from suggested retail prices or volume discounts from set selling prices. Companies may also give **ad hoc discounts** reflecting price concessions that do not relate to volume but simply to real or imagined competition. Such discounts are not usually subject to detailed legal justification.

price discrimination

Other discounts may be indicative of some type of **price discrimination,** or charging different prices for the same product to different groups of buyers when those prices are not reflective of cost differences. Cost differences must result from actual variations in the cost to manufacture, sell, or distribute a product due to differing methods of production or quantities sold. Many types of price discrimination exist, such as senior citizens' discounts for pharmaceuticals and children's discounts for movies. Discrimination of this sort is generally illegal under the **Robinson-Patman**

Robinson-Patman Act

Act of 1936, unless the seller is meeting a competitive situation.

Regulated Prices

fair-return pricing

A regulated firm such as a utility company often has its prices set by a governmental rate-making body. This type of price regulation reflects **fair-return pricing** in which a firm is allowed to charge a high enough price to make a "normal" return but nothing more than that. The rates are based on several factors including "approved" costs. Allowable rates of return are specified on the firm's assets. Allowable net income is derived by multiplying the rate times the asset base. The allowable net income is added to the firm's operating expenses to derive the company's allowable revenue. The allowable revenue is then apportioned to the firm's various classes of customers. For an electric utility, apportionment is generally based on kilowatt hours of power used and on the class of customer (such as residential, commercial, governmental, and not-for-profit).

As indicated in the News Note at the top of page 423, regulated pricing is not necessarily reasonable, nor ethical, pricing. While apparently many places are paying too much for milk, the farmers in Wisconsin, on the average, "are getting $2.59 less than they pay to produce 100 pounds of milk, or losing about 20 cents for every $1 of milk they sell, the U.S. Department of Agriculture says." [7]

OPERATING ENVIRONMENT

The operating environment of a firm consists of the market structure in which it exists, the government regulations under which it must act, the behavior exhibited by the consumers of its products and services, and the laws of supply and demand. Each of these factors plays a large part in determining how a company establishes prices.

Market Structure

The degree to which a firm can control a product's price is affected by the nature of the market and the degree of competition the firm has. There are four basic market structures: pure competition, monopolistic competition, monopoly, and oligopoly.

---

[7]P. B. Seymour, "Dairyland Alarmed Over Low Prices," *Reno Gazette-Journal* (June 16, 1991), p. E1.

NEWS NOTE

Regulated Prices Can Cost Consumers

The decades-old program for setting the price of milk, which requires 500 people to administer, works something like this: First, government experts survey about 70 cheese and butter plants to find out what they are paying dairy farmers in Minnesota and Wisconsin. Then they feed this data into an equation to set the minimum price for milk at the farm in various "marketing areas" across the country. On top of this, they add a bonus based on a farmer's distance from one city: Eau Claire, Wisconsin.

Milk is the only commodity for which the Secretary of Agriculture can dictate the minimum price a buyer must pay a farmer. Critics, however, assail the system for stimulating inefficient production, discouraging the use of new processing technology and creating surpluses that the government then has to buy. In Florida, historically among the least efficient places to produce milk because of the climate, many dairies survive only because of price advantages in the Eau Claire rule.

Ultimately, consumers wind up paying more. The Agriculture Department itself has calculated that consumers and taxpayers could have saved as much as $1.7 billion in certain years if milk pricing had been freer. In some cities, less regulation could have meant a price drop of close to 20%, it's estimated.

SOURCE: Scott Kilman, "Why the Price of Milk Depends on Distance from Eau Claire, Wis.," *Wall Street Journal* (May 20, 1991), p. A1. Reprinted by permission of *The Wall Street Journal*, © 1991 Dow Jones & Company, Inc. All rights reserved worldwide.

In a **pure competition** market structure, there are many firms and each has a small market share and produces identical products. Firms are price takers; each firm accepts the price for its product as set by the interaction of market demand for and supply of the product. It is unlikely that any large industry in the United States meets all the requirements of a purely competitive market, but farming approximates such a structure.

pure competition

When many firms have slightly differentiated products and services, there is **monopolistic competition.** Because the products and services differ, some people are willing to pay more for one firm's products than for similar products of other firms. Such a consumer attitude allows each firm to have some control over its products' selling prices. Since product differentiation is crucial, monopolistically competitive firms use advertising to create brand loyalty and consumer recognition. Small, independent retailers, especially in large cities, are generally viewed as part of a monopolistic competitive structure.

monopolistic competition

A **monopoly** exists when there is only one seller of a product or provider of a service. The monopolistic firm has total control over the price of its products and is a price maker, setting both market price and output level to maximize its profit. In the United States, federal antitrust laws restrict most monopolies; those that are allowed to exist are regulated and their prices controlled by various levels of government. Local telephone and utility companies and local TV cable franchises are regulated monopolies.

monopoly

In an **oligopoly,** there are only a few firms whose products and services may be differentiated or standardized. If the goods can be differentiated (such as spaghetti sauce or airline flights), oligopolistic firms spend large sums of money on advertising

oligopoly

Pricing in the oligopolistic airline industry seems to be in a constant state of flux. Whenever one major airline takes the initiative to adjust prices, the others typically follow suit. Rarely, however, do the price changes seem to be connected with cost changes.

and product development. Because of firm interdependence, prices tend to be rigid and price leadership is typical. Once price changes are announced by a dominant firm, others in the industry typically match the announced price. Price decreases are almost always matched immediately; occasionally, price increases are not followed and the announcing firm is forced to return prices to previous levels.

International Dimensions

At one time, most domestic companies were concerned only with competing within national boundaries. With the world becoming more accessible politically, economically, and technically for international trade, domestic companies face new opportunities and greater competitive pressures. The new opportunities involve access to more markets with vast numbers of new customers. The pressures come from the need to at least meet selling prices charged by international competitors and the greater risks involved in selling in global markets. Often, selling prices of goods produced internationally are lower than those of goods produced domestically because (1) foreign competitors may pay their workers substantially lower wages than those paid in the United States; (2) foreign governments either provide subsidies to and/or own part of producing firms; (3) to maintain market share, foreign exporters may not raise prices when the dollar depreciates against foreign currencies; and (4), as indicated in the following News Note, some foreign companies' productivity may be higher than that of some domestic companies.

dumping   Foreign competitors may also engage in **dumping,** which refers to selling products abroad at lower prices than the ones charged in the home country or in other national markets. When practiced to force domestic producers out of business so that

The Efficiency of Japanese Automakers Is Worldclass

Not all of Japan's automakers are equally efficient, but the top tier perform remarkable feats. Not only do they build cars with half the man-hours and one-third the defects in half the factory space of traditional mass producers, but they also get by with one-quarter of the finished unit inventories and one-tenth of in-process inventories. In the Eighties they developed new models in an average of 46 months rather than 60 months. That makes them worldclass in every measurable area of automotive production.

Taking longer to build a car doesn't necessarily make it any better. In European plants, assembly defects average 76.4 per 100 cars vs. 52.1 per 100 cars in Japan. Given these findings, it is easy to understand why the European Community is vigorously devising new barriers to the sale of Japanese cars that will extend to 1998.

SOURCE: Alex Taylor III, "New Lessons from Japan's Carmakers," *FORTUNE* (October 22, 1990), p. 166. © 1990 The Time Inc. Magazine Company. All rights reserved.

the foreign competitor becomes the primary source of supply and can then raise prices, this technique is referred to as **predatory dumping.** Domestic governments usually establish stiff import duties on goods that are dumped in their countries to eliminate the domestic-foreign price differential.

predatory dumping

Regulation

Domestic companies are also subject to government regulations. These regulations seek to maintain a market environment in which healthy competitive forces provide consumers with the best quality products at the lowest prices and companies with a viable business community in which to succeed. Regulatory agencies monitor prices and trade practices on a fairly continuous basis to detect activities believed to be detrimental to healthy commerce. Examples of some of these "unhealthy" activities follow.

When competing firms conspire to set the price of a good or service at a specified level, they are engaging in **price fixing.** Buyers who purchase the good or service must do so at the specified price because no suppliers are offering the item at a lower price. Price fixing may be horizontal or vertical.

price fixing

In **horizontal price fixing,** competitors attempt to regulate prices through an agreement or conspiracy. By cooperating with each other, the competitors deprive customers of the normal benefits of seeking lower prices through market forces. Price regulation may be accomplished through agreeing either on a selling price or on the quantity of goods that may be produced or offered for sale. Airlines, oil companies, and the NCAA have all been accused of horizontal price fixing. Now, as indicated in the following News Note, physicians are added to the list.

horizontal price fixing

Horizontal price fixing differs from certain independent business behavior by competitors. The act of competitors independently engaging in the same or similar courses of action because of simple business judgment is called **conscious parallelism.** Since there has been no conspiracy, such practices are considered legal.

conscious parallelism

Do Doctors Fix Prices?

Dr. Gregory Whitaker had no idea he was breaking the law when he attended a series of meetings with 21 other obstetricians in Savannah, Ga., to discuss fees for delivering babies. But he soon found himself before a federal grand jury facing possible criminal charges. Whitaker learned the hard way what doctors nationwide are learning—the government expects them to compete with each other like any other business.

To violate the law, doctors must conspire to fix their prices. If doctors independently set fees, there is no violation, even if they are uniform. The reimbursement levels paid by insurers tend to set a price level for many services.

SOURCE: Hugh Vickery, "Price-fixing Doctors Caught by Courts," [*New Orleans*] *Times-Picayune* (April 21, 1991), p. A-13.

vertical price fixing

Vertical price fixing (or resale price maintenance) involves agreements by businesses and their distributors to control the prices at which products may be sold to consumers. Manufacturers may set a suggested retail price (SRP) for goods; they may also specify that their products cannot be sold below the SRP and refuse to do business with any firm that has not maintained those prices.[8] However, an agreement between the manufacturer and the distributor is illegal.

Consumer Behavior

Consumers are a major factor in a business's operating environment. Company management needs market research to determine the factors that influence purchasers' rationale for paying certain prices. Customers may buy because of product features, product quality, and/or company service, reliability, and ethical reputation. Having numerous considerations in the purchasing decision makes pricing decisions much more difficult than if customers bought solely on the basis of price.

Most consumers, however, must consider price in making a purchase because they are trying to make efficient use of their scarce resources. If they think a product is priced too high, they will seek similar products that meet their needs at lower prices. If they don't find these, they may then seek alternatives. For example, if a shopper decides that ground sirloin is priced too high, that shopper may buy ground chuck or beef as a substitute. Alternatively, the shopper may decide that turkey legs are a better value than any of the ground meats. Ultimately, satisfaction of needs and desires governs consumer purchases. This can be met by an initial choice (ground sirloin), a substitute (ground chuck or ground beef), or an alternative (turkey legs).

price elasticity of demand

When consumer demand responds quickly and strongly to a change in price, demand for that product is said to be elastic with respect to price. For any good or service, **price elasticity of demand** reflects the percentage change in the quantity demanded relative to the percentage change in price. The closer the elasticity value is to 0, the more inelastic the demand is said to be. However, the degree of elasticity must exceed 1.00 before demand can be thought to be elastic—referring to a situation in

---

[8]United States v. Colgate & Co., 250 U.S. 300 (1919).

which a price decrease causes an increase in total revenue. Calculations of demand elasticity, however, are valid only for the ranges of quantities and prices used in the calculation. If the ranges are changed, a different result will occur.

The drug industry is one in which there is little relationship between price and demand, as shown in the above News Note. Because of the price increases on drugs being approximately three times the inflation rate over the last ten years, one U.S. senator has called for a federal law to regulate drug prices.[9]

Supply

When product demand exceeds product supply, both buyers and sellers will bid the price up. In addition, the higher price often stimulates greater production which, in turn, increases supply (unless production is constrained by cost factors). When demand is less than supply, buyers and sellers will bid the price down. In turn, this lower price should motivate lower production, which lowers supply. Therefore, price is consistently and circularly influenced by the relationship of supply to demand. As supply increases or decreases and demand increases or decreases because of changing prices, supply and demand find a point at which they are equal. At this point, price will stabilize as long as other factors (such as new technology or changing consumer incomes) do not intervene.

All of the previous considerations affect external prices. In contrast, companies also may sell to other organizational units or segments using an internal pricing structure called transfer pricing.

---

[9]Michael Waldholz, "Drug Prices Rise Three Times Rate of Inflation," *Wall Street Journal* (September 15, 1991), p. B4.

TRANSFER PRICING

transfer price

Intracompany sales of goods and services involve the use of transfer pricing.[10] A **transfer price** (or charge-back system) is an internal charge established for the exchange of goods or services between organizational units of the same company. Transfer prices are often used for internal reporting purposes in a company that has independent segments or divisions.[11] Internal company transfers should be presented on external financial statements at the producing segment's costs. Thus, if transfers are "sold" at an amount other than cost, any intersegment profit, expense, and/or revenue accounts must be eliminated.

A number of different approaches are used to establish transfer prices. Intracompany transfers should be made only if they are in the best interest of the whole organization. Within this context, the general rules for choosing a transfer price are as follows:[12]

incremental cost

- The maximum price should be no greater than the lowest market price at which the buying segment can acquire the goods or services externally.
- The minimum price should be no less than the sum of the selling segment's incremental production costs plus the opportunity cost of the facilities used. (**Incremental cost** refers to the additional cost of producing a contemplated quantity of output, which generally means variable costs of production.)

From the company's perspective, any transfer price set between these two limits is generally considered appropriate.

To illustrate use of this model, assume that a product is available from external suppliers at a price below the lower limit (incremental costs plus opportunity cost). The producing division has two choices. First, it can stop production of the product and buy it from the external suppliers. This decision is reasonable since, compared to those suppliers, the division does not appear to be cost efficient in its production activities. Stopping production would release the facilities for other, more profitable purposes. Or, the producing division could try to improve its efficiency and reduce the internal cost of making the product.

The difference between the model's upper and lower limits is the corporate "profit" (or savings) generated by producing internally rather than buying externally. The transfer price acts to "divide the corporate profit" between the buying and selling segments.

After the transfer price range limits have been determined, one criterion used to choose a price within the range is the ease by which the price can be determined. Managers should be able to understand the computation of a transfer price and to evaluate how that transfer price will affect their divisions' profits. Three traditional methods are used for determining transfer prices: cost-based prices, market-based

---

[10]Transfer prices for services are discussed in the appendix to this chapter.
[11]Such companies are referred to as decentralized operations, which are discussed in detail in chapter 15.
[12]These rules are more difficult to implement when the selling division is in a captive relationship and not able to sell its products outside the corporate entity. In such situations, opportunity cost must be estimated to provide the selling division an incentive to transfer products.

Demand for pharmaceuticals is only slightly related to price. People who need medications will purchase them, but may request generic substitutes if they are available.

prices, and negotiated prices. Following is a discussion of each method and its advantages and disadvantages.

Assume that Hugo Auto Company is composed of a radio manufacturing division (managed by Mr. Lew) and an automobile manufacturing division (managed by Ms. Randall). The managers are attempting to establish a transfer price for the radios that are installed in the automobiles. Radio Division data (shown in Exhibit 10–6) are used to illustrate various transfer pricing approaches. Note that the Radio Division is capable of supplying all external and internal production needs.

Standard unit production cost		
Direct materials (DM)	$40	
Direct labor (DL)	12	
Variable overhead (VOH)	18	
Variable selling & administrative	2	
Total variable costs		$ 72
Fixed overhead (FOH)*	$18	
Fixed selling & administrative*	4	22
Total costs		$ 94
Normal markup on variable cost (50%)		36
List selling price		$130

Estimated annual production: 400,000 units
Estimated sales to outside entities: 150,000 units
Estimated intracompany transfers: 250,000 units

*Fixed costs are allocated to all units produced based on estimated annual production.

EXHIBIT 10–6
▼▼▼▼▼▼▼▼▼▼▼

HUGO AUTO
COMPANY RADIO
MANUFACTURING
DIVISION

Cost-based Transfer Prices

As mentioned earlier in the chapter, the term *cost* can be defined in a variety of ways. The definition used must be agreed upon by the managers engaging in the intracompany transfer. The absorption cost for the radios is $88 ($40 DM + $12 DL + $18 VOH + $18 FOH). A transfer price equal to absorption cost provides a contribution toward covering the selling division's fixed production overhead. Such a transfer price does not produce the same amount of income that would be generated if the transferring division sold the goods externally, but it does provide for coverage of all production costs.

Cost can also be defined as variable cost. Using the data in Exhibit 10–6, a transfer price for radios based on variable cost is either $70 or $72. The difference depends on whether variable cost is defined as variable production cost or total variable cost. Using either of these costs as the transfer price, however, will not provide Mr. Lew much incentive to transfer the radios internally. Fixed costs of the Radio Division are not being reduced by selling internally and no contribution margin is being generated by the transfers to help cover these fixed expenses.

Market-based Transfer Prices

To eliminate the problems of defining "cost," some companies simply use a market price approach to setting transfer prices. Market price is believed to be an objective measure of value and simulates the selling price that would exist if the segments were independent companies. If a selling division is operating efficiently relative to its competition, it should ordinarily be able to show a profit when transferring products or services at market prices. An efficiently operating buying division should not be troubled by a market-based transfer price because that is what would have to be paid for the goods or services if the alternative of buying internally did not exist.

Still, several problems may exist with using market prices for intracompany transfers. The first problem is that transfers may involve products that have no exact counterpart in the external market. Second, market price may not be entirely appropriate because of internal cost savings arising from reductions in bad debts and in packaging, advertising, or delivery expenditures. Third, difficulties can arise in setting a transfer price when the market is depressed because of a temporary reduction in demand for the product. Should the current depressed price be used as the transfer price, or should the expected long-run market price be used? Lastly, a question exists as to what is the "right" market price to use. Different prices are quoted and different discounts and credit terms are allowed to different buyers. Therefore, it may not be possible to determine which market price is the most appropriate transfer price to charge.

Negotiated Transfer Prices

negotiated transfer prices

Because of the problems associated with both cost- and market-based prices, **negotiated transfer prices** are often set through a process of bargaining between the selling and purchasing unit managers. Such prices are normally below the external sales price of the selling unit, but above that unit's incremental costs plus opportunity cost. The negotiated price would also be below the market purchase price of the buying unit. A negotiated price meeting these specifications falls within the range limits of the transfer pricing model.

A negotiated transfer price for the Radio Division of Hugo Auto Company would be less than the $130 list selling price or the Automobile Division's buying price, if lower. The price would also be set greater than the $72 incremental variable costs. If some of the variable selling costs could be eliminated, the incremental cost would even be less. If the Radio Division could not sell any additional radios externally nor downsize its facilities, there would be no opportunity cost involved. Otherwise, an opportunity cost would need to be determined, which could increase total costs to as much as the $130 list selling price (if all units could be sold externally).

Ability to negotiate a transfer price implies that division managers have the autonomy to sell or buy products externally if internal negotiations fail. To encourage cooperation between the transferring divisions, top management may consider allowing each party to set a different transfer price.

Dual Pricing

Since a transfer price is used to satisfy internal managerial objectives, **dual pricing arrangements** can be used that allow a different transfer price for the selling and the buying segments. Such an arrangement would allow a selling division to record the transfer of goods or services at a market or negotiated market price and a buying division to record the transfer at a cost-based amount. Use of dual prices would provide a profit margin on the goods transferred and, thus, reflect a "profit" for the selling division. The arrangement would also provide a minimal cost to the buying division. Dual pricing eliminates the problem of having to artificially divide the profits between the selling and buying segments. Dual transfer pricing policies allow managers to have the most relevant information for decision making and performance evaluation.

dual pricing arrangements

The final determination of which transfer pricing system to use should reflect the circumstances of the organizational units and corporate goals. No one method of setting a transfer price is best in all instances. Also, transfer prices are not permanent; they are frequently revised in relation to changes in costs, supply, demand, competitive forces, and other factors. Such cost adjustments will allow a department "to stimulate consumption during its slack times and ration consumption during peak demand times, thus encouraging efficient use of resources." [13]

Regardless of what method is used, a thoughtfully set transfer price will provide the following advantages:

- An appropriate basis for the calculation and evaluation of segment performance
- The rational acquisition or use of goods and services between corporate divisions
- The flexibility to respond to changes in demand or market conditions
- A means of motivating managers in decentralized operations

Setting a reasonable transfer price and measuring divisional performance are not easy tasks. Everyone involved in the process must be aware of the positive and negative aspects of each type of transfer price and be responsive to suggestions of change if the need is indicated.

---

[13]Leon B. Hoshower and Robert P. Crum, "Controlling Service Center Costs," *Management Accounting* (November 1987), p. 45.

EXHIBIT 10–7
▼▼▼▼▼▼▼▼▼▼

MULTINATIONAL
COMPANY
TRANSFER PRICING
OBJECTIVES

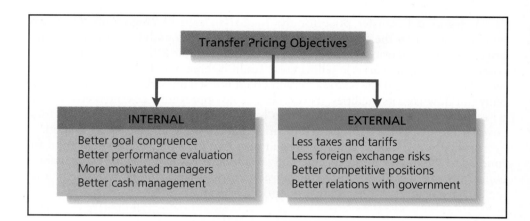

Multinational Settings

Because of the differences in tax systems, customs duties, freight and insurance costs, import/export regulations, and foreign exchange controls, setting transfer prices for products and services becomes extremely difficult when the company is engaged in multinational operations. In addition, as shown in Exhibit 10–7, the internal and external objectives of transfer pricing policies in multinational enterprises (MNEs) differ.

Because of these differences, there is no simple answer to setting transfer prices in these entities. Multinational companies may use one transfer price when a product is sent to or received from one country and a different transfer price for the same product when it is sent to or received from another country. However, some guidelines as to transfer pricing policies should be set by the company and followed on a consistent basis. For example, a company should not price certain parent services to host country subsidiaries in a manner that would send the majority of those costs to the subsidiary in the country with the highest tax rate unless that method of pricing were reasonable and equitable to all subsidiaries.

Multinational companies must be able to determine the effectiveness of their transfer pricing policies. To do so,

> two criteria can be used: (a) does the system achieve economic decisions that positively affect MNE performance, including international capital investment decisions, output level decisions for both intermediate and final products, and product pricing decisions for external customers? and (b) do subsidiary managers feel that they are being fairly evaluated and rewarded for their divisional contributions to the MNE as a whole?[14]

If the answers to both of these questions are yes, then the company appears to have a transfer pricing system that appropriately coordinates the underlying considerations, minimizes the internal and external goal conflicts, and balances short- and long-range perspectives of the multinational company.

---

[14]Wagdy M. Abdallah, "Guidelines for CEOs in Transfer Pricing Policies," *Management Accounting* (September 1988), p. 61.

PRICING ETHICS

While the law establishes some pricing rules, there are also some ethical questions involved—both positive and negative—especially in the area of discriminatory pricing. Should discriminatory pricing be acceptable in either the goods or services markets? This issue is not one that is accounting oriented, but it is definitely business oriented. Corporate management or managing partners in professional firms must address this issue, arrive at a policy on it, and be able to justify whatever stance is taken—from both a legal and an ethical point of view. The above News Note reflects some concerns for the ethical implications of pricing.

SITE ANALYSIS

Kraft General Foods (KGF) recognized its pricing mistakes for cheese products after a significant downturn in sales. KGF also experienced declining sales in its Oscar Mayer processed-meat business as consumers began making healthier food choices. When pork prices dropped in 1991, the company reduced selling prices for products made from pork. The company now intends to keep prices flat and use advertising to spur market growth. Marketing expenses were increased 23 percent in 1990 and 16 percent in 1991; no additional increases were projected for 1992.[15] In addition, cost-cutting techniques such as consolidated purchasing and limiting the number of suppliers used are being introduced.

continued

---

[15]Patricia Sellers, "Can He Keep Philip Morris Growing?" *FORTUNE* (April 6, 1992), p. 91.

It is clear that over the long run, revenues must exceed expenses by a sufficient amount that a satisfactory profit is earned. Thus, managers need to know what their costs are so products can be priced above these costs. Managers must be able to control costs and keep them in line with those of competitors, so the competitors will not have a pricing advantage resulting from lower costs. Managers must also estimate what consumers will pay and competitors will charge.

Why do firms not price correctly? There are a variety of reasons including the following two: "The data needed to make smart pricing decisions either don't exist in many companies or are not readily accessible [and] managers give in to emotionalism—especially to the fear of losing sales volume."[16] Managers need to think about pricing in relation to three things: industry supply and demand, product market strategy, and individual transactions. Systematic observation and analysis are important to managers to help them be alert to and aware of changes in their internal and external environment. Understanding what a customer wants and how a company's product meshes with those wants is essential. Lastly, managers must investigate reasons behind downward trends in prices, including decreases resulting from discounts and favorable credit terms.

In some way, pricing affects everyone in an organization. Therefore, it is imperative that, regardless of functional discipline, all managers must understand the importance of proper pricing, as is noted in the Applications Strategies section on page 435.

CHAPTER SUMMARY

Finding the right price is an art, not a science. Pricing first depends upon company objectives and strategies, which should follow from the entity's goals. Specific pricing objectives include achieving a target return on investment, achieving a target share of the market, stabilizing prices, and meeting the competition's prices. Additionally, factors such as the product life cycle stage and cost and the operating environment in which the company exists need to be considered. The company's operating environment includes the influences of customers, competitors, and the government.

Managers ordinarily try to set prices to cover product and period costs and provide a satisfactory contribution to profits. Depending on the circumstances, different versions of cost may be used ranging from variable cost to full product cost plus a share of period expenses.

The degree to which a firm can control the price of a product to external parties is determined by the nature of the market and the firm's competition. There are four basic market structures: pure competition, monopolistic competition, monopoly, and oligopoly. New global markets are providing sales opportunities, but these markets are also creating pricing pressures for domestic firms. Government regulations have been implemented to prevent activities such as price discrimination and price fixing, while import duties have been imposed to prevent dumping of products by foreign competitors.

Customers may buy goods because of product features, product quality, and/or company service, reliability, and ethical reputation. Most customers must also, however, consider price in making a purchase because they are trying to make efficient

---

[16]Michael Marn, "When the Price Is Not Right," *Wall Street Journal* (February 12, 1990), p. A10.

Discipline	Applications
Accounting	Accurate costs are imperative for appropriate product pricing; prices must be supportable by accounting in cost-plus contracts and fair trade pricing.
Economics	Pricing is basic to making competition and the economic factors of supply and demand work properly; pricing strategies will affect how quickly equilibrium points are reached; setting prices at their optimal level will maximize firm profits; pricing strategies affect the extent to which the firm is able to attain its goals and must be based on both demand and cost conditions; relevant costs will differ from one pricing decision to another.
Finance	Proper pricing affects sales and profitability which, in turn, affect the ability to obtain financing; understanding which customers are being charged which prices and the resulting profits being generated from those sales can help direct attention to the most profitable customer mix.
Management	Awareness of legal restrictions on pricing is essential to operations; may use transfer pricing to evaluate performance; pricing objectives and strategies should follow from overall entity goals.
Marketing	The various cost definitions must be understood to properly bid orders; knowledge of product life cycles can help in effectively pricing products; monitoring and analyzing product differences, supply and demand factors, and customer profiles are critical to proper pricing; prices have a direct impact on sales volume and commissions; marketing generally sets the pricing strategy within the company's pricing objectives; pricing decisions must combine knowledge of costs, product life cycle, target markets, idea of fair price, demand function, and psychological factors.

APPLICATIONS STRATEGIES FOR PRICING

use of their scarce resources. If they believe a price is too high, they will seek a lower-priced similar product or substitute.

Transfer prices are intracompany charges for goods or services exchanged between segments of a company. Product transfer prices are typically cost-based, market-based, or negotiated. A dual pricing system that assigns different transfer prices to the buying and selling units may also be used. Management should promote a transfer pricing system that is in the best interest of the whole company, motivates managers to strive for segment effectiveness and efficiency, and is practical.

Setting transfer prices in multinational enterprises is a complex process because of the differences that exist in tax structures, import/export regulations, customs duties, and other factors associated with international subsidiaries and divisions. A valid transfer price for a multinational firm is one that achieves economic benefit for the entire company and generates support from the domestic and international managers utilizing the system.

APPENDIX

Transfer Prices for Service Departments

The idea of setting transfer prices for products moving between one organizational unit and another is a well-established practice. Instituting transfer prices for services is a less common but effective technique for some types of service departments. Common applications of transfer prices for services are in governmental (such as for the motor pool and computer operations services) and in not-for-profit organizations.

Setting Transfer Prices

If management is considering setting a transfer price for a service department, the questions in Exhibit 10–8 should first be answered. Depending on the answers to the questions, the exhibit also presents some suggestions as to how the transfer price should be set. Questions should be answered simultaneously and the suggestions combined to form a reasonable transfer price.

Application of the suggestions in Exhibit 10–8 is demonstrated in the following example related to the Management Information System (MIS) Department of Fisher

EXHIBIT 10–8
▼▼▼▼▼▼▼▼▼▼▼

SETTING A
TRANSFER PRICE
FOR SERVICES

	If Response Is:	
Questions	**Yes**	**No**
Is the service department to be considered a "money maker"?	Set using market-based, negotiated, or dual pricing	Set using cost-based prices
Does a user department have significant control over the quantity and quality of service used?	Use a base that reflects total quantity of activity of service department	Transfer prices are not particularly useful
Do opportunities exist to use external services rather than internal services?	Use a base that reflects the typical manner in which external purchases are made	Set by negotiation or upper level management; use a base that reflects the quantity of activity of service department
Is there a reasonable alternative (or surrogate) measure of service benefits provided to users?	Use a base representing total volume of alternative measure produced by service department	Transfer prices are not particularly useful
Are the services provided of a recurring nature?	Use a fixed price for each service use	Use a price that reflects degree of use; constrained by whether the user can bear the cost
Are all services provided of a similar nature?	Use a fixed price based on a single factor of use	Use a price that reflects degree of use; constrained by whether the user can bear the cost
Are the services performed typically expensive?	Use market-based or negotiated prices; base may be more complex than typical; constrained by whether the user can bear the cost	Use cost-based or negotiated price; base should be easy to understand and simple to compute

& Millet, Attorneys at Law.[17] The firm's managing partners have decided that the MIS Department will be evaluated as a "money-making" operation. Therefore, a cost-based transfer price is not appropriate, because no departmental "profits" would be generated from such a price. The user departments in the law firm are allowed to obtain data processing services externally, and all departments have control over the quantity of MIS services used. A transfer price should be set by negotiation and be based on the quantity of services typically performed by the MIS Department. In most instances, an alternative or surrogate measure of benefit provided by the department is machine time used.

Whether services are recurring or not depends upon the nature of the user department. For example, a typical MIS application for the law firm's Accounting Department is a biweekly payroll. A fixed charge could be established for this service at the beginning of the year and reviewed for appropriateness at specified intervals. Once a year, however, accounting has the MIS Department process W-2 forms for all employees. The transfer price for this activity should be based on the charge established per minute of machine time.

The MIS Department also does case searches for all lawyers in the firm. These searches are all similar in nature, although each takes a different amount of time depending upon the type of case involved. A fixed charge per minute of machine time used could be charged to the individual attorney for use in billing the individual clients involved.

The MIS Department is sometimes asked to write a specific program application for use by a single user. For example, a tax attorney in the firm has just been engaged by Mr. Trump, a client who has extensive real estate holdings. The attorney asks the MIS Department to develop a program applicable to Mr. Trump's tax situation. If the client is billed for the actual cost of development, he is likely to take his tax (and other potential legal) business elsewhere. A transfer price needs to be developed that is reasonable, yet does not discourage the acquisition of new types of client business.

In setting a transfer price for services, a department must decide on a capacity level to use in price development. This decision is equivalent to that made in setting a predetermined overhead rate. For example, a service department may use expected capacity or practical capacity.

If expected capacity is chosen, the transfer price per unit of service will be higher than if practical capacity is chosen. If the service department uses expected capacity and performs more services than expected, a favorable volume variance will arise.[18] Users, however, will not necessarily benefit from reduced charges because the transfer price is not normally changed. Use of practical capacity would, on the other hand, create a lower price and, hopefully, encourage more internal services use, and may generate ideas as to how to use the additional capacity to fill outside needs. In addition, if practical capacity is not used, an unfavorable volume variance is noted, and the opportunity cost of underutilization is clearly identifiable.

In developing transfer prices for services, it is essential that general costs be allocated to the various departments equitably and that the underlying reason for cost incurrence be determined. As indicated in the following News Note, Bellcore decided

---

[17]This illustration is based, in part, on suggestions provided in "Allocation of Information Systems Costs," *Statements on Management Accounting Number 4F* (Montvale, N.J.: Institute of Management Accountants [formerly National Association of Accountants], December 15, 1986), pp. 3–5.
[18]Volume variances are covered in chapter 5 on standard costing.

NEWS NOTE

Transfer Pricing Systems Need to Look for Cost Drivers

When we designed our charge-back system in 1983, it was state-of-the-art. But within a few years, the system's imperfections began to manifest themselves. For one thing, we had researchers and engineers spending an increasing amount of their time typing documents and making overhead slides because they couldn't abide the high prices the word processing, graphics, technical publications, and secretarial departments were charging. Those in-house departments tried to contain their costs but, in spite of the large work volume, couldn't seem to perform as efficiently as small, independent service companies could. Even as they reduced their work force, costs kept spiraling up.

We eventually discovered that the main problem for certain services lay with our transfer pricing system—specifically, with the way it allocated overhead and rent. Word processing, graphics, technical publications, and secretarial services were paying more than their share. We had to find a fairer way to distribute overhead and rent charges, which meant tracking what was actually driving them.

SOURCE: An excerpt from "Getting Transfer Prices Right: What Bellcore Did," by Edward J. Kovac and Henry P. Troy (September–October 1989), p. 148. Reprinted by permission of *Harvard Business Review.* Copyright © 1989 by the President and Fellows of Harvard College; all rights reserved.

Simply establishing a transfer pricing system does not guarantee its success. At Bellcore, the system charges needed to be revised to reflect the true cost drivers of the various departments.

to focus attention on determining service department cost drivers to improve its transfer pricing system. By addressing the issues of cost drivers, Bellcore changed the system to one that is fairer and only slightly more complex than the original system.

Advantages of Transfer Prices

Transfer prices are useful when service departments provide distinct, measurable benefits to other areas or provide services having a specific cause-and-effect relationship. Transfer prices in these circumstances can provide certain advantages to the organization in both the revenue-producing and service departments. These advantages are listed in Exhibit 10–9 and discussed next.

First, transfer prices can encourage more involvement between the user and service departments. Users are more likely to suggest ways for the service department to improve its performance, since improved performance could result in lower transfer prices. Service departments are more likely to interact with users to find out the specific types of services that are needed and to eliminate or reduce those that are not cost beneficial.

Second, use of a transfer price for services should cause managers to be more cost conscious. Managers of user departments should attempt to eliminate wasteful usage. For example, if the MIS Department charged recipients in other departments for the number of reports received, managers would be less likely to request reports simply to be "on the receiving list," as sometimes occurs. For managers of the service departments, cost consciousness would be directed at monitoring the cost to provide services. If excessive costs are incurred, a reasonable transfer price may not cover costs or a high transfer price may not be justifiable to users.

Weyerhaeuser and Bell Atlantic are strong proponents of the use of transfer prices for service departments. Weyerhaeuser began a transfer price program in 1985, and the program is now effective for all fourteen corporate headquarter departments. All operating managers are allowed to obtain outside bids and are free to use those outside services if they wish. The Information Systems Department found its users complaining about the high cost of computer services; to remain competitive with outside sources, the department "dropped prices, laid off staff and began covering

	User Departments	Provider Departments
User Involvement	Suggestions of ways to improve services to benefit users	Promotes development of services more beneficial to users
Cost Consciousness	Relates to services used; restrict usage to those necessary and cost beneficial	Relates to cost of services provided; must justify transfer price established
Performance Evaluations	If control over amount of services used exists, costs can be included in making performance evaluations	Can provide "revenues" to the service department and give managers more ways to evaluate departmental performance

EXHIBIT 10–9
▼▼▼▼▼▼▼▼▼▼▼
ADVANTAGES OF
TRANSFER PRICES
FOR SERVICES

costs by selling laser printing services on the open market."[19] The CEO at Bell Atlantic believes transfer pricing for services can cut costs by approximately 25 percent in addition to providing "an absolute flood of creativity and responsiveness."[20]

Lastly, transfer prices can result in information useful for evaluating managerial performance. A department report on operations would show a service department cost that was related to the quantity of actual services used rather than showing either no assigned cost for services or arbitrarily assigned amounts. Use of transfer prices can also allow service departments to be treated as "money-making" operations rather than simply cost-generating operations. But, although transfer prices for service departments are effective tools, their disadvantages must be considered before their implementation.

Disadvantages of Transfer Prices

Using transfer prices, whether for products or services, has certain disadvantages. The first is that there can be, and most often is, disagreement among unit managers as to how the transfer price should be set. The second disadvantage is that implementing transfer prices into the accounting system requires additional organizational costs and employee time. Third, transfer prices do not work equally well for all types of service departments. Service departments that do not provide measurable benefits or cannot show a distinct cause-and-effect relationship between cost incurrence and service use by other departments should not use transfer prices. Lastly, depending on how the transfer price is set, a transfer price may cause dysfunctional behavior among the organizational units, and certain services may be under- or overutilized.

A company should weigh the advantages and disadvantages of using transfer prices. If the company decides that a transfer pricing system will enhance effectiveness and efficiency, transfer prices for services can take the same forms as those for products: cost-based, market-based, negotiated, or dual. A Price Waterhouse survey on transfer prices for services indicated that "[m]ost companies (72 percent) reported that transfer prices are negotiated between buyer and seller. This is especially true for services because value is often added by means that cannot be measured effectively—such as expertise, reliability, convenience and responsiveness."[21] The decision as to which type of transfer price to use should depend on the cost and volume level of the service as well as whether there are comparable substitutes available. Setting transfer prices for services require that internal guidelines be developed that are practical and provide meaningful information for both the user and provider.

GLOSSARY

Ad hoc discount   a price concession made under competitive pressure, real or imaginary, that does not relate to quantity

Conscious parallelism   the act of competitors independently engaging in the same or similar courses of action because of simple business judgment

---

[19]Terence P. Pare, "How to Cut the Cost of Headquarters," *FORTUNE* (September 11, 1989), p. 192.
[20]Ibid., p. 196.
[21]Daniel P. Keegan and Patrick D. Howard, "Transfer Pricing for Services: A Price Waterhouse Survey," *Journal of Accountancy* (March 1988), p. 98.

Cost-plus pricing setting a price as a defined cost plus a designated markup (either an agreed-upon amount or percentage)

Differential costs costs that vary in amount among the alternatives being considered

Dual pricing arrangement an arrangement that allows a selling division to record the transfer of goods or services at a market or negotiated market price and a buying division to record the transfer at a cost-based amount

Dumping the selling abroad of products at prices lower than those charged in the producing country or in other national markets

Fair-return pricing price regulation in which a firm is allowed to charge a price that will provide a normal return but nothing more than that (i.e., no economic profit)

Horizontal price fixing a situation in which competitors attempt to regulate prices through an agreement or conspiracy

Incremental cost the additional cost of producing a contemplated quantity of output, which generally means variable costs of production

Labor loading charge an add-on to labor cost per hour to cover labor-related charges plus provide a desired profit rate

Materials loading charge an add-on to materials cost to cover ordering, handling, and carrying costs of the parts inventory plus provide a profit margin

Monopolistic competition a market structure in which there are many firms having slightly differentiated products and services

Monopoly a market structure in which there is only one seller of a product or provider of a service

Negotiated transfer price an intracompany charge for goods or services that has been set through a process of negotiation between the selling and purchasing unit managers

Oligopoly a market structure in which there are only a few firms, whose products/services may be either differentiated or standardized

Opportunity cost a monetary benefit that is given up because one course of action is chosen over another

Out-of-pocket costs current or near-current cash expenditures

Penetration pricing setting a price that is significantly below the current market price for a similar product or service; the lower price is then often raised as the product moves into its growth stage

Predatory dumping dumping that is practiced to force domestic producers out of business so that the foreign competitor becomes the primary source of supply and can then raise prices

Price discrimination charging different prices for the same product to different groups of buyers when those prices are not reflective of cost differences

Price elasticity of demand a relationship that reflects the percentage change in the quantity demanded relative to the percentage change in price

Price fixing a practice in which firms conspire to set the price of a good at a specified level

Price maker a firm that determines the level of output and the corresponding price that will maximize its profits

Price skimming setting an introductory price that is higher than what exists for similar, but potentially lower-quality, products in the market or setting a high introductory price because there are no similar products or services in the market

Price taker a firm that accepts the market price as given by the industry supply and demand

Pure competition a market structure in which there are many firms, each with a small market share, producing identical products

Relevant costs all costs that are logically associated with a specific problem

Robinson-Patman Act the 1936 law that prohibits price discrimination

Special order pricing setting a sales price for manufacturing or service jobs that are outside the company's normal production/service realm

Substitute good a good that can be used in place of another to satisfy the same wants or needs of the consumer

Time and material pricing a common practice in service organizations that allows prices to be set using separate rates for the direct labor time involved and the direct materials used

Transfer price an internal charge established for the exchange of goods or services between organizational units of the same company

Vertical price fixing collusion between producing businesses and their distributors to control the prices at which their products may be sold to consumers

---

SELECTED BIBLIOGRAPHY

Aranoff, Gerald. "Transfer Pricing for Short-Run Profit Maximization in Manufacturing." *Journal of Cost Management for the Manufacturing Industry* (Fall 1990), pp. 37–43.

Coy, Peter. "For PBX Makers, the Future Is Later." *Business Week* (February 25, 1991), pp. 88–89.

Deveny, Kathleen. "After Some Key Sales Strategies Go Sour, Kraft General Foods Gets Back to Basics." *Wall Street Journal* (March 18, 1992), p. B1.

Harrington, Mark. "New York in Forefront of Price-Fixing Battle." *CES [Consumer Electronic Show] Daily* (June 2, 1991), p. 52Aff.

Saporito, Bill. "Why the Price Wars Never End." *FORTUNE* (March 23, 1992), pp. 68–71ff.

Schiller, Zachary, et al. "The Humana Flap Could Make All Hospitals Feel Sick." *Business Week* (November 4, 1991), p. 34.

Shields, Michael D., and S. Mark Young. "Managing Product Life Cycle Costs: An Organizational Model." *Journal of Cost Management for the Manufacturing Industry* (Fall 1991), pp. 39–52.

SOLUTION STRATEGIES

Time and Material Pricing

(a) Hourly billing for time = Hourly wage + (Time rate for support costs* + Desired profit per hour)

*Estimated annual DL support costs ÷ Estimated annual DLHs

(b) Billing for materials = Cost of job materials + (Materials loading charge** ×
Materials cost)

**(Estimated DM annual support costs ÷ Estimated annual DM$) + Desired profit
per $1 of DM cost

(c) Total price to customer = [(a) × DLHs] + (b)

Transfer Prices   (Cost-based, market-based, negotiated, dual)
Upper limit: Lowest price available from external suppliers

Feasible region for
setting a reasonable
transfer price

Lower limit: Incremental costs of producing and selling the transferred goods or services plus the opportunity cost for the facilities used

END-OF-CHAPTER MATERIALS

Questions

1. Why must companies be aware of where their products are in their life cycle?

2. Why are decisions made during the development stage of a product so important?

3. Name the four primary pricing goals. Would these goals ever conflict with one
another? If so, how? If not, why not?

4. Define and contrast *price maker* with *price taker*. Give three examples of each.

5. In a cost-plus contract, why must the definition of cost be strictly delineated in
advance?

6. Present the approach managers have traditionally taken to setting a product's
price.

7. For normal, ongoing sales, what items are prices ordinarily set to cover and why?

8. Some people refer to absorption costing as full costing. Is there a cost that is more
"full" than absorption costing? If so, discuss.

9. Why is variable costing considered an acceptable method of defining product cost
even though it considers fixed production overhead a period cost?

10. Explain what is meant by time and materials pricing.

11. Discuss the approach normally taken for special order pricing.

12. How are special prices set and when are they used?

13. In a special order decision, the minimum selling price a company should charge
is the sum of all the incremental costs of production and sale in order not to lose
money on the order. Is this a true statement? Discuss the rationale for your
answer.

14. In considering a special order that will enable a company to make use of currently
idle capacity, which costs are likely to be relevant? Irrelevant?

15. Compare the two common pricing strategies often used in the introduction stages of products' life cycles. Give three illustrations of the use of these strategies.

16. What is meant by discriminatory pricing? Is it legal? Is there discriminatory pricing in the marketplace? If so, provide some examples.

17. For a given company, who sets or influences the price of its products and how?

18. What factors determine the degree to which a firm can control the price of its products?

19. What are the four basic market structures? Describe how a firm in each of the respective markets would normally decide on the price for a standard product in an ongoing sales situation.

20. How does horizontal price fixing differ from vertical price fixing?

21. Airlines tend to play "follow the leader" when one drops its prices for particular periods of time or to particular market segments. Discuss the rationale for this behavior.

22. What motivates some companies to engage in dumping?

23. Why are transfer prices not appropriate for external financial statements?

24. What are the maximum and minimum limits for a transfer cost? Why should the transfer cost fall between these limits?

25. Name three alternative bases for transfer prices. As the manager of a selling division, which would you prefer and why? As the manager of a buying division, which would you prefer and why?

26. (Appendix) What bases are normally used to set transfer prices for services? Who should have input into the transfer price set and why?

■ **Exercises**

27. *(Terminology)* Match the numbered items on the right to the lettered terms on the left.

a.	Relevant cost	1.	An attempt to limit buyers' access to prices at or above a given level
b.	Transfer price	2.	A firm that can set the level of output and price to maximize its profits
c.	Dumping	3.	An internal price set by managers for the transfer of goods or services
d.	Differential cost	4.	Cost logically associated with a problem or decision
e.	Vertical price fixing	5.	A firm that accepts, as given, the market price resulting from industry supply and demand
f.	Robinson-Patman Act	6.	Setting an initial price for a new product which is high with the expectation of lowering it later
g.	Price fixing	7.	A cost that varies among alternatives being considered
h.	Price skimming	8.	Generally makes price discrimination illegal unless justified by differences in cost or to meet already existing competition in a locality
i.	Price maker	9.	Engaging in agreements to control retail selling prices
j.	Price taker	10.	Selling abroad at prices lower than those charged in the producing country

28. *(Terminology)* Match the numbered items on the right to the lettered terms on the left.

a. Absorption costing	1.	Current or near-current cash expenditure
b. Out-of-pocket cost	2.	Product cost only includes variable costs
c. Cost-plus contract	3.	Market includes only a few firms
d. Dual pricing arrangement	4.	Product cost includes all production costs including fixed factory overhead
e. Relevant cost	5.	An often used method of pricing for government contracts
f. Monopolistic competition	6.	Setting an initial low price in the early stages of a product life cycle which is often raised later
g. Oligopoly	7.	A market structure having many small firms, each having only a small market share and producing identical products
h. Penetration pricing	8.	A market structure with many firms having slightly differentiated products
i. Pure competition	9.	A cost logically related to a decision
j. Variable costing	10.	Using different transfer prices for the buying and selling divisions of a company

29. *(Terminology)* Match the numbered items on the right to the lettered terms on the left.

a. Monopoly	1.	A product that may be used in place of another to satisfy the same wants or needs
b. Predatory dumping	2.	An add-on cost used to cover ordering, handling, and carrying materials and to provide a profit margin
c. Price discrimination	3.	Concessions made under competitive pressure that relate to factors other than volume
d. Price elasticity of demand	4.	A market with only one seller
e. Substitute good	5.	Setting low prices for goods sold in another country in order to become the primary source of supply and subsequently raise prices
f. Ad hoc discount	6.	The benefit foregone by choosing one alternative over another
g. Charge-back system	7.	Independently following similar courses of business action
h. Conscious parallelism	8.	Measures the purchase responsiveness of buyers to price changes
i. Material loading charge	9.	Transfer pricing
j. Opportunity cost	10.	Charging different prices for the same product when those prices do not reflect cost differences

30. *(Different types of costs)* Mark Hennen Enterprises has the following costs associated with its 30-second egg poacher:

Product costs (per unit)

Direct materials	$11.00
Direct labor	2.00

Variable production overhead	1.00
Allocated fixed production overhead	.60

Period Expenses

Variable expenses per unit	.40
Fixed expenses per unit ($282,000 total divided by expected production and sales of 940,000 units)	.30
Opportunity cost ($235,000 averaged over production and sales of 940,000 units)	.25

Determine the following, on a per-unit basis:

a. variable product cost
b. full product cost
c. total variable cost per unit
d. total full recorded cost per unit
e. total full recorded and unrecorded cost per unit

31. *(Pricing based on costs)* Given the data in Exercise 30 and your solutions to that exercise, provide responses to the following:

a. Assume that Mr. Hennen, company president, has previously stated that he wants a 25 percent markup on cost. Determine a selling price for each of the levels of cost determined in Exercise 30.
b. Which price calculated above in part (a) would you normally choose for the long-run price for ongoing sales, assuming that such price is competitive and acceptable to consumers?
c. Assume that Mark Hennen Enterprises is already profitable and has an opportunity to bid on a sale outside of its normal, ongoing business. Competition is very tight, and Mr. Hennen wants to know the lowest price he can justify, assuming that ongoing business is covering all fixed costs and opportunity costs.

32. *(Special order)* Hurry-Hurry-Hurry produces a plastic circus set that includes a tent, circus figures, and animals. The set is sold to exclusive children's toy stores for $200. Plant capacity is 20,000 sets per year. Production costs are as follows:

Direct materials cost per set	$20
Direct labor cost per set	30
Variable overhead per set	40
Variable selling cost per set	10
Fixed overhead per year	$1,100,000

A prominent British store, which has not previously purchased from Hurry-Hurry-Hurry, has approached the marketing manager about buying 5,000 sets for $170 each. No selling expenses would be incurred on this offer, but the British store wants its name in gold on a green package. This request means that Hurry-Hurry-Hurry will incur an additional $2 cost per unit. The company is currently selling 18,000 circus sets, so acceptance of this job would require the company to reject some of its current business.

a. What is the current operating income of Hurry-Hurry-Hurry?
b. If the company accepted this offer, what would be its operating income? Should the company accept the offer?
c. If Hurry-Hurry-Hurry were currently selling only 10,000 sets per year and wanted to earn $150,000 of income for the year, what selling price would the company have to quote the British store?

33. *(Special order)* The manufacturing capacity of Houle Company's plant is 60,000 units of product per year. A summary of operations for the year ended December 31, 1993, is as follows:

Sales (36,000 units @ $75)		$2,700,000
Variable manufacturing costs	$1,440,000	
Variable selling costs	180,000	1,620,000
Contribution margin		$1,080,000
Fixed costs		990,000
Operating income		$ 90,000

A Canadian distributor has offered to buy 20,000 units at $60 per unit during 1994. Assume all costs (including variable selling expenses) will be at the 1993 level during 1994. If Houle accepts this offer and also sells as many units to regular customers as it did in 1993, what would be the total operating income for 1994? Normal variable selling costs will be incurred on this and all transactions as a result of a sales contract.

34. *(Transfer price)* Alexandra Manufacturing's Athens Lens Division sells a tiny lens called the Iota to its Sparta Camera Division. The Iota has the following per-unit characteristics:

Direct labor	$ 2.50
Direct materials	.25
Variable factory overhead	1.75
Fixed factory overhead	2.40
Opportunity cost	.30
Sparta's external market purchase price	12.80

a. Determine the limits of the transfer price.
b. Set the transfer price by dividing the "profit" equally between the Athens and Sparta divisions.

35. *(Transfer price)* Use the data contained in Exhibit 10–6 (page 429) to answer the following questions.

a. Assume that the Radio Division uses an $88 absorption cost as its transfer price to the Automobile Division. What will the division's income (loss) be if external and internal sales and all costs are as shown in the exhibit?
b. Assume that the Radio Division uses an $88 absorption cost as its transfer price to the Automobile Division. Suppose that the Automobile Division can purchase radios externally from Real Sound, Inc., for $85 and the externally purchased radios are of the same quality and specifications as those produced internally. External sales by the Radio Division are at 150,000 units. Is the Automobile Division better off acquiring the radios internally or externally? Is the company better off if the Automobile Division acquires the radios internally or externally? By how much?
c. Use the same facts as in part (b), but assume that the Radio Division can sell all its production externally. Is the company better off if the Automobile Division acquires the radios internally or externally? By how much?
d. Assume that the Radio Division uses a $72 variable cost as its transfer price to the Automobile Division. What will the division's income (loss) be if external and internal sales and all costs are as shown in the exhibit? What would the division's income (loss) have been if all units were sold externally?

36. *(Transfer price)* Gibbs Division of Deloitte Corporation is trying to determine what transfer price to charge for each component transferred to the Tate Division

of the company. The following per-unit production cost information has been gathered:

Direct materials	$ 3.20
Direct labor	7.50
Variable overhead	5.20
Fixed overhead	2.80
Total	$18.70

Fixed overhead results entirely from facility depreciation for which Gibbs Division has no alternative use. The Tate Division managers have recently received external offers to provide the division with components; these offers range from $30 to $46. Determine the upper and lower limits for the transfer price Gibbs should ask from the Tate Division.

37. *(Transfer price)* Gahagan Enterprises manufactures steel blades for sale to other company divisions as well as to outside entities. As part of the Andersen Corporation, Gahagan Enterprises is expected to generate a profit as would a separate company. The selling price for a set of blades is $6; costs for each set are as follows:

Direct material	$1.00
Direct labor	.70
Variable overhead	.40
Fixed overhead (based on production of 350,000 sets)	1.40
Variable selling expense	.25

Tucei Division wants to purchase 12,500 sets of blades from Gahagan during the next year. No selling costs are incurred between divisions.

a. If Gahagan's manager can sell all the sets of blades produced by the division externally, what should the transfer price be? Why?

b. Gahagan Enterprises is experiencing a slight decrease in external demand and will only be able to sell 300,000 sets of blades to nonrelated entities next year at the $6 selling price. What selling price should Gahagan set for the blades going to Tucei Division so that Gahagan's net income will be the same as if all production were sold externally for the regular price?

c. Ms. Carlyle, the manager of Tucei Division, offers to pay Gahagan Enterprises the production cost plus 25 percent for each set of blades. She receives an invoice for $54,687.50, and she was planning on a cost of $32,812.50. How were each of these amounts determined and why?

38. *(Transfer price)* The Stamping and Assembly divisions are part of the Ernst Company. The Stamping division manufactures Part 135, which can be sold externally and is also used in making metal desks by the Assembly division. The following information is available about Part 135:

Total production annually—500,000 units; internal requirements are
   300,000 units; all others are sold externally
List selling price—$23.80
Variable production costs—$10
Fixed overhead—$1,000,000; allocated on the basis of units of production
Variable selling costs—$4; includes $1 per unit in advertising cost
Fixed selling costs—$500,000

Determine the transfer price under each of the following methods:

a. Total variable cost
b. Full production cost
c. Total variable production cost plus necessary selling costs
d. Market price

39. *(Transfer price)* Brechtel Division produces large metal clamps. All production of Brechtel Division is sold to another division of the Marwick Corporation at the market price of $20. Annual production and sales are 20,000 clamps. Production costs for the clamps are as follows:

Variable production costs	$11
General fixed overhead ($6 per hour; one-half hour for production time)	3
Direct fixed overhead ($40,000 ÷ 20,000)	2
Unit cost	$16
Variable shipping expenses	1
Total unit cost	$17

General fixed overhead is composed of executive salaries and allocated production costs relating to the building. Discontinuing production of the clamps would save Brechtel Division $5,000 in annual direct fixed overhead.

a. Determine the incremental cost of producing one clamp.
b. Assume Brechtel Division is operating at full capacity. What is the appropriate unit cost to be used to set a minimum transfer price for selling clamps to the other division of the Marwick Corporation?

Problems

40. *(Special order)* Steve Watts Manufacturing produces and sells auxiliary electric generators for businesses. Business has been good, and the firm has been consistently profitable. Unit costs are as follows:

Product costs	
Direct materials	$72
Direct labor	88
Variable overhead	26
Fixed overhead	15
Period expenses	
Variable	18
Fixed	16

The company has no alternative use for the facilities used to make the generators. The price to the firm's regular customers is $300.

The U.S. Army Procurement Office has asked Mr. Watts to bid on providing 1,000 modified generators for front-line command posts. The modification would involve adding an additional "hush" muffler so that the units could not be heard by enemy troops more than fifty yards away. This muffler would cost the company $25. In addition, fixed production costs would increase by $10,000 in total during the production run that would make the additional 1,000 generators. The ad hoc commission on the sale would be $1,000 total, and the normal variable period expense would drop to $8 because the normal sales commission of $10 per unit would be replaced by the flat $1,000 ad hoc commission.

Required: Determine the minimum bid price that could be submitted to yield a satisfactory profit of $40 per unit.

41. *(Special order)* Cathy Newmann makes and sells the "Huggable Brown," her famous stuffed puppy for young children. They are sold to department stores for $50. The capacity of the plant is 20,000 Huggables per year. Costs to make and sell each stuffed animal are as follows:

Direct materials	$ 5.50
Direct labor	7.00
Variable overhead	10.00
Fixed overhead	12.00
Variable selling expenses	3.00

An Australian import/export company has approached Cathy about buying 2,000 Huggables. Cathy is currently making and selling 20,000 Huggables per year. The Australian firm wants its own label attached to each stuffed animal, which will raise costs by $.50 each. No selling expenses would be incurred on this offer. Cathy feels she must make an extra $1 on each stuffed animal to accept the offer.

Required:

a. What is the opportunity cost per unit of selling to the Australian firm?
b. What is the minimum selling price Cathy should set?
c. Predict how much more operating profit Cathy will have if she accepts this offer at the price specified in (b).
d. Prove your answer to (c) by providing operating profits without and with the new offer.

42. *(Special order)* Filbert Wilmore makes wax figurines for various holidays to be sold in gift shops. His selling price is $1.25 each. His costs are as follows:

Variable production cost per unit	$.45
Fixed production cost per unit	.15

Wilmore pays his salespeople a 10 percent commission on all sales. Other period expenses are all fixed in total at $20,000 per year. A large department store has asked Wilmore to bid on providing 1,000 figurines during the Christmas season. He has sufficient unused capacity to fill the order. Wilmore's company has already done sufficient business to be profitable for the year prior to the bid request.

Required:

a. What is the lowest bid price that would not lose money?
b. What price should Wilmore bid to make a 10 percent profit on the order?
c. What price should he bid if he expects the additional 1,000 figurines to also increase fixed expenses by $200 and he wants 5 percent profit on the order?

43. *(Special pricing)* Powell-Storey Ltd. builds custom motor homes, which range in price from $100,000 to $400,000. For the past twenty-five years, the company's owner, Jessica Storey, has determined the selling price of each vehicle by estimating the costs of materials, labor, and prorated overhead, and adding 25 percent to these estimated costs.

For example, a recent price quotation was determined as follows:

Direct materials	$ 50,000
Direct labor	80,000
Overhead	20,000
Cost	$150,000
Plus 25%	37,500
Selling price	$187,500

Overhead is allocated to all orders at 25 percent of direct labor. The company has traditionally operated at 80 percent of full capacity. Occasionally, a customer would reject a price quote and, if the company were in a slack period, Ms. Storey would often be willing to reduce the markup to as little as 10 percent over estimated costs. The average markup for the year is estimated to be 20 percent.

Ms. Storey has recently completed a course on pricing with an emphasis on the contribution margin approach to pricing. She thinks that such an approach would be helpful in determining the selling prices of her custom vehicles.

Total overhead, which includes selling and administrative costs for the year, is estimated to be $1,500,000. Of this amount, $900,000 is fixed and the remainder is variable in direct proportion to direct labor.

Required:

a. Assume the customer in the example rejected the $187,500 bid and also rejected a $165,000 bid. The customer countered with a $150,000 offer.
1. What is the difference in net income for the year (assuming no replacement offer) between accepting and rejecting the customer's offer?
2. What is the minimum selling price Ms. Storey could have quoted the customer without reducing or increasing net income for the year?
b. What advantage does the contribution margin approach to pricing have over the approach Ms. Storey is currently using?
c. What pitfalls are there, if any, to contribution pricing?

(CMA adapted)

44. *(Transfer price)* Robin Division produces a computer chip that is sold to Hood Division at a price of $19. Robin does not sell any chips externally. Annual production and sales are 40,000 chips. Robin's costs of production and shipping per chip are as follows:

Variable production costs	$11
Fixed production overhead ($200,000 ÷ 40,000)	5
Variable shipping expense	1

Of the $200,000 fixed overhead, $40,000 has been allocated to the production of chips but would be incurred regardless of whether Robin made chips. The rest of the fixed overhead is directly associated with making the chips. Hood could buy the chips externally for $22. Robin has no other use for the facilities.

Required:

a. What is the incremental cost of producing one chip?
b. Explain how the $19 transfer price was derived.

45. *(Transfer price)* Pecuniary Segment makes and sells engine gaskets to other internal segments as well as to external customers. Corporate management expects

Pecuniary to make a profit. The external sales price is $18 per gasket. Pecuniary's costs per gasket follow:

Direct materials	$3.00
Direct labor	2.10
Variable overhead	1.20
Fixed overhead (based on production of 700,000 gaskets)	4.10
Variable selling expense	.75

Largesse Division wants to buy 25,000 gaskets from Pecuniary. There are no selling expenses incurred on internal sales. Largesse can buy at an external price of $18 per gasket.

Required:

a. If Pecuniary can sell all the gaskets externally, what should the transfer price be? Why?
b. If Pecuniary expects a 25,000 unit downturn in external sales and agrees to split the "profit" with Largesse on the internal sales, what will the transfer price be?
c. If corporate management permits use of dual pricing under the conditions described in (b) and Largesse uses the lowest price while Pecuniary uses the highest price, what are those prices?

46. *(Transfer prices)* Porter Division sells a component to Kazmier Division, another division of Lybrand Company. Kazmier uses the component in making one of Lybrand Company's finished products. Kazmier obtained three prices from external suppliers for the component: $89, $72, and $78. Examination of Porter Division's records for component production reveals the following costs: direct materials, $18; direct labor, $12; variable overhead, $3; and fixed overhead, $5. Porter Division has no other opportunities available for the facilities used to make the component. Of the fixed overhead unit cost, $2 would be avoided if Porter did not make the component.

Required:

a. What is the savings (or profit) to Lybrand Company if Kazmier Division buys the component internally?
b. What would the transfer price be if the two divisions agreed to split the total company savings evenly between the two divisions?
c. If dual transfer pricing were used, set the maximum realistic price for Porter Division and the minimum realistic price for Kazmier Division.

47. *(Transfer prices)* In the two cases presented next, the Attaya Division can sell all of its production to outside customers or can sell some units to the Payne Division and the remainder to outside customers. Attaya Division's capacity for production is 200,000 units annually. The data related to each independent case are as follows:

	Case #1	Case #2
Attaya Division		
Production costs per unit		
Direct materials	$30	$20
Direct labor	10	8
Variable overhead	3	2
Fixed overhead (based on capacity)	1	1
Other variable selling & delivery costs per unit*	6	4
Selling price to outside customers	75	60

Payne Division

Number of units needed annually	40,000	40,000
Current unit price being paid to outside supplier	$65	$52

*In either case, $1 of the selling expenses will not be incurred on intracompany transfers.

Required:

a. For each case, determine the upper and lower limits for a transfer price for the units.

b. For each case, determine a transfer selling price for Attaya Division that will provide a $10 contribution margin per unit.

c. Using the information developed for part (b), determine a dual transfer price for Case #1 assuming that Payne is able to acquire the units from Attaya at $10 below Payne's purchase price from outsider suppliers.

48. *(Appendix)* For each of the following, indicate whether transfer pricing constitutes an advantage (A), a disadvantage (D), or neither (N):

1. Useful in evaluating the performance of different organizational units
2. Encourages suggestions by users of how to improve products or service
3. Causes disagreements among managers
4. Implementing a transfer pricing system requires time and costs
5. Causes buying departments to "buy" no more than needed
6. Causes selling departments to develop goods and services more beneficial to users
7. Allows service departments to be treated as money-making segments rather than simply cost-generating operations
8. Is not uniformly useful in all departments
9. May cause dysfunctional behavior among organizational units
10. May require adjustments of the accounts for presentation in external financial statements
11. May increase the desire to waste resources

49. *(Transfer price; essay)* MHR has divisions throughout the United States. Each division has its own sales force and production facilities. Each division is operated as a money-making operation, and top management uses the rate of return on the assets invested to evaluate divisional managers' performance.

The Mitchell Division has just been awarded a contract for a product that uses a component that is manufactured by the Reeves Division as well as by outside suppliers. Mitchell used a cost figure of $3.80 for the component when the bid was prepared for the new product. This cost figure was supplied by Reeves in response to Mitchell's request for the average variable cost of the component.

Reeves has an active sales force that is continually soliciting new customers. Reeves' regular selling price for the component Mitchell needs for the new product is $6.50. Sales of the component are expected to increase. Reeves management has the following costs associated with the component:

Standard variable manufacturing cost	$3.20
Standard variable selling and distribution expenses	.60
Standard fixed manufacturing cost	1.20
Total	$5.00

The two divisions have been unable to agree on a transfer price for the component. Corporate management has never established a transfer price policy because interdivisional transactions have never occurred. The following suggestions have been made for the transfer price:

- Regular selling price;
- Regular selling price less variable selling and distribution expenses;
- Standard manufacturing cost plus 15%; and
- Standard variable manufacturing cost plus 20%.

a. Compute each of the suggested transfer prices.
b. Discuss the effect each of the transfer prices might have on the Reeves Division management's attitude toward intracompany business.
c. Is the negotiation of a price between the Mitchell and Reeves Divisions a satisfactory method to solve the transfer price problem? Explain your answer.
d. Should the corporate management of MHR become involved in this transfer controversy? Explain your answer.

(CMA adapted)

50. *(Essay)* One of the big gripes about the airline industry in recent years has been a fare structure that looks as if it was designed by someone who couldn't read maps. Until recently, for instance, Texas Air Corp's Eastern Airlines subsidiary was charging $99 to fly 230 miles from New York to Washington—but only $70 to fly 1,100 miles from New York to Orlando, Florida. Such fares clearly don't make sense.

(SOURCE: John Koten, "Airlines Pushing Fares Linked to Mileage," *Wall Street Journal* [January 13, 1989], p. B1.) Reprinted by permission of *The Wall Street Journal*, © 1989 Dow Jones and Company, Inc. All rights reserved worldwide.

Regardless of what has happened to Eastern Airlines, most airline fares have been constructed in apparently the same manner.

a. Discuss the reasons why airline fares would be set in what appears to be a haphazard way.
b. Would changing fares to reflect a mileage-based structure be appropriate from a consumer point of view? From the airline's point of view?
c. What cost factors could be considered relevant in setting air fares?

51. *(Essay)* Deregulation, the removal or scaling down of the regulatory authority and activities of the government, was advocated during the late 1970s and early 1980s. Many economists and politicians believed that consumers would benefit from freedom of choice, lower prices, and improved services if regulated industries were subjected to the vagaries of the competitive marketplace. Among the major segments of the U.S. economy affected were banking, communications, energy, and transportation.

As financial institutions and corporations were set free from regulatory restraints, the managements of regulated industries had to change their ways. No longer could management be complacent, hiding behind the regulatory blankets that previously provided order, equity, and antitrust immunity. With barriers relaxed, new entities emerged, seeking new opportunities and threatening the existence of many well-known companies. As competitive pressures intensified, the financial policies and strategies needed for success and survival in a deregulated environment centered on improving profitability and maintaining or expanding market share.

a. Discuss how deregulation has affected the way prices are set in industries that have been deregulated.
b. Describe the strategic considerations that would concern the management of a company in a recently deregulated industry.

c. Discuss the positive and negative changes that have occurred in the previously mentioned industries since deregulation.

(CMA adapted)

Cases

52. Bonn Company recently reorganized its computer and data processing activities. The small installations located within the accounting departments at its plants and subsidiaries have been replaced with a single data processing department at corporate headquarters responsible for the operations of a newly acquired large-scale computer system. The new department has been in operation for two years and has been producing reliable and timely data for the past twelve months.

Because the department has focused its activities on converting applications to the new system and producing reports for the plant and subsidiary managements, little attention has been devoted to the costs of the department. Now that the department's activities are operating relatively smoothly, company management has requested that the department manager recommend a cost accumulation system to facilitate cost control and the development of suitable rates to charge users for service.

For the past two years, the departmental costs have been recorded in one account. The costs have then been allocated to user departments on the basis of computer time used. The following schedule reports the costs and charging rate for the calendar year 1993:

1. Salaries and benefits	$ 622,600
2. Supplies	40,000
3. Equipment maintenance contract	15,000
4. Insurance	25,000
5. Heat and air-conditioning	36,000
6. Electricity	50,000
7. Equipment and furniture depreciation	285,400
8. Building improvements depreciation	10,000
9. Building occupancy and security	39,300
10. Corporate administrative charges	52,700
Total costs	$1,176,000
Computer hours for user processing*	2,750
Hourly rate ($1,176,000 ÷ 2,750) (rounded)	$428

*Use of available computer hours:

Testing and debugging programs	250
Setup of jobs	500
Processing jobs	2,750
Downtime for maintenance	750
Idle time	742
Total hours of usage	4,992

The department manager recommends that the department costs be accumulated by five activity centers within the department: Systems Analysis, Programming, Data Preparation, Computer Operations (processing), and Administration. He then suggested that the costs of the Administration activity should be allocated to the other four activity centers before a separate rate for charging users is developed for each of the first four activities. The manager made the following observations regarding the charges to the several subsidiary accounts within the department after reviewing details of the accounts:

1. Salaries and benefits—records the salary and benefit costs of all employees in the department.
2. Supplies—records forms costs, paper costs for printers, and a small amount for miscellaneous other costs.
3. Equipment maintenance contracts—records charges for maintenance contracts; all equipment is covered by maintenance contracts.
4. Insurance—records costs of insurance covering the equipment and furniture.
5. Heat and air-conditioning—records a charge from the corporate heating and air-conditioning department estimated to be the incremental costs to meet the special needs of the computer department.
6. Electricity—records the charge for electricity based upon a separate meter within the department.
7. Equipment and furniture depreciation—records the depreciation charges for all owned equipment and furniture within the department.
8. Building improvements—records the amortization charges for the building changes required to provide proper environmental control and electrical service for the computer equipment.
9. Building occupancy and security—records the computer department's share of the depreciation, maintenance, heat, and security costs of the building; these costs are allocated to the department on the basis of square feet occupied.
10. Corporate administrative charges—records the computer department's share of the corporate administrative costs. They are allocated to the department on the basis of number of employees in the department.

a. For each of the ten cost items, state whether it should be distributed to the five activity centers, and for each cost item that should be distributed, recommend the basis upon which it should be distributed. Justify your conclusion in each case.

b. Assume the costs of the Computer Operations (processing) activity will be charged to the user departments on the basis of computer hours. Using the analysis of computer utilization shown, determine the total number of hours that should be employed to determine the charging rate for Computer Operations (processing). Justify your answer.

(CMA adapted)

53. Frederica Firewater, a management accountant, has recently been employed by International Traveler, Inc. The company is organized on a divisional basis with considerable vertical integration. Frederica is assigned as controller in the Cosmopolitan Division.

Cosmopolitan Division makes several luggage products, one of which is a slim leather portfolio. Sales of the case have been steady, and the marketing department expects continued strong demand. Frederica is looking for ways in which Cosmopolitan Division can contain its costs and thus boost its earnings from future sales. She discovered that Cosmopolitan Division has always purchased its supply of high-quality tanned leather from another division of International Traveler, the Vagabond Division. Vagabond Division has been providing the three square feet of tanned leather needed for each case for $9 per square foot.

Frederica wondered if it might be possible to purchase Cosmopolitan's leather needs from a supplier other than Vagabond at a lesser price for comparable quality. Top management at International Traveler reluctantly agreed to allow Cosmopolitan Division to consider purchasing outside the company.

Cosmopolitan Division will need leather for 100,000 portfolios during the coming year. Cosmopolitan management has requested bids from several leather suppliers. The following bids have been received: $8 and $7 per square foot from Rover and Peltry, respectively. Frederica has been informed that another subsidiary of International Traveler, Conundrum Chemical, supplies Peltry with chemicals that have been an essential ingredient of the tanning process for Peltry. Conundrum Chemical charges Peltry $2 for enough chemicals to prepare three square feet of leather. Conundrum's profit margin is 30 percent.

Finally, Vagabond Division has put into writing its desire to supply Cosmopolitan's leather needs. It will continue to charge $9 per square foot as it has in the past. Bob Trout, Vagabond's controller, has made it clear that he believes Cosmopolitan should continue to purchase all its needs from Vagabond in order to preserve Vagabond's healthy profit margin of 40 percent of sales.

You, as International Traveler's vice-president of finance, have called a meeting of the controllers of Cosmopolitan and Vagabond. Frederica is eager to accept Peltry's bid of $7. She points out that Cosmopolitan's earnings will show a significant increase if the division can buy from Peltry.

Bob Trout, however, wants International to keep the business within the company and suggests that you require Cosmopolitan to purchase its needs from Vagabond. He emphasizes that Vagabond's profit margin should not be lost to the company.

From whom should Cosmopolitan Division buy the leather? Consider both Cosmopolitan's desire to minimize its costs and International's corporate goal of maximizing profit on a companywide basis.

("Management Accounting Case Study: International Traveler, Inc.," *Management Accounting Campus Report* [Spring 1989]; copyright © 1989 IMA [formerly NAA])

54. Klein Corporation is a diversified manufacturing company with corporate headquarters in Kansas City. The three operating divisions are the Aerospace Division, the Ceramic Products Division, and the Glass Products Division. Much of the manufacturing activity of the Aerospace Division is related to work performed for the government space program under negotiated contracts.

Klein Corporation headquarters provides general administrative support and computer services to each of the three operating divisions. The computer services are provided through a computer time-sharing arrangement whereby the central processing unit (CPU) is located in Kansas City and the divisions have remote terminals that are connected to the CPU by telephone lines. One standard from the Cost Accounting Standards Board provides that the cost of general administration may be allocated to negotiated defense contracts. Further, the standards provide that, in situations in which computer services are provided by corporate headquarters, the actual costs (fixed and variable) of operating the computer department may be allocated to the defense division based on a reasonable measure of computer usage.

The general managers of the three divisions are evaluated based on the before-tax performance of each division. The November 1993 income statement (in millions of dollars) for each division is as follows:

	Aerospace Division	Ceramic Products Division	Glass Products Division
Sales	$23.0	$15.0	$55.0
Cost of goods sold	13.0	7.0	38.0
Gross profit	$10.0	$ 8.0	$17.0

Selling & administrative			
Division selling & administration costs	$ 5.0	$ 5.0	$ 8.0
Corporate general administration costs	1.0	—	—
Corporate computing	1.0	—	—
Total	$ 7.0	$ 5.0	$ 8.0
Profit before taxes	$ 3.0	$ 3.0	$ 9.0

Without a charge for computing services, the operating divisions may not make the most cost-effective use of the resources of the Computer Systems Department of Klein Corporation. Outline and discuss a method for charging the operating divisions for use of computer services that would promote an attitude of cost awareness by the operating divisions and operating efficiency by the Computer Systems Department.

(CMA adapted)

55. Wildwood, Inc., manufactures a combination fertilizer/weed-killer under the name Fertikil. This is the only product Wildwood produces at the present time. Fertikil is sold nationwide through normal marketing channels to retail nurseries and garden stores. Westford Nursery plans to sell a similar fertilizer/weed-killer compound through its regional nursery chain under its own private label. Westford has asked Wildwood to submit a bid for a 25,000 pound order of the private brand compound. While the chemical composition of the Westford compound differs from Fertikil, the manufacturing process is very similar.

The Westford compound would be produced in 1,000-pound lots. Each lot would require 60 direct labor hours and the following chemicals:

CW-3	400 lbs.
JX-6	300 lbs.
MZ-8	200 lbs.
BE-7	100 lbs.

The first three chemicals are all used in the production of Fertikil.

BE-7 was used in a compound that Wildwood has discontinued. This chemical was not sold or discarded because it does not deteriorate and there have been adequate storage facilities. Wildwood could sell BE-7 at the prevailing market price less $.10 per pound selling expenses.

Wildwood also has on hand a chemical called CN-5, which was manufactured for use in another product that is no longer produced. CN-5, which cannot be used in Fertikil, can be substituted for CW-3 on a one-for-one basis without affecting the quality of the Westford compound. The quantity of CN-5 in inventory has a salvage value of $500.

Inventory and cost data for the chemicals that can be used to produce the Westford compound are as follows:

Material	Pounds in Inventory	Price per Pound When Purchased	Current Market Price per Pound
CW-3	22,000	$ .80	$ .90
JX-6	5,000	.55	.60
MZ-8	8,000	1.40	1.60
BE-7	4,000	.60	.65
CN-5	5,500	.75	(salvage)

The current direct labor rate is $7 per hour. The manufacturing overhead rate is established at the beginning of the year and is applied consistently throughout the year using direct labor hours (DLHs) as the base. The predetermined overhead rate for the current year, based on a two-shift capacity of 400,000 total DLHs with no overtime, follows:

Variable manufacturing overhead	$2.25 per DLH
Fixed manufacturing overhead	3.75 per DLH
Combined rate	$6.00 per DLH

Wildwood's production manager reports that the present equipment and facilities are adequate to manufacture the Westford compound. However, Wildwood is within 800 hours of its two-shift capacity this month before it must schedule overtime. If need be, the Westford compound could be produced on regular time by shifting a portion of Fertikil production to overtime. Wildwood's rate for overtime hours is one and one-half the regular pay or $10.50 per hour. There is no allowance for any overtime premium in the manufacturing overhead rate.

Wildwood's standard markup policy for new products is 25 percent of full manufacturing cost.

Required:

a. Assume Wildwood has decided to submit a bid for a 25,000 pound order of Westford's new compound. The order must be delivered by the end of the current month. Westford has indicated that this is a one-time order which will not be repeated. Calculate the lowest price Wildwood should bid for the order and not reduce its net income.

b. Without prejudice to your answer to (a), assume that Westford Nursery plans to place regular orders for 25,000-pound lots of the new compound during the coming year. Wildwood expects the demand for Fertikil to remain strong again in the coming year. Therefore, the recurring orders from Westford will put Wildwood over its two-shift capacity. However, production can be scheduled so that 60 percent of each Westford order can be completed during regular hours, or Fertikil production could be shifted temporarily to overtime so that the Westford orders could be produced on regular time. Wildwood's production manager has estimated that the prices of all chemicals will stabilize at the current market rates for the coming year and that all other manufacturing costs are expected to be maintained at the same rates or amounts. Calculate the price Wildwood should quote Westford Nursery for each 25,000-pound lot of the new compound, assuming that there will be recurring orders during the coming year.

(CMA adapted)

Ethics Discussion

56. The Gordon Company has several plants, one of which produces military equipment for the federal government. Many of the contracts are negotiated on a cost-plus basis. Some of the other plants have been only marginally profitable, and the home office has engaged a consultant, Mr. Shifty, to meet with top management. Shifty observes that the company isn't using some of the more "creative" accounting techniques to shift costs toward the plant serving the federal government and away from the marginally profitable plants. He notes that "transfer pricing and service department allocations involve a lot of subjectivity. There is plenty of room to stack the deck and let the taxpayer foot the bill. Taxpayers will never know, and even if the government suspects, it can't prove motive if we

document the procedures with contrived business jargon." One of the staff stated that "this would be a way to get back some of those exorbitant income taxes we have had to pay all these years." The company president ended the meeting and asked for some time to consider the matter.

a. What is the purpose of setting transfer prices and making service department allocations?

b. Can or should transfer prices and service department allocations be used to shift income from one plant to another? If so, under what conditions?

c. Do you think that what the consultant is suggesting is legal? Ethical? Ever been done? Discuss your reasoning for each answer.

57. Competitive pricing and marketing can be an ethical minefield. Obviously we want to get all the business we can, and obviously we want to do it at profitable margins. But competition stands in our way. Discussing price with competitors is unthinkable, but studying their price lists and trying to figure out their strategies is essential. Then the new product is priced and marketed in a fashion slightly more to the consumer's advantage.

(SOURCE: Barbara Ley Toffler, "Interview with Robert Smith," *Managers Talk Ethics* [New York: Wiley, 1991], pp. 263–64.)

Some companies enter markets with cheap prices and then raise the prices if the product is successful.

a. Can all types of companies use such penetration pricing techniques? If so, how? If not, discuss why not.

b. Is it ethical to lure a customer into buying a product based on a low price and then raise the prices later? Discuss the rationale for your answer.

58. A News Note in the chapter discussed the way in which milk prices were set. Another article indicates that Wisconsin farmers are losing money for every one hundred pounds of milk produced.

a. Discuss the rationale of paying farmers more for milk depending on how far from Eau Claire, Wisconsin, the production operations are.

b. Discuss the ethical implications of this price-setting policy.

c. Discuss the rationale and ethical implications behind other types of regulated pricing, such as for electricity.

59. An innovative method of effectively increasing prices without appearing to do so is downsizing, which refers to reducing the package size or contents while charging the same price as before. While downsizing is not a pricing technique per se, such a technique may be used after the product has gained a customer following with high brand loyalty. Although practiced by many companies, some people wonder about its legitimacy, as seen in the following excerpt:

Consumer advocates charge that downsizing is an increasingly common way of raising prices without telling consumers they're paying more for less. New York State Attorney General Robert Abrams will issue a report charging that such practices are deceptive. Mr. Abrams also plans to press for a bill in the state legislature requiring marketers to signal such changes on the package.

For more than 30 years, StarKist Seafood put 6½ ounces of tuna—the industry standard—into its regular-sized can. Today, though, you'll find StarKist's cans weigh ⅜ of an ounce less—for exactly the same price. The result: a nearly invisible 5.8% price increase. StarKist defends its downsizing, saying that the new can handles and stacks better and uses less steel—a boon to the environment. But other manufacturers acknowledge that downsizing has more to do with pricing than anything else. "It's a price increase any way you slice it," says Scott Stewart, a spokesman for Procter &

Gamble Co.'s diaper division. Over the past few months, both Procter & Gamble and Kimberly-Clark Corp. have cut the number of diapers in their packages, leaving prices the same. A package that used to contain 88 diapers now has 80, effectively a 9.1% price increase, while the old 28-count package now has 26, for a 7.1% increase.

(SOURCE: John B. Hinge, "Critics Call Cuts in Package Size Deceptive Move," *Wall Street Journal* [February 5, 1991], p. B1.)

a. As a manufacturing executive, if costs were increasing but you did not want to raise prices, would you consider downsizing as a viable alternative strategy? Discuss the rationale for your answer.

b. If you downsized your product, how would you address this issue with consumers of your product?

c. What are the ethical implications of downsizing products without appropriate consumer information?

60. Amid grumblings that contract change orders have spun out of control in Jefferson Parish, Councilman Nick Giambelluca is spearheading a move to cap cost increases on public projects [by making a] motion to limit change orders to 25 percent of the original contract amount. Most recently, Giambelluca was incensed by a fifth change order on a contract for paving at Lafreniere Park . . . that put the job about 46 percent over budget. Taxpayers have now paid $3.2 million on the park's Scenic Loop Improvement project—$1 million more than the original contract amount.

   Under the terms of the contract, concrete at the park's scenic loop road must be 7 inches thick and [concrete] poured on parking lots must be 5 inches thick. The contract states that no payment will be made for areas where the concrete is too thin. Nevertheless, York Construction Co. (the contractor) was paid for long stretches of roadway that do not meet specifications. [An inspection] report shows areas with deficient depths that run for more than 1,500 feet in places, and sections of the road and the parking lot where roughly 60 percent of the concrete did not meet specifications.

(SOURCE: James Varney, "Contract Cost Increases Blasted," [*New Orleans*] *Times-Picayune* [March 31, 1992], p. B1.)

a. After a government contract has been bid and accepted, should additions to the project simply be added on to the original contract, or should they be put out for additional bid?

b. Is it ethical for a contractor to accept payments for work that did not meet contract standards?

c. Is it ethical for a governmental unit to make payments for substandard work?

d. Assuming that this case is not an isolated instance of substandard work being performed for governmental entities, how are the taxpayers affected by such occurrences? As a taxpayer, discuss your perceptions of cost-plus contracts issued by governmental entities.

C H A P T E R   11

MANAGERIAL
ASPECTS
OF
BUDGETING

LEARNING OBJECTIVES

After completing this chapter, you should be able to do the following:

1. Understand the importance of the budgeting process
2. Differentiate between strategic and tactical planning
3. Relate strategic and tactical planning to the budgeting process
4. Compare the benefits and disadvantages of imposed budgets and participatory budgets
5. Explain how a budget manual facilitates the budgeting process
6. Compute budget variances and use them to analyze differences between budgeted and actual revenues
7. Understand how the managerial function of control is related to budgeting
8. Recognize why managers should use achievable budget targets

Financial Planning at The Placers Inc.

No matter how successful a company's products, the bottom line will be greatly affected by how wisely it manages its assets. Forecasting, planning and budgeting are often the last things on the mind of the entrepreneur struggling to keep his company going. But they are the blocks on which a sturdy financial structure is built. Should the company introduce an additional product? Add staff? Go into a new market? Build a new warehouse? Such decisions can involve major—and risky—financial commitments.

Savvy planning has been the key to the financial success of The Placers Inc., a temporary-personnel and job-search firm in Wilmington, Del. CEO Alan Burkhard meets with his senior management team to discuss the company's outlook and plans for the coming year. Over the next month, department heads and other key employees generate detailed information about current and projected sales and expenditures, client by client. They also come up with a wish list of anticipated capital expenditures [for plant and equipment items].

At the end of each month of the budget year, employees receive updates comparing forecasted sales and expenses with actual results. Says Burkhard, "We tell people we expect them to stay on target. And if they're not meeting their forecasted numbers, they've got to figure out how to adjust their performance."

SOURCE: "Managing Working Capital," *Inc.* (September 1991), p. 38. Reprinted with permission, *Inc.* magazine. Copyright © by Goldhirsch Group Inc., 38 Commercial Wharf, Boston, Mass. 02110.

P lanning is the cornerstone of effective management, and one vital part of good planning is budgeting. Alan Burkhard and his managers at The Placers Inc. project future sales and expenditures so that they can use the plans to guide their actions and compare actual performance against the plans—a process of budgetary control. While financial planning is important if future conditions will be roughly the same as current conditions, such planning is critical when conditions are expected to change. Managers at The Placers Inc. would not, for instance, come to work one morning and decide to open a day-care center for workers' children; such a major decision would require consideration of the impact on income, cash flow, and debt structure.

During the planning process, managers attempt to agree on company goals and objectives and how to achieve them. Typically, goals are stated in abstract terms, while objectives are quantifiable for a period of time. Achievement of goals and objectives requires undertaking complex activities and providing diverse resources that, in turn, typically demand a formalized planning or budgeting process.

Planning should include qualitative narratives of goals, objectives, and means of accomplishment. However, if plans were limited to qualitative narratives, the process of comparing actual results to expectations would only allow generalizations, and trying to measure how well the organization met its specified objectives would be impossible. Therefore, management translates qualitative narratives into a quantitative format, or **budget**.

The budget expresses an organization's commitment to planned activities and resource acquisition and use. "A budget is more than a forecast. A forecast is a prediction of what may happen and sometimes contains prescriptions for dealing with future events. A budget, on the other hand, involves a commitment to a forecast to make an agreed-on outcome happen." [1]

BUDGETING AND MANAGEMENT FUNCTIONS

budgeting

The process of devising a financial plan for future operations (**budgeting**) is an important part of an organization's planning and controlling processes. Budgeting has many different purposes and can be performed in many different ways. The basics of the budgeting process are illustrated in the flow diagram in Exhibit 11–1; the individual steps are discussed in the remainder of this chapter and in chapter 12.

Purposes of Budgeting

As with any other planning activity, budgeting helps provide a focused direction or a chosen path from among many future alternatives. Management generally indicates the direction chosen through some accounting measure of financial performance, such as net income, earnings per share, or sales level in dollars or units. Such accounting-based measures provide specific quantitative criteria against which future performance (also recorded in accounting terms) can be compared. Budgets, then, are a type of standard, and variances from a budget can be computed.

Budgeting can also help identify potential problems of achieving the specified goals and objectives. For example, assume The Placers Inc. has the 1994 objectives of generating $1,000,000 of revenues and $150,000 of net income. The budget might indicate that, based on current costs and forecasted inflation rates, such a bottom line could not be obtained. Managers could then brainstorm to find ways to reduce costs or increase revenues so that the $150,000 income objective could be reached. By quantifying potential difficulties and making them visible, budgets can help stimulate managers to think of ways to overcome those difficulties.

The News Note on page 466 indicates how the American Institute of CPAs addressed its 1992 budget problems—a decline in membership has to be made up with an increase in membership dues.

A well-prepared budget can be an effective device to communicate objectives, constraints, and expectations to people throughout an organization. Such communication promotes the understanding of exactly what is to be accomplished, how those accomplishments are to be achieved, and the manner in which resources are to be allocated. Determination of resource allocations is made, in part, from a process of obtaining information, justifying requests, and negotiating compromises. Allowing managers to participate in the budgeting process helps produce a spirit of cooperation, motivates employees, and instills a feeling of teamwork. Employee participation is needed to effectively integrate necessary information from various sources as well as to obtain individual managerial commitment to the resulting budget.

---

[1] Neil C. Churchill, "Budget Choice: Planning vs. Control," *Harvard Business Review* (July–August 1984), p. 150.

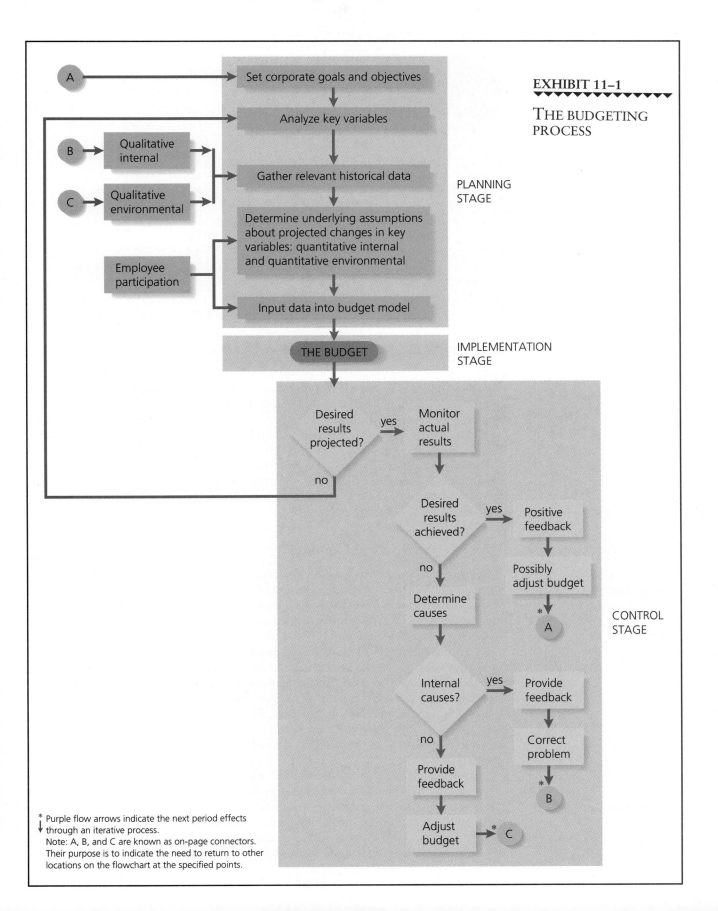

EXHIBIT 11–1

THE BUDGETING PROCESS

A → Set corporate goals and objectives

Analyze key variables

B → Qualitative internal

C → Qualitative environmental

Gather relevant historical data

Determine underlying assumptions about projected changes in key variables: quantitative internal and quantitative environmental

Employee participation

Input data into budget model

THE BUDGET

PLANNING STAGE

IMPLEMENTATION STAGE

Desired results projected? — yes → Monitor actual results

no

Desired results achieved? — yes → Positive feedback

no

Determine causes

Possibly adjust budget

* A

Internal causes? — yes → Provide feedback

no

Correct problem

Provide feedback

* B

Adjust budget → * C

CONTROL STAGE

* Purple flow arrows indicate the next period effects through an iterative process.
Note: A, B, and C are known as on-page connectors. Their purpose is to indicate the need to return to other locations on the flowchart at the specified points.

Even Accountants Can't Always Budget for Profits

AICPA council members approved a budget calling for a $500,000 shortfall for the year ending July 1992, on revenue of $117.5 million. In 1990–91, the AICPA lost $2.9 million on revenue of $107.5 million.

The Institute planned no 1991–92 dues increase, but the members could face a possible 230% dues increase for 1992–93—the first one in four years. Without the dues increase, the Institute treasurer projects a $3.9 million deficit that could rise to $7 million by 1995.

The financial strains are coming at a time when the AICPA's public accounting membership is slipping. During 1990–91, for instance, there were only 130,080 accountants in public practice compared to 131,500 the previous year.

SOURCE: Adapted from "New Budget Keeps AICPA in the Red," *Accounting Today* (November 11, 1991), p. 3.

The budget indicates the resource constraints under which managers must operate for the upcoming budget period. Thus, the budget becomes the basis for controlling activities and resource usage. Periodic budget-to-actual comparisons allow managers to determine how well they are doing and to assess how well they understand their operations.

While budgets are typically expressed in financial terms, the budgeting and planning processes are concerned with all organizational resources—raw materials, inventory, supplies, personnel, and facilities. These processes can be viewed from a long-term or a short-term perspective.

Strategic and Tactical Planning

strategic planning

When managers plan on a long-term basis (five to ten years), they are engaged in **strategic planning.** This process is generally performed only by top level management with the assistance of several key staff members. The result of the process is a statement of long-range goals for the organization and of the strategies and policies that will help in the achievement of those goals.

Expressing long-term goals first requires an acknowledgement of the organization's business. Sometimes, the obvious function is not the true function. For example, the TLC Group (Zeeland, Michigan) owned warehouses in which goods were stored by others. Thus, company management believed the company was in the warehousing business. Upon review, however, TLC management found that the company was a logistics firm which also provided a warehousing function. The new strategic outlook helped TLC increase its sales from $2.4 million in 1985 to $30 million in 1990.

key variables

Strategic planning is not concerned with day-to-day operations, although the strategic plan will be the foundation on which short-term planning is based. Managers engaging in strategic planning should identify **key variables,** or critical factors believed to potentially be direct causes of the achievement or nonachievement of organizational goals and objectives. Key variables can be internal or external. Exhibit 11–2 provides the results of one study about the external factors considered to be the

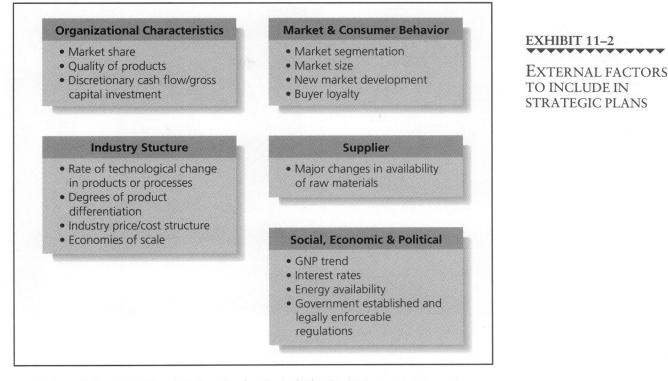

SOURCE: James F. Brown, Jr., "How U.S. Firms Conduct Strategic Planning," *Management Accounting* (February 1986), p. 55. Published by Institute of Management Accountants, Montvale, N.J.

most critical in determining the strategic plans of manufacturing companies. One conclusion from the survey was that a "firm's long-term success is dependent on the integration of the forces in its environment into its own planning process so that the firm *influences* its own destiny instead of constantly *reacting* to environmental forces."[2] Internal key variables are under the control of management, while external key variables are normally noncontrollable.

For example, when oil prices decreased dramatically, a major portion of Moody-Price's customer base was eliminated. This Baton Rouge (Louisiana)-based company knew that the price of oil was a key external variable that company management could not change. Therefore, the company focused on providing good customer service and obtaining new customers—factors that Moody-Price could impact.

After the key variables have been identified, information related to them can be gathered. Much of this information will be historical and qualitative and provides a useful starting point for tactical planning activities.

The process of determining the specific objectives and means by which strategic plans will be achieved is called **tactical** (or operational) **planning.** Although some tactical plans, such as corporate policy statements, exist for the long term and address repetitive situations, most tactical plans are short-term (one to eighteen months). Such short-term tactical plans are considered "single use" plans and have been developed to address a given set of circumstances or for a specific time frame.

tactical planning

---

[2]James F. Brown, Jr., "How U.S. Firms Conduct Strategic Planning," *Management Accounting* (February 1986), p. 55.

When making strategic and tactical plans, managers should gather data about the past and expected trends for the future. The more information that is obtained, the better the ability to make informed decisions rather than simply "guess-timates."

The annual budget is an example of a single use tactical plan. While a budget's focus is on a twelve-month period, intermediate (quarterly and monthly) plans should also be included for the budget to work effectively. Remember that at The Placers Inc., budget-to-actual comparisons are performed monthly to keep people on track with the established plan.

A well-prepared budget "translates the strategic plans of the organization and [the company's] implementation programs into period-oriented operational guides to

EXHIBIT 11–3
▼▼▼▼▼▼▼▼▼▼▼▼

RELATIONSHIPS
AMONG PLANNING
PROCESSES

Who?	What?	How?	Why?
Top management	Strategic planning	Statement of organizational mission, goals, and strategies; long-range (five to ten years)	Establish a long-range vision of the organization and provide a sense of unity and commitment to specified purposes
Top and mid-management	Tactical planning	Statement of organizational objectives and operational plans; short-range (twelve to eighteen months)	Provide direction for the achievement of strategic plans; state strategic plans in terms that can be acted on; furnish a basis against which results can be measured
Top, mid- and operational management	Budgeting	Quantitative and monetary statements that coordinate company activities for periods of twelve months or less	Allocate resources effectively and efficiently; indicate a commitment to objectives; provide a monetary control device

NEWS NOTE

Life Cycle Stage of Product Affects Budgeting Process

[A product life cycle] budgeting system improves the traditional process because the assumptions used in any budgeting system should depend on a product's life cycle stage—start-up, growth, maturity, or harvest. Most managers, however, budget as if all products are always in the maturity stage.

Budgeting has three main functions: planning, control, and motivation. For planning purposes, managers want the most realistic outcome. For motivational purposes, managers want the budget to be difficult yet attainable. For control purposes, a manager wants a budget to be the optimal one.

In the start-up and growth stages, planning is the most important budgetary function. Control ranks second. Motivation is the least important budget function during these stages because, for the product to survive, employees must be internally motivated.

Planning remains the most important function during product maturity, but motivation replaces control in second place. As the product matures, the process becomes standardized. Therefore, employees need more motivation because their job tasks do not provide it. The controls should have been formalized by this stage or the product probably would not have made it this far.

In the harvest stage, motivation is the most important function. The product is dying, so employees are shifted around or terminated. Employees, then, need a reason to keep on producing. Planning is now in second place, but continues to be important. If the product is canceled too soon, the company loses potential future revenue. If the product is canceled too late, extra expenses are incurred for producing, storing, and disposing of obsolete goods. Control is basically unimportant at this point because there is now a relatively small product investment.

Managers who understand which function is most important to budgetary success in a particular stage can allocate company resources more efficiently.

SOURCE: Alan B. Czyzewski and Rita P. Hull, "Improving Profitability With Life Cycle Costing," (Summer 1991), p. 20ff. Adapted with permission from the *Journal of Cost Management for the Manufacturing Industry*. Warren, Gorham & Lamont, a division of Research Institute of America, 210 South Street, Boston, Mass. 02111. All rights reserved.

company activities." [3] Exhibit 11–3 illustrates the relationships among strategic planning, tactical planning, and budgeting.

Both strategic and tactical planning require that information regarding the economy, environment, technological developments, and available resources be incorporated into the setting of goals and objectives. As indicated in the preceding News Note, managers must also take into consideration the product life cycle (PLC) stages (see chapter 10) at which the company's products exist. Each stage requires a different budgetary focus. These planning processes also demand that, as activity takes place and plans are implemented, a monitoring system be in place to provide feedback so that the control function can be operationalized.

---

[3]Churchill, "Budget Choice," p. 151.

NEWS NOTE

Different Stages of Life, Different Ways of Budgeting

Not all budget processes are created equal. High-tech start-up companies know this all too well. Unlike the usual operating budget, the high-tech variety must take into account many factors not faced by mature companies. The budgeting process traditionally has been viewed as a measurement tool with revenue and expense tracked in the accounting department. But Photon Technology International, Inc. had a distance to go before it could share this perspective.

[For example,] the time and resources devoted to product improvement use up limited resources, and staying within the R&D budget is of major concern to companies already tight on cash. Photon developed three "what-if" scenarios: (1) a best-case budget that assumed everything was going according to plan; (2) a worst-case budget that predicted just the opposite and the necessary corrective action that would be taken; and (3) a most-likely-to-happen budget that examined each variable against each level of sales and projected the amount over or under budget and an appropriate reaction.

Photon is now beginning to move out of the woods. Although [its] budget is made up of "bits and pieces" of budgets from the various stages of its life, budgeting for Photon now is progressing toward a more traditional operating budgeting process. The company looks closely at quotes from the sales force, the time required to close on a sale, the number of calls, the cost-benefit of trade shows, and so on. [After-sales service and support is also] included in the budget [because the company believes that] proper application support and follow-up cements a long-term relationship.

SOURCE: Janine S. Pouliot, "High-Tech Budgeting," *Management Accounting* (May 1991), pp. 30–31. Published by Institute of Management Accountants, Montvale, N.J.

THE BUDGETING PROCESS

Once management has decided upon the organization's strategic plan, budgeting activity should begin for future periods. The budgeting process requires carefully integrating a complex set of facts and projections with human relationships and attitudes. Most budgeting literature notes that an "appropriate" budgeting system (development, implementation, and control) can only be defined within the context of a specific organization's structure, goals and objectives, management leadership style, and employee attitudes.[4] In other words, as shown in the above News Note, one system of budgeting is not right for all organizations. However, it is recognized that there are basically two ways by which the budgets can be derived: from the top down (**imposed budgets**) or from the bottom up (**participatory budgets**). Each of these types is discussed in the following section.

imposed budgets
participatory budgets

---

[4]Mary T. Soulier, "A Psychological Model of the Budgetary Process," *The Woman CPA* (January 1980), p. 3.

Best Times to Use?

- In start-up organizations
- In extremely small businesses
- In times of economic crises
- When operating managers lack budgetary skills or perspective
- When the organizational units require precise coordination of efforts

Advantages Of:

- Increase probability that organization's strategic plans are incorporated in planned activities
- Enhance coordination among divisional plans and objectives
- Utilize top management's knowledge of overall resource availability
- Reduce the possibility of input from inexperienced or uninformed lower-level employees
- Reduce the time frame for the budgeting process

Disadvantages Of:

- May result in dissatisfaction, defensiveness, and low morale among individuals who must work under them
- Reduce the feeling of teamwork
- May limit the acceptance of the stated goals and objectives
- Limit the communication process among employees and management
- May create a view of the budget as a punitive device
- May result in unachievable budgets for international divisions if the local operating and political environment is not adequately considered
- May stifle initiative of lower-level managers

EXHIBIT 11–4
▼▼▼▼▼▼▼▼▼▼▼▼
IMPOSED BUDGETS

Participation

For decades, budgets have been used in governmental and not-for-profit organizations and have had the goals of monetary control and fiscal responsibility. Business budgets, when they were first used, followed such governmental ideas and were prepared by top management with little or no input from operating personnel. Such budgets were then simply imposed upon the individuals who had to work within the budgeted figures. After the imposed budget is developed, operating personnel are informed of budget goals and constraints. While operating personnel may sometimes be given an opportunity to suggest changes to the budget, such suggestions may or may not be accepted. As indicated in Exhibit 11–4, there are certain times when imposed budgets are effective and provide some distinct benefits; the disadvantages of imposed budgets are also listed.

Businesspeople soon recognized the dissatisfaction caused by and the disadvantages of imposed budgets, and the idea of participation by various management levels was introduced. From the standpoint of operational managers, participation could

Working under imposed budgets is similar to living under a dictator. Lower level managers have no opportunity to integrate their experience and knowledge of conditions into the budget whose objectives those managers are expected to achieve.

be viewed on a spectrum from having a right to comment on budgets before their implementation by top management to having the ultimate right to set budgets. Neither end of that spectrum is quite feasible. Simply commenting on the handed-down budget still reflects an imposed budgeting system, while each individual manager setting his or her own budget ignores the fact that cooperation and communication among areas are essential to the functioning of a cohesive organization.

Thus, a participatory budget is generally defined as one that has been developed through a process of *joint decision making* by top management and operating personnel, similar to the one described in the next News Note. The degree to which lower-level operating management is allowed to participate in budget development usually depends on two factors: top management's awareness of and agreement with the advantages (listed in Exhibit 11–5, page 474) of the participation process. Participatory budgets also have disadvantages that are provided in Exhibit 11–5.

budget slack

Managers may introduce **budget slack** (the intentional underestimation of revenues and/or overestimation of expenses) into the budgeting process. Slack, if it exists, is usually built into the budget during the participation process; it is not often found in imposed budgets. Having slack in the budget allows subordinate managers to achieve their objectives with less effort than would be necessary if there were no slack. Budget slack creates problems because of the significant interaction of the budget factors. If sales are understated, problems can arise in the production, purchasing, and personnel areas.

Since the functions of operating personnel are affected by the budget and these individuals must work under the budget guidelines, input from the operating level is often invaluable in the planning process. While there is no concrete evidence as to how well participatory budgeting works in all circumstances, such participation in

NEWS NOTE

Participation Is Important

The success of the budgeting process is directly related to the level of involvement of the company's CEO and senior managers. Without the CEO's full support and understanding, the result will always be less than could have been achieved. Worse, the budgeting process will be meaningless and extremely frustrating for all managers involved. If company management complains about the ineffectiveness of their budgets, an honest evaluation would show that their budget is little more than the finance manager's forecast shown on a combined (lumping) basis, which is no more than a set of figures. To be meaningful, the budget must be prepared starting at the lowest identifiable manager level. A budget is most effective if each manager in the company agrees to the identifiable portions relative to his/her unit—and all the way up to the CEO.

SOURCE: Lon Addams, "Back to Budgets," *Grant Thornton Tax Planner* (August 1988), p. 5.

budget development by operating managers also seems to create a higher commitment to the budget's success. Additionally,

> [t]he more that a budgetary system can be used to encourage the flow of relevant information to decision makers, the greater is the system's ability to diminish uncertainty. Should participation release more information to the budget planner, then the uncertainty surrounding their projections will be diminished and their plans will be based more upon informed, rational judgments and less upon guesswork.[5]

The budgeting process represents a continuum with imposed budgets on one end and participatory budgets on the other. Currently, most business budgets are prepared through a coordinated effort of input from operating personnel and revision by top management. In this manner, the plans of all levels can be considered. Top management first sets strategic objectives for lower-level management; then, lower-level managers suggest and justify their operations' performance targets. Upper-level managers combine all component budgets, evaluate the overall results, and provide feedback on any needed changes to the lower-level managers. In addition, some companies have a **budget committee**, composed of top management and the chief financial officer, which reviews and approves, or makes adjustments to, the budgets submitted from operational managers and/or the master budget (which is discussed in the next chapter).

budget committee

Regardless of whether the process is top-down or bottom-up, management must first review the complete budget before approving and implementing it to first determine if the underlying assumptions on which the budget is based are reasonable. Budgeted figures are only as reasonable as the assumptions on which they are based. Second, management must determine if the budgeted results are acceptable and realistic. The budget may indicate that the results expected from the planned activities do not achieve the desired objectives. In this case, planned activities should be reconsidered and revised to more appropriately represent the desired outcomes (assuming they are not overly ambitious) that were expressed during the tactical planning stage.

[5]Lee D. Parker, "Participation in Budget Planning: The Prospects Surveyed," *Accounting and Business Research* (Spring 1979), pp. 123–37.

EXHIBIT 11–5
▼▼▼▼▼▼▼▼▼▼▼

PARTICIPATORY
BUDGETS

Best Times to Use?

- In well-established organizations
- In extremely large businesses
- In times of economic affluence
- When operating managers have strong budgetary skills and perspectives
- When the organizational units are quite autonomous

Advantages of:

- Provide information from those persons most familiar with the needs and constraints of organizational units
- Integrate knowledge that is diffused among various levels of management
- Lead to better morale and higher motivation
- Provide a means to develop fiscal responsibility and budgetary skills of employees
- Develop a high degree of acceptance of and commitment to organizational goals and objectives by operating management
- Are generally more realistic
- Allow organizational units to coordinate with one another
- Allow subordinate managers to develop operational plans that conform to organizational goals and objectives
- Include specific resource requirements
- Blend overview of top management with operating details
- Provide a social contract that expresses expectations of top management and subordinates

Disadvantages of:

- Require significantly more time
- Effects of managerial participation may be negated by top management changes, creating a level of dissatisfaction with the process approximately equal to that occurring under imposed budgets
- Managers may be ambivalent about or unqualified to participate, creating an unachievable budget
- May cause managers to introduce "slack" into the budget
- May support "empire building" by subordinates
- May require starting the budgeting process earlier in the year when there is more uncertainty about the future year

Timing

The budget is normally prepared on an annual basis and detailed first by quarters and, next, by months within those quarters. The *minimum* time to begin budget preparation is two to three months in advance of the period to be covered, but management must remember two things: (1) participatory budget development will take longer than an imposed budget process and (2) the larger and more complex the company is, the longer the budgeting process will take.

Some companies use a **continuous** (or rolling) **budget** that presents an ongoing twelve-month budget by successively adding a new budget month (twelve months into the future) as each current month expires. As shown in Exhibit 11–6, at any point in time, management is working within the present one-month component of a full twelve-month annual budget. Continuous budgets make the planning process less sporadic and disruptive. Rather than having managers "go into the budgeting period" at a specific point in time, they are continuously involved in planning and budgeting. Continuous budgets also provide a longer-range focus, so that surprises do not occur at year-end. Surprises within the budgeting process can also be minimized through the use of a detailed budget manual.

continuous budget

Budget Manuals

A well-prepared budget requires a substantial amount of time and effort by the persons engaged in preparing it. This process can be improved by the availability of an organization **budget manual,** or detailed set of documents that provides information and guidelines about the budgetary process. It should include the following:

budget manual

1. statements of the budgeting purpose and its desired results;
2. a listing of specific budgetary activities to be performed;
3. a calendar of scheduled budgetary activities;
4. sample budget forms; and
5. original, revised, and approved budgets.

EXHIBIT 11–6
▼▼▼▼▼▼▼▼▼▼▼▼

CONTINUOUS
BUDGET

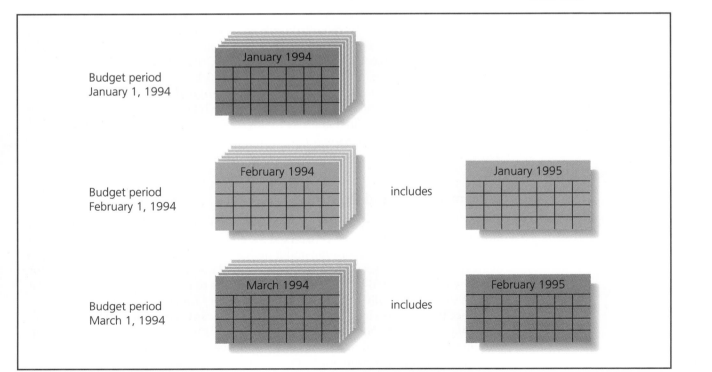

The *statements of budgeting purpose and desired results* communicate the reasons behind the process and should flow from general to specific details. An example of a general statement of budgeting purpose is: "The cash budget provides a basis for planning, reviewing, and controlling cash flows from and for various activities; this budget is essential to the preparation of a pro forma Statement of Cash Flows." Specific statements regarding the cash budget could include references to minimum desired cash balances and periods of high cash needs. These needs would be taken into consideration when preparing the cash budget portion of the master budget.

Budgetary activities should be listed by job rather than by person because the responsibility for actions should be delegated to the individuals holding the specific jobs when the budget manual is being implemented. This section of the manual should indicate who has the final authority for revising and approving the budget. Budget approval may be delegated to a budget committee or reserved by one or several members of top management.

The *budget calendar* is needed to coordinate the budgetary process and should include a timetable for all budget activities. The timetable for the budget process is unique to each organization. The larger the organization, the more time will be needed to gather information, coordinate that information, identify weak points in the process or the budget itself, and take corrective action. The calendar should also indicate control points for the upcoming periods, when budget-to-actual comparisons will be made, and when and how feedback will be provided to managers responsible for operations.

Sample forms are very useful because they provide for a consistent presentation of budget information from all individuals. Consistent presentations make summarizations of information easier, quicker, and more effective. The sample forms should be easy to understand and can include standardized worksheets that allow managers to update historical information to arrive at budgetary figures. This section of the budget manual may also provide standard cost tables for items on which the organization has specific guidelines or policies. For example, in estimating employee fringe benefit costs, the company rule of thumb may be 30 percent of base salary. Or, a company policy may exist that the meal per diem allowance for salespersons is $30; in estimating meal expenses for the future period, the salesmanager would simply need to multiply total estimated travel days times $30.

The last section of the manual includes the *original and revised budgets*. It is helpful for future planning to understand how the revision process works and why changes were made. The final approved budget is composed of many individual budgets and is known as the master budget (discussed in chapter 12). The master budget serves as a control document for budget-to-actual comparisons.

Implementation and Control

After a budget is prepared and accepted, it is implemented. Budget implementation means that the budget is now considered a standard against which performance can be measured. Managers operating under budget guidelines should be provided copies of all appropriate budgets. These managers should also be informed that their performance will be evaluated by comparing actual results to budgeted amounts. Such evaluations should generally be made by budget category for specific periods of time.

Once the budget is implemented, the control phase begins. Control includes making actual-to-budget comparisons, determining variances, providing feedback to operating managers, investigating the causes of the variances, and taking any necessary corrective action. This control process indicates the cyclical nature of the budgeting

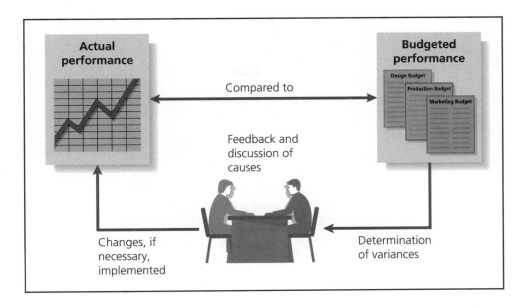

EXHIBIT 11–7
▼▼▼▼▼▼▼▼▼▼▼▼

NATURE OF THE
BUDGETING PROCESS

process (see Exhibit 11–7). Feedback (both positive and negative) is essential to the control process and must be provided in a timely manner to be useful.

Sales Price and Sales Volume Variances

In making actual-to-budget comparisons, managers are held accountable for the revenues (if any) and the costs in the operating areas over which those managers have authority and responsibility. The actual performance of the operating area should be compared to budgeted performance to determine variances from expectations. In

JC Penney cannot simply budget for total sales. The company must also set budget figures for specified operational areas, such as each individual store, and by region.

making such comparisons, however, management needs to be certain that it is considering results in a proper perspective.

If a manager's operating area is one in which revenues are being generated (for example, the Jersey City location of JC Penney or the Chevrolet Division of General Motors), comparisons should first be made on the revenue level to determine how closely projected sales are being met. As discussed in chapter 5 on standard costing, a total variance from standard can have both a price (or cost) and a quantity element. Thus, revenue variance calculations should be made for both these elements.

sales price variance

Calculating the difference between actual and budgeted selling prices and multiplying by the actual number of units sold will provide the **sales price variance**. This variance indicates the portion of the total variance that is related to a change in the selling price of the goods. A variance is also created by the difference between actual and budgeted sales volumes; multiplying this difference by the budgeted selling price indicates the **sales volume variance**. The sales variance model is as follows:[6]

sales volume variance

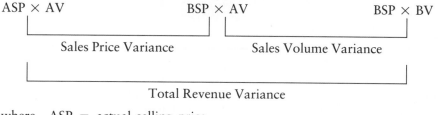

where ASP = actual selling price
       AV = actual volume
       BSP = budgeted selling price
       BV = budgeted volume

To illustrate these computations, assume that the Doll Division of Mendoza Company budgets 1994 sales at 10,000 units per month and a selling price of $35. Thus, monthly budgeted sales are $350,000. Actual January sales were $306,000, creating a total unfavorable revenue variance of $44,000. To make a valid comparison, it is also necessary to know that the $306,000 of revenues was composed of a sales volume of 10,200 units sold at $30. Thus, the following variance calculations can be made:

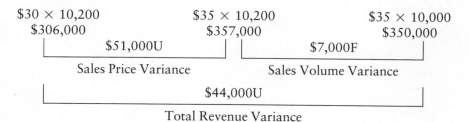

Company managers should be pleased with the increased volume but displeased with the reduced selling price. Discussions with the responsible division managers might indicate that the dolls were placed on sale after Christmas to avoid incurring

---

[6]These computations assume a single product for the company. If the company sells multiple products, another variance will exist called the sales mix variance. This variance explains the change in budgeted revenue caused by selling a different mix of products than was expected. Sales mix is discussed in chapter 9 on cost-volume-profit analysis. Variance computations would require information on the estimated percentage of total expected sales for each product.

costs for warehousing and paying beginning-of-the-year inventory tax. Such reasons should be discussed and examined as to acceptability. If the warehousing costs and inventory tax would have exceeded $44,000, then the division manager made a good decision.

Analyzing Cost Variances

After revenue variances have been explained, managers can focus on analyzing cost variances. It is important that costs should be analyzed in relation to the *actual* volume of sales rather than the *budgeted* volume of sales. Such analysis requires the use of flexible budgets and flexible budget formulas.

For example, assume that Mendoza's Doll Division has a flexible budget formula for selling expenses of $1,000 per month plus 5 percent of sales dollars. The original selling expense budget estimate for January would have been $18,500 [$1,000 + .05(10,000 × $35)]. However, since the Doll Division only achieved an actual sales level of $306,000, the division should only expect selling expenses of $16,300 [$1,000 + .05($306,000)]. If actual selling expenses were $18,500, the division did not perform up to expectations; it should recognize a $2,200 unfavorable variance for selling expenses. Comparing actual expenses to budgeted expenses that were calculated *at a different level of sales* will not provide valid information on how well costs were controlled during a period.

In addition to determining whether costs were controlled, managers need to analyze the ways in which money was spent. Donald A. Curtis, a senior partner at the international public accounting firm of Deloitte & Touche, emphasizes, "Just because a budget was not overspent doesn't mean it was well spent." [7] Spending analysis should focus on individual line items, not just totals, and on spending within categories. Oftentimes, money is spent simply because it is available for spending—not because there was a need for spending.

As with any variance computations, the reason for making income statement actual-to-budget comparisons is to determine why the actual results differed from those that were planned. To determine the underlying reasons for variances requires that comparisons be made as early as possible. Delaying variance computations until the end of a period may impede a manager's ability to detect and, therefore, control variance causes. Providing useful variance computations requires that an effective and prompt variance reporting system must be maintained.

Management should also consider the effects that current changes in conditions may have on future operations and on the types and extent of future budgetary variances. Will increased sales currently mean reduced sales in later periods? Could a current selling price reduction spur product demand sufficiently to increase revenues to total projected levels? Does the increased cost of a raw material make the use of an alternative, higher-quality material more cost beneficial? These are just some of the possible questions that management needs to consider when making actual-to-budget comparisons.

Exhibit 11–8 indicates some possible problems and causes of poor actual-to-budget performance. This figure is not intended to be a comprehensive list, and some factors may work together in performance problems. Once the causes of the performance deviations are known, management may wish to consider budget revisions.

---

[7]Thomas A. Stewart, "Why Budgets Are Bad for Business," *FORTUNE* (June 4, 1990), p. 179.

EXHIBIT 11–8
▼▼▼▼▼▼▼▼▼▼▼

PROBLEMS AND
CAUSES OF POOR
PERFORMANCE

Problem	Possible Causes (or lack of consideration given to):
Sales significantly less than expected	Weakening economic conditions that reduced company product sales volume or necessitated a lower selling price
Direct materials cost significantly higher than expected	Inflation rate that caused direct materials cost to increase; use of higher-quality materials
Compensation cost higher than expected	Changes in labor contract rates or increases in minimum wage law
Overhead cost higher than expected	Increased fringe benefit costs, insurance costs, or utility rates
Severe cash flow difficulties	Declining collection patterns, increases in interest rates and costs, or weakened money supply
Selling expenses higher than expected	Advertising rates increased or media changes were made (substituted TV spots for print advertising)
Interest cost higher than expected	Inflation; tightened money supply
Production not able to keep up with demand	Shortages of critical direct material or supplies

Budget Revisions

Arrangements cannot usually be made rapidly enough to revise the current month's budget. However, under certain circumstances and if they so desire, management may decide to revise future months' budgets. If actual performance is substantially less than what was expected, the budget may or may not be adjusted depending on the causes of the variances. If the causes are beyond the organization's control (such as when the Gulf War caused oil prices to increase dramatically), management may decide to revise budget estimates upward to more realistically reflect costs. If the causes are internal (sales staff simply is not selling the product), management may leave the budget in its original form so that the lack of operational control is visible in the comparisons.

If actual performance is substantially better than expected, budget alterations may be made. However, sometimes when positive results occur, management may not alter the budget so that the positive performance is highlighted. Regardless of whether the budget is revised, managers should commend those responsible and communicate the effects of such performance to related departments. For example, if the sales force has been very effective and has sold significantly higher quantities of product than expected (at the expected selling price), the production and purchasing areas will need to be notified to increase the number of units manufactured and materials bought.

Performance Evaluation

One important reason that management must decide whether to revise is that the budget is often used to evaluate performance. When things do not turn out the way they were expected, management must communicate to those people being evaluated how or if budget revisions will affect their performance evaluations. While revised budgets may provide more accurate information, they also create a fluctuating measure against which people may be uncertain of their performance. Thus, if revised budgets are prepared, top management may want to compare performance to both the original and the revised budgets and then use multiple evaluation tools to judge the quality as well as the quantity of performance.

The possibility that operating managers may attempt to introduce budgetary slack into their budgets was mentioned earlier in the chapter. One method that top management can use to try to reduce slack is to evaluate actual performance against budgeted performance through a bonus system. Operating managers would be rewarded with large bonuses for budgeting relatively high performance levels and achieving those levels. If performance is set at a low or minimal level, achievement of that performance is either not rewarded or only minimally rewarded. Top management must remember that the "most important effect [of budget slack] probably is its detrimental impact on effectiveness and efficiency." [8]

In addition to including budget slack in the process, managers may play other "budget games." Budget games may be played by top management or by lower-level management; some of these games are discussed in Exhibit 11–9. These games exist because of human nature. If managers (either top-level or subordinate) are playing one or more of these games in the budgeting process, performance evaluations will become very ineffective, since many of the numbers become more sham, than real, projections. Company management often expects that good budgets will result simply because participation is allowed and encouraged. Good budgets result only from having responsible individuals involved in the process and from creating an atmosphere of sound interpersonal relationships. In other words, good budgeting relies heavily on trust among the parties involved.

If budgets are to be used in effectively evaluating performance, they should be challenging but achievable. The advantages of using achievable budget targets include the following:[9]

1. Managers' commitment to achieve the budget targets is increased because the managers will have little reason not to be able to meet the targets.

2. Managers' confidence remains high; achievement of the target is perceived as successful performance.

3. Organizational control costs decrease because there is less necessity to apply the management by exception principle when targets are achieved.

4. The risk of managers engaging in harmful short-term "income management" practices (such as delaying maintenance or shifting sales between years) is reduced.

5. Effective managers are allowed greater operating flexibility because they may be able to accumulate some additional resources on the basis of good performance.

6. The corporation is somewhat protected against the costs of optimistic projections, such as overproduction and warehousing.

7. The predictability of corporate earnings is increased because the probability of target achievement is high.

---

[8] Gary J. Mann, "Reducing Budget Slack," *Journal of Accountancy* (August 1989), p. 118.
[9] Kenneth A. Merchant, "How Challenging Should Profit Budget Targets Be?" *Management Accounting* (November 1990), pp. 46–48. Published by Institute of Management Accountants, Montvale, N.J.

EXHIBIT 11–9
▼▼▼▼▼▼▼▼▼▼▼▼▼

BUDGET GAMES

1. The Dictator Game
This game is simply imposed budgeting. The budget is developed by top management and is handed down to lower levels with no room for discussion.

2. The Father-Knows-Best Game
In this game, input is requested from lower-level managers, but either is not used or is changed with no reasons provided. This game allows people to believe at first that they are important to the process, but they recognize in the end that they are not.

3. The Do-What-You-Want (and Fail) Game
In this game, lower-level managers submit their own budgets, which are then used for performance evaluation purposes. Unfortunately, individual managers are not informed of the "big picture" and then at year-end, fail to measure up because their budget figures were (a) too high and unachievable to begin with or (b) too low and not acceptable to begin with.

4. The It's-Not-in-the-Budget Game
In this game, a manager submits a worthwhile project that is turned down because money is unavailable. Then, when the manager's performance level is low, he or she may be criticized for not justifying the project convincingly.

5. The Cut-Everything-10-Percent Game
This game is a favorite of all organizations. Rather than allowing managers to decide to cut certain expenditures and have the opportunity to justify why others need to be raised, the mandate is simply handed down. Managers get to figure out how to play with what remains. A problem with this game, if played too often by top management, is that lower-level managers simply increase their budget requests by 10 percent and, therefore, are not disturbed by the reduction.

6. The End-of-Year (or Spend-It-or-Lose-It) Game
Lower-level managers, recognizing that the end-of-period is near, evaluate the remaining budget dollars per category and spend everything that is left. In this way, they can justify budget increases next year, because "I used everything I was budgeted for this year, and you know costs will increase."

   (The opposite of this game is played by top managers. Budget dollars that were not spent this period are lost, regardless of the reasons. This is a tough game when played with personnel budgets—a person not replaced is a position lost.)

7. The It-Wasn't-My-Fault Game
The object of this game is for a manager to try to shift the blame for failure to meet the budget on someone or something else. This game probably allows for the most creativity. (Hint: The "economy" is always a good target because it's hard to prove or disprove.)

8. The Accounting Change Game
This game requires a high degree of understanding of accounting rules but can work wonders on income statements. Unfortunately, you are only allowed one play for any given accounting change.

9. The Sell-It-No-Matter-What Game
Managers who play this game are probably headed for a transfer and wanting to make a final name for themselves. They should be aware of CVP relationships; if the contribution margin is high and fixed costs are low, then increased volume will pad the bottom line substantially. But if the sales were accomplished using high-pressure techniques or by reducing quality, watch out for returns next period.

(continued)

10. The Build-a-Kingdom Game
This game allows managers to use budgets to create their own kingdoms. The larger the budget that can be obtained, the more "possessions" (equipment, personnel, etc.) the kingdom has. This game provides many opportunities to win friends by helping others maintain or increase their budget requests while extracting promises from those who helped you maintain or increase your kingdom. However, these relationships can only work for a limited period of time before the kingdoms are in competition for the same budget dollars. Then war occurs.

In preparing budgets, managers often create their own kind of Fantasyland by playing a variety of budget games. Budget targets for both revenues and costs should be grounded in reality—not wishful thinking.

The degree of "achievability" needed in budgets to obtain the previous seven benefits depends, of course, on the organization's stage of life, its environmental considerations (past performance, need for sales, types of products, and product life cycles), and its management personnel and their motivation levels.

As indicated in the page 485 News Note, managers must be careful to judge performance (and to engage in the budgeting process itself) with a realistic attitude. Budgets are not the "be-all, end-all" managerial accounting technique. If used properly, they can provide significant benefits; if used improperly, they can cause serious organizational problems.

SITE ANALYSIS

Unlike financial statements for publicly held companies, budgets are not *required* for any businesses (although they are often required for not-for-profit organizations). There are no standardized guidelines as to how budgets should be prepared or in what depth. No survey indicates that *X* percent of all companies prepare formal budgets or companies that do budget fare *Y* percent better in their operations than companies not preparing budgets. But it just seems logical that companies undertaking the budget process encounter some distinct benefits over companies that do not budget.

"A well-designed system of financial controls . . . gives the business owner the information [needed] to track operating performance and squeeze the maximum productivity from the company's cash and other assets. This is as important for the start-up [company] with five employees as it is for a $50 million-a-year enterprise."[10] The information provided allows all managers to focus their attention on areas of success and areas that need improvement.

Successful budgeting must involve people in all organizational disciplines who, as indicated in the Applications Strategies on page 485, also receive the benefits of the process.

CHAPTER SUMMARY

A budget is the primary basis and justification for financial operations in a firm. Budget preparation is part of the tactical planning function. Implementing and administering a budget are parts of the control function. A well-prepared budget provides the following benefits:

1. a detailed path for managers to follow to achieve organizational goals;
2. improved planning and decision making;
3. an allocation of resources among departments;
4. a better understanding of key business variables;
5. a means of employee participation and influence;

---

[10] "Managing Working Capital," *Inc.* (September 1991), pp. 38–39. Reprinted with permission, *Inc.* magazine. Copyright © by Goldhirsch Group Inc., 38 Commercial Wharf, Boston, Mass. 02110.

NEWS NOTE

Budgets Should Direct, Not Control, the Organization

Budgets, forecasts, plans—whatever you call them, you cannot escape the annual ritual. Think of a budget as being like a detailed golf scorecard: It can tell you what clubs you used, how far you hit each drive, whether you made par on the ninth hole, and whether you shot a 72 or an 84. But it cannot tell you if your backswing is lousy or your grip is wrong—knowledge you require to help you play better next Saturday. For tracking where the money goes, budgets are dandy. They become iniquitous when they are made to do more—when the budget becomes management's main tool to gauge performance, or when it distorts long-term planning or blocks managers from shifting resources when they need to. Then the budget becomes an end in itself. Managers lock their radar onto the signals it sends out. "Making the numbers" becomes their overriding goal.

SOURCE: Thomas A. Stewart, "Why Budgets Are Bad for Business," *FORTUNE* (June 4, 1990), p. 179ff. © 1990 The Time Inc. Magazine Company. All rights reserved.

APPLICATIONS STRATEGIES OF MANAGERIAL ASPECTS OF BUDGETING	Discipline	Applications
	Accounting	Integrating budgets and standards into the accounting system is necessary for capturing and reporting variances for cost control purposes; clarity in budget manual is heightened by standardized accounting input
	Economics	Assists managers in using resources effectively and efficiently to provide customers with goods and services at competitive prices; allows persons working within budget guidelines to analyze the allocation of limited resources (especially important in governmental budgeting circumstances); flexible budgets cause recognition of relationships between volume and costs; achievability of budget targets is affected by total economic constraints of supply and demand
	Finance	Provides recognition of necessity for integration among areas' resource wants, needs, and availability; knowledge of achievability (or lack thereof) of budget targets can help future assessment of performance
	Management	Promotes awareness of resource scarcities; strengthens organization's capacity to mobilize internal and external resources; promotes the "art of persuasion" ability in managers through justifying budget requests; forces choices as to goals and objectives; process creates interdisciplinary and interdepartmental discussion and cooperation
	Marketing	Can assess achievability of budget sales targets; targets should reflect media promotion choices; budget manual should provide guidelines on cost standards for various sales techniques; participation in process should motivate sales staff to achieve budget targets

6. a means to determine troublesome or hard-to-control cost areas;

7. a recognition of departmental interrelationships;

8. a means of responding more rapidly to changing economic conditions; and

9. a means by which managerial performance can be judged.

Budgets may be imposed or participatory, but top management is responsible for assuring that the budget is attainable and acceptable. The common budget period is one fiscal year, segmented for quarterly and monthly periods. Continuous budgets may be used to ensure an ongoing, full one-year planning cycle.

Actual operating results should be compared to budget figures to measure how effectively and efficiently organizational goals were met. Sales price and sales volume variances should be calculated before attempting to make expense comparisons. Expense comparisons should be made using budgetary amounts based on the actual level of sales volume achieved rather than originally anticipated budgetary volume. Significant unfavorable differences dictate that managers either attempt to alter behavior of personnel or alter the budget if it appears to be unrealistic. Significant favorable differences may not cause the budget to be adjusted, but should cause communication to affected departments regarding possible consequences. Regardless of whether variances are unfavorable or favorable, feedback to operating personnel is an important part of the budget process.

Budget manuals may be used to assure that procedures are standardized and understood by all parties involved in the process.

To use budgets for performance evaluation, care should be taken that the budget itself is achievable and that managers understand the process by which they will be evaluated. Recognize that budget games may be played and strive to minimize or eliminate their occurrence.

APPENDIX

Zero-Based Budgeting

Traditional budgeting is often limited in its usefulness as a control tool because poor budgeting techniques are often used. That is, many managers preparing budgets begin with the prior year's funding levels and treat these as given and essential to operations. Decisions are then made about whether and by what percentage to incrementally raise existing **appropriations,** which represent maximum allowable expenditures. Such an approach has often resulted in what is known as the "creeping commitment syndrome" in which activities are funded without systematic annual regard for priorities or alternative means for accomplishing objectives.

appropriations

To help eliminate the creeping commitment syndrome, **zero-based budgeting** (ZBB) was originally developed for the government. ZBB is a comprehensive budgeting process that systematically considers the priorities and alternatives for current and proposed activities in relation to organizational objectives. Annual justification of programs and activities is required to have managers rethink priorities within the context of agreed-upon objectives. ZBB does not necessarily mean that each operation is specified from a zero-cost base, since this would be unrealistic and extreme. However, ZBB requires that managers reevaluate all activities at the start of the bud-

zero-based budgeting

Traditional Budgeting	Zero-Based Budgeting
Starts with last year's funding appropriation	Starts with a minimal (or zero) figure for funding
Focuses on money	Focuses on goals and objectives
Does not systematically consider alternatives to current operations	Directly examines alternative approaches to achieve similar results
Produces a single level of appropriation for an activity	Produces alternative levels of funding based on fund availability and desired results

EXHIBIT 11–10
▼▼▼▼▼▼▼▼▼▼▼
DIFFERENCES BETWEEN TRADITIONAL BUDGETING AND ZBB

geting process to make decisions about which activities should be continued, eliminated, or funded at a lower level. Differences between traditional budgeting and zero-based budgeting are shown in Exhibit 11–10.

Zero-based budgeting is applicable in all business organizations, especially in the support and service areas where nonmonetary measures of performance are available. However, zero-based budgeting does not provide measures of efficiency; also, it is difficult to implement because of the significant amount of effort necessary to investigate the causes of prior costs and justify the purposes of budgeted costs.

After deciding upon organizational goals and objectives, there are three steps to the ZBB process: (1) converting the company activities into decision packages; (2) ranking each decision package; and (3) allocating resources based on priorities. A decision package contains information about the activity: objectives and benefits, consequences of not funding, and necessary costs and staffing requirements. The decision packages are then ranked and prioritized on the basis of need, costs, and benefits.

Zero-based budgeting is a rigorous exercise that demands considerable time and effort to be effectively employed. It also requires a wholehearted commitment by the organization's personnel to make it work. Without the time, effort, and commitment needed, ZBB should not be attempted. With these ingredients, an organization can be more effective in planning for and controlling costs. One of the major benefits of zero-based budgeting is that managers focus on identifying non-value-added activities and working to reduce items that cause money to be spent unnecessarily or ineffectively.

An entity should assess whether the benefits of ZBB are worth the costs. Management may consider "zero-basing" certain segments of the company on a rotating basis over a period of years as an alternative to applying the approach to the entire firm annually.

GLOSSARY

Appropriation   a maximum allowable expenditure for a budget item (from appendix)

Budget   the quantitative expression of an organization's commitment to planned activities and resource acquisition and use

Budget committee   a committee, usually composed of top management and the chief financial officer, that reviews and approves, or makes adjustments to, the master budget and/or the budgets submitted from operational managers

Budget manual   a detailed set of documents that provides information and guidelines about the budgetary process

Budget slack   the intentional underestimation of revenues and/or overestimation of expenses

Budgeting   the process of determining a financial plan for future operations

Continuous budget   an ongoing twelve-month budget that is created by successively adding a new budget month (twelve months into the future) as each current month expires

Imposed budget   a budget that is prepared by top management with little or no input from operating personnel, who are simply informed of the budget goals and constraints

Key variable   a critical factor believed to be a direct cause of the achievement or nonachievement of organizational goals and objectives; can be internal or external

Participatory budget   a budget that has been developed through a process of joint decision making by top management and operating personnel

Sales price variance   the difference between actual and budgeted selling prices multiplied by the actual number of units sold

Sales volume variance   the difference between actual and budgeted volumes multiplied by the budgeted selling price

Strategic planning   the process of developing a statement of long-range (five to ten years) goals for the organization and defining the strategies and policies that will help the organization achieve those goals

Tactical planning   the process of determining the specific objectives and means by which strategic plans will be achieved; are short-term (one to eighteen months), single use plans that have been developed to address a given set of circumstances or for a specific time frame

Zero-based budgeting   a comprehensive budgeting process that systematically considers the priorities and alternatives for current and proposed activities in relation to organizational objectives (from appendix)

Selected Bibliography

Appleyard, A. R., et al. "Multi-Currency Budgeting by Multinational Companies." *British Accounting Review* 12, no. 2 (1991), pp. 105–21.

Chenhall, R. H., and P. Brownell. "The Effects of Participative Budgeting on Job Satisfaction and Performance: Role Ambiguity as an Intervening Variable." *Accounting, Organizations, and Society* 13, no. 3 (1988), pp. 225–33.

Collins, Frank, et al. "The Budgeting Games People Play." *The Accounting Review* (January 1987), pp. 29–49.

Finch, Gerald L. "Improving the Bottom Line." *Management Accounting* (October 1987), pp. 42–43ff.

Koehler, Kenneth G. "Link Budget to Overall Plan." *CMA* [published in Canada] (May–June 1987), p. 17.

SOLUTION STRATEGIES

Budget Manual

Should include:

1. statements of the budgetary purpose and its desired results;
2. a listing of specific budgetary activities to be performed;
3. a calendar of scheduled budgetary activities;
4. sample budgetary forms; and
5. original, revised, and approved budgets.

Revenue Variances

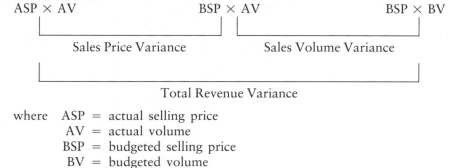

where
ASP = actual selling price
AV = actual volume
BSP = budgeted selling price
BV = budgeted volume

END-OF-CHAPTER MATERIALS

Questions

1. Why is budgeting important? Discuss the reasons why it would be more important in some organizations than in others.

2. Briefly describe the basic budgeting process. Which steps would you consider the most critical?

3. How do goals and objectives differ? Give three examples in which a goal could be quantifiable.

4. How is the budget an effective communication device?

5. Explain how strategic and tactical planning differ.

6. How are strategic and tactical planning related to budgeting? Present a model that depicts the relationship.

7. When are imposed budgets appropriate? Why?

8. Why do most organizations use participatory budgets? Discuss the disadvantages of using such budgets.

9. Define budget slack. Why does it occur and what might be done to reduce or eliminate it?

10. What is meant by the comment, ". . . good budgeting relies on trust"?

11. What is a continuous budget?

12. List the various sections of the budget manual and briefly explain the reasons for each section.

13. Explain how managerial control is related to budgeting.

14. Why is it important that budget targets be achievable?

15. (Appendix) What is zero-based budgeting? Why do you think it was started in the government sector rather than in the business sector?

▌ Exercises

16. *(Terminology)* Match the numbered item on the right with the lettered term on the left.

a. Key variable	1. Developed through joint decision making of top managers and operating personnel
b. Goal	2. A quantitative expression of a commitment to planned activities and resource acquisition and use
c. Budgeting	3. A desired abstract achievement
d. Objective	4. Prepared by top managers with little or no input from operating personnel
e. Imposed budget	5. Critical causal factor in achievement of organizational goals and objectives
f. Budget	6. A desired quantifiable achievement for a period of time
g. Participatory budget	7. Developing a quantitative plan in financial terms to satisfy company goals and objectives

17. *(Terminology)* Match the numbered item on the right with the lettered term on the left.

a. Tactical planning	1. Difference in revenue caused by the difference between actual and budgeted selling prices
b. Budget slack	2. Developing long-term goals, strategies, and policies
c. Sales volume variance	3. Difference in revenue caused by the difference between actual and budgeted demand
d. Strategic planning	4. Determining short-term (twelve to eighteen months) specific objectives and the means by which strategic plans will be achieved
e. Sales price variance	5. Intentional budgetary underestimation of revenues or overestimation of expenses
f. Appropriation (appendix)	6. Systematically (re)considers current or proposed activities in light of priorities and alternatives for achievement of organizational goals and objectives
g. Zero-based budgeting (appendix)	7. Maximum allowable expenditure for an item in the budget

18. *(Imposed vs. participatory budgets)* Indicate which of the following is an advantage of imposed budgets (AI), an advantage of a participatory budget (AP), or neither (N).

1. Develops fiscal responsibility and budgetary skills of operating personnel
2. Blends overview of top management with operating details
3. Reduces budgeting to inputting data into a computer program
4. Increases chances that strategic plans are incorporated into planned activities
5. Allows operating managers to completely take over the budgeting process
6. Incorporates top management's knowledge of overall resource availability
7. Produces more realistic budgets
8. Improves morale and motivation
9. Encourages operating managers to establish the long-run company goals
10. Incorporates inputs from persons most familiar with the needs and constraints of organizational units

19. *(Sales variances)* Cristin Company planned 1994 sales of 360,000 units at a $30 unit selling price. In early 1995, the company president asked why budgeted revenue had not been achieved. Investigation revealed the following:

Actual sales volume	365,000
Actual average sales price	$29

Analyze the previous facts and provide an explanation for the president.

20. *(Sales variances)* The manager of a small vineyard has been asked by the company owner why sales of grapes were below budget by $736. Review of the budget reveals that revenue from grape sales was $21,000, based on expected sales of 30,000 pounds at $.70 per pound. Inspection of the records shows that 29,800 pounds were actually sold at $.68 per pound. Analyze sales and explain what happened.

21. *(Sales variances)* John Foster delivers two-day motivational seminars for management leaders. Each program normally brings John a $3,000 fee, and last year he presented 30 such seminars. He budgeted a 20 percent increase in programs to be presented in the current year. At the end of the current year, he was disappointed that actual revenue was only $103,600. He presented 37 programs.

a. What was Mr. Foster's expected revenue for the current year?
b. Analyze why he did not achieve the budgeted revenue.

22. *(Budget-to-actual comparison)* Phil Preddy does wedding photography on weekends. He has been charging $225 for a complete album, and his costs have averaged $78 each. He believes he can book 30 weddings in 1994, and on that basis he prepared the following budget:

Revenue (30 × $225)	$6,750
Costs (30 × $78)	2,340
Projected profits	$4,410

In 1995, Phil was contemplating his results and was disappointed that his profits were only $4,256. He asks your help in understanding the shortfall. Review of his journal shows that his fee averaged $218 per wedding and that his costs averaged $85. Phil photographed 32 weddings in 1994.

Explain to Phil why he made less than he budgeted. (Hint: With regard to costs, analyze them using the same model as was presented in the chapter to analyze revenues.)

23. *(Causes of poor performance)* Match the numbered best possible causes on the right with the lettered problems on the left in assessing poor performance (more

than one numbered cause may be appropriately matched with a problem, and a cause can be used more than once).

a. Compensation cost higher than expected	1. Shortage in supply of direct materials was greater than expected
b. Sales volume less than expected	2. Increased rates for fringe benefits, insurance, or utilities
c. Severe cash flow difficulties	3. Increase in labor contract rates or minimum wage law
d. Overhead cost higher than expected	4. Recessionary economic conditions
e. Production cannot keep up with demand	5. Inflation
f. Selling expense higher than expected	6. Declining collection patterns
g. Direct materials cost higher than expected	7. Operations are at a maximum capacity
h. Interest cost higher than expected	8. Advertising rates increased

24. *(Budget games)* Match the numbered descriptions on the right with the lettered names of budget games on the left.

Name of Game	Description
a. It-Wasn't-My-Fault	1. Trying to increase the bottom line without regard to reducing customer satisfaction and subsequent sales returns
b. It's-Not-in-the-Budget	2. Imposed budgeting with no room for discussion
c. The Accounting Change	3. Mandated across-the-board cuts without opportunity to justify selected increases and decreases
d. Build-a-Kingdom	4. Inputs by operating personnel are encouraged but subsequently ignored
e. Sell-It-No-Matter-What	5. Worthwhile projects are rejected, and manager is later blamed for low performance because the project was not adequately justified
f. The Dictator	6. Changing accounting methods to influence calculated net income
g. Father-Knows-Best	7. Shifting blame for failure to achieve budget to someone else or something else
h. Cut-Everything-10-Percent	8. Pushing for larger budgets to gain power
i. Spend-It-or-Lose-It	9. Withholding support information; allowing a subordinate manager to undertake budgetary projects that are probably destined to fail
j. Do-What-You-Want	10. Spending everything left at end of period in a budget so that next period's budget will not be reduced

25. *(Essay)* Discuss the contents, need for, and advantages of a budget manual.

26. *(Essay)* Discuss what is likely to occur in a large firm that decides not to prepare an annual budget.

27. *(Essay)* Successful business organizations appear to be those that have clearly defined long-range goals and a well-planned strategy to reach those goals. These

successful organizations understand the markets in which they do business as well as their internal strengths and weaknesses. These organizations take advantage of this knowledge to grow (through internal development or acquisitions) in a consistent and disciplined manner.

a. Discuss the need for long-range goals for business organizations.

b. Discuss how long-range goals are set.

c. Define the concepts of strategic planning and management control. Discuss how they relate to each other and contribute to the progress toward the attainment of long-range goals.

(CMA)

28. *(Essay)* Rouge Corporation is a medium-size company in the steel fabrication industry with six divisions located in different geographical sectors of the United States. Considerable autonomy in operational management is permitted in the divisions, due in part to the distance between corporate headquarters in St. Louis and five of the six divisions. Corporate management establishes divisional budgets using prior year data adjusted for industry and economic changes expected for the coming year. Budgets are prepared by year and by quarter, with top management attempting to recognize problems unique to each division in the divisional budget-setting process. Once the year's divisional budgets are set by corporate management, they cannot be modified by division management.

The budget for calendar year 1993 projects total corporate net income before taxes of $3,750,000 for the year, including $937,500 for the first quarter. Results of first-quarter operations presented to corporate management in early April showed corporate net income of $865,000, which was $72,500 below the projected net income for the quarter. The St. Louis Division operated at 4.5 percent above its projected divisional net income, while the other five divisions showed net incomes with variances ranging from 1.5 to 22 percent below budgeted net income.

Corporate managers are concerned with the first-quarter results because they believe strongly that differences between divisions had been recognized. An entire day in late November of last year had been spent presenting and explaining the corporate and divisional budgets to the division managers and their division controllers. A mid-April meeting of corporate and division management has generated unusual candor. All five out-of-state division managers cited reasons why first-quarter results in their respective divisions represented effective management and was the best that could be expected. Corporate management has remained unconvinced and informs division managers that "results will be brought into line with the budget by the end of the second quarter."

a. Identify and explain the major disadvantages in the procedures employed by Rouge Corporation's corporate management in preparing and implementing the divisional budgets.

b. Discuss the behavioral problems that may arise by requiring Rouge Corporation's division managers to meet the quarterly budgeted net income figures as well as the annual budgeted net income.

(CMA)

29. *(Essay)* Lymar Products is a divisionalized corporation in the agribusiness industry with its corporate headquarters in Philadelphia. The R&D Division is located in central Illinois and is responsible for all of the corporation's seed, fertilizer, and insecticide research and development. The R&D is conducted primarily for the benefit of Lymar's other operating divisions. The R&D Division conducts

contract research for outside firms when such research does not interfere with the division's regular work or does not represent work that is directly competitive with Lymar's interests.

Lymar's annual budget preparation begins approximately five months before the beginning of the fiscal year. Each division manager is responsible for developing the budget for his or her division within the guidelines provided by corporate headquarters. Once the annual budget procedure is completed and the budget is accepted and approved, the division managers have complete authority to operate within the limits prescribed by the budget.

The budget procedures apply to the R&D Division. However, because this division does work for other Lymar divisions and for the corporate office, careful coordination between the R&D Division and the other units is needed to construct a good budget for the R&D Division. Further, the costs associated with the contract research require special consideration by Lymar's management. In the past, there has been good cooperation that has resulted in sound budget practices.

R&D's management always has presented well-documented budgets for both the internal and external contract research. When the submitted budget has been changed, the revisions are the result of review, discussion, and agreement between R&D's management and corporate management.

Staff travel is a major item included in R&D's budget. Some twenty-five to thirty-five trips are made annually to corporate headquarters for meetings by R&D's employees. In addition, the division's technical staff make trips related to their research projects and are expected to attend professional meetings and seminars. These trips always have been detailed in a supporting schedule presented with the annual budget.

Lymar's performance for the current year is considered reasonable in light of current and expected future poor economic conditions, but corporate management has become extremely cost conscious. Divisions have been directed to cut down on any unnecessary spending. A specific new directive has been issued stating that any travel in excess of $500 must now be approved in advance by corporate headquarters. In addition, once a division's total dollar amount budgeted for travel has been spent, no budget overruns would be allowed. This directive is effective immediately, and corporate management has indicated that it will continue to be in effect for at least the next two years.

The R&D manager is concerned because this directive appears to represent a change in budget policy. Now, travel that was thought already approved because it was included in the annual budget must be reapproved before each trip. In addition, some scheduled trips previously approved may have to be canceled because travel funds are likely to run out before the end of the year. R&D staff members already have had to make five special trips to corporate headquarters that were not included in the current year's budget.

The new directive will probably increase costs. The approval process may delay the purchase of airline tickets, thus reducing the opportunity to obtain the lowest fares. Further, there will be a major increase in paperwork for the R&D Division because virtually every trip exceeds the $500 limit.

a. The directive requiring the reapproval of all travel in excess of $500 could have far-reaching effects for Lymar Products.

    1. Explain how this directive could affect the entire budget process, especially the validity of the annual budget.

   2. Explain what effect this directive is likely to have on the care with which divisions prepare their annual travel budgets in the future.

   b. Explain what effect the directive on reapproval of travel costs is likely to have on the morale and motivation of the division manager and research staff of the R&D Division.

(CMA)

Cases

30. Following is a list of typical questions that are raised and dealt with during the process of strategic planning. Assume that you are part of top management in one of the following types of organizations: a major automotive manufacturer; a major charitable organization; a major pharmaceutical company; a major airline; a major advertising agency; or a major hospital chain. Obtain several current annual reports (if available) from a particular company of your choice, perform some library (or other type of) research, and do some creative thinking to prepare a research paper that answers these questions about that company.

   • What is the company's justification for existence?
   • What will be the environment in which the company will operate?

      Nature of the industry
      Nature of the competitive situation
      Nature of the general economy
      Political situation in markets served and potential markets

   • What are the key variables to being successful in this industry?
   • What product, product lines, and market should the company be in?

      What is the company good at doing?
      What directions should the company take in relation to: new products, new markets, development of existing products, and development of existing markets?

   • What are the company's strengths and weaknesses?

      In organization
      In facilities
      In finance

   • Where is the company now and where does it appear to be heading?

      What has the company accomplished?
      How does it stand financially, organizationally, and in its industry?
      Should it consider any acquisitions? Which ones and why?

   • What assumptions should be made about the future with respect to sales, profit, growth, return on investment, and other factors?

(Questions adapted from Clarence B. Nickerson, *Accounting Handbook for Nonaccountants* [Boston: Cahners Books International, 1975], pp. 533–34. Used with permission of Cahners Publishing Company, a division of Reed Publishing [USA] Inc.)

31. *(Note: Includes variances and sales mix)* The Markley Division of Rosette Industries manufactures and sells patio chairs. The chairs are manufactured in two versions—a metal model and a plastic model of a lesser quality. The company uses its own sales force to sell the chairs to retail stores and to catalog outlets. Generally, customers purchase both the metal and the plastic versions.

   The chairs are manufactured on two different assembly lines located in adjoining buildings. The division management and sales department occupy the third building on the property. The division management includes a division controller responsible for the divisional financial activities and the preparation of reports explaining the differences between actual and budgeted performance. The controller structures these reports such that the sales activities are distinguished from cost factors so that each can be analyzed separately.

The operating results for the first three months of the fiscal year as compared to the budget follow. The budget for the current year was based upon the assumption that Markley Division would maintain its present market share of the estimated total patio chair market (plastic and metal combined). A status report had been sent to corporate management toward the end of the second month indicating that divisional operating income for the first quarter would probably be about 45 percent below budget; this estimate was just about on target. The division's operating income was below budget even though industry volume for patio chairs increased by 10 percent more than was expected at the time the budget was developed.

	Actual	Budget	Favorable (Unfavorable) Relative to the Budget
Sales in units			
Plastic model	60,000	50,000	10,000
Metal model	20,000	25,000	(5,000)
Sales revenue			
Plastic model	$630,000	$500,000	$130,000
Metal model	300,000	375,000	(75,000)
Total sales	$930,000	$875,000	$ 55,000
Less variable costs			
Manufacturing (at standard)			
Plastic model	$480,000	$400,000	$(80,000)
Metal model	200,000	250,000	50,000
Selling			
Commissions	46,500	43,750	($2,750)
Bad debt allowance	9,300	8,750	($550)
Total variable costs (except variable manufacturing variances)	$735,800	$702,500	$(33,300)
Contribution margin (except variable manufacturing variances)	$194,200	$172,500	$ 21,700
Less other costs			
Variable manufacturing cost variances from standard	$ 49,600	$ 0	$(49,600)
Fixed manufacturing costs	49,200	48,000	(1,200)
Fixed selling & administrative costs	38,500	36,000	(2,500)
Allocation of corporate office costs	18,500	17,500	(1,000)
Total other costs	$155,800	$101,500	$(54,300)
Divisional operational income	$ 38,400	$ 71,000	$(32,600)

The manufacturing activities for the quarter resulted in the production of 55,000 plastic chairs and 22,500 metal chairs. The costs incurred by each manufacturing unit follow. The raw materials quantities are stated in terms of the equivalents of finished chairs; for example, although 55,000 plastic chairs were produced, the company purchased enough material for 60,000 chairs and used enough material to make 56,000 chairs.

	Quantity	Price	Plastic Model	Metal Model
Purchases				
Plastic	60,000	$5.65	$339,000	
Metal	30,000	$6.00		$180,000
Usage				
Plastic	56,000	$5.00	280,000	
Metal	23,000	$6.00		138,000
Direct labor				
9,300 hours @ $6.00 per hour			55,800	
5,600 hours @ $8.00 per hour				44,800
Manufacturing overhead				
Variable				
Supplies			43,000	18,000
Power			50,000	15,000
Employee benefits			19,000	12,000
Fixed				
Supervision			14,000	11,000
Depreciation			12,000	9,000
Property taxes & other items			1,900	1,300

The standard variable manufacturing costs per unit and the budgeted monthly fixed manufacturing costs established for the current year are presented next.

	Plastic Model	Metal Model
Raw material	$5.00	$ 6.00
Direct labor		
⅙ hour @ $6.00 per DLH	1.00	
¼ hour @ $8.00 per DLH		2.00
Variable overhead		
⅙ hour @ $12.00 per DLH	2.00	
¼ hour @ $8.00 per DLH		2.00
Standard variable manufacturing cost per unit	$8.00	$10.00
Budgeted fixed costs per month		
Supervision	$4,500	$3,500
Depreciation	4,000	3,000
Property taxes & other fixed costs	600	400
Total budgeted fixed costs for month	$9,100	$6,900

a. Explain the variance in Markley Division's contribution margin attributable to sales activities by calculating the:
   1. sales price variance.
   2. sales mix variance. Hint: Compute as (actual total units sold × {budgeted UCM − [(actual TCM − price variance) ÷ actual units sold]}).
   3. sales volume variance.
b. What portion of the sales volume variance, if any, can be attributed to a change in Markley Division's market share?
c. Analyze the variance in Markley Division's variable manufacturing costs ($49,600) in as much detail as the data permit.

d. Based upon your analyses prepared for parts a, b, and c:
   1. Identify the major cause of Markley Division's unfavorable profit performance.
   2. Did Markley's management attempt to correct this problem? Explain your answer.
   3. What other steps, if any, could Markley's management have taken to improve the division's operating income. Explain your answer.

(CMA)

▌ Ethics Discussion

32. Many managers believe that if all amounts in their budgets are not spent during a period, they will lose allocations in future periods and little or no recognition will result from cost savings. The following figure indicates results of a survey of IMA (formerly NAA) members about the motivating factors behind budgeting issues:

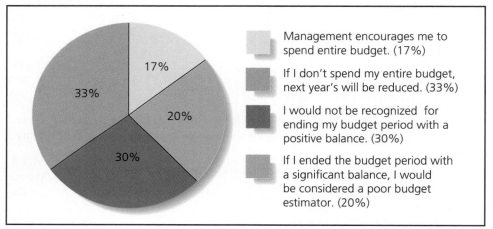

SOURCE: Gerald L. Finch and William Mihal, "Spend It or Lose It," *Management Accounting* (March 1989), p. 45. Published by Institute of Management Accountants, Montvale, N.J.

Discuss the behavioral and ethical issues involved in a "spend it or lose it" attitude. Include in your discussion the issue of negotiating budget allocation requests before the beginning of the period.

33. Assume that you are a top manager in an advertising firm with eight regional locations. Kim Taylor is the manager in charge of the Denver office of the firm.

In 1993, Kim worked diligently with her staff on creating an optimal budget for her office; she believed the amounts for revenues and expenses were as precisely forecasted as they could be. When you received her 1993 budget, you immediately increased her expected revenues 15 percent and reduced all expense categories by 10 percent. You informed her that you believed her office capable of dealing with both adjustments. Near the end of 1993, it was obvious that Kim's office would probably come in about 12 percent below her increased budget in revenues and almost exactly equal to her original estimates in regard to costs.

Although 1993 is not over yet, it is time for Kim to prepare the 1994 budget. She again elicits substantial information from her staff and prepares a detailed budget. Before sending it to you, however, she reduces revenues by 20 percent and increases costs by 15 percent in each category.

a. What justifications might you have had for making the 1993 changes to Kim's budget? How ethical was it of you to make the changes to her budget without consulting her after asking for her input?

b. Why would Kim not have sent the same type of accurate forecast to you in 1994 as she did in 1993? How ethical is it of her to have made the budget misstatements?

c. Since advertising firms are not manufacturing products, would Kim's attitude about understanding her revenues have any effects on other offices of the firm?

34. Norton Company, a manufacturer of infant furniture and carriages, is in the initial stages of preparing the annual budget for 1994. Scott Ford has recently joined Norton's accounting staff and is interested to learn as much as possible about the company's budgeting process. During a recent lunch with Marge Atkins, sales manager, and Pete Granger, production manager, Ford initiated the following conversation:

Ford: "Since I'm new around here and am going to be involved with the preparation of the annual budget, I'd be interested to learn how the two of you estimate sales and production numbers."

Atkins: "We start out very methodically by looking at recent history, discussing what we know about current accounts, potential customers, and the general state of consumer spending. Then we add that usual dose of intuition to come up with the best forecast we can."

Granger: "I usually take the sales projections as the basis for my projections. Of course, we have to make an estimate of what this year's closing inventories will be, which is sometimes difficult."

Ford: "Why does that present a problem? There must have been an estimate of closing inventories in the budget for the current year."

Granger: "Those numbers aren't always reliable, since Marge makes some adjustments to the sales numbers before passing them on to me."

Ford: "What kind of adjustments?"

Atkins: "Well, we don't want to fall short of the sales projections, so we generally give ourselves a little breathing room by lowering the initial sales projection anywhere from 5 to 10 percent."

Granger: "So, you can see why this year's budget is not a very reliable starting point. We always have to adjust the projected production rates as the year progresses and, of course, this changes the ending inventory estimates. By the way, we make similar adjustments to expenses by adding at least 10 percent to the estimates. I think everyone around here does the same thing."

a. Marge Atkins and Pete Granger have described the use of budgetary slack.
   1. Explain why Atkins and Granger behave in this manner, and describe the benefits they expect to realize from the use of budgetary slack.
   2. Explain how the use of budgetary slack can adversely affect Atkins and Granger.

b. As a management accountant, Scott Ford believes that the behavior described by Marge Atkins and Pete Granger may be unethical and that he may have an obligation not to support this behavior. By citing the specific standards of competence, confidentiality, integrity, and/or objectivity from *Statements on Management Accounting*, "Standards of Ethical Conduct for Management Accountants" (Exhibit 1–6 in your text), explain why the use of budgetary slack may be unethical.

(CMA)

C H A P T E R   12

THE MASTER BUDGET

LEARNING OBJECTIVES

After completing this chapter, you should be able to do the following:

1. Determine the starting point of a master budget and why this item is chosen
2. Prepare the various master budget schedules
3. Relate the various master budget schedules to one another
4. Understand why the cash budget is so important in the master budgeting process
5. Relate the statement of cash flows to the income statement and the cash budget

U.S. Catholic Church Benefits from Budgets

For years, the U.S. Catholic Church hummed along without much concern for the bottom line. Budgets were perfunctory. Contributions declined while costs rose. The Chicago Archdiocese, after a $47 million deficit in 1989, closed 47 churches and schools in 1990. The Cardinal's financial advisory committee recommended consolidating parishes and schools, reining in spending, and tracking costs more closely. Parishes must now submit three-year budgets and quarterly financial reports. Pastors exceeding their budgets are called in for consultation and urged to cut expenses.

Adapted from Kevin Kelly, "Chicago's Catholic Church: Putting Its House in Order," *Business Week* (June 10, 1991), p. 60ff.

R egardless of the type of endeavor in which you engage, it is necessary at some point to visualize the future, imagine what results you want to occur, and determine the activities and resources required to achieve those results. If the process is complex, the means by which results are to be obtained should be written. Writing out complex plans is necessary because of the human tendency to forget and the difficulty of mentally processing many facts and relationships at the same time. Written plans that are monetarily enumerated are called budgets. While budgeting is important for everyone, organizations (such as the Catholic church, IBM, New York City, or Circuit City electronics stores) that have significant amounts of cash and other resources should prepare and use detailed budgets for both planning and control purposes.

Chapter 11 covers the managerial aspects of the budgeting process. This chapter covers the quantitative aspects of the budgeting process and the preparation of a master budget.

THE MASTER BUDGET

The budgeting process culminates, from an accounting standpoint, in the preparation of a **master budget,** or comprehensive set of all budgetary schedules and the pro forma financial statements of an organization. The master budget is composed of both operating and financial budgets. **Operating budgets** are expressed in both units and dollars. When an operating budget is related to revenues, the units are those expected to be sold and the dollars reflect selling prices. When an operating budget relates to expense items, the units are those expected to be used and the dollars reflect costs.

master budget

operating budgets

Monetary details from the operating budgets are aggregated to prepare **financial budgets** that reflect the funds to be generated or consumed during the budget period. Financial budgets include the company's cash and capital budgets as well as its pro-

financial budgets

501

Budgets are important planning and control tools. The Archdiocese of Chicago recognizes that revenue and cost budgets would help determine the viability of its various organizational programs.

jected or pro forma financial statements. These budgets are the ultimate focal points for the firm's top management.

The master budget is prepared for a specific period and is static rather than flexible. It is static in that it is based on a single, most probable level of output demand. Expressing the budget on a single level of output is necessary to facilitate the many time-consuming financial arrangements that must be made before beginning operations for the budget period. Such arrangements include hiring an adequate number of people, obtaining needed production and/or storage space, obtaining suppliers, and confirming prices, delivery schedules, and quality of resources.

The output level of sales or service quantities selected for use in the master budget preparation affects all organizational components. It is essential that all the components interact in a coordinated manner. Exhibit 12–1 indicates the budgetary interactions among the primary departments of a manufacturing organization. A budget developed by one department is commonly an essential ingredient in the development of another department's budget.

The budgetary process shown in Exhibit 12–1 begins with the Sales Department's estimates of the types, quantities, and timing of demand for the company's products. This information is needed by both Production and Accounts Receivable. The production manager combines sales estimates with information from Purchasing, Personnel, Operations, and Capital Facilities to be able to specify the types, quantities, and timing of products to be manufactured and transferred to finished goods. Accounts Receivable uses sales estimates, in conjunction with estimated collection patterns, to determine the amounts and timing of cash receipts. Cash receipts information is necessary for the treasurer to properly manage the organization's flow of funds. All areas create cash disbursements that must be matched with cash receipts so that cash is available when it is needed.

Note that certain information must flow back into a department from which it began. For example, the Sales Department must receive finished goods information to know if goods are in stock (or can be produced to order) before selling products. The treasurer must receive continual input information on cash receipts and disbursements as well as provide output information to various organizational units on the availability of funds so that proper funds management can be maintained.

EXHIBIT 12–1
▼▼▼▼▼▼▼▼▼▼▼

THE BUDGETARY
PROCESS IN A
MANUFACTURING
ORGANIZATION

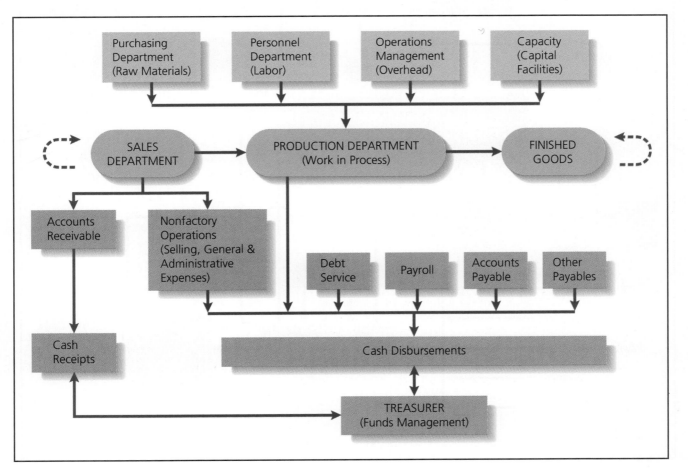

Assuming that top management is engaging in participatory budgeting, each department in the budgetary process either prepares its own budget or provides information for inclusion in a budget. Master budget preparation begins with a sales budget (provided by the marketing area) based on expected demand. Production activities and cash flows are planned using the chosen level of sales and, ultimately, pro forma financial statements are prepared.

Exhibit 12–2 presents an overview of the master budget preparation sequence and component budgets, indicates the department responsible for each budget's preparation, and illustrates how the budgets relate to one another. While the flow of in-

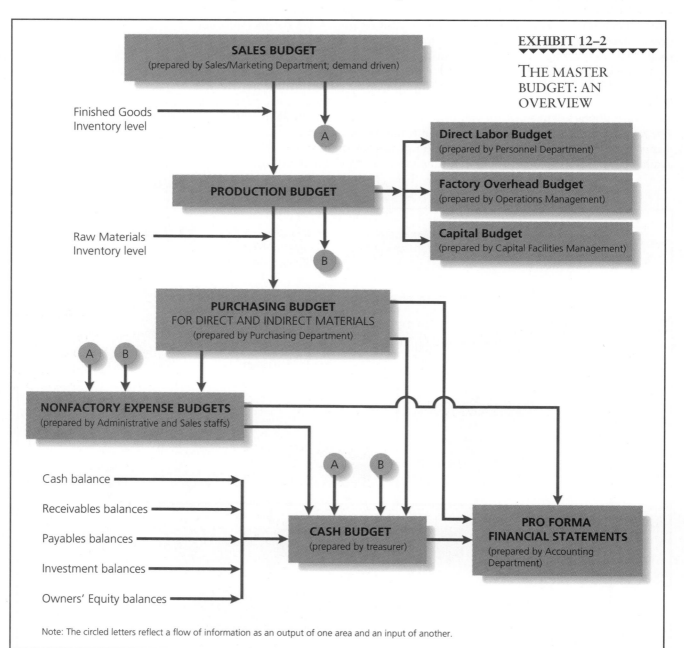

EXHIBIT 12–2

THE MASTER BUDGET: AN OVERVIEW

Note: The circled letters reflect a flow of information as an output of one area and an input of another.

formation is visible from Exhibit 12–2, the quantitative and monetary implications are not. The remainder of the chapter reflects these implications through the preparation of a master budget.

THE MASTER BUDGET ILLUSTRATED

Tidewater Production Company is used to illustrate the process of preparing a master budget for 1994. The company produces a single product called "McMonsters," which are small, bendable creatures in a variety of colors. The master budget is prepared for the entire year and then subdivided into quarterly and monthly periods. Tidewater's marketing division has estimated total sales for the year at 4,000,000 creatures. While annual sales would be detailed on a monthly basis, the Tidewater illustration focuses only on the first-quarter budgets. The process of developing the master budget is the same regardless of whether the time frame is one year or one quarter.

The December 31, 1993, balance sheet presented in Exhibit 12–3 provides the account balances needed to prepare the master budget. The December 31 balances are really estimates rather than actual figures because the budget process for 1994 must begin significantly before December 31, 1993. A company's budgetary time schedule depends on many factors including its size and degree of forecasting sophistication. Tidewater starts its budgeting process in November 1993 when the sales forecast is received by management or the budget committee.

EXHIBIT 12–3

▼▼▼▼▼▼▼▼▼▼▼

TIDEWATER PRODUCTION COMPANY BALANCE SHEET (ESTIMATED) DECEMBER 31, 1993

Assets		
Current Assets		
Cash		$ 5,050
Accounts Receivable	$ 84,000	
Less Allowance for Uncollectibles	(1,200)	82,800
Inventories		
Direct Materials	$ 8,758	
Finished Goods (30,800 units @ $.35)	10,780	19,538
Total Current Assets		$107,388
Plant Assets		
Property, Plant & Equipment	$540,000	
Less Accumulated Depreciation	(180,000)	360,000
TOTAL ASSETS		$467,388

Liabilities & Stockholders' Equity		
Current Liabilities		
Accounts Payable		$ 48,757
Dividends Payable (due 1/15/94)		15,000
Total Current Liabilities		$ 63,757
Stockholders' Equity		
Common Stock	$300,000	
Retained Earnings	103,631	403,631
TOTAL LIABILITIES AND STOCKHOLDERS' EQUITY		$467,388

	January	February	March	Total for Quarter	April	May
Sales in units	440,000	410,000	387,000	1,237,000	360,000	390,000
Sales in dollars	$220,000	$205,000	$193,500	$ 618,500	$180,000	$195,000

EXHIBIT 12–4
▼▼▼▼▼▼▼▼▼▼▼▼

TIDEWATER
PRODUCTION
COMPANY SALES
BUDGET (FOR THE
THREE MONTHS
AND QUARTER
ENDING MARCH 31,
1994)

Sales Budget

The sales budget is prepared in terms of both units and sales dollars. The selling price set for 1994 is $.50 per McMonster, and the price is the same for all sales territories and all customers. Monthly sales demand and revenue for the first five months of 1994 are shown in Exhibit 12–4. Dollar sales figures are computed by multiplying sales quantities by product selling price. April and May information is presented because it is needed later to determine production information for the March budget. The "Total for Quarter" column reflects sales for only January, February, and March.

The following News Note indicates the importance of analyzing the characteristics associated with the market when preparing a sales budget. While such analysis is important domestically, it is absolutely essential when the company is involved in international operations.

Stockpiled inventory ties up facility space and slows down cash flow. Minimizing the time between production/purchase and sale of goods reduces the non-value-added activities as well as the possibility of market value declines due to inventory deterioration or obsolescence.

Budgeting Sales on an International Basis is a Complex Task

Budgeting is impacted by conditions tied to a multinational's international business operations. Multinationals must be aware of and respond to the conditions of each market they serve, including the level of economic development, degree of government price control, cost of sales in each market, product pricing decisions for each market (e.g., standard mark-up, market prices), available channels of distribution and promotion, and import/export controls.

Dawson/Berg Corporation is a multinational entity that does business in several areas of the world. In preparing its sales budget, the following analysis might occur:

Region/Country	Dominant and Distinctive Market Characteristic
Canada	U.S./Canada Free Trade Agreement
Denmark	Strong local competition
Eastern Europe	Recent democratization and uncertain trade regulations
European Community	Upcoming EC92 economic integration
France	Price controls
Germany	New and uncertain situation caused by the reunification of the country
Japan	Complex distribution system
Pacific Rim	New area with many developing countries offering a growing consumer base
United States	Specific market penetration is desired in a highly segmented market

[Factors requiring consideration may] arise from a specific nation's characteristics [or] from international forces. Whatever their origin, [t]he existence of these differences indicates that marketing strategies and the resulting sales budget cannot be transplanted merely from domestic operations to a foreign operation.

SOURCE: Paul V. Mannino and Ken Milani, "Budgeting for an International Business," *Management Accounting* (February 1992), p. 39. Published by Institute of Management Accounting, Montvale, N.J.

Production Budget

The production budget follows naturally from the sales budget and uses the information regarding the type, quantity, and timing of units to be sold. Sales information is combined with information on beginning and ending inventories so that managers can schedule the necessary production.

Ending inventory policy (as to quantity of units) is generally specified by company management. Desired ending inventory is normally a function of the quantity and timing of demand in the upcoming period as related to the capacity and speed of the firm to produce goods. Before making a decision about how much inventory to keep on hand, managers should consider the high costs of stockpiling inventory. Management may stipulate that ending inventory be a given percentage of the next period's projected sales. Other alternatives include a constant amount of inventory, a

EXHIBIT 12–5

TIDEWATER
PRODUCTION
COMPANY
PRODUCTION
BUDGET (FOR THE
THREE MONTHS
AND QUARTER
ENDING MARCH 31,
1994)

	January	February	March	Total
Sales in units				
(from Exhibit 12–4)	440,000	410,000	387,000	1,237,000
+ Desired ending inventory	28,700	27,090	25,200	25,200
Total needed	468,700	437,090	412,200	1,262,200
− Beginning inventory	30,800	28,700	27,090	30,800
Units to be produced	437,900	408,390	385,110	1,231,400

Note: January's beginning inventory is from Exhibit 12–3. April's production would be 360,000 + 27,300 − 25,200 = 362,100.

buildup of inventory for future high-demand periods, or near-zero inventory under a just-in-time system. The decision about ending inventory levels affects whether a firm has constant production with varying inventory levels or variable production with constant inventory levels. And, as indicated in the following quote, the size of the inventory is also directly related to cash flow.

> Mismanagement of your company's inventory can create a financial hemorrhage that may cripple the business for life. Excessive inventory purchases, slow-moving inventory, and the inability to reorder in a timely fashion can all wreak havoc on your cash flow. Remember that inventory is "cash" sitting on your shelves without earning any interest. Actually, it may be one of your firm's larger expenditures, depending on the type of business and industry you are in.[1]

Demand for McMonsters varies throughout the year, and Tidewater carries very little inventory. Production time is short, so company management has a policy that Finished Goods Inventory need be only 7 percent of the next month's sales. Implementing the ending inventory policy and using the sales information from Exhibit 12–4, the production budget shown in Exhibit 12–5 is prepared.

The beginning inventory balance shown for January is the number of units on hand at December 31, 1993. This inventory figure is 30,800 units, which represents 7 percent of January's estimated 440,000 units of sales. March's ending inventory balance is 7 percent of April's estimated 360,000 units of sales. Tidewater Production has no Work in Process Inventory because all units placed into production are fully completed each period.[2]

Purchases Budget

Direct materials are essential to production and must be purchased each period in sufficient quantities to meet production needs and to conform with the company's ending inventory policies. Tidewater's management has established that raw mate-

---

[1] Leslie N. Masonson, ed., *Cash Management Performance Report* (Boston: Warren, Gorham & Lamont, January 1991), p. 1.
[2] Most manufacturing entities do not produce only whole units during the period. Normally, partially completed beginning and ending Work in Process Inventories will exist. Consideration of partially completed inventories is covered in chapter 7 on process costing.

rials be 10 percent of the following month's production needs. This inventory level is slightly higher than that of the finished goods because the raw materials are petroleum-based and oil supplies affect both availability and price.

The purchases budget is first stated in whole units of finished products. It is subsequently converted to individual direct material component requirements. Production of a McMonster requires two ounces of rubberized plastic. The quantity of coloring dye and its cost are insignificant, so the dye is treated as an indirect material. Unit material cost has been estimated by the purchasing agent at $.10 per ounce. The "whole unit" and component purchases budgets for each month of the first quarter of 1994 are shown in Exhibit 12–6. The beginning inventory for January is 10 percent of January production.

Overhead Budget

Overhead is another production cost that must be estimated by management. Exhibit 12–7 presents Tidewater Production Company's monthly cost of each overhead item for the first quarter of 1994. The company has determined that machine hours are the best predictor of overhead costs.

In estimating overhead, all costs must be specified and mixed costs must be separated into their fixed (a) and variable (b) elements. Each overhead amount shown is calculated using the $y = a + bX$ formula for a mixed cost, in which X refers to the number of units of activity (in this case, machine hours). For example, February maintenance cost is the fixed amount of $2,600 plus ($5.80 multiplied by 160 estimated machine hours), or $2,600 + $928 = $3,528. Both total cost and cost net of depreciation are shown in the budget. The cost net of depreciation is the amount that is expected to be paid in cash during the month and will, therefore, affect the cash budget.

Selling, General, and Administrative (SG&A) Budget

Selling, general, and administrative expenses for each month can be predicted in the same manner as overhead costs. Exhibit 12–8 on page 511 presents the SG&A budget. Note that sales figures rather than production levels are used as the measure

EXHIBIT 12–6
▼▼▼▼▼▼▼▼▼▼▼▼

Tidewater
PRODUCTION
COMPANY
MATERIALS
PURCHASES BUDGET
(FOR THE THREE
MONTHS AND
QUARTER ENDING
MARCH 31, 1994)

	January	February	March	Total
Units to be produced (from Exhibit 12–5)	437,900	408,390	385,110	1,231,400
+ EI units (10% of next month's production)	40,839	38,511	36,210	36,210
= Total whole unit quantities needed	478,739	446,901	421,320	1,267,610
− Beginning inventory units (10% of current production)	43,790	40,839	38,511	43,790
= Purchases required in whole unit quantities	434,949	406,062	382,809	1,223,820
× Ounces per unit	× 2	× 2	× 2	× 2
Total ounces to be purchased	869,898	812,124	765,618	2,447,640
× Price per ounce	× $.10	× $.10	× $.10	× $.10
Total cost of plastic	$86,989.80	$81,212.40	$76,561.80	$244,764.00

Note: All dollar amounts will be rounded to the nearest whole dollar when used in computations later in the chapter.

			January	February	March	Total
Estimated Machine Hours (X) (given)			180	160	150	490
	Value of					
Factory Overhead Item:	a	b				
Depreciation	$14,000	$10.00	$15,800	$15,600	$15,500	$ 46,900
Indirect materials	—	.10	18	16	15	49
Indirect labor	7,000	.50	7,090	7,080	7,075	21,245
Utilities	3,000	1.60	3,288	3,256	3,240	9,784
Property taxes	5,000	—	5,000	5,000	5,000	15,000
Insurance	6,500	—	6,500	6,500	6,500	19,500
Maintenance	2,600	5.80	3,644	3,528	3,470	10,642
Total cost (y)	$38,100	$18.00	$41,340	$40,980	$40,800	$123,120
Total cost net of depreciation			$25,540	$25,380	$25,300	$ 76,220

EXHIBIT 12–7
▼▼▼▼▼▼▼▼▼▼▼▼

TIDEWATER
PRODUCTION
COMPANY FACTORY
OVERHEAD BUDGET
(FOR THE THREE
MONTHS AND
QUARTER ENDING
MARCH 31, 1994)

of activity in preparing this budget. The company's sales force consists of a manager with a monthly salary of $5,000 and four salespeople who receive $500 per month plus a 10 percent commission on sales. The general and administrative staff are paid salaries totaling $18,000 per month.

Personnel Compensation Budget

Given expected production, the Engineering and Personnel Departments can work together to determine the necessary labor requirements for the factory, sales force, and office staff. Labor requirements are stated in total number of people, specific number of types of people (skilled laborers, salespeople, clerical personnel), as well as production hours needed for factory employees. Labor costs are computed from union labor contracts, minimum wage laws, fringe benefit costs, payroll taxes, and bonus arrangements.

Tidewater's management has reviewed the staffing requirements and has developed the compensation estimates shown in Exhibit 12–9 for the first quarter of 1994. Factory labor costs are based on the standard labor time needed to produce the number of units shown in the production budget. Remember that even though they are shown in different budgets, direct materials, direct labor, and overhead are all product costs. The indirect labor cost, while a part of overhead, is included in the compensation budget for the purpose of estimating total labor needs. The amounts for indirect labor charges were determined in Exhibit 12–7. Salespeople's and general and administrative staff compensation were calculated in Exhibit 12–8. All compensation is paid in the month in which it is incurred and, for simplicity in this illustration, payroll taxes and fringe benefit costs are ignored (even though these items usually add between 25 and 30 percent to the base rate).

Capital Budget

The budgets included in the master budget focus on the short-term or upcoming fiscal period. Managers, however, must also consider long-term needs in the area of plant and equipment purchases. The process of assessing such needs and budgeting for the

	Value of		January	February	March	Total
Predicted Sales (from Exhibit 12–4)			$220,000	$205,000	$193,500	$618,500
SG&A Items	*a*	*b*				
Supplies	$ 350	$.02	$ 4,750	$ 4,450	$ 4,220	$ 13,420
Depreciation	3,800	—	3,800	3,800	3,800	11,400
Utilities	200	—	200	200	200	600
Miscellaneous	500	—	500	500	500	1,500
Salaries						
Sales manager	5,000	—	5,000	5,000	5,000	15,000
Salespeople	2,000	.10	24,000	22,500	21,350	67,850
General & administrative	18,000	—	18,000	18,000	18,000	54,000
Total cost (*y*)	$29,850	$.12	$ 56,250	$ 54,450	$ 53,070	$163,770
Total cost net of depreciation			$ 52,450	$ 50,650	$ 49,270	$152,370

EXHIBIT 12–8

▼▼▼▼▼▼▼▼▼▼

TIDEWATER PRODUCTION COMPANY SELLING, GENERAL, AND ADMINISTRATIVE BUDGET (FOR THE THREE MONTHS AND QUARTER ENDING MARCH 31, 1994)

capital budgeting

expenditures is called **capital budgeting**.[3] The capital budget is prepared separately from the master budget, but since expenditures are involved, capital budgeting does affect the master budgeting process. As shown in Exhibit 12–10 on page 513, Tidewater managers have decided that only one capital asset will be acquired in the first quarter of 1994. This asset, a molding machine, will be purchased and placed into service at the beginning of January at a cost of $40,000. The company will pay for the machine at the end of February. The depreciation on this machine was included in the overhead calculation in Exhibit 12–7. No machines will be sold or scrapped when the new machine is purchased.

Cash Budget

After all the preceding budgets have been developed, a cash budget can be constructed. The cash budget may be the most important schedule prepared during the budgeting process because, as indicated in the following News Note, without cash a company cannot survive. "Market growth cannot materialize, expansion will stag-

	January	February	March	Total
Factory labor				
Direct labor	$21,895	$20,420	$19,256	$ 61,571
Indirect labor	7,090	7,080	7,075	21,245
Sales force				
Sales manager	5,000	5,000	5,000	15,000
Salespeople's base salaries	2,000	2,000	2,000	6,000
Estimated sales commissions				
(based on Exhibit 12–4)	22,000	20,500	19,350	61,850
General & administrative	18,000	18,000	18,000	54,000
Total personnel compensation	$75,985	$73,000	$70,681	$219,666

EXHIBIT 12–9

▼▼▼▼▼▼▼▼▼▼▼

TIDEWATER PRODUCTION COMPANY PERSONNEL COMPENSATION BUDGET (FOR THE THREE MONTHS AND QUARTER ENDING MARCH 31, 1994)

[3]Chapter 17 covers the concepts and techniques of capital budgeting.

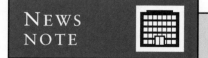

A Corporation's Oxygen Is Its Cash!

Any company, no matter how big or small, moves on cash, not profits. You can't pay bills with profits, only cash. You can't pay employees with profits, only cash. And when anyone asks you, "Did you make any profits?" all they probably want to know is whether you've got any cash.

Those may sound like extreme statements, but time and again I've heard managers complain, "If I'm making such big profits, why don't I have any money?" It doesn't matter whether your industry is high tech or low, smokestack or service. In the end, you need to have enough money to pay your obligations or you'll go out of business.

SOURCE: An excerpt from "When Is There Cash in Cash Flow?" by James McNeill Stancill (March–April 1987), p. 2. Reprinted by permission of *Harvard Business Review*. Copyright © 1987 by the President and Fellows of Harvard College; all rights reserved.

nate, capital expansion programs cannot occur, and R&D programs cannot be achieved without adequate cash flow." [4] "[O]f the 60,432 businesses that failed in 1990, more than 60% blamed their demise on economic factors linked to cash flow. And according to a study by the accounting firm of BDO Seidman, 26% of small to medium-sized companies rank their inability to control their cash flow as problem No. 1." [5] Luckily, GBC of Honolulu was not one of these companies. After suffering a $170,000 receivable write-off, George Chu (the company's owner) took steps to speed up other receivables collection and slow down payables disbursements. His efforts produced a manageable cash flow situation within one year of the write-off.

The following model can be used to summarize cash receipts and disbursements in a manner that assists managers to devise appropriate financing measures to meet company needs.

CASH BUDGET MODEL

Beginning cash balance
+ Cash receipts from collections
= Cash available for disbursements exclusive of financing
− Cash needed for disbursements
= Cash excess or deficiency (a)
− Minimum desired cash balance
= Cash (needed) or available for investment or repayment

Financing methods:
± Borrowings (repayments)
± Issue (reacquire) capital stock
± Sell (acquire) investments or plant assets
± Receive (pay) interest or dividends
        Total impact (+ or −) of planned financing (b)
= Ending cash balance (c), where $c = a \pm b$

[4]Cosmo S. Trapani, "Six Critical Areas in the Budgeting Process," *Management Accounting* (November 1982), p. 54.
[5]Shelly Branch, "Go With the Flow—Or Else," *Black Enterprise* (November 1991), p. 77.

	January	February	March	Total
Acquisitions				
Molding machine	$40,000	$ 0	$0	$40,000
Cash payments				
Molding machine	$ 0	$40,000	$0	$40,000

EXHIBIT 12–10
▼▼▼▼▼▼▼▼▼▼

TIDEWATER PRODUCTION COMPANY CAPITAL BUDGET (FOR THE THREE MONTHS AND QUARTER ENDING MARCH 31, 1994)

Financing methods:
± Borrowings (repayments)
± Issue (reacquire) capital stock
± Sell (acquire) investments or plant assets
± Receive (pay) interest or dividends
      Total impact ($+$ or $-$) of planned financing (b)
= Ending cash balance (c), where $c = a \pm b$

Cash budgets can be used to predict seasonal variances in any potential cash flow. Such predictions can indicate a need for short-term borrowing and a potential schedule of repayments. The cash budget may also show the possibility of surplus cash that could be used for investment. Cash budgets can be used to measure the performances of the accounts receivable and accounts payable departments by comparing actual to scheduled collections, payments, and discounts taken.

Cash Receipts and Accounts Receivable   Once sales revenues have been determined, managers translate that information into actual cash receipts through the use of an expected collection pattern. This pattern considers the actual collection patterns experienced in recent past periods and management's judgment about changes that

To prepare a cash receipts budget, customers must be segmented into groups with similar payment habits. Quality Croutons' owner George Johnson (on right) found out that all customers do not pay as promptly as McDonald's Corporation.

could disturb current collection patterns. For example, changes that could weaken current collection patterns include recessionary conditions, increases in interest rates, less strict credit granting practices, or weakened collection practices.

In specifying collection patterns, managers should recognize that different types of customers pay in different ways. Any sizeable, unique category of clientele should be segregated. For example, at Quality Croutons, the company in the News Note on the next page, George Johnson should show separate collection patterns for receivables from McDonald's and receivables from other businesses.

Tidewater has two different types of customers. Forty percent of the customers pay cash and receive a 2 percent discount. The remaining 60 percent of the customers purchase products on credit and have the following collection pattern: 30 percent in the month of sale and 69 percent in the month following the sale. One percent of credit sales are uncollectible. Tidewater's collection pattern is diagrammed in Exhibit 12–11.

Using the sales budget, information on December 1993 sales, and the collection pattern, management can estimate cash receipts from sales during the first three months of 1994. Management must have December sales information because collections for credit sales extend over two months, meaning that some collections from the $200,000 of December 1993 sales occur in January 1994. Projected monthly collections for the first quarter of 1994 are shown in Exhibit 12–12. The individual calculations relate to the alternative collection patterns and corresponding percentages presented in Exhibit 12–11. All amounts have been rounded to the nearest dollar.

The December collection amounts can be reconciled to the December 31, 1993, balance sheet (Exhibit 12–3) that indicated an Accounts Receivable balance of $84,000. This amount appears in the collection schedule as follows:

January collections of December sales	$82,800
January write-off of December bad debts	1,200
December 31, 1993, balance in Accounts Receivable	$84,000

January 1994 sales of $220,000 are used as an example of the collection calculations in Exhibit 12–12. The (A) line of the diagram in Exhibit 12–11 represents cash sales of 40 percent, or $88,000. These sales will be collected net of the 2 percent discount:

EXHIBIT 12–11
▼▼▼▼▼▼▼▼▼▼▼▼

TIDEWATER
PRODUCTION
COMPANY
COLLECTION
PATTERN FOR SALES

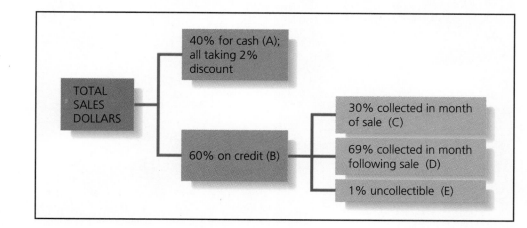

NEWS NOTE

Who Pays When?

Like many a confident entrepreneur, George Johnson failed to brace himself for cash-flow glitches. It was 1987 when his fledgling company, Quality Croutons, nabbed McDonald's Corp. as its sole customer. With its pay-in-10-days policy, the fast food giant proved a good partner indeed. Cash, it seemed, flowed into Johnson's coffers as quickly as his machines could dice bread.

Before long, the Chicago entrepreneur was signing up new customers. But instead of getting fatter, Quality Croutons' cash accounts crumbled.

"We were spending money to make additional sales, but the receipts were lagging behind by 30 to 45 days," Johnson recalls. "We tried financing new customers internally, but the float time [the time between the check's deposit and payment] was killing us."

SOURCE: Shelly Branch, "Go With the Flow—Or Else," *Black Enterprise* (November 1991), p. 77. Copyright November 1991, The Earl G. Graves Publishing Co., Inc., 130 Fifth Avenue, New York, N.Y. 10011. All rights reserved.

EXHIBIT 12–12
▼▼▼▼▼▼▼▼▼▼

TIDEWATER PRODUCTION COMPANY CASH COLLECTIONS FIRST QUARTER 1994

	January	February	March	Total	Discount	Uncollectible
From:						
December 1993 Sales:						
$200,000(60%)(69%)	$ 82,800			$ 82,800		
$200,000(60%)(1%)						$1,200
January 1994 Sales:						
$220,000(40%)	86,240N			86,240	$1,760	
$220,000(60%)(30%)	39,600			39,600		
$220,000(60%)(69%)		$ 91,080		91,080		
$220,000(60%)(1%)						1,320
February 1994 Sales:						
$205,000(40%)		80,360N		80,360	1,640	
$205,000(60%)(30%)		36,900		36,900		
$205,000(60%)(69%)			$ 84,870	84,870		
$205,000(60%)(1%)						1,230
March 1994 Sales:						
$193,500(40%)			75,852N	75,852	1,548	
$193,500(60%)(30%)			34,830	34,830		
$193,500(60%)(1%)						1,161
Totals	$208,640	$208,340	$195,552	$612,532	$4,948	$4,911

Note: "N" stands for "Net of discount." The total amount of cash sales is the sum of the net of discount collection plus the amount shown on the same line in the Discount column.

Sales to customers allowed discount (40% × $220,000)	$88,000
Discount taken by customers (.02 × $ 88,000)	1,760
Net collections from customers allowed discount	$86,240

The next three January calculations in Exhibit 12–12 represent customers who buy on credit (60 percent; line [B] in Exhibit 12–11) and who pay (1) within the month of the sale (line C), (2) in the month after the sale (line D), or (3) do not pay (line E):

Sales to customers on credit (60% × $220,000)	$132,000
Collections in month of sale (30% × $132,000)	39,600
Collections in month after sale (69% × $132,000)	91,080
Uncollectible from January credit sales (1% × $132,000)	1,320

The remaining amounts are computed in the same manner. Note that the collection in the month after the sale is 69 percent of the *original* credit sale, and uncollectibles are 1 percent of the *original* credit sales, not of the remaining balance.

Once the schedule of cash collections is prepared, the balances of the Accounts Receivable and Allowance for Uncollectibles accounts can be projected. The T-accounts for Tidewater Production are shown next and will be used to prepare pro forma year-end 1994 financial statements. Note that the Allowance account balance indicates that Tidewater has not written off any accounts receivable since December 1993. The company may still believe some of these accounts are collectible or may simply choose to write them off at the end of the first quarter of 1994.

ACCOUNTS RECEIVABLE

12/31/93 Balance (Ex. 12–3)	84,000		
Jan. 1994 Sales (Ex. 12–4)	220,000	Jan. collections (Ex. 12–12)	208,640
		Jan. discounts	1,760
Feb. 1994 Sales (Ex. 12–4)	205,000	Feb. collections (Ex. 12–12)	208,340
		Feb. discounts	1,640
March 1994 Sales (Ex. 12–4)	193,500	March collections (Ex. 12–12)	195,552
		March discounts	1,548
3/31/94 Balance	85,020		

ALLOWANCE FOR UNCOLLECTIBLES

		12/31/93 Balance (Ex. 12–3)	1,200
		Jan. estimate (Ex. 12–12)	1,320
		Feb. estimate (Ex. 12–12)	1,230
		March estimate (Ex. 12–12)	1,161
		3/31/94 Balance	4,911

Cash Disbursements and Accounts Payable   Using the purchases information from Exhibit 12–6, management can prepare an estimated cash disbursements schedule for Accounts Payable. All purchases of direct materials are made on account by Tidewater Production. The company pays for 40 percent of each month's purchases in the month of purchase, taking a 2 percent cash discount. The remaining 60 percent of each month's purchases are paid in the month following the month of purchase; no discount is available for these payments.

Exhibit 12–13 presents the cash disbursements information related to purchases for the first quarter of 1994. The December 31, 1993, accounts payable balance of $48,757 (Exhibit 12–3) represents the 60 percent remaining payment required for December purchases. All amounts have been rounded to whole dollars.

The accounts payable activity is summarized in the following T-account. The March 31 balance represents 60 percent of March purchases that will be paid during April.

ACCOUNTS PAYABLE

		12/31/93 Balance (Ex. 12–3)	48,757
Jan. payments (Ex. 12–13)	82,857	Jan. purchases (Ex. 12–6)	86,990
Jan. discounts taken	696		
Feb. payments (Ex. 12–13)	84,029	Feb. purchases (Ex. 12–6)	81,212
Feb. discounts taken	650		
March payments (Ex. 12–13)	78,739	March purchases (Ex. 12–6)	76,562
March discounts taken	613		
		3/31/94 Balance	45,937

Given the cash receipts and disbursements information for Tidewater Production, the cash budget model is used to prepare the cash budget shown in Exhibit 12–14. The company has established $5,000 as its desired minimum cash balance.

	January	February	March	Discounts
Payment for purchases from:				
December 1993	$48,757			
January 1994 (from Exhibit 12–6)				
$86,990(.40)(.98)	34,100N			$696
$86,990(.60)		$52,194		
February 1994 (from Exhibit 12–6)				
$81,212(.40)(.98)		31,835N		650
$81,212(.60)			$48,727	
March 1994 (from Exhibit 12–6)				
$76,562(.40)(.98)			30,012N	613
Total disbursements for Accounts Payable	$82,857	$84,029	$78,739	

Note: "N" stands for "Net for discount." The total amount of gross purchases being paid for the month of purchase is the sum of the net of discount payment plus the amount shown on the same line in the Discount column.

EXHIBIT 12–13
▼▼▼▼▼▼▼▼▼▼▼▼

TIDEWATER PRODUCTION COMPANY CASH DISBURSEMENTS— ACCOUNTS PAYABLE (FOR THE THREE MONTHS ENDING MARCH 31, 1994)

EXHIBIT 12–14
▼▼▼▼▼▼▼▼▼▼▼▼▼

TIDEWATER
PRODUCTION
COMPANY CASH
BUDGET (FOR THE
THREE MONTHS
AND QUARTER
ENDING MARCH 31,
1994)

	January	February	March	Total
Beginning cash balance	$ 5,050	$ 5,048	$ 5,070	$ 5,050
Cash collections (Ex. 12–12)	208,640	208,340	195,552	612,532
Cash available exclusive of financing	$213,690	$213,388	$200,622	$617,582
Disbursements:				
Accounts payable (Ex. 12–13)	$ 82,857	$ 84,029	$ 78,739	$245,625
Direct labor (Ex. 12–9)	21,895	20,420	19,256	61,571
Overhead (Ex. 12–7)*	25,540	25,380	25,300	76,220
SG&A expenses (Ex. 12–8)*	52,450	50,650	49,270	152,370
Total planned disbursements	$182,742	$180,479	$172,565	$535,786
Cash excess or (inadequacy)	$ 30,948	$ 32,909	$ 28,057	$ 81,796
Minimum cash balance desired	5,000	5,000	5,000	5,000
Cash available or (needed)	$ 25,948	$ 27,909	$ 23,057	$ 76,796
Financing:				
Borrowings (repayments)	0	1,200	(1,200)	0
Issue (reacquire) stock	0	0	0	0
Sell (acquire) investments	(10,900)	10,900	(21,800)	(21,800)
Sell (acquire) plant assets (Ex. 12–10)	0	(40,000)	0	(40,000)
Receive (pay) interest or dividends**	(15,000)	61	(12)	(14,951)
Total impact of planned financing	$(25,900)	$(27,839)	$(23,012)	$(76,751)
Ending cash balance	$ 5,048	$ 5,070	$ 5,045	$ 5,045

*These amounts are the net of depreciation figures.
**Dividends payable on the December 31, 1993, balance sheet were shown as being owed on January 15, 1994. Interest on investments is calculated assuming an 8 percent rate, and interest on borrowings is calculated assuming a 12 percent rate. Borrowings are made at the beginning of the month, and repayments or investments are made at the end of the month. For February, interest received is $73 ($10,900 × .08 × 1/12), and interest owed is $12 ($1,200 × .12 × 1/12). In March, interest owed is $12 ($1,200 × .12 × 1/12).

The primary reason for having a desired minimum cash balance is the uncertainty associated with the budgeting process. If management had perfect certainty about cash inflows and outflows, there would be no need for this cash "cushion."

All borrowings by Tidewater Production are assumed to take place in increments of $100 at the beginning of a month. All repayments and investments are made in $100 amounts and are assumed to occur at the end of a month. These assumptions are simplistic, since management would not actually borrow until the need for funds arose and would repay as quickly as it was able so as to minimize interest expenditures. Interest on any company investments is assumed to be added to the company's bank account at the end of each month.

Exhibit 12–14 indicates that Tidewater has $30,948 excess of cash available over disbursements in January. This excess not only meets the specified $5,000 minimum balance and the dividend payment requirement from the December 1993 balance sheet, but also provides an opportunity to invest $10,900. In February, Tidewater expects to have enough cash to meet its desired minimum cash balance, but not enough to pay for the machine purchased in January. The January investment must be liquidated and an additional $1,200 borrowed. Since the machine did not have to be paid for until the end of the month, the investment could continue to draw interest until that time. The borrowing has been *assumed*, however, to occur at the beginning of the month for consistency with the previously specified plan. Thus, Tidewater earns interest on the investment, but must pay interest on the borrowings for February. In March, there is enough cash available to meet budgeted disbursements, pay off the February borrowings, and make a $21,800 investment. Interest on borrowings and investments is calculated at the bottom of Exhibit 12–14. Changes in the interest rate will affect any future budget-to-actual comparisons.

Several things should be specially noted involving the total column in Exhibit 12–14. First, the beginning cash balance is not the total of the three months, but is the balance at January 1. Second, the monthly minimum cash balance is $5,000, not $15,000 for the quarter. Lastly, the ending cash balance should be the same as what appears in the final month of the quarter. These figures (beginning, minimum, and ending cash balances), cash available exclusive of financing, cash excess/inadequacy, and cash available/needed are the only ones that are not summed across from the three-month information; all other figures are totals. These figures can be updated monthly; a spreadsheet program is very useful for this function.

Budgeted Financial Statements

The final step in the budgeting process is the development of budgeted or pro forma financial statements for the period. These statements reflect the results that will be achieved *if the estimates and assumptions used for all previous budgets actually occur.* Such statements allow management to determine if the predicted results are acceptable for the period. If the predicted results are not acceptable, management has the opportunity to change and adjust items before beginning the period.

For example, if expected net income is not considered to be a reasonable amount, management may discuss raising selling prices or finding ways to decrease costs. Any specific changes considered by management may have related effects that must be included in the revised projections. For example, if selling prices are raised, volume may decrease. Alternatively, reductions in costs from using lesser quality of materials could have an effect on spoilage during production or could cause a decline in demand. Computer spreadsheet programs are used to make the recalculations necessary from such changes in assumptions quickly and easily.

Cost of Goods Manufactured Schedule   Before an income statement can be drafted, management must prepare a schedule of cost of goods manufactured, which is necessary to determine cost of goods sold.[6] Using information from previous budgets, Tidewater's accountant has prepared the budgeted cost of goods manufactured schedule shown in Exhibit 12–15. Since there were no beginning or ending Work in Process Inventories, cost of goods manufactured is equal to the manufacturing costs of the period.

Income Statement   The projected income statement for Tidewater Production Company for the first quarter of 1994 is presented in Exhibit 12–16. This statement uses much of the information previously developed in determining the revenues and expenses for the period.

---

[6]Discussion of a cost of goods manufactured schedule is given in chapter 2.

EXHIBIT 12–15
▼▼▼▼▼▼▼▼▼▼▼▼

TIDEWATER
PRODUCTION
COMPANY PRO
FORMA COST OF
GOODS
MANUFACTURED
SCHEDULE FOR THE
FIRST QUARTER OF
1994

Beginning work in process			$ 0
Cost of direct materials used			
Beginning balance of direct materials (Ex. 12–3)		$ 8,758	
Purchases (net of $1,959 of discounts taken) (from Accounts Payable, p. 517)		242,805	
Total direct materials available		$251,563	
Ending balance of direct materials (Note A)		7,242	
Cost of direct materials used		$244,321	
Direct labor (Ex. 12–9)		61,571	
Factory overhead (Ex. 12–7)		123,120	
Total costs to be accounted for			429,012
Ending work in process			0
Costs of goods manufactured			$429,012

Note A

Ending balance (Ex. 12–6) in units	36,210
Ounces per unit	× 2
Total ounces needed	72,420
Price per ounce	× $.10
Ending balance	$7,242

Computers have helped make the budgeting process less time-consuming than when they were prepared manually. Preparing useful and credible budgets, however, still takes considerable time and effort.

Sales (Ex. 12–4)		$618,500
Less: Sales discounts (from Accounts Receivable account, p. 516)		4,948
Net sales		$613,552
Cost of goods sold		
Finished goods—12/31/93 (Ex. 12–3)	$ 10,780	
Cost of goods manufactured (Ex. 12–15)	429,012	
Cost of goods available for sale	$439,792	
Finished goods—3/31/94 (Note A)	8,820	430,972
Gross margin		$182,580
Expenses		
Bad debts expense (Note B)	$ (3,711)	
SG&A expenses (Ex. 12–8)	(163,770)	
Interest expense/income (net) (Ex. 12–14)	49	167,432
Income before income taxes		$ 15,148
Income taxes (assumed rate of 30%)		4,544
Net income		$ 10,604

Note A:

Beginning finished goods (Ex. 12–5)		30,800
Production (Ex. 12–5)		1,231,400
Units available for sale		1,262,200
Sales (Ex. 12–4)		1,237,000
Ending finished goods		25,200
Costs per unit		
Materials	$ .20	
Conversion (assumed)	.15	× $.35
Cost of ending inventory		$8,820

Note B:

Total sales	$618,500
× % credit sales	× .60
Credit sales	$371,100
× % estimated uncollectible	× .01
Estimated bad debts	$ 3,711

EXHIBIT 12–16
▼▼▼▼▼▼▼▼▼▼▼

TIDEWATER PRODUCTION COMPANY PRO FORMA INCOME STATEMENT FOR THE FIRST QUARTER OF 1994

Balance Sheet   Upon completion of the income statement, Tidewater accountants can prepare a March 31, 1994, balance sheet (Exhibit 12–17). The letters in parentheses after some of the items in Exhibit 12–17 refer to the calculations shown at the bottom of the exhibit.

Statement of Cash Flows (SCF)   The information found on the income statement, balance sheet, and cash budget is used in preparing a Statement of Cash Flows. This statement is a principal internal, as well as external, report. The SCF explains the change in the cash balance by reflecting the company's sources and uses of cash. Such knowledge can assist in judging the company's ability to handle fixed cash outflow commitments, adapt to adverse changes in business conditions, and undertake new commitments. Further, because the cash flow statement identifies the relationships between net income and net cash flow from operations, it assists managers in judging the quality of the company's earnings.

EXHIBIT 12–17
▼▼▼▼▼▼▼▼▼▼▼▼

TIDEWATER
PRODUCTION
COMPANY PRO
FORMA BALANCE
SHEET MARCH 31,
1994

Assets

Current Assets

Cash (Ex. 12–14)		$ 5,045
Investments (Ex. 12–14)		21,800
Accounts Receivable (p. 516)	$ 85,020	
Less Allowance for Uncollectibles (p. 516)	(4,911)	80,109
Inventory		
Direct Materials (Ex. 12–15, Note A)	$ 7,242	
Finished Goods (Ex. 12–16, Note A)	8,820	16,062
Total Current Assets		$123,016

Plant Assets

Property, Plant & Equipment (a)	$580,000	
Less Accumulated Depreciation (b)	(238,300)	341,700
TOTAL ASSETS		$464,716

Liabilities and Stockholders' Equity

Current Liabilities

Accounts Payable (p. 517)		$ 45,937
Income Taxes Payable (Ex. 12–16)		4,544
Total Current Liabilities		$ 50,481

Stockholders' Equity

Common Stock	$300,000	
Retained Earnings (c)	114,235	414,235
TOTAL LIABILITIES AND STOCKHOLDERS' EQUITY		$464,716

(a)	Beginning balance (Ex. 12–3)	$540,000
	Purchased new molding machine	40,000
	Ending balance	$580,000
(b)	Beginning balance (Ex. 12–3)	$180,000
	Factory depreciation (Ex. 12–7)	46,900
	SG&A depreciation (Ex. 12–8)	11,400
	Ending balance	$238,300
(c)	Beginning balance (Ex. 12–3)	$103,631
	Net income (Ex. 12–16)	10,604
	Ending balance	$114,235

While the cash budget is essential to current cash management, the budgeted SCF gives managers a more global view of cash flows by rearranging them into three distinct major activities (operating, investing, and financing). Such a rearrangement permits management to judge whether the specific anticipated flows are consistent with the company's strategic plans. In addition, the SCF incorporates a schedule or narrative about significant noncash transactions, such as an exchange of stock for land, that are ignored in the cash budget.

It is acceptable for external reporting to present the operating section of the Statement of Cash Flows on either a direct or an indirect basis. The direct basis uses pure cash flow information—cash collections and cash disbursements for operating activities. The indirect basis begins the operating section with net income and makes reconciling adjustments to arrive at cash flow from operations. Exhibit 12–18 provides a Statement of Cash Flows for Tidewater Production using the information from the cash budget in Exhibit 12–14; the second, indirect presentation of the operating section uses the information from the income statement in Exhibit 12–16 and the balance sheets in Exhibits 12–3 and 12–17.

It is interesting to note that Tidewater generates a very high cash flow from operations, but is only earning 1.7 percent on sales dollars. However, both cash flow from operations *and* net income are necessary for long-run success in business. It appears that Tidewater either is not charging enough for its product or is not controlling costs well. As indicated in the following News Note, even major corporations like Chrysler experience cash flow difficulties at times.

When goods are sold on credit, payment is not received until some future time. The Statement of Cash Flows prepared on a direct basis converts accrual-based sales to cash receipts.

Operating Activities:			
Cash collections			
From sales		$612,532	
From interest		49	$612,581
Cash payments			
For inventory:			
Direct materials	$245,625		
Direct labor	61,571		
Overhead	76,220	$383,416	
For nonfactory costs:			
Salaries	$136,850		
Supplies	13,420		
Other SG&A expenses	2,100	152,370	535,786
Net cash inflow from operating activities			$ 76,795
Investing Activities:			
Purchase of plant asset		$ (40,000)	
Short-term investment		(21,800)	
Net cash outflow from investing activities			(61,800)
Financing Activities:			
Issuance of short-term note payable		$ 1,200	
Repayment of short-term note payable		(1,200)	
Payment of dividends (owed at 12/31/93)		(15,000)	
Net cash outflow from financing activities			(15,000)
Net decrease in cash			$ (5)
Alternative (Indirect) Basis			
Operating Activities:			
Net income			$ 10,604
+ Depreciation expense ($46,900 + $11,400)			58,300
+ Decrease in Accounts Receivable ($82,800 − $80,109)		$ 2,691	
+ Decrease in Inventory ($19,538 − $16,062)		3,476	
− Decrease in Accounts Payable ($48,757 − $45,937)		(2,820)	
+ Increase in Taxes Payable		4,544	7,891
Net cash inflow from operating activities			$ 76,795

EXHIBIT 12–18
▼▼▼▼▼▼▼▼▼▼

Tᴉᴅᴇᴡᴀᴛᴇʀ PRODUCTION COMPANY PRO FORMA STATEMENT OF CASH FLOWS FOR THE FIRST QUARTER OF 1994

Negative Cash Flow Takes Its Toll at Chrysler

Although Chrysler has $3 billion in the bank, its finances are precarious. Years of running on a shoestring have left it with an aging work force, tired facilities, and a dated product line. Capital spending to relieve the worst of these problems, along with expected losses, will likely add up to negative cash flow from operations of more than $1 billion in 1991. To function "comfortably" under normal circumstances, the company needs $800 million in the bank. That leaves roughly $1 billion in reserve—not much of an air bag, if times grow harder, for a business Chrysler's size.

SOURCE: Alex Taylor III, "Can Iacocca Fix Chrysler Again?" *FORTUNE* (April 8, 1991), p. 51. © 1991 The Time Inc. Magazine Company. All rights reserved.

CONCLUDING COMMENTS

Because of its fundamental nature in the budgeting process, demand must be predicted as accurately and with as many details as possible. Sales forecasts must indicate type and quantity of products to be sold, geographic locations of the sales, types of buyers, and points in time the sales are to be made. Such detail is necessary because different products require different production and distribution facilities; different customers have different credit terms and payment schedules; and different seasons or months may necessitate different shipping schedules or methods.

Estimated sales demand has a pervasive impact on the master budget. To arrive at a valid prediction, managers use as much information as is available and may combine several estimation approaches. Combining prediction methods provides managers with corroboration of estimates, which reduces uncertainty. Some ways of estimating future demand are (1) asking sales personnel for a subjective consensus; (2) making simple extrapolations of past trends; (3) using market research; and (4) employing statistical and other mathematical models. Models are programmed so that, after changing one or more factors, repetitive computer simulations can be run. These simulations permit managers to review results that would be obtained under various circumstances.

After the master budget and all of its pro forma financial statements have been developed, they can and should be used for a variety of purposes. One common use of the master budget is to help in obtaining bank loans, as indicated in the following News Note.

Banks also need to be kept informed after loans are obtained. When the bank used by Transamerica Energy Associates Inc. (TEA of Atlanta) got "cold feet" because the company was going to have problems meeting payroll, the company looked for and found another bank. Company management and the bank are now in constant communication about the business' financial situation.

Additionally, master budgets can be used to monitor performance by comparing budgeted figures to actual results. Variances, as they occur, should be investigated so

Loan Officers Aren't Receptive to Cold Calls

With today's economic downturn and regulatory measures to increase bank capitalization, banks are getting even more selective. Prepare written material on the nature of your business, your company's philosophy, position, and objectives. This should be included in your business plan. Make sure your business plan is detailed and includes certified financial statements, such as a balance sheet that lists all assets, liabilities and net worth; financial status for the last three years; profit and loss statements; cash flow and revenue projections and accounts receivable and payable listing and aging. Put in writing any funding requests based on seasonal swings. For example, if you are a retailer and you know your industry always has a terrible first quarter, let your banker know.

SOURCE: Adapted from Carolyn M. Brown, "Advice Your Company Can Bank On," *Black Enterprise* (June 1991), p. 259ff. Copyright June 1991, The Earl G. Graves Publishing Co., Inc., 130 Fifth Avenue, New York, N.Y. 10011. All rights reserved.

that the underlying causes can be determined. Understanding the reasons for not meeting a budget can be useful in controlling future operations within the budget period, evaluating performance, and budgeting more accurately in the future.

SITE ANALYSIS

Budgets are an essential part of planning no matter what business you are in or what endeavor you are striving to succeed. Even the Catholic church is finding that instituting budgets and financial reports is successful. In 1991, the Chicago Archdiocese finance director John Benware indicated that the church has simply started implementing basic business practices. "Such changes helped to slice the [1990] deficit by 40% to $29 million." [7] That may still sound like a lot of red ink, but the archdiocese would have been facing a $71 million deficit by 1993 if action had not been taken!

As discussed in chapter 11, the budgeting process and the impacts of budgeting affect all organization members. How the master budget applies to the various disciplines is discussed in the Applications Strategies shown on the next page.

CHAPTER SUMMARY

Planning is the process of setting goals and objectives and translating them into activities and resources required for accomplishment within a specified time horizon. Budgeting is the quantifying of a company's financial plans and activities. Budgets

[7]Kevin Kelly, "Chicago's Catholic Church: Putting Its House in Order," *Business Week* (June 10, 1991), p. 61.

	Discipline	Application
APPLICATIONS STRATEGIES OF THE MASTER BUDGET	Accounting	Provides a basis against which actual accounting information can be compared; translates management plans into quantitative and monetary information; the budgetary process organizes management's plans according to the accountant's chart of accounts so that plans can conform to the way financial statement results will be presented, thus allowing accounting to assist managers in performance evaluation
	Economics	Enhances efforts to use resources in the most efficient and effective ways; reflects process that is similar to that existing in all-level governmental units
	Finance	Helps indicate the need for and ability to repay borrowings so that advance arrangements can be made; can assist in developing dividend strategy; provides information on future earnings that may affect stock prices or new issues of capital
	Management	Enhances communication of authority, provides a basis for performance evaluation, and promotes teamwork; illustrates hiring implications; indicates resource allocations among areas; serves as an organizational plan for the upcoming period
	Marketing	Requires an astute assessment of market demand as the key variable on which entire budgeting process is based; provides individual salesperson's sales quotas for budget period; helps prioritize how marketing resources will be spent (advertising, sales expenses, trade shows) to generate projected sales level; marketing inputs on budgets are critical because many expenditures drive or are driven by sales volume (such as sales salaries and commissions, advertising, promotions, inventory, delivery trucks) and should be correlated with the desired sales volume

facilitate communication, coordination, and teamwork. A master budget is the comprehensive set of projections (pro forma financial statements) for a specific budget period. It is composed of operating and financial budgets and is usually detailed by quarters and months.

Sales demand is the proper starting point for the master budget. Once sales demand is determined, managers forecast revenues, production, costs, and cash flows for the firm's activities for the upcoming period. These expectations reflect the firm's input and output of resources and are used in preparing the master budget. When budgeting, managers need to remember that the various organizational departments interact with each other, and the budget for one department may form the basis of or have an effect on the budgets in other departments.

Pro forma financial statements will help managers determine if their plans will provide the desired results, in terms of both net income and cash flow. Inadequate results should cause a reevaluation of the objectives that have been set, and appropriate changes should be made.

GLOSSARY

Capital budgeting the process of making decisions and budgeting for expenditures on long-term plant and equipment items

Financial budget a budget that reflects the funds to be generated or used during the budget period; includes the cash and capital budgets and the projected or pro forma financial statements

Master budget the comprehensive set of all budgetary schedules and the pro forma financial statements of an organization

Operating budget a budget that is expressed in both units and dollars

SELECTED BIBLIOGRAPHY

Archer, Simon, and David Otley. "Strategy, Structure, Planning and Control Systems, and Performance Evaluation—Rumenco Ltd." *Management Accounting Research* (December 1991), pp. 263–303.

Cook, Donald. "Strategic Plan Creates a Blueprint for Budgeting." *Healthcare Financial Management* (May 1990), pp. 20–24ff.

Czyzewski, Alan B., and Donald W. Hicks. "Hold Onto Your Cash." *Management Accounting* (March 1992), pp. 27–30.

SOLUTION STRATEGIES

Sales Budget

    Units of sales
$\times$ Selling price per unit
= Dollars of sales

Production Budget

    Units of sales
+ Units desired in ending inventory
− Units in beginning inventory
= Units to be produced

Purchases Budget

    Units to be produced
$\times$ Appropriate quantity measure per unit
= Units needed for production
+ Units desired in ending inventory
− Units in beginning inventory
= Units to be purchased

Personnel Compensation Budget

    Number of people or direct labor hours
$\times$ Salaries per month or Wages per hour
= Cost of compensation

Overhead Budget (excluding compensation)

    Predicted activity base
$\times$ VOH rate per unit of activity
= Total variable OH cost
+ Fixed OH cost
= Total OH cost

Selling, General & Administrative Budget (excluding compensation)

    Predicted sales dollars (or other variable measure)
$\times$ Variable SG&A rate per dollar (or other variable measure)
= Total variable SG&A cost
+ Fixed SG&A cost
= Total SG&A cost

Schedule of Cash Collections (for sales on account)

    Dollars of credit sales for month
$\times$ Percent collection for month of sale
= Credit to A/R for month's sales
− Allowed and taken sales discounts
= Receipts for current month's sales
+ Current month's cash receipts for prior months' sales
= Cash receipts for current month

Schedule of Cash Payments for A/P
   Units to be purchased
× Cost per unit
= Total cost of purchases
× Percent payment for current
   purchases
= Debit to A/P for month's purchases
− Purchase discounts taken
= Cash payments for current month's
   purchases
+ Current month's payments for prior
   months' purchases
= Cash payments for A/P for current
   month

Cash Budget
   Beginning cash balance
+ Cash receipts
= Cash available for disbursements
− Cash needed for disbursements:
   Cash payments for A/P for month
   Cost of compensation
   Total cost of OH less depreciation
   Total SG&A cost less depreciation
= Cash excess or deficiency
− Minimum desired cash balance
= Cash needed or available for
   investment or financing

   Cash excess or deficiency
+ or − Various financing amounts
= Ending cash balance

END-OF-CHAPTER MATERIALS

Questions

1. Why is it more necessary for businesses to formalize plans in writing than it is for individuals?

2. How are operating and financial budgets different? How are they related?

3. Why is the master budget said to be a static budget? Why is it necessary for the master budget to be static?

4. Why must the beginning of the budget year balance sheet be estimated? Why is it needed in the master budget process?

5. Why is the sales budget the first of the operating budgets prepared?

6. Explain the purposes of the production budget and of the purchases budget. How are they similar and how are they different?

7. Since the capital budget is not a component within the master budget, how does it relate to the master budget preparation?

8. Explain the importance of the cash budget.

9. How are cash collections from sales determined? What part do cash collections play in the budgeting process?

10. What justifies maintaining a minimum cash balance?

11. Why are pro forma statements included in the master budget?

12. Since there is already a cash budget, what does the budgeted statement of cash flows add?

13. What is the relationship between the budgeted statement of cash flows and the budgeted balance sheet?

14. Give some examples of items included in the financing section of a Statement of Cash Flows and their cash flow effects.

15. List the schedules and statements that make up the master budget in the sequence they would normally be prepared. If more than one schedule can be prepared simultaneously, so indicate.

Exercises

16. *(Production budget)* Clemon Company has budgeted its second-quarter unit sales for 1995 as follows:

April	7,000
May	12,000
June	10,500

Clemon desires an ending inventory of 8 percent of sales of the following month. July's sales are expected to be 8,000 units. Produce a second-quarter production budget by month and in total.

17. *(Production budget)* Rotation Tires' quarterly unit sales for 1995 are:

1st	200,000
2nd	150,000
3rd	250,000
4th	180,000

The firm expects to begin 1995 with 80,000 tires. Desired ending balances are to be 40 percent of the subsequent quarter's sales. Sales in the first quarter of 1996 are expected to be 220,000 tires. Prepare a production budget by quarter, and in total, for 1995.

18. *(Purchases budget)* Fantastic Flippers expects to sell 12,200 pairs of swim flippers during June. It requires two pounds of rubber to make each pair. The company has a beginning June inventory of 3,300 pairs of flippers and 12,800 pounds of rubber. The company desires to end June with 8,200 pairs of flippers and 17,000 pounds of rubber. Because flippers can be made very quickly from heated rubber, the firm does not have Work in Process Inventories. How much rubber should Fantastic buy?

19. *(Purchases budget)* Kim Company expects to sell 37,000 units of its major product in November 1995. Each unit requires two pounds of Material A and five pounds of Material B. Material A costs $4.80 per pound and Material B costs $2.10 per pound. Expected beginning and ending inventories are as follows:

	November 1	November 30
Finished goods (units)	7,000	6,300
Material A (pounds)	4,000	4,800
Material B (pounds)	6,200	6,200

a. How many pounds of Material A does Kim plan to purchase in November? What is the expected cost of those purchases?

b. How many pounds of Material B does Kim plan to purchase in November? What is the expected cost of those purchases?

20. *(Mixed overhead cost budget)* Allesandro, Inc., wants to estimate the cost of laundering employee uniforms in preparing its manufacturing overhead portion of the master budget. Laundering is a mixed cost with the following flexible budget formula:

$$y = \$13,800 + \$.07X$$

where X = direct labor hours

Total laundering cost includes $3,200 of depreciation.

a. Calculate the laundering cost if Allesandro plans to incur 120,000 direct labor hours for the coming year.

b. Determine how much cash will be spent for laundering uniforms if Allesandro incurs the 120,000 direct labor hours.

21. *(Cash collections)* Shipman, Inc., is experiencing difficulty in estimating cash collections for the second quarter of 1996. Inspection of records and documents reveals the following sales information:

February	March	April	May	June
$126,000	$116,000	$124,000	$146,000	$136,000

Analysis of past collection patterns helped to develop the following:

- 30 percent of each month's sales are for cash, with no discount.
- Of the credit sales, 50 percent are collected in the month of sale on which a 2 percent discount is taken.
- 40 percent of credit sales are collected in the month following the sale.
- 10 percent of credit sales are collected in the second month after the sale. Bad debts are negligible and should be ignored. Shipman's Accounts Receivable balance at April 1 is estimated at $49,420.

a. Prepare a table of cash received from sales for each month in the second quarter.

b. Calculate the Accounts Receivable balance at the end of the second quarter.

22. *(Cash collections)* Steve Watts Engineering's records revealed an accounts receivable balance of $388,000 at April 1, 1996. Analysis shows that $280,000 of the April first balance is the amount remaining from March billings. April billings are expected to be $420,000. The company's pattern of collections is 30 percent in the month of billing for services, 40 percent in the month following the service, 29 percent in the second month following the service, and 1 percent uncollectible. No write-off of bad debts has been made for February or March billings.

a. What were the February billings?

b. What amount of the March billings is expected to be uncollectible?

c. What are the projected cash collections in April?

23. *(Cash collections)* Holly, Inc., expects sales of $200,000, $150,000, and $180,000 respectively for January, February, and March. Holly has determined the following collection profile from its sales, all of which are on account:

Collections from	
Current month's sales	22%
Prior month's sales	60%
Second month after sale	16%
Uncollectibles	2%

A bank loan is coming due in March, so Holly managers want to be sure that they have done a good job of predicting collections. How much cash can Holly expect to collect in March?

24. *(Cash collections)* Royland Enterprises has established a collection profile as follows:

> 75 percent of every month's sales is on credit
> For credit sales:
> > 40 percent is collected in the month of sale
> > 36 percent is collected in the month following the sale
> > 24 percent is collected in the 2nd month following the sale

Sales for December are expected to be $330,000. The Accounts Receivable balance at November 30 is $190,350. Of that amount, $141,750 represents the balance due on November credit sales. There are no receivables from months prior to October.

a. What were October's total sales?
b. Calculate November's cash sales.
c. Estimate December's cash collections.
d. Determine the December 31 Accounts Receivable balance.

25. *(Cash payments)* Augeletty, Inc., is trying to budget the June 1996 cash payments for Accounts Payable. Management believes that of a given month's purchases, 40 percent is paid in the month of purchase with a 2 percent discount on one-half of what is paid in that month. The remaining 60 percent is paid in the following month. Expected unit purchases for May and June of 1996 are 45,600 and 38,300, respectively. The cost per unit is $2.80.

What are expected cash payments for accounts payable in June?

26. *(Cash budget)* Darren Huitt Enterprises expects to begin 1996 with a cash balance of $16,000. Cash collections from sales and on account are expected to be $768,600. The firm wants to maintain a minimum cash balance of $14,000. Cash disbursements are projected as follows:

Payoff of notes payable	$ 26,000
Interest on notes payable	2,200
Purchase of computer system	12,800
Payments on account for operating costs and purchases	180,000
Direct labor payments	140,000
Overhead payments	270,000
Selling, general & administrative payments	130,000

Using the format for a cash budget presented in the chapter, prepare the 1996 cash budget.

27. *(Cost of goods manufactured schedule)* Stanley Company is trying to complete preparation of its 1996 master budget and asks you to prepare a pro forma cost of goods manufactured schedule. The firm provides you with the following expected data:

Work in Process—January 1	$ 28,600
Work in Process—December 31	24,300
Direct Materials Inventory—January 1	37,300
Direct Materials Inventory—December 31	38,800
Purchases of direct materials on purchases budget	387,700
Direct labor—from personnel compensation budget	176,700
Factory overhead—from factory overhead budget	425,500

Problems

28. *(Production and purchases budgets)* Janet Stern Company has budgeted unit sales monthly for the first quarter of 1996 as follows:

	January	February	March	Total
Sales in units	36,000	32,000	30,000	98,000

April's sales are expected to be 28,000 units.

The following are estimates of finished units and direct materials in pounds at various points in time:

	12/31/95	1/31/96	2/29/96	3/31/96
Finished units	9,000	8,000	7,500	7,000
Direct Material M	6,750	6,000	5,625	5,250
Direct Material N	4,500	4,000	3,750	3,500
Direct Material O	9,000	8,000	7,500	7,000

The production process requires three pounds of Material M, two pounds of Material N, and four pounds of Material O.

Required: Prepare a monthly production and purchases budget for the first quarter of 1996.

29. *(Purchases and cash payments)* Jungsen Coffee Company expects to sell 100,000 one-pound bags of coffee in November and 120,000 one-pound bags of coffee in December 1996. Each one-pound bag contains fifteen ounces of coffee and one ounce of additional ingredients, such as chicory. The company expects to begin November with the following inventories:

Finished goods	10,000 units
Bags—unused	24,000
Coffee beans	28,000 pounds
Additional ingredients	2,200 pounds

Based on a recent study, Jungsen has decided, as of November 30, to carry 10 percent of the subsequent month's sales in finished goods. Enough direct materials are also to be carried to produce 10 percent of the next month's sales. Bags cost $.14, coffee beans cost $.92 per pound, and the additional ingredients cost $.20 per pound. Management normally pays for 60 percent of a month's purchases in the month of purchase and takes a 2 percent discount on those payments.

Required:

a. How many bags must be acquired during November?

b. How many pounds of coffee beans must be purchased during November?

c. How many pounds of additional ingredients should be acquired in November?

d. Calculate the dollar amount of November purchases.

e. Determine the cash payments in November for November purchases.

30. *(Estimate various amounts)* Wright, Inc., expects its May 1995 Cost of Goods Sold to be $210,000. Included in this amount is $12,000 of fixed overhead. Total variable cost approximates 70 percent of sales. Wright's gross margin percentage averages 35 percent of sales and net income runs 10 percent of sales. Depreciation is $3,500 per month. All other expenses and purchases are paid 75 percent in the month incurred and 25 percent in the following month. Wright purchases only enough to satisfy sales of any given month.

Required:

a. Estimate Wright's expected May sales.
b. Estimate for May, Wright's expected variable selling, general, and administrative costs.
c. How much are Wright's total fixed costs for May expected to be?
d. Wright normally collects 60 percent of its sales in the month of sale and 40 percent in the following month. Estimate cash collections and cash payments in May related only to May transactions.

31. *(Multiple budgets)* Digger Douglas makes shovels. Sales and collections for the first quarter of 1996 are as follows:

	January	February	March	Total
Sales				
Quantity	6,400	5,200	7,400	19,000
Revenue	$73,600	$59,800	$85,100	$218,500
Collections	$76,200	$61,300	$81,100	$218,600

The December 31, 1995, estimated balance sheet contains the following balances: Cash, $18,320; Direct Materials, $8,230; Finished Goods, $23,200; and Accounts Payable, $5,800. The direct materials balance represents 2,000 pounds of scrap iron and 3,200 shovel handles. Finished Goods consists of 4,220 shovels.

Each shovel requires two pounds of scrap iron. Scrap iron costs $2 per pound, and shovel handles are made at a local lumber mill at a cost of $1.80 to the company. Beginning in 1996, management wants ending direct materials to equal 25 percent of the following month's production requirements. Management also wants ending finished goods equal to 20 percent of the next month's sales. Sales for April and May are expected to be 8,000 shovels each month.

The payment pattern for purchases is 75 percent in the month of purchase with a 1 percent discount and the remainder paid in the next month with no discount.

Direct labor is budgeted at $.70 per shovel while out-of-pocket plant overhead runs $24,000 monthly plus $1.30 per shovel. Total monthly out-of-pocket period costs run $13,600 plus 10 percent of sales revenue. All out-of-pocket costs are paid in the month of incurrence, with the exception of materials purchases as discussed earlier. Management wants a minimum cash balance of $15,000. The company has a policy of borrowing funds in multiples of $1,000 at the beginning of a month, while repaying borrowed funds in multiples of $1,000 plus interest on amounts repaid at the rate of 12 percent per annum.

Required:

a. Prepare a monthly production budget for the first quarter of 1996.
b. Prepare a monthly direct materials purchases budget for the first quarter of 1996.
c. Prepare a monthly schedule of cash payments for purchases for the first quarter of 1996.
d. Prepare a combined payments schedule for factory overhead and period costs on a monthly basis for the first quarter of 1996.
e. Prepare a cash budget for each month and in total for the first quarter of 1996.

32. *(Cash collections and payments)* The Wise Quack, which operates in the New York City area, is a wholesale distributor of joke books and other humorous types of books for light entertainment. The company is preparing its budget for the first three months of 1995. At the end of 1994, the following balances are estimated:

Accounts Receivable	$376,560	Accounts Payable	$83,400
Inventory	105,750	Other payables	14,240

Management has agreed upon the following guidelines in preparing the budget:

Collections

- Credit sales are billed on the last day of each month
- Cash customers and credit customers who pay by the tenth of the month are allowed a 1 percent discount.
- Ten percent of sales are for cash. Of the credit sales, 10 percent are received within the discount period; another 40 percent are received during the rest of the month after billing; 40 percent are received in the second month after billing; and 10 percent are received in the third month after billing.

Payments

- Forty percent of purchases are paid for in the month of purchase. The rest is paid in the next month.
- Of the operating expenses incurred, 60 percent are paid in the month incurred and the remainder is paid in the next month.

Other Operating Statistics

- All sales are made at 200 percent of cost.
- Desired ending inventory is set at 75 percent of the following month's Cost of Goods Sold.
- Actual and projected sales are estimated at:

October	$244,000
November	256,000
December	266,000
January	282,000
February	278,000
March	248,000
April	254,000

- Selling, general, and administrative expenses run 10 percent of sales plus $12,000 monthly. Included in the monthly SG&A expenses are $3,000 of depreciation.

Required:

a. Determine total monthly cash receipts for the first quarter.
b. Determine monthly purchases for the first quarter.
c. Determine monthly cash disbursements for the first quarter.

33. *(Cash budget)* Livingston, Inc.'s September 30, 1995, balance sheet follows:

Assets		Liabilities & Stockholders' Equity	
Cash	$ 20,000	Accounts payable	$136,000
Accounts receivable (net of $3,800 allowance for doubtful accounts)	72,200		
Inventory	54,000		
Plant assets (net of $40,000 accumulated depreciation)	160,000	Common stock	60,000
		Retained earnings	110,200
		Total liabilities & stockholders'	
Total assets	$306,200	equity	$306,200

Other information about the company follows:

- The company wants a minimum cash balance of $20,000.
- Revenues of $180,000 and $240,000 are expected for October and November, respectively.
- The collection pattern is 60 percent in the month of sale, 38 percent in the next month, and 2 percent uncollectible.
- Cost of goods sold is 75 percent of sales.
- Purchases each month are 60 percent of the current month's sales and 40 percent of the following month's sales. All purchases are paid for in the month following the purchase.
- Other monthly expenses are $24,000, which include $1,000 of depreciation, but does not include bad debt expense.

Required:

a. Forecast the October cash collections.
b. Forecast the October 31 inventory balance.
c. Forecast the October 31 retained earnings balance.
d. Prepare the October cash budget including the amount available for investment or to be borrowed during October.

34. *(Cash budget and pro forma income statement)* Francee's Fancy Pastries makes large quantities of pastries for wholesale to supermarket chains in metropolitan Chicago. Company records reveal the following for the first four months of 1994:

	Purchases	Sales
January	$33,000	$51,000
February	29,000	46,000
March	39,800	58,000
April	22,500	54,000

Francee expects that May purchases and sales will be $40,000 and $60,000, respectively. Francee usually pays 60 percent of any month's purchases in the month of purchase, on which an average 2 percent discount is taken. The remaining amount is paid in the following month with no discount. Other monthly payments for expenses run $12,000 plus 12 percent of sales. Depreciation is $2,000 per month. Francee wants a minimum cash balance of $14,000 and starts May with $18,000 cash.

Francee experiences the following collection pattern for sales: 25 percent in the month of sale, 60 percent in the month after the sale, and 15 percent in the second month after the sale. Francee has no debt other than what is currently owed for purchases on account.

Required:

a. Calculate the April 30 balances for Accounts Receivable and Accounts Payable.

b. Calculate the cash collections expected in May.

c. Calculate the expected total cash disbursements in May.

d. Present a cash budget for May. Assume management wants no more cash on hand at May 31 than the minimum cash balance desired.

e. Prepare an income statement for May. Assume an average gross margin percentage of 40 percent. Ignore income taxes.

35. *(Cash budget)* Cullum Company's accounting records show the following information related to purchases and sales during the first four months of 1995:

	Purchases	Sales
January	$65,000	$100,000
February	58,000	91,000
March	79,500	115,000
April	43,000	110,200

Cullum estimates that its May 1995 purchases and sales will be $78,700 and $103,400, respectively. The company pays for 45 percent of its purchases in the month of purchase, taking a 3 percent cash discount. The remainder of the purchases is paid for in the following month, and no discount is allowed. The cash collection pattern for Cullum is 30 percent in the month of sale, 55 percent in the month following the sale, 11 percent in the second month following the sale, and 4 percent uncollectible. Other expenses each month are normally 10 percent of sales plus $28,000, which includes $5,000 of depreciation and $1,500 of goodwill amortization. No Accounts Receivable have been written off.

Required:

a. If January 1995 was Cullum's first month in business, what is the April 30 balance in Accounts Receivable? Accounts Payable?

b. What are total cash collections expected in May 1995?

c. What are total cash disbursements expected in May 1995?

d. What is the expected cash balance at May 31, 1995, if the cash balance on May 1, 1995, was $23,000?

e. What is the expected income for May 1995 if the normal gross profit margin is 40 percent on sales?

36. *(Cash budget)* Warren Manufacturing has incurred substantial losses for several years and has decided to declare bankruptcy. The company petitioned the court for protection from creditors on March 31, 1995, and submitted the following balance sheet:

WARREN MANUFACTURING
BALANCE SHEET
MARCH 31, 1995

	Book Value	Liquidation Value
Assets		
Accounts receivable	$100,000	$ 50,000
Inventories	90,000	40,000
Plant assets (net)	150,000	160,000
Totals	$340,000	$250,000

Total liabilities and stockholders' equity of Warren at this date are:

Accounts payable—general creditors	$600,000
Common stock	60,000
Retained earnings (deficit)	(320,000)
Total	$340,000

Warren's management informed the court that the company has developed a new product and that a prospective customer is willing to sign a contract for the purchase (at a firm price of $90 per unit for all units) of 10,000 units of the product during the year ending March 31, 1996; 12,000 units during the year ending March 31, 1997; and 15,000 units during the year ending March 31, 1998. The product can be manufactured using Warren's present facilities. Monthly production with immediate delivery is expected to be uniform within the year. Receivables are expected to be collected during the calendar month following sales.

Unit production costs of the new product are estimated at

Direct materials	$20
Direct labor	30
Variable overhead	10

Fixed costs of $130,000 (excluding depreciation) are estimated per year.

Purchases of direct materials will be paid during the calendar month following purchase. Fixed costs, direct labor, and variable overhead will be paid as incurred. Inventory of direct materials will be equal to sixty days' usage. After the first month of operations, thirty days' usage will be ordered each month.

The general creditors have agreed to reduce their total claims to 60 percent of their March 31, 1995, balances under the following conditions:

- Existing accounts receivable and inventories are to be liquidated immediately, with the proceeds turned over to the general creditors.
- The balance of reduced accounts payable is to be paid as cash is generated from future operations, but in no event later than March 31, 1997. No interest will be paid on these obligations.

Under this proposed plan, the general creditors would receive $110,000 more than the current liquidation value of Warren's assets. The court has engaged you to determine the feasibility of this plan.

Required: Ignoring any need to borrow and repay short-term funds for working capital purposes, prepare a cash budget for the years ending March 31, 1996 and 1997, showing the cash expected to be available to pay the claims of the general creditors, the payments to general creditors, and the cash remaining after payment of claims.

(AICPA)

37. *(Comprehensive)* The Skelle Company produces and sells two products, rachets and sprachets. In July 1995, Skelle's budget department gathered the following data to project budgeted requirements for 1996:

1996 Projected Sales

Product	Units	Price
Rachets	60,000	$ 70
Sprachets	40,000	100

1996 Inventories—Units

Product	Expected 1/1/96	Desired 12/31/96
Rachets	20,000	25,000
Sprachets	8,000	9,000

To produce one of each product, the following raw materials are used:

Raw Material	Measure	1 Rachet	1 Sprachet
A	pounds	4	5
B	pounds	2	3
C	units		1

Projected data for 1996 with respect to raw materials are as follows:

Raw Material	Anticipated Purchase Price	Expected Inventory 1/1/96	Desired Inventory 12/31/96
A	$8	32,000 lbs.	36,000 lbs.
B	$5	29,000 lbs.	32,000 lbs.
C	$3	6,000 units	7,000 units

Projected direct labor requirements for 1996 and rates are as follows:

Product	Hours Per Unit	Rate Per Hour
Rachet	2	$6
Sprachet	3	$8

Overhead is applied at a rate of $5 per direct labor hour.

Required: Based on the previous projections and budget requirements for 1996 for Skelle Company, prepare the following budgets for 1996 for each product, and in total, for Skelle Company:

a. sales budget (in dollars)
b. production budget (in units)
c. raw materials purchases budget (in quantities)
d. raw materials purchases budget (in dollars)
e. direct labor budget (in dollars)
f. budgeted Finished Goods Inventory at December 31, 1996 (in dollars)

(AICPA adapted)

38. *(Comprehensive)* Captain Quirk Enterprises (CQE) makes an environmentally safe space-age cat litter called Pooh Wars. You have been asked to prepare CQE's 1996 master budget and have been provided with the following:

1. The 12/31/95 estimated balance sheet data follows:

Assets

Cash		$ 5,260
Accounts Receivable		16,900
Direct Materials Inventory (6,952 pounds)		1,390
Finished Goods Inventory (6,400 pounds)		6,208
Plant & Equipment	$440,000	
Accumulated Depreciation	112,000	328,000
Total assets		$357,758

Liabilities & Stockholders' Equity

Accounts Payable		$ 2,218
Note Payable		40,000
Total liabilities		$ 42,218
Common Stock	$200,000	
Retained Earnings	115,540	
Total stockholders' equity		315,540
Total liabilities & stockholders' equity		$357,758

2. Each pound of litter requires the following standards for direct materials and labor:

   - 1.1 pounds of materials mix (.1 pound is discarded as waste) at $.20 $.22
   - 2 minutes of labor time; direct labor averages $7.20 per hour   .24

   Variable overhead is applied on the basis of oven baking time. One and one-half hours of baking time is required for each finished pound of litter processed. The variable overhead is $.10 per finished pound per hour of baking time. Annual fixed production overhead of $86,400 is applied using an expected annual capacity of 240,000 pounds to be processed. The total fixed factory overhead comprises the following:

Salaries	$46,000
Insurance	1,800
Fixed portion of utilities	10,600
Depreciation	28,000

   Fixed overhead is incurred evenly throughout the year.

3. Expected sales in pounds for the first five months of 1996 are:

January	32,000
February	30,000
March	30,000
April	26,000
May	20,000

   CQE grants no discounts and all sales are on credit at $2 per pound. CQE's collection pattern is 80 percent in the month of sale, 15 percent in the month following the sale, and 5 percent in the second month following the sale. The Accounts Receivable balance in the balance sheet data shown earlier represents amounts remaining due from November sales, which were $66,000, and December sales of $68,000.

4. CQE completes all production each day. The desired ending Direct Materials Inventory balance is 10 percent of the amount needed to satisfy the next month's production for finished goods. Direct materials are carried at $.20 per pound. Finished litter is carried at $.97 (DM, $.22; DL, $.24; VOH, $.15; and FOH, $.36). Desired ending finished goods balances are 20 percent of the next month's sales.

5. Purchases are without discount and paid 70 percent in the month of purchase and 30 percent in the month following the purchase. The note payable has a 12 percent interest rate, and the interest is paid at the end of each month. The $40,000 balance of the principal on the note is due on March 31, 1996.

6. CQE's minimum cash balance desired is $5,000. The firm may borrow at the beginning of a month and repay at the end of the month in $500 increments. Interest on these short-term loans, if any, is payable monthly. Investments and investment liquidations are made only in $500 amounts at the end of a month and earn 12 percent per annum, collected monthly at month's end.

7. Period (SG&A) expenses, paid as incurred, run $18,000 per month plus 1 percent of revenue. Direct labor and overhead are paid as incurred.

8. The company accrues income taxes at a 40 percent rate, which will be paid in a quarterly installment on April 15, 1996.

Required: Prepare master budget schedules on a monthly basis for the first quarter of 1996 and pro forma financial statements as of the end of the first quarter. Round all numbers in schedules and pro forma statements to the nearest whole dollar.

39. *(Essay)* Royal Container, a privately held firm founded in 1991, specializes in the packaging of toys and games. The company's administrative offices are in Chicago, and the regional packaging plants are located in Seattle, Little Rock, Nashville, and Hartford. Royal Container expects 1995 sales to exceed $25 million, and the company is forecasting its first profitable year.

Because of its rapid growth, Royal Container has had ongoing requirements for additional working capital. The bank that participated in the initial financing of the company has continued to be supportive by arranging for additional long-range loans and extending a $3 million line of credit to the company. However, the bank is now reluctant to enter into a new loan agreement and has declined to increase the company's line of credit.

The board of directors of Royal Container is concerned about the company's capital position and has recently hired Jim Wilson as treasurer of the company. Wilson has been directed to improve the company's working capital position. Since joining Royal Container, Wilson has gathered the following information about the company's operations.

- Based on sales data received from the regional plants, all invoices are prepared at the Chicago office during the last week of each month. All sales are made on a credit basis, and payment terms are net thirty days.

- Customers' checks are sent to the Chicago office for processing and are deposited in the bank at 3:00 P.M. each afternoon. Approximately one and one-half days are required to process and deposit a check once it is received at the Chicago office.

- The collection effort on past-due accounts is haphazard and consists entirely of phone calls made by the controller when time allows. The company does not charge interest on past-due accounts.

- Royal Container has a strict credit policy, but it is not applied evenly. Because sales are made from all five locations, credit is often granted by the individual making the sale.
- Each of Royal Container's regional plants has its own bank account for disbursements, which includes payroll, inventory purchases, and repair and maintenance of equipment. These accounts are replenished by wire transfer of funds from the Chicago office.
- Because each plant controls its own disbursements, payment procedures are not standardized. Some locations take advantage of vendor discounts while others pay in thirty days.
- Royal Container has yet to develop inventory policies and procedures. Each plant does its own purchasing and maintains its own inventory records. New toys and games are continually being developed to keep up with changing tastes, and Royal Container must keep pace. Therefore, new items are frequently being added to inventories.

   Royal Container's board is concerned about the company's working capital position; however, they do not wish to make a public offering to raise cash unless it becomes absolutely necessary.

a. Discuss how Jim Wilson could improve Royal Container's working capital position by addressing the following areas of cash management:
   1. Acceleration of cash receipts
   2. Deceleration of cash disbursements
   3. Generation of cash
b. Describe how Royal Container's cash management might differ between a period of high interest rates and a period of low interest rates.

(CMA)

Cases

40. CrossMan Corporation, a rapidly expanding crossbow distributor to retail outlets, is in the process of formulating plans for 1994. Joan Caldwell, director of marketing, has completed her 1994 forecast and is confident that sales estimates will be met or exceeded. The following sales figures show the growth expected and will provide the planning basis for other corporate departments.

Month	Forecasted Sales	Month	Forecasted Sales
January	$1,800,000	July	$3,000,000
February	2,000,000	August	3,000,000
March	1,800,000	September	3,200,000
April	2,200,000	October	3,200,000
May	2,500,000	November	3,000,000
June	2,800,000	December	3,400,000

   George Brownell, assistant controller, has been given the responsibility for formulating the cash flow projection, a critical element during a period of rapid expansion. The following information will be used in preparing the cash analysis:

- CrossMan has experienced an excellent record in accounts receivable collections and expects this trend to continue. Sixty percent of billings are collected in the month after sale and 40 percent in the second month after the sale. Uncollectible accounts are nominal and will not be considered in the analysis.

- The purchase of the crossbows is CrossMan's largest expenditure; the cost of these items equals 50 percent of sales. Sixty percent of the crossbows are received one month prior to sale and 40 percent are received during the month of sale.
- Prior experience shows that 80 percent of accounts payable are paid by CrossMan one month after receipt of the purchased crossbows, and the remaining 20 percent are paid the second month after receipt.
- Hourly wages, including fringe benefits, are a factor of sales volume and are equal to 20 percent of the current month's sales. These wages are paid in the month incurred.
- General and administrative expenses are projected to be $2,640,000 for 1994. The composition of the expenses is given next. All of these expenses are incurred uniformly throughout the year except the property taxes. Property taxes are paid in four equal installments in the last month of each quarter.

Salaries	$ 480,000
Promotion	660,000
Property taxes	240,000
Insurance	360,000
Utilities	300,000
Depreciation	600,000
Total	$2,640,000

- Income tax payments are made by CrossMan in the first month of each quarter based on income for the prior quarter. CrossMan's income tax rate is 40 percent. CrossMan's net income for the first quarter of 1994 is projected to be $612,000.
- CrossMan has a corporate policy of maintaining an end-of-month cash balance of $100,000. Cash is invested or borrowed monthly, as necessary, to maintain this balance.
- CrossMan uses a calendar year reporting period.

a. Prepare a pro forma schedule of cash receipts and disbursements for CrossMan Corporation, by month, for the second quarter of 1994. Be sure that all receipts, disbursements, and borrowing/investing amounts are presented on a monthly basis. Ignore the interest expense and/or interest income associated with the borrowing/investing activities.

b. Discuss why cash budgeting is particularly important for a rapidly expanding company such as CrossMan Corporation.

(CMA)

41. Watson Corporation manufactures and sells extended keyboard units to be used with microcomputers. Robin Halter, budget analyst, coordinated the preparation of the annual budget for the year ending August 31, 1993. The budget was based on the prior year's sales and production activity. The pro forma statements of income and cost of goods sold are as follows:

WATSON CORPORATION
PRO FORMA STATEMENT OF INCOME
FOR THE YEAR ENDING AUGUST 31, 1993
($000 OMITTED)

Net sales		$25,550
Cost of goods sold		16,565
Gross profit		$ 8,985
Operating expenses		
Marketing	$3,200	
General and administrative	2,000	5,200
Income from operations before income taxes		$ 3,785

WATSON CORPORATION
PRO FORMA STATEMENT OF COST OF GOODS SOLD
FOR THE YEAR ENDING AUGUST 31, 1993
($000 OMITTED)

Direct materials		
Materials inventory, 9/1/92	$ 1,200	
Materials purchased	11,400	
Materials available for use	12,600	
Materials inventory, 8/31/93	1,480	
Direct materials used		$11,120
Direct labor		980
Factory overhead		
Indirect materials	$ 1,112	
General factory overhead	2,800	3,912
Cost of goods manufactured		$16,012
Finished goods inventory, 9/1/92		930
Cost of goods available for sale		$16,942
Finished goods inventory, 8/31/93		377
Cost of goods sold		$16,565

On December 10, 1992, Halter met with Walter Collins, vice-president of finance, to discuss the first quarter's results (the period September 1 to November 30, 1992). After their discussion, Collins directed Halter to reflect the following changes to the budget assumptions in revised pro forma statements.

- The estimated production in units for the fiscal year should be revised from 140,000 to 145,000 units, with the balance of production being scheduled in equal segments over the last months of the year. The actual first quarter's production was 25,000 units.
- The planned inventory for finished goods of 3,300 units at the end of the fiscal year remains unchanged and will be valued at the average manufacturing cost for the year. The finished goods inventory of 9,300 units on September 1, 1992, had dropped to 9,000 units by November 30, 1992.
- Due to a new labor agreement, the labor rate will increase 8 percent effective June 1, 1993, the beginning of the fourth quarter, instead of the previously

anticipated effective date of September 1, 1993, the beginning of the next fiscal year.

- The assumptions remain unchanged for direct materials inventory at 16,000 units for beginning inventory and 18,500 units for ending inventory. Direct materials inventory is valued on a first-in, first-out basis. During the first quarter, direct materials for 27,500 units of output were purchased for $2,200,000. Although direct materials will be purchased evenly for the last nine months, the cost of the direct materials will increase by 5 percent on March 1, 1993, the beginning of the third quarter.
- Indirect material costs will continue to be projected at 10 percent of the cost of direct materials consumed.
- One-half of general factory overhead and all of the marketing and general and administrative expenses are considered fixed.

a. Based on the revised data presented, calculate Watson Corporation's projected sales for the year ending August 31, 1993, in
   1. number of units to be sold.
   2. dollar volume of net sales.
b. Prepare the pro forma statement of costs of goods sold for the year ending August 31, 1993.

(CMA)

42. Collegiate Management Education, Inc. (CME), is a nonprofit organization that sponsors a wide variety of management seminars throughout the Southwest. In addition, it is heavily involved in research into improved methods of teaching and motivating college administrators. The seminar activity is largely supported by fees and the research program from membership dues.

CME operates on a calendar year basis and is in the process of finalizing the budget for 1993. The following information has been taken from approved plans, which are still tentative at this time:

Seminar Program

Revenue—The scheduled number of programs should produce $12,000,000 of revenue for the year. Each program is budgeted to produce the same amount of revenue. The revenue is collected during the month the program is offered. The programs are scheduled during the basic academic year and are not held during June, July, August, and December. Twelve percent of the revenue is generated in each of the first five months of the year, and the remainder is distributed evenly during September, October, and November.

Direct expenses—The seminar expenses are made up of three types:

- Instructors' fees are paid at the rate of 70 percent of seminar revenue in the month following the seminar. The instructors are considered independent contractors and are not eligible for CME employee benefits.
- Facilities fees total $5,600,000 for the year. Fees are the same for each program and are paid in the month the program is given.
- Annual promotional costs of $1,000,000 are spent equally in all months except June and July when there is no promotional effort.

Research Program

Research grants—The research program has a large number of projects nearing completion. The other main research activity this year includes feasibility studies for new projects to be started in 1993. As a result, the total grant expense of $3,000,000 for 1993 is expected to be paid out at the rate of $500,000 per month during the first six months of the year.

Salaries and Other CME Expenses

Office lease—Annual amount of $240,000 paid monthly at the beginning of each month.

General administrative expenses—$1,500,000 annually or $125,000 per month. These are paid in cash as incurred.

Depreciation expense—$240,000 per year.

General CME promotion—Annual cost of $600,000, paid monthly.

Salaries and benefits—

Number of Employees	Monthly Cash Salary	Total Annual Salaries
1	$50,000	$ 50,000
3	40,000	120,000
4	30,000	120,000
15	25,000	375,000
5	15,000	75,000
22	10,000	220,000
50		$960,000

Employee benefits amount to $240,000, or 25 percent of annual salaries. Except for the pension contribution, the benefits are paid as salaries are paid. The annual pension payment of $24,000, based on 2.5 percent of salaries (including total benefits and the 25 percent rate), is due on April 15, 1993.

Other Information

Membership income—CME has 100,000 members who each pay an annual fee of $100. The fee for the calendar year is invoiced in late June. The collection schedule is as follows: July, 60 percent; August, 30 percent; September, 5 percent; and October, 5 percent.

Capital expenditures—The capital expenditures program calls for a total of $510,000 in cash payments to be spread evenly over the first five months of 1993.

Cash and temporary investments at January 1, 1993, are estimated at $750,000.

a. Prepare a budget of the annual cash receipts and disbursements for 1993.
b. Prepare a cash budget for CME, Inc., for January 1993.
c. Using the information developed in (a) and (b), identify two important operating problems of CME, Inc.

(CMA)

43. The Mason Agency, a division of General Service Industries, offers consulting services to clients for a fee. The corporate management at General Service is pleased with the performance of the Mason Agency for the first nine months of the current year and has recommended that the division manager of the Mason Agency, Richard Howell, submit a revised forecast for the remaining quarter, as the division has exceeded the annual plan year-to-date by 20 percent of operating income. An unexpected increase in billed hour volume over the original plan is the main reason for this gain in income. The original operating budget for the first three quarters for the Mason Agency is as follows:

1993–1994 Operating Budget

	1st Quarter	2d Quarter	3d Quarter	Total Nine Months
Revenue:				
Consulting fees				
Management consulting	$315,000	$315,000	$315,000	$ 945,000
EDP consulting	421,875	421,875	421,875	1,265,625
Total	$736,875	$736,875	$736,875	$2,210,625
Other revenue	10,000	10,000	10,000	30,000
Total	$746,875	$746,875	$746,875	$2,240,625
Expenses:				
Consultant salaries	$386,750	$386,750	$386,750	$1,160,250
Travel and entertainment	45,625	45,625	45,625	136,875
General and administration	100,000	100,000	100,000	300,000
Depreciation	40,000	40,000	40,000	120,000
Corporate allocation	50,000	50,000	50,000	150,000
Total	$622,375	$622,375	$622,375	$1,867,125
Operating income	$124,500	$124,500	$124,500	$ 373,500

When comparing the actuals for the first three quarters to the original plan, Howell analyzed the variances and will reflect the following information in his revised forecast for the fourth quarter:

- The division currently has twenty-five consultants on staff—ten for management consulting and fifteen for EDP consulting, and has hired three additional management consultants to start work at the beginning of the fourth quarter in order to meet the increased client demand.
- The hourly billing rate for consulting revenues is market acceptable and will remain at $90 per hour for each management consultant and $75 per hour for each EDP consultant. However, due to the favorable increase in billing hour volume when compared to plan, the hours for each consultant will be increased by fifty hours per quarter. New employees are equally as capable as current employees and will be billed at the current rates.
- The budgeted annual salaries and actual annual salaries, paid monthly, are the same at $50,000 for a management consultant and 8 percent less for an EDP consultant. Corporate management has approved a merit increase of 10 percent at the beginning of the fourth quarter for all twenty-five existing consultants, while the new consultants will be compensated at the planned rate.
- The planned salary expense includes a provision for employee fringe benefits amounting to 30 percent of the annual salaries; however, the improvement of some corporatewide employee programs will increase the fringe benefit allocation to 40 percent.
- The original plan assumes a fixed hourly rate for travel and other related expenses for each billing hour of consulting. These are expenses that are not reimbursed by the client, and the previously determined hourly rate has proven to be adequate to cover these costs.
- Other revenues are derived from temporary rentals and interest income and remain unchanged for the fourth quarter.
- General and administrative expenses have been favorable at 7 percent below the plan; this 7 percent savings on fourth-quarter expenses will be reflected in the revised plan.
- Depreciation for office equipment and microcomputers will stay constant at the projected straight-line rate.

- Due to the favorable experience for the first three quarters and the division's increased ability to absorb costs, the corporate management at General Service Industries has increased the corporate expense allocation by 50 percent.

a. Prepare a revised operating budget for the fourth quarter for the Mason Agency, which Richard Howell will present to General Service Industries. Be sure to furnish supporting calculations for all revised revenue and expense amounts.

b. Discuss the reasons why an organization would prepare a revised forecast.

(CMA adapted)

▌ Ethics Discussion

44. Comet Company is in the process of acquiring a $10,000,000 bank loan that is vital to the continuation of the business. Comet submitted its 1995 pro forma financial statements to the bank two weeks ago. Caspari Pacioli, the loan officer, informed Comet's CFO that the pro formas would be a primary ingredient in determining whether the loan would be granted.

    After the pro forma statements were submitted, Comet's CFO learned that a major customer (which accounts for 35 percent of annual sales) is being absorbed by a larger national chain. Because the national chain has the capability of providing Comet's customer with the same type of products that Comet now provides, Comet's CFO believes that the customer will be lost to the national chain.

    Comet's sales manager believes that the lost sales can be replaced over the next two years. Loss of the customer will, however, most likely result in a poor cash flow situation that could easily affect the scheduled bank loan repayment. The company president is concerned that if the bank is told of the situation at this time, the loan will not be made and Comet Company will be forced out of business. Comet's president reasons that, when the pro forma information was submitted, the expected figures were provided in good faith. Had the loss of the customer been known at the time of the preparation of the pro formas, other arrangements might have been made.

a. Does the company have a legal or a moral obligation to immediately inform the bank of the customer's acquisition?

b. What are the implications of telling the loan officer at the bank?

c. What are the implications of not telling the loan officer at the bank?

d. What do you recommend and why?

PART FOUR

USING MANAGERIAL ACCOUNTING INFORMATION FOR CONTROLLING

C H A P T E R   13

PRODUCTION AND INVENTORY MANAGEMENT TECHNIQUES

LEARNING OBJECTIVES

After completing this chapter, you should be able to do the following:

1. Calculate and use economic order quantity and reorder point
2. Differentiate between material requirements planning and the economic order quantity model
3. Evaluate the workings of the push and pull systems of production control
4. Explain the JIT philosophy and how it affects production
5. Explain how the traditional accounting system would change if a JIT inventory system were adopted
6. Understand why managers use ABC inventory control systems
7. (Appendix) Calculate reorder point
8. (Appendix) Understand why a company carries safety stock and how the appropriate amount is estimated

Harley-Davidson Gets Help From JIT

America was wild about motorcycles in the mid-1970s, which should have been great for Harley-Davidson. But Harley-Davidson, then owned by AMF, was in trouble. AMF had almost tripled production to 75,000 units annually over four years. Quality had deteriorated sharply—more than half the cycles came off the line missing parts, and dealers often had to fix them up to sell.

Though Harley's sales remained strong, its market share dwindled steadily . . . [and by] 1980, AMF was losing interest in the company. In 1981, thirteen Harley executives took the company over in an $81.5 million leveraged buyout. But manufacturing was still a major problem. Management had done everything it knew to boost quality and cut costs, but the Japanese were still producing better bikes at lower cost.

In October, 3½ months after the buyout, the manufacturing team began a pilot just-in-time inventory program in the Milwaukee engine plant. When that showed promise, Tom Gelb, senior VP of operations, called a series of meetings with employees to explain his plan to convert to JIT; many managers at the York, Pennsylvania, assembly plant reacted with disbelief. Some workers laughed out loud. After all, York already had a computer-based control system with overhead conveyors and high-rise parts storage—and the new system would replace all this with push carts. The new owners appeared to be taking the company back to 1930.

Just-in-time, however, eliminates the mountains of costly inventory that require elaborate handling systems and at the same time clears away many other manufacturing problems. For example, parts at York were made in large batches for long production runs, stored until needed, then loaded onto the 3.5-mile conveyor that rattled endlessly around the plant. "Sometimes we couldn't even find the parts we needed," says Gelb. "Or if we found them they were rusted or damaged. Or there had been an engineering change since the parts were made and they didn't even fit."

SOURCE: Peter C. Reid, "How Harley Beat Back the Japanese," FORTUNE (September 25, 1989), p. 155ff. © 1989 The Time Inc. Magazine Company. All rights reserved.

I n recent years, questions have been raised as to the productivity and efficiency of American companies—especially in comparison to their counterparts in Japan. Like Harley-Davidson Motor Company, many U.S. companies have begun concentrating on ways to improve productivity and use available technology. These efforts are often directed at reducing the costs of producing and carrying inventory.

Other than the amount spent on plant assets, the amount spent on inventory can be the largest investment made by a company. This is especially true in retail companies. Unfortunately, investment in inventory provides no return until that inventory is sold. Chapters 11 and 12 discuss the budgeting process and the importance of inventory management. This chapter deals with a variety of techniques that minimize organizational investment in inventory. These techniques include: economic order quantity (EOQ); material requirements planning (MRP); the just-in-time (JIT) philosophy; and ABC inventory analysis. Additionally, the appendix covers the concepts of reorder point and safety stock.

COSTS ASSOCIATED WITH INVENTORY

Most organizations that engage in any type of conversion use some inputs and produce some outputs that are tangible or physical in nature. Inputs and outputs that have a physical presence can be stored or inventoried. For example, raw materials and finished goods can be stockpiled for later use. Nonphysical inputs and outputs, such as direct labor and cleaning services, are simultaneously consumed as they are supplied. The potential for physical items to be placed in, or withdrawn from, inventory creates opportunities for managers to improve organizational effectiveness and efficiency by manipulating the quantities in which items are purchased, produced, and stored.

Good inventory management largely relies on cost-minimizing strategies. As indicated in Exhibit 13–1, there are four basic costs associated with inventory: (1) purchasing/production; (2) ordering or setup; (3) carrying goods in stock; and (4) not

EXHIBIT 13–1
▼▼▼▼▼▼▼▼▼▼▼

CATEGORIES OF INVENTORY COSTS

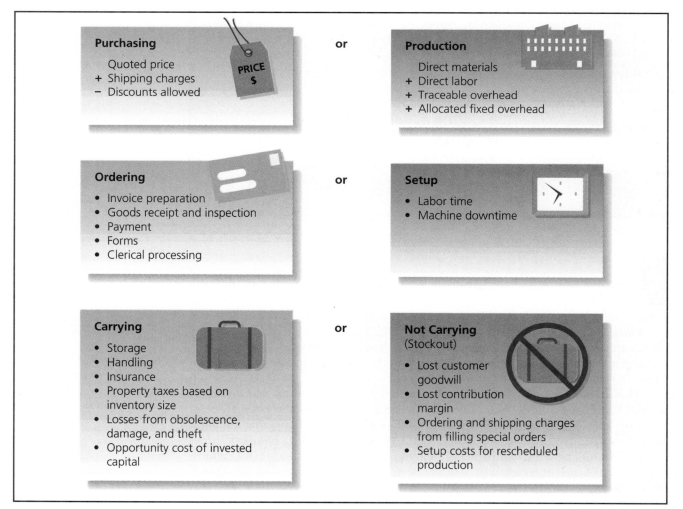

Purchasing

   Quoted price
+ Shipping charges
− Discounts allowed

or

Production

   Direct materials
+ Direct labor
+ Traceable overhead
+ Allocated fixed overhead

Ordering

• Invoice preparation
• Goods receipt and inspection
• Payment
• Forms
• Clerical processing

or

Setup

• Labor time
• Machine downtime

Carrying

• Storage
• Handling
• Insurance
• Property taxes based on inventory size
• Losses from obsolescence, damage, and theft
• Opportunity cost of invested capital

or

Not Carrying
(Stockout)

• Lost customer goodwill
• Lost contribution margin
• Ordering and shipping charges from filling special orders
• Setup costs for rescheduled production

carrying goods in stock. The **cost of purchasing** inventory is the quoted purchase price minus any discounts allowed plus any shipping charges. In a manufacturing company, the cost of production refers to the costs associated with purchasing direct materials, paying for direct labor, incurring traceable overhead, and having allocated fixed overhead.

Purchasing/production cost is the amount to be recorded in the inventory account. Purchasing cost size is commonly a factor in the degree of control that is maintained over the inventory item. As the unit cost increases, internal controls (such as inventory access) are typically tightened and a perpetual inventory system is more often used.

The incremental, variable costs associated with preparing, receiving, and paying for an order are called **ordering costs**. These costs include the cost of forms and a variety of clerical costs. Ordering costs are traditionally expensed as incurred, although under an activity-based costing system (discussed in chapter 4), these costs could be traced to the items ordered as an additional direct cost. Retailers incur ordering costs for all their merchandise inventory. In manufacturing companies, ordering costs are incurred for raw material purchases. If the company intends to produce rather than order a part, direct and indirect **setup costs** would be created as equipment was readied for each new production run; these costs would be incurred in lieu of ordering costs.

Inventory **carrying costs** consist of storage, handling, insurance charges, and ad valorem property taxes. Carrying costs can be estimated using information from various budgets, special studies, or other analytical techniques. One estimate of the size of the annual carrying cost is between 20 and 30 percent of the inventory's value.[1]

Carrying cost should also include the opportunity cost of the capital invested in inventory. Inventory is one of many organizational investments and should be ex-

cost of purchasing

ordering costs

setup costs

carrying costs

When a company produces as wide a variety of tube fittings, valves, and adapters as does the Fluid Connector Group at Parker Hannifin, reducing setup time is essential for fast delivery of parts to customers.

[1]Leslie N. Masonson, ed., "The Inventory Cardiogram: Unlocking an Overlooked Cash Flow Generator," *Cash Management Performance Report* (January 1991), p. 1.

pected to earn a rate of return similar to other investments.[2] One opportunity cost often ignored is any possible loss that might result from inventory obsolescence or damage. For example, a write-off of inventory cut Nike's profits by 40 percent in 1987.[3]

stockout

While carrying excess inventory generates costs, so can a fully depleted inventory. When a company does not have inventory available upon customer request, a **stockout** occurs. Stockout cost is not easily determinable or recordable, but includes lost customer goodwill, lost contribution margin from not being able to fill a sale, and the ordering and shipping charges incurred from filling special orders. The News Note on the next page indicates that the U.S. government is extremely concerned about not having a stockout on some items it may need.

All of the costs associated with inventory should be considered when purchasing decisions are made—and purchases should be made in "reasonable" quantities.

ECONOMIC ORDER QUANTITY

The first decision a purchasing manager needs to make is "from whom to buy." This decision should be based on which supplier can offer the appropriate quality of goods at the best price in the most reliable manner. While purchase cost is considered at this time, it must be viewed in relation to quality and reliability. The lowest-cost supplier is not necessarily the best supplier.

After the supplier is selected, the next decision is that of how many to buy at a time. The purchasing manager's objective is to buy in the most economical quantity possible, which requires consideration of the ordering and carrying costs of inventory. A tool used in this decision process is the **economic order quantity** (EOQ) model. EOQ is an estimate of the least costly number of units per order that would provide the optimal balance between ordering and carrying costs. The EOQ formula is

economic order quantity

$$EOQ = \sqrt{\frac{2QO}{C}}$$

where   EOQ = economic order quantity in units
Q = estimated annual quantity used (in units)
O = estimated cost of placing *one* order
C = estimated cost to carry *one* unit in stock for one year

The EOQ formula does not include purchase cost, since that amount relates to the decision of "from whom to buy" rather than to "how many to buy." Purchase cost does not affect ordering and carrying costs, except to the extent that opportunity cost is calculated on the basis of cost.

---

[2]The rate of return expected should be the weighted average cost of capital, which is discussed in chapter 17.
[3]Kathleen Kerwin and Mark Landler, "L.A. Gear Is Tripping Over Its Shoelaces," *Business Week* (August 20, 1990), p. 39.

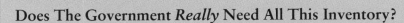
Assume that SABRINA produces crystal atomizers. The company purchases cardboard boxes in which to pack its various products. Boxes must be available at all times because of product breakage. The purchasing manager, Bill Withers, has found several suppliers who can continuously provide the proper quality of boxes at a cost of $2 each. Exhibit 13–2 provides information for use in calculating economic order quantity and uses a flexible budget to show the total costs of purchasing 750,000 boxes per year in various order sizes.

The EOQ model assumes that orders will be filled exactly when needed, so when the order arrives, the inventory on hand is zero units. Thus, the average inventory is half of any given order size. The number of times an order must be placed depends on how many units are ordered each time. The total number of orders equals total annual quantity of units needed divided by size of the order placed.

EXHIBIT 13–2

SABRINA YEARLY PURCHASING COST FOR BOXES

Annual quantity needed (Q) = 750,000
Cost of ordering (O) = $4.00 per order
Cost of carrying (C) = $ .60 per unit

Size of order	500	1,000	2,000	3,000	4,000	5,000
Average inventory	250	500	1,000	1,500	2,000	2,500
Number of orders	1,500	750	375	250	187.50	150
Annual:						
Ordering cost	$6,000	$3,000	$1,500	$1,000	$ 750	$ 600
Carrying cost	150	300	600	900	1,200	1,500
Total cost	$6,150	$3,300	$2,100	$1,900	$1,950	$2,100

Exhibit 13–2 indicates that as order size increases, the number of orders and the total annual ordering costs decline. At the same time, the total annual cost of carrying inventory increases because more units are being held in inventory at any given point. Alternatively, smaller size orders reduce carrying costs, but increase annual ordering costs. Total annual costs for SABRINA decline through an order size of 3,000 units; then, they begin to rise.

Based on total costs, Exhibit 13–2 indicates that SABRINA's most economical order size is between 3,000 and 4,000 units. Using the formula, the economic order quantity is found to be 3,162 units:

$$EOQ = \sqrt{\frac{2(750,000)\ (4)}{.60}}$$

$$EOQ = \sqrt{10,000,000}$$

$$EOQ = 3,162 \text{ (rounded)}$$

The total annual cost to place and carry orders of 3,162 units is $1,897.48, calculated as follows:

Average inventory (3,162 ÷ 2)	1,581
Number of orders (750,000 ÷ 3,162)	237 (rounded)
Cost of ordering (237 × $4.00)	$ 948
Cost of carrying (1,581 × $.60)	949 (rounded)
Total cost	$1,897

Note that this total cost does not include the $2 purchase cost per unit.

Managers must remember that the EOQ formula contains *estimated* values. However, in most instances, small errors in estimating costs will not cause a major impact on total cost. If the cost of ordering quantities close to the EOQ level is not significantly different from the cost of ordering at the EOQ level, factors such as cash availability and storage space constraints should be considered.

In a manufacturing company, managers are concerned with "how many units to produce" in addition to "how many units (of a raw material) to buy." The EOQ formula can be modified to calculate the appropriate number of units to manufacture in an **economic production run** (EPR). The EPR quantity minimizes the total costs of setting up a production run and carrying a unit in stock for one year. In the EPR formula, the terms of the EOQ equation are simply defined as manufacturing costs rather than purchasing costs:

economic production run

$$EPR = \sqrt{\frac{2QS}{C}}$$

where EPR = economic production run
     Q = estimated annual quantity to be produced (in units)
     S = estimated cost of setting up *a* production run
     C = estimated cost of carrying *one* unit in stock for one year

Like the answer provided by the EOQ model, the differences in costs among various run sizes around the EPR may not be significant. If such costs are insignificant, management would have a range of acceptable, economical production run quantities.

MATERIALS REQUIREMENTS PLANNING

The basic EOQ model determines what quantity of inventory to order. One problem with this model is that relationships among inventory items are ignored. For example, Harley-Davidson might require four lug nuts to install a tire on a motorcycle. If the EOQs for tires and lug nuts are computed independently, this interrelationship could be overlooked. Harley might find that, at a time when four thousand tires are on hand, there are only fourteen thousand lug nuts. Computer techniques known as MRP or MRP II overcome this deficiency in the EOQ model by integrating interrelationships of units into the ordering process.

MRP, or **materials requirements planning,** was developed to answer the questions of what items are needed, how many of them are needed, and when they are needed. MRP is a computer simulation system "to help companies plan by calculating the future availability of raw materials, parts, subassemblies, and end products based on a master production schedule [MPS]."[4] The MPS is developed using budgeted sales information and would be essentially equivalent to the production budget shown in chapter 12, although with significantly more detail as to time horizons. The master production schedule is then converted into individual schedules that indicate the raw materials and components needed to produce the finished goods in the specified time.

materials requirements planning

Once projected sales and production for a product have been estimated, the MRP computer model accesses the product's bill of materials to determine all production components. Quantities needed are compared to current inventory balances and, if purchases are necessary, the estimated lead times for each purchase are accessed from supplier information contained in the data base. The model then generates a time-sequenced schedule for purchases and production component needs.

The MPS is integrated with the operations flow documents to project the work load on each work center that would result from the given master schedule. The work loads are then compared to the work center's capacity to determine whether meeting the master schedule is feasible. Potential bottlenecks are identified so that changes in input factors (such as the quantity of a particular component) can be made, and the MRP program is run again. This process is reiterated until the schedule compensates for all potential bottlenecks in the production system.

A fully integrated MRP system, known as MRP II (**manufacturing resource planning**), plans production jobs using the usual MRP method and also calculates resource needs such as labor and machine hours. MRP II involves manufacturing, marketing, and finance in determining the master production schedule. While manu-

manufacturing resource planning

---

[4]Lakshmi U. Tatikonda and Rao J. Tatikonda, "Success in MRP," *Management Accounting* (May 1989), p. 34.

facturing is primarily responsible for carrying out the master schedule, it is essential that appropriate levels of resource and sales support be available to make the plan work.

The MRP models extend, rather than eliminate, the economic order quantity concept. EOQ indicates the most economical quantity to order at one time, and MRP indicates which items of inventory to order at what points in time. Because of lead time or economic production/order quantity requirements, these two models may cause inventory to be purchased or produced that is not currently needed. Such inventory would have to be stored until it is needed by other work centers. Exhibit 13–3 depicts the relationship of inventory to production processes in such a traditional **push system** production environment.

push system

As discussed in the next News Note, many firms have achieved the significant benefits of reduced inventories, improved labor and space utilization, improved communications, and streamlined scheduling from using MRP and MRP II. In addition, companies report better customer service because of the elimination of erratic production and back orders.

MRP and MRP II also have their problems, some of which are caused by their less-than-realistic underlying assumptions. These assumptions are not unique to MRP/MRP II and can also cause difficulties when they are used in other decision-making situations. The following are five "problem" assumptions:

1. The bill of materials and operations flow documents are assumed to be complete and totally accurate. If they are not, small inconsistencies or distortions in quantities or labor times may become cumulatively significant over time.
2. MRP assumes that there are no "bottleneck" operations in the factory even though most production processes include one or more operations that can-

EXHIBIT 13–3
▼▼▼▼▼▼▼▼▼▼▼

PUSH SYSTEM OF
PRODUCTION
CONTROL

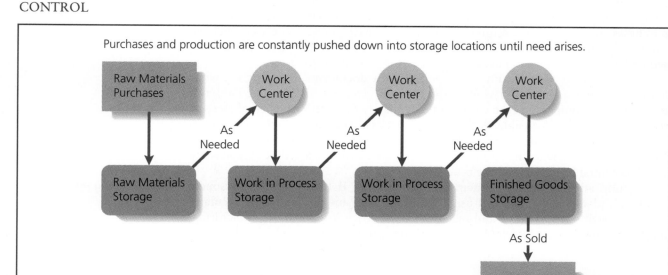

Purchases and production are constantly pushed down into storage locations until need arises.

NEWS
NOTE

MRP Helps in Inventory Planning

[MRP and MRP II have] played a key role in the success of the AccuRate Division of Mosknes Manufacturing Co. by alleviating inventory shortages and by refining production scheduling. Even though production and sales of [AccuRate's] machines increased 45% during 1987, on-time delivery, with a shortened lead time, was still achieved.

The ability to time-phase demand has had a positive effect on inventory planning in the Division. With MRP, shortages are no longer a rampant problem. MRP also has allowed attention to be focused on other problems such as the quality of vendor-supplied material, so that vendor quality and delivery performance have improved significantly.

The top-down planning inherent in MRP II facilitates the effective use of all manufacturing resources. Starting at the highest executive level, all officers and functional heads formulate a strategic plan that becomes a part of the master production schedule and is translated into work orders and projects for execution at the lower levels.

Cooperation is needed from all functional areas to secure accurate data. The common database shared by the entire company must have accurate data at all levels to ensure that the vital data elements in the database are available and usable. If the numbers are correct and generate valid schedules, all in the manufacturing plant can work together as a team.

In MRP II systems, information is the link between: strategic planning and shop floor control; the functional areas of marketing, engineering, and manufacturing; and the firm and its vendors.

SOURCE: Joseph R. Biggs and Ellen J. Long, "Gaining the Competitive Edge with MRP/MRP II," *Management Accounting* (May 1988), p. 27ff. Published by Institute of Management Accountants, Montvale, N.J.

not be eliminated. (Remember, the MRP system is run successively until the bottlenecks are eliminated on the computer model—which does not necessarily eliminate them in the workplace.)

3. MRP is based on the EOQ model that employs fixed estimates for annual usage, carrying and ordering cost, and lead time. These estimates may be imprecise and actual cost factors may be quite volatile. For example, carrying cost is often simply estimated as the direct financing cost of holding inventory. This type of estimate fails to include indirect costs such as additional space requirements, higher obsolescence, and so on. One source estimates that if the financing cost of holding inventory "is 10%, then a more accurate estimate of the total cost may be 20 to 25%."[5] Such a significant understatement in carrying cost may cause firms to purchase in much larger quantities than are cost beneficial.

4. Current inventory levels are assumed to be the amounts reflected by the accounting records. These records can be incorrect for a variety of reasons, such

[5]Robert A. Howell and Stephen R. Soucy, "The New Manufacturing Environment: Major Trends for Management Accounting," *Management Accounting* (July 1987), p. 22.

Bar codes provide information to managers about the sales that have occurred. This information can then be used to indicate what products are most popular and which ones need to be reordered. EOQ techniques can assist in determining order sizes.

as shortages from theft, breakage, or (in Harley-Davidson's case) rust, or from human errors in counting or recording.

5. MRP assumes that the system will be in effect and used at all times. Managers, however, often use less formalized systems to achieve objectives and may not fully implement MRP.

The no-bottleneck assumption made by the MRP model often provides unrealistic schedules of processing. "MRP survives by building excess lead time into the system. This approach allows MRP to work but at a cost of higher inventories and unreliable schedules."[6] Thus, many companies are now attempting to reduce inventory levels and purchase order quantities through the introduction of just-in-time inventory systems.

---

[6]James B. Edwards, "At the Crossroads," *Management Accounting* (September 1985), p. 48.

JUST-IN-TIME SYSTEMS

At least two major problems are associated with the use of the EOQ model. First, identifying all the relevant inventory costs (especially carrying costs) is very difficult. Second, the EOQ model does not provide any direction for managers attempting to control all the separate costs that collectively make up purchasing and carrying costs. By considering only trade-offs between purchasing and carrying costs, the EOQ model does not lead managers to consider inventory management alternatives that may simultaneously reduce both categories of costs.

Just-in-time (JIT) is a philosophy about when to do something. The *when* is "as needed" and the *something* is a production, purchasing, or delivery activity. The JIT philosophy is applicable in any type of organization (retail, service, and manufacturing). The basic purpose of the JIT philosophy is to minimize wasted activities and excess costs; its elements are outlined in Exhibit 13–4.

Regardless of the type of organization in which it exists, a just-in-time system has three primary goals:

- elimination of any production process or operation that does not add value to the product/service;
- continuous improvement in production/performance efficiency; and
- reduction in the total cost of production/performance.

For example, in a **JIT manufacturing system,** the company attempts to acquire components and produce inventory units only as they are needed, minimize product defects, and reduce lead/setup times for acquisition and production. Production has traditionally been dictated by the need to smooth operating activity over a period of time. Smooth production allows a company to maintain a steady work force and

JIT manufacturing system

Inventory is a liability, not an asset; eliminate it to the extent possible.

Storage space is directly related to inventories; eliminate it in response to the elimination of inventories.

Long lead times cause inventory buildup; keep lead times as short as possible by using frequent deliveries.

Creative thinking doesn't cost anything; use it to find ways to reduce costs before making expenditures for additional resources.

Quality is essential at all times; work to eliminate defects and scrap.

Suppliers are essential to operations; establish and cultivate good relationships with them including the use of long-term contracts.

Employees often have the best knowledge of ways to improve operations; listen to them.

Employees generally have more talents than are being used; train them to be multiskilled and increase their productivity.

Ways to improve operations are always available; look for them constantly, being certain to make fundamental changes rather than superficial ones.

EXHIBIT 13–4
▼▼▼▼▼▼▼▼▼▼

ELEMENTS OF JIT PHILOSOPHY

generate continuous machine use. However, while smooth production fulfills the underlying EOQ assumptions of average use and size of inventory, managers recognize that EOQ is based on estimates and build in a buffer safety stock in the EOQ model to have parts "on hand" in case they are needed. Also, as discussed in the following News Note, smooth production often creates products that are stored for future sales.

EXHIBIT 13–5

DEPICTION OF
TRADITIONAL AND
JIT PRODUCTION
PHILOSOPHIES

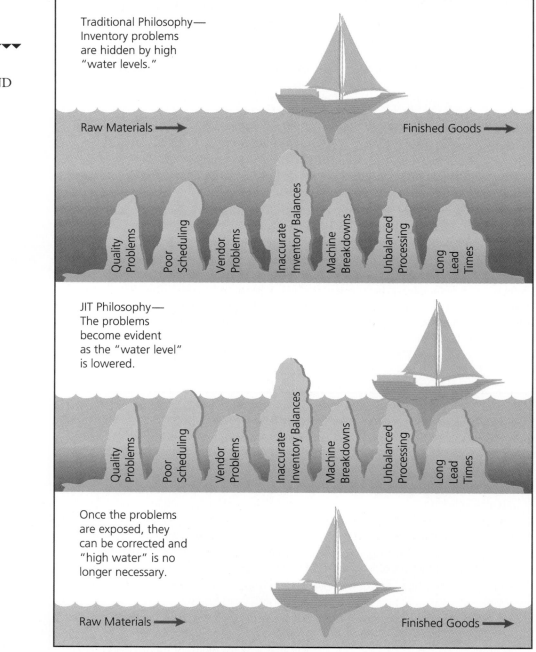

Reprinted with permission of Ernst & Young. © Ernst & Young, 1987.

NEWS NOTE

The Big Box Theory

You've heard of the "big bang theory," now hear about the "big box theory." The big box is our factory. We put costs into the box and out come products. For too long we have been analyzing the individual costs within the box and forgetting about the number of products coming out. We played games like building inventory to lower our unit costs, but the product stayed in the box. We appeared to be very efficient in labor and machine utilization, but what good is it if the product stays in the box?

We also soon realized our box was not big enough to hold all the products we produced. So we built other boxes, called warehouses, to store them in. Most companies became very efficient at producing products with low unit costs. Unfortunately, the products sat in the warehouses.

While we were filling up the boxes with products we did not need, we were simultaneously missing our customer delivery promise dates. The factory was very efficient with long production runs but the wrong product was being produced.

SOURCE: John F. Towey, ed., "What is JIT and FMS?" *Management Accounting* (May 1988), p. 71. Published by Institute of Management Accountants, Montvale, N.J.

Thus, the various types of inventory (raw materials, components, supplies, and work in process) have generally been maintained at high enough levels to cover up for inefficiencies in acquisition and/or production. Exhibit 13–5 depicts these inefficiencies or problems as "rocks" in a stream of "water" representing inventory. The traditional philosophy is that the "water level" (inventory) should be kept high enough for the "rocks" (problems) to be so deeply submerged that there will be "smooth sailing" in production activity. This technique is intended to avoid the original problems, but it creates a new one. By covering up the problems, the excess inventory adds to the difficulty of making corrections. The JIT manufacturing philosophy is to lower the water level (inventory), expose the rocks (problems), and eliminate them to the extent possible. The shallower stream will then flow more smoothly and rapidly than the deep river.

Just-in-time manufacturing has many names, including zero-inventory production systems (ZIPS) and **Kanban** (pronounced "kahn bahn," which is the Japanese word for *card*). The Kanban system originated from the use of cards to control the flow of materials between work centers. In a JIT system, no manufacturing occurs unless it is needed by the next work center in the production line. This factor makes JIT a pull system of production control rather than a push system.

Kanban

In a **pull system** of production, parts are delivered or manufactured only as they are needed by the work center for which they are intended. There are basically no storage areas to which work is "pushed" when it is completed but not needed to meet current sales orders or production demands. Exhibit 13–6 illustrates a pull system of production, and the News Note at the top of page 564 provides an excellent example of such a system.

pull system

Since JIT is a pull system, forecasted sales demand is the controlling production force. Once demand is estimated, the production schedule is set for an extended period (such as a month), and schedule changes should be minimal. Level scheduling

NEWS NOTE

We Could Have It To You Quicker, But . . .

The National Bicycle Industrial Co. of Kokubu, Japan, makes custom-made, hand-assembled bicycles one by one. With 20 employees and a computer capable of design work, this small factory is ready to produce any of 11,231,862 variations on 18 models of bikes in 199 color patterns and about as many sizes as there are people. Production doesn't start until a customer places an order, but within two weeks a one-of-a-kind machine is available. From individually-taken measurements and specifications, a CAD [computer-aided design] system creates blueprints in three minutes that would take a draftsman 60 times as long. A custom bike requires 3 hours to make and sells for $545 to $3,200, compared with 90 minutes for a mass-produced model that sells for $250 to $510. Margins are fat, workers proud, and customers happy with their unique machines. With a 3-hour production time, why the two-week wait? Says Koji Nishikawa, head of sales: "We could have made the time shorter, but we want people to feel excited about waiting for something special."

SOURCE: Adapted from Susan Moffat, "Japan's New Personalized Production," *FORTUNE* (October 22, 1990), p. 132. © 1990 The Time Inc. Magazine Company. All rights reserved.

creates a constant rate of use for component materials, labor, equipment, materials handling, maintenance, and support functions. Slack time found in the schedule is not treated as idle time. If workers are not needed for production activities, time is used for employee training, machine maintenance, and workplace organization.

EXHIBIT 13–6
▼▼▼▼▼▼▼▼▼▼▼▼

PULL SYSTEM OF
PRODUCTION
CONTROL

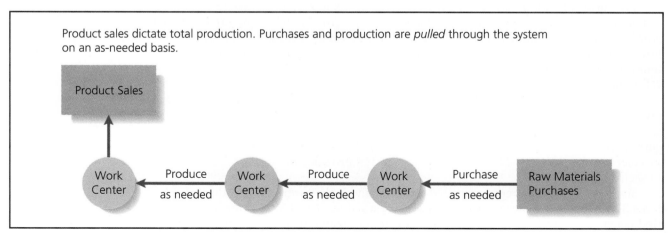

Product sales dictate total production. Purchases and production are *pulled* through the system on an as-needed basis.

CHANGES NEEDED TO IMPLEMENT JIT

Implementing a just-in-time system does not occur overnight; it took Toyota over twenty years to develop its system and realize significant benefits from it. While JIT techniques are becoming more well known and more quickly and easily implemented, the most impressive benefits are normally reached only after the system has been operational for five to ten years. "Japanese companies that have used [JIT] for five or more years are reporting close to a 30% increase in labor productivity, a 60% reduction in inventories, a 90% reduction in quality rejection rates, and a 15% reduction in necessary plant space." [7] Hewlett-Packard (an American company that successfully uses JIT in its Fort Collins, Colorado, plant) has shown "an increase in work in process [turnover] from 5 to 45 times per year, a decrease in required space of 20% while output increased 29%, and both scrap and rework decreases of more than 50%." [8]

For any company to achieve the JIT goals, certain modifications must be made in purchasing, supplier relationships, and distribution. Manufacturers must additionally address product design, product processing, and plant layout. Product design is discussed in chapter 10; the remaining topics are discussed in the following sections.

Purchasing, Supplier Relationships, and Distribution

When applying JIT to purchasing, it must first be recognized that the lowest quoted purchase price does not necessarily mean the lowest cost. "Once the cost of poor quality is factored in—downtime on the line, rework, scrap, warranty work, legal fees, and so on—the cheapest may well be the most costly." [9] To assure high quality, good vendor relationships are essential.

The optimal JIT situation would be to have only one vendor for all items. Such an ideal, however, creates the risk of not having alternative sources (especially for critical products or materials) in the event of vendor production strikes, unfair pricing, or shipment delays. Thus, it is often more feasible and realistic to reduce the number of vendors to a limited number. The selected vendors would be certified as to quality and reliability.

Certifying vendors as to quality and reliability means substantial effort on the purchasing company's part. People from various areas must decide on the factors by which the vendor will be rated and, then, weigh these factors as to relative importance. Evaluations should be made and discussed with the vendors so they will understand their strong and weak points and how they compare to their competitors. Vendors should be monitored after selection to assure continued compliance. Thus, rather than performing quality inspections to find defective products, ideally JIT managers can concentrate on providing quality service to customers.

---

[7]Sumer C. Aggarwal, "MRP, JIT, OPT, FMS? Making Sense of Production Operations Systems," *Harvard Business Review* (September–October 1985), p. 9.
[8]Thomas E. Vollman, William Lee Berry, and D. Clay Whybark, *Manufacturing Planning and Control Systems,* 2nd ed. (Homewood, Ill.: Dow-Jones Irwin/APICS Series in Production Management, 1988), p. 271.
[9]David N. Burt, "Managing Suppliers Up to Speed," *Harvard Business Review* (July–August 1989), p. 127.

Working with fewer vendors on a long-term basis provides the opportunity to develop better communications, assure quality and service (including delivery), obtain quantity discounts, and reduce operating costs. As shown in the News Note opposite, Baylor University Medical Center is in the process of establishing at least one closer supplier relationship that should reduce costs and improve service.

One unit is the ideal economic order quantity in a JIT system. While this quantity is normally not a feasible ordering level, the closer a company can get to it, the more effective the JIT system is. A reduction in ordering levels means more frequent orders and deliveries. Ford, for example, has some deliveries made every two hours! [10] Thus, vendors chosen by the company should be located close to the company to minimize both shipping costs and delivery time.

The ability to obtain suppliers close to the plant is easy in a country the size of Japan. Such an objective is not so readily accomplished in the United States where a plant can be located in New Jersey and a critical parts vendor in California. UPS, though, recognizes the critical nature of prompt delivery and is using it as an important marketing tool:

> Is just-in-time, low inventory logistics the reason for guaranteed UPS 2nd Day Air? Or is it 2nd Day Air that makes JIT practical and profitable? Whichever it is, the two are a perfect match. UPS 2nd Day Air provides the guaranteed time-definite delivery that is the backbone (or, more accurately, the circulatory system) of any minimum-inventory logistics program.[11]

In the heart of downtown Dallas, Baylor Medical Center seeks to implement the Japanese-inspired JIT philosophy. The hospital and its supplier, Owens & Minor, are committed to a long-term relationship that will benefit both the two parties involved and the hospital's patients.

---

[10]Ibid., p. 128.
[11] "Delivering Like Clockwork—Second Day Air," *RoundUPS* (Fall 1991), p. 8. © United Parcel Service of America. Reprinted with permission.

NEWS NOTE

Team Up with Your Suppliers

In partnership with Owens & Minor, Baylor University Medical Center is testing a new total quality supply management process to reduce total delivered costs. Lee Majewski, Baylor's Director of Material Services, said the new process has the potential to change the industry from the cost-plus system of pricing to a system based on clearer identification of the true costs of supply and distribution.

"This process identifies the hospital's individual costs, not industry standards. We can no longer tolerate commonly accepted levels of delay, stock-outs, back-orders, etc., because of the costs associated with such inefficiencies." Majewski believes that establishing long-term, trusting and, where appropriate, single source relationships with suppliers is a key part of the Baylor commitment to continuous improvement. He also said that requiring statistical evidence of quality from trading partners will lend itself to the selection of the lowest cost provider of services.

"By forming partnerships with all members of the supply chain, we can eliminate redundancies in warehousing, packaging, labeling, transportation, inventories, etc., that will provide continuous savings instead of one-time inventory buy-backs or other current industry gimmicks and fads," Fred Ricker, Vice President of Logistics, of O&M said.

SOURCE: "Baylor University Medical Center Teams Up with O&M," *The [Owens & Minor, Inc.] Community Post* (Fall 1991), pp. 1, 3.

Firms have implemented numerous techniques that embrace JIT concepts relative to purchasing and vendors. Large trucks are being traded for smaller, more efficient ones for the limited delivery quantities. Suppliers are being asked to deliver materials "ready for use" with little packaging or with packaging that can be alternately-used or reused. Long-term supplier contracts are negotiated with continuance based on delivery reliability. Vendors missing a certain number of scheduled deliveries by more than a specified number of hours are dismissed.

Focused factory arrangements are often adopted to connect a vendor more closely to a JIT manufacturer's operations. A **focused factory arrangement** is one in which a vendor agrees to provide a limited number of products according to specifications or to perform a limited number of unique services for the JIT company. "The supplier, in effect, becomes a specialized maker and functional specialist to a major manufacturer." [12] Such an arrangement may involve relocation or plant modernization by the vendor, and financial assistance from the JIT manufacturer may be available to recoup such investments. In addition, the vendor benefits from long-term supply contracts. Simpson Industries, Inc., which signed a nine-year supplier agreement with Consolidated Diesel, is a partner in such a relationship. From a $9 million investment, Simpson has gained $145 million in additional business and believes that the supplier agreement will be extended. [13]

focused factory arrangement

---

[12]A. T. Sadhwani, M. H. Sarhan, and Roger A. Camp, "The Impact of Just-in-Time Inventory Systems on Small Businesses," *Journal of Accountancy* (January 1987), p. 122.
[13] "Managing Suppliers," p. 131.

Another example of a focused factory arrangement is between Air Relief Inc. and America Machine Inc., both of Mayfield, Kentucky. Air Relief provides the facilities for America Machine. In return, America Machine makes quality parts exclusively for Air Relief, which engages in the marketing and service functions. Profitability and cost control for both companies have benefitted.

Production Processing

In making processing improvements, a primary JIT consideration is to reduce machine setup time. Setup time reduction allows processing to shift rapidly among different types of units. Increases in setup cost and time have been found to be more than recovered by the savings derived from reducing downtime, WIP inventory, and materials handling, as well as increasing safety, flexibility, and ease of operation.

Most companies implementing rapid setup procedures have been able to obtain setup times of ten minutes or less. These companies use many low-cost setups rather than using the traditional processing approach of a small number of more expensive setups. Under JIT, setup cost is considered almost purely variable rather than fixed, as it was in the traditional manufacturing environment.

Another essential part of JIT product processing is implementing high quality standards that result in zero quality errors. Zero defects is a difficult goal. One Connecticut company (Seitz Corporation), which had only 3 to 4 percent product returns, saw its business decline by 10 to 15 percent per year. It implemented a total quality program that now has returns from defects of only a fraction of one percent—and business has increased.

High quality is essential because inferior quality causes the additional costs mentioned earlier in relation to vendors.[14] Under JIT systems, quality is determined on a continual basis rather than at quality control checkpoints. Continuous quality is achieved by first assuring vendor product quality more often and at a lower cost. Even if quality is assured at receipt of goods, some machines (such as optical scanners or chutes for size dimensions) monitor quality while production is in process.

Often, the traditional cost accounting system buries quality control costs and costs of scrap in the standard cost of production. For instance, allowing excess materials or labor time to be added into the standard quantities is a "buried cost of quality." Such costs are often 10 to 30 percent of total production cost. Consider a company making a $10 product that has quality control/scrap costs of 10 percent or $1 per unit. If that company has $10,000,000 of cost of goods sold annually, its quality control/scrap costs are $1,000,000! When quality is controlled on an ongoing basis, costs of obtaining good quality may be significantly reduced. It is less costly in many manufacturing situations to avoid mistakes rather than correct them. For example, Fel-Pro, Inc. (Skokie, Illinois) implemented over one thousand recommendations for quality improvements that have, collectively, saved $3 for every $1 invested.[15]

---

[14]In Philip Crosby's book, *Quality Is Free* (New York: New American Library, 1979), the premise is that quality itself costs nothing—it is only poor quality that has a cost. Quality costs are discussed in more detail in chapters 3 and 5.

[15]Jacob H. Brooks, "Manufacturing the Future," KPMG Peat Marwick *World* (Spring 1988), p. 14.

Plant Layout

In an effective JIT system, the physical plant is arranged in a way that is conducive to the flow of goods and the organization of workers. The layout would have equipment placed in a rational arrangement according to the materials flow. Such a layout would reduce material handling cost and the lead time to get work in process from one point to another. Streamlined design allows more visual controls to be instituted for problems such as excess inventory, product defects, equipment malfunctions, and out-of-place tools.

One way to minimize cycle time through the plant is to establish linear or U-shaped groupings of workers or machines, commonly referred to as **manufacturing cells.** These cells reduce inventory storage, improve materials handling and flow, increase machine utilization rates, maximize communication among workers, and result in better quality control. Manufacturing cells create an opportunity for workers to broaden skills and deepen their workplace involvement.

manufacturing cells

As equipment is automated, it is often able to run without direct labor involvement—requiring workers to "stand by and watch" while the machine performs its various functions. Amazing results are reported by Tellabs, Inc., a telecommunications equipment company in Lisle, Illinois, in the News Note on the next page.

Cross-training is also useful in companies that do not engage in high automation. At Eagle Bronze Foundry in Lander, Wyoming, employees originally had no training in foundry work. Now, they are cross-trained in numerous tasks to produce high-quality sculptures for collectors and hand-made castings for the aerospace industry. The cross-training allowed production to continue even when employees were sick or on vacation.

Training multiskilled workers is valid even in nonmanufacturing companies. For instance, USAA (a San Antonio insurance and financial services company), after in-

USAA is a leader in training its employees to perform numerous tasks. Whether in a service, retail, or manufacturing company, upgrading worker skills results in employees who are more satisfied with their jobs and customers who are served faster and better.

NEWS NOTE

Moving Furniture for Production Increases

Using JIT enabled the largest Tellabs' Digital Systems division production facility to triple its output in less than 18 months. During the initial three-month pilot of the JIT process in 1986, Tellabs experienced incredible increases in efficiency and quality:

- The number of defective boards produced dropped 55%,
- Production lead time plunged 96%,
- Work-in-process inventory fell 95%,
- Manufacturing floor space shrunk by 50%, and
- Labor costs dropped 54%.

At the same time, product quality increased 20% and the company increased its manufacturing capacity and improved its customer service.

All this amazing increase was due to changing production from the traditional batch, assembly line processing to the use of JIT manufacturing.

Prior to implementing JIT, the company manufactured large quantities of one product at a time. During the various stages of manufacturing, these products would lie untouched as they waited to be processed, inspected, or shipped. They would tie up inventory, labor, and time, not to mention cluttering the aisles of the factory. Nor would products be inspected until they had gone through the entire manufacturing process. So, if one module was defective, chances were that hundreds, or even thousands, were. All had to be reworked or scrapped, a tremendous waste.

Now, instead of sitting along an assembly line, soldering part A to part B, workers are now organized in product groups and build entire products by themselves. They sit in small, U-shaped work areas, solving most of the problems that come up in the manufacture of their product themselves.

SOURCE: "Tellabs: Working Smarter, Not Harder," *Grant Thornton Manufacturing Issues* (Winter 1990), p. 5.

stalling a huge network of automated equipment, consolidated its various departments and trained its salespeople to handle every aspect of processing insurance policies. Although the cost of training can be substantial and workers often resent change, in the long run, employers have a more viable work force and workers seem to be more satisfied with their jobs. Additionally, companies may find that workers, by knowing more about the process as a whole, are better able to provide helpful suggestions about process improvement.

Overall, the just-in-time philosophy is more than a cost-cutting endeavor or a matter of reducing personnel.[16] It requires good human resource management and a

[16]For example, Philips Corporation (a building materials producer in Ohio) has an employee program to generate ideas on cost-saving measures. The program saved the company $62 million in six years—with no personnel layoffs! John McCormick and Bill Powell, "Management for the 1990s," *Newsweek* (April 25, 1988), p. 48.

1. Determine how well products, materials, or services are delivered now.

2. Determine what customers consider superior service and set priorities accordingly.

3. Establish specific priorities for distribution (and possibly purchasing functions to meet customer needs).

4. Collaborate with and educate managers and employees to refine objectives and to prepare for implementation of JIT.

5. Execute a pilot implementation project and evaluate its results.

6. Refine the JIT delivery program and execute it companywide.

7. Monitor progress, adjust objectives over time, and always strive for excellence.

SOURCE: Gene R. Tyndall, "Just-in-Time Logistics: Added Value for Manufacturing Cost Management," (Spring 1989), pp. 57–59. Reprinted with permission from the *Journal of Cost Management for the Manufacturing Industry*. Warren, Gorham & Lamont, a division of Research Institute of America, 210 South Street, Boston, Mass. 02111. All rights reserved.

EXHIBIT 13–7
▼▼▼▼▼▼▼▼▼▼▼▼

SEVEN STEPS TO IMPLEMENT JIT

dedication to teamwork. In fact, when Minarik Electric Company of Glendale, California, combined some JIT measures such as a more efficient production plant with robotic equipment, the number of workers increased from 35 to 90 and production output went up 600 percent.

Exhibit 13–7 provides an action plan for implementing JIT, and the News Note on page 572 discusses a possible side benefit of JIT implementation.

ACCOUNTING IMPLICATIONS OF JIT

The implementation of a comprehensive JIT inventory system will have significant accounting implications for manufacturers. Because of the simplification of the process, the accounting techniques will also be simplified.

First, companies adopting a just-in-time system would no longer need a separate raw materials inventory classification. Since the majority of the needed materials are acquired as production occurs, JIT companies can use a new account called RIP (raw and in process).

Another accounting change that may occur in a JIT system is the use of one or more "conversion" categories for purposes of cost accumulation rather than separate labor and overhead categories. A conversion category is useful because direct labor is becoming a progressively less important part of total manufacturing cost.

Companies may also be able to adopt **backflush accounting** procedures that focus on the **throughput** (or customer output) and work backward through the system to allocate costs between cost of goods sold and inventory.[17] Since each sequential area is dependent upon the previous area, any problems will quickly cause the system to "backflush," or stop the production process. Individual daily accounting for the costs of production will no longer be necessary because all costs should be at standard, as variations will be observed and corrected almost immediately.

backflush accounting
throughput

---

[17]A company may want to measure output of each manufacturing cell or work center rather than throughput. While this measurement may indicate problems in a given area, it does not correlate with the JIT philosophy of the team approach, plantwide attitude, and total cost picture.

NEWS NOTE

Implement JIT with a Charitable Donation!

The changes that a JIT philosophy requires cannot be achieved immediately. While reducing inventory at the raw materials and in-process stages is a natural by-product of the JIT approach, reducing finished goods inventory is affected by product demand. Logically, demand must exceed production for a time until the buffer stocks of finished goods are reduced to their practical near-zero levels. Reducing finished inventory by stopping work would seriously, negatively affect work force attitudes. Because positive work force attitudes are critical [to JIT's] success, this alternative is not practical. However, depending on slow attrition to reduce inventory will delay the elimination of unnecessary costs. The most desirable way to reduce finished goods would be to have an instantaneous spike in demand exactly equivalent to the amount of excess inventory. The market is seldom so accommodating, but charitable donation of excess inventory is an often overlooked method of inventory reduction that may produce results approaching those of a momentary spurt in demand. Besides solving the tactical problem of quick inventory reduction, it also carries what may be strategic public relations benefits.

SOURCE: Alfred J. Nanni, Jr., and W. Robert Smith, "Charity and JIT: One Can Help the Other," *Management Accounting* (December 1990), pp. 37–40. Published by Institute of Management Accountants, Montvale, N.J.

In backflush accounting, purchases of raw materials would be recorded and actual conversion costs would be accumulated during the period. At either completion of production or sale of goods, an entry is made to allocate the total costs incurred to cost of goods sold and to finished goods inventory using standard production costs.

The journal entries needed in a backflush costing system are illustrated in Exhibit 13–8. Nordtvedt Company's standard production cost is $25.90. The company has a long-term contract with its direct materials supplier at $7.50, so there is no material price variance upon purchase. Nordtvedt's JIT inventory system has minimum inventories that basically remain constant from period to period. Beginning inventories for June are assumed to be zero.

Three other alternatives are also possible for the Exhibit 13–8 entries. First, if Nordtvedt's production time were extremely short, it might not journalize raw material purchases until completion of production. In that case, the entry would be:

Raw and In Process Inventory	3,000	
Finished Goods	518,000	
Accounts Payable		153,000
Conversion Costs		368,000

If goods were immediately shipped to customers upon completion, Nordtvedt could use an alternative in which the entries to complete and remove the goods from inventory would be combined:

Finished Goods	1,813	
Cost of Goods Sold	516,187	
Raw and In Process Inventory		150,000
Conversion Costs		368,000

The third alternative reflects the ultimate JIT system, in which only one entry (other than recording actual conversion costs and the sales revenue) is made. For Nordtvedt, this entry would be:

Raw and In Process Inventory (minimal overpurchases)	3,000	
Finished Goods (minimal overproduction)	1,813	
Cost of Goods Sold	516,187	
Accounts Payable		153,000
Conversion Costs		368,000

In a just-in-time system, fewer costs will need to be arbitrarily allocated to products, since more costs can be traced directly to their related output. Costs are incurred in specified cells on a per-hour or per-unit basis. Total production for each period is determinable under JIT (or MRP) because of the required constant (frozen) scheduling. Energy costs are direct to production in a comprehensive JIT system because there should be only minimum machine downtime. Virtually the only costs to be

---

EXHIBIT 13–8
▼▼▼▼▼▼▼▼▼▼▼▼

BACKFLUSH COSTING

Nordtvedt Company's standard production cost per unit:

Direct materials	$ 7.50
Conversion	18.40
Total cost	$25.90

Purchased $153,000 of direct materials in June:

Raw and In Process Inventory	153,000	
Accounts Payable		153,000

Incurred $368,700 of conversion costs for June:

Conversion Costs	368,700	
Various accounts		368,700

The various accounts would include wages payable for direct and indirect labor, accumulated depreciation, supplies, etc.

Completed 20,000 units of production in June:

Finished Goods Inventory (20,000 × $25.90)	518,000	
Raw and In Process Inventory (20,000 × $7.50)		150,000
Conversion Costs (20,000 × $18.40)		368,000

Sold 19,930 units in June for $42:

Cost of Goods Sold (19,930 × $25.90)	516,187	
Finished Goods		516,187
Accounts Receivable	837,060	
Sales		837,060

Ending Inventories:

Raw and In Process ($153,000 − $150,000)	$3,000	
Finished Goods ($518,000 − $516,187)	1,813	

In addition, there are underapplied conversion costs of $700 ($368,700 − $368,000)

allocated are costs associated with the building (depreciation, rent, taxes, and insurance). Machinery depreciation may be traced directly to products using the units-of-production method and a bar code system. Fewer allocations ultimately provide more useful measures of cost control and performance evaluation than have traditionally been available.

Another primary difference in the JIT accounting system is in the area of variance analysis. Under a JIT system, long-term price agreements have been made with vendors, so material price variances should be minimal. While the idea of long-term price agreements is neither new nor always possible, such arrangements are emphasized under JIT. The JIT accounting system should be designed so that purchase orders cannot be cut for an amount greater than the designated price without manager approval.[18] In this way, the variance amount and its cause are known in advance to provide an opportunity to eliminate the excess expenditure before it occurs. Calls can be made to the vendor to negotiate the price or other vendors can be contacted for quotes.

The ongoing use of specified vendors also provides the ability to control the quality of materials. Thus, little or no material usage variances should be caused by substandard materials. If usage standards are accurate, there should be virtually no favorable usage variance of materials during production. Excess usage should be promptly detected because of ongoing machine and/or human observation of processing. When an unfavorable variance occurs, the JIT system is stopped and the error causing the unfavorable materials usage is corrected.

Labor variances in a just-in-time system should also be minimal if standard rates and times have been set appropriately. And, if a separate labor category is not used, a standard departmental or manufacturing cell conversion cost per unit of cost driver may be calculated rather than individual standards for labor and overhead. Variances would be determined by comparing actual cost to the designated standard.

One goal of variance analysis in a traditional standard cost system is to find and remove the variance cause at the point of its occurrence rather than spending time and money calculating variances on an after-the-fact basis. In practice, however, traditional variance analysis is sometimes historical in nature, providing information later than desirable for correcting the problem. A JIT system reemphasizes that variances should be determinable on the spot so that causes can be ascertained and, if possible, promptly removed. JIT workers are trained and expected to monitor quality and efficiency continually *while production occurs* rather than just at the end of production.

Inventory implementation of the just-in-time philosophy can cause significant cost reductions, productivity improvements, and (as pointed out in the following News Note) possible deterrents to recession. However, all inventory situations do not necessarily have to be on a just-in-time system. The costs and benefits of any inventory control system must be evaluated before management should install the system.

ABC INVENTORY ANALYSIS

ABC analysis

Companies cannot always devote the same degree of control to all inventory items because of the cost/benefit relationship. One method of controlling inventory is through **ABC analysis,** which separates inventory into three groups based on annual

---

[18]This procedure can be implemented under a traditional standard cost system but it is not common, whereas it is required under JIT.

cost-to-volume usage.[19] Items that are the highest value are referred to as A items, while C items represent the lowest dollar volume usage. All inventory items in between these two categories are designated as B items. The most rigorous control procedures are assigned to A items. Exhibit 13–9 provides the results of a typical ABC inventory analysis—20 percent of the inventory items account for 80 percent of the

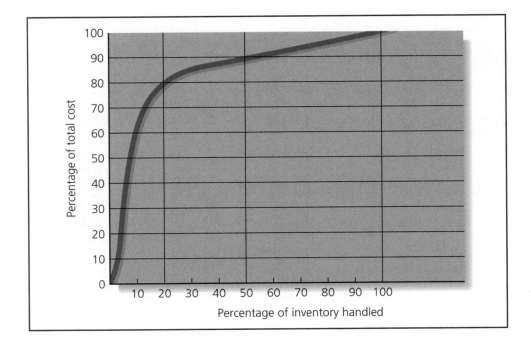

EXHIBIT 13–9

ABC INVENTORY ANALYSIS

---

[19]ABC inventory analysis should not be confused with activity-based costing (also called ABC), which is covered in depth in chapter 4.

cost; 30 percent of the items account for another 10 percent of the cost; and 50 percent of the items account for the remaining 10 percent of the cost. These results are consistent with Pareto's 20/80 Law, which reflects the observation that 20 percent of the customers accounts for 80 percent of the business, 20 percent of the parts accounts for 80 percent of the cost, and so on.

Once inventory is categorized as an A, B, or C item, management can determine the best inventory control method for that type of item. A-type inventory would definitely have a perpetual inventory system and would be a highly likely candidate for just-in-time purchasing techniques to minimize the capital investment. Items that fall into the C category may only require periodic inventory procedures and may use the simplistic, but cost-effective, two-bin or red-line techniques. Under a **two-bin system,** two containers or stacks of inventory are available for production needs. When production begins to use materials in the second bin, a purchase order is placed to refill the first bin. In a **red-line system,** a single container or stack of inventory is available for production needs. A red line is painted on the inventory container (or on the wall for a stack) at a point deemed to be the reorder point. Both of these systems require that production needs and delivery times can be fairly accurately estimated. Having the additional stock on hand is considered to be reasonable based on the insignificant dollar amount of investment involved.

two-bin system

red-line system

SITE ANALYSIS

Following are the kinds of changes that Harley-Davidson has made to compete more effectively with the Japanese.[20]

Harley parts are now assembled a few hours or days after being made, and flaws are spotted quickly and corrected. The plant no longer accumulates excessive engine parts inventories. The key to the smaller production runs was making it easy and fast to change over machines so small lots go directly to assembly rather than to storage.

The company rearranged its factory, grouping the machines in cells so that all machines needed to make a particular part are together, overseen by one operator. This rearrangement eliminated the old practices of hauling parts around the factory, sending them through one machine, putting them back in storage, and taking them out later for another processing step.

Engineers modified components to reduce or eliminate changeover time. Traditionally, motors and their components were designed without regard for manufacturing efficiency. For instance, Harley was making two similar crankpins, one having an oil hole drilled at a forty-five-degree angle and the other at a forty-eight-degree angle. Repositioning the machines to make these different crankpins required about two hours. Engineers designed a common angle on both parts and common tools for drilling the holes. This cut changeover time for that process to three minutes.

With such dramatic changeover-time reductions, Harley embraced short production runs with frequent changeovers. Now, Harley maintains about a ten-day supply of parts

continued

---

[20]The remainder of this section is adapted from Jon Van's "Leaks No Longer Stain Harley-Davidson Name" (November 4, 1991), p. 6. © Copyrighted 1991, Chicago Tribune Company, all rights reserved, used with permission.

rather than the old three-month supply. Employees deliver parts to assembly-line workers every few hours, usually directly from production elsewhere in the plant. "I'm like a milkman on a route," says employee Greg Nordquist. "I bring materials as needed, good and fresh."

About 90 percent of Harley's production costs are tied to overhead and materials, so reducing the space devoted to inventory storage and materials has cut costs tremendously.

It seems that all of the changes Harley's made have been worthwhile—overseas sales have increased from 13 percent of total revenues in 1983 to 31 percent in 1991. This increase occurred even though Harley could meet only half of its product demand in Europe. To help ease this problem, a new $26 million plant was opened in York, Pennsylvania, "in which workers can paint as many as 300 bikes per shift—more than three times the old rate." [21] Controlling inventory production time and costs can certainly lead to economic victory.

Good inventory management techniques apply to all types of managers, regardless of discipline or area of expertise. Some of these applications are given in the set of applications strategies that appear on page 578.

CHAPTER SUMMARY

Costs associated with inventory can be significant for any company, and sound business practices seek to limit the amount of those costs. Inventory costs include the cost of purchasing, ordering, carrying, and not carrying inventory. The economic order quantity (EOQ) model determines the purchase order size that minimizes, in total, the costs of ordering and carrying inventory. This model can also be adapted to find the most economical production run (EPR).

The EOQ model ignores relationships among product components. To overcome this shortcoming, MRP (material requirements planning) can be used to generate master production and time-sequenced purchasing schedules. MRP II (manufacturing resource planning) implements MRP on a companywide basis and includes top management input. MRP is a push system of production control dictated by delivery lead times and EOQ/EPR requirements. Purchased and produced goods must be stored until needed.

In contrast, a pull system of production control (such as just-in-time manufacturing) involves the purchase and/or production of inventory only as needs arise. Storage is basically eliminated except for a minimal level to hold safety stock.

The JIT philosophy can be applied to some extent in any company having inventories. JIT requires that purchases be made in small quantities and that deliveries be frequent. Production lot sizes are minimized so that many different products can be made on a daily basis. Products are designed for quality, and component parts are standardized to the extent possible. Machine setup time is reduced so that production runs can be easily shifted between products. To eliminate the need for, or buildup of, buffer inventories between operations, plant layout emphasizes manufacturing cells and the operating capabilities of all factory equipment are considered.

[21]Clint Willis, "Cash in on U.S. Companies that Are Hammering the Japanese," *Money* (April 1992), p. 72.

	Discipline	Applications
APPLICATIONS STRATEGIES FOR PRODUCTION AND INVENTORY MANAGEMENT	Accounting	Under JIT, combine raw materials with work in process to form one inventory account known as RIP; the number and magnitude of variances from standard are minimized; taking inventory should be streamlined; with ABC analysis, use of different inventory techniques for different items can minimize recordkeeping
	Economics	JIT can make companies more "recession-proof" by reducing the need to have production cutbacks in response to declining sales; implementing JIT and advanced production management systems assists in lowering costs and increasing quality; EOQ involves a trade-off between inventory carrying costs and ordering costs, with the objective being to minimize the sum of these costs
	Finance	Strong production and inventory management reduces costs and the investment in inventory, resulting in improved financial ratios; lower costs and higher quality enhance operating results and facilitate obtaining additional financing for expanded future operations
	Management	Managers can perform more efficiently and effectively with tools such as MRP, JIT, and ABC analysis; better use of workers and other resources permits management to better serve customers, owners, and the public
	Marketing	Advantages of higher quality and lower costs and prices permit stronger market position for promotion and competitive advantages; shorter lead times mean servicing sales orders faster; sales staff needs to: give input on the acceptable delay in delivery to customers of various products to help determine ABC level analysis, determine customer needs, and interface with customers setting up own JIT inventory systems to determine needs and priorities; sales forecasts are critical to determine needed delivery dates and allow decrease in inventory levels

Instituting a JIT system will have accounting implications. JIT implementation may allow the use of a merged raw materials and work in process inventory (RIP) classification because raw materials are basically only acquired as needed in production. A conversion cost category may take the place of direct labor and overhead. Backflush accounting techniques may be used that basically eliminate the need for journal entries to trace production costs through the process. In addition, more costs may be directly traceable to production under a JIT system. Variances from standards should be negligible under JIT; however, variances should be recognized earlier in the process so that causes may be found and corrective action taken quickly.

The process of classifying inventory into ABC categories allows management to establish controls over inventory items that are related to the cost and volume of those items. Two-bin and red-line systems are acceptable for inventory items in the C category because of the limited financial investment.

APPENDIX

Order Point and Safety Stock

While the EOQ model indicates how many units to order, managers are also con-cerned with the **order point,** which reflects the inventory level that triggers the place-ment of an order. Order point is based on usage (the amount of inventory used or sold each day) and **lead time** (the time from order placement to order arrival). Many companies can project a constant figure for both usage and lead time, in which case the order point is calculated as:

order point

lead time

$$\text{Order Point} = \text{Daily Usage} \times \text{Lead Time}$$

Assume that SABRINA (the company introduced in the chapter's EOQ example) uses 2,500 boxes per day and the company's supplier can deliver boxes in three days. When the stock of boxes reaches 7,500 units (2,500 × 3), SABRINA's purchasing manager should reorder.

The prior order point formula minimizes the funds a company has invested in its inventory. Orders would arrive at precisely the time the inventory reached zero. How-ever, this formula does not take into consideration unusual events. For example, var-iations occur in production or use; some products provided by the supplier are defec-tive; supplier shipping schedules are erratic; or units shipped do not arrive on schedule. To provide for such events, a **safety stock** of inventory is carried to act as a buffer to protect the company against the possibility of stockouts. When a safety stock is maintained, the order point formula is

safety stock

$$\text{Order Point} = (\text{Daily Usage} \times \text{Lead Time}) + \text{Safety Stock}$$

Safety stock size should be determined on how crucial the item is to the business, the item's purchase cost, and the amount of uncertainty related to both usage and lead time.

One way to estimate safety stock size is to allow one factor to vary from the norm. For example, either excess usage during normal lead time or normal usage during an excess lead time can be considered in the safety stock calculation. Assume that SABRINA never uses more than 2,600 boxes in one day. One estimate of the necessary safety stock is 300 boxes, computed as follows:

Maximum daily usage	2,600 boxes
Normal daily usage	2,500 boxes
Excess usage	100 boxes
Lead time	3 days
Safety stock	300 boxes

Using this estimate of safety stock, SABRINA would reorder boxes when 7,800 boxes (7,500 original order point + 300 safety stock) were on hand.

Instead of assuming that only one factor can be out of the ordinary, the purchas-ing manager can estimate the necessary amount of safety stock by using probabilities and weighing the cost of carrying safety stock against the cost of having a stockout. Stockout probability estimates can be based on historical data for usage and lead time. Such probabilities are related to each purchase order because it is possible to have a stockout before every order arrives. A model can be developed to determine the optimal quantity of safety stock. The optimal quantity of safety stock is the amount that balances the cost of carrying with the cost of not carrying safety stock units.

Mathematical determination of economic order quantity and optimal quantity of safety stock will help a company control its investment in inventory. However, such models are only as valid as the estimates used in the formula. For example, projections of costs such as lost customer goodwill may be extremely difficult. In some cases, the degree of inaccuracy may not be important; in other cases, it may be critical.

GLOSSARY

ABC analysis an inventory control method that separates items into three groups based on annual cost-to-volume usage; items having the highest value are referred to as A items, while C items represent the lowest dollar volume

Backflush accounting a costing system that focuses on company output and works backward through the system to allocate costs to cost of goods sold and inventory

Carrying cost the variable costs of carrying one unit of inventory in stock for one year; consists of storage, handling, insurance charges, property taxes based on inventory size, possible losses from obsolescence or damage, and opportunity cost

Economic order quantity an estimate of the least costly number of units per order that would provide the optimal balance between ordering and carrying costs

Economic production run the quantity of units to produce that minimizes the total costs of setting up a production run and of carrying costs

Focused factory arrangement an arrangement in which a vendor agrees to provide a limited number of specified products or to perform a limited number of unique services for the JIT company; providers can be internal segments (or divisions) or non-related companies

Just-in-time manufacturing system a production system that attempts to acquire components and produce inventory units only as they are needed, minimize product defects, and reduce lead/setup times for acquisition and production

Kanban the Japanese word for *card;* a production system that originated from the use of cards to indicate a work center's need for additional components

Lead time the quantity of time from the placement of an order to the arrival of the goods (from appendix)

Manufacturing cells linear or U-shaped groupings of workers and/or machines

Manufacturing resource planning a fully integrated MRP system that involves the functional areas of marketing, finance, and manufacturing in planning the master production schedule using the usual MRP method; is also able to calculate resource needs such as labor and machine hours

Materials requirements planning a computer simulation system that helps companies plan by calculating the future availability of raw materials, parts, subassemblies, and end products based on a master production schedule

Order point   the inventory level that triggers the placement of an order (from appendix)

Ordering cost   the variable costs associated with preparing, receiving, and paying for an order

Pull system   a production system in which parts are delivered or manufactured only as they are needed by the work center for which they are intended

Purchasing cost   the quoted purchase price minus any discounts allowed plus shipping charges

Push system   a production system in which work centers may produce inventory that is not currently needed because of lead time or economic production/order quantity requirements; the excess inventory is then stored until it is needed by other work centers

Red-line system   an inventory system in which a single container (or stack) of inventory is available for production needs, and a red line is painted on the inventory container (or on the wall for a stack) at a point deemed to be the reorder point

Safety stock   the quantity of inventory kept on hand by a company to compensate for potential fluctuating usage or unusual delays in lead time (from appendix)

Setup costs   the direct and indirect labor costs of getting equipment ready for each new production run

Stockout   a condition in which a company does not have inventory available upon customer request or production demand

Throughput   the output of the plant to the customer

Two-bin system   an inventory system in which two containers or stacks of inventory are available for production needs; when production begins to use materials in the second bin, a purchase order is placed to refill the first bin

---

SELECTED BIBLIOGRAPHY

Bailes, Jack C., and Ilene K. Kleinsorge. "Cutting Waste with JIT." *Management Accounting* (May 1992), pp. 28–32.

Dumaine, Brian. "Earning More by Moving Faster." *FORTUNE* (October 7, 1991), pp. 89–90, 94.

Green, Forrest B., and Felix E. Amenkhienan. "Accounting Innovations: A Cross-Sectional Survey of Manufacturing Firms." *Journal of Cost Management for the Manufacturing Industry* (Spring 1992), pp. 58–64.

Henkoff, Ronald. "The Ultimate Nuts and Bolts Co." *FORTUNE* (July 16, 1990), pp. 70–73.

Hopson, James F., et al. "Simplifying the Use of the Economic Order Quantity Formula to Control Inventory Costs." *Journal of Cost Management for the Manufacturing Industry* (Winter 1990), pp. 8–13.

Inman, Anthony. "Quality Certification of Suppliers by JIT Manufacturing Firms." *Production and Inventory Management Journal* (2nd quarter 1990), pp. 58–61.

Jones, Daniel J. "JIT and EOQ Model: Odd Couple No More." *Management Accounting* (February 1991), pp. 54–57.

Knowlton, Christopher. "Can Europe Compete?" *FORTUNE* (December 2, 1991), pp. 147–48ff.

MacArthur, John B. "The ABC/JIT Costing Continuum." *Journal of Cost Management for the Manufacturing Industry* (Winter 1992), pp. 61–63.

Miltenburg, G. J. "Changing MRP's Costing Procedures to Suit JIT." *Production and Inventory Management Journal* 31, no. 2 (1990), pp. 77–83.

Primrose, P. L. "The Economics of MRP II." *BPICS Control* (October 1990), p. 43ff.

Turk, William T. "Management Accounting Revitalized: The Harley-Davidson Experience." *Journal of Cost Management for the Manufacturing Industry* (Winter 1990), pp. 28–39.

Zipkin, Paul H. "Does Manufacturing Need a JIT Revolution?" *Harvard Business Review* (January–February 1991), pp. 40–50.

SOLUTION STRATEGIES

Economic Order Quantity

$$EOQ = \sqrt{\frac{2QO}{C}}$$

where EOQ = economic order quantity in units
  Q = estimated annual quantity used in units (can be found in the annual purchases budget)
  O = estimated cost of placing one order
  C = estimated cost to carry one unit in stock for one year

Economic Production Run

$$EPR = \sqrt{\frac{2QS}{C}}$$

where EPR = economic production run
  Q = estimated annual quantity produced in units
  S = estimated cost of setting up a production run
  C = estimated cost of carrying one unit in stock for one year

Order Point

Order Point = (Daily Usage × Lead Time) + Safety Stock

Backflush Accounting
  Upon purchase of direct materials:
    Raw and In Process Inventory (at standard cost)
      Accounts Payable (at actual cost)
    A material price variance account will be debited (if actual is greater than standard) or credited (if actual is less than standard) for the difference.
  Upon incurrence of conversion costs:
    Conversion Costs (at actual cost)
      Various Accounts (at actual cost)

Upon completion of units:
> Finished Goods Inventory (at standard cost)
>> Raw and In Process Inventory (at standard cost)
>> Conversion Costs (at standard cost)

Upon sale of units:
> Cost of Goods Sold (at standard cost)
>> Finished Goods (at standard cost)
> Accounts Receivable (at selling price)
>> Sales (at selling price)

Material and Labor Variances under JIT

Generally firms will have minimal, if any, material price variances, since prices are set by long-term contract. A labor rate variance may exist and would be calculated in the traditional manner.

END-OF-CHAPTER MATERIALS

Questions

1. List four costs included in each of the following: ordering inventory, carrying inventory, and not carrying inventory. How does incurring costs in one of these categories affect the costs of the other categories?

2. Why is the purchasing cost of an item not included in the economic order quantity formula?

3. Assuming that all costs in the EOQ formula could be determined with *absolute precision,* discuss some reasons that one might not buy at the economic order quantity amount.

4. Although MRP is based on EOQ and safety stock models, it overcomes an inherent deficiency in those models. What is this deficiency and how does MRP overcome it?

5. Why is MRP said to be a push system?

6. What significant benefits have many firms achieved using MRP? Discuss some of the problems associated with using MRP.

7. It is recognized that MRP does not, in fact, eliminate bottlenecks. How are bottlenecks treated in an MRP system?

8. Why would it be said that JIT views inventory as a liability rather than an asset?

9. What are the primary goals of a JIT philosophy, and how does JIT attempt to achieve these goals?

10. Discuss the differences between push and pull inventory systems.

11. What are the advantages and disadvantages of having only one (or very few) supplier sources?

12. Discuss the meaning and benefits of a focused factory arrangement.

13. What are manufacturing cells and what are their benefits?

14. In what areas of accounting can a company implementing a JIT manufacturing system expect changes? Why will such changes arise?

15. "Philosophically, JIT is aimed at minimizing time, space, and energy." Discuss what you think the person making this statement meant.

16. How can JIT be used by nonmanufacturers?

17. Are MRP and JIT systems compatible? Explain your answer.

18. What is backflush accounting? What are its advantages?

19. What is ABC inventory analysis?

20. List four accounting and/or management tools you could suggest to exert strong controls over the A-type items identified using ABC inventory analysis.

21. List four accounting and/or management tools you could suggest to minimize the cost and effort of controlling C-type items identified using ABC inventory analysis.

22. *(Appendix)* Why would a company carry safety stock of an item? Discuss how the size of that safety stock might be determined.

Exercises

23. *(Types of costs)* Classify each of the following items as a cost of ordering (O), carrying (C), or not carrying (N) inventory. Use N/A for any items not fitting any of the categories.

    a. contribution margin lost on a sale due to stockout
    b. spoilage of products in storage
    c. opportunity cost of capital invested in inventory
    d. inventory storage cost
    e. wages of staff in purchasing agent's office
    f. long-distance calls to vendor to get prices
    g. property tax on inventory
    h. freight-out on sales of inventory
    i. purchase order forms, receiving report forms, disbursement voucher forms
    j. insurance on warehouse and its inventory contents
    k. extra freight on rush orders caused by stockouts
    l. freight-in on purchases
    m. postage to send purchase orders
    n. handling costs for products on hand
    o. purchase price of products

24. *(EOQ)* Natalie Locke manages a regional hotel chain headquartered in Charleston, South Carolina. She has been wondering how many monogrammed towels should be ordered at a time and when should an order be placed. She wants a safety stock of 1,000 towels and has determined that the chain uses 40,000 towels each year. Placing an order costs $2.50, and she estimates that the carrying cost of a towel is $1.80 annually. The chain operates 365 days a year. It takes 10 days from the time an order is placed until it arrives. Calculate the EOQ.

25. *(EOQ)* Enrique Castro has misplaced some of his working papers, which originally were used to calculate an EOQ of 340 units of item Z. He determined that order costs are $3.20 and carrying costs are $4.46. Identify the missing statistic and calculate its value.

26. *(EOQ)* The following represent five independent situations, each with a missing item of data.

	(E) EOQ	(Q) Annual Quantity	(O) Ordering Costs	(C) Carrying Costs
a.	34	?	$ 2.70	$ 1.20
b.	?	600	$ 1.85	$ .48
c.	72	750	$ 7.80	?
d.	162	3,678	?	$ 4.38
e.	30	?	$12.00	$16.50

Required: Provide the missing numbers.

27. *(Error in estimating ordering cost)* Use the basic information for SABRINA in Exhibit 13–2, but assume that the true cost of ordering is $5 rather than $4.

    a. Compute the true economic order quantity.

    b. Compute the total cost of ordering and carrying inventory.

    c. Compare your answers with the ones in the chapter using the $4 ordering cost. Discuss the effects of using an incorrect amount on SABRINA's total inventory cost.

28. *(EPR)* Henri Harfleur is trying to determine the best size of a batch to be produced on each production run of tires. Annual demand is 65,000 tires. Setup costs per run are $66 and annual carrying costs per tire are estimated at $2.25. Calculate the EPR.

29. *(Terminology)* Match the numbered items on the right to the lettered items on the left:

a. push system	1. Generates an interrelated purchase order and production schedule.
b. ABC analysis	2. Time duration from placing an order to receiving the goods
c. MRP	3. U-shaped groupings of workers or machines
d. lead time	4. Supplier agrees to become a specialized maker or functional specialist to a manufacturer
e. focused factory arrangement	5. Segregates inventory into three groups based on cost and volume
f. two-bin system	6. Inventory is acquired/produced no sooner than it is needed/sold
g. pull system	7. Inventory is produced and stored before it is sold
h. set up costs	8. Direct and indirect labor cost of getting equipment ready for a production run
i. Kanban	9. As materials are starting to be withdrawn from the second bin, a purchase order is issued to refill the first bin
j. manufacturing cell	10. A system using cards to indicate a work center's need for additional components

30. *(JIT; types of costs)* David Fernandez Company uses a highly automated system in which products are bar coded and tracked electronically through each manufacturing cell. Following are some factory costs incurred by Fernandez:

   a. Raw materials

   b. Electricity

   c. Depreciation of the machinery

   d. Setup costs

   e. Labor costs for the cell workers, who are paid hourly

   f. Repairs to machinery

   g. Lubricants for machinery

   h. Worker training

   i. Worker recreation facilities

   j. Engineering change orders

   k. Employee brainstorming sessions

   l. Machine malfunction adjustments

   m. Insurance on equipment

   n. Product design

   o. Night security guard

For each of the previous costs, indicate whether it is a traceable (T) or an indirect (I) product cost.

31. *(Journal entries)* Hal Gray Enterprises makes fine china. The company uses a just-in-time inventory system. The following transactions occurred during July 1994:

   a. Raw materials of $93,000 were purchased on account.

   b. Conversion costs of $141,000 were incurred.

   c. Conversion costs of $140,940 were applied.

   d. The cost of goods manufactured during July was $234,000.

   e. July sales were $322,000 on account, with the cost of sales being $230,000.

Beginning of July balances were: Raw and In Process, $3,000; Finished Goods, $6,000.

   a. Journalize the previous transactions using a perpetual inventory system.

   b. Determine the July balances in the inventory accounts.

32. *(ABC inventory)* Following is a list of techniques used to control inventories.

   a. Perpetual inventory system

   b. Daily inventory counts

   c. Monthly inventory counts

   d. Annual inventory count

   e. Limited access to storage areas

   f. Open access display areas

   g. Red-line system

   h. Two-bin system

   i. Specific identification inventory tracking

   j. Weighted-average cost flow

   k. Rigorous, in-depth demand estimation (EOQ, lead time, order point, safety stock)

For each of the techniques just listed, indicate whether it would most likely be used for A-, B-, or C-type inventory items. More than one type of inventory item may be indicated for a given technique.

33. *(Variances with conversion cost classification)* Hank Hawkins, president of Technology R Us, has asked you to work with the company controller in analyzing the newly combined direct labor and variable overhead conversion account. The new variable conversion account is to be analyzed in the same way as the traditional variable overhead account. In addition, the fixed conversion account replaces the former account known as fixed overhead and is to be analyzed in the same manner as fixed overhead has been analyzed. The following data has been gathered to accomplish the above-requested analysis:

Standards per unit
Variable conversion cost
    2.5 machine hours @ $7.60 $19.00
Fixed conversion cost
    2.5 machine hours @ $8.20   20.50
       (based on budgeted machine
       hours of 219,512 annually)

Actual operations
Production, 87,680 units
Actual variable conversion cost $1,652,300
Actual fixed conversion cost $1,801,500
Actual machine hours run   219,400 hours

Prepare the variance analysis for variable and fixed conversion costs.

34. *(Appendix)* Heinrick Bauer is a Pennsylvania farmer who raises pheasants. His birds eat approximately 7,300 pounds of feed per annum. It requires 18 days on the average from the time he places an order until the feed is delivered. It costs Henrick $.75 for each order placed and an estimated $.48 in annual carrying cost per pound.

a. What is Heinrick's EOQ?
b. Assuming no safety stock, calculate Heinrick's order point.
c. If the lead time varies ± 3 days, calculate a safety stock.
d. If the average daily consumption varies ± 10 percent, calculate a safety stock.
e. Combine the safety stock calculated in (c) and (d) and redetermine a conservative order point.

35. *(Appendix)* Using the data in Exercise 24, calculate the order point (round upward to the next whole number).

Problems

36. *(EPR, EOQ)* Enrico Ferrari makes desktop models of a popular style of the real Ferrari. He uses two raw materials: a pound of plastic and 6 ounces of a metal alloy. Enrico sells approximately 3,000 cars annually. The following information is available:

	Cars	Plastic	Alloy
Carrying cost	$ 2.50 per unit	$ .30 per pound	$ .06 per ounce
Ordering costs (per order)	—	$8.50	$7.00
Setup cost (per setup)	$40.00	—	—

Required:

a. What is the economic production run for model cars?
b. How many production runs should Enrico Ferrari make annually?
c. What is the EOQ for the plastic and the alloy?
d. How many orders should Enrico Ferrari place annually for the plastic? The alloy?
e. What is the total annual cost of ordering, carrying, and setting up for these model cars?

37. *(Using EOQ, EPR figures to solve for missing numbers)* Alexander Allejandro is utilizing a computer game in one of his senior management courses. The professor won't provide the class with particular information that would assist in producing optimum results for teams playing the game. Alexander's teammates have asked him to try to figure out sales revenue for each of the game's two products (K and L).

Alexander determines the following: (1) production is equal to sales; (2) the annual carrying cost of Product K is $1.80 and of Product L is $2.20; setup costs for Product K production runs are $22 and for Product L are $20; EPR for Product K is 275 and for Product L is 420; Product K sells for $32 and Product L sells for $26.

Required: Assist Alexander in estimating the sales revenue for Product K and for Product L.

38. *(JIT features)* Given the following features concerning just-in-time systems, indicate by letter which of the three categories shown next applies to that item. If more than one category apply, indicate with the additional letter.

D—desired intermediate result of using JIT
U—ultimate goal of JIT
T—technique associated with JIT

a. Reducing setup costs
b. Reducing total cost of producing and carrying inventory
c. Focused factory arrangement
d. Designing products to minimize design changes after production starts
e. Monitoring quality on a continuous basis
f. Use of manufacturing cells
g. Minimizing inventory stored
h. Using backflush accounting
i. Having workers and machines continuously monitor quality during processing
j. Purchases and production are pulled through the system based on sales demand

39. *(Journal entries for JIT standard costing system)* Henrietta Manufacturing has implemented a just-in-time system for production of its one-half-inch plastic pipe. Inventories of raw materials and work in process are very small, so Henrietta uses a Raw and In Process (RIP) account. In addition, the company has become highly automated and includes labor and overhead in a single conversion category. Production standards for 1995 for 100 yards of pipe are:

Direct material, 100 pounds @ $2.00	$200
Conversion, 4 machine hours @ $35	140
Total	$340

The conversion cost of $35 per machine hour was estimated on the basis of 500,000 machine hours for the year and $17,500,000 of conversion costs. 1995 activities are as follows:

1. Direct materials purchased and placed into production were 12,452,000 pounds. All except 8,000 pounds were purchased at standard. The other 8,000 pounds were purchased at a cost of $2.06 per pound when the regular vendor was unable to meet demand. All purchases are on account. The accounts payable were paid within the period.

2. From January 1 to February 28, Henrietta made 2,080,000 yards of pipe. Conversion costs for this period were $2,918,000. Of this amount, $321,000 was for depreciation. The remaining costs were either paid in cash ($103,000) or were acquired on account. The accounts payable were paid within the period.

3. Conversion costs were applied to the RIP account from January 1 to February 28.

4. Total production for the remainder of 1995 was 10,320,000 yards of pipe. Conversion costs from March through December were $14,432,000. Of this amount, $4,000,000 is depreciation, $9,325,000 is cash, and $1,107,000 is on account. The accounts payable were paid within the period.

5. Standard costs for conversion costs were applied to the RIP account for the period of March through December 1995.

Required: Prepare the journal entries to record the events just presented.

40. *(Changes from implementing JIT)* Using the symbols for each of the following areas where changes are implemented using JIT, categorize the lettered items a.–s. by associating the appropriate symbol with each of the items:

Symbol	Area of Change Using JIT
PSR&D	Purchasing, Supplier Relationships, and Distribution
PD	Product Design
PP	Production Processing
PL	Plant Layout
JP	JIT Philosophy
AI	Accounting Implications of JIT

a. Recognizing that employees often know best how to improve operations
b. A single RIP account replaces two inventory accounts
c. Focused factory arrangement
d. The ideal is one vendor for each part or raw material
e. Reduction of setup time
f. Layout intended to minimize throughput time
g. Long-term contracts are negotiated
h. Physical arrangement conducive to a worker handling a greater number of tasks
i. Inventory is a liability
j. A single conversion account combines direct labor and overhead
k. Fewer costs need to be arbitrarily allocated
l. Workers and machines monitor quality while processing
m. U-shaped groupings of workers and machines
n. Perform many setup tasks while machines are running
o. Layout assists visual controls
p. Plan to use fewest number of parts (reduce product complexity)
q. Recognizing that creative thinking doesn't cost anything
r. Standardize as many parts as possible
s. Careful design minimizes the number of subsequent changes

41. *(Backflush accounting)* Dutchgirl Company has a standard cost per pair of its famous Dutchgirl shoes as follows:

Direct materials	$11.20
Conversion	8.80
Total	$20.00

The company had no beginning inventories on April 1. During April, the following occurred:

- Purchased $450,000 of direct materials on account at standard cost
- Incurred $353,900 of actual conversion costs
- Completed 40,000 pairs of Dutchgirl shoes
- Sold 39,800 pairs of shoes on account. These shoes sell for $36 per pair.

Required: Using backflush accounting, journalize the prior events.

42. *(ABC inventory analysis)* The following twenty items, along with unit costs and volumes of sales last year, are part of an ABC analysis of Skipper's Dive Shop:

Items		Unit Cost	Volume Sold
(Pr.) Flippers:	Men's	$ 3.00	320
	Women's	2.50	210
	Children's	1.80	66
Masks:	Men's	4.00	280
	Women's	3.40	172
	Children's	2.80	40
Weight belts:	Men's	1.80	63
	Women's	1.70	46
	Children's	1.20	12
Snorkels		1.20	420
Air tanks		36.00	42
Meters & connections		42.00	36
Wet suits:	Men's	60.00	170
	Women's	52.00	102
	Children's	42.00	12
Weights:	Large	2.00	160
	Medium	1.50	180
	Small	1.25	64
Underwater watches		25.00	32
Ear plugs		.25	120

Required:

a. Rearrange the items in descending order of magnitude according to the product of cost times volume. Use these headings: Items; Unit Cost; Volume Sold; Cost × Volume.

b. Classify the items in three groups: A items including 20 percent of the total volume sold; B items including the next 30 percent of the total volume sold; and C items including the lowest 50 percent of the volume sold.

c. Recommend three techniques to control each group.

43. *(Appendix)* Each of the following independent cases has a missing amount.

	Case A	Case B	Case C	Case D	Case E
Order point	200	(b)	88	120	350
Daily usage	10	10	(c)	6	(e)
Lead time	12	20	7	(d)	10
Safety stock	(a)	52	4	30	60

Required: Supply the missing amounts for the lettered spaces.

44. *(Essay)* Paul Li is the CEO of Alexander Company, which makes small airplanes. Paul has asked you to write a brief report explaining the following:

a. the advantages and disadvantages of using an MRP system and

b. some potential barriers that might exist to effectively implementing an MRP system.

45. *(Essay)* You have been employed for two years by the Wm. Pickering Dental Tools Company, and the president, Bill Pickering, has called you into his office to ask if you would prepare a brief report on what JIT manufacturing is about. Pickering has observed that the company has experienced increased difficulty in meeting competitor prices and quality in recent years and has heard that JIT manufacturing should be considered.

a. Prepare a brief report describing JIT.

b. After reading your report, Mr. Pickering asked you to prepare another brief report recommending ways in which the firm can implement JIT.

46. *(Essay)* Ed Smith's dad is the controller of a small furniture manufacturing firm in Baltimore, Maryland. Ed is home from college, has gotten a job with his dad's company, and has been assigned to assist his dad on special projects. Ed's dad wears many hats at the company and doesn't have a lot of time for reading and research. The president of the company has expressed an interest in adopting a JIT system. Ed's dad asks Ed to review the literature on JIT and draft a brief report on the accounting implications of JIT. Assume the role of Ed and draft such a report.

47. *(Essay)* Experts believe that we are far behind the Japanese in JIT for demographic and cultural reasons, and cannot possibly achieve JIT in the near future. Demographic differences can be related to the geographical vastness of the United States in comparison with Japan, an island which is only two hundred miles across. Cultural differences between the two countries include the fact that the Japanese culture places high regard on dependability, concern for quality, cooperative behavior, and respect for authority. This work ethic carries over into the typical six-day work week. Obvious difficulties exist in translating a system that works for such a culture to the American worker, who puts in a five-day work week in anticipation of two days off for private pursuits.

(SOURCE: Michael A. Muchnik, Margaret F. Shipley, and Hugh M. Shane, "Why JIT Can't Bear Fruit in American Plants," *Business Forum* [Summer 1990], p. 13.)

a. Do you believe the basic premises made by these authors? Discuss the reasoning behind your answer.

b. Which aspects of JIT might be more difficult to implement in the United States than in Japan?

c. Do you think that the previous passage may be relevant for some businesses but not others? Why or why not? If so, to what businesses might it relate?

d. Assume that you believe the previous passage to be true and you are the manager of a medium-sized manufacturer that wants to implement a JIT system. How would you go about trying to reduce the impacts of the problems just mentioned?

48. *(Essay)* The management at Megafilters, Inc., has been discussing the possible implementation of a just-in-time (JIT) production system at its Illinois plant, where oil filters and air filters for heavy construction equipment and large, off-the-road vehicles are manufactured. The Metal Stamping Department at the Illinois plant has already instituted a JIT system for controlling raw materials inventory, but the remainder of the plant is still discussing how to proceed with the

implementation of this concept. Some of the other department managers have grown increasingly cautious about the JIT process after hearing about the problems that have arisen in the Metal Stamping Department.

Robert Goertz, manager of the Illinois plant, is a strong proponent of the JIT production system, and recently made the following statement at a meeting of all departmental managers. "Just-in-time is often referred to as a management philosophy of doing business rather than a technique for improving efficiency on the plant floor. We will all have to make many changes in the way we think about our employees, our suppliers, and our customers if we are going to be successful in using just-in-time procedures. Rather than dwelling on some of the negative things you have heard from the Metal Stamping Department, I want each of you to prepare a list of things we can do to make a smooth transition to the just-in-time philosophy of management for the rest of the plant."

a. The just-in-time (JIT) management philosophy emphasizes objectives for the general improvement of a production system. Describe several important objectives of this philosophy.

b. Discuss several actions that Megafilters, Inc., can take to ease the transition to a just-in-time production system at the Illinois plant.

c. In order for the JIT production system to be successful, Megafilters, Inc., must establish appropriate relationships with its vendors, employees, and customers. Describe each of these three relationships.

(CMA)

49. *(Essay)* Henry Higgins was asked by his boss, Horace Hogarty, to write a brief report on the advantages of ABC inventory analysis. Take the place of Henry and prepare that report.

50. *(Essay; includes appendix materials)* John Holster, controller for ProCorp, Inc., has been examining all phases of ProCorp's manufacturing operations in order to reduce costs and improve efficiency. The reason for urgency is that the company's sales force has been complaining about lost sales caused by product stockouts, and the production people are unhappy about downtime caused by shortages of raw materials. Holster believes the company may be losing as much as $220,000 in revenue as a result of these problems.

ProCorp manufactures only one product: boomerangs (trademark, Boomers). The single raw material used in making Boomers is plastic, with each Boomer requiring 8 ounces of red plastic. ProCorp expects to manufacture 300,000 Boomers this year with a steady demand through the entire year. The ordering costs for clerical processing are $30 per order of plastic. There is a three-day delay between placement of an order and receipt of the inventory. The carrying costs for storage, handling, insurance, and interest are $.72 per Boomer unit per year.

a. Discuss the general benefits of a well-managed inventory policy.

b. By using the economic order quantity formula, ProCorp, Inc., determined that the optimal economic order quantity is 2,500 pounds of plastic, which will produce 5,000 units.

1. Discuss how an increase in each of the following components will impact the economic order quantity:

- Annual sales demand;
- The ordering costs; and
- The carrying costs for storage, handling, insurance, and interest.

2. Determine the number of times ProCorp will order plastic during the year.

c. ProCorp, Inc., while reviewing its safety stock policy, has determined that an appropriate safety stock is 1,250 pounds of plastic, which will produce 2,500 units.

   1. Describe the factors that affect an appropriate safety stock level.

   2. List the effects of maintaining an appropriate safety stock level on ProCorp's short-term and long-term profitability.

   3. Identify the effect that a well-implemented just-in-time inventory procedure will have on safety stock level and explain why.

(CMA)

Cases

51. Systrack Systems produces a private brand of compact disc player. The company makes only one type of player, which is sold through different distribution organizations who resell them under their own brand names. Systrack Systems' product is high quality, equal to that of nationally branded competitors.

The compact disc industry is highly concentrated with three major players holding the lion's share of the market. A half-dozen other suppliers, such as Systrack Systems, hold small and about equal market shares. All three of the major suppliers have high quality products. Consumers are aware of this, leading to a tendency for consumers to see all brands, including private brands, as being about the same. As a result, price competition is intense, making manufacturing and the introduction of new technology as soon as possible, very important elements of marketing strategy.

Systrack Systems has significant compact disc player production experience, having produced an average of 500,000 units per year over the past three years. During manufacturing, compact disc players go through three major processes: cutting, assembly, and finishing. Historically, the manufacturing costs of producing one compact disc player are as follows:

Direct material	$ 80
Direct labor	60
Variable overhead	40
Fixed overhead	20
Total manufacturing costs	$200

At the present time, Systrack Systems operates at 80 percent of production capacity. The product is sold at $300 in the market.

Andrea Chicoine, president of Systrack Systems, is very interested in converting the company's conventional current accounting system to an activity-based costing system and also introducing just-in-time into her manufacturing system. To get some movement on this, Chicoine asked her controller, John Russ, to submit a comparison of the manufacturing costs under the present system and a just-in-time system to meet a special 100,000-unit order from one of its dealers at a price of $220 per unit. The company has the capacity to meet the special order at no increase in fixed costs. Russ's report revealed the following manufacturing costs using a JIT system and the allocation of manufacturing overhead based on an activity-based costing system:

Direct material	$ 80
Direct labor	70
Variable overhead	30
Fixed overhead	10
Total manufacturing costs	$190

A JIT manufacturing system requires the establishment of manufacturing cells in the plant. The company has to adopt the philosophy of total quality control (TQC). No scrap or waste is allowed. Inventory levels should be zero (because JIT is a demand pull approach). Workers in each cell are trained to perform various tasks within the cell. Therefore, idle time is not permissible. Finally, each cell is considered a separate unit.

Under an activity-based costing system, manufacturing overhead costs are applied to products based on cost drivers and not on departmental overhead rates. Plant layout should be changed. Manufacturing cells should be developed to manufacture a company's product. Many costs that are considered indirect costs under the current system will be considered direct costs that are easy to trace to the final product and are measured precisely. A JIT system considers direct labor costs as fixed costs and not as variable costs as they are under conventional accounting systems. This is legitimate because workers are trained to perform various jobs within a given work cell. Chicoine is convinced that a JIT manufacturing system, even though it would result in changing many indirect common product costs to direct traceable product costs, will more accurately determine product costs.

a. Should the special order be accepted or rejected? Show computations under the conventional and JIT systems.

b. If the cost activities described in the case will result in different cost estimates and different contribution margins, which cost accounting system is preferable for pricing this special order?

(From Nabil Hassan, Herbert E. Brown, and Paula M. Saunders, "Management Accounting Case Study: Systrack Systems," *Management Accounting Campus Report* [Spring 1991], copyright © 1991 IMA [formerly NAA].)

52. AgriCorp is a manufacturer of farm equipment that is sold by a network of distributors throughout the United States. A majority of the distributors are also repair centers for AgriCorp equipment and depend on AgriCorp's Service Division to provide a timely supply of spare parts.

In an effort to reduce the inventory costs incurred by the Service Division, Richard Bachman, division manager, implemented a just-in-time inventory program on June 1, 1993, the beginning of the company's fiscal year. Since JIT has been in place for a year, Bachman has asked the division controller, Janice Grady, to determine the effect the program has had on the Service Division's financial performance. Grady has been able to document the following results of JIT implementation.

• The Service Division's average inventory declined from $550,000 to $150,000.

• Projected annual insurance costs of $80,000 declined 60 percent because of the lower average inventory.

• A leased 8,000 square foot warehouse, previously used for raw material storage, was not used at all during the year. The division paid $11,200 annual rent for the warehouse and was able to sublet three-quarters of the building to several tenants at $2.50 per square foot, while the balance of the space remained idle.

- Two warehouse employees whose services were no longer needed were transferred on June 1, 1993, to the Purchasing Department to assist in the coordination of the JIT program. The annual salary expense for these two employees totaled $38,000 and continued to be charged to the indirect labor portion of fixed overhead.
- Despite the use of overtime to manufacture 7,500 spare parts, lost sales caused by stockouts totaled 3,800 spare parts. The overtime premium incurred amounted to $5.60 per part manufactured. The use of overtime to fill spare parts orders was immaterial prior to June 1, 1993.

Prior to the decision to implement the JIT inventory program, AgriCorp's Service Division had completed its 1993–94 fiscal budget. The division's pro forma income statement, without any adjustments for JIT inventory, is presented next. AgriCorp's borrowing rate related to inventory is 9 percent after income taxes. All AgriCorp budgets are prepared using an effective tax rate of 40 percent.

AGRICORP SERVICE DIVISION
PRO FORMA INCOME STATEMENT
FOR THE YEAR ENDING MAY 31, 1994

Sales (280,000 spare parts)		$6,160,000
Cost of goods sold		
Variable	$2,660,000	
Fixed	1,120,000	3,780,000
Gross profit		$2,380,000
Selling & administrative expense		
Variable	$ 700,000	
Fixed	555,000	1,255,000
Operating income		$1,125,000
Other income		75,000
Income before interest & taxes		$1,200,000
Interest expense		150,000
Income before income taxes		$1,050,000
Income taxes		420,000
Net income		$ 630,000

a. Calculate the after-tax cash savings (loss) for AgriCorp's Service Division that resulted during the 1993–94 fiscal year from the adoption of the JIT program.
b. Identify and explain the factors, other than financial, that should be considered before a company implements a JIT program.

(CMA)

Ethics Discussion

53. Shelby Lessons is the production manager for the Su-it Company, located in a small town in Mississippi. Su-it is the only major employer in the county, which has substantial unemployment.

Shelby is in the process of trying to introduce manufacturing cells in the company. Of the 150 employees at Su-it, approximately 80 percent have little formal education, but have worked for the company for fifteen years or more. Some of these employees are close to retirement, but not all.

In talking with the employees, Shelby determines that most would require substantial training before they would be able to change from their current single-task production jobs to being able to handle multifunctional tasks.

A neighboring county has a vocational-technical school that is educating many young people in the use of the new types of multitask equipment that could be used at Su-it. Shelby has discussed the company's plans with the head of the vo-tech school, who has indicated that the school could easily provide a cadre of 150 well-trained employees within the next ten months—approximately the time it will take the equipment to arrive and be installed.

Shelby is excited to hear this, because Su-it would not have to pay for training and would be able to hire new graduates at a slightly lower hourly wage because of "lack of experience." Her only difficulty is trying to determine how to remove the older work force from the plant. She decides to institute a rigorous training program that would be intolerable for most of the less-educated employees.

a. Discuss the business sense of hiring graduates with the necessary skills rather than paying for on-location training.
b. Discuss the ethics of the plan to "remove" the current work force.
c. Why should Shelby and Su-it be concerned about the welfare of the current work force if it makes good business sense to hire the graduates of the vo-tech school?

C H A P T E R   14

CONTROLLING NONINVENTORY COSTS

LEARNING OBJECTIVES

After completing this chapter, you should be able to do the following:

1. Recognize why cost consciousness is of great importance to all members of an organization
2. Differentiate between committed and discretionary costs
3. Understand how the benefits from discretionary cost expenditures can be measured
4. Determine when standards are applicable to discretionary costs
5. Explain how a budget helps in controlling discretionary costs
6. (Appendix) Understand how program budgeting is used for cost control in not-for-profit entities

Corporate Travel Costs Are Flying High

Today's companies face a tough, competitive environment. Travel and entertainment spending typically represents the third largest controllable expense for companies. If your company is in the service sector, it may be number two. The annual cost per business traveler is approximately $10,000 and, depending on the industry your company is in, the figure could be as high as $15,000 to $25,000.

One Chicago-based Fortune 500 company spent somewhere between $5 million and $15 million in travel annually, used over 100 travel agencies, and had not considered consolidating suppliers. The company had six basic travel-related cost problems: there was no detailed corporate-wide information on total travel costs; the company did not effectively negotiate rates with travel vendors; the travel policy was over six years old; adequate use was not being made of travel agencies; employees had the "it's other people's money" attitude; and there was no internal travel manager in the company. A rational approach to travel spending management could save 10%–30% annually and make the organization more cost effective, productive and efficient at every level.

SOURCE: Adapted from Denis W. Day, "How to Cut Travel Costs," *Management Accounting* (August 1990), p. 36ff. Published by Institute of Management Accountants, Montvale, N.J.

here is no doubt that travel cost is a major factor for many organizations. But then, so are health costs, advertising costs, and utility costs. Any business wanting to succeed must not only generate reasonable levels of revenues, but also control the costs that are matched against those revenues.

Previous chapters presented various ways to control costs. For example, direct materials and direct labor cost control are typically linked to the development and implementation of a standard cost system. Additionally, just-in-time inventory techniques can significantly reduce the cost of warehousing and purchasing.

This chapter focuses on three topics related to cost control. The first topic is the **cost control system,** which is used to analyze and evaluate how well expenditures were managed during a period. This system covers all the formal and informal activities related to controlling costs. The second topic focuses on costs, such as advertising, that are set by management at specific levels *each* period. Often, these costs are difficult to control because their benefits are harder to measure than those provided by costs that are fixed from long-term commitments. Third, the use of flexible, rather than static, budgets to control costs is discussed. The chapter appendix considers an alternative budgeting method (program budgeting) used in governmental and not-for-profit entities because of the unique nature of their output.

cost control system

COST CONTROL SYSTEMS

A good control system should provide three functions: control before an event; control during an event; and control after an event. An event could be a period of time, the manufacture of a product, or the performance of a service. Exhibit 14–1 indicates the ways in which an effective cost control system can address each of these three functions.

Because individuals collectively compose an organization, managers should consider the attitudes and efforts of those individuals in determining how an organization's costs may be controlled. Managers alone cannot control costs. Cost control is a continual process that requires the support of *all* employees at *all* times. Thus, a good control system would encompass the functions shown in Exhibit 14–1 as well as include the ideas about **cost consciousness** shown in Exhibit 14–2. Cost consciousness refers to a companywide employee attitude about the topics of cost understanding, cost containment, cost avoidance, and cost reduction. Each of these topics is important at different stages of the control system.

cost consciousness

Cost Understanding

Cost control is first exercised when the budget is prepared because control requires that a set of expectations exist. Budgets allow formal comparisons of expected and actual costs. But budgets can be properly prepared only when the reasons for periodic cost changes are understood, and cost control can be achieved only with an understanding of why costs may differ from the budgeted amounts.

Costs may change from previous periods or differ from budget expectations for many reasons. Some costs change because of their underlying behavior. Total variable cost increases or decreases with increases or decreases in activity level. If the current period activity level differs from a prior period's activity level or the budgeted activity level, total actual variable cost will differ from the prior period or the budget. A flexible budget can compensate for such differences by providing expected variable costs at the actual activity level. Managers can then make valid budget-to-actual cost comparisons to determine if total variable costs were properly controlled.

In addition to variable cost reactions to changes in activity levels, the factors listed on page 602 can cause costs to differ from prior periods or the budget.

Function	Reason	Cost Control Methods
Control before an event	Preventive; reflects planning	Budgets; standards; policies concerning approval for deviations; expressions of quantitative and qualitative objectives
Control during an event	Corrective; ensures that the event is being pursued according to plans; can correct problems as they occur	Periodic monitoring of ongoing activities; comparing activities and costs to budgets and standards and avoiding excessive expenditures
Control after an event	Diagnostic; guides future actions	Feedback, variance analysis; responsibility reports (discussed in chapter 15)

EXHIBIT 14–1
▼▼▼▼▼▼▼▼▼▼▼▼

FUNCTIONS OF AN
EFFECTIVE COST
CONTROL SYSTEM

Controlling costs was not of any importance when this castle was built. However, present economic conditions necessitate that almost all individuals and businesses be concerned with how costs can be controlled and what benefits are obtained by cost incurrence.

EXHIBIT 14–2
▼▼▼▼▼▼▼▼▼▼▼

COST CONTROL
SYSTEM

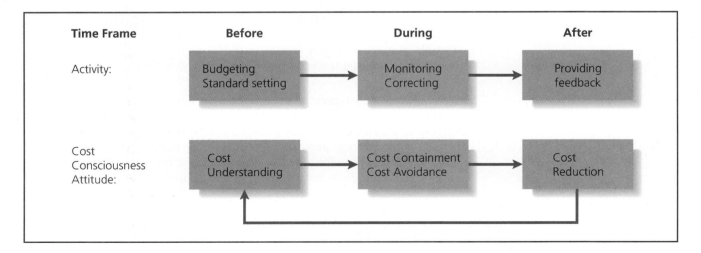

Time Frame	Before	During	After
Activity:	Budgeting Standard setting	Monitoring Correcting	Providing feedback
Cost Consciousness Attitude:	Cost Understanding	Cost Containment Cost Avoidance	Cost Reduction

1. *Cost changes due to inflation/deflation.* Fluctuations in the value of the dollar are called general price level changes. When the general price level changes, the cost of goods and services that the dollar can purchase also changes. General price level changes affect almost all costs approximately equally and in the same direction, if all other factors are constant.

2. *Cost changes due to technology advances.* As a general rule, if the technology of producing a good or service advances, the cost of that good or service declines. The result of this type of change is referred to as a specific price level change.

3. *Cost changes due to supply and demand.* The relationship of the availability of goods and services to the demand for these items affects costs. If supply of a good is low and demand is high relative to the past, the cost of the goods or services increases. Or, if demand for a good falls but supply remains constant, the cost of the good will fall. Like cost changes related to technology, changes related to supply and demand also cause specific price level changes that may move in the same or opposite direction as general price level changes. At American Airlines, for example, a one-cent-per-gallon increase in fuel prices is reflected as a $25 million increase in costs.[1]

4. *Cost changes due to tax or regulatory adjustments.* As taxes or regulations increase, costs will increase. Companies must pass their increased costs on to the next consumer in the supply chain. For example, airlines are continuously faced with more stringent noise-abatement, clean-air, and required maintenance legislation. Complying with these regulations increases costs for the airline company that must (1) be passed along in the form of ticket-price increases to maintain the same income level, (2) force decreases in other costs to maintain the same income level, or (3) cause a decline in net income.

5. *Cost changes due to quantity of competition.* The number of organizational competitors can also create a specific price level change. As the number of suppliers of a good or service increases, the competitive environment causes the cost of that good or service to fall. A change in the quantity of suppliers is not the same as a change in the quantity of supply. If the supply of an item is large, one normally expects the price to be low, but if there is only one supplier, the price can remain high because of supplier control. Air fares could be expected to increase as more airlines declare bankruptcy and, thus, reduce the number of suppliers.

6. *Cost changes due to seasonality or other timing factors.* Certain goods and services cost more at certain times of the year because of use or demand. For example, it is generally less expensive to travel on the airlines at "nonpeak" times, such as on the weekend or during January or February after the holiday rush.

7. *Cost changes due to quantity purchased.* Firms are normally given quantity discounts, up to some maximum level, when purchases are made in bulk. Therefore, a cost per unit may change because quantities are purchased in different lot sizes from previous periods or other than as projected. Companies using one airline for all their business travel may be able to negotiate substantial discounts because of the volume of purchases.

---

[1]Kenneth Labich, "American Takes on the World," *FORTUNE* (September 24, 1990), p. 44.

While the preceding seven reasons indicate why costs change, they do not indicate what managers can do to contain the upward effects of the changes. The next section discusses some concepts of cost containment.

Cost Containment

To the extent possible, managers should attempt to practice **cost containment** through minimizing period-by-period increases in per-unit variable and total fixed costs. Some cost changes are more easily contained than others.

cost containment

Causes #1–4   Cost containment is difficult for changes resulting from inflation, technology, supply and demand adjustments, and taxes/regulatory increases because these factors exist outside the organizational structure. Managers may, however, be able to practice cost avoidance (discussed in the next section) in hopes of minimizing the effects that these causes have on the organization's costs.

Costs that rise because of causes 5 through 7 (reduced competition, seasonality, and quantities purchased) are subject to cost containment activities. Companies should look for ways to cap the upward changes in these costs. An example of a cost containment activity is given next for each type of cost change that is controllable.

Cause #5—Quantity of Competition   Companies should be aware of the quantity of suppliers for needed goods and services. The purchasing agent should investigate new suppliers to determine which companies can provide needed items in the quantity, quality, and time desired. Comparing costs and finding new sources of supply can increase buying power and reduce costs. If bids are used to select suppliers, the

The airline industry exhibits a perfect example of changes in the quantity of competition. While the number of suppliers has declined tremendously in the past few years, fare wars have kept the prices of tickets from skyrocketing.

purchasing agent should remember that a bid is merely the first step in negotiating. A low bid is made to eliminate the competition from consideration. It is possible that negotiations with the supplier can actually cause the goods or services to be provided at a cost lower than the bid amount or that concessions (such as better delivery) can be obtained.

Companies can view travel agents as suppliers. The intriguing aspect of this relationship, however, is that the companies do not have to pay these suppliers; travel agents are paid by the airline, hotel, and rental car agencies that the company uses. Because of this dual relationship, companies should be certain that the agency works for them and not for the travel partners. Using one travel agency (or one agency per region) allows a company to receive detailed, consistent information about travel expenditures and to make certain that the agency understands and carries out the company's travel policies. For instance, to obtain such benefits, Price Waterhouse, a Big Six public accounting firm, uses a single travel agency that has "about 50 agents assigned exclusively to [its] account."[2] If one agency cannot or will not cooperate in a company's cost containment program, many other suppliers of this service are available.

Cause #6—Seasonality or Other Timing Factors A company may circumvent seasonal cost changes by postponing or advancing purchases of goods and services. However, such purchasing changes should not mean buying irresponsibly or incurring excessive carrying costs. The concepts of economic order quantities, safety stock levels, materials requirements planning, and the just-in-time philosophy should be considered when making purchases. These concepts are discussed in the previous chapter.

Many opportunities for cost containment exist for some services. For example, travel plans might need to include a Saturday stay to obtain a better airline fare if the ticket savings are greater than the extra night's hotel cost. Occasionally, travel can be postponed to low-peak times of the year when airlines, hotels, and car rental companies offer special discounts. Or off-airport car companies might be used to reduce the daily rental rate by 15 to 25 percent.

Cause #7—Quantity Purchased Buying in bulk is not a new or unique idea, but it is often not applied on an extended basis for related companies or enterprises. In a corporation, one division could take the responsibility for obtaining a supplier contract for items (such as computer disks) that are necessary to all divisions. The savings resulting from buying in a quantity appropriate for all divisions might offset the additional shipping costs to get the disks to the divisions.

In regard to travel, the more business a company can do with a specific carrier, the more negotiating power that company has. Over 20 percent of corporate tickets in the first quarter of 1991 were bought for negotiated fares that saved companies 45 to 60 percent off regular coach fares.[3] It is also important to know whether the carrier can serve the company's needs adequately. For example, a company may be able to negotiate very low fares with a carrier that has only two flights a day to or from a destination to which company members often travel. The savings in ticket prices may be eroded because of the wait delays and lack of convenience for the travelers.

---

[2]Carl E. Schwab, "Price Waterhouse's Experience," *Management Accounting* (August 1990), p. 37.
[3]Alan Deutschman, "Smart Ways to Cut Travel Costs," *FORTUNE* (June 3, 1991), p. 79.

Nonrelated organizations can even improve cost control by group purchasing of necessary items that do not directly enter into any product or service on which they may be competing. For example, several companies in an area that do not individually have a significant amount of travel volume could negotiate as one "entity" with a travel agency to obtain the best airline, hotel, and car rental rates.

Cost Avoidance

Cost containment activities can prove very effective if they can be implemented. In some instances, cost containment may not be possible although **cost avoidance** might be. Cost avoidance means finding acceptable alternatives to high cost items and not spending money for unnecessary goods or services. Avoiding one cost may require that an alternative, lower cost be incurred.

cost avoidance

The most effective way to reduce travel costs is, quite obviously, to travel less. One reasonable substitute to travel is the telephone and, as indicated in the News Note on the next page, part of the telephone system is videoconferencing. The cost of videoconferencing includes either purchasing in-house facilities or renting room space from one of the telephone companies.

An attitude of cost avoidance should have managers and employees seeking to eliminate unnecessary expenditures. Assume that the Management Department in the College of Business at State University has always purchased videotapes for classroom use. This year, because of cutbacks in state funding, the department has significantly fewer dollars available in its media budget. One way the department can implement cost avoidance is to rent the videotapes needed this year rather than buying them. In this manner, the faculty has avoided a significant outlay of $100–$500 per videotape, but still provided the films to classes.

Cost Reduction

Closely related to the concept of cost avoidance is **cost reduction,** which means lowering current costs—especially those in excess of what is necessary. For example, it is not possible for a company to control increases in utility cost per kilowatt hour nor to avoid using electricity, but it is possible for employees to reduce some of the organization's energy costs by using sound energy conservation techniques.

cost reduction

Cost reduction often focuses on the activities that are causing the costs to occur. As discussed in chapter 4 on activity-based management, companies engage in both value-added and non-value-added activities. If it is possible to reduce or eliminate the non-value-added activities, the corresponding costs will also be reduced or eliminated. The following example indicates the importance of analyzing activities (in this case, producing computer reports) to uncover those that add no value and recognizing the amount of cost reduction that can occur when such activities are eliminated.

At one 2,000-person manufacturing company, data processing produced 321 copies of 41 reports containing 140,000 pages and distributed these copies to 63 persons each month. Interviews revealed that only 2 copies of 9 reports were needed. Changes were made and manufacturing removed 300+ filing cabinets, sold them, and freed up over 3,000 sq. ft. of floor space. The floor space was then used to store materials, saving $30,000 per year of rent for an outside warehouse. Giving up the warehouse eliminated the need for a driver and truck (operating costs about $4,000 per year) used to move goods to and from the warehouse. Two file clerks' and a printer operator's positions were eliminated. Purchase orders for 42 new file cabinets were cancelled, as were appropriations for $38,000 in additional equipment. No one

"Face-to-Face" No Longer Necessarily Means Travel

In this age of rampant technology, cost control has become the mother of invention. And while companies have for years been using teleconferencing to cut [travel and entertainment] expenses, it was fear of terrorism that made the technology—first introduced at the 1964–65 New York World's Fair—an idea whose boom has finally come.

As the Persian Gulf conflict erupted [in January 1991], AT&T reported a 100% increase in requests for video linkups; US Sprint's Meeting Channel reported a 600% increase. By the time the skies were safe again, videoconferencing had quietly grown into a $1 billion megabusiness—with a staggering $8.3 billion predicted for 1995, according [to] the New York market research firm Frost & Sullivan. And videoconferencing is predicted to grow as more people become accustomed to the format and usage becomes ever more cost-effective.

Videoconferencing still can't be called inexpensive, but costs are falling. A coast-to-coast videoconference once cost up to $5,000 an hour; the price [in late 1991] averages $400 an hour.

Renting facilities for a 12-person, two-hour video meeting between New York and Paris costs well under $2,000 on US Sprint's Meeting Channel. To compare, Ed Coering, financial officer with Elizabeth Arden Inc., notes that "one round-trip business-class ticket to Paris averages $4,000; add hotel and meals and you're well over $5,000."

SOURCE: Julie Moline, "Managing Business Travel Costs: Preparing for 1992," *FORTUNE* (December 2, 1991), p. 26. From a paid advertising section, *FORTUNE* magazine, 1991.

ever bothered to figure out how much was saved in computer paper or report folders. Because the cause was eliminated, a $100,000+ permanent cost reduction per year was achieved. All costs are results, not causes, and costs can be reduced or eliminated only by attacking their causes.[4]

Sometimes money must be spent to generate cost savings. Although many companies believe that eliminating jobs and labor is an effective way to reduce costs, sometimes (as indicated in the following News Note about StarKist) cutting costs by cutting people merely creates other problems. The people may be performing a value-added activity and, by eliminating the people, a company eliminates its ability to do the necessary tasks.

Cost reduction is also possible when companies begin to use part-time rather than full-time employees or external providers of services rather than maintaining internal departments. In 1988, for example, almost 17 percent of Apple Computer's work force was employed on a "temp" basis. If the quantity of work in an area fluctuates substantially, part-time employees can be hired for peak periods. Airlines, for instance, often hire part-time ground personnel because of the "bunching" nature of the airline schedule (early morning, mid-day, and early evening flights). Use of these

---

[4]Donald J. Byrum, "The Right Way to Control Period Expense," *Management Accounting* (September 1990), pp. 55ff. Published by Institute of Management Accountants, Montvale, N.J.

Just Cutting Costs Won't "Cut" It

If any company has earned the right to crow about cost-cutting, it is Pittsburgh-based H. J. Heinz, the king of ketchup. Chief Executive Anthony O'Reilly, renowned for his relentless attention to costs, has closed factories, laid off workers, and speeded up production lines. Then Heinz discovered that overzealous cost cutting can injure product quality.

Under its low-cost operator programs, Heinz had cut the work force at its StarKist tuna canning factories in Puerto Rico and American Samoa by 5%. But the fish cleaners were so overworked that they were leaving tons of meat on the bone every day. Says J. Wray Connolly, a senior vice president who heads the company's total quality management effort: "We discovered that we had to add people, not subtract them. In the past, we just wouldn't have done that."

StarKist managers slowed down the production lines, hired 400 hourly workers and 15 supervisors, and retrained the entire workforce. They installed four more lines to take some of the load off each worker and to expand volume. All told, StarKist increased labor costs by $5 million but cut out $15 million in waste. Net saving: $10 million annually.

SOURCE: Ronald Henkoff, "Cost Cutting: How to Do It Right," *FORTUNE* (April 9, 1990), p. 46. © 1990 The Time Inc. Magazine Company. All rights reserved.

part-timers has dramatically reduced airlines' labor and fringe benefit costs. There is even a company (CompHealth of Salt Lake City) that provides temporary physicians for hospitals and clinics nationwide.

Management-level employees are extremely important in cost reduction programs. Not only can these individuals provide important input on cost reduction measures, but their attitude also sets the tone for the entire department or organization. Cost-conscious managers generally have cost-conscious employees. The reverse is also true.

While management is an important part of a cost control system, employees cannot be overlooked. Managers need to communicate the need for cost consciousness to employees and indicate that such an attitude is not desired only so that the company can have higher profits. Employees often do not mind engaging in cost control efforts if such efforts will provide the employees some benefit either monetarily or at performance review time. For example, companies may want to pay employees to stay at a friend's house when traveling rather than at a hotel. "At Unisys, employees who use their frequent-flyer points to travel on business now get paid half what those tickets would have cost the company."[5] Government employees in Phoenix, Arizona, receive bonuses of up to 10 percent of the amount saved by their suggestions, with a $2,500 limitation.[6] Nonmonetary rewards could include new equipment to do a job better or to make a job easier.

[5]Deutschman, p. 80.
[6]Ronald Henkoff, "Some Hope for Troubled Cities," *FORTUNE* (September 9, 1991), p. 128.

Most companies that have instituted employee suggestion programs have found that employees are able to contribute significantly to improvement ideas. The News Note opposite discusses the monetary benefits that Philips Corporation has obtained from its employee suggestion program. Employees who are listened to (and rewarded in some way) are more likely to be motivated to provide useful cost-cutting tips.

Recognizing that they are responsible for the costs in their area, managers should have a five-step method of implementing a cost control system. First, the types of costs incurred by an organization must be understood. Second, for it to be effective, the need for cost consciousness must be communicated to all employees. Third, employees must be motivated by education and incentives to embrace the concepts. Managers must also be flexible enough to allow for changes from the current method of operation. Fourth, reports must be generated that indicate actual results, budget-to-actual comparisons, and variances. These reports must be evaluated by management to improve future performance. And lastly, the cost control system should be viewed as a long-run process, not a short-run solution. "To be successful, organizations must avoid the illusion of short-term, highly simplified cost-cutting procedures. Instead, they must carefully evaluate proposed solutions to insure that these are practical, workable, and measurable changes based on realities, not illusions." [7]

Following these five steps will provide an atmosphere conducive to controlling costs to the fullest extent possible as well as deriving the most benefit from the costs that are incurred. All costs incurred should be subjected to appropriate value-added/non-value-added and cost-benefit analyses. However, distinct differences exist in the cost control system between committed and discretionary costs.

COMMITTED VERSUS DISCRETIONARY COSTS

Managers are charged with planning and controlling the types and amounts of costs needed to conduct business activities. Many activities necessary to achieve business objectives involve fixed costs. All fixed costs (and the activities that create them) can be categorized as either committed or discretionary. The difference between the two categories is primarily the time period for which management binds itself to the activity and the cost.

Committed Costs

committed costs

The costs associated with basic plant assets or with the personnel structure that an organization must have to operate are known as **committed costs**. The amount of committed costs is normally dictated by long-run management decisions involving the desired level of operations. Committed costs include depreciation, lease rentals, and property taxes. Such costs cannot easily be reduced even during periods of temporarily diminished activity.

Control of committed costs is first provided during the evaluation process of comparing the expected benefits of having plant assets (or human resources) to the expected costs of such investments. Managers must decide on the activities needed to attain company objectives and determine which (and how many) assets are needed to support those activities. Once the assets are acquired, managers are committed to

---

[7]Mark D. Lutchen, "Cost-Cutting Illusions," *Today's CPA* (May/June 1989), p. 46.

NEWS NOTE

Cost Cutting with No Layoffs

Philips Corp. is a small Dayton, Ohio–based building-materials producer. The company runs a Japanese-style, how-can-we-save-some-money program, in which nearly everyone can participate. It has saved Philips $62 million in six years. The program allows groups of five employees, from various departments, to work together for five days to improve Philips products. [N]o team effort has ever failed to yield some savings. Even better, not once has the group decided to save money by laying people off.

SOURCE: John McCormick and Bill Powell, "Management for the 1990s," *Newsweek* (April 25, 1988), p. 48.

both the activities and the costs associated with those activities for the long run. However, regardless of how good an asset investment appears on the surface, managers need to understand how committed fixed costs could affect income in the event of changes in operations.

The managers of Garigh Company are considering the following two investments: a corporate jet and a fleet of twenty company cars for executives. Both investments have been evaluated and found to be acceptable, since their benefits would exceed their costs. The jet will cost $1,200,000 and produce $240,000 of depreciation expense per year. The cars will cost $800,000 in total and produce depreciation expense of $200,000 per year. Garigh's capital budget can support both expenditures. The company's cost relationships indicate that variable costs are 60 percent of sales, giving a contribution margin of 40 percent. Exhibit 14–3 illustrates the potential effects on net income of these long-term commitments, if revenues either increased by 20 percent or decreased by 20 percent.

EXHIBIT 14–3
▼▼▼▼▼▼▼▼▼▼▼▼▼

RISK EFFECTS
RELATED TO
COMMITTED COSTS

	Current Level of Operations	(a) Current Level of Revenues & Increase in Depreciation	(b) Increase in Revenues of 20% & Increase in Depreciation	(c) Decrease in Revenues of 20% & Increase in Depreciation
Revenues	$7,000,000	$7,000,000	$8,400,000	$5,600,000
Variable costs	4,200,000	4,200,000	5,040,000	3,360,000
Contribution margin	$2,800,000	$2,800,000	$3,360,000	$2,240,000
Fixed costs	2,000,000	2,440,000	2,440,000	2,440,000
Net income	$ 800,000	$ 360,000	$ 920,000	$ (200,000)

Each change from the original income level to the new income level is explained as the change in the contribution margin minus the increase in fixed costs:

Change to (a) = Increase in CM − Increase in FC = $0 − $440,000 = $(440,000)

Change to (b) = Increase in CM − Increase in FC = $560,000 − $440,000 = +$120,000

Change to (c) = Decrease in CM − Increase in FC = $(560,000) − $440,000 = $(1,000,000)

Note that the $440,000 increased depreciation expense affects the income statement more significantly when sales decline than when sales increase. This effect is caused by the operating leverage factor discussed in chapter 9. Companies that have fairly high contribution margins can withstand large increases in fixed costs as long as revenues increase. However, these same companies feel the effects of decreases in revenue more strongly because the margin available to cover fixed costs erodes so rapidly. As the magnitude of committed fixed costs increases, so does the risk of incurring an operating loss in the event of a downturn in demand. Therefore, managers must be extremely careful about the level of fixed costs to which they commit the organization.

The second method of controlling committed costs is through comparing actual and expected results from plant asset investments. During this process, managers are able to see and evaluate the accuracy of their cost and revenue predictions relative to the investment. This comparison is called a post-investment audit and is discussed in chapter 17.

Discretionary Costs

discretionary cost

In contrast to committed costs, a **discretionary cost** is one "that a decision maker must periodically review to determine that it continues to be in accord with ongoing policies." [8] A discretionary cost is a fixed cost that reflects a management decision to fund an activity at a specified amount for a specified period of time. *The decision to fund an activity as discretionary is based on organizational policy or management preference.* Although advertising, public relations, and research and development are typical examples of discretionary costs, there are no specific activities whose costs will, in all organizations, be considered discretionary.

For example, while equipment is typically considered a committed cost, a 1972 cash shortage at Southwest Airlines forced the sale of one airplane. Pilots were told to continue the same flight schedule with three planes rather than four. The piece of equipment that was sold proved to be less than necessary, and selling it allowed the company to gain a competitive advantage as to airport turn-around time.

Discretionary costs relate to activities that are important to the company, but that are viewed as optional. Discretionary cost activities are usually service-oriented and include employee travel, repairs and maintenance, advertising, research and development, and employee training and development. There is no "correct" amount at which to set funding for discretionary costs and, as indicated in the following News Note, in the event of cash flow shortages or forecasted operating losses, managers may reduce these expenditures. Managers believe that, in the short run, reductions can be made in discretionary costs without impairing the organization's long-range profitability or capacity. (Unfortunately, not painting the planes did not help Midway. The airline went bankrupt in November 1991.)

To illustrate the ease with which discretionary costs can be reduced, consider what occurred after Iraq's invasion of Kuwait. The travel business saw bookings decline approximately 50 percent in early 1991. Morton Ehrlich, president of Lifeco Services Corporation (a travel company which deals primarily with corporate

---

[8]Institute of Management Accountants (formerly National Association of Accountants) *Statements on Management Accounting: Management Accounting Terminology* (Montvale, N.J.: National Association of Accountants, June 1, 1983), p. 35.

NEWS NOTE

"Naked" Planes Are Less Costly

In what the cash-strapped carrier calls a cost-cutting move that will also reduce environmental concerns, Midway [Airlines] said it plans to stop painting its traditionally red-and-white aircraft.

Midway, operating under Chapter 11 bankruptcy-law protection, said flying naked-aluminum planes—bearing only logos on their sides and tails—will save the company about $1.4 million annually or about $20,000 a year for each plane in its fleet of 70.

As for the paintless planes, the new look will satisfy environmental concerns that are involved during the process of stripping and repainting planes, which involves chemicals that face "more and more restrictive" regulations.

Midway notes that the bare look will make it easier for maintenance crews to run routine airframe checks. In the past, other carriers have eliminated the usage of paint to lighten the weight of the plane and reduce fuel usage.

SOURCE: Brett Pulley, "Midway Airlines Will Discontinue Painting Aircraft," *Wall Street Journal* (July 12, 1991), p. A7. Reprinted by permission of the *Wall Street Journal*, © 1991 Dow Jones & Company, Inc. All rights reserved worldwide.

clients), said that as of mid-March 1991, overseas travel booked by the company was still down by nearly a third even though the war had ended.[9] Companies started "traveling" by telephone and fax machines rather than by air.

Part of the difference in management attitude between committed and discretionary activities and costs has to do with ability to measure the benefits provided by those items. Management must acknowledge that the company cannot operate without some level of commitment to plant and human assets. Thus, considerable control exists over the process of committing to certain activities and their related fixed costs.

Discretionary costs, on the other hand, relate to activities that are relatively unstructured, and results from the activities are oftentimes not measurable in terms of money. This situation is in contrast to the benefits of committed fixed activities, where costs can be predicted and later compared to actual results.

Benefits from Discretionary Cost Incurrence

Discretionary cost activities vary in type and magnitude from day to day. The output quality of discretionary cost activities may also vary according to the tasks and skill levels of the persons performing those activities. Because of these two factors (varying activities and varying quality levels), discretionary costs are not usually susceptible to the precise planning and control measures available for variable production costs or to the cost/benefit evaluation techniques available to control committed fixed costs.

---

[9]Wendy Zellner, "The Travel Business Still Has an Altitude Problem," *Business Week* (March 18, 1991), p. 30.

Management does not generally know how much discretionary cost is the optimal amount for the activity involved. In regard to some discretionary costs, the common opinion exists that "less is better" and that a lower cost indicates efficiency. But because of the nature of other discretionary cost activities, less is not necessarily better. As an example of "less is not better," consider the cost of preventive maintenance. This cost can be viewed as discretionary, but reducing it could result in production breakdowns or machine inefficiency. American Airlines believed the "less is not better" concept when, in 1987, it spent over $1.8 million a day on maintenance, or an average of $1.5 million per year per plane.[10] This amount far exceeded government requirements because company management made a commitment to maintenance excellence. Although the benefits from conducting this level of maintenance could not be quantified, American felt that less maintenance cost was not desirable.

Many discretionary costs, although significant, cannot normally be closely tied to outcomes. For example, in 1992, Merck & Company increased the company's research and development budget 16 percent to $1.1 billion.[11] How long will it take the pharmaceutical company to develop new products from this R&D? In 1990, "Tokyo announced a $370 million Japan–U.S. Global Partnership Fund to enhance Japan's image, primarily in the United States, and to pay for joint research on problems between the two nations."[12] How will the Japanese government know if this fund did enhance Japan's image? And in 1989, News Corporation began a $10 million advertising campaign for its *TV Guide* magazine.[13] If *TV Guide* sales increase, how can News Corporation know that the advertising spurred those sales? Expenditures of this magnitude require that management have some idea of the benefits that are expected, but measuring those results is often difficult. Because of this difficulty, discretionary cost activities are often some of the first costs to be cut when profits are lagging.

Before top management can address the issue of discretionary costs, company goals must be translated into specific objectives and policies that management believes will be conducive to organizational success. Then, management needs to decide what discretionary activities are necessary to accomplish the chosen objectives. These activities are "value-added." Funding levels should be set only after prioritizing the discretionary cost activities and reviewing cash flow and income expectations for the coming period. Management tends to be more generous in making discretionary cost appropriations during periods of strong economic outlook for the organization than during periods of weak economic outlook.

Based on the total budgeted amount of discretionary costs, management should fund activities in a way that corresponds to the level of operations projected for the period. At UPS, for example, one policy is "Our planes fly clean." The money spent on washing planes is believed by management to reduce maintenance costs, improve morale, and build a positive public image. All three benefits are believed to be impor-

---

[10]"Do Mechanical Delays Have You Stuck on the Ground?" American Airlines *AAdvantage Newsletter* (September 1987), p. 1.

[11]Elyse Tanouye, "Merck to Increase R&D Budget 16 Percent to $1.1 Billion," *Wall Street Journal* (March 17, 1992), p. B12.

[12]Ronald E. Yates, "Japan launches PR campaign," *(Honolulu) Sunday Star-Bulletin & Advertiser* (January 6, 1991), p. A24.

[13]Patrick M. Reilly, "*TV Guide*, Its Circulation Lagging, Initiates $10 Million Ad Campaign," *Wall Street Journal* (September 5, 1989), p. B4.

Incurring the costs of keeping planes clean may be appropriate while UPS is profitable. Such time and costs may be considered less value-added in the face of lowered profits.

tant to achieve the company's goals. UPS may budget a specified dollar amount each year for washing planes. However, if revenues, profits, or cash flows were reduced, the discretionary expenditures for washing planes could be reduced. Management may determine that spending money on maintenance achieves a higher priority goal (safety) than spending money to clean planes.

In developing discretionary cost budgets, top management often relies on the advice of specialists or project managers. For example, the budget for advertising expenditures would normally be set after considering input from the marketing and research staff. Information from such specialists is necessary to decision making, since these people have more detailed knowledge of the specific discretionary cost area. Top management should be aware, however, that the advice received from specialists is sometimes biased in favor of "pet" projects.

The value of the outputs produced by most discretionary costs is difficult to determine. Nonmonetary surrogate measures may be devised, but the effort requires time and creativity. Exhibit 14–4 presents some surrogate measures that could be used to determine the effectiveness of various types of discretionary costs. Some of these surrogates can be documented and gathered quickly and easily, while others are abstract and require a longer time horizon before they can be measured. As discussed in the next chapter, surrogates are often what is needed to measure and evaluate performance.

EXHIBIT 14–4
▼▼▼▼▼▼▼▼▼▼▼▼

NONMONETARY
MEASURES OF
OUTPUTS FROM
DISCRETIONARY
COSTS

Discretionary Cost Activity	Surrogate Measure of Results
Executive training seminar on leadership	• Reduction in subordinate complaints • Increased productivity of department • Decrease in staff absenteeism
Research and development	• Number of patents applied for • Number of engineering changes issued for cost reduction purposes
Guest lecturer at a university	• Increased enrollments in related courses • Length of coverage on lecture in various news media • Quantity of positive feedback about lecture
Special programming on public television	• Number of subscribers • Number of calls about program • Change in market share for periods of program • Decrease in subscriber "gifts" in station's inventory
Charitable contribution to local shelter for homeless	• Number/quality of letters received from sponsors • Positive employee feedback • Decrease in homeless persons in the city
Employee health club	• Decrease in health insurance claims • Improved employee morale • Decrease in number of sick days

Measuring Discretionary Cost Efficiency and Effectiveness

The amounts spent on discretionary activities are the inputs to a process that should provide some desired monetary or surrogate output. Comparisons of input costs and output results are used to determine if there is a reasonable cost/benefit relationship between the two. Managers can judge this cost/benefit relationship by how efficiently costs were used and how effectively those costs achieved their purposes. These relationships can be seen in the following model:

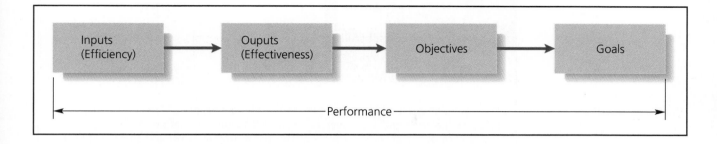

The degree to which a satisfactory relationship occurs when comparing outputs to inputs reflects the **efficiency** of an activity. Thus, efficiency is a yield concept and is usually measured by a ratio of output to input. For instance, one measure of automobile efficiency is the number of miles the car gets per gallon of gas consumed. The higher the number of miles per gallon, the greater the efficiency. Comparing actual output results to desired results indicates the **effectiveness** of an activity, which is the measure of how well the firm's objectives and goals were achieved.

efficiency

effectiveness

Determination of both efficiency and effectiveness requires a valid measure of output. When such an output measure is available, efficiency and effectiveness can be measured as follows:

Actual Result	*compared to*	Desired Result
Efficiency $= \dfrac{\text{Actual Output}}{\text{Actual Input}}$		$\dfrac{\text{Planned Output}}{\text{Planned Input}}$
or		
Efficiency $= \dfrac{\text{Actual Input}}{\text{Actual Output}}$		$\dfrac{\text{Planned Input}}{\text{Planned Output}}$
Effectiveness $= \dfrac{\text{Actual Output}}{\text{Planned Output}}$		Preestablished Standard

However, as illustrated in the News Note on the next page about Johnson & Johnson, one or more characteristics of a discretionary cost activity must often be stated as a nonmonetary, rather than a monetary, measure.

A reasonable measure of efficiency can exist only when inputs and outputs can be both measured quantitatively and matched in the same period and when there is a credible causal relationship between them. These factors make measuring the efficiency of discretionary activities very difficult. First, several years may pass before the output of a discretionary activity may be noticeable. Consider, for example, the time that might elapse between making expenditures for research and development or a drug rehabilitation program and when results of these expenditures are visible. Secondly, there is frequently a dubious cause-effect relationship between discretionary cost inputs and resulting outputs. For instance, there is a Folgers cents-off coupon in the Sunday paper. You clip it out and use it to buy a can of coffee. Can Folgers assume that it was the advertising and the coupon that caused you to buy the product, or might you have purchased the coffee anyway?

NEWS NOTE

The Surrogate Measure Is Absenteeism

Cost containment has been a major goal of J&J's wellness program since day one—and that goal has apparently been met. Johnson & Johnson says that [in 1989] the program saved $378 per employee by lowering absenteeism and by slowing the rise in the company's health-care expenses. The cost of the program, which offers checkups and encourages healthier eating and exercise habits, is $200 per employee.

J&J is one of only a handful of companies that have made comprehensive examinations of the costs and benefits of their programs. It is precisely because of this lack of hard data that many other corporate wellness programs are vulnerable to cost-cutting pressure, one expert says. "In a rough economic climate, one of the first things that is cut is a health program or a wellness program," says Roger Reed, who supervises wellness programs for Blue Cross and Blue Shield of Indiana. "The reason is a lot of wellness-program administrators haven't done a good job of documenting the results."

SOURCE: Neal Templin, "Johnson & Johnson 'Wellness' Program for Workers Shows Healthy Bottom Line," *Wall Street Journal* (May 21, 1990), p. B1. Reprinted by permission of the *Wall Street Journal*, © 1990 Dow Jones & Company, Inc. All rights reserved worldwide.

Effectiveness, on the other hand, is determined for a particular period by comparing the results achieved with the results desired. Determination of an activity's effectiveness is not affected by whether the designated measure of output is stated in monetary or nonmonetary terms. But management can only subjectively attribute some or all of the effectiveness of the cost incurrence to the results. Subjectivity is required because the comparison of actual output to planned output is not indicative of a perfect causal relationship between activities and output results. *Measurement of effectiveness does not require the consideration of inputs, but measurement of efficiency does.*

Assume that last month Prieto Company increased its expenditures on quality control and, during that period, merchandise returns dropped by 15 percent. The planned decrease in returns was 20 percent. Management was 75 percent effective (.15 ÷ .20) in achieving its goal of decreased returns. However, it cannot be presumed that the discretionary costs spent on the quality control program were totally responsible. It is possible that the decline in returns was caused partially or entirely by other factors, such as use of better raw materials or improved production efforts. Thus, it is not known for certain whether the expenditure on the quality control program was the most efficient way in which to decrease merchandise returns.

Measuring the efficiency of discretionary costs in achieving their desired results is tenuous at best. The effectiveness of discretionary costs can only be inferred from the relationship of actual output to desired output. Since the benefits of discretionary costs cannot be assessed in any definitive manner, reliance on proper planning for discretionary activities and costs is essential. Planning may be more important than subsequent control measures. Control after the planning stage is often relegated to monitoring expenditures to assure conformity with budget classifications and preventing managers from overspending their budgeted amounts.

BUDGETING DISCRETIONARY COSTS

Budgets are described in chapters 11 and 12 as both planning and controlling devices. Budgets serve to officially communicate a manager's authority to spend up to a maximum amount (appropriation) or rate for each budget item. Budget appropriations serve as a basis for comparison with actual costs. Accumulated expenditures in each budgetary category are periodically compared with appropriated amounts to determine whether funds have been under- or overexpended.

Discretionary cost appropriations are generally based on three factors: the activity's perceived significance to the achievement of objectives and goals; the upcoming period's expected level of operations; and managerial negotiations in the budgetary process. For some discretionary costs, managers are expected to spend the full amount of their appropriations within the specified time frame. For other discretionary cost activities, the "less is better" adage is appropriate.

Consider the differences in the following discretionary cost activities: machine maintenance versus executive travel and entertainment. Top management would probably not consider money "saved" by not doing preventive maintenance to be a positive measure of cost control. In fact, spending (with supervisory approval) more than originally appropriated in these areas might be necessary or even commendable—assuming that positive results are indicated. However, spending less than budgeted on travel and entertainment (while achieving the desired results) would probably be considered positive performance.

Public television stations typically offer special programming during their subscription drives. An increased number of subscribers would indicate the drive was, to some degree, effective. However, the station may never know whether the subscriptions resulted from the special programming or whether another technique would have been more effective (or even efficient).

No Checking, Less Cheating

"Why do we check all our sales peoples' expense accounts?" "To keep them honest, of course." But that is hardly a business objective. The right answer is: "To keep sales expenses under control." And this is best done—and at a fraction of the cost—by determining expense standards based, for instance, on a sales person's need to travel and on the number of nights spent away from home. All that is needed to arrive at these standards is for a small number of experienced sales people to keep a record of their actual expenses twice a year for one week.

The previous system in the company—the system that thought its purpose was morality—kept 11 clerks busy the year round. The new system employs not even one full-time person. And it further enabled the company—a large national wholesaler of builders' supplies—to cut its sales force to 158 people from 167, despite a steady growth in sales volume. Sales people have more time to sell, when they no longer misuse selling time filling out lengthy "swindle sheets."

SOURCE: Peter Drucker, "Permanent Cost Cutting," *Wall Street Journal* (January 11, 1991), p. A8. Reprinted by permission of the *Wall Street Journal,* © 1991 Dow Jones & Company, Inc. All rights reserved worldwide.

Managers may often view discretionary activities and costs as though they were committed. A manager who states that a particular activity's cost will not be reduced during a period has chosen to view that activity and cost as committed. However, this viewpoint does not change the underlying discretionary nature of the item. In such circumstances, top management must have a high degree of faith in the ability of lower-level management to perform the specified tasks in an efficient manner. For example, a discretionary expenditure may be budgeted on an annual basis as a function of planned volume of company sales. Once this appropriation has been justified, management's intention may be that it is not to be reduced within that year regardless of whether actual sales are less than planned sales.

Managers should also be aware that there are alternative ways to manage fixed cost incurrences for certain types of discretionary cost activities. Some discretionary cost activities occur in a particular pattern and are repetitive enough to allow the development of standards, as discussed in the preceding News Note relative to salespersons' expenses. Such activities result in **engineered costs,** which are those that have been found to bear observable and known relationships to a quantifiable activity base. An engineered cost can be treated as a variable, rather than a fixed, cost.

engineered costs

CONTROLLING ENGINEERED COSTS

Discretionary cost activities that can fit into the engineered cost category are usually geared to a performance measure relative to work accomplished. For example, in some instances, quality control can be considered an engineered cost. Taken as a whole, quality control inspections may be enough alike to develop a standard time for an average inspection. If a company has access to quality control inspectors who can be paid on an hourly basis only for the hours they work, the company can determine how many inspection clerks to hire and can compare actual cost to a standard cost each month. The activity base of this engineered cost is the number of inspections performed. Budget appropriations for engineered costs are based on the static master budget level, but control can be exerted through the use of flexible budgets if the expected level of activity is not achieved.

The Kim Company is used to demonstrate how quality control costs can be evaluated under both possible cost categories. Kim Company has found that quality control can be treated as an engineered instead of a discretionary cost. Company management, in a cost reduction effort, is willing to contract with part-time, experienced quality control workers during peak-load times and retain only a minimal number of inspectors in the company's full-time labor force. Company management, through statistical analysis of past quality control inspections, has found that product inspections average slightly less than five minutes. Thus, an inspector should be able to perform approximately twelve inspections per hour. From this information, Kim's managers can obtain a fairly valid estimate of what inspection costs should be, based on a particular level of activity and, therefore, have a basis against which to compare actual costs.

In March, Kim predicts that 7,800 inspections will be needed so 650 inspection hours should be provided. If the standard hourly rate for inspectors is $10, the March budget would be $6,500. In March, 8,136 inspections are made at a cost of $6,765 for 660 actual hours. Using the generalized cost analysis model for variance analysis presented in chapter 5, the following calculations can be made:

AQ × AP	AQ × SP	SQ × SP
		(8,136 ÷ 12) = 678
660 hours × $10.25	660 hours × $10	678 hours × $10
$6,765	$6,600	$6,780
	$165 U	$180 F
	Price Variance	Efficiency Variance

$15 F

Total Inspection Cost Variance

Note: The actual and standard quantities in this model reflect hours of time; the actual and standard prices reflect rates.

This analysis is predicated on the company being willing and able to hire personnel to provide the exact number of inspection hours needed. If the firm has to employ only full-time salaried employees, analyzing inspection costs in the previous manner is not very useful. In this instance, quality control inspections become a discretionary fixed cost, and Kim Company may prefer the following type of fixed overhead variance analysis:

Actual Cost	Budgeted Fixed Cost	Standard Hours Allowed X Standard Fixed Rate
	Spending Variance	Volume Variance

Total Inspection Cost Variance

In this analysis, an assumption must be made about expected capacity to determine the application rate. Assume again the following facts: (1) the standard hourly rate is $10; (2) the standard quantity of work is 12 inspections per hour; (3) employees made 8,136 inspections; and (4) actual payroll was $6,600. Budgeted fixed costs are $6,500. This amount is based on total quality inspectors' salaries and an expected 650 hours of work in the month. Such expectations result in an average wage rate of $10 per hour. The following variances can be computed:

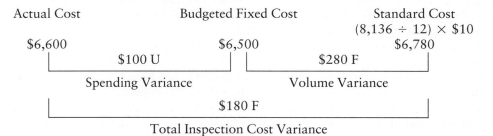

Actual Cost	Budgeted Fixed Cost	Standard Cost
		(8,136 ÷ 12) × $10
$6,600	$6,500	$6,780
	$100 U	$280 F
	Spending Variance	Volume Variance
	$180 F	

Total Inspection Cost Variance

The $100 unfavorable spending variance could have been incurred because of a change in salary structure during the month. The $280 favorable volume variance reflects the increase in capacity utilization of 28 hours multiplied by the $10 average wage rate per hour.

The method of variance analysis and, thus, cost control must be appropriate to the cost category and management information needs. But regardless of the variance levels or the explanations provided, managers should always consider whether the activity itself and, therefore, the cost incurrence was sufficiently justified.

For instance, assume that $70,000 is spent on the salary of an additional research chemist in the R&D department. During the year, research and development activities take place, but there is no measurable output such as a new product or a new patent. Before determining that the discretionary cost expenditure was justified, top management should review the R&D manager's activity reports for the chemists in the department. The discretionary activity (hiring the additional chemist) would not be considered effective if the new chemist spent a significant portion of the period doing menial tasks. In other words, post-incurrence audits of discretionary activities are important in determining the value of the activity and the related expenditure.

CONTROLLING DISCRETIONARY COSTS USING THE BUDGET

Once discretionary cost appropriations have been made, monetary control is effected through the use of budget-to-actual comparisons. Discretionary costs are not treated any differently from other costs in the budget. Actual results are compared to expected results, and explanations should be provided for variances. Explanations for variances can often be found by recognizing cost consciousness attitudes. The following illustration (which includes two discretionary cost activities) provides a budget-to-actual comparison that demonstrates employee cost consciousness.

The Fisher Advertising Agency has prepared the condensed budget shown in Exhibit 14–5 for the first quarter of 1994. Don Dozier, the controller for the agency, estimates 250 clients with an average billing of $5,000 each during that period. Ex-

Revenues		
Client fees		$1,250,000
Expenses		
Salaries and fringe benefits	$200,000	
Media expenses	500,000	
Travel and entertainment	25,000	
Advertising	3,000	
Utilities	3,900	
Wages and fringe benefits	29,900	
Rent	12,000	
Supplies	4,800	
Mailing	5,000	
Depreciation	10,000	793,600
Income before taxes		$ 456,400
Taxes (estimated at 30%)		136,920
Net income		$ 319,480

EXHIBIT 14–5
▼▼▼▼▼▼▼▼▼▼

FISHER
ADVERTISING
AGENCY BUDGET—
FIRST QUARTER 1994

penses have been estimated on the basis of the last quarter charges for 1993 and include expected increases, such as personnel raises.

The primary expenses for the agency are salaries and media expenses. Media expenses are budgeted at 40 percent of client fees. Travel and entertainment is a discretionary activity, and the related costs are budgeted at 2 percent of sales revenues. Advertising is another discretionary activity; its cost is budgeted at $1,000 per month. Utility cost is variable and is budgeted at $7.50 per hour that the agency is open. The agency operates 40 hours per week, and there are 13 weeks in the budget quarter. Wages are for the five hourly paid secretarial and other staff. These wages are totally variable at $11.50 per hour—of which $3.00 relates to fringe benefits. The salaries and fringe benefits are for the marketing executives and, like supplies, mailings, and depreciation, are fixed monthly amounts.

Exhibit 14–6 provides the actual revenue and expense data collected by Mr. Dozier during the first quarter of 1994. Fisher Advertising acquired a new account in late February that required agency employees to work 20 hours of overtime at time and a half pay.

After reviewing the actual results, Caroline Fisher, the agency's president, requested a budget-to-actual comparison from Mr. Dozier and explanations for the cost differentials. Ms. Fisher was of the opinion that costs had not been properly controlled. Mr. Dozier's comparison is presented in Exhibit 14–7, and he provided the following explanations for the budget cost variances. Each explanation is preceded by the related budget item number.

The following explanations were provided:

1. The agency replaced one marketing executive with a new person having a $4,000 higher salary. The increase was justified by the new person's level of experience and the client base acquired by Fisher. This explanation reflects an understanding of supply and demand relationships and their effects on costs. (An alternative justification could have been inflationary trends in salaries.)

2. The decrease in media cost was because of a switch in advertising medium from high-priced television spots to more print ads. Several clients determined that the print ads were more specifically directed at the target audiences. This

EXHIBIT 14–6
▼▼▼▼▼▼▼▼▼▼▼

FISHER
ADVERTISING
AGENCY ACTUAL
RESULTS—FIRST
QUARTER 1994

Revenues		
Client fees		$1,300,000
Expenses		
Salaries and fringe benefits	$204,000	
Media expenses	514,000	
Travel and entertainment	24,000	
Advertising	3,000	
Utilities	4,300	
Wages and fringe benefits	31,475	
Rent	10,000	
Supplies	4,800	
Mailing	3,800	
Depreciation	10,050	809,425
Income before taxes		$ 490,575
Taxes		147,173
Net income		$ 343,402

EXHIBIT 14–7
▼▼▼▼▼▼▼▼▼▼▼

FISHER
ADVERTISING
AGENCY
FLEXIBLE BUDGET—
ACTUAL
COMPARISON—
FIRST QUARTER 1994

	Budget Item #	Original Budget	Budget Based on Actual Results	Actual	Variances*
Revenues					
Client fees		$1,250,000	$1,300,000	$1,300,000	$ 0
Expenses					
Salaries and fringe benefits	(1)	$ 200,000	$ 200,000	$ 204,000	(4,000)
Media expenses	(2)	500,000	520,000	514,000	6,000
Travel and entertainment	(3)	25,000	26,000	24,000	2,000
Advertising		3,000	3,000	3,000	0
Utilities	(4)	3,900	4,050	4,300	(250)
Wages and fringe benefits	(5)	29,900	31,475	31,475	0
Rent	(6)	12,000	12,000	10,000	2,000
Supplies		4,800	4,800	4,800	0
Mailing	(7)	5,000	5,000	3,800	1,200
Depreciation	(8)	10,000	10,000	10,050	(50)
Total expenses		$ 793,600	$ 816,325	$ 809,425	6,900
Income before taxes		$ 456,400	$ 483,675	$ 490,575	
Taxes		136,920	145,103	147,173	
Net income		$ 319,480	$ 338,572	$ 343,402	

*Note: Unfavorable variances are shown as negative amounts; favorable variances are shown as positive amounts.

cost adjustment is indicative of a cost reduction that provides the same (or better) results for fewer dollars of expenditure.

3. The difference in travel and entertainment costs was caused by two factors: airline fare increases caused by increases in oil prices and ticket price decreases through using a consortium of ticket buyers. The first explanation reflects an understanding of supply and demand relationships and their effects on costs; the second represents cost reduction techniques. Had Fisher not joined the consortium, its travel and entertainment costs would have increased by approximately $3,500.

4. The utility cost increase was caused by three factors: the additional 20 hours of operation; an increase in local utility rates; and the use of a fax machine that the company purchased in January. This explanation reflects an understanding of the nature of variable costs. Since the company had more hours of operations and used more equipment, more utility costs were incurred. The increase in utility rates could have been caused by inflation.

5. The large increase in wages was because of two factors: additional operating hours and time-and-a-half pay for overtime. The agency had a total of 540 hours of operation:

540 hours × $11.50 per hour × 5 people	$31,050
20 hours of overtime × ($8.50 ÷ 2) × 5 people	425
Total wages cost	$31,475

Each of these increases reflects the nature of variable costs. Had the agency known overtime would be needed, those costs could have been budgeted.

6. The rent decrease resulted from a lease renegotiation. The city in which Fisher operates had excess rental properties, and landlords were willing to decrease rents to maintain tenants. This factor reflects supply and demand relationships.

7. Mailing cost declined because the agency was able to fax some of its paperwork rather than using express mail services as it previously had. This change represents cost avoidance of higher-priced services.

8. The depreciation increase was caused by the fax machine. Managers approved the purchase when another business went bankrupt during the quarter and had a liquidation sale. The fax purchase had been included in the capital budget for the end of 1994, not during the first quarter.

Acquiring the fax machine is a good example of the cost containment concept. The agency wanted to buy the machine and had an opportunity to buy it at a substantial savings, but earlier than anticipated. This purchase created an unfavorable cost variance for depreciation in the first quarter, but it shows an instance of planning, foresight, and flexibility. The benefits of this purchase are threefold. First, a favorable variance will be shown in the capital budget when the cost of this machine is compared to the cost that was expected. Secondly, in future periods, the budgeted committed cost for depreciation will be less than if the purchase not been made at the bargain price. Third, the acquisition of the machine caused a favorable decline in mailing expenditures.

Note that the variance computations in Exhibit 14–7 are based on comparisons between a revised budget that uses actual sales as the base and the actual revenues and costs incurred. When comparing budgeted and actual expenditures, managers should always analyze variances using an equitable basis of comparison. Comparisons between the original budget and actual results for the variable cost items would not have been useful for control purposes because total variable costs automatically rise with increases in activity.

If, however, management wants to consider total variances from plans, actual results should be compared to the original (rather than a flexible) budget. Such a comparison is usually made when revenues (in units or dollars) are lower than expected and provides managers a perspective on the magnitude of the deviations between expected and actual results. Original budget-to-actual results comparisons should not be used to judge cost control, because control should be judged on the basis of what costs should have been for the level of activity *actually* achieved.[14]

Another possible comparison of expected and actual results can be based on actual activity and after-the-fact information about the new factors influencing costs. This comparison would require that formulae be developed showing the relationships between costs and various causal factors. Regression analysis could then be used to calculate the dependent variables for control purposes. While using a flexible budget developed on a regression basis "is a superior tool for controlling . . . costs, the master budget or the flexible budget based on actual usage is often employed in practice because the preparation costs are less."[15]

The discretionary charges for advertising, supplies, and mailings in the previous illustration were constant amounts. Therefore, in the budget-to-actual comparisons, the budgeted amounts shown for these activities were not changed. If engineered costs are used for discretionary activities, the costs are treated as variable and control is focused on a flexible, rather than static, budget figure.

SITE ANALYSIS

One estimate of the 1991 spending by U.S. companies on domestic travel and entertainment was $125 billion![16] All rational attempts by companies to understand, control, and reduce their T&E costs should help produce a measurable improvement in those companies' income pictures.

The Fortune 500 company discussed in the opening segment investigated a variety of solutions to manage its travel costs.[17] These solutions included first gaining an understanding of the categories and the level of companywide spending on travel and entertainment. This information was obtained by beginning to deal with one travel agent who provided detailed records of the types and quantities of travel expenditures. Once the company understood the volume of its spending, it was also aware of the significance of

continued

continued

---

[14]Revenue variances are discussed in chapter 11.
[15]John K. Harris and James M. Shirley, "Performance Reports for Energy Costs," *CPA Journal* (June 1986), p. 114.
[16]Julie Moline, "Managing Business Travel Costs: Preparing for 1992," *FORTUNE* (December 2, 1991), p. 24.
[17]The solutions provided in this site analysis are adapted from Denis W. Day, "How to Cut Travel Costs," *Management Accounting* (August 1990), p. 37ff.

its negotiation power and was able to obtain about $500,000 in savings. The company next provided all employees and the travel agency with the new travel policy that was both understandable and strictly enforced. The policy is periodically updated and provides the underlying rationale of the requirements. The policy was provided to the agency so that the agents were informed as to the corporate requirements and could provide better service that conformed to company policy. Company management sought a team spirit to eliminate the "other people's money" attitude. Employees typically understand the need to economize their personal environments; developing the team spirit requires that such an understanding be brought into the job environment. And, last, the company employed a travel manager whose job is to take advantage of all possible savings opportunities and who views travel as a significant business activity that needs, like other areas of the business, to be properly managed.

Travel is only one area at which cost control must be continuously directed. Controlling costs means controlling activities that cause those costs. This requires that all organizational disciplines (as indicated in the Applications Strategies) be involved, and emphasis should be placed on planning, communicating, motivating, and inspiring the need for cost consciousness throughout the company. Pareto's Law (as discussed in chapter 13) is applicable here: 80 percent of the cost problems in an organization are caused by 20 percent of the activities and people. Managers must focus their cost control efforts where those efforts will be most effective.

CHAPTER SUMMARY

Cost control over an organization's expenditures is essential to that organization's long-run success. An effective cost control system encompasses efforts before, during, and after a cost is incurred. Regardless of the cost involved, managers and employees must exercise attitudes of cost consciousness to provide the best means of cost control. Cost consciousness reflects cost understanding, cost containment, cost avoidance, and cost reduction.

People and organizations engage in activities to provide results, and those activities create costs. Comparing actual outputs to actual inputs reflects efficiency, while comparing actual outputs to desired results reflects effectiveness. Efficiency plus effectiveness indicates performance. Measuring the outputs generated by cost inputs, however, is not always easy. Such measurement difficulty is most frequently encountered with discretionary costs.

Most discretionary costs are incurred to provide service-type activities that are considered optional in the short run. Discretionary costs are appropriated annually for the conduct of activities that could be temporarily reduced without impairing the firm's capacity to function. The outputs of discretionary cost activities are often nonmonetary and qualitative in nature. Surrogate measures of output can be developed; however, it is often questionable to ascribe a cause-and-effect relationship between the result and the current amounts of input costs. Discretionary activities should be planned to achieve results that fit within an overall management philosophy. Managers must avoid making expenditures for discretionary activities that may be conducted efficiently, but for which the results are of dubious effectiveness.

Some discretionary costs may be treated as engineered costs because they are routine and structured enough to allow for the computation of standards. These en-

APPLICATIONS STRATEGIES FOR COST CONTROL	Discipline	Applications
	Accounting	Requires analysis of budget expenditures by category and amount; can use value analysis performed for activity-based costing to determine excess spending; accounting should formally assist managers in their control efforts before, during, and after all activities
	Economics	Analysis can help explain profitability of different types of customers and sizes of orders; cost understanding requires knowledge of supply and demand relationships; recognizes trade-offs and relationship between efficiency and effectiveness; cost consciousness is essential to providing goods and services to customers at competitive prices and quality
	Finance	Capital expenditures for technology can be justified by other cost reductions and/or by increases in income and cash flow; requires budget preparation for proper planning and comparison
	Management	Requires justification of budget expenditures; focuses on controlling the cause of a cost (activity) rather than the result (the cost itself); instilling cost consciousness in all workers helps managers to achieve their objectives of a profitable organization: providing jobs in a community, paying bills promptly, and paying dividends to shareholders
	Marketing	Creates a focus on product "benchmarking" and analyzing how other products cost-compare to yours; lower costs result in lower selling prices that will typically increase market share; can help focus on cost effects of product clutter (variety) strategies

gineered cost standards can be used to determine the appropriate amount of planned expenditures to achieve a given result. One aspect of control over engineered costs can be provided by performing variance analysis similar to that used for variable factory overhead.

Budgeting is a primary tool in planning and controlling discretionary activities and costs. Budget appropriations provide both authorization for spending and the bases against which actual costs are compared. Care must be taken that appropriate levels of activity are used to make budget-to-actual comparisons, so that cost control can be effective. Since discretionary costs are fixed, they will not change with changes in activity levels within the relevant range.

APPENDIX

Program Budgeting

The problems of controlling discretionary costs have been particularly acute in governmental and other not-for-profit entities. In addition, activities performed by these organizations produce results that are often difficult to measure in monetary terms or that may take several years to be measurable while the related activities must be funded annually. Traditional budgeting often takes the current year's spending levels as givens in setting the budget for the next year. Additions to the budget each year may lead to nonprioritized and ever-increasing spending levels (the creeping commitment syndrome). **Program budgeting** is useful for cost control purposes in certain types of organizations. Resource inputs are related to service outputs and, thereby, managers can focus on the cost/benefit relationships.

program budgeting

Program budgeting starts by defining objectives in terms of output results rather than quantity of input activities. For instance, an input measure of an executive development program would be a statement of the target number of courses each person must complete by year-end. An output measure would state the objective in terms of expected improvement rates on executive annual performance evaluations. Once output results have been defined in some measurable terms, effectiveness can be measured. Program budgeting involves a thorough analysis of alternative activities to achieve a firm's objectives. This analysis includes projecting both quantitative and qualitative costs and benefits for each alternative and selecting those alternatives that, in the judgment of top management, yield a satisfactory result at a reasonable cost. These choices are then translated into budget appropriations to be acted on by the manager responsible for the related programs.

Program budgeting requires the use of detailed surrogate measures of output that necessitate answers to the following questions:

1. When should results be measured? Since many not-for-profit programs are effective only after some period of time, multiple measurements are necessary to determine effectiveness. When should these measures begin to be made, and how often should they be made thereafter?

2. What results should be chosen as output measures? Many not-for-profit programs have multiple results. For example, reading programs for the adult illiterate can impact employment, overall crime reduction statistics, welfare dollar reductions, and so on. Should a determination be made of which results are more important than others, or should all results be given equal weight?

3. What program actually caused the result? There are questions about the legitimacy of cause-and-effect relationships when measuring the results of not-for-profit programs. For example, did an adult literacy program cause the decrease in unemployment statistics, or was that decrease more the result of money spent for job placement programs?

4. Did the program actually impact the target population? An adult literacy program may be aimed at the unemployed. If the majority of the persons attending the program already have jobs, the program did not impact the target group. However, it could still be considered effective if the participants increased their job skills and employment levels.

Program budgeting can be useful in government and not-for-profit organizations as well as for service activities in for-profit businesses. Program budgeting can help managers evaluate and control discretionary activities and costs, avoid excessive cost expenditures, and make certain that expenditures are used for programs and activities that generate the most beneficial results.

GLOSSARY

Committed cost   the cost of basic plant assets or personnel structure that an organization must have to operate

Cost avoidance   a process of finding acceptable alternatives to high-cost items and not spending money for unnecessary goods or services

Cost consciousness   companywide employee attitude about the topics of cost understanding, cost containment, cost avoidance, and cost reduction

Cost containment   the process of attempting, to the extent possible, to minimize period-by-period increases in per-unit variable and total fixed costs

Cost control system   a logical structure of formal and/or informal activities designed to influence costs and to analyze and evaluate how well expenditures were managed during a period

Cost reduction   a process of lowering current costs, especially those in excess of what is necessary

Discretionary cost   an optional cost that a decision maker must periodically review to determine that it continues to be in accord with ongoing policies

Effectiveness   a measure that compares actual output results to desired results and indicates how well the firm's objectives and goals were achieved.

Efficiency   the degree to which a satisfactory relationship occurs when comparing outputs to inputs

Engineered cost   any cost that has been found to bear an observable and known relationship to a quantifiable activity base

Program budgeting   an approach to budgeting that relates resource inputs to service outputs and, thereby, focuses on the relationship of benefits to cost expenditures (from appendix)

SELECTED BIBLIOGRAPHY

Ames, B. C., and J. D. Hlavacek. "Vital Truths about Managing Your Costs." *Harvard Business Review* (January–February 1990), pp. 140–47.

"Companies Learn Valuable Lessons from Lean Times." *Grant Thornton Tax & Business Adviser* (January/February 1992), pp. 4–5.

Dudick, Thomas S. "Why SG&A Doesn't Always Work." *Harvard Business Review* (January–February 1987), pp. 30–33.

Power, William. "Firms Get Stingy with Quarterly Reports." *Wall Street Journal* (February 13, 1992), pp. C1, C19.

Rice, Faye. "Where the Bargains Are in Hotels." *FORTUNE* (April 20, 1992), pp. 91–92ff.

Shields, Michael D., and S. Mark Young. "Effective Long-Term Cost Reduction: A Strategic Perspective." *Journal of Cost Management for the Manufacturing Industry* (Spring 1992), pp. 16–30.

Templeman, John, and Patrick Oster. "Why Eaton Got Noticed." *Business Week* (March 30, 1992), pp. 25–26.

Trost, Cathy. "To Cut Costs and Keep the Best People, More Concerns Offer Flexible Work Plans." *Wall Street Journal* (February 18, 1992), pp. B1, B6.

Turney, Peter B. B. "How Activity-Based Costing Helps Reduce Costs." *Journal of Cost Management for the Manufacturing Industry* (Winter 1991), pp. 29–35.

SOLUTION STRATEGIES

Determination of efficiency:
Relationship of inputs and outputs

$$\text{Actual yield ratio} = \frac{\text{Actual output} \div \text{Actual input}}{\text{Actual input} \div \text{Actual output}} \quad \text{or}$$

$$\text{Desired yield ratio} = \frac{\text{Planned output} \div \text{Planned input}}{\text{Planned input} \div \text{Planned output}} \quad \text{or}$$

Determination of effectiveness:
Actual output compared to Desired output

Efficiency + Effectiveness = Performance

Cost variances
Actual costs compared to budgeted costs—allows management to compare absolute cost discrepancies from the original plan

Actual costs compared to budgeted costs at actual activity level—allows management to make determinations as to the degree to which costs were controlled; makes use of a flexible budget

Variance analyses using standards for discretionary costs—allow for the computation of variances for routine, structured discretionary costs.

For discretionary costs susceptible to engineered cost treatment:

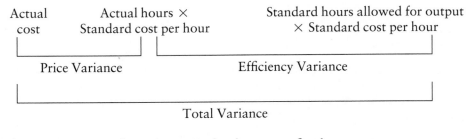

For discretionary costs that are managed as lump-sum fixed costs:

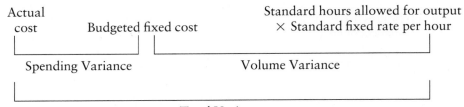

END-OF-CHAPTER MATERIALS

 Questions

1. What are the points in time of an activity when control can be exerted?

2. Explain the meaning and significance of cost consciousness.

3. Since committed costs are in place for the long run, how can they be controlled?

4. How do discretionary and committed costs differ? Does management's attitude toward a cost affect whether it is classified as discretionary or committed?

5. Define *efficiency* and *effectiveness* and distinguish the one from the other.

6. Management performance is evaluated by how efficiently and effectively the company's goals are achieved. Describe the linkages from inputs to goals by which management performance can be described and measured.

7. If a manager having responsibility for a discretionary cost spends less than is budgeted for that discretionary cost, should that manager be praised? Discuss the rationale for your answer.

8. Why is it difficult to measure the output of activities funded by discretionary costs?

9. Define surrogate output measures. Explain their use in conjunction with discretionary costs.

10. Explain why it is often difficult to measure the efficiency of discretionary costs. How can discretionary cost effectiveness be measured?

11. Of what importance is budgeting in the control of discretionary costs?

12. What questions should be asked and answered by managers when developing discretionary cost budgets?

13. What is an engineered cost? How can the concept of engineered costs be used to control some discretionary costs?

14. (Appendix) What is program budgeting? How does it differ from traditional budgeting?

Exercises

15. *(Type of cost consciousness)* An architectural firm hires temporary staff to work on certain jobs. The firm compensates these employees at $20 per hour with no fringe benefits. However, if a temporary employee works more than 1,600 hours in a year, that employee is also given a 15 percent bonus above normal compensation.

   Permanent staff receive $32,000 annually, to which fringe benefits of 24 percent are added.

   a. Is the practice of hiring part-time staff an example of cost containment, cost avoidance, or cost reduction? Explain.

   b. At what level of hours of work should the firm hire permanent staff rather than part-time employees?

16. *(Cost consciousness)* Inez Chapman has just been promoted to director of admissions at a small university in Arizona. The admissions office operates a phone bank to facilitate the admissions process, which is staffed by admissions counse-

lors. Indicate whether the following actions represent cost understanding, cost containment, cost avoidance, or cost reduction. If an action represents more than one implication, indicate what the additional implication is and briefly discuss.

a. Negotiated a new agreement for telephone service; the university will now pay a constant monthly charge of $160 instead of $15 per phone, regardless of the number of phones on the phone banks. Ms. Chapman expects to increase the number of phones from eight to twelve.

b. Purchased blank notepads; the former stock of pads (now depleted) had the university emblem, name, and address.

c. Increased budgeted salary figures because more admissions staff is about to be hired.

d. Exchanged multibutton executive phones for simpler, minimum-function phones.

e. Eliminated call waiting feature because more staff and phones are available to handle calls.

f. Acquired a microcomputer system to process admissions data. The data have been processed by hand, and Ms. Chapman has determined that in the absence of the computer system, two more admissions staff would have to be hired.

17. *(Terminology)* Match the numbered items on the right with the lettered items on the left.

a. Discretionary cost
b. Committed cost
c. Engineered cost
d. Cost containment
e. Cost consciousness
f. Efficiency
g. Effectiveness
h. Cost avoidance
i. Cost reduction
j. Cost control system

1. any cost that bears a known and observable relationship to an activity base
2. an attitude regarding cost understanding, cost containment, and cost reduction
3. a measure of input-output yield
4. an optional fixed cost incurred to fund an activity for a specified period
5. unit variable costs and total fixed costs are held at prior-period levels
6. a cost incurred to provide physical or organizational capacity
7. a logical structure of activities designed to analyze and evaluate how well expenditures were managed during a period
8. finding acceptable alternatives for high priced items and not buying unnecessary goods or services
9. a process of lowering current costs
10. determining how well a firm's goals and objectives are achieved

18. *(Committed vs. discretionary costs)* Indicate with the letter C (committed cost) or D (discretionary cost) the type of cost to which each of the following sentences best relates. Explain the rationale for your choice.

a. Temporary reductions can usually be made without impairing the firm's long-range capacity or profitability.

b. Control is first provided during the capital budgeting process.

c. The cost is primarily affected by long-range decisions regarding desired capacity levels.

d. Examples include property taxes, depreciation, and lease rentals.

e. This type of cost often provides benefits that are not monetarily measurable.

f. Examples include research and development, quality control, and advertising.
g. This type of cost cannot be easily reduced, even during temporary slowdowns in activity.
h. It is often difficult to ascribe outcomes as being closely correlated with this type of cost.
i. This type of cost usually relates to service activities.
j. There is usually no "correct" amount at which to set funding levels.

19. *(Committed vs. discretionary costs)* Following is a list of specific discretionary and committed costs:

a. property taxes
b. marketing research
c. quality control
d. depreciation of equipment
e. insurance on equipment
f. research and development
g. secretarial pool
h. executive training
i. advertising
j. interest expense
k. preventive maintenance
l. salary of legal staff

a. Classify each of the previous costs as ordinarily being either committed (C) or discretionary (D).
b. Provide a monetary or nonmonetary surrogate measure of output for any of the items you designated as discretionary (D).
c. Which of these costs can be classified as either committed or discretionary, depending upon management attitude?

20. *(Efficiency vs. effectiveness)* Andrew Turner has a fleet of deep-sea fishing excursion vessels operating out of Plymouth, Massachusetts. He is considering outfitting an older vessel with an inboard diesel engine. He has two diesel engines in his shop, and he wants to install the more efficient of the two. These engines have been used in vessels similar to the one for which he intends to make the installation. Records show that engine A ran 21,600 miles and consumed 3,176 gallons of fuel, and engine B ran 18,650 miles and consumed 3,272 gallons of fuel. Diesel fuel is expected to cost $.88 per gallon next year. The refitted boat is expected to run 9,600 nautical miles next year.

a. Which engine has demonstrated the most efficiency?
b. How much would be spent next year on diesel fuel if engine A were installed?
c. How much would be spent next year on diesel fuel if engine B were installed?
d. How much savings would there be if the more efficient engine were installed?

21. *(Efficiency vs. effectiveness)* Mercy Hospital administration has concluded that the number of form letters word-processed is a good measure of output for its secretarial pool. The hospital included $54,000 for the pool in its 1995 budget. George Chapman, chief administrator of the hospital, has estimated that 6,000 letters will be processed in 1995.

Review of the actual 1995 results showed that 5,400 letters had been processed by the pool and that the payroll for the pool was $52,000. Another 800 letters were prepared by an external agency at an additional cost of $7,600.

a. What were the secretarial pool's planned and actual degrees of efficiency? What was the company's degree of efficiency in having letters processed?

b. What was the secretarial pool's degree of effectiveness?

22. *(Efficiency vs. effectiveness)* The Escambia County director of public records, George Lehman, has been granted a $180,000 budget for the salaries in that department for the 1995 fiscal year. The director has estimated that each entry to the public records should require 30 minutes to prepare, input, and review. The county expects 24,000 entries for the year. The director can hire part-time employees during periods of peak activity.

Early in the 1996 fiscal year it was determined that actual payroll in the prior year was $176,000 and that 22,600 entries in the public record had been made. Review has shown that all transactions were promptly, completely, and accurately recorded.

a. Was the department efficient? Prove your answer.

b. Was the department effective? Discuss your answer.

23. *(Surrogate measures of output)* The Finance Department in the College of Business at Indiana University plans to expend funds during 1996 for several purposes:

a. library acquisitions

b. a statistics lab to be taught by graduate assistants to tutor finance majors

c. professional development courses for faculty

d. a finance faculty computer lab

e. a funding supplement to establish a "chair" for a research professor

Provide nonmonetary surrogate measures that would help evaluate the potential effectiveness of these purposes.

24. *(Engineered cost variances)* Franklin Engines is instituting a quality control program. Management estimates that each inspector should make an average of six inspections per hour. Retired production workers are well acquainted with the company's products and are expected to do well as quality control inspectors. A standard hourly rate of $10 has been established for these part-time inspectors.

In the first month of the program, 6,310 inspections were made, and the inspectors were paid $10,610 for 1,045 hours.

a. Analyze variances for quality control labor.

b. If Franklin could hire three full-time inspectors, each to work 200 hours monthly at a salary of $3,000 each, and use the part-time inspectors for the needed extra inspections, how much better or worse off would the company be than with entirely part-timers doing the standard performance at the standard pay?

25. *(Engineered cost variances)* Hannibal Wreckers operates an auto wrecker service in Hannibal, Missouri. The firm employs three drivers who are each paid an average of $7 per hour for regular time and $10.50 for overtime. A pickup and delivery averages an hour each. Drivers are paid for a 40-hour week because they must be on call all day. One driver stands by for after-hour deliveries.

During one week in July, the company picked up 112 cars during the day and had 9 after-hour pickups. The payroll for drivers for that week was $924. The employees worked 120 hours regular time and 8 hours overtime.

Analyze the labor costs for the week.

 **Problems**

26. *(Type of cost consciousness)* Will Shear is a broker with a good income, but he and his wife Nelda still have to shave expenses to stay within their budget. They have a three-year-old child, Shearson. Will's nephew and niece (Hans and Hedda) are seventeen-year-old twins who are coming from Austria to spend July in Milwaukee with the Shears. The following is a list of budget decisions made by the Shear family:

    a. Will and Nelda postpone the weekend excursion to Williamsburg for the July 4th weekend (expected cost of $400).
    b. The Shears decide to rent the video *The Sound of Music* for $5 instead of going to see a local production of the play, which would have cost $32 a person.
    c. Nelda budgets $150 in additional grocery costs.
    d. Nelda budgets an additional $60 for utilities.
    e. Nelda budgets $50 less in sitter costs for Shearson.
    f. Nelda budgets to buy ground beef to grill hamburgers each weekend rather than eating steak.
    g. Rather than paying the regular yard maintenance company, Nelda budgets $80 rather than the normal $100 for yard maintenance so that Hans and Hedda can earn some spending money.
    h. Nelda decides to buy generic brand foods in larger quantities to offset the larger amount of food the teenagers will consume.
    i. The family agrees to cut back on long-distance telephone calls to relatives by $40 during July because more gasoline for the car will be needed to take the visitors around town.

    Required: For each budget decision listed, indicate whether it is indicative of cost understanding (CU), cost containment (CC), cost avoidance (CA), or cost reduction (CR). Some decisions may have more than one answer.

27. *(Cost consciousness)* Temporary or part-time employees are sometimes used in each of the following ways:

    a. To write material for a monthly magazine
    b. To tailor men's suits for a local department store
    c. To sell clothing in a department store during the Christmas season
    d. To conduct classes as substitute teachers in the absence of the regular teachers
    e. To teach evening courses at the local university
    f. To work as medical doctors at the emergency room of a local hospital
    g. To prepare tax returns for a local CPA firm
    h. To draw house plans for a construction company
    i. To do legal research for a law firm

    Required: For each way listed, suggest potential advantages and disadvantages of using temporary or part-time employees from both the employer's and the user's perspective.

28. *(Committed vs. discretionary cost)* Champion Sports Products is concerned about proper staffing in the expansion of its purchasing department. Analysis shows that the historical average time needed to prepare purchase orders is 20 minutes. Management believes that the predicted number of purchase orders is highly correlated with the predicted sales for any future year. The average revenue for the past three years is $12,000,000, and the average number of purchase orders in those years is 40,000. Full-time purchasing staff cost $36,600 annually. Part-time purchasing staff can be hired at $14 per hour.

Full-time employees work 8 hours per day, 5 days per week, 50 weeks annually. Budgeted revenue for 1996 is $12,600,000.

Required:

a. How many purchase orders are predicted for 1996?

b. If only part-timers were used, estimate what it would cost to staff the department for 1996.

c. If only full-timers were used, estimate what it would cost to staff the department for 1996.

d. Assume that management wants to have 4 full-time employees and to staff the remaining hours needed with part-timers. What would the staff costs be?

29. *(Efficiency vs. effectiveness)* Bill Brown, who has just graduated from Summa University with a degree in management, has been asked to evaluate the efficiency of his employer's newly acquired plastics forming machine. The machine forms plastic sheets for a variety of purposes (cars, boats, tanks, etc.) and is guaranteed to form 80 sheets per kilowatt hour (kwh). The rate of defects in the forming operation is expected to be 8 percent. The new machine is equipped with a monitor that measures and records the kwh used.

The machine was first used in June 1996 and formed 29,872 plastic sheets of which 2,748 were defective. The kwh used that month were 365. Top management wants effectiveness measured on the basis of how well the machine formed nondefective sheets given the kilowatt hours used in June. Efficiency is to be measured on the basis of nondefective output per kwh compared to the guaranteed output per kwh. The power company is currently charging $5.12 per kwh.

Required:

a. How effective was the new machine in June?

b. What is the efficiency standard for nondefective output?

c. What is the achieved efficiency for June?

d. Calculate the dollar energy savings or excess energy cost in June due to the machine efficiency.

e. If you were a boat manufacturer purchasing formed sheets for hulls, how much quality control would you want your vendor to have?

30. *(Efficiency vs. effectiveness; variance analysis)* Matthew Construction has budgeted $140,000 for its bid department for making bids on potential road and bridge-building contracts. The company expects to issue 800 bids in 1996. In analyzing 1996 activity in the following year, the following statistics were ascertained:

Actual bids prepared	880
Actual bid department expenses	$146,000

Required:

a. Was the bid department effective? Present calculations.

b. Was the bid department efficient? Present calculations.

c. Did the bid department stay within its budget? If not, discuss what bid department personnel might have done before overspending their budget.

d. Prepare a variance analysis of the bid department costs.

31. *(Cost control)* South Bend Watch Company top management observed that the EDP department was justifying ever-larger budget requests on the basis of ever-larger usage by the company's various departments. User departments are not charged for EDP services and state that EDP personnel are "always very generous in recommending ways the EDP department can be of greater service."

Operating statistics for the EDP department for 1995 follow:

Budget—$97,600 based on 2,200 hours of run time; of this amount, $57,600 relates to fixed costs

Actual—$38,600 variable cost (incurred for 2,100 hours of run time); $58,500 fixed cost

Required:

a. Did the EDP department operate within its approved budget? Present calculations.
b. Calculate the department's effectiveness and comment.
c. Was the department efficient in usage of its variable costs? Fixed costs?
d. Calculate variable and fixed cost variances.
e. Prepare an hourly rate to charge EDP users. Do you think charging for EDP services will slow expansion of the EDP department budget?

32. *(Cost control)* Summit Airlines budgeted $2.2 million per day in 1995 for maintenance to service 420 planes. The company's maintenance crew was composed of 7,200 employees.

Required:

a. Do you believe maintenance to be a discretionary or committed cost for Summit Airlines? Explain.
b. If the company acquired another airline that could potentially increase its fleet by 300 planes, what would the company's annual maintenance cost be assuming it could put all 300 additional planes into service? Show calculations.
c. For 1996, the company estimates that it would have a total of 600 planes flying and that its maintenance crew would number 7,600, each person being paid an average of $32,000 annually. Other fixed maintenance costs total $120,000,000. The remainder of the maintenance costs are variable. Prepare the 1996 budget based upon these estimates.

33. *(Appendix)* Select the letter of the budget category from the following list that best corresponds to items a through j:

T—traditional budgeting
P—program budgeting

After identifying the appropriate type of budgeting, discuss how the other budgeting method would differ.

a. Is especially useful in government and not-for-profit entities and for service activities in for-profit firms
b. Begins with amounts budgeted in prior year and builds on those numbers based on expansion of resources to fund greater input activity
c. Begins by defining objectives in terms of output results rather than quantity of input activities
d. Is concerned with alternative approaches to achieve similar results
e. Treats prior year's funding levels as given and essential to operations
f. Requires the use of surrogate measures of output
g. Focuses on budgeted monetary levels rather than on goals, objectives, and outputs
h. Is particularly well suited to budgeting for discretionary cost expenditures
i. Requires an analysis of alternative activities to achieve a firm's objectives
j. Is concerned with choosing the particular results that should be used as output measures

34. *(Essay)* When the going gets tough, Americans go to the library. They go to scan the help-wanted ads. They go to borrow books they can no longer afford to buy. If they have no home, they go to warm up, wash up, doze off, and get treated with a dignity hardly any place else accords them. They go, but more and more often the library is closed. People want to use library books to train themselves for new careers; they want to use typewriters to type resumes so that they may search for jobs. In small towns, libraries serve as a place to pick up the latest romance novel and gossip. Rural libraries are often the only source of information and culture in small counties. The public libraries are the people's universities.

    (Adapted from Jonathan Tilove, "Budgets Dwindle When Libraries Are Needed Most," [*New Orleans*] *Times–Picayune* [February 10, 1991], p. A-10.)

    a. Organizations (especially governmental agencies) cannot find money for specific activities when money does not exist. Using the factors (cost behavior and causes 1–7) listed in the chapter as a guide to your discussion, provide some explanations of the problems facing American city libraries.
    b. Assume you are a local politician seeking reelection. Your city is faced with library cuts and/or closure. Discuss some ways in which the benefits of keeping the libraries open can be measured against the continuously rising costs.

35. *(Essay)* The Stevenson Works is a medium-sized manufacturing plant in a capital-intensive industry. The corporation's profitability is very low at the moment. As a result, investment funds are limited and hiring is restricted. These consequences of the corporation's problems have placed a strain on the plant's repair and maintenance program. The result has been a reduction in work efficiency and cost control effectiveness in the repair and maintenance area.

    The assistant controller proposes the installation of a maintenance work order system to overcome these problems. This system would require a work order to be prepared for each repair request and for each regular maintenance activity. The maintenance superintendent would record the estimated time to complete a job and send one copy of the work order to the department in which the work was to be done. The work order would also serve as a cost sheet for a job. The actual cost of the parts and supplies used on the job as well as the actual labor costs incurred in completing the job would be recorded directly on the work order. A copy of the completed work order would be the basis of the charge to the department in which the repair or maintenance activity occurred.

    The maintenance superintendent opposes the program on the grounds that the added paperwork will be costly and nonproductive. The superintendent states that the departmental clerk who now schedules repairs and maintenance activities is doing a good job without all the extra forms the new system would require. The real problem, in the superintendent's opinion, is that the department is understaffed.

    a. Discuss how such a maintenance work order system would aid in cost control.
    b. Explain how a maintenance work order system might assist the maintenance superintendent in getting authorization to hire more mechanics.

    (CMA)

36. *(Essay)* Write a short answer to each of the following questions. Discuss each in relation to (1) a manufacturing plant, (2) a professional service firm (e.g., accounting or law), and (3) a charitable organization.

    a. When is a variance uncontrollable? Discuss the underlying factors that make it uncontrollable.

b. Which is more important, efficiency or effectiveness? Why?

c. Is planning of discretionary costs more important than controlling them? Discuss the reasoning for your answer.

 Cases

37. Wagner Company employs flexible budgeting techniques to evaluate the performance of its activities. The selling expense flexible budgets for three representative monthly activity levels are as follows:

Representative Monthly Flexible Budgets—Selling Expenses

Activity			
Unit sales volume	400,000	425,000	450,000
Dollar sales volume	$10,000,000	$10,625,000	$11,250,000
Number of orders	4,000	4,250	4,500
Number of salespersons	75	75	75
Monthly Expenses			
Advertising & promotion	$ 1,200,000	$ 1,200,000	$ 1,200,000
Administrative salaries	57,000	57,000	57,000
Sales salaries	75,000	75,000	75,000
Sales commissions	200,000	212,500	225,000
Salesperson travel	170,000	175,000	180,000
Sales office expense	490,000	498,750	507,500
Shipping expense	675,000	712,500	750,000
Total	$ 2,867,000	$ 2,930,750	$ 2,994,500

The following assumptions were used to develop the selling expense flexible budgets:

- The average size of Wagner's sales force during the year was planned to be 75 people.
- Salespersons are paid a monthly salary plus commission on gross dollar sales.
- The travel costs have both a fixed and a variable element. The variable portion tends to fluctuate with gross dollars of sales.
- Sales office expense is a mixed cost, with the variable portion related to the number of orders processed.
- Shipping expense is a mixed cost, with the variable portion related to the number of units sold.

A sales force of 80 persons generated a total of 4,300 orders, resulting in a sales volume of 420,000 units during November. The gross dollar sales amounted to $10.9 million. The selling expenses incurred for November were as follows:

Advertising & promotion	$1,350,000
Administrative salaries	57,000
Sales salaries	80,000
Sales commissions	218,000
Salesperson travel	185,000
Sales office expense	497,200
Shipping expense	730,000
Total	$3,117,200

a. Explain why the selling expense flexible budget just presented would not be appropriate for evaluating Wagner's November selling expense, and indicate how the flexible budget would have to be revised.

b. Determine the budgeted variable cost per salesperson and variable cost per sales order for Wagner Company.

c. Prepare a selling expense report for November that Wagner Company can use to evaluate its control over selling expenses. The report should have a line for each selling expense item, showing the appropriate budgeted amount, the actual selling expense, and the monthly dollar variation.

d. Determine the actual variable cost per salesperson and variable cost per sales order for Wagner Company.

e. Comment on the effectiveness and efficiency of the salespersons during the month of November.

(CMA adapted)

38. The financial results for the Continuing Education Department of BusEd Corporation for November 1993 are presented in the schedule at the end of the case. Mary Ross, president of BusEd, is pleased with the final results but has observed that the revenue and most of the costs and expenses of this department exceeded the budgeted amounts. Barry Stein, vice-president of the Continuing Education Department, has been requested to provide an explanation of any amount that exceeded the budget by 5 percent or more.

Stein has accumulated the following facts to assist in his analysis of the November results:

1. The budget for calendar year 1993 was finalized in December 1992, and at that time, a full program of continuing education courses was scheduled to be held in Chicago during the first week of November 1993. The courses were scheduled so that eight courses would be run on each of the five days during the week. The budget assumed that there would be 425 participants in the program and 1,000 participant days for the week.

2. BusEd charges a flat fee of $150 per day of course instruction, so the fee for a three-day course would be $450. BusEd grants a 10 percent discount to persons who subscribe to its publications. The 10 percent discount is also granted to second and subsequent registrants for the same course from the same organization. However, only one discount per registration is allowed. Historically, 70 percent of the participant day registrations are at the full fee of $150 per day, and 30 percent of the participant day registrations receive the discounted fee of $135 per day. These percentages were used in developing the November 1993 budgeted revenue.

3. The following estimates were used to develop the budgeted figures for course-related expenses.

Food charges per participant day (lunch/coffee breaks)	$ 27
Course materials per participant	8
Instructor fee per day	1,000

4. A total of 530 individuals participated in the Chicago courses in November 1993, accounting for 1,280 participant days. This included 20 persons who took a new, two-day course on pension accounting that was not on the original schedule; thus, on two of the days, nine courses were offered, and an additional instructor was hired to cover the new course. The breakdown of the course registration was as follows:

Full fee registrations	704
Discounted fees	
Current periodical subscribers	128
New periodical subscribers	128
Second registrations from the same organization	320
Total participant day registrations	1,280

5. A combined promotional mailing was used to advertise the Chicago program and a program in Cincinnati that was scheduled for December 1993. The incremental costs of the combined promotional price were $5,000, but none of the promotional expenses ($20,000) budgeted for the Cincinnati program in December will have to be incurred. This earlier-than-normal promotion for the Cincinnati program has resulted in early registration fees collected in November as follows (in terms of participant days):

Full fee registrations	140
Discounted registrations	60
Total participant day registrations	200

6. BusEd continually updates and adds new courses, and includes $2,000 in each monthly budget for this purpose. The additional amount spent on course development during November was for an unscheduled course that will be offered in February for the first time.

Barry Stein has prepared the following quantitative analysis of the November 1993 variances:

BusEd Corporation
STATEMENT OF OPERATIONS
CONTINUING EDUCATION DEPARTMENT

	Budget	Actual	Favorable/ (Unfavorable) Dollars	Favorable/ (Unfavorable) Percent
Revenue				
Course fees	$145,500	$212,460	$66,960	46.0
Expenses				
Food charges	$ 27,000	$ 32,000	$ (5,000)	(18.5)
Course materials	3,400	4,770	(1,370)	(40.3)
Instructor fees	40,000	42,000	(2,000)	(5.0)
Instructor travel	9,600	9,885	(285)	(3.0)
Staff salaries & benefits	12,000	12,250	(250)	(2.1)
Staff travel	2,500	2,400	100	4.0
Promotion	20,000	25,000	(5,000)	(25.0)
Course development	2,000	5,000	(3,000)	(150.0)
Total expenses	$116,500	$133,305	$(16,805)	(14.4)
Revenue over expenses	$ 29,000	$ 79,155	$ 50,155	172.9

BusEd Corporation
ANALYSIS OF NOVEMBER 1993 VARIANCES

Budgeted revenue		$145,500
Variances:		
Quantity variance		
[(1,280 − 1,000) × $145.50]	$40,740 F	
Mix variance		
[($143.25 − $145.50) × 1,280]	2,880 U	
Timing difference ($145.50 × 200)	29,100 F	66,960 F
Actual revenue		$212,460
Budgeted expenses		$116,500
Quantity variances		
Food charges [(1,000 − 1,280) × $27]	$ 7,560 U	
Course materials [(425 − 530) × $8]	840 U	
Instructor fees (2 × $1,000)	2,000 U	10,400 U
Price variances		
Food charges [($27 − $25) × 1,280]	$ 2,560 F	
Course materials [($8 − $9) × 530]	530 U	2,030 F
Timing differences		
Promotion	$ 5,000 U	
Course development	3,000 U	8,000 U
Variances not analyzed (5% or less)		
Instructor travel	$ 285 U	
Staff salaries and benefits	250 U	
Staff travel	100 F	435 U
Actual expenses		$133,305

After reviewing Barry Stein's quantitative analysis of the November variances, prepare a memorandum addressed to Mary Ross explaining the following:

1. The cause of the revenue mix variance
2. The implication of the revenue mix variance
3. The cause of the revenue timing difference
4. The significance of the revenue timing difference
5. The primary cause of the unfavorable total expense variance
6. How the favorable food price variance was determined
7. The impact of the promotion timing difference on future revenues and expenses
8. Whether or not the course development variance has an unfavorable impact on the company

(CMA)

Ethics Discussion

39. Cost containment is especially critical in the health-care field because of continuously rising costs of providing services and stable or decreasing revenues from third-party payors (such as insurance companies and Medicare). Hospital expenses rose almost 35 percent from 1985 to 1988. But during that same period, Medicare established DRGs (diagnostic-related groups) that pay only a flat rate for an illness regardless of costs incurred by the health-care facility. To help in managing this trend, some hospitals have established cost containment committees that address (among other issues) the budget, cost control systems, and purchasing policies and practices.

   a. Discuss some of the reasons why hospital costs are increasing at such a rapid pace.

   b. The use of DRGs is allowing, in essence, a third party to set "selling prices" for a hospital by stating the amounts that will be paid for procedures. Provide arguments for positions both for and against the use of DRGs.

   c. Discuss the ethical issues involved when hospitals are forced to keep costs under a level specified by the DRGs.

40. The St. Bernard Parish Sheriff's Office habitually sidesteps state bid laws—costing taxpayers thousands of extra dollars—at a time when the office is hurting for money, public records show.

    Among the examples turned up by a *Times-Picayune* review of Sheriff's Office spending since 1985:

- The office paid $4.37 for an eight-inch pair of scissors—about 500 percent more than the 69 cents it could have paid.
- The office could have paid $1,844 for a Macintosh computer. Instead, it paid $2,375—about 29 percent more.
- The office could have bought four high-speed, steel-belted radial tires for $233.96—instead of the $423.76 it paid, or 81 percent more.

    Those are just some examples of what happens when Sheriff Jack Stephens does shopping but doesn't follow the procedures used by other parish agencies or by the state.

(SOURCE: Chris Adams, "Sheriff's Office Pays Top Dollar" [*New Orleans*] *Times-Picayune*, August 5, 1991, p. A1.)

   a. Are there instances in which bid laws should be sidestepped? If so, describe such instances. If not, discuss why.

   b. Discuss the ethical problems of violating state bid laws.

   c. Assume that you are Sheriff Stephens. Prepare a news release justifying your "shopping" habits.

   d. Do bid laws adequately provide a good cost control mechanism for governmental agencies? Explain the reasoning behind your answer.

CHAPTER 15

DECENTRALIZATION AND RESPONSIBILITY ACCOUNTING

LEARNING OBJECTIVES

After completing this chapter, you should be able to do the following:

1. Discuss the reasons that decentralization is appropriate for some companies but not for others
2. Describe the advantages and disadvantages of decentralized operations
3. Relate responsibility accounting to decentralization
4. Differentiate among and compute performance measures for the four types of responsibility centers
5. Understand why cash flows are a useful tool in performance measurement
6. Distinguish between return on investment and residual income
7. Discuss the concept and effects of suboptimization
8. Describe some of the difficulties encountered in trying to measure performance for multinational firms
9. Calculate throughput as a performance measurement

Alcoa Decentralizes for "Freedom"

William Evancho figured he was in for the usual ordeal. In previous years when he presented the business plan for the Aluminum Co. of America joint venture he heads, Mr. Evancho suffered for months while five Alcoa management layers scrutinized every detail. But this time, after just one brief out-of-town management meeting, Mr. Evancho was on his way back to his office, approved plan in hand.

Such tales of freedom have been ringing throughout this $11 billion company since Chairman Paul H. O'Neill wiped out layers of management so Alcoa's 25 businesses would report directly to him. Already, Alcoa managers say they are moving faster to please customers and jumping to meet new two-year targets that could determine the fate of their careers at the company.

But with the new sense of freedom comes an equally potent dose of confusion. Around the company, people are wondering who's in charge, as managers struggle to find new ways to handle strategic planning, budgeting, purchasing and sales.

While Mr. O'Neill's plan is perhaps the most aggressive and rapid attempt by an old-line manufacturer to push decision making down to lower levels, it isn't the first. General Electric Co. Chairman John F. Welch has thinned management from as many as nine layers to as few as four in the past decade, and he maintains direct contact with each of GE's 14 business groups. Du Pont Co. abolished its executive committee [in the fall of 1990], which had overseen every major decision for 87 years, so its 19 businesses could report directly to a five-person office of the chairman.

SOURCE: Dana Milbank, "Changes at Alcoa Point Up Challenges and Benefits of Decentralized Authority," *Wall Street Journal* (November 7, 1991), p. B1. Reprinted by permission of the *Wall Street Journal*, © 1991 Dow Jones & Company, Inc. All Rights Reserved Worldwide.

A lcoa, like many other companies, grew over the years until, apparently, it had a corporate structure that was hurting rather than helping it achieve organizational goals and objectives. Thus, that structure needed to be changed so that the company could most effectively use its resources and employee talents. Alcoa's chairman, Paul O'Neill, stated that the company organization needed change in spite of the major improvements in financial and operating performance since 1987. He commented that, "Waiting until outside events force change is, at best, reactive administration and, at worst, management cowardice." [1]

An organization's structure naturally evolves as its goals, technology, and employees change, and the progression is typically from highly centralized to highly decentralized. The degree of centralization reflects a chain of command, authority and responsibility relationships, and decision-making capabilities. This chapter discusses the degree to which top managers delegate authority to subordinate managers and how the performance of those subordinates is measured.

---

[1] Remarks by Paul O'Neill at Alcoa Organizational Meeting, Pittsburgh Hilton Hotel, August 9, 1991, p. 2.

DECENTRALIZATION

centralization
decentralization

The extent to which authority is retained by top management (**centralization**) or released from top management and passed to lower managerial levels (**decentralization**) can be viewed as a continuum. In a completely centralized firm, a single individual (usually the company owner or president) performs all decision making and retains full authority and responsibility for that organization's activities. On the other hand, a purely decentralized organization would have virtually no central authority, and each subunit would act as a totally independent entity. Either end of the continuum represents a clearly undesirable arrangement. In the totally centralized company, the single individual may not have the expertise or sufficient and timely information to make decisions in all areas. In the totally decentralized firm, subunits may act in ways that are not consistent with the goals of the total organization.

Each organization tends to structure itself in light of the pure centralization versus pure decentralization factors presented in Exhibit 15–1. Alcoa, for example, is a mature, large firm that has moved along the continuum toward more and more decentralization. Most businesses are, to some extent, somewhere within the continuum because of practical necessity. This continuum does not exist only in U.S. companies. The following News Note discusses Lucky-Goldstar, a Korean company that has existed since 1947 and is making the move toward decentralization.

While almost every organization is decentralized to some degree, quantifying the extent of decentralization may not be possible. Some subunits may have more autonomy than others. In addition to top management philosophy, decentralization depends on the type of organizational units. For example, a unit, segment, or division that operates in a turbulent environment and must respond quickly to new and unanticipated problems is likely to be a prime candidate for decentralization.

EXHIBIT 15–1
▼▼▼▼▼▼▼▼▼▼▼▼

CONTINUUM OF
AUTHORITY IN
ORGANIZATIONAL
STRUCTURES

	Continuum	
Factor	Pure Centralization ⟶	Pure Decentralization
Age of firm	Young ⟶	Mature
Size of firm	Small ⟶	Large
Stage of product development	Stable ⟶	Growth
Growth rate of firm	Slow ⟶	Rapid
Expected impact on profits of incorrect decisions	High ⟶	Low
Top management's confidence in subordinates	Low ⟶	High
Historical degree of control in firm	Tight ⟶	Moderate or loose

NEWS
NOTE

Loosening the Reins

Lucky-Goldstar Group is into everything from shampoos to semiconductors to solar power systems. The founding Koo family has dominated virtually every facet of decision-making. Inevitably, the group became too unwieldy for the Koo family to manage well. As sales from 31 separate companies hit the $25 billion mark, quality slipped—and so did innovation. Critics said Chairman Koo's hierarchical decision-making style was in part to blame. Now, Koo is giving more decision-making authority to his frontline managers. "We are becoming more efficient in management, quicker in decision-making," says Byun Kyu-Chill, president of the Lucky's trading arm.

SOURCE: Adapted from Laxmi Nakarmi, "At Lucky-Goldstar, the Koos Loosen the Reins," *Business Week* (February 18, 1991), p. 72.

Top management must also consider the subunit managers' personalities and perceived abilities. Managers in decentralized environments must be goal-oriented, assertive, decisive, and creative. While these employee traits are always desirable, they are *essential* for decentralized company managers. Managers in decentralized companies must also be willing to accept the authority delegated by top management and to be judged on the outcomes of the decisions that they make. Some subunit managers may be either reluctant or unable to accept this authority or responsibility. Therefore, a company may allow some units to be highly decentralized, while others are only minimally decentralized. Since managerial behaviors change and managers are replaced, supervisors should periodically reassess their decisions about a unit's extent of decentralization.

Decentralization does not necessarily mean that a unit manager has the authority to make all decisions concerning that unit. Top management selectively determines the types of authority to delegate and the types to withhold. For example, Alcoa considers safety, environmental factors, quality processes, insurance, and information strategy to be "central resource" capabilities. Chairman O'Neill believes that centralization is the most sensible and cost-effective method of handling these functions.

Advantages of Decentralization

Decentralization has many personnel advantages. Managers have the need and occasion to develop their leadership qualities, creative problem-solving abilities, and decision-making skills. Decentralized units provide excellent settings for training personnel and for screening aspiring managers for promotion. Managers can be judged on job performance and on the results of their units relative to those headed by other managers; such comparisons can encourage a healthy level of organizational competition. Decentralization also often leads to greater job satisfaction for managers because it provides for job enrichment and gives a feeling of increased importance to the organization. Employees are given more challenging and responsible work that provides greater opportunities for advancement.

The new organizational structure at Alcoa is sure to cause some significant changes at headquarters. Chairman O'Neill believes decentralization will create faster decision making by, and more entrepreneurship among, divisional managers.

In addition to the personnel benefits, decentralization is generally more effective than centralization in accomplishing organizational goals and objectives. The decentralized unit manager has more knowledge of the local operating environment, which means the following: (1) reduction of the time it takes to make decisions; (2) minimization of difficulties that may result from attempting to communicate problems

NEWS NOTE

Hanson Prefers a "Hands Off" Structure

It's only common sense that the right people to run a successful company are, of course, the experts who run it already. And that knowledge and expertise learned at the operating level are invaluable and impossible to gain sitting only at "corporate headquarters." We also believe that too much meddling only serves to demoralize staff and management alike. In short, to operate a "puppet regime" is bad business. Currently, at Hanson, we own more than 150 companies worldwide [such as Jacuzzi, Smith Corona, Faberware, and Universal Gym]. And they operate in sectors as basic and diverse as shovels and shoes. In every one of those companies we employ the same tried and trusted principles. We look closely at any new ideas or proposed plans. We talk over budgets until we come to agreement. Then we step aside and leave the operating managers free to run their day to day operations.

SOURCE: "The Problem with 'Hands On' Management Is What Happens When You Take the Hands Off," *Wall Street Journal* (January 18, 1989), p. C9.

and instructions through an organizational chain of command; and (3) quicker perceptions of environmental changes than is possible for top management. As discussed in the above News Note, the manager of a decentralized unit not only is in closest contact with daily operations but also is charged with making decisions about those operations.

A decentralized structure also allows the management by exception principle to be implemented. Top management, when reviewing divisional reports, can address issues that are out of the ordinary rather than dealing with operations that are proceeding according to plans.

Disadvantages of Decentralization

All aspects of a decentralized structure are not positive. For instance, the authority and responsibility for making decisions may be divided among too many individuals. This division of authority and responsibility may result in a lack of goal congruence among the organizational units. (**Goal congruence** exists when the personal and organizational goals of decision makers throughout a firm are consistent and mutually supportive.) In a decentralized company, unit managers are essentially competing with one another since the results of unit activities are compared. Unit managers may make decisions that positively affect their own units, but are detrimental to other organizational units or to the whole company. This process results in **suboptimization,** which is discussed later in the chapter.

goal congruence

suboptimization

A decentralized organization requires that more effective methods of communicating plans, activities, and achievements be established because decision making is removed from the central office. Top management has delegated the authority to make decisions to unit managers, but still retains the responsibility for the ultimate effects of those decisions. Thus, to determine if operations are progressing toward established goals, top management must be continuously aware of events occurring at lower levels. The following News Note indicates a decentralized situation at Daewoo, a Korean company, that got totally out of control before top management had to step in to make corrections.

NEWS NOTE

$8 Million Worth of Haircuts!

At Daewoo, day-to-day-control was ceded by Chairman Kim Woo-Choong to the presidents of individual Daewoo companies. It didn't work.

At Daewoo Shipbuilding, labor costs had risen tenfold over a decade and no attempt had been made to trim other expenses. Workers received free haircuts in the shipyard at a cost of $60 each a month, including lost hours. Kim personally took over Daewoo Shipbuilding for 18 months. Removing the barber shops saved $8 million a year. For bigger savings, Kim eliminated thousands of positions. From near-bankruptcy, the unit projects a $144 million profit for 1991.

SOURCE: Adapted from Laxmi Nakarmi, "At Daewoo, a 'Revolution' at the Top," *Business Week* (February 18, 1991), pp. 68–69.

Some employees may be disrupted when top management attempts to introduce decentralization policies. Top managers often have difficulty relinquishing the control they previously held over the segments or may be unwilling or unable to delegate effectively.

A final disadvantage of decentralization is that it may be extremely costly. In a large company, it is unlikely that all subordinate managers have equally good decision-making skills. Thus, the first cost is for training lower-level managers to make better decisions. Second, there is the potential cost of poor decisions. As discussed in the following quote, decentralization implies the willingness of top manage-

The introduction of decentralization policies may cause some confusion and disruption in the organization. Some managers may not want to give up their control; others may not wish to accept new responsibilities.

ment to let subordinates make some mistakes. The potentially adverse consequences of poor decisions by subordinates can (or might) cause some top managers to resist a high degree of decentralization.

> Decentralization of authority in itself has ethical consequences. It absolutely requires trust and latitude for error. The inability to monitor the performance—especially when measurement of results is the only surveillance—of executives assigned to tasks their superiors cannot know in detail results inexorably in delegation. The leaders of a corporation are accustomed to reliance upon the business acumen of . . . managers, whose results they watch with a practiced eye. Those concerned with the maintenance of the ethical standards of the corporation are dependent just as much on the ethical judgment and moral character of the managers to whom authority is delegated. Beyond keeping our fingers crossed, what do we do?[2]

Decentralization can also create a duplication of activities that could be quite expensive in terms of both time and money. To illustrate this possibility, the head of a Du Pont division remarked, "We don't want to have 25 divisions working with 25 consultants, each one getting $100,000 from the company." [3]

Another cost of decentralization relates to developing and operating a more sophisticated planning and reporting system. Since top management delegates decision-making authority, but retains ultimate responsibility for decision outcomes, a reporting system must be implemented that will provide top management with the ability to measure the overall accountability of the subunits. This reporting system is known as a **responsibility accounting** system.

responsibility accounting

RESPONSIBILITY ACCOUNTING

Responsibility accounting refers to an accounting system that provides information to top management about the performance of an organizational subunit. As companies became more decentralized, responsibility accounting systems evolved from the increased need to communicate operating results through the managerial hierarchy.

A responsibility accounting system produces **responsibility reports** that assist each successively higher level of management in evaluating the performances of its subordinate managers and their respective organizational units. These reports reflect the revenues and/or costs *under the control* of a specific unit manager. Any revenues or costs that are *not* under the control of a specific unit manager should not be shown on his or her responsibility reports. Much of the information communicated on these reports is monetary, although some nonmonetary data may be included.

responsibility reports

The number of responsibility reports issued at a specific point in time for a decentralized unit depends on the degree of influence that unit's manager has on the unit's day-to-day operations and costs. If a manager strongly influences all operations and costs of a unit, one report will suffice for both the manager and the unit. Normally, however, some costs are not controlled (or are only partially or indirectly controlled)

---

[2]Kenneth R. Andrews, ed., *Ethics in Practice: Managing the Moral Corporation* (Boston: Harvard Business School Press, 1989), p. 7.
[3]Richard Koenig, "Du Pont to Abolish Executive Committee, in Bid to Push More Authority into Ranks," *Wall Street Journal* (October 1, 1990), p. B6.

by the unit manager. In such instances, the responsibility report will take one of two forms. First, a single report can be issued that shows all costs incurred in the unit, separately classified as either controllable or noncontrollable by the manager. Alternatively, separate reports can be prepared for the manager and the organizational unit. The manager's report would include only costs under his or her control, while the unit's report would include all costs.

A responsibility accounting system is an important tool in making decentralization work effectively. The responsibility reports about unit performance are primarily tailored to fit the planning, controlling, and decision-making needs of subordinate managers. Top managers review these reports to evaluate the efficiency and effectiveness of each unit and each manager.

RESPONSIBILITY ACCOUNTING AND CONTROL SYSTEMS

One purpose of a responsibility accounting system is to "secure control at the point where costs are incurred instead of assigning them all to products and processes remote from the point of incurrence."[4] This purpose agrees with the concepts of standard costing and activity-based costing. In standard costing, variances are traced to the person (or machine) having responsibility for the variance (such as tracing the material purchase price variance to the purchasing agent). Activity-based costing attempts to trace as many costs as possible to the activities that caused the costs rather than using highly aggregated allocation techniques.

Control procedures are implemented for the following three reasons:

- Managers attempt to cause actual operating results to conform to planned results. This conformity is known as effectiveness.

- Managers attempt to cause, at a minimum, the standard output yield to occur from the actual input costs incurred. This conformity is known as efficiency.

- Managers need to ensure, to the extent possible, a reasonable utilization of plant and equipment. Utilization is primarily affected by product or service demand. At higher volumes of activity or utilization, fixed capacity costs can be spread over more units, resulting in a lower unit cost. Utilization is appropriate even in service businesses, as indicated in the next News Note.

Responsibility accounting implies acceptance of *communicated* authority from top management by subordinate managers. Budgets are used to officially communicate output expectations (sales, production, and so forth) and, through budget appropriations, delegate the authority to spend. Ideally, subunit managers will negotiate budgets and standards for their units with top management for the coming year. Involvement in the budgeting process is essential for those whose performance will be evaluated on budget-to-actual comparisons.

The responsibility accounting system is designed so that actual data are captured in conformity with budgetary accounts. During the year, the accounting system is used to record and summarize data for each organizational unit. Operating reports

---

[4]W. W. Cooper and Yuji Ijiri, eds., *Kohler's Dictionary for Accountants* (Englewood Cliffs, N.J.: Prentice-Hall, 1983), p. 435.

NEWS NOTE

Credit Cards Need Volume to be Profitable

Credit cards are the current, often-lucrative fad among big banks. Citicorp, the nation's largest credit-card issuer, earned $600 million in 1989 from credit cards. But a successful card operation requires huge investments in technology and huge outlays for marketing. Over the past five years or so, the credit-card business "has become a game of economies of scale," says Robert H. Burke, general manager of Bank of New York's credit-card operation. "In effect, you're running a factory, and the more volume you can push through your fixed costs, the better the profits are."

SOURCE: Douglas R. Sease and Robert Guenther, "Big Banks Are Plagued by a Gradual Erosion of Key Profit Centers," *Wall Street Journal* (August 1, 1990), p. A14. Reprinted by permission of the *Wall Street Journal,* © 1990 Dow Jones & Company, Inc. All Rights Reserved Worldwide.

that compare actual account balances with budgeted, standard, or target amounts are prepared periodically and issued to managers. Because of day-to-day contact with operations, managers should have been aware of these significant variances *before* they are reported, identified variance causes, and attempted to correct causes of the problems. Top management, on the other hand, may not know about operational variances until responsibility reports are received. By the time top management receives the reports, the problems causing the variances should have been corrected, or subordinate managers should have explanations as to why the problems were not or could not have been resolved.

The responsibility reports received by top management may compare actual performance to the master budget. Such a comparison can be viewed as yielding an overall performance evaluation, since the master budget reflects management's expectations about sales prices, volume and mix, as well as costs. However, using the budget as a comparison may be inappropriate in some cases. For example, if the budget had an allowance for scrap built into the materials usage estimated, making comparisons to the budget figure does not cause companies to focus on total quality. A "budget-versus-actual variance analysis may result in the conclusion that a positive variance relative to budget is favorable performance, even if significant scrap still is being produced. Using zero scrap as a target results in any variance being identified as unfavorable." [5]

A more appropriate form of responsibility report may be that of the flexible budget, which provides information at various levels of activity. This report form would compare actual information about controllable items (revenues and/or costs) with both the master budget and with amounts based on the actual achieved level of activity. This secondary comparison is more useful for control purposes, since both operating results and budget figures are based on the same activity level.

Regardless of the types of comparisons provided, responsibility reports reflect the upward flow of information from operational units to top management. These reports indicate the broadening scope of managerial responsibility. Managers receive

---

[5]Robert A. Howell and Stephen R. Soucy, "Management Reporting in the New Manufacturing Environment," *Management Accounting* (February 1988), p. 24. Published by Institute of Management Accountants, Montvale, N.J.

detailed information on the performance of their immediate areas of control and summary information on all other organizational units for which they are responsible. Summarizing results causes a pyramiding of information. Reports at the lowest-level units are highly detailed, while detail is less specific at the top of the organization. Upper-level managers desiring more specific information than that provided in summary reports can review the responsibility reports prepared for their subordinates.

Exhibit 15–2 illustrates a partial year set of performance reports for Margol Ltd. The Cutting and Assembly Department's actual costs are compared to those in the flexible budget. Data for Cutting and Assembly are then aggregated with data of other departments under the production vice-president's control. These combined data are shown in the middle section of Exhibit 15–2. In a like manner, the total costs

EXHIBIT 15–2
▼▼▼▼▼▼▼▼▼▼▼▼

MARGOL LTD.—
PERFORMANCE
REPORTS FOR 1993
YEAR-TO-DATE
COSTS

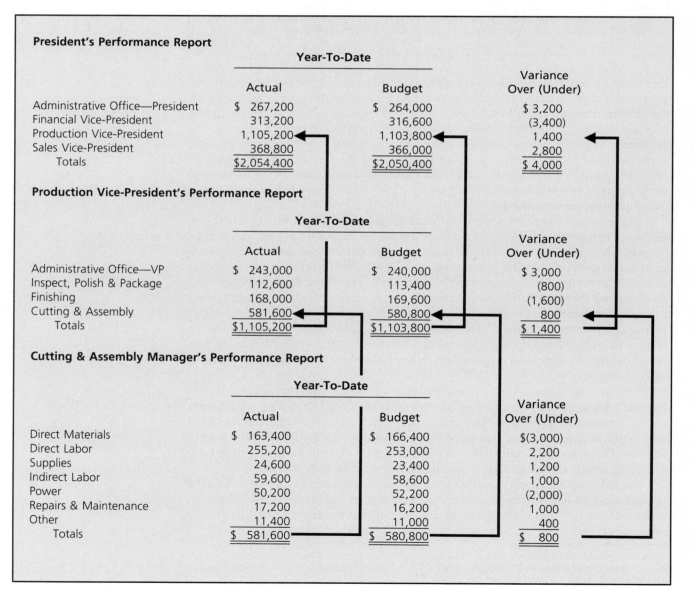

President's Performance Report

	Year-To-Date		Variance
	Actual	Budget	Over (Under)
Administrative Office—President	$ 267,200	$ 264,000	$ 3,200
Financial Vice-President	313,200	316,600	(3,400)
Production Vice-President	1,105,200	1,103,800	1,400
Sales Vice-President	368,800	366,000	2,800
Totals	$2,054,400	$2,050,400	$ 4,000

Production Vice-President's Performance Report

	Year-To-Date		Variance
	Actual	Budget	Over (Under)
Administrative Office—VP	$ 243,000	$ 240,000	$ 3,000
Inspect, Polish & Package	112,600	113,400	(800)
Finishing	168,000	169,600	(1,600)
Cutting & Assembly	581,600	580,800	800
Totals	$1,105,200	$1,103,800	$ 1,400

Cutting & Assembly Manager's Performance Report

	Year-To-Date		Variance
	Actual	Budget	Over (Under)
Direct Materials	$ 163,400	$ 166,400	$(3,000)
Direct Labor	255,200	253,000	2,200
Supplies	24,600	23,400	1,200
Indirect Labor	59,600	58,600	1,000
Power	50,200	52,200	(2,000)
Repairs & Maintenance	17,200	16,200	1,000
Other	11,400	11,000	400
Totals	$ 581,600	$ 580,800	$ 800

of the production vice-president's area of responsibility are combined with other costs for which the company president is responsible and are shown in the top section of Exhibit 15–2.

Variances are the responsibility of the manager under whose direct supervision those variances occurred. Variances are individually itemized in performance reports at the lower levels so that the appropriate manager has the necessary details to take any required corrective action related to significant variances.[6] Under the management by exception principle, major deviations from expectations are highlighted under the subordinate manager's reporting section to assist upper-level managers in making decisions about when to become involved in subordinates' operations. If no significant deviations exist, top management is free to devote its attention to other matters. In addition, such detailed variance analysis alerts operating managers to items that may need to be explained to superiors.

The performance reports of each management layer are reviewed and evaluated by each successive layer of management. Managers are likely to be more careful and alert in controlling operations knowing that the reports generated by the responsibility accounting system reveal financial accomplishments and problems. Thus, in addition to providing a means for control, responsibility reports can motivate managers to influence operations in ways that will reflect positive performance.

While a focus of cost accounting is on product costing, the focus of responsibility accounting is on people. The people emphasized are the managers responsible for an organizational unit such as a department, division, or geographic region. The subunit under the control of a manager is called a **responsibility center**.

responsibility center

Types of Responsibility Centers

Responsibility accounting systems identify, measure, and report on the performance of people who control the activities of responsibility centers. There are four classifications of responsibility centers based on the manager's scope of authority and type of financial responsibility: cost, revenue, profit, and investment. Each is illustrated in Exhibit 15–3 and discussed in the following sections.

Cost Centers

In a **cost center**, the manager only has the authority to incur costs and is specifically evaluated on the basis of how well costs are controlled. In many cost centers, revenues do not exist because the organizational unit does not engage in any revenue-producing activity. For example, the placement center in a university may be a cost center, since it does not charge for the use of its services, but it does incur costs.

cost center

In other instances, revenues may exist for a particular subunit, but they either are not under the manager's control or are not effectively measurable. The first type of situation exists in a governmental agency that is provided a specific proration of sales tax dollars, but has no authority to levy or collect the related taxes. The second situation could exist in engineered and discretionary cost centers in which the outputs

---

[6]In practice, the variances shown in Exhibit 15–2 would be further separated into their respective price and quantity elements as shown in chapter 5 on standard costing.

EXHIBIT 15-3
▼▼▼▼▼▼▼▼▼▼▼

TYPES OF
RESPONSIBILITY
CENTERS

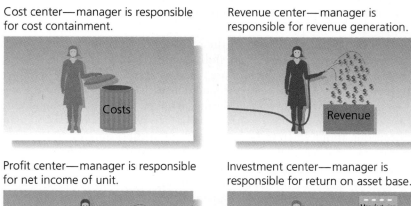

(revenues or benefits generated from the cost inputs) are not easily measured.[7] In these situations, revenues should not be included in the manager's responsibility accounting report. As discussed in the News Note on page 657, an individual's performance should be judged only in relation to that individual's specific duties and responsibilities.

In the traditional manufacturing environment, a standard costing system is generally used and variances are reported and analyzed. In such an environment, the highest priority in a cost center is often the minimization of unfavorable cost variances. Top management may often concentrate only on the unfavorable variances occurring in a cost center and ignore the efficient performance indicated by favorable variances. To illustrate this possibility, January operating results for Division A, a cost center of the Lenox Company, are given in Exhibit 15–4.

During the month, the division produced 10,000 units of product at a cost of $69,800. The standard production cost for these units is $70,000. Top management analysis of the responsibility report issued for Division A for January might focus on the unfavorable materials variance rather than on the favorable variances for the other costs of production. Sandy Withers, the manager of Division A, is the person responsible for controlling costs, and she did so in two of the three cost areas. A considered evaluation by her superiors should recognize this fact.

Significant favorable variances should not be ignored if the management by exception principle is applied appropriately. Using this principle, top management should investigate all variances (both favorable and unfavorable) that fall outside the range of acceptable deviations. The unfavorable materials variance in Division A should be investigated further to find its cause. It is possible that substandard materials were purchased and caused excessive usage. If this is the case, the purchasing

---

[7]Engineered and discretionary costs are discussed in chapter 14.

Performance Measurements Must Correlate with Jobs

Measuring individual processes with overall gross indicators is analogous to measuring a professional baseball player on his team's overall performance. It isn't fair to say that a player is no good because his team has a losing record. It is fair, however, to measure that player on RBIs, batting average, or on base percentage because he can influence those measures directly. In the manufacturing process, it is not fair to measure a line foreman on cost of production as a percentage of sales because he cannot control sales price, sales volume, or many elements of cost. It is fair to measure that foreman on utility usage, cycle time, and schedule attainment, which he can control and influence directly.

SOURCE: Mark E. Beischel and K. Richard Smith, "Linking the Shop Floor to the Top Floor," *Management Accounting* (October 1991), p. 26. Published by Institute of Management Accountants, Montvale, N.J.

agent, not Ms. Withers, should be assigned the responsibility for the variance. Other possible causes for the unfavorable materials variance include increased materials prices, excess waste, or some combination of all causes. Only additional inquiry will determine if the variance could have been controlled by Ms. Withers.

The favorable direct labor variance should also be analyzed for causes. Ms. Withers may have used inexperienced personnel who were being paid lower rates. This cause might explain the favorable direct labor variance and, to some extent, the unfavorable direct materials variance (because of their lack of skill and possible overuse of materials). Alternatively, the people working in Division A could have simply been very efficient this period.

EXHIBIT 15–4
▼▼▼▼▼▼▼▼▼▼

JANUARY PRODUCTION COSTS—DIVISION A OF LENOX COMPANY

Units produced: 10,000

Standard cost per unit of production:

Direct materials	$4.50
Direct labor	2.00
Overhead	.50
Total	$7.00

	Actual cost incurred	Standard cost allowed	Variance
Direct materials	$47,600	$45,000	$2,600 U
Direct labor	18,000	20,000	2,000 F
Overhead	4,200	5,000	800 F
Total	$69,800	$70,000	$ 200 F

The performance of the New York Mets cannot be judged solely by Howard Johnson's performance. Organizational performance is a group effort and should be evaluated by global measurements, while an individual's performance should be evaluated on measurements related to his or her specific duties and responsibilities.

Revenue Centers

revenue center

A **revenue center** is strictly defined as an organizational unit for which a manager is accountable only for the generation of revenues and has no control over setting selling prices or budgeting costs. Practically speaking, however, pure revenue centers do not often exist. Managers of "revenue centers" not only are typically responsible for revenues, but also are involved in the planning and control over at least some of the costs incurred in the center.

For example, Jessica Evans is a district sales manager for Best Publishing Company and is responsible for the sales revenues generated in her territory. In addition, she is also accountable for controlling the mileage and other travel-related expenses of her sales force. Jessica is not, however, able to influence the types of cars her sales staff obtain because cars are acquired on a fleetwide basis by top management.

Salaries, if directly traceable to the center, are often a cost responsibility of the "revenue center" manager. This situation reflects the traditional retail environment in which a sales clerk was assigned to a specific department and was only allowed to check out customers wanting to purchase that department's merchandise. Most stores, however, have found such a checkout situation to be detrimental to business because customers were forced to wait for the appropriate clerk. Clerks in many stores are now allowed to assist all customers with all types of merchandise. Such a change in policy causes what was a traceable departmental cost to be reclassified as an indirect cost. Those stores carrying high-cost, high-selling-price merchandise normally still retain the traditional system. Managers of such departments are able to trace sales salaries as a direct departmental cost.

Profit Centers

In a **profit center,** managers are responsible for generating revenues and for planning and controlling all expenses. A profit center manager's goal is to maximize the center's net income. Profit centers should be independent organizational units whose managers have the ability to obtain resources at the most economical prices and to sell products at prices that will maximize revenue. If managers do not have complete authority to buy and sell at objectively determined costs and prices, it is difficult to make a meaningful evaluation of the profit center. Like cost and revenue centers, profit centers do not generally have control over any investment base.

profit center

The revenues and expenses of profit centers are not always provided by manufacturing divisions or branches of retail stores. In Greensboro, North Carolina, for instance, managers at Trailco Leasing use truck trailers as the revenue-generators of profit centers. These managers are given the authority and accounting information to allow them to make responsible decisions about acquiring trailers and clients.

Investment Centers

An **investment center** is an organizational unit in which the manager is responsible not only for generating revenues and planning and controlling costs, but also for acquiring, using, and disposing of plant assets in a manner that seeks to earn the highest feasible rate of return on the investment base. Many investment centers are independent, freestanding divisions or subsidiaries of a firm. This independence allows investment center managers the opportunity to make decisions about all matters affecting their organizational units and to be judged on the outcomes of those decisions.

investment center

Companies may define their organizational units in various ways based on management accountability for one or more income-producing factors—costs, revenues, and/or assets. Because of their closeness to daily divisional activities, responsibility center managers should have more current and detailed knowledge about sales prices, costs, and other market information than top management has. If the responsibility centers are designated as profit or investment centers, their managers are encouraged, to the extent possible, to operate those subunits as separate economic entities that exist for the same basic organizational goal.

MEASURING PERFORMANCE TOWARD THE ULTIMATE GOAL

Regardless of the size, type of ownership, or product or service being sold, one basic goal for any business is to generate profits. For other organizations, such as a charity or a governmental entity, the ultimate financial goal may be to break even. The ultimate goal is achieved when the organization satisfies its **critical success factors**—those items that are so important that, without them, the organization would cease to exist. Most organizations would consider quality, customer service, efficiency, controlling costs, and responsiveness to change as five critical success factors. If all of these factors are managed properly, the organization should be financially successful; if they are not, sooner or later the organization will fail. The following News Note stresses the need for quality as a critical success factor.

critical success factors

Quality Means Zero Defects at Senco

Senco Products in Cincinnati embraced the policy of total quality as its number one priority. William Been, director of fastener manufacturing for Senco, thinks that having such a policy "is not only worth doing, but is mandatory for success." The commitment to quality pays off, Been says. Senco has seen its defect rates plunge, customer satisfaction climb, and employee morale improve. On average, scrap and rework costs have been reduced more than 40 percent. Senco has adopted the total quality concept not only in manufacturing, but in all aspects of the business. The company is devoting itself to quality not because the company has problems with defects, but because management sees a commitment to quality as necessary to remain competitive.

SOURCE: "Quality Equals Perfection at Cincinnati Fastener Systems Company," *Grant Thornton Manufacturing Issues* (Winter 1990), p. 8.

A profit-making company's financial success accrues *over the long run* to its owners (stockholders) and cannot be truly known until the company no longer exists. Stockholders, however, use short-term surrogate performance measures (such as current year net income or return on assets employed) to provide indicators of success. In a like manner, each successive level of management within the organization makes performance judgments about those individuals working for them. The bases for the judgments may be quantitative or nonquantitative, monetary or nonmonetary. But the means by which individuals are judged should be reflective of how they have contributed to the ultimate goals of the organization.

To encompass the numerous considerations involved in performance evaluation, it may be necessary to use "[a] pyramid of measures . . . to ensure that every element of the organization that is relevant to business strategy implementation is covered." [8] The "performance pyramid" depicted in Exhibit 15–5 indicates the types of measures needed at different organizational levels and for different purposes. Within the pyramid are measures that consider both long- and short-term organizational considerations. These measures can be financially based (net income or return on assets employed) or market based (number of warranty claims or length of lead time from order to delivery). Some of the more common measures are discussed in the following section of the chapter.

PERFORMANCE MEASUREMENTS

Responsibility center managers can only be evaluated using measures of performance that relate to the types of authority and responsibility they have. Therefore, different performance measurements are applicable to different types of responsibility centers.

---

[8]Kelvin Cross and Richard Lynch, "Accounting for Competitive Performance," *Journal of Cost Management for the Manufacturing Industry* (Spring 1989), p. 22.

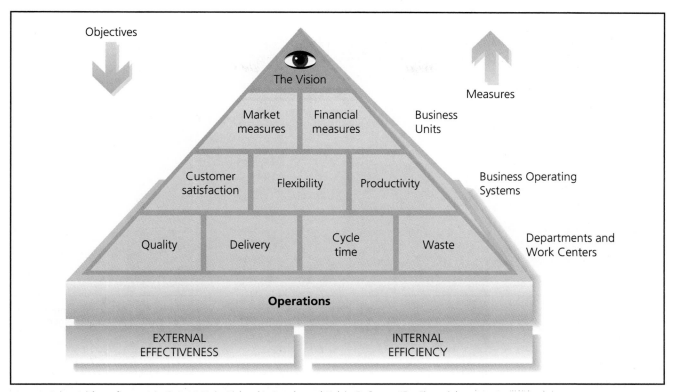

SOURCE: Adapted from figure 1 in C. J. McNair, Richard L. Lynch, and Kelvin F. Cross, "Do Financial and Nonfinancial Performance Measures Have to Agree?" *Management Accounting* (November 1990), p. 30. Published by Institute of Management Accountants, Montvale, N.J.

EXHIBIT 15–5
▼▼▼▼▼▼▼▼▼▼▼▼
THE PERFORMANCE
PYRAMID

Performance measurement has typically relied on information generated during the management control process. Exhibit 15–6 provides a diagram of the basic management control process and indicates the point at which performance has traditionally been evaluated. While this type of measurement system has been fairly easy to implement, it has focused, in some ways, on aspects that are not always the most conducive to a sound competitive position.

For example, assume that top management at Chrysler engages in management by exception and investigates variances only when they are outside an "acceptable range." While this technique allows top management to ignore many variances, it also delivers the statement to employees that a certain amount of error is acceptable. That degree of error results in additional costs and, possibly, lower quality.

Managers will normally act specifically in accordance with how they are to be measured. Thus, performance measurements should have the following characteristics:

- they must be designed to reflect organizational goals and objectives;
- they must be specific and understandable;
- they must promote harmonious operations between and among units; and
- if financial, they must reflect an understanding of how the use of accounting information might affect the quality of the measurement.

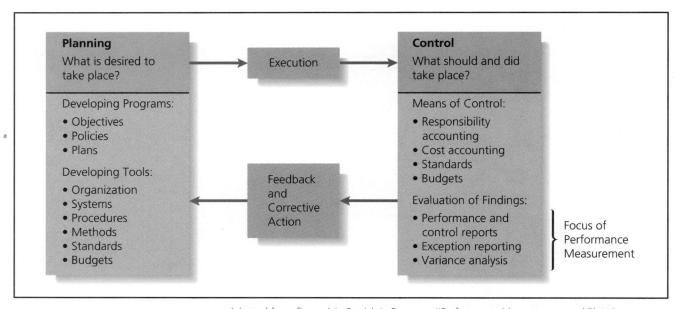

SOURCE: Adapted from figure 1 in Patrick L. Romano, "Performance Measurement and Planning—Revisited," *Management Accounting* (January 1989), p. 62. Published by Institute of Management Accountants, Montvale, N.J.

EXHIBIT 15–6
▼▼▼▼▼▼▼▼▼▼▼▼

DIAGRAM OF
MANAGEMENT
CONTROL

All pyramids require a sound foundation upon which to build. Everyone involved needs to move toward the same ultimate vision, and their performance must be judged relative to their success at the tasks assigned.

Managerial performance can and should be evaluated using both qualitative and quantitative measures. Qualitative measures are very often subjective. For example, a manager may be evaluated using simple low-to-high rankings on job skills, such as knowledge, quality of work, and need for supervision. The rankings can be given for an individual on a stand-alone basis, in relationship to other managers, or on a group or team basis. While such qualitative measures provide useful information, at some point and in some way, performance should also be compared to a quantitative standard.

Managers are generally more comfortable with and respond better to quantitative measures of performance because such measures provide a defined target at which to aim. Quantifiable performance measures are of two types: nonfinancial and financial. Nonfinancial measures "rely on data outside of a conventional financial or cost system, such as on-time delivery, manufacturing cycle time, set-up time, productivity for the total work force and various measures of quality." [9] According to *Statement on Management Accounting 4D,* nonfinancial performance measures have two distinct advantages over financial performance measures:

- Nonfinancial indicators directly measure an entity's performance in the activities that create shareholder wealth, such as manufacturing and delivering quality goods and services and providing service for the customer. . . .

- Because they measure productive activity directly, nonfinancial measures may better predict the direction of future cash flows. For example, the long-term financial viability of some industries rests largely on their ability to keep promises of improved product quality at a competitive price.[10]

The advantages provided by nonfinancial measures should be considered when establishing a performance measurement system. The appendix to this chapter presents a variety of nonfinancial performance measures that can also be viewed as the cost drivers of an activity-based costing system (as discussed in chapter 4).

A well-designed performance measurement system should encompass more than one performance measure, as stressed in the News Note at the top of the next page. It is essential, however, that the number of performance measurements used for any area be limited. Top management should choose several measures on which to concentrate during a period; those measures should be the ones most reflective of the company's objectives for that time frame.

In addition to using more than one measure, the system should include various *types* of measures. Traditionally, top management has tended to focus on quantitative *financial* measures of performance. Numerous financial performance measures exist including the following: divisional profits, achievement of budget objectives, individual and total variances from budget or standard, and cash flow. Each of these measures provides different information that can be used by top management to analyze the effectiveness and efficiency of subordinate managers' performances. Exhibit 15–7 (on page 665) provides some ideas for judging the managerial performance in four areas of operations.

---

[9]Peter R. Santori, "Manufacturing Performance in the 1990s: Measuring for Excellence," *Journal of Accountancy* (November 1987), p. 146.
[10]Institute of Management Accountants (formerly National Association of Accountants), "Measuring Entity Performance," *Statements on Management Accounting 4D* (Montvale, N.J.: National Association of Accountants, January 3, 1986), p. 12.

NEWS NOTE

Even More Than One Financial Performance Measure Exists

Let us pierce the myth of the single bottom line and acknowledge that there are really three bottom lines—cash, profit, and return on assets. If they all are held as part of the corporate goal and *kept in balance,* a company's employee team really can manage to connect the managerial inputs (sales, expense, and assets) more easily to reach financial goals. For instance, poor inventory management might have little impact on profit but could have a powerful and surprisingly negative impact on cash and return-on-assets.

SOURCE: Karen K. Kalkbrenner, W. Chuck Kremer, and Dennis D. Smith, "Why Managers Need Three Bottom Lines," *Management Accounting* (July 1989), p. 22. Published by Institute of Management Accountants, Montvale, N.J.

The type of responsibility center being evaluated affects the performance measure(s) that can be used. In a cost center, the fundamental financial performance measure is the materiality of the variances from budgeted or target costs. Performance can be judged in a pure revenue center primarily by comparing budgeted with actual revenues. Since these two responsibility centers are accountable for only one type of monetary object (costs and revenues, respectively), there are few financial measurements that can be used to evaluate managerial performance.

While performing quality control inspections is generally not perceived as a value-added activity, the number of quality parts produced is an important non-financial performance measure. Quality should be built into the process so that zero defects becomes a more achievable standard.

	Qualitative	Quantitative	
		Nonfinancial	Financial
Personnel	• Acceptance of additional responsibility • Generation of new ideas • Increased job skills • Need for supervision • Interaction with upper- and lower-level employees	• Proportion of direct to indirect labor (low or high depending on degree of automation) • Diversity of ethnic background in hiring and promotion • Hours of continuing professional education • Scores on standardized examinations	• Comparability of pay levels of personnel with those of competitors • Savings from using part-time personnel
Market	• Addition of new product features • Increased product durability • Improved efficiency of product • Improved effectiveness of product	• Number of customer complaints • Number of days to deliver an order • Proportion of repeat business • Number of new patents obtained	• Increase in revenue from previous period • Percentage of total market revenues • Revenue generated per advertising dollar
Costs	• Better traceability of costs • Increased cost consciousness • Better employee suggestions for cost reductions • Increased usage of automated equipment for routine tasks	• Time to design new products • Number of engineering change orders issued for new products • Proportion of product defects • Number of different product parts • Number of days of inventory in stock • Length of processing time • Proportion of materials generated as scrap or waste • Reduction in setup time since prior period	• Reduction in production cost since prior period (individually for materials, labor, and overhead, and collectively) • Reduction in distribution and scrap/waste cost since prior period • Cost of engineering changes • Variances from standard
Returns (profitability)	• Customer satisfaction • Product brand loyalty	• Proportion of on-time deliveries • Degree of accuracy in sales figures • Frequency of customer willingness to accept an exchange rather than a refund	• Increase in market price per share • Return on investment • Increase in net income • Increase in cash flow

EXHIBIT 15–7
▼▼▼▼▼▼▼▼▼▼▼▼

EXAMPLES OF
PERFORMANCE
MEASUREMENTS

Profit and investment center managers are responsible for both revenues and expenses. Given this greater accountability, additional performance measures (such as divisional profits and cash flows for both types of centers and return on investment and residual income for investment centers) can be used in addition to the measures used by cost and revenue centers. Each of these measures is discussed next.

Divisional Income

Income of a profit or investment center is a frequently used measure of divisional performance. The amount of income generated by the center is compared with its budgeted income objective, and variances are computed to determine where objectives were exceeded or were not achieved. One problem with using income to measure performance is that the individual components used to derive income are subject to manipulation. Net income manipulation can take many forms; the following are some examples:

- If the center is using a cost flow method other than FIFO, inventory purchases can be accelerated or deferred at the end of the period. Advancing or delaying these purchases will increase or decrease the inventory base from which cost of raw materials used or cost of goods sold is computed for the period.
- Replacement of workers who have resigned or been terminated can be deferred to minimize salary expense for the period.
- Routine maintenance can be delayed or eliminated to reduce expenses.
- If actual overhead is being allocated to inventory, an increase in production will cause cost per unit to decline.
- Sales can be shifted between periods.
- Advertising expenses or other discretionary costs can be delayed.
- Depreciation methods may be changed, resulting in higher or lower depreciation charges and net income amounts.

All the listed tactics can be used to "cause" reported income to conform to budget expectations. However, such manipulations are normally not in the best long-run interest of the center because they may create offsetting changes later. For example, delaying current maintenance until next period simply shifts the cost from one period to the next; eliminating current maintenance could also result in long-term equipment problems.

Divisional income represents a short-term, rather than a long-term, objective. Most reward systems (promotion, pay raises, bonuses) are based on short-term performance. While it is necessary to promote short-run efficiency, companies should not use the quarterly or annual income of a profit or investment center as the only measure of the performance of that center's manager. A year is often too short a time span over which to judge a manager's performance. The performance measurement period should coincide with the time it takes to evaluate the quality of the center manager's decisions.

Cash Flow

For an entity to succeed, managers who have authority over operations and investments know that two requirements must be met: (1) long-run profitability must be attained, and (2) liquidity must be preserved on a continuous basis. Continuous cash flow is essential, even in a seasonal business such as boating. Norton's Shipyard and Marina Inc. (of Rhode Island) instituted a quarterly payment schedule for customers to ensure an on-going supply of cash rather than having high cash inflows in the summers and zero inflows in the off-season.

Since external financial statements use accrual-based accounting figures, management's attention can be diverted from the liquidity aspect. The Statement of Cash Flows (SCF) focuses on the size and direction of cash inflows and outflows. This statement provides information about the cash impacts of the three major categories of business activities (operating, investing, and financing). When this statement is used for divisional reporting, some items that would appear on the companywide SCF will not appear on the division's. For example, the divisional statement would never show a dividend payout or the effects of issuing or retiring capital stock.

The SCF explains the change in the cash balance by indicating sources and uses of cash. This information allows managers to determine the entity's ability to provide for scheduled payments, enter into new obligations for cash outflows, and react to other business circumstances that might affect cash flows. For instance, an investment center's manager should have the ability to change credit discount terms, extend credit, negotiate payment of payables, and buy and sell equipment.

Like profits, cash flow can be manipulated and relates to the short run rather than to the long run. Thus, as a performance measure, cash flow suffers from some of the same problems as divisional profits. Regardless of its deficiencies in measuring performance, adequate cash flow is a necessity for carrying on business activities. Inadequate cash flow or too much cash on hand may reflect poor judgment and decision making on the part of the profit or investment center manager.

Two other financial measures often used to evaluate divisional performance in an investment center are return on investment and residual income.

Return on Investment

The difference between a profit center and an investment center is that the investment center manager has responsibility for assets under the center's control. Giving the manager the responsibility for acquisition, use, and disposal of assets increases the number of financial performance measurements available, since another dimension of accountability is added. For example, managers can be judged in relation to the **return on investment** earned by their organizational units. Return on investment (ROI) is a ratio that relates income generated by the investment center to the resources (or asset base) used to produce that income. The ROI formula is: **return on investment**

$$\text{Return on Investment} = \frac{\text{Income}}{\text{Assets Invested}}$$

Before the return on investment computation can be used effectively as a performance measure, both terms in the formula must be specifically defined. Exhibit 15–8 provides several definitional questions and answers about this ratio. Once definitions have been assigned to the terms, ROI can be used to evaluate an investment center and to make intracompany, intercompany, and multinational comparisons. However, managers making these comparisons must consider differences in the compared entities' natures (including size and stages of growth and product development) and accounting methods employed.

Segment margin is defined as segment sales minus (direct variable expenses and avoidable fixed expenses). This amount is preferred to operating income in the ROI calculation because the investment center manager does not, in the short run, have **segment margin**

EXHIBIT 15–8
▼▼▼▼▼▼▼▼▼▼▼

ROI DEFINITIONAL
QUESTIONS AND
ANSWERS

Question	Preferable Answer
Is income defined as segment margin or operating income?	Segment margin
Is income on a before- or after-tax basis?	Before-tax
Should assets be defined as	
• total assets used	
• total assets under the control of the investment center manager and available for use; or	
• net assets (equity)?	Total assets available for use
Should plant assets be included at original cost or depreciated book value?	Original cost
Should plant assets be included at historical costs or at current values?	Current values
Should beginning, ending, or average assets be used?	Average assets

EXHIBIT 15–9
▼▼▼▼▼▼▼▼▼▼▼

DINAH
CORPORATION 1994
INFORMATION

	Atlanta	Hartford	Seattle	Total
Revenues	$1,350,000	$ 860,000	$ 6,400,000	$8,610,000
Direct costs				
Variable	(621,000)	(344,000)	(2,240,000)	(3,205,000)
Fixed (avoidable)	(235,000)	(120,000)	(1,100,000)	(1,455,000)
Segment income	$ 494,000	$ 396,000	$ 3,060,000	
Unavoidable fixed				
and allocated costs	(156,000)	(100,000)	(744,000)	(1,000,000)
Operating income	$ 338,000	$ 296,000	$ 2,316,000	$2,950,000
Taxes (35%)	118,300	103,600	810,600	1,032,500
Net income	$ 219,700	$ 192,400	$ 1,505,400	$1,917,500
Current assets	$ 66,250	$ 40,000	$ 97,000	
Plant assets	9,220,000	975,000	12,358,000	
Accumulated depreciation	(6,540,000)	(125,000)	(2,465,000)	
Total assets	$2,746,250	$ 890,000	$ 9,990,000	
Liabilities	1,200,000	325,000	4,260,000	
Net assets	$1,546,250	$ 565,000	$ 5,730,000	
Percentage of total assets used	92 %	95 %	100 %	
Value of assets used	$2,526,550	$ 845,500	$ 9,990,000	
Current value of plant assets	$2,566,250	$1,240,000	$ 9,200,000	

Note: A summarized corporate balance sheet would not balance with the investment center balance sheets because of the existence of general corporate assets and liabilities.

control over unavoidable fixed expenses and allocated corporate costs. Therefore, unavoidable fixed expenses and allocated corporate costs should not be a part of the performance evaluation criteria. The same logic applies to the exclusion of taxes (or corporate interest) from investment center income. Corporate tax rates are determined based on companywide income, and investment centers might pay higher or lower rates if they were separate taxable entities.

Total assets available for use is preferable to total assets used if the objective is to measure how well the manager performed with the assets that were committed to him or her. If the objective is to measure return on the quality of the entire investment center, then net assets are preferable.

Use of original cost of plant assets is more appropriate than net book value in determining the amount of assets invested. As net book value declines, an investment center earning the same income each year would show a continuously increasing return on investment solely because the asset base would steadily diminish. Such apparent increasing returns could cause managers to make improper assessments of the investment center's performance. The use of current plant asset values is preferable to historical costs because current values measure the opportunity cost of using the assets. However, current values are more difficult to obtain and may be subject to low levels of assurance regarding the inherent subjectivity of the amount. Finally, regardless of which asset base is selected, that base should be an average for the year. Since income (the numerator of the ROI formula) is earned over the period, assets (as the denominator) should be reflective of this same time frame.

Data for the Dinah Corporation (Exhibit 15–9) for 1994 are used to illustrate return on investment computations. The company has three investment centers located in Atlanta, Hartford, and Seattle.

Return on investment computations (using a variety of bases) for the Dinah Corporation investment centers are shown in Exhibit 15–10. Note that average assets cannot be used, as only one balance sheet figure was provided. This exhibit illustrates

EXHIBIT 15–10
▼▼▼▼▼▼▼▼▼▼▼▼▼

DINAH CORPORATION ROI COMPUTATIONS

	Atlanta		Hartford		Seattle	
Operating Income	$ 338,000		$ 296,000		$ 2,316,000	
Assets Utilized	$2,526,550		$ 845,500		$ 9,990,000	
ROI		13.4%		35.0%		23.2%
Operating Income	$ 338,000		$ 296,000		$ 2,316,000	
Asset Current Value	$2,566,250		$1,240,000		$ 9,200,000	
ROI		13.2%		23.9%		25.2%
Segment Income	$ 494,000		$ 396,000		$ 3,060,000	
Total Assets	$9,286,250		$1,015,000		$12,455,000	
ROI		5.3%		39.0%		24.6%
Segment Income	$ 494,000		$ 396,000		$ 3,060,000	
Asset Book Value	$2,746,250		$ 890,000		$ 9,990,000	
ROI		18.0%		44.5%		30.6%
Segment Income	$ 494,000		$ 396,000		$ 3,060,000	
Asset Current Value	$2,566,250		$1,240,000		$ 9,200,000	
ROI		19.2%		31.9%		33.3%
Segment Income	$ 494,000		$ 396,000		$ 3,060,000	
Net Assets	$1,546,250		$ 565,000		$ 5,730,000	
ROI		31.9%		70.1%		53.4%

that ROI figures, and sometimes the rankings, differ dramatically depending on the definitions used for the terms in the formula. Therefore, the way in which the numerator and denominator in the ROI computation are to be determined must be precisely specified before making computations or comparisons.

The return on investment formula can be restated to provide useful information about individual factors that compose the rate of return. This restatement is referred to as the **Du Pont model,** which indicates that ROI is affected by both profit margin and asset turnover. **Profit margin** is the percentage of income to sales. This percentage indicates what proportion of each sales dollar is not used for expenses and, thus, becomes profit. **Asset turnover** measures asset productivity and shows the number of sales dollars generated by each dollar of assets. The restatement of the ROI formula in terms of its component elements is:

Du Pont model

profit margin

asset turnover

$$\text{ROI} = \text{Profit Margin} \times \text{Asset Turnover}$$
$$= \frac{\text{Income}}{\text{Sales}} \times \frac{\text{Sales}}{\text{Assets Invested}}$$

Use of component elements in the ROI formula provides refined information about opportunities for improvement by an investment center. Profit margin can be used to judge operating leverage or management's efficiency in regard to the relationship between sales and expenses. Asset turnover can be used to judge marketing leverage in regard to the effectiveness of asset use to revenue production.

Calculations showing the ROI components using the Dinah Corporation information are given in Exhibit 15–11. The calculations are provided using segment income and total historical cost asset valuation rather than the other alternatives.

Assessments about whether profit margin, asset turnover, and return on investment are favorable or unfavorable can be made only by comparing actual results for each component with some valid basis. Bases of comparison include expected results, prior results, or results of other similar entities.

EXHIBIT 15–11
▼▼▼▼▼▼▼▼▼▼▼▼▼▼

DINAH
CORPORATION ROI
COMPONENTS

Atlanta Investment Center:
ROI = (Income ÷ Sales) × (Sales ÷ Assets)
    = ($494,000 ÷ $1,350,000) × ($1,350,000 ÷ $9,286,250)
    = .366 × .145
    = 5.3%

Hartford Investment Center:
ROI = (Income ÷ Sales) × (Sales ÷ Assets)
    = ($396,000 ÷ $860,000) × ($860,000 ÷ $1,015,000)
    = .46 × .847
    = 39%

Seattle Investment Center:
ROI = (Income ÷ Sales) × (Sales ÷ Assets)
    = ($3,060,000 ÷ $6,400,000) × ($6,400,000 ÷ $12,455,000)
    = .478 × .514
    = 24.6%

It appears that the Hartford investment center has an extremely high asset turn-over rate at 84.7 times. Examination reveals that, based on the proportions of accumulated depreciation to plant assets, Hartford is also the center with the newest assets. The Atlanta center seems to have fairly old plant assets because the relationship of accumulated depreciation to historical cost (shown in Exhibit 15–9) is high. (This relationship could also have been created by using an accelerated depreciation method.) This center's plant assets are not generating substantial sales dollars relative to the asset base. The Atlanta investment center manager might consider purchasing more modern facilities to generate more sales dollars and greater profits. Such an acquisition could, however, cause ROI to decline, since the asset base would be increased. Rate of return computations encourage managers to retain and use old plant assets to keep ROIs high as long as those assets are effective in keeping revenues up and expenses down. This type of encouragement is obviously a problem when ROI is used as the sole performance criterion.

Many companies establish target rates of return either for the company or, alternatively, for the division based on the nature of the industry or market in which that division operates. Favorable results should promote rewards to investment center managers. Unfavorable rates of return should be viewed as managerial opportunities for improvement, and factors used in the computation should be analyzed for more information. For example, if asset turnover is low, additional calculations can be made for inventory turnover, accounts receivable turnover, and level of machine utilization time. Such calculations should help to indicate to the manager the direction of the problem(s) involved so that causes may be determined and adjustments made.

ROI is affected by decisions involving sales prices, volume and mix of products sold, expenses, and capital asset acquisitions and dispositions. Return on investment can possibly be increased through various management options including: (1) improving profit margins by raising sales prices without impairing demand; (2) decreasing expenses; and (3) decreasing dollars invested in assets, especially if those assets are no longer productive. Managerial action should be taken only after considering all the interrelationships that determine ROI. A change in one of the component elements will affect many of the others.

Another performance measurement often used for investment centers is its amount of residual income.

Residual Income

An investment center's **residual income** (RI) is the income earned that exceeds an amount "charged" for funds committed to the center. The amount charged for funds is equal to the asset base multiplied by a specified rate of return. The residual income computation is:

residual income

$$\text{Residual Income} = \text{Income} - (\text{Target Rate} \times \text{Asset Base})$$

Top management establishes a minimum acceptable rate of return against which the investment center's ROI can be judged. This target rate is comparable to an imputed rate of interest on the assets used by the division. The rate can be changed from period to period consistent with market rate fluctuations or to compensate for risk.

The advantage of residual income over return on investment is that RI is concerned with a dollar figure rather than a percentage. It would always be to a company's advantage to obtain new assets if they would earn more dollars of return than the dollars required by the rate charged for the additional investment.

EXHIBIT 15–12
▼▼▼▼▼▼▼▼▼▼▼▼

DINAH
CORPORATION
RESIDUAL INCOME

Income − (Target Rate × Asset Base) = Residual Income

Atlanta:
$$\$\ 494{,}000 - .12(\$\ 9{,}286{,}250) = \$\ 494{,}000 - \$1{,}114{,}350 = \$\ (620{,}350)$$

Hartford:
$$\$\ 396{,}000 - .12(\$\ 1{,}015{,}000) = \$\ 396{,}000 - \$\ 121{,}800 = \$\ 274{,}200$$

Seattle:
$$\$3{,}060{,}000 - .12(\$12{,}455{,}000) = \$3{,}060{,}000 - \$1{,}494{,}600 = \$1{,}565{,}400$$

Continuing the Dinah Corporation example, residual income is calculated for each of the investment centers. Dinah has established 12 percent on total assets as the target rate of return on assets invested and has defined income as segment income. The RI calculations are shown in Exhibit 15–12.

The Atlanta investment center's residual income computation indicates that income is being significantly underproduced relative to the asset investment. The division manager should be informed of the problem, so that investigations can be made to discover the cause of the problem and take steps to correct it. The other investment centers show positive residual incomes. Expansion (or additional investments in assets) could occur in all of these centers as long as positive residual income is expected on the additional investments.

One difficulty in using residual income as a performance measure is that it is difficult to make comparisons among divisions of various sizes. Larger divisions should, simply because of their size, have larger residual incomes. One evaluative criterion in such a case should be budgeted residual income by organizational unit.

As mentioned earlier, performance should be evaluated using several measures rather than a single one. Each performance measure has certain limitations. The following section addresses some limitations that should be considered when return on investment and residual income are used as performance measures.

LIMITATIONS OF RETURN ON INVESTMENT AND RESIDUAL INCOME

Return on investment and residual income have three primary limitations. The first limitation of these measures is, itself, a triple problem related to income. Income can be manipulated on a short-run basis. This possibility was previously explained in regard to the use of divisional profit as a performance measure. Income also depends on the accounting methods used, such as inventory cost flow or depreciation. For perfectly valid ROI and RI comparisons to be made among investment centers, all centers would have to use the same accounting methods. Finally, income is based on accrual accounting, which some analysts believe limits the usefulness of ROI and RI. Accrual accounting may not always provide the best basis for evaluating investment center performance because it does not consider the pattern of cash flows or the time value of money.

The second limitation is also a triple problem related to the asset base on which both measures rely. Asset investment is difficult to properly measure and assign to center managers. Some expenditures are made that have value beyond the accounting period but, for accounting purposes, are not capitalized (for example, R&D costs).[11] Also, assets included in the investment base might be the result of decisions made by previous investment center managers. Thus, current managers can potentially be judged on investment decisions over which they have or had no control. Third, "[w]hen fixed assets and inventory are not restated for [rising] price level changes after acquisition, net income is overstated and investment is understated. Thus managers who retain older, mostly depreciated assets [often] report much higher ROIs than managers who invest in new assets." [12]

The third limitation of these measures is a potentially critical problem. Use of ROI and RI may motivate suboptimal managerial behavior. Suboptimization exists when individual managers pursue goals and objectives that are in their own and their segments' particular interests rather than in the best interests of the company. Investment center managers must remember that their operations are integral parts of the corporate structure. Therefore, all actions taken should be in the best long-run interest of both the investment center and the organization. Subunit managers should be aware of and accept the need for goal congruence throughout the entity.

Unfortunately, the use of ROI and RI focuses attention on how well an investment center performs in the short run and does not consider how well that investment center performs in regard to the entity's long-run objectives. Such a focus can result in a suboptimization of resources, meaning that the firm is not maximizing its operational effectiveness and efficiency.

The Regan Division of Extendo Corporation is used to illustrate the effects of suboptimization. Regan has revenues of $2,300,000, expenses of $940,000, and an asset base of $7,000,000. ROI for the division is 19.4 percent ($1,360,000 ÷ $7,000,000). Regan Division has an opportunity to increase income by $195,000 from sales of a new product, which requires an additional $1,120,000 capital investment. Considered separately, this venture would result in a return on investment of 17.4 percent ($195,000 ÷ $1,120,000). If Regan Division acts on this opportunity, the divisional return on investment will decrease slightly, as shown below:

$$\text{ROI} = \frac{\$1,360,000 + \$195,000}{\$7,000,000 + \$1,120,000} = \frac{\$1,555,000}{\$8,120,000}$$

$$= 19.15 \% \text{ (rounded)}$$

If top management evaluates investment centers' managers on the ROIs of their divisions, the Regan Division manager would choose not to accept this investment opportunity.

If, however, Extendo has a target rate of return of 16 percent on investment dollars, the decision by Regan's manager to reject the new opportunity suboptimizes companywide returns. This project should have been accepted since it provides a return higher than the firm's target rate and the division's residual income would increase (see Exhibit 15–13). Top management should be informed of such opportuni-

---

[11]Use of life cycle accounting, as discussed in chapter 4, could help to eliminate this problem.
[12]Robert S. Kaplan, "Yesterday's Accounting Undermines Production" *Harvard Business Review* (July–August 1984), p. 99.

EXHIBIT 15–13
▼▼▼▼▼▼▼▼▼▼▼▼

REGAN DIVSION
RESIDUAL INCOME
CALCULATION

Residual Income without New Investment
RI = ($2,300,000 − $940,000) − .16 ($7,000,000)
  = $1,360,000 − $1,120,000
  = $240,000

Residual Income with New Investment
RI = ($1,360,000 + $195,000) − .16($7,000,000 + $1,120,000)
  = $1,555,000 − $1,299,200
  = $255,800

EXHIBIT 15–14
▼▼▼▼▼▼▼▼▼▼▼▼

PERFORMANCE
MEASURES TO LIMIT
SUBOPTIMIZATION

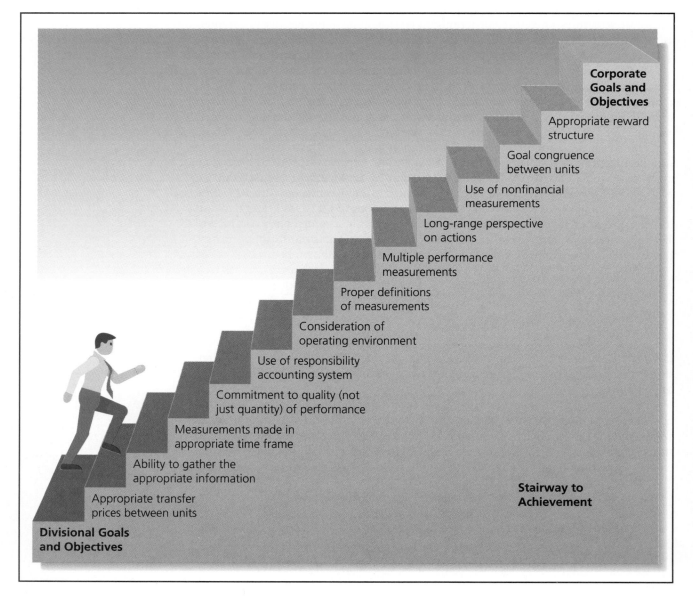

Corporate Goals and Objectives

Appropriate reward structure

Goal congruence between units

Use of nonfinancial measurements

Long-range perspective on actions

Multiple performance measurements

Proper definitions of measurements

Consideration of operating environment

Use of responsibility accounting system

Commitment to quality (not just quantity) of performance

Measurements made in appropriate time frame

Ability to gather the appropriate information

Appropriate transfer prices between units

Divisional Goals and Objectives

Stairway to Achievement

ties, made aware of the effects that acceptance would have on divisional performance measurements, and be willing to reward such project acceptance based on its impact on company performance.

After recognizing that suboptimization can occur, a primary way managers can try to limit it is by communicating corporate goals to all organizational units, regardless of the types of responsibility centers. Other ways to limit suboptimization effects are depicted in Exhibit 15–14 as stairsteps to the achievement of corporate goals. These steps are not in a hierarchical order. If any steps are missing, the climb toward corporate goals and objectives becomes more difficult for divisional managers.

PERFORMANCE EVALUATION IN MULTINATIONAL SETTINGS

Many large, decentralized companies are involved in overseas operations. Upper-level managers, in attempting to measure and evaluate such operations, often focus on income as the primary criterion for all subunits, regardless of their locales. Such a single focus is not appropriate for comparing domestic responsibility centers, and it is extremely inappropriate for multinational segments.

Income comparisons between multinational units may be invalid because of material differences in trade tariffs and income tax rates between countries, currency fluctuations of a country, and the possibility of restrictions on the transfer of goods or currency from a country. In addition, within the constraints of moral and social responsibility, managers may be able to transfer goods between segments at prices that minimize profits or tariffs in locations where taxes are high by shifting profits or cost values to more advantageous climates from a tax or tariff perspective. As the following News Note indicates, transfer pricing *abuses* are illegal.

Companies operating in multinational settings must be concerned about host country laws, income tax rates, and currency fluctuations. All of these items can affect the performance of the international segment and the evaluation of that segment's manager.

NEWS NOTE

Use Transfer Prices—But Don't Abuse Them

By manipulating the prices charged among their own subsidiaries, the multinationals can concentrate profits in countries with low corporate rates and thus get away with a smaller total tax bite. Abuses in pricing across borders—"transfer pricing," in corporate jargon—are illegal, if they can be proved. Corporations dealing with their own subsidiaries are required to set prices at "arm's length," just as they would for unrelated customers. And there's no question that abuses can be enormous. In its biggest known victory, the IRS made its case that Japan's Toyota had been systematically overcharging its U.S. subsidiary for years on most of the cars, trucks and parts sold in the United States. What would have been profits from the United States had wafted back to Japan. Toyota denied improprieties but agreed to a reported $1 billion settlement, paid in part with tax rebates from the government of Japan.

SOURCE: Larry Martz and Rich Thomas, "The Corporate Shell Game," *Newsweek* (April 15, 1991), p. 48.

U.S. firms having multinational profit or investment centers (or subsidiaries) must establish a flexible system of measuring profit performance for those units. Such a system should recognize that income may be based on amounts outside the control of the unit's manager. In such cases, qualitative factors may become significantly more useful.

Performance evaluations can include measures such as market share increases, quality improvements and related customer satisfaction, waste and defect reduction, on-time delivery, processing or cycle time, establishment of just-in-time inventory systems with the related reduction in working capital, and new product development. Some of these same factors have been presented in the stairsteps of Exhibit 15–14. Another important factor in measuring performance is the throughput of an organizational unit.

THROUGHPUT AS A PERFORMANCE MEASURE

throughput

The use of **throughput** as a performance indicator is gaining acceptability. Throughput refers to the number of good units or quantity of services that an organization produces and *sells* within a time period. The important part of this definition is that the company must sell the units and not simply produce them for inventory stockpiles. Since the goal of a profit-oriented organization is to make money, inventory must be sold for that goal to be achieved. All endeavors that help an organization

synchronous management

achieve its goal are considered to be **synchronous** (or synchronized) **management** techniques. "Synchronous management's strategic objective is to simultaneously increase throughput, while reducing inventory and operating expenses." [13]

[13]Victor Lippa, "Measuring Performance with Synchronous Management," *Management Accounting* (February 1990), p. 54.

One way to measure throughput is to view it as made up of component elements similar to the expanded rate of return formula. Those component elements are productive capacity, productive processing time, and yield.[14]

$$\frac{\text{Productive}}{\text{Capacity}} \times \frac{\text{Productive}}{\text{Processing Time}} \times \frac{\text{Process}}{\text{Yield}} = \text{Throughput}$$

$$\frac{\text{Total Units}}{\text{Processing Time}} \times \frac{\text{Processing Time}}{\text{Total Time}} \times \frac{\text{Good Units}}{\text{Total Units}} = \frac{\text{Good Units}}{\text{Total Time}}$$

The total units that could be produced based on the equipment available during a period is called **productive capacity.** This measure assumes that all units that were started could have been completed, and ignores downtime and spoiled units.

productive capacity

The amount of total time from beginning to completion of production or service performance that is value-added is called **productive processing time.** (Value-added time indicates that activities took place that increased the worth of the product to the customer.) A useful performance measure in regard to value-added inventory production time is **dollar days,** which measures the value of inventory and the time that inventory stays in an area. Dollar days of inventory "treats inventory as a loan from the bank." [15] To illustrate how this measure is calculated, assume that $25,000 of inventory enters Department 1 and stays there four days. Department 1 would be charged with $100,000 dollar days of inventory. If the inventory remains in Department 1 because of a bottleneck, the manager is made more aware of the cost of having that bottleneck and is motivated to take actions to reduce the dollar days cost assigned to the department. Measuring dollar days is also useful in nonmanufacturing areas. In marketing, the concept could be used to encourage prompt sale of finished goods inventory; in purchasing, dollar days could be used to encourage the use of just-in-time purchasing techniques.

productive processing time

dollar days

Production activities serve to produce both good and defective units. The proportion of good units that resulted from the activities expended is the **process yield.** This measure reflects the quality of the production process. Thus, if 10,000 units were produced during a period and 9,500 of those were good units, the company would have had a 95 percent process yield for the period.

process yield

Throughput can be increased by increasing the productive capacity, decreasing the unit processing time (which would increase the productive processing time), and/ or increasing yield. One useful way to measure performance is to determine how well the company's goal of increasing profits is being met by having rapid and high-quality throughput.

Using the following information, throughput and its elements for Glawor, Inc., are computed for 1994:

Total units processed	500,000
Good units	472,000
Processing time	1,200,000 hours
Total time available	1,420,000 hours

[14]These terms and formulae are based on Carole Cheatham's "Measuring and Improving Throughput," *Journal of Accountancy* (March 1990), pp. 89–91. One assumption that must be made in regard to this model is that the quantity labeled "throughput" is sold.
[15]Robert E. Fox, "Coping with Today's Technology: Is Cost Accounting Keeping Up?" *Cost Accounting for the 90s* (Montvale, N.J.: National Association of Accountants, 1986), p. 21.

$$\frac{\text{Productive}}{\text{Capacity}} \times \frac{\text{Productive}}{\text{Processing Time}} \times \frac{\text{Process}}{\text{Yield}} = \text{Throughput}$$

$$\frac{500,000}{1,200,000} \times \frac{1,200,000}{1,420,000} \times \frac{472,000}{500,000} = \frac{472,000}{1,420,000}$$

$$.4167 \times .8451 \times .944 = .3324$$

Throughput for Glawor, Inc., for 1994 was slightly better than one-third of a unit per hour, or one unit every three hours.

SITE ANALYSIS

Changing performance measurement systems is a difficult task—one that requires significant employee involvement. At Alcoa, experts say that the key to the plan "is to encourage entrepreneurship without causing chaos." [16] Mr. O'Neill has eliminated the position of corporate president and has, instead, instituted "three executive vice presidents who would, along with headquarters staff, advise but not direct the presidents of Alcoa's 25 businesses." [17] Each divisional president has the authority to spend a maximum of $5 million; funding requests go directly to Mr. O'Neill—not to the three executive VPs. Mr. O'Neill's contention is that, when divisional presidents send in requests for funding approval, the appropriate investigation has been made to determine the legitimacy and justification of the need for funding.

Company divisions are attempting to cut costs, produce higher returns on investment, shorten product development times, and establish joint ventures with foreign partners. While most Alcoa executives say that the changes were needed, other managers are afraid that there might be significant suboptimization and confusion.

> The result could be business units under cutting each other and a fragmented company without a cohesive strategy for building and shrinking businesses. Alcoa must be sure, for example, that its fabricating units don't spurn their Alcoa counterparts and buy metal from rivals, and that Alcoa's raw material businesses don't call for production halts that would cut off supplies to other business units. [18]

Mr. O'Neill intends to keep such problems from occurring by requiring weekly reports on business activities and rewarding managers only for actions that are beneficial to the entire company. He has also set a target rate of 15 percent return on equity for each business enterprise. Only time will tell whether the new structure has accomplished its objectives of pushing power down the organizational ladder.

Some applications of organizational structure and performance evaluation follow.

---

[16] Dana Milbank, "Changes at Alcoa Point Up Challenges and Benefits of Decentralized Authority," *Wall Street Journal* (November 7, 1991), pp. B1, B5.
[17] Ibid., p. B5.
[18] Ibid.

Discipline	Applications
Accounting	Provide accurate, prompt information for performance evaluations; provide nonmonetary and nontraditional measures of operation; help managers in developing the degree of detail provided in responsibility reports
Economics	Addressing critical success factors can help determine resource allocations and reward systems; understand the economic diversity among foreign subsidiaries to develop appropriate performance measures
Finance	Responsibility reporting is essential to determining the financial needs of individual operations
Management	Need to recognize potential limitations of single performance measures and that financial performance measures can be manipulated; need to develop both monetary and nonmonetary performance measures; use of transfer prices for service departments can make those departments profit or investment centers rather than cost centers and provide more performance measurements; responsibility reports emphasize management by exception; attempt to limit suboptimization in decentralized units
Marketing	Decentralization allows quicker decisions about pricing, product line development, advertising, etc.; responsibility reports provide detailed information about marketing area costs; knowledge of desired ROI (and other organizational objectives) can impact the setting of prices and deciding what market segments to pursue

APPLICATIONS STRATEGIES OF ORGANIZATIONAL STRUCTURE AND PERFORMANCE EVALUATION

CHAPTER SUMMARY

Centralization refers to having management control at high organizational levels, while decentralization refers to the downward delegation of decision-making authority to subunit managers. Thus, a decentralized organization is composed of operational units led by managers who have some autonomy in decision making. The degree to which a company is decentralized depends on top management philosophy and the unit managers' abilities to perform independently. Decentralization provides the opportunity for managers to develop leadership qualities, creative problem-solving abilities, and decision-making skills. It also lets the individual most closely in tune with the operational unit and its immediate environment make the decisions for that unit and reduces the time spent in communicating and making decisions.

In a decentralized structure, subunit managers are partially evaluated using responsibility reports. Responsibility reports reflect the upward flow of information from each decentralized unit to the top of the organization. Managers receive information regarding the activities under their immediate control and under the control of their direct subordinates. The information is successively aggregated, and the reports allow the application of the management by exception principle.

Responsibility centers are classified as cost, revenue, profit, or investment centers. Each classification reflects the degree of authority managers have for financial items within their subunit. The type of responsibility center also affects the kind of performance measurements that can be used for the center and its manager.

Two major financial measures of performance for investment centers are return on investment and residual income. ROI is net income divided by invested assets. RI is the amount of net income in excess of income calculated by using an imputed interest charge on the asset base. While both measures provide important information about the efficiency and effectiveness of managers, neither should be used alone nor without recognizing the limitations inherent in the measure.

Top management should recognize that when profit and investment centers exist, there is a possibility of suboptimization of resources. Performance measurements should be designed so that all subunit managers work toward the maximization of organizational goals and objectives.

Performance measures of multinational units may be more difficult to establish than those of domestic units because of differences in taxes, tariffs, currency exchange rates, and transfer restrictions. Top management may wish to consider extending the use of qualitative performance measures because of such differences.

One important nonfinancial measure of performance is throughput, or the goods or services started and sold by an organization during a period. When throughput is increased, the company goal of financial success is enhanced.

APPENDIX

Performance Measurement Areas and Cost Drivers

Exhibit 15–15 provides information from a joint study by the National Association of Accountants (now the Institute of Management Accountants) and the international accounting firm of Coopers & Lybrand. The exhibit indicates some activity cost drivers that could be measured to determine performance in the six specified areas. Many of these cost drivers and performance measures are affected by or, possibly, are direct outcomes of operating in a just-in-time environment.

GLOSSARY

Asset turnover   a ratio that measures asset productivity and shows the number of sales dollars generated by each dollar of assets

Centralization   an organizational structure in which top management makes most decisions and controls most activities of the organizational units from the company's central headquarters

Cost center   a responsibility center in which the manager only has the authority to incur costs and is specifically evaluated on the basis of how well costs are controlled

Critical success factors   those items that are so important to a company that, without them, the company would fail; typically include quality, customer service, efficiency, cost control, and responsiveness to change as five basic success factors

Decentralization   an organizational structure in which top management grants subordinate managers a significant degree of autonomy and independence in operating and making decisions for their organizational units

EXHIBIT 15–15
▼▼▼▼▼▼▼▼▼▼▼▼

PERFORMANCE
MEASUREMENTS

Performance Measurement Area: **Design for Manufacturability**

Key Characteristics	*Cost Drivers/Measures*
Quantity and quality of engineering changes	Number of engineering changes
	Severity of engineering changes
Test results	First pass reject rate
	Materials used versus design specification
	Manufacturing skills required
Part standardization	Number of products
	Percentage of common parts per product
Engineering cycle time	Lead time to engineer (design) a finished product
	Start-up time from design to production
Product complexity	Number of components per finished product
	Number of manufacturing operations per finished product
	Number of tools required per finished product

Performance Measurement Area: **Zero Defects**

Key Characteristics	*Cost Drivers/Measures*
Product specification	Tolerances of critical components
	Historical capability of process versus current performance
Parts quality	First pass reject rate versus test results
	Units scrapped by cell
	Cell downtime caused by quality problems
	Yield of finished product per raw material batch
	Units reworked by cell
Quality control checkpoints	Sampling requirements for incoming materials
	Time required for sample/test procedures
	Production time loss caused by quality control procedures/queues
	Number of checkpoints
	Effectiveness—number of returned units

Performance Measurement Area: **Minimize Raw and In Process Inventory**

Key Characteristics	*Cost Drivers/Measures*
Supplier performance	Number and location of vendors
	Number/frequency of deliveries
	Lead time from order initiation to delivery
	Flexibility in order quantity, delivery, and variety
Component standardization	Complexity of components
	Number of components to support total production
Market characteristics	Demand variation
	Forecast accuracy
	Availability/accuracy of information

(continued)

Performance Measurement Area: Zero Lead Time

Key Characteristics	Cost Drivers/Measures
Velocity of units through cell	Actual production time
	Queue time between operations
	Move, setup, and inspection times
	Value-added time percentage
Quality of components	Scrap percentage
	Rework percentage
	Yield percentage
Customer service levels	Late deliveries
	On-time deliveries
	Back orders
	Canceled orders
Complexity of flow	Mix of products
	New product introductions
	Routing required per product

Performance Measurement Area: Minimize Process Time

Key Characteristics	Cost Drivers/Measures
Product design	Number of components
Complexity	Number of manufacturing procedures/steps
Tolerance	Required tolerance versus matching optimum
Materials	Maximum tolerance range per component
Producibility	Quality of components
	Availability/ease of use
	Skills necessary to meet engineering requirements
Process capabilities and limitations	Information system capabilities
	Plant layout: optimum versus current
	Work rules: percentage changed

Performance Measurement Area: Optimize Production

Key Characteristics	Cost Drivers/Measures
Resource limitations	Bottleneck capacity level
	Setup time
	Lot size constraints
	Labor availability, qualifications, flexibility
	Material resources (e.g., availability, lead time, quality, proximity)
	Number of distribution centers
	Number of storerooms
Demand fluctuation	Volume variations (total units produced)
	Mix changes (number and magnitude)
	Schedule changes (number and magnitude)
Configuration of plant	Plant layout (e.g., move time, move distance, number of total moves)
Information processing constraints	Information accuracy and availability
	Data accuracy in planning execution (routing, bills, standards)

SOURCE: C. J. McNair, William Mosconi, and Thomas Norris, *Meeting the Technology Challenge: Cost Accounting in a JIT Environment* (Montvale, N.J.: IMA, 1988), pp. 199–210. Copyright by Institute of Management Accountants (formerly National Association of Accountants), Montvale, N.J.

Dollar days   a performance measure that multiplies the value of inventory by the time that inventory remains in an area and, essentially, assigns a charge for that amount to the area manager

Du Pont model   a restatement of the return on investment formula that multiplies profit margin by asset turnover

Goal congruence   a condition that exists when the personal and organizational goals of decision makers throughout a firm are consistent and mutually supportive

Investment center   an organizational unit in which the manager is responsible for generating revenues, planning and controlling costs, and acquiring, disposing of, and using plant assets to earn the highest feasible rate of return on the investment base

Process yield   the proportion of good units that resulted from the activities expended

Productive capacity   the total units that could be produced during a period from value-added processing time on the equipment available

Productive processing time   the proportion of total processing time that is value-added

Profit center   an organizational unit in which managers are responsible for generating revenues and planning and controlling all expenses

Profit margin   the percentage of income to sales

Residual income   the profit earned that exceeds an amount charged for funds committed to the center

Responsibility accounting   an accounting system that provides information to top management about segment or subunit performance

Responsibility center   the cost object under the control of a manager; in the case of a decentralized company, the cost object is an organizational unit such as a division, department, or geographical region

Responsibility reports   reports that reflect the revenues and/or costs under the control of a specific unit manager

Return on investment   a ratio that relates income generated by the investment center to the resources (or asset base) used to produce that income; income divided by assets invested

Revenue center   an organizational unit for which a manager is accountable only for the generation of revenues and has no control over setting selling prices or budgeting costs

Segment margin   an amount equal to segment sales minus (direct variable expenses and avoidable fixed expenses)

Suboptimization   a situation in which unit managers make decisions that positively affect their own units, but are detrimental to other organizational units or to the company as a whole

Synchronous management   a technique that has the strategic objective to simultaneously increase throughput while reducing inventory and operating expenses; includes all techniques that help an organization achieve its goal(s)

Throughput   the number of good units or quantity of services that an organization produces and sells within a time period

SELECTED BIBLIOGRAPHY

Ballanger, Ned B. "Developing a Performance Appraisal System." *Management Accounting* (September 1990), pp. 52–54.

Dearden, John. "Measuring Profit Center Managers." *Harvard Business Review* (September–October 1987), pp. 84–88.

Eccles, Robert G. "The Performance Measurement Manifesto." *Harvard Business Review* (January–February 1991), pp. 131–37.

Green, F. B., et al., "Performance Measures and JIT." *Management Accounting* (February 1991), pp. 50–53.

Greene, Alica H., and Peter Flentov. "Managing Performance: Maximizing the Benefit of Activity-Based Costing." *Journal of Cost Management for the Manufacturing Industry* (Summer 1990), pp. 50–59.

Harr, David J., and James T. Godfrey. "Making Government Profitable," *Management Accounting* (February 1992), pp. 52–57.

Kanter, Rosabeth Moss. "The New Managerial Work." *Harvard Business Review* (November–December 1989), pp. 85–92.

Kaplan, Robert S. "Measures for Manufacturing Excellence." *Journal of Cost Management for the Manufacturing Industry* (Fall 1990), pp. 22–29.

Lippa, Victor. "Measuring Performance with Synchronous Management." *Management Accounting* (February 1990), pp. 54–59.

Ostrenga, Michael R. "Return on Investment through the Cost of Quality." *Journal of Cost Management for the Manufacturing Industry* (Summer 1991), pp. 37–44.

Schaffer, Robert H. "Demand Better Results—And Get Them." *Harvard Business Review* (March–April 1991), pp. 142–49.

Sellenheim, Michael R. "Performance Measurement." *Management Accounting* (September 1991), pp. 50–53.

Sellers, Patricia. "Does the CEO Really Matter?" *FORTUNE* (April 22, 1991), pp. 80–82ff.

Son, Young K. "A Performance Measurement Method Which Remedies the 'Productivity Paradox'." *Production and Inventory Management Journal* 31, no. 2 (1990), pp. 38–43.

Stewart, Thomas A. "The Search for the Organization of Tomorrow." *FORTUNE* (May 18, 1992), pp. 92–98.

Walsh, Francis J. *Measuring Business-Unit Performance: Research Bulletin #206* (New York: The Conference Board, 1987).

Wanner, David L., and Richard W. Leer. "Managing for Shareholder Value—From Top to Bottom." *Harvard Business Review* (November–December 1989), pp. 52–60.

SOLUTION STRATEGIES

Performance Measurements for Responsibility Centers

- Cost Center

  Budgeted costs
  − Actual costs
  Variances (consider materiality)

- Revenue Center

    Budgeted revenues
    − Actual revenues
    Variances (consider materiality)

- Profit Center

    Budgeted divisional profits
    − Actual divisional profits
    Variances (consider materiality)

    Cash inflows
    − Cash outflows
    Net cash flow (adequate for operations?)

- Investment Center

    Budgeted investment center profits
    − Actual investment center profits
    Variances (consider materiality)

    Cash inflows
    − Cash outflows
    Net cash flow (adequate for operations?)

    Return on Investment = Income ÷ Assets Invested
            (high enough rate?)

Du Pont model:
ROI = Net Margin × Asset Turnover

    = (Net Income ÷ Sales) (Sales ÷ Average Total Assets)
            (high enough rate?)

Residual Income = Income − (Target Rate × Asset Base)

OR

Residual Income = Asset Base × (ROI − Target Rate)
            (positive or negative?; high enough amount?)

Measuring Throughput

$$\frac{\text{Productive}}{\text{Capacity}} \times \frac{\text{Productive}}{\text{Processing Time}} \times \frac{\text{Process}}{\text{Yield}} = \text{Throughput}$$

$$\frac{\text{Total Units}}{\text{Processing Time}} \times \frac{\text{Processing Time}}{\text{Total Time}} \times \frac{\text{Good Units}}{\text{Total Units}} = \frac{\text{Good Units}}{\text{Total Time}}$$

DEMONSTRATION PROBLEM

One of several operating divisions of the Global Technology Company is the Engineered Instruments Division. Engineered Instruments produces and sells various pieces of equipment (such as temperature and pressure sensors, X-ray technology, and lasers) that are used to monitor and control the quality of production processes. The division and its management are evaluated by senior corporate executives based on investment center concepts. The following is information pertaining to operations of the Engineered Instruments Division for 1993:

Total revenues	$42,500,000
Direct variable costs	17,500,000
Direct fixed costs	15,000,000
Allocated corporate costs	7,875,000
Allocated corporate income taxes	0

	Book Values		Current Market Values	
	12/31/92	*12/31/93*	*12/31/92*	*12/31/93*
Current assets	$ 2,500,000	$ 3,600,000		
Fixed assets	20,500,000	23,400,000		
Accumulated depreciation	(2,500,000)	(3,500,000)		
Total assets	$20,500,000	$23,500,000	$19,000,000	$21,000,000
Liabilities	6,000,000	7,000,000		

Required:

For the 1993 operations of the Engineered Instruments Division, compute:

1. the segment income and operating income.
2. the profit margin, asset turnover, and ROI based on operating income and the book value of average total assets.
3. the ROI based on segment income and average current asset value.
4. the residual income based on operating income and the book value of average net assets. Assume the target rate of return is 10 percent.

Solution to Demonstration Problem

1.
Total revenue	$42,500,000
Direct variable costs	(17,500,000)
Direct fixed costs	(15,000,000)
Segment income	$10,000,000
Allocated costs	(7,875,000)
Operating income	$ 2,125,000

2. Profit margin $= \dfrac{\$2,125,000}{\$42,500,000} = 5\%$

Asset turnover $= \dfrac{\$42,500,000}{(\$20,500,000\ +\ \$23,500,000)\ \div\ 2} = 1.932$

ROI $= 1.932 \times 5\% = 9.66\%$

3. $\text{ROI} = \dfrac{\$10,000,000}{(\$19,000,000 \ + \ \$21,000,000) \ \div \ 2} = 50\%$

4. First determine the value of net assets:

	12/31/92	12/31/93
Total assets	$20,500,000	$23,500,000
Less liabilities	(6,000,000)	(7,000,000)
Net assets	$14,500,000	$16,500,000

Next determine target return and subtract from operating income:

Operating income	$ 2,125,000
Target return [($14,500,000 + $16,500,000) ÷ 2] × .10	(1,550,000)
Residual income	$ 575,000

END-OF-CHAPTER MATERIALS

Questions

1. Would a very young company, or a large mature company, be a more likely candidate to employ decentralized management? Explain.

2. The top managers at Global Manufacturing Company are pondering the possibility of decentralizing control of all foreign operating divisions. The firm has traditionally maintained very tight central control over these operations. What are some of the major costs of decentralization that Global's top managers should consider in making their decision?

3. Some activities in an organization are more likely to be decentralized than others. What activities are most likely to be decentralized? Least likely?

4. In evaluating performance, why is a segment manager's performance evaluated separately from the performance of the segment?

5. Are all managers equally suited to function in either a decentralized or centralized organization? Explain.

6. Describe the four types of responsibility centers. For each type, describe how performance can be measured.

7. What is the major role of responsibility accounting in decentralized organizations?

8. Describe how suboptimization is related to the performance measures that are used to evaluate segment managers and segment performance.

9. Consider the statement, "In a decentralized company, competition between segment managers should always be encouraged." Do you agree? Explain.

10. What is meant by the term *variance*, and how are variances used by managers in controlling the organization?

11. How is the philosophy of management by exception employed in responsibility accounting?

12. Is managerial performance always evaluated solely on financial measures? Explain.

13. In evaluating the performance of managers, how are the performance measures related to the scope of authority of the manager?

14. Which type of responsibility center would be evaluated based on a residual income measure?

15. What is the Du Pont model? Describe each of the two ratios that make up the Du Pont model.

16. Why is performance often evaluated based on cash flow measures as well as accrual-based accounting measures?

17. List two quantitative, but nonfinancial, measures that could be used to evaluate the quality of the performance of the outpatient care division of a major public hospital. Why would these measures be useful?

18. What is throughput and how is it measured?

19. What is the primary objective of synchronous management techniques? Why is this objective important?

Exercises

20. *(Centralized vs. decentralized control)* Each of the following independent descriptions characterizes some trait of an organization. For each description, indicate whether the firm would be more likely to adopt a centralized (C) or decentralized (D) control structure.

   a. The firm is growing very rapidly.
   b. The firm has just been established.
   c. The firm's entrepreneurial CEO is the firm's founder and wants to maintain involvement in all aspects of the business.
   d. The firm's operations span the globe. Many of the foreign divisions have operations that are very sensitive to volatility in local economic conditions.
   e. Top management expresses sincere doubts about the capability of lower-level managers to make sound economic decisions.

21. *(Terminology)* Match each of the lettered items on the left with the number of the best matching item on the right.

   a. Centralized organization
   b. Return on investment
   c. Suboptimization
   d. Residual income
   e. Responsibility center
   f. Decentralized organization
   g. Cost center

   1. Decisions in this type of company are made by division managers
   2. Manager is primarily responsible for generating revenues, controlling costs, and managing assets
   3. Manager is primarily responsible for controlling operating costs
   4. Making decisions that may not be in the best interest of the entire firm
   5. Profit margin multiplied by asset turnover
   6. Profits that exceed a normal return on assets
   7. Manager is responsible for revenue generation and controlling operating costs

h. Investment center

i. Profit center

j. Revenue center

8. Manager is primarily responsible for revenue generation

9. The organizational cost object under the control of a manager

10. Decisions in this type of company are generally made by top management

22. *(ROI)* The managers of Marquette Ltd. are trying to calculate return on invested assets. The following information is available:

Average assets invested	$ 3,600,000
Revenues	13,200,000
Expenses	12,600,000

a. Calculate profit margin.
b. Calculate asset turnover.
c. Calculate return on investment in two different ways.

23. *(Missing numbers)* Your managerial accounting class has been assigned a case, but the teacher only provides partial information. You have been told that Cilantro Company has an ROI of 15 percent, average total assets of $1,860,000, and total expenses of $386,000. You have been asked to:

a. determine net income
b. determine revenues
c. determine asset turnover
d. determine net margin percentage
e. prove that ROI is 15 percent from the amounts calculated in parts (a) to (d).

24. *(ROI)* Hextel Company relies on a residual income measure to evaluate the performance of certain segment managers. The target rate of return for all segments is 12 percent. One segment, East Shore Engineering, generated net income of $800,000 for the year just ended. For the same period, East Shore's residual income was $320,000.

a. Compute the amount of average assets employed by East Shore Engineering.
b. Compute the return on investment for East Shore Engineering.

25. *(ROI)* Ramona Helpsmee owns the Hardlee Motel. She is uncertain whether she is doing well or poorly in her business and asks you to make some calculations that will help her understand her business's financial condition. The following information is available:

Assets, January 1, 1993	$280,000
Assets, December 31, 1993	364,000
1993 revenues	97,000
1993 expenses	60,000

Ramona has estimated that her variable expenses are 30 percent of total revenues; the remaining expenses are fixed.

a. Compute average assets for the year.
b. Compute the 1993 profit margin.
c. Compute the 1993 asset turnover.
d. Compute the 1993 return on investment.
e. Ramona thinks she could increase her revenues next year by 15 percent if she spent another $1,000 on advertising. Assuming no other changes, what would be her new rate of return?

26. *(Residual income)* Universe Enterprises operates with two investment centers. Following is some financial information about each of these investment centers:

	Satellite Division	Planet Division
Sales	$2,400,000	$4,200,000
Total variable costs	600,000	2,730,000
Total fixed cost	1,400,000	500,000
Average assets invested	2,200,000	6,100,000

a. What is each division's residual income if the company has established a 14 percent target rate of return on invested assets?
b. Which division is doing a better job?
c. What will each division's residual income be, assuming no changes other than a 10 percent increase in sales? Which division would be doing a better job at that time?
d. Explain why the answers to parts (b) and (c) differed or did not differ.

27. *(Missing numbers)* Fill in the missing numbers in the following three independent cases.

	Case #1	Case #2	Case #3
Revenue	$110,000	e	$104,167.50
Expenses	a	$135,000	$ 94,167.50
Net income	$ 40,000	$ 15,000	i
Average total assets	b	$ 50,000	$ 41,667.00
Asset turnover	.55	f	j
Profit margin	36.4%	g	9.6%
Achieved ROI	c	30%	k
Residual income	d	h	($833)
Expected ROI	14%	20%	l

28. *(Missing numbers)* XYZ Corporation has a target rate of return of 15 percent. X Division is analyzing a new investment that promises to generate an ROI of 25 percent and a residual income of $20,000.

a. What is the acquisition cost of the investment that X Division is considering?
b. What is the estimated net income from the new project?

29. *(Performance measures)* The Picket Company evaluates division managers based on the return they generate on division assets. For 1994, the North Division generated a segment margin of $500,000 on sales of $2,000,000 using an average asset base of $1,800,000. For the North Division for 1994, compute:

a. return on investment
b. asset turnover
c. profit margin
d. return on investment using the Du Pont model

30. *(Performance measures)* For the most recent fiscal year, the Business Software Division of Macro Company generated an asset turnover ratio of 6 and a profit margin (as measured by the segment margin) ratio of 3 percent on sales of $400,000. Compute:

a. average assets employed by Business Software
b. segment margin
c. return on investment

31. *(Performance measures)* Agracompany has a target rate of return of 10 percent for its Ranching Division. For 1993, the Ranching Division generated sales of $4,000,000 on average assets of $2,000,000. The Ranching Division's variable costs were 35 percent of sales, and fixed costs were $1,500,000. For 1993, compute the division's:

a. return on investment
b. residual income
c. profit margin
d. asset turnover

Problems

32. *(Responsibility reports)* To respond to increased competition and a reduction in profitability, a nationwide law firm, U.S. Law, recently instituted a responsibility accounting system. One of the several responsibility centers established was the Civil Litigation Division. This division is treated as a cost center for control purposes. In the first year (1994) after responsibility accounting was put in place at U.S. Law, the responsibility report for the Civil Litigation Division contained the following comparisons:

	Budgeted	Actual	Variance
Variable costs:			
Professional labor	$1,000,000	$ 940,000	$60,000 F
Travel	50,000	40,000	10,000 F
Supplies	100,000	90,000	10,000 F
Fixed costs:			
Professional labor	400,000	405,000	5,000 U
Facilities cost	250,000	265,000	15,000 U
Insurance	80,000	78,000	2,000 F
Totals	$1,880,000	$1,818,000	$62,000 F

For 1994, the Civil Litigation Division projected it would handle 1,000 cases. It actually processed 900 cases.

Required:

a. What are the major weaknesses in the responsibility report above?
b. Recast the responsibility report in a more meaningful format for cost control evaluation.
c. If U.S. Law utilizes a management by exception philosophy, which costs are likely to receive additional evaluation? Explain.

33. *(Evaluating variances)* On January 1, 1993, fast-tracker Michael Malicon was promoted to the production manager position in Salmon Company. The firm purchases raw fish, cooks and processes the fish, and then cans the fish in single-portion containers. The canned fish is sold to several wholesalers who specialize in providing food to school lunch programs in the Northwest region of the United States and certain areas in Canada. All processing is conducted in the firm's single (highly automated) plant in Seattle, Washington. Performance of the production manager is evaluated on the basis of a comparison of actual costs to standard costs. Only costs that are controllable by the production manager are included in the comparison (all are variable). The cost of fish is noncontrollable. Standard costs per pound of canned fish for 1993 were set as follows:

Direct labor	$0.25
Repairs	.05
Maintenance	.30
Indirect labor	.05
Power	.10

For 1993, the company purchased 5,000,000 pounds of fish and canned 3,000,000 pounds. There were no beginning or ending inventories of raw, in-process, or canned fish. Actual 1993 costs were:

Direct labor	$600,000
Repairs	160,000
Maintenance	650,000
Indirect labor	155,000
Power	315,000

Required:

a. Prepare a performance report for Michael Malicon for 1993.
b. Evaluate Michael Malicon's performance based on your report.
c. Michael feels that his 1993 performance is so good that he should be considered for immediate promotion to the position of vice-president of operations. Do you agree? Defend your answer.
d. Should additional performance measures (other than standard cost variances) be added to evaluate the production manager's performance? If so, identify the measures you would recommend.

34. *(Evaluating cash flow)* Shilika Currency, the controller of Texoma Meat Products, has become increasingly disillusioned with the company's system of evaluating the performance of profit centers and their managers. The present system focuses on a comparison of budgeted to actual income from operations. Shilika's major concern with the current system is the ease with which the measure "income from operations" can be manipulated by profit center managers. The "basic business" of Texoma Meat Products consists of purchasing live hogs and cattle, slaughtering the purchased animals, and then selling the various meat products and by-products to regional wholesalers and large retail chains. Most sales are made on credit, and all live animals are purchased for cash. The profit centers consist of geographical segments of Texoma Meat Products, and all profit center segments conduct both production and sales activities within their geographical territories. Following is a typical quarterly income statement for a profit center that appears in the responsibility report for the profit center:

Sales	$2,500,000
Cost of goods sold	1,500,000
Gross profit	$1,000,000
Selling & administrative expenses	750,000
Income from operations	$ 250,000

Shilika has suggested to top management that the company replace the accrual income evaluation measure, "income from operations," with a measure called "cash flow from operations." Shilika suggests that this measure will be less susceptible to manipulation by profit center managers. To defend her position, she compiles a cash flow income statement for the same profit center:

Cash receipts from customers	$2,200,000
Cash payments for production labor, livestock, and overhead	(1,600,000)
Cash payments for selling and administrative activities	(400,000)
Cash flow from operations	$ 200,000

Required:

a. If Shilika is correct about profit center managers manipulating the income measure, where are manipulations likely taking place?

b. Is the proposed cash flow measure less subject to manipulation than the income measure?

c. Could manipulation be reduced if both the cash flow and income measures were utilized? Explain.

d. Do the cash and income measures reveal different information about profit center performance?

e. Could the existing income statement be used more effectively in evaluating performance? Explain.

35. *(ROI)* Avante, Bellmane, and Coloa are three companies that operated in the sporting goods industry. Some information on each of these companies for 1993 is presented below:

	Avante	Bellmane	Coloa
Average total assets	$1,050,000	$ 900,000	$1,200,000
Revenues	2,100,000	2,700,000	2,400,000
Expenses	1,890,000	2,535,000	2,070,000

Required:

a. For each company, calculate profit margin, asset turnover, and return on investment.

b. Based on the computations in part (a), which company appears strongest? Which company appears weakest?

c. Is there any indication how any of the companies could improve their performance?

36. *(ROI)* The 1993 income statement for the Talley-Ho Division of Thames Enterprises is as follows:

Sales	$1,600,000
Variable expenses	800,000
Contribution margin	$ 800,000
Fixed expenses	400,000
Net income	$ 400,000

Assets at the beginning of 1993 for Talley-Ho were $1,800,000; because of various capital investments during the year, Talley-Ho ended 1993 with $2,200,000 of assets. Overall, Thames Enterprises experienced a 15 percent return on investment for 1993. It is a Thames policy to reward year-end bonuses to managers whose divisions show the highest ROIs.

The chief operating officer of Talley-Ho is investigating a new product line of English saddles for the division. The new line is expected to show the following approximate annual results: sales, $800,000; variable expenses, $400,000; and fixed expenses, $200,000. The saddle line would require a $1,240,000 investment in plant assets.

Required:

a. What was Talley-Ho's 1993 ROI?
b. What is the expected ROI on the new product line?
c. If Talley-Ho had invested in the new product line in 1993 and the approximated results occurred, what would have been the division's ROI?
d. Is the Talley-Ho Division manager likely to want to add the new product line? Would the president of Thames Enterprises want Talley-Ho to add the new product line? Discuss the rationale of each of the individuals.

37. *(Missing numbers)* The following numbers (1–9) identify missing data for three divisions of Elk Industries.

	Deer Division	Antelope Division	Moose Division
Sales	$1,000,000	$8,000,000	$4,000,000
Segment income	$ 200,000	(4)	$ 500,000
Sales margin	(1)	15%	(7)
Asset turnover	(2)	1.4	(8)
Average assets	(3)	(5)	$2,000,000
Return on investment	10%	(6)	(9)

Required:

a. Determine the values for each of the missing items.
b. Relative to the other divisions, identify the area where each division's performance is weakest.

38. *(ROI, RI)* Strike Three Industries manufactures various sports equipment items for professional sports teams. For 1994, the company's Baseball Division had the following performance targets:

Asset turnover	1.6
Profit margin	8%

Information about the Baseball Division is summarized below:

Total assets at year-end 1993	$2,400,000
Total assets at year-end 1994	3,200,000
Sales for 1994	3,600,000
Operating expenses for 1994	3,200,000

Required:

a. For 1994, did the Baseball Division achieve its target objectives for ROI, asset turnover, and profit margin?
b. Where, as indicated by the performance measures, are the most likely areas to improve performance?
c. If Strike Three Industries has an overall target return of 14 percent, what was the Baseball Division's residual income for 1994?

39. *(Transaction effects on ROI, RI)* The following are a number of transactions affecting a specific division within a multiple-division company. For each described transaction, indicate whether the transaction would increase (IN), decrease (D), have no effect (N), or have an indeterminate (I) effect on the following measures: asset turnover, profit margin, ROI, and RI for the present fiscal year. Each transaction is independent.

Required:

a. The division writes down an inventory of obsolete finished goods. The journal entry is:

Cost of Goods Sold	$40,000	
Finished Goods Inventory		$40,000

b. A special overseas order is accepted. The sales price for this order is well below the sales price on normal business but is sufficient to cover all costs traceable to this order.

c. A piece of equipment is sold for $50,000. The equipment's original cost was $400,000. At the time of sale, the book value of the equipment is $60,000. The sale of the equipment has no effect on product sales.

d. The division fires its R&D manager. The manager will not be replaced during the current fiscal year.

e. The company raises its target rate of return for this division from 12 percent to 13 percent.

f. At midyear, the divisional manager decides to increase scheduled annual production by 1,000 units. This decision has no effect on scheduled sales.

g. Also at midyear, the division manager spends an additional $50,000 on advertising. Sales immediately increase thereafter.

h. The divisional manager replaces a labor-intense operation with machine technology. This action has no effect on sales, but total annual expenses of the operation are expected to decline by 12 percent.

40. *(Decisions based on ROI)* Hank is a division manager of Moody Company. Hank's performance as a division manager is evaluated primarily on the following measure: divisional segment income divided by gross book value of total divisional assets. For the existing operations in Hank's division, projections for 1993 are as follows:

Sales	$40,000,000
Expenses	35,000,000
Segment income	$ 5,000,000

The gross book value of total assets for existing operations is $25,000,000.

At this moment, Hank is evaluating an investment in a new product line that would, according to Hank's projections, increase 1993 segment income by $400,000. The cost of the investment has not yet been determined.

Required:

a. Ignoring the new investment, what is Hank's projected ROI for 1993?

b. In light of your answer in part (a), what is the maximum amount that Hank would be willing to invest in the new product line?

c. Assuming the new product line would require an investment of $2,200,000, what would be the revised projected ROI for Hank's division in 1993 after making the investment?

d. If the new product line requires an investment of $2,200,000, will Hank invest in the new product line? If the cost was only $1,500,000, would Hank invest in the product line?

41. *(Decisions based on ROI, RI)* The Myopic Company evaluates the performance of its two division managers using a ROI formula. For the forthcoming period, divisional estimates of relevant measures are:

	Division 1	Division 2	Total Company
Sales	$3,000,000	$12,000,000	$15,000,000
Expenses	2,700,000	10,500,000	13,200,000
Divisional assets	2,500,000	7,500,000	10,000,000

The managers of both operating divisions have the autonomy to make decisions regarding new investments. The manager of Division 1 is presently contemplating an investment in an additional asset that would generate an ROI of 14 percent and the manager of Division 2 is considering an investment in an additional asset that would generate an ROI of 18 percent.

Required:

a. Compute the projected ROI for each division disregarding the contemplated new investments.

b. Based on your answer in part (a), which of the managers is likely to actually invest in the additional assets under consideration?

c. Are the outcomes of the investment decisions in part (b) likely to be consistent with overall corporate goals? Explain.

d. If Myopic Company evaluated the division managers' performance using a residual income measure with a target return of 17 percent, would the outcomes of the investment decisions be different from those described in part (b)? Explain.

42. *(Throughput)* The Vaya Del Sol Company has historically evaluated divisional performance exclusively on financial measures. Top managers have become increasingly concerned with this approach to performance evaluation and are now actively seeking alternative measures. Specifically, they are looking for measures that more accurately assess success in the activities that generate value for customers. One promising measure is throughput. To experiment with the annual throughput measure, management has gathered the following historical information on one of its larger operating divisions:

Units started into production	100,000
Total good units completed	65,000
Total hours of processing time	40,000
Total hours of division time	60,000

Required:

a. What is the productive capacity of the division?

b. What is the process yield of the division?

c. What is the percentage productive processing time?

d. What is the total throughput per hour?

e. Which of the previous measures (part a, b, or c) reflects the possible existence of a production bottleneck?

f. Which of the previous measures (part a, b, or c) reflects potentially poor quality in the production process as measured by the number of defective units?

43. *(Essay)* For the past three years, the highest divisional ROI within Mountain Corporation has been generated by Hill Division, a very high-tech manufacturing division. The segment income and ROI for each year appear below:

	1991	1992	1993
Segment income	$200,000	$195,000	$193,500
ROI	20%	23%	27%

a. Why do you think Hill Division has been so successful as measured by its ROI?

b. What change(s) would you recommend to control the continued escalation in the ROI?

44. *(Essay)* You have been assigned the task of defining "income" and "assets" as they will be used to evaluate investment center performance in your firm. Assume your firm comprises multiple investment centers, and explain how you will treat each of the following in your definitions:

a. allocated corporate costs
b. corporate income taxes
c. the salary of the investment center manager
d. idle assets under the control of the investment center manager
e. direct fixed costs of the investment center
f. current values or historical values for assets

45. *(Essay)* For a firm to utilize an ROI performance measure, it must first define the terms in the ROI ratio. Identify ways in which divisional managers can manipulate the following:

a. the income measure
b. the asset measure

46. *(Essay)* Explain how each of the following items would affect the asset turnover ratio of a corporate division if asset amounts are determined by their net book values.

a. A new labor contract is negotiated, which reduces labor costs by 10 percent.
b. Unused assets are carried on the books. These assets could be sold.
c. Obsolete inventory is carried on the books.
d. Uncollectible accounts receivable are maintained on the books.
e. The rate of depreciation on plant and equipment is increased.
f. Fixed costs allocated to the division drop by 4 percent.

47. *(Essay)* Worldwide Corporation has two divisions operating in the trucking industry. One division, Here, is a domestic U.S. division; the other division, There, is a foreign-based division operating exclusively in Europe and Asia. Both divisions are evaluated, in part, based on a measure of ROI. For the most recent year, Here's ROI was 14 percent and There's ROI was 8 percent. One of the tasks of upper management is to evaluate the relative performance of the divisions so that an appropriate performance pay bonus can be determined for each manager. In evaluating relative performance, provide arguments as to why the determination of relative performance should

a. involve a comparison of the ROI measures in the two divisions.
b. not include a comparison of ROI measures in the two divisions.

48. *(Essay)* In 1993, the lead story in your college newspaper reports the details of the hiring of your new football coach. Your old football coach was fired for failing to win games (in his last season his record was one win and ten losses) or attract fans. The news story states that the new coach's contract provides for a base salary of $100,000 per year plus an annual bonus computed as follows:

Win less than five games	$ 0
Win five to seven games	25,000
Win eight games or more	75,000
Win eight or more games and conference championship	95,000
Win eight or more games, win conference, get a bowl bid	150,000

There are essentially no other features or clauses in the coach's contract.

The first year after the new coach is hired, the football team wins three games and loses eight. The second year the team wins six games and loses five. The third year the team wins nine games and a conference championship and is invited to a prestigious bowl. Shortly after the bowl game, articles appear on the front page of several national sports publications, announcing your college football program has been cited by the National Collegiate Athletic Association (NCAA) for nine major rule violations including cash payoffs to players, playing academically ineligible players, illegal recruiting tactics, and illegal involvement of alumni in recruiting. All of the national news publications agree that your football program will be disbanded by the NCAA. One article also mentioned that over the past three years, only 13 percent of senior football players managed to graduate on time. Additional speculation suggests the responsible parties, including the coaching staff, athletic director, and college president, will be dismissed by the board of trustees.

a. Did the performance measures in the coach's contract foster goal congruence? Explain.

b. Would the coach's actions have been different if other performance measures were added to the contract? Explain.

c. What performance measures should be considered for the next coach's contract, assuming the football program could be kept alive?

d. Even with the existing contract, why might another coach have been more restrained in the actions he took to win games than the coach referenced in this situation?

49. *(Essay)* The National Association of Accountants (now the Institute of Management Accountants) issued *Statements on Management Accounting 4D*, "Measuring Entity Performance," to help management accountants deal with the issues associated with measuring entity performance. Managers can use these measures to evaluate their own performance or the performance of subordinates, to identify and correct problems, and to discover opportunities. To assist management in measuring achievement, there are a number of performance measures available. To present a more complete picture of performance, it is strongly recommended that several of these performance measures be utilized and that they be combined with nonfinancial measures such as market share, new product development, and human resource utilization. Five commonly used performance measures that are derived from the traditional historical accounting system are listed next.

• Gross profit margin (percentage)
• Cash flows
• Return on the investment in assets
• Residual income
• Total asset turnover

For each of the five performance measures just identified,

a. describe how the measure is calculated,
b. describe the information provided by the measure, and
c. explain the limitations of this information.

(CMA)

Cases

50. Raddington Industries produces tool and die machinery for manufacturers. The company expanded vertically in 1989 by acquiring one of its suppliers of alloy steel plates, Reigis Steel Company. In order to manage the two separate businesses, the operations of Reigis are reported separately as an investment center.

    Raddington monitors its divisions on the basis of both unit contribution and return on average investment (ROI), with investment defined as average operating assets employed. Management bonuses are determined based on ROI. All investments in operating assets are expected to earn a minimum return of 11 percent before income taxes.

    Reigis's cost of goods sold is considered to be entirely variable, while the division's administrative expenses are not dependent on volume. Selling expenses are a mixed cost with 40 percent attributed to sales volume. Reigis's ROI has ranged from 11.8% to 14.7% since 1989. During the fiscal year ended November 30, 1994, Reigis contemplated a capital acquisition with an estimated ROI of 11.5 percent; however, division management decided that the investment would decrease Reigis's overall ROI.

    The 1994 operating statement for Reigis follows. The division's operating assets employed were $15,750,000 at November 30, 1994, a 5 percent increase over the 1993 year-end balance.

REIGIS STEEL DIVISION
OPERATING STATEMENT
FOR THE YEAR ENDED NOVEMBER 30, 1994
($000 OMITTED)

Sales revenue		$25,000
Less expenses		
Cost of goods sold	$16,500	
Administrative expenses	3,955	
Selling expenses	2,700	23,155
Income from operations		
before income taxes		$ 1,845

   a. Calculate the unit contribution for Reigis Steel Division if 1,484,000 units were produced and sold during the year ended November 30, 1994.
   b. Calculate the following performance measures for 1994 for the Reigis Steel Division:
      1. Pretax return on average investment on operating assets employed (ROI)
      2. Residual income calculated on the basis of average operating assets employed
   c. Explain why the management of the Reigis Steel Division would have been more likely to accept the contemplated capital acquisition if residual income rather than ROI was used as a performance measure.
   d. The Reigis Steel Division is a separate investment center within Raddington Industries. Identify several items that Reigis should control if it is to be evaluated fairly by either the ROI or residual income performance measures.

   (CMA)

51. Family Resorts, Inc., is a holding company for several vacation hotels in the northeast and mid-Atlantic states. The firm originally purchased several old inns, restored the buildings, and upgraded the recreational facilities. The inns have been well received by vacationing families as many services are provided that accommodate children and afford parents time for themselves. Since the completion of the restorations ten years ago, the company has been profitable.

Family Resorts has just concluded its annual meeting of regional and district managers. This meeting is held each November to review the results of the previous season and to help the managers prepare for the upcoming year. Prior to the meeting, the managers have submitted proposed budgets for their districts or regions as appropriate. These budgets have been reviewed and consolidated into an annual operating budget for the entire company. The 1994 budget has been presented at the meeting and was accepted by the managers.

To evaluate the performance of its managers, Family Resorts uses responsibility accounting. Therefore, the preparation of the budget is given close attention at headquarters. If major changes need to be made to the budgets submitted by the managers, all affected parties are consulted before the changes are incorporated. The following are two pages from the budget booklet that all managers received at the meeting.

FAMILY RESORTS, INC.
RESPONSIBILITY SUMMARY
($000 OMITTED)

Reporting Unit: Family Resorts	
Responsible Person: President	
Mid-Atlantic Region	$605
New England Region	365
Unallocated costs	(160)
Income before taxes	$810
Reporting Unit: New England Region	
Responsible Person: Regional Manager	
Vermont	$200
New Hampshire	140
Maine	105
Unallocated costs	(80)
Total contribution	$365
Reporting Unit: Maine District	
Responsible Person: District Manager	
Harbor Inn	$ 80
Camden Country Inn	60
Unallocated costs	(35)
Total contribution	$105
Reporting Unit: Harbor Inn	
Responsible Person: Innkeeper	
Revenue	$600
Controllable costs	(455)
Allocated costs	(65)
Total contribution	$ 80

The budget for Family Resorts, Inc., follows.

FAMILY RESORTS, INC.
CONDENSED OPERATING BUDGET—MAINE DISTRICT
FOR THE YEAR ENDING DECEMBER 31, 1994
($000 OMITTED)

	Family Resorts	Mid-Atlantic	New England	Not Allocated[1]	Vermont	New Hampshire	Maine	Not Allocated[2]	Harbor	Camden Country
Net sales	$7,900	$4,200	$3,700		$1,400	$1,200	$1,100		$600	$500
Cost of sales	4,530	2,310	2,220		840	720	660		360	300
Gross margin	$3,370	$1,890	$1,480		$ 560	$ 480	$ 440		$240	$200
Controllable expenses										
Supervisory expense	$ 240	$ 130	$ 110		$ 35	$ 30	$ 45	$ 10	$ 20	$ 15
Training expense	160	80	80		30	25	25		15	10
Advertising expense	500	280	220	$ 50	55	60	55	15	20	20
Repairs & maintenance	480	225	255		90	85	80		40	40
Total controllable expenses	$1,380	$ 715	$ 665	$ 50	$ 210	$ 200	$ 205	$ 25	$ 95	$ 85
Controllable contribution	$1,990	$1,175	$ 815	$(50)	$ 350	$ 280	$ 235	$(25)	$145	$115
Expenses controlled by others										
Depreciation	$ 520	$ 300	$ 220	$ 30	$ 70	$ 60	$ 60	$ 10	$ 30	$ 20
Property taxes	200	120	80		30	$ 30	20		10	10
Insurance	300	150	150		50	50	50		25	25
Total expenses controlled by others	$1,020	$ 570	$ 450	$ 30	$ 150	$ 140	$ 130	$ 10	$ 65	$ 55
Total contribution	$ 970	$ 605	$ 365	$(80)	$ 200	$ 140	$ 105	$(35)	$ 80	$ 60
Unallocated costs[3]	160									
Income before taxes	$ 810									

[1]Unallocated expenses include a regional advertising campaign and equipment used by the regional manager.
[2]Unallocated expenses include a portion of the district manager's salary, district promotion costs, district manager's car.
[3]Unallocated costs include taxes on undeveloped real estate, headquarters expense, legal, audit fees.

a. Responsibility accounting has been used effectively by many companies, both large and small.
   1. Define responsibility accounting.
   2. Discuss the benefits that accrue to a company using responsibility accounting.
   3. Describe the advantages of responsibility accounting for the managers of a firm.
b. Family Resorts, Inc.'s budget was accepted by the regional and district managers. Based on the facts presented, evaluate the budget process employed by Family Resorts by addressing the following:
   1. What features of the budget preparation are likely to result in the managers adopting and supporting the budget process?
   2. What recommendations, if any, could be made to the budget preparers to improve the budget process? Explain your answer.

(CMA)

52. Pittsburgh-Walsh Company (PWC) is a manufacturing company whose product line consists of lighting fixtures and electronic timing devices. The Lighting Fixtures Division assembles units for the upscale and midrange markets. The Electronic Timing Devices Division manufactures instrument panels that allow elec-

tronic systems to be activated and deactivated at scheduled times for both efficiency and safety purposes. Both divisions operate out of the same manufacturing facilities and share production equipment.

PWC's budget for the year ending December 31, 1994, shown at the top of page 703, was prepared on a business segment basis under the following guidelines:

- Variable expenses are directly assigned to the incurring division.
- Fixed overhead expenses are directly assigned to the incurring division.
- Common fixed expenses are allocated to the divisions on the basis of units produced, which bear a close relationship to direct labor. Included in common fixed expenses are costs of the corporate staff, legal expenses, taxes, staff marketing, and advertising.
- The production plan is for 8,000 upscale fixtures, 22,000 midrange fixtures, and 20,000 electronic timing devices.

PWC established a bonus plan for division management that requires meeting the budget's planned net income by product line, with a bonus increment if the division exceeds the planned product line net income by 10 percent or more.

Shortly before the year began, the CEO, Jack Parkow, suffered a heart attack and retired. After reviewing the 1994 budget, the new CEO, Joe Kelly, decided to close the lighting fixtures midrange product line by the end of the first quarter and use the available production capacity to increase the remaining two product lines. The marketing staff advised that electronic timing devices could grow by 40 percent with increased direct sales support. Increases above that level and increasing sales of upscale lighting fixtures would require expanded advertising expenditures to increase consumer awareness of PWC as an electronics and upscale lighting fixture company. Kelly approved the increased sales support and advertising expenditures to achieve the revised plan. Kelly advised the divisions that for bonus purposes, the original product line net income objectives must be met, but he did allow the Lighting Fixtures Division to combine the net income objectives for both product lines for bonus purposes.

Prior to the close of the fiscal year, the division controllers were furnished with preliminary actual data for review and adjustment, as appropriate. These preliminary year-end data reflect the revised units of production amounting to 12,000 upscale fixtures, 4,000 midrange fixtures, and 30,000 electronics timing devices and are presented after the budget on page 703.

The controller of the Lighting Fixtures Division, anticipating a similar bonus plan for 1995, is contemplating deferring some revenues into the next year on the pretext that the sales are not yet final, and accruing in the current year expenditures that will be applicable to the first quarter of 1995. The corporation would meet its annual plan, and the division would exceed the 10 percent incremental bonus plateau in the year 1994 despite the deferred revenues and accrued expenses contemplated.

PITTSBURGH-WALSH COMPANY
BUDGET FOR THE YEAR ENDING DECEMBER 31, 1994
(AMOUNTS IN THOUSANDS)

| | Lighting Fixtures | | Electronic Timing | |
	Upscale	Midrange	Devices	Totals
Sales	$1,440	$770	$800	$3,010
Variable expenses				
Cost of goods sold	(720)	(439)	(320)	(1,479)
Selling & administrative	(170)	(60)	(60)	(290)
Contribution margin	$ 550	$271	$420	$1,241
Fixed overhead expenses	(140)	(80)	(80)	(300)
Segment margin	$ 410	$191	$340	$ 941
Common fixed expenses				
Overhead	(48)	(132)	(120)	(300)
Selling & administrative	(11)	(31)	(28)	(70)
Net income (loss)	$ 351	$ 28	$192	$ 571

PITTSBURGH-WALSH COMPANY
PRELIMINARY ACTUALS FOR THE YEAR
ENDING DECEMBER 31, 1994
(AMOUNTS IN THOUSANDS)

| | Lighting Fixtures | | Electronic Timing | |
	Upscale	Midrange	Devices	Totals
Sales	$2,160	$140	$1,200	$3,500
Variable expenses				
Cost of goods sold	(1,080)	(80)	(480)	(1,640)
Selling & administrative	(260)	(11)	(96)	(367)
Contribution margin	$ 820	$ 49	$ 624	$1,493
Fixed overhead expenses	(140)	(14)	(80)	(234)
Segment margin	$ 680	$ 35	$ 544	$1,259
Common fixed expenses				
Overhead	(78)	(27)	(195)	(300)
Selling & administrative	(60)	(20)	(150)	(230)
Net income (loss)	$ 542	$(12)	$ 199	$ 729

a. 1. Outline the benefits that an organization realizes from segment reporting.
   2. Evaluate segment reporting on a variable cost basis versus an absorption cost basis. (You may want to refer to chapter 8.)
b. 1. Segment reporting can be developed based on different criteria. What criteria must be present for division management to accept being evaluated on a segment basis?
   2. Why would the management of the Electronic Timing Devices Division be unhappy with the current reporting, and how should the reporting be revised to gain their acceptance?

c. Explain why the adjustments contemplated by the controller of the Lighting Fixtures Division are unethical by citing the specific standards of competence, confidentiality, integrity, and/or objectivity from "Standards of Ethical Conduct for Management Accountants" (Exhibit 1–6).

(CMA)

∎ Ethics Discussion

53. Bobbie Pilkington, a United Air Lines flight attendant from Chicago, went five years without a pay raise while watching [the value of] her new shares of stock plunge right along with the company's 71 percent drop in profits.

    UAL chairman Stephen Wolf had no such problems. Despite the company's poor performance, he earned $18.3 million [in 1990], or about 610 times more than Pilkington and 1,272 times more than a newly hired flight attendant.

    (SOURCE: Mary Kane, "CEO Pay, Perks Foster Resentment," [*New Orleans*] *Times-Picayune* [November 3, 1991], p. F1.)

    a. Plato said that the highest-paid worker should earn no more than five times the lowest-paid worker. Do you agree with Plato? Justify your answer.
    b. Should corporate executives have their compensation packages (total cash and noncash elements) tied in some way to company performance? If so, why? If not, why not?
    c. Discuss the ethics of allowing corporate executives to be paid extremely well, when the companies for which they work are laying off employees, deferring payments to creditors, and not declaring dividends to stockholders.
    d. Many companies also have "golden parachutes" for their executives that require substantial payments to the executives when they leave the firm involuntarily and, sometimes, voluntarily. Assume that you are the CEO of a company that has just been taken over by another company. The new company board of directors has decided to replace you because your company has not been performing at what they believe is a "reasonable" level. Discuss why you would want a golden parachute and why the stockholders may disagree.

54. A large American corporation participates in a highly competitive industry. In order to meet this competition and achieve profit goals, the company has chosen the decentralized form of organization. Each manager of a decentralized profit center is measured on the basis of profit contribution, market penetration, and return on investment. Failure to meet the objectives established by corporate management for these measures was unacceptable and usually resulted in demotion or dismissal of a profit center manager.

    An anonymous survey of managers in the company revealed that the managers felt pressure to compromise their personal ethical standards to achieve corporate objectives. For example, at certain plant locations there was pressure to reduce quality control to a level which could not assure that all unsafe products would be rejected. Also, sales personnel were encouraged to use questionable sales tactics to obtain orders, including gifts and other incentives to purchasing agents.

    The chief executive officer is disturbed by the survey findings. In his opinion, such behavior cannot be condoned by the company. He concludes that the company should do something about this problem.

a. Discuss what might be the causes for the ethical problems described.

b. Outline a program that could be instituted by the company to help reduce the pressures on managers to compromise personal ethical standards in their work.

(CMA)

55. Nason Corporation manufactures and distributes a line of toys for children. As a consequence, the corporation has large seasonal variations in sales. The company issues quarterly financial statements, and first-quarter earnings were down from the same period last year.

During a visit to the Preschool and Infant Division, Nason's president expressed dissatisfaction with the division's first-quarter performance. As a result, John Kraft, division manager, felt pressure to report higher earnings in the second quarter. Kraft was aware that Nason Corporation uses the LIFO inventory method, so he had the purchasing manager postpone several large inventory orders scheduled for delivery in the second quarter. Kraft knew that the use of older inventory costs during the second quarter would cause a decline in the cost of goods sold and, thus, increase earnings.

During a review of the preliminary second-quarter income statement, Donna Jensen, division controller, noticed that the cost of goods sold was low relative to sales. Jensen analyzed the inventory account and discovered that the scheduled second-quarter material purchases had been delayed until the third quarter. Jensen prepared a revised income statement using current replacement costs to calculate cost of goods sold and submitted the income statement to John Kraft, her superior, for review. Kraft was not pleased with these results and insisted that the second-quarter income statement remain unchanged. Jensen tried to explain to Kraft that the interim inventory should reflect the expected cost of the replacement of the liquidated layers when the inventory is expected to be replaced before the end of the year. Kraft did not relent and told Jensen to issue the income statement using LIFO costs. Jensen is concerned about Kraft's response and is contemplating what her next action should be.

a. Determine whether the actions of John Kraft are ethical and explain your position.

b. Referring to the "Standards of Ethical Conduct for Management Accountants" (Exhibit 1–6), (1) describe the specific standards that would apply in Donna Jensen's evaluation of the actions of her superior, and (2) recommend a course of action that Donna Jensen should take in proceeding to resolve this situation.

(CMA)

PART FIVE

USING MANAGERIAL ACCOUNTING INFORMATION FOR DECISION MAKING

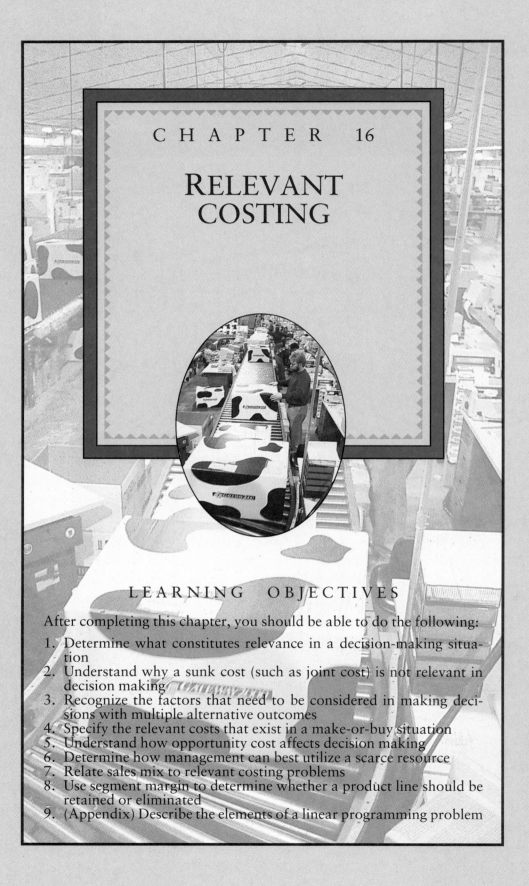

C H A P T E R   16

RELEVANT COSTING

LEARNING OBJECTIVES

After completing this chapter, you should be able to do the following:

1. Determine what constitutes relevance in a decision-making situation
2. Understand why a sunk cost (such as joint cost) is not relevant in decision making
3. Recognize the factors that need to be considered in making decisions with multiple alternative outcomes
4. Specify the relevant costs that exist in a make-or-buy situation
5. Understand how opportunity cost affects decision making
6. Determine how management can best utilize a scarce resource
7. Relate sales mix to relevant costing problems
8. Use segment margin to determine whether a product line should be retained or eliminated
9. (Appendix) Describe the elements of a linear programming problem

I t is hard to believe that Gateway, which assembles but does not manufacture parts, could sell more computers than any other company by phone. How did Ted Waitt and his co-founder decide on such an unusual plan of operation? Gateway's managers made a "buy" choice in what is commonly referred to as a make-or-buy decision. They had to determine and compare the costs of setting up manufacturing operations to the costs of engaging only in assembly. This comparison was made on the basis of **relevant costs,** which are those costs that are pertinent to or logically associated with a specific problem or decision.

Gateway's choice reflects a common type of business decision—that of trying to competently allocate the limited, available organizational resources so that company goals and objectives are achieved. As indicated in the following quote, making decisions in today's business environment is not an easy task.

> Decision making in the 1990s will be more of an art and less of a science. Not only is the world growing more complex and uncertain at a faster and faster pace, but the old decision-making models are failing, and we can expect their failure to accelerate as well.
>
> If executives once imagined they could gather enough information to read the business environment like an open book, they have had to dim their hopes. The flow of information has swollen to such a flood that managers are in danger of drowning; extracting relevant data from the torrent is increasingly a daunting task.[1]

Accounting information can improve, but not perfect, management's understanding of the consequences of various resource allocation decisions. To the extent that accounting information can reduce management's uncertainty about the eco-

relevant costs

---

[1]An excerpt from "Humble Decision Making," by Amitai Etzioni (July–August 1989), p. 122. Reprinted by permission of *Harvard Business Review*. Copyright © 1989 by the President and Fellows of Harvard College; all rights reserved.

relevant costing

nomic facts, outcomes, and relationships involved in various courses of action, such information is valuable for decision making purposes and necessary for conducting business.

As discussed in chapter 9, many decisions are made on the basis of incremental analysis. This type of analysis encompasses the concept of **relevant costing,** which allows managers to focus on pertinent facts and disregard extraneous information. This chapter illustrates the use of relevant costing in decisions about replacing an asset, making or buying a product or part, allocating scarce resources, and determining the appropriate sales and/or production mix. While these decisions are often viewed by managers as short-run, each decision has significant long-run implications that must be considered.

The concept of relevance

When managers make choices among alternatives, all relevant costs and revenues associated with each alternative should be considered. Relevant information is associated with the decision or question under consideration, is important to a decision maker, and has a connection to or bearing upon some future endeavor.

Association with Decision

Relevant information supports decision making. Information is relevant when it is logically related to the decision. In this regard, different costs exist that can be used for many different purposes. No single cost can be relevant in all decisions or to all

At a state fair, each passenger on a ride or participant in a game of skill creates an incremental revenue for the ride or booth owner. Because many of the ride and booth costs are fixed, there are few incremental costs associated with each additional unit of activity.

managers. Accountants can assist managers in determining which costs are relevant to the objectives and decisions at hand.

To the extent possible and practical, relevant costing compares the differential, incremental revenues and differential, incremental costs of alternative decisions. Differential means that the costs differ between or among the choices, while incremental means the additional or extra amount associated with some action. Thus, **incremental revenue** is the additional revenue resulting from a contemplated sale or provision of service. An **incremental cost** is the additional cost of producing or selling a contemplated quantity of output.

incremental revenue

incremental cost

Incremental costs can be either variable or fixed. Two general rules are that (1) most variable costs are relevant and (2) most fixed costs are not. The reasoning behind this rule is that, as sales or production volume changes, variable costs change but fixed costs do not. As with most general rules, however, there are some exceptions that must be acknowledged in the decision-making process.

The difference between the incremental revenue and incremental cost of a particular alternative is the positive or negative incremental benefit of that course of action. Management can compare the incremental benefits of possible alternatives to decide on the most profitable or least costly alternative or set of alternatives. While such a comparison may appear simple on the surface, it is not always so easy, because the concept of relevance is an inherently individual determination. For example, an investment proposal might provide a high rate of return for a company, but might also create a future potential environmental hazard. One unit manager might view the potential hazard as very relevant, while another manager may minimize the relevance of that possibility.

Some relevant factors, such as sales commissions and the prime costs of production (direct materials and direct labor), are easily identified and quantified. These factors are integral parts of the accounting system. Other factors, such as opportunity costs, may be relevant and quantifiable, but are not part of the accounting system. (Remember that an opportunity cost represents the benefits foregone because one course of action is chosen over another.) Such factors cannot be overlooked simply because they may be more difficult to obtain or may require the use of estimates.

An example of a relevant, quantifiable opportunity cost in a labor-intensive company is the labor savings that would result from replacing employees with robots. Company managers should, however, weigh potential future cost reductions and increases in productivity against the possible short- and long-range negative public reaction toward the company because of unemployment increases resulting from the layoffs. Although public reaction is difficult to measure and quantify and it may take some time to become noticeable, such reactions should still be factored into the decision. In addition, there may be very relevant but highly unquantifiable costs resulting from ethical considerations, such as the moral obligations the firm has toward the displaced workers. Such costs must be estimated in a reasonable manner if the decision to automate is to be based on a truly valid analysis.

Importance to Decision Maker

The need for specific information depends on how important that information is relative to management objectives. If all other factors are equal, more precise information is given greater weight in the decision-making process. However, if information is important but less precise, the manager must weigh importance against precision. The following News Note illustrates the need for qualitative information and management's ethical duty to weigh important but imprecise, qualitative information (risk to consumers and company) against company profits.

NEWS NOTE

Are the Profits Worth the Costs?

Halcion was the first benzodiazepine (medicine for sleep disorders) that seemed to . . . put people to sleep quickly and left the body so rapidly that users experienced virtually no grogginess the next day.

Belgium and Holland approved 1-milligram doses of Halcion in 1977, but the drug soon ran into trouble. By early 1979, a handful of users had reported "peculiar psychiatric changes." In August 1979 Dutch authorities suspended the drug's license for six months to study the problem, and the reports kept mounting. By year-end, Dutch doctors had reported 1,100 such reactions. In early 1980, quarter-milligram doses were authorized, but the Dutch government permanently banned higher doses. Upjohn left the Dutch market, but reintroduced Halcion there in 1990.

Halcion was also applying at the FDA for U.S. approval. In 1980, Dr. Theresa Woo, the medical review officer handling Halcion's application, wrote a series of evaluations recommending against approval. Woo's superiors decided to approve the drug despite her concerns. Halcion was licensed in November 1982, and in early 1983 the half-milligram dose hit the American market. During its first 3 years on the U.S. market, Halcion had 8 to 30 times as many adverse-reaction reports (to the FDA) as did other sleeping aids in its same category. In 1990, FDA analysts compared the numbers of violent acts associated with 329 prescription drugs; Halcion ranked first. In 1991, Upjohn settled out-of-court with Ilo Grundberg who had been on Halcion and killed her mother. Ms. Grundberg was not convicted of the murder. The civil suit had been filed for $21 million.

As of August 1991, Halcion is Upjohn's second biggest money-maker, having annual sales of $250 million—$100 million in the United States. American pharmacists fill about 500,000 Halcion prescriptions every month.

SOURCE: Geoffrey Cowley, et al., "Sweet Dreams or Nightmare?" *Newsweek* (August 19, 1991), p. 44ff.

Bearing on the Future

Information can be based on past or present data, but it can be relevant only if it pertains to and will be differential in relation to a future choice. All managerial decisions are made to affect future events, so the information on which decisions are based should reflect future conditions. The future may be the short-run (two hours from now or next month) or the long-run (five years or more from now).[2]

Future costs are the only costs that can be avoided, and the longer into the future a decision's time horizon, the more costs are controllable, avoidable, and relevant. *Only information that has a bearing on future events is relevant in decision making.* But people too often forget this basic fact and try to make decisions using inapplicable data. One common error is trying to use a previously purchased asset's acquisition cost to make current decisions. This error reflects the misconception that sunk costs are relevant costs.

---

[2]Short-run decisions typically focus on a measure of accounting income that excludes some past costs, such as depreciation on old assets. Long-range decision analysis commonly uses cash flow as its decision criterion; this topic is covered in chapter 17.

SUNK COSTS AND JOINT PROCESSES

Current costs (such as replacement or budgeted costs) are assumed to be accurate for the time period involved in a decision. As such, these costs represent information that is relevant and should be considered in the decision-making process. In contrast, historical costs that were incurred in the past for the acquisition of an asset or a resource are called **sunk costs** because they cannot be changed, no matter what future course of action is taken. Past expenditures are not recoverable, no matter what current

sunk costs

The process of obtaining sides of beef from cattle requires the incurrence of many joint costs. These costs should be allocated to the primary output produced, such as steaks, ground beef, and roasts.

circumstances exist. A current or future selling price may be obtained for an asset, but that is the result of current or future conditions and is not a recouping of a historical cost. Joint costs are used to illustrate why sunk costs are not relevant costs.

Almost every company produces and sells more than one type of product. While companies often have to engage in multiple production processes to produce a variety of products, it is possible for a single process to simultaneously generate several different outputs. A single process in which one product cannot be manufactured without producing others is known as a **joint process.** Industries that produce multiple products from a single process include oil refining, lumber milling, and chemical and food processing.

joint products
by-products
scrap

waste

A company undertakes a joint production process to generate outputs known as **joint products.** Each type of joint product has substantial revenue-generating ability. In contrast, **by-products** and **scrap** are incidental outputs of a joint process. Both are salable, but their sales values alone would not be enough for management to justify undertaking the joint process. By-products are viewed as having a higher sales value than scrap. A final output from a joint process is waste. **Waste** is a residual output that has no sales value. A normal amount of waste is considered a production cost that cannot be avoided.

A corn processing plant can be used to illustrate the types of outputs resulting from a joint process. Outputs may include corn-on-the-cob and whole-kernel corn (joint products), corn kernels (by-products) used for cornmeal, inferior kernels (scrap) for sale to producers of animal food, and cobs (waste) that are discarded.

split-off point

The point at which the outputs of a joint process are first identifiable as individual products is called the **split-off point.** A joint process may have one or more split-off points, depending on the number and types of output produced. Output may be sold at the split-off point, if a market exists for products in that condition. Alternatively, some or all of the products may be processed further after exiting the joint process.

joint cost

The costs incurred for materials, labor, and overhead during a joint process (up to the split-off point) are referred to as the **joint cost** of the production process. For managers to engage in a joint process, they should expect that total revenues from product sales will exceed total costs. Since the joint process results in a "basket" of products, managers must be aware that some of the joint process output may require additional processing to make it salable. Once joint process costs have been incurred, they become sunk costs regardless of whether the output is salable at the end of the joint process or at what amount.

If any of the joint process outputs are processed after the split-off point, additional costs will be incurred. Costs after split-off are assigned to the separate products for which those costs are incurred. Thus, management must consider total joint costs plus separate processing or selling costs expected to be incurred at or after the end of the joint process before making the decision to commit resources to the joint process.

The joint cost is allocated, at the split-off point, to the primary output of the production process. Joint cost is a necessary and reasonable cost of producing the joint products and, based on the cost principle, should be attached to them for external financial statement purposes. Joint cost is allocated only to primary products because these products are the reason that management undertook the production process. Allocation of the joint cost to joint products is not relevant to decision making.

To illustrate, assume that a joint product has a selling price of $10 at split-off, but its selling price after further processing is $16. If the additional processing costs are less than $6, the $6 incremental revenue ($16 − $10) exceeds the incremental costs and additional processing should occur. Notice that the joint cost is not considered in this decision process. Once the products have reached the split-off point, the joint cost has already been incurred and is a sunk cost. Additionally, the joint cost is a common cost of all joint products and is irrelevant to the sell-or-process-further decision. The only relevant items in the decision to sell or process further are the incremental revenues and incremental costs after the split-off point.

This example introduces the difference between relevant and irrelevant costs. The next section shows how the concepts of relevant costing are applied in making some common managerial decisions.

RELEVANT COSTS FOR SPECIFIC DECISIONS

Managers routinely make decisions on alternatives that have been identified as feasible solutions to problems or feasible methods for the attainment of objectives. In doing so, managers weigh the costs and benefits of alternative courses of action and determine which course is best. Incremental revenues, costs, and benefits of all courses of action are measured from a base that corresponds to current conditions. This statement means that managers must provide some mechanism for including the inherently nonquantifiable considerations. Inclusion can be made by attempting to quantify items or by simply making instinctive value judgments about nonmonetary benefits and costs, as indicated in the following discussion.

> Perhaps the overriding concern in any determination of what should be done to improve the environment is a calculation of what it will cost. A technique that plays a major role in determining whether it's worthwhile to incur a particular cost (such as the cost of employing a pollution-control device) is cost-benefit analysis. The approach takes a project and evaluates its direct and indirect costs and benefits, the difference being the net positive or negative result.
>
> Consider, for example, a national project undertaken to clean up the air. . . . Cost-benefit analysis does not consider costs and benefits only in monetary terms. [And] benefits related to environmental matters are especially difficult to calculate because they often take the form of an aesthetic enhancement.
>
> Although cost-benefit analysis may be necessary for determining the soundness of a pollution-control project, it seems inevitable that an assessment of costs and benefits will be significantly influenced by the values one holds.[3]

When evaluating alternative courses of action, managers should select the alternative that provides the highest incremental benefit to the company. In some instances, all alternatives result in incremental losses, and managers must choose the one that creates the smallest incremental loss. One alternative course of action often considered is defensive avoidance, or the "change nothing for the moment" option.

While other alternatives have certain incremental revenues and costs associated with them, the "change nothing" alternative has a zero incremental benefit because it represents current conditions from which all other alternatives are measured. The "change nothing" alternative should be chosen only when it is perceived to be the

---

[3]Adapted from William Shaw and Vincent Barry, *Moral Issues in Business* (Belmont, Calif.: Wadsworth Publishing, 1989), pp. 445–447.

If a company is cited for pollution, it may not realistically be able to employ a "change nothing" strategy. Two incremental benefits of the costs incurred for clean-up would be the ability to continue in business and a lack of future fines assessed against the company.

best alternative solution. Often, the "change nothing" alternative is selected only because it is easier than making changes. At other times, "change nothing" is chosen because of a lack of information. The lack of information may be seen by decision makers as causing the risk of making a change to be greater than the risk of continuing the current course of action. When this condition exists, the results achieved from the "change nothing" alternative (current results) are thought to be more advantageous than the potential incremental benefit of any other alternative.

In regard to specific government regulations or mandates, there are some situations in which a "change nothing" alternative does not truly exist. For example, if a company were polluting river water and a governmental regulatory agency issued an injunction against it, the company (assuming it wishes to continue in business) would be forced to correct the pollution problem. The company could, of course, delay installation of the pollution control devices at the risk of fines or closure—creating additional incremental cost effects that would need to be considered. Managers must make decisions using a "now-versus-later" attitude and, as shown in the following News Note, may determine that "now" is better regardless of the cost.

Since a comprehensive evaluation of the monetary and nonmonetary effects of all alternative courses of action is part of rational management behavior, the chosen course should be the one that will make the business better off in the future.

Equipment Replacement Decisions

Many business decision situations relate to assets. After an asset or resource is acquired, managers may find that the product produced or service performed by that asset is no longer marketable or that the asset is no longer adequate for the intended purposes, does not perform to expectations, or is not technologically current. Decisions must then be made whether to keep or dispose of the old asset and, if disposed, whether to replace it. While asset acquisition decisions are covered in depth in the next chapter, the following illustration provides an excellent starting point to introduce the concept of using relevant cost information for making asset replacement decisions.

Assume that Debbie Wisnowski purchases a computer system for $3,200 on December 28, 1993, from a company that was going out of business. Debbie expects the computer to last for her three years in law school and, at that time, to have no salvage value. This computer will be referred to as the "old" computer. One week later, on January 4, 1994, Debbie notices an advertisement for a similar computer for $2,300 at one of the major electronics discount stores. This computer also has an estimated life of three years and no salvage value. This "new" computer will perform as well as the "old" computer and, in addition, has a larger hard drive memory for faster processing time. The new computer will save $300 per year in operating, maintenance, and repair costs over the old computer. Upon investigation, Debbie discovers that she can sell her week-old computer for only $2,200—the "going out of business" price had not been such a bargain, and she was unable to return it to the store since it no longer existed. Data on the old and new computers are shown in Exhibit 16–1.

Debbie has two options: (1) use the old computer or (2) sell the old computer and buy the new one. Exhibit 16–2 presents the relevant costs Debbie should consider in making her asset replacement decision. As shown in the computations in Exhibit 16–2, the $3,200 purchase price of the old computer does not affect the decision process. This amount was "gone forever" when Debbie bought the computer. However, if she sells the old computer, she will be able to effectively reduce the net cash outlay for the new computer to $100 because she will have $2,200 more money than she has currently. Using either computer, Debbie will spend money over the next three years for operating costs, but she will spend $900 less using the new computer ($300 savings per year × 3 years).

EXHIBIT 16–1
▼▼▼▼▼▼▼▼▼▼▼

DEBBIE
WISNOWSKI'S
COMPUTER
INFORMATION

	Old Computer (purchased 12/28)	New Computer (available 1/4)
Cost	$3,200	$2,300
Annual Operating Cost	$1,200	$ 900
Salvage Value	0	0
Current Resale Value	$2,200	Not applicable
Life in Years	3	3

The $1,000 difference between the $3,200 original cost and the $2,200 resale value is either a current period loss or, if she keeps the computer, future period depreciation. Thus, the $1,000 loss or its equivalent in depreciation charges is the same in magnitude whether Debbie disposes of the old computer and buys the new one or retains the old computer and uses it. This $1,000 cannot be avoided under either alternative; it will be either a loss or an expense. Since the amount is the same under both alternatives, it is not relevant to the decision process. The relevant factors in deciding whether to purchase the new computer are the:

1. cost of the new computer ($2,300);
2. current resale value of the old computer ($2,200); and
3. annual savings of the new computer ($300) and the number of years (three) the savings would be enjoyed.

The common tendency is to initially believe that Debbie should not purchase the new computer because she will incur a $1,000 loss on an asset that she has only had for seven days. Even if Debbie received only $1,500 from its sale, the choice would have remained the same. In this case, she would save a total of $100 by buying the new computer and abandoning the old, as shown in the following computation:

Operating cost of old computer		$3,600
Cost of new computer:		
Purchase price ($2,300 − $1,500)	$ 800	
Operating cost	2,700	3,500
Savings by purchasing new computer		$ 100

EXHIBIT 16–2
▼▼▼▼▼▼▼▼▼▼▼

RELEVANT COSTS
RELATED TO
WISNOWSKI'S
ALTERNATIVES

Alternative (1): Use old computer	
Operating cost over life of old computer ($1,200 × 3 years)	$3,600
Alternative (2): Sell old computer and buy new	
Cost of new computer	$2,300
Resale value of old computer	2,200
Effective net outlay for new computer	$ 100
Operating cost over life of new computer ($900 × 3 years)	2,700
Total cost of new computer	$2,800
Incremental benefit from purchasing new computer	$ 800

Debbie must resign herself to accept the past as a fact and make new choices given her set of future alternatives.

Relevant costing techniques are also appropriate in make-or-buy decisions.

Make-or-Buy Decisions

Managers involved in manufacturing are continuously concerned about whether the right quality components will be available at the right time and at a reasonable price to assure production. Companies often assure the availability of a component by manufacturing it themselves. In some cases, this decision may be made because the company is interested in embarking on a vertical integration path, in which one division or subsidiary can serve as a supplier to others within the same company. Other companies, like Gateway 2000, believe that the better way is to purchase some or all components from others.

This type of **make-or-buy decision** should be made only after proper analysis. **make-or-buy decision** Managers should compare the cost of internally manufacturing a product component to the cost of purchasing it from outside suppliers (or from another division at a specified transfer price) and, then, assess the best uses of the available facilities. (Consideration of a "make" option implies that the company has the available capacity for that purpose.) Relevant information for this decision includes both quantitative and qualitative factors.

Exhibit 16–3 presents some factors that should be considered in a make-or-buy decision. Several of the quantitative factors (such as incremental prime production cost per unit and the purchase price quoted by the supplier) are known with a high degree of certainty. Other factors, such as the opportunity cost associated with production facilities, must be estimated. The qualitative factors should be evaluated by more than one individual so that personal biases do not cloud valid business judgment.

Relevant Quantitative Factors:
Incremental production costs for each unit
Unit cost of purchasing from outside supplier (price less any discounts available plus shipping, etc.)
Availability of production capacity to manufacture components
Opportunity costs of using facilities for production rather than for other purposes
Availability of storage space for units and raw materials

Relevant Qualitative Factors:
Reliability of source(s) of supply
Ability to control quality when units are purchased from outside
Nature of the work to be subcontracted (such as the importance of the part to the whole)
Number of available suppliers
Impact on customers and markets
Future bargaining position with supplier(s)
Perceptions regarding possible future price changes
Perceptions about current product prices (are the prices appropriate or, in some cases with international suppliers, is product dumping involved?)

EXHIBIT 16–3
▼▼▼▼▼▼▼▼▼▼▼

MAKE-OR-BUY
CONSIDERATIONS

Exhibit 16–4 provides information about a mirror produced by Miso Production Company and installed into the company's camcorders. The total cost to manufacture one mirror is $5. The company can purchase mirrors from a supplier for $4.75 per unit. Miso's accountant is trying to determine if the company should make the mirrors or buy them from the outside supplier.

Relevant costs are those costs that are pertinent and avoidable, regardless of whether they are variable or fixed. In a make-or-buy decision, variable costs of production are relevant. Fixed production costs may be relevant if they can be avoided if production is discontinued. Production of each mirror requires a cost outlay of $4.40 per unit for materials, labor, and variable overhead. In addition, $.20 of the fixed overhead is considered a relevant product cost because it specifically relates to the manufacture of mirrors. This $.20 is an incremental cost, since it could be avoided if mirrors were not produced. The remaining $.40 of fixed overhead is not relevant to the decision of whether to make or buy the mirrors. The $.40 of fixed overhead is a common cost that cannot be associated with mirror production and is incurred because of general production activity. Because this portion of the fixed cost would continue under either alternative, it is not relevant.

The relevant cost for the "make" alternative is $4.60, or the cost that would be avoided if the product was not made. This amount should be compared to the $4.75 price quoted by the supplier under the "buy" alternative. Each amount is the incremental cost of production and purchase, respectively. Based solely on the quantitative information, management should choose to manufacture the mirrors rather than buy them, since $.15 will be saved on each mirror produced rather than purchased.

The opportunity cost of the facilities being used by production may also be relevant in a make-or-buy alternative. Miso's management should review the company's continuing needs for the mirrors and determine if an alternative purpose exists for the facilities now being used to manufacture the mirrors. If a more profitable alternative is available, management should consider diverting the capacity to this alternative use.

For example, assume that Miso Production Company has an opportunity to rent to an outside tenant, the building now used to produce mirrors for $176,000 per year. The company produces 800,000 mirrors annually. There is an opportunity cost of $.22 per unit ($176,000 ÷ 800,000 mirrors) from using rather than renting the

EXHIBIT 16–4
▼▼▼▼▼▼▼▼▼▼▼▼

MISO PRODUCTION COMPANY MAKE-OR-BUY COST INFORMATION

	Present Manufacturing Cost Per Mirror	Relevant Cost to Manufacture Per Mirror
Direct materials	$1.60	$1.60
Direct labor	2.00	2.00
Variable factory overhead	.80	.80
Fixed factory overhead*	.60	.20
Total unit cost	$5.00	$4.60
Quoted price from supplier	$4.75	

*Of the $.60 fixed factory overhead, only $.20 is actually caused by mirror production. This amount is related to the production supervisor's salary and could be avoided if the firm chooses not to produce mirrors. The remaining $.40 of fixed factory overhead is an allocated indirect (common) cost that would continue even if mirror production ceases.

Gateway 2000 has chosen a partial "buy" strategy in the production of its computers. Company management believes that components can be purchased less expensively than they could be made in-house—leaving Gateway employees to assemble those components.

building. There are two ways to treat this opportunity cost. Both methods provide the same selection decision.

First, the $.22 per unit can be treated as a reduction in the purchase cost because the facilities can be rented only if the component is purchased. Second, $.22 per unit can be added to the production cost, since the company is giving up this amount by choosing to make the component. (This treatment is more consistent with the definition of an opportunity cost.) The giving up of inflows is as much a cost as the incurrence of an outflow. Exhibit 16–5 shows these two treatments on a per-unit basis as well as illustrates the computations on a total cost basis. Under all formats, the comparison indicates that there is a $.07 per-unit advantage to purchasing rather than producing.

Miso Production Company's accountant should inform management that, based on the information shown in Exhibit 16–5, it is more economical to buy mirrors from a supplier for $4.75 than to manufacture them. This information is the typical starting point of the decision process—determining whether an alternative satisfies the quantitative considerations of a problem. If it does, managers then use judgment to assess the qualitative aspects of the decision.

Assume that Miso's purchasing agent read in the *Wall Street Journal* that the supplier being considered for mirror manufacturing was in poor financial condition and there was a high probability of a bankruptcy filing. In this case, management would likely decide to continue producing rather than purchasing the mirrors from this supplier. In this instance, quantitative analysis supports the purchase of the units, but qualitative judgment suggests this would not be a wise course of action, since the stability of the supplying source is questionable.

This additional consideration also indicates that there are many potential long-run effects of a theoretically short-run decision. If Miso had stopped mirror produc-

EXHIBIT 16–5
▼▼▼▼▼▼▼▼▼▼▼▼

MISO PRODUCTION
COMPANY
OPPORTUNITY COST
IN A MAKE-OR-BUY
DECISION

	Make	Buy	*or*	Make	Buy
Per unit:					
Direct production costs	$4.60			$4.60	
Opportunity cost (revenue)		$ (.22)		.22	
Purchase cost		4.75			$4.75
Cost per mirror	$4.60	$4.53		$4.82	$4.75

	Make	Buy	Difference in Favor of Purchasing
In total:			
Revenue from renting capacity	$ 0	$ 176,000	$176,000
Cost for 800,000 mirrors	(3,680,000)	(3,800,000)	(120,000)
Net (cost) or revenue	$(3,680,000)	$(3,624,000)	$ 56,000 *

*The $56,000 represents the net purchase benefit of $.07 per unit multiplied by the 800,000 units to be purchased during the year.

tion and rented its facilities and the supplier had gone bankrupt, Miso could be faced with high start-up costs to revitalize its mirror production process. This was essentially the situation faced by Stoneyfield Farm, a New Hampshire-based yogurt company. Stoneyfield Farm subcontracted its yogurt production and, one day, found its supplier bankrupt—creating an inability to fill customer orders. It took Stoneyfield two years to acquire necessary production capacity and regain market strength. The next News Note indicates that many companies are beginning to analyze make-or-buy decisions on the basis of longer-range impacts than basic incremental analyses.

Make-or-buy decisions are not confined to manufacturing entities. Many service organizations must also make the same kinds of choices. For example, accounting and law firms must decide whether to prepare and present in-house continuing education programs or to rely on external sources such as professional organizations or consultants. Private schools must determine whether to have their own school buses or hire independent contractors. Doctors investigate the differences in cost, quality of results, and convenience to patients between having blood work drawn and tested in the office or in separate lab facilities. These examples simply indicate that the term *make* in make-or-buy decisions does not necessarily require converting a raw material to a finished component. It can also mean providing an in-house service.

Make-or-buy decisions consider the opportunity costs of utilized facilities because those facilities are in limited supply. If capacity is occupied in one way, it cannot be used at the same time for another purpose. Limited capacity is only one type of scarce resource that managers need to consider when making decisions.

Scarce Resources Decisions

scarce resources

Managers are frequently confronted with the short-run problem of making the best use of **scarce resources** that are essential to production activity, but are available only in limited quantity. Scarce resources create constraints on producing goods or providing services and can include money, machine hours, skilled labor hours, raw materials, and (as mentioned earlier) production capacity. Management may, in the long

NEWS NOTE

Is Make-or-Buy a Short-Run Decision?

Contrary to what one would expect from reading textbook discussions, make versus buy decisions at six large industrial companies surveyed were rarely treated as incremental decisions made on the basis of differential costing techniques. In the short term, firms apparently buy because they do not have the ability to make. In the long term, they decide whether or not they want to be in a particular business. The decision becomes an investment decision rather than a make/buy decision. Differential cost analyses are omitted not out of concern about integrity of the information but because the make/buy decisions are made on other grounds. For example, one firm makes rather than buys on any operation deemed critical to product quality or customer service. Another executive said that his firm made anything that it could if the company could meet its contract deadlines.

SOURCE: Bernard A. Coda and Barry G. King, "Manufacturing Decision-making Tools," (Spring 1989), pp. 32–33. Reprinted with permission from *Journal of Cost Management for the Manufacturing Industry*. Warren, Gorham & Lamont, a division of Research Institute of America, 210 South Street, Boston, Mass., 02111. All rights reserved.

run, desire and be able to obtain a greater abundance of a scarce resource. For instance, additional machines could be purchased to increase availability of machine hours. However, in the short run, management must make the best current use of the scarce resources it has.

Determining the best use of a scarce resource requires that specific company objectives be recognized. If management's objective is to maximize company contribution margin and profits, the best use of a scarce resource is for the production and sale of a product that has the highest contribution margin *per unit of the scarce resource*. This strategy assumes that the company is faced with only one scarce resource.

Exhibit 16–6 presents information on two products being manufactured by the Tipgos Company. The company's scarce resource is its access to machine time; only 4,000 machine hours are available per month to make either Product A or Product B

	Product A	Product B
Selling price per unit (a)	$ 30	$ 24
Variable production cost per unit:		
Direct materials	$ 6	$ 5
Direct labor	8	4
Variable overhead	6	2
Total variable cost (b)	$ 20	$ 11
Unit contribution margin [(c) = (a) − (b)]	$ 10	$ 13
Times units of output per machine hour (d)	80	40
Contribution margin per machine hour [(a) × (d)]	$800	$520

EXHIBIT 16–6

▼▼▼▼▼▼▼▼▼▼▼▼▼

TIPGOS COMPANY
PRODUCT
INFORMATION

or some combination of both. Demand is unlimited for both products. There are no variable selling, general, or administrative costs related to either product.

Product A's $30 unit selling price minus its $20 unit variable cost provides a contribution margin of $10 per unit. Product B's contribution margin per unit is $13 ($24 selling price less $11 variable cost). Fixed overhead totals $320,000 and is allocated to products on a per-unit basis for purposes of inventory valuation. However, fixed overhead does not change with production levels within the relevant range and, therefore, is not a relevant cost for a scarce resource mix decision.

Since fixed overhead per unit is not relevant in the present case, unit contribution margin rather than unit gross margin is the appropriate measure of profitability of the two products.[4] Unit contribution margin is multiplied by the number of units of output per unit of the scarce resource (in this case, machine hours) to obtain the contribution margin per unit of scarce resource. The last line in Exhibit 16–6 shows the $800 contribution margin per machine hour ($10 × 80) for Product A compared to $520 for Product B ($13 × 40). Product A is the more profitable item for Tipgos Company to produce.

At first glance, it would appear that Product B would be the more profitable, since its $13 contribution margin per unit is higher than A's $10 contribution margin per unit. However, since one hour of machine time produces twice as many units of A as B, a greater amount of contribution margin per hour of scarce resource is generated by the production of A. If the Tipgos Company wants to achieve the highest possible profit, it would dedicate all machine time to the production of Product A. Such a strategy would provide a total contribution margin of $3,200,000 per month, if all units produced were sold.

When one limiting factor is involved, the outcome of a scarce resource decision will always indicate that a single type of product should be manufactured and sold. Most situations, however, involve several limiting factors that compete with one another in the process of striving to attain business objectives. One method used to solve problems that have several limiting factors is **linear programming** (LP). LP finds the optimal allocation of scarce resources when there is one objective and multiple restrictions on achieving that objective.[5]

linear programming

In addition to concern about the quantitative effects of scarce resources, managers must remember that all factors involved in the decision alternatives cannot be readily quantified. Company management must also consider qualitative aspects of the problem in addition to the quantitative ones. For example, to achieve the maximum possible profit, Tipgos Company would have to produce only Product A during the available machine time. Before choosing such a strategy, company managers would need to assess the potential damage to reputation and image of limiting its market assortment of products to customers by providing one product to the exclusion of another. If the two products under consideration were family and single-serving sizes of breakfast cereal, Tipgos might be eliminating restaurants as part of its customer base because they would not be likely to purchase the product in the single-serving size.

Concentrating on a single product could create market saturation. In Montana, the owners of the Havre Culligan Water Conditioning franchise found that finally

---

[4]Gross margin is unit selling price minus total production cost per unit. Total production cost includes allocated fixed overhead.

[5]LP is briefly discussed in the appendix to this chapter and is covered in depth in most management science courses.

NEWS NOTE

Dollars Pour in from Barbie Accessory Sales

"Barbie is the great strength of our company," says John W. Amerman, Chairman & CEO of Mattel, Inc. By early 1990, more than half a billion Barbies have been manufactured and sold; the doll sells at a rate in excess of 100,000 a day.

Amerman's management team saw an opportunity in the fact that most consumers considered Barbie as simply a doll—albeit the world's best-known one—for youngsters aged three to 11. Mattel might be able to sell more dolls, but there was more. Rather than just sell Barbie dolls, Amerman opted to merchandise the "Barbie Lifestyle" and added Barbie-theme accessories.

Amerman's "Barbie" strategy is paying off. Sales of Barbie and her accessory items increased from $430 million in 1987 to $590 million in 1989. Mattel expects to do even better in the years ahead. "Around here, we like to call her 'Billion Dollar Barbie'," he says with a vision in his eye.

SOURCE: Mike Sheridan, "John W. Amerman" (June 1989), pp. 46–47. This article has been excerpted through the courtesy of Halsey Publishing Co., publishers of Delta Airlines' *SKY* magazine.

everyone in the area had water softening equipment. The company then focused on diversifying its product line.

It is also possible that multiple products may be complementary, that one product cannot be used without the other, or that one product will be the key to revenue generation in future periods. To illustrate the first possibility, consider Cross's well-known ballpoint pen and mechanical pencil sets—a standard graduation gift. As to the second possibility, consider Drexel Furniture, which makes both dining room tables and dining room chairs. And, thirdly, consider Mattel, Inc., the producer of Barbie dolls. Would it be reasonable for Mattel to produce only Barbie dolls and none of her related accessories (clothes, dream house, car, camper, and so forth)? While the sale of Barbie dolls makes money, the flows from the total group of Barbie products are enormous, as indicated in the above News Note.

Thus, company management may decide that production and sale of some number of less profitable products are necessary parts of the company's product mix to maintain either customer satisfaction or sales of another product. Production mix translates into sales mix on the revenue side. The next section addresses the issue of sales mix.

Sales Mix Decisions

Management continuously strives to satisfy a variety of company objectives such as maximization of company profit, improvement of relative market share, and generation of customer goodwill and loyalty. These objectives are achieved through selling products or performing services. Regardless of whether the company is a retailer, manufacturer, or service organization, **sales mix** refers to "the relative combination of quantities of sales of the various products that make up the total sales of a com-

sales mix

EXHIBIT 16–7

STRUVE COMPANY PRODUCT INFORMATION

	Economy	Standard	Deluxe
Unit selling price	$90	$120	$150
Variable unit costs:			
Direct materials	$15	$ 20	$ 36
Direct labor	10	15	31
Variable factory overhead	3	7	17
Total variable production cost	$28	$ 42	$ 84
Variable selling expense*	9	12	15
Total variable costs	$37	$ 54	$ 99
Contribution margin per unit	$53	$ 66	$ 51

Total fixed costs:	
Production	$ 750,000
Selling & administrative	375,000
Total	$1,125,000

*The only variable selling expense is for sales commissions, which are always set at 10 percent of the selling price per unit.

pany." [6] Some important factors affecting the appropriate sales mix of a company are product selling prices, sales force compensation, and advertising expenditures. A change in one or all of these factors may cause a company's sales mix to shift.

Supportive Homecare Corporation of Oshkosh, Wisconsin, can be used to illustrate a shift in sales mix. The company began business by providing in-home nursing services. However, when health care reimbursement for home health aides declined substantially, Terri Hanson decided to expand her sales mix to include markets that did not require health care funding, such as hospital temporary personnel services and home management services for executives. Revenues, profits, and number of employees all increased for the company.

The Struve Company data presented in Exhibit 16–7 are used to illustrate the effects on sales mix of the three factors mentioned earlier. The company produces three types of briefcases: economy, standard, and deluxe.

Sales Price Changes and Relative Profitability of Products   Managers must continuously monitor the relative selling prices of company products, in respect to each other as well as to competitors' prices. This process may provide information that causes management to change one or more selling prices. For example, if Struve Company found that deluxe briefcases sold better during the spring (because of graduations) than at other times, the sales price of these briefcases might be increased during this period. Factors that might influence price changes include fluctuations in demand, production/distribution costs, economic conditions, and competition. Any shift in the selling price of one product in a multiproduct firm will normally cause a change in sales mix of that firm because of the economic law of demand elasticity with respect to price.[7]

---

[6]Institute of Management Accountants (formerly National Association of Accountants), "Management Accounting Terminology," *Statements of Management Accounting Number 2* (Montvale, N.J.: June 1, 1983), p. 94.

[7]The law of demand elasticity is discussed in chapter 10 and indicates how closely price and demand are related. Product demand is highly elastic if a small price reduction generates a large demand increase. If demand is less elastic, large price reductions are needed to bring about moderate sales volume increases.

Mattel has established a firm hold on related product sales for its Barbie dolls. While the doll herself retails for less than $25, the entire product line generates sales in the several hundred-million-dollar range each year.

Struve's management has set profit maximization as the primary corporate objective. This strategy does not necessarily mean selling as many units as possible of the product with the highest selling price and as few as possible of the products with the lower selling prices. The product with the highest selling price per unit does not necessarily yield the highest contribution margin per unit or per unit of scarce resource. In Struve Company's case, deluxe briefcases yield the lowest unit contribution margin of the three products. It is also probable that one deluxe case requires both more direct labor and more machine time, based on the large costs shown for direct labor and variable overhead. But even making the simplistic assumption of no scarce resources, it is more profit-beneficial to sell standard cases than either economy or deluxe, since a standard briefcase provides the highest unit contribution margin of the three products. Even the economy briefcases are more profitable than the deluxe, because although the economy case has the lowest unit selling price, its unit contribution margin is greater than that of the deluxe case.

If profit maximization is a company's goal, a product's sales volume and unit contribution margin should be considered. Total company contribution margin is equal to the combined contribution margins provided by all the products' sales. Exhibit 16–8 indicates the respective total contribution margins of Struve's three types of briefcases. While the economy cases do not have the highest unit contribution margin, they do generate the largest total company contribution margin because of their sales volume. To maximize profits, Struve management must maximize total contribution margin rather than per-unit contribution margin.

EXHIBIT 16–8
▼▼▼▼▼▼▼▼▼▼▼▼

STRUVE COMPANY
RELATIONSHIP
BETWEEN
CONTRIBUTION
MARGIN AND SALES
VOLUME

	Unit Contribution Margin (from Exhibit 16–7)	Current Sales Volume in Units	Contribution Margin Information
Economy briefcases	$53	20,000	$1,060,000
Standard briefcases	$66	13,000	858,000
Deluxe briefcases	$51	8,000	408,000
Total contribution margin of product sales mix			$2,326,000
Fixed costs (from Exhibit 16–7)			1,125,000
Net income at present volume and sales mix			$1,201,000

The sales volume of a product or service is almost always intricately related to its selling price. Generally, when the selling price of a good is increased and demand is elastic with respect to price, demand for that good decreases.[8] Thus, if Struve management, in an attempt to increase profits, decides to raise the price of the economy briefcases to $100, there should be some decline in demand. Assume that consultation with the marketing research personnel indicates that such a price increase would cause demand for that product to drop from 20,000 cases to 17,000 cases per period. Exhibit 16–9 shows the effect of this pricing decision on total net income of the Struve Company.

Even though the contribution margin per unit of the economy cases increased from $53 to $62, the total dollar contribution margin generated by sales of that product declined because of the decrease in sales volume. This example assumed that customers did not switch their purchases from economy cases to other Struve Company briefcases when the price of the economy case was raised. Price increases will normally cause customers to switch from a company's high-priced products to its lower-priced products or to a competitor's product. Switching within the company was ignored in this instance because the economy cases were the lowest-priced briefcase sold by the Struve Company. It is *unlikely* that customers would stop buying economy briefcases because of a $10 price increase and begin buying standard cases that would have cost even more—but that situation could occur. Customers might believe that the difference in quality between the economy and standard cases is worth the $20 (rather than $30) difference and make such a purchasing switch.

In making decisions to raise or lower prices, the relevant quantitative factors include: (1) prospective or new contribution margin per unit of product; (2) both short-term and long-term changes in product demand and production volume because of the price increase or decrease; and (3) best use of any scarce resources faced by the company. Some relevant qualitative factors involved in pricing decisions are: (1) impact of changes on customer goodwill toward the company; (2) customer loyalty toward company products; and (3) competitors' responses to the firm's new pricing structure.[9]

---

[8]Such a decline in demand would generally not occur when the product in question has no close substitutes or is not a major expenditure in consumers' budgets.

[9]In regard to this last item, consider what occurs when one airline raises or lowers its fares between cities. It typically does not take very long for all the other airlines flying that route to adjust their fares accordingly. Thus, any competitive advantage is often only for a short time span.

EXHIBIT 16–9

▼▼▼▼▼▼▼▼▼▼▼▼▼

STRUVE COMPANY
RELATIONSHIP
BETWEEN SALES
PRICE AND DEMAND

	Unit Contribution Margin	New Sales Volume in Units	Contribution Margin Information
Economy briefcases	$62*	17,000	$1,054,000
Standard briefcases	$66	13,000	858,000
Deluxe briefcases	$51	8,000	408,000
Total contribution margin of product sales mix			$2,320,000
Fixed costs			1,125,000
Net income at new volume of sales			$1,195,000

*New selling price of $100 minus [total variable production cost of $28 plus variable selling expense of $10 (10% of new selling price)].

When managers decide to make price changes for current products or introduce new products that will compete with and potentially impact sales volumes of current products, they need to be certain that their assumptions about consumer behavior are rational. The News Note on the next page discusses the idea of the rational "base case" scenario.

Compensation Changes   Many companies compensate their salespeople by paying a fixed rate of commission on gross sales dollars. If Struve Company uses this type of commission structure, sales personnel will be motivated to sell deluxe briefcases, rather than economy or standard. Sales of the deluxe cases will not achieve the company's profit maximization objective, since these cases provide the lowest unit contribution margin. If management wants to motivate salespeople so that the company is able to achieve its profit maximization objective, a change in the commission compensation structure is needed.

Struve is considering a new commission policy of paying salespeople a commission of 18 percent on **product contribution margin** rather than 10 percent on sales price. Product contribution margin is equal to selling price minus total variable production costs; it does not consider variable selling costs. The per-unit product contribution margins of each of Struve's products are as follows:

product contribution margin

	Selling Price	Total Variable Production Cost	Product Contribution Margin
Economy briefcases	$ 90	$28	$62
Standard briefcases	120	42	78
Deluxe briefcases	150	84	66

This policy change should motivate sales personnel to sell more of the product that would produce the highest commission, which, in turn, will shift the original sales mix toward sales of products most profitable to the company.

Exhibit 16–10 compares Struve's total contribution margin using the original sales mix and commission structure (repeated from Exhibit 16–8) with total contribution margin provided under a newly assumed sales mix and commission structure. The new commission policy is beneficial for the company because it shifts sales mix

Make Sure Your "Base Case" Is an Appropriate Comparison

Finance theory assumes that a project will be evaluated against its base case, that is, what will happen if the project is not carried out. Managers tend to explore fully the implications of adopting the project but usually spend less time considering the likely outcome of not making the investment. Yet unless the base case is realistic, the incremental cash flows—the difference between the "with" and the "without" scenarios—will mislead.

Often companies implicitly assume that the base case is simply a continuation of the status quo, but this assumption ignores market trends and competitor behavior. It also neglects the impact of changes the company might make anyway, like improving operations management. Using the wrong base case is typical of product launches in which the new product will likely erode the market for the company's existing product line. Take Apple Computer's introduction of the Macintosh SE. The new PC had obvious implications for sales of earlier generation Macintoshes. To analyze the incremental cash flows arising from the new product, Apple would have needed to count the lost contribution from sales of its existing products as a cost of the launch.

Wrongly applied, however, this approach would equate the without case to the status quo: it would assume that without the SE, sales of existing Macintoshes would continue at their current level. In the competitive PC market, however, nothing stands still. Competitors like IBM would likely innovate and take share away from the earlier generation Macintoshes—which a more realistic base case would have reflected.

SOURCE: An excerpt from "Must Finance and Strategy Clash?" by Patrick Barwise, Paul R. Marsh, and Robin Wensley (September–October 1989), p. 86. Reprinted by permission of *Harvard Business Review*. Copyright © 1989 by the President and Fellows of Harvard College; all rights reserved.

from the high-priced, low contribution margin deluxe briefcases toward the lower-priced, but more profitable standard cases. In this case, some shifting will also take place away from the economy briefcase.

Fixed costs are not considered in setting sales commissions. All sales and production volumes of the respective products are assumed to be within the relevant range of activity for the company. Therefore, regardless of a shift in activity levels, total fixed costs will remain constant.

Advertising Budget Changes Another factor that may cause shifts in the sales mix involves either adjusting the proportion of the advertising budgets respective to each product the company sells or increasing the total company advertising budget. This discussion uses the original data for the Struve Company and examines a proposed increase in the company's total advertising budget.

Struve's advertising manager, Lee Mundell, has proposed doubling the advertising budget from $30,000 to $60,000 per year. Lee thinks the increased advertising will result in the following additional unit sales during the coming year: Economy, 200 cases; Standard, 500 cases; and Deluxe, 100 cases.

If the company spends the additional $30,000 for advertising, will the additional 800 units of sales produce larger profits than Struve is currently experiencing? The original fixed costs as well as the contribution margin generated by the old sales level

Old Policy—Commissions equal to 10 percent of selling price per unit

	Product Contribution Margin	Commission	Contribution Margin After Commission	Old Volume	Total Contribution Margin
Economy cases	$62	$ 9.00 (.1 × $ 90)	$53.00	20,000	$1,060,000
Standard cases	78	12.00 (.1 × $120)	66.00	13,000	858,000
Deluxe cases	66	15.00 (.1 × $150)	51.00	8,000	408,000
Total contribution margin for product sales					$2,326,000

New Policy—Commissions equal to 18 percent of product contribution margin per unit

	Product Contribution Margin	Commission	Contribution Margin After Commission	New Volume	Total Contribution Margin
Economy cases	$62	$11.16 (.18 × $62)	$50.84	17,600	$ 894,784
Standard cases	78	14.04 (.18 × $78)	63.96	17,900	1,144,884
Deluxe cases	66	11.88 (.18 × $66)	54.12	5,500	297,660
Total contribution margin for product sales					$2,337,328

EXHIBIT 16–10

STRUVE COMPANY
IMPACT OF CHANGE
IN COMMISSION
STRUCTURE

are irrelevant to the decision. The relevant items are the increased sales revenue, increased variable costs, and increased fixed cost—the incremental effects of the change. The difference between incremental revenues and incremental variable costs is the incremental contribution margin. Incremental contribution margin minus the incremental fixed cost is the incremental benefit (or loss) of the decision.[10]

Exhibit 16–11 on page 732 shows the expected increase in contribution margin if the increased advertising expenditures are made. The $48,700 of additional contribution margin far exceeds the $30,000 incremental cost for advertising, so the Struve Company should definitely increase its advertising by $30,000.

Increasing advertising may cause changes in the sales mix or the number of units sold. Sales can also be affected by opportunities that allow companies to obtain business at a sales price that differs from the normal price. Such special pricing situations are discussed in chapter 10.

Product Line Decisions

To make better performance evaluations, operating results of multiproduct environments are often presented in a format that indicates separate product lines. In reviewing these disaggregated statements, managers must distinguish relevant from irrelevant information, in a manner that relates to the individual product lines. If all costs (variable and fixed) are allocated to product lines, a product line or segment may be perceived to be operating at a loss when actually it is not. Such perceptions may be caused by the commingling of relevant and irrelevant information on the statements.

Exhibit 16–12 presents basic earnings information for the Lanai Corporation, which manufactures silk products. The company has three product lines: ties, scarves, and lingerie. The format of the information given in the top of the exhibit makes it

[10]This same type of incremental analysis is shown in chapter 9 in relation to CVP computations.

EXHIBIT 16–11

STRUVE COMPANY
INCREMENTAL
ANALYSIS OF
INCREASED
ADVERTISING COST

	Economy	Standard	Deluxe	Total
New volume	20,200	13,500	8,100	41,800
Old volume	20,000	13,000	8,000	41,000
Increase in volume	200	500	100	800
Contribution margin per unit	× $53	× $66	× $51	
Incremental contribution margin	$10,600	$33,000	$5,100	$48,700
Incremental fixed cost of advertising				30,000
Incremental benefit of increased advertising expenditure				$18,700

appear that the tie and scarf lines are each operating at a net loss ($16,500 and $5,250, respectively). Managers reviewing such results might reason that the firm would be $21,750 more profitable if both of these products were eliminated. Such a conclusion may be premature because of the mixture of relevant and irrelevant information in the income statement presentation. This mixture results from the fact that all fixed expenses have been allocated to the individual product lines.

Fixed cost allocations are traditionally based on one or more measures that are presumed to provide an "equitable" division of costs. These measures might include square footage of the manufacturing plant occupied by each product line, number of machine hours incurred for production of each product line, or number of employees directly associated with each product line. Regardless of the allocation base, allocations may force fixed costs into specific product line operating results even though those costs may not have actually been caused by the making and/or selling of the specific product line. This inequity results from the fact that most cost allocation schemes currently used by managers are arbitrary.

The detail in Exhibit 16–12 separates Lanai's fixed expenses into three categories: (1) those that are avoidable if the particular product line is eliminated; (2) those that are directly associated with a particular product line, but are unavoid-

EXHIBIT 16–12

LANAI
CORPORATION
PRODUCT LINE
INCOME
STATEMENT

	Ties	Scarves	Lingerie	Total
Sales	$150,000	$85,000	$380,000	$615,000
Total direct variable expenses	87,500	55,250	228,000	370,750
Total contribution margin	$ 62,500	$29,750	$152,000	$244,250
Total fixed expenses	79,000	35,000	76,000	190,000
Net income (loss)	$ (16,500)	$ (5,250)	$ 76,000	$ 54,250
Fixed expenses are detailed below:				
1. Avoidable fixed expenses	$ 50,000	$32,000	$ 48,000	$130,000
2. Unavoidable fixed expenses	9,000	1,000	6,000	16,000
3. Allocated common costs	20,000	2,000	22,000	44,000
Total	$ 79,000	$35,000	$ 76,000	$190,000

	Ties	Scarves	Lingerie	Total
Sales	$150,000	$85,000	$380,000	$615,000
Total direct variable expenses	87,500	55,250	228,000	370,750
Total contribution margin	$ 62,500	$29,750	$152,000	$244,250
(1) Avoidable fixed expenses	50,000	32,000	48,000	130,000
Segment margin	$ 12,500	$ (2,250)	$104,000	$114,250
(2) Unavoidable direct fixed expenses (see Exhibit 16–12)				16,000
Total product line operating results				$ 98,250
(3) Common costs				44,000
Net income (loss)				$ 54,250

EXHIBIT 16–13
▼▼▼▼▼▼▼▼▼▼▼▼

LANAI
CORPORATION
SEGMENT MARGIN
INCOME
STATEMENT

able; and (3) those that are incurred for the company as a whole (common costs) and that are allocated to the individual product lines. The latter two categories are irrelevant to the question of whether to eliminate a product line.

An unavoidable cost will be shifted to another product line if the product line with which it is associated is eliminated. For example, Lanai has several senior employees who work in the tie area. If that product line were eliminated, those employees would be transferred to scarves or lingerie. Depreciation on factory equipment used to manufacture a specific product is an irrelevant cost in product line decisions. If the equipment will be kept in service and used to produce other products, the depreciation expense on it is unavoidable and irrelevant to the decision. However, if the equipment can be sold, the selling price is relevant to the decision because it would increase the marginal benefit of the decision to discontinue the product line.

Common costs will be incurred regardless of which product lines are retained. One example of a common cost is the insurance premium on a manufacturing facility that houses all product lines.

If Lanai eliminated both ties and scarves, total company profit would decline by $10,250. This amount represents the combined lost **segment margin** of the two product lines shown in Exhibit 16–13. Segment margin represents the excess of revenues over direct variable expenses and avoidable fixed expenses. It is the amount remaining to cover unavoidable direct fixed expenses and common costs and, then, to provide profits.[11] The segment margin figure is the appropriate one on which to base continuation or elimination decisions, since that figure measures the segment's contribution to the coverage of indirect and unavoidable costs. This decrease in total company income can be shown in the following alternative computations:

segment margin

Current net income	$ 54,250
Increase in income due to elimination of scarf product line (segment margin)	2,250
Decrease in income due to elimination of tie product line (segment margin)	(12,500)
New net income	$ 44,000
or	

---

[11]It is assumed here that all common costs are fixed costs; this is not always the case. Some common costs are variable, such as costs of processing purchase orders or computer time-sharing expenses for payroll or other corporate functions.

NEWS NOTE

Consider the Potential As Well As the Costs

If an ailing business is to grow again, tinkering around the edges won't make it happen. You've got to challenge the deepest assumptions on which the business is based. Consider Jell-O gelatin, which for years had been considered a cash cow to be milked for profits, not a business to invest in. As a result its sales over the last two decades had been allowed to shrink about 2% a year. Believing Jell-O to be a star in disguise, Richard Mayer (president of General Foods) broke with old wisdom and, in 1989, invested most of the product's $50 million marketing budget in Jigglers—Jell-O to hold in your hand and eat as a snack. By April 1990, Jell-O sales were up 40% over 1989 and profits were wiggling upwards.

But what if Jell-O really had been a mature business with no growth left? That $50 million was a big bet to place. Leo McKernan of Clark Equipment (a business near collapse in 1986) suggests breaking a business down into its basic parts and then analyzing how many of them need fixing. He developed the idea in the late 1970s while trying to turn around Clark's money-losing crane division. Then a vice president, he did his analysis and found the business needed a total overhaul: upgraded factories, stronger distribution channels, and a new generation of product. His conclusion: "The cost of fixing that business was too high. With only a 50% chance of turning it around, it wasn't worth it." Instead, Clark liquidated the division.

SOURCE: Brian Dumaine, "The New Turnaround Champs," *FORTUNE* (July 16, 1990), p. 40. © 1990 The Time Inc. Magazine Company. All rights reserved.

Total contribution margin of lingerie product line	$152,000
Minus avoidable fixed expenses of lingerie product line	48,000
Segment margin of the lingerie product line	$104,000
Minus all remaining expenses shown on Exhibit 16–13 ($16,000 + $44,000)	60,000
Remaining income with one product line	$ 44,000

Based on the information in Exhibit 16–13, Lanai should eliminate the scarf line. That product line is generating a negative segment margin and, thus, is not even covering its own costs. If the scarf line were eliminated, total company profit would increase by $2,250, the amount of negative segment margin.

Before making spontaneous decisions to discontinue a product line, management should carefully consider what it would take to "turn that product line or division around." The preceding News Note indicates two sides of the discontinuance issue.

┌─────────────────────────────────┐
│   SITE ANALYSIS   │
└─────────────────────────────────┘

Decision making by managers is not an easy task. Because management is a social rather than a natural science, there are no fundamental "truths," and few problems are susceptible to black-or-white solutions. Relevant costing is a process of making human approximations of the costs of alternative decision results. The implications and applications of relevant costing to decision making are extensive (as shown in the Applications Strategies). But be aware that relevant costing will foster good decision making only if the details of the decision are understood by all involved and an interdisciplinary approach to decision making is taken.

> Rationalist decision makers simply need to know much more than ever before. Of course, with computers our capacity to collect and to semiprocess information has grown, but information is not the same as knowledge. The production of knowledge is analogous to the manufacture of any other product. We begin with the raw material of facts (of which we often have a more than adequate supply). We pretreat these by means of classification, tabulation, summary, and so on, and then proceed to the assembly of correlations and comparisons. But the final product, conclusions, does not simply roll off the production line. Indeed, without powerful overarching explanatory schemes (or theories), whatever knowledge there is in the mountain of data we daily amass is often invisible.[12]

For Gateway 2000, the decision to assemble but not manufacture is a critical one. This decision has produced some problems. For example, in 1991, the company ran out of one type of monitor and was forced to ship a more expensive one for the same price to maintain customer relations and provide prompt delivery. Also, only first-year on-site repairs are available for customers—a problem that Gateway is attempting to negotiate with its suppliers. Waitt also wants to have a laptop for sale by 1992. In other companies, this choice would require capital investment and R&D; at Gateway, this decision means detailed negotiation with suppliers.[13]

Whether Gateway will ever opt to make any or all of its components is unknown, but Waitt knows that service and delivery time are critical. If he can keep his suppliers on top of these qualitative issues, the decision to rely on the quantitative benefits of low overhead may prove an excellent one.

CHAPTER SUMMARY

Management's task is to effectively and efficiently allocate its finite stock of resources to accomplish its chosen set of corporate objectives. Managers should explain how requested information will be used, so that accountants can make certain relevant information is provided in an appropriate form. In this way, managers will have a reliable quantitative basis on which to analyze problems, compare viable solutions, and choose the best course of action.

---

[12]"Humble Decision Making," p. 123.
[13]Andrew Kupfer, "The Champ of Cheap Clones," *FORTUNE* (September 23, 1991), p. 120.

	Discipline	Applications
APPLICATIONS STRATEGIES OF RELEVANT COSTING	Accounting	Helps to distinguish relevant costs for purposes of decision making; reinforces the idea that past costs are sunk costs
	Economics	Is a form of the economic concept of marginal costing, which advises that rational decisions for short-run problems are made on the basis of marginal revenue versus marginal cost; understanding the concept of relevant costs will help the decision maker avoid two common pitfalls: ignoring opportunity cost and ascribing significance to sunk costs; decisions should be made on the basis of incremental revenues versus incremental (relevant and opportunity) costs
	Finance	Helps in making major financial decisions about expansion or contraction of product lines
	Management	Helps to indicate the critical nature of differentiating among avoidable fixed, unavoidable fixed, and allocated common costs to make valid product decisions; helps to differentiate between costs that are useful for short-run versus long-run decisions; helps to make scarce resource allocation decisions
	Marketing	Helps to indicate the reasons behind basing sales commissions on contribution margin rather than sales price, basing special prices on incremental costs to win the business, and justifying additional advertising costs by comparing the increase in fixed costs with the incremental contribution generated by the advertising

For information to be relevant, it must (1) relate to the decision at hand, (2) be important to the decision, and (3) have a bearing upon a future endeavor. Relevant costing compares the incremental or additional revenues and/or costs associated with alternative decisions.

Relevant information may be both quantitative and qualitative. Variable costs are generally relevant to a decision; they are irrelevant only when they cannot be avoided under any possible alternative or when they do not differ between (or among) alternatives. Direct avoidable fixed costs are also relevant to decision making. Sometimes costs give the illusion of being relevant when they actually are not. Examples of such irrelevant costs include sunk costs, arbitrarily allocated common costs, and nonincremental fixed costs that have been averaged on a per-unit basis.

Managers use relevant cost information to determine the incremental benefits of alternatives. One option often available is to "change nothing." This option provides zero incremental benefit to the company. After rigorous analysis of the quantifiable factors associated with each alternative, a manager must assess the merits and potential risks of the qualitative factors involved, so that the best possible course of action is chosen.

Situations in which relevant costing is essential include further processing decisions, asset replacement problems, make-or-buy decisions, scarce resource allocations, sales mix distributions, and questions about retention or elimination of product lines. The following points are important to remember:

1. In a further processing decision about products at split-off, ignore the total or allocated joint cost. The only relevant items are the incremental revenues and costs of processing further.

2. In an asset replacement decision, costs paid in the past are not relevant because they have already been incurred; therefore, ignore sunk costs.

3. In a make-or-buy decision, include the opportunity costs associated with the buy alternative; the buy alternative potentially allows management an opportunity to make plant assets and personnel available for other purposes.

4. In a single scarce resource decision, if the objective is to maximize company contribution margin and profits, then production and sales should be focused toward the product with the highest contribution margin per unit of the scarce resource.

5. In a sales mix decision, changes in selling prices and advertising will normally affect sales volume, thus changing the company's total contribution margin. Also, tying sales commissions to contribution margin will motivate salespeople to sell products that are most beneficial to the company's profit picture.

6. In a product line decision, product lines should be evaluated on their segment margins rather than on their income amounts. Segment margin includes any relevant direct costs, but excludes any allocated common costs of the entity.

The quantitative analysis presented in this chapter is short-range in perspective. Additional qualitative factors should be reviewed by management in each case. Some of these qualitative factors may have long-range planning and policy implications. Other qualitative factors may be short-range in nature. Managers must decide the relevance of individual factors based on experience, judgment, knowledge of economic theory, and use of logic.

APPENDIX

Linear Programming

Linear programming (LP) is a method used to solve problems with one objective and multiple limiting factors. LP is used to find the optimal allocation of scarce resources when the objective and restrictions on achieving that objective can be stated as linear equations. This technique is also useful in determining the appropriate amount of scarce resources to allocate to other than the single product that would be chosen if the "maximize the scarce resource" criterion is used.

The objective in an LP problem will be to either maximize or minimize some measure of performance. The mathematical equation stating that objective is called the **objective function.** For example, a company's objective could be to maximize contribution margin or to minimize product cost. A linear programming problem can have only one goal expressed as the objective function.

objective function

A restriction that hampers management's pursuits of its objective is a **constraint.** There are several types of constraints. Resource constraints involve limited availability of labor time, machine time, raw materials, space, or production capacity. De-

constraint

mand or marketing constraints restrict the quantity of the product that can be sold during a time period. Constraints can also be in the form of technical product requirements. For example, management may be constrained in the production requirements for frozen meals by caloric or vitamin content. A final constraint in all LP problems is a non-negativity constraint. This constraint specifies that there cannot be negative values of physical quantities. Constraints, like the objective function, are specified in mathematical equations and represent the limits imposed on optimizing the objective function.

feasible solutions

Almost every allocation problem has a multiple number of **feasible solutions** that do not violate any of the problem constraints. Different solutions will generally give different values for the objective function. In some cases, a problem may have several solutions that provide the same value for the objective function. Solutions may also be generated that contain fractional values. The **optimal solution** to a maximization or minimization goal is the one that provides the best answer to the allocation problem. Some LP problems may have more than one optimal solution.

optimal solution

simplex

Linear programming problems may be solved by a graphical approach, or the **simplex** method. Graphs are simple to use and provide a visual representation of the problem. However, because of the inability to accurately draw and interpret graphs in three or more dimensions, graphical approaches to solving LP problems lose their appeal when the number of unknowns exceeds two. In such cases, the computer-adaptable simplex method can be used.

Simplex is an iterative (sequential) algorithm used to solve multivariable, multi-constraint LP problems. (An algorithm is a logical step-by-step problem-solving technique that continuously searches for an improved solution from the one previously computed.) Simplex solutions also provide valuable additional information that may be used in budgeting and production analyses.

Detailed solutions to linear programming problems are beyond the scope of this text.

Glossary

By-product   an incidental output of a joint process; has a higher sales value than scrap

Constraint   a restriction that hampers the ability to reach an objective (from appendix)

Feasible solution   an answer to a linear programming problem that does not violate any of the problem constraints (from appendix)

Incremental cost   the additional cost of producing or selling a contemplated quantity of output

Incremental revenue   the additional revenue resulting from a contemplated sale of a quantity of output

Joint cost   the cost incurred, up to the split-off point, for materials, labor, and overhead during a joint process

Joint process   a single process in which one product cannot be manufactured without producing others

Joint products   the primary outputs of a joint process, each of which has substantial revenue-generating ability

Linear programming   a method used to solve problems with one objective and multiple limiting factors; finds the optimal allocation of scarce resources when the objective and restrictions on achieving that objective can be stated as linear equations

Make-or-buy decision   a decision that compares the cost of internally manufacturing a product component to the cost of purchasing it from outside suppliers or from another division at a specified transfer price and, thus, attempts to assess the best uses of available facilities

Objective function   the mathematical equation that states the maximization or minimization goal of a linear programming problem (from appendix)

Optimal solution   the solution to a linear programming problem that provides the best answer to the allocation problem without violating any problem constraints (from appendix)

Product contribution margin   an amount equal to selling price minus total variable production costs; does not consider variable selling costs

Relevant cost   a cost that is pertinent to or logically associated with a specific problem or decision

Relevant costing   a process that allows managers to focus on pertinent facts and disregard extraneous information by comparing, to the extent possible and practical, incremental revenues and incremental costs of alternative decisions

Sales mix   the relative combination of quantities of sales of the various products that make up the total sales of a company

Scarce resource   an item that is essential to production activity, but that is available only in a limited quantity

Scrap   an incidental output of a joint process; has a lower sales value than a by-product

Segment margin   the excess of revenues over direct variable expenses and avoidable fixed expenses; the amount remaining to cover unavoidable direct fixed expenses and common costs and, then, to provide profits

Simplex   an iterative, step-by-step technique used to solve multi-variable, multi-constraint linear programming problems; usually requires the aid of a computer (from appendix)

Split-off point   the point at which the outputs of a joint process are first identifiable as individual products

Sunk cost   the historical or past cost that is associated with the acquisition of an asset or a resource and that has no future recovery value

Waste   a residual output of a joint process that has no sales value

SELECTED BIBLIOGRAPHY

Allen, Michael. "Low-Cost PC Makers Have Come on Strong But Difficulties Loom." *Wall Street Journal* (May 11, 1992), pp. A1, A4.

Keller, John J. "More Firms 'Outsource' Data Networks." *Wall Street Journal* (March 11, 1992), pp. B1, B7.

Primrose, P. L. "Is Anything Really Wrong with Cost Management?" *Journal of Cost Management for the Manufacturing Industry* (Spring 1992), pp. 48–57.

Speir, Robert E. "Make or Buy: A Winner's Guide." *Purchasing World* (February 1989), pp. 32–33.

Verschoor, Curtis C. "Evaluating Outsourcing of Internal Auditing." *Management Accounting* (February 1992), pp. 27–30.

SOLUTION STRATEGIES

General rule of decision making: Choose the alternative that yields the greatest incremental benefit (or provides the smallest incremental loss).

$$\begin{array}{r} \text{Incremental (additional) revenues} \\ - \;\underline{\text{Incremental (additional) costs}} \\ \text{Incremental benefit (positive or negative)} \end{array}$$

Relevant Costs

Direct materials and direct labor

Variable production overhead

Variable selling expenses related to each alternative (may be greater or less than under the "change nothing" alternative)

Avoidable fixed production overhead

Avoidable fixed selling/administrative costs (if any)

Opportunity cost of choosing some other alternative (will either increase one alternative's cost or reduce the cost of the other)

Single Scarce Resource

1. Determine the scarce resource.
2. Determine the production per unit of the scarce resource.
3. Determine the contribution margin (CM) per unit of the scarce resource.
4. Multiply production times CM to obtain total CM provided by the product per unit of the scarce resource. Production and sale of the product with the highest CM per unit of scarce resource will maximize profits.

Product Lines

$$\begin{array}{r} \text{Sales} \\ - \;\underline{\text{Direct variable expenses}} \\ \text{Product line contribution margin} \\ - \;\underline{\text{Avoidable fixed expenses}} \\ \text{Segment (product line) margin*} \end{array}$$

*Make decision to retain or eliminate based on this line item.

DEMONSTRATION PROBLEM

Crestline Sports Products is a multiple product manufacturing firm serving the sports and leisure industry. One of the company's product lines consists of outboard motors for water craft. The company produces three different models of outboard motors. Crestline is presently considering a proposal from a vendor who wishes to supply the company with propellers for the outboard motor line.

The company currently produces the propellers it requires. Because customers have differing preferences in the types of propellers they want attached to their motors, Crestline now offers three alternative propellers for each of the outboard motor models (therefore, the company now must produce a total of nine different types of propellers). The vendor has indicated it would produce five different types of propellers for each of the outboard models, thus expanding the variety of propellers that could be offered to the customer. Irrespective of the type of propeller required, the vendor would charge Crestline $25 per propeller.

Crestline produces its propellers in its outboard motor factory in St. Paul, Minnesota, along with all the other outboard motor components. For the coming year, Crestline has projected the costs of propeller production as follows (based on projected volume of 10,000 units):

Direct materials	$ 75,000
Direct labor	65,000
Variable overhead	55,000
Fixed overhead	
Depreciation on equipment[1]	50,000
Property taxes on production space and equipment[2]	15,000
Factory supervision[3]	35,000
Total production costs	$295,000

[1]The equipment utilized to produce the propellers has no alternative use and no material market value.
[2]The space occupied by propeller production activities will remain idle if the company purchases rather than makes the propellers.
[3]The factory supervision cost reflects the salary of a production supervisor who oversees propeller production. This individual would be dismissed from the firm if propeller production ceased.

Required:

a. Relative to producing the propellers, determine the net advantage or disadvantage of purchasing the propellers required for outboard motor production in the coming year.

b. Determine the level of outboard motor production where Crestline would be indifferent between buying and producing the propellers. If the volume of future production is expected to increase, would the firm be more likely to make or buy?

c. For this part only, assume that the space presently occupied by propeller production could be leased to another firm for $45,000 per year. How would this affect the make-or-buy decision?

d. What other factors should the company take into account in determining whether it should make or buy the propellers?

Solution to Demonstration Problem

a. Relevant costs to make 10,000 propellers:

Direct materials	$ 75,000
Direct labor	65,000
Variable overhead	55,000
Factory supervision	35,000
Total	$230,000
Cost to buy: 10,000 × $25	250,000
Net advantage of in-house production	$ 20,000

Note that the only fixed cost that is relevant to the decision is the cost of factory supervision. The other fixed costs would be unaffected by the decision.

b. The relevant costs to make the propellers could be expressed as:

$$\$35{,}000 + \$19.50X$$

where X represents production volume.

The term $\$19.50X$ represents the total variable costs and the term $\$35,000$ is the relevant fixed costs. The variable unit cost of $\$19.50$ was found by dividing the total projected variable production costs by the projected production volume: ($\$75,000 + \$65,000 + \$55,000$) ÷ 10,000.

The total costs to buy the required propellers can be expressed as $\$25X$, where X represents production volume.

By setting the production cost equation equal to the purchase cost equation, the point of indifference can be found:

$$\$35{,}000 + \$19.50X = \$25X$$

$$X = 6{,}364 \text{ units}$$

As production volume goes up, the company would favor in-house production because average costs would be lower and rise only at a rate of $19.50 per unit rather than $25 per unit.

c. Referring to the solution to part (a), the net advantage of in-house production is $20,000. The possibility of renting the production space for $45,000 per year increases the cost of in-house production (because an opportunity cost of $45,000 is incurred to continue in-house production). Consequently the balance would shift to favor the purchase of the propellers:

Original advantage of producing in-house	$ 20,000
Additional opportunity cost (lost rent)	(45,000)
Net cost of producing the propellers (or net advantage of purchasing)	$(25,000)

d. Among the additional factors that might be considered would be: the quality of the propellers produced relative to the quality of the propellers purchased; the reliability of the vendor; the number of competing vendors; the effect of the additional variety of propellers on customer demand; the likelihood of price increases from the vendor in the future; and alternative (cost-reducing or income-generating) uses of the space currently utilized to produce propellers.

END-OF-CHAPTER MATERIALS

Questions

1. What are the three characteristics that a cost must possess to be relevant to a decision? Why are these characteristics important?

2. What is meant by the term *incremental* as it applies to costs and revenues?

3. Are future variable costs always relevant costs? Discuss the rationale for your answer.

4. Which category of costs is often relevant in making a decision, but would probably never be directly recorded in a company's cost records? Explain.

5. On November 13, 1993, Bill paid Jim $25 for a concert ticket which Jim had originally purchased for $50. On December 15, 1993, Ted offers Bill $30 for the ticket. Which of the costs mentioned are relevant in Bill's decision regarding whether he should sell the ticket to Ted or attend the concert? What is the opportunity cost that Bill will incur if he decides to attend the concert? Explain.

6. What is the term used to describe historical costs? Are such costs relevant in making decisions?

7. In an asset replacement decision, which of the following costs would typically be relevant?

   a. the purchase cost of the new machine
   b. the purchase cost of the old machine
   c. the cost of electricity to run the old machine
   d. the cost of electricity to run the new machine
   e. the annual depreciation expense on the old machine

   Explain the reasons for your answers.

8. What are some of the qualitative factors that should be considered in make-or-buy decisions?

9. In a make-or-buy decision, is it possible that some of the fixed costs associated with the "make" option could be relevant? Explain.

10. Evaluate the merit of the following statement: "In the long run the only binding constraint on a firm's output is capital; in the short run nearly any resource can be a binding constraint."

11. In production decisions that involve the allocation of a single scarce production resource to multiple products, which of the following would be relevant?

    a. sales demand for each product
    b. sales price of each product
    c. fixed production costs
    d. variable selling costs for each product
    e. variable production costs for each product

    Explain the reasons for your answers.

12. In allocating a scarce production resource in a multiproduct corporation whose goal is to maximize the total corporate contribution margin, why would the corporation not simply produce the product that generates the highest contribution margin per unit?

13. In a multiproduct company, what is meant by the term *sales mix?*

14. What factors are most likely to be manipulated in managerial attempts to induce a change in a company's sales mix?

15. Would you expect a greater relative change in sales volume to accompany a price change for a product whose demand is characterized as "very elastic" or "very inelastic"? (Elasticity is discussed in chapter 10.) Explain the reasons for your answer.

16. When management is considering the elimination of a product line, why are some direct fixed costs irrelevant to the decision?

17. What is "segment margin," and how is it related to the decision to keep or delete a product line?

18. In the short run, which of the following must be non-negative in order to retain a product line?

   a. product line contribution margin
   b. product line segment margin
   c. product line net income

   Why?

19. (Appendix) Why is linear programming used in business organizations?

20. (Appendix) What is the difference between a feasible solution and an optimal solution?

▉ Exercises

21. *(Process further)* A certain joint process yields two joint products, A and B. The joint cost for June 1993 is $64,000 and the sales value of the output at split-off is $172,000 for Product A and $54,000 for Product B. Management is trying to decide whether to process its products further. If the products are processed beyond split-off, the final sales value will be $200,000 for Product A and $76,000 for Product B. The additional costs of processing are expected to be $32,000 for A and $8,000 for B.

   a. Should management process the products further? Show computations.
   b. Are there any revenues and/or costs that are not relevant to the decision? If so, what are they and why are they not relevant?

22. *(Cost identification)* Managers at Harry's Mutt & Cutt are trying to decide whether they should keep their old dog-grooming equipment or invest in new energy-efficient equipment. Some data on both groups of equipment follow:

	Old Equipment	New Equipment
Original cost	$12,000	$21,000
Remaining life	5 years	5 years
Accumulated depreciation	$ 4,000	$ 0
Annual cash operating costs	$ 7,000	$ 3,000
Current salvage value	$ 2,000	$21,000
Salvage value in 5 years	$ 0	$ 0

   a. Identify any sunk costs listed above.
   b. Identify any irrelevant (nondifferential) future costs.
   c. Identify all relevant costs to the equipment replacement decision.

d. What are the opportunity costs associated with the alternative of keeping the old machine?

e. What is the incremental cost to purchase the new machine?

23. *(Incremental analysis)* Two years ago, Roses R Us Flower Shop purchased a two-ton delivery truck. Because of increases in fuel prices and the other high costs of operating this truck, the company is considering replacing this truck with a smaller, more efficient pickup. Data on the existing and proposed trucks follow:

	Old Truck	Proposed Truck
Original cost	$20,000	$10,000
Market value now	$ 5,000	$10,000
Remaining life	3 yrs.	3 yrs.
Salvage value in 3 years	$ 0	$ 0
Annual cash operating costs	$ 6,000	$ 4,500
Annual depreciation	$ 4,000	$ 3,333

a. What is the incremental cost of the proposed truck?

b. What are the incremental savings in annual operating costs?

c. What should the company do? Support your decision with calculations.

24. *(Make-or-buy)* The Big Track Shoe Company manufactures various types of shoes for sports and recreational use. Several types of shoes require a built-in air pump. Presently, the company makes all of the air pumps it requires for production. However, management is evaluating an offer from Slippery Supply Company to provide air pumps at a cost of $3 each. Big Track's management has estimated that the variable production costs of the air pump amount to $2 per unit. The firm also estimates that it could avoid $30,000 per year in fixed costs if it purchased rather than produced the air pumps.

a. If Big Track requires 20,000 pumps per year, should it make them or buy them from Slippery Supply Company?

b. If Big Track requires 40,000 pumps per year, should it make them or buy them?

c. Assuming all other factors are equal, at what level of production would Big Track be indifferent between making and buying the pumps? Show computations.

25. *(Scarce resource)* Merry Melodies manufactures holiday bells. The firm produces three types of bells: dings, dongs, and tingalings. Because of political turmoil in Africa, a critical raw material, bellinium, is in very short supply and is restricting the number of bells the firm can produce. For the coming year, the firm will be able to purchase only 30,000 pounds of bellinium (at a cost of $4 per pound). The firm needs to determine how to allocate the bellinium to maximize profits. The following information has been gathered for your consideration:

	Dings	Dongs	Tingalings
Sales price per unit	$15.00	$10.00	$4.00
Bellinium cost	5.00	4.00	2.00
Direct labor cost	6.00	3.00	1.00
Variable overhead cost	2.00	1.00	0.25
Sales demand in units	200,000	300,000	1,000,000

Fixed production costs total $100,000 per year, fixed selling costs are $38,000, and there are no variable selling costs.

a. How should Merry Melodies allocate the scarce bellinium?
b. Based on the optimal allocation, what is the company's projected contribution margin for the coming year?

26. *(Scarce resource)* Big Jim's Accounting Emporium provides two types of services: tax and financial accounting. All company personnel can perform either service equally well. In efforts to market its services, Big Jim's relies heavily on radio and billboard advertising. Information on Big Jim's projected operations for 1993 follows:

	Taxes	Financial Accounting
Revenue per billable hour	$ 30	$ 25
Variable cost of professional labor	20	15
Material costs per billable hour	1	2
Allocated fixed costs per year	100,000	200,000
Projected billable hours for 1993	12,000	8,000

a. What is Big Jim's projected profit or (loss) for 1993?
b. If $1 spent on advertising could increase either tax services revenue by $20 or financial accounting services revenue by $20, on which service should the advertising dollar be spent?
c. If $1 spent on advertising could increase tax services billable time by one hour or financial accounting services billable time by one hour, on which service should the advertising dollar be spent?

27. *(Product line)* Megatalent Marketing is in the business of hiring celebrities and marketing their services. The firm has three operating segments: rock & roll (R & R) entertainment, after dinner speakers, and political action (Politics) speakers. Projected income statements for the fourth quarter of this fiscal year follow:

	R & R	After Dinner	Politics
Sales	$ 300,000	$ 500,000	$ 600,000
Variable costs of professional services	(100,000)	(300,000)	(325,000)
Variable marketing costs	(50,000)	(75,000)	(100,000)
Direct fixed costs	(100,000)	(150,000)	(125,000)
Allocated fixed costs	(15,000)	(30,000)	(30,000)
Net income	$ 35,000	$ (55,000)	$ 20,000

a. Assuming that all but $25,000 of the direct fixed costs of the After Dinner segment could be avoided if the segment is eliminated, what would be the effect of its elimination on Megatalent's overall net income?
b. Before the After Dinner segment is eliminated, what qualitative factors should be considered?

28. *(Segment margin)* The projected quarterly operating expenses at normal volume levels for the Western Division of Global Company are given below. These quarterly expense patterns are expected to hold for the next few years.

Variable production (50% of sales)	$800,000
Variable selling (18.75% of sales)	300,000
Direct fixed	600,000
Allocated fixed	250,000

The direct fixed costs represent the salary of the division manager, $200,000; depreciation on equipment, $300,000; and the quarterly rental payment on leased facilities, $100,000. The division manager has a contract that guarantees her a job at her present salary for the next five years. The lease on the facilities can be canceled, without penalty, six months after notifying the owner of the facility by Global Company and the $300,000 of quarterly depreciation applies to equipment that has no alternative use or tangible market value.

a. Assuming next quarter's projected sales are $1,600,000, develop an income statement that identifies the Western Division's projected segment margin and net income or loss for next quarter.
b. What is the minimum acceptable level of sales for the upcoming quarter for the Western Division to be retained?
c. For a quarter commencing more than six months from the present time (but less than five years from now), what is the minimum acceptable level of sales that must be achieved in order to keep the division operating? (As indicated earlier, assume total variable costs will be equal to 68.75 percent of sales revenue.)

Problems

29. *(Asset replacement)* The Funky Chicken Conglomerate offers products and services to various restaurants under a franchising arrangement. For operating purposes, the Funky Chicken has three autonomous divisions: Steamed, Fried, and Barbecued. For the fourth quarter of 1993, the Steamed Division has projected its net income at $1.2 million.

One of the Steamed Division's most important operations involves a water boiler that is used to steam the chickens. The division's management has recently asked its controller to prepare a comparative financial analysis of a newer steam-generating technology with the existing boiler. The following information was presented by the controller to division management:

	Old Boiler	New Technology
Original cost	$3,000,000	$2,000,000
Market value now	$ 200,000	—
Remaining life	8 years	8 years
Quarterly operating costs	$ 400,000	$ 50,000
Salvage value in 8 years	$ 0	$ 0
Accumulated depreciation	$1,000,000	—

After allowing the Steamed divisional manger to examine the previous information for a few moments, the divisional controller said, "As this financial information clearly indicates, we must invest in the new technology."

Required:

a. Identify the costs that are relevant to the Steamed Division's equipment replacement decision.
b. Do you agree with the controller's conclusions? Provide your own computations based only on relevant costs.
c. For this part only, assume that the cost of the new technology is unknown. What is the maximum amount that the division could pay for the new technology and be no worse off financially?

30. *(Asset replacement)* Bama Beans, Inc., has operations in thirteen states. Bama Beans is in the business of growing soybeans and processing the beans into two products: soybean oil and soybean meal. These products are then sold for various commercial uses. Operations in each state are under the control of an autonomous state manager whose performance is evaluated (in large part) based on the magnitude of annual profit. State managers typically receive an annual bonus equal to one-half of 1 percent of net state profits.

The manager of North Carolina operations is Beano DuMars. Beano is sixty-three years old and has been with Bama Beans for thirty-nine years. He would like to sell his existing bean crusher and purchase a new, technologically superior one. To evaluate the feasibility of such a move, Beano's controller prepared the following information. This information has created a tremendous dilemma for Beano.

Incremental cost of the new crusher		$2,000,000
Expected remaining life of the old crusher		5 years
Expected life of the new crusher		5 years
Expected effect of the new crusher on net profit for the next 5 years:		
Year 1: Decrease in operating costs	$ 600,000	
Loss on disposal of old crusher	1,500,000	
Net decrease in profit		$ (900,000)
Year 2: Net increase in profit		400,000
Year 3: Net increase in profit		500,000
Year 4: Net increase in profit		510,000
Year 5: Net increase in profit		600,000

Required:

a. What is the source of Beano's dilemma?

b. Is the expected book loss on the disposal of the old equipment relevant to Beano's decision?

c. Is Beano's age likely to be an important factor in his decision? Why or why not?

d. What should Beano do?

31. *(Make or buy)* The New Visions Lighting Company manufactures various types of household light fixtures. Most of the light fixtures require sixty-watt light bulbs to operate. Historically, the company has produced its own light bulbs. The costs to produce a bulb (based on capacity operation of 3,000,000 bulbs per year) are:

Direct materials	$.10
Direct labor	.05
Variable factory overhead	.01
Fixed factory overhead	.03
Total	$.19

The fixed factory overhead includes $60,000 of depreciation on equipment for which there is no alternative use and no external market value. The balance of the fixed factory overhead pertains to the salary of the production supervisor. While the production supervisor of the light bulb operation has a lifetime employment contract, she has skills that could be used to displace another manager (the supervisor of electrical cord production) who draws a salary of $15,000 per year but is due to retire from the company.

The Specific Electric Company has recently approached New Visions with an offer to supply all the light bulbs New Visions requires at a price of $.18 per bulb. Anticipated sales demand for the coming year will require 2,000,000 bulbs.

Required:

a. Identify the costs that are relevant in this make-or-buy decision.
b. What is the total annual advantage or disadvantage (in dollars) of buying the bulbs rather than making the bulbs?
c. What qualitative factors should be taken into account in this make-or-buy decision?

32. *(Make or buy)* Sportway, Inc., is a wholesale distributor supplying moderately priced sporting equipment to large chain stores. About 60 percent of Sportway's products are purchased from other companies while the rest are manufactured by Sportway. The company's Plastics Department currently manufactures molded fishing tackle boxes. Sportway manufactures and sells 8,000 tackle boxes annually, making full use of its direct labor capacity at available work stations. Following are the selling price and costs associated with Sportway's tackle boxes:

Selling price per box	$86.00
Costs per box	
Molded plastic	$ 8.00
Hinges, latches, handle	9.00
Direct labor ($15 per hour)	18.75
Manufacturing overhead	12.50
Selling and administrative cost	17.00
Total cost	$65.25
Profit per box	$20.75

Sportway believes it could sell 12,000 tackle boxes if it had sufficient manufacturing capacity. The company has looked into the possibility of purchasing the tackle boxes for distribution. Maple Products, a steady supplier of quality products, would be able to provide up to 9,000 tackle boxes per year at a price of $68.00 per box delivered to Sportway's facility.

Bart Johnson, Sportway's product manager, has suggested that the company could make better use of its Plastics Department by manufacturing skateboards. A market report indicates an expanding skateboard market and a need for additional suppliers. Johnson believes that Sportway could sell 17,500 skateboards per year at $45.00 per skateboard. Manufacturing cost estimates follow:

Selling price per skateboard	$45.00
Costs per skateboard	
Molded plastic	$ 5.50
Wheels, hardware	7.00
Direct labor ($15 per hour)	7.50
Manufacturing overhead	5.00
Selling and administrative cost	9.00
Total cost	$34.00
Profit per skateboard	$11.00

In the Plastics Department, Sportway uses direct labor as the application base for manufacturing overhead. This year, the Plastics Department has been allocated $50,000 of factorywide fixed manufacturing overhead. Every unit of product that Sportway sells, whether purchased or manufactured, is allocated $6.00 of fixed overhead cost for distribution; this amount is included in the selling and administrative cost. Total selling and administrative costs for the purchased tackle boxes would be $10.00 per unit.

Required: To maximize the company's profitability, prepare an analysis based on the data presented that will show which products Sportway, Inc., should manufacture and/or purchase and will show the associated financial impact. Support your answer with appropriate calculations.

(CMA)

33. *(Purchase or lease)* The Delaware Grocery Company manufactures twelve kinds of breakfast cereal. The company has recently expanded its operations into the western half of the United States and Canada. To provide a stable supply of product to its wholesalers in the new market area, the firm wants to maintain in a central warehouse a quantity of approximately 12 million boxes of cereal. Its primary dilemma at the present time involves the decision as to whether it will build warehouse space or rent warehouse space. To build and operate its own warehouse facility (capable of holding up to 22 million boxes), the company projects the costs would be as follows:

Initial cost of the building & equipment	$7,000,000
Variable costs	
Insurance	$.0020 per box
Labor	.0030 per box
Utilities	.0010 per box
Repairs	.0015 per box
Fixed costs	
Depreciation	$72,917
Supervision & security	$ 5,000
Other information	
Life expectancy of the warehouse	8 years
Expected salvage value in 8 years	$0

Alternatively, The Big Warehouse Leasing Company has agreed to store and safeguard the cereal for the Delaware Grocery Company at a cost of $.02 per box per month.

Required:

a. Identify the relevant costs for making the purchase or lease decision.
b. Based on an expected storage level of 12 million boxes, what should the Delaware Grocery Company do?
c. If the required quantity of cereal boxes to be stored is expected to rise in the future, would the company be more inclined or less inclined to build a facility? Why?
d. Assume the company decides to build the facility. After the facility is operational, which costs are then relevant in a decision as to whether the company should "operate the facility or rent warehouse space"?

34. *(Scarce resource)* The Mid-City Bakery produces three types of cakes: birthday, wedding, and special occasion. The cakes are made from scratch and baked in a special cake oven. During the holiday season (roughly November 15–January 15), total demand for the cakes exceeds the capacity of the cake oven. The cake oven is available for baking 690 hours per month, but because of the size of the cakes, it can bake only one cake at a time. Management must determine how to ration the oven time among the three types of cakes. Information on costs, sales prices, and product demand follows:

	Birthday Cakes	Wedding Cakes	Special Occasion Cakes
Sales price	$ 25	$100	$40
Variable costs			
Direct materials	5	30	10
Direct labor	5	15	8
Variable overhead	2	5	4
Variable selling	3	12	5
Required oven time per cake	10 min.	80 min.	18 min.
Fixed costs (monthly)			
Factory		$1,200	
Selling & administrative		800	

Required:

a. If demand is essentially unlimited for all three types of cakes during the holiday season, which cake or cakes should Mid-City bake during the holiday season? Why?

b. Based on your answer in part (a), how many cakes of each type will be produced? What is the projected level of monthly profit for the holiday season?

35. *(Scarce resource)* Sally has been studying the role of relevance in making decisions. She has decided that she may be able to employ the concepts she has learned to allocate her limited time in reviewing for final exams. Allowing adequate time for meals and rest, she has estimated that she has twenty-six hours available to review for final exams. As a first step, she has determined that her goal should be to maximize her semester grade point average. Her grade point average is measured on a four-point scale where an A is worth four points, a B is worth three points, a C is worth two points, and a D is worth one point. She is currently enrolled in five courses (each course is worth three semester credit hours). She has estimated, for each course, the review time that she must spend to maintain her existing semester grade (failure to invest this review time will result in her semester grade dropping by one letter), and the total time that she would have to study to actually raise her semester grade by one letter. The following table summarizes her estimates:

Course	Existing Grade	Review Time Required to Maintain Existing Grade	Total Review Time Required to Raise Grade by One Letter Grade
Geology	B	3 hours	6 hours
Accounting	C	3 hours	7 hours
Chemistry	B	4 hours	9 hours
Marketing	B	4 hours	10 hours
Spanish	C	3 hours	5 hours

Required:

a. Determine how Sally should allocate her time in reviewing for final exams to maximize her grade point average.

b. Based on your solution to part (a), what is Sally's expected grade point average for the semester?

c. What other factors should Sally consider in deciding how to allocate her time?

36. *(Sales commissions)* One year ago, Freddy Mac purchased the rights (under a five-year contract) to sell concessions at a local municipal football stadium. After analyzing the results of his first-year operations, Freddy is somewhat disappointed. His two main products are "dogs" and "burgers." He had expected to sell about the same number of each product over the course of the year. However, his sales mix was approximately two-thirds dogs and one-third burgers. Freddy feels this combination is less profitable than a balanced mix of dogs and burgers. He is now trying to determine how to improve profitability for the coming year and is considering strategies to improve the sales mix. His first year operations are summarized below:

Dogs

Sales (100,000 @ $1.50)	$150,000
Less: Direct materials	(40,000)
Direct labor	(15,000)
Fixed costs	(45,000)
Net profit	$ 50,000

Burgers

Sales (50,000 @ $2.50)	$125,000
Less: Direct materials	(55,000)
Direct labor	(10,000)
Fixed costs	(15,000)
Net profit	$ 45,000
Total profit	$ 95,000

If Freddy takes no action to improve profitability, he expects sales and expenses in the second year to mirror the first-year results. Freddy is considering two alternative strategies to boost profitability.

Strategy #1: Add point of sale advertising to boost burger sales. The estimated cost per year for such advertising would be $23,000. Freddy estimates such advertising would have the effect of decreasing dog sales by 5,000 units and increasing burger sales by 20,000 units.

Strategy #2: Provide a sales commission to his employees. The commission would be paid at a rate of 10 percent on all sales less variable production costs. Freddy estimates this strategy would increase dog sales by 5 percent and burger sales by 20 percent.

Required: Determine what action Freddy should take: No action, Strategy #1, or Strategy #2. Show your supporting calculations.

37. *(Product lines)* The Canadian Paper Company produces three types of consumer products: sticky note pads, tablets, and custom stationery. The firm has become increasingly concerned about the profitability of the custom stationery line. A segmented income statement for the most recent quarter follows:

	Sticky Notes	Tablets	Custom Stationery
Sales	$800,000	$400,000	$1,000,000
Variable costs:			
Production	(200,000)	(150,000)	(550,000)
Selling	(150,000)	(100,000)	(200,000)
Fixed costs:			
Production	(160,000)	(80,000)	(300,000)
Selling	(200,000)	(60,000)	(180,000)
Net income	$ 90,000	$ 10,000	$ (230,000)

Because of the significance of the loss on custom stationery products, the company is considering the elimination of that product line. Of the fixed production costs, $400,000 are allocated to the product lines based on relative sales value; likewise, $250,000 of fixed selling expenses are allocated to the product lines based on relative sales value. All of the other fixed costs charged to each product line are direct and would be eliminated if the product line was dropped. Required: Recast the above income statements in a more meaningful format for deciding whether the custom stationery product line should be eliminated. Based on the new income statements, determine whether any product line should be eliminated.

38. *(Product lines)* The Hardware Emporium has two operating divisions: wholesale and retail. Sales in the Wholesale Division are generated by salespeople who visit professional mechanics and carpenters. Such salespeople drive trucks which are fully stocked with inventory. The Retail Division comprises two traditional store outlets. Income statements for each segment covering the most recent fiscal year follow:

	Wholesale	Retail
Sales	$2,000,000	$950,000
Cost of merchandise sold	(1,200,000)	(600,000)
Commissions to salespeople	(200,000)	(100,000)
Truck-related costs	(250,000)	(0)
Real estate taxes, insurance	(0)	(50,000)
Depreciation on real estate	(0)	(100,000)
Salaries of division managers	(80,000)	(75,000)
Allocated corporate salaries	(100,000)	(65,000)
Net income (loss)	$ 170,000	$(40,000)

Management is concerned about profitability in the Retail Division, and the company is considering the possibility of closing the retail stores and renting the space. Management estimates that the stores could generate combined rent of $60,000 per year. If the stores were rented, the Retail Division manager would be dismissed. The depreciation, taxes, and insurance on the real estate would be unaffected by renting the stores.
Required:

a. Recast the previous income statements in a format that provides more information for making this decision regarding the retail stores.
b. What is the net advantage or disadvantage (change in total company profits) of continuing to operate the retail stores as opposed to renting the space?

39. *(Essay)* Teddy Edwards and his friend Donald Thump visit several Las Vegas casinos over spring break to gamble. Donald disappears for the entire afternoon but returns to the hotel room around dinnertime looking haggard and dejected. Before Teddy gets a chance to speak, Donald says, "Look, pal, I've been shoving quarters in the same slot machine all afternoon. I've invested $300 in this machine, but I've run out of money. Please loan me $50 so I can get back to the casino. I've got that slot primed, and the odds are now in my favor to win a ton of money."

a. Using concepts learned from this chapter, briefly describe how Teddy would inform his friend that the $300 should simply be forgotten.
b. If Teddy agrees to loan Donald $50, will the odds of winning go up with each additional quarter placed in the slot machine? Explain.

40. *(Essay)* The following are costs associated with a product line of Tennessee Technologies, Inc. The costs reflect capacity-level production of 12,000 units per year.

Variable production costs	$5
Fixed production costs	3
Variable selling costs	2
Fixed selling and administrative costs	3

a. Assuming these costs apply to a product line that is yet to be developed, which of the costs would likely be relevant in a decision as to whether the company should invest in the product line? Explain.
b. Assuming these costs apply to an existing inventory of obsolete products, which costs are relevant in setting the minimum acceptable sales price? Explain.

41. *(Essay)* Sally S. Smart is about to graduate from Private University. She is currently trying to decide whether she should stay at the university and obtain a master's degree or enter the job market with only a bachelor's degree. She has asked for your help and provided you with the following information:

Costs incurred for the bachelor's degree	$48,000
Out-of-pocket costs to get a master's degree	20,000
Estimated starting salary with B.A.	29,500
Estimated starting salary with M.A.	33,000
Estimated time to complete master's degree	2 years
Estimated time from the present to retirement	40 years

a. Which of the previous factors are relevant in Sally's decision?
b. Is $20,000 the best measure of the cost of getting a master's degree? Why or why not?
c. What other factors should Sally consider?

42. *(Essay)* FarmChem, Inc., is a multinational firm that provides agricultural chemicals to farmers and chemical wholesalers. One of the many autonomous divisions is the Western Ag Services Division. The manager of Western Ag Services, Janice Duvall, was recently overheard discussing a vexing problem with her controller, Huey Packard. The topic of discussion was whether the division should replace its existing chemical handling equipment with newer technology that is safer, more efficient, and cheaper to operate.

According to an analysis by Packard, the cost savings over the life of the new technology would pay for the initial cost of the technology several times over. However, Duvall remained reluctant to invest. Her most fundamental concern involved the disposition of the old processing equipment. Because this equipment has only been in use for two years, it has a very high book value relative to its current market value. To illustrate, Duvall noted that if the new technology were not purchased, the division would anticipate a net income of $4,000,000 for the year. However, if the new technology is purchased, the old equipment would have to be sold; Duvall noted that the division could probably sell the equipment for $1.2 million. This equipment had an original cost of $8 million, and $1.5 million in depreciation has been recorded. Thus, a book loss of $5.3 million would have to be recorded on the sale. Duvall concluded, "The corporate folks would swallow their teeth if we booked that kind of loss!"

Required:

a. Is the book value of the old equipment, $6.5 million, relevant to this decision? Is Duvall's analysis flawed? Explain.

b. As an advisor to Duvall and Packard, what action would you advise Janice to take in this equipment decision? Be sure you address the concerns she has about the corporate-level managers.

Cases

43. Stac Industries is a multiproduct company with several manufacturing plants. The Clinton Plant manufactures and distributes two household cleaning and polishing compounds, regular and heavy duty, under the Cleen-Brite label. The forecasted operating results for the first six months of 1994, when 100,000 cases of each compound are expected to be manufactured and sold, are presented in the following statement:

CLEEN-BRITE COMPOUNDS—CLINTON PLANT
FORECASTED RESULTS OF OPERATIONS
FOR THE SIX-MONTH PERIOD ENDING JUNE 30, 1994
($000 OMITTED)

	Regular	Heavy Duty	Total
Sales	$2,000	$3,000	$5,000
Cost of sales	1,600	1,900	3,500
Gross profit	$ 400	$1,100	$1,500
Selling and administrative expenses			
Variable	$ 400	$ 700	$1,100
Fixed*	240	360	600
Total selling and administrative expenses	$ 640	$1,060	$1,700
Income (loss) before taxes	$ (240)	$ 40	$ (200)

*The fixed selling and administrative expenses are allocated between the two products on the basis of dollar sales volume on the internal reports.

The regular compound sold for $20 per case and the heavy-duty compound sold for $30 per case during the first six months of 1994. The manufacturing costs by case of product are presented in the following schedule:

	Cost Per Case	
	Regular	Heavy Duty
Raw materials	$ 7.00	$ 8.00
Direct labor	4.00	4.00
Variable manufacturing overhead	1.00	2.00
Fixed manufacturing overhead*	4.00	5.00
Total manufacturing cost	$16.00	$19.00
Variable selling and administrative costs	$ 4.00	$ 7.00

*Depreciation charges are 50 percent of the fixed manufacturing overhead of each product.

Each product is manufactured on a separate production line. Annual normal manufacturing capacity is 200,000 cases of each product. However, the plant is capable of producing 250,000 cases of regular compound and 350,000 cases of heavy-duty compound annually.

The following schedule reflects the consensus of top management regarding the price/volume alternatives for the Cleen-Brite products for the last six months of 1994. These are essentially the same alternatives management had during the first six months of 1994.

Regular Compound		Heavy-Duty Compound	
Alternative Prices (per case)	Sales Volume (in cases)	Alternative Prices (per case)	Sales Volume (in cases)
$18	120,000	$25	175,000
20	100,000	27	140,000
21	90,000	30	100,000
22	80,000	32	55,000
23	50,000	35	35,000

Top management believes the loss for the first six months reflects a tight profit margin caused by intense competition. Management also believes that many companies will be forced out of this market by next year and profits should improve.

a. What unit selling price should Stac Industries select for each of the Cleen-Brite compounds for the remaining six months of 1994? Support your answer with appropriate calculations.

b. Without prejudice to your answer to part (a), assume the optimum price/volume alternatives for the last six months were a selling price of $23 and volume level of 50,000 cases for the regular compound and a selling price of $35 and volume of 35,000 cases for the heavy-duty compound.

1. Should Stac Industries consider closing down its operations until 1995 to minimize its losses? Support your answer with appropriate calculations.

2. Identify and discuss the qualitative factors that should be considered in deciding whether the Clinton Plant should be closed down during the last six months of 1994.

(CMA adapted)

44. Auer Company had received an order for a piece of special machinery from Jay Company. Just as Auer Company completed the machine, Jay Company declared bankruptcy, defaulted on the order, and forfeited the 10 percent deposit paid on the selling price of $72,500.

Auer's manufacturing manager identified the costs already incurred in the production of the special machinery for Jay as follows:

Direct materials used		$16,600
Direct labor incurred		21,400
Overhead applied:		
Variable	$10,700	
Fixed	5,350	16,050
Fixed selling and administrative		5,405
Total cost		$59,455

Another company, Kaytell Corporation, would be interested in buying the special machinery if it is reworked to Kaytell's specifications. Auer offered to sell the reworked special machinery to Kaytell as a special order for a net price of $68,400. Kaytell has agreed to pay the net price when it takes delivery in two months. The additional identifiable costs to rework the machinery to the specifications of Kaytell are as follows:

Direct materials	$ 6,200
Direct labor	4,200
Total	$10,400

A second alternative available to Auer is to convert the special machinery to the standard model. The standard model lists for $62,500. The additional identifiable costs to convert the special machinery to the standard model are:

Direct materials	$2,850
Direct labor	3,300
Total	$6,150

A third alternative for the Auer Company is to sell, as a special order, the machine as is (e.g., without modification) for a net price of $52,000. However, the potential buyer of the unmodified machine does not want it for sixty days. The buyer offers a $7,000 down payment with final payment upon delivery.

The following additional information is available regarding Auer's operations:

- Sales commission rate on sales of standard models is 2 percent, while the sales commission rate on special orders is 3 percent. All sales commissions are calculated on net sales price (i.e., list price less cash discount, if any).
- Normal credit terms for sales of standard models are 2/10, net/30. Customers take the discounts except in rare instances.
- The application rates for manufacturing overhead and the fixed selling and administrative costs are as follows:

  Manufacturing
Variable	50% of direct labor cost
Fixed	25% of direct labor cost

  Selling and administrative
Fixed	10% of the total of direct materials, direct labor, and manufacturing overhead costs

- Normal time required for rework is one month.
- A surcharge of 5 percent of the sales price is placed on all customer requests for minor modifications of standard models.
- Auer normally sells a sufficient number of standard models for the company to operate at a volume in excess of the breakeven point.

Auer does not consider the time value of money in analyses of special orders and projects whenever the time period is less than one year because the effect is not significant.

a. Determine the dollar contribution that each of the three alternatives will add to the Auer Company's before-tax profits.
b. If Kaytell makes Auer a counteroffer, what is the lowest price Auer Company should accept for the reworked machinery from Kaytell? Explain your answer.

c. Discuss the influence fixed factory overhead costs should have on the sales prices quoted by Auer Company for special orders when:
1. a firm is operating at or below the breakeven point.
2. a firm's special orders constitute efficient utilization of unused capacity above the breakeven volume.

(CMA adapted)

45. The Sommers Company, located in southern Wisconsin, manufactures a variety of industrial valves and pipe fittings that are sold to customers in nearby states. Currently, the company is operating at about 70 percent capacity and is earning a satisfactory return on investment.

Management has been approached by Glascow Industries Ltd. of Scotland with an offer to buy 120,000 units of a pressure valve. Glascow Industries manufactures a valve that is almost identical to Sommers's pressure valve; however, a fire in Glascow Industries' valve plant has shut down its manufacturing operations. Glascow needs the 120,000 valves over the next four months to meet commitments to its regular customers; the company is prepared to pay $19 each for the valves, FOB shipping point.

Sommers's product cost, based on current attainable standards, for the pressure valve is:

Direct materials	$ 5
Direct labor	6
Manufacturing overhead	9
Total cost	$20

Manufacturing overhead is applied to production at the rate of $18 per standard direct labor hour. This overhead rate is made up of the following components:

Variable factory overhead	$ 6
Fixed factory overhead—direct	8
Fixed factory overhead—allocated	4
Applied manufacturing overhead rate	$18

Additional costs incurred in connection with sales of the pressure valve include sales commissions of 5 percent and freight expense of $1 per unit. However, the company does not pay sales commissions on special orders that come directly to management.

In determining selling prices, Sommers adds a 40 percent markup to product cost. This provides a $28 suggested selling price for the pressure valve. The Marketing Department, however, has set the current selling price at $27 in order to maintain market share.

Production management believes that it can handle the Glascow Industries order without disrupting its scheduled production. The order would, however, require additional fixed factory overhead of $12,000 per month in the form of supervision and clerical costs.

If management accepts the order, 30,000 pressure valves will be manufactured and shipped to Glascow Industries each month for the next four months. Shipments will be made in weekly consignments, FOB shipping point.

a. Determine how many additional direct labor hours would be required each month to fill the Glascow Industries order.

b. Prepare an incremental analysis showing the impact of accepting the Glascow Industries order.

c. Calculate the minimum unit price that Sommers's management could accept for the Glascow Industries order without reducing net income.

d. Identify the factors, other than price, that Sommers Company should consider before accepting the Glascow Industries order.

(CMA)

Ethics Discussion

46. Sunk costs are said to be irrelevant for decision-making purposes. However, sunk costs may have behavioral effects. For example, if a manager knows that he will be charged with a loss resulting from a decision to scrap obsolete inventory that he purchased, the manager may decide to do nothing even though the cost of the inventory is a sunk cost.

a. Is this an instance of suboptimization? (Hint: See chapter 15.)

b. Is the manager, by doing nothing, behaving in an ethical manner? Why or why not?

c. By making managers responsible for such losses, is the company behaving in an ethical manner? Why or why not?

47. Lundy's Computers manufactures computers and all their components. The purchasing agent informed the company owner, George Lundy, that another company has offered to supply keyboards for Lundy's computers at prices below the variable costs at which Lundy can make them. Incredulous, Mr. Lundy hired an industrial consultant to explain how the supplier could offer the keyboards at less than Lundy's variable costs.

It seems that the competitor supplier is suspected by the consultant of using many illegal aliens to work in that plant. These people are poverty stricken and will take such work at substandard wages. The purchasing agent and the plant manager feel that Lundy should buy the keyboards from the competitor supplier, as "no one can blame us for the competitor's hiring practices and will not even be able to show that we knew of those practices."

a. What are the ethical issues involved in this case?

b. What are the advantages and disadvantages of buying from this competitor supplier?

c. What do you think Mr. Lundy should do and why?

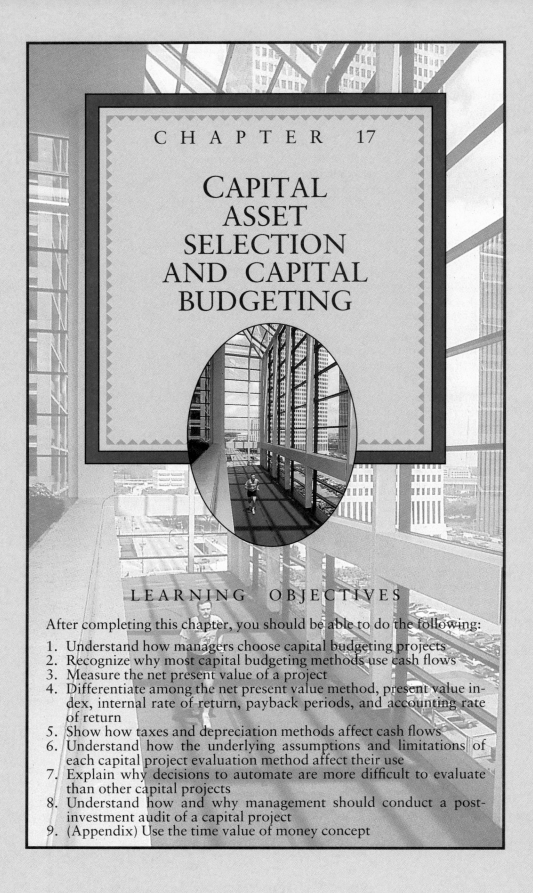

C H A P T E R   17

CAPITAL ASSET SELECTION AND CAPITAL BUDGETING

LEARNING OBJECTIVES

After completing this chapter, you should be able to do the following:

1. Understand how managers choose capital budgeting projects
2. Recognize why most capital budgeting methods use cash flows
3. Measure the net present value of a project
4. Differentiate among the net present value method, present value index, internal rate of return, payback periods, and accounting rate of return
5. Show how taxes and depreciation methods affect cash flows
6. Understand how the underlying assumptions and limitations of each capital project evaluation method affect their use
7. Explain why decisions to automate are more difficult to evaluate than other capital projects
8. Understand how and why management should conduct a post-investment audit of a capital project
9. (Appendix) Use the time value of money concept

Wellness Programs Are Businesses' Newest Investments

Health-related problems are reaching crisis proportions for American companies—draining corporate coffers and employee energy and morale. In the past decade corporations have been faced with rising costs in health and worker's compensation insurance, as well as employee absenteeism, sickness, accidents, injuries, and turnover rates. To reduce these steadily increasing costs, companies have begun to implement health, fitness, and wellness programs at the worksite or at nearby facilities. These programs integrate exercise, education, and peer support and usually are offered free, or nearly free, to employees.

Such programs can be costly, and intangible benefits can be hard to measure, so how does a company know if it is in its best interest to establish and/or continue these programs? Is the company actually benefiting by having more healthy and fit employees, or is it simply incurring hefty expenses and low, if any, short-term returns on investment?

A few major wellness program leaders are Control Data Corp.; PepsiCo, Inc.; Kimberly-Clark Corp.; Johnson & Johnson; IBM; Xerox; Sentry Insurance; and Tenneco Inc. Wellness programs are not inexpensive for the companies that offer them. Conoco's new fitness center cost the company $3 million. Tenneco's two-story 100,000-square-foot facility in Houston cost $11 million. Mannington Mills joined the fitness fad with its new $1.8 million physical fitness center. PepsiCo, Inc.'s $2 million fitness and health complex is located at its New York headquarters.

A company incurs operations costs in addition to set-up costs in fitness programs. For example, McNeil Consumer Products, a division of Johnson & Johnson, estimates that the company allocated $150,000 in its 1987 annual budget for health screening and programs for 900 participants, and it incurred expenses to provide incentives for participation in the program. Johnson & Johnson awards health-oriented prizes to employees adhering to good health practices, such as seat belts, workshops, smoke detectors, and so on. Hospital Corporation of America pays participants 24 cents for each mile run or walked, each one-quarter mile swum, or every four miles biked. SpeedCall Corporation gives employees $7 a week for not smoking at work. A medium-sized firm such as Mattel estimated its fitness program costs the company from $75 to $100 per person. Are these monies well spent?

SOURCE: Otto H. Chang and Cynthia Boyle, "Fitness Programs: Hefty Expense or Wise Investment?" *Management Accounting* (January 1989), pp. 45–46. Published by Institute of Management Accountants, Montvale, N.J.

hy would a company spend millions of dollars to invest in fitness facilities for employees and then incur hundreds of thousands of dollars of expense each year after the facilities are built to encourage good health? Such a choice is just one type of capital budgeting decision that managers must continuously face in regard to long-term expenditures of corporate funds.

One of the most important and basic tasks managers face is choosing the investments that a firm will make. Investments are made in short-term working capital assets (such as inventory) and in long-term **capital assets**, which are used to generate revenues or cost savings. Capital assets provide production, distribution, or service

capital assets

capabilities for more than one year. Capital assets may be tangible, such as machinery or buildings, or intangible, such as capital leases or patents. Fitness centers are tangible assets that provide service to employees.

As noted in the opening vignette, capital asset acquisition decisions involve long-term commitments of large expenditures. Managers typically find that the availability of projects that meet investment criteria exceeds the availability of resources. Making the most economically beneficial investments within resource constraints is critical to the organization's long-range well-being. Capital budgeting techniques are designed to enhance mangement's success in making capital investment decisions.

This chapter presents five basic methods used to analyze capital projects: net present value, present value index, internal rate of return, payback period, and accounting rate of return. Also covered in the chapter are some complexities of acquiring automated equipment and the need for post-investment audits. The appendix discusses some basic concepts about time value of money.

THE INVESTMENT DECISION

capital budgeting

project

When managers evaluate proposed long-range investments, they are engaged in the process of **capital budgeting.** Capital budgeting helps managers efficiently and effectively allocate the company's limited resources to the most desirable long-range projects. Any course of future activity can be referred to as a **project** and will typically include the purchase, installation, and operation of a capital asset. Managers generally have a choice among several capital assets that can perform the same function. A manager's job is to make the best possible investment choice of projects and assets.

Management must identify the best asset(s) for the firm to acquire to fulfill the company's goals and objectives. This process requires answers to the following four basic questions discussed.

Is the Activity Worth an Investment?

A company acquires assets when they have value in relation to specific activities in which the company is engaged. For example, jet airplanes are acquired by an airline because they are necessary to provide flight services (the activity). Before making decisions to acquire assets, company management must be certain that the activity for which the assets will be needed is worth an investment.

An activity's worth is initially measured by monetary cost/benefit analysis. If an activity's financial benefits exceed its costs, the activity is, to that extent, considered worthwhile. In some cases, however, benefits cannot be measured by money, or it is known in advance that the financial benefits will not exceed the costs. An activity meeting either of these criteria may still be judged worthwhile for some qualitative reason(s).

For example, a company may decide to invest in a day-care center for its employees' children. Company management may not be able to objectively measure the monetary benefits of the center, but it is believed to be worth the cost because of reductions in employee time off and turnover. Another example is a rural hospital that invests in a kidney dialysis machine even though there are only a limited number of kidney patients in the area. Hospital administrators may believe the goodwill generated by such an acquisition justifies the cost. If an activity is deemed worthwhile enough, the question of cost may become secondary—as is oftentimes the case with employee fitness center investments.

Which Assets Can Be Used for the Activity?

Determining the available and suitable assets for conducting the intended activity is closely related to the consideration of an activity's worth. Management must have an idea of how much the needed assets will cost to determine if the activity should be pursued. To answer this second question, and as shown in Exhibit 17–1 (page 764), managers should gather, for each asset, specific monetary and nonmonetary information about: initial cost, estimated life and salvage value, raw material and labor requirements, operating costs (both fixed and variable), output capability, service availability and cost, maintenance expectations, and revenues to be generated (if any).

Of the Available Assets for Each Activity, Which Is the Best Investment?

Using all available information, management should select the best asset from the candidates and exclude all others from consideration. Deciding which asset is the best investment requires the use of one or more of the evaluation techniques discussed later in the chapter.

In judging the acceptability of capital projects, managers should recognize that there are two types of capital budgeting decisions to be made: screening and preference decisions. A **screening decision** indicates whether a capital project is desirable   **screening decision**

Nuclear reactors (such as those at Three Mile Island) are appropriate assets for generating electricity. In making a choice among available alternatives, however, power companies would need to evaluate all the ramifications of their choice of capital investment.

EXHIBIT 17–1
▼▼▼▼▼▼▼▼▼▼▼▼

CAPITAL
INVESTMENT
INFORMATION

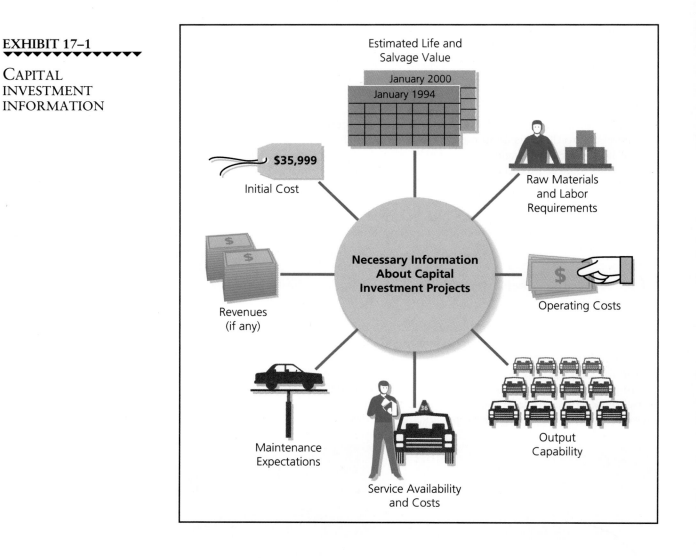

based on some previously established minimum criterion or criteria. If the project does not meet the minimum standards, it is excluded from further consideration.

preference decision

The second decision that must be made is a **preference decision** in which projects are ranked according to their impact on the achievement of company objectives. Many companies set up ranking categories for projects such as those shown in Exhibit 17–2. Projects are first screened and placed into an appropriate category. Monetary resources are allocated to projects in a top-to-bottom fashion. Within each category, projects are ranked using some established criterion or criteria. Management's goal should be to select those projects that, within budget constraints, will maximize shareholder wealth over the long run.

Some techniques may be used to screen the projects as to those that are acceptable from those that are unacceptable. Other techniques may be used to rank the projects in order of preferability. Different companies will use different techniques for screening and ranking purposes. In most instances, large companies will have standing committees to discuss, evaluate, and approve capital projects.

EXHIBIT 17–2
▼▼▼▼▼▼▼▼▼▼▼

RANKING CATEGORIES FOR CAPITAL PROJECTS

Category 1—Required by Legislation

Includes items, such as pollution control equipment, that have been mandated by law. Most companies can ill afford the fines or penalties that can be assessed for lack of installation; however, these capital acquisitions may not meet the company's minimum established economic criteria.

Category 2—Essential to Operations

Includes capital assets without which the primary functions of the organization could not continue. This category could include new purchases of capital assets or replacements of broken or no longer usable assets. For example, the purchase of a kiln for a ceramics manufacturer would fall into this category.

Category 3—Nonessential but Income Generating

Includes capital assets that would improve organizational operations by providing cost savings or supplements to revenue. Robots in an automobile manufacturer would be included in this group.

Category 4—Optional Improvements

Includes capital assets that do not provide any cost savings or revenue increases but would make operations run more smoothly or make working conditions better. The purchase of computer hardware or software that is faster than that currently being used and the installation of a microwave oven in the employees' lounge would be included here.

Category 5—Miscellaneous

Includes "pet projects" that might be requested. Such acquisitions may be more for the benefit of a single individual and not to the whole organization. Such projects may not even be related to organizational objectives. The installation of new carpeting in a manager's office could be an example of this group of investments. Items in this category will normally be chosen only when the organization has substantial, unencumbered resources at its disposal.

Some enacted legislation (such as that related to pollution control) basically requires companies to make certain types of capital investments. When this occurs, those investments rise to the top ranking category in making "preference" decisions.

In small companies, the owner-managers may simply decide on capital projects. For example, Michael Kelly, the owner of Kelly Truck Lines (Pittsburgh, Kansas) made some capital budgeting decisions that showed an out-of-the-ordinary thinking style. Even though the company was debt-heavy after a leveraged buy-out, Kelly decided to upgrade his fuel-inefficient truck fleet and install more comfort features for the drivers. The new, improved fleet made it easier for KTL to hire and retain drivers, generate increased revenues, and pay off the debt.

Of the "Best Investments" for All Worthwhile Activities, in Which Ones Should the Company Invest?

While many worthwhile investment activities exist, each company has a limited quantity of resources to invest at any point in time. Therefore, after choosing the best asset for each activity, management must decide which activities and assets to fund. Investment activities may be classified as mutually exclusive, independent, or mutually inclusive.

mutually exclusive projects

In **mutually exclusive projects,** there are many projects that perform the same basic task. From this set of proposed projects, one is chosen which causes all of the others to be rejected. Mutually exclusive projects may be used to replace current assets or to provide new or additional capabilities. Replacement assets may have the same or different capabilities and/or operating costs as the old asset. If the company keeps the old asset, it will not buy the new one; if the new one is purchased, the old will be sold. Thus, the two assets are mutually exclusive.

For example, the Byt Company plans to install a new telephone system. Company managers want to purchase a telecommunications network that would provide all the standard telephone features and allow videoconferencing and electronic mail service. After identifying all technologically appropriate equipment, Byt's managers must select one system from the multiple candidate group and exclude the others since benefit can only be obtained from one system.

independent projects

Other investment projects may be **independent projects** in that they have no specific bearing on one another. For example, the acquisition of an office microcomputer system is not related to the purchase of a factory machine. These project decisions are analyzed and accepted or rejected independently from one another. While limited resources may preclude the acquisition of all acceptable projects, the projects themselves are not mutually exclusive.

mutually inclusive projects

Management may be considering certain investments that are all related to a primary project, or are **mutually inclusive.** In a mutually inclusive situation, when the primary project is chosen, all related projects are also selected. Alternatively, rejection of the primary project requires rejection of the others. For instance, when the accounting firm of KPMG Peat Marwick selected Macintosh computers for its personnel, that selection dictated the acquisition of compatible brands of software and peripheral equipment.

Note that capital investment decisions do not simply include purchasing a fixed asset or constructing a building. Decisions to lease assets rather than purchase them are also capital budgeting decisions, as are decisions to expand a plant or institute cost reduction efforts. Any decision that will involve long-term assets is an investment decision.

Exhibit 17–3 shows the typical investment decision process. To assure that capital funds are invested in the best projects available, managers must carefully evaluate all projects and decide which ones represent the most effective and efficient use of resources—a difficult determination. The evaluation process should consider and rank projects based on business activity priorities, project risk, and project cash flows.

EXHIBIT 17–3
▼▼▼▼▼▼▼▼▼▼▼▼

TYPICAL
INVESTMENT
DECISION PROCESS

Activity—Provide transportation for a ten-person sales force

1. Is the activity worth an investment?
   Yes; this decision is based on a cost analysis of providing transportation in relationship to the revenue dollars to be generated by the sales force.

2. Which assets can be used for the activity?
   Available: Bus passes, bicycles, motorcycles, automobiles (purchased), automobiles (leased), automobiles (currently owned), small airplanes.
   Infeasible: Bus passes, bicycles, and motorcycles are infeasible because of inconvenience and inability of the sales force to carry a reasonable quantity of sample merchandise; airplanes are infeasible because of inconvenience of landing sites to customers.
   Feasible: Various types of automobiles to purchase (assume asset options A through G); various types of leasing arrangements (assume availability of leases 1 through 5); current fleet.
   Gather all relevant quantitative and qualitative information on feasible assets (A–G; 1–5; current fleet).

3. Which asset is the best investment?
   Compare all relevant information and choose the best asset candidate from the purchase group (assume Asset D) and the lease group (assume Asset 2).

4. Which investment should the company make?
   Compare the best asset candidate from the purchase group and the lease group; this represents a mutually exclusive project decision. The best candidate is found to be Asset D. Compare the Asset D costs and benefits to those of currently owned fleet; this is a mutually exclusive project relating to a replacement decision. The best choice is to sell the currently owned autos and purchase ten new type D autos.

USE OF CASH FLOWS IN CAPITAL BUDGETING

Capital budgeting investment decisions can be made using a variety of techniques including net present value, present value index, internal rate of return, payback period, and accounting rate of return. All but the last method focus on the amounts and timing of **cash flows,** which reflect receipts or disbursements of cash.

cash flows

Any investment is expected to earn some type of rate of return or interest. Using cash flows allows analysts to equate an investment in a bank (a savings account or a certificate of deposit), an investment in marketable securities (bonds or stocks), and an investment in an operating asset. In each case, money is spent and money (interest, dividends, or cash flows from use or sale) is hopefully returned. Accounting income is an accrual-based measure of various types of flows, only some of which may be in the form of current cash flows. Thus, accrual-based revenues and expenses must be converted into cash receipts and cash disbursements for use in any of the cash-flow-based capital budgeting techniques.

Cash flows arise from the purchase, operation, and disposition of capital assets. Cash receipts include project revenues that have been earned and collected, savings generated by reduced project operating costs, and inflows from the asset's sale and/or release of working capital at the end of the asset's useful life. Cash disbursements include expenditures to acquire the asset, additional working capital investments, and amounts paid for related operating costs.

financing decision

investing decisions

Interest is a cash flow caused by the method of financing the project and is not a factor that should be considered in project evaluation. The manner in which projects are funded is a financing, not an investing, decision and cash flows of the two types of decisions should not be combined. A **financing decision** is a judgment regarding the method of raising funds that will be used to make an acquisition. Financing is based on the entity's ability to issue and service debt and equity securities. On the other hand, **investing decisions** are judgments about which assets will be acquired by an entity to achieve its stated objectives. Company management must justify the acquisition and use of an asset *prior to* justifying the method of financing that asset.

Cash flows from a capital project are received and paid at different times in a project's life. Some cash flows occur at the beginning of a period (a payment on a leased asset) and some at the end (a payment on a mortgaged asset). Other cash flows occur during the period but, to simplify capital budgeting analysis, analysts assume that occurrence takes place at either the beginning or the end of the time period during which they actually occur. *Assumed* end-of-period cash flows include inflows provided by contribution margins from product sales and outflows for repair expenditures and property taxes on the capital asset. The following example illustrates the treatment of cash flows in capital budgeting situations.

Cash Flows Illustrated

The Newmann Company is considering the purchase of a machine to manufacture a new product. Basic data about the asset and its acquisition appear in Exhibit 17–4. This detailed information can be simplified into two basic cash flows: a net negative

The New South Wales government established a lottery to finance its capital investment in the $102 million Sydney Opera House. The building (started in 1959) was paid for in July 1975 and, since then, 40 percent of the lottery profits have been used to maintain and operate the complex.

EXHIBIT 17–4
▼▼▼▼▼▼▼▼▼▼▼▼

NEWMANN
COMPANY
MACHINERY
ACQUISITION
DECISION

Purchase price of machine: $62,000 (terms allow a 10% cash discount)
Installation costs: $8,000
Life of new machine: 5 years; no salvage value
Sales price of old machine: $3,800

Selling price per unit of product manufactured by new machinery: $7.00
Expected units of sales each year: 5,000
Production cost per unit:

Direct materials	$2.00	
Direct labor	1.00	
Overhead	.70	(including $.30 per unit depreciation)
	$3.70	

Assumptions: All sales are collected in cash and all costs (other than depreciation) are paid in cash. Also, in this case, administrative and marketing costs are insignificant and not considered.

flow representing the initial expenditure for the acquisition and a positive flow representing the net annual receipts from the sale of units produced by the machine. These net outflows and inflows are as follows.

Purchase price of new machine		$(62,000)
Less discount (10%)		6,200
Cash cost of new machine		$(55,800)
Installation costs		(8,000)
Total cash outflows for new machine		$(63,800)
Less sales price of old machine		3,800
Net cash outflow for new machine		$(60,000)
Product sales (5,000 per year × $7)		$35,000
Cash cost per unit:		
Direct materials	$2.00	
Direct labor	1.00	
Cash overhead (excludes depreciation)	.40	
	$3.40 × 5,000	(17,000)
Net annual cash inflow from product sales		$ 18,000

Note that depreciation is excluded in these cash flow computations. Depreciation is not a cash flow item; it is important in capital budgeting only to the extent that it reduces the amount of taxable income and, thus, the cash outflow for income taxes payable. Income taxes and the related depreciation effect are important elements in capital budgeting analysis, but add unnecessary complexities at this point. These elements are discussed after the initial illustrations.

The information about the Newmann Company's machine acquisition can be used to prepare a cash flow timeline.

Timelines

One helpful tool for analyzing cash flows of a capital investment proposal is a **timeline,** which illustrates the timing of expected cash receipts and payments. On a timeline, cash inflows are shown as positive amounts and cash outflows are shown as negative amounts.

timeline

The following timeline represents the cash flows from Newmann Company's potential machinery purchase. Although individual cash flows can be shown in a timeline, it is easier to use net cash flows. Thus, only two types of cash flows are shown below: the net negative flow for the acquisition and the net positive flow each year from product sales.

Time Point:	t0	t1	t2	t3	t4	t5
Date:	3/1/94	3/1/95	3/1/96	3/1/97	3/1/98	3/1/99
Amount:	−$60,000	+$18,000	+$18,000	+$18,000	+$18,000	+$18,000

On a timeline, the acquisition date represents time point 0. Each year after acquisition is represented as a full time period. Periods only serve to separate the times at which flows occur. Cash flows each year from product sales are treated according to the conventional assumption of end-of-period cash flows because of the difficulty in assigning them within the period.

DISCOUNTING FUTURE CASH FLOWS

discounting

Money has a time value associated with it because interest is paid or received on money.[1] Because of this fact, most capital budgeting techniques use discounted cash flows to determine the value of expected receipts and expenditures. **Discounting** means removing the portion of the future cash flows that represents interest and reducing those flows to present value amounts. The flow's imputed interest amount is based on how long a receipt or payment is delayed and on the interest rate assumed. After discounting, all future values are stated in a common base of current dollars and managers can, therefore, view all project amounts in terms of their present values. Cash flows incurred immediately are already stated in terms of their present values and are not discounted.

The capital budgeting discounting process requires the use of several estimates. First, the project cost must be estimated and should include purchase price, installation, and additional investments in working capital items such as inventory. These items constitute the cash outflows relating to the project. It is extremely important to have the best possible estimates of these current expenditures, since the full impact of these undiscounted dollars is used in the project evaluation process.

Next, the amounts and timing of future cash inflows and outflows must be estimated. Managers need to consider all future cash flows—those that are obvious and those that might be hidden. Companies installing computer systems, for example, find that the most expensive costs are those that are not readily apparent: supplies, support, training, maintenance, and opportunity costs.

discount rate

cost of capital

Last, managers must estimate the rate of return on capital investments required by the company. This rate of return is called the **discount rate** and is used to determine the imputed interest portion of future cash receipts and expenditures. The discount rate should equal or exceed a company's **cost of capital,** or the weighted average rate that reflects the costs of the various sources of funds making up a firm's debt and

---

[1]Time value of money and present value computations are reviewed in the appendix to this chapter. These concepts should have been covered in depth in Principles of Accounting or Financial Accounting and are essential to understanding the rest of this chapter; be certain they are clear before continuing.

equity (common and preferred stock) structure.[2] For example, if a company has a cost of capital of 10 percent, it annually costs the company an average of $.10 of each dollar to finance capital projects. The company would use a minimum rate of 10 percent to discount all future cash flows from a capital project to determine if the project is a worthwhile investment.

The News Note on page 772 indicates that the cost of capital has a significant influence on the acceptance or rejection of capital investments; possibly that influence is too strong. As discussed in other chapters, managers must remember that decisions should be made based on *both* quantitative and qualitative factors.

While use of the cost of capital rate helps managers toward their objective of maximizing shareholder wealth, managers must be diligent to calculate the rate appropriately and to compensate for qualitative factors and project risk or uncertainty. In addition, managers in multinational operations need to determine whether they will use the same cost of capital discount rate for international and domestic investments. Foreign capital investments are often subject to more risks than domestic investments, such as foreign exchange fluctuations and potential political intervention.

In analyzing cash flows, managers need to differentiate between cash flows that represent a return *of* capital and those that represent a return *on* capital. A **return of capital** is recovery of the original investment, while a **return on capital** represents income. The return on capital is computed for each investment period and equals the discount rate times the investment amount. Companies are only better off by making an investment when, over the life of the investment, it produces cash inflows greater than the investment made. To determine if a project meets a company's desired rate of return, one of several discounted cash flow methods can be used.

return of capital

return on capital

DISCOUNTED CASH FLOW METHODS

Three discounted cash flow techniques are the net present value method, present value index, and internal rate of return. Each of these methods is defined and illustrated in the following sections.

Net Present Value Method

The **net present value method** uses discounted cash flows to determine if the rate of return on a project is equal to, higher than, or lower than the desired rate of return. Each cash flow is discounted to its present value using the desired rate of return specified by the company. A project's **net present value** (NPV) is the difference between the present values of all its cash inflows and cash outflows.

net present value method

net present value

The possible purchase of machinery by Cawton, Inc., is used to illustrate the computation of net present value. The machine, which will be used to produce nylon-belt pouches, costs $75,000 and has an expected life of five years. The machine can

[2]Some managers believe the discount rate should reflect the opportunity cost of capital, which is the highest rate of return that could be earned by using capital for the most attractive, alternative project available. Using the opportunity cost of capital to discount project cash flows reflects the benefits that could have been realized from the foregone opportunity. Use of this rate has theoretical merit, but its application is generally not feasible. Therefore, most companies use the overall cost of capital as the discount rate. The computations involved in calculating the cost of capital are covered in finance textbooks and are beyond the scope of this text.

NEWS NOTE

Use Cost of Capital Cautiously

[T]hroughout the 1980s the U.S. [had] the highest cost of capital of the leading industrialized economies. Approximate rates were as follows: Japan, 2.9%; Britain, 3.5%; West Germany, 4.4%; and the United States, 5.5%. Simply put, . . . American companies can afford to wait just half as long as their Japanese competitors for capital investments to reach an acceptable level of profitability.

Expensive money forces U.S. managers to expend enormous mental energy on capital allocation decisions. Most managers use tools of financial analysis that seek to maximize investment returns on a project-by-project basis. But investing strictly by the numbers leads to perverse effects that stifle many worthwhile investments. With high capital costs setting a high discount rate, safe long-term projects that offer lower returns are often spurned. Riskier projects make the cut because they promise bigger paybacks. Projects with quick payoffs sail through.

SOURCE: Louis S. Richman, "How Capital Costs Cripple America," *FORTUNE* (August 14, 1989), p. 51. © 1989 The Time Inc. Magazine Company. All rights reserved.

produce 100 pouches per day and will be used 260 days per year. Exhibit 17–5 presents the information and net present value calculations, assuming a 16 percent discount rate, related to Cawton, Inc.'s prospective investment.

The factors used to compute the net present values are obtained from the present value tables provided in Appendix A at the end of the text. The first set of computations uses the net cash flows for each period; the second set shows each individual type of cash flow. Each lump-sum cash flow uses a factor from Table 1 (PV of $1) for 16 percent and the appropriate number of years designated for the cash flow. For example, maintenance cost uses the factor for the third period, while salvage value uses the factor for the fifth period. Continuous amounts each period (annuities) use factors from Table 2 in Appendix A. For example, the contribution margin cash flow uses the Table 2 factor at 16 percent for five periods.

The machine's net present value to Cawton is a positive $4,680. NPV represents the net cash benefit or cost to a company acquiring and using the investment asset. Using this criterion, whenever the NPV is zero or greater, the project is acceptable. *If the NPV is zero, the actual rate of return on the project is equal to the desired rate of return. If NPV is positive, the actual rate is greater than the desired rate. If NPV is negative, the actual rate is less than the desired rate of return.* If all estimates are correct, the machine being considered by Cawton, Inc., will provide a rate of return over 16 percent. The exact rate of return is not determined by the net present value method unless the NPV happens to be exactly equal to zero.

Had Cawton, Inc., chosen any rate other than 16 percent and used that rate in conjunction with the same basic facts, a different net present value would have resulted. For example, if Cawton had set 20 percent as the discount rate, a negative $2,227 NPV would have resulted for the project (see Exhibit 17–6). Net present values at other selected discount rates are also given. The computations for these values are made in a similar manner as those at 16 percent and 20 percent. (To indicate your understanding of the NPV method, you may want to prove these computations.)

Discount rate: 16%
Cost of machine: $75,000
Life: 5 years
Salvage: $2,000
Maintenance required: $10,000 at end of the third year

Production and sales: 26,000 pouches per year		
Sales price per pouch		$2.75
Cash production cost per pouch		
Direct materials	$ .70	
Variable labor and overhead cost	1.05	1.75
Cash contribution margin per pouch		$1.00

Cash Outflows
Cost of machinery (now): $75,000
Cost of maintenance (end of 3rd year): $10,000

Cash Inflows
Cash contribution margin per year: $26,000 (26,000 × $1.00)
Salvage value (end of fifth year): $2,000

Timeline

t0	t1	t2	t3	t4	t5
−$75,000	+$26,000	+$26,000	+$26,000	+$26,000	+$26,000
			−$10,000		+$ 2,000

Time Period	Item	Present Value
t0	Cost: −$75,000 × 1.000	−$75,000
t1	Contribution margin: +$26,000 × .8621 [16%; year 1]	22,415
t2	Contribution margin: +$26,000 × .7432 [16%; year 2]	19,323
t3	Contribution margin − Maintenance:	
	+$26,000 − $10,000 = $16,000; $16,000 × .6407 [16%; year 3]	10,251
t4	Contribution margin: +$26,000 × .5523 [16%; year 4]	14,360
t5	Contribution margin + Salvage:	
	+$26,000 + $2,000 = $28,000; $28,000 × .4761 [16%; year 5]	13,331
Net present value		$ 4,680

or alternatively

Cost: −$75,000 × 1.00	−$75,000
Contribution margin: +$26,000 × 3.2743 [16%; 5-year annuity]	+ 85,132
Maintenance: −$10,000 × .6407 [16%; year 3]	− 6,407
Salvage: +$2,000 × .4761 [16%; year 5]	+ 952
Net present value	+$ 4,677

Note: The difference in the computations results from rounding the factors in the present value tables.

EXHIBIT 17–5
▼▼▼▼▼▼▼▼▼▼▼▼

CAWTON, INC.
MACHINERY
PURCHASE

    The table in Exhibit 17–6 indicates the NPV is not a single, unique amount. Net present value is a function of several factors. First, changing the discount rate while holding the amounts and timing of cash flows constant affects the NPV. Increasing the discount rate causes the NPV to decrease; decreasing the discount rate causes NPV to increase.[3] Second, any changes in the estimated amounts and/or timing of

[3]As an interest rate is increased, fewer dollars of investment are needed to obtain the same ultimate outcome over the same time period because more interest will be earned.

EXHIBIT 17–6
▼▼▼▼▼▼▼▼▼▼▼▼

CAWTON, INC.
MACHINERY
PURCHASE—NPVs
FROM ALTERNATIVE
DISCOUNT RATES

Using a 20% discount rate and factors from Tables 1 and 2 in Appendix A

Cost: −$75,000 × 1.00	− $75,000
Contribution margin: +$26,000 × 2.9906 [20%; 5-year annuity]	+ 77,756
Maintenance: −$10,000 × .5787 [20%; year 3]	− 5,787
Salvage: +$2,000 × .4019 [20%; year 5]	+ 804
Net present value	− $ 2,227

For various other discount rates:

Discount Rate	Net Present Value
2%	+ $39,939
5%	+ $30,495
8%	+ $22,233
12%	+ $12,740
18%	+ $ 1,095

cash inflows and outflows also affect the net present value of a project. The effects on the NPV of cash flow changes depend on the nature of the changes themselves. For example, decreasing the estimate of cash outflows causes NPV to increase; reducing the stream of the cash inflows causes NPV to decrease. When amounts and timing of cash flows change in conjunction with one another, it is impossible to predict the effects of the changes without calculating the results.

The net present value method, while not providing the actual rate of return on a project, provides information on how the actual rate compares to the desired rate. This information allows managers to eliminate from consideration any projects on which the rates of return are less than the desired rate and, therefore, not acceptable. Cawton can use a table such as the one in Exhibit 17–6 to compare various alternative investments.[4]

The NPV method can be used to select the best project when choosing among investments that can perform the same task or achieve the same objective. Net present value should not, however, be used to compare independent investment projects that do not approximately have the same original asset cost. Such comparisons favor projects having higher net present values over those with lower net present values *without regard to the capital invested in the project.* As a simplistic example of this fact, assume that Cawton could spend $75,000 on the pouch-making machine or $35,000 on a bar-code scanner. The two projects' net present values are $4,678 and $3,980, respectively. If only NPVs were compared, Cawton would conclude that the machine was a "better" investment because it has a larger NPV. However, the machine provides a NPV of only 6.2 percent ($4,678 ÷ $75,000) on the investment, while the

---

[4]When making investment comparisons, managers must use the same project life span for all projects under consideration. Life-span equality is necessary because the funds released from a shorter-lived project could be used for another investment that would generate additional dollars of revenues and cause additional dollars of costs. If the alternative projects' lives are not equal, they are treated for computational purposes as if they were. For example, if Cawton could purchase the machine (having a five-year life) or lease the machine for two and one-half years, a comparison of the two alternatives could be made either by using only two and one-half years of cash flows on the purchase alternative or by assuming that another machine will be leased for two and one-half years at the end of the first lease term. If the latter assumption is made, appropriate estimates must be made relating to cash flows that may vary from the first two-and-one-half-year period. Computer packages are available to quickly do "what if" or sensitivity analysis.

scanner provides an 11.4 percent ($3,980 ÷ $35,000) NPV on its investment. Logically, companies should invest in projects that produce the highest return per investment dollar.

Present Value Index

Projects with uneven investments can be compared by using a variation of the NPV method known as the present value index. The **present value index** (PVI) is a ratio that compares the present value of net cash inflows to the present value of the net investment. The PVI is calculated as

present value index

$$PVI = \frac{\text{Present Value of Net Cash Inflows}}{\text{Present Value of Investment}}$$

The present value of the net cash inflows represents an output measure of the project's worth. This amount is equal to the cash benefit provided by the project or the present value of future cash inflows minus the present value of future cash outflows. The present value of the investment represents an input measure of the project's cost. By relating these two measures, the present value index gauges the firm's efficiency at using its capital. The higher the index, the more efficient the firm's capital investments are.

The following information about Commercial Bank is used to illustrate the calculation and use of a present value index. The bank is considering purchasing a computer system for $600,000 or a high-speed check sorter for $375,000. The following present values of net cash inflows have been calculated using a 15 percent discount rate: $770,000 for the computer system and $525,000 for the check sorter. Dividing the present value of the net inflows by the equipment cost gives the present value index. Subtracting asset cost from the present value of the inflows gives NPV. Results of these computations are as follows:

	PV of Inflows	Cost	Present Value Index	NPV
Computer system	$770,000	$600,000	1.28	$170,000
Check sorter	525,000	375,000	1.40	150,000

Although the computer system's net present value is higher, the present value index indicates that the check sorter is a more efficient use of bank capital. The higher PVI reflects a higher rate of return on the check sorter than on the computer system.

Two conditions must exist for the PVI to provide better information than the NPV method. First, the projects must be mutually exclusive. Accepting one project must require rejecting the other. This condition does not necessarily exist for Commercial Bank, since the two machines do not perform the same functions. Buying one would not automatically exclude buying the other. Second, there must be limited availability of investment funds. If the bank's total capital budget is $600,000, buying the computer system would preclude buying the check sorter. But buying the check sorter would leave $225,000 that the bank could invest in another capital asset. In this case, the check sorter and any alternative projects are considered as various "packaged" investments, and the benefits of each package must be determined and compared.

If a firm is making capital budgeting decisions on a profitability basis, a project's PVI should be equal to or greater than 1.00. Such a PVI would indicate that the present value of the net cash inflows would be at least equal to or greater than the cost of the investment. Sometimes, however, firms make decisions on a least-cost, rather than most-profit, basis.

Like the net present value method, the present value index does not indicate the project's expected rate of return. However, another discounted cash flow method (the internal rate of return) computes the expected rate of return to be earned on an investment.

Internal Rate of Return

internal rate of return

A project's **internal rate of return** (IRR) is its expected rate of return. The IRR is the discount rate at which the present value of the cash inflows minus the present value of the cash outflows equals zero. This computation is shown in the following formula:

$$NPV = -\text{Investment} + \text{PV of cash inflows} - \text{PV of other cash outflows}$$

$$0 = -\text{Investment} + \text{Cash inflows (PV factor)} - \text{Cash outflows (PV factor)}$$

Capital project information includes investment amount, cash inflows, and cash outflows. Thus, the only missing items in the previous formula are the present value factors. In annuity situations, these factors can be determined algebraically, as shown next, and then be found in the present value tables. The columns under which the present value factors are found in the tables provide the internal rate of return.

The internal rate of return is computed as follows for projects having equal annual net cash flows. When such an annuity exists, the NPV formula can be restated as:

$$NPV = -\text{Investment} + \text{PV of annuity}$$

$$0 = -\text{Investment} + \text{Annuity cash flow (PV factor)}$$

To determine the internal rate of return, substitute known amounts (investment and annuity) into the formula, rearrange terms, and solve for the unknown (the present value factor):

$$NPV = -\text{Investment} + (\text{Annuity} \times \text{PV Factor})$$

$$0 = -\text{Investment} + (\text{Annuity} \times \text{PV Factor})$$

$$\text{Investment} = (\text{Annuity} \times \text{PV Factor})$$

$$\text{Investment} \div \text{Annuity} = \text{PV Factor}$$

The solution yields a present value factor for the number of annuity periods of project life at the internal rate of return. Looking up this factor in the PV of an annuity table provides the internal rate of return.

A project of the Ziggy Company is used to illustrate an annuity IRR computation. The project will cost $226,008 and produce annual net cash inflows of $40,000 for ten years. The NPV equation is solved for the present value factor.

$$NPV = -\text{Investment} + (\text{Annuity} \times \text{PV Factor})$$
$$0 = -\$226,008 + (\$40,000 \times \text{PV Factor})$$
$$+\$226,008 = (\$40,000 \times \text{PV Factor})$$
$$+\$226,008 \div \$40,000 = \text{PV Factor}$$
$$5.6502 = \text{PV Factor}$$

The present value of an ordinary annuity table (Table 2, Appendix A) is examined to find the internal rate of return. A present value factor is a function of time and discount rate. In the table, find the row representing the project's life (in this case, ten periods). Look across the table in that row for the present value factor found upon solving the equation. The IRR (or its approximation) is found at the top of the column containing the factor. The 5.6502 factor on row 10 appears under the column headed 12 percent. This rate is the expected rate of return on Ziggy Company's project if all assumed project information holds true.

Manually finding the IRR of a project that does not have equal annual cash flows requires an iterative trial-and-error process. An initial estimate is made of a rate believed to be close to the IRR and the NPV is computed. If the resulting NPV is negative, a lower rate is estimated and the NPV is computed again. If the NPV is positive, a higher rate is tried. This process is continued until the net present value equals zero, at which time the internal rate of return has been found.

t0	t1	t2	t3	t4	t5
$75,000	+ $26,000	+ $26,000	+ $26,000	+ $26,000	+ $26,000
			− $10,000		+ $ 2,000

If the initial IRR estimate is 18%, all present value factors are at an 18% rate and the NPV calculation is:

NPV = − Investment + (PV of cash inflows) − (PV of other cash outflows)
   = − $75,000 + ($26,000 × PV of an annuity factor for 5 periods) + $2,000 × PV of $1 factor at end of 5 periods) − ($10,000 × PV of $1 factor at end of 3 periods)
   = − $75,000 + ($26,000 × 3.1272) + ($2,000 × .4371) − ($10,000 × .6086)
   = − $75,000 + $81,307 + $874 − $6,086
   = + $1,095

Since 18% yields a positive NPV, a higher rate should be tried. The present value factors for a 20% rate are attempted next:

NPV = − $75,000 + ($26,000 × 2.9906) + ($2,000 × .4019) − ($10,000 × .5787)
   = − $75,000 + $77,756 + $804 − $5,787
   = − $2,227

The IRR is between 18% and 20%. At 19%, NPV is

NPV = − $75,000 + ($26,000 × 3.0576) + ($2,000 × .4190) − ($10,000 × .5934)
   = − $75,000 + $79,498 + $838 − $5,934
   = − $598

Thus, the IRR is between 18% and 19%.

EXHIBIT 17–7
▼▼▼▼▼▼▼▼▼▼▼▼

CAWTON COMPANY MACHINERY PURCHASE DETERMINATION OF INTERNAL RATE OF RETURN—UNEQUAL CASH FLOWS

NEWS NOTE

Japan Must Now Begin to Consider Hurdle Rates

Japan's industrial leaders approached 1991 with trepidation. For many, their cost of capital was more than three times higher than it was a year prior. Faced with higher capital costs, Japanese managers are beginning to embrace such previously little-known Western concepts as "hurdle rates" and "required rate of return." That's a big switch for executives who once concerned themselves only with market share. Says Tsunehiko Ishibashi, who is general manager of finance for Mitsubishi Kasei, a major petrochemical company: "As a result of the higher cost of capital, the profitability standards for new investments must be raised."

SOURCE: John J. Curran, "Japan Tries to Cool Money Mania," *FORTUNE* (January 28, 1991), p. 66. © 1991 The Time Inc. Magazine Company. All rights reserved.

Exhibit 17–7 (previous page) uses Exhibit 17–5 data for the Cawton machinery purchase to demonstrate the process of searching for the internal rate of return. The machinery investment was previously shown to have an expected rate of return over 16 percent, since a positive NPV resulted after discounting the cash flows at 16 percent. Exhibit 17–7 indicates a first estimate of 18 percent as the IRR for this project, but the NPV is still positive at this discount rate. A second estimate of 20 percent is made, resulting in a negative NPV. A third attempt using 19 percent is made that also produces a negative net present value. Thus, the internal rate of return falls between 18 percent and 19 percent. **Interpolation,** a computer program, or a programmable calculator gives 18.65 percent as the IRR for this project.[5]

interpolation

hurdle rate

Once the internal rate of return on a project is known, it is compared to the company's discount rate or to a preestablished hurdle rate. A company's **hurdle rate** is the rate of return deemed by management to be the lowest acceptable return on investment. This rate should at least be equal to the cost of capital and is typically the discount rate used in computing net present value amounts. As indicated in the News Note above, hurdle rates are no longer simply an American concept.

If a project's IRR is equal to or greater than the hurdle rate, the project is considered a viable investment. The higher the internal rate of return, the more financially attractive the investment proposal is. In choosing among alternative investments, however, managers cannot look solely at the internal rates of return on projects. The rate does not reflect the dollars involved. An investor would normally rather have a 10 percent return on $1,000 than a 100 percent return on $10!

---

[5]Interpolation is the process of finding a term between two other terms in a series. The difference in the NPVs at 18 percent and 19 percent is $1,693 [$1,095 − (−$598)]. The interpolation process gives the following computation:

$$\text{Actual rate} = 18\% + [(\$1,095 \div \$1,693)(1.0)]$$
$$= 18\% + (.647)(1.0)$$
$$= 18.65\% \text{ (rounded)}$$

The 1.0 represents the 1 percent difference between the 18 percent and 19 percent rates.

NONDISCOUNTING METHODS

Unlike the NPV, PVI, and IRR methods, not all capital budgeting techniques use the time value of money concept. Two methods that do not discount future cash flows are the payback period and the accounting rate of return. Both methods are simple to use and provide useful information, but for different reasons are not as helpful in evaluating capital projects as discounted cash flow methods.

Payback Period

A project's **payback period** is the time required to recoup the original investment through cash flows from a project. In one sense, payback period measures a dimension of project risk by focusing on timing of cash flows. Since longer-term future cash flows are more uncertain than current or relatively current cash flows, the assumption is that the longer it takes to recover the initial investment, the greater the project's risk. Another reason for concern about long payback periods relates to capital reinvestment. The faster capital is returned from an investment, the more rapidly it can be invested in other projects; consider how quickly the company discussed in the News Note on page 780 could reinvest its $34,000!

payback period

When the cash flow of a project is a simple annuity, the payback period is determined as follows:

$$\text{Payback Period} = \text{Investment} \div \text{Annuity}$$

The cash flows for Ziggy Company's project (investment cost, $226,008; annuity, $40,000) are used to compute the payback period for an investment returning an annuity amount. The payback period is 5.65 years ($226,008 ÷ $40,000). Note that 5.65 was also the present value factor needed to approximate Ziggy's internal rate of return. Thus, when the project is a simple annuity situation, knowledge of the payback period can also be used to determine the internal rate of return.

The payback period for a project having unequal cash inflows is determined by accumulating cash flows until the original investment is recovered. A project costing $58,000 and providing the following cash flows over its life is used to illustrate a situation of unequal cash flows:

Year	Amount
1	$12,000
2	24,000
3	32,000
4	36,000
5	24,000
6	5,000

The payback is calculated by obtaining a yearly cumulative total of the above inflows:

Year	Amount	Cumulative Total	
1	$12,000	$ 12,000	
2	24,000	36,000	← Payback point
3	32,000	68,000	

NEWS NOTE

Investment's Payback Occurs in Less Than a Half-Year

In one company, the controller conducted a cost-benefit analysis to determine the payback period of an investment in a bar code system that combined inventory control, production scheduling, and cost accounting. Bar coding eliminated the manual calculation of direct labor cost per part that was recorded on time cards and the posting of these costs into the ledger. It also eliminated the need for quality inspectors to count parts without defects. When the total cost savings of $1,370 per week was compared to the cost of equipment and services for implementing the system ($34,104 net of depreciation), payback was achieved in about 25 weeks.

SOURCE: Arjan T. Sadhwani and Thomas Tyson, "Does Your Firm Need Bar Coding?" *Management Accounting* (April 1990), p. 47. Published by Institute of Management Accountants, Montvale, N.J.

Year	Amount	Cumulative Total
4	36,000	104,000
5	24,000	128,000
6	5,000	133,000

Since $36,000 will be received by the end of the first two years, $22,000 more is needed to recover the original $58,000 investment. If the $32,000 inflow in the third year is assumed to occur evenly throughout the year, it should take approximately .6875 percent ($22,000 ÷ $32,000) of the third year to cover the rest of the original investment, giving a payback period for this project of approximately 2 years and 8 months (.6875 × 12 months). It is important to note that most managers would minimize the significance of the decimal points in this payback calculation. While the division itself is accurate, cash flows do not arise perfectly evenly throughout a year and, thus, the precision of such a calculation may be considered unfounded.

Company management often sets a maximum acceptable payback period as part of its evaluation techniques for capital projects. Most companies use payback period as only one way of judging an investment project—usually as a screening technique. Normally, after being found acceptable in terms of payback period, a project is subjected to evaluation by another capital budgeting technique. This secondary evaluation is performed because the payback period method ignores three important things: inflows occurring after the payback period has been reached; the company's desired rate of return; and the time value of money. In periods of high uncertainty, however, payback is quite useful because shortening the desired payback period helps to compensate for risk.

Accounting Rate of Return

accounting rate of return

The **accounting rate of return** (ARR) measures the expected rate of earnings obtained on the average capital investment over a project's life. This evaluation method uses the projected net income amount shown on accrual-based financial statements and is a return on investment formula for a single project. It is the one evaluation technique that is not based on cash flows. The formula to compute the accounting rate of return is:

$$ARR = \frac{\text{Average Annual Profits from Project}}{\text{Average Investment in Project}}$$

Project investment includes original cost and project support costs, such as those needed for working capital items (for example, inventory). Investment, salvage value, and working capital released at the end of the project's life are summed and divided by two to obtain the average investment.[6]

To illustrate the computation of the accounting rate of return, information for a piece of equipment being considered by the Wilson Company is available. Data on the potential investment are as follows:

Beginning investment:	
Initial cost of equipment	$200,000
Additional working capital needed for the project	70,000
Return at end of project:	
Salvage value of equipment at the end of ten years	20,000
Working capital released at the end of ten years	70,000
Return over life of project:	
Average incremental company profits after taxes	44,000

Solving the formula for the accounting rate of return gives:

$$ARR = \frac{\$44,000}{(\$270,000 + \$90,000) \div 2}$$

$$= \frac{\$44,000}{\$180,000}$$

$$= 24.4\%$$

The project's 24.4 percent ARR can be compared with a preestablished hurdle rate set by management. This hurdle rate may not be the same as the desired discount rate, since the data used in calculating the accounting rate of return are not cash flow data. Management may set the ARR hurdle rate at a higher level than the discount rate because the method does not include the time value of money. In addition, the 24.4 percent accounting rate of return for this project should be compared to ARRs on other investment projects being considered by the Wilson Company to determine which projects have the highest accounting rates of return.

Considering the various benefits and drawbacks of each of the various capital budgeting techniques, the results given in the following News Notes are interesting.

---

[6]Sometimes ARR is computed using initial cost rather than average investment as the denominator. Such a computation ignores the return of funds at the end of the project life and is less appropriate than the computation shown.

Comparing U.S., Japanese, and Korean Techniques

In a recent survey, payback was found to be the most popular among the quantitative methods commonly used to justify long-term investments in the U.S., Japan, and Korea. As many as 86% of the Japanese, 75% of the Korean, and 71% of U.S. corporations surveyed use this naive approach as an important criterion in long-term investment decisions. While the payback method is theoretically inferior to discounted cash flow techniques, in an environment where technology changes rapidly and new products become obsolete quickly, corporations should look for investment opportunities that pay back within a short period of time. Corporations using payback period were asked about the number of years in which investments in advanced technology were expected to be recovered. The majority considered less than five years as the minimum payback period.

Approximately the same percentage of Korean and U.S. corporations use the three other quantitative methods: accounting rate of return, internal rate of return, and net present value. Surprisingly, not many Japanese corporations use discounted cash flow techniques. Only 20% of the Japanese sample corporations use the internal rate of return as an important criterion in making investment decisions, and only 28% use net present value.

Qualitative factors are also considered. For Korea, competing in the marketplace and operational performance improvements were at the top of the list of extremely important investment justifications—mentioned by 52% and 49%, respectively. The U.S. (43%) and Japanese (41%) companies agreed on the assessment of marketplace competitiveness. Forty-six percent of the Japanese companies agreed with Korean ones that operational performance improvements were extremely important investment justifications. In the U.S., however, only 18% of the companies surveyed ranked it at that level.

SOURCE: Adapted from Il-Woon Kim and Ja Song, "U.S., Korea, and Japan: Accounting Practices in Three Countries," *Management Accounting* (August 1990), pp. 26–27. Published by Institute of Management Accountants, Montvale, N.J.

ASSUMPTIONS AND LIMITATIONS OF METHODS

Each capital budgeting evaluation technique has its own underlying assumptions and limitations on usefulness; these are summarized in Exhibit 17–8. To derive the most success from the capital budgeting process, managers should understand the basic similarities and differences of the various methods and use several techniques to evaluate a project.

All of the methods have two identical limitations: (1) they do not consider management preferences about the timing of cash flows, and (2) they use a single, deterministic measure of cash flow amounts rather than ranges of cash flow values based on probabilities. The former limitation can be compensated for by subjectively favoring projects whose cash flow profiles better suit management's preferences, assuming other project factors are equal. The second limitation can be overcome by using prob-

EXHIBIT 17–8
▼▼▼▼▼▼▼▼▼▼▼▼

SELECTED
ASSUMPTIONS AND
LIMITATIONS OF
CAPITAL BUDGETING
METHODS

Assumptions	Limitations

Net Present Value

• Discount rate used is valid	• Basic method treats cash flows and project life as deterministic without explicit consideration of probabilities
• Timing and size of cash flows are accurately predicted	
• Life of project is accurately predicted	• Alternative project rates of return are not known
• If the shorter-lived of two projects is selected, the proceeds of that project will continue to earn the discount rate of return through the theoretical completion of the longer-lived project	• Cash flow pattern preferences are not explicitly recognized
	• IRR on project is not reflected

Present Value Index

• Same as NPV	• Same as NPV
• Size of PV of net inflows relative to size of present value of investment measures efficient use of capital	• Gives a relative answer but does not reflect dollars of NPV

Internal Rate of Return

• Hurdle rate used is valid	• Projects are ranked for funding using the IRR rather than dollar size
• Timing and size of cash flows are accurately predicted	• Does not reflect dollars of NPV
• Life of project is accurately predicted	• Basic method treats cash flows and project life as deterministic without explicit consideration of probabilities
• If the shorter-lived of two projects is selected, the proceeds of that project will continue to earn the IRR through the theoretical completion of the longer-lived project	• Cash flow pattern preferences are not explicitly recognized
	• It is possible to calculate multiple rates of return on the same project

Payback

• Speed of investment recovery is the key consideration	• Ignores cash flows after payback
• Timing and size of cash flows are accurately predicted	• Basic method treats cash flows and project life as deterministic without explicit consideration of probabilities
• Risk (uncertainty) is lower for a shorter payback project	• Ignores time value of money
	• Cash flow pattern preferences are not explicitly recognized

Accounting Rate of Return

• Effect on company accounting earnings relative to average investment is key consideration	• Does not consider cash flows
	• Does not consider time value of money
• Size and timing of increase in company earnings, investment cost, project life, and salvage value can be accurately predicted	• Treats earnings, investment, and project life as deterministic without explicit consideration of probabilities

ability estimates of cash flows. These estimates can be input into a computer program to determine a distribution of cash flows for each method under various conditions of uncertainty.

All of the previous examples of capital budgeting analysis have ignored one major influence—that of depreciation and its effects on cash flows. This topic is covered in the following section.

THE EFFECT OF DEPRECIATION ON AFTER-TAX CASH FLOWS

Income taxes are a significant aspect of the business environment. Tax planning is a central part of management planning and overall business profitability. Managers should give thorough recognition to tax implications of all company decisions. In evaluating capital projects, managers should use after-tax cash flows to determine project acceptability. Like interest on debt, depreciation on capital assets is deductible in computing taxable income. As taxable income decreases, so do the taxes that must be paid and, thus, cash flow is affected.

tax shield

tax benefit

Continuously profitable businesses generally find it advantageous to claim depreciation deductions as rapidly as permitted by tax law. Depreciation expense is *not* a cash flow item. Companies neither pay nor receive any funds for depreciation. However, by reducing the amount of taxable income, depreciation expense is a **tax shield** against revenues in regard to the payment of taxes. The amount of the tax shield depends on asset cost, asset life, asset salvage value, and depreciation method chosen. This tax shield produces a **tax benefit** equal to the depreciation amount multiplied by the tax rate.

The concepts of tax shield and tax benefit are shown on the following income statements. The tax rate is assumed to be 35 percent.

No Depreciation Deduction		Depreciation Deduction	
Income Statement		Income Statement	
Sales	$1,100,000	Sales	$1,100,000
Cost of goods sold	(450,000)	Cost of goods sold	(450,000)
Gross margin	$ 650,000	Gross margin	$ 650,000
Expenses other than depreciation	(150,000)	Expenses other than depreciation	(150,000)
Depreciation expense	0 ⬌	Depreciation expense	(200,000)
Income before taxes	$ 500,000	Income before taxes	$ 300,000
Tax expense (35%)	(175,000) ⬌	Tax expense (35%)	(105,000)
Net income	$ 325,000	Net income	$195,000

The tax shield is the depreciation expense amount of $200,000. The tax benefit is $70,000 ($200,000 × 35%), or the difference between $175,000 of tax expense on the first income statement and $105,000 of tax expense on the second income statement. Since taxes are reduced by $70,000, less cash must be spent and, thus, the pattern of cash flows is improved.

Income tax laws regarding depreciation deductions are subject to annual revision. In analyzing capital investments, managers should use the most current depreciation regulations to calculate cash flows from projects. Different depreciation methods may have significant impacts on after-tax cash flows. For a continuously profitable company, an accelerated method of depreciation will produce higher tax benefits in the early years of asset life than will the straight-line method. These higher tax benefits will translate into a higher net present value over the life of the investment project.

Capital projects are analyzed and evaluated before investments are made, and managers should be aware of the inherent risk of tax law changes. It is possible that a tax depreciation method assumed in making the capital project evaluation may not be available by the time an investment is actually made and an asset is placed into service. Such changes may cause dramatic effects on projected after-tax cash flows. However, once purchased and placed into service, an asset can generally be depreciated using the method and tax life allowed when the asset was placed into service *regardless* of the tax law changes occurring after that time.

Changes may also occur in the tax rate structure. Rate changes may be relatively unpredictable. For example, the maximum federal corporate tax rate for many years was 46 percent; then, the Tax Reform Act of 1986 lowered this rate to 34 percent. A reduction in the tax rates lowers the tax benefit provided by the depreciation tax shield because the cash flow impact is lessened. Tax rate changes can cause the expected outcomes from the original capital investment analysis to vary from the actual outcomes achieved by the project.

ILLUSTRATION OF AFTER-TAX CASH FLOWS IN CAPITAL BUDGETING

Mary Applewhite is considering the purchase of a new tractor for her ten-acre farm. Basic information relative to this investment is presented in Exhibit 17–9. The cash flows shown are only a small part of the farm's total cash flows. However, the portion of the company's total tax caused by this project must be estimated, as this portion must be included in project analysis.

Estimated life		6 years
Cost		$20,000
Salvage value		$ 2,000
Estimated additional annual revenue per acre	$10,000	
Estimated annual cost to operate tractor	4,000	
Net cash flow (CF)		$ 6,000
Tax rate for farm		35%
Discount rate		10%
Hurdle rate for ARR		13%
Minimum payback period		4 years

Depreciation deduction for tax purposes (using double-declining balance):
Year 1   2/6 ($20,000 − $0)   = $6,667
Year 2   2/6 ($20,000 − $6,667) = $4,444
Year 3   2/6 ($20,000 − $11,111) = $2,963
Year 4   2/6 ($20,000 − $14,074) = $1,975
Year 5   2/6 ($20,000 − $16,049) = $1,317
Year 6 $ 634*

*This amount forces the remaining book value of the asset to be equal to the salvage value. If the book and tax methods of depreciation have been the same over the asset's life, the salvage value of $2,000 will not be taxable.

EXHIBIT 17–9

▼▼▼▼▼▼▼▼▼▼▼▼

APPLEWHITE TRACTOR OPERATING STATISTICS

The incremental income tax each year is added to the other cash outflows in a capital budgeting project. The amount of incremental, net after-tax cash flow can be estimated on the project as follows:

$$NATCF = t(D) + (1 - t)(NOCF)$$

$$T = t(NOCF - D)$$

where

$$
\begin{aligned}
NATCF &= \text{net after-tax cash flows} \\
t &= \text{tax rate} \\
D &= \text{depreciation for period} \\
NOCF &= \text{net operating cash flows} \\
T &= \text{income tax for period}
\end{aligned}
$$

The net after-tax cash flows from the tractor would be as follows:

Year	(a) Depreciation	(b) Tax Benefit From Depreciation $(a)(t)$	(c) Net of Tax Cash Inflows $(CF)(1 - t)$	(d) Net After-Tax Cash Inflows $(b) + (c)$
1	$6,667	$2,333	$3,900	$6,233
2	4,444	1,555	3,900	5,455
3	2,963	1,037	3,900	4,937
4	1,975	691	3,900	4,591
5	1,317	461	3,900	4,361
6	634	222	3,900	4,122

The net after-tax cash flow timeline is:

Time	t0	t1	t2	t3	t4	t5	t6
Net operating cash flows		$6,233	$5,455	$4,937	$4,591	$4,361	$4,122
Other cash flows	$(20,000)						2,000
Totals	$(20,000)	$6,233	$5,455	$4,937	$4,591	$4,361	$6,122

The net present value of the investment is calculated as follows:

Time	Cash Flow	10% Discount Factor	Present Value
0	$(20,000)	1.0000	$(20,000)
1	6,233	.9091	5,666
2	5,455	.8265	4,509
3	4,937	.7513	3,709
4	4,591	.6830	3,136
5	4,361	.6209	2,708
6	6,122	.5645	3,456
		NPV	+$ 3,184

Since the NPV is positive, the tractor will earn a rate higher than the 10 percent discount rate.

The PVI for the investment is determined as follows:

$$PVI = \frac{\$23,184}{\$20,000} = 1.16$$

This statistic exceeds 1.00 and, thus, indicates that the investment earns more than the discount rate.

The internal rate of return for the tractor must exceed 10 percent because there is a positive $3,184 NPV. The following schedule shows that, at 15.5 percent, the NPV is an extremely small negative amount, meaning that the actual rate is slightly below 15.5 percent.

Time	Cash Flow	15.5% Discount Factor	Present Value
0	$(20,000)	1.0000	$(20,000)
1	6,233	.8658	5,397
2	5,455	.7496	4,089
3	4,937	.6490	3,204
4	4,591	.5619	2,580
5	4,361	.4865	2,122
6	6,122	.4212	2,579
		NPV	$ (29)

A programmable calculator indicates that the IRR is 15.4 percent.
Payback is found as follows:

Year	Inflows	Cumulative Total
1	$6,233	$ 6,233
2	5,455	11,688
3	4,937	16,625
4	4,591	21,216
5	4,361	25,577
6	6,122	31,699

It should take approximately 73.5 percent of the fourth year [($20,000 − $16,625) ÷ $4,591] to recover the initial $20,000. The payback, then, is approximately three years and nine months, which is less than the minimum payback period desired.

Last, the ARR is found as follows:

Step 1: Calculate the average annual net income:

Year	Net After Tax Cash Inflows	−	Depreciation	=	Net Income
1	$ 6,233		$ 6,667		$ (434)
2	5,455		4,444		1,011
3	4,937		2,963		1,974
4	4,591		1,975		2,616
5	4,361		1,317		3,044
6	4,122		634		3,488
	$29,699		$18,000		$11,699

$$\text{Average annual net income} = \frac{\$11,699}{6} = \$1,950$$

Step 2: Calculate the average investment:

$$\frac{\text{Beginning investment} + \text{Salvage value}}{2} = \frac{\$20,000 + \$2,000}{2} = \$11,000$$

Step 3: Divide results of Step 1 by those of Step 2:

$$\text{ARR} = \frac{\$1,950}{\$11,000} = 17.7\%$$

This rate is higher than the 13 percent minimum acceptable ARR hurdle rate established by Mary Applewhite.

Based solely on quantitative investment criteria, each of the previous techniques indicates that purchasing the tractor is a viable investment for Mary Applewhite. If the farm has limited funds available, this project should be compared to all other acceptable, alternative uses of funds to determine which investment(s) would provide the best return to the farm and the most efficient use of resources. Additionally, Ms. Applewhite should consider all important qualitative factors before making her investment decision.

LINK BETWEEN PAYBACK PERIOD AND ACCOUNTING RATE OF RETURN

When taxes are included, payback period is computed as the original investment divided by annual after-tax cash flows. Accounting rate of return is found by dividing annual after-tax net income from the investment by the amount of the investment. In other words, payback period focuses on cash-basis income, while ARR focuses on accrual-basis income. Because most revenues and expenses except depreciation are cash-based, depreciation is usually the primary difference between accrual-based net income and the net cash inflow generated by a capital budgeting project. Because of this singular difference, the "link" or relationship between a project's payback period and its accounting rate of return can be expressed by the following model:

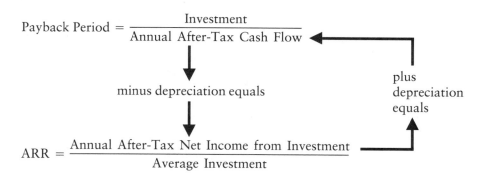

This relationship is presented in the following simplified illustration in which a 30 percent tax rate has been assumed for Beatle Company. The company is considering purchasing a machine costing $120,000 and lasting ten years with no salvage value.

Before-tax cash flow	$21,000
Depreciation	(12,000) (straight line)
Income before tax	$ 9,000
Tax	(2,700)
Net income after tax	$ 6,300 (use as numerator in ARR)
Depreciation	12,000 (link between ARR & payback)
Cash flow after tax	$18,300 (use as denominator in payback)

Using this model, Beatle Company's anticipated payback period and ARR for the machine are calculated as follows:

$$\text{Payback} = \frac{\$120,000}{\$18,300} = 6.56 \text{ years}$$

less $12,000 depreciation

$$\text{ARR} = \frac{\$6,300}{(\$120,000 \ + \ \$0) \ \div \ 2} = \frac{\$6,300}{\$60,000} = 10.5\%$$

Managers will do a better job justifying capital investments if the effect of depreciation on taxes is understood and the assumptions and limitations of the various capital budgeting techniques are recognized. An important area of business investment that requires managers to understand all aspects (quantitative vs. qualitative, tax impacts, opportunity costs, etc.) of capital budgeting is that related to high-technology equipment.

HIGH-TECH INVESTMENTS

Some of the most pressing investment decisions currently facing American companies are those related to the purchase of automated and robotic equipment. In many instances, the decision is more a question of "how much" and "when" rather than "whether." High-technology equipment generally requires massive investments, and significant thought should be given to the tangible and intangible benefits generated by such investments. In addition, management must consider the interdependent relationships of such investments, including significantly reduced labor costs, increased quality and quantity of production, shortened processing time, and increased utility and maintenance costs. In such a spirit, Northern Telecom (a subsidiary of Canada's

At Masco Industries, highly automated equipment is used to ensure consistent, part-to-part workpiece quality. Quality improvements should be considered when evaluating the feasibility of equipment purchases.

Northern Telecom Limited) decided to change its capital justification procedures to allow managers to justify projects on the basis of quality improvements and time savings rather than simply financial payback periods.[7]

Through the late 1980s, the major "high-tech" capital investments made by American businesses were in office equipment. However, outlays for factory automation are expected to increase substantially during the 1990s. The rationale for the slowness by companies to invest in automated equipment is multifaceted. One reason has been a desire to minimize worker displacement and, thus, the corresponding increase in unemployment. A basic robot can do the work of up to six employees depending upon the tasks involved.

A second concern has been morale problems of employees who retain their jobs after some degree of automation has occurred. These employees often feel guilty because they kept their jobs and feel uneasy at learning new skills. Third, after companies have installed some automated equipment, management has found that the equipment often did not work correctly, was difficult to integrate with nonautomated equipment, or did not do as good a job as had been done by humans. A fourth concern is that automated equipment is computer-driven, and some senior managers still do not regard computers as competitive assets. But, as can be seen from the next News Note, probably the most significant reason behind the lack of acquisition of automated equipment is that it is often difficult to justify the major capital investment required.

This mindset is also illustrated in the following example. Japan's Yamazaki Manufacturing Company spent $18 million to install a flexible manufacturing system. The

---

[7]Roy Merrills, "How Northern Telecom Competes on Time," *Harvard Business Review* (July–August 1989), p. 114.

number of machines went from sixty-eight to eighteen; production floor space declined from 103,000 square feet to 30,000; and average processing (throughput) time was reduced from 35 to 1.5 days. But the total savings after two years was only $6.9 million, and $3.9 million of that amount came from a one-time inventory reduction. "Even if the system continued to produce annual labor savings of $1.5 million for 20 years, the project's return would be less than 10 percent per year." [8] Many U.S. companies would not consider 10 percent a reasonable rate of return in spite of the huge savings in fixed assets and time. Additionally, the payback period for the investment would extend far beyond the norms set by most firms.

Traditional capital budgeting analysis may need some modifications to be more useful to managers making automated equipment investment decisions. Four modifications to the analysis process are suggested. First, managers need to be careful in setting the discount rate used to determine present value figures. This rate is often set somewhere between 12 and 18 percent. Such high rates "penalize long-term investments with heavy front-end costs and delayed project startups that take many years to achieve their mature rate of return." [9] Whether such high discount rates are even reasonable is currently under debate. One survey indicated that most companies have a cost of capital between 9 and 12 percent; however, as indicated in the following News Note, companies are using rates 30 to 40 percent higher than that! [10]

Second, more weight needs to be given to the qualitative benefits to be provided by the capital expenditure. This point is appropriate for all investment decisions, but especially for high-tech ones. Oftentimes, justification in such investments has required a "leap of faith" because of the inability to quantify some of the new key elements of such investment projects. [11] Benefits, such as quality and delivery time,

[8] Robert S. Kaplan, "Must CIM Be Justified by Faith Alone?" *Harvard Business Review* (March–April 1986), p. 87.

[9] Richard L. Engwall, "Investment Justification Issues," *Journal of Cost Management* (Spring 1989), p. 52.

[10] Allen H. Seed III and Randell G. Wagner, "Investment Justification of Factory Automation," *Cost Accounting for the Nineties: Responding to Technological Change* (Montvale, N.J.: National Association of Accountants, 1988), p. 88.

[11] Thornton Parker and Theodore Lettes, "Is Accounting Standing in the Way of Flexible Computer-integrated Manufacturing?" *Management Accounting* (January 1991), p. 34.

NEWS NOTE

High Hurdle Rates Bias Investment Decisions

Regarding hurdle rates, surveys have indicated that it is not unusual for U.S. firms to require payback periods of less than two to three years, which roughly corresponds to internal rates of return in excess of 30% to 50% (after taxes) to justify investments. Such arbitrarily high hurdle rates force U.S. managers to focus on the short term.

For example, if you have a 10-year annuity and you plot it against a discount rate of 5%, 10%, 15%, and so on, as the discount rate assumption increases to 30%, the percentage of the total present value added to the justification of the project increases to approximately 80% in the first five years. In other words, at a 30% discount rate, 80% of the hypothetical project's value is accrued in the first five years, and the remaining 20% accrues in the last five years. Consequently, the high investment justification hurdles mean that only certain kinds of investments will be considered worthwhile. Projects having large savings in their early years will tend to dominate the typically more strategic investments that are characterized by large cash flows in the mid to late part of the useful project life.

SOURCE: William G. Sullivan and James M. Reeve, "Xventure: Expert Systems to the Rescue," *Management Accounting* (October 1988), p. 51. Published by Institute of Management Accountants, Montvale, N.J.

have typically been assigned a zero dollar value in making investment decisions because of the difficulty in determining their worth. The improved competitive position that can result from higher product quality or shorter throughput time is another qualitative benefit that is often overlooked. Exhibit 17–10 indicates the results of a survey showing various qualitative factors and the percentages of respondent companies that considered such factors in investment justification. Note that some respondents attempted to quantify these qualitative factors in their analyses.[12]

A third item to consider in regard to high-tech investments is that such projects are not "free-standing."

> Investments should be considered as interrelated elements of an integrated strategy rather than as individual projects. The benefits of many advanced manufacturing technologies accrue when several of the manufacturing activities are integrated. Because these activities are synergistic, the benefits that accrue when they are linked may far outweigh the simple sum of the individual benefits of the separate activities (if not linked).[13]

---

[12]Companies may also choose to use the Analytic Hierarchy Process (AHP) developed by Thomas Saaty. AHP provides a decision framework that reduces the decision into component elements and organizes those elements into levels of importance. Managers can focus on the process and incorporate uncertainty into the decision model. See, for example, "Decision Support Software for Capital Budgeting," by David E. Stout, Matthew J. Liberatore, and Thomas F. Monahan in *Management Accounting* (July 1991), pp. 50–53.

[13]Callie Berliner and James A. Brimson, eds., *Cost Management for Today's Advanced Manufacturing* (Boston, Mass.: Harvard Business School Press, 1988), p. 176.

EXHIBIT 17–10

BASES OF
JUSTIFYING
INVESTMENTS

	Qualitatively Considered Only	Quantified in Dollars
Improved competitive position	70%	18%
Consistency with business strategy	70%	8%
Improved delivery and service	68%	11%
Improved product quality/reliability	65%	27%
Reduced product development time	61%	7%
Additional manufacturing capabilities and flexibility	59%	23%

SOURCE: Robert A. Howell et al., *Management Accounting in the New Manufacturing Environment* (Montvale, N.J.: National Association of Accountants and Computer Aided Manufacturing-International, 1987), p. 24.

Exhibit 17–11 on the next page illustrates the synergistic benefits of interrelated operations. This exhibit indicates the potential benefits to be obtained from the installation of a computer-integrated manufacturing (CIM) system consisting of a network of computers and machines.

Finally, consideration should be given to the opportunity cost of *not* acquiring automated equipment. The opportunity cost of nonautomation refers to the competitive disadvantage a company will experience when its competitors acquire such equipment and experience the qualitative benefits mentioned earlier.

In making capital budgeting decisions, managers should quantify all benefits and costs that can be quantified with any reasonable degree of accuracy. Such quantifications are especially necessary when evaluating high-technology equipment expenditures. Managers can also attempt to quantify the *qualitative* benefits using probabilities and recalculate the investment's net present value and/or internal rate of return to check for financial acceptability. If the more uncertain benefits and costs "aren't quantified, many viable automation projects may be rejected—to the long-run detriment of the company and the U.S. economy." [14] Alternatively, management can try to subjectively evaluate nonquantifiable items so that they are properly weighed in the decision model. For example, using traditional capital budgeting models, a satellite being considered by Hibernia Bank is shown to be unacceptable, and an additional $250,000 of cash inflow per year is needed to make the rate of return acceptable. However, Hibernia knows that some overseas banks have satellites that will send information from Tokyo to New York five seconds quicker than Hibernia can. A subjective decision can be made as to whether the qualitative benefits of the investment make it acceptable. If so, the investment should be made; if not, the company should use its funds in another manner. [15]

---

[14] Robert E. Bennett and James A. Hendricks, "Justifying the Acquisition of Automated Equipment," *Management Accounting* (July 1987), p. 46.
[15] A recent survey indicated that upper-level managers may be placing more reliance on qualitative information and intuition than on analytical techniques. While they understand and know how to use such techniques, managers indicated that such tools were more important in making lower-level decisions. Managers are using more judgment "because they are unwilling to trust engineers or financial personnel to apply a concept like opportunity cost." Bernard A. Coda and Barry G. King, "Manufacturing Decision-making Tools," *Journal of Cost Management* (Spring 1989), p. 30.

EXHIBIT 17–11
▼▼▼▼▼▼▼▼▼▼▼▼▼

POTENTIAL SAVINGS
FROM A CIM SYSTEM

Savings	Function
5%– 15%	Reduction in personnel costs
15%– 30%	Reduction in engineering design costs
30%– 60%	Reduction in overall lead time
40%– 60%	Reduction in work in process
40%– 70%	Gain in overall production
200%– 300%	Gain in capital equipment uptime
200%– 300%	Gain in product quality
300%–3,500%	Gain in engineering productivity

SOURCE: Joel C. Polakoff, "Computer Integrated Manufacturing: A New Look at Cost Justifications," *Journal of Accountancy* (March 1990), p. 24.

Exhibit 17–12 illustrates a CAD/CAM equipment acquisition decision under consideration by Toro Engineering. (CAD/CAM stands for computer-aided design/computer-aided manufacturing.) The system costs $690,000. Management has set 10 percent as the discount rate to be used and requires a payback period no greater than two-thirds the life of the investment project. Using these criteria, Part A of the exhibit indicates that the system is not an acceptable acquisition. However, Toro's marketing vice-president estimates that customer goodwill will increase because of the quickness with which design changes can be made and she values that increase at $50,000 per year. This amount is added to the annual cash flow, and a new net present value and payback period are computed in Part B of the exhibit. By including an estimated value for the qualitative goodwill benefit, the CAD/CAM system meets Toro's selection criteria.

EXHIBIT 17–12
▼▼▼▼▼▼▼▼▼▼▼▼▼

TORO ENGINEERING
CAD/CAM SYSTEM
ACQUISITION

Cost: $690,000
Annual maintenance: $200,000
Life: 5 years

Efficiency: three times as efficient as manual design
Manual equivalent of system: 6 draftspersons
Annual salary per draftsperson: $60,000
Labor cost savings of system: $360,000 ($60,000 × 6)

Part A—Traditional Capital Budgeting Technique
Annual net cash flows of system

Maintenance (additional cost)	− $200,000
Labor savings (reduced cost)	+ 360,000
Net cash flow	$160,000

NPV @ 10% = (− $690,000) + ($160,000 × 3.7908) = − $83,472
Payback period = 4.3 years

Part B—Adjustment for Qualitative Value-Added
Estimated value of customer goodwill from increased speed of design changes ($50,000 per year) raises "cash flow" to $210,000.

NPV @ 10% = (− $690,000) + ($210,000 × 3.7908) = + $106,068
Payback period = 3.3 years

The "hottest" high-tech investment being made by Japanese companies is **flexible manufacturing systems** (FMSs) that can produce numerous high-quality varieties of a product through the use of computer-controlled robots. These systems are used in modular factories and can manufacture basically customized units at a low per-unit cost. The keys to customization are small lot sizes, rapid set-up and lots of information; the ability to be flexible is useful only if a company understands its customers and sales market. Salespeople working for a company that has an FMS will soon be able to ask customers what they want rather than telling them what the company has available.

flexible manufacturing systems

FMSs are not inexpensive, but the investment can pay for itself through increased sales at higher prices as well as lower costs. The News Note on page 796 provides some indications of the benefits of flexible manufacturing systems.

Regardless of the type of investment project being considered, the capital budgeting selection and investment process should not end with project acquisition. At some point (or points) in time, management should perform post-investment audits of projects.

POST-INVESTMENT AUDIT

In a **post-investment audit** of a capital project, information on actual project results is gathered and compared to expected results. This process is intended

post-investment audit

> to accomplish at least four primary objectives: serve as an important financial control mechanism, provide information for future capital expenditure decisions, remove certain psychological and/or political impediments usually associated with asset control and abandonment, and have a psychological impact on those proposing capital investments.[16]

Comparisons should be made using the same technique or techniques as were originally used to determine project acceptance. Actual data should be extrapolated to future periods where such information would be appropriate. In cases where significant learning or training is necessary, start-up costs of the first year may not be appropriate indicators of future costs. Such projects should be given a chance to stabilize before making the project audit.

As the size of capital expenditures increases, post-investment audits become more crucial. Although an audit cannot change the past investment decision, it can be used to pinpoint areas of operations that are not in line with expectations for the purpose of correcting problems before they get out of hand. It is not enough to make only actual-to-expected cash flow comparisons. Management should take action to find the causes of the adverse differences and the means, if possible, to remedy them.

Comparison will also help managers evaluate the accuracy of the cost and benefit predictions given in support of capital budgeting projects. Project sponsors may be biased in favor of their projects. Such bias may result in overly optimistic forecasts of

---

[16]Lawrence A. Gordon and Mary D. Myers, "Postauditing Capital Projects," *Management Accounting* (January 1991), p. 39.

Flexibility Means Profitability

Japan's flexibility drive was fueled by a boom in capital spending—$3 trillion in domestic plant and equipment from 1986 to 1991. . . . The plunging cost of computing power, combined with low-cost capital, put flexibility within reach even of second-tier companies in Japan. [For example,] Fuji Electric, Japan's fourth-largest maker of electrical machinery, [began investing in FMS in 1987]—the effort consumes 30 percent of the capital budget. When Fuji gets an order for an electric motor switch, 20 percent of the time the buyer wants—and gets—twenty-four hour delivery. Another 40 percent gets delivery within two days. Fuji didn't narrow its product line; those schedules are for customized work.

Beginning in 1988, Fuji installed flexible, computer-integrated lines where setup, parts selection, and assembly are all automated using bar codes that tell the machines what to do. Before those lines, Fuji filled orders in three days. Now Fuji needs twenty-four hours, using one-third as many workers and almost one-third less inventory, while making about 8,000 varieties, three times more than before.

Japanese carmakers are rebuilding the heart of their factories to become even more versatile and labor-efficient—an effort that could once again give them fundamental cost advantages and protect their lead in the time and cost of bringing new cars to market. While many American auto plants still devote a production line to a single model, Toyota began installing flexible lines in the mid-Eighties. Toyota director Mikio Kitano says there is no theoretical limit to how many body types these lines can handle, "but four is good enough." Counting sunroofs and other options, that might mean twenty variations. The secret: "intelligent pallets," computer-controlled fixtures each programmed to hold the body panels for a different model. The pallets work in rotation, picking up parts for various models as they come down the line and holding them together to be tack-welded by robots. A line can weld a Camry one minute, a Lexus the next, then a Crown, with no pause.

The new lines cost more to build (10 percent more at Toyota, 20 percent at Nissan), but a single model change pays more than the difference due to lower tooling and other costs. Toyota claims a 60 percent saving compared with its old lines. Greater capacity utilization has saved Toyota the cost of building five production lines, and the company predicts that the number of workers on the body lines will fall 30 percent by 1994 from its level in 1986. By then Toyota says, total savings will top half a billion dollars.

Just having the right equipment isn't enough, though; more important is how you use it. In 1986 Harvard business school professor Ramchandran Jaikumar reported that the typical American company with an FMS used it to turn out ten different items, while Japanese companies produce ninety-three.

Japanese companies [say that they] plan to emphasize both lower-priced products and those with high R&D content—a formidable pairing. Hitachi, Toshiba, Fujitsu, Canon, and others now spend more on R&D than on plant and equipment. They can afford to because of flexible factories, says Fumio Kodama, professor of innovation policy at Saitama University. "The introduction of FMS has paradoxically brought about the situation in which we will not have to worry about manufacturing anymore."

[It is said that] manufacturing follows an unavoidable progression from product quality (doing it right) through reliability (always doing it right) and only then to flexibility—adding variety and speed. American companies must acknowledge that quality is just a start. The flexibility wars are coming.

Investments in downtown high-rises that appeared during the analysis stage to be justifiable may, with an economic downturn, be unprofitable. Projected revenues from leased space may have been overestimated, while expected construction and other costs may have been underestimated. A post-investment audit will highlight differences between expectations and reality.

future revenues, cost savings, or expenses. Individuals providing unrealistic estimates should be required to explain all major differences. However, knowing that post-investment audits will be made may cause project sponsors to provide realistic cash flow forecasts for capital requests.

Performing a post-investment audit is not easy, for the following reasons. Actual information may be in a different form from the original estimates. Some project benefits may be difficult to quantify. Project returns vary considerably over time, so results gathered at one point in time may not be representative of the project. But regardless of the difficulties involved, post-investment audits provide management with information that can help to make better capital investment decisions in the future, as discussed in the following News Note.

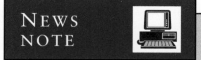

Why Do Post-Investment Audits?

Larger, longer-term, and more uncertain returns heighten the importance of conducting post-investment audits. These audits serve as an important control mechanism over the cash flows associated with investments in advanced automation. While an audit will have no direct impact on any investment decision, there are a number of substantive indirect benefits that warrant the effort. A post-investment audit . . . provides valuable information that can be used to correct problems before the success of the investment is undermined and to provide management with feedback on how well the cash outlays and inflows associated with the investment were estimated.

[T]he post-investment audit [should] include both an audit of the financial cash flows generated by the investment and the operating benefits forecasted. The financial expectations should be assessed against the actual cash flows. The operational expectations, such as the flexibility provided by the investment, are evaluated against the results achieved. The operating expectations often provide the most direct comparison of expected versus realized performance.

SOURCE: Robert A. Howell and Stephen R. Soucy, "Capital Investment in the New Manufacturing Environment," *Management Accounting* (November 1987), pp. 31–32. Published by Institute of Management Accountants, Montvale, N.J.

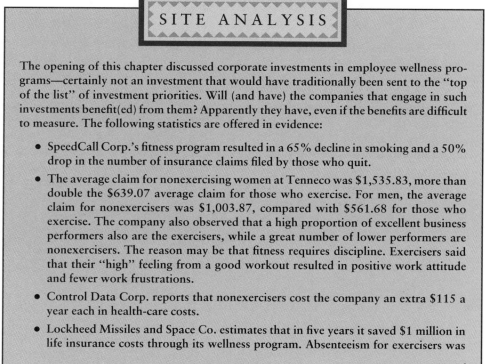

SITE ANALYSIS

The opening of this chapter discussed corporate investments in employee wellness programs—certainly not an investment that would have traditionally been sent to the "top of the list" of investment priorities. Will (and have) the companies that engage in such investments benefit(ed) from them? Apparently they have, even if the benefits are difficult to measure. The following statistics are offered in evidence:

- SpeedCall Corp.'s fitness program resulted in a 65% decline in smoking and a 50% drop in the number of insurance claims filed by those who quit.
- The average claim for nonexercising women at Tenneco was $1,535.83, more than double the $639.07 average claim for those who exercise. For men, the average claim for nonexercisers was $1,003.87, compared with $561.68 for those who exercise. The company also observed that a high proportion of excellent business performers also are the exercisers, while a great number of lower performers are nonexercisers. The reason may be that fitness requires discipline. Exercisers said that their "high" feeling from a good workout resulted in positive work attitude and fewer work frustrations.
- Control Data Corp. reports that nonexercisers cost the company an extra $115 a year each in health-care costs.
- Lockheed Missiles and Space Co. estimates that in five years it saved $1 million in life insurance costs through its wellness program. Absenteeism for exercisers was

continued

60% lower than for nonexercisers. It also reports that the turnover rate is 13 percent lower among regular exercisers.

- Weyerhaeuser Co. in Tacoma, Wash., said it saved about $4 million in each of the last two years through a communications-based program to enhance employee health.

- Dallas school teachers who enrolled in a fitness program took an average of three fewer sick days per year, a savings of almost a half-million dollars a year in substitute teacher pay.

- The evidence accumulated thus far strongly indicates that fitness programs pay off not only in monetary terms—such as savings in health insurance, life insurance, and sick pay—but also in intangible ways such as productivity, morale, retention, and recruiting.[17]

Thus, what is good for employees in a fitness sense also seems to be good for the employers financially. Good project evaluation considers all the relevant factors, including hard-to-quantify costs and benefits, and takes into account the commonly neglected consequences of not investing. Managers need to recognize the value of keeping investment options open and avoid undervaluing long-term projects by not arbitrarily restricting the time horizon or setting discount rates too high. Understanding project evaluation is easy. Doing it effectively is the real challenge. Application strategies related to capital budgeting are provided on the next page for each business discipline.

CHAPTER SUMMARY

Capital budgeting is concerned with evaluating long-range projects involving the acquisition, operation, and disposition of one or more capital assets. Management should select investment projects that will help to achieve the organization's objectives, provide a reasonable rate of return on invested capital, and help maximize shareholder wealth. The company must determine whether the activities in which it wishes to engage are worth an investment and which assets can be used for those activities. Then, decisions must be made about the best investments to accept from all the ones available.

The most common capital budgeting evaluation techniques are net present value (NPV), present value index (PVI), internal rate of return (IRR), payback period, and accounting rate of return (AROR). NPV, PVI, and IRR are discounted cash flow methods. The minimum rate at which the discount rate should be set is the cost of capital, but setting this rate requires management judgment based on the amount of capital employed and the risk involved.

Depreciation expense and changes in tax rates affect after-tax cash flows. Depreciation expense, although not a cash flow, provides a tax shield for revenues. For the best computations, discounted cash flow methods should use after-tax cash flows. The tax rates and allowable depreciation methods estimated when an investment is

---

[17]Otto H. Chang and Cynthia Boyle, "Fitness Programs: Hefty Expense or Wise Investment?" *Management Accounting* (January 1989), p. 47.

APPLICATIONS STRATEGIES OF CAPITAL BUDGETING	Discipline	Application
	Accounting	Provide financial data in the form needed for capital project analysis and for post-investment audits; can help to find ways to meaningfully quantify qualitative investment factors
	Economics	Is concerned with maximization of the use of scarce resources; capital investments play an important part of the viability of the domestic economy; capital investments in automated equipment could impact unemployment and worker morale; investment projects involve cost reductions, revenue generation or some combination of both and, hence, are designed to enhance the profit potential of the firm; capital investments are also important for economic growth and, therefore, play an important part in the vitality of the economy
	Finance	Determine which capital projects are the most beneficial to the entity; allocate resources most efficiently; determine methods of financing for projects once they are deemed to be acceptable; understand the impact of capital investments on cash flows, taxes, and profitability
	Management	Recognize and seek to infuse decision making with the impacts of replacing human workers with machines; must be able to select the activities that are best suited for investment and the assets to best achieve target goals; analyze the costs and benefits of various projects
	Marketing	Provide significant market research input about estimated sales volumes when investments are to be made in equipment needed to produce new products or to protect market share through higher-quality, lower-cost products; while marketing may have impressive "ideas" for new products, presenting these ideas to management requires more than simply sales volume and market share predictions—it requires showing that customer needs can be met in a way that makes the firm more profitable

analyzed may not be the same as when the project is implemented. Such changes can cause a significant difference in the actual NPV and IRR amounts from those originally estimated on the project.

Each capital project evaluation technique is based on certain assumptions and, therefore, has certain limitations. To compensate for these limitations, many managers subject capital projects to more than one evaluation technique.

Installation of high-technology equipment is one type of capital investment currently being considered by many company managers. While significantly reducing labor cost, increasing quality and quantity of production, and shortening throughput time, such equipment is often not justifiable under traditional capital budgeting evaluation techniques because of its long payback period and numerous nonquantifiable benefits.

After a capital project is accepted and implemented, a post-investment audit should be undertaken to compare actual with expected results. The audit will help managers identify and correct any problems that may exist, evaluate the accuracy of estimates used for the original investment decision, and help improve the forecasts of future investment projects.

APPENDIX

Time Value of Money

The time value of money can be discussed in relationship to its future or its present value. **Future value** (FV) refers to the amount to which one or more sums of money invested at a specified interest rate will grow over a specified number of time periods. **Present value** (PV) is the amount that one or more future cash flows are worth currently, given a specified rate of interest. Thus, future and present values depend on three things: (1) amount of the cash flow; (2) rate of interest; and (3) timing of the cash flow. Only present values are discussed in this appendix, since they are most relevant to the types of management decisions discussed in this text.

future value

present value

In computing future and present values, simple or compound interest may be used. **Simple interest** means that interest is earned only on the original investment or principal amount.[18] **Compound interest** means that interest earned in prior periods is added to the original investment so that, in each successive period, interest is earned on both principal and interest. The time between each interest computation is called the **compounding period.** The more often interest is compounded, the higher the actual rate of interest being received is relative to the stated rate. All of the following discussion assumes compound interest, since most transactions use this method.

simple interest

compound interest

compounding period

Interest rates are typically stated for an annual period. If compounding occurs more often, divide the annual interest rate by the number of compounding periods per year and multiply the number of years times the number of compounding periods per year. For example, if 14 percent interest is to be received each year for five years and the compounding period is semiannual, the effective rate per compounding period is 7 percent (14% ÷ 2) and the number of interest periods would be ten (5 years × 2).

Present Value of a Single Cash Flow

Assume that Bob Glover knows that his bank pays interest at 12 percent per year compounded semiannually. Bob wants to have $1,418 in three years and wants to know what amount to invest now. A table of factors for the present value of $1 (Table 1 in Appendix A to the text) for a variety of *i* and *n* values can be used to solve this problem:

$$PV = FV \text{ (PV factor)}$$

where PV = present value of a future amount
       FV = future value of a current investment

The PV factor is obtained from Table 1 using the known interest rate of 6 percent and the six discount periods. Substituting known values into the formula gives the following:

$$PV = \$1,418 \text{ (.7050)}$$

$$= \$1,000 \text{ (rounded)}$$

---

[18]Interest can be earned or owed, received or paid. To simplify the discussion for definitional purposes, the topic of interest is viewed only from the inflow standpoint.

discount rate

Future and present values are distinctly related. A present value is simply a future value discounted back the same number of periods at the same rate of interest as it would require to compound from the resulting present value to the same future value. The rate of return used in present value computations is called the **discount rate.** In capital budgeting, future value amounts need to be converted to present values.

Present Value of an Annuity

annuity
ordinary annuity
annuity due

rent

An **annuity** is a series of equal cash flows per period. In an **ordinary annuity** (such as bond interest), the first cash flow is at the end of a period. In contrast, the cash flows from an **annuity due** occur at the beginning of a period. A lease payment made at the beginning of the month for the upcoming month is one rent of an annuity due. Each equal cash flow of an annuity is called a **rent.**

To illustrate the computation of the present value of an annuity, consider the following situation. Casey Leftwich is planning to give her alma mater $1,000 at the end of each of the next five years. The university would prefer to have the money now to invest in a project that will earn 10 percent compounded annually. Casey is willing to give the university some money now, but refuses to give the entire $5,000. University administrators need to know what amount represents a current equivalent of the $1,000 per year cash flow in the future. The following diagram presents the situation:

Time in Years	0	1	2	3	4	5
Future Value		$1,000	$1,000	$1,000	$1,000	$1,000
Present Value		? (assuming a 10 percent interest rate)				

The present value of each single cash flow can be found using 10 percent discount factors from Table 1 as follows:

PV of first receipt	= $1,000 (.9091)	$ 909.10
PV of second receipt	= $1,000 (.8265)	826.50
PV of third receipt	= $1,000 (.7513)	751.30
PV of fourth receipt	= $1,000 (.6830)	683.00
PV of fifth receipt	= $1,000 (.6209)	620.90
Total present value		$3,790.80

The present value factor for an ordinary annuity can be determined by adding the present value factors for all periods having a future cash flow. Alternatively, Table 2 in Appendix A provides factors for the present value of ordinary annuity at various interest rates and time periods. From this table, the factor of 3.7908 can be obtained and is multiplied by $1,000 to yield the same result as before.

If this had been an annuity due problem, the ordinary annuity PV factors can be converted to annuity due PV factors by using one less time period and adding 1.000 to the annuity factor given. For example, assume that Casey wanted to give the university $1,000 per year for five years, beginning immediately. The following timeline reflects the cash outflows, and the calculation for the present value (using 10 percent and four periods) is also given.

Time in Years	0	1	2	3	4
Future Value	$1,000	$1,000	$1,000	$1,000	$1,000
Present Value	? (assuming a 10 percent interest rate)				

$$PV = \$1,000 \,(4.1699) = \$4,169.90$$

Nested Annuities

Situations often exist in which an annuity is "nested," or surrounded by unequal flows. The present value of each rent could be found separately using the factors for the present value of $1 (Table 1). The alternative is to use Table 2 (PV of a $1 annuity) which is more direct, but does require a slight modification.

The Duckworth Company is considering a $12,000 investment project with the following ten years of cash flows. Note that there is a nested annuity of $5,000 from 1997 to 2001. Duckworth's discount rate is 10 percent.

Current investment:	1/ 1/94	($12,000)
Returns at year-end:	12/31/94	+$ 3,000
	12/31/95	+ 4,000
	12/31/96	+ 4,500
	12/31/97	+ 5,000
	12/31/98	+ 5,000
	12/31/99	+ 5,000
	12/31/00	+ 5,000
	12/31/01	+ 5,000
	12/31/02	+ 3,000
	12/31/03	+ 8,000

The present value of each annual rent, including the five annuity installments, could be computed separately by multiplying each rent times the PV factor for that period. Annual computations for the present value of the $5,000 annuity are as follows:

Year	Cash Flow	Present Value Factor	Present Value
4	+$5,000	.6830	$ 3,415
5	+$5,000	.6209	3,104
6	+$5,000	.5645	2,822
7	+$5,000	.5132	2,566
8	+$5,000	.4665	2,333
		Total present value	$14,240

The previous approach requires that five factors be extracted from the PV table and five multiplications be made. Alternatively, the five factors could be summed (2.8481) and multiplied by $5,000 to provide the same result. Because the situation involves an annuity, there is another method of making this computation. It is possible to use Table 2 (PV of an ordinary annuity of $1) to find the present value at a 10 percent rate. Since the $5,000 annuity stops at the end of the eighth year, find the PV factor for eight periods (5.3349). Because the annuity did not begin until after the end of the third period, subtract the PV factor for three periods (2.4869). This computation gives a factor of 2.848 (slightly off due to rounding), representing the present value of an ordinary annuity occurring for five periods between periods 4 through 8.

GLOSSARY

Accounting rate of return   the rate of accounting earnings obtained on the average capital investment over a project's life

Annuity   a series of equal cash flows at equal time intervals

Annuity due   an annuity in which the cash flows occur at the beginning of a period (from appendix)

Capital asset   an asset used to generate revenues or cost savings by providing production, distribution, or service capabilities for more than one year

Capital budgeting   a process for evaluating proposed long-range projects or courses of future activity for the purpose of allocating limited resources to desirable projects

Cash flow   the receipt or disbursement of cash

Compound interest   interest earned in prior periods is added to the original investment so that, in each successive period, interest is earned on both principal and interest (from appendix)

Compounding period   the time between each interest computation (from appendix)

Cost of capital   the weighted average rate that reflects the costs of the various sources of funds making up a firm's debt and equity structure

Discount rate   the rate of return on capital investments required by the company; the rate of return used in present value computations (from appendix)

Discounting   the process of removing the portion of the future cash flows that represents interest, thereby reducing those flows to present value amounts

Financing decision   a judgment regarding the method of procuring funds that will be used to make an acquisition

Flexible manufacturing system   an integrated production system that uses computer-controlled robots to produce immense varieties of a product at a low cost; flexibility is promoted through rapid changeover times

Future value   the amount to which one or more sums of money invested at a specified interest rate will grow over a specified number of time periods (from appendix)

Hurdle rate   the rate of return deemed by management to be the lowest acceptable return on investment

Independent project   an investment project that has no specific bearing on any other investment project

Internal rate of return   the discount rate at which the present value of the cash inflows minus the present value of the cash outflows equals zero

Interpolation   the process of finding a term between two other terms using the method of ratio and proportion

Investing decision   a judgment about which assets will be acquired by an entity to achieve its stated objectives

Mutually exclusive projects   a set of proposed projects for which there is a group of available candidates that all perform essentially the same function or meet the same objective; from this group, one is chosen causing all of the others to be rejected

Mutually inclusive projects   a set of proposed investments that are all related to a primary project; when the primary project is chosen, all related projects are also selected

Net present value the difference between the present values of all the cash inflows and cash outflows of an investment project

Net present value method an investment evaluation technique that uses discounted cash flows to determine if the rate of return on a project is equal to, higher than, or lower than the desired rate of return

Ordinary annuity an annuity in which the first cash flow is at the end of a period (from appendix)

Payback period the time required to recoup the original investment through cash flows from a project

Post-investment audit a management comparison of information on actual project results to the results that were expected at the inception of the project

Preference decision a choice in which projects are ranked according to their impact on the achievement of company objectives

Present value the amount that one or more future cash flows are worth currently, given a specified rate of interest (from appendix)

Present value index a ratio that compares the present value of net cash inflows to the present value of the net investment

Project a course of future investment activity that will typically include the purchase, installation, and operation of a capital asset

Rent each equal cash flow of an annuity (from appendix)

Return of capital recovery of the original investment

Return on capital income; equals the discount rate times the investment amount

Screening decision a choice that indicates whether a capital project is desirable based on some previously established minimum criterion or criteria

Simple interest interest is earned only on the original investment or principal amount (from appendix)

Tax benefit (of depreciation) the depreciation provided by a capital investment multiplied by the tax rate

Tax shield (of depreciation) the amount of the reduction of taxable income provided by depreciation expense

Timeline a visual tool that illustrates the timing of expected cash receipts and payments; used for analyzing cash flows of a capital investment proposal

SELECTED BIBLIOGRAPHY

Azzone, Giovanni, and Umberto Bertele. "Planning and Controlling Investments in Computer Based Automation." *Journal of Cost Management* (Summer 1991), pp. 28–36.

Berndt, Jerry. "Accounting for Technology Costs." *Enterprise* (Winter 1990), pp. 9–12.

Bromwich, Michael, and Al Bhimani. "Strategic Investment Appraisal." *Management Accounting* (March 1991), pp. 45–48.

Discenza, Richard, and Brian Gurney. "New Considerations for Evaluating Capital Equipment Purchases." *Production and Inventory Management Journal* (2nd Quarter, 1990), pp. 33–37.

Engwall, Richard L. "Cost/Benefit Analysis." *Journal of Cost Management* (Fall 1989), pp. 64–68.

Harrar, G. "To Justify or Not to Justify." *Enterprise* (Winter 1990), pp. 13–18.

Hendricks, James A., et al. "Bundle Monitoring of Strategic Projects." *Management Accounting* (February 1992), pp. 31–35.

Ho, Simon S. M., and Richard H. Pike. "Risk Analysis in Capital Budgeting Contexts: Simple or Sophisticated?" *Accounting and Business Research* (Summer 1991), pp. 227–38.

King, Alfred M. "Let's Make America Competitive." *Management Accounting* (May 1992), pp. 24–27.

Lender, Gerald H., and Mohamed E. Bayou. "Does ROI Apply to Robotic Factories?" *Management Accounting* (May 1992), pp. 49–53.

Romano, Patrick, et al. "The Capital Investment Decision—How to Make It." *Financial Executive* (July/August 1991), pp. 40–47.

Troxler, Joel W. "Estimating the Cost Impact of Flexible Manufacturing." *Journal of Cost Management* (Summer 1990), pp. 26–32.

SOLUTION STRATEGIES

- Prepare a timeline to illustrate all moments in time when cash flows are expected to occur.
- Use the cost of capital rate as the discount rate to determine PVs.

Net Present Value

Current investment (always valued at a factor of 1.000)
+ PV of future cash inflows or cost savings
− PV of future cash outflows
= NPV

If NPV is equal to or greater than zero, the project is returning a rate equal to or greater than the discount rate. The project is acceptable.

Present Value Index

+ PV of future cash inflows or cost savings
− PV of future cash outflows
= PV of net future cash flows

PVI = (PV of net future cash flows) ÷ PV of net investment

If PVI is 1.00 or greater, the project is returning a rate equal to or greater than the discount rate. The project is acceptable.

Internal Rate of Return

1. For projects with equal annual cash flows:

PV factor = Investment outlay ÷ Annuity amount

Find the PV factor (or the one closest to it) in the table on the row for the number of periods of the cash flows. The percentage at the top of the column where this factor is found will approximate the IRR.

2. For projects with unequal annual cash flows:
    Make estimate of rate provided by project; compute NPV. If NPV is positive (negative), try a higher (lower) rate until the NPV is zero.

Compare IRR to the discount or preestablished hurdle rate. If the IRR equals or is greater than that rate, the project is acceptable.

Payback Period

1. For projects with an equal annual cash flow:

$$\text{Payback period} = \text{Investment} \div \text{Annuity amount}$$

2. For projects with unequal annual cash flows:
    Sum the annual cash flows until investment is reached to find payback period.

If payback period is equal to or less than a preestablished maximum number of years, the project is acceptable.

Accounting Rate of Return

$$\text{ARR} = \frac{\text{Average Annual Income from Project}}{\text{Average Investment in Project}}$$

$$\text{Average Investment} = \frac{\text{Investment} + \text{Salvage}}{2}$$

Compare calculated ARR to hurdle ARR. If it is greater, the project is acceptable.

Tax Benefit of Depreciation = Depreciation amount × Tax rate

Link Between Payback Period and Accounting Rate of Return

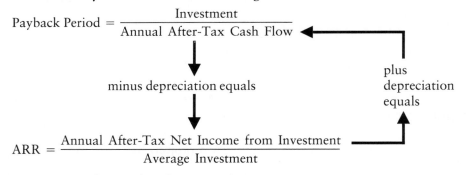

Basic Concepts of Capital Budgeting Techniques

	NPV	PVI	IRR	Payback	ARR
Uses time value of money?	Yes	Yes	Yes	No	No
Provides a *rate* of return?	No	No	Yes	No	Yes
Uses cash flows?	Yes	Yes	Yes	Yes	No
Considers returns throughout life of project?	Yes	Yes	Yes	No	Yes
Discount rate used in calculation?	Yes	Yes	No*	No	No

*Discount rate is not used in the calculation, but it may be used as the hurdle rate indicating acceptability under the IRR method.

DEMONSTRATION PROBLEM

The Consumer Products Company is considering an investment in a new product line. The company produces a variety of consumer products from various plastic materials. The new product under consideration is a high-tech frisbee-boomerang.

To produce the product, the company would need to acquire additional production and marketing equipment with an investment of $1,000,000. The equipment would have an expected life of six years, at which time it would have no market value. The company would also need to invest $200,000 in additional working capital (primarily to support an increase in accounts receivable).

Over the six-year life of the equipment, the company projects the following production and sales volume:

	Sales Volume
Year 1	200,000
Year 2	300,000
Year 3	400,000
Year 4	300,000
Year 5	200,000
Year 6	200,000

The company projects the sales price for the new product to be $2.75 for all years and estimates all variable costs would sum to $1.30 per unit. Furthermore, fixed cash expenses are projected at $125,000 per year. For tax purposes, the original cost of the equipment would be depreciated at the following rates (consistent with cost recovery rules in the tax code):

Year 1	15%
Year 2	22%
Year 3	21%
Year 4	21%
Year 5	21%
Year 6	0%
Total	100%

For financial accounting purposes, the equipment would be depreciated based on the straight-line method over six years.

The company's marginal tax rate is expected to remain at the current rate of 40 percent over the life of the equipment. The company uses a hurdle rate of 8 percent (its cost of capital) to evaluate projects of this type.

Required:

a. Compute the after-tax NPV of the proposed project. Based on the NPV, is the project acceptable?
b. Compute the present value index.
c. Compute the payback period for the proposed project.
d. Without computing the IRR, determine whether the IRR is greater than the discount rate.

Solution to Demonstration Problem

a. Compute the net income and tax expense for each year:

	Year 1	Year 2	Year 3	Year 4	Year 5	Year 6
Sales	$550,000	$825,000	$1,100,000	$825,000	$550,000	$550,000
Variable costs	(260,000)	(390,000)	(520,000)	(390,000)	(260,000)	(260,000)
CM	$290,000	$435,000	$ 580,000	$435,000	$290,000	$290,000
Cash FC	(125,000)	(125,000)	(125,000)	(125,000)	(125,000)	(125,000)
Depreciation	(150,000)	(220,000)	(210,000)	(210,000)	(210,000)	0
Pretax income	$ 15,000	$ 90,000	$ 245,000	$100,000	$(45,000)	$165,000
Taxes	(6,000)	(36,000)	(98,000)	(40,000)	18,000	(66,000)
NI	$ 9,000	$ 54,000	$ 147,000	$ 60,000	$(27,000)	$ 99,000

Items to note:

- The investment in working capital is not depreciable.
- The pretax loss in year 5 results in a tax refund.
- The investment in working capital is not deductible for tax purposes.
- The relevant depreciation is the amount for tax purposes rather than the financial accounting amount.

Convert the NI for each year to a net annual cash flow after-tax (CFAT):

	Year 1	Year 2	Year 3	Year 4	Year 5	Year 6
NI	$ 9,000	$ 54,000	$147,000	$ 60,000	$(27,000)	$99,000
Add depreciation	150,000	220,000	210,000	210,000	210,000	0
CFAT	$159,000	$274,000	$357,000	$270,000	$183,000	$99,000

Using the present value tables provided in the text, compute the NPV of the project:

Cash Flow Description	Time	CFAT Amount	Discount Factor	Present Value
Required investment	t0	$(1,200,000)	1.0000	$(1,200,000)
Annual earnings	t1	159,000	.9259	147,218
Annual earnings	t2	274,000	.8573	234,900
Annual earnings	t3	357,000	.7938	283,387
Annual earnings	t4	270,000	.7350	198,450
Annual earnings	t5	183,000	.6806	124,550
Annual earnings	t6	99,000	.6302	62,390
Return of working capital	t6	200,000	.6302	126,040
Net present value				$(23,065)

Note: Working capital is returned at the end of the project's life.

Because the NPV is less than zero, the project is unacceptable.

b. The present value index is:

$$\frac{(\$147,218 + \$234,900 + \$283,387 + \$198,450 + \$124,550 + \$62,390 + \$126,040)}{\$1,200,000} = .981$$

c. The payback period is:

		Remaining Cost to Recapture
Original cost		$1,200,000
Year 1 cash flow	$159,000	1,041,000
Year 2 cash flow	274,000	767,000
Year 3 cash flow	357,000	410,000
Year 4 cash flow	270,000	140,000

After year 4, there is $140,000 of investment remaining to be recaptured. We assume that the fifth-year cash flow of $183,000 will flow evenly throughout the year. Therefore, it will take a fraction equal to $140,000 ÷ $183,000 of the fifth year to completely recapture the original investment. Thus, the payback period would be 4.765 years or approximately 4 years and 9 months.

d. The IRR must be less than 8 percent because an 8 percent discount rate causes the NPV to be less than zero, whereas the IRR, when used as the discount rate, would cause the NPV to be exactly zero.

END-OF-CHAPTER MATERIALS

Questions

1. What is a capital asset? How is it distinguished from other assets?
2. What is the objective of capital budgeting? Why is this an important business consideration?
3. Discuss some reasons why managers might use different techniques to screen projects and evaluate project preferences.
4. In the capital budgeting context, what are mutually exclusive projects? Give three examples.
5. In the capital budgeting context, what are independent projects? Give three examples.
6. Of the five capital budgeting techniques discussed in the chapter, which ones consider the time value of money? Discuss the concept of time value of money.
7. What is the difference between the financing decision for a project and the investment decision in a project? Are the decisions related? If so, how? If not, why not?
8. When and why is it necessary to discount future cash flows?
9. "When cash flows are received in the future, a company has a return on capital." Discuss the validity of this statement.
10. How is an interest rate selected for discounting the cash flows associated with a project?
11. What is the difference between an annuity and an ordinary cash flow?
12. When using the NPV method, how does one determine if the actual rate of return on a project is greater than or less than the discount rate?
13. If a project's net present value is equal to zero, what can be said about the internal rate of return of the project? Discuss the reasoning behind your answer.

14. Relative to the NPV method, what is the primary strength of the present value index method of evaluating capital projects?

15. What are the major weaknesses of the internal rate of return method of project evaluation?

16. Differentiate between the discount rate and the hurdle rate that might be selected by a company.

17. Each of the following three measures (NPV, PVI, IRR) can be used as a criterion in an accept/reject decision regarding a capital project. What types of values for each of these measures would make a project acceptable?

18. What does the payback period of a project represent? Why is the payback method commonly used in conjunction with other methods rather than as a stand-alone evaluation measure?

19. A project provides an annuity of $15,000 every year for ten years. How are the payback period and the internal rate of return on the project related?

20. Which method of evaluating capital projects uses accrual accounting information rather than cash flows? How does net income differ from net cash flows?

21. What are the two identical limitations of all the capital budgeting techniques discussed in the chapter? How can these limitations be overcome?

22. How does depreciation expense, which is an accounting expense rather than a cash flow, become relevant in the capital budgeting analysis when the effects of income taxes are considered?

23. Why can the method of depreciation affect the present value of the depreciation tax shield for a project?

24. If all other factors are equal, which of the following changes would increase the present value of the depreciation tax shield?

a. an increase in the tax rate
b. an increase in the discount rate
c. an increase in the rate of depreciation

25. Based on an analysis which relies on the capital budgeting techniques discussed in this text, why are high-technology projects often rejected?

26. Why is it important to perform a post-investment audit?

27. (Appendix) If a sum of $1 is to be received at some point in the future, what are the factors that affect its present value?

■ **Exercises**

28. *(Return of and on capital)* Billy has recently invested $25,313 in a project that promises to pay him $10,000 per year for the next three years.

a. What is Billy's expected annual rate of return on the project?
b. Based on the rate computed in part (a), compute for each year the: (1) amount of return on capital and (2) the amount of capital returned by the project.

29. *(NPV)* Bill Harbaugh recently purchased an annuity contract which will pay him $250,000 per year for the next seven years. According to Bill's calculations, the estimated internal rate of return on this investment is 14 percent. If Bill's cost of capital is 10 percent, what is the estimated net present value of the annuity investment?

30. *(NPV)* Jonathon Rawlins is considering the purchase of a machine costing $1,063,559 to manufacture brass and wooden bird cages. Mr. Rawlins has learned from marketing research that no more than 100,000 of these cages can be sold. Mr. Rawlins is sure that he can sell all of the bird cages at $100 each and estimates the following costs associated with each bird cage:

Direct labor	$16
Direct materials	8
Other out-of-pocket costs	6
Commissions and royalties	40
Total	$70

Mr. Rawlins provides you with the following schedule of cash sales and states that he plans to produce the bird cages according to the same schedule:

Year	Sales in Units
1	10,000
2	25,000
3	32,000
4	28,000
5	5,000

At the end of the five years, the machine will have no salvage value. Using a discount rate of 14 percent, determine the NPV of the machine investment.

31. *(PVI)* The Metropolitan Transport Company (MTC) is considering replacing a bus with a new one that will last ten years, cost $160,000, and have no salvage value. A $24,000 trade-in can be obtained on the old bus. The MTC uses a 10 percent required rate of return. Annual operating costs would be reduced each year by $18,000 if the new bus is acquired.

a. Compute the present value index. Does this indicate that the purchase of the new bus is acceptable?

b. Should the MTC buy the new bus? Discuss other points that the MTC should consider.

32. *(IRR)* Fayetteville Can Works is considering the purchase of a new canning machine. One machine was proposed that costs $180,000 and would save $30,000 annually for ten years over current manual methods. No salvage value is expected on the machine at the end of its useful life. The firm's cost of capital and discount rate is 12 percent.

a. Calculate the internal rate of return for the proposed machine. Does this indicate that the purchase is an acceptable investment?

b. Should the company purchase the machine? Discuss other points that the company should consider.

33. *(Payback)* A project under consideration by the New Wave Company has an estimated present value index of 1.40. This project requires an initial investment of $2,000,000 and has an estimated life of eight years. The only cash inflow associated with this project is an annuity with an eight-year life. If the company's cost of capital is 12 percent, what is the payback period for this investment?

34. *(NPV, payback)* The Cycle and Fitness Company recently purchased a new machine that is used to straighten bicycle frames that have been bent in collisions. The machine required an initial investment of $12,000, and the company estimated over the machine's five-year life it would generate net additional annual cash inflows of $4,000.

a. What is the net present value of the investment in the machine if the company's discount rate is 12 percent?

b. What is the expected payback period?

c. If the company determined the investment in the new machine generated a net present value of $1,409 (rounded to the nearest dollar), what was the company's discount rate?

35. *(Investment amount, payback)* Managers at the Smith Brothers Museum are evaluating the feasibility of purchasing the rights to display certain Elvis memorabilia. The rights would give the museum the exclusive license to display specific personal items owned by Elvis (cars, clothes, etc.) for a period of six years. According to estimates by the museum's accounting staff, the Elvis display would increase net annual cash receipts by $180,000 in each of the six years.

a. Assuming the museum's cost of capital is 12 percent, what is the maximum the museum would pay for the display rights?

b. Based on your answer in part (a), compute the payback period.

36. *(ARR, payback)* The Empire Manufacturing Company is considering an investment in a solar-powered electricity generator. The generator would cost $1,000,000 and have an expected life of ten years. The company would depreciate the generator using the straight-line method. At the end of its life, the generator would have no value. The generator would reduce the company's annual power costs by $200,000.

a. Compute the accounting rate of return on the generator investment. (Ignore income taxes.)

b. Compute the payback period for the investment.

37. *(All methods; no depreciation)* AeroStar is considering purchasing a robot to assemble its rice cookers. The robot will cost $600,000 and will produce annual cost savings of $100,000. The robot is expected to last ten years and have no salvage value.

a. If AeroStar's discount rate is 10 percent, what is the net present value?

b. What is the present value index?

c. What is the internal rate of return?

d. What is the payback period?

e. What is the accounting rate of return? (Ignore income taxes.)

38. *(Depreciation effects)* The HealthCare Management Corporation is a profit-oriented firm that operates hospitals in three states. The firm is presently considering an investment in a new mainframe computer to manage accounts receivable and patient billings. The computer would cost $2,000,000 and have an expected life of ten years. For tax purposes, the computer can be depreciated using the straight-line method over ten years or over five years at a rate of 15 percent in year 1, 22 percent in year 2, and 21 percent in years 3–5. No salvage value is recognized under either method. The company's cost of capital is 12 percent and its tax rate is 35 percent.

a. Compute the present value of the depreciation tax shield if the company uses the straight-line depreciation method.

b. Compute the present value of the depreciation tax shield if the company uses the alternative method.

c. If the company expected its annual tax rate to rise over the ten-year life of the computer, would it be more likely to choose straight-line depreciation? Explain.

39. *(After-tax; payback; ARR)* Mumford Publishing is evaluating the purchase of a desktop publishing system that costs $7,200. The company purchasing agent advises the owner, Stacey Mumford, that the system will generate $24,000 of annual cash receipts for six years. At the end of that time, the system will have zero salvage value because of technological obsolescence. The purchasing agent also estimates that cash operating costs will be $6,000 annually. The company tax rate is expected to be 30 percent during the life of the asset, and the company uses straight-line depreciation.

a. Determine the annual after-tax cash flows from the project.
b. Determine the payback period for the project.
c. Determine the accounting rate of return for the project.

40. *(After-tax; NPV, PVI)* Use the facts from Exercise 39 and assume that the company estimates its cost of capital at 7 percent.

a. Calculate the net present value of the project.
b. Calculate the present value index for the project.

41. *(After-tax; payback; ARR)* CareCorp operates a rehabilitation center for physically disabled individuals. The company is considering the purchase of a new piece of equipment that costs $950,000, has a life of nine years, and an estimated salvage value of $50,000. CareCorp depreciates assets on a straight-line basis, and its tax rate is 20 percent per year. The expected annual cash flow on a before-tax basis for this piece of equipment is $400,000. CareCorp requires that an investment be recouped in less than five years and have an accounting rate of return of at least 16 percent.

a. Compute the payback period and the accounting rate of return for this piece of equipment.
b. Quantitatively, is this piece of equipment an acceptable investment for CareCorp? Why or why not?
c. Regardless of your answer to part (b), what (if any) other factors should CareCorp management take into consideration relating to this purchase?

42. *(Appendix)* On January 1, 1991, Dalton Company invested some funds in a project that will mature on December 31, 1993. The controller of Dalton Company determined that the firm would earn 14 percent interest (compounded annually) on this investment. If the maturity value of the investment is $18,000, how much did Dalton Company invest?

43. *(Appendix)* Ted Johnson recently purchased a new car. He financed the entire purchase cost on an installment credit plan. According to the credit agreement, Ted agreed to pay $250 per month for a period of fifty months.

a. If the credit agreement was based on a monthly interest rate of 1 percent, what was the cost of the car?
b. If the cost of the car was $7,856, what is the monthly interest rate in the credit agreement?

▌ Problems

44. *(NPV)* Custom Metalworks, Inc., manufactures body panels for automobiles. One of its main manufacturing processes involves bending sheet metal into various shapes. At the current time, this process is performed manually by a staff of ten workers. The company is considering mechanizing this process with a computer-driven bending machine. The machine would cost $1,200,000 and would be operated by a single person. If this machine is purchased, it would have an estimated life of ten years and a salvage value of $100,000 at the end of its life. Following are estimates of the annual labor savings as well as the additional costs associated with the operation of the new machine:

Annual labor cost savings (nine workers)	$220,000
Annual maintenance costs	22,000
Annual property taxes	14,000
Annual insurance costs	14,000

Required:

a. Assuming the company's cost of capital is 14 percent, compute the net present value of the investment in the computer-driven bending machine. Ignore taxes.
b. Based on the NPV, should the company invest in the new machine?
c. What other factors should the company consider in evaluating this investment?

45. (NPV) The Pittsburgh Sports Equipment Company operates retail stores throughout Pennsylvania. The company maintains a central warehouse of merchandise to stock the various stores. Because of increased customer demand, the company has found it necessary to acquire an additional warehousing facility. The owner of one warehouse has offered to lease space to the company under two alternative arrangements. Under the first arrangement, the company would be required to pay $50,000 per year for a twenty-year lease agreement. The owner would provide all insurance, maintenance, and other such costs. Under the second alternative, the company would assume total management of the facility and would pay $400,000 in advance for a twenty-year lease. This alternative would also require the company to pay the estimated $10,000 annual operating expenses.

Required:

a. Assuming the company's cost of capital is 10 percent and using the net present value method, determine which lease option would be the most appealing to the Pittsburgh Sports Equipment Company.
b. Assume the company is uncertain as to its true cost of capital. Find the cost of capital, rounded to the nearest whole percent, where the company would be indifferent between the two lease alternatives.

46. (NPV; probabilities) The Arizona Sand & Gravel Company is in the business of supplying materials to construction companies for purposes of building roads and bridges. The company has been searching for a location to "mine" gravel for a new major interstate road project. The owner of one location is willing to allow the company to mine all the gravel it needs for the road project, provided the firm reclaims the land (which essentially involves building a road and a small lake, and planting trees) after the road project is completed. The firm would also be required to post a $1,000,000 damage deposit which would be refunded (without interest) at the end of the reclamation. The road project is expected to last three years, and the reclamation of the mining location would require an additional year. To evaluate the feasibility of this offer, the company has estimated cash expenses and cash income under a pessimistic and an optimistic scenario:

	Pessimistic	Optimistic
Costs to relocate mining equipment	$ 100,000	$ 100,000
Damage deposit	1,000,000	1,000,000
Year 1 gravel sales	2,000,000	2,200,000
Year 2 gravel sales	2,000,000	2,200,000
Year 3 gravel sales	3,000,000	3,500,000
Costs of reclamation (year 4)	500,000	350,000
Annual fixed cash expenses	400,000	400,000
Annual variable expenses	70% of sales	65% of sales

The annual fixed and variable expenses would be incurred only in years 1 through 3 when the mine is operational.

Required:

a. Assuming the company's cost of capital is 14 percent, compute the net present value under both the pessimistic and the optimistic alternatives. Ignore taxes.

b. If the company estimates the probability of the pessimistic scenario occurring is .7 and the probability of the optimistic scenario occurring is .3, what should the company do?

47. *(Timeline; NPV; payback)* Realistic Taxi Company is considering the purchase of a new car to replace one it has been leasing. The new car would cost $10,000 and would last eight years and have no salvage value at that time. Annual incremental operating costs on the new car are expected as follows:

Year	Amount
1	$2,700
2	2,800
3	3,000
4	4,000
5	4,000
6	4,100
7	4,200
8	4,500

The annual lease rental cost is $6,000. Realistic uses a 10 percent discount rate.

Required:

a. Construct a timeline for the purchase of the car.
b. Calculate the net present value of the project.
c. Determine the payback period.

48. *(NPV, IRR)* John Honaker is trying to decide whether to purchase (for $300,000) the land and building where his business is located or to continue to rent it for $48,000 annually. The present owner assures John that he can continue to rent for the next twenty years. At the end of twenty years, the property would have such an uncertain salvage value that John wishes to ignore it in his calculations. John's cost of capital (which he uses to discount cash flows) is 12 percent. If John buys the property, he will have property taxes of $2,000 and maintenance costs of $1,000 annually.

Required:

a. Should John buy or continue to rent? Base your answer on the net present value of the property.

b. Based on your answer to part (a), what is the present value index of the investment?

c. What is the internal rate of return on the investment?

49. *(NPV; payback)* The Thurston Animal Clinic is considering the acquisition of an X-ray machine that could be used to diagnose injuries in large animals. The machine would cost $200,000 and have an expected life of fifteen years with no salvage value. The annual cash operating costs of the machine are estimated at $18,000. The manager of the clinic is uncertain as to how much the new machine would increase annual cash revenues.

Required:

a. Assuming the clinic's cost of capital is 16 percent, compute the minimum amount by which cash receipts would need to increase to induce the manager to purchase the new machine.

b. Based on your answer in part (a), compute the payback period for the new investment.

50. *(NPV; PVI; payback)* John Adams is the division manager of the Metalworks Division of the Big Apple Company. One of John's assistants, Deanna Ross, has heard about a new machine on the market that could replace one of their existing machines. Deanna told John that she thinks the new machine should be purchased because it would save $500,000 per year in the costs of galvanizing raw metal. Deanna asked John to look at the following information which summarized her analysis:

Old machine:	
Original cost new	$1,500,000
Present book value	1,000,000
Annual cash operating costs	1,000,000
Market value now	200,000
Market value in 5 years	0
Remaining useful life	5 years
New machine:	
Cost	$1,800,000
Annual cash operating costs	500,000
Market value in 5 years	0
Useful life	5 years

John explained to Deanna that such a decision cannot be made by looking at operating cost savings alone; both costs and benefits of the new machine must be considered.

Required:

a. Assume that the cost of capital in this company is 14 percent, which is the rate to be used in a discounted cash flow analysis. Compute the NPV and PVI for investing in the new machine. Ignore taxes. Should the machine be purchased? Why or why not?

b. Compute the payback period for the investment in the new machine. Ignore taxes.

51. *(AROR)* Big Bill's Auto Auction sells cars by auction three days each week. Cars are consigned for sale by both individuals and car wholesalers. Likewise, cars are purchased by both individuals and car wholesalers. Currently, all of the book-

keeping associated with each sale is performed manually by a staff of three people. Big Bill is considering the possibility of purchasing a computer system that would allow all of the sale day transactions to be processed by a single individual. To evaluate the feasibility of a computer system, Big Bill has gathered the following information:

Initial cost of the hardware and software	$40,000
Annual depreciation	8,000
Annual labor savings	10,000
Expected salvage value in 5 years	0
Expected life of the computer system	5 years

Required:

a. Compute the accounting rate of return on this investment. If Big Bill requires projects to generate an accounting rate of return of 13 percent or greater, is the project acceptable from a quantitative perspective?
b. Based on your knowledge of computers, do you think Big Bill has captured all of the relevant costs and benefits associated with the installation of the computer system? Explain.

52. *(Comprehensive; no taxes)* The management of Essen Manufacturing Company is evaluating a proposal to purchase a new drill press as a replacement for a less efficient piece of similar equipment that would then be sold. The cost of the new drill press including delivery and installation is $175,000. If the equipment is purchased, Essen will incur $5,000 of costs in removing the present equipment and revamping service facilities.

The present equipment has a book value of $100,000 and a remaining useful life of ten years. Because of new technical improvements that have made the equipment outmoded, it presently has a resale value of only $40,000.

Management has provided you with the following comparative manufacturing cost tabulation:

	Present Equipment	New Equipment
Annual production in units	400,000	500,000
Revenue from each unit	$.30	$.30
Annual costs:		
Labor	$30,000	$25,000
Depreciation (10% of asset book value or cost)	10,000	17,500
Other cash operating costs	48,000	20,000

Management believes that if the present equipment is not replaced now, the company will have to wait seven years before replacement is justified. The company uses a 15 percent discount or hurdle rate in evaluating capital projects and expects that all capital project investments recoup their costs within five years.

Both pieces of equipment are expected to have a negligible salvage value at the end of ten years.

Required:

a. Determine the net present value of the new equipment.
b. Determine the payback period for the new equipment.
c. Determine the accounting rate of return for the new equipment.
d. Using an incremental approach, determine whether the company should keep the present equipment or purchase the new.

(CPA adapted)

53. *(Comprehensive; no taxes)* Ramirez Construction Company is considering purchasing a dragline for $300,000. Expectations are for a ten-year life and salvage value of $30,000. The firm currently has a similar piece of equipment. If the new dragline is purchased, Ramirez will sell its old equipment for $20,000.

Ramirez Construction Company management has the following policies regarding acceptability of capital projects: (1) the rate of return must equal or exceed a discount rate of 10 percent; (2) the accounting rate of return must equal or exceed a hurdle rate of 17 percent; and (3) the payback period cannot be longer than six years.

Required:

a. Prepare a timeline for this project.
b. Compute the net present value.
c. Compute the present value index.
d. Compute the internal rate of return.
e. Compute the payback period.
f. Compute the ARR using the following additional information:
   1. The $20,000 received from selling the old equipment equals the old dragline's book value, so there is no accounting gain or loss on the sale.
   2. The project will produce average annual accounting profits of $30,700.
g. For each of the methods, discuss whether your computations showed that the project is quantitatively acceptable.

54. *(NPV; different depreciation methods)* Eli Wallace, president of Wallace Enterprises, asked his accountant to evaluate a proposal for a new press that will cost $52,000. The purchase would be made at the beginning of the company's fiscal year. The press has an estimated life of eight years and will have no salvage value at the end of its life. Wallace's accountant estimated that the press will save $18,000 annually in operating costs. The firm uses a discount rate of 7 percent and has a tax rate of 30 percent.

Required:

a. Using straight-line depreciation, calculate the net present value of the press.
b. Mr. Wallace asks how much the NPV would differ if the sum-of-the-years-digits (SYD) depreciation method were used. Assume for this problem that the SYD method is acceptable for tax purposes in the fiscal year of the purchase. (Round all calculations to the nearest dollar.)
c. Which NPV is higher and why?
d. Referring to your answer in part (a), how much margin for error is there in the 7 percent discount rate that would still allow the project to be quantitatively acceptable?

55. *(After-tax; NPV)* Joanna Lipscomb is a division manager of Westshore Corporation. She is presently evaluating a potential revenue-generating investment that has the following characteristics:

Initial cost	$1,000,000
Net annual increase in cash receipts:	
Year 1	100,000
Year 2	200,000
Year 3	250,000
Year 4	800,000
Year 5	800,000

The project would have a five-year life with no salvage value. Westshore's cost of capital is 12 percent and its income tax rate is 35 percent. All assets are depreciated using the straight-line method.

Required:

a. Compute the NPV of the potential investment.
b. Based on the NPV, will Joanna invest in the project?
c. Assume Joanna is evaluated based on the amount of pretax profit her division generates. Compute the effect of the new investment on the level of divisional profits for years 1 through 3.
d. Based on your computations in part (c), will Joanna want to invest in the new project? Explain.

56. *(After-tax; NPV; PVI; payback)* Philadelphia Glassworks is considering adding a new product line. The new product line would consist of glass Christmas ornaments and would require the following investment:

Production equipment	$200,000
Working capital	100,000
Marketing equipment and displays	50,000
Total	$350,000

The production and marketing equipment, as well as the displays, would have an expected life of ten years. All equipment and displays would be depreciated over the ten-year life using the straight-line method (no salvage value would be recognized in computing depreciation deductions). At the end of ten years, it is expected the equipment and displays could be sold for a total of $10,000. Following are the expected operating cash receipts and cash expenses by year for the proposed product line:

	Cash Receipts	Cash Expenses
Year 1	$ 40,000	$50,000
Year 2	80,000	50,000
Year 3	100,000	55,000
Year 4	120,000	65,000
Year 5	150,000	70,000
Years 6–10	160,000	75,000

The company's tax rate is 30 percent and its cost of capital is 8 percent.

Required:

a. Compute the after-tax NPV and PVI for the proposed investment.
b. Compute the after-tax payback for the proposed investment.
c. Based on the NPV, should the investment be made?

57. *(After-tax; IRR; payback)* The Laredo Shoe Company manufactures work boots for farmers and ranchers. Currently the company relies on a system of carts and pallets to move materials between work stations. The company is now considering the installation of a conveyor belt system to move the materials. Some of the summary financial characteristics of the proposed investment follow:

Required initial investment	$900,000
Net annual savings in cash operating costs	160,000
Annual depreciation expense	60,000
Expected salvage value	0
Expected life	15 years

The company's combined state and federal income tax rate is 40 percent.

Required:

a. To the nearest whole percentage point, compute the internal rate of return on the investment in the conveyor system.

b. If the company's cost of capital is 11 percent, and using only quantitative considerations, should the firm invest in the conveyor system? Are there any qualitative factors that might need to be considered?

c. Compute the after-tax payback period for the investment.

58. *(Essay)* Andiron Steel is a relatively small manufacturing company with a total market value of approximately $100,000,000. The total value of the outstanding common shareholders' equity is $1,000,000, and the total value of outstanding debt claims is about $99,000,000 (the debt-to-equity ratio is, therefore, 99:1). The president of Andiron Steel, Mr. T. Sipper, has approached a private lender for a $20,000,000 loan to finance expansion. The expansion project involves the opening of another plant. According to Mr. T. Sipper's data, the expansion project has a net present value of $2,000,000. Based on this data, the lender has agreed to provide the funds.

Before Mr. T. Sipper has an opportunity to invest in the project (but after acquiring the lender's funds), his friend, Mr. Chugger, suggests to T. Sipper that he invest in an alternative project (a highly speculative research and development project) that also will require an initial investment of $20,000,000 and will have a useful life similar to the first project. Mr. Chugger admits that there is a great deal of uncertainty about the net present value of this alternative project because the net present value is highly correlated with the future state of the economy. Based on his forecasts of the future state of the economy, Mr. Chugger believes that the net present value of his project is $0. He arrived at this conclusion by determining the net present value of the project in each of the possible future states of the economy and multiplying each of those net present values by its probability of occurring. His computations follow:

State of the Economy	Resulting NPV	Probability	Expected Value
Great	$10,000,000	.5	$5,000,000
Fair	5,000,000	.4	2,000,000
Lousy	(70,000,000)	.1	(7,000,000)
Overall expected NPV			$ 0

The net present value of the first project that Mr. T. Sipper is considering (plant expansion) is not influenced by the state of the economy.

Required: *Independently* assess the influence of each of the following factors on Mr. T. Sipper's decision as to the project in which he will invest:

a. the debt-to-equity ratio of Andiron Steel
b. ethics
c. the preference of the common shareholders of Andiron Steel
d. a management bonus plan based on a measure of corporate profit
e. the overall calculated NPVs: $2 million on the first project and $0 on the alternative project

59. *(Essay)* Clewash Linen Supply Company provides laundered items to various commercial and service establishments in a large metropolitan city. Clewash is scheduled to acquire some new cleaning equipment in mid-1994 that should provide some operating efficiencies. The new equipment would enable Clewash to

increase the volume of laundry it handles without any increase in labor costs. In addition, the estimated maintenance costs in terms of pounds of laundry would be reduced slightly with the new equipment.

The new equipment was justified not only on the basis of reduced cost but also on the basis of expected increase in demand starting in late 1994. However, since the original forecast was prepared, several potential new customers have either delayed or discontinued their own expansion plans in the market area that is serviced by Clewash. The most recent forecast indicates that no great increase in demand can be expected until late 1995 or early 1996.

Identify and explain the factors that Clewash Linen Supply Company should consider in deciding whether to delay the investment in the new cleaning equipment. In the presentation of your response, distinguish between those factors that tend to indicate that the investment should be made as scheduled versus those that tend to indicate that the investment should be delayed.

(CMA)

60. *(Essay)* Dickson, Inc., has formal policies and procedures to screen and ultimately approve capital projects. Proposed capital projects are classified as one of the following types:

- Expansion requiring new plant and equipment
- Expansion by replacement of present equipment with more productive equipment
- Replacement of old equipment with new equipment of similar quality

All expansion projects and replacement projects that will cost more than $50,000 must be submitted to the top management capital investment committee for approval. The investment committee evaluates proposed projects considering the costs and benefits outlined in the supporting proposal and the long-range effects on the company.

The projected revenue and/or expense effects of the projects, once operational, are included in the proposal. Once a project is accepted, the committee approves an expenditure budget for the project from its inception until it becomes operational. The expenditures required each year for the expansions or replacements are also incorporated into Dickson's annual budget procedure. The budgeted revenue and/or cost effects of the projects, for the periods in which they become operational, are incorporated into the five-year forecast.

Dickson, Inc., does not have a procedure for evaluating projects once they have been implemented and become operational. The vice-president of finance has recommended that Dickson establish a post-investment audit program to evaluate its capital expenditure projects.

a. Discuss the benefits a company could derive from a post-investment audit program for capital expenditure projects.
b. Discuss the practical difficulties in collecting and accumulating information that would be used to evaluate a capital project once it becomes operational.

(CMA)

▌ Cases

61. Top Flight is a limousine service operating in Chicago. The owner is considering the purchase of five new white stretch limos at a cost of $75,000 each. Each limo will have a useful life of five years and a salvage value of $15,000. Estimated revenues and operating costs for each limo are as follows:

Rental Fees

First two years: $150 per hour; 20 hours per week for 52 weeks
Next three years: $100 per hour; 15 hours per week for 52 weeks

Operating Costs

Driver's annual salary: $12,000 (increases $1,000 each year)
Uniform: $200 (at the beginning of the first, third, and fifth years)
Annual insurance: $5,000 each year; annual rate decreases for age are offset
by annual increases in premium rates (paid at the beginning of each year)
Annual personalized license plate and inspection fees: $100 (paid at the
beginning of each year)
Annual gas and oil: $36,850 (increases 10% each year of use)
Annual repairs and maintenance: $10,000 (increases 10% each year of use)
Major repairs at end of third year: $2,000
Tires at end of second and fourth years: $400

a. Determine the net cash flows for each year of the five-year period.
b. Using a 14 percent discount rate, what is the net present value? Is the purchase
quantitatively acceptable?
c. Using a 16 percent discount rate, what is the net present value? Is the purchase
quantitatively acceptable?
d. What other factors should be considered by Top Flight's management before
acquiring the limos, assuming a positive net present value?

62. The board of directors of Miami Hospital is attempting to decide whether to
purchase or lease a CAT scanner. The cost of the equipment is $1,200,000, and
its estimated useful life is seven years. The lease period is only for five years and
would have to be renewed for the additional two years; the renewal rate is 10
percent of the original lease rate of $100,000 per year.

All costs of operating the CAT scanner are the same under either alternative.
Therefore, they are not relevant to this decision. In addition, all revenues (except
those generated by Medicare reimbursements) are the same under both alternatives. Medicare reimbursement is based on either the amount of depreciation or
the amount of lease payment. Medicare patients are assumed to use the CAT
scanner 30 percent of the time, and Medicare will reimburse that percentage of
equipment cost. Equipment cost is defined in the Medicare reimbursement policy
as annual straight-line depreciation or out-of-pocket lease payments. Miami
Hospital has a discount rate of 8 percent.

a. Assume that there is no salvage value for the CAT scanner if it is purchased.
Lease payments and Medicare reimbursements occur at the end of each year.
What is the net present value of the purchase and the lease alternative? Should
the board purchase or lease the CAT scanner?
b. Assume that there is no salvage value for the CAT scanner if it is purchased.
Lease payments are made at the beginning of the year, and Medicare reimbursements occur at the end of the year. What is the net present value of the
purchase and the lease alternative? Should the board purchase or lease the
CAT scanner?
c. Assume that there is a 5 percent salvage value for the CAT scanner if it is
purchased. Lease payments and Medicare reimbursements occur at the end of
each year. What is the net present value of the purchase and the lease alternative? Should the board purchase or lease the CAT scanner?
d. Assume that there is a 5 percent salvage value for the CAT scanner if it is
purchased. Lease payments are made at the beginning of the year, and Medi-

care reimbursements occur at the end of the year. What is the net present value of the purchase and the lease alternative? Should the board purchase or lease the CAT scanner?

63. HMG Corporation is a for-profit health-care provider that operates three hospitals. One of these hospitals, Metrohealth, plans to acquire new X-ray equipment that management has already decided will be cost beneficial and will enhance the technology available in the outpatient diagnostic laboratory. Before Metrohealth prepares the requisition to corporate headquarters for the purchase, Paul Monden, Metrohealth's controller, has to prepare an analysis to compare financing alternatives.

The equipment is a Supraimage X-ray 400 machine priced at $1,000,000, including shipping and installation; it would be delivered January 2, 1994. Under the tax regulations, this machine qualifies as "qualified technological equipment" with a five-year recovery period. It will be depreciated over five years for tax purposes using the double-declining balance method, with a switch to straight-line at a point in time to maximize the depreciation deduction. The machine will have no salvage value at the end of five years. The three financing alternatives Metrohealth is considering are described next.

- **Finance Internally**

  HMG Corporation would provide Metrohealth with the funds to purchase the equipment. The supplier would be paid on the day of delivery.

- **Finance with a Bank Loan**

  Metrohealth could obtain a bank loan to finance 90 percent of the equipment cost at 10 percent annual interest, with five annual payments of $237,420 each due at the end of each year, with the first payment due on December 31, 1994. The loan amortization schedule is presented next. Metrohealth would provide the remaining $100,000, which would be paid upon delivery.

Year	Beginning Balance	Payment	Interest	Principal Reduction
1	$900,000	$237,420	$90,000	$147,420
2	752,580	237,420	75,258	162,162
3	590,418	237,420	59,042	178,378
4	412,040	237,420	41,204	196,216
5	215,824	237,420	21,596	215,824

- **Lease from a Lessor**

  The equipment could be leased from MedLeasing, with an initial payment of $50,000 due on equipment delivery and five annual payments of $220,000 each, commencing on December 31, 1994. At the option of the lessee, the equipment can be purchased at the fair market value at lease termination (the lessor is currently estimating a 30 percent salvage value). The lease satisfies the requirements to be an operating lease for both FASB and income tax purposes. This means that all lease payments are deductible for tax purposes each year. Because of expected technological changes in medical equipment, Metrohealth would not plan to purchase the X-ray equipment at the end of the lease commitment.

  Both HMG Corporation and Metrohealth have an effective income tax rate of 40 percent, an incremental borrowing rate of 10 percent, and an after-tax corporate hurdle rate of 12 percent. Income taxes are paid at the end of the year.

a. Prepare a present value analysis as of January 1, 1994, of the expected after-tax cash flows for each of the three financing alternatives available to Metrohealth to acquire the new X-ray equipment. As part of your present value analysis, (1) justify the discount rates you used and (2) identify the financing alternative most advantageous to Metrohealth.

b. Discuss the qualitative factors Paul Monden should include for management consideration before a final decision is made regarding the financing of this new equipment.

(CMA)

Ethics Discussion

64. Heidi Swenson, the plant manager of the St. Paul plant of the Nordtvedt Manufacturing Company, has submitted a capital budgeting proposal for a new CAD/CAM system for her plant. She is excited about the acquisition, as it almost perfectly meets the plant's needs and she has received approval from the home office. However, Heidi was reading the local newspaper this morning only to realize that Nordtvedt's purchasing agent happens to be the sister of the vendor of the CAD/CAM system.

Nordtvedt Manufacturing has a strict policy that prohibits purchasing from relatives. If this relationship comes to light, the purchasing agent could be fired and Heidi could potentially not get the system that is best, in her judgment, for the plant. Since the purchasing agent is married, her name is different from her brother's and it is unlikely that a connection will be made. Heidi is concerned about what to do—abide by the policy or acquire the necessary system at the reasonable price quoted from the vendor.

a. Why would a company have a policy of this nature?
b. What are the ethical conflicts in this situation?
c. What are the potential risks for Heidi? For the company?
d. What do you recommend and why?

65. The Fore Corporation has operations in over two dozen countries. Fore's headquarters are in Chicago, and company executives frequently travel to visit Fore's foreign and domestic operations.

Fore owns two business jets with international range and six smaller aircraft for shorter flights. Company policy is to assign aircraft to trips based on cost minimization, but practice is to assign aircraft based on organizational rank of the traveler. Fore offers its aircraft for short-term lease or for charter by other organizations whenever Fore employees do not plan to use the aircraft. Fore surveys the market often to keep its lease and charter rates competitive.

William Earle, Fore's vice-president of finance, claims that a third business jet can be justified financially. However, some people in the controller's office think the real reason for a third business jet is because people outranking Earle keep the two business jets busy. Thus, Earle usually must travel in the smaller aircraft.

The third business jet would cost $11 million. A capital expenditure of this magnitude requires a formal proposal with projected cash flows and net present value computations using Fore's minimum required rate of return. If Fore's president and finance committee approve the proposal, it would be submitted to the full board. The board has final approval on capital expenditures exceeding $5 million and has established a policy of rejecting any discretionary proposal that has a negative net present value.

Earle asked Rachel Arnett, assistant corporate controller, to prepare a proposal on a third business jet. Arnett gathered the following information:

- Acquisition cost of the jet, including instrumentation and interior furnishings
- Operating cost of the jet for company use
- Projected avoidable commercial airfare and other avoidable costs from company use of the plane
- Projected value of executive time saved by using the third business jet
- Projected contribution margin from incremental lease and charter activity
- Estimated resale value of the jet
- Estimated income tax effects of the proposal

When Earle reviewed Arnett's completed proposal and saw the large negative net present value figure, he returned the proposal to Arnett and insisted she had made an error in her calculations.

Feeling some pressure, Arnett checked her computations and found no errors. However, Earle's message was clear. Arnett discarded her projections and estimates and replaced them with figures that had a remote chance of actually occurring but were more favorable to the proposal. For example, she used first-class airfares to refigure the avoidable commercial airfare costs, even though the company policy is to fly coach. She found revising the proposal to be distressing.

The revised proposal still had a negative net present value. Earle's anger was evident as he told Arnett to revise the proposal again, and to start with a $100,000 positive net present value and work backward to compute supporting estimates and projections.

a. Explain whether Rachel Arnett's revision of the proposal was in violation of the Standards of Ethical Conduct for Management Accountants. (Refer to Exhibit 1–6.)

b. Was William Earle in violation of the Standards of Ethical Conduct for Management Accountants by telling Arnett specifically to revise the proposal? Explain your answer.

c. What elements of the projection and estimation process would be compromised in preparing an analysis for which a preconceived result is sought?

d. Identify specific controls over the capital budgeting process that Fore Corporation could implement to prevent unethical behavior on the part of the vice-president of finance.

(CMA)

66. Andy Vickers was reprimanded by the home office for recommending a pollution abatement project because the project did not meet the standard financial criterion of a 10 percent rate of return. However, Andy had concluded that the $60,000 piece of equipment was necessary to prevent small amounts of arsenic from seeping into the city's water system. No EPA warnings have been issued for the company.

a. Discuss the company requirement of a 10 percent rate of return on all projects.

b. What might be the ultimate consequence to Vickers's company if it fails to prevent future arsenic seepage into the groundwater system?

c. How should (or can) Vickers justify the purchase of the equipment to the home office?

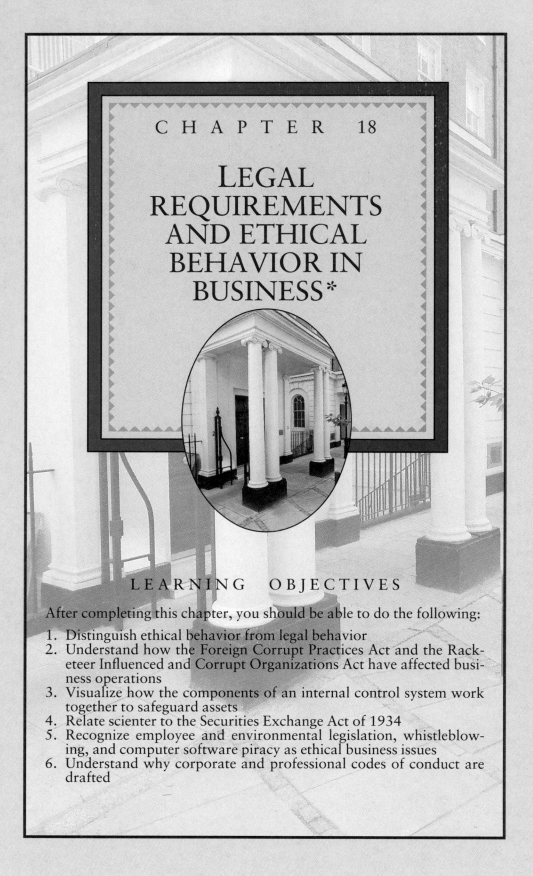

C H A P T E R   18

LEGAL REQUIREMENTS AND ETHICAL BEHAVIOR IN BUSINESS*

LEARNING OBJECTIVES

After completing this chapter, you should be able to do the following:

1. Distinguish ethical behavior from legal behavior
2. Understand how the Foreign Corrupt Practices Act and the Racketeer Influenced and Corrupt Organizations Act have affected business operations
3. Visualize how the components of an internal control system work together to safeguard assets
4. Relate scienter to the Securities Exchange Act of 1934
5. Recognize employee and environmental legislation, whistleblowing, and computer software piracy as ethical business issues
6. Understand why corporate and professional codes of conduct are drafted

Cadbury Owner Faced Many Ethical Dilemmas

In 1900 Queen Victoria sent a decorative tin with a bar of chocolate inside to all of her soldiers who were serving in South Africa. At the time, the order faced my grandfather with an ethical dilemma. He owned and ran the second-largest chocolate company [Cadbury's] in Britain, so he was trying harder and the order meant additional work for the factory. Yet he was deeply and publicly opposed to the Anglo-Boer War. He resolved the dilemma by accepting the order, but carrying it out at cost. He therefore made no profit out of what he saw as an unjust war, his employees benefitted from the additional work, the soldiers received their royal present, and I am still sent the tins.

My grandfather was able to resolve the conflict between the decision best for his business and his personal code of ethics because he and his family owned the firm which bore their name. Certainly his dilemma would have been more acute if he had had to take into account the interests of outside shareholders, many of whom would no doubt have been in favor both of the war and of profiting from it. But even so, not all my grandfather's ethical dilemmas could be as straight-forwardly resolved.

So strongly did my grandfather feel about the South African War that he acquired and financed the only British newspaper which opposed it. He was also against gambling, however, and so he tried to run the paper without any references to horse racing. The effect on the newspaper's circulation was such that he had to choose between his ethical beliefs. He decided, in the end, that it was more important that the paper's voice be heard as widely as possible than that gambling should thereby receive some mild encouragement.

SOURCE: An excerpt from "Ethical Managers Make Their Own Rules," by Sir Adrian Cadbury (September–October 1987), p. 69. Reprinted by permission of *Harvard Business Review*. Copyright © 1987 by the President and Fellows of Harvard College; all rights reserved.

E thical choices are part of everyday life. Children are faced with the choice of lying or telling the truth when their parents ask questions such as, "Did you break this?" or "Did you hit your brother?" Students face the choice of cheating or not cheating on exams. Most universities have basic honor codes. For example, the overriding ethical code at Texas A&M is: An Aggie does not lie, cheat, or steal, nor does he tolerate those who do. On the other hand, Texas A&M also has a body of rules and regulations (perhaps one hundred pages or more) that provide legal definitions and consequences when, in fact, an Aggie does lie, cheat, or steal. Unfortunately, these rules are needed because one survey indicated that, of 6,096 students responding to a poll at thirty-one of the country's most prestigious universities, "75% of those planning business careers said they had cheated on at least one test, and 19% admitted to cheating on four or more tests."[1] That statistic is frightening.

---

*The authors wish to thank Dinah Payne, J.D., M.B.A., of the University of New Orleans for her assistance in writing this chapter. Some of the information in this chapter has been taken from "Corporate Codes of Conduct: A Collective Conscience and Continuum," by Cecily Raiborn and Dinah Payne, published in the *Journal of Business Ethics* 9 (1990), pp. 879–89. Reprinted by permission of Kulwer Academic Publishers.
[1]Rick Tetzeli, "Business Students Cheat Most," *FORTUNE* (July 1, 1991), p. 14.

Business people are no different from children or students. They face ethical choices in decisions concerning product safety, stock transactions, and obtaining business in a foreign country. Some of these choices have legal right-and-wrong answers. Some choices only serve to indicate the potential need for legislation to clear up the gray areas. Choosing the right or wrong solution to an ethical dilemma, however, is more often a choice one makes based on one's own personal ethical code. And, it is important to note, there is a difference between what is legal and what is ethical.

DISTINGUISHING LEGAL FROM ETHICAL BEHAVIOR

ethics

Law is the written form of what society as a whole thinks is morally correct. Law is jurisdictional in that it is valid and applicable only for the particular locale that enacted it. On the other hand, **ethics** reflects the moral law, is a system of value principles or practices, and defines right and wrong. Ethics is not jurisdictional; it represents moral rights that people have no matter where or what time they live, whether these rights are recognized or not. For example, the legal right to free speech is recognized fully in the United States, but is only now becoming a reality in the former Soviet Union. The ethical right to free speech always existed in the former Soviet Union—it was simply not legally recognized.

Another example that highlights the distinction of legal and ethical rights was the system of slavery before the Civil War. The legal right of slaves to be free was not recognized until the Emancipation Proclamation. The moral right to be free, though in existence, was not recognized until even later. Thus, what is legal may or may not equate to what is ethical. To provide a foundation upon which to subjectively gauge the ethics of decisions, two basic theories of ethics are explained.

Sir Adrian Cadbury is proud of his grandfather's ethical behavior during the Boer War. The decision to send chocolate tins to the soldiers, but not make a profit on the order, could have resulted from either a utilitarian or Kantian analysis perspective.

BASIC ETHICAL THEORIES

There are two major categories of ethical theory. The first category approaches ethics by considering the outcomes or consequences of the ethical choice. The second is the approach that duty dictates the morality of the action, regardless of consequences.

Utilitarianism

A primary theory that looks at outcomes is **utilitarianism.** This approach, which reflects a type of cost/benefit analysis, is probably a familiar one for anyone who has had a basic course in economics. The premise of this theory is that actions or policies are right or ethical if they produce other actions or experiences that people value. Utilitarianism is the most commonly used ethical theory because most people use a form of this review without even knowing that an ethical "theory" is being used.

utilitarianism

For example, assume you are a salesperson who is preparing an expense report for the week. You are, at that time, faced with the ethical question of whether to provide accurate information or to cheat. Most salespeople would quickly come to the conclusion that cheating is probably not worthwhile. The steps used to arrive at this conclusion are basically as follows. First, you determine the alternatives (be truthful or cheat), the possible outcomes of each alternative (keep your job or lose it), and the people or groups potentially affected by the alternatives (you, your family, your customers, your friends, the company stockholders, and so forth). Next, you attach some measures of relative importance to the previous elements—the costs and benefits accruing to each. Lastly, you choose the alternative that produces either the greatest good or the least harm for all concerned. This type of analysis is suggested in the News Note on page 832.

While utilitarianism may provide extremely ethical decisions, there are a number of pitfalls in using only such an analytical process. First, it may be difficult to identify *all* of the people affected by the decision and the degree to which they are affected. Measuring costs and benefits is also not always easy: what one person might regard as a cost, another person may regard as a benefit. Nevertheless, in most situations, some of the benefits and costs are fairly obvious. Would you be able to steal enough on an expense report (the benefit) to compensate for the possibility of a lost job (the cost)?

The most critical downfall of the utilitarian theory is that it has a tendency to disregard individual rights. For example, assume that you are new at your sales job. Your supervisor has made the assumption that "everybody" cheats on their expense reports and, therefore, reduces all requests for reimbursement by 15 percent. You turn in your actual expenses; have you been treated justly when you get your reimbursement check for 15 percent less than you requested? To prevent such a disregard for individual rights, **Kantian analysis** can be applied.

Kantian analysis

Kantian Analysis

The second category of ethical theory was devised by Immanuel Kant, a German philosopher, and is based on duty. Actions are deemed to be intrinsically either right or wrong, regardless of the possible consequences. This theory is familiar to most people as the golden rule: do unto others as you would have them do unto you. If everyone acted in a rational manner using Kantian analysis, no one would be treated unfairly, simply because he or she personally would not want to be treated unfairly.

NEWS NOTE

Managers Need to Perform Ethical Analysis

In most companies, the manager is the person who understands, interprets, and communicates the corporate value system. Effective managers have a strong sense of purpose and ethics for themselves and their organizations.

A system of ethics provides principles by which we make decisions. To effectively weigh a decision, you must identify and understand the facts and the options available to you:

- Do you have all the information you need? Do you need to speak to someone else, such as the legal staff, to obtain what you need?

- Identify your options. Are they legal? Do they violate any company policy or standard?

- Do the options support your values and personal ethics?

- What are the short-term and long-term consequences of each option? Who benefits? Who is harmed?

- Are you comfortable with the options? How will they be perceived by others? Could they embarrass the company?

Leaders in any group must establish the ethical tone for the organization. If leaders act beyond reproach, if they reward correct behavior, and if they refuse to tolerate wrongdoing, there is a much greater chance that the entire organization will behave ethically.

SOURCE: Patricia Haddock and Marilyn Manning, "Ethically Speaking" (March 1990), p. 128ff. This article has been excerpted through the courtesy of Halsey Publishing Co., publishers of Delta Air Lines' *SKY* magazine.

Theories of justice and rights are also based on Kantian analysis. Justice requires benefits and burdens to be distributed in an equitable fashion. The theory of justice requires that people make decisions based on equity, fairness, and impartiality. The theory of justice, therefore, requires that people who are similar must be treated in a similar manner, but it allows that people who are different in a *relevant* way be treated differently. For example, the concept of nondiscrimination on non-job-related criteria in employment is based on the theory of justice.

The concept of rights asserts that people have some fundamental rights that must be respected in all types of decisions. Rights advocates suggest that there are liberty rights and welfare rights for all persons. Liberty rights are basically those that have been embedded in the United States Constitution. Welfare rights reflect the right of all people to some minimum standard of living; these rights typically have fallen into the realm of governmental or corporate social responsibilities. Privileges (or duties to perform) are allocated to people based on society's perception of individuals' entitlements.

Theories promoting duty, justice, and rights as the bases of right or wrong are helpful in making business decisions. People are far less willing to engage in activity that is morally questionable if they realize that the same activity may be perpetrated against them or if they perceive that the activity may, at some time, inhibit their own rights or privileges.

This short discussion of ethical theories provides a frame of reference or a starting point for the following discussion of the laws affecting businesspeople and accountants.

CONCERN FOR LEGALITY IS ESSENTIAL

Managers must, by necessity, consider what is and what is not legal when making decisions. However, if business is to function effectively within society, managers should attempt to behave in a moral manner *regardless of the law*. Thus, managers should attempt to make decisions that respect not only the letter of the law, but also the spirit of the law. In most cases, the law represents what society thinks is morally right; so, generally, what the individual thinks is right corresponds to what society views as correct.

Numerous laws impact the functioning of businesses in the United States. Many of these laws affect accounting because noncompliance has two major ramifications. Noncompliance with the law can create expensive consequences in the form of fines and penalties that will cause the values reflected on the financial statements to diminish. Besides the direct reduction of income on the income statement, fines and penalties related to legal violations are not deductible for tax purposes. Further, noncompliance with the law can bring society's moral censure down on the wrongdoer. Following is a discussion of some laws that are important from both a financial and a moral standpoint.

Foreign Corrupt Practices Act

The **Foreign Corrupt Practices Act** (FCPA) was passed in 1977 after discoveries that hundreds of American corporations had been giving bribes and other improper payments in connection with foreign and domestic business activities. The following quote indicates the pre-FCPA business attitude about making bribery payments.

Foreign Corrupt Practices Act

> In many countries, corporate payoffs are seen as venial sins or even normal courtesies, and the line between sales commissions and outright kickbacks is fuzzy or nonexistent.
>
> To multinational businessmen, [making overseas bribes illegal] is a simplistic response; they operate in a world where ethical standards vary almost as much as wage rates, and with much the same practical effect. In this view, it's foolish not to offer a bribe if a bribe is expected.[2]

Exhibit 18–1 shows the "top ten" in questionable payment spenders in the year *prior* to the enactment of the FCPA.

The FCPA was enacted to prevent bribes from being offered or given (directly or indirectly) to foreign officials to influence those individuals (or to cause them to use their influence) to obtain or retain business. The act is directed at payments that cause officials to act in a way specified by the firm rather than in a way that the official has

---

[2]Larry Martz, et al., "Payoffs: The Growing Scandal," *Newsweek* (February 23, 1976), p. 26ff.

EXHIBIT 18–1
▼▼▼▼▼▼▼▼▼▼▼

TEN OF THE
BIGGEST SPENDERS
IN 1976

Nearly forty large American corporations have been accused of paying bribes or questionable "commissions" to win contracts overseas. Ten of the biggest admitted spenders:

Ashland Oil, Inc.	Admits paying more than $300,000 to foreign officials, including $150,000 to President Albert Bernard Bongo of Gabon to retain mineral and refining rights.
Burroughs Corp.	Admits that $1.5 million in corporate funds may have been used in improper payments to foreign officials.
Exxon Corp.	Admits paying $740,000 to government officials and others in three countries. Admits its Italian subsidiary made $27 million in secret but legal contributions to seven Italian political parties.
Gulf Oil Corp.	Admits paying $4 million to South Korea's ruling political party. Admits giving $460,000 to Bolivian officials—including a $110,000 helicopter to the late President René Barrientos Orutño—for oil rights.
Lockheed Aircraft Corp.	Admits giving $202 million in commissions, payoffs and bribes to foreign agents and government officials in the Netherlands, Italy, Japan, Turkey and other countries. Admits that $22 million of this sum went for outright bribes.
McDonnell Douglas Corp.	Admits paying $2.5 million in commissions and consultant fees between 1970 and 1975 to foreign government officials.
Merck & Co., Inc.	Admits giving $3 million, largely in "commission-type payments," to employees of 36 foreign governments between 1968 and 1975.
Northrop Corp.	Admits in part to SEC charges that it paid $30 million in commissions and bribes to government officials and agents in Holland, Iran, France, West Germany, Saudi Arabia, Brazil, Malaysia, and Taiwan.
G. D. Searle & Co.	Admits paying $1.3 million to foreign governmental employees from 1973 to 1975 to "obtain sales of products or services."
United Brands Co.	Admits paying a $1,250,000 bribe to Honduran officials for a reduction in the banana export tax. Admits paying $750,000 to European officials. Investigators say the payment was made to head off proposed Italian restrictions on banana imports.

SOURCE: Larry Martz, et al., "Payoffs: The Growing Scandal," *Newsweek* (February 23, 1976), p. 26ff.

grease payments

a duty to act. "**Grease** (or facilitating) **payments**" to minor employees (such as payments made to customs officials to expedite the rapid processing of the goods on the dock) are excluded from the act.

In some countries, paying bribes seems to be considered a necessary and, in some circumstances, legal way to do business. Such practices could result because people's wages cannot produce an adequate standard of living or because leaders are corrupt and people are simply doing what they see being done. While such activity may be commonplace somewhere else, doing it does not make it right or ethical. American culture tends to frown on the use of bribery. In fact, in most cultures, bribery has a very negative connotation—people think that it is a foul, rather than a fair, means to achieve the desired result. The News Note on the following page indicates Sir Adrian Cadbury's views on paying bribes.

Cultural differences regarding the rightness or wrongness of paying bribes might be seen as causing domestic firms competing internationally to suffer hardships in obtaining and retaining business. U.S. firms are prohibited by U.S. law from giving bribes in foreign countries, while non-U.S. companies operating in foreign countries may not be similarly restricted. Therefore, adherence to the FCPA could make competing with non-U.S. firms more difficult in foreign countries. A necessary question is whether bribery is so repugnant to the American system of ethics that companies should be asked to forgo a foreign custom of using bribes and, thus, the profits that could be obtained through such a custom. There are managers in many multinational U.S. companies that do not believe in the appropriateness of the Foreign Corrupt Practices Act. Legally, however, these managers are compelled to abide by the law, regardless of whether they believe that law is ethical or right.

This managerial quandary points out the difficulty in knowing what is and is not ethical. There are large gray areas in making ethical decisions; the concept of ethical relativism, or **situational ethics,** is relevant here. Most people have a tendency to engage in situational ethics, which simply viewed means determining "right or wrong" based on the circumstances at the time the decision is being made. Different cultures have different social mores and taboos—such as on the morality of bribery as a business tool. The question becomes how to determine, at any one time or place, which decisions are right or wrong. Does one gauge the ethics of bribery using the consequence-based or the duty-based approach, and how does one know that the final decision is right? In such situations, it is best to rely on the law, which presumably evolved in a rational, discussion-based manner. And while the law may reflect the current general moral consensus, it is also best to be tolerant of alternative viewpoints in the event that the law is later deemed ineffectual or inappropriate.

situational ethics

Being convicted of making illegal foreign bribes is expensive and carries a fine of up to $1 million for the firm. Additionally, officers and directors who are convicted of "willfully" violating the bribery provisions are subject to fines of up to $10,000 and jail terms of up to five years. The FCPA also prohibits the fines to be paid by the firm with which that officer or director is associated. And, if those penalties aren't enough, disclosure of violations must be made, creating more company costs. For example, in a report that cost the company stockholders $3 million, Gulf Oil admitted to payment (prior to the FCPA) of some $12.3 million to politicians at home and abroad.[3]

A second, less ethically oriented requirement was added to the Foreign Corrupt Practices Act to help strengthen the antibribery provisions. This portion of the FCPA requires companies registered under the Securities Exchange Act of 1934 to devise and maintain good **internal control systems** and to keep financial records that, in reasonable detail, accurately and fairly reflect financial activities. An internal control system is a set of procedures that are concerned with authorizing transactions, protecting assets, and promoting the accuracy of financial information. Protecting assets is also an essential part of an internal control system. Assets include both inventory and information. When a fire destroyed its manufacturing plant, Fox Manufacturing

internal control systems

---

[3]Peter Brimelow, "Courting Disaster," *Barron's* (July 27, 1981), p. 7.

NEWS NOTE

How Much to "Buy" Business?

If what would be considered corruption in the company's home territory is an accepted business practice elsewhere, how are local managers expected to act? Companies could do business only in countries in which they feel ethically at home, provided always that their shareholders take the same view. But this approach could prove unduly restrictive, and there is also a certain arrogance in dismissing foreign codes of conduct without considering why they may be different. If companies find, for example, that they have to pay customs officers in another country just to do their job, it may be that the state is simply transferring its responsibilities to the private sector as an alternative to using taxation less efficiently to the same end.

Nevertheless, this example brings us to one of the most common ethical issues companies face—how far to go in buying business? I use two rules of thumb to test whether a payment is acceptable from the company's point of view: Is the payment on the face of the invoice? Would it embarrass the recipient to have the gift mentioned in the company newspaper?

The first test ensures that all payments, however unusual they may seem, are recorded and go through the books. Listing a payment on the face of the invoice may not be a sufficient ethical test, but it is a necessary one; payments outside the company's system are corrupt and corrupting.

The second [test] is aimed at distinguishing bribes from gifts, a definition which depends on the size of the gift and the influence it is likely to have on the recipient.

SOURCE: An excerpt from "Ethical Managers Make Their Own Rules," by Sir Adrian Cadbury (September–October 1987), pp. 71–72. Reprinted by permission of *Harvard Business Review*. Copyright © 1987 by the President and Fellows of Harvard College; all rights reserved.

Company of Albuquerque learned the importance of the protection afforded by fire-proof vaults—furniture plans and accounting records were stored in one, but people left the door open when they went home at night. Now, the company realizes that an internal control feature is not only *having* the vault, but *using* it appropriately.

A recent study conducted by the international accounting firm of Coopers & Lybrand provided the following, more specific definition of internal control:

> [It] is the process by which an entity's board of directors, management and/or other personnel obtain reasonable assurance as to achievement of specified objectives [such as financial reporting and compliance with laws and regulations]; it consists of nine interrelated components, with integrity, ethical values, and competence . . . serving as the foundation for the other components.[4]

The nine components detailed in the study are: (1) integrity, ethical values, and competence; (2) the control environment (including organizational structure and manage-

---

[4]Richard M. Steinberg and Robert J. Faulk, "Internal Control—A Question of Integrity, Ethics, and Competence," *Journal of Corporate Accounting and Finance* (Summer 1991), p. 396.

ment philosophy and operating style); (3) financial reporting and compliance objectives; (4) internal and external risk assessment; (5) the information system in place; (6) the control procedures taken; (7) communication of responsibility for internal control; (8) mechanisms to identify and effectively deal with change; and (9) ongoing monitoring activities. These components should interact to form a basic internal control framework as depicted in Exhibit 18–2.

Designing and installing an internal control system requires that company managers compare the costs of installing controls with the benefits to be provided by those controls. Thus, managers need to assign some estimates of the costs and benefits of integrity, ethical values, and competence. For example, to control theft or excess waste, company managers could make employees sign for each item of office supplies used. Such a policy would not be very expensive to enforce, but it could make employees feel as though they were thought to be thieves. The quantitative cost of enforcement and the qualitative assessment of employees' feelings would need to be compared to the savings generated by the policy. Since, however, precise measurements of costs and benefits are impossible, it is difficult to know how much to spend on installing internal controls in order to minimize the associated risks of not having those controls.

The risks of not having internal controls relate to the probabilities of having losses associated with three items: (1) the issuance of misleading financial statements; (2) improper disposition or use of assets; and (3) alleged or actual violations under the Foreign Corrupt Practices Act. The intentions of the FCPA accounting provisions

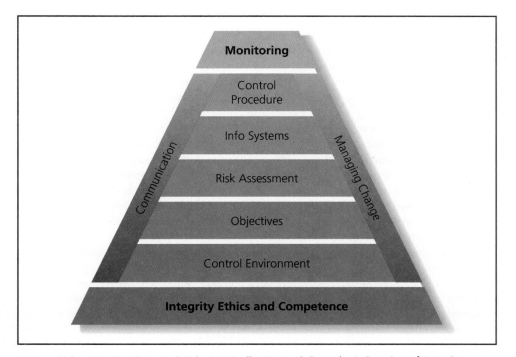

EXHIBIT 18–2
▼▼▼▼▼▼▼▼▼▼▼

INTERNAL
CONTROL
COMPONENTS

Inventory controls for non-prescription medications are much more lax than those for prescription drugs. This situation is primarily due to regulation rather than monetary value. Access to prescription medication is restricted to authorized pharmacy staff, while everyone has access to over-the-counter medicines.

were that control systems would prevent or detect foreign bribes and would assure that all transactions entered into by the firm were properly accounted for and legal.

Evaluating whether an internal control system is sufficient to meet the responsibilities placed on it by the FCPA is a subjective process. Different evaluators could arrive at different conclusions. This fact should be relatively unimportant, though, if the foundations (integrity, ethical values and competence) of a good internal control system are in place. If each firm and each individual within the firm were to abide by the spirit of the law, then all actions would promote the good of the firm, the individual, and society in general, and the need for internal controls would be minimized.

Unfortunately, even the best system of internal control may not prevent or detect circumstances that arise from employee or management collusion or circumvention of the system. During testimony before the House subcommittee concerned with the FCPA legislation, an American Institute of CPAs spokesperson "noted that most published reports of illegal or questionable payments indicated that the problem did not involve the adequacy of internal control, but rather the circumvention of the system." [5]

While the FCPA mandates publicly held companies to have internal control systems that provide reasonable assurance of meeting the objectives specified in existing accounting literature, all businesses should have some type of internal control system. Again, the controls implemented should be based on rational cost/benefit analysis. As the following News Note indicates, even small businesses can take some simple steps that will help meet the objectives of making certain transactions are authorized, financial statements are fairly presented, and assets are accounted for.

---

[5]Ernst & Ernst, *Foreign Corrupt Practices Act of 1977* (E&E: Financial Reporting Developments, Retrieval No. 38748, February 1978), p. 14.

NEWS NOTE

Internal Controls for Small Business

Could someone be ripping off your business? [C]onsider how a few "trusted" employees cheated small companies.

A bookkeeper diverted $750,000 of bill payments to her bank account in three years. Another bookkeeper made off with $80,000 in less than a year by drawing checks to herself and forging the owner's signature on them. A fellow in charge of paying bills paid himself $250,000 of company money. An employee of 28 years, who was a crackerjack at filling and shipping orders, shipped thousands of dollars of merchandise to himself.

Small companies can be easy prey. Their accounting systems usually lack tight controls because of the extra expense involved. A few employees normally do a number of critical jobs, weakening the first line of defense against employee dishonesty: segregating duties.

Some simple precautions can make larceny difficult.

- Segregation of duties is the biggest single deterrent.
- Nothing moves in or out of inventory without documents, such as purchase orders, receiving tickets, bills of lading, invoices, sales orders, and shipping tickets.
- Paper work should tie into the books.
- Pay employees a fair wage; poorly paid employees may feel justified in "ripping off" their employer.
- Inventory safeguards should be installed based on the value of goods.
- Don't expect your bank to spot forgeries.
- The person trusted the most often is the one who can embezzle with the least effort.

SOURCE: Stanford L. Jacobs, "How to Prevent an Employee from Ripping Off the Firm," *Wall Street Journal* (May 10, 1982), p. 21. Reprinted by permission of the *Wall Street Journal* © 1982 Dow Jones & Company, Inc. All rights reserved worldwide.

Racketeer Influenced and Corrupt Organizations Act

The second significant law addressed in this chapter is the **Racketeer Influenced and Corrupt Organizations Act** (RICO). This act was designed to discourage organized crime from investing profits from illegal activities into legitimate business. There are three elements to a RICO violation: (1) commission of racketeering offenses; (2) a pattern of such offenses (established by the conviction of at least two of such prohibited offenses within a ten-year period); and (3) involvement in the acts by an enterprise (for example, a corporation or partnership). Racketeering offenses include the following wide variety of crimes called **predicate acts:** mail, wire and bankruptcy fraud, extortion, arson, murder, interference with interstate commerce by violence or threat thereof, securities fraud, and bribery. Because of the inclusion of so many different criminal offenses (over thirty are covered by the act), almost any type of business fraud activity can be alleged to be a "racketeering" activity.

Civil suits involving RICO have become increasingly popular (see Exhibit 18–3). Examples of the range of civil actions include industrial espionage, government contracting, labor relations, and insurance fraud. Accountants and brokers, in addition to officers, directors, and management, have been sued under civil RICO.

Racketeer Influenced and Corrupt Organizations Act

predicate acts

EXHIBIT 18–3
▼▼▼▼▼▼▼▼▼▼▼

RICO
PROSECUTIONS

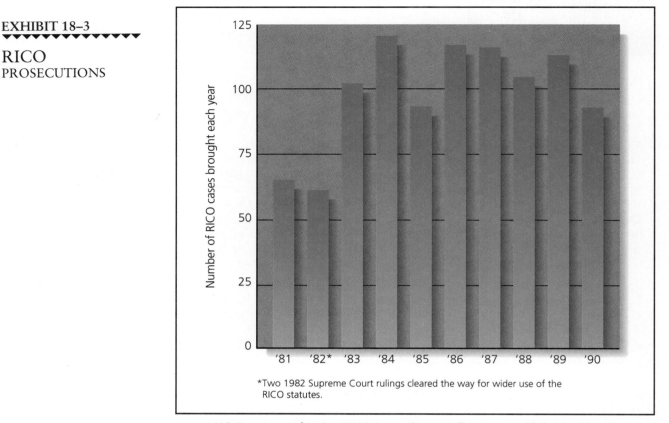

*Two 1982 Supreme Court rulings cleared the way for wider use of the RICO statutes.

SOURCE: U.S. Department of Justice, "RICO Prosecutions," *Wall Street Journal* (July 7, 1991), p. B1. Reprinted by permission of the *Wall Street Journal* © 1991 Dow Jones & Company, Inc. All rights reserved worldwide.

The breadth of the bill's use has created a major controversy. Proponents of the RICO Act believe that it is a useful and appropriate method of addressing a variety of unethical business practices. Opponents of the act believe that Congress did not intend for such broad application of the law. Opponents also think the use of the RICO statutes often needlessly victimizes people and taints reputations. When people are indicted under the RICO law, they have their property seized and frozen *prior to* trial and are essentially branded as racketeers *prior to* trial.

Opposition has been so vocal for so long that a bill (H.R. 1717) has been introduced to alter the RICO Act and make its reach less intrusive to business activities not commonly thought of as racketeering acts. "The measure would preserve the use of civil RICO actions for those cases in which egregious criminal conduct exists, but remove the availability of civil RICO from ordinary commercial transactions."[6] However, whether the bill will ever be passed (or in what form) is debatable, as is indicated by the following News Note. The U.S. Supreme Court did provide some relief from the RICO provisions in March 1992 when it unanimously ruled that plaintiffs must prove they had been directly harmed by the alleged wrongdoing.

---

[6]"Hughes Introduces Bill in House to Reform RICO Act," *The CPA Letter* (May 1991), p. 3.

NEWS NOTE

An Attempt to Alter RICO

In introducing HR 1717, Congressman William J. Hughes said Congress has been work-ing for over six years to reform civil RICO—ever since the U.S. Supreme Court warned that civil RICO provisions were being used in ways never envisioned by Congress. According to Hughes, extensive hearings over the years have "established beyond dis-pute that civil RICO's powerful treble damages remedy, designed for use against crimi-nal racketeering, is being used with increasing frequency as a tool in everyday civil liti-gation to leverage extraordinary settlements from and to damage the reputations of adversaries."

Specifically, the bill includes a judicial "gatekeeper" provision, allowing courts to dis-miss suits that do not meet the "egregious criminal conduct" standard. The bill main-tains treble damages for actions that pass that gatekeeper test (including criminal fraud related to savings and loan failures), and will maintain civil RICO for major white-collar frauds. The proposed legislation also . . . makes it clear that RICO is not available as a remedy in nonviolent free speech and assembly situations.

SOURCE: "RICO Reform Bill Introduced by Congressman Hughes," *Journal of Accountancy* (June 1991), p. 31.

Managers must be aware of the consequences of engaging in RICO offenses, for the law provides both criminal and civil penalties. Criminal penalties include fines of up to $25,000 per violation, jail terms of up to twenty years per violation, and the forfeiture of all ill-gotten gains. Civil penalties can be equally harsh, if not more so. The person injured by racketeering activities can choose remedies such as treble dam-ages (a tripling of the original damage amount), loss of the defendant's holdings in the legitimate business, and payment of attorney's fees.

The numerous possibilities that exist under the RICO law for potential harm to businesses—in terms of both money and reputation—must be recognized by man-agers. Unless a RICO reform bill is passed, perfectly rational, legal, and ethical ac-tions taken in the normal course of business could be viewed by others as predicate acts that justify a RICO violation.

To discourage distortion of the moral law through misuse of written law, the RICO Act was broadly written. The language of the act, however, is *so* broad that it has been used in many cases that have nothing to do with organized crime. The moral question is whether such a law is itself a morally acceptable method of uncovering organized crime. Is society prepared to use legal technicalities to further its perceived moral goal? In this case, does the end (which may not even be achieved) justify the means? Using either utilitarian or Kantian analysis, such outcomes are neither cost beneficial nor just.

Referring back to basic ethical theories, utilitarian analysis would not tolerate such an unfair law. While the common good seems to benefit when the true culprits are caught, consider the incidental harm done to the innocent individuals who were erroneously trapped by the law. Use of laws such as RICO could, in the long run, cause irreparable damage to a society. One question is sufficient to show why: if a society accepts the use of one overly broad law, couldn't any number of other such overly broad laws be justified? Kantian analysis would also not accept a law written in such a manner. The duty of the law is to protect a society and individuals within that society. The disregard of individual rights that can occur through indiscriminate use of RICO is inherently not fair or equitable. This situation effectively punishes everyone simply because the guilty cannot be distinguished from the innocent.

The Securities Exchange Act of 1934

Securities Exchange Act of 1934

Another body of law that particularly relates to management is securities regulations. The Securities and Exchange Commission (SEC) issues regulations that control both the issuance of securities and their continued sales on the various stock markets. The SEC was created by the **Securities Exchange Act of 1934.** This law was designed to regulate the securities market after the original issuance of the securities.

scienter

The 1934 law contains sections 10(b) and 16 that are applicable to insider trading. Section 10(b) outlaws the use of interstate instruments (such as telephones and the United States mail) in the purchase or sale of securities if there is any manipulation or deception involved. One important aspect of this law is that the manipulation or deception must have been committed with **scienter,** or the intent to defraud, or intentional misconduct that amounts to more than mere negligence.

insider

Section 16 defines an **insider** as any director, officer, or owner who holds more than 10 percent of the shares of any one class of stock of a company registered under the 1934 act. Persons who have been entrusted with information for solely corporate purposes (such as lawyers, accountants, and underwriters) are also considered insiders. Insiders may be prosecuted for using **material** inside (nonpublic) information to trade securities for financial gain.[7] Before insiders can trade using this information, it must first be made available to the public.

material

tippees

Persons who receive inside information from an insider, regardless of whether the insider used the information, are called **tippees.** A tippee is subject to the 1934 act sanctions when the information is received and the tippee knew or should have known that the insider had breached a duty of trust and confidence to the corporation.

Penalties for violating the 1934 act can be either criminal or civil. For example, a willful violation of the 1934 act is subject to a fine of up to $100,000 and imprisonment of up to five years. Civil damages under the securities acts vary and include reimbursement for losses suffered by those trading in the stock, loss of trading profits, and injunctions to prohibit further similar practices. In 1984, the 1934 act was amended to allow the SEC to ask for a civil penalty of treble the profit gained or loss avoided from using inside information in trades. This amount is paid to the U.S. Treasury and has no effect on the amount of damages that can be recovered by private individuals. A common measure of monetary damages is the difference between the price paid for the stock at issuance and the price either at the time of the suit or at the time the buyer sold the stock.

It is interesting to note, however, in the case of *U.S. v. Arthur Lang and Thomas Trexler,* lawyers will be arguing that insider trading is not a criminal activity. The arguments that will be used are included in the following News Note.

---

[7]"Material" basically means important in relation to some standard of comparison. Relative to securities regulations, "material" means any information that might make a difference to a reasonable investor. It is not necessary that the final decision *be* any different, it is only necessary that the decision *could have been* different. Some examples of material items include dividend adjustments, acquisition or loss of a major client, a takeover attempt by another company, and the discovery of a new product, process, or natural resource reserve.

Is Insider Trading *Not* a Crime?

In 1942, a lawyer (Milton V. Freedman) at the SEC got a call complaining that a company president bought stock after telling shareholders that earnings were down when he knew business was good. Wasn't there anything the agency could do about it? Freedman then, in one day, drafted Rule 10b-5, which everyone thinks made insider trading a crime. But everyone doesn't include Mr. Freedman, who denies that the rule had anything to do with criminal penalties or even private lawsuits against insider trading.

Mr. Freedman's recollections have been cited in papers filed in December 1990 in Baltimore federal court on behalf of two accused inside traders. Lawyers argue that the SEC never had the power to outlaw insider trading, indeed that "Congress made an explicit legislative decision not to criminalize insider trading." If so, there is no crime as insider trading and the Lang and Trexler indictment must be dismissed. Mr. Trexler's lawyers, who include a former SEC official, say that when the 1934 Securities Act was passed, Congress considered making insider trading a crime, but rejected the idea. Then Rule 10b-5 used broad language and prohibited "any device, scheme, or artifice to defraud."

Chief Justice William Rehnquist wrote that Rule 10b-5 is a "judicial oak which has grown from little more than a legislative acorn." The SEC didn't use the rule until 1961 and 1978, respectively, to bring a civil and a criminal case. No insider trading case that has been tried (almost all are plea-bargained) has raised the point that the SEC didn't have the authority to make the tactic a crime. The outcome will be interesting.

SOURCE: Adapted from L. Gordon Crovitz, "Insider Trading a Crime or SEC Overstepping?" *Wall Street Journal* (December 19, 1990), p. A17. Reprinted with permission of the *Wall Street Journal* © 1990 Dow Jones & Company, Inc. All rights reserved worldwide.

The ethical issue associated with the 1934 law is fairness of market transactions. To be ethical, persons engaging in securities transactions should be fair. Fairness is achieved through equal bargaining power and the ability to make a well-informed decision. When an insider manipulates the market, other investors are not being treated fairly, as they do not have access to all the information necessary to make a good decision. If the markets are perceived as being unfair, investors will not invest and, thus, investors, the market, and the market economy will not flourish. Now the full circle has been covered: (1) the practical problem was to safeguard the market from future depressions; (2) the ethical problem was to assure fairness in transactions; so that (3) investors, the market, and the market economy would flourish. This example indicates that oftentimes actions that are practical and legal in society are, additionally, ethical actions.

Legislation Related to Employees

There are far too many laws affecting employee rights to review all of them. However, there are two classes of laws that should be addressed. The first is the body of law protecting employees' rights and benefits. The second relates to laws about discrimination in employment. The importance of these laws is as significant as a job is to an individual. Practically and morally, employees owe certain duties to their employers. These duties correspond to the rights the employees can expect from their employers. Conversely, employers have the right to expect that employees perform their duties and have some obligations to those employees for such performance.

Following are three examples of employer–employee rights and duties. First, an employee (Ann Rivet) works diligently on a project that requires evening and week-end time (the accomplishment of the duty owed by Ann to her employer). In return, Ann expects her employer to reward her in some way—a pat on the back, a day off, or a raise recommendation. Second, employers have the duty to provide their employees with a safe workplace. Since an employer would not want to be injured at work, he or she should not place employees at risk of injury. Employees also have a right to expect safety unless they have been warned about, and have agreed to accept, job hazards. Third, employees have the right to expect nondiscriminatory treatment by their employers in the workplace, and they have the duty not to discriminate against others.

Occupational Safety and Health Act

One law that addresses worker rights is the **Occupational Safety and Health Act.** OSHA was designed to protect the health and safety of employees while on the job. This law indicates that a company has the duty to provide safe working conditions and requires that the workplace be free from recognized hazards that could cause death or serious injury to workers. But sometimes it is difficult, if not impossible, for

The computer has both positive and negative workplace impacts. On the positive side, many detailed and mundane tasks are now completed more efficiently. Constant keyboard usage has, however, created a new job-related complaint: repetitive strain injury.

workers or companies to know of the risks they face on various jobs. For example, who knew when asbestos was originally installed that it could cause cancer? Is it possible to make a safe workplace for computer keyboard operators or supermarket checkout clerks who suffer from "repetitive strain injury" caused by a continued repetition of awkward hand and arm movements? How will OSHA eliminate the most recent work-related complaint—stress? "Three quarters of Americans say their jobs cause them stress; stress now accounts for 14 percent of workers' compensation claims and costs business an estimated $150 billion annually." [8]

In addition to employers taking basic safety precautions, the National Institute for Occupational Safety and Health told the U.S. Senate that workers should be told if they are being exposed to hazardous materials that are governmentally regulated. This position was affirmed by OSHA in the mid-1980s. While both state and federal legislation is in place to provide such information to workers, that legislation is not consistent and no general agreement exists about employers' legal or ethical obligations to disclose such information. The News Note on the next page discusses a situation in which an employee is informed of health hazards and is allowed to choose a dangerous job. The costs of such a choice, however, are potentially very high to the firm and to society.

Violations of health and safety laws carry both civil and criminal penalties. Fines can be as high as $1,000 a day per violation and $10,000 for some intentional violations. For example, Boise Cascade's Rumsford, Maine pulp and paper mill has often been cited for worker safety and health violations. In 1989, the Labor Department proposed fines totaling $1.6 million for 535 different types of violations—of which 241 were related to health and safety standards.[9]

The second category of laws dealing with employer–employee relationships is that of discrimination. The Civil Rights Act of 1964 is the cornerstone of laws preventing discrimination in employment on a variety of bases. This law makes it illegal to discriminate on the basis of race, religion, color, creed, sex, or national origin. Other laws have been designed to deal more specifically with different kinds of discrimination.

For instance, the Equal Pay Act requires that, all things being equal, men and women who do the same job should be paid the same salary. This law was enacted to stop the practice of paying women less than men with the same qualifications for doing the same job.

The Pregnancy Discrimination Act of 1978 is another law directed originally at gender. Women of childbearing years were being discriminated against because employers were afraid that those women would become pregnant and want to take maternity leave. The benefits associated with pregnancy and maternity leave are expensive, and employers believed that they could avoid incurring those expenses if they simply did not hire women in childbearing range. This act outlaws such exclusions in hiring.

The Age Discrimination in Employment Act makes it illegal to refuse to hire someone who is more than forty years old. Because the American work force is aging and there is a growing trend for workers to start second, different careers, it is necessary to protect those older workers actually in the work force and those entering the work force for the first time from age discrimination.

---

[8]William H. Shaw, *Business Ethics* (Belmont, Calif.: Wadsworth, 1991), p. 238.
[9]Albert R. Karr, "Boise Cascade Faces Penalties of $1.6 Million," *The Wall Street Journal* (September 14, 1989), p. C5.

NEWS NOTE

Mandatory Protection No Longer an Employer Option

[In 1982] Gloyce Qualls was a 32-year-old cog on the assembly line at the Johnson Controls battery plant in Milwaukee. As a "burner," she made roughly $350 a week. . . . In the process, she inhaled oxide from the melting lead. (When the concentration of lead in her blood got too high, she was moved to a cleaner area until the level decreased.) Since lead is toxic, particularly to fetuses, the company in earlier years allowed women to transfer to jobs that were less hazardous—and that often paid less. But in 1982, Johnson Controls imposed a mandatory protection policy. Women of child-bearing age could either prove that they were sterile or be forced to change jobs. Several months after being transferred to a $200-a-week position, Gloyce Qualls had her tubes tied. "I had no choice," she says. "I had bills to pay. I had to live."

. . . In 1991, the U.S. Supreme Court unanimously struck down Johnson Controls' mandatory exclusion of fertile women from hazardous jobs, a ruling that immediately affected other companies such as Du Pont, General Motors, Gulf Oil, and Monsanto. . . .

Beyond the women involved, the justices' ruling leaves employers in a bind. Companies adopted fetal protection policies at least in part to protect themselves from lawsuits brought after infants were born with defects. "It's been a Catch-22 all along," says a spokeswoman for Johnson Controls. "We're horsewhipped when we're perceived as waiting for a tragedy to occur before taking a proactive stance. But here we were willing to make a tough choice to avoid a tragedy." . . . Now what? Clearly, employers will make Herculean efforts to warn workers and warn them again of hazards. [Justice Harry] Blackmun tried to reassure corporate America. If a plant "fully informs the woman of the risk and the employer has not acted negligently," the justice wrote, the basis for liability "seems remote at best."

[However,] even though mothers might not be able to bring winning lawsuits against companies, their *offspring* could. Indeed, as Justice Byron White noted in a concurring opinion, all states permit children to sue for prenatal injuries. . . .

In addition to issuing thorough warnings, companies might consider making the plants safer. . . . [Implementation of many safety measures] would drive up costs, complain representatives of various companies, and put American business at a competitive disadvantage. At Johnson Controls, safety measures include medical screening and sophisticated ventilation systems. "We don't know how to make it any safer," says [the company representative.] "And, if we did, it would be fabulously expensive." . . .

SOURCE: David A. Kaplan, Bob Cohn, and Karen Springen, "Equal Rights, Equal Risks, " *Newsweek* (April 1, 1991), pp. 56, 58.

These laws are all designed to protect the employee from being treated unfairly with regard to employment criteria. Only job-related criteria should be used to make decisions to hire, promote, or compensate, or for any other aspect of employment. The smart businessperson should be asking which prospective employee will do the best job, not what that employee looks like or espouses. Use of non-job-related criteria is not only unfair according to ethical standards, but also such action may represent poor business judgment because the employer may not be getting the best person for the job. According to the utilitarian theory, a good businessperson perceives the usefulness of getting the best person for the job no matter what other extrinsic characteristics exist.

Environmental Legislation

One final area of protective law should be reviewed because of its significant monetary and ethical considerations: laws to protect the environment. As with the other bodies of law mentioned, a tremendous number of laws exist that deal with a business's ability to "interact" with the environment. The underpinning of environmental laws is in the **National Environmental Policy Act** (NEPA), which requires that an environmental impact statement be prepared for major federal activities that significantly affect the quality of the environment. Enforcement is housed in the **Environmental Protection Agency** (EPA), which assures that the environmental impact statement, if necessary, is completed and acceptable before the federal activity can proceed. Environmental impact statements review how the federal activity will affect the environment, as well as what possible alternative courses of action may be available that might have a less detrimental impact on the environment.

National Environmental Policy Act

Environmental Protection Agency

Even with the knowledge that polluting is harmful, businesses often pollute for two reasons. First, business managers may regard the environment as a free good. Disposing of waste into the air or water costs nothing, but disposing of such waste in an environmentally safe manner usually requires cost incurrence. Second, businesses may pollute because managers believe that their company's pollution levels are insignificant. However, with many firms each thinking they are only polluting "a little bit," the total pollution level can rise quite significantly.

Managers should also be aware of the increasing harshness of the EPA's attitude in regard to their firm's complicity in environmental pollution. In May 1990, John Borowski, the owner of a small defense plant, was convicted on charges of knowingly violating the Clean Water Act by dumping nitric acid waste down the sink. The acid waste ultimately ended up in Boston Harbor. Mr. Borowski faces a prison term for his violations. "A person who mugs a city by polluting should receive at least as strong a punishment as the person who mugs an individual," says the EPA's criminal

Air pollution is one of the most visible forms of pollution. Although the costs of clean-up might be high, the cost of continuance may be higher considering the size of some of the judgments against violators.

enforcement chief, James M. Strock.[10] The courts, apparently, agree. "In fiscal 1989, federal courts handed out prison terms totaling about 37 years and $11.1 million in fines for environmental crimes, compared with less than two years of sentences and $198,000 in fines five years earlier, EPA figures show." [11]

Addressing pollution problems creates additional costs for businesses, which then attempt to pass those costs on to consumers through higher product costs. How extensive are environmental costs? The following headlines from *The Wall Street Journal* help illustrate the seriousness of the situation.

- Oil Spill Trial Yields $2.5 Million Award
  (September 11, 1991)
- GE Faces $270 Million in Cleanup Costs in EPA Scrutiny of Hudson River PCBs
  (December 13, 1990)
- PPG to Pay New Jersey $82.5 Million for Chromium-Waste Cleanups, Fine
  (July 20, 1990)
- EPA Sets Toxic-Waste Cleanup Rules; Heavy Costs Likely for Chemical Firms
  (July 10, 1990)
- Kodak Pays $2 Million in Environmental Fines
  (April 6, 1990)
- Clean-Air Legislation Will Cost Americans $21.5 Billion a Year
  (March 28, 1990)

The manner in which a company conducts business is of concern to all of the company stakeholders (stockholders, employees, and creditors). Stockholders want to make profits and, thus, would prefer to keep costs low. Employees want to keep their jobs, which is not possible if the company is not profitable or is closed down for pollution violations. Creditors want debts to be repaid and, therefore, are also interested in the profit picture as well as the potential risks (as indicated in the following News Note).

While cleaning up previous problems can cost money, many companies are finding that there are economic benefits to making the adjustments. Steel mills have found this to be true in regard to the oil used to lubricate machinery. Oil Technology Inc. of Gary, Indiana provides on-site recycling of the mills' oil at a lower cost to the mills than what was previously paid to haul the oil away. Exhibit 18–4 indicates the bottom-line improvements shown by some companies after making environmentally beneficial changes.

The ethical issues of environmental pollution are twofold: (1) should the environment be kept clean for its own sake, and (2) how clean does the environment need to be kept? Some people believe that the environment is intrinsically valuable or has value apart from any human interest in it. These people insist that the integrity of the environment should be maintained for the sake of all its inhabitants, not just for humans. Thus, water would be kept clean because of all the life associated with it, not simply to provide people with seafood or a pleasant beach. For example, blue

---

[10]David Stipp, "Environmental Crime Can Land Executives in Prison These Days," *Wall Street Journal* (September 10, 1990), p. A1.
[11]Ibid.

Cleanup Costs Can Create Credit Concerns

As I understand it, the environmental risk can hit a bank in two different ways:

1. A borrower's cleanup problem can be so costly in relation to its financial capacity that it weakens the credit, turning it into a problem loan or a loss, and

2. Cleanup costs can become the direct liability of the lending bank, sometimes the ironic consequence of the bank taking prudent action to protect its position. For example, foreclosure of collateral can make the bank the "current owner" of a polluted site, or efforts to work with a troubled borrower can lead to a determination that the bank has become an "operator" of the polluted site and thus responsible for cleanup costs.

SOURCE: T. Carter Hagaman, "Environmental Risks Worry Bankers," *Management Accounting* (November 1990), p. 20. Published by Institute of Management Accountants, Montvale, N.J.

EXHIBIT 18–4

CLEANING UP
PAYS OFF

Company	Manufacturing Change	Benefit
AT&T	Redesigned circuit-board cleaning process	Eliminated use of ozone-depleting chemicals, slashed cleaning costs by $3 million annually
Carrier	Revamped metal cutting and redesigned air conditioner parts	Eliminated toxic solvents, cut manufacturing cost by $1.2 million annually
Clairol	Switched to foam balls from water to flush pipes in hair-care product manufacturing	Reduced waste water 70 percent, saving $240,000 annually in disposal costs
W. R. Grace	Reformulated solvents and changed process in sealant and gasket operation	Reduced toxic waste by 50 percent
3M	Developed adhesive for box-sealing tapes that doesn't require solvent	Eliminated the need for $2 million worth of pollution control equipment
Polaroid	Eliminated mercury from battery. Streamlined photographic chemical plants	The batteries are now recyclable. Cut waste generation 31 percent and cut disposal costs by $250,000 annually
Reynolds Metals	Replaced solvent-based ink with water-based in packaging plants	Cut emissions 65 percent, saved $30 million in pollution equipment
Union Carbide	Developed system that replaces solvents with carbon dioxide as medium for spraying paint	Cut volatile organic emissions 72 percent

SOURCE: Amal Kumar Naj, "Some Companies Cut Pollution by Altering Production Methods," *Wall Street Journal* (December 24, 1990), p. A28. Reprinted by permission of the *Wall Street Journal* © 1990 Dow Jones & Company, Inc. All rights reserved worldwide.

sharks were being killed with alarming frequency in the nets of commercial swordfish and tuna fishermen. Until environmental groups expressed concern, the plight of the then commercially useless shark was ignored.

If the environment has intrinsic value, the environment should be treated with even more respect than if it is kept clean only for the sake of the people who exist in it. To determine how clean this might be, cost/benefit analysis can be applied. For example, if it would cost $100,000 to have the environment 65 percent clean, and it would cost an additional $100,000 to have the environment 66 percent clean, is it worth the extra $100,000 to have the environment 1 percent cleaner? Unfortunately, such a question brings back the original question of why keep the environment clean: for people only or for all the environment's inhabitants whether animate or, like land-scapes, inanimate?

Environmental concern is necessary for businesses to pursue profits and provide jobs. Customers may be faced with the hard choices of paying more for products so that the environment can be protected. A final business question about environmental protection must be asked: what environmental standards should be placed on the foreign operations of multinational companies? Should these operations be held to U.S. standards, or would such standards impose too high a cost relative to other companies? In addition, some developing countries believe that they have sufficient environmental resources upon which to draw without endangerment at the current time. Should pollution be allowed because environmental endangerment currently does not exist?

Whistleblowing

whistleblowing

A final topic related to employer–employee relationships is whistleblowing. This subject can be addressed in conjunction with the concept of employment at will. **Whistleblowing** can be defined as alerting the proper authorities to a firm's improper or illegal action. The proper authorities can be internal or external. Although some environmental and workplace safety laws include whistleblower provisions, there is only one major federal law on the subject and its scope is not very broad.

There are few, if any, protections for those employees who perceive an illegal or immoral action occurring in their firms. Most states still use employment at will contracts, which allow the employer and the employee the respective rights to fire or quit at any time, without even the usual two-week notice. Thus, employers are perfectly within their legal rights in the majority of states when they fire an employee for refusing to do an immoral or illegal act. Maine, for example, "will protect private-sector whistleblowers only if they follow strictly defined procedures. Mississippi and Georgia offer almost no protection."[12] While the concept of employment at will is declining, it is not doing so at a rate sufficient to prevent would-be whistleblowers from being fired for refusing to do an immoral or illegal action for the firm.

Five conditions have been suggested as those under which whistleblowing is (with the first three) permissible and (with the addition of the last two) morally obligatory.[13] First, to avoid the "cry wolf" syndrome, the employee must be certain that the behavior in question is of serious consequence. Second, the employee must alert his or her immediate supervisor of the problem to avoid the problems arising by going

---

[12]Joan Hamilton, "Blowing the Whistle Without Paying the Piper," *Business Week* (July 3, 1991), p. 138.
[13]Richard T. De George, *Business Ethics* (New York: Macmillan, 1986), pp. 230–34.

over the supervisor's head. Third, the employee should contact each member in the chain of command until he or she achieves the correction of the problem. If the previous three conditions are met, whistleblowing is permitted; however, only if the next two conditions are met would whistleblowing be considered an employee's moral obligation: (1) there must be access to documented evidence of the immorality or illegality; and (2) there must be a reasonable expectation that the whistleblowing will produce some good.

Blowing the whistle on corporate wrongdoing requires a high measure of regard for ethical principles. As indicated in the News Note on page 852, an employee must weigh the costs (generally to the employee) against the benefits of publicly recounting the corporate errors. In addition, the employee violates a duty (loyalty) owed to the employer in making the disclosures. Viewed from the "golden rule" perspective, however, most people would prefer truth to lies.

COMPUTER SOFTWARE PIRACY

One relatively new activity, believed by many individuals and managers not to be a crime, is the illicit copying of computer software. The most obvious cost is the loss of revenue in the firms whose software programs are copied rather than sold. The expense of software piracy is estimated, respectively, at $2 billion and $6 billion annually in the United States and internationally. Secondarily, software piracy could result in substantial penalties or settlements from copyright infringement lawsuits.

The primary law protecting software is the 1976 Copyright Law, as amended in 1980. Copyright law grants a legal monopoly to the tangible forms of original ideas for a specified period of time. There are some circumstances in which copyright infringement is deemed not to occur. One limitation is the fair use doctrine, which allows the public to use copyrighted material in a *reasonable* manner without the consent of the copyright holder. The second limitation allows the reproduction of *one* backup copy of copyrighted materials for archival or library purposes.

From a business standpoint, the ethical issue is fairly straightforward. Engaging in software piracy is, in fact, the same thing as stealing. Anytime one person takes something that belongs to another without permission or without paying for it, that person has engaged in both illegal and unethical activity. Such activity makes both the individual and the organization for which he or she works subject to punishment. The fines associated with suits under the Copyright Law include $100,000 per violation.

CODES OF CONDUCT

Numerous corporations have begun to recognize their various responsibilities for both ethical and legal behavior. A typical and highly visible means by which corporations are indicating their recognition is through the adoption of a corporate code of conduct or code of ethics. Johnson & Johnson's Credo is a well-known example of a corporate ethics code as well as a corporate responsibility statement; it is shown in Exhibit 18–5 on page 853.

The Good in Whistleblowing

Whistleblowers challenge the assumption that what is good for the organization is good for the larger public. Whistleblowers have decided that the value of loyalty to the group has to be superseded by other values, such as the dignity of life and equality and efficiency. Non-conformity is a laudable value when the group's norms or activities are of an extremely low ethical quality, but the whistleblower has to prove this. . . . This whistleblower, of course, may believe that the public revelations will actually in the long run help the organization. That is, once it is cleansed of its sins, its errors corrected, its financial accounting straightened out, its safety measures installed, its new leadership in place, it will go forward to greater accomplishments, greater profits, and greater credibility.

SOURCE: J. Vernon Jensen, "Ethical Tension Points in Whistleblowing," *Journal of Business Ethics* 6 (1987), p. 324.

Many companies prepare codes of conduct for three "wrong" reasons: (1) they are being pressured to do so by external forces; (2) they have agreed to do so under a project called the Defense Industry Initiative on Business Ethics and Conduct; and (3) they believe it is the "in" thing to do. Codes oftentimes seem to focus on illegal acts (for example, overcharging, bribing, and manipulating accounting records), but fail to address unethical acts or issues related to items such as executive character, product quality, or civic responsibilities. Very few of the codes indicate what behavior is acceptable under specific situations.

Codes instead should be developed to affect the behavior of all employees in the organization and to communicate management's concern for high-level ethical standards of behavior and corporate social responsibility. Regardless of *why* a company establishes a code of conduct, one intended primary benefit of the process is the development of a positively stated code that can act as the underlying basis for all corporate policies, activities, and employee behavior. Exhibit 18–6 (pages 854–855) provides some guidelines for developing corporate codes of ethics.

The desire to acknowledge responsibility for ethical behavior has transcended United States domestic businesses and been elevated to a concern at the United Nations. The appendix to this chapter provides a summary of the United Nations' guidelines to regulate the relationships between transnational (multinational) corporations (TNCs) and their host countries.

In addition to corporate codes of conduct, many employees are subject to professional codes of ethics. These codes typically contain two types of norms: obligations and permissions. Obligations refer to things that are requirements. Obligations can encompass character traits, responsibilities, or duties. The difference between a responsibility and a duty is that the former allows room for professional judgment and discretion. Permissions allow professionals to do or not do as they desire; for example, accountants may choose to accept or reject clients.

A professional code of conduct sets limits of acceptable behavior for the members of that profession. Individuals violating the rules of professional conduct are judged by their peers. Depending on the seriousness of the violation, punishments could in-

EXHIBIT 18–5
▼▼▼▼▼▼▼▼▼▼▼▼

JOHNSON &
JOHNSON'S CREDO

Our Credo

We believe our first responsibility is to the doctors, nurses, and patients,
to mothers and fathers and all others who use our products and services.
In meeting their needs everything we do must be of high quality.
We must constantly strive to reduce our costs
in order to maintain reasonable prices.
Customers' orders must be serviced promptly and accurately.
Our suppliers and distributors must have an opportunity
to make a fair profit.

We are responsible to our employees,
the men and women who work with us throughout the world.
Everyone must be considered as an individual.
We must respect their dignity and recognize their merit.
They must have a sense of security in their jobs.
Compensation must be fair and adequate,
and working conditions clean, orderly and safe.
We must be mindful of ways to help our employees fulfill
their family responsibilities.
Employees must feel free to make suggestions and complaints.
There must be equal opportunity for employment development
and advancement for those qualified.
We must provide competent management,
and their actions must be just and ethical.

We are responsible to the communities in which we live and work
and to the world community as well.
We must be good citizens—support good works and charities
and bear our fair share of taxes.
We must encourage civic improvements and better health and education.
We must maintain in good order
the property we are privileged to use,
protecting the environment and natural resources.

Our final responsibility is to our stockholders.
Business must make a sound profit.
We must experiment with new ideas.
Research must be carried on, innovative programs developed
and mistakes paid for.
New equipment must be purchased, new facilities provided
and new products launched.
Reserves must be created to provide for adverse times.
When we operate according to these principles,
the stockholders should realize a fair return.

SOURCE: Johnson & Johnson.

clude being chastised, being required to take continuing education courses, or being expelled from the profession.

From all of the previous discussions, it should become clear that any decision has some ethical dimensions. Most of the time, these dimensions are so cut and dried that decision makers never even consider that the dimensions exist. However, managers should never lose sight of the fact that ethics is a fundamental aspect of choice and all business decisions involve choice.

EXHIBIT 18–6
▼▼▼▼▼▼▼▼▼▼▼▼▼▼

GUIDELINES FOR
CORPORATE CODES
OF ETHICS

Preamble	This set of standards constitutes the Company's Code of Ethics (Code), which represents our current ethical consensus regarding the maintainable ethical level of business conduct, as ascertained and approved by the Board of Directors. Some of the standards supplement ethics-related provisions of various Company policies and procedures, but the standards take precedence in matters of interpretation and compliance. Changes in the Code are to be recommended exclusively by the Audit Committee. No employee, regardless of position or function in the Company is allowed to tamper with or to downgrade the significance of any standard, either explicitly or implicitly, by his or her behavior. In case of doubt as to proper application of a standard, written opinion of the Legal Department can be obtained.
Standard 1	It is the policy of the Company to comply strictly in all respects with all applicable laws and regulations. Diligent observance of the law is a requirement from which there can be no exception. Supervisors must make sure that all applicable laws are known by them and by the personnel under their supervision.
Standard 2	It is the overall policy of the Company to organize and carry out its activities toward the goal of a sustainable successful performance in the best interest of shareholders and other constituencies, with an overriding concern for observance of the highest ethical principles as they apply to business policies and practices.
Standard 3	The Company will promote fair competition and candid treatment of its customers or clients. Integrity of information communicated in soliciting business or in marketing products and services is the obligation of all those involved in such efforts, including Company-authorized nonemployee representatives, dealers, and contractors. No one is authorized to make a promise or commitment that the Company cannot or does not intend to meet.
Standard 4	The Company will always act honorably toward those who do business with the Company and are otherwise parties in a mutual relationship with the Company.
Standard 5	The Company is committed to support and contribute to the efforts undertaken in public interest, especially those affecting its community, its employees, its industry, or business at large. The Company will not participate, directly or indirectly, in any program or activity where the Company role is not or appears not to be ethically sound.
Standard 6	The Company's continued success and good reputation depend on a consistently reliable high-quality performance of its employees in every situation and under all circumstances. Every employee should have the working knowledge and competence needed to achieve and maintain satisfactory performance. No employee should knowingly be given an assignment involving unwarranted ethical, physical, or professional risks.
Standard 7	Every supervisor's task is to create and maintain an on-the-job atmosphere conducive to self-esteem and care about the job and other employees, and an experience-based confidence on the part of the employees that good performance is given due recognition.
Standard 8	Employees are expected to uphold the spirit as well as the letter of the Code and be guided by the Code in all business dealings and relationships—toward one another, with government, shareholders, customers, suppliers, competitors, community, and everyone else affected by their behavior or performance in any way or to any degree.
Standard 9	The Company's property encompasses monetary values reflected in the Company's records as well as any other tangible or intangible items, rights, or claims whose loss would diminish the Company's

(continued)

value or adversely affect its earning potential. Every employee shall safeguard the Company's property. No misappropriation, neglect, or waste is to be tolerated. No employee is entitled to use the Company's property in ways not intended to serve the Company's legitimate interests.

Standard 10   Every employee is subject to complete, accurate, and timely financial accountability and/or reporting requirements as needed to assure the integrity of the Company's accounting records, financial statements, and disclosures. This includes candid cooperation with auditors, internal and external.

In particular, with respect to the Company's accounting records, employees will not knowingly:
(a) make or cause to be made any false, artificial, or misleading entry that does not accurately and properly record, in accordance with supporting facts or documents, a transaction, acquisition, or disposition of assets.
(b) fail to make or cause another person to fail to make any entry necessary to make the Company's accounting records accurate and fairly reflecting transactions, acquisitions, or dispositions of assets, or tamper with the integrity of financial reporting by making or causing another person to make false or misleading statements in presenting or interpreting the Company's performance or financial condition.

Standard 11   Any information developed or acquired by the Company is proprietary and should be safeguarded and used, like any other Company property, solely for the proper conduct of the Company's business.

All information pertaining to the Company's business that an employee obtains in the course of his or her employment is confidential unless the Company has made such information public. Unauthorized disclosure is prohibited.

Any employee who is uncertain whether something is confidential should presume that it is. No employee should attempt to obtain confidential information that does not relate to his or her employment duties.

Standard 12   The payment of normal discounts and allowances, commissions, and fees and the extension of customary courtesies in the ordinary course of business are permissible, provided that they are (1) reasonable in nature, frequency, and amount and consistent with applicable laws, and (2) properly recorded and of sufficiently limited value so they cannot be construed as bribes, payoffs, or kickbacks or as having the purpose to influence the recipients to give favored treatment to the Company's business.

Standard 13   All employees are to be treated equitably. This is a general responsibility of the Company's Chief Executive Officer. No employee is to be treated arbitrarily in a materially different way from other comparable employees. No employee should be subject to exemplary punishment, and no employee who has committed a serious violation is to be granted immunity from the enforcement of this Code.

Standard 14   This Code is not intended to impose any burdensome requirements on the personal affairs of the employees. Every employee should ensure that there is no real or apparent conflict between his or her interests and the Company's interests. Any employee having an interest or relationship requiring disclosure under the Company's conflict-of-interest policy, as currently in effect, has an affirmative duty to comply with its provisions.

Standard 15   All employees are encouraged to seek advice of their immediate superiors. Any observed violations of the Code are to be reported—through their superiors or directly to the person designated by the Company.

The Company will protect from any harmful consequences all employees who act in good faith either to comply or to assure or promote compliance with this Code.

Standard 16   Except for the protection clause in Standard 15, this Code does not constitute or grant a legal right of any nature to anyone in the Company and no standard is to be interpreted to have conferred any kinds of rights or privileges upon any employee or group of employees.

SOURCE: Stephen Landekich, *Corporate Codes of Conduct* (Montvale, N.J.: Institute of Management Accountants, 1989), pp. 95–98.

Sir Adrian Cadbury reflects on his grandfather's ethical conflicts:

> In the first place, the possibility that ethical and commercial considerations will conflict has always faced those who run companies. It is not a new problem. The difference now is that a more widespread and critical interest is being taken in our decisions and in the ethical judgments which lie behind them.
>
> Secondly, as the newspaper example demonstrates, ethical signposts do not always point in the same direction. My grandfather had to choose between opposing a war and condoning gambling. The rule that it is best to tell the truth often runs up against the rule that we should not hurt people's feelings unnecessarily. There is no simple, universal formula for solving ethical problems. We have to choose from our own codes of conduct whichever rules are appropriate to the case in hand; the outcome of those choices makes us who we are.
>
> Lastly, while it is hard enough to resolve dilemmas when our personal rules of conduct conflict, the real difficulties arise when we have to make decisions which affect the interests of others. We can work out what weighting to give to our own rules through trial and error. But business decisions require us to do the same for others by allocating weights to all the conflicting interests which may be involved.
>
> There is always a temptation to postpone difficult decisions, but it is not in society's interests that hard choices should be evaded because of public clamor or the possibility of legal action. Companies need to be encouraged to make the decisions which face them; the responsibility for providing that encouragement rests with society as a whole.[14]

Cadbury Schweppes seems to be continuing its solid traditions. Cadbury's nonexecutive chairman, Sir Graham Day, says the company "won't be motivated by the 'corporate ego' and 'national pride' that he says pushed some competitors to make acquisitions too rapidly in risky places such as Eastern Europe." [15]

Laws and ethics often overlap. Managers will face decisions that may appear to conflict with one or the other or both. Accountants may be asked to help justify positions through the process of analyzing the figures associated with the decision. Cost/benefit analysis is very important in all business endeavors, but in some cases when the issue is not clear-cut (such as many legal versus ethical decisions), the solution must be made on the basis of an underlying set of values and principles that reflect a choice of the universal right rather than the societal legal right.

CHAPTER SUMMARY

Laws are designed to protect all of the stakeholders in a business, which includes the stockholders, creditors, employees, customers, and society as a whole. Laws form a basis of what a particular society perceives as morally correct and reflect a society's

---

[14]An excerpt from "Ethical Managers Make Their Own Rules," by Sir Adrian Cadbury (September–October 1987), p. 69. Reprinted by permission of *Harvard Business Review.* Copyright © 1987 by the President and Fellows of Harvard College; all rights reserved.
[15]E. S. Browning, "Cadbury Schweppes Has No Appetite for Big Growth as '91 Profit Rises 13 Percent," *Wall Street Journal* (March 5, 1992), p. A13.

attitudes and desires about the culture in which it wishes to exist. Ethics, on the other hand, is a system of value principles or practices that form a definition of right and wrong. Thus, sometimes society may condone an act as legal although that act, in itself, may be viewed as immoral or unethical.

The laws discussed in this chapter could have immediate accounting implications because of the huge fines and penalties that can be involved. All future managers should be aware of both the legal and moral effects of a decision when choosing among alternative actions. Utilitarianism and Kantian analysis are two primary ethical theories that can be used to make ethical choices. Utilitarianism is basically a cost/benefit analysis, while Kantian analysis concentrates on performance of duty without regard to consequences and views outcomes in their relationship to fairness or justice.

The Foreign Corrupt Practices Act has two major components: it prohibits payment of bribes to foreign officials and requires maintenance of an adequate system of internal control. The Racketeer Influenced and Corrupt Organizations Act was passed to discourage organized crime from investing illegal gains in legitimate businesses. The language of the act, however, has been interpreted so broadly that many of the suits brought under it have nothing to do with organized crime. The Securities Exchange Act of 1934 puts forth regulations about stock transactions and also includes Rule 10b-5, which has been interpreted to criminalize insider trading.

Numerous laws address employer–employee relationships because of the rights and duties that exist between these parties. The Occupational Safety and Health Act requires that a company have safe working conditions; this law has significant managerial implications in terms of cost of implementation. Employee rights are also addressed in the multiple discrimination acts that are designed to prevent bias in job-related actions.

In considering their obligations to society, businesses must acknowledge the environment as part of the society in which it operates. Environmental laws have been passed that, in some instances, dictate precisely what constitutes an acceptable level of pollution.

Whistleblowing occurs when an employee exposes an illegal or unethical practice of an organization. Unfortunately, legal protections for the employee are limited. Software piracy, while illegal, is engaged in by a substantial number of people—probably because it is easy to do and hard to detect. Many companies, however, have adopted corporate codes of conduct to address the numerous issues of legal and ethical actions. Professional codes of conduct also exist for many groups of employees.

APPENDIX

Summary of the United Nations Code of Conduct[16]

1. TNCs shall respect the national sovereignty of the host country and are subject to its laws.
2. TNCs shall operate in conformity with the development policies set out by host governments and shall work seriously in contributing to achieving national goals.

[16]Source: G. R. Bassiry, "Business Ethics and the United Nations: A Code of Conduct," *SAM Management Journal* (Autumn 1990), p. 39.

3. TNCs and host countries shall negotiate contracts and agreements in good faith.

4. TNCs shall respect the social and cultural values and traditions of host countries and shall avoid practices and products which cause detrimental effects on cultural and social norms.

5. TNCs shall respect human rights and fundamental freedoms.

6. TNCs shall not interfere in host country internal affairs or engage in political activities not permitted by host countries.

7. TNCs shall not interfere in inter-governmental relations.

8. TNCs shall refrain from corrupt practices such as offering bribes or other payments to public officials of host countries.

9. TNCs shall provide for effective participation in decision-making by host country citizens.

10. TNCs shall contribute to managerial and technical training of host country citizens.

Codes of conduct are often established for professions and organizations. The United Nations decided that a code of conduct would also be appropriate for transnational companies (TNCs).

11. TNCs shall contribute to solving major problems in the balance of payments of host countries.

12. TNCs shall contribute to promoting exports.

13. TNCs shall not engage in short-term financial transfers that cause serious balance of payments difficulties.

14. TNCs shall strengthen the scientific and technological capacities of developing countries.

15. TNCs shall conform to national laws regarding consumer protection in terms of preventing health and safety hazards.

16. TNCs shall take steps to protect the environment.

17. TNCs shall disclose to the public of host countries financial and nonfinancial information regarding their activities.

18. TNCs shall receive fair and equitable treatment in host countries.

19. Host countries shall make public all laws and regulations affecting TNCs.

20. TNCs are entitled to transfer all payments legally due, subject to host country laws.

21. Host countries have the right to nationalize or expropriate TNC assets, provided that TNCs are given appropriate compensation.

22. States agree not to use TNCs as instruments to intervene in the affairs of other states.

23. Government action on behalf of TNCs shall be subject to the principle of "exhaustion of local remedies" provided in the host country. Any such action should not include coercive measures not consistent with the United Nations Charter.

GLOSSARY

Environmental Protection Agency   the agency that assures that the environmental impact statement is prepared, if necessary, and that it is acceptable for the federal activity to proceed

Ethics   the moral law; is a system of value principles or practices, and defines right and wrong

Foreign Corrupt Practices Act   a law designed to serve the basic purpose of preventing bribes from being offered or given to foreign officials (directly or indirectly) for the purpose of influencing that person (or causing that person to use his or her influence) to obtain or retain business

Grease payments   facilitating payments to minor employees

Insider   any director, officer, or owner of more than 10 percent of the shares of any one class of stock of a company registered under the Securities Exchange Act of 1934

Internal control system   a set of procedures that are concerned with authorizing transactions, protecting assets, and promoting the accuracy of financial information

Kantian analysis   an ethical theory that is based on duty and determining whether an action is intrinsically right or wrong, without regard to possible consequences; basically reflects the "golden rule"

Material   important in relation to some standard of comparison

National Environmental Policy Act   the law that requires an environmental impact statement be done for major federal activities that significantly affect the quality of the environment

Occupational Safety and Health Act   a law designed to protect the health and safety of employees while actually on the job and from job-related health effects

Predicate acts   a wide variety of racketeering crimes that include mail, wire and bankruptcy fraud, extortion, arson, murder, interference with interstate commerce by violence or threat thereof, securities fraud, and bribery

Racketeer Influenced and Corrupt Organizations Act   a law designed to discourage organized crime from investing profits from illegal activities in legitimate business

Scienter   the intent to defraud or intentional misconduct that amounts to more than mere negligence

Securities Exchange Act of 1934   a law that created the Securities and Exchange Commission and designed to regulate the secondary securities market

Situational ethics   the process of determining "right or wrong" based on the circumstances at the time and place the decision is being made

Tippees   persons who receive inside information from an insider, regardless of whether the insider used the information

Utilitarianism   an approach to ethics that considers the outcomes or consequences of the ethical choice; basically is a cost/benefit analysis

Whistleblowing   alerting the proper authorities of a firm's improper or illegal action

SELECTED BIBLIOGRAPHY

Anderson, Jack. "A Haven for Whistleblowers." *Parade Magazine* (August 18, 1991), pp. 16–17.

Axline, Larry L. "The Bottom Line on Ethics." *Journal of Accountancy* (December 1990), pp. 87–91.

Bailey, Jeff. "Concerns Mount Over Operating Methods of Plants That Incinerate Toxic Waste." *Wall Street Journal* (March 20, 1992), pp. B1, B3.

Barrett, Paul M. "Supreme Court Makes It Harder to File Civil Lawsuits Under Racketeering Law." *Wall Street Journal* (March 25, 1992), p. A3.

Carmichael, Sheena, and John Drummond. *Good Business: A Guide to Corporate Responsibility and Business Ethics* (London: Business Books Limited, 1989).

McKee, Bradford. "The Best Defense Against Pollution." *Nation's Business* (November 1991), pp. 53–54, 56.

Milken, Michael, as told to James W. Michaels and Phyllis Berman. "My Story—Michael Milken." *Forbes* (March 16, 1992), pp. 78–84ff.

Pickering, John. "Ernst Takes RICO Battle to Supreme Court." *Accounting Today* (March 16, 1992), pp. 1, 23.

Schiff, Jonathan B., and Claire B. May. "What Is Internal Control? Who Owns It?" *Management Accounting* (November 1990), pp. 37–40.

Shaw, Bill. "Foreign Corrupt Practices Act: A Legal and Moral Analysis." *Journal of Business Ethics* 7 (1988), pp. 789–95.

Singer, Andrew W. "Ethics: Are Standards Lower Overseas?" *Across the Board* (September 1991), pp. 31–34.

Stock, Gregory. *The Book of Questions: Business, Politics, and Ethics* (New York: Workman, 1991).

Surma, John P., and Albert A. Vondra. "Accounting for Environmental Costs: A Hazardous Subject." *Journal of Accountancy* (March 1992), pp. 51–55.

Sweeney, Robert B., and Howard L. Siers. "Survey: Ethics in Corporate America." *Management Accounting* (June 1990), pp. 34–35, 38–40.

Zuber, George R., and Charles G. Berry. "Assessing Environmental Risk." *Journal of Accountancy* (March 1992), pp. 43–46, 48.

END-OF-CHAPTER MATERIALS

Questions

1. Distinguish between business scandals, legal misdeeds, and ethical failures.

2. Describe the difference between legal rights and moral rights and the significance of the difference. Give three examples of how legal and moral rights differ.

3. Describe utilitarian analysis: the basic philosophy behind it, the steps necessary to successful completion of the analysis, and the flaws in the system.

4. Briefly describe Kantian analysis and how it applies to your actions toward others and others' actions toward you.

5. The FCPA requires business compliance with two major provisions. What are they?

6. List the nine interrelated components of internal control system developed in the study by Coopers & Lybrand.

7. Should U.S. multinationals be allowed to compete under the customary terms of the foreign countries in which they operate? Or should they be restricted by the FCPA, even though by doing so, those firms are placed at a disadvantage in relation to their competitors? Discuss the reasons for your choice.

8. Should other countries be pressured to pass equal or substantially equivalent FCPAs to make certain that corruption and cheating have no place in their business culture? Why or why not?

9. Discuss the implementation difficulties associated with the Racketeer Influenced and Corrupt Organizations Act.

10. List the three elements necessary to prove a RICO violation.

11. Does RICO violate, as some people have inferred, some basic principles of American justice by making the indictment the punishment?

12. As noted in the chapter, the RICO Act has been used in widely diverse situations. Do you think the RICO Act should be modified to address a more narrow spectrum of crimes? Discuss.

13. Does, in fact, either the Foreign Corrupt Practices Act or the Racketeer Influenced and Corrupt Organizations Act fulfill its mission? If so, how? If not, discuss the reasons for your answer.

14. Explain the market motivation for passage of the Securities Exchange Act of 1934.

15. Why is scienter required for prosecution under the Securities Exchange Act of 1934?

16. Discuss the concept of "material" as it relates to securities and financial statements.

17. Describe the relationship between employer and employee concerning the rights and duties each owes to the other. Give three examples of each of these rights and duties to the parties.

18. Briefly describe the wide variety of groups harmed by the various types of discrimination and the nature and extent of the harm.

19. The chapter provided two reasons for keeping the environment clean. Explain each and the results that each philosophy could have on the environment.

20. Discuss two possible justifications for businesses polluting the environment.

21. Should whistleblowers be protected by law? Why or why not?

22. Discuss the difficulties of employees who are employed at will in refusing to participate in illegal corporate activities.

23. Why is computer software copyrighted?

24. Discuss the benefits of having a corporate code of conduct.

Exercises

25. *(Terminology)* Match the numbered item on the right with the lettered term on the left:

a. Environmental Protection Agency	1. System of ethics dealing with outcomes
b. Employment at will	2. Payments made to quicken administrative procedures in foreign countries
c. Utilitarianism	3. Crimes considered to be racketeering offenses for the purposes of RICO
d. Kantian analysis	4. Alerting the proper authorities to improper or illegal business activity
e. Grease payments	5. System of ethics dealing with moral duty, regardless of consequences
f. Internal control systems	6. Set of procedures to monitor transactions protecting assets and promoting accuracy of financial information
g. Predicate acts	7. Document reviewing impact of major federal action and possible effects on the environment
h. Whistleblowing	8. Right of either employer or employee to fire or quit, respectively, at any time
i. Environmental impact statement	9. Agency charged with enforcement of federal environmental laws

26. *(Terminology)* Match the numbered item on the right with the lettered item on the left:

a. Equal Pay Act

b. Racketeer Influenced and Corrupt Organizations Act

c. Occupational Health and Safety Act

d. National Environmental Policy Act

e. Foreign Corrupt Practices Act

f. Pregnancy Discrimination Act

g. Age Discrimination in Employment Act

h. Civil Rights Act of 1964

1. Law designed to prevent discrimination on the basis of race, religion, color, creed, sex, or national origin

2. Law designed to protect the health and safety of employees while on the job and from job-related health effects

3. Law requiring an environmental impact statement before major federal action can be taken

4. Law designed to discourage organized crime from investing profits from illegal activities into legitimate businesses

5. Law designed to prevent discrimination against persons over forty years of age

6. Law designed to prevent bribes to obtain or retain business from being offered to foreign officials

7. Law designed to assure that women are paid at the same rate as men for the same job

8. Law designed to prevent discrimination against women in their childbearing years

27. *(Essay)* When companies were found to have been engaging in bribery and kickbacks in the late 1970s, many people wondered whether the firms' accountants had known of the actions and, if so, why those actions had not been reported. Accountants are also typically heavily involved in establishing the internal control procedures for organizations.

a. Should accountants (either internal or external) have the obligation of reporting to the external public any improper activities engaged in by the firm? Why or why not?

b. If accountants were required to be whistleblowers and report any corporate wrongdoing, to whom should such reports be given and why?

28. *(Essay)* One of the News Notes in the chapter indicated that insider trading was never meant to be a crime.

a. Do you believe insider trading is unethical? Why or why not?

b. Do you think insider trading should be illegal? Why or why not?

c. A janitor at a printing company finds some information on a tender offer that has not yet been provided to the public. This information is in the form of badly printed copy and was in the company's trash. The janitor buys some of the stock of the company that is going to be purchased. Is this insider trading? Discuss.

29. *(Essay)* You are the president of a major oil company. While transporting oil in international waters, one of your company's tankers began leaking. Significant damage was done to foreign shores when the oil washed up on the beaches.

    a. Should your company be held liable to foreign countries for pollution effects caused by your company? Explain your reasoning.

    b. Should American society be held liable for damage to foreign countries from non-company-specific pollution (for example, acid rain)? Discuss the rationale for your answer.

30. *(Essay)* Most consumers have some responsibility for pollution problems because of our consumption preferences. For example, we use disposable diapers because they are convenient; unfortunately, these items are not biodegradable and help create landfill problems.

    a. What are the costs and benefits of using disposable diapers?

    b. Should businesses not be allowed to make a product that is so popular? Explain.

    c. Should businesses attempt to raise prices on products that are not environmentally safe so that consumers would make alternative choices? Why or why not?

31. *(Essay)* You have just been elected president of the United States. One of your most popular platforms was that you would reduce the costs of doing business in the United States. When asked how you intended to accomplish this, you replied, "By seeking to repeal all laws that create unnecessary costs. In this manner, not only will business be better off, but the consumer will be also, since product prices will be reduced." Congress heard the message being sent and has decided to repeal all environmental protection laws. Discuss the short-term and long-term implications of such a policy.

32. *(Essay)* You are the head of a small firm in Atlanta that provides continuing education courses. One of your employees, for whom you have scheduled several finance courses in multiple locations during the next nine months, unexpectedly (but cordially) leaves the firm. He informs you that he knows some extremely competent individuals who are ready and willing to take on his lecturing responsibilities. You, however, have just recently found out that one of your old friends, Rudy Gere, has moved back to Atlanta.

    Rudy was laid off from his former job and is now unemployed. Rudy has a degree in business, but not in finance. He has never taught any finance courses. The day after you learn of your employee's resignation, you and Rudy are sitting in the sauna at your house, and he reiterates his need to find a job because of the house payment, the children's school clothes, and so forth. You ask if he is interested in teaching the finance courses for you, and he says, "That would be great! I'm sure I can get up to speed in the next three weeks before the first class."

    a. Should you have offered the job to Rudy, knowing that he was less qualified than some of the other people recommended by your previous employee? Why or why not?

    b. Assume that you did hire Rudy. At the end of each course, participants are asked to do evaluations of the course, the facilities, and the course leader (or teacher). Reading Rudy's evaluations, you learn that the participants perceive him to be "less than adequate" in terms of course knowledge and rigor. What should you do?

    c. Assume the same facts as in part (b). You discuss the matter with Rudy, and the two of you agree that he will not continue with the company. While Rudy is teaching the last of his scheduled finance courses, an employee who normally teaches the health-care courses becomes ill. Again you find yourself needing someone to go on the lecture circuit. Rudy mentions that he thinks he would do a better job in the health-care courses. Do you hire Rudy to replace the employee who is ill? Discuss the reasoning behind your answer.

33. Charity Hospital in New Orleans is losing millions of dollars each year by not billing patients for treatment or medicine they receive, according to state legislative auditor Dan Kyle. In addition, Charity cannot account for $882,742 of supplies and inventory, including almost $542,000 in drugs from the hospital pharmacy. Kyle said that in the past four years, about $4 million in drugs has been unaccounted for.

    Kyle stated that Charity "has not maintained adequate controls over charges incurred by patients. . . . Our audit revealed that effective procedures have not been developed and implemented to provide management with assurance that all charges incurred by patients are accurate and billed."

    The report also said that Charity is lacking an "effective internal audit function" to track its $50.6 million in assets and $159.2 million in operating revenues. "If they would organize and get accounting controls in place that would [save] enough money to pay for itself," Kyle said.

    (SOURCE: Ed Anderson, "Audit: Charity Losing Millions with Bad Billing Procedures" [*New Orleans*] *Times-Picayune* [March 6, 1990], p. B3.)

    Draft some recommendations for internal controls related to drugs, other supplies, and patient billings.

Cases

34. Within the last two decades, United States businesses moved from an era of minimal regulation limited to antitrust and employment legislation to the current environment that includes compliance with numerous social regulations. Businesses no longer have the freedom to design and produce products without regard to social considerations, nor do they have complete control over marketing practices and pricing policies. Social regulations have had an enormous impact on businesses, causing economic and continuity concerns. Despite the fact that there has been criticism against overregulation by the government, polls indicate that the majority of Americans continue to support most forms of social regulation.

    Listed next are five agencies that have been created for the implementation and administration of social regulations.

- Food and Drug Administration (FDA)
- Consumer Product Safety Commission (CPSC)
- Environmental Protection Agency (EPA)
- Occupational Safety and Health Administration (OSHA)
- Equal Employment Opportunity Commission (EEOC)

Required:

a. Discuss the general reasons for the dramatic increase in the social regulation of business during the last two decades.

b. For each of the five areas of social regulation administered by the agencies just listed,
    1. describe the social concerns that gave rise to each area of social regulation.
    2. discuss how each area of social regulation has impacted the business community.

(CMA)

35. According to one source, improper activities in regard to government contracts typically fall into six categories:

- outright bribery of officials involved in procurement;
- inclusion, in billings, of unallowable costs;
- defective pricing (pricing that is inaccurate, incomplete, or not current);
- overpricing of spare parts;
- mischarging of costs (costs included in wrong job); and
- delivery of hardware known to be not in compliance with contract specifications.

(SOURCE: J. D. Eiland, "And the Whistle Blows and Blows and Blows," *Today's CPA* [July/August 1989], p. 30. Published by the Texas Society of CPAs.)

a. Discuss some methods that would help alleviate each of the previous procurement improprieties.

b. Do you believe it is proper to pay people to blow the whistle on such activities? Why?

c. What difficulties could result from paying people to blow the whistle?

36. JRD Corporation, a medium-sized firm in the artificial intelligence industry, has just hired a new president, Walter Dean. With the downturn in the economy, Dean has decided that the two best methods of increasing efficiency are to downsize the firm, rather than using current physical and human resources to increase market share, and to decrease the safety elements at the plant. Among the persons he must consider for termination are: Jim Clay, a white thirty-five-year-old man with a family of four; Marie Patutsky, a white thirty-two-year-old woman engaged to be married; Steve Pine, a white forty-nine-year-old man; and Lea Green, a fifty-four-year-old African-American woman. None of these employees has ever been disciplined for any work-related problem; in fact, all of them are good employees. You are the corporate attorney for JRD, and Dean has consulted you about the legal ramifications of terminating these employees. None of them is working under contract, but they have all been with the firm for at least four years. Additionally, Dean is concerned about government interference over the reduced use of safety devices at the plant.

a. Write an opinion letter describing for Dean the possible lawsuits that could be brought by any interested party and make an estimation of the probability of success of each claim.

b. Discuss the ethics involved in dismissing any of these employees, as well as the reduction of the safety devices.

37. A number of things are rotten in the firm of Denmark, Inc., a small furniture manufacturing company. Hamlet Shakespeare is the manager of the management information system center for Denmark and, over time, has realized that the firm is engaging in a variety of what he suspects are illegal activities. As the manager of the MIS center, virtually all information concerning the enterprise is known to him, while it is available in its entirety to almost no one else. Because all of this information is at his disposal, he has been able to piece together a frightening picture of wrongdoing by the firm. From the accounting system, he has learned of three expensive gifts given to top officials in the Customs Department of Japan to facilitate the process of importing the goods into Japan. Further, such gifts were not properly recorded in the accounting records.

Hamlet also found that at least three times, Denmark was the recipient of moneys obtained through mail and wire fraud. To top it all off, the CEO of Denmark, Richard T. Third, was aware of these irregularities and, in an attempt to keep it all straight, asked Hamlet to make a copy of the spreadsheet Lotus 1-2-3 (against its license agreement) to project future profits generated by these activities. Hamlet is beside himself with worry: he faces a legal and ethical dilemma.

a. Should he tell anyone of these irregularities, and if so, whom?

b. If Hamlet does not tell anyone, will he be implicated in the misdeeds?

c. If he does tell anyone, will he be fired or lauded as an honest and loyal employee?

38. Customized Openings, Inc. is a one-hundred-year-old, family-owned company that produces high-quality windows and doors. Yearly sales revenues have averaged $80 million over the last eight years.

   John Weller and Michael Fox have both been with the company for about thirty years. Over the years, they have built a strong personal and working relationship. Having been chairperson of the board for over ten years, Weller wished to continue working at Customized Openings but in a lesser role. Hence, he asked to be appointed VP of long-term planning, with no reduction in his current salary. The board quickly approved both his appointment and his salary request, appointing Fox chairperson in the process.

   The board then turned to an executive recruiting firm to find a replacement for Fox. The best candidate was Eric Witt, who was hired as president of Customized Openings. In addition to his technical qualifications, Witt believed that unless business adheres to a minimum standard of justice, giving recognition to the rights of those engaged in business, business practice becomes impossible; therefore, practices in advertising, hiring, and so on, need to be guided by moral norms.

   Two years after Witt's arrival, Customized Openings' sales volume had grown from $80 to $100 million. This was easily traceable to Witt's efforts in cost efficiency, productivity, cost/benefit analysis, performance evaluation, elimination of non-value-added activities, and the like.

   In his third year, Witt asked the VP of human resources to evaluate the performance of every VP to determine if any VP was being paid more or less than the market suggested appropriate. The VP reported that Weller was being paid significantly higher than any other VP in both this type of business and in the company. In confidence, the VP of human resources recommended that Weller's salary be reduced.

   Witt's secretary (who had previously been Weller's) leaked the news to Weller. Upset and angry, Weller asked Fox to fire Witt. So despite positive performance, Witt was fired.

   Deciding that discussion with Fox would lead nowhere, Witt did not challenge Fox's decision. Witt did, however, feel that what had happened to him was immoral. This feeling persisted even though he'd seen the same thing happen to others in the business world. The ambitious simply learn to tolerate it (so it is commonly held) if they seek success as a business executive.

   While looking for another position, Witt spent some of his leisure time reading several articles on business morality. One question often seen was: "Would you like to see it on TV tomorrow morning? If not, what you're about to do, or have done, undoubtedly violates your moral principles." Another read: "Would the boy or girl in you be proud of the man or woman you have become? If not, what you're doing or about to do undoubtedly violates your moral principles."

Witt became even further intrigued when he discovered a piece on Kohlberg's three stages of moral development: the preconventional, the conventional, and the postconventional. The first is often the perspective of children where the self only is considered. Avoiding punishment is their only motivation. A person with a conventional perspective makes his or her group norms the justification for behavior. Witt realized that this is the viewpoint from which Fox (and Weller) see the world. Finally, the postconventional perspective follows a universal outlook, looking to general moral principles. The article concluded that a preconventional (self) or conventional (group) perspective provides no means for the resolution of conflict. The only way to avoid win-lose conflicts was to appeal to moral principles.

a. What are the relevant facts in this case?
b. What are the ethical issues?
c. Who are the primary stakeholders?
d. What were the possible alternative management solutions to the case—from the point of view of Fox, the chairperson of the board?
e. What are the ethics of each of the management solution alternatives?
f. What actions should have been taken?

(From Nabil Hassan, Herbert E. Brown, and Paula M. Saunders, "Management Accounting Case Study: Customized Openings, Inc.," *Management Accounting Campus Report* [Spring 1992], pp. 4–5. Copyright © 1992 IMA [formerly NAA].)

▌ Ethics Discussion

39. "Few trends could so thoroughly undermine the very foundation of our free society," writes Milton Friedman in *Capitalism and Freedom,* "as the acceptance by corporate officials of a social responsibility other than to make as much money for their shareholders as possible."

a. Discuss your reactions to this quote from a legal standpoint.
b. Discuss your reactions to this quote from an ethical standpoint.
c. How would you resolve any conflicts that exist between your two answers?

40. Many individuals, when asked, say that they know that unauthorized copying of computer software is illegal, but they either do not care or justify their behavior by referencing the "high" cost of the software.

a. Discuss the legitimacy of such rationale.
b. Assume, as a manager, you either pirate software or allow pirating to occur in your organization. Discuss the ethical message you are sending to your employees.

41. The Tara Corporation has adopted a corporate code of conduct that discusses a variety of legal and ethical issues. The code has been duplicated and distributed among all the employees.

Scarlett O'Hara (the head of the computer department) has recently purchased a variety of computer software packages on a trial basis for the firm. Several of the packages are exactly what the company needs. Rhett Butler (Tara's chief financial officer) has asked Scarlett to simply make an appropriate number of copies and distribute them to everyone in the MIS area.

Scarlett demurs and tells Rhett that she will not engage in such activity for two reasons: (1) it is illegal and (2) it is against the spirit of the code of conduct (although not mentioned specifically). Rhett charmingly informs Scarlett that Georgia is an employment at will state and unemployment is very high at the moment.

a. What options does Scarlett have?
b. What are the costs and benefits of each option?
c. What is the best choice for Scarlett?

42. S. Stewart Joslin figured he was being a good citizen when he let the Internal Revenue Service know his bosses weren't forwarding the income taxes they had withheld from employees' paychecks. Instead, Joslin, the operations manager for a defunct New Orleans computer firm, said he is being held liable for the taxes, totaling $69,000. For nearly nine months in 1987 and 1988, Joslin said, he persistently pressed the computer firm's executives to pay [the taxes]. And when that failed he arranged to let the IRS know about the delinquency. Joslin was apparently cited for the tax liability because he had the authority to sign payroll checks.

The case against Joslin is not unique. Recently, columnist Jack Anderson wrote about the comptroller for a landscaping firm in Austin, Texas, who quit and notified the IRS after her bosses refused to turn over unpaid withholding taxes. Anderson reported that the IRS still held her liable for the $120,000 tax bill.

[There is also] a case in which a personnel manager for a San Francisco firm has been held responsible for $600,000 in unpaid taxes after the company declared bankruptcy and its owners left for England.

(SOURCE: Bruce Alpert, "Whistleblowers Get IRS Sting," [*New Orleans*] *Times-Picayune* [September 25, 1991], p. C1.)

a. Do you believe that it was Joslin's responsibility to see that the taxes were paid?
b. Under the circumstances, do you think Joslin and the others should have blown the whistle? Why or why not?
c. If you found yourself in similar circumstances, knowing what happened to Mr. Joslin and the others, would you blow the whistle? Why or why not?

PRESENT VALUE TABLES

TABLE 1 PRESENT VALUE OF $1

Period	1.00%	2.00%	3.00%	4.00%	5.00%	6.00%	7.00%	8.00%	9.00%	9.50%	10.00%	10.50%	11.00%
1	0.9901	0.9804	0.9709	0.9615	0.9524	0.9434	0.9346	0.9259	0.9174	0.9132	0.9091	0.9050	0.9009
2	0.9803	0.9612	0.9426	0.9246	0.9070	0.8900	0.8734	0.8573	0.8417	0.8340	0.8265	0.8190	0.8116
3	0.9706	0.9423	0.9151	0.8890	0.8638	0.8396	0.8163	0.7938	0.7722	0.7617	0.7513	0.7412	0.7312
4	0.9610	0.9239	0.8885	0.8548	0.8227	0.7921	0.7629	0.7350	0.7084	0.6956	0.6830	0.6707	0.6587
5	0.9515	0.9057	0.8626	0.8219	0.7835	0.7473	0.7130	0.6806	0.6499	0.6352	0.6209	0.6070	0.5935
6	0.9421	0.8880	0.8375	0.7903	0.7462	0.7050	0.6663	0.6302	0.5963	0.5801	0.5645	0.5493	0.5346
7	0.9327	0.8706	0.8131	0.7599	0.7107	0.6651	0.6228	0.5835	0.5470	0.5298	0.5132	0.4971	0.4817
8	0.9235	0.8535	0.7894	0.7307	0.6768	0.6274	0.5820	0.5403	0.5019	0.4838	0.4665	0.4499	0.4339
9	0.9143	0.8368	0.7664	0.7026	0.6446	0.5919	0.5439	0.5003	0.4604	0.4419	0.4241	0.4071	0.3909
10	0.9053	0.8204	0.7441	0.6756	0.6139	0.5584	0.5084	0.4632	0.4224	0.4035	0.3855	0.3685	0.3522
11	0.8963	0.8043	0.7224	0.6496	0.5847	0.5268	0.4751	0.4289	0.3875	0.3685	0.3505	0.3334	0.3173
12	0.8875	0.7885	0.7014	0.6246	0.5568	0.4970	0.4440	0.3971	0.3555	0.3365	0.3186	0.3018	0.2858
13	0.8787	0.7730	0.6810	0.6006	0.5303	0.4688	0.4150	0.3677	0.3262	0.3073	0.2897	0.2731	0.2575
14	0.8700	0.7579	0.6611	0.5775	0.5051	0.4423	0.3878	0.3405	0.2993	0.2807	0.2633	0.2471	0.2320
15	0.8614	0.7430	0.6419	0.5553	0.4810	0.4173	0.3625	0.3152	0.2745	0.2563	0.2394	0.2237	0.2090
16	0.8528	0.7285	0.6232	0.5339	0.4581	0.3937	0.3387	0.2919	0.2519	0.2341	0.2176	0.2024	0.1883
17	0.8444	0.7142	0.6050	0.5134	0.4363	0.3714	0.3166	0.2703	0.2311	0.2138	0.1978	0.1832	0.1696
18	0.8360	0.7002	0.5874	0.4936	0.4155	0.3503	0.2959	0.2503	0.2120	0.1952	0.1799	0.1658	0.1528
19	0.8277	0.6864	0.5703	0.4746	0.3957	0.3305	0.2765	0.2317	0.1945	0.1783	0.1635	0.1500	0.1377
20	0.8195	0.6730	0.5537	0.4564	0.3769	0.3118	0.2584	0.2146	0.1784	0.1628	0.1486	0.1358	0.1240
21	0.8114	0.6598	0.5376	0.4388	0.3589	0.2942	0.2415	0.1987	0.1637	0.1487	0.1351	0.1229	0.1117
22	0.8034	0.6468	0.5219	0.4220	0.3419	0.2775	0.2257	0.1839	0.1502	0.1358	0.1229	0.1112	0.1007
23	0.7954	0.6342	0.5067	0.4057	0.3256	0.2618	0.2110	0.1703	0.1378	0.1240	0.1117	0.1006	0.0907
24	0.7876	0.6217	0.4919	0.3901	0.3101	0.2470	0.1972	0.1577	0.1264	0.1133	0.1015	0.0911	0.0817
25	0.7798	0.6095	0.4776	0.3751	0.2953	0.2330	0.1843	0.1460	0.1160	0.1034	0.0923	0.0824	0.0736
26	0.7721	0.5976	0.4637	0.3607	0.2812	0.2198	0.1722	0.1352	0.1064	0.0945	0.0839	0.0746	0.0663
27	0.7644	0.5859	0.4502	0.3468	0.2679	0.2074	0.1609	0.1252	0.0976	0.0863	0.0763	0.0675	0.0597
28	0.7568	0.5744	0.4371	0.3335	0.2551	0.1956	0.1504	0.1159	0.0896	0.0788	0.0693	0.0611	0.0538
29	0.7493	0.5631	0.4244	0.3207	0.2430	0.1846	0.1406	0.1073	0.0822	0.0719	0.0630	0.0553	0.0485
30	0.7419	0.5521	0.4120	0.3083	0.2314	0.1741	0.1314	0.0994	0.0754	0.0657	0.0573	0.0500	0.0437
31	0.7346	0.5413	0.4000	0.2965	0.2204	0.1643	0.1228	0.0920	0.0692	0.0600	0.0521	0.0453	0.0394
32	0.7273	0.5306	0.3883	0.2851	0.2099	0.1550	0.1147	0.0852	0.0634	0.0058	0.0474	0.0410	0.0355
33	0.7201	0.5202	0.3770	0.2741	0.1999	0.1462	0.1072	0.0789	0.0582	0.0500	0.0431	0.0371	0.0319
34	0.7130	0.5100	0.3660	0.2636	0.1904	0.1379	0.1002	0.0731	0.0534	0.0457	0.0391	0.0336	0.0288
35	0.7059	0.5000	0.3554	0.2534	0.1813	0.1301	0.0937	0.0676	0.0490	0.0417	0.0356	0.0304	0.0259
36	0.6989	0.4902	0.3450	0.2437	0.1727	0.1227	0.0875	0.0626	0.0449	0.0381	0.0324	0.0275	0.0234
37	0.6920	0.4806	0.3350	0.2343	0.1644	0.1158	0.0818	8.0580	0.0412	0.0348	0.0294	0.0249	0.0210
38	0.6852	0.4712	0.3252	0.2253	0.1566	0.1092	0.0765	0.0537	0.0378	0.0318	0.0267	0.0225	0.0190
39	0.6784	0.4620	0.3158	0.2166	0.1492	0.1031	0.0715	0.0497	0.0347	0.0290	0.0243	0.0204	0.0171
40	0.6717	0.4529	0.3066	0.2083	0.1421	0.0972	0.0668	0.0460	0.0318	0.0265	0.0221	0.0184	0.0154
41	0.6650	0.4440	0.2976	0.2003	0.1353	0.0917	0.0624	0.0426	0.0292	0.0242	0.0201	0.0167	0.0139
42	0.6584	0.4353	0.2890	0.1926	0.1288	0.0865	0.0583	0.0395	0.0268	0.0221	0.0183	0.0151	0.0125
43	0.6519	0.4268	0.2805	0.1852	0.1227	0.0816	0.0545	0.0365	0.0246	0.0202	0.0166	0.0137	0.0113
44	0.6455	0.4184	0.2724	0.1781	0.1169	0.0770	0.0510	0.0338	0.0226	0.0184	0.0151	0.0124	0.0101
45	0.6391	0.4102	0.2644	0.1712	0.1113	0.0727	0.0476	0.0313	0.0207	0.0168	0.0137	0.0112	0.0091
46	0.6327	0.4022	0.2567	0.1646	0.1060	0.0685	0.0445	0.0290	0.0190	0.0154	0.0125	0.0101	0.0082
47	0.6265	0.3943	0.2493	0.1583	0.1010	0.0647	0.0416	0.0269	0.0174	0.0141	0.0113	0.0092	0.0074
48	0.6203	0.3865	0.2420	0.1522	0.0961	0.0610	0.0389	0.0249	0.0160	0.0128	0.0103	0.0083	0.0067
49	0.6141	0.3790	0.2350	0.1463	0.0916	0.0576	0.0363	0.0230	0.0147	0.0117	0.0094	0.0075	0.0060
50	0.6080	0.3715	0.2281	0.1407	0.0872	0.0543	0.0340	0.0213	0.0135	0.0107	0.0085	0.0068	0.0054

11.50%	12.00%	12.50%	13.00%	13.50%	14.00%	14.50%	15.00%	15.50%	16.00%	17.00%	18.00%	19.00%	20.00%
0.8969	0.8929	0.8889	0.8850	0.8811	0.8772	0.8734	0.8696	0.8658	0.8621	0.8547	0.8475	0.8403	0.8333
0.8044	0.7972	0.7901	0.7832	0.7763	0.7695	0.7628	0.7561	0.7496	0.7432	0.7305	0.7182	0.7062	0.6944
0.7214	0.7118	0.7023	0.6931	0.6839	0.6750	0.6662	0.6575	0.6490	0.6407	0.6244	0.6086	0.5934	0.5787
0.6470	0.6355	0.6243	0.6133	0.6026	0.5921	0.5818	0.5718	0.5619	0.5523	0.5337	0.5158	0.4987	0.4823
0.5803	0.5674	0.5549	0.5428	0.5309	0.5194	0.5081	0.4972	0.4865	0.4761	0.4561	0.4371	0.4191	0.4019
0.5204	0.5066	0.4933	0.4803	0.4678	0.4556	0.4438	0.4323	0.4212	0.4104	0.3898	0.3704	0.3521	0.3349
0.4667	0.4524	0.4385	0.4251	0.4121	0.3996	0.3876	0.3759	0.3647	0.3538	0.3332	0.3139	0.2959	0.2791
0.4186	0.4039	0.3897	0.3762	0.3631	0.3506	0.3385	0.3269	0.3158	0.3050	0.2848	0.2660	0.2487	0.2326
0.3754	0.3606	0.3464	0.3329	0.3199	0.3075	0.2956	0.2843	0.2734	0.2630	0.2434	0.2255	0.2090	0.1938
0.3367	0.3220	0.3080	0.2946	0.2819	0.2697	0.2582	0.2472	0.2367	0.2267	0.2080	0.1911	0.1756	0.1615
0.3020	0.2875	0.2737	0.2607	0.2483	0.2366	0.2255	0.2149	0.2049	0.1954	0.1778	0.1619	0.1476	0.1346
0.2708	0.2567	0.2433	0.2307	0.2188	0.2076	0.1969	0.1869	0.1774	0.1685	0.1520	0.1372	0.1240	0.1122
0.2429	0.2292	0.2163	0.2042	0.1928	0.1821	0.1720	0.1625	0.1536	0.1452	0.1299	0.1163	0.1042	0.0935
0.2179	0.2046	0.1923	0.1807	0.1699	0.1597	0.1502	0.1413	0.1330	0.1252	0.1110	0.0986	0.0876	0.0779
0.1954	0.1827	0.1709	0.1599	0.1496	0.1401	0.1312	0.1229	0.1152	0.1079	0.0949	0.0835	0.0736	0.0649
0.1752	0.1631	0.1519	0.1415	0.1319	0.1229	0.1146	0.1069	0.0997	0.0930	0.0811	0.0708	0.0618	0.0541
0.1572	0.1456	0.1350	0.1252	0.1162	0.1078	0.1001	0.0929	0.0863	0.0802	0.0693	0.0600	0.0520	0.0451
0.1410	0.1300	0.1200	0.1108	0.1024	0.0946	0.0874	0.0808	0.0747	0.0691	0.0593	0.0508	0.0437	0.0376
0.1264	0.1161	0.1067	0.0981	0.0902	0.0830	0.0763	0.0703	0.0647	0.0596	0.0506	0.0431	0.0367	0.0313
0.1134	0.1037	0.0948	0.0868	0.0795	0.0728	0.0667	0.0611	0.0560	0.0514	0.0433	0.0365	0.0308	0.0261
0.1017	0.0926	0.0843	0.0768	0.0700	0.0638	0.0582	0.0531	0.0485	0.0443	0.0370	0.0309	0.0259	0.0217
0.0912	0.0826	0.0749	0.0680	0.0617	0.0560	0.0509	0.0462	0.0420	0.0382	0.0316	0.0262	0.0218	0.0181
0.0818	0.0738	0.0666	0.0601	0.0543	0.0491	0.0444	0.0402	0.0364	0.0329	0.0270	0.0222	0.0183	0.0151
0.0734	0.0659	0.0592	0.0532	0.0479	0.0431	0.0388	0.0349	0.0315	0.0284	0.0231	0.0188	0.0154	0.0126
0.0658	0.0588	0.0526	0.0471	0.0422	0.0378	0.0339	0.0304	0.0273	0.0245	0.0197	0.0160	0.0129	0.0105
0.0590	0.0525	0.0468	0.0417	0.0372	0.0332	0.0296	0.0264	0.0236	0.0211	0.0169	0.0135	0.0109	0.0087
0.0529	0.0469	0.0416	0.0369	0.0327	0.0291	0.0258	0.0230	0.0204	0.0182	0.0144	0.0115	0.0091	0.0073
0.0475	0.0419	0.0370	0.0326	0.0289	0.0255	0.0226	0.0200	0.0177	0.0157	0.0123	0.0097	0.0077	0.0061
0.0426	0.0374	0.0329	0.0289	0.0254	0.0224	0.0197	0.0174	0.0153	0.0135	0.0105	0.0082	0.0064	0.0051
0.0382	0.0334	0.0292	0.0256	0.0224	0.0196	0.0172	0.0151	0.0133	0.0117	0.0090	0.0070	0.0054	0.0042
0.0342	0.0298	0.0260	0.0226	0.0197	0.0172	0.0150	0.0131	0.0115	0.0100	0.0077	0.0059	0.0046	0.0035
0.0307	0.0266	0.0231	0.0200	0.0174	0.0151	0.0131	0.0114	0.0099	0.0087	0.0066	0.0050	0.0038	0.0029
0.0275	0.0238	0.0205	0.0177	0.0153	0.0133	0.0115	0.0099	0.0086	0.0075	0.0056	0.0043	0.0032	0.0024
0.0247	0.0212	0.0182	0.0157	0.0135	0.0116	0.0100	0.0088	0.0075	0.0064	0.0048	0.0036	0.0027	0.0020
0.0222	0.0189	0.0162	0.0139	0.0119	0.0102	0.0088	0.0075	0.0065	0.0056	0.0041	0.0031	0.0023	0.0017
0.0199	0.0169	0.0144	0.0123	0.0105	0.0089	0.0076	0.0065	0.0056	0.0048	0.0035	0.0026	0.0019	0.0014
0.0178	0.0151	0.0128	0.0109	0.0092	0.0078	0.0067	0.0057	0.0048	0.0041	0.0030	0.0022	0.0016	0.0012
0.0160	0.0135	0.0114	0.0096	0.0081	0.0069	0.0058	0.0049	0.0042	0.0036	0.0026	0.0019	0.0014	0.0010
0.0143	0.0120	0.0101	0.0085	0.0072	0.0060	0.0051	0.0043	0.0036	0.0031	0.0022	0.0016	0.0011	0.0008
0.0129	0.0108	0.0090	0.0075	0.0063	0.0053	0.0044	0.0037	0.0031	0.0026	0.0019	0.0013	0.0010	0.0007
0.0115	0.0096	0.0080	0.0067	0.0056	0.0046	0.0039	0.0033	0.0027	0.0023	0.0016	0.0011	0.0008	0.0006
0.0103	0.0086	0.0077	0.0059	0.0049	0.0041	0.0034	0.0028	0.0024	0.0020	0.0014	0.0010	0.0007	0.0005
0.0093	0.0077	0.0063	0.0052	0.0043	0.0036	0.0030	0.0025	0.0020	0.0017	0.0012	0.0008	0.0006	0.0004
0.0083	0.0068	0.0056	0.0046	0.0038	0.0031	0.0026	0.0021	0.0018	0.0015	0.0010	0.0007	0.0005	0.0003
0.0075	0.0061	0.0050	0.0041	0.0034	0.0028	0.0023	0.0019	0.0015	0.0013	0.0009	0.0006	0.0004	0.0003
0.0067	0.0054	0.0044	0.0036	0.0030	0.0024	0.0020	0.0016	0.0013	0.0011	0.0007	0.0005	0.0003	0.0002
0.0060	0.0049	0.0039	0.0032	0.0026	0.0021	0.0017	0.0014	0.0011	0.0009	0.0006	0.0004	0.0003	0.0002
0.0054	0.0043	0.0035	0.0028	0.0023	0.0019	0.0015	0.0012	0.0010	0.0008	0.0005	0.0004	0.0002	0.0002
0.0048	0.0039	0.0031	0.0025	0.0020	0.0016	0.0013	0.0011	0.0009	0.0007	0.0005	0.0003	0.0002	0.0001
0.0043	0.0035	0.0028	0.0022	0.0018	0.0014	0.0012	0.0009	0.0007	0.0006	0.0004	0.0003	0.0002	0.0001

Period	1.00%	2.00%	3.00%	4.00%	5.00%	6.00%	7.00%	8.00%	9.00%	9.50%	10.00%	10.50%	11.00%
1	0.9901	0.9804	0.9709	0.9615	0.0524	0.9434	0.9346	0.9259	0.9174	0.9132	0.9091	0.9050	0.9009
2	1.9704	1.9416	1.9135	1.8861	1.8594	1.8334	1.8080	1.7833	1.7591	1.7473	1.7355	1.7240	1.7125
3	2.9410	2.8839	2.8286	2.7751	2.7233	2.6730	2.6243	2.5771	2.5313	2.5089	2.4869	2.4651	2.4437
4	3.9020	3.8077	3.7171	3.6299	3.5460	3.4651	3.3872	3.3121	3.2397	3.2045	3.1699	3.1359	3.1025
5	4.8534	4.7135	4.5797	4.4518	4.3295	4.2124	4.1002	3.9927	3.8897	3.8397	3.7908	3.7429	3.6959
6	5.7955	5.6014	5.4172	5.2421	5.0757	4.9173	4.7665	4.6229	4.4859	4.4198	4.3553	4.2922	4.2305
7	6.7282	6.4720	6.2303	6.0021	5.7864	5.5824	5.3893	5.2064	5.0330	4.9496	4.8684	4.7893	4.7122
8	7.6517	7.3255	7.0197	6.7327	6.4632	6.2098	5.9713	5.7466	5.5348	5.4334	5.3349	5.2392	5.1461
9	8.5660	8.1622	7.7861	7.4353	7.1078	6.8017	6.5152	6.2469	5.9953	5.8753	5.7590	5.6463	5.5371
10	9.4713	8.9826	8.5302	8.1109	7.7217	7.3601	7.0236	6.7101	6.4177	6.2788	6.1446	6.0148	5.8892
11	10.3676	9.7869	9.2526	8.7605	8.3064	7.8869	7.4987	7.1390	6.8052	6.6473	6.4951	6.3482	6.2065
12	11.2551	10.5753	9.9540	9.3851	8.8633	8.3838	7.9427	7.5361	7.1607	6.9838	6.8137	6.6500	6.4924
13	12.1337	11.3484	10.6350	9.9857	9.3936	8.8527	8.3577	7.9038	7.4869	7.2912	7.1034	6.9230	6.7499
14	13.0037	12.1063	11.2961	10.5631	9.8986	9.2950	8.7455	8.2442	7.7862	7.5719	7.3667	7.1702	6.9819
15	13.8651	12.8493	11.9379	11.1184	10.3797	9.7123	9.1079	8.5595	8.0607	7.8282	7.6061	7.3938	7.1909
16	14.7179	13.5777	12.5611	11.6523	10.8378	10.1059	9.4467	8.8514	8.3126	8.0623	7.8237	7.5962	7.3792
17	15.5623	14.2919	13.1661	12.1657	11.2741	10.4773	9.7632	9.1216	8.5436	8.2760	8.0216	7.7794	7.5488
18	16.3983	14.9920	13.7535	12.6593	11.6896	10.8276	10.0591	9.3719	8.7556	8.4713	8.2014	7.9452	7.7016
19	17.2260	15.6785	14.3238	13.1339	12.0853	11.1581	10.3356	9.6036	8.9501	8.6496	8.3649	8.0952	7.8393
20	18.0456	16.3514	14.8775	13.5903	12.4622	11.4699	10.5940	9.8182	9.1286	8.8124	8.5136	8.2309	7.9633
21	18.8570	17.0112	15.4150	14.0292	12.8212	11.7641	10.8355	10.0168	9.2922	8.9611	8.6487	8.3538	8.0751
22	19.6604	17.6581	15.9369	14.4511	13.1630	12.0416	11.0612	10.2007	9.4424	9.0969	8.7715	8.4649	8.1757
23	20.4558	18.2922	16.4436	14.8568	13.4886	12.3034	11.2722	10.3711	9.5802	9.2209	8.8832	8.5656	8.2664
24	21.2434	18.9139	16.9355	15.2470	13.7986	12.5504	11.4693	10.5288	9.7066	9.3342	8.9847	8.6566	8.3481
25	22.0232	19.5235	17.4132	15.6221	14.0939	12.7834	11.6536	10.6748	9.8226	9.4376	9.0770	8.7390	8.4217
26	22.7952	20.1210	17.8768	15.9828	14.3752	13.0032	11.8258	10.8100	9.9290	9.5320	9.1610	8.8136	8.4881
27	23.5596	20.7069	18.3270	16.3296	14.6430	13.2105	11.9867	10.9352	10.0266	9.6183	9.2372	8.8811	8.5478
28	24.3164	21.2813	18.7641	16.6631	14.8981	13.4062	12.1371	11.0511	10.1161	9.6971	9.3066	8.9422	8.6016
29	25.0658	21.8444	19.1885	16.9837	15.1411	13.5907	12.2777	11.1584	10.1983	9.7690	9.3696	8.9974	8.6501
30	25.8077	22.3965	19.6004	17.2920	15.3725	13.7648	12.4090	11.2578	10.2737	9.8347	9.4269	9.0474	8.6938
31	26.5423	22.9377	20.0004	17.5885	15.5928	13.9291	12.5318	11.3498	10.3428	9.8947	9.4790	9.0927	8.7332
32	27.2696	23.4683	20.3888	17.8736	15.8027	14.0840	12.6466	11.4350	10.4062	9.9495	9.5264	9.1337	8.7686
33	27.9897	23.9886	20.7658	18.1477	16.0026	14.2302	12.7538	11.5139	10.4664	9.9996	9.5694	9.1707	8.8005
34	28.7027	24.4986	21.1318	18.4112	16.1929	14.3681	12.8540	11.5869	10.5178	10.0453	9.6086	9.2043	8.8293
35	29.4086	24.9986	21.4872	18.6646	16.3742	14.4983	12.9477	11.6546	10.5668	10.0870	9.6442	9.2347	8.8552
36	30.1075	25.4888	21.8323	18.9083	16.5469	14.6210	13.0352	11.7172	10.6118	10.1251	9.6765	9.2621	8.8786
37	30.7995	25.9695	22.1672	19.1426	16.7113	14.7368	13.1170	11.7752	10.6530	10.1599	9.7059	9.2870	8.8996
38	31.4847	26.4406	22.4925	19.3679	16.8679	14.8460	13.1935	11.8289	10.6908	10.1917	9.7327	9.3095	8.9186
39	32.1630	26.9026	22.8082	19.5845	17.0170	14.9491	13.2649	11.8786	10.7255	10.2207	9.7570	9.3299	8.9357
40	32.8347	27.3555	23.1148	19.7928	17.1591	15.0463	13.3317	11.9246	10.7574	10.2473	9.7791	9.3483	8.9511
41	33.4997	27.7995	23.4124	19.9931	17.2944	15.1380	13.3941	11.9672	10.7866	10.2715	9.7991	9.3650	8.9649
42	34.1581	28.2348	23.7014	20.1856	17.4232	15.2245	13.4525	12.0067	10.8134	10.2936	9.8174	9.3801	8.9774
43	34.8100	28.6616	23.9819	20.3708	17.5459	15.3062	13.5070	12.0432	10.8380	10.3138	9.8340	9.3937	8.9887
44	35.4555	29.0800	24.2543	20.5488	17.6628	15.3832	13.5579	12.0771	10.8605	10.3322	9.8491	9.4061	8.9988
45	36.0945	29.4902	24.5187	20.7200	17.7741	15.4558	13.6055	12.1084	10.8812	10.3490	9.8628	9.4163	9.0079
46	36.7272	29.8923	24.7755	20.8847	17.8801	15.5244	13.6500	12.1374	10.9002	10.3644	9.8753	9.4274	9.0161
47	37.3537	30.2866	25.0247	21.0429	17.9810	15.5890	13.6916	12.1643	10.9176	10.3785	9.8866	9.4366	9.0236
48	37.9740	30.6731	25.2667	21.1951	18.0772	15.6500	13.7305	12.1891	10.9336	10.3913	9.8969	9.4449	9.0302
49	38.5881	31.0521	25.5017	21.3415	18.1687	15.7076	13.7668	12.2122	10.9482	10.4030	9.9063	9.4524	9.0362
50	39.1961	31.4236	25.7298	21.4822	18.2559	15.7619	13.8008	12.2335	10.9617	10.4137	9.9148	9.4591	9.0417

11.50%	12.00%	12.50%	13.00%	13.50%	14.00%	14.50%	15.00%	15.50%	16.00%	17.00%	18.00%	19.00%	20.00%
0.8969	0.8929	0.8889	0.8850	0.8811	0.8772	0.8734	0.8696	0.8658	0.8621	0.8547	0.8475	0.8403	0.8333
1.7012	1.6901	1.6790	1.6681	1.6573	1.6467	1.6361	1.6257	1.6154	1.6052	1.5852	1.5656	1.5465	1.5278
2.4226	2.4018	2.3813	2.3612	2.3413	2.3216	2.3023	2.2832	2.2644	2.2459	2.2096	2.1743	2.1399	2.1065
3.0696	3.0374	3.0056	2.9745	2.9438	2.9137	2.8841	2.8850	2.8263	2.7982	2.7432	2.6901	2.6386	2.5887
3.6499	3.6048	3.5606	3.5172	3.4747	3.4331	3.3922	3.3522	3.3129	3.2743	3.1994	3.1272	3.0576	2.9906
4.1703	4.1114	4.0538	3.9976	3.9425	3.8887	3.8360	3.7845	3.7341	3.6847	3.5892	3.4976	3.4098	3.3255
4.6370	4.5638	4.4923	4.4226	4.3546	4.2883	4.2236	4.1604	4.0988	4.0386	3.9224	3.8115	3.7057	3.6046
5.0556	4.9676	4.8821	4.7988	4.7177	4.6389	4.5621	4.4873	4.4145	4.3436	4.2072	4.0776	3.9544	3.8372
5.4311	5.3283	5.2285	5.1317	5.0377	4.9464	4.8577	4.7716	4.6879	4.6065	4.4506	4.3030	4.1633	4.0310
5.7678	5.6502	5.5364	5.4262	5.3195	5.2161	5.1159	5.0188	4.9246	4.8332	4.6586	4.4941	4.3389	4.1925
6.0698	5.9377	5.8102	5.6869	5.5679	5.4527	5.3414	5.2337	5.1295	5.0286	4.8364	4.6560	4.4865	4.3271
6.3406	6.1944	6.0535	5.9177	5.7867	5.6603	5.5383	5.4206	5.3069	5.1971	4.9884	4.7932	4.6105	4.4392
6.5835	6.4236	6.2698	6.1218	5.9794	5.8424	5.7103	5.5832	5.4606	5.3423	5.1183	4.9095	4.7147	4.5327
6.8013	6.6282	6.4620	6.3025	6.1493	6.0021	5.8606	5.7245	5.5936	5.4675	5.2293	5.0081	4.8023	4.6106
6.9967	6.8109	6.6329	6.4624	6.2989	6.1422	5.9918	5.8474	5.7087	5.5755	5.3242	5.0916	4.8759	4.6755
7.1719	6.9740	6.7848	6.6039	6.4308	6.2651	6.1063	5.9542	5.8084	5.6685	5.4053	5.1624	4.9377	4.7296
7.3291	7.1196	6.9198	6.7291	6.5469	6.3729	6.2064	6.0472	5.8947	5.7487	5.4746	5.2223	4.9897	4.7746
7.4700	7.2497	7.0398	6.8399	6.6493	6.4674	6.2938	6.1280	5.9695	5.8179	5.5339	5.2732	5.0333	4.8122
7.5964	7.3658	7.1465	6.9380	6.7395	6.5504	6.3701	6.1982	6.0342	5.8775	5.5845	5.3162	5.0700	4.8435
7.7098	7.4694	7.2414	7.0248	6.8189	6.6231	6.4368	6.2593	6.0902	5.9288	5.6278	5.3528	5.1009	4.8696
7.8115	7.5620	7.3257	7.1016	6.8889	6.6870	6.4950	6.3125	6.1387	5.9731	5.6648	5.3837	5.1268	4.8913
7.9027	7.6447	7.4006	7.1695	6.9506	6.7429	6.5459	6.3587	6.1807	6.0113	5.6964	5.4099	5.1486	4.9094
7.9845	7.7184	7.4672	7.2297	7.0049	6.7921	6.5903	6.3988	6.2170	6.0443	5.7234	5.4321	5.1669	4.9245
8.0578	7.7843	7.5264	7.2829	7.0528	6.8351	6.6291	6.4338	6.2485	6.0726	5.7465	5.4510	5.1822	4.9371
8.1236	7.8431	7.5790	7.3300	7.0950	6.8729	6.6629	6.4642	6.2758	6.0971	5.7662	5.4669	5.1952	4.9476
8.1826	7.8957	7.6258	7.3717	7.1321	6.9061	6.6925	6.4906	6.2994	6.1182	5.7831	5.4804	5.2060	4.9563
8.2355	7.9426	7.6674	7.4086	7.1649	6.9352	6.7184	6.5135	6.3198	6.1364	5.7975	5.4919	5.2151	4.9636
8.2830	7.9844	7.7043	7.4412	7.1937	6.9607	6.7409	6.5335	6.3375	6.1520	5.8099	5.5016	5.2228	4.9697
8.3255	8.0218	7.7372	7.4701	7.2191	6.9830	6.7606	6.5509	6.3528	6.1656	5.8204	5.5098	5.2292	4.9747
8.3637	8.0552	7.7664	7.4957	7.2415	7.0027	6.7779	6.5660	6.3661	6.1772	5.8294	5.5168	5.2347	4.9789
8.3980	8.0850	7.7923	7.5183	7.2613	7.0199	6.7929	6.5791	6.3776	6.1872	5.8371	5.5227	5.2392	4.9825
8.4287	8.1116	7.8154	7.5383	7.2786	7.0350	6.8060	6.5905	6.3875	6.1959	5.8437	5.5277	5.2430	4.9854
8.4562	8.1354	7.8359	7.5560	7.2940	7.0482	6.8175	6.6005	6.3961	6.2034	5.8493	5.5320	5.2463	4.9878
8.4809	8.1566	7.8542	7.5717	7.3075	7.0599	6.8275	6.6091	6.4035	6.2098	5.8541	5.5356	5.2490	4.9898
8.5030	8.1755	7.8704	7.5856	7.3193	7.0701	6.8362	6.6166	6.4100	6.2153	5.8582	5.5386	5.2512	4.9930
8.5229	8.1924	7.8848	7.5979	7.3298	7.0790	6.8439	6.6231	6.4156	6.2201	5.8617	5.5412	5.2531	4.9930
8.5407	8.2075	7.8976	7.6087	7.3390	7.0868	6.8505	6.6288	6.4204	6.2242	5.8647	5.5434	5.2547	4.9941
8.5567	8.2210	7.9090	7.6183	7.3472	7.0937	6.8564	6.6338	6.4246	6.2278	5.8673	5.5453	5.2561	4.9951
8.5710	8.2330	7.9191	7.6268	7.3543	7.0998	6.8615	6.6381	6.4282	6.2309	5.8695	5.5468	5.2572	4.9959
8.5839	8.2438	7.9281	7.6344	7.3607	7.1050	6.8659	6.6418	6.4314	6.2335	5.8713	5.5482	5.2582	4.9966
8.5954	8.2534	7.9361	7.6410	7.3662	7.1097	6.8698	6.6450	6.4341	6.2358	5.8729	5.5493	5.2590	4.9972
8.6058	8.2619	7.9432	7.6469	7.3711	7.1138	6.8732	6.6479	6.4364	6.2377	5.8743	5.5502	5.2596	4.9976
8.6150	8.2696	7.9495	7.6522	7.3754	7.1173	6.8761	6.6503	6.4385	6.2394	5.8755	5.5511	5.2602	4.9980
8.6233	8.2764	7.9551	7.6568	7.3792	7.1205	6.8787	6.6524	6.4402	6.2409	5.8765	5.5517	5.2607	4.9984
8.6308	8.2825	7.9601	7.6609	7.3826	7.1232	6.8810	6.6543	6.4418	6.2421	5.8773	5.5523	5.2611	4.9986
8.6375	8.2880	7.9645	7.6645	7.3855	7.1256	6.8830	6.6559	6.4431	6.2432	5.8781	5.5528	5.2614	4.9989
8.6435	8.2928	7.9685	7.6677	7.3881	7.1277	6.8847	6.6573	6.4442	6.2442	5.8787	5.5532	5.2617	4.9991
8.6489	8.2972	7.9720	7.6705	7.3904	7.1296	6.8862	6.6585	6.4452	6.2450	5.8792	5.5536	5.2619	4.9992
8.6537	8.3010	7.9751	7.6730	7.3925	7.1312	6.8875	6.6596	6.4461	6.2457	5.8797	5.5539	5.2621	4.9993
8.6580	8.3045	7.9779	7.6752	7.3942	7.1327	6.8886	6.6605	6.4468	6.2463	5.8801	5.5541	5.2623	4.9995

ABC analysis an inventory control method that separates items into three groups based on annual cost-to-volume usage; items that are the highest value are referred to as A items, while C items represent the lowest dollar volume usage

Absorption costing a cost accumulation method that treats the costs of all manufacturing components (direct materials, direct labor, variable overhead, and fixed overhead) as inventoriable or product costs; also known as full costing

Accounting rate of return the rate of accounting earnings obtained on the average capital investment over a project's life

Activity an action performed in fulfillment of business functions

Activity-based costing an accounting information system that identifies the various activities performed in an organization and collects and assigns costs on the basis of the underlying nature and extent of those activities

Activity-based management a discipline that focuses on the activities incurred during production/performance process as the way to improve the value received by a customer and the resulting profit achieved by providing this value

Activity center a segment of the production or service process for which management wants to separately report the costs of the activities performed

Actual cost system a method of accumulating product or service costs that uses actual direct materials, actual direct labor, and actual overhead costs

Administrative department an organizational unit that performs management activities that benefit the entire organization

Ad hoc discount a price concession made under competitive pressure, real or imaginary, which does not relate to volume

Allocate to assign based on the use of a cost predictor or an arbitrary method

Annuity a series of equal cash flows at equal time intervals

Annuity due an annuity in which the cash flows occur at the beginning of a period

Applied overhead the amount of overhead assigned to Work in Process Inventory as a result of incurring the activity that was used to develop the application rate; computed by multiplying the measure of actual activity by the predetermined rate

Appraisal costs quality control costs that are incurred for monitoring or inspection; compensate for mistakes not eliminated through prevention

Appropriation a maximum allowable expenditure for a budget item

Asset turnover a ratio that measures asset productivity and shows the number of sales dollars generated by each dollar of assets

Authority the right (usually by virtue of position or rank) to use resources to accomplish a task or achieve an objective

Backflush accounting a costing system that focuses on company output and works backward through the system to allocate costs to cost of goods sold and inventory

Batch level cost a cost that is caused by a group of things made, handled, or processed at a single time

Benefits-provided ranking a listing of service departments in an order that begins with the one providing the most service to all other corporate areas and ends with the service department that provides the least service to all but the revenue-producing areas

Bill of materials a document that contains information about product material components, their specifications (including quality), and the quantities needed for production

Bottleneck any resource whose ability to process is less than the need for processing; a constraint

Breakeven chart a graphical depiction of the relationships among revenues, variable costs, fixed costs, and profits (or losses)

Breakeven point the level of activity, in units or dollars, at which total revenues equal total costs

Budget the quantitative expression of an organization's commitment to planned activities and resource acquisition and use

Budget committee a committee, composed of top management and the chief financial officer, that reviews and approves, or makes adjustments to, the master budget and/or the budgets submitted from operational managers

Budget manual a detailed set of documents that provides information and guidelines about the budgetary process

Budget slack the intentional underestimation of revenues and/or overestimation of expenses

Budgeting the process of determining the financial plan for future operations

By-product an incidental output of a joint process; has a higher sales value than scrap

Capacity a measure of production volume or some other cost driver

Capital asset an asset used to generate revenues or cost savings by providing production, distribution, or service capabilities for more than one year

Capital budgeting a process for evaluating an entity's proposed long-range projects or courses of future activity for the purpose of allocating limited resources to desirable projects

Carrying cost the variable cost of carrying one unit of inventory in stock for one year; consists of storage, handling, insurance charges, property taxes based on inventory size, possible losses from obsolescence or damage, and opportunity cost

Cash breakeven point a sales volume necessary to cover all cash expenses for a period

Cash flow the receipt or disbursement of cash

Centralization an organizational structure in which top management makes most decisions and controls most activities of the organizational units from the company's central headquarters

Committed cost the cost of basic plant assets or personnel structure that an organization must have to operate

Compound interest a situation in which interest earned in prior periods is added to the original investment so that, in each successive period, interest is earned on both principal and interest

Compounding period the time between each interest computation

Conscious parallelism a case in which competitors independently engage in the same or similar courses of action simply because of business judgment

Constraint anything that confines or limits the ability to perform a project or function or reach an objective

Continuous budget an ongoing twelve-month budget that is created by successively adding a new budget month (twelve months into the future) as each current month expires

Contribution margin an amount equal to selling price per unit minus all variable production, selling, and administrative costs per unit; can also be computed as revenues minus total variable costs

Contribution margin ratio contribution margin divided by revenue; indicates what proportion of selling price remains after variable costs have been covered

Controller the person who supervises operations of the accounting system, but does not handle or negotiate changes in actual resources

Controlling the exerting of managerial influence on operations so that they will conform to plans

Conversion cost the sum of direct labor and factory overhead costs; the cost incurred in changing direct materials or supplies into finished products or services

Cost accounting an area of management accounting that focuses on determining the cost of making products or performing services

Cost Accounting Standards Board (CASB) a public-sector board established first in 1970 (terminated in 1980; reestablished in 1988) that has the power to promulgate uniform cost accounting standards for defense contractors and federal agencies

Cost avoidance a process of finding acceptable alternatives to high-cost items or not spending money for unnecessary goods or services

Cost center a responsibility center in which the manager has only the authority to incur costs and is specifically evaluated on the basis of how well costs are controlled

Cost consciousness a companywide attitude about the topics of cost understanding, cost containment, cost avoidance, and cost reduction

Cost containment an attempt, to the extent possible, to minimize period-by-period increases in per-unit variable and total fixed costs

Cost control system a logical structure of formal and/or informal activities designed to influence costs and to analyze and evaluate how well expenditures were managed during a period

Cost driver analysis the process of investigating, quantifying, and explaining the relationships of cost drivers and their related costs

Cost driver a factor that has a direct cause-effect relationship to a cost

Cost object anything to which costs attach or are related

Cost of capital the weighted average rate that reflects the costs of the various sources of funds making up a firm's debt and equity structure

Cost of goods manufactured the total cost of the goods that were completed and transferred to Finished Goods during the period

Cost-plus pricing a method of setting selling price in which the price is specified as a defined cost basis plus a designated markup (either an agreed-upon amount or percentage)

Cost pool a grouping of all costs that are associated with the same activity or cost driver

Cost reduction the process of lowering current costs, especially those in excess of what is necessary

Cost tables data bases that provide information about the effects on product costs of using different input resources, manufacturing processes, and product designs

Cost-volume-profit analysis a process of examining the relationships among revenues, costs, and profits for a relevant range of activity and for a particular time frame

Critical success factors those items that are so important to a company that, without them, the company would fail; typically include quality, customer service, efficiency, cost control, and responsiveness to change

Decentralization an organizational structure in which top management grants subordinate managers a significant degree of autonomy and independence in operating and making decisions for their organizational units

Decision making a process of choosing among the alternative solutions available for a particular course of action

Degree of operating leverage a measure of how a percentage change in sales, from the current level, will affect company profits

Differential costs costs that vary in amount among the alternatives being considered

Direct cost a cost that is distinctly traceable to a particular cost object

Direct labor the time spend by individuals who work specifically on manufacturing a product or performing a service; the wages paid to these workers

Direct material a readily identifiable part of a product

Direct method (of service department allocation) an allocation technique that uses a specific base to assign service department costs directly to revenue-producing departments with no other intermediate cost allocations

Discount rate the rate of return on capital investments required by the company; the rate of return used in present value computations

Discounting a process of removing the portion of the future cash flows that represents interest, thereby reducing those flows to present value amounts

Discretionary cost an optional cost that a decision maker must periodically review to determine whether it continues to be in accord with ongoing policies

Distribution cost any cost incurred to market a product or service; includes all money spent on advertising, warehousing, and shipping products to customers

Dollar days a performance measure that multiplies the value of inventory by the time that inventory remains in an area and, essentially, assigns a charge for that amount to the area manager

Dual pricing arrangement an agreement that allows a selling division to record the transfer of goods or services at a market or negotiated market price and a buying division to record the transfer at a lower cost-based amount

Dumping the selling abroad of products at prices lower than those charged in the producing country or in other national markets

Du Pont model a restatement of the return on investment formula that multiples profit margin by asset turnover

Economic order quantity an estimate of the least costly number of units per order that would provide the optimal balance between ordering and carrying costs

Economic production run an estimate of the quantity of units to produce that minimizes the total costs of setting up a production run and carrying costs

Effectiveness a comparison of actual output results to desired results to indicate how well the firm's objectives and goals were achieved; the successful accomplishment of a task

Efficiency the performance of tasks to produce the best outcome at the lowest cost from the resources used; the degree to which a satisfactory relationship occurs when comparing outputs to inputs

Employee time sheet a source document that indicates, for each employee, what jobs were worked on during the day and for what amount of time

Engineered cost a discretionary cost that has been found to bear an observable and known relationship to a quantifiable activity base

Environmental Protection Agency the agency that assures that a company prepares, if necessary, an environmental impact statement and decides whether it is acceptable for the activity to proceed

Equivalent units of production an approximation of the number of whole units of output that could have been produced during a period from the actual effort expended during that period

Ethics the moral law; a system of value principles or practices that defines right and wrong

Expected activity a short-run concept representing the anticipated level of activity for the upcoming year

Expected standards norms that reflect what is actually expected to occur in the future period

Failure costs quality control costs that are associated with goods or services that have been found not to conform or perform to the required standards, as well as all related costs (such as that of the complaint department); may be internal or external

Fair-return pricing price regulation in which a firm is allowed to charge a price that will provide a normal return but nothing more than that (i.e., no economic profit)

Feasible solution an answer to a linear programming problem that does not violate any of the problem constraints

FIFO method a method of process costing that computes an average cost per equivalent unit of production using only current period production and cost information; units and costs in beginning inventory are separately sent to the next department or to Finished Goods Inventory, as appropriate

Financial budget a budget that reflects the funds to be generated or consumed during the budget period; includes the cash and capital budgets and the projected or pro forma financial statements

Financing decision a judgment regarding the method of procuring funds that will be used to make an acquisition

Fixed cost a cost that remains constant in total within a specified range of activity

Fixed overhead spending variance the difference between actual and budgeted fixed overhead

Flexible budget a series of financial plans that detail the individual cost factors composing total cost and present those costs at different levels of activity according to cost behavior

Flexible manufacturing system an integrated production system that uses computer-controlled robots to produce immense varieties of a product at a low cost; flexibility is promoted through rapid changeover times

Focused factory arrangement an arrangement in which a vendor agrees to provide a limited number of products according to specifications or to perform a limited number of unique services for the JIT company; vendors can be internal segments or divisions

Foreign Corrupt Practices Act a law designed to serve the basic purpose of preventing bribes from being offered or given to foreign officials (directly or indirectly) for the purpose of influencing that person (or causing that person to use his or her influence) to obtain or retain business

Functional classification a group of costs that were all incurred for the same basic purpose

Future value the amount to which one or more sums of money invested at a specified interest rate will grow over a specified number of time periods

Goal a desired result or condition contemplated in qualitative terms

Goal congruence exists when the personal and organizational goals of decision makers throughout a firm are consistent and mutually supportive

Grease payments facilitating payments to minor employees

High-low method a mixed cost separation technique that uses actual observations of a total cost at the highest and lowest levels of activity and calculates the change in both activity and cost; the levels chosen must be within the relevant range

Horizontal price fixing when competitors attempt to regulate prices through a contract, combination, or conspiracy

Hurdle rate the rate of return deemed by management to be the lowest acceptable return on investment

Ideal standards norms that allow for no inefficiency of *any* type; are sometimes also called perfection or theoretical standards

Idle time time spent in storage or waiting at a production operation for processing

Imposed budget a budget that is prepared by top management with little or no input from operating personnel, who are simply informed of the budget goals and constraints

Incremental analysis a process that focuses only on factors that change from one course of action or decision to another

Incremental cost the additional cost of producing a contemplated quantity of output; generally reflects the variable costs of production

Incremental revenue the additional revenue resulting from a contemplated sale

Independent project an investment project that has no specific bearing on any other investment project

Indirect cost a cost that cannot be traced explicitly to a particular cost object; a common cost

Insider any director, officer, or owner of more than 10 percent of the shares of any one class of stock of a company registered under the Securities Exchange Act of 1934

Inspection time the time taken to perform quality control

Internal control any measure used by management to protect assets, promote the accuracy of records, ensure adherence to company policies, or promote operational efficiency

Internal control system a set of procedures that are concerned with authorizing transactions, protecting assets, and promoting the accuracy of financial information

Internal rate of return the discount rate at which the present value of the cash inflows minus the present value of the cash outflows equals zero

Interpolation the process of finding a term between two other terms using the method of ratio and proportion

Inventoriable cost see product cost

Investing decision a judgment about which assets will be acquired by an entity to achieve its stated objectives

Investment center an organizational unit in which the manager is responsible for generating revenues, planning and controlling costs, and acquiring, disposing of, and using plant assets to earn the highest feasible rate of return on the investment base

JIT (just-in-time) inventory see just-in-time

Job a single unit or group of like units identifiable as being produced to distinct customer specifications

Job order cost sheet a source document that provides virtually all the financial information about a particular job; the set of all job order cost sheets for uncompleted jobs composes the Work in Process subsidiary ledger

Job order product costing the product costing system used by entities that produce tailor-made goods or services in limited quantities that conform to specifications designated by the purchaser of these goods or services

Joint cost the total cost incurred, up to the split-off point, for materials, labor, and overhead during a joint process

Joint process a single process in which one product cannot be manufactured without producing others

Joint products the primary outputs of a joint process, each of which has substantial revenue-generating ability

Just-in-time (JIT) the idea that inventory is manufactured (or purchased) only as the need for it arises or in time to be sold or used; a philosophy about how things are done

Just-in-time manufacturing system a production system that attempts to acquire components and produce inventory units only as they are needed, minimize product defects, and reduce lead/setup times for acquisition and production

Kanban the Japanese word for *card;* a production system that originated from the use of cards to indicate a work center's need for additional components

Kantian analysis an ethical theory that is based on duty and determining whether an action is intrinsically right or wrong, without regard to possible consequences

Key variable a critical factor believed to be a direct cause of the achievement or nonachievement of organizational goals and objectives; can be internal or external

Labor efficiency variance the difference between the number of actual direct labor hours worked and the standard hours allowed for the actual output times standard labor rate per hour

Labor loading charge an add-on to labor cost per hour to cover labor-related charges plus provide a desired profit rate

Labor rate variance the difference between the total actual direct labor wages for the period and the standard rate for all hours actually worked during the period

Lead time the quantity of time from the placement of an order to the arrival of the goods

Least-squares regression analysis a statistical technique that mathematically determines the cost formula of a mixed cost by considering all representative data points; investigates the association or relationship between or among dependent and independent variables

Linear programming a method used to solve problems with one objective and multiple limiting factors; finds the optimal allocation of scarce resources when the objective and restrictions on achieving that objective can be stated as linear equations

Line employee a person who is directly responsible for achieving an organization's goals and objectives

Long-term variable cost a cost that has traditionally been viewed as a fixed cost

Make-or-buy decision a decision that compares the cost of internally manufacturing a product component to the cost of purchasing it from outside suppliers or from another division at a specified transfer price and, thus, attempts to assess the best uses of available facilities; can also relate to services

Management accounting the process of identification, measurement, accumulation, analysis, preparation, interpretation, and communication of financial information used by management to plan, evaluate, and control within an organization and to assure appropriate use of and accountability for its resources

Management by exception a technique in which managers set upper and lower limits of tolerance for deviations and only investigate those deviations that fall outside those tolerance ranges

Manufacturing cells linear or U-shaped groupings of workers and/or machines

Manufacturing cycle efficiency (MCE) a measure of processing efficiency in which actual value-added production time is divided by total lead time

Manufacturing resource planning (MRP II) a fully integrated materials requirements planning (MRP) system that involves the functional areas of marketing, finance, and manufacturing in planning the master production schedule using the usual MRP method; is also able to calculate resource needs such as labor and machine hours

Margin of safety the excess of the budgeted or actual sales of a company over its breakeven point

Master budget the comprehensive set of all budgetary schedules and the pro forma financial statements of an organization

Material important in relation to some standard of comparison; a component or ingredient in a product

Materials loading charge an add-on to materials cost to cover ordering, handling, and carrying costs of the parts inventory plus provide a profit margin

Materials price variance the difference between the actual and standard cost of the quantity of materials purchased or used

Materials quantity variance the difference between the actual quantity of material used and the standard quantity of material allowed for the goods produced during the period times the standard material price

Materials requirements planning (MRP) a computer simulation system that helps companies plan by calculating the future availability of raw materials, parts, subassemblies, and end products based on a master production schedule

Materials requisition a source document that indicates the types and quantities of materials to be placed into production or used in performing a service; causes materials and their costs to be released from the Raw Materials warehouse and sent to Work in Process

Matrix structure an organizational structure in which functional departments and project teams exist simultaneously so that the resulting lines of authority resemble a grid

Mean the arithmetic average, calculated by dividing the sum of the observations by the number of observations

Mixed cost a cost that has both a variable and a fixed component; does not fluctuate in direct proportion to changes in activity nor does it remain constant with changes in activity

Monopolistic competition a market structure in which there are many firms having slightly differentiated products and services

Monopoly a market structure in which there is only one seller of a product or provider of a service

Multiple regression a process that uses two or more independent variables to predict the dependent variable in the least-squares regression

Mutually exclusive projects a set of proposed projects for which there is a group of available candidates that all perform essentially the same function or meet the same objective; from this group, one is chosen causing all of the others to be rejected

Mutually inclusive projects a set of proposed investments that are all related to a primary project; when the primary project is chosen, all related projects are also selected

National Environmental Policy Act the law requiring an environmental impact statement to be prepared for major federal activities that significantly affect the quality of the environment

Negotiated transfer price an intracompany charge for goods or services that has been set through a process of negotiation between the selling and purchasing unit managers

Net present value the difference between the present values of all the cash inflows and cash outflows of an investment project

Net present value method an investment evaluation technique that uses discounted cash flows to determine if the rate

of return on a project is equal to, higher than, or lower than the desired rate of return

Non-value-added activity an activity that increases the time spent on a product or service but does not increase its worth

Normal capacity the long-run (5 to 10 years) average activity of the firm that gives effect to historical and estimated future production levels and to cyclical and seasonal fluctuations

Normal cost system a method of accumulating product or service cost that uses actual direct materials and direct labor cost, but assigns overhead costs to Work in Process through the use of a predetermined overhead rate

Objective a target to be achieved during a preestablished period or by a specified date; can be expressed in quantitative terms

Objective function the mathematical equation that states the maximization or minimization objective of a linear programming problem

Occupational Safety and Health Act a law designed to protect the health and safety of employees while on the job from job-related health effects

Oligopoly a market structure in which there are only a few firms, whose products/services may be differentiated or standardized

Operating budget a budget for on-going company performance that is expressed in both units and dollars

Operating leverage a factor that reflects the relationship of a company's variable and fixed costs

Operations flow document a listing of all tasks necessary to make a unit of product or perform a service and the corresponding time allowed for each operation

Opportunity cost a potential benefit that is given up because one course of action is chosen over another

Optimal solution the solution to a linear programming problem that provides the best answer to the problem without violating any problem constraints

Order point the inventory level that triggers the placement of an order

Ordering cost the variable cost associated with preparing, receiving, and paying for an order

Ordinary annuity an annuity in which the first cash flow is at the end of a period

Organizational level cost a cost incurred to support the on-going facility operations

Organization chart a visual illustration of the functions, divisions, and positions in a company and how these are related

Outlier a nonrepresentative point that falls outside the relevant range

Out-of-pocket costs current or near-current cash expenditures

Overapplied overhead the excess of overhead applied to Work in Process over actual overhead cost

Overhead the indirect or supporting costs of converting materials or supplies into finished products or services; does not include direct materials or direct labor

Participatory budget a budget that has been developed through a process of joint decision making by top management and operating personnel

Payback period the time required to recoup the original investment through cash flows from a project

Penetration pricing a price that is set significantly below the current market price for a similar product or service; the lower price is then often raised as the product moves into its growth stage

Performance evaluation the process of determining the degree of success in accomplishing a task; equates to both effectiveness and efficiency

Period cost any cost not associated with making or acquiring inventory

Planning translating goals and objectives into the specific activities and resources required to achieve those goals and objectives

Post-investment audit a management comparison of information on actual project results to the results that were expected at the project inception

Practical capacity the activity level that could be achieved during normal working hours giving consideration to ongoing, regular operating interruptions such as holidays, downtime, and start-up time

Practical standards norms that allow for normal, unavoidable time problems or delays such as machine downtime and worker breaks; can be reached or slightly exceeded approximately 60 to 70 percent of the time with reasonable effort by workers

Predatory dumping dumping that is practiced to force domestic producers out of business so that the foreign competitor is the primary source of supply and can raise prices

Predetermined overhead rate an estimated constant charge per unit of activity used to assign overhead costs to production or services based on the actual quantity of the related activity base incurred

Predicate acts a wide variety of racketeering crimes that include mail, wire and bankruptcy fraud, extortion, arson, murder, interference with interstate commerce by violence or threat thereof, securities fraud, and bribery

Predictor an activity measure that, when changed, is accompanied by consistent, observable changes in another item

Preference decision a choice in which projects are ranked according to their impact on the achievement of company objectives

Present value the amount that a future cash flow is currently worth, given a specified rate of interest

Present value index a ratio that compares the present value of net cash inflows to the present value of the net investment

Prevention costs quality control costs that are incurred to improve quality by preventing defects from occurring

Price discrimination the practice of charging different prices for the same product to different groups of buyers when those prices are not reflective of cost differences

Price elasticity of demand a measure that reflects the percentage change in the quantity demanded relative to the percentage change in price

Price fixing a practice in which firms conspire to set the price of a good at a specified level

Price maker a firm that determines the level of output and the corresponding price that will maximize its profits

Price skimming the practice of setting an introductory price higher than what exists for similar, but potentially lower-quality, products in the market or setting a high price because there are no similar products or services in the market

Price taker a firm that accepts the market price as given by the industry supply and demand

Prime cost the sum of direct materials cost and direct labor cost

Process costing a method of accumulating and assigning costs to units of production in companies that make large quantities of homogeneous products

Process costing system a costing system in which costs are accumulated by cost component in each department and assigned to all of the units that flowed through the department; used by entities that produce large quantities of homogeneous goods

Process map a flowchart or diagram that indicates every step of making a product or providing a service

Process yield the proportion of good units that resulted from the activities expended to the total units produced

Product complexity a reflection of the number of components or operations included in a product or the number of processes through which a product flows

Product contribution margin selling price minus total variable production costs; does not consider variable selling costs

Product cost a cost associated with making or acquiring inventory

Product level cost a cost that is caused by the development, production or acquisition of different items

Product variety the number of different types of products produced

Production and cost report a document used in a process costing system that details all manufacturing quantities and costs, shows the computation of cost per EUP, and indicates the cost assignment to goods produced during the period

Production time the time needed to perform the manufacturing functions necessary to production; includes value-added and non-value-added time

Productive capacity a measure of the total units that could be produced during a period from value-added processing time on the equipment available

Productive processing time the proportion of total processing time that is value-added

Profit center an organizational unit in which managers are responsible for generating revenues and planning and controlling all expenses

Profit margin the percentage of income to sales

Profit-volume graph a visual presentation that reflects the amount of profit or loss associated with each level of sales

Program budgeting an approach to budgeting that relates resource inputs to service outputs and, thereby, focuses on the relationship of benefits to cost expenditures

Project a course of future investment activity that will typically include the purchase, installation, and operation of a capital asset

Pull system a production system in which parts are delivered or manufactured only as they are needed by the work center for which they are intended; a just-in-time system

Purchase price variance the difference between the actual cost of the quantity of materials purchased and the standard cost of the materials purchased

Purchasing cost the quoted purchase price minus any discounts allowed plus shipping charges

Pure competition a market structure in which there are many firms, each with a small market share, producing identical products

Push system a production system in which work centers may produce inventory that is not currently needed because of lead time or economic production/order quantity requirements; excess inventory is stored until it is needed by other work centers

Racketeer Influenced and Corrupt Organizations Act a law designed to discourage organized crime from investing profits from illegal activities into legitimate business

Red-line system an inventory system in which a single container or stack of inventory is available for production needs; a red line is painted on the inventory container (or on the wall for a stack) at a point deemed to be the reorder point

Regression line a line that represents the cost formula for a set of cost observations

Relevant cost a cost that is pertinent to or logically associated with a specific problem or decision

Relevant costing a technique that allows managers to focus on pertinent facts and disregard extraneous information by comparing, to the extent possible and practical, incremental revenues and incremental costs of alternative decisions

Relevant costs all costs that are logically associated with a specific problem or decision

Relevant range the specified range of activity over which a variable cost per unit remains constant or a fixed cost remains fixed in total

Rent each equal cash flow of an annuity

Repetitive manufacturing a manufacturing process in which company output consists of a large volume of homogeneous products that have been fabricated, machined, assembled, and tested

Resale price maintenance see vertical price fixing

Residual income the profit earned that exceeds an amount charged for funds committed to the center

Responsibility the obligation to accomplish a task or achieve an objective

Responsibility accounting an accounting system that provides information to top management about segment or subunit performance

Responsibility center the cost object under the control of a manager; in the case of a decentralized company, the cost object is an organizational unit such as a division, department, or geographical region

Responsibility reports reports that reflect the revenues and/or costs under the control of a specific unit manager

Return of capital recovery of the original investment

Return on capital the income from an investment

Return on investment a ratio that relates income generated to the resources (or asset base) used to produce that income; income divided by assets invested

Revenue center an organizational unit in which a manager is accountable only for the generation of revenues and has no control over setting selling prices or budgeting costs

Robinson-Patman Act the 1936 law that prohibits price discrimination

Safety stock the quantity of inventory kept on hand by a company to compensate for potential fluctuating usage or unusual delays in lead time

Sales mix the relative combination of sales quantities of the various products that make up a company's total sales

Sales price variance the difference between actual and budgeted selling price multiplied by the actual number of units sold

Sales volume variance the difference between actual and budgeted sales volume multiplied by the budgeted selling price

Scarce resource an item that is essential to production activity, but that is available only in a limited quantity

Scienter the intent to defraud or intentional misconduct that amounts to more than mere negligence

Scrap an incidental output of a joint process; has a lower sales values than a by-product

Screening decision a choice that indicates whether a capital project is desirable based on some previously established minimum criterion or criteria

Securities Exchange Act of 1934 the law that created the Securities and Exchange Commission and was designed to regulate the secondary securities market

Segment margin the excess of segment sales over direct variable expenses and avoidable fixed expenses; the amount remaining to cover unavoidable direct fixed expenses and common costs and, then, to provide profits

Service department an organizational unit that provides one or more specific functional tasks for other internal units

Setup costs the direct and indirect costs of getting equipment ready for each new production run

Simple interest interest that is earned only on the original investment or principal amount

Simple regression the process of using only one independent variable to predict the dependent variable in least-squares regression

Simplex an iterative, step-by-step technique used to solve multi-variable, multi-constraint linear programming problems; usually requires the aid of a computer

Situational ethics a system of determining "right or wrong" based on the circumstances at the time and place the decision is being made

Special order pricing the process of determining a sales price to charge for manufacturing or service jobs that are outside the company's normal production/service realm

Split-off point the point at which the outputs of a joint process are first identifiable as individual products

Staff employee a person who is responsible for providing advice, guidance, and service to line personnel

Standard a benchmark or norm against which actual results may be compared

Standard cost a budgeted or estimated cost

Standard cost card a document that summarizes the direct material and direct labor standard quantities and prices needed to complete one unit of product as well as the overhead allocation bases and rates

Standard cost system a product costing system that uses norms for direct materials and direct labor quantities and/or costs and a predetermined rate for overhead; these standards are used to value inventories and to compare with actual costs to determine deviations; a system in which standards are developed and used for planning and control purposes; both standard and actual costs are recorded in the accounting records

Standard quantity allowed a measure of quantity that translates the actual output achieved into the standard input quantity that should have been used to achieve that output

Statements on Management Accounting (SMAs) nonbinding guidelines for cost and management accounting issued by the Institute of Management Accountants

Step method (of service department cost allocation) the process of assigning service department costs to cost objects through the use of a specific base after the interrelationships of the service departments and the revenue-producing departments have been considered

Stockout a condition in which a company does not have inventory available upon customer request or production demand

Strategic planning the process of developing a statement of long-range (five to ten years) goals for the organization and defining the strategies and policies that will help the organization achieve those goals

Suboptimization a situation in which unit managers make decisions that positively affect their own units, but are detrimental to other organizational units or to the company as a whole

Substitute good an item that can be used in place of another to satisfy the same wants or needs

Sunk cost the historical or past cost that is associated with the acquisition of an asset or a resource and that has no future recovery value

Synchronous management a situation in which management has the strategic objective of simultaneously increasing throughput while reducing inventory and operating expenses; includes all techniques that help an organization achieve its goal

Tactical planning the process of determining the specific objectives and means by which strategic plans will be achieved; are short-term (one to eighteen months), single use plans that have been developed to address a given set of circumstances or for a specific time frame

Target costing a method of determining the maximum allowable cost of a product before it is designed, engineered, or produced by subtracting an acceptable profit margin rate from a forecasted selling price

Tax benefit the reduction in taxes provided by noncash deductions; the amount is equal to the amount of the noncash charge multiplied by the tax rate

Tax shield (of depreciation) the amount of the reduction of taxable income provided by depreciation expense

Theoretical capacity the estimated maximum potential activity that could occur during a specific time frame

Theory of constraints a concept stating that production or performance cannot take place at a rate faster than the slowest machine or person in the process

Throughput the number of good units or quantity of services that an organization produces and sells within a time period; the output of the plant to the customer

Time and material pricing a common practice in service organizations that allows prices to be set using separate rates for the direct labor time involved and the direct materials used

Timeline a visual illustration of the timing of expected cash receipts and payments; used for analyzing cash flows of a capital investment proposal

Tippees persons who receive inside information from an insider, regardless of whether the insider used the information

Total contribution margin an amount equal to revenue minus all variable costs regardless of the area of incurrence (production or nonproduction)

Total cost to account for the balance in Work in Process at the beginning of the period plus all current costs for direct materials, direct labor, and overhead

Total units to account for all units that were worked on in a department during the current period; consists of beginning inventory units plus units started

Total variance the difference between total actual cost incurred and total standard cost for the output produced during the period; can also be designated by cost component

Transfer price an internal charge established for the exchange of goods or services between organizational units of the same company

Transfer time the time it takes to move products or components from one place to another

Treasurer the person who generally handles the actual resources in an organization but who does not have access to the accounting records

Two-bin system an inventory system in which two containers or stacks of inventory are available for production needs; when production begins to use materials in the second bin, a purchase order is placed to refill the first bin

Underapplied overhead the excess of actual overhead over the overhead applied to Work in Process Inventory

Unexpired costs assets

Uniform capitalization rules IRS rules that require certain indirect costs to be included in inventory; for manufacturers, these inclusions cover all costs that directly benefit or are incurred because of production, including some general and administrative costs; wholesalers and retailers must inventory costs for items such as off-site warehousing, purchasing agents' salaries, and repackaging; is also known as super-full absorption costing

Unit level cost a cost that is caused by the production or acquisition of a single unit of product or the delivery of a single unit of service

Units started and completed the total units completed during the period minus the units in beginning inventory

Usage price variance the difference between the total cost of the materials used during the period and the standard cost of those materials

Utilitarianism an approach to ethics that considers the outcomes or consequences of the ethical choice; basically is a cost-benefit analysis

Value-added activity an activity that increases the worth of a product or service to the consumer and for which the customer is willing to pay

Value chart a visual representation that indicates the value-added and non-value-added activities and time spent in those activities from the beginning to the end of a process

Variable cost a cost that varies in total in direct proportion to changes in activity; is constant per unit within the relevant range

Variable costing a cost accumulation method that includes only variable production costs (direct materials, direct labor, and variable overhead) as product or inventoriable costs; fixed overhead is treated as a period cost; also known as direct costing

Variable overhead efficiency variance the difference between budgeted variable overhead at actual input activity and budgeted variable overhead at standard input allowed

Variable overhead spending variance the difference between actual variable overhead and budgeted variable overhead based on actual input

Variance any difference between actual and standard costs

Variance analysis the process of categorizing the nature (favorable or unfavorable) of the differences between standard and actual costs and seeking the reasons for those differences

Vertical price fixing a requirement by a producing business and its distributors that establishes the prices at which products may be sold to consumers

Volume variance the difference between budgeted and applied fixed overhead

Waste a residual output of a joint process that has no sales value

Weighted average method a method of process costing that computes an average cost per equivalent unit of production; combines beginning inventory units and costs with current production of units and costs, respectively, to compute that average

Whistleblowing the process of alerting the proper authorities of a firm's improper or illegal action

Zero-based budgeting a comprehensive budgeting process that systematically considers the priorities and alternatives for current and proposed activities in relation to organizational objectives

A U T H O R I N D E X

Abdallah, Wagdy M., 432
Adams, Chris, 642
Addams, Lon, 473
Adkins, Lynn, 414
Aggarwal, Sumer C., 565
Allen, Michael, 739
Alpert, Bruce, 869
Amenkhienan, Felix E., 581
Ames, B. Charles, 139, 396, 628
Anderson, Ed, 865
Anderson, Jack, 860
Andrews, Kenneth R., 651
Appleyard, A. R., 488
Aranoff, Gerald, 442
Archer, Simon, 527
Ashton, James E., 250
Axline, Larry L., 860
Azzone, Giovanni, 805

Bailes, Jack C., 581
Bailey, Jeff, 860
Ballanger, Ned B., 684
Barrett, Paul M., 860
Barton, Thomas L., 245
Barwise, Patrick, 730
Bassiry, G. R., 858
Bayou, Mohamed E., 806
BDO Seidman, 511
Begley, Sharon, 120
Beischel, Mark E., 657
Bennett, Robert E., 793
Berk, Richard F., 240
Berlant, Debbie, 84
Berliner, Callie, 131, 792
Berndt, Jerry, 805
Berry, Charles G., 861
Berry, William Lee, 565

Berry, Vincent, 715
Bertele, Umberto, 805
Bhimani, Al, 805
Biggs, Joseph R., 559
Blanchard, Kenneth, 23
Boer, Germain B., 209
Bonsack, Robert A., 197
Borthick, A. Faye, 104, 168
Bowles, Jerry G., 386
Boyle, Cynthia, 761, 799
Branch, Shelly, 511, 515
Brandt, Richard, 250
Brausch, John M, 155
Brignall, T. J., 254
Brimelow, Peter, 835
Brimson, James, 46, 59, 131, 155, 792
Bromwich, Michael, 805
Brooks, Jacob H., 568
Brown, Carolyn M., 525
Brown, Herbert E., 162, 594, 868
Brown, James F. Jr., 467
Brownell, P., 488
Browning, E. S., 858
Browning, Reese, 84
Brunton, Nancy M., 104
Bryant, Keith Jr., 19
Burgess, Michele, 231, 241
Burt, David N., 565, 566
Busher, John R., 43
Byrum, Donald J., 606

Cadbury, Sir Adrian, 829, 836, 856
Callan, John P., 104
Calonius, Erik, 59
Calvasina, Eugene J., 201
Calvasina, Richard V., 201
Caminiti, Susan, 155

Camp, Roger A., 567
Canadian Press, 394
Cardullo, J. Patrick, 170
Carmichael, Sheena, 860
Cetron, Marvin, 6
Chakravarty, Subrata N., 3
Chang, Otto H., 761, 799
Cheatham, Carole, 189, 677
Cheney, Glenn Alan, 94
Chenhall, R. H., 488
Christensen, Linda F., 341
Churchill, Neil C., 464, 469
Clausing, Neal, 104, 319, 336
Coda, Bernard A., 723, 793
Cohn, Bob, 846
Cole, Frederick M., 245
Collins, Don E., 300
Collins, Frank, 155, 488
Cook, Donald, 527
Cook, Frank X., Jr., 250
Cook, James, 380
Cooper, Robin, 59, 85, 142, 144, 145, 152, 384
Cooper, W. W., 652
Coopers & Lybrand, 158, 836
Cornick, Michael, 341
Coulter, Carlton III, 254
Cowley, Geoffrey, 712
Cox, Jeff, 150, 151
Coy, Peter, 442
Crosby, Philip B., 149, 150, 568
Cross, Kelvin, 660, 661
Crovitz, L. Gordon, 843
Crum, Robert P., 431
Curran, John J., 778
Curtis, Donald A., 479
Czyzewski, Alan B., 469, 527

Davis, Bob, 31, 55, 555
Day, Denis W., 599, 624
Dearden, John, 684
DeGeorge, Richard T., 850
Deloitte & Touche, 8
Deutschman, Alan, 604, 607
Deveny, Kathleen, 442
Discenza, Richard, 805
Doney, Lloyd D., 254
Doost, Robert K., 209
Drucker, Peter, 618
Dudick, Thomas S., 396, 628
Dumaine, Brian, 413, 581, 734
Drummond, John, 860

Eccles, Robert G., 684
Edwards, Donald E., 279

Edwards, Gary, 26,
Edwards, James B., 560
Edwards, James Don, 209
Eiland, J. D., 866
Elliott, Robert K., 23
Engwall, Richard L., 791, 806
Ernst & Ernst (see Ernst & Young)
Ernst & Young, 562, 838
Etzioni, Amitai, 709, 735

Falhaber, Thomas A., 300
Faulk, Robert J., 836, 837
Finch, Gerald L., 488, 498
Flentov, Peter, 684
Fordham, Gregory L, 254
Foster, George, 84
Fox, Robert E., 151, 677
Fremgen, James M., 339

Garrett, Linda, 294, 295
Garrett, Thomas M., 433
Gaumnitz, Bruce R., 203
Gibson, Richard, 413
Godfrey, James T., 684
Goldratt, Eliyahu, 150, 151
Gordon, Lawrence A., 795
Grant Thornton, 7, 9, 48, 570, 628, 660
Green, Forrest B., 581
Greene, Alicia H., 684
Guenther, Robert, 653
Gulledge, Jo, 273

Haddock, Particia, 832
Hagaman, T. Carter, 849
Hager, Bruce, 23
Hall, John, 374
Hamilton, Joan, 850
Harr, David J., 684
Harrar, G., 806
Harrell, Horace W., 209
Harrington, Mark, 442
Harris, John K., 624
Hassan, Nabil, 162, 224, 594, 868
Hauser, Rex C., 279
Hendricks, James A., 793, 806
Henkoff, Ronald, 581, 607
Hinge, John B., 461
Hirsch, Maurice L. Jr., 155
Hlavacek, James D., 139, 396, 628
Ho, Simon S. M., 806
Hooper, Laurence, 38
Hopson, James F., 581
Hoshower, Leon B., 431
Howard, Patrick D., 440

Howell, Robert A., 33, 50, 77, 126, 559, 653, 793, 798
Hubbard, Robert B., 15
Hughlett, Mike, 73, 94
Hull, Rita P., 469
Hunt, Rick, 294, 295

Inman, Anthony, 581
Institute of Management Accountants, 3, 19, 46, 49, 74,
        437, 610, 663,698,726
Ijiri, Yuji, 652

Jacobs, Stanford L., 839
Jacobson, Peter D., 23
Jaouen, Pauline R, 209
Jensen, J. Vernon, 852
Johnson, H. Thomas, 125, 146, 148
Jones, Daniel J., 581
Jones, Lou F., 125, 138

Kalkbrenner, Karen K., 663
Kane, Mary, 704
Kant, Immanuel, 831
Kanter, Rosabeth Moss, 23, 25, 684
Kaplan, David A., 846
Kaplan, Robert S., 13, 23, 59, 85, 125, 139, 145, 152, 194,
        330, 337, 384, 673, 684, 791
Karr, Albert R., 845
Keegan, Daniel P., 440
Keller, John J., 740
Kelly, Kevin, 149, 501, 525
Kerwin, Kathleen, 554
Kilman, Scott, 423
Kim, Il-Woon, 782
King, Alfred M., 806
King, Barry G., 723, 793
Kirkpatrick, David, 37, 717
Kleinsorge, Ilene K., 147, 581
Klonoski, Richard J., 433
Knowlton, Christopher, 581
Koenig, Richard, 651
Kollaritsch, Felix P., 203
Koehler, Kenneth G., 488
Koehler, Robert W., 321, 334
Koten, John, 454
Kovac, Edward J., 438
Koziol, David S., 252
Krantz, K. Theordor, 59
Kremer, W. Chuck, 663
Kupfer, Andrew, 232, 709, 735

Labich, Kenneth, 602
Landekich, Stephen, 855
Landler, Mark, 554
Lanzillotti, Robert F., 414

Leer, Richard W., 684
Leinster, Colin, 34
Lender, Gerald H., 806
Lettes, Theodore, 791
Liberatore, Matthew J., 792
Lippa, Victor, 676, 684
Loewe, Dennis A., 146
Long, Ellen J., 559
Lutchen, Mark D., 608
Lynch, Richard, 660, 661

MacArthur, John B., 582
Main, Jeremy, 387, 396
Mann, Gary J., 481
Manning, Marilyn, 832
Mannino, Paul V., 507
Marn, Michael, 434
Marsh, Barbara, 27
Marsh, Paul R., 730
Martz, Larry, 676, 833
Masonson, Leslie N., 508, 553
May, Claire, B., 860
McCormick, John, 570
McFadden, David, 121, 122
McKee, Bradford, 367, 860
McNair, C. J., 661, 682
Merchant, Kenneth A., 481
Melloan, George, 385
Mendes, Joshua, 396
Merz, C. Mike, 294, 295
Mihal, William, 498
Milani, Ken, 507
Milbank, Dana, 645, 646, 678
Milken, Michael, 860
Miller, John A., 104
Miltenburg, G.J., 582
Moellenberndt, Richard A., 170
Moffat, Susan, 564
Moline, Julie, 606, 624
Monahan, Thomas F., 792
Moore, L. Ted, 341
Moore, Marcus, 152
Mosconi, William, 682
Muchnik, Michael A., 591
Myers, Henry F., 575
Myers, Mary D., 795

Naj, Amal Kumar, 849
Nakarmi, Laxmi, 647, 650
Nanni, Alfred J., 572
National Association of Accountants (see Institute of
        Management Accountants)
Neumann, Bruce R., 209
News Corp., Ch. 113

Nibbelin, Michael C., 155
Nickerson, Clarence B., 495
Noreen, Eric, 134
Norris, Thomas, 682

O'Brien, Thomas, 149
O'Reilly, Brian, 427
Oliver, Joseph R., 336
Oster, Patrick, 628
Ostrenga, Michael R., 148, 684
Otley, David, 527

Paegelow, Richard S., 341
Palmer, Sarah, 224
Papas, Evans, 209
Pare, Terence P., 440
Parker, Lee D., 473
Parker, Thornton, 791
Payne, Dinah, 828
Peale, Norman Vincent, 23
Pederson, R. Brian, 209
Pickering, John, 402, 860
Pike, Richard H., 806
Polakoff, Joel C., 794
Poneman, Lawrence A., 49
Pouliot, Janine, 470
Powell, Bill, 570
Power, William, 628
Primrose, P. L., 582, 740
Pryor, Tom E., 131, 142
Pulley, Brett, 611

Quinn, James Brian, 47

Raffish, Norm, 155
Raiborn, Cecily, 828
Reeve, James M., 792
Reichheld, Frederick F., 385
Reid, Peter C., 551
Reilly, Patrick M., 612
Rice, Faye, 628
Richards, Bill, 409
Richman, Louis S., 772
Roach, Stephen S., 575
Robinson, Leonard A., 249
Robinson, Loudell Ellis, 249
Robotic Industries Association, 8
Romano, Patrick L., 148, 662, 806
Roth, Harold P., 104, 168

Saaty, Thomas, 792
Sadhwani, Arjan T., 567, 780
Sakurai, Michiharu, 209
Sandretto, Michael J., 247

Santori, Peter, 341, 663
Saporito, Bill, 442
Sarhan, M. H., 567
Sasser, W. Earl, Jr., 385
Saunders, Paula M. 162, 594, 868
Schaffer, Robert H., 684
Schiff, Jonathon B. 860
Schiller, Zachary, 442
Schine, Eric, 24
Schlesinger, Jacob M., 104
Schwab, Carl E., 604
Sease, Douglas R., 653
Seed, Allen H. III, 791
Sellenheim, Michael R., 684
Sellers, Patricia, 24, 411, 433, 684
Seymour, P. B., 422
Shane, Hugh M., 591
Shao, Maria, 120
Sharman, Paul, 341
Sharp, Douglas, 341
Shaw, William, 715, 845, 860
Shenkir, William G., 24
Sheridan, Mike, 725
Shields, Michael D., 442, 628
Shipley, Margaret F., 591
Shirley, James, M., 624
Siers, Howard L., 24, 861
Singer, Andrew W., 861
Smith, Dennis D., 663
Smith, K. Richard, 657
Smith, W. Robert, 572
Son, Young K., 684
Song, Ja, 782
Soulier, Mary T., 470
Soucy, Stephen R., 33, 50, 152, 559, 653, 798
Sourwine, Darrel A., 24
Speir, Robert E., 740
Sprohge, Hans, 173, 203
Springen, Karen, 846
Stancill, James McNeill, 512
Steinberg, Richard M., 836, 837
Stewart, Thomas A., 47, 130, 133, 479, 485, 684, 791, 796
Stipp, David, 848
Stock, Gregory, 861
Stout, David E., 792
Sullivan, William G., 792
Surma, John P., 861
Susman, Gerald I., 414
Sweeney, Robert B., 861
Swift, Paul, 59
Swoboda, Frank, 48

Talbot, John, 173, 204
Tanner, Ray D., 147

Tanouye, Elyse, 612
Tatikonda, Lakshmi U., 200, 557
Tatikonda, Rao J., 557
Taylor, Alex III, 55, 425, 524
Templeman, John, 628
Templin, Neal, 616
Tetzeli, Rick, 829
Thomas, Rich, 676
Tilove, Jonathan, 637
Towey, John F., 563
Trapani, Cosmo S., 511
Treece, James B., 250
Trost, Cathy, 628
Troxler, Joel W., 806
Troy, Henry P., 438
Turk, William T, 582
Turney, Peter B. B., 146, 155, 628
Tyndall, Gene R., 43, 571
Tyson, Thomas, 239, 780

United States Department of Justice, 840
Urbancic, Frank R., 279

Van, Jon, 576
Varney, James, 461
Verschoor, Curtis C., 740

Vickery, Hugh, 426
Vollman, Thomas E., 565
Vondra, Albert A., 861

Wagner, Randell G., 791
Walden, Steven, 209
Waldholz, Michael, 427
Walleigh, Richard C., 254
Walsh, Francis J., 684
Wanner, David L, 684
Weber, Joseph V., 341
Wensley, Robin, 730
Whybark, D. Clay, 565
Willis, Clint, 577
Worthy, Ford S., 178
Wright, John W., 6
Wucinich, William, 361, 389

Yates, Ronald E., 612
Youde, Richard Y., 396
Young, S. Mark, 442, 628

Zellner, Wendy, 611
Zipkin, Paul H., 582
Zuber, George R., 861

AccuRate Division (see Mosknes Manufacturing Co.)
Air Relief, 568
Alcoa, 645–648, 678
Allen-Bradley, 50
America Machine Inc., 568
American Airlines, 602, 612
American Institute of CPAs, 464, 465
Andersen Consulting, 36
Apple Computer, 606, 730
AT&T, 36, 606, 849

Bank of New York, ch. 15
Baylor University Medical Center, 566, 567
Bearings, Inc., 378
Bell Atlantic, 439, 440
Bellcore, 437–439
Black & Decker, 413
Boise Cascade Corporation, 845
Braun, 412
BTG Inc., 232

Cadbury Schweppes, 274, 829, 858
Canon, 796
Carrier, 849
Caterpillar, 125, 138, 141, 152, 153
Charity Hospital (New Orleans), 865
Catholic Church, 501, 525
Chrysler, 524
Citicorp, 653
Clairol, 849
Clark Equipment, 734
Coca-Cola, 386
Commercial Nuclear Fuel, 387
CompHealth, 607
Conner Peripherals, 232
Consolidated Diesel, 567

Continental Traffic Service, 8
Control Data Corp., 761, 798
Cost Accounting Standards Board, 14
Cummins Engine, 36

Daewoo, 649, 650
Delta Wire Company, 181
Dinamation International Corporation, 231, 241, 244, 252

E. McIlhenny Sons, 273, 277, 282, 292, 296
Eagle Bronze Foundry, 569
Eastern Airlines, 454
EDS, 37
Enron, 37
Entenmann's, 274

Falcon Products Inc., 6
Federal Express, 387
Financial Accounting Standards Board, 14, 126, 321
First State Bank of Lake Lillian, 409
FM Corporation, 250
Ford, 566
Fox Manufacturing Company, 835
Freeport McMoRan, 374, 375
Fresh From Texas, 367
Fuji Electric, 796
Fujitsu, 796

Gateway 2000, 709, 719, 721, 735
GBC, 511
General Electric, 130
General Foods (see Philip Morris)
Gulf Oil, 835

Hanson, 649
Harley-Davidson, 551, 576, 577

Havre Culligan Water Conditioning, 724
Hewlett-Packard, 84, 295, 565
Hitachi, 796
H.J. Heinz, 460, 607
Hospital Corporation of America, 761

IBM, 36–38, 761
Institute of Management Accountants, 15–19
Internal Revenue Service, 321, 335

Japan-U.S. Global Partnership Fund, 612
Jefferson Parish (Louisiana), 461
Johnson & Johnson, 616, 761, 851, 852
Johnson Controls, 846

Kelly Truck Lines, 766
Kiamichi Railroad, 415
Kimberly-Clark Corp., 461, 761
KL Spring & Stamping, 143
Kodak, 36
KPMG Peat Marwick, 36
Kraft General Foods (see Philip Morris)

LaPorte State Bank, 9
Lifeco Services Corp., 610
Lifeline Systems Inc., 48
Lockheed Missiles and Space Co., 798
Lucky-Goldstar Group, 647

Mannington Mills, 761
Masco Industries, 790
Massachusetts Mutual Life Insurance Co., 36
Mattel, 725, 727, 761
McIlhenny (see E. McIlhenny Sons)
McNeil Consumer Products (see Johnson & Johnson)
Merck & Co., 612
Midway Airlines, 610, 611
Minarik Electric Company, 571
Minnesota Mining & Manufacturing (3M), 717, 849
Moody-Price, 467
Mosknes Manufacturing Co., 559
Motorola, 387

National Association of Accountants (see Institute of
        Management Accountants)
National Bicycle Industrial Co., 564
National Car Rental, 36
New England Patriots, 361, 389
New York Life Insurance Co., 36
News Corp., 612
Nike, 554
Nissan, 796
Northern Telecom, 789
Norton Manufacturing, 232
Norton's Shipyard and Marina, 667

Office of Technology Assessment, 31
Owens & Minor, 567

PepsiCo, Inc., 761
Philip Morris, 411, 413, 414, 433, 734
Philips Corporation, 570, 608, 609
Philips Industries, 413, 414
Photon Technology International Inc., 470
Polaroid, 849
Price Waterhouse, 604
Proctor & Gamble, 460, 461

Quality Croutons, 515

Reynolds Metals, 849
Richtman's Printing, 232
Royal Canadian Mint, 394

Sally Industries, Inc., 245
Securities and Exchange Commission, 12, 321
Seitz Corporation, 568
Senco Products, 660
Sentry Insurance, 761
Simpson Industries, Inc., 567
Southwest Airlines, 3, 4, 5, 8, 19, 610
SpeedCall Corp., 761, 798
St. Bernard Parish Sheriff's Office, 642
StarKist (see H. J. Heinz)
Stoneyfield Farm, 722
Strategic Defense Initiative Office, 55
Supportive Homecare Corporation, 726
Sydney Opera House, 768

Tellabs Inc., 570
Tenneco, 761, 798
The Placers, Inc., 463
TLC Group, 466
Toshiba, 796
Toyota, 796
Trailco Leasing, 659
Trans Gulf Inc., 73
Transamerica Energy Associates, 524
Transamerica Telemarketing, 131

Union Carbide, 849
Unisys, 607
United Air Lines, 704
United States Government, 555
United States Postal Service, 380
Upjohn, 712
UPS, 566, 612, 613
USAA, 569
US Sprint, 606

Valmont/ALS, 251, 252
Viking Penguin, 402

Wallace Co., 387
Weyerhaeuser, 146, 439, 440, 799
W. R. Grace, 849

Xerox, 761

Yamazaki Manufacturing Company, 790
York Construction Company, 461

SUBJECT INDEX

ABC (see Activity-based costing)

ABC analysis (for inventory control), 574

Ability to bear (see Allocation, criteria)

Absorption costing
  advantages, 339
  comparison of variable and absorption costing, 324ff, 333
  cost-volume-profit relationship analysis, 332
  defined, 320ff, 416, 417
  effect of capacity levels, 86, 87, 325
  effect on accounting records, 333
  models, 322
  professional and regulatory requirements, 321
  system, 335
  theoretical justification, 339, 340
  use in transfer pricing, 430

Accounting information, 12

Accounting rate of return (see also Capital budgeting), 780, 781, 787–789

Activity (see also Capacity), 127, 133
  differences causing under/overapplied overhead, 76
  horizontal flow, 140, 141
  levels of, 86ff, 133ff
  non-traditional measures of (see Cost drivers)

Activity accounting (see Activity-based costing)

Activity base (see Cost driver; Predictor)

Activity-based costing, 139, 141–146, 148, 149, 196

Activity-based management, 127, 128, 605

Activity center, 139

Actual cost system, 74, 174, 175

Ad hoc discount, 422

Administrative department (see also Service department), 99

Advertising budget changes, 730, 731

Age Discrimination Employment Act, 845

Allocate, 44

Allocation(s)
  ability-to-bear, 99
  bases, 84, 93, 94
  behavioral aspects (see Decision making; Motivation)
  criteria, 99
  defined, 44
  indirect costs, 44
  joint cost, 714
  multi-tier systems of, 133ff
  of overhead cost, 44
  of standard cost variances, 207
  reasons for, 99
  scarce resources, 710, 724
  service department costs (see Service department, cost allocation)

Alternative courses of action, 715

American Institute of Certified Public Accountants, 464, 466

Analytic hierarchy process, 792

Annuity, 802

Applied overhead (see also Overhead, application), 88, 182

Appropriation, 486

Approximated net realizable value at split-off method (see Joint cost allocation)

Asset turnover, 670

Attachability (see Cost, direct; Predetermined overhead rates)

Authority, 645, 646, 652

Automation
  impact on capital budgeting models, 789ff
  impact on cost accounting, 46
  impact on overhead allocations, 73, 84, 85
  impact on production, 46, 73, 790ff
  impact on types of costs, 73
  in job shops, 250, 251
  opportunity cost of not automating, 793

Average costing methods (in process costing), 275ff
Avoidable cost (see Cost, avoidable)

Backflush accounting (production system), 571
Bar coding, 238ff
Behavior patterns (see Cost, fixed; mixed; and variable)
Behavioral factors (implications of profit and cost centers), 655ff
Benefits-provided ranking (see Service department cost allocation)
Bill of materials, 180, 558
Bottleneck, 150, 151, 558–560
Breakeven (see also Cost-volume-profit analysis)
    assumptions and limitations, 361, 362
    automation, impact, 378, 379, 384
    cash-flow breakeven, 390, 391
    chart, 392, 393
    contribution margin, 362
    formula approach, 364ff
    income statement approach, 371ff
    incremental analysis, 373, 374
    margin of safety, 377
    point, 361, 363ff
    profit-volume graph, 394, 395
Bribes, 833, 834
Budget
    advantages of achievable targets, 481, 484
    appropriation, 486
    basis for control, 466, 652–655
    calendar, 476
    capital (see also Capital budgeting), 501, 510, 511
    cash, 476, 511ff, 518
    committee, 473
    constraints, 466
    continuous, 475
    defined, 463, 464, 468
    financial, 501, 519ff
    flexible, 81–83, 86, 87, 192, 600, 602, 624, 653
    implementation, 476
    imposed, 488
    master, 501, 653
    operating, 501
    overhead, 509
    participatory (see Participatory budgeting; Participation)
    personnel compensation, 510, 512
    preparation of, 464, 468, 475
    production, 507
    purchases, 508, 509
    rolling (see continuous)
    sales, 506
    sample forms, 476

    selling, general and administrative, 509, 510
    static, 502
Budget games, 481–483
Budget manual, 475
Budget revisions, 480
Budget slack, 472, 481
Budget variance, 653
Budgetary activities, 476
Budgeted cost (see Cost, standard)
Budgeted financial statements, 519ff
Budgeting, 464
    administrative expenses, 509
    advantages of, 464, 466, 484, 485
    behavior, 464
    continuous, 475
    defined, 464, 525
    for discretionary costs, 617, 618, 620–624
    implementation and control, 464ff
    in multinational companies, 507
    overview, 464, 465, 504
    participatory (see Participatory budgeting; Participation)
    process, 464, 465, 470, 476, 477, 503, 613
    program, 626ff
    purposes of, 464ff
    traditional, 486, 487
    use of equivalent units, 508
    zero-base, 486, 487
Business environment, 6ff
By-products, 714

Capacity
    concepts of, 86ff
        expected annual, 87
        ideal (see theoretical)
        normal, 87, 88
        practical, 87
        theoretical, 87
    defined, 87
    utilization, 198
Capital asset, 761
Capital budgeting (see also Discounted cash flow methods), 510, 511, 762
    assumptions and limitations of techniques, 782, 783
    automation impact, 789ff
    basis for justifying investments, 762
    categories for ranking projects, 765
    investment decision, 762ff
    leasing assets, 766
    under uncertainty, 782, 783
Capital expenditure analysis
    discounting techniques, 771–778
    non-discounting techniques, 779ff

Carrying costs (see Inventory costs)
CASB (see Cost Accounting Standards Board)
Cash flow
  in breakeven, 390, 391
  in budgeting, 511–519, 521–524
  in capital budgeting, 767, 770, 782, 783
  in performance measurement, 663, 666, 667, 672
Centralization, 645, 646
Certificate in Management Accounting, 19
Change nothing alternative, 715, 716
Changes in American business, 6
Charge-back system (see Service department allocation; Transfer price)
Civil Rights Act of 1964, 845
Clean Water Act, 847
Cleanup costs, 848, 849
Clock card (see Employee time sheet)
Code of ethics (see also Ethical conduct), 16ff
Codes of conduct, 851ff
Compensation changes, 729
Competition (see Monopolistic competition; Pure competition)
Complementary products, 725
Compound interest, 801
Compounding period, 801
Computer-aided design/computer-aided manufacturing, 794, 796
Computer department cost allocation (see Service department allocation; Transfer pricing)
Computer-integrated manufacturing (CIM), 793, 794
Computer software pirarcy, 851
Concern for legality, 833
Confidentiality, 16, 17
Constraints (see also Bottleneck), 150, 151, 737
Consumer behavior (see also Pricing), 426
Continuous budgeting (see Budget, continuous)
Continuous improvement (see also Quality), 143
Contribution income statements (see Variable costing income statements)
Contribution margin, 362, 363
  per unit of limited resources, 727
  ratio, 365
Control (see also Cost analysis and control)
  activities, 146, 148
  defined, 476
  function, 469
  internal (see Internal control)
  role of management accounting, 3, 4
Controllable cost (see Cost, controllable)
Controller, 22
Controlling (see also Planning), 4
Conventional costing (see Absorption costing)
Conversion, 39, 40, 552
Conversion cost (see Cost, conversion)
Cost,
  administrative, 99

appraisal, 48
avoidable, 720, 732
batch level, 133, 134, 137
budgeted (see Standard cost)
committed, 608–611
common, 44
controllable, 652–655
conversion, 49, 50, 281
differential (see also incremental), 419
direct, 44
discretionary, 610–624
distribution, 42–44
engineered, 618–620
expired, 40, 42
failure, 48
fixed (see also Cost behavior), 33, 608
fringe benefit, 6
full, 321
historical (see also Cost, sunk), 32
incremental, 428, 711
indirect (see also Overhead), 44, 46
inventoriable (see Cost, product)
irrelevant (see Cost, sunk)
joint, 714
mixed, 35, 36, 78–80
noncontrollable, 652, 667, 669
opportunity, 417, 669, 711, 721
organizational level, 133, 134, 136, 137
out-of-pocket, 419
outside processing, 36, 33
overhead (see Overhead)
period, 39, 41–43
prevention, 48
prime, 49, 50
product (see also Direct materials; Direct labor; Overhead; Absorption costing; Variable costing), 39, 40, 42, 43, 73, 74, 126, 127, 146, 321ff
product/process level, 133–135, 137
quality (see also Quality), 48, 49
reaction to changes in activity (see Cost behavior)
relevant, 419, 420, 709
replacement, 32, 713
semivariable (see mixed)
separable, 553
setup (also setup time), 134, 135, 137, 140
standard (see Standard cost)
step, 36
sunk, 713, 716ff
target, 176–178, 412
total, 33, 36
unexpired, 40, 42
unit, 33, 284, 285
unit level, 133–135, 137
variable (see also Cost behavior), 33
Cost accounting

comparison with financial accounting, 13, 14
comparison with managerial accounting, 13, 14
defined, 12, 13
functions (or goals), 12, 13
pull systems, 563, 564, 571–574
push systems, 558
reporting cost information (see Responsibility reports)
standards, 14, 15
systems development, 336, 337
tomorrows' factories, 6–9
traditional reporting system (see Absorption costing)
Cost Accounting Standards Board, 14, 15
Cost accumulation, 51, 320
Cost allocations (see Allocations; Service department
    allocation; Transfer pricing)
Cost analysis, 600ff
    breakeven analysis, 361, 363ff
    cost-volume-profit analysis, 365ff
    differential cost analysis (see Relevant costing)
    marketing (see also Cost, distribution), 729–731
    standards and variance analysis (see Variance analysis)
Cost avoidance, 605
Cost behavior (see also Cost, variable; Cost, fixed; Relevant
    range), 33, 36, 37, 77, 322ff
Cost-benefit analysis, 147, 715
Cost center (see Responsibility center, cost)
Cost categories, 32
Cost components (see Direct materials; Direct labor;
    Overhead)
Cost composition (agreement in defining), 417, 418
Cost consciousness, 439, 600
Cost containment, 603–605, 623
Cost control, 146, 193, 245, 279, 600, 651
Cost control system, 193, 599–624, 652–655
Cost driver, 37, 84, 127, 139, 141, 281, 437–439, 680–682
Cost driver analysis, 133, 663–665, 680–682
Cost estimation (see High-low method; Scattergraph;
    Regression analysis)
Cost flow assumptions, 278, 279, 286ff
Cost formula for a straight line, 78
Cost function, 322
Cost management (see Cost control system)
Cost object, 44, 232
Cost of capital (see Weighted average cost of capital)
Cost of goods manufactured, 52, 53, 519, 520
Cost of goods sold, 53
Cost of production report (see Process costing, production
    and cost report)
Cost of services rendered, 40, 41
Cost-plus contract (see Pricing, cost-plus)
Cost pool, 75, 84, 85, 94, 281
Cost presentation, 320
Cost reduction, 605–607
Costing system (see also Actual costing system; Job order
    costing system; Normal costing system; Process
    costing system; Standard costing system), 296

Cost tables, 176
Cost understanding, 600, 602
Cost-volume-profit analysis, 365ff
    assumptions, 366, 383, 384
    breakeven point (see also Breakeven), 366
    effects of quality, 385–387
    in a multiproduct environments, 380ff
    income statement approach, 371ff
    incremental analysis, 373ff
    related to demand elasticity, 726
    target profit, 367ff
Criminal penalties, 841, 842
Critical success factors (see also Key variables), 659
Cultural differences, 835
Currently attainable standard (see Standards)
CVP (see Cost-volume-profit)

Decentralization, 645–659
Decision making, 710, 735
    costs used in, 32, 709, 710, 715ff
    in decentralized units, 647–651
    relationship to joint costs (products), 714, 755
    relationship to standard costs, 176
Decision package (see also Budgeting, zero-based), 487
Degree of operating leverage, 379
Demand (sales) estimation, 524
Denominator level of activity, 277, 278
    effect on volume variance, 198
    in relationship to absorption costing, 325, 326
    in setting fixed cost per unit, 76
Departmental versus plantwide rates of applying overhead
    (see also Predetermined overhead), 92–94
Dependent variable, 96
Depreciation
    comparison of tax effects of different methods, 784
    in accounting rate of return, 788, 789
    in discounted cash flow techniques, 769
    part of overhead, 47
    tax benefit of, 391, 784
    tax shield of, 784
Deregulation, 8
Different uses of costs, 44
Differential cost (see Cost, differential)
Differential revenue (see Incremental revenue)
Direct cost (see Cost, direct)
Direct costing (see Variable costing)
Direct labor,
    as a basis for applying overhead, 94, 281
    cost, 6, 44
    defined, 45
    in master budget, 510, 512
    in process costing, 276, 281ff
    quality, 188
    standards, 180–182
    variances
        efficiency, 187, 188, 192, 195

mix, 195
rate, 187, 188, 192, 195
use of temporaries, 606
Direct materials
cost, 44
defined, 44
in master budget, 508, 509
in process costing, 276, 279, 280
issuance of (see Materials requisition forms)
multiple, 280, 281
standards, 179, 180
variances
price, 186, 192
purchase price, 187, 193ff
quantity, 186, 192ff
usage (see quantity)
usage price, 187
Direct method of allocation (see Service department cost allocation)
Discount rate, 770
Discounted cash flow methods,
alternatives (see Payback period and Accounting rate of return)
internal rate of return, 776–778, 782, 787
net present value method, 771, 786
present value (or profitability) index, 774, 787
Discounting, 770
Discrete project (see Independent project)
Discretionary costs,
budgeting for, 617ff
control of, 618–620
fixed, 618
nonmonetary measures of output, 613, 614
Discrimination, 845
Distribution cost (see Cost, distribution)
Documents
bill of materials, 180
employee time sheet, 238
job cost record, 236
materials requisition form, 235
operations flow document, 181
production and cost report, 287, 289
standard cost card, 183
Dollar days (of inventory), 677
Dumping (see Pricing, dumping)
DuPont model (see also Return on investment), 670, 671
Dysfunctional decision making (see Suboptimization)

Economic order quantity (EOQ), 554–557, 559, 562
Economic production run, 556, 557
Effectiveness, 5, 614–616, 663–666
Efficiency, 5, 614–616, 663–666
Efficiency variance (see also Direct labor; Variable overhead), 188, 190
Employee suggestion programs, 607
Employee time sheet, 181, 237–239

Engineered cost (see Cost, engineered)
Environmental legislation and issues, 847
Equal Pay Act, 845
Equivalent units of production (see Process costing system, equivalent units of production)
Estimated cost (see Standard cost)
Ethical conduct, 16, 17, 651, 711, 712, 830–832, 835, 841
Excess capacity, 419
Excess material requisitions, 194
Expected annual capacity (see Capacity, expected annual)
Expected standard (see Standard, expected)
Expenses (see Period cost; Product cost)
Experience curve (see Learning curve)
Expired cost (see Cost, expired)

FCPA (see Foreign Corrupt Practices Act)
Feasible region, 738
Feasible solution, 738
Feedback, 469
FIFO method (see also Process costing), 278, 279, 286, 291
Financial accounting, 12, 13
Financial Accounting Standards Board (FASB), 14, 126, 321
Financial budget (see Budget, financial)
Financial measures of performance, 663–675
Financing decision, 768
Finished goods , 10, 11, 54, 240, 278, 280
Fixed cost (see Cost, fixed)
Fixed overhead
controllability, 196–198
spending variance, 189, 191
volume variance, 189, 191
Flexibility, 12
Flexible budget (see Budget, flexible)
Flexible manufacturing system, 203, 790, 791, 795, 796
Flow of cost through production, 275
Focused factory arrangement (see also Just-in-time), 567
Forecasting (see Budgeting)
Foreign Corrupt Practices Act, 18, 833ff
Fringe benefit costs (see Cost, fringe benefit)
Full costing (see Absorption costing)
Functional classification, 321, 322
Future value (of a dollar), 801

Goal, 4, 20, 463, 466, 645, 675, 676
Goal congruence, 649, 661, 675
Goods in process (see Work in Process)
Grease payments, 834

High-low method, 79, 80, 96
Historical cost, 32
Homogeniety, 84
Hurdle rate (see also Discount rate; Weighted average cost of capital), 778, 792

Ideal capacity (see Capacity, theoretical)
Idle time, 129
Imposed budget, 471

Income under absorption and variable costing, 331, 332
Income statement comparisons, 56–58
Income taxes
    in cost-volume-profit analysis, 368–370
    in capital budgeting, 784ff
    in transfer pricing, 432
Incremental analysis (see also Cost-volume-profit analysis), 374
Incremental cost (see Cost, incremental)
Incremental revenue, 711
Ideal standard (see Standard, ideal)
Independent projects, 766
Independent variable, 96
Indirect cost (see Cost, indirect)
Indirect labor, 6
Indirect materials, 45–47
Information, 4
    qualitative vs. quantitative, 12
Input-output relationships, 611, 612
    surrogate measures of output, 627
Insider, 842
Inspection time, 129
Institute of Management Accountants, 3, 16, 18, 19
Integrity, 16, 17
Interest rate, 801
Internal control, 18, 835ff
Internal rate of return (see Discounted cash flow methods, internal rate of return)
Internal Revenue Service, 126, 321
International companies (see Multinational companies)
International marketplace, 8, 203
Interpolation, 778
Inventoriable cost (see Cost, product)
Inventory costs (see also Economic order quantity; Economic production run; Order point; Safety stock), 553, 554
    categories, 552
    cost of carrying, 553, 554
    cost of ordering, 553
    cost of purchasing, 553
    flow assumptions (see Cost flow assumptions)
    methods of valuation, 174, 319, 320
    stockout cost, 554
Inventory models
    ABC, 574
    economic order quantity (see Economic order quantity)
    MRP/MRP II, 557ff
    red-line method, 576
Investing decision, 766–768
Investment center (see Responsibility center, investment)
IRR (see Internal rate of return)

JIT (see Just-in-time)
Job, 231, 232
Job cost record (see Job order cost sheet)
Job enrichment, 569, 570

Job order cost sheet, 236, 237
Job order costing system, 174, 231ff, 238–250, 273
    entries for, 241
    using standard costs, 246ff
    subsidiary ledger accounts, 232, 233
Job time ticket, 238
Joint process, 714
Joint products, 714
Journal entries
    for backflush accounting, 572, 573
    for converting variable costing to absorption costing, 324
    for job-order costing, 241ff, 244
    for overhead variances, 89, 90, 206, 243
    for perpetual inventory system, 51, 52
    for process costing, 298
    for standard cost systems, 205–207
Just-in-time
    changes needed to implement, 251, 565, 570, 571
    cross-training employees, 569
    impact on accounting and costs, 571ff
    manufacturing systems, 561
    philosophy and goals, 131, 251, 561, 562
    plant layout, 569
    production processing, 568
    purchasing, supplier relationships, and distribution, 565–567
    quality control, 565

Kanban (see Just-in-time)
Key variable, 466, 467

Labor (see Direct labor; Indirect labor)
Labor variances (see Direct labor variances)
Law, 830
Lead time, 131, 149, 150
Least squares regression analysis, 96–98
Legal and ethical behavior compared, 830
Level scheduling, 563,564
Life cycle costing, 673
Line employee, 21
Linear programming, 724, 732
Long-term variable cost, 139, 140

Machine clocks or counters, 238
Machine hours, 93, 94, 281, 282
Make-or-buy decision (see Cost analysis)
Malcolm Baldrige National Quality Awards, 386, 387
Managed cost (see Cost, discretionary)
Management accounting, 3, 12, 13, 14
    standards (see Cost accounting, standards; Cost Accounting Standards Board; Statements on Management Accounting)
Management by exception, 202, 203, 661
Management control process, 600, 601, 662
Management functions, 4

Manufacturer (manufacturing companies), 9, 10, 40
Manufacturing cells (see also Just-in-time), 569
Manufacturing cycle efficiency, 131
Manufacturing overhead (see Overhead)
Manufacturing resource planning (see MRP II)
Margin of safety, 377
Master budget (see Budget, master)
Master production schedule, 557
Material costs (see Direct materials; Indirect materials)
Material requisition form, 194, 234–236, 276
Materials requirements planning (see MRP)
Materials variances (see Direct materials variances)
Matrix structures (of organizations), 22
Mean, 97, 98
Merchandising companies, 9, 40, 41
Mixed cost (see Cost, mixed)
Monopolistic competition, 423
Monopoly, 423
Motivation, 661
MRP/MRP II, 557ff
Multinational companies, 432, 507, 675, 676, 771, 835
Multiple regression, 96
Multiproduct companies (using CVP analysis), 380ff

National Association of Accountants (NAA) (see Institute of
        Management Accountants)
National Environmental Policy Act, 847
Negotiated transfer price, 430, 431
Net income
    absorption vs. variable costing (see Income under
            absorption and variable costing)
    cost-volume-profit relationships, 367ff
    manipulation, 333, 666
Net margin on sales, 369ff
Net present value (see Discounted cash flow methods, net
        present value)
Net realizable value method (see Joint cost allocation)
Noncontrollable cost (see Cost, noncontrollable)
Nonfinancial measures of performance, 663–666, 676–678,
        680–682
Non-value-added activity, 127–129, 131, 132, 146, 487
Normal capacity (see Capacity, normal)
Normal cost system, 74, 175, 232ff

Objective, 4, 463, 612, 645, 725
Objective function, 737
Occupational Safety and Health Act, 844, 845
Office of Federal Procurement Policy, 15
Oligopoly, 423, 424
Operating budget (see Budget, operating)
Operating leverage, 378
Operations flow document, 181
Opportunity cost (see Cost, opportunity)
Opportunity cost of capital, 771
Optimal solution, 738
Order point, 579

Ordering cost, 553
Ordinary annuity, 802
Organization chart, 21
Organizational structure (see also Centralization;
        Decentralization), 20, 21, 645, 646
Outliers, 96
Out-of-pocket cost (see Cost, out-of-pocket)
Outside processing cost (see Cost, outside processing)
Outsourcing, 36
Overhead
    analysis- 189ff, 195ff, 277
    application (see also Predetermined overhead rate), 88
    budgeted, 191
    control of, 73, 74, 195–197
    defined, 10, 47
    fixed, 47, 48, 86, 190, 191, 724
    generally accepted accounting principles, 90
    in master budget, 509
    in product cost, 239, 277, 281
    pool (see Cost pool)
    standards, 182
    under- and overapplied, 89, 190
        disposition of, 89, 90, 243
        reasons for, 89
    recording, 239
    variable, 47, 82, 83
    variances, 189–192, 195ff
Overtime premium, 46

Participation, 464, 471ff
Participatory budgeting, 470ff, 474, 504
Past cost (see Sunk cost)
Payback period, 779, 780, 782, 787
Performance, 5
Performance evaluation (measurement), 4, 149, 176, 464,
        480, 481, 615, 660–678, 680–682
Performance motivation, 661, 673
Performance reports (see Responsibility reports)
Period cost (see Cost, period)
Perpetual inventory system, 51, 52, 553
Physical measurement method of joint cost allocation (see
        Joint cost allocation)
Physical units in process costing, 283
Planning (see also Controlling), 4, 463, 525, 616
Planning relationships, 468, 469
Plant layout, 569
Plantwide versus departmental overhead application rates
        (see also Predetermined overhead), 92–94
Post-investment audit (of a capital project), 795ff
Practical capacity (see Capacity, practical)
Practical standard (see Standard, practical)
Predecessor department cost, 292
Predetermined overhead
    activity (capacity) bases used in computing FOH rate, 87,
            88
    allocation bases, 86

combined rate (see single rate)
multiple rates (see separate rates)
rate, 74
reasons for, 75, 76, 91, 245, 246
separate rates, 76, 77, 82, 83, 86, 91, 94
single rate, 91, 92
use in product costing, 239, 277
Predicate acts, 839
Predictor, 37, 38, 84
Preference decision, 764
Pregnancy Discrimination Act of 1978, 845
Present value index (see Discounted cash flow methods,
present value index)
Present value (of a dollar), 801
Previous department costs (see Predecessor department cost)
Price discrimination, 422
Price fixing, 425, 426
Price maker, 414, 415
Price taker, 414
Pricing,
changes, 726ff
cost-plus, 246
dumping, 424, 425
effect of market structure, 422ff
effect of mispricing, 415
effect of supply, 427
elasticity of demand, 426
ethics, 422, 423, 433
factors affecting, 411, 415, 416
fair return, 422
goals, 411, 414, 415
international dimensions, 424, 425
labor loading charge, 419
low-ball bidding, 420
materials loading charge, 419
multiple products, 420, 421
penetration, 421
regulated, 422
skimming, 421
special order, 419–421
time and materials, 418, 419
transfer (see Transfer pricing)
Primary output (products) (see Joint products)
Prime cost (see Cost, prime)
Process costing, 273
Process costing system
cost of goods transferred out, 286, 287
defined, 174, 273
differences from job order costing, 274, 275
entries for, 298
equivalent units of production, 277, 278, 286
estimating degree of completion, 278
FIFO, 273, 286ff
multidepartmental setting, 292–294
production and cost report, 286, 287, 289
steps to assign costs, 290

unit costs, 285, 288
units started and completed, 283
using standard costs, 291
weighted average, 273, 278, 279, 282ff
Process map, 129, 132
Process yield, 677, 729
Product complexity, 140
Product contribution margin, 323
Product costing, methods of (see also Absorption costing;
Job order costing; Process costing; Variable
costing; Standard costing), 231
Product cost (see Cost, product)
Product design, 178, 179, 412, 413
Product life cycle, 412ff, 469
Product life cycle stages, 412–414
Product line decisions, 731ff
Product quality (see Quality)
Product variety, 9, 140, 143
Production and cost report (see Process costing, production
and cost report)
Production center, 40, 41
Production costs (see Costs, product)
Production time, 129
Productive processing time, 677
Professional examinations, 19
Profitability, 659
Profitability index (see Present value index)
Profit center (see Responsibility center, profit)
Profit margin, 670
Profit planning (see Budgeting)
Profit-volume graph, 394, 395
Pro forma financial statements, 501, 502, 519ff, 524
Program budgeting, 626, 627
Programmed costs (see Cost, discretionary)
Proration, 207
Pull system (of inventory), 563ff
Purchase order lead time, 477
Purchase price variance (see Direct materials, variances)
Purchasing agent, 180, 193, 194
Purchasing costs, 553
Purchasing practices (see Just-in-time, purchasing, supplier
relationships, and distribution)
Pure competition, 423
Push system (of inventory), 558

Quality (see also Cost, quality), 48, 77, 94, 143, 149, 178,
179, 189, 385–387, 412, 479, 565, 568, 659, 660,
661
circles, 143
control, 129, 151

Racketeer Influenced and Corrupt Organizations Act, 839
Raw and In Process (RIP), 572, 573
Raw materials, 54
Red-line system, 576
Regression analysis (see Least squares regression analysis)

Relevant cost (see Cost, relevant)
Relevant costing, 710ff
Relevant range, 32
Rent (annuity cash flow), 802
Reorder point (see Order point)
Repetitive manufacturing, 294, 319
Replacement cost, 32, 713
Required rate of return (see Hurdle rate)
Resale price maintenance (see Price fixing, vertical)
Residual income, 671–675
Resources, scarce, 737
Responsibility (see also Variance responsibility), 21
Responsibility accounting, 651–682
Responsibility center, 655, 656
    cost, 655–657, 664
    investment, 659, 666–675
    performance measurements, 653, 657, 659–682
    profit, 659, 666, 667
    revenue, 658, 664
Responsibility reports, 651–655
Retail companies (see Merchandising companies)
Return on capital, 771
Return on investment, 667–671, 672–675
Revenue center (see Responsiblity center, revenue)
Revenue variance, 376
RICO (see Racketeer Influenced and Corrupt Organizations Act)
Robinson-Patman Act, 422
Robotics, 7, 8, 46
ROI (see Return on investment)

Safety stock, 579, 580
Sales budget (see Budget, sales)
Sales demand, 524
Sales mix, 380–384, 725ff
Scarce resource, 710, 722, 724
Scienter, 842
Scrap, 714
Screening decision, 763
Securities and Exchange Commission, 12, 126, 321
Securities Exchange Act of 1934, 842
Segment margin, 667, 733, 734
Separable costs (see Split-off point)
Service company, 11, 40, 41, 45
Service department (see also Administrative department), 99
    cost allocation, 99
        bases for, 99
        benefits-provided ranking, 100
        direct method, 100, 101
        reasons for, 99
        step method, 100–102
Setup costs (see Cost, setup)
Setup times, 561, 568
Short-run financial performance, 673
Simple interest, 801
Simple regression, 96

Simplex method, 738
Situational ethics, 835
Special order decision (see Pricing, special order)
Split-off point, 714
Staff employee, 21
Stages of production, 10
Standard, 175, 464
    dimensions (appropriateness; attainability), 198ff
    expected, 201
    ideal, 201–203
    practical, 201
Standard cost
    card, 182, 183
    defined, 175, 178
    system, 175, 176
    treatment of end-of-period variances (see Variance, treatment of end-of-period)
    used in job order costing systems, 246
    used in process costing systems, 291, 292
    used in responsibility accounting systems, 652
Standard hours allowed, 188
Standard overhead application rates, 182
Standard quantity allowed, 184
Standards (see also Direct labor; Direct material; Overhead), 175, 198ff
    of ethical conduct (see Ethical conduct)
Started and completed (see Units started and completed)
Statement of cash flows, 521–523, 667
Statements on Management Accounting, 15
Step allocation method (see Service department cost allocations, step method)
Step cost (see Cost, step)
Stockout costs, 554, 579
Stockpiling inventory, 507, 508
Strategic planning, 466, 467
Suboptimization (see also Goal congruence), 673, 674
Substitute goods, 413
Sunk cost (see Cost, sunk)
Super-full absorption costing (see Uniform capitalization rules)
Support activites (see Administrative department; Service department; Service department cost allocations)
Surrogate measures of activity, 613, 614, 616
Sychronous management, 676

Tactical planning, 467
Target costing, 176
Tax benefit (of depreciation), 391
Theoretical capacity (see Capacity, theoretical)
Theory of constraints, 150, 151, 251
Throughput, 571, 676, 677
Time and motion studies, 181
Time sheet (see Employee time sheet)
Time value of money, 672, 770, 801
Timeline, 769
Tippee, 842

Total contribution margin, 323, 324
Total cost to be accounted for, 284
Total units to account for, 283
Traceable cost (see Cost, direct)
Transfer price, 428
Transfer pricing, 428ff
    advantages of, 431, 439, 440
    cost-based, 428, 430
    disadvantages, 431, 440
    dual pricing arrangement, 431
    general rules, 428
    hybrid (see dual)
    in multinational companies, 432
    market-based, 430
    negotiated, 430, 431
Transfer time, 129
Transnational companies (see Multinational companies)
Travel costs, 599, 604, 606, 607, 624, 625
Treasurer, 21
Two-bin system, 574
Two stage allocation, 139, 140

Unexpired cost (see Cost, unexpired)
Uniform capitalization rules, 44, 335ff
Unit costs, 275, 284, 285
United Nations Code of Conduct, 857–859
Units started and completed, 283
Usage variance, 184, 185

Valuation (methods of), 174, 175, 319, 320
Value-added activity, 127–129, 146, 612
Value chart, 129
Variable cost (see Cost, variable)
Variable costing
    advantages, 329, 340
    comparison with absorption costing, 324ff, 333, 340
    cost-volume-profit relationship analysis, 322

defined, 320–322, 417
    effects on accounting records, 333
    income statements, 323, 324
    model, 323
Variable overhead (see also Overhead, variable), 189
    efficiency variance, 190, 192, 195, 196
    spending variance, 190, 192, 195, 196
Variance (see also Direct material variances; Direct labor variances; Management by exception; Overhead variances), 176, 182, 464, 653
    analysis, 186–188, 193, 202, 479, 480
    favorable vs. unfavorable, 184
    price, 184, 185, 195
    responsibility, 193–195, 655
    sales price, 478
    sales volume, 478
    total, 183, 184, 190
    treatment at end-of-period, 207
    usage, 184, 185
Volume variance, 191, 192, 325

Wages (for factory labor), 6
Weighted average cost of capital, 770
Weighted average method (of process costing), 278, 279, 282ff
Whistleblowing, 850, 851
Work in process, 10, 54, 237
Work not started, 10
World markets (see International marketplace)

Zero-base budgeting (see Budgeting, zero-based)
Zero-defects (see Continuous improvement; Just-in-time; Quality)
Zero inventory production systems (ZIPS) (see Just-in-time)
Zero volume inventory (see Just-in-time)

Photo Credits

v Eddie Hironaka, Image Bank. vi Photo courtesy of the National Aeronautics and Space Administration. vii Seth Resnick, Stock Boston. viii Photo courtesy of Caterpillar, Inc. x Mark Gibson, The Stock Market. xi © 1989, Michele Burgess and Dinamation International Corp. xii Photo courtesy of McIlhenny Co., Avery Island, LA 70513. xiii Photo courtesy of the Audubon Institute, New Orleans. xv Photo courtesy of National Institute of Standards and Technology. xvi Photo by Cathy Blaivas. xviii Andrew Sacks, Tony Stone Worldwide. xix Murray Alcosser, Image Bank. xx David Brownell, Image Bank. xxi Jeffrey Mark Dunn, Stock Boston. xxiii Cecily Raiborn. xxiv Photo courtesy of Gateway 2000. xxv Photo courtesy of Tenneco, Inc. xxvii Photo courtesy of Cadbury Schweppes. 1 Robert Rathe, Stock Boston. 2 Eddie Hironaka, Image Bank. 5 Courtesy of Southwest Airlines. 11 (middle) Jeffrey Grosscup. 11 (bottom) Jeffrey Grosscup. 30 Courtesy of the National Aeronautics and Space Administration. 31 Charles Gupton, The Stock Market. 38 Sobel-Klonsky, The Image Bank. 45 Courtesy of the Haggar Apparel Company. 49 Craig Hammell, The Stock Market. 54 Chris Jones, The Stock Market. 72 Seth Resnick, Stock Boston. 73 Cecily Raiborn. 76 Cecily Raiborn. 83 Photo by Tom Gigliotti. 86 Courtesy of Masco Corporation. 124 Courtesy of Caterpillar, Inc. 128 Courtesy of Symbol Technologies, Inc., Bohemia, NY. 132 Paul Chauncey, The Stock Market. 135 Courtesy of Nintendo of America. 141 Courtesy of Caterpillar, Inc. 147 Logos courtesy of International Business Machines, Inc.; Caterpillar, Inc.; Owens Corning; and Gen Corp. Polymer Products. 171 Bob Stein, Firth Photobank. 172 Mark Gibson, The Stock Market. 175 Tom Bean, The Stock Market. 179 Jake Rajs, The Image Bank. 192 Cecily Raiborn. 195 Cecily Raiborn. 199 (top) Photo courtesy of USAA. 199 (bottom) Photo courtesy of USAA. 230 © 1989, Michele Burgess and Dinamation International Corp. 235 Jeffrey Muir Hamilton, Stock Boston. 241 © 1989, Michele Burgess and Dinamation International Corporation. 244 © 1989, Michele Burgess and Dinamation International Corporation. 245 Photo courtesy of Sally Industries, Inc. 249 Photo courtesy of Carver Boat Company. 272 Photo courtesy of McIlhenny Co., Avery Island, LA 70513. 274 Photo courtesy of Cadbury Schweppes. 277 Photo courtesy of McIlhenny Co., Avery Island, LA 70513. 282 Photo courtesy of McIlhenny Co., Avery Island, LA 70513. 292 Photo courtesy of McIlhenny Co., Avery Island, LA 70513. 318 Photo courtesy of the Audubon Institute, New Orleans. 320 Jim Corwin, Stock Boston. 324 Cecily Raiborn. 328 Lionel Deleringne, Stock Boston. 332 Photo courtesy of the Minneapolis Convention Center. 359 William Johnson, Stock Boston. 360 Photo courtesy of National Institute of Standards and Technology. 362 Photo courtesy of the New England Patriots. 366 Jon Feingersh, The Stock Market. 375 Photo courtesy of Freeport-McMoran Global Resource Companies. 378 Photo courtesy of Bearings, Inc. 386 (left) Photo courtesy of National Institute of Standards and Technology. 386 (right) Photo courtesy of National Institute of Standards and Technology. 410 Photo by Cathy Blaivas. 415 Cecily Raiborn. 424 Baine Harrington III, The Stock Market. 429 Bob Daemmrich, Stock Boston. 438 Photo courtesy of Bell Communications Research (Bellcore). 462 Andrew Sacks, Tony Stone Worldwide. 468 Jon Feingersh, The Stock Market. 472 Lou Jones, Image Bank. 477 Photo courtesy of J.C. Penney Co. 483 David Hundley, The Stock Market. 500 Murray Alcosser, Image Bank. 502 Archdiocese of Chicago. 506 Photos used with permission of Mattel, Inc. 513 Howard D. Simmons Photography, Chicago. 520 Courtesy of International Business Machines, Inc. 523 Julie Houck, Stock Boston. 549 John Zoiner, Firth Photobank. 550 David Brownell, Image Bank. 553 Photo courtesy of Parker Hannifin Corporation. 560 Tom Tracy, The Stock Market. 566 Photo courtesy of Baylor University Medical Center. 569 Photo courtesy of USAA. 598 Jeffrey Mark Dunn, Stock Boston. 601 Mike Mazzcischi, Stock Boston. 603 Cynthia Matthews, Stock Market. 613 Photo courtesy of United Parcel Service. 617 Photo courtesy of Channel 10/36 Friends, Inc., Milwaukee. 644 Cecily Raiborn. 648 Photo courtesy of Aluminum Company of America. 650 Gabe Palmer, The Stock Market. 658 Mark Levine/New York Mets. 662 Egyptian Tourist Authority. 664 Brownie Harris, The Stock Market. 675 Wendy Chan, Image Bank. 706 Patti McConville, Image Bank. 707 Photo courtesy of Gateway 2000. 710 Minnesota State Fair. 713 Jan Staller, The Stock Market. 716 © Dorreboom/Greenpeace. 721 Photo courtesy of Gateway 2000. 726 Photo used with permission of Mattel Inc. 760 Photo courtesy of Tenneco, Inc. 763 Brownie Harris, Stock Market. 765 Architect of the Capital. 768 Cecily Raiborn. 790 Photo courtesy of Masco Corporation. 797 Chicago Tourism Bureau. 828 Photo courtesy of Cadbury Schweppes. 830 Photo courtesy of Cadbury Schweppes. 838 Photo courtesy of Supermarkets General Corporation. 844 Photo courtesy of USAA. 847 Chris Mihulka, The Stock Market. 858 United Nations.